The Rand McNally
Concise Atlas
of the
Earth

The Rand McNally
Concise Atlas of the Earth

RAND McNALLY & COMPANY

New York   Chicago   San Francisco

In association with Mitchell Beazley Ltd. London

The Rand McNally Concise Atlas of the Earth
Copyright © 1976 by Rand McNally & Company
Map pages 48-194, World Political Information Tables and
Index pages 196-240 © Rand McNally and Company from
The International Atlas © 1969 Rand McNally and Company,
further re-edited for *The Earth and Man* © 1976 Rand
McNally and Company

The Good Earth section, pages 6-47 inclusive,
Copyright © by Mitchell Beazley Publishers Limited 1973
Fully revised 1976

Library of Congress number: **76-3070**
Printed in the United States of America

Contents

THE GOOD EARTH

THE PLANET EARTH

The Life and Death of the Earth	8–9
The Solar System	10–11
Earth's Companion: The Moon	12–13
Anatomy of Earth	14–15
The Active Earth	16–17
The Evolution of Land and Sea	18–19
The Earth Under the Sea	20–21
The Atmosphere	22–23
The Structure of Weather Systems	24–25

MAN ON EARTH

Earth's Water Resources	28–29
Minerals under the Land	30–31
Earth's Energy Resources	32–33
The Ocean's Living Resources	34–35
The Food Resource: 1	36–37
The Food Resource: 2	38–39
The Settled World	40–41
Religion, Language	42–43
The Population Problem	44–45
The Abuse of the Earth	46–47

MAPS

LOCATOR MAPS AND LEGENDS

	49, 50–51
World—Physical	52–53
Europe and Africa—Physical	54–55
Asia—Physical	56–57
Australia—Physical	58–59
North America—Physical	60–61
South America—Physical	62–63

EUROPE AND THE SOVIET UNION

Europe	64–65
Northern Europe	66–67
Southern Scandinavia	68–69
British Isles	70–71
Central Europe	72–73
France and the Alps	74–75
Spain and Portugal	76–77
Italy	78–79
Southeastern Europe	80–81
Western and Central Soviet Union	82–83
Eastern and Central Soviet Union	84–85
Baltic and Moscow Regions	86–87

ASIA

China, Japan, and Korea	88–89
Japan	90–91
Southeast Asia	92–93
Burma, Thailand, and Indochina	94–95
Malaysia and Western Indonesia	96–97
Philippines	98–99
India, Pakistan, and Southwest Asia	100–101
Northern India and Pakistan	102–103
Middle East	104–105

AFRICA

Western North Africa	106–107
Eastern North Africa	108–109
Southern Africa	110–111
Egypt and Sudan	112–113
West Africa	114–115
Southern Africa and Madagascar	116–117

AUSTRALIA AND NEW ZEALAND

Australia	118–119
Eastern Australia	120–121
Western and Central Australia	122–123
Northern Australia and New Guinea	124–125
New Zealand	126–127

LATIN AMERICA

Middle America	128–129
Mexico	130–131
Caribbean Region	132–133
Northern South America	134–135
Southern South America	136–137
Ecuador, Venezuela, and Guyana	138–139
Central Argentina and Chile	140–141

ANGLO AMERICA

Canada	142–143
United States	144–145
Alaska and Yukon	146–147
Southwestern Canada	148–149
Southeastern Canada	150–151
Northeastern United States	152–153
Great Lakes Region	154–155
Southeastern United States	156–157
Mississippi Valley	158–159
Southern Great Plains	160–161
Northern Great Plains	162–163
Southern Rocky Mountains	164–165
Northwestern United States	166–167
California and Nevada	168–169
Hawaii	170

CITY MAPS

LEGEND TO CITY MAPS

	171
Paris	172
Berlin • Wien • Budapest	173
Moscow • Leningrad	174
Rome • Athinai • Istanbul • Tehran	175
London	176
Delhi • Bombay • Calcutta	177
Beijing (Peking) • Sŏul • Singapore • Hong Kong	178
Tōkyō–Yokohama	179
Krung Thep (Bangkok) • Sai-gon • Djakarta • Shanghai • T'aipei • Manila	180
Sydney • Melbourne	181
Ciudad de México • La Habana • Caracas • Lima • Santiago	182
Rio de Janeiro • São Paulo	183
Montréal • Toronto	184
Boston	185
New York	186–187
Philadelphia	188
Buffalo • Niagara Falls • Baltimore • Washington	189
Cleveland • Pittsburgh	190
San Francisco–Oakland–San Jose	191
Detroit–Windsor	192
Chicago	193
Los Angeles	194

INDEXES

ACKNOWLEDGMENTS AND CREDITS

	195
World Political Information Table	196–200
Largest Metropolitan Areas	201

GEOGRAPHICAL INDEX

	202–240

The Planet Earth

Our home the Earth is a small planet revolving round the Sun. The Sun is a star, but only one of the hundred thousand million which exist in the local system of stars, or galaxy, of which we are a part. Our own galaxy, we now know, is just one of millions of other galaxies in the universe, all almost unbelievably remote. The light now reaching us from the most distant observable star-systems began its journey towards us even before the Earth came into existence more than 4500 million years ago.

It is inconceivable that other stars in the universe do not have planetary systems like our own Sun. Although our neighbors in the Sun's family seem barren of life, some of those planets in other systems must support life in some form. Yet, barring some revolutionary new insight into the problems of time and space travel, it is difficult to realize that man will some day be able to explore the depths of the universe to find such life. For the present we on this Earth are alone.

Nebula in Sagittarius
The Trifid nebula in the constellation Sagittarius is so called because dark dust clouds appear to divide the glowing gas into three segments. The Trifid, which forms a typical emission nebula, contains hot early-type stars. Its distance from us is 2300 light-years.

The Life and Death of the Earth

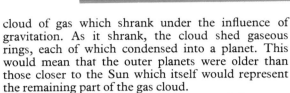

3 The gas cloud begins to assume the form of a regular disk. The infant Sun begins to shine - by the energy from gravitational shrinkage.

4 Material is thrown off from the Sun to join that already in the solar cloud, whose condensations have become more noticeable.

1 According to the most widely accepted theory, (the 'accretion' theory) the solar system originally consisted only of a mass of tenuous gas, and dust. There was no true Sun, and there was no production of nuclear energy. The gas was made up chiefly of hydrogen, with occasional random condensations.

2 Gravitational forces now cause the cloud to shrink and assume a more regular shape. Its density and mass near the center increase, but there are still no nuclear processes.

How did the Earth come into existence? This question has intrigued mankind for centuries but it was not until the start of true science that plausible theories were advanced. Although some theories held sway for many years, they were eventually deposed by the discovery of some fatal flaw. Even today, it is impossible to be sure that the main problem has been solved, but at least some concrete facts exist as a guide. It is now reasonably certain that the age of the Earth is of the order of 4550-4700 million years. The other planets are presumably about the same age, since they were probably formed by the same process in the same epoch.

Several centuries ago Archbishop Ussher of Armagh maintained that the world had come into being at a definite moment in the year 4004 BC. This estimate was made on purely religious grounds, and it soon became clear that the Earth is much older. In 1796 the French astronomer Laplace put forward the famous Nebular Hypothesis, according to which the Sun and the planets were formed from a rotating

cloud of gas which shrank under the influence of gravitation. As it shrank, the cloud shed gaseous rings, each of which condensed into a planet. This would mean that the outer planets were older than those closer to the Sun which itself would represent the remaining part of the gas cloud.

The Nebular Hypothesis was accepted for many years, but eventually serious mathematical weaknesses were found in it. Next came a number of tidal theories according to which the Earth and other planets were formed from a cigar-shaped tongue of matter torn from the Sun by the gravitational pull of a passing star. The first plausible theory of this kind came from the English astronomer Sir James Jeans, but this too was found to be mathematically untenable and the idea had to be given up.

Most modern theories assume that the planets were formed by accretion from a rotating solar cloud of gas and finely-dispersed dust. If the Sun were originally attended by such a cloud, this cloud would, over a sufficiently long period of time, become a flat disk.

If random concentration had become sufficiently massive, it would draw in extra material by virtue of its gravitational attraction. When the Sun began to radiate strongly, part of the mass of each proto-planet would be driven off due to the high temperatures, leaving a solar system of the kind that exists today.

The fact that such an evolutionary sequence can be traced emphasizes that in talking about the origin of the Earth we are considering only a small part of a continuous story. What will become of the Earth in the far future? The Sun is radiating energy because of the nuclear process within it: hydrogen is being converted into helium causing mass to be lost with a resulting release of energy. However, when the supply of hydrogen begins to run low, the Sun must change radically. It will move towards a red giant stage swelling and engulfing the Earth. Fortunately, this will not happen for at least another 6000 million years, but eventually the Sun which sustains our planet will finally destroy it.

Alternative theories

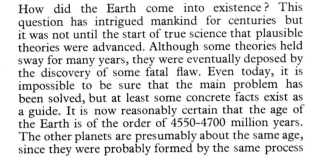

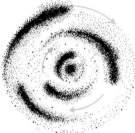

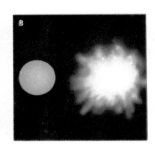

Contracting nebula *above* Laplace suggested that a contracting nebula might shed gas which then condensed.

Tidal theories *above* In 1901 Sir James Jeans postulated that Sun A was attracted to

another star B which passed at close range. A cloud of matter was drawn off by their gravitational

attraction. Star B moved on while the cloud condensed to form planets circling our Sun at C.

A violent beginning *above* One of the theories of how the solar system came to be formed assumes that the Sun

once had a binary companion star. This exploded as a supernova (above) and was blown off as a white dwarf

15 By now all the inner planets will have long since been destroyed. The Sun will become unstable, reaching the most violent stage of its career as a red giant, with a vast, relatively cool surface and an intensely hot, dense core.

14 When the center of the Sun has reached another critical temperature, the helium will begin to 'burn' giving the so-called 'helium flash'. After a temporary contraction the Sun will then swell out to a diameter 400 times that at present.

16 As the 'fuel' runs out, the radiation pressure falls, and under internal gravity the Sun will collapse inwards changing in only 50000 years from a red giant into a super-dense white dwarf.

17 As a white dwarf, the Sun will continue to radiate feebly for an immense period. At last all radiation must cease, and the Sun will remain as a dead, dark globe - a black dwarf.

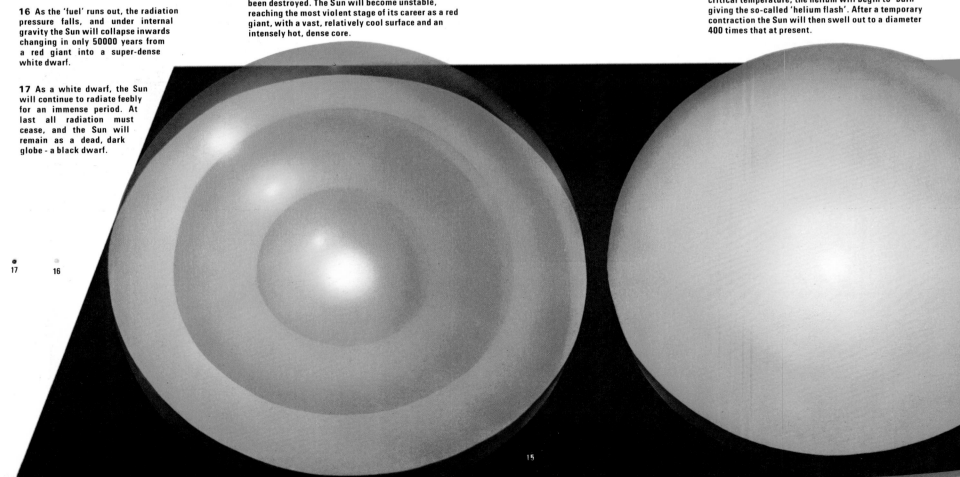

5 The Sun, still contracting, continues to radiate because of gravitational effects. More and more of the solar cloud collects into the condensations.

6 The Sun, surrounded by a system of regularly-shaped proto-planets, shrinks to about its present size, though its surface is only half as bright.

7 By now the solar system becomes recognizable, though the Sun is still orange and slowly contracting. Much of the material in the solar cloud has been absorbed.

8 The core of the Sun reaches the critical temperature to start the nuclear reaction that converts hydrogen into helium. There are relatively few proto-planets left.

9 As the Sun settles down to a period of stable radiation, the proto-planets assume a spherical shape. The four largest, Jupiter, Saturn, Uranus and Neptune, are over 400 million miles from the Sun.

Birth of the solar system

60000 million years Sun as a black dwarf

Outer planets

4500 million years Conditions on Earth favourable to life

Sun consumes inner planets

Sun as white dwarf

Timescale of the solar system *above*
Taking the vertical 12 o'clock position as the time when the Sun and solar system were created (illustration 1 in the main sequence, above left) the present time appears at about the 1 o'clock position. By half-past two the Sun will flare up and consume its inner planets, thereafter dying a slow death.

10 The solar system today is made up of the Sun (which is the central remnant of the original cloud), the nine principal planets, of which four are giants, and various smaller bodies. The Sun's rate of rotation has been considerably reduced, and the interplanetary material is largely restricted to the main plane of the system.

star (above), leaving behind a cloud of fragments. These then coalesced into the planets as we know

them today, having organized themselves into heliocentric orbits (above). Few subscribe to this theory now.

13 The expansion of the Sun will continue, with the hydrogen-burning region approaching the surface. After another 600 million years, the Sun will be fifty times its present diameter. It will have become a red giant, engulfing the inner planets, including Earth.

11 When the supply of hydrogen at the Sun's core runs low, as will happen in perhaps 6000 million years, the region of the hydrogen-burning will move out towards the surface. The Sun will become larger, with a lower surface temperature but greater output.

12 The change in the Sun will continue as the hydrogen-burning region inside its globe moves farther and farther away from the core. The overall increase in energy output will raise the temperatures of the planets considerably, and the inner planets will become intolerably hot.

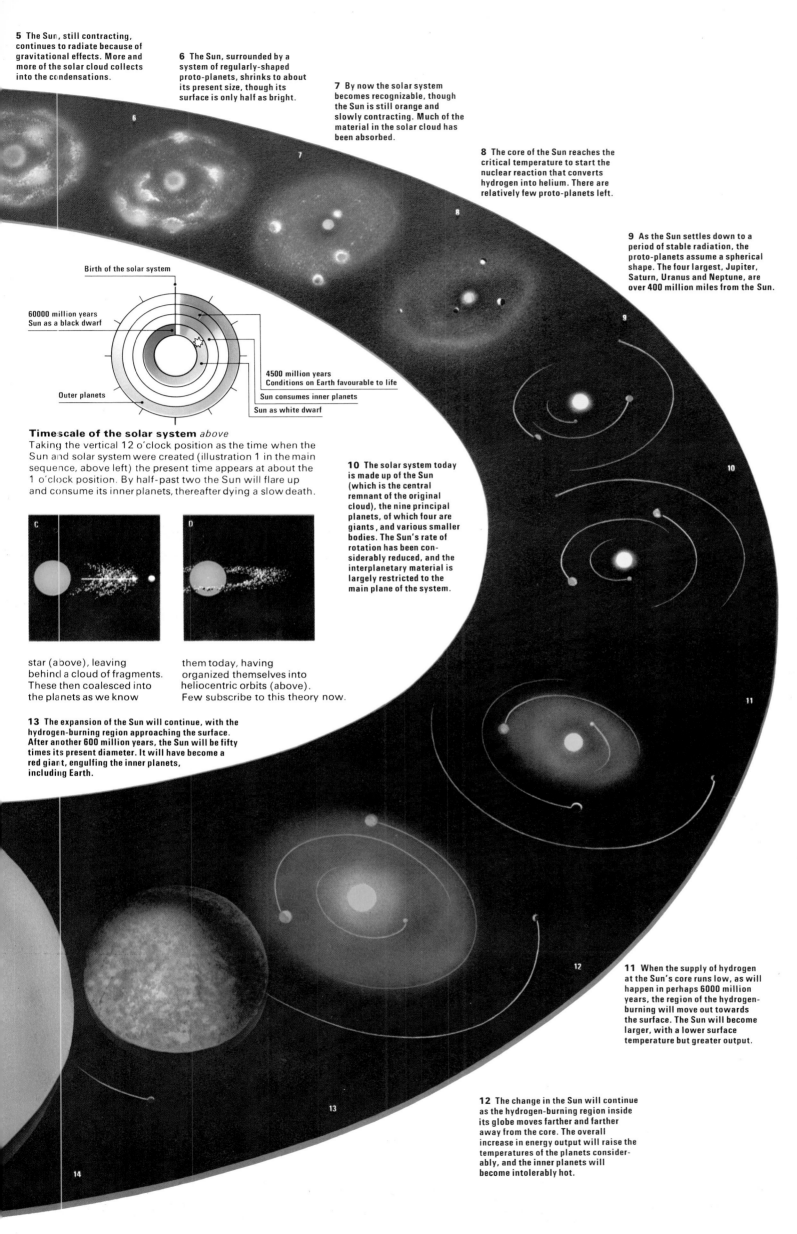

The lifespan of the Earth

The Earth was produced from the solar cloud (1-6 on main diagram). It had no regular form, but, as more and more material was drawn in, it began to assume a spherical shape (7-8).

When it had reached its present size (9), the Earth had a dense atmosphere; not the original hydrogen atmosphere but one produced by gas from the interior. Life had not started.

The Earth today (10), moving in a stable orbit, has an equable temperature and oxygen-rich atmosphere, so that it alone of all the planets in the solar system is suitable for life.

When the Sun nears the red giant stage (11-13), the Earth will be heated to an intolerable degree. The atmosphere will be driven off, the oceans will boil and life must come to an end.

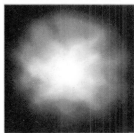

As the Sun reaches the peak of its violence (14-15), it will swell out until the Earth is engulfed. Its natural life is probably no more than 8000 million years; its end is certain

The Solar System

The Sun is the controlling body of the solar system and is far more massive than all its planets combined. Even Jupiter, much the largest of the planets, has a diameter only about one-tenth that of the Sun. The solar system is divided into two main parts. The inner region includes four relatively small, solid planets: Mercury, Venus, the Earth and Mars. Beyond the orbit of Mars comes a wide gap in which move many thousands of small minor planets or asteroids, some of which are little more than rocks. Further out come the four giants: Jupiter, Saturn, Uranus and Neptune. Pluto, on the fringe of the system, is a curious little planet; it appears to be in a class of its own, but at present very little is known about it and even its size is a matter for conjecture. Maps of the solar system can be misleading in that they tend to give a false idea about distance. The outer planets are very widely separated. For example, Saturn is further away from Uranus than it is from the Earth.

The contrasting planets

The inner, or terrestrial, planets have some points in common, but a greater number of differences. Mercury, the planet closest to the Sun, has no atmosphere and that of Mars is very thin; but Venus, strikingly similar to the Earth in size and mass, has a dense atmosphere made up chiefly of carbon dioxide, and a surface temperature of over 400°C. The giant planets are entirely different. At least in their outer layers they are made up of gas, like a star; but, unlike a star, they have no light of their own, and shine only by reflecting the light of their star, the Sun. Several of the planets have moons. The Earth has one (or it may be our partner in a binary system), Jupiter has 14, Saturn 10 (discounting its rings), Uranus five and Neptune two. Mars also has two satellites, but these are less than 15 miles (24 km) in diameter and of a different type from the Earth's Moon. The Earth is unique in the solar system in having oceans on its surface and an atmosphere made up chiefly of nitrogen and oxygen. It is the only planet suited to life of terrestrial type. It is not now believed that life can exist on any other planet in the Sun's family, though it is still possible that some primitive vegetation may grow on Mars.

Observing the planets

Five of the planets, Mercury, Venus, Mars, Jupiter and Saturn, were known to the inhabitants of the Earth in very ancient times. They are starlike in aspect but easy to distinguish because, unlike the stars, they seem to wander slowly about the sky whereas the true stars appear to hold their position for century after century. The so-called proper motions of the stars are too slight to be noticed by the naked eye, but they can be measured by modern techniques. Mercury and Venus always appear to be in the same part of the sky as the Sun. Mercury is never prominent but Venus is dazzlingly bright, partly because its upper clouds are highly reflective and partly because it is close; it can come within 25,000,000 mi (40,000,000 km), only about 100 times as far as the Moon. Jupiter is generally very bright, as is Mars when it is well placed. Saturn is also conspicuous to the naked eye, but Uranus is only just visible and Neptune and Pluto are much fainter.

The Sun's active surface *right*

The structure of a star, such as the Sun, is immensely complex. The very concept of its surface is hard to define, and the size of the Sun depends on the wavelength of the light with which it is viewed. Using the 'hydrogen alpha' wavelength the bright surface of the Sun, known as the photosphere, appears as shown right. The surface, at about 6000 °C, is dotted with light and dark patches as a result of the violent upcurrents of hotter gas and cooler areas between them. Larger, darker regions are sunspots (right), temporary but very large disturbances.

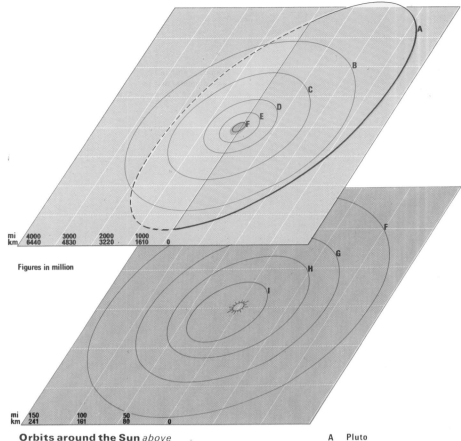

Orbits around the Sun *above*
The Sun's nine known planets, and the asteroids, describe heliocentric orbits in the same direction. But some planetary orbits are highly eccentric, while some asteroids are both eccentric and steeply inclined. The outermost planet, Pluto, passes within the orbit of Neptune, while one asteroid reaches almost to the radius of Saturn. Over 350 years ago Johannes Kepler showed that the planets do not move in perfect circles, and found that the line joining each planet to the Sun sweeps out a constant area in a given time so that speed is greatest close to the Sun.

Figures in million

A	Pluto
B	Neptune
C	Uranus
D	Saturn
E	Jupiter
F	Mars
G	Earth
H	Venus
I	Mercury

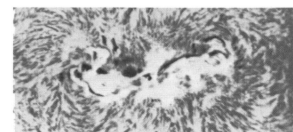

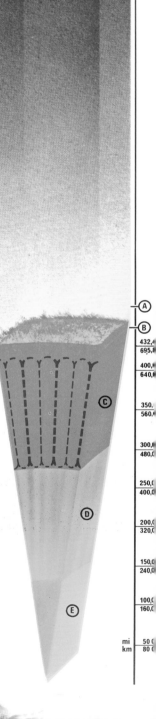

The Sun's structure *right*
The Sun is made up of highly dissimilar regions. This narrow sector includes the inner part of the corona (A) which, though very diffuse, has a temperature of some 1,000,000 °C. Into it leap solar prominences, 'flames' thousands of miles long which arch along the local magnetic field from the chromosphere (B), the outer layer of the Sun proper, which covers the visible photosphere with a layer of variable, highly mobile and rarefied gas about 6000 mi (10000 km) thick. Inside the Sun the outer layer (C) of gas is in constant movement and transfers heat from the interior. Inner region D is thought to transfer energy mainly by radiation. The innermost zone of all (E), the conditions of which can only be surmised but are thought to include a temperature of some 14,000,000 °C, sustains the energy of the Sun (and its planets) by continuous fusion of hydrogen into helium.

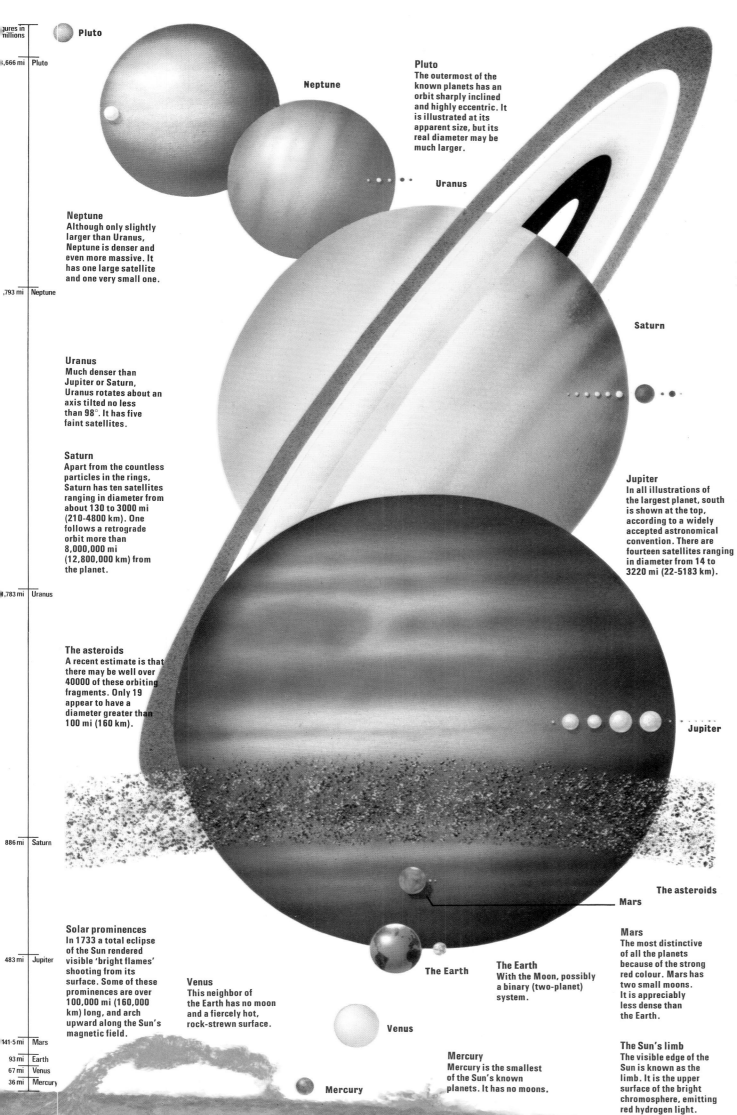

Pluto

Pluto
The outermost of the known planets has an orbit sharply inclined and highly eccentric. It is illustrated at its apparent size, but its real diameter may be much larger.

Neptune

Uranus

Neptune
Although only slightly larger than Uranus, Neptune is denser and even more massive. It has one large satellite and one very small one.

Saturn

Uranus
Much denser than Jupiter or Saturn, Uranus rotates about an axis tilted no less than 98°. It has five faint satellites.

Saturn
Apart from the countless particles in the rings, Saturn has ten satellites ranging in diameter from about 130 to 3000 mi (210-4800 km). One follows a retrograde orbit more than 8,000,000 mi (12,800,000 km) from the planet.

Jupiter
In all illustrations of the largest planet, south is shown at the top, according to a widely accepted astronomical convention. There are fourteen satellites ranging in diameter from 14 to 3220 mi (22-5183 km).

The asteroids
A recent estimate is that there may be well over 40000 of these orbiting fragments. Only 19 appear to have a diameter greater than 100 mi (160 km).

Jupiter

The asteroids

Mars

Solar prominences
In 1733 a total eclipse of the Sun rendered visible 'bright flames' shooting from its surface. Some of these prominences are over 100,000 mi (160,000 km) long, and arch upward along the Sun's magnetic field.

Venus
This neighbor of the Earth has no moon and a fiercely hot, rock-strewn surface.

Venus

The Earth
With the Moon, possibly a binary (two-planet) system.

The Earth

Mars
The most distinctive of all the planets because of the strong red colour. Mars has two small moons. It is appreciably less dense than the Earth.

Mercury
Mercury is the smallest of the Sun's known planets. It has no moons.

Mercury

The Sun's limb
The visible edge of the Sun is known as the limb. It is the upper surface of the bright chromosphere, emitting red hydrogen light.

The solar system *left*
The Sun is the major body in the solar system. It lies 30000 light-years from the center of our galaxy and takes 225 million years to complete one journey around it. There are nine planets and their satellites in the system, as well as comets and various minor bodies such as meteoroids. The diagram on the left shows the upper limb of the Sun (bottom) and the main constituent members of the solar system very greatly condensed into a smaller space. To indicate the amount of the radial compression, the limb of the Sun is drawn for a near-sphere of 5 ft (1.52 m) diameter. On this scale the Earth would be about 420 ft (127 m) away and the outermost planet Pluto, no less than 3 mi (4.9 km) distant.

Pluto, discovered in 1930, has a very eccentric orbit, with a radius varying between 2766 and 4566 million mi (4500 and 7400 million kilometers). Being so far from the Sun, it is extremely cold, and probably has no atmosphere.

Neptune, discovered in 1846, has a diameter of 31500 mi (50700 km) and is made up of gas, although little is known of its interior. It orbits the Sun once in 164¾ years. Seen through binoculars it is a small bluish disk.

Uranus, discovered in 1781, is apparently similar to Neptune, but less massive. Although faintly visible to the naked eye, even large telescopes show little detail upon its greenish surface.

Saturn is the second largest planet, its equatorial diameter being 75100 mi (122,300 km). Visually it is unlike any other heavenly body, because of its equatorial system of rings made up of particles of various sizes. The planet itself is less dense than water and at least its outer layers are gaseous.

Jupiter, the largest planet, has an equatorial diameter of 88700 mi (142,750 km), but its rapid spin, once every 9¾ hours, makes it very flattened at the poles. It appears to have cloud belts, possibly of liquid ammonia, and various spots, of which the great red spot seems to be semi-permanent.

The asteroids, a mass of apparent planetary material ranging in size from dust up to one lump about as large as the British Isles, orbit mainly between Mars and Jupiter, though some have eccentric orbits which approach the Earth.

Mars is about 4200 mi (6760 km) in diameter. It has a thin atmosphere, mainly of carbon dioxide, and its surface is pitted with Moon-like craters. It is not thought today that the planet contains any life.

The Earth/Moon system is today regarded as a double planet rather than a planet and satellite. The Moon has an average distance from Earth of 239,000 mi (385,000 km) and it is now known that it has never contained life.

Venus is almost the twin of the Earth in size and mass. It is too hot to contain life, and its very dense atmosphere is mainly carbon dioxide. It has a 'year' of 224¾ Earth days, and it spins on its axis once every 243 Earth days.

Mercury, the innermost planet, is only about 3000 mi (4800 km) in diameter, and has lost whatever atmosphere it had. Like Venus it shows phases, but it is always close to the Sun when viewed from the Earth and cannot be seen clearly.

gures in
millions

,666 mi | Pluto

,793 mi | Neptune

M mi | Uranus

886 mi | Saturn

483 mi | Jupiter

141·5 mi | Mars
93 mi | Earth
67 mi | Venus
36 mi | Mercury

,783 mi | Uranus

Earth's Companion: The Moon

The Moon is our companion in space. Its mean distance from the Earth is less than a quarter of a million miles – it varies between 221,460 miles (356,410 km) and 252,700 miles (406,685 km) – and it was the first world other than our Earth to come within the range of man's space probes. At first mere masses, these then became instrument packages and finally spacecraft carrying men. With their aid our knowledge of the Moon has been vastly increased in the past decade. Astronauts Neil Armstrong and Edwin Aldrin made the first human journey to the lunar surface in July 1969, and the Moon has since been subjected to detailed and direct investigation.

The mean diameter of the Moon is 2158 miles (3473 km), and its mass is 1/81st as much as that of the Earth. Despite this wide difference the ratio is much less than that between other planets and their moons, and the Earth/Moon system is now widely regarded as a double planet rather than as a planet and satellite. The Moon's mean density is less than that of the Earth, and it may lack a comparable heavy core. Escape velocity from the lunar surface is only 1.5 mi/sec (2.4 km/sec), and this is so low that the Moon has lost any atmosphere it may once have had. To Earth life it is therefore an extremely hostile world. Analysis of lunar rock brought back to Earth laboratories and investigated by Soviet probes on the Moon has so far revealed no trace of any life. The Moon appears to have always been sterile.

Much of the surface of the Moon comprises large grey plains, mis-called 'mare' (seas), but most of it is extremely rough. There are great ranges of mountains, isolated peaks and countless craters which range from tiny pits up to vast enclosures more than 150 miles (240 km) in diameter. Many of the craters have central mountains or mountain-groups. Some of the larger craters show signs of having been produced by volcanic action, while others appear to have resulted from the impacts of meteorites.

The Moon rotates slowly, performing one complete turn on its axis every 27.3 days. This is the same as its period of revolution around the Earth, so it always presents the same face to us. But in October 1959 the Soviet probe *Lunik 3* photographed the hidden rear hemisphere and it has since been mapped in detail. It contains no large 'seas'. The appearance of the lunar surface depends strongly on the angle at which it is viewed and the direction of solar illumination. In the photograph on the right, taken from a height of about 70 miles (115 km) with the Earth having once more come into full view ahead, the lunar surface looks deceptively smooth; in fact, there is practically no level ground anywhere in the field of vision. The lunar horizon is always sharply defined, because there is no atmosphere to cause blurring or distortion. For the same reason, the sky seen from the Moon is always jet black.

Full Moon *below*
This striking photograph was taken by the *Apollo 11* astronauts in July 1969. It shows parts of both the Earth-turned and far hemispheres. The dark plain near the center is the Mare Crisium.

Earthrise *above*
This view of the Earth rising was visible to the crew of
Apollo 10 in May 1969 as they orbited the Moon 70 miles
(115 km) above the surface. They had just come round
from the Moon's rear hemisphere.

Eclipses

Once regarded as terrifying actions of angry gods,
eclipses are today merely useful. They provide a
different view of the Sun and Moon that opens up
fresh information. In a lunar eclipse the Earth passes
directly between the Sun and Moon; in a solar eclipse
the Moon passes between Sun and Earth. Both the
Earth and Moon constantly cast a shadow comprising
a dark inner cone surrounded by a region to which
part of the sunlight penetrates. A body passing
through the outer shadow experiences a partial
eclipse, while the inner cone causes a total eclipse in
which all direct sunlight is cut off.

A total solar eclipse is magnificent. The bright star
is blocked out by a black Moon, but around it the
Sun's atmosphere flashes into view. The pearly
corona of thin gas can be seen extending a million
miles from the Sun. Closer to the surface huge
'prominences' of red hydrogen leap into space and
curve back along the solar magnetic field. In a partial
solar eclipse these things cannot be seen, while in a
total eclipse caused by the Moon at its greatest
distance from Earth a ring of the Sun is left visible.
As the Moon's orbit is not in the same plane as the
Earth's, total solar eclipses occur very rarely, on
occasions when the tip of the Moon's dark shadow
crosses the Earth as a spot 169 miles (272 km) wide.

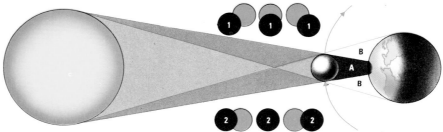

Eclipses *left and below*
When the Moon passes in
front of the Sun as in
sequence 1 its shadow B
causes a partial solar
eclipse (below, left, taken
21 November 1966).
But in the case of sequence
2, shadow cone A gives a
total eclipse (below, right,
15 February 1961).

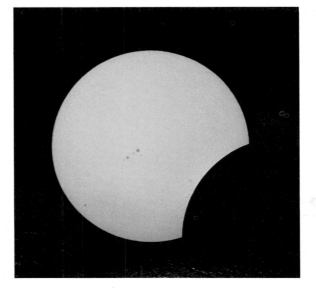

Anatomy of the Earth

A fundamental mystery that still confronts science even today is the detailed internal structure of the planet on which we live. Although Jules Verne's intrepid Professor Otto Lindenbrock was able to journey to the center of the Earth, this is one scientific fantasy that will never be achieved. The deepest boreholes and mines do little more than scratch the surface and so, deprived of direct observation, the geologist is forced to rely almost entirely on indirect evidence (pages 16-17) to construct his picture of the Earth's anatomy. In spite of these drawbacks, he can outline with some confidence the story of the planet's development from the time of its formation as a separate body in space some 4550 million years ago.

Since that time the Earth has been continuously evolving. The crust, mantle and inner core developed during its first 1000 million years, but there is only scant evidence of how they did so. Probably the original homogenous mass then partly or completely melted, whereupon gravitational attraction caused the densest material to form a part-liquid, part-solid central core overlaid by the less dense mantle. The extremely thin outermost layer of 'scum' began to form at an early stage and as long ago as 3500 million years parts of it had reached almost their present state. But most of the crust evolved in a complex way through long-term cyclic changes spanning immense periods of time. The evidence of today's rocks can be interpreted in different ways; for example, the core, mantle and crust could have separated out quickly at an early stage or gradually over a longer period.

Today's restless Earth

Many of the changes which have taken place in the Earth's structure and form have been very gradual. For example, although it may well be that our planet has been getting larger (as illustrated below), the rate of increase in radius has been no more rapid than $2\frac{1}{2}$ inches (65 mm) per century. But this does not alter the fact that the Earth is very far from being a mere inert sphere of matter. Although it is not possible faithfully to portray it, almost the whole globe is at brilliant white heat. If the main drawing were true to life it would contain no color except for a thin band, about as thick as cardboard, around the outer crust in which the color would change from white through yellow and orange to red. With such high temperatures the interior of the Earth is able to flow under the influence of relatively small differences in density and stress. The result is to set up convection currents which are now believed to be the main driving force behind the formation of mountain ranges and the drifting apart of continents. But the fact remains that our knowledge of the interior of our planet is derived almost entirely from indirect evidence, such as the passage of earthquake shock waves through the mantle (see page 17). Direct exploration is confined to the surface and to boreholes which so far have never penetrated more than five miles (8 km) into the crust. It is difficult to imagine how man could ever devise experiments that would greatly enhance and refine his knowledge of the Earth's interior. Indeed, he knows as much about the Moon and other much more distant heavenly bodies as he does about the Earth below a depth of a mere 20 miles (32 km).

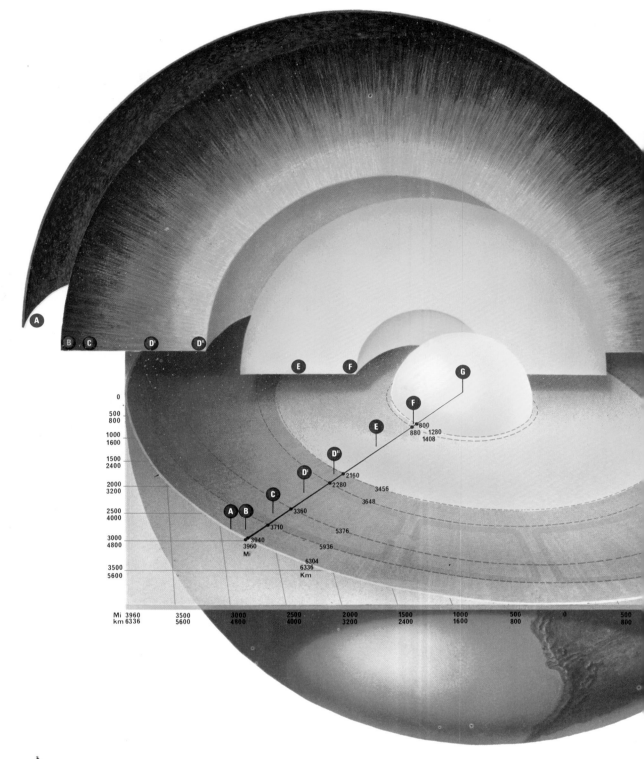

The crust (A)
This varies in thickness from 25 miles (40 km) in continental regions, where it is largely granitic, to 3 miles (5 km) under the oceans, where it is basaltic.

The upper mantle (B, C)
From the crust down to 375 miles (600 km), this layer is divided into upper and lower zones with differing P wave speeds (see page 17).

The lower mantle (D¹, D²)
Made of peridotite, as is the upper mantle, this zone extends down to a depth of 1800 miles (2900 km). P wave speeds increase still further.

The outer core (E, F)
Largely iron and nickel, this molten zone reaches to 2900 miles (4700 km). Dynamo action of convection currents may cause the Earth's magnetic field.

Not a true sphere *below*
The Earth's shape is controlled by equilibrium between inward gravitational attraction and outward centrifugal force. This results in the average radius at the equator of 3963 miles (6378 km) slightly exceeding that at the poles of 3950 miles (6356 km).

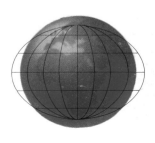

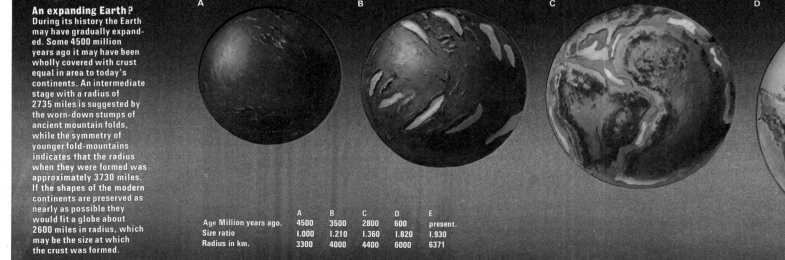

An expanding Earth?
During its history the Earth may have gradually expanded. Some 4500 million years ago it may have been wholly covered with crust equal in area to today's continents. An intermediate stage with a radius of 2735 miles is suggested by the worn-down stumps of ancient mountain folds, while the symmetry of younger fold-mountains indicates that the radius when they were formed was approximately 3730 miles. If the shapes of the modern continents are preserved as nearly as possible they would fit a globe about 2600 miles in radius, which may be the size at which the crust was formed.

	A	B	C	D	E
Age Million years ago.	4500	3500	2800	600	present.
Size ratio	1.000	1.210	1.360	1.820	1.930
Radius in km.	3300	4000	4400	6000	6371

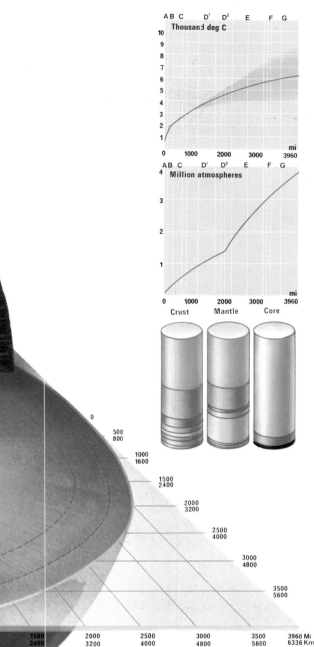

Temperature *left*
Temperature inside the Earth increases with depth, initially at a rate of 48°C per mile (30°C/km) so that 60 miles (100 km) down it is white hot. The rate of increase then falls, and the shaded area indicates how uncertain is man's knowledge of great depths.

Pressure *left*
This likewise increases with depth. Only 200 miles (320 km) down it reaches 100,000 atmospheres, 1200 times the pressure at the deepest point in the ocean. A change of state at the discontinuity between the mantle and core shows as a kink on the graph.

O₂	OXYGEN
Si	SILICON
Al	ALUMINUM
Fe	IRON
Ni	NICKEL
Co	COBALT
Mg	MAGNESIUM
Ca	CALCIUM
Na	SODIUM
K	POTASSIUM

Chemical composition *above*
The crust is made of mainly light elements and has relatively low density. Towards the base of the crust the composition is probably richer in iron and magnesium. The mantle is composed of heavier elements and the core is probably of iron and nickel.

The inner core (G)
The pressure of 3½ million atmospheres (35000 kg/mm²) keeps this a solid ball of 750 miles (1200 km) radius. Its density varies from 14 to about 16.

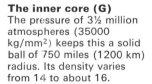

Density *left*
Virtually all man's knowledge of the interior of the Earth stems from measuring the transit of earthquake waves. The resulting data indicate sharp increases in density at the boundaries of both the outer core and the 'solid' inner core, with several intermediate zones.

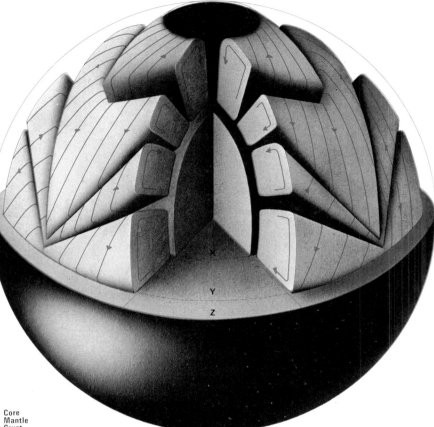

Convection currents
The fundamental pattern of movement in the mantle (A) is modified by the Earth's rotation (B) and also by friction between adjacent cells as shown in the main figure, below, in which core (X) and mantle (Y) are shown but crust (Z) is removed.

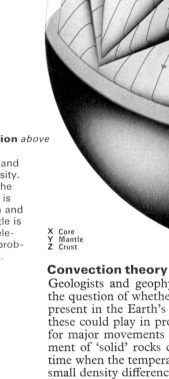

X Core
Y Mantle
Z Crust

Convection theory

Geologists and geophysicists are not unanimous on the question of whether there are convection currents present in the Earth's mantle or not, nor on the part these could play in providing the driving mechanism for major movements of the continents. Slow movement of 'solid' rocks can occur over long periods of time when the temperature is high and only relatively small density differences would be required to trigger them. Another matter for debate is whether convection is confined to the upper mantle or is continuous throughout the whole. It is not certain whether changes of physical state at different levels would constitute barriers to mantle-wide convection. The convection cells above are highly schematic but could largely explain the formation of some of the major geosynclinal fold mountains in the crust over the past thousand million years. Large-scale convection current systems in the mantle could also be the driving force for sea floor spreading and the associated continental drift.

The watery Earth *below*
Almost three-quarters of the Earth is covered by water. Basically the continents are rafts of relatively light crust 'floating' on generally denser oceanic crust. They comprise not only the visible land but also the adjacent continental shelves covered by shallow water. Oceanic crust underlies the deep sea platforms and ocean trenches. The areas of the major lands and seas (below, left) do not take into account the continental shelves but are the gross areas reckoned in terms of the land and water distribution at mean sea level. Extra area due to terrain is not included.

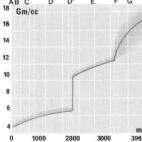

The watery Earth *right*
Key to numbered areas.

	Area (x 1000)	
Oceans	Sq mi	km²
1 Arctic	5541	14350
2 Pacific	63986	165750
3 Atlantic	31530	81660
4 Indian	28350	73430
Continents		
5 Americas	16241	42063
6 Europe (excluding USSR)	1903	4929
7 Asia (excluding USSR)	10661	27611
8 USSR	8649	22402
9 Africa	11683	30258
10 Oceania	3286	8510
11 Antarctica	5500	14245

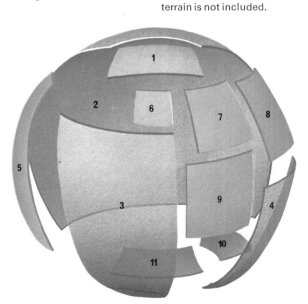

The Active Earth

Man's most powerful nuclear weapons pale into insignificance beside the violence of an earthquake or the destructive and indiscriminate force of a volcano. These cataclysmic phenomena frequently occur along the same belts of instability in the Earth's crust and are often only different manifestations of the same fundamental processes. About 800 volcanoes are known to have been active in historical times, and many are extremely active today. All the mid-ocean ridges are volcanic in origin, and many underwater eruptions occur along these submarine mountain ranges. Spectacular volcanic eruptions sometimes break the ocean surface, such as during the formation in 1963 of the island of Surtsey, south of Iceland (photograph, right). Some islands, such as Iceland itself, are the products of continued outpourings of lava along the crest of the mid-ocean ridge.

Oceanic earthquakes caused by sudden sea-floor displacements may result in tsunamis or giant sea waves. About 80 per cent of the shallow earthquakes and almost all deep ones take place along the belt around the Pacific. Clear evidence of the large scale movements of the mantle are provided by the zones within which earthquake shocks are generated along some Pacific island arc systems. These zones plunge down from sea-floor level to depths of 440 miles (700 km) beneath the adjacent continents and mark the positions of downward flow of the mantle convection currents (page 15). The corresponding upwelling regions lie along the mid-ocean ridges, where new basic volcanic material is continually being added to the ocean crust as outward movement takes place away from the ridges.

These sea-floor spreading movements act as 'conveyor belts' for the continents, and constitute the basic mechanism for the large displacements involved in continental drifting. Geological data confirm the former close fits of the margins of the reassembled continental jig-saw puzzle, and also corroborate the detailed paleomagnetic evidence visible in today's rocks of the movements of the continents relative to the geographic poles.

Geysers
Ground water and mud heated by volcanic activity can lie on the surface as puddles and hot springs, rendered colorful by dissolved minerals, or be pumped out in the form of geysers. The latter are connected to extensive underground reservoirs in which steam pressure builds up above the hot water. Intermittently the system discharges high into the air.

Fissure eruption
In this type of eruption freely flowing molten basaltic material exudes from apertures forced in the crust. The surface crack may be several miles in length and the more or less horizontal flow has on occasion covered more than 200 square miles (500 km^2).

Hawaiian-type eruption
In this case large, shallow cones, often containing lakes of molten lava, generally release gas and vapor in a relatively passive way. But sometimes glowing lava is expelled as a fine spray which in a high wind can be drawn out into fine threads called Pelée's hair.

Emissions
Incandescent lava issues from the main cone or from side vents, while dense vapors pour from every crevice. Water vapor is the main gaseous component, but nitrogen and sulphur dioxide are also important.

Layering
Most volcanoes have a history extending back thousands or even millions of years. Over this time the main cone has built up in many stratified layers, sometimes of contrasting types of lava. Each fresh eruption produces at least one additional layer.

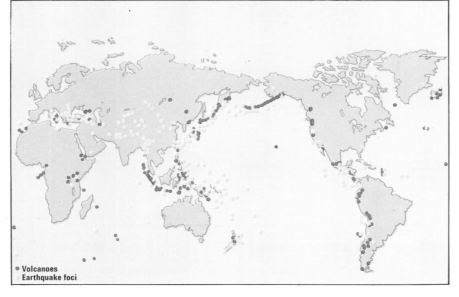

Underground water
Heated beyond normal boiling point, the pressurized water issues in a rush when pressure is relieved.

Magma chamber
Underlying every volcano is a volume of intensely hot fluid under high pressure.

Laccolith
Above the pipes and sills of the hot magma lies a giant lens-shaped intrusion of cold rock.

Metamorphic rock
The strata adjacent to the fiery magma are physically and chemically altered by the heat.

Where the Earth seems active *right*
Although we live on a white-hot globe with a thin cool crust, the fierce heat and energy of the interior is manifest only along fairly clearly defined belts. Around the Pacific, volcanoes and earthquakes are frequent. Another belt traverses the mountains from southeast Asia through the Middle East to the Mediterranean. Every site is an external expression of activity within the crust and upper mantle. The underlying cause is a slow flowing of the rocks of the mantle in response to changes in temperature and density.

• Volcanoes
• Earthquake foci

Types of eruption *above*
Volcanic cones differ in both shape and activity. The Strombolian (1) erupts every few minutes or hours; the Peléan form (2) gives a hot avalanche; the Vesuvian (3) is a fierce upward expulsion, while the Plinian (4) is the extreme form.

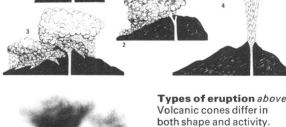

A caldera *left*
Expulsion of lava (A) from the magma chamber (B) may leave the central core (C) without support. A collapse results in a large, steep-sided caldera (D). The magma chamber may cool and solidify (E), and water may collect inside the caldera (F).

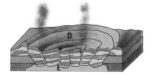

Earthquake *right*

Along lines of potential movement, such as fault planes, stresses may build up over many years until the breaking strength of some part of the rock is exceeded (A). A sudden break occurs and the two sides of the fault line move, generating shock-waves which travel outward in all directions from the focus at the point of rupture (B). The point on the surface directly above the focus is the epicenter (C). While the fault movement reaches its fullest extent, the shockwaves reach the surface (D). Far right the aftermath of an earthquake.

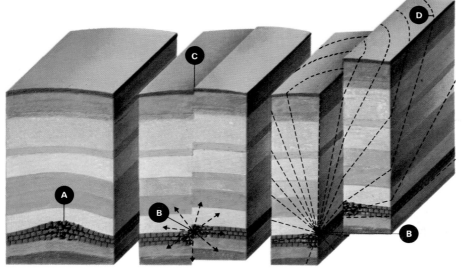

Destructive waves *right*

The Japanese, who have suffered severely from them, have given the name tsunami to the terrifying waves which follow earthquakes. Their character depends on the cause. In the case of a sudden rift and slump in the ocean bed (A) the wave at the surface is initially a trough, which travels away to both sides followed by a crest and subsequent smaller waves (B). A fault causing a sudden changed level of sea bed (C) can generate a tsunami that starts with a crest (D). Travelling at 400 miles (650 km) per hour or more the tsunami arrives at a beach as a series of waves up to 200 feet (60 m) high (E), the 'trough first' variety being heralded by a sudden withdrawal of the ocean from the shore. Warning stations ring the Pacific (far right) and the concentric rings show tsunamic travel time from an earthquake site to Hawaii at the center.

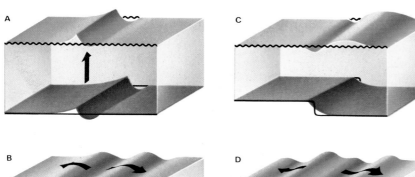

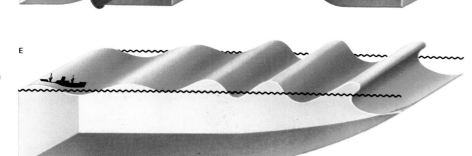

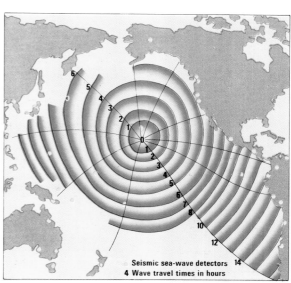

Seismic sea-wave detectors
4 Wave travel times in hours

Tsunami warning *above*

Numerous seismographic warning stations around the earthquake belt of the Pacific Ocean maintain a continuous alert for earthquake shocks and for the tsunami waves that may follow it. Possible recipients of such waves plot a series of concentric rings, such as these centered on the Hawaiian Islands, which show the time in hours that would be taken for a tsunami to travel from any earthquake epicenter. Aircraft and satellites are increasingly helping to create a globally integrated life-saving system.

Seismic waves *right*

An earthquake caused by a sudden movement in the crust at the focus (A) sends out a pattern of shock waves radiating like ripples in a pond. These waves are of three kinds. Primary (P) waves (full lines) vibrate in the direction of propagation, and thus are a rapid succession of high and low pressures. Secondary (S) waves (broken lines), which travel only 60 per cent as fast, shake from side to side. Long waves (L) travel round the crust. In a belt around the world only waves of the L-type occur, giving rise to the concept of a shadow zone (B and shaded belt in inset at lower right). But intermittent records of P waves in this zone led seismologists to the belief that the Earth must have a very dense fluid core (D, lower drawing) capable of strongly refracting P waves like a lens. Seismic waves are almost man's only source of knowledge about the Earth's interior.

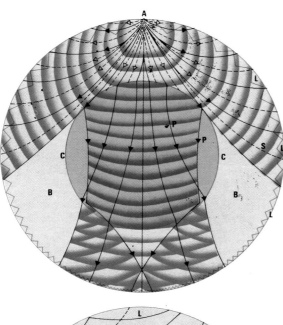

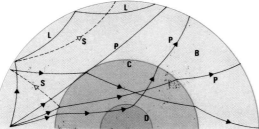

Seismology *right*

Seismic waves of all three types (P, S and L) are detected and recorded by seismographs. Usually these contain a sprung mass which, when an earthquake shock passes, stays still while the rest of the instrument moves. Some seismographs detect horizontal waves (A) while others detect vertical ones (B). The pen in the instrument leaves a distinctive trace (P-S-L). P (primary) waves are a succession of rarefactions and compressions, denoted by the packing of the dots; S (secondary) waves are a sideways shaking, shown here in plan view.

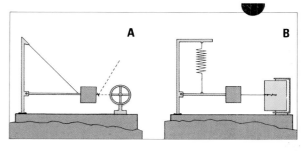

P. waves (longitudinal)

← Rarefaction   Compression

Direction of travel →

S. waves (transverse)

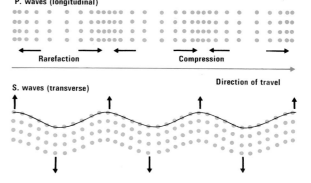

17

The Evolution of Land and Sea

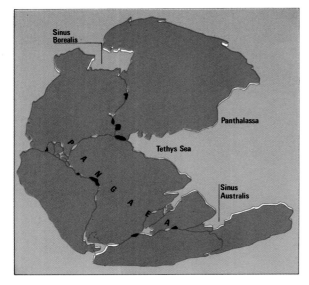

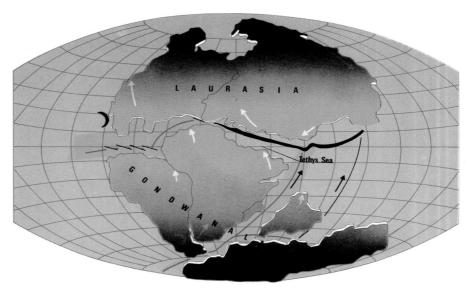

180 million years ago
At this time the original Pangaea land mass had just begun to break up. The continents first split along the lines of the North Atlantic and Indian Oceans. North America separated from Africa and so did India and Antarctica. The Tethys Sea, between Africa and Asia, closed somewhat, and the super continents of Laurasia to the north and Gondwanaland to the south became almost completely separated. In effect the Earth possessed three super landmasses, plus an India that had already begun to move strongly northward.

Pangaea *above*
About 200 million years ago there was only a single land mass on Earth, named Pangaea. The map shows how today's continents can be fitted together, with the aid of a computer, at the edge of the continental shelf at a depth of 1000 fathoms (6000 ft, 1830 m).

Although land and water first appeared on the Earth's surface several thousand million years before anyone could be there to watch, modern man has a very good idea of how it came about. The Earth's gravitational field caused the lighter, more volatile elements gradually to move outwards through the mantle and form a solid crust on the surface. By far the largest proportion of material newly added to the crust is basaltic volcanic rock derived from partial melting of the mantle beneath; in fact the oceanic crust which underlies the Earth's great water areas is made of almost nothing else. So the earliest crust to form was probably volcanic and of basaltic composition.

Air and water appear
The earliest records of the existence of an atmosphere of air and a hydrosphere of water are to be found in sediments laid down some 3300 million years ago from the residue of erosion of previously existing rocks. These sediments could not have been formed without atmospheric weathering, water transport and water deposition. The atmosphere was probably originally similar to the fumes which today issue from volcanoes and hot springs and which are about three-quarters water vapor. Once formed, the primitive atmosphere and oceans could erode the crust to produce vast layers of sediments of new chemical compositions. Gradually the oceans deepened and the land took on a more varied form. Convection in the mantle produced mountain ranges which in turn eroded to generate new sedimentary rocks. The ceaseless cycles of growth and decay had started, causing continually changing patterns of seas, mountains and plains. And in the past few years man has discovered how the continents and oceans have developed over the most recent 200 million years of geological time. The results of this research are to be seen in the maps on this page.

135 million years ago
After a further 45 million years of drifting, the world map had still not taken on a form that looks familiar today. But the two original splits, the North Atlantic and the Indian Ocean, have continued to open out. The North Atlantic is now about 600–650 miles (1000 km) wide. Rifting is extending towards the split which opened up the Labrador Sea and this will eventually separate Greenland from North America. India has firmly launched itself on its collision course with the southern coast of Asia, which is still 2000 miles (3200 km) away.

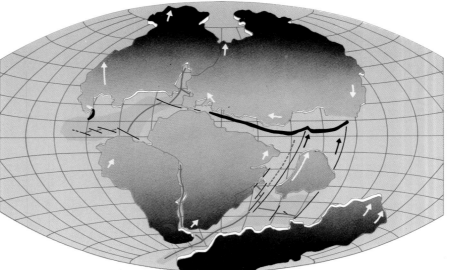

65 million years ago
Some 135 million years after the start of the drifting process the continents have begun to assume their present configuration. South America has at last separated from Africa and in Gondwanaland only Australia and Antarctica have yet to move apart. A continuation of the North Atlantic rifting will shortly bring about another big separation in Laurasia. Greenland will move apart from Europe and eventually North America will separate completely from the Eurasian landmass. The pink area (below) shows the extent of the crustal movements.

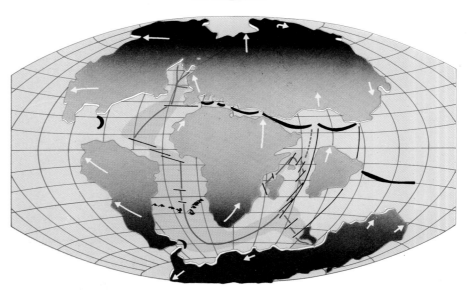

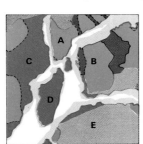

Another arrangement *left*
India (A) may have been separated by Australia (B) from East Antarctica (E) more than 200 million years ago on the evidence of today's geological deposition zones. Africa (C) and Madagascar (D) complete this convincing fit.

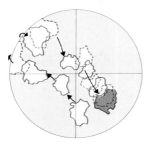

Migrant Australia *left*
By measuring the direction of magnetization of old Australian rocks it is possible to trace successive positions of that continent with respect to the Earth's magnetic pole. It appears to have moved across the world and back during the past 1000 million years.

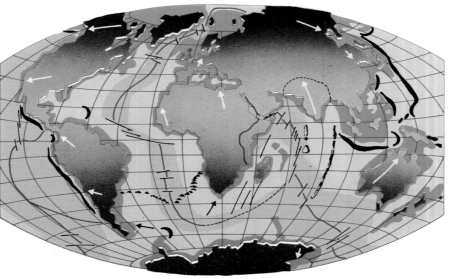

Today's positions
The Atlantic is now a wide ocean from Arctic to Antarctic, the Americas have joined and Australia has separated from Antarctica and moved far to the north. India has likewise moved northwards and its collision with Asia and continued movement has given rise to the extensive uplift of the Himalayas. All the continents which formerly made up the great land mass of Pangaea are now separated by wide oceans. Comparison of areas shows how much of India has been submerged by sliding underneath the crust of Asia (see facing page, far right).

Plate tectonics

This theory has revolutionized the way the Earth's crust – continents and oceans – is interpreted on a global scale. The crust is regarded as being made up of huge plates which converge or diverge along margins marked by earthquakes, volcanoes and other seismic activity. Major divergent margins are the mid-ocean ridges where molten lava forces its way upward and escapes. This causes vast regions of crust to move apart at a rate of an inch or two (some centimeters) per year. When sustained for up to 200 million years this means movements of thousands of miles or kilometers. The process can be seen in operation today in and around Iceland. Oceanic trenches are margins where the plates are moving together and the crust is consumed downward. The overall result is for the crustal plates to move as relatively rigid entities, carrying the continents along with them as if they were on a giant conveyor belt. Over further considerable periods of geologic time this will markedly change today's maps.

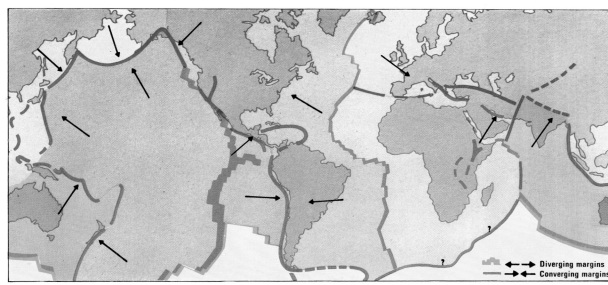

← → Diverging margins
→ ← Converging margins

Sea-floor spreading *left*
Arrows show how the lava flows on the ocean bed spread out on each side of a mid-ocean ridge. Evidence for such movement is provided by the fact the rock is alternately magnetized in opposing directions (coloured stripes).

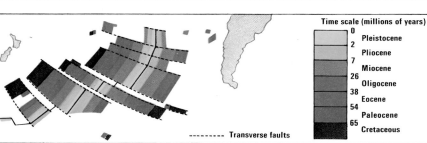

Time scale (millions of years)

0	
2	Pleistocene
7	Pliocene
	Miocene
26	Oligocene
38	Eocene
54	Paleocene
65	Cretaceous

-------- Transverse faults

Plate movements
above and left
The Earth's crust is a series of large plates 'floating' on the fluid mantle. At their edges the plates are either growing or disappearing. Magnetic measurements in the S. Pacific (left) show rock ages on each side of the mid-ocean ridges.

Plate movements in cross-section *above*

The basic mechanism of plate movements is illustrated above in simplified form with the vertical scale greatly exaggerated. This figure is explained in detail in both of the captions below.

Crustal divergence

above and right
The Earth's crust (1) behaves as a series of rigid plates which move on top of the fluid mantle (2). At their mating edges some of these plates are moving apart (3). This was the mechanism that separated North America (A) from Europe (B). The plates moved to the north and also away from each other under the influence of convection currents in the mantle (C). Between the land areas appeared an oceanic gap with a mid-ocean ridge (D) and lateral ridges (E). The movements continued for some 200 million years, fresh volcanoes being generated by igneous material escaping through the plate joint (F) to add to the lateral ridges which today cross the Atlantic (G). The volcanoes closest to the median line in mid-Atlantic are still young and active, whereas those nearer to the continents are old and extinct.

Crustal convergence

above and right
Diverging plate margins occur only in the centers of the major oceans (see map above) but plates are converging on both sea and land. Where an oceanic plate (4, above) is under-riding a continental plate (5) a deep ocean trench is the result (6). Such trenches extend around much of the Pacific; those around the northwest Pacific include the deepest on Earth where the sea bed is almost seven miles below the ocean surface. The continental margin is squeezed upward to form mountains such as the Andes or Rockies (7). If continental masses converge, such as India (A, right) and Asia (B), the convection in the mantle (C) pulls the plates together so hard that the upper crust crumples (D). Sedimentary deposits between the plates (E) are crushed and squeezed out upward (F), while the mantle on each side is turned downward, one side being forced under the other (G). Continued movement causes gross deformation at the point of collision. The static or slow-moving crust is crushed and tilted, and giant young mountains (the Himalayas, H) are thrust upward along the collision just behind the edge of the crumpled plate.

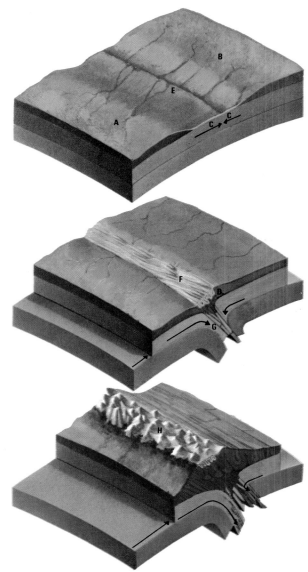

The Earth under the Sea

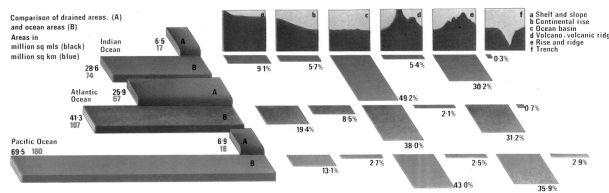

		a Shelf and slope
		b Continental rise
		c Ocean basin
		d Volcano: volcanic ridge
		e Rise and ridge
		f Trench

Comparison of drained areas. (A)
and ocean areas (B)
Areas in
million sq mls (black)
million sq km (blue)

Indian Ocean 6·5 / 17
28·6 / 74
Atlantic Ocean 25·9 / 67
41·3 / 107
Pacific Ocean 69·5 / 180
6·9 / 18

9·1% 5·7% 5·4% 0·3%
30·2%
49·2%
8·5% 2·1% 0·7%
19·4% 31·2%
38·0%
13·1% 2·7% 2·5% 2·9%
43·0% 35·9%

The water planet *left*
From directly over Tahiti the Earth appears to be covered by water. The Pacific averages 2.5 miles (4 km) deep, with great mountains and trenches.

Ocean drainage *above*
The ratio between the areas of the oceans and the land they drain varies greatly. Many large rivers feed the Atlantic but few discharge into the Pacific.

Ocean proportions *above*
The major oceans show a similarity in the proportions of their submarine topography. By far the greatest areas contain deep plains with rises and ridges. More prominent features, the mid-ocean volcanic ridges and trenches, occupy much smaller areas. About one tenth of each ocean is continental shelf.

At present the sea covers about 71 per cent of the Earth's surface. But if the continents could be sliced away and put into the deep oceans to make a perfectly uniform sphere the sea would have an average depth of about 8000 feet (2500 m) over the whole planet. In the distant past the level of the sea has fluctuated violently. The main cause has been the comings and goings of the ice ages. Glaciers and ice-caps lock up enormous volumes of water and the advance and recession of ice has alternately covered the continental shelves with shallow seas and revealed them as dry land. If the Earth's present polar ice-caps and glaciers were to melt, the mean sea level would rise by about 200 feet (60 m), which would submerge half the world's population. Average depth of the sea is more than 12000 feet (3600 m), five times the average height of the land above sea level.

The deep oceans
Below the level of the continental shelf lies the deep ocean floor with great topographical contrasts ranging from abyssal plains at a depth of about 13000 feet (4 km) to towering submarine mountain ranges of the mid-ocean ridges which reach far up toward the surface. Great advances have recently been made in exploring the ocean floors which were previously unknown. Most of the ocean area is abyssal plain which extends over about 78 million square miles (200 million km²). But a more remarkable feature of the deep ocean is the almost continuous mid-ocean mountain range which sweeps 40000 miles (64000 km) around the globe and occasionally – as at Iceland – is seen above sea level in the form of isolated volcanic islands. The basic symmetry of the oceans is the central ridge flanked by abyssal plain sloping up to the continental shelves. On the deep floor sediments accumulate at a rate of 30–35 feet (10 m) per million years; they also build up more slowly at the central ridges. No ocean sediments have been found older than 150 million years, which suggests that the material which now makes up the floors of the deep oceans was formed comparatively recently. Exploration and detailed mapping of the ocean bed is still in its infancy.

Submarine landscape
Principal features of the bed of the oceans can be grouped into a much smaller space than they would actually occupy. Although each ocean differs in detail, all tend to conform to the general layout of a central volcanic ridge (which can break the surface in places), broad abyssal plains with occasional deep trenches and shallow slopes and shelves bordering the continents.

Submarine relief *below*
The bottom of the sea is very far from being flat. If the ocean waters were removed a new landscape would become visible, with immense relief features.

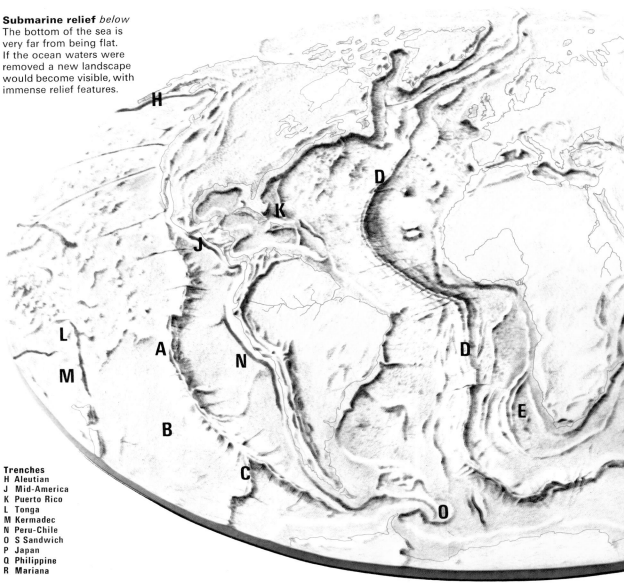

Trenches
H Aleutian
J Mid-America
K Puerto Rico
L Tonga
M Kermadec
N Peru-Chile
O S Sandwich
P Japan
Q Philippine
R Mariana

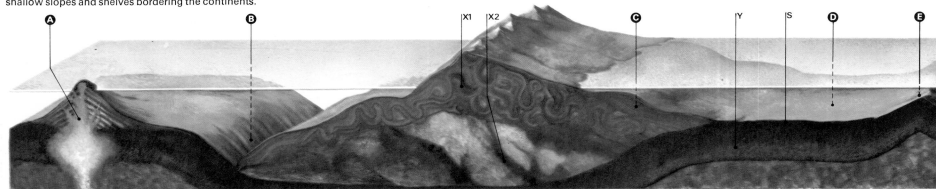

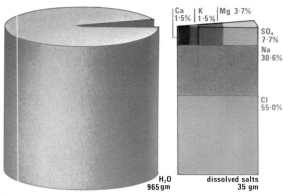

Composition of sea-water *above*
The water of the Earth's oceans is an exceedingly complex solution of many organic and inorganic salts, together with suspended solid matter. In a typical kilogram of sea-water there are 35 grams of chlorine, sodium, sulphates, magnesium, potassium and calcium.

Ca 1·5% | K 1·5% | Mg 3·7%
SO₄ 7·7%
Na 30·6%
Cl 55·0%
H₂O 965 gm
dissolved salts 35 gm

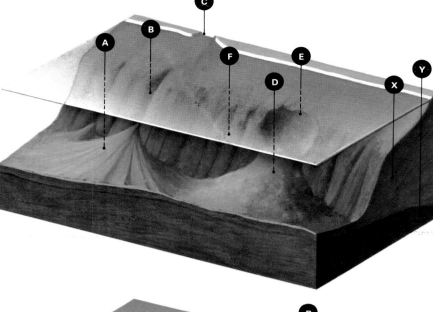

Continental shelf *left*
The submerged continental fringes lie at depths to about 450 feet (135 m) and have a total area of some 11 million square miles (28 million km²). The surface of the land is eroded and carried by rivers to form sedimentary deposits on the shelf. At its outer margin it slopes down to the abyssal plains of the deep ocean at about 2½ miles (4 km) below sea level.

A Scree fan
B Gully opposite river
C River delta
D Slump (turbidite) mass
E Scar left by (D)
F Continental slope
X Granite
Y Basalt

Rises and Ridges
A E Pacific
B SE Pacific
C Pacific-Antarctic
D Mid-Atlantic
E Walvis
F Indian Ocean
G SE Indian

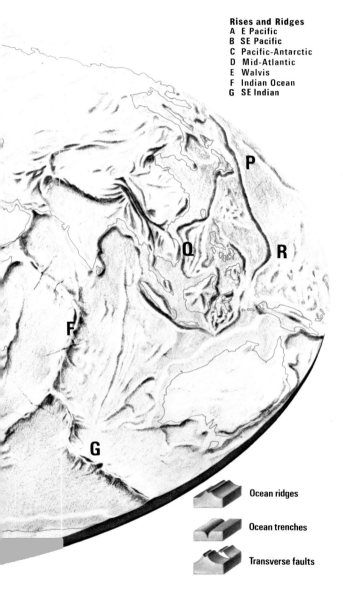

Ocean ridges

Ocean trenches

Transverse faults

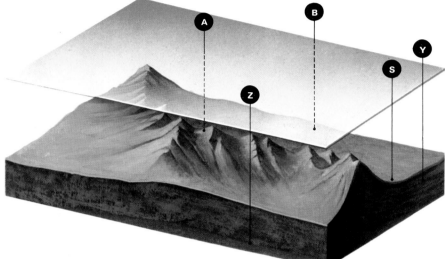

Mid-ocean ridge *left*
Well-marked ridges are found along the centers of the major oceans and form an extensive worldwide system. The central part of the ridge may have a double crest with an intervening deep trough forming a rift valley, or there may be several ridges. They are volcanic in nature and along them is generated new basaltic ocean crust. The volcanoes become progressively younger as the mid-ocean ridge is approached.

A Mid-ocean ridge
B Abyssal plain
S Ocean floor sediments
Y Basalt crust
Z Mantle

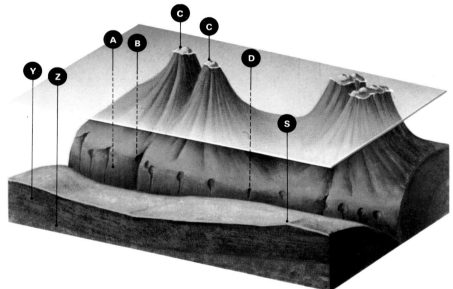

Oceanic trench *left*
These long and relatively narrow depressions are the deepest portions of the oceans, averaging over 30,000 feet (10 km) below sea level. Around the Pacific they lie close to the continental margins and in the western Pacific are often associated with chains of volcanic islands. Some trenches are slowly becoming narrower as the ocean floor plates on either side converge.

A Trench wall
B Canyon
C Island arc
D Trench
S Sediment
Y Basalt
Z Mantle

A Volcano in mid-ocean ridge
B Deep oceanic trench
C Continental shelf
D Abyssal plain
E Mid-ocean ridge
F Guyots
G Oceanic islands
X1 Upper granitic crust and sediments
X2 Lower granitic crust
Y Basaltic crust
Z Mantle

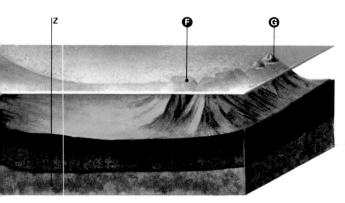

A sinking island *below*
A pre-requisite to the formation of a coral atoll is an island that is becoming submerged by the sea. Such islands are formed by the peaks of the volcanic mountains which are found on the flanks of the great mid-oceanic ridges.

Coral grows *below*
Millions of polyps, small marine animals, secrete a substance which forms the hard and often beautiful coral. The structure grows round the island in shallow water and extends above the sinking island to form an enclosed and shallow salt-water lagoon.

The mature atoll *below*
Continued submergence of the volcano results in the disappearance of the original island, but the upward growth of the coral continues unabated. The reef is then worn away by the sea and the coral debris fills in the central part of the lagoon.

A guyot *below*
Eventually the coral atoll itself begins to sink beneath the ocean surface. By this time the lagoon is likely to have become completely filled in by debris eroded from the reef, and the result is a submerged flat island, known as a guyot.

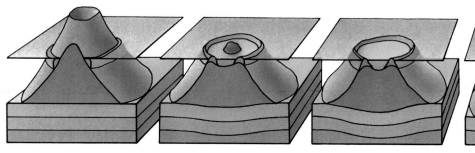

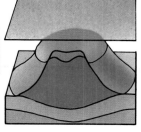

The Atmosphere

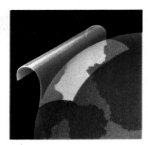

A thin coating *left*
The protective atmospheric shell around the Earth is proportionately no thicker than the skin of an apple. Gravity compresses the air so that half its mass lies within 3.5 miles (5.5 km) of the surface and all the weather within an average depth of 12 miles (20 km).

Space exploration has enabled man to stand back and take a fresh look at his Earth. Even though we, like all Earth life, have evolved to suit the Earth environment, we can see today as never before how miraculous that environment is. And by far the most important single factor in determining that environment is the atmosphere.

The Earth orbits round the Sun in a near-total vacuum. So rarefied is the interplanetary medium that it contains little heat energy, but the gas molecules that are present are vibrating so violently that their individual temperature is over 2000°C. And the surface of the Sun, at some 6000°C, would melt almost everything on the surface of the Earth, while the tenuous chromosphere around the Sun is as hot as 1,000,000°C. From the chromosphere, and from millions of other stars and heavenly objects, come radio waves. Various places in the universe, most of them far beyond the solar system, send us a penetrating kind of radiation known as cosmic rays. The Earth also receives gamma rays, X-rays and ultra-violet radiation, and from the asteroid belt in the solar system (see pages 10-11) comes a stream of solid material. Most of these are small micrometeorites, no more than flying specks, but the Earth also receives meteors and meteorites.

A meteorite is a substantial mass that strikes the Earth; fortunately, none has yet hit in a populous area. Apart from these extremely rare objects, every other influence from the environment that would be dangerous to life is filtered out by the atmosphere. Meteors burn up through friction as they plunge into the upper parts of the atmosphere. To avoid burning up in the same way, spacecraft designed to return to the Earth from lunar or interplanetary flight require a special re-entry shield.

Much of the ultraviolet radiation is arrested many miles above the Earth and creates ionized layers known as the ionosphere which man uses to reflect radio waves. Much of the infra-red (heat) radiation is likewise absorbed, lower down in the atmosphere, and most of the cosmic radiation is broken up by collisions far above the ground into such particles as 'mu-mesons'. Only a few cosmic rays, harmless radio waves and visible light penetrate the blanket of air to reach the planetary surface and its teeming life.

Credit for our vital atmosphere rests with the Earth's gravitational attraction, which both prevents the molecules and atoms in the atmosphere from escaping into space and also pulls them down tightly against the Earth. As a result nearly all the atmosphere's mass is concentrated in a very thin layer; three-quarters of it lies below 29000 feet (8840 m), the height of Mount Everest. The highest-flying aircraft, 19 miles (30 km) up, are above 99 per cent of the atmosphere. The total weight of the atmosphere is of the order of 5000 million million tons. In the lower parts are some 17 million million tons of water vapor.

The water vapor plays a great part in determining the weather on Earth, the only way in which the atmosphere consciously affects daily human life. All the weather is confined to the lower parts of the atmosphere below the tropopause. In this region, called the troposphere, temperature falls away sharply with increasing altitude. The Sun heats up the Earth's surface, water is evaporated from the surface of the oceans and an immensely complicated pattern of global and local weather systems is set up. Every part of the air in the troposphere is in motion. Sometimes the motion is so slow as to be barely perceptible, while on other occasions, or at the same time in other places, the air roars over the surface with terrifying force at speeds of 200 miles (320 km) per hour or more. It erodes the land, lashes the surface with rain and clogs cold regions with snow. Yet it is man's shield against dangers, an ocean of air without which we could not exist.

Characteristics of the atmosphere *right*

Basically the Earth's atmosphere consists of a layer of mixed gases covering the surface of the globe which, as a result of the Earth's gravitational attraction, increases in density as the surface is approached. But there is very much more to it than this. Temperature, composition and physical properties vary greatly through the depth of the atmosphere. The Earth's surface is assumed to lie along the bottom of the illustration, and the various major regions of the atmosphere—which imperceptibly merge into each other—are indicated by the numbers on the vertical scale on the facing page.

Exosphere (1)
This rarefied region is taken to start at a height of some 400 miles (650 km) and to merge above into the interplanetary medium. Atomic oxygen exists up to 600 mi (1000 km); from there up to about 1500 mi (2400 km) helium and hydrogen are approximately equally abundant, with hydrogen becoming dominant above 1500 mi. The highest auroras are found in this region. Traces of the exosphere extend out to at least 5000 mi (8000 km).

Ionosphere (2)
This contains electrically conducting layers capable of reflecting radio waves and thus of enabling radio signals to be received over great distances across the Earth. The major reflecting layers, designated D, E, F1 and F2, are at the approximate heights shown. Meteors burn up brightly at heights of around 100 mi (160 km). Charged particles coming in along the lines of force of the Earth's magnetic field produce aurorae in the ionosphere at high latitudes, some of them of the corona type with a series of radial rays; and the ionosphere's structure alters from day to night and according to the influence of the solar wind and incoming streams of other particles and radiation.

Stratosphere (3)
This lies above the tropopause which varies in altitude from about 10 mi (16 km) over the equator to just below 7 mi (11 km) in temperate latitudes. The lower stratosphere has a constant temperature of −56°C up to 19 mi (30 km); higher still the 'mesosphere' becomes warmer again. One of the vital properties of the stratosphere is its minute ozone content which shields the Earth life from some harmful short-wave radiations which, before the Earth's atmosphere had developed, penetrated to the surface.

Troposphere (4)
Within this relatively very shallow layer is concentrated about 80 per cent of the total mass of the atmosphere, as well as all the weather and all the Earth's life. The upper boundary of the troposphere is the tropopause, which is about 36000 ft (11000 m) above the surface in temperate latitudes; over the tropics it is higher, and therefore colder, while it is at a lower altitude over the poles. Air temperature falls uniformly with increasing height until the tropopause is reached; thereafter it remains constant in the stratosphere. Composition of the troposphere is essentially constant, apart from the vital factor of clouds and humidity.

Structure and features

Temperature

Pressure

450mi / 720km		10⁻⁴³mb
400mi / 640km		10⁻³³mb
350mi / 560km		10⁻³²mb
300mi / 480km		10⁻²⁷mb
250mi / 400km	2227°C	10⁻²²mb
200mi / 320km	1487°C	10⁻¹⁷mb
150mi / 240km	739°C	10⁻¹²mb
100mi / 160km	−12°C / −183°C / −63°C	10⁻⁷mb
50mi / 80km	2°C	10⁻²mb
8mi / 11km	−38°C / −55°C / −63°C / −56°C / 15°C	10³mb

Chemical composition
- Nitrogen
- Oxygen
- Argon
- Carbon dioxide
- Water vapour
- Ozone

Temperature
The mean temperature at the Earth's surface is about 15°C. As height is gained the temperature falls swiftly, to −56°C at the tropopause. It remains at this value to 19 miles (30 km), becomes warmer again, and then falls to a very low value around 60 miles (100 km). It rises once again in space.

Pressure
At sea level the pressure is some 1000 millibars, or about 14.7 pounds per square inch. The total force acting on the surface of an adult human body is thus of the order of 20 tons. But only 10 miles (16 km) above the Earth the pressure, and the atmospheric density, have both fallen by some 90 per cent.

Composition
Chemical composition of the atmosphere varies considerably with altitude. In the troposphere the mixture of nitrogen, oxygen and other gases is supplemented by water vapor, which exerts a profound influence on the weather. Ozone in the stratosphere shields life from harmful ultraviolet rays.

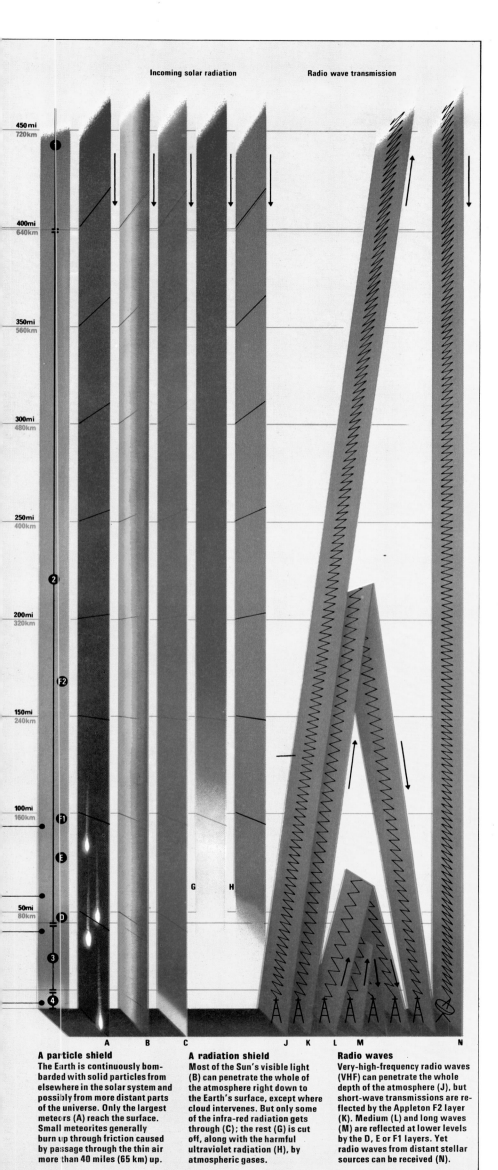

Incoming solar radiation

Radio wave transmission

450 mi
720 km

400 mi
640 km

350 mi
560 km

300 mi
480 km

250 mi
400 km

200 mi
320 km

150 mi
240 km

100 mi
160 km

50 mi
80 km

A B C   J K L M   N

A particle shield
The Earth is continuously bombarded with solid particles from elsewhere in the solar system and possibly from more distant parts of the universe. Only the largest meteors (A) reach the surface. Small meteorites generally burn up through friction caused by passage through the thin air more than 40 miles (65 km) up.

A radiation shield
Most of the Sun's visible light (B) can penetrate the whole of the atmosphere right down to the Earth's surface, except where cloud intervenes. But only some of the infra-red radiation gets through (C); the rest (G) is cut off, along with the harmful ultraviolet radiation (H), by atmospheric gases.

Radio waves
Very-high-frequency radio waves (VHF) can penetrate the whole depth of the atmosphere (J), but short-wave transmissions are reflected by the Appleton F2 layer (K). Medium (L) and long waves (M) are reflected at lower levels by the D, E or F1 layers. Yet radio waves from distant stellar sources can be received (N).

The circulation of the atmosphere *left*

The atmosphere maintains its equilibrium by transferring heat, moisture and momentum from low levels at low latitudes to high levels at high latitudes where the heat is radiated to space. This circulation appears to comprise three distinct 'cells' in each hemisphere. In the tropical (A) and polar (B) cells the circulations are thermally direct — warm air rises and cold air sinks — but the mid-latitude circulation, the Ferrel cell (C), is distorted by the polar front as shown in greater detail below.

Frontal systems *left*

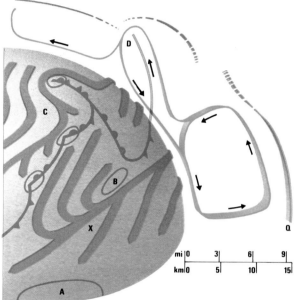

Although the figure above shows a true general picture, the actual circulation is more complicated. A portion of the Earth on a larger scale shows how frontal systems develop between the polar and tropical air masses. The tropopause, the demarcation between the troposphere in which temperature falls with height, and the strato-sphere above, is much higher in the tropics than in the polar cell. Between the cells the polar front causes constant successions of warm and cold fronts and changeable weather. Surface winds are shown, together with areas of low pressure and high pressure. The scale along the bottom, although exaggerated, indicates the greater height of the tropical tropopause compared with that in polar regions. Conventional symbols indicate warm and cold fronts.

Warm front

Cold front

A Area of low pressure   D Polar front
B Area of high pressure   P Polar cell tropopause
C Area of low pressure   Q Tropical tropopause

Precipitation *left*

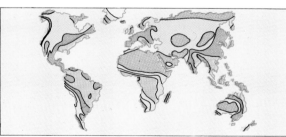

This map shows the mean annual rain, hail and snow over the Earth.

0	Cm per year
25	
50	
100	
200	

Evaporation *left*

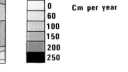

Accurate estimates of evaporation can be made only over the oceans.

0	Cm per year
60	
100	
150	
200	
250	

Net surface radiation *left*

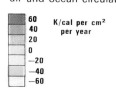

Variations in heat output over the Earth's surface affect air and ocean circulations.

60	K/cal per cm²
40	per year
20	
0	
−20	
−40	
−60	

The Structure of Weather Systems

Until recently there were few scientists in the tropics or the polar regions, and the science of meteorology therefore evolved in the mid-latitudes. Likewise, the early concepts of meteorology were all based on observations of the mid-latitude atmosphere. Originally only two types of air mass were recognized: polar and tropical. Today a distinct equatorial air mass has been identified, as well as Arctic and Antarctic masses at latitudes even higher than the original polar ones. The concept of a 'front' between dissimilar air masses dates from as recently as 1919, and three years later the development of a cyclone – a large system of air rotating around an area of low pressure– was first described. Today satellite photographs have confirmed the validity of these early studies and enable the whole Earth's weather to be watched on daily computer processed photo-charts as it develops.

Why the weather varies

Anywhere in the Earth's mid-latitudes the climate is determined mainly by the frequency and intensity of the cyclones, with their frontal systems and contrasting air masses, which unceasingly alter the local temperature, wind velocity, air pressure and humidity. In turn, the frequency of the cyclonic visits is governed principally by the behavior of the long waves in the upper westerlies. When these waves change their shape and position the cyclonic depressions follow different paths. The major changes are seasonal, but significant variations also occur on a cycle of 5–6 weeks. It is still proving difficult to investigate the long wave variations. As a front passes, a fairly definite sequence of cloud, wind, humidity, temperature, precipitation and visibility can be seen. The most obvious change is the type of cloud, of which nine are shown opposite. Each cyclone contains numerous cloud types in its structure. Within these clouds several forms of precipitation can form; raindrops are the most common, but ice precipitation also forms, with snow in winter and hail in the summer when intense atmospheric instability produces towering cumulonimbus clouds topped by an 'anvil' of ice crystals.

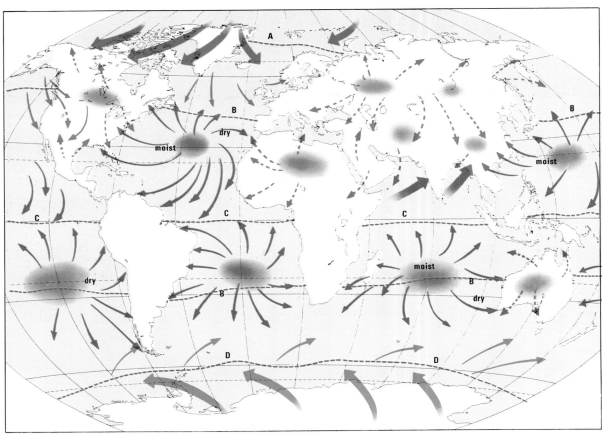

Air masses and convergences *above*
An air mass is an extensive portion of the atmosphere in which, at any given altitude, the moisture and temperature are almost uniform. Such a mass generally arises when the air rests for a time on a large area of land or water which has uniform surface conditions. There are some 20 source regions throughout the world. A second pre-requisite is large-scale subsidence and divergence over the source region. The boundary between air masses is a convergence or front. (A Arctic, B Polar, C Equatorial, D Antarctic.) The polar front is

Arctic	Equatorial
Polar maritime	Tropical maritime
Polar continental	Tropical continental
Cold air masses	Warm air masses

particularly important in governing much of the weather in mid-latitudes. The pattern depicted provides a raw framework for the world's weather. It is considerably modified by the air's vertical motion, by surface friction, land topography, the Earth's rotation and other factors.

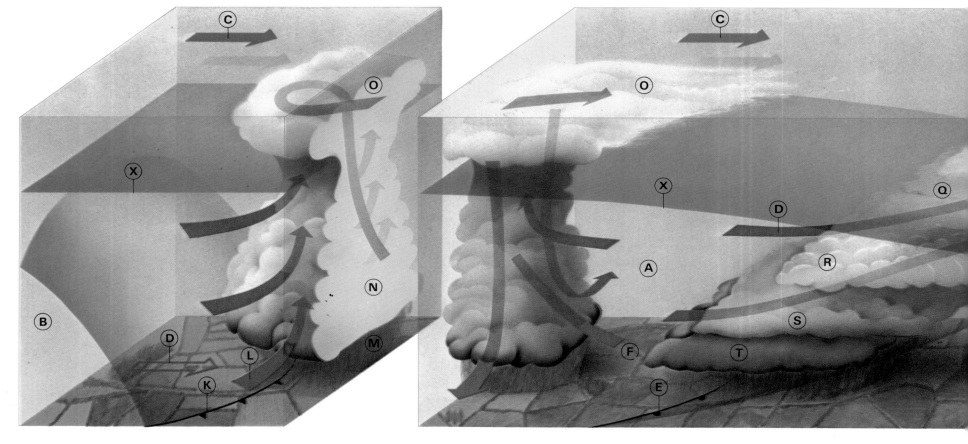

Anatomy of a depression

Seen in cross section, a mature mid-latitude cyclone forms a large system which always follows basically the same pattern. Essentially it comprises a wedge of warm air (A) riding over, and being undercut by, cold air masses (B). The entire cyclone is moving from left to right, and this is also the basic direction of the winds (C) and (D). To an observer on the ground the warm front (E) may take 12-24 hours to pass, followed by the warm sector (F) perhaps 180 miles (300 km) wide.

The cold front (K)

As this frontal zone, about one mile (1-2 km) wide, passes overhead the direction of the wind alters (L) and precipitation (M) pours from cumuliform clouds (N). If the air above the frontal surface is moving upwards then giant cumulonimbus (O) may grow, with heavy rain or hail. Cirrus clouds then form in air above the freezing level (X). Sometimes the front is weak with subsidence of air predominant on both sides of it. In this case there is little cloud development and near-zero surface precipitation.

The warm front (E)

The front is first heralded by cirrus clouds (P), followed by cirrostratus (Q), altocumulus (R), stratus (S) and finally nimbostratus (T). The descending layers are due partly to humidity distribution and partly to the warm air rising over the sloping frontal surface. Precipitation may be steady and last for hours. Alternatively some warm fronts have a predominantly subsident air motion, with the result that there is only a little thin cloud and negligible precipitation. Air temperature increases as the front passes.

24

Development of a depression *right*

Most mid-latitude depressions (cyclones) develop on the polar front (map above). An initial disturbance along this front causes a fall in pressure and a confluence at the surface, deforming the front into a wave (1, right). The confluence and thermal structure accelerate the cyclonic spin into a fully developed depression (2). The depression comprises a warm sector bounded by a sharp cold front (A) and warm front (B). The fast-moving cold front overtakes the warm front and eventually the warm sector is lifted completely clear of the ground resulting in an occlusion (3). The continued overlapping of the two wedges of cold air eventually fills up the depression and causes it to weaken and disperse (4). By the time this occurs the warm sector has been lifted high in the atmosphere. In this way, depressions fulfil an essential role in transferring heat from low to high levels and from low to high latitudes.

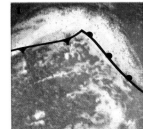

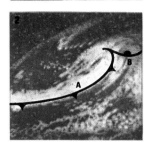

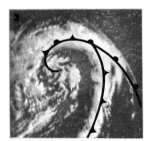

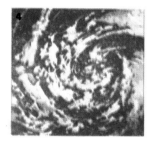

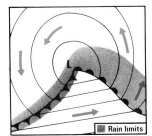

Plan view *left*

A developing cyclone will appear this way on the 'synoptic' weather chart. Lines of equal pressure (isobars) are nearly straight within the warm sector but curve sharply in the cold sector to enclose the low pressure focus of the system.

Rain limits

Examples of the three major cloud groups

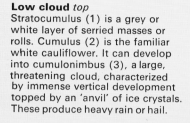

Low cloud *top*
Stratocumulus (1) is a grey or white layer of serried masses or rolls. Cumulus (2) is the familiar white cauliflower. It can develop into cumulonimbus (3), a large, threatening cloud, characterized by immense vertical development topped by an 'anvil' of ice crystals. These produce heavy rain or hail.

Medium cloud *left*
Nimbostratus (4) is a ragged grey layer producing drizzle or snow. Altocumulus (5) comprises rows of 'blobs' of ice and water forming a sheet at a height of 1.5-4.5 miles (2-7 km). Altostratus (6) occurs at similar heights but is a water/ice sheet either uniform, striated or fibrous in appearance.

High cloud *right*
Cirrus (7) is the highest cloud and appears as fine white ice filaments at 8–10 miles (13–16 km), often hair-like or silky. Cirro-cumulus (8) forms into thin white layers made up of very numerous icy globules or ripples. Cirrostratus (9) is a high-level veil of ice crystals often forming a halo round the Sun.

Four kinds of precipitation

Rain
Although raindrops are often melted snow, most rain results from the coalescence of microscopic droplets (1) which are condensed from vapour on to nuclei such as small particles of salt from sea spray. The repeated merging eventually forms water droplets (2) which are too large to be kept up by the air currents.

Glaze
In completely undisturbed air it is possible for water to remain liquid even at temperatures well below freezing point. So air above the freezing level (X) may contain large quantities of this 'supercooled water'. This can fall as rain and freeze on impact with objects, coating them with ice.

Dry snow
The origin of snow differs from that of rain in that the vapour droplets (1) settle on microscopic crystals of ice and freeze. The result is the growth of a white or translucent ice crystal having a basically hexagonal form (photomicrograph below). The crystals then agglomerate into flakes (2).

Hail
In cumulonimbus clouds raindrops (formed at 1,2) may encounter up-currents strong enough to lift them repeatedly back through a freezing level (X). On each pass (3) a fresh layer of ice is collected. The hailstone builds up like an onion until it is so heavy (4) that it falls to the ground.

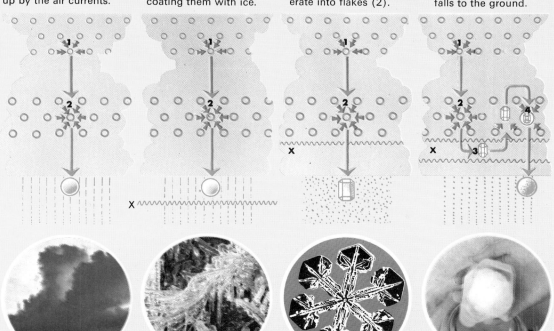

Man on Earth

The vast geographical expanse of the Earth has beguiled man into believing that its resources could never be exhausted. Only with the dramatic growth in man's industrial and agricultural demands has it become obvious that not only does his home planet have limits, but in some instances these limits are being fast approached. Of course some new supplies remain to be discovered and others will be replaced from man-made sources, but there is no room for complacency when man continues to squander his terrestrial heritage. If all nations were ever to enjoy the same standard of life as the privileged few, the demand for energy and minerals would generate an industrial 'famine' that would bring a world-wide crisis. Already excessive demands have led in some instances to over-exploitation and dereliction of the land. If a world disaster is to be averted, man must discover a new relationship with the Earth and learn to manage and to conserve its vital resources.

Monitoring Earth's resources
With Earth's known resources under pressure, a complete global picture of them, using techniques such as infra-red photography shown here, becomes urgent. In the photo, healthy vegetation is red, stubble in a harvested field pink over blue, while roads and buildings are blue.

Earth's Water Resources

Without water there would be no life as we know it on the Earth. Life began in the oceans and the life of the land, both plant and animal, still remains utterly dependent on water for its survival. The atmosphere plays a vital role in the terrestrial water system. Spurred by the energy of the Sun, the moist layer surrounding the globe forms a vast heat engine, operating at a rate of billions of horsepower. All the exposed water surface is constantly being converted into vapor. Eventually the air holding the vapor cools, and the vapor condenses as rain, hail or snow. Most of this precipitation falls into the sea, but nearly a quarter of it falls on the land. Altogether about two-thirds of it evaporates back into the air, or is transpired by plants; the rest runs off in rivers, or filters through the ground to the water table beneath.

Satisfying the collective thirst of man and his industry grows daily more difficult. Almost always the demand is for fresh water; but the proportion of the Earth's water in rivers and streams is less than one part in a million. If the Antarctic ice cap were to melt, it would feed all the rivers for 800 years. Although schemes have been suggested for towing giant freshwater icebergs from Antarctica to the Californian coast, man is unlikely to make extensive use of the ice cap. Far more promising is the large supply of subterranean water. At the same time great strides are being made in desalination of sea water, using a variety of methods. Management of the Earth's water resources is seen ever more clearly as a technical challenge of the greatest magnitude.

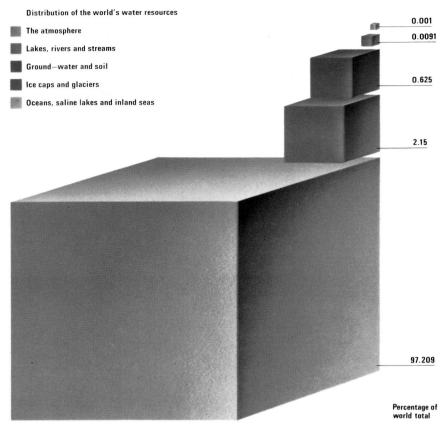

Distribution of the world's water resources

- The atmosphere
- Lakes, rivers and streams
- Ground-water and soil
- Ice caps and glaciers
- Oceans, saline lakes and inland seas

0.001
0.0091
0.625
2.15
97.209

Percentage of world total

The world's water *left*
The total volume of the Earth's water is 317 million cubic miles (1330 million km³). Practically all of it is in the oceans, in a form rich in dissolved salts. Solar heating is constantly evaporating this mass, converting it ultimately into precipitation of fresh water which falls back to the surface. Run-off from the surface in rivers and streams is one of the forms of terrestrial water most visible to man, but it accounts for a negligible fraction of the total. Some 80 times as much water lies in salt lakes and inland seas, 90 times as much in fresh-water lakes, more than 6000 times as much in ground water beneath the land surface, and almost a quarter-million times as much in ice caps and glaciers. So far man has made little attempt to use these sources of fresh water. Instead he interrupts the hydrologic cycle in the easy places: the rivers and lakes, where, because of the small volumes and flows available, he causes significant pollution.

A valued resource *above*
Shiupur head, the head-waters of the Gang canal in Rajasthan province, India. This and other canal systems are gradually bringing to this arid province an assured supply of irrigation water from the Himalayas.

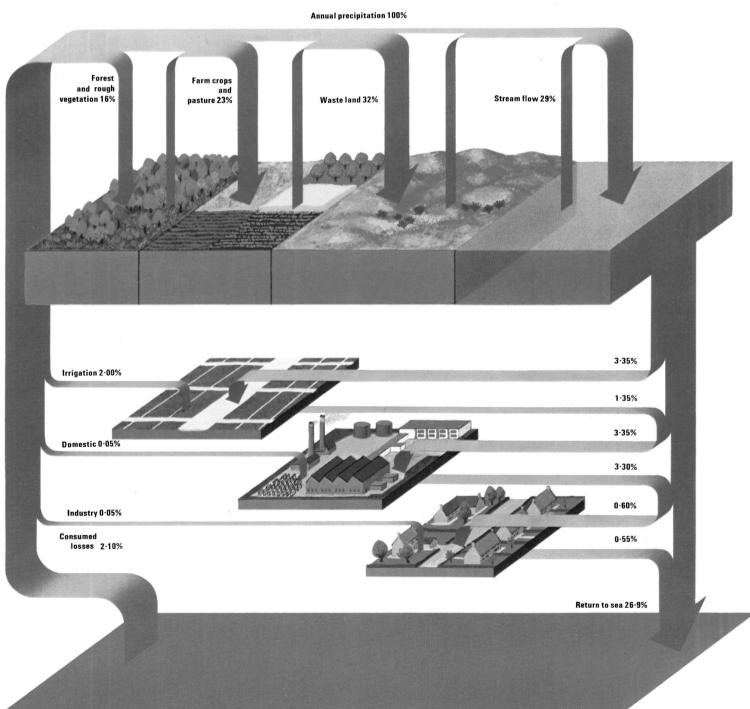

Annual precipitation 100%

Forest and rough vegetation 16%

Farm crops and pasture 23%

Waste land 32%

Stream flow 29%

Irrigation 2·00%

Domestic 0·05%

Industry 0·05%

Consumed losses 2·10%

3·35%
1·35%
3·35%
3·30%
0·60%
0·55%

Return to sea 26·9%

The hydrologic cycle *left*
This diagram is drawn for United States, but the basic features of the cycle are common to most of the Earth's land. Just over three-quarters of the rain snow and hail falls on the oceans. The usual measure for water in huge quantities is the acre-foot (one acre of water, one foot deep). Each year about 300 thousand million acre-feet of water falls on the oceans and 80 thousand million on the land. In the diagram all the figures are percentages. In the US, which is not unusual in its proportion of farmland, less than one-quarter of the water falling on the land falls directly on crops or pasture. A greater amount falls into rivers and streams, from which man takes varying small fractions for his own purposes. It can be seen that, even in the US, the total quantity of water withdrawn for use is only 7.3 per cent of the fraction of water falling on the land. Yet, to attain even this performance, Americans spend more than $10000 million each year on improving their water supplies.

Domestic use of water

In some countries the total consumption of water is less than one gallon per head, but in the United States more than 70 US gallons are consumed by each person daily, on average, in domestic use alone. The way this consumption is split up varies greatly, but these percentages, for 'an average home in Akron, Ohio' are typical for modern urban areas having piped water to flush toilets. Total domestic water consumption in the industrially advanced countries is usually between five and 30 per cent of the national total.

Flushing toilet 41%

Washing and bathing 37%

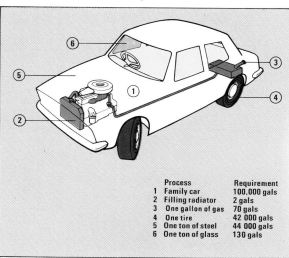

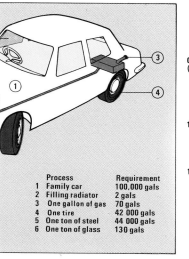

Process	Requirement
1 Family car	100,000 gals
2 Filling radiator	2 gals
3 One gallon of gas	70 gals
4 One tire	42 000 gals
5 One ton of steel	44 000 gals
6 One ton of glass	130 gals

Kitchen use 6%

Drinking 5%

Laundry 4%

Household cleaning 3%

Garden 3%

Cleaning car 1%

Consumption of water (m³ x 1000)

Irrigation
Public
Rural domestic
Industry
Electricity

Rising demand *above*
Civilized man needs more water every year. Plotted graphically, the rising demand for water in the United States is startling; the rate of increase is about three times the rate of population growth. Rural domestic supplies are from wells; others are piped.

Irrigation *below*
Irrigation of land by man is at least 7000 years old, yet still in its infancy. The grey areas on the world map are virtually without irrigation. The last column of data shows the percentage of each continent irrigated. Only Japan and the UAR exceed 50 per cent.

Most liquid wastes are generated by mixed human concentrations including habitations, businesses and industry. Before reclamation, any wastes having excessive or toxic mineral content must be segregated from the main flow.

Oilfields on the land invariably generate large and varied liquid wastes, particularly including concentrated brines, which must be excluded from conventional reclamation processes.

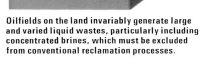

This water reclamation plant accepts mainly residential effluent. Water reclaimed is returned for re-use, while sludge and grease are returned to the sewer and piped to the main sewage treatment plant. A proportion of the output is supplied to spreading grounds at the coast (below) to replenish the ground water table.

Liquid wastes from residential and business areas normally comprise sewage suitable for reclamation without pre-treatment or segregation.

This water reclamation plant supplies water to the city (above) and to agriculture and industry (below, right). Sludge and grease are returned to the sewer (route, far right).

Reclaimed waters may be used to maintain underground supplies by spreading them on percolation beds (above), where the water filters down to the storage basin.

Below, the main sewage treatment plant can operate by a variety of methods, including long-term open storage, aeration, mechanical filtration and softening.

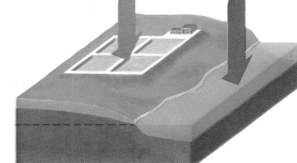 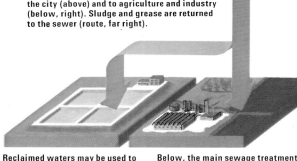

Reclaiming used water
In almost every country the quality of the water pumped into domestic supplies is subject to precise controls, and the proportion of some substances may not exceed one or two parts per million. National water systems make maximum use of water reclaimed close to the point of consumption by plant which returns the heavy sludges and greases to the sewer for treatment at a large sewage works. This facilitates effluent quality control and also provides an emergency outlet for a temporarily overloaded or faulty reclamation plant. In the example here the main treatment plant discharges wastes into an ocean outfall (left), while the fresh water spreading grounds just inshore replenish the water table and thus prevent infiltration by the ocean water.

Continent	Area : million acres (1 acre = 4047m²) Total	Cultivated (A)	Irrigated (B)	Ratio of B to A (x 100)
Africa	898	37	11.2	30
Asia	5062	1289	296.9	23
Australia	1900	38	3	8
Europe	288	122	5.8	5
N America	2809	485	49	10
S America	4620	187	13	7
USSR	5540	568	23	4
Grand total	21117	2726	401.9	15

Desalination
Man's growing demand for fresh water cannot readily be met without an enormous increase in his capacity to desalinate salt water. A choice between several ways of doing this is invariably made on economic grounds. Nearly all the large installations in use are multi-stage flash evaporators in which some form of heat – if possible, heat otherwise wasted - is used to convert sea water to steam which is condensed by the incoming salt water. But in some circumstances more economic results can be obtained by freezing, reverse osmosis or other methods.

GROWTH OF DESALTING CAPACITY 1961 TO 1968

Year Ending	Municipal water use M gal per day	Industrial/other uses M gal per day	Total
1961	17.6	42.2	59.8
1962	20.9	45.5	66.4
1963	28.4	50.4	78.8
1964	32.5	53.5	86.0
1965	39.3	58.9	98.2
1966	52.6	101.6	154.2
1967	102.2	115.3	217.5
1968	121.4	125.8	247.2
Historical annual growth %	32	17	23
Projection to 1975	835	415	1250
Projected annual growth %	32	19	26

SIZE RANGES OF THE WORLD'S DESALTING PLANTS

Size range M gal per day	Number of Plants	Total capacity M gal per day
0.025–0.1	351	17.8
0.1–0.3	218	35.3
0.3–0.5	34	13.0
0.5–1.0	31	21.3
1.0–5.0	46	95.4
5.0–7.5	3	17.5
over 7.5	3	46.9
TOTAL	686	247.2

Minerals under the Land

Of about 2000 minerals in the Earth's crust only 100 or so are of economic importance. These are distributed very irregularly, so that no country today can boast all the minerals it needs. As a result minerals are a source of great national wealth, exploitation and even of rivalry. And the strife is likely to intensify as man's demands grow, because the total of the Earth's minerals is limited.

Against this background of uneven distribution, economic warfare and sharply increasing demand, man's use of minerals constantly changes. Coal, in 1920 the most important mineral in the world on a tonnage basis, is today unable to compete in several of its former markets because of the high cost of transporting it, and its use is increasingly changing from that of a fuel to that of a raw material for plastics and chemicals. Nitrates for fertilizers and explosives sustained the economy of Chile until 1914, when Germany found a way to 'fix' nitrogen from the atmosphere. Aluminum, one the most abundant minerals, was costly and little used until a large-scale refining process was discovered which made use of cheap hydroelectricity.

Taking the broad view, the Earth's minerals are seen as a stern test of man's ability to make proper use of the resources available to him. Already some nations have amassed enormous stockpiles of what are today considered to be strategically important minerals. Nickel is one such metal, and the bulk of the world's supply comes from Canada. Another is manganese, and in this case the dominant supplier is the Soviet Union; but manganese is one of the many minerals which might be dredged from the sea bed.

Uneven distribution of minerals is paralleled by uneven consumption. Paradoxically, the industrialized countries which owed their original development to the presence of mineral resources, particularly iron and coal, now rely for their continued prosperity on developing nations. If the latter were to develop a similar demand for materials a mineral famine would ensue which would have repercussions throughout the world.

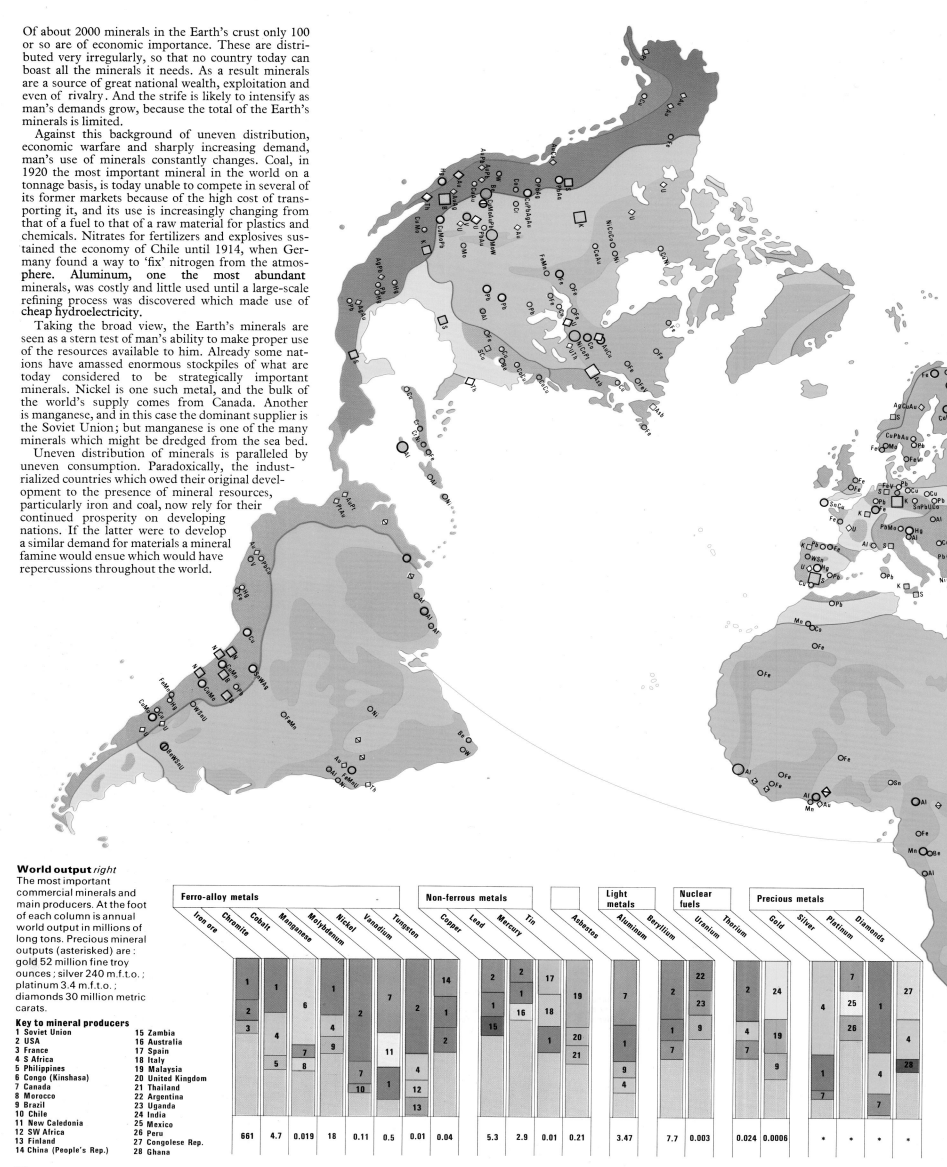

World output *right*
The most important commercial minerals and main producers. At the foot of each column is annual world output in millions of long tons. Precious mineral outputs (asterisked) are : gold 52 million fine troy ounces ; silver 240 m.f.t.o. ; platinum 3.4 m.f.t.o. ; diamonds 30 million metric carats.

Key to mineral producers

1 Soviet Union	15 Zambia
2 USA	16 Australia
3 France	17 Spain
4 S Africa	18 Italy
5 Philippines	19 Malaysia
6 Congo (Kinshasa)	20 United Kingdom
7 Canada	21 Thailand
8 Morocco	22 Argentina
9 Brazil	23 Uganda
10 Chile	24 India
11 New Caledonia	25 Mexico
12 SW Africa	26 Peru
13 Finland	27 Congolese Rep.
14 China (People's Rep.)	28 Ghana

	Ferro-alloy metals								Non-ferrous metals					Light metals		Nuclear fuels		Precious metals			
Iron ore	Chromite	Cobalt	Manganese	Molybdenum	Nickel	Vanadium	Tungsten	Copper	Lead	Mercury	Tin	Asbestos	Aluminum	Beryllium	Uranium	Thorium	Gold	Silver	Platinum	Diamonds		
	1	1					14	2	2	17		7	22		2	24		7	25	1	27
	2		6		7		2	1	16	18			23		1	9	4	4	26		4
	3	4	7	4			2	15			20				7		7	19			28
		5	8	9	11		4			21		9				9		1	4	
					7		12					4						7	7	
				10	1		13													
661	4.7	0.019	18	0.11	0.5	0.01	0.04	5.3	2.9	0.01	0.21	3.47	7.7	0.003	0.024	0.0006	*	*	*	*		

30

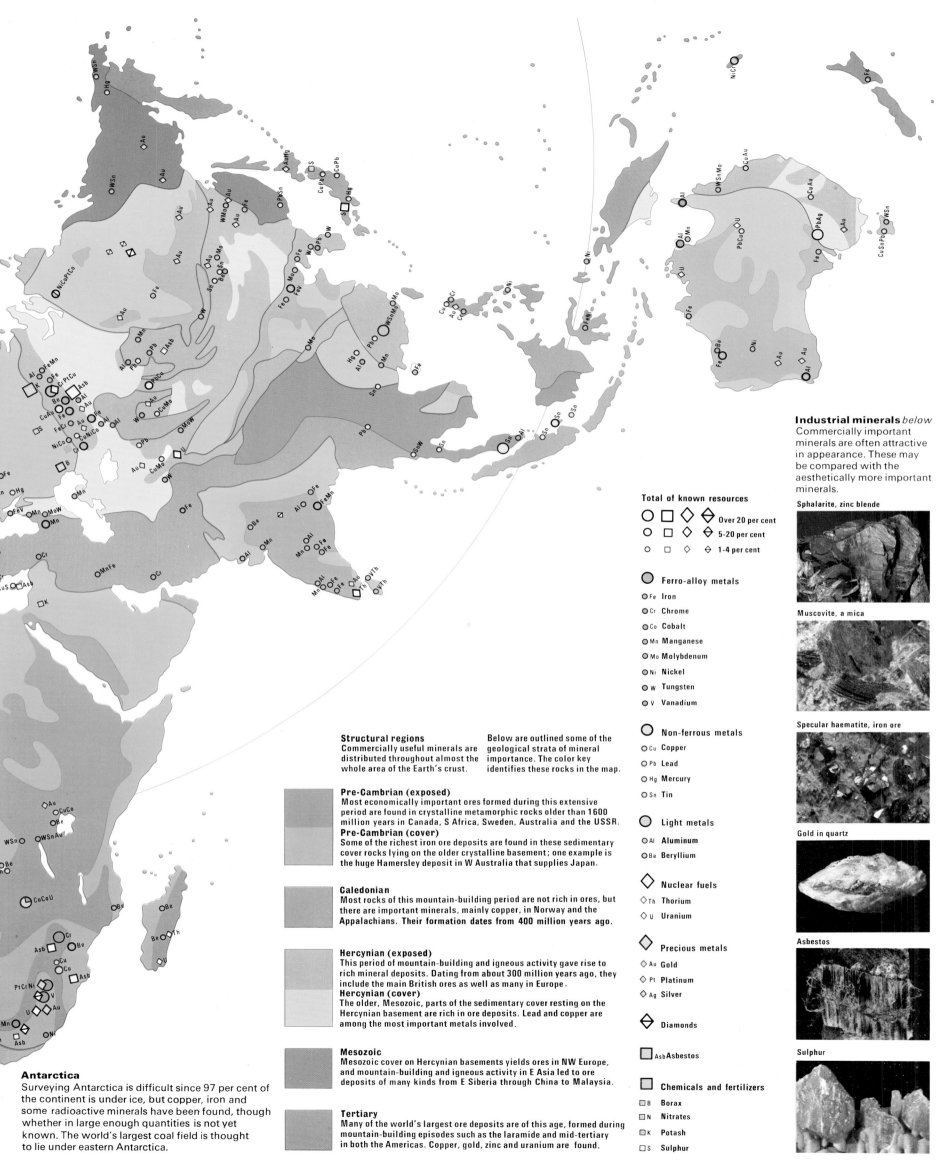

Antarctica
Surveying Antarctica is difficult since 97 per cent of the continent is under ice, but copper, iron and some radioactive minerals have been found, though whether in large enough quantities is not yet known. The world's largest coal field is thought to lie under eastern Antarctica.

Structural regions
Commercially useful minerals are distributed throughout almost the whole area of the Earth's crust.

Below are outlined some of the geological strata of mineral importance. The color key identifies these rocks in the map.

Pre-Cambrian (exposed)
Most economically important ores formed during this extensive period are found in crystalline metamorphic rocks older than 1600 million years in Canada, S Africa, Sweden, Australia and the USSR.
Pre-Cambrian (cover)
Some of the richest iron ore deposits are found in these sedimentary cover rocks lying on the older crystalline basement; one example is the huge Hamersley deposit in W Australia that supplies Japan.

Caledonian
Most rocks of this mountain-building period are not rich in ores, but there are important minerals, mainly copper, in Norway and the Appalachians. Their formation dates from 400 million years ago.

Hercynian (exposed)
This period of mountain-building and igneous activity gave rise to rich mineral deposits. Dating from about 300 million years ago, they include the main British ores as well as many in Europe.
Hercynian (cover)
The older, Mesozoic, parts of the sedimentary cover resting on the Hercynian basement are rich in ore deposits. Lead and copper are among the most important metals involved.

Mesozoic
Mesozoic cover on Hercynian basements yields ores in NW Europe, and mountain-building and igneous activity in E Asia led to ore deposits of many kinds from E Siberia through China to Malaysia.

Tertiary
Many of the world's largest ore deposits are of this age, formed during mountain-building episodes such as the laramide and mid-tertiary in both the Americas. Copper, gold, zinc and uranium are found.

Total of known resources

◯	▢	◇	◈	Over 20 per cent
○	▫	◇	◈	5-20 per cent
○	▫	◇	◈	1-4 per cent

Ferro-alloy metals
- ⊘Fe Iron
- ⊘Cr Chrome
- ⊘Co Cobalt
- ⊘Mn Manganese
- ⊘Mo Molybdenum
- ⊘Ni Nickel
- ⊘W Tungsten
- ⊘V Vanadium

Non-ferrous metals
- ○Cu Copper
- ○Pb Lead
- ○Hg Mercury
- ○Sn Tin

Light metals
- ○Al Aluminum
- ○Be Beryllium

Nuclear fuels
- ◇Th Thorium
- ◇U Uranium

Precious metals
- ◇Au Gold
- ◇Pt Platinum
- ◇Ag Silver

Diamonds
◇

AsbAsbestos

Chemicals and fertilizers
- ▫B Borax
- ▫N Nitrates
- ▫K Potash
- ▫S Sulphur

Industrial minerals *below*
Commercially important minerals are often attractive in appearance. These may be compared with the aesthetically more important minerals.

Sphalarite, zinc blende

Muscovite, a mica

Specular haematite, iron ore

Gold in quartz

Asbestos

Sulphur

31

Earth's Energy Resources

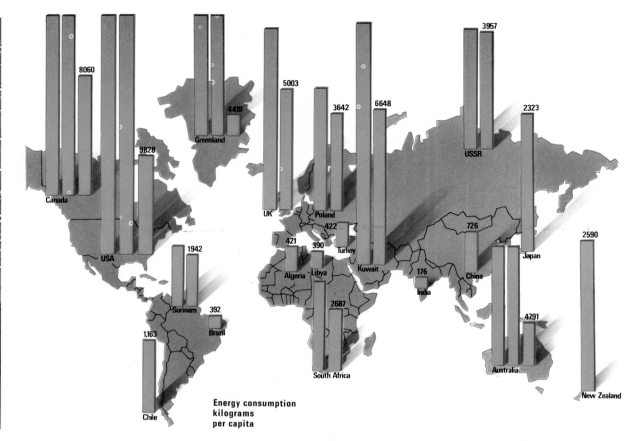

Energy consumption
kilograms
per capita

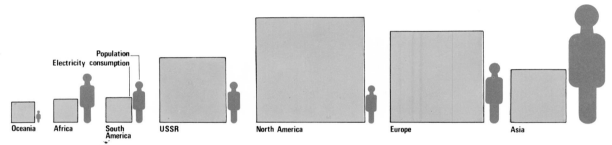

The concept of energy arose only very recently in the period of man's life on Earth, but already it dominates the whole quality of this life. Early man had no mechanical energy but that of his muscles. By about 2500 years ago he had learned to harness draft animals, such as the ox and horse, and to devise crude water wheels to harness part of the energy of the flow of water in a river. Soon afterwards he added sails to make the fickle wind propel his ships, and by 1000 years ago had started to dot his landscape with windmills. By this time he was adept at burning combustible materials, and during the past 500 years his energy has been increasingly based upon fire, first using wood, and subsequently coal, gas made from coal, petroleum, and natural gas.

All these energy sources, including animal muscle and the wind, are based on the energy radiated by the Sun. Although modern man has begun to use this energy directly in a few trivial installations in hot countries, almost all his energy is derived from solar heat locked up in fossil fuels. The known reserves of these fuels are tending to increase, as a result of prospecting, even faster than man is burning them up. But if no more were discovered most of man's world would come to a halt inside 20 years.

But there should be no energy gap. The promise of nuclear energy is such that, by using fast reactors that breed more fuel than they consume, energy should become one of the very few really plentiful and cheap commodities in man's world of the future. The challenges reside in extracting the fuels and using them effectively.

Power and people *above*
World consumption of energy is very uneven. One way of measuring it is to reduce all forms of energy to an equivalent weight of coal burned. The columns on the world map are proportional to the 'coal equivalent' of selected national consumptions expressed in kilograms per head. Electricity consumption is even more disproportionate, as witness the square areas and figure heights immediately above.

Fuels and energy *right*
The caloric value of a fuel is the quantity of heat generated by burning a unit mass. Figures are in British Thermal Units per pound. The surrounding curve shows the increase in the rate at which man is consuming energy; one joule (j) per second is equal to one watt.

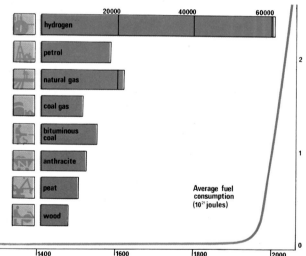

Average fuel consumption (10^{21} joules)

Sources of power *below*
For many centuries the only alternative sources of power to muscles were wood fires, waterwheels and windmills – and the latter had too slight an effect to be shown on the figure below. The left portion shows the way in which, since 1850, the United States has enjoyed successive new sources of energy. In 1920 the US economy was not untypical in being based on coal, but since then more energetic, cleaner and more efficiently used fuels have dominated the picture. In the future, nuclear power, shown in the right-hand figure, promises to make good shortages of fossil fuels.

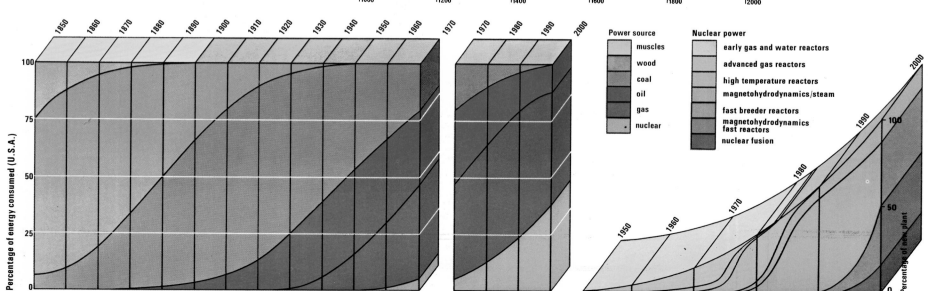

Power source	Nuclear power
muscles	early gas and water reactors
wood	advanced gas reactors
coal	high temperature reactors
oil	magnetohydrodynamics/steam
gas	fast breeder reactors
nuclear	magnetohydrodynamics/fast reactors
	nuclear fusion

Coal into electricity
To reduce costs modern coal-fired generating stations are sited on coalfields ; Lea Hall colliery feeds Rugeley power station (background).

Flare in the desert
Once oil has been struck, harmful gases are burned off in the atmosphere. Similar 'flares' are a prominent feature of petroleum refineries.

Drilling for gas
To reach natural gas trapped in submarine strata a drill rig is used to bore a hole at a location determined by the prospectors.

Nuclear power station
Nearly all today's nuclear energy is used to generate electricity. One of the largest stations is Wylfa, Wales, rated at 1180 million watts.

Coal
For three centuries the most important of the fossil fuels, coal is the result of some 300 million years of subterranean decay of vegetation. Many thousands of generations of the Carboniferous trees have become compressed and hardened, first into peat, then into lignite, then into bituminous coal and finally into anthracite. Until this century coal was used inefficiently as a source of heat. Today it is becoming equally important as a raw material producing plastics, heavy chemicals, insecticides, perfumes, antiseptics, road surfaces and many other products. Great advances have been made in automating the mining of coal, but it remains a laborious task and is therefore becoming increasingly expensive. However, coal mining remains a worldwide industry that passes on to modern man the products of the solar energy captured by a younger Earth.

Petroleum
Like coal, oil is a mixture of fossil remains, but yields few clues as to its origin. Crude oil, from the locations shown on the map at right, is carried by tanker ships to refineries in the user countries. Here it is heated in pipe stills until the various constituent 'fractions' are boiled off. The result is a wide range of products from gasoline through kerosene and gas oil to heavy fuel oils, lubricants and vaseline, with a wide range of other by-products used in many thousands of chemicals and plastics materials. Petroleum fuels are replacing coal in heating and transport applications, partly owing to their easier handling and partly to reduce air pollution by sulphurous compounds. LPG, liquefied pertroleum gas, is even cleaner burning and may become more important than gasoline and kerosene in road vehicles and aircraft over the next 25 years.

Gas
In 1807 a London street was lit by town gas, a mixture of hydrogen (about 50%), methane, carbon monoxide and dioxide and other gases, formed by cooking coal at high temperature in a retort. By 1950 this manufactured gas was an important fuel, but in many advanced countries its place is now being taken by natural gas, a primary fuel consisting mainly of methane piped straight from deposits sometimes conveniently sited from the user's point of view (right). Intensive prospecting is discovering natural gas faster than it is being used, and during the past 20 years natural gas has become man's largest single source of energy. In refrigerated form as a compact liquid, it promises to become an attractive fuel for transport vehicles. A major benefit is that the exhaust from such a vehicle would contain less pollutants than from those using gasoline.

Nuclear energy
In 1956 Britain opened the world's first electricity generating station using the heat of nuclear fission. It was fuelled with rods of natural uranium, a heavy silvery metal containing a small proportion of atoms capable of spontaneous fission when struck by a free neutron. Fission releases further neutrons capable of sustaining a continuous chain reaction. Such a reaction generates heat which is used to provide steam for turbines. The prime advantage of nuclear power is that the fuel is used extremely slowly. Now the fast reactor, which uses raw 'fast' neutrons instead of ones artificially slowed down, has been developed. Not only can the fast reactor generate great energy from a small bulk but it creates fresh fuel faster than the original (plutonium) fuel is consumed. Fast reactors, using uranium from granite, could provide limitless cheap energy.

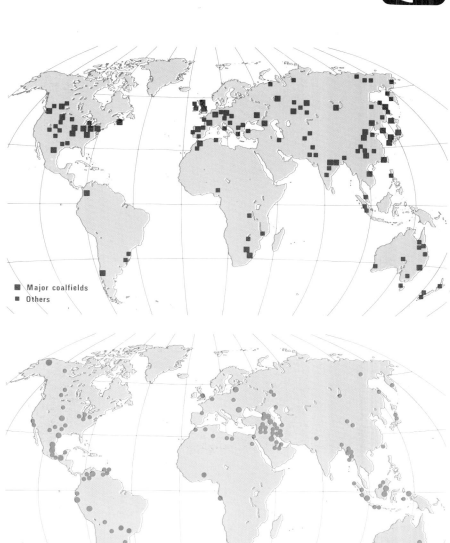

■ Major coalfields
■ Others

● Massive producers
● Smaller oilfields

● Gas-producing areas

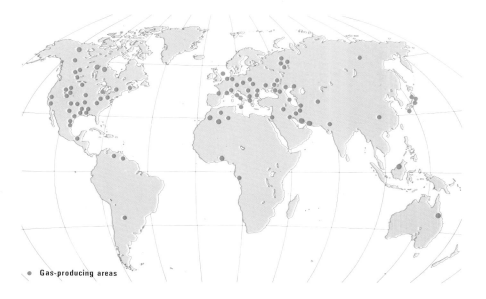

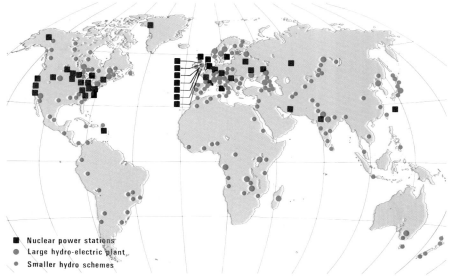

■ Nuclear power stations
● Large hydro-electric plant
● Smaller hydro schemes

The Oceans' Living Resources

Fish and shellfish were probably the first marine resources to be exploited by man. Many of his early settlements in coastal and estuarine areas bear witness to this with their ancient mounds of oyster and mussel shells. Even now, coastal fisheries remain a vital source of high quality protein for numerous primitive communities. And yet, in spite of this long history of coastal fishing, the commercial fisheries have been dominated by a mere handful of nations until recent times. Three-quarters of the world fish catch is still accounted for by only 14 countries.

The world fish catch is the only source of food that has managed to increase dramatically since the end of World War 2. In the decade from 1958-68 alone, it rose from below 34 million tons to 64 million tons. Although the catch fell by two per cent in 1969, it is expected to continue to improve and may even top the 120 million ton mark by the mid-1980s.

The steady growth of the commercial fisheries since the war has relied on improvements in technology and boats, and the spread of these modern techniques from traditional northern fisheries to newer ones being developed in the southern oceans. Peru, for example, now has the world's largest single species fishery, catching some 10 million tons of anchoveta a year: in 1958 the catch was only 960,000 tons. However, the time is fast approaching when few fish stocks will remain unexploited.

Already many established fisheries are beginning to suffer from the effects of over-fishing with too many boats pursuing too few fish, leading to the capture of younger, smaller fish and a decline in the fish stocks and the fisheries that they support. Only the briefest respite may be needed for the fish to recover: a single female fish can lay thousands of eggs in a single season. Over-exploitation of the whales and turtles is a much more serious matter. Already several species of whale are on the verge of extinction and, with one young born to a female every two years, the prospects for their recovery are poor.

The living resources of the oceans must be conserved and managed if they are to continue to provide mankind with food. It is now clear that the world fish catch has a finite limit, possibly about 200 million tons. With adequate international agreement and controls, this limit might one day be approached. The productivity of the oceans could be increased further only by harvesting animals lower than fish in the marine food chain or by artificially fertilizing and farming the seas. Some of the first steps in this direction are now in progress. Perhaps in the future a new pattern of exploitation will emerge, with fleets harvesting the oceanic fish while other fish, shellfish and crustaceans such as lobster and prawn are farmed in the shallow coastal waters.

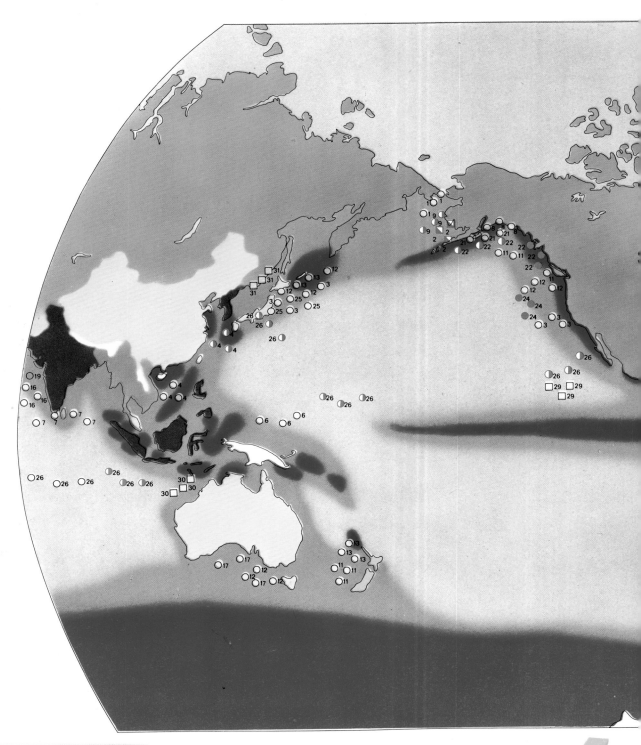

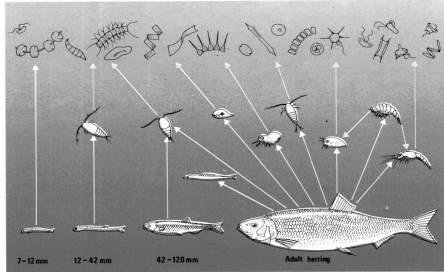

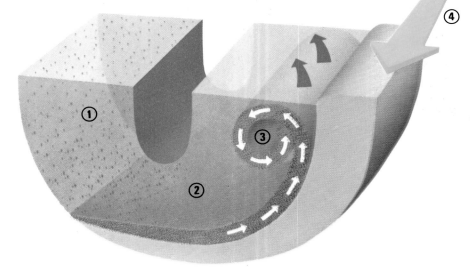

Marine food web *above*
The path leading to food fish such as the herring involves a succession of feeding and energy levels. The plants drifting in the plankton first convert the Sun's energy into a usable form through the process of photosynthesis (top band). The plants are then eaten by small planktonic animals (middle band). These in turn are eaten by the fish during its growth (bottom band). However, as the arrows indicate, the path from plant to fish is far from simple. At each point in the web, energy is exchanged and lost so that the adult fish receives less than a thousandth of the original energy captured in photosynthesis. This loss of energy has prompted suggestions for short-circuiting the process by harvesting members of the plankton itself – either the plants or the small crustaceans and other animals that feed on them.

Upwelling *above*
Most of the world's great fisheries occur in regions of upwelling where nutrient-rich water rises to the surface and supports prolific marine life. Deep ocean waters accumulate the remains of dead and decaying organisms (1) that rain down from the surface. When this nutrient-rich water (2) rises to the surface (3) it contains all the minerals and salts necessary for plant growth in approximately the ratio best suited to stimulate maximum growth. The actual mechanism which causes the water to rise to the surface can vary, but a common source is the interaction between surface winds and ocean currents running along the edge of continents. The wind (4) causes the surface water to move away from the coast, enabling the deep water to swirl up to the surface where it renews the supplies of plant nutrients.

World fisheries *left*
With more nations claiming a share of the oceans' living resources few productive regions remain unexplored by fishing fleets. Already many fisheries show signs of over-exploitation and some coastal states are demanding exclusive rights to very large areas of sea, e.g. Iceland's demand for a 50 mile limit.

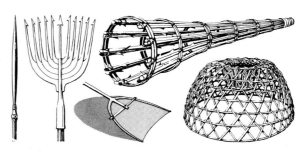

Fishing gear
Primitive fisheries use a wide range of techniques (above) including spears, nets and basket traps.

Mainstays of the modern commercial fisheries (below) are the gill net (top), the seine net and the otter trawl (bottom).

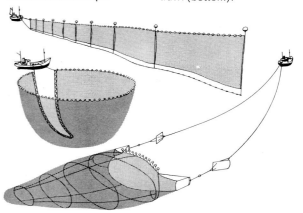

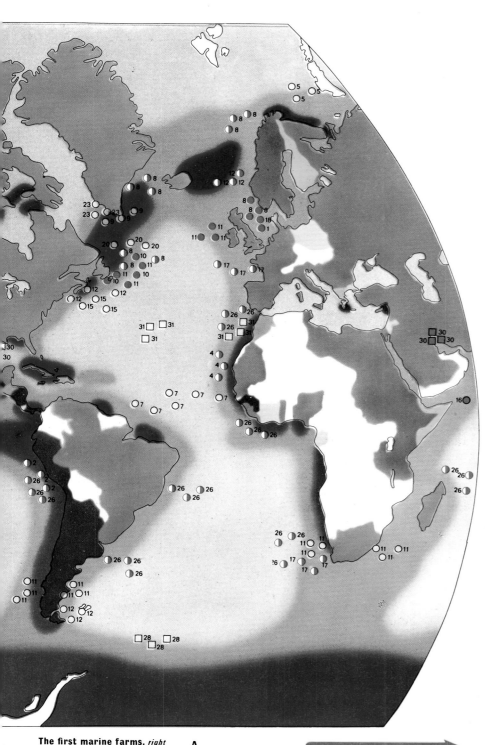

Biological productivity

■ Very favorable conditions for the growth of marine life

▨ Moderately favorable conditions for the growth of marine life

Exploitation of fish stocks

● Over-exploited by 1949

◐ Over-exploited by 1968

○ Under-exploited

Exploitation of crustaceans

◪ Over-exploited by 1968

□ Under-exploited

Key to numbers
1 Alaska pollack	16 Pelagic
2 Anchoveta	17 Pilchard
3 Anchovy	18 Plaice
4 Demersal fish	19 Pomfret
5 Capelin	20 Red fish
6 Carangidae	21 Rock fish
7 Clupeidae	22 Salmon
8 Cod	23 Sand eel
9 Flat fish	24 Sardine
10 Haddock	25 Saury
11 Hake	26 Tuna
12 Herring	27 King crab
13 Jack Mackerel	28 Krill
14 Mackerel	29 Crab
15 Menhaden	30 Shrimp
	31 Squid

Fishing limits

▢ Nations claiming a 3 mile exclusive zone

▨ Nations claiming a 6 mile exclusive zone

▩ Nations claiming a 12 mile exclusive zone

■ Nations claiming more than 12 miles

Commercial fish
Although the oceans contain many thousands of different fish species, very few of these support large commercial fisheries. The anchoveta supplies the largest single species fishery in the world with an annual catch of about 10 million tons. This is slightly greater than the total catch of the other species illustrated here.

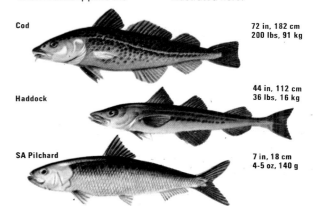

Anchoveta — 5 in, 13 cm / 2-3 oz, 85 g

Herring — 12 in, 30 cm / 8 oz, 227 g

Cod — 72 in, 182 cm / 200 lbs, 91 kg

Haddock — 44 in, 112 cm / 36 lbs, 16 kg

SA Pilchard — 7 in, 18 cm / 4-5 oz, 140 g

The first marine farms, *right*
An early use of marine stockades was to keep alive fish caught at sea until they were needed for eating (A). An advance on this is to catch young fish and then fatten them in fertile coastal waters (B). But marine farming really begins with the production of 'seed fish' which can be reared until they are large enough to survive at sea (C). Such a scheme was proposed in the early 1900s as a means of increasing the productivity of the North Sea fisheries. The proposal was rejected, although marine fish hatcheries existed at the time. These hatcheries, however, were unable to feed their young fish once the yolk sacs had become exhausted. Success became possible with the discovery that brine shrimps, hatched in large numbers, could be used as fish food and that antibiotics would prevent marine bacteria from coating the eggs and killing or weakening the fish embryos inside. The point has now been reached at which fish farming is possible, although fish reared in this way are still too expensive to compete with those caught at sea. In one scheme, eggs collected from adult fish kept in ponds are hatched and the young fed on diatoms and brine shrimps until large enough to be put into marine enclosures (D).

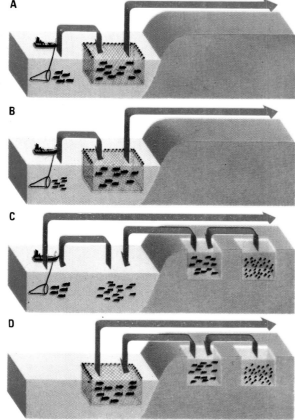

A

B

C

D

Enriching the sea *right, below*
Some marine farms in the future will exploit the store of nutrients that lie in the cold, deep ocean water. The value of this marine 'fertilizer' is clearly seen in areas where deep water rises to the surface. One project to create an artificial upwelling was started in the Virgin Islands in 1970. When completed it could include both a marine farm and provide fresh water supplies. In this system the cold nutrient-rich water (1) would be raised to the surface by a pump (2) driven by the warm, humid, prevailing winds (3). The cold water would then pass through a condenser (4) where it would be used to cool the wind and release its store of fresh water (5). Finally, the water, now warmed to the temperature of the surface waters, would be used to promote the growth of marine plants and animals such as shellfish, prawn and valuable food fish within net enclosures in the lagoon (6). Deep ocean water may also be used to combat thermal pollution, particularly in tropical areas where marine organisms live close to their upper temperature limit. The cold water would cool down the warm effluent discharged from power stations as well as provide valuable nutrients for marine aquiculture.

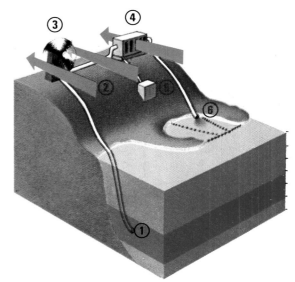

The Food Resource : 1

Combine harvester discharging wheat into trailer

Agriculture has always been a cornerstone of human civilization. Until man was able to give up the life of a nomadic hunter he could not be called civilized, and it was the settled life based on the land which enabled progress toward modern society to begin. Today agriculture is the occupation of more people than all other industries, but the pattern of their work varies greatly. In poor or developing lands as many as 90 per cent of the population live directly off the land, whereas in the most industrialized countries the proportion can be as low as three per cent.

The underlying purpose of farming is to convert the energy of sunlight into a form in which it can be assimilated by humans. Initially this can be done only by photosynthesis in green plants, and here the efficiency of the conversion process – expressed in terms of assimilable food energy obtained from a given amount of sunlight – varies from about two per cent down to less than one part in 1000. Further stages involve the consumption of plants by livestock to provide meat and other food for man, or the direct consumption of fruit, vegetables and cereals by man himself. Each additional step in this food chain involves large losses in energy, lowering the overall 'efficiency' of the process.

For many years research has led to improved methods of producing crops, by developing new plant strains with a higher edible yield or greater resistance to disease, by increasing both the area of land under cultivation and the nutritional value of the soil, by devising swifter and surer techniques of cultivation and by reducing the labor effort needed. Improved methods are especially needed in regions of poor farming. The 'Green Revolution' of SE Asia has already shown how yields can be increased dramatically, although at a greater cost in terms of agricultural chemicals and water supplies. Another promising way of increasing food supplies is to extract protein from plants such as soybean and even grass, and to convert them into forms that have the texture and taste of meat. For the more distant future there are prospects of growing single-cell protein and other revolutionary foods which in theory could at least double the Earth's ability to produce food.

World crop production and trade *right above*
In the large map, symbols and shading indicate the pattern of distribution of a selection of the most important crops used for human food. The distribution shown is that of growing area. This is often far removed from the plant's original center, and today the world crop pattern is being subjected to dramatic changes. For example, enormous increases have taken place in Italy's yield of maize (corn) and the United States' production of rice. Pie diagrams are used to show world crop trade, the pie area giving output and the color segments the products (key, far right).

Some important crops *right*
Eight of the world's chief human food crops are described individually at right. The figure below the name is the aggregate world production expressed in metric tons (1 m. ton is 0.984 British ton and 1.12 US tons). The pie diagrams in the form of segmented drums show the percentage of the world total raised by the three largest producing countries (in each case China is the People's Republic). The sketches illustrate the mature plant and its fruit, a form often unfamiliar to consumers. Similar panels on the next two pages deal with livestock, fish and oils.

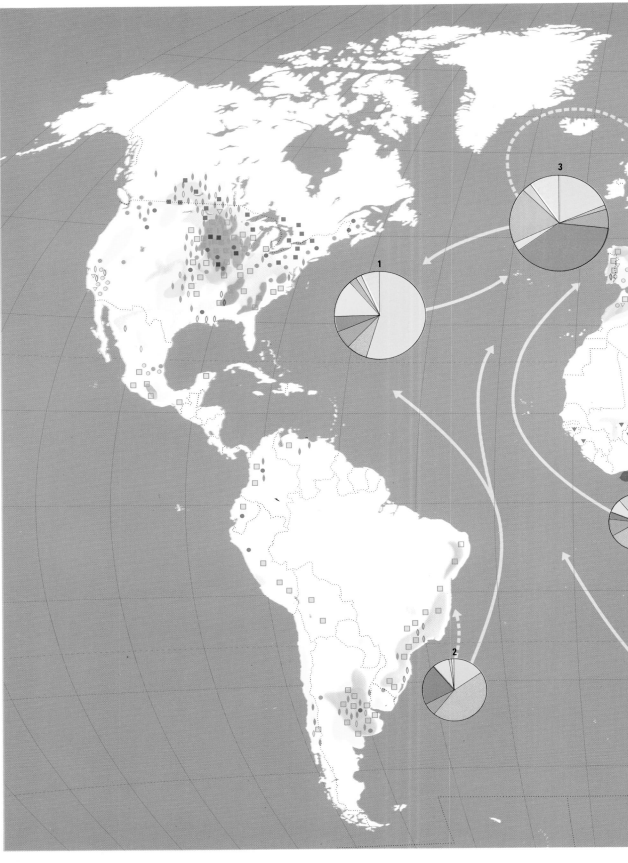

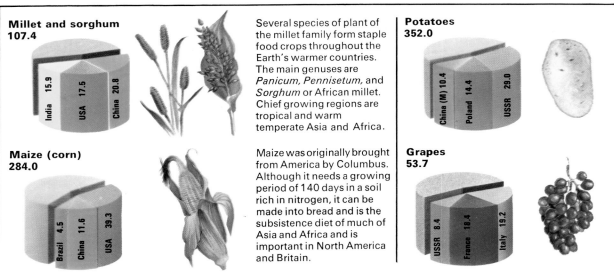

Millet and sorghum
107.4
India 15.9 | USA 17.5 | China 20.8

Maize (corn)
284.0
Brazil 4.5 | China 11.6 | USA 39.3

Several species of plant of the millet family form staple food crops throughout the Earth's warmer countries. The main genuses are *Panicum, Pennisetum,* and *Sorghum* or African millet. Chief growing regions are tropical and warm temperate Asia and Africa.

Maize was originally brought from America by Columbus. Although it needs a growing period of 140 days in a soil rich in nitrogen, it can be made into bread and is the subsistence diet of much of Asia and Africa and is important in North America and Britain.

Potatoes
352.0
China (M) 10.4 | Poland 14.4 | USSR 29.0

Grapes
53.7
USSR 8.4 | France 18.4 | Italy 19.2

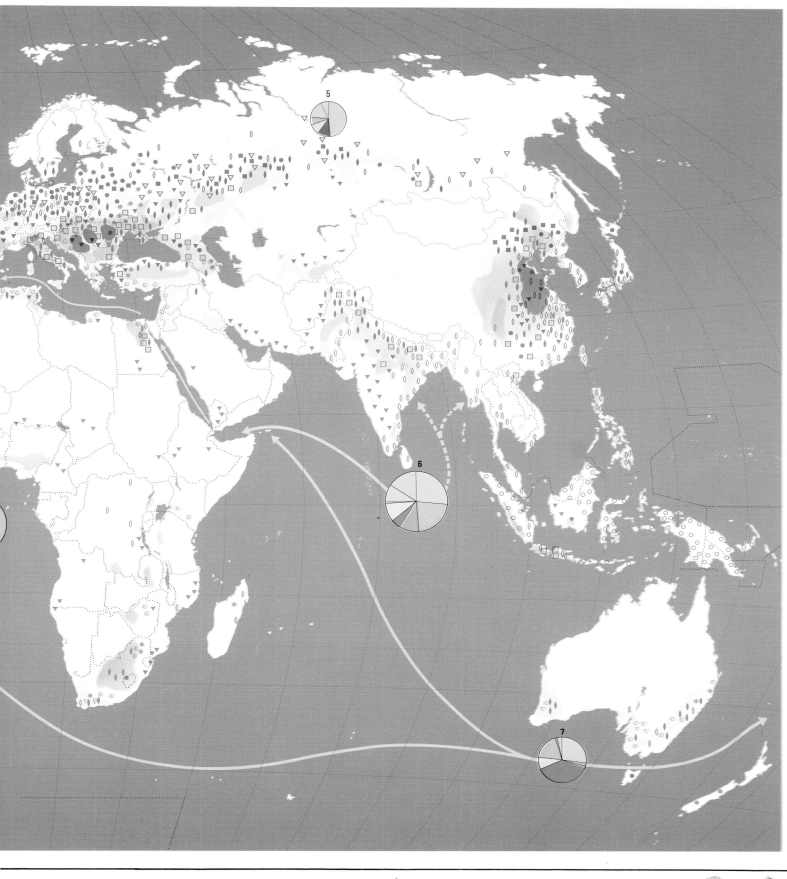

The circular 'pie diagrams'
depict world trade in selected
agricultural products in 1968:
1 N and Central America;
2 S America 3 Europe 4 Africa;
5 Soviet Union 6 Asia
7 Oceania Products considered
are cereals, beverages, meat
and meat products, fish and fish
products, dairy products, fruit
and vegetables, vegetable oils
and sugar.

Cereals
Beverages
Fruit
Meat and meat products
Sugar
Dairy products
Vegetable oils
Fish and fish products

Total trade US$ million

5000

2500

1250

Native to South America,
the potato was introduced
by Spanish explorers to an
intrigued Europe about
1572. Although it needs a
long, cool growing season,
and a high nutrient level. it
yields more food per area of
land than cereals. It is a
source of alcohol.

The vine thrives in warm,
temperate areas, although
the quality of its rootstock
is critical to its nutrient
demand and its resistance
to disease and drought.
About 80 per cent of the
world crop is made into
wine, but large quantities
are dried for raisins.

Rice
284.2

Pakistan 7.1   India 21.0   China 32.0

Rye
33.4

W Germany 9.5   Poland 25.5   USSR 42.2

Grown in Asia for at least
5000 years, rice was
introduced into Europe by
the Arabs. Irrigation or a
very heavy rainfall is
essential for growing rice,
with the fields being flooded
for most of the season. The
main source of vitamins, the
husk, is removed in milling.

Gradually giving way to
other cereals, rye is
important where soils are
sandy and acid and the
winters long and harsh.
From Britain deep into
Siberia it remains a staple
foodstuff used for animal
feeds, for various forms of
bread and for whisky.

Wheat
332.5

China 8.1   USA 12.9   USSR 28.1

Barley
145.1

USA 6.3   China 9.9   USSR 19.9

Wheat is the most basic
human food of the
temperate zone. It flourishes
in well-drained, fertile
conditions, but can rapidly
exhaust the soil. New breeds
have been genetically
tailored to improve yield
and resistance to disease.

Barley has a very short
growing season and so can
be produced further north
and at a higher altitude than
any other cereal. It needs
good drainage and non-
acid soil. More than half the
world crop is eaten by
livestock, and 12 per cent
goes into making beer.

The Food Resource:2

Unloading frozen lamb carcasses.

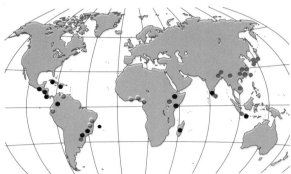

Beverages
Coffee, cocoa and tea are grown in the tropics for export to economically advanced countries where their chief role is to add flavor rather than to provide nutrition. Tea is the cheapest at present.

- ● Coffee
- ● Cocoa
- ● Tea

Spices
Invariably these are pungent, aromatic vegetable products. They have been important European imports since pre-Roman times, and a major source today is Indonesia. Spices are extracted from buds, bark and pods.

- ■ Pimento
- ▲ Ginger
- ◆ Nutmeg
- ● Mace
- ■ Pepper
- ◆ Cloves
- ● Cinnamon
- ■ Cassia
- ▲ Vanilla

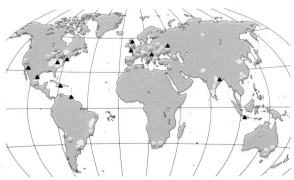

Alcohol and tobacco
Originally native to South America, tobacco was brought to Europe by the Spanish 400 years ago. Today, it is grown all over the world in various climates and soils. The US is the biggest producer.

- ■ Beer
- ● Wine
- ▲ Spirits
- ■ Tobacco

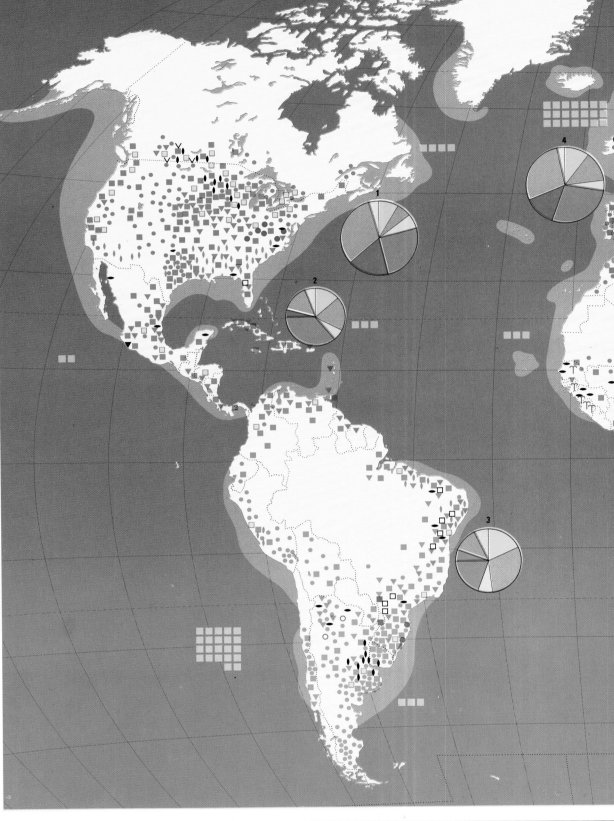

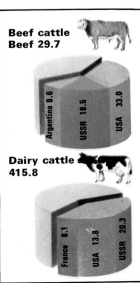

**Beef cattle
Beef 29.7**

Argentina 8.6 | USSR 18.5 | USA 33.0

The two principal types of domestic cattle, the Europoean and the tropical Zebu or humped type, are found all over the world in every type of climate. There is an urgent need in the developing countries for better breeding, disease control and management.

**Dairy cattle
415.8**

France 8.1 | USA 13.8 | USSR 20.3

Specialized dairy farming takes place mainly near densely populated urban areas with a high standard of living, though there is an increasing trend towards combined milk/meat herds. Various forms of processing, such as canning and freezing, extend product life.

**Sheep
Mutton 4.5**

India 8.2 | Australia 15.0 | USSR 22.3

Sheep are kept mainly for meat and wool, although in southern Europe they may be milked and in the tropics the hides are the most important product. Sheep do not lend themselves readily to 'factory farming' and are raised on marginal land only.

**Pigs
Pork 24.5**

China 11.0 | USSR 16.7 | USA 24.1

Because they are often kept indoors, the distribution of pigs depends more on food supply than on the climate. They are often found on mixed farms where they are fed on by-products such as skim milk. Their breeding cycle is complete in about six months.

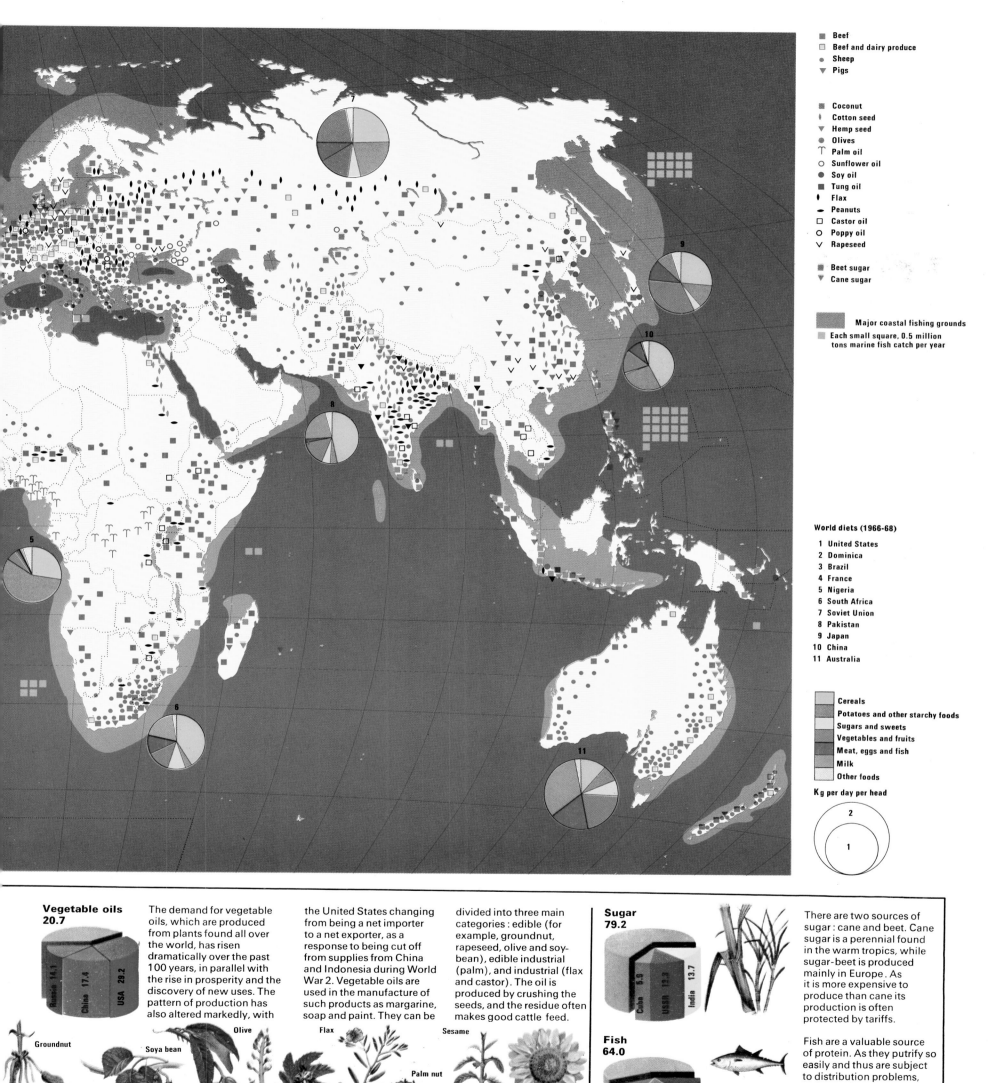

■ Beef
□ Beef and dairy produce
● Sheep
▼ Pigs

■ Coconut
✝ Cotton seed
▼ Hemp seed
● Olives
⊤ Palm oil
○ Sunflower oil
● Soy oil
■ Tung oil
♦ Flax
➖ Peanuts
□ Castor oil
○ Poppy oil
∨ Rapeseed

■ Beet sugar
▼ Cane sugar

▨ Major coastal fishing grounds
▨ Each small square, 0.5 million tons marine fish catch per year

World diets (1966-68)

1 United States
2 Dominica
3 Brazil
4 France
5 Nigeria
6 South Africa
7 Soviet Union
8 Pakistan
9 Japan
10 China
11 Australia

Cereals
Potatoes and other starchy foods
Sugars and sweets
Vegetables and fruits
Meat, eggs and fish
Milk
Other foods

Kg per day per head

2

1

Vegetable oils 20.7

Russia 14.1 China 17.4 USA 29.2

The demand for vegetable oils, which are produced from plants found all over the world, has risen dramatically over the past 100 years, in parallel with the rise in prosperity and the discovery of new uses. The pattern of production has also altered markedly, with the United States changing from being a net importer to a net exporter, as a response to being cut off from supplies from China and Indonesia during World War 2. Vegetable oils are used in the manufacture of such products as margarine, soap and paint. They can be divided into three main categories: edible (for example, groundnut, rapeseed, olive and soybean), edible industrial (palm), and industrial (flax and castor). The oil is produced by crushing the seeds, and the residue often makes good cattle feed.

Groundnut Soya bean Olive Flax Sesame

Cotton Castor Not to scale Palm nut Sunflower

Sugar 79.2

Cuba 6.9 USSR 13.3 India 13.7

There are two sources of sugar: cane and beet. Cane sugar is a perennial found in the warm tropics, while sugar-beet is produced mainly in Europe. As it is more expensive to produce than cane its production is often protected by tariffs.

Fish 64.0

China 11.8 Japan 13.5 Peru 16.4

Fish are a valuable source of protein. As they putrify so easily and thus are subject to distribution problems, an increasing amount of the world catch is converted into meal for use in animal feeds. Most fish are caught near the coasts over the continental shelves.

The Settled World

Man is the most mobile of animals and has adapted himself to life in almost every part of the Earth's land surface. The earliest adaptations involved bodily changes giving rise to three main racial groups: one was peculiar to Africa; a second group, adapted to colder conditions, arose in central and northern Asia and eventually spread to the Americas; and, finally, a third group ranged from northern Europe to Oceania. Nevertheless, this early settlement still remains a matter of debate. The more recent migrations of man are much easier to trace and to explain.

Although the expansion of population and the need for food are a major underlying reason for migration, the movement of people around the world is not always voluntary. The most spectacular forced movement was that of West Africans caught up in the slave trade. Anything from ten to fifteen millions reached America, but many millions more did not survive the journey. Only modern warfare has caused comparable movement. In World War 2 about 60 million people were forced to move by such means as

Neanderthal man

The spread of mankind *right, above*
Early hominid fossils have been discovered throughout the eastern hemisphere, but on present evidence the birthplace of mankind appears to lie somewhere in central Africa. From here, and possibly from other centres, man has spread across the entire land surface of the Earth. Ancestral man may have been a relatively adaptable animal whose physical make-up changed according to climate. In Africa the negro is well adapted to strong sunlight, while Mongoloids appear to have been adapted to cold before they spread from Asia to the Americas.

deportation, evacuation and transfer of minority groups. After the partition of India, a million Hindus left Pakistan and almost as many Moslems left India. Forced movement has therefore played a large part in determining the shifting pattern of population.

In modern times the overwhelming movements are voluntary, whether for short distances or long. Although there are examples of small communities moving for ideological reasons, the vast majority of people move for economic or social reasons. The movement from Europe to the United States was that of an impoverished peasantry trying to improve its lot. The classic example is that of the Irish movement after the potato famine of the 1840s. Industrialization, which brought more prosperity to Europe, helped to stem the movement away. Even voluntary movement is generally controlled when it involves migration from one country to another. Sometimes states are reluctant to allow emigration because it depletes their manpower, while states often control immigration in an effort to protect the indigenous populations or to secure some particular social or economic goal.

Migrations bring many social problems. Migrants have to adapt to a new society and possibly learn a new language; and the problems are even worse for the society which receives them, especially if the migrants come from a variety of sources. In the past the United States has tried to absorb migrants completely, minimizing their differences, and aiming to Americanize them thoroughly. This is difficult when the differences are cultural; when they are racial then it becomes almost impossible.

The great migrations *right*
In historic times migrations were principally a story of the movement of people from heavily populated areas to relatively empty ones. Some of these great mass movements were forced, an outstanding example of this kind being the transport of millions of slaves from West Africa to North America. But overpopulation and economic pressure caused an even greater voluntary movement to the New World, in this case from Europe. It was by such migrations that man was able to open up the continental interiors in North America and Asiatic Russia.

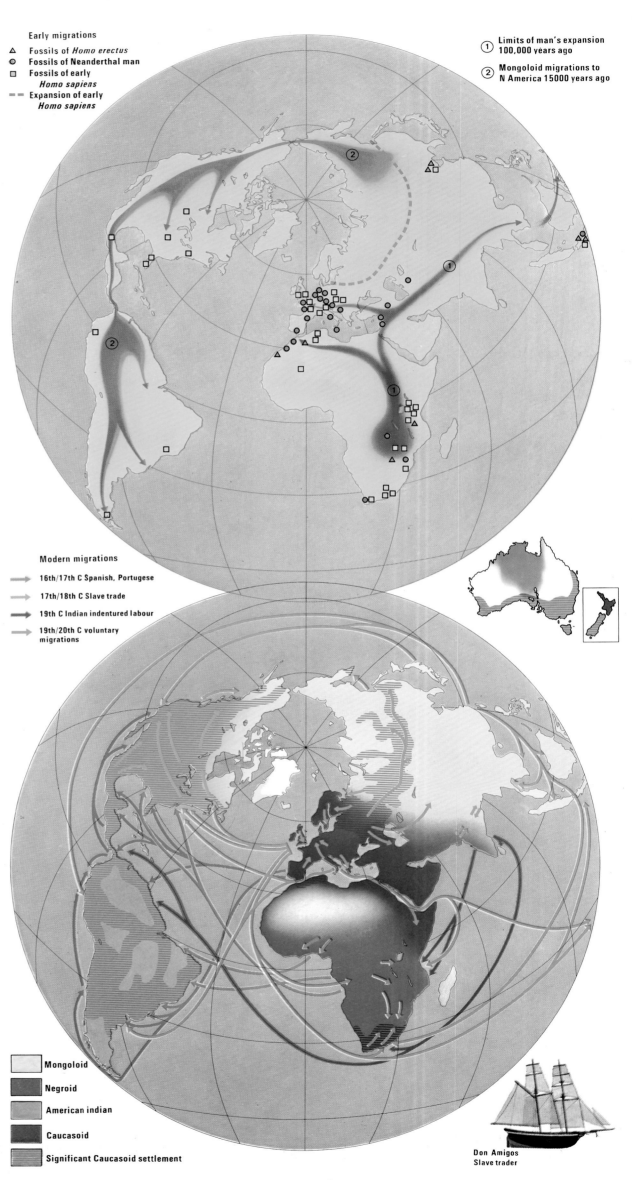

Early migrations
△ Fossils of *Homo erectus*
◎ Fossils of Neanderthal man
□ Fossils of early *Homo sapiens*
- - - Expansion of early *Homo sapiens*

① Limits of man's expansion 100,000 years ago
② Mongoloid migrations to N America 15000 years ago

Modern migrations
➡ 16th/17th C Spanish, Portugese
➡ 17th/18th C Slave trade
➡ 19th C Indian indentured labour
➡ 19th/20th C voluntary migrations

Mongoloid
Negroid
American indian
Caucasoid
Significant Caucasoid settlement

Don Amigos
Slave trader

The 'known world' *left*
To the classic civilizations and medieval Europe the known world comprised most of Europe and the north coast of Africa. Beyond this region knowledge was very sketchy. So-called world maps were bordered by pure speculation, apart from China. Early men may have explored other distant regions, but the only sure evidence that has survived tells of voyages by the Norse (Vikings) to Iceland and Greenland.

→ Norsemen c 1000 AD
→ Marco Polo 1271-95
→ Ibn Batuta 1324-55

A spherical world *left*
Until after 1450 most men took it for granted the world was flat . But the notion of a spherical world, was courageously assumed by navigators such as Columbus, who were in a position to test it. There ensued the greatest age of terrestrial discovery, which opened up all the continents to exploration – and to exploitation – by the Western Europeans. By 1900 little of the Earth remained to be discovered.

→ Columbus 1492-3
→ DaGama 1497-99
→ Magellan 1519-22
→ Tasman 1642-44
→ Cook 1768-71

Leif the Lucky
Norse longship

Marco Polo
Overland routes

Christopher Columbus
Santa Maria

Vasco da Gama
San Gabriel

Ferdinand Magellan
Victoria

James Cook
Endeavour

Great Britain

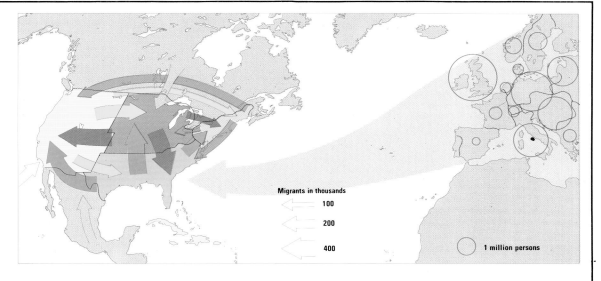

Colonizing America *right and above*
The greatest voluntary movement in the history of man was the colonization of North America in the 19th century. It involved about 36 million people, and almost all of them came from Western Europe. Until the 1890s the majority came from the British Isles, Germany and Scandinavia, but in the early 20th century the main sources shifted to Eastern Europe and the Mediterranean. Within the US itself there has also been further massive migration.

Migrants in thousands
100
200
400

1 million persons

Urbanization

Today there are several localized areas in which refugees are seeking to escape from war, civil strife or a discriminatory administration, but there are no massive population movements such as were common in the past. By far the biggest movement in terms of numbers and ultimate social consequence is the steady drift from the countryside to the cities. In 1900, about one person in every six in the so-called advanced countries lived in a large city; by 1950 the proportion had risen to one in three, and the movement had become worldwide. Until this century there were very few 'million cities', but today there are more than 130 distributed across the globe, with the fastest-growing examples often lying in developing lands. Until this century cities, such as Rome (above, left), grew naturally without imposing any insuperable problems. Today's cities, such as Tokyo (above, right), are the sites of problems of congestion, pollution, transport and almost every other facet of human life on a scale so large that there is no simple solution.

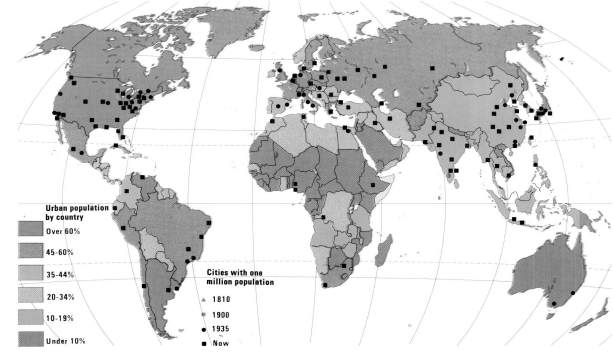

Urban population
by country
Over 60%
45-60%
35-44%
20-34%
10-19%
Under 10%

Cities with one
million population
▲ 1810
● 1900
● 1935
■ Now

The growing cities *above*
The biggest modern migration is the move from the country into the cities.

Spurred by prospects of a richer life, this movement usually involves quite short distances but extremely

large numbers of people. Ultimately nearly the entire human population will probably live in huge urban

regions, each housing many millions, with the intervening spaces used for food production and leisure.

Religion

The earliest religions, still strong among pre-civilized peoples, were animistic and identified with the forces of nature. Even when these have crystallized into systems of beliefs centered on gods there often is still a close identification with a restricted territory. These ethnic religions are confined to specific peoples having a limited range of movement. Such a territorial concept of a deity is apparent in the earlier parts of Jewish and Christian scripture. In the religions of the East beliefs of this kind became more diffuse and the system more philosophical. The teaching of Gautama Buddha (563-483 BC) was a denial of materialism, in the face of the miseries of life in a part of the world where existence is still equated with hardship. Confucius (551-478 BC) was more concerned with defining social relationships and was able to absorb primitive ancestor worship, which still survives. In India Hinduism is a comprehensive system embracing a range of beliefs in numbers of gods but welding the whole together by fundamental attitudes such as the doctrine of rebirth, worship of cattle and the caste system. The last is a practical social element based on occupation and very different from the philosophical elements of Hinduism.

Ethnic religions in the Near East took on a totally different aspect by becoming monotheistic: the tribal god of the Jews became for them the only god. To Christianity, which emerged from Judaism, monotheism was central, and so it became in Islam, which owed much to both Judaism and Christianity. Judaism was dispersed, but retained its strength until Israel was re-established in 1948. But Christianity and Islam became the great 'saving' religions whose aim was the conversion of mankind. The early history of Christianity is of proselytizing, and later of conquest. And within a short time of the death of Mohammed (AD 632), his beliefs also had been carried far.

But a characteristic of both these religions is the deep schisms which have appeared. In Islam there is sharp disagreement between Sunni and Shia. Equally marked is the division of Christianity into Roman Catholics and Protestants, with a strong third element in the Eastern Orthodox Church.

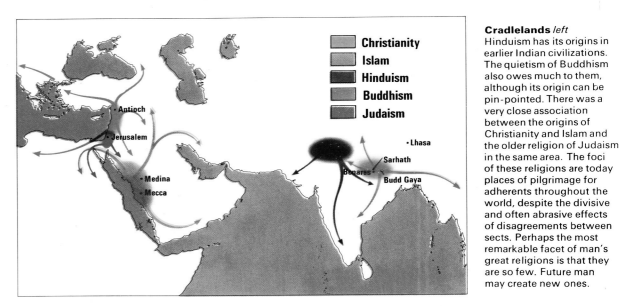

Christianity
Islam
Hinduism
Buddhism
Judaism

Cradlelands *left*
Hinduism has its origins in earlier Indian civilizations. The quietism of Buddhism also owes much to them, although its origin can be pin-pointed. There was a very close association between the origins of Christianity and Islam and the older religion of Judaism in the same area. The foci of these religions are today places of pilgrimage for adherents throughout the world, despite the divisive and often abrasive effects of disagreements between sects. Perhaps the most remarkable facet of man's great religions is that they are so few. Future man may create new ones.

Hindu *left*
While most Hindus worship at home, often to local or to family deities, they may passively watch ceremonies conducted by priests in temples for their gods. In Jinja, Uganda, priests pour ghee (clarified butter) into a fire in supplication to the terrible god Amba (Durga).

Islam *left*
Seated in the open court-yard of a mosque an Indian reads the Koran. This holy book, about as long as the Christian New Testament, is the scripture revealed to Mohammed. It is the basis of Moslem teaching and social behaviour; mosques are also schools.

Buddhism *left*
Buddhist temples are ornate and richly decorated. Here in Singapore an assistant priest studies the scriptures. His white robe distinguishes him from a monk who would wear saffron yellow (and be prohibited from having any possessions apart from vestments, razor and bowl).

Christianity *left*
Central to the belief in Christianity is the observance of the sacraments, such as baptism, confirmation, matrimony, burials, and other rites considered to have been instituted by Jesus. Shown here is a baptism of baby being performed by a priest.

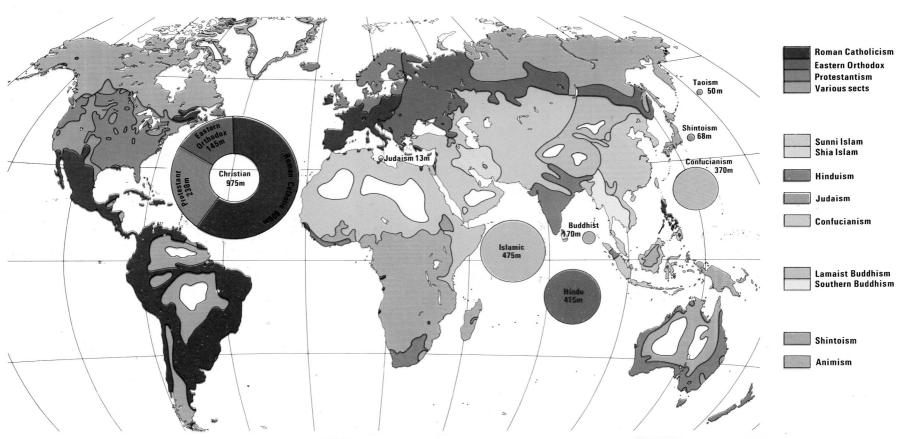

Roman Catholicism
Eastern Orthodox
Protestantism
Various sects

Sunni Islam
Shia Islam

Hinduism

Judaism

Confucianism

Lamaist Buddhism
Southern Buddhism

Shintoism

Animism

Contrasting beliefs
Christianity is numerically the strongest religion, with Roman Catholicism the largest of its many sects. Islam is next largest (overwhelmingly Sunni), and Hinduism is growing with the Indian population. Animism and ethnic religions prevail where Western influences are slight or where, as in Central Africa, there is a very large indigenous population. The most remarkable spread has been that of the great proselytizing religions, Christianity and Islam. The former is world-wide, while the latter is restricted to hot, dry lands of the Old World. Many minor sects are urban.

Shinto *left*
This religion is based on a multitude of small shrines dedicated to numerous deities. Its priests were government officials until 1945. The Japanese temple in the background contains an inner sanctuary where these priests recite, pray and conduct the purification rites.

Judaism *left*
Inside the West London Synagogue the Rabbi holds up the richly decorated Torah (Law) which contains the five Books of Moses. Behind him is the Ark. Judaism emphasizes the transcendence of God, whose name it avoids by substituting some epithet (such as 'the Holy One').

Language

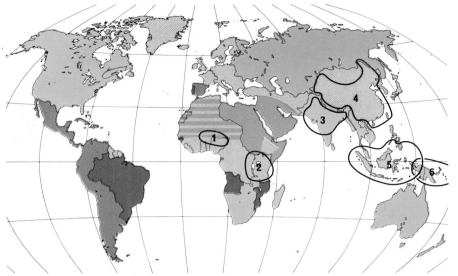

Of all those things which tend to divide mankind into groups, language is possibly the most important. While it binds together those who speak a common language, it imposes a major handicap upon communication between different groups. Language is the medium by which ideas are transmitted, and this tends to give a cultural homogeneity to each language group. For example, the 'English-speaking world' identifies people with common culture and sympathetic beliefs. Language also has very strong emotional connotations, because it is associated with the individual's earliest memories. Consequently a great amount of tension can arise between contiguous language groups, or when a majority language is given precedence in a multi-language state. The subdivision of India, largely on a language basis, produced many riots. The dividing line between Flemish and Walloon in Belgium is marked by constant tensions. Language is the main basis of the claims of the French Canadians to independence.

World languages and their distribution are extremely complex. Even the major groups of languages, such as Latin or Teutonic, do not mean much in practical terms because to the layman it is the minor differences which count and not the basic similarities. Differences even of dialect are enough to divide people: the least nuance will serve to identify group antipathies. 'Speaking another language' can apply to subtleties of meaning even within one language. One way of overcoming this problem is to encourage second languages of international standing. Many of the world's peoples are bilingual—a fact which makes the mapping of distributions very difficult. Even so it is difficult to overcome a person's emotional link with his first language. There are over 30 languages in Europe alone. Many of the minor languages are in danger of disappearing. This is partly because they cannot cope with the language of modern technology, and partly because fluent knowledge of a major language is an essential. Within the British Isles, for example, the Celtic languages could not hope to compete with English and some such as Cornish and Manx have virtually disappeared.

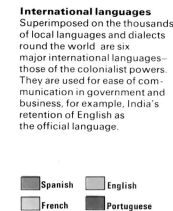

Spanish	English
French	Portuguese
Russian	Arabic

1 Hausa   4 Chinese
2 Swahili   5 Malay
3 Hindi/Urdu   6 Melanesian pidgin

The written word
left and foot of page
The invention of writing has proved one of the most potent of all human tools. Some of the earliest written forms show clear derivation from pictures; indeed Nasi (foot of page) is still a major language in the Yunnan province of China. But most modern languages have become streamlined into simpler forms. Even Chinese is being simplified, although its hieroglyphic form remains. Modern Burmese, based on curved characters, contrasts with the angular Sanskrit which is an ancient script pictorially resembling Hindi and other languages of modern India.

Russian
Идея использования квантовых систем для генерадиоволн оказалась весьма плодотворной и недостижимые для обычной радиотехники резу.

Burmese
ဗုဒ္ဓဘုန်းကရိယာများ ရှိပြီးဖြစ်လေသည်။ အလယ်တွင်ရ ပုဂ္ဂိုလ်များအတွက် အထူးသင်တန်းများ

Greek
Ὁ Ὀδυσσεὺς καὶ οἱ σύντροφοι αὐτοῦ πλοῖα, τὰ ὁποῖα ἦσαν πλήρη λαφύρων, αἰ Τρῳάδος, ἐπιθυμοῦντες νὰ φθάσωσιν ὅσο

Hebrew
יהודים שְׁמָרדי בָּךְ. כְּמָן שֶׁהוֹיַע לְאָנְטּפֹטְרֶם זְרחָה בֵן שֶׁרָאָה אֶת שִׁמְעוֹן הַצַּדִּיק יָרַד מִמֶּרְכַּבְתּוֹ וְהָשְׁתַּחֲוָה

Sanskrit
संस्कृत नाम देवी वाग् ह्वानुव्याना महर्षिभिः। तद्वस्य तत्तमो देशोत्रिये अनेकं प्राक्तकम्॥ प्राभेरादिगिरः काव्यव्यपदेश इति स्मृता। शास्त्रम् तु सैस्कृत्य मन्यद् प्रयोगतयोदितम्॥ रूपेयं प्रसाद समता माधुर्य मुकुमारता। अर्थव्यापितर

Chinese
是
停業。光是倫敦一地，過去一年來停

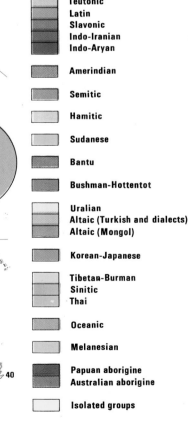

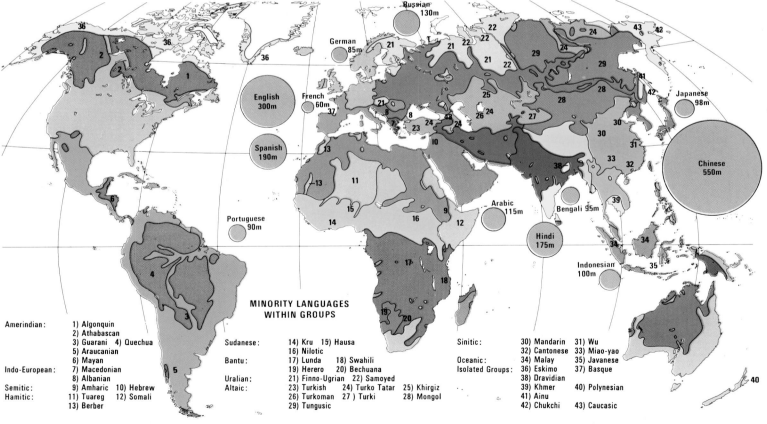

Russian 130m
German 85m
English 300m
French 60m
Spanish 190m
Portuguese 90m
Arabic 115m
Bengali 95m
Hindi 175m
Chinese 550m
Japanese 98m
Indonesian 100m

MINORITY LANGUAGES
WITHIN GROUPS

Amerindian: 1) Algonquin
              2) Athabascan
              3) Guarani 4) Quechua
              5) Araucanian
              6) Mayan
Indo-European: 7) Macedonian
              8) Albanian
Semitic: 9) Amharic 10) Hebrew
Hamitic: 11) Tuareg 12) Somali
              13) Berber

Sudanese: 14) Kru 15) Hausa
          16) Nilotic
Bantu: 17) Lunda   18) Swahili
          19) Herero 20) Bechuana
Uralian: 21) Finno-Ugrian 22) Samoyed
Altaic: 23) Turkish   24) Turko Tatar 25) Khirgiz
          26) Turkoman 27) Turki   28) Mongol
          29) Tungusic

Sinitic: 30) Mandarin 31) Wu
                32) Cantonese 33) Miao-yao
Oceanic: 34) Malay   35) Javanese
Isolated Groups: 36) Eskimo   37) Basque
                38) Dravidian
                39) Polynesian
                40) Ainu
                41) Ainu
                42) Chukchi   43) Caucasic

	Teutonic
	Latin
	Slavonic
	Indo-Iranian
	Indo-Aryan
	Amerindian
	Semitic
	Hamitic
	Sudanese
	Bantu
	Bushman-Hottentot
	Uralian
	Altaic (Turkish and dialects)
	Altaic (Mongol)
	Korean-Japanese
	Tibetan-Burman
	Sinitic
	Thai
	Oceanic
	Melanesian
	Papuan aborigine
	Australian aborigine
	Isolated groups

Contrasting languages
The biggest language group is Chinese, but this is really a profusion of dialects. English, Spanish and Portuguese have spread with colonization, while Russian has become a uniform language from Europe to the Pacific. Easy communications will increase the domination of the great international languages for education, commerce and cultural exchange. This means that many more people will have to become at least bilingual, although minor languages may survive indefinitely. It is unlikely that cultural diversity, which depends so much on language, will be submerged.

Nasi   New Assyrian   Mayan

Egyptian hieroglyphic

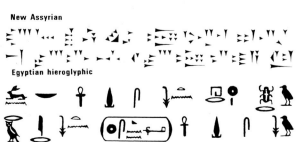

The Population Problem

In the year 1000 there were about 300 million people. In the last century the population reached 1000 million. Today it exceeds 3600 million. In 2000 it is predicted to reach 7000 million, and in 2050 something between 12000 and 20000 million. The main reason is that even with generally improved survival rates for children, little attempt has been made in many countries to curb the size of families.

The distribution of humans over the Earth has always been grossly uneven, and it appears likely to stay that way. While man has never ceased to open up and exploit new regions, a process of urbanization has become clearly evident in recent years. The more advanced the development of a nation, the more its cities attract people from the surrounding countryside. In most industrialized countries the proportion of the population living in cities has risen to 60 or 70 per cent. Modern cities pose severe social and environmental problems; they have to be considered as living, adaptable organisms in themselves if human life is not to become increasingly frustrating.

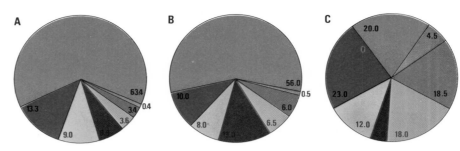

A   B   C

Asia   USSR
Africa   North America
Latin America   Oceania
Europe

People and land area *left*
Nearly two-thirds of the births (percentages per continent, A) and half the population (B) are in only quarter of the area (C).

World population density *below*
Humanity is distributed over the Earth's land surface in a most uneven way. Dividing the population of each country by its area yields such diverse figures (for 1965) as 3.8 inhabitants per square mile for Australia and almost 10000 per square mile for Hong Kong (1.46 and 3900 per square kilometer, respectively). This map indicates density in proportion to the heights of the columns.

North America and Europe
Europe has for centuries housed about one-sixth of the world's population, but the developing countries are reducing this proportion. Despite massive migrations and wars, the pattern of settlement has changed little in 500 years. In contrast North America was almost uninhabited 200 years ago, but the westward migration of the white man opened up the continent. But most of the population is still concentrated along the coasts and Great Lakes.

Latin America
In 1750 Central and South America had more than six times as many inhabitants as the north. Although North America surged ahead in 1860, S America is today the fastest growing continent in the world, mainly on or near the coast.

An overcrowded world *right and above*
Of all the problems facing man today the most intractable and persistent is the basic fact that his numbers are growing in an excessive and uncontrolled manner. When the total human population is plotted graphically the result is frightening in its implications. Cold statistics (right), projected to the year 2000, bring home the desperate problems of an overcrowded world.

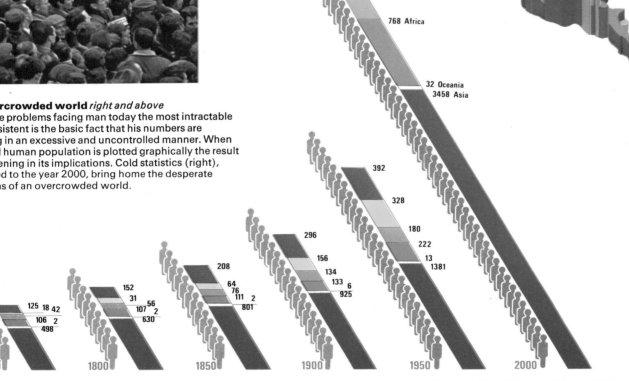

527 Europe
992 North and South America
353 USSR
768 Africa
32 Oceania
3458 Asia

392
328
180
222
13 1381

296
156
134
133 6
925

208
64
76 2
111
801

152
31 56
107 2
630

125 18 42
106 2
498

1750   1800   1850   1900   1950   2000

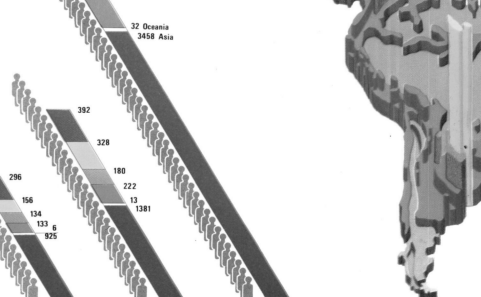

UK births and deaths *left*
The basic reason for the population explosion is an excess of births over deaths. In the UK both birth and death rates have declined during the past 100 years, but over five year periods births have always exceeded deaths, though in the 1930s the margin was very small.

Population in millions

33 35 52
29 38 45
20
10

Births per thousand living
Deaths per thousand living

1841-50 1971-80 1901-05 1931-35 1991-95

23 23 15 12 11

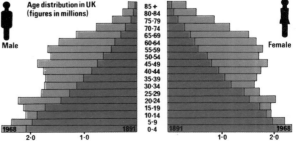

Age distribution in UK (figures in millions)

Male   Female

85+
80-84
75-79
70-74
65-69
60-64
55-59
50-54
45-49
40-44
35-39
30-34
25-29
20-24
15-19
10-14
5-9
0-4

1968   1891   1891   1968
2·0   1·0   1·0   2·0

Age groups: Mexico   Sweden

85+
80-84
75-79
70-74
65-69
60-64
55-59
50-54
45-49
40-44
35-39
30-34
25-29
20-24
15-19
10-14
5-9
0-4

Age distribution *right*
British population growth is about 0.5 per cent, or 250,000 people, per year. This is a modest rate and gives an age distribution where the old are almost as numerous as the young (right above). Sweden (far right) is an even more marked case of slow growth.

Large families *above*
Big families are no longer common in the U.K. But in many parts of the world the tradition of large families persists. Allied with much lower child mortality, the result is booming population. The age distribution then looks like that of Mexico (left).

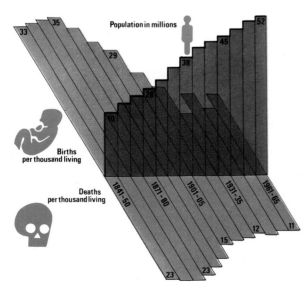

Europe

Population per sq mi
- 0–5
- 5–25
- 25–250
- over 250

Migration to the cities
In every part of the world people are congregating in the cities, searching for a better standard of living. Many of the world's larger cities, unable to accommodate this rapid influx, have become marred by largely unplanned settlements. The most densely packed city in the world, Hong Kong, is home to over three million people. The fortunate ones live in tenements (right); the rest have built shanties (left). Man's population is thus becoming increasingly an urban one.

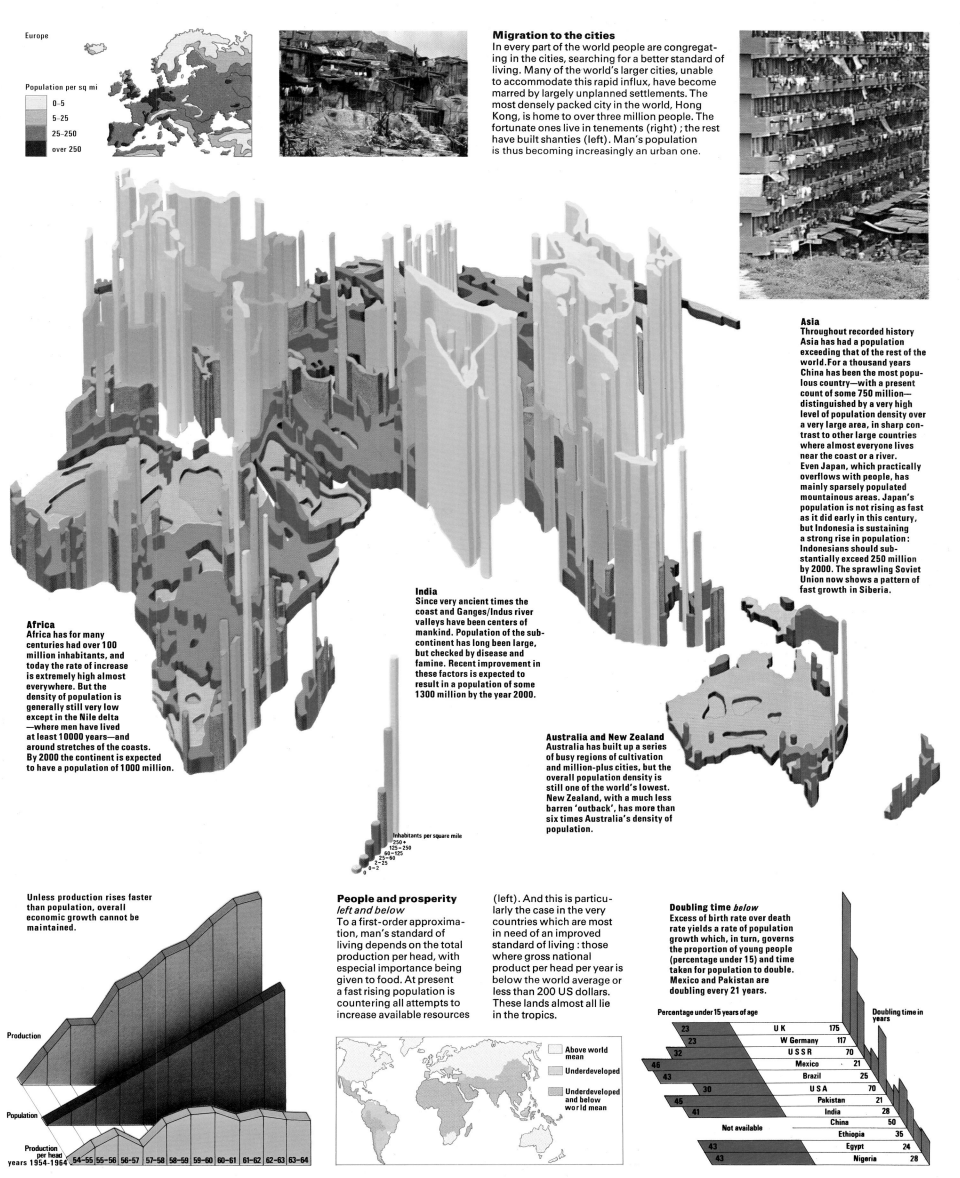

Asia
Throughout recorded history Asia has had a population exceeding that of the rest of the world. For a thousand years China has been the most populous country—with a present count of some 750 million—distinguished by a very high level of population density over a very large area, in sharp contrast to other large countries where almost everyone lives near the coast or a river. Even Japan, which practically overflows with people, has mainly sparsely populated mountainous areas. Japan's population is not rising as fast as it did early in this century, but Indonesia is sustaining a strong rise in population: Indonesians should substantially exceed 250 million by 2000. The sprawling Soviet Union now shows a pattern of fast growth in Siberia.

India
Since very ancient times the coast and Ganges/Indus river valleys have been centers of mankind. Population of the sub-continent has long been large, but checked by disease and famine. Recent improvement in these factors is expected to result in a population of some 1300 million by the year 2000.

Africa
Africa has for many centuries had over 100 million inhabitants, and today the rate of increase is extremely high almost everywhere. But the density of population is generally still very low except in the Nile delta —where men have lived at least 10000 years—and around stretches of the coasts. By 2000 the continent is expected to have a population of 1000 million.

Australia and New Zealand
Australia has built up a series of busy regions of cultivation and million-plus cities, but the overall population density is still one of the world's lowest. New Zealand, with a much less barren 'outback', has more than six times Australia's density of population.

Inhabitants per square mile
- 250+
- 125–250
- 60–125
- 25–60
- 2–25
- 0–2

Unless production rises faster than population, overall economic growth cannot be maintained.

Production

Population

Production per head

years 1954–1964 | 54–55 | 55–56 | 56–57 | 57–58 | 58–59 | 59–60 | 60–61 | 61–62 | 62–63 | 63–64

People and prosperity
left and below
To a first-order approximation, man's standard of living depends on the total production per head, with especial importance being given to food. At present a fast rising population is countering all attempts to increase available resources (left). And this is particularly the case in the very countries which are most in need of an improved standard of living : those where gross national product per head per year is below the world average or less than 200 US dollars. These lands almost all lie in the tropics.

- Above world mean
- Underdeveloped
- Underdeveloped and below world mean

Doubling time *below*
Excess of birth rate over death rate yields a rate of population growth which, in turn, governs the proportion of young people (percentage under 15) and time taken for population to double. Mexico and Pakistan are doubling every 21 years.

Percentage under 15 years of age	Country		Doubling time in years
23	U K	175	
23	W Germany	117	
32	U S S R	70	
46	Mexico	21	
43	Brazil	25	
30	U S A	70	
45	Pakistan	21	
41	India	28	
Not available	China	50	
	Ethiopia	35	
43	Egypt	24	
43	Nigeria	28	

The Abuse of the Earth

Pollution is harmful waste. All living creatures produce waste, often with marked effects on the environment. Pine leaves blanket out the flowers which would otherwise grow on the forest floor; the droppings of seabirds can cover nesting islands meters deep in guano. Plants as well as road vehicles give off carbon dioxide; volcanoes as well as power stations emit sulphur dioxide.

What turns man's waste into pollution? First, we produce too much waste: only man lives in such vast communities that his excreta de-oxygenates whole rivers. Secondly, the unwanted by-products of man's industrial metabolism change so rapidly that the environment has little hope of accommodating it. African grassland has evolved over millions of years to accept piles of elephant dung, with many species of animals specially adapted to living inside dungheaps and helping to decompose them. But the ecosystem is often unable to cope with our latest pollutants: few bacteria are able to digest plastics. Thirdly, man's waste is often extremely persistent: DDT may remain unchanged for decades, passing from one animal to another, poisoning and weakening them all.

Pollution may harm man directly: smoke causes bronchitis, and fouled drinking water can spread typhoid. Pollution may harm us indirectly, reducing the capacity of the land, rivers and seas to supply us with food. But perhaps the most insidious effects are the least obvious. Small doses of separate pollutants, each harmless by itself, may together weaken wild populations of animals so that they cannot recover from natural disasters. Acute pollution kills tens of thousands of animals; chronic pollution gradually reduces the quality of the entire human environment.

Pollution is wasteful. Too often modern technology painstakingly extracts a metal from the crust, uses it once and then discards it. For example, once unwanted chromium or mercury is released into the seas it will be diluted many millions of times and is unlikely ever to be recoverable except at prohibitive expense. If man is not to face raw material famines in the foreseeable future, he must learn to recycle everything from air and water to the rarer elements.

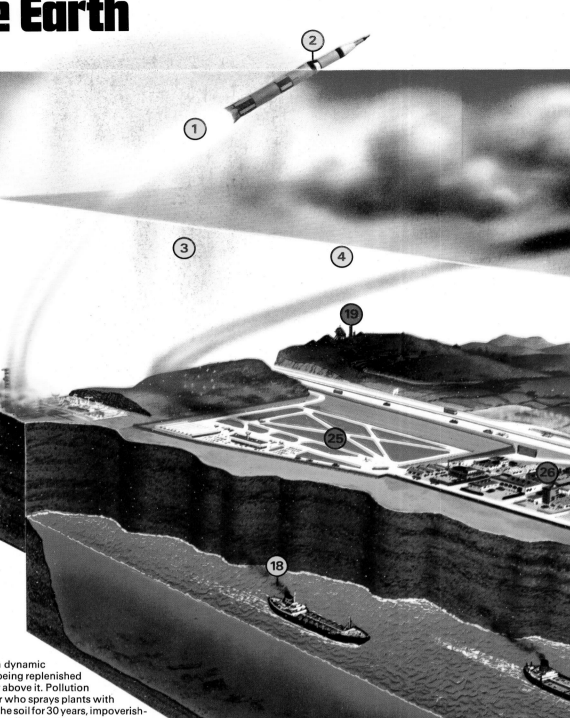

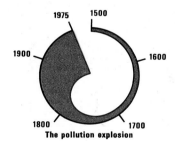

The pollution explosion

Pollution of the land

The soil is a living organic layer, in dynamic equilibrium with, and continually being replenished by, the rocks beneath it and the air above it. Pollution affects it in many ways. The farmer who sprays plants with insecticides may leave residues in the soil for 30 years, impoverishing the micro-organisms which contribute to the ecology on which his crops depend. The delicate chemical balance of the soil may be disrupted by rain loaded with nitrates and sulphates from polluted air. But the land is also a de-pollutant. Some substances can be buried in the knowledge that before they can re-appear they will have been oxidized to harmless compounds.

Pollution of the air

1 Rocket exhaust contains a variety of combustion products.

2 Space launchings leave jettisoned propellants and other debris orbiting above the atmosphere.

3 Nuclear weapon testing can leave fall-out on a global scale.

4 Increased air traffic creates noise pollution over wide areas.

5 Jet efflux contains kerosene combustion products, unburned fuel and particles of soot.

6 Nuclear weapons can cause radioactive contamination; together with chemical and biological devices they could eradicate all life on Earth.

7 Jet aircraft cause intense local noise, and supersonic aircraft create a shock-wave boom.

8 Large-scale aerial transport of pollutants distributes particles and gaseous matter.

9 Carbon dioxide build-up and 'greenhouse effect' traps solar heat within the atmosphere.

10 Pesticide spraying can cause widespread contamination, and organochlorine residues (such as DDT) can build up in animals and disrupt natural food chains.

11 Nuclear power station is potential source of escaping radioactive or liquid coolant.

12 Thermal (coal or oil fired) power station causes thermal and chemical pollution from exhaust stacks.

13 Power station cooling towers transfer waste heat to the air.

14 Sulphur dioxide from high roof-level chimneys falls into 'canyon streets' causing irritation to eyes and lungs.

15 Refinery waste gases burned in the air cause heavy pollution unless the flame is extremely hot.

16 Road vehicle exhausts and crankcase gases contain lead, unburned hydrocarbons, carbon monoxide and oxides of nitrogen, and can cause widespread pollution; action of sunlight on nitrogen oxides causes smog.

17 Most domestic fuels are very inefficiently burned, causing smoke and chemical pollution.

18 Steam boilers or diesel smoke can cause persistent trails of gaseous and particulate matter.

Pollution of the land

19 Coal mining leaves unsightly and potentially dangerous tips.

20 Electricity transmission pylons are a classic of visual pollution.

21 Powerful air-conditioning cools buildings in summer by heating the immediate surroundings.

22 Visual pollution of highways is accentuated by billboards.

23 Unreclaimed wastes are often dumped and not recycled.

24 Quarrying leaves unsightly scars.

25 Growth of air traffic is reflected in increasing size and number of airports which occupy otherwise valuable land.

26 Even modern industrial estates invariably cause chemical and thermal pollution, and pose waste-disposal problems.

27 Large motorways, especially intersections, occupy large areas of land.

28 Caravan and chalet sites may cause severe local chemical, as well as visual, pollution.

29 Modern litter includes high proportion of non-biodegradable plastics materials.

Pollution of the water

30 Nuclear power station discharges waste heat into river and can cause radioactive contamination.

31 Industrial wastes are often poured into rivers without treatment.

32 Cooling water from thermal power stations can cause very large-scale heating of rivers, changing or destroying the natural fauna and flora.

33 Refinery and other chemical plants generate waste heat and liquid refuse which may be discharged directly into the river.

34 Oil storage installation can cause intermittent pollution.

35 When it reaches the sea the river is heavily polluted by nitrates and phosphates from fertilizers and treated sewage, as well as by heavy toxic metals.

36 Tanker too close inshore risks severe beach pollution from accidental release of cargo.

37 Radioactive and corrosive wastes often dumped without enough knowledge of local conditions to insure that the containers will not leak before contents have decomposed; nothing should be dumped on continental shelf and adequate dilution is essential.

38 The main influx of pollutants into the sea is via rivers; typical categories include agricultural and industrial chemicals, waste heat, treated and untreated sewage and solid matter.

39 Excess nutrients from untreated sewage, agricultural chemicals and nuclear wastes can lead to 'blooms' of toxic marine plankton or, through their oxidation and decay, to severely reduced oxygen levels in the water.

40 Sewage sludge dumped at sea contains persistent chemicals such as PCB (polychlorinated biophenyl) compounds, toxic heavy metals and nutrients.

41 Large oil slicks are released by tanker accidents or deliberate washing at sea, and by oil-rig blow-outs.

42 Sediments stirred by mineral exploitation, dumped from ships or carried by rivers may form thick layers on the ocean floor which suffocate the organisms living there.

43 Clouds of particulate matter, both organic and inorganic wastes, reduce the penetration of sunlight and sharply curtail marine productivity.

44 Oil rigs suffer explosive blow-outs, a serious problem off the California coast.

45 In some waters wrecks, many of them uncharted, pose hazards to shipping which may lead to further pollution.

Pollution of the air
Most atmospheric pollutants are gases or dusts emitted when coal, oil and natural gas are burned. DDT and other organochlorine pesticides are distributed mainly by air, since they readily evaporate but are extremely insoluble in water. Some pollutants, such as the particles of carbon we call smoke, fall to the ground within 100 mi (160 km) of emission. Others, particularly minute radioactive particles, can circle the globe for months. Some pollutants undergo chemical change in the air; sulphur dioxide is oxidized and then hydrolyzed to fall in rain as dilute sulphuric acid.

46 Apart from the direct effect of pollutants on marine life, many are less obvious. For example, traces of organic chemicals may confuse or disrupt the mating behavior of fish that normally make use of related chemicals that occur naturally.

Pollution of the water
Water is a great transporter. Agricultural run-off joins sewage and industrial effluent down the rivers. While some organic pollutants decay or settle into mud, most end up in lakes, estuaries and shallow seas. These are the very waters which have the highest productivity, and already the spawning grounds of fish and shellfish have been seriously damaged in some enclosed waters. Today man treats the deep seas as his final dump. Radioactive wastes are dumped in containers, and drums of sulphuric acid are tipped overboard. The sea is also the main transport route for bulk materials, notably crude petroleum. As the size and speed of bulk carriers increase, so does accidental pollution of busy waterways become more frequent and more severe. Exploitation of submarine minerals will pose yet another pollution hazard involving new materials and locations.

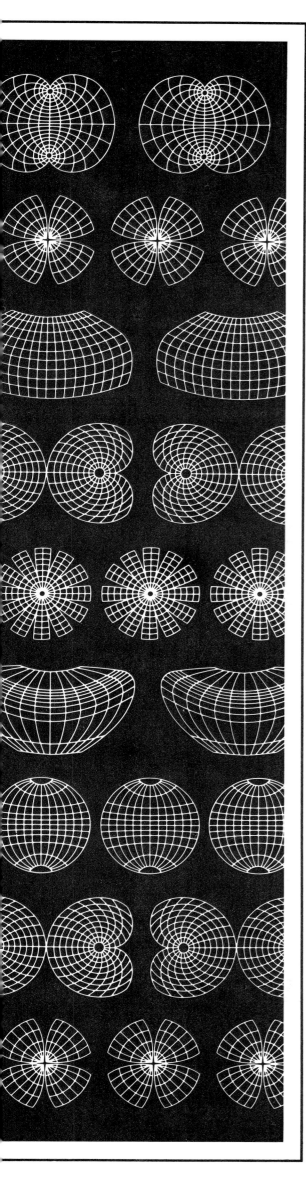

Maps

For many centuries, during the Age of Discovery, our earthly home seemed to be expanding. With each new voyage or exploration the known world became larger. In recent years, with the coming of air and space travel, our Earth seemed to shrink as the speed of flight increased.
Now the Earth can be encircled in minutes and full views of our planet have become a familiar sight.

In this section, except for the first group of specialized maps, the atlas maps emphasize national boundaries and the effects of man on the Earth spread out on the physical background provided by nature. The map selection also has been made with man in mind, and emphasis has been placed on the more congested areas of the world.
The major urbanized areas and communities contiguous to them are shown on a larger scale. These maps show transportation and drainage patterns in great detail plus a large number of place names.

Legend to Physical Maps

Submarine Features

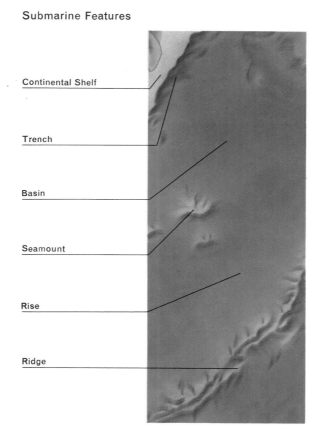

Continental Shelf

Trench

Basin

Seamount

Rise

Ridge

Land Features

Ice and Snow

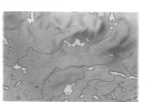
High Barren Area

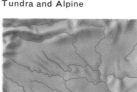
Tundra and Alpine

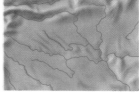
Needleleaf Trees

Broadleaf Trees

Tropical Rainforest

Grassland

Dry Scrub

Desert

The Spherical Earth Flattened
The curved surface of the Earth is transferred to a flat surface by means of a projection.
This is an orderly system of parallels and meridians upon which a map can be drawn.
Many different map projections are used today, and the most appropriate ones have been chosen for the maps that follow.

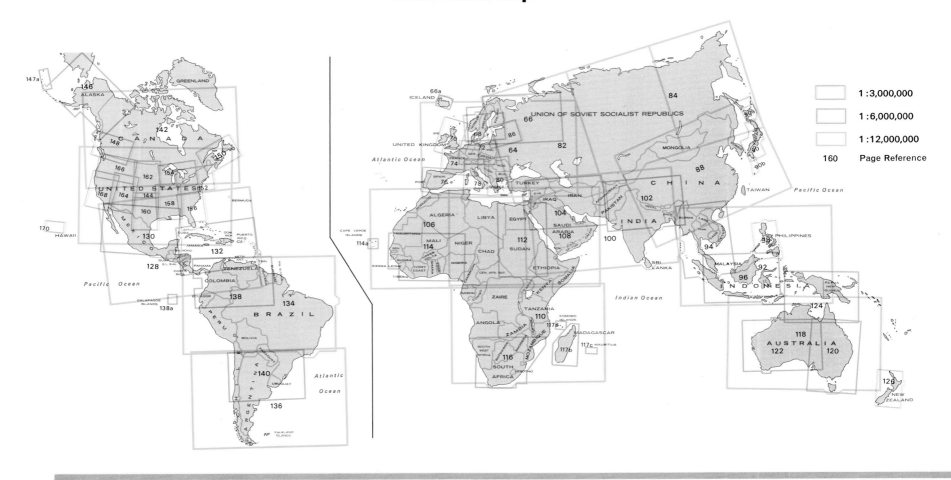

☐	1:3,000,000
☐	1:6,000,000
☐	1:12,000,000
160	Page Reference

Legend to Maps

Inhabited Localities

The symbol represents the number of inhabitants within the locality

1:3,000,000	•	0—10,000	1:12,000,000	• 0—50,000
1:6,000,000	○	10,000—25,000		⊛ 50,000—100,000
	⊛	25,000—100,000		⊞ 100,000—250,000
	⊡	100,000—250,000		▣ 250,000—1,000,000
	▣	250,000—1,000,000		■ >1,000,000
	■	>1,000,000		

Urban Area (area of continuous industrial, commercial, and residential development)

The size of type indicates the relative economic and political importance of the locality

Écommoy	Lisieux	**Rouen**
Trouville	**Orléans**	**PARIS**

Hollywood ◻   Section of a City, Neighborhood
Westminster

Bi'r Safâjah °   Inhabited Oasis   Kurudan °   Uninhabited Oasis

Capitals of Political Units

BUDAPEST   Independent Nation

Cayenne   Dependency (Colony, protectorate, etc.)

GALAPAGOS   Administering Country
(Ecuador)

Villarica   State, Province, etc.

White Plains   County, Oblast, etc.

Alternate Names

Basel	**MOSKVA**	English or second official language names are shown
Bâle	MOSCOW	in reduced size lettering
Ventura	Volgograd	Historical or other alternates in the local language
(San Buenaventura)	(Stalingrad)	are shown in parentheses

Political Boundaries

International (First-order political unit)

1:3,000,000
1:6,000,000
1:12,000,000

—··—··—··—   Demarcated, Undemarcated, and Administrative

— ·· — ·· —   Disputed de jure

════════   Indefinite or Undefined

————————   Demarcation Line
(used in Korea and Vietnam)

Internal

▬▬▬▬▬   State, Province, etc. (Second-order political unit)
GUAIRA

————————   County, Oblast, etc. (Third-order political unit)
W E S T C H E S T E R

ANDALUCIA   Historical Region (No boundaries indicated)

Miscellaneous Cultural Features

PARQUE NACIONAL CANAIMA ▲	National or State Park or Monument		STEINHAUSEN ⊥	Church, Monastery
FORT CLATSOP NAT. MEM. ▲	National or State Historic(al) Site, Memorial		UXMAL ∴	Ruins
BLACKFOOT IND. RES.	Indian Reservation		WINDSOR CASTLE ⌐	Castle
			AMISTAD DAM	Dam
FORT DIX ▪	Military Installation			
TANGLEWOOD ▲	Point of Interest (Battlefield, cave, historical site, etc.)			

Regional Index Maps

Transportation

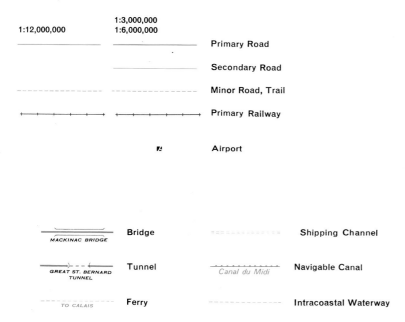

1:12,000,000	1:3,000,000 1:6,000,000	
		Primary Road
		Secondary Road
		Minor Road, Trail
		Primary Railway
		Airport

MACKINAC BRIDGE	Bridge		Shipping Channel
GREAT ST. BERNARD TUNNEL	Tunnel	Canal du Midi	Navigable Canal
TO CALAIS	Ferry		Intracoastal Waterway

Metric-English Equivalents

Areas represented by one square centimeter at various map scales

1:3,000,000 900 km² 348 square miles	1:6,000,000 3,600 km² 1,390 square miles	1:12,000,000 14,400 km² 5,558 square miles

Meter=3.28 feet
Kilometer=0.62 mile

Meter² (m²)=10.76 square feet
Kilometer² (km²)=0.39 square mile

Hydrographic Features

	Shoreline	The Everglades	Swamp
	Undefined or Fluctuating Shoreline	SEWARD GLACIER	Glacier
Amur	River, Stream	L. Victoria	Lake, Reservoir
	Intermittent Stream	Tuz Gölü	Salt Lake
	Rapids, Falls		Intermittent Lake, Reservoir
	Irrigation or Drainage Canal		Dry Lake Bed
	Reef	(395)	Lake Surface Elevation
764 ▽	Depth of Water		

Topographic Features

			Lava
Mt. Kenya △ 5199	Elevation Above Sea Level		Sand Area
76 ▽	Elevation Below Sea Level		Salt Flat
Mount Cook ▲ 3764	Highest Elevation in Country	A N D E S KUNLUNSHANMAI	Mountain Range, Plateau, Valley, etc.
Khyber Pass ⊰ 1067	Mountain Pass		
133 ▼	Lowest Elevation in Country	BAFFIN ISLAND NUNIVAK ISLAND	Island

Elevations and depths are given in meters
Highest Elevation and Lowest Elevation of a continent are underlined

POLUOSTROV KAMČATKA CABO DE HORNOS	Peninsula, Cape, Point, etc.

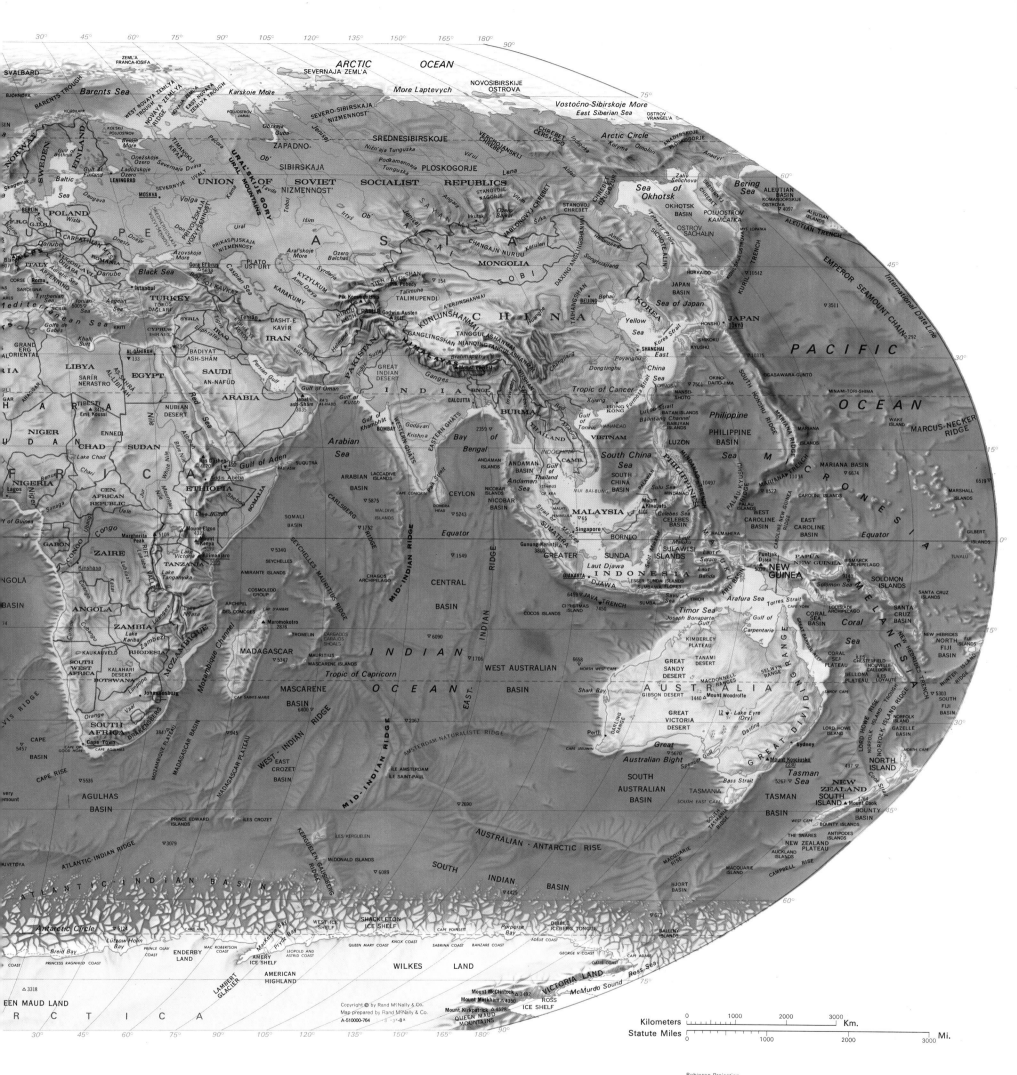

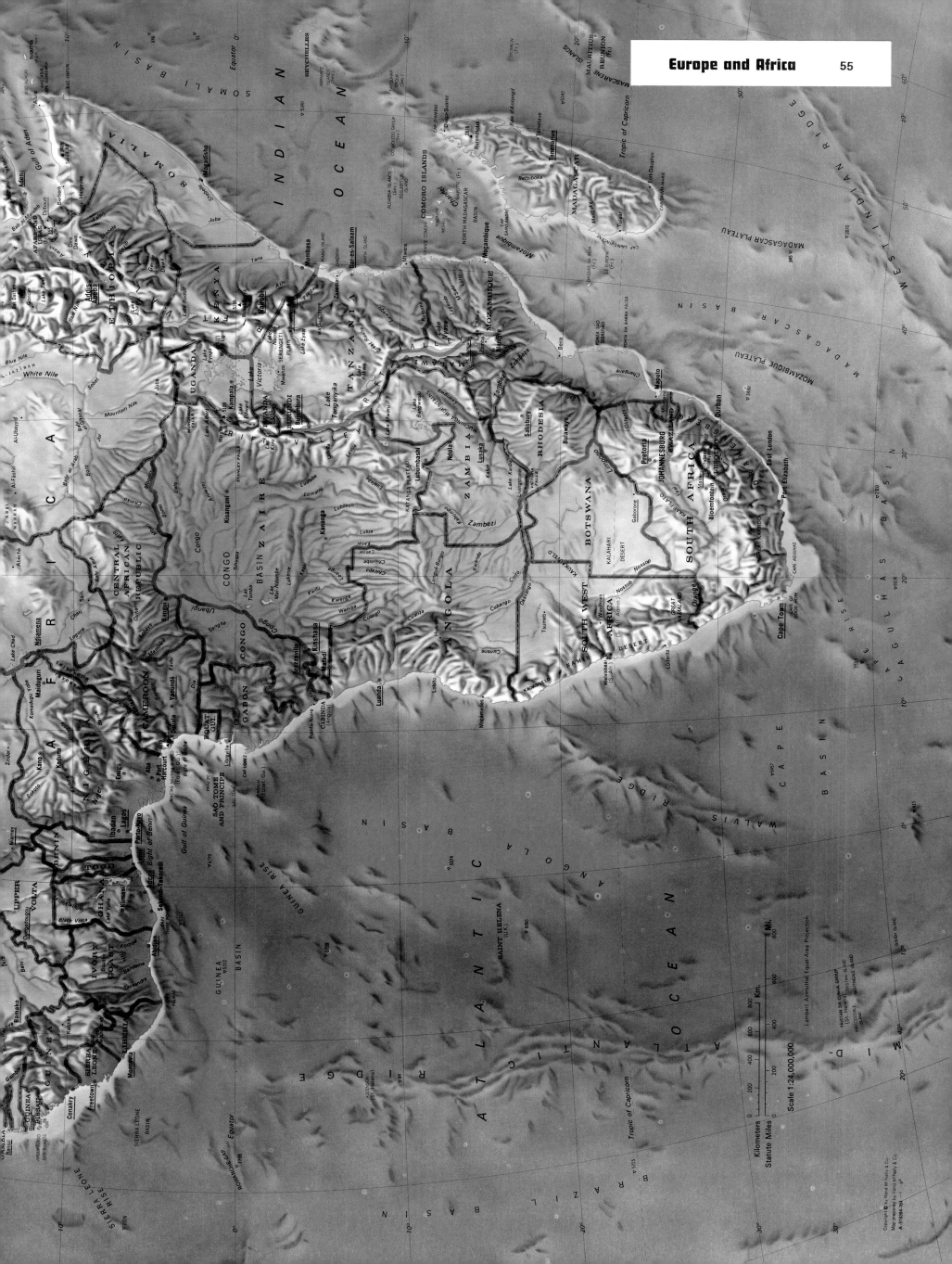

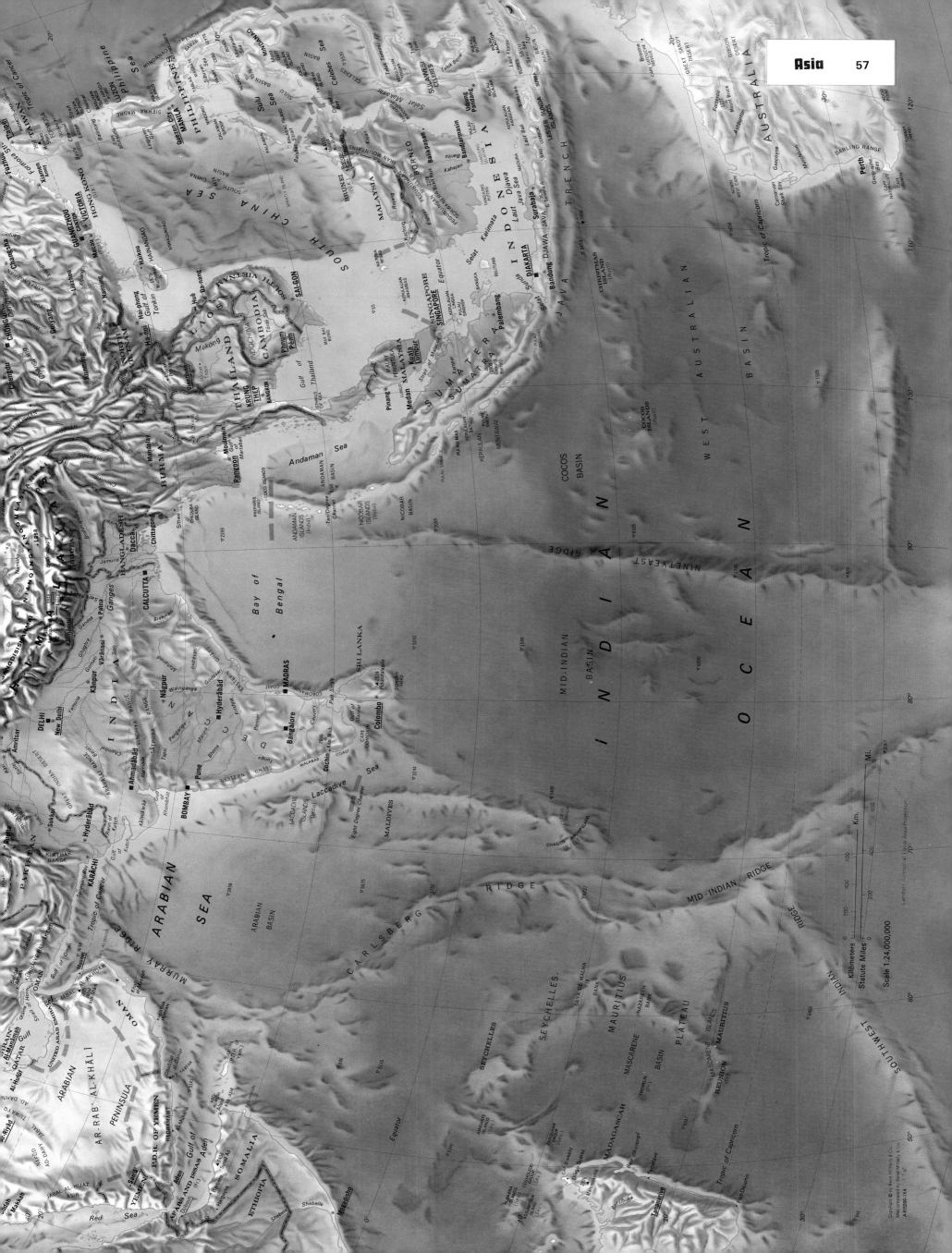

160° 170° 180° 170° 160° 150°

Tropic of Cancer

MIDWAY
ISLANDS
(U.S.)

PEARL AND
HERMES REEF

HAWAIIAN ISLANDS (U.S.)

Guadalupe
Seamount

LAYSAN
ISLAND

LISIANSKI
ISLAND

Gardner
Pinnacles

NECKER
ISLAND

NIHOA

KAUAI
NIIHAU
OAHU MOLOKAI
LANAI MAUI
KAHOOLAWE
Honolulu

HAWAIIAN RIDGE

Horizon
Tablemount

Mauna Loa
4170 Hilo
HAWAII
K.A LAE

20°

∇1316

∇1477

MARCUS-NECKER RIDGE

∇6890

WAKE ISLAND
(U.S.)

∇859

Hess
Tablemount

Paul
Seamount

RIONAL
REEF

RENE
REEF

Cape
Johnson
Seamount

Karin Seamount

JOHNSTON
ISLAND (U.S.)

Swordfish
Seamount

Pensacola
Seamount

∇1057

4809

PACIFIC ISLANDS
TRUST TERRITORY
(U.S.)

TAONGI

SCHUETMAN
REEF

EAST PACIFIC BASIN

RATAK CHAIN

BIKAR

UTIRIK

BIKINI

RONGELAP

AILUK

ENIWETOK

WOTHO

UJAE

LAE

KWAJALEIN

WOTJE

MALOELAP

ARNO

WILDER
SHOAL

CENTRAL ∇6519

P A C I F I C   O C E A N

UELANG

NAMU

MAJURO

PACIFIC

∇5349

MARSHALL
ISLANDS

10°

MOKIL

PINGELAP

JALUIT

MILI

NORTHWEST CHRISTMAS ISLAND RIDGE

KUSAIE

EBON

RALIK CHAIN

BASIN

KINGMAN
REEF

PALMYRA
ISLAND
(U.S.)

WASHINGTON
ISLAND
(U.K.)

FANNING
ISLAND
(U.K.)

Winslow
Seamount ∇11

MAKIN

CHRISTMAS
ISLAND
(U.K.-U.S.)

∇4462

TARAWA

ABEMAMA

GILBERT
ISLANDS

HOWLAND ISLAND (U.S.)

(U.K.)

NAURU

KURIA

OCEAN ISLAND

NONOUTI

BERU

NIKUNAU

BAKER ISLAND (U.S.)

CANTON AND ENDERBURY
(U.K.-U.S.)

JARVIS
ISLAND
(U.S.)

Equator 0°

NUKUMANU
ISLANDS

∇1737

TABITEUEA

ONOTOA

TAMANA

ARORAE

PHOENIX
ISLANDS
(U.K.-U.S.)

CANTON
ENDERBURY

BIRNIE

HULL

PHOENIX

SYDNEY

MALDEN
ISLAND
(U.K.-U.S.)

FILIPPO
REEF

ONTONG
JAVA
RISE

BRITISH SOLOMON
SOLOMON   ISLANDS

TUVALU
(U.K.)

NANUMEA
NIUTAO

NANUMANGA

NIU

PHOENIX
TROUGH

NORTH TOKELAU TROUGH

∇6469

STARBUCK
ISLAND
(U.K.-U.S.)

Merlin
Seamount

SANTA
CRUZ
ISLANDS

MALAITA

SANTA CRUZ
ISLANDS

MELANESIAN   BORDER

VAITUPU
NUKUFETAU
FUNAFUTI

PENRHYN

Honiara

GUADALCANAL

NDENI
UTUPUA

NURAKITA

PLATEAU

TOKELAU
ISLANDS
(N.Z.)

ATAFU
NUKUNONO

FAKAOFU

 VOSTOK
ISLAND
(U.K.-U.S.)

CAROLINE
ATOLL

CRISTOBAL
TRENCH

SAN CRISTOBAL

VANIKORO

ROTUMA

Combe Seamount

Home
Seamount

SWAINS
ISLAND

NASSAU
ISLAND

MANIHIKI

∇6879

SANTA CRUZ
BASIN

RENNELL
ISLAND

LES WALLIS

Pasco
Seamount

AMERICAN
SAMOA
ISLANDS

FLINT
ISLAND
(U.K.-U.S.)

NEW HEBRIDES
(Fr.-U.K.)

∇1188

TORRES
ISLANDS

VANUA LAVA

SANTA MARIA
ISLAND

WALLIS AND
FUTUNA
(Fr.)

ÎLES DE
HORNE

SAVAII

WESTERN
SAMOA

Apia
UPOLU

Pago
Pago

SOUVOROV
ISLANDS

∇4846

NEW
HEBRIDES
BASIN

ESPIRITU
SANTO

PENTECOST
ISLAND

AMBRIM

MAEWO

NORTH

FIJI

TUTUILA

MANUA ISLANDS

MANIHIKI

SELLINGSHAUSEN
SCILLY

MATAIVA
TAHAA

TAKAPOTO

ÎLES DU DÉSAPPOINTEMENT

ÎLES DU
ROI GEORGES

MALEKULA

NEW
HEBRIDES

NEW

FIJI

FIJI ISLANDS

VANUA
LEVU

VANUALEVU

TAVEUNI

LAU
GROUP

TAFAHI

∇7314

MOPELIA

BORA-BORA
RAIATEA

SOCIETY

MAKATEA

ILES DE
LA SOCIÉTÉ
SOCIETY ISLANDS

RAIATEA
MOOREA
TAHITI

TUPAI

MAKATEA
FAKARAVA

MAKEMO

KAUKURA
FAKAHINA

HARAIKI

RAROIA

NENGONENGO

ILES TUAMOTU
TUAMOTU ARCHIPELAGO

ANAA
HIKUERU
MARUTEA

AHUNUI

HAO

ÎLES
CHESTERFIELD

∇al

NEW
CALEDONIA
(Fr.)

LOYALTY

ILE UVEA

ÎLE OUVEA

VITI
LEVU

Suva

KORO
Sea

KANDAVU

VANJA
LEVU

EFATE

EROMANGA

TANNA

ANEITYUM

LOYALTY
ISLANDS
ILES LOYAUTÉ

NORTH
FIJI
BASIN

FIJI

∇3580

ONO-I-LAU

SOUTH FIJI TROUGH

TONGATAPU
GROUP

VAVAU
GROUP

TOFUA

NIUAFOU

TONGA
ISLANDS

NIUE
(N.Z.)

COOK ISLANDS
(N.Z.)

PALMERSTON

COOK
RIDGE

AITUTAKI
MANUAE

MITIARO

ATIU
MAUKE

Papeete

TARAVAI

MEHETIA

MARUTEA

PUKAPUKA

MANGAREVA

NGONENGO

MANUHANGI

MAKEMO

VANAVANA

FRENCH
POLYNESIA

ILES GAMBIER

Noumea

HUNTER
RIDGE

ÎLE MARÉ

TONGA RIDGE

SOUTH FIJI RIDGE

Nukualofa

EUA

ONO-I-LAU

TONGATAPU

ISLAND RIDGE

HUNTER
TRENCH

TONGA

TONGA TRENCH

RAROTONGA

MANGAIA

MARIA
RIMATARA

TUBUAI

∇10882

ÎLES
TUBUAI

RURUTU

∇5303

SOUTH

FIJI

BASIN

∇3580

Ozbourn
Seamount

FABERT
SHOAL

TEMATAGI

AUSTRAL SEAMOUNT CHAIN

RAEVAVAE

TEMATAGI

RAPA

LORD
HOWE
ISLAND
(Austl.)

NORFOLK
RIDGE

WANGANELLA
BANK

GAZELLE
BASIN

NORFOLK
ISLAND
(Austl.)

NORTH CAPE RISE

Monongahela
Seamount

KERMADEC
ISLANDS

CURTIS ISLAND

∇10047

RAOUL ISLAND

Currituck Seamount
Seafos Seamount

Louisville Seamount

E. ORNE BANK

ERNEST
LEGOUVE
REEF

Tropic of Capricorn

LORD HOWE
RISE

NORFOLK
ISLAND TROUGH

THREE KINGS IS.

NORTH CAPE

TAURUA
POINT

∇1518

GREAT BARRIER ISLAND

KERMADEC RIDGE

KERMADEC TRENCH

LOUISVILLE RIDGE

Burton Seamount

∇1088

WACHUSETT SHOAL

∇8009

Auckland

Bay of
Plenty

EAST CAPE

INTERNATIONAL DATE LINE

30°

Tasman

∇5267

Sea

NEW

New
Plymouth

∇2797
Ruapehu

Napier

Hawke Bay

NORTH ISLAND

SOUTHWESTERN

∇497

CAPE
EGMONT
CAPE
FAREWELL

ZEALAND

Mount Cook
3764

Wellington

CAPE PALLISER

COOK Strait

CHATHAM
RISE

CHATHAM

CHATHAM
ISLAND

CHATHAM
ISLANDS
(N.Z.)

PACIFIC BASIN

Christchurch

SOUTHERN ALPS

SOUTH ISLAND

Canterbury
Bight

BOUNTY

BASIN

ASIN

WEST CAPE

Dunedin

Invercargill

SOUTHWEST CAPE

STEWART ISLAND

THE SNARES

NEW ZEALAND
PLATEAU

ANTIPODES
ISLANDS
(N.Z.)

BOUNTY
ISLANDS
(N.Z.)

160° 170° 180° 170° 160° 150° 140° 130° 40°

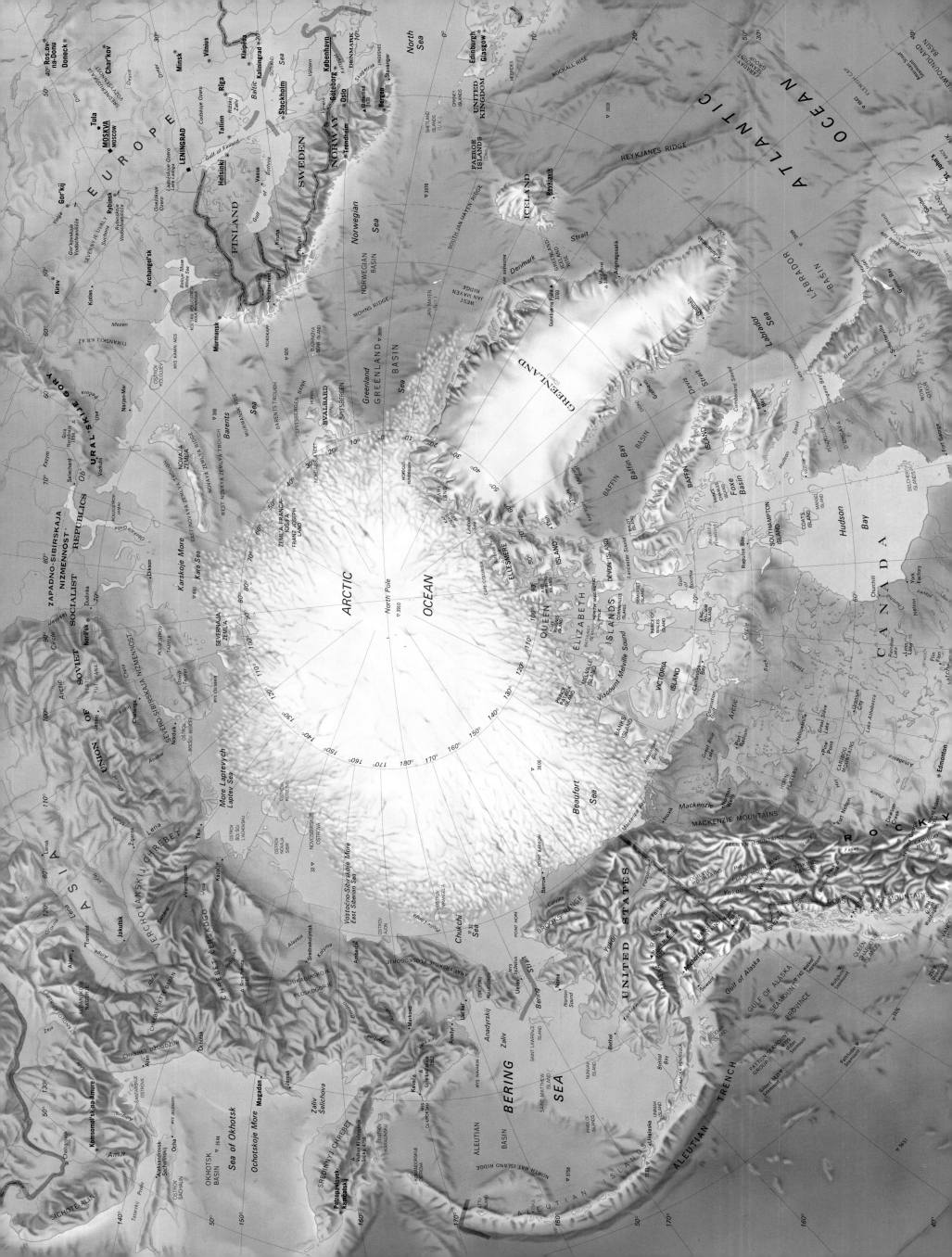

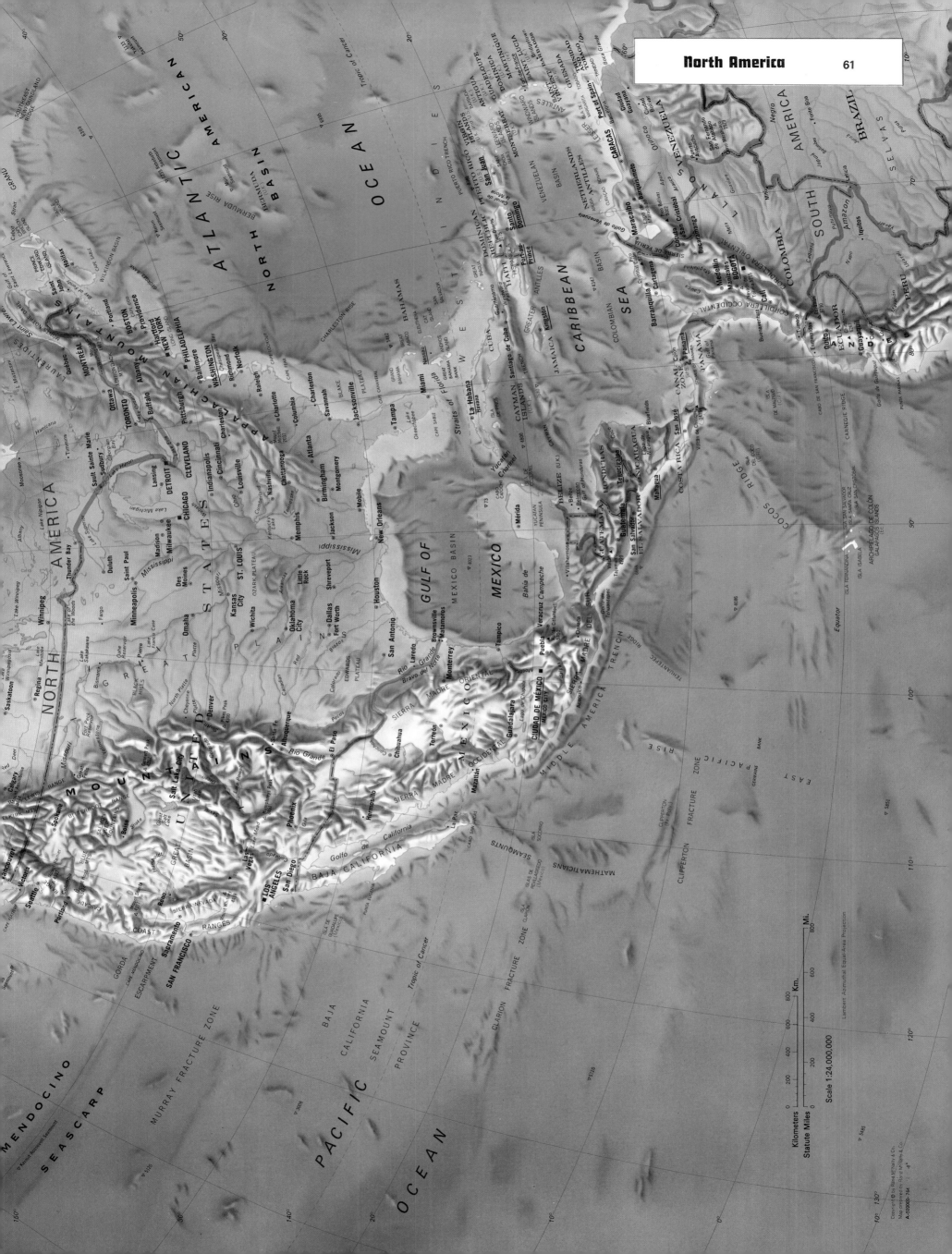

NORTH AMERICA

UNITED STATES

ATLANTIC OCEAN

MID-ATLANTIC RIDGE

AZORES RIDGE

CANARY BASIN

CAPE VERDE BASIN

NORTH AMERICAN BASIN

BERMUDA RISE

SOUTHEAST NEWFOUNDLAND RIDGE

GEORGES BANK

LONG ISLAND

Tropic of Cancer

Equator

SOUTH AMERICA

BRAZIL

VENEZUELA

COLOMBIA

GUYANA

SURINAM

FRENCH GUIANA

ECUADOR

PERU

PANAMA

COSTA RICA

NICARAGUA

HONDURAS

EL SALVADOR

GUATEMALA

BELIZE

MEXICO

GULF OF MEXICO

CARIBBEAN SEA

BAHAMAS

CUBA

JAMAICA

HAITI

DOMINICAN REPUBLIC

HISPANIOLA

PUERTO RICO

VIRGIN ISLANDS (U.K. and U.S.)

LEEWARD ISLANDS

WINDWARD ISLANDS

NETHERLANDS ANTILLES

LESSER ANTILLES

GREATER ANTILLES

WEST INDIES

ANTIGUA (U.K.)

GUADELOUPE (Fr.)

DOMINICA (U.K.)

MARTINIQUE (Fr.)

SAINT LUCIA (U.K.)

SAINT VINCENT (U.K.)

BARBADOS (U.K.)

GRENADA

TRINIDAD AND TOBAGO

CAYMAN ISLANDS (U.K.)

CANAL ZONE (U.S.)

ISTHMUS OF PANAMA

YUCATAN PENINSULA

YUCATAN CHANNEL

Straits of Florida

PUERTO RICO TRENCH

APPALACHIAN MOUNTAINS

ROCKY MOUNTAINS

GREAT PLAINS

SIERRA MADRE ORIENTAL

SIERRA MADRE DEL SUR

OZARK PLATEAU

EDWARDS PLATEAU

CHARLESTON RISE

BLAKE PLATEAU

MIDDLE AMERICA TRENCH

COCOS RIDGE

CARNEGIE RIDGE

COLOMBIAN BASIN

VENEZUELAN BASIN

GUIANA BASIN

CORDILLERA OCCIDENTAL

CORDILLERA ORIENTAL

CORDILLERA CENTRAL

SELVAS

LLANOS

SERRA GRANDE

SERRA DO RONCADOR

CHAPADA DAS MANGABEIRAS

SA. GERAL DE GOIAS

PLANALTO DO MATO GROSSO

PINHAGO

Cities and places:
CHICAGO, CLEVELAND, NEW YORK, PHILADELPHIA, Baltimore, WASHINGTON, Norfolk, Pittsburgh, Cincinnati, Louisville, ST. LOUIS, Kansas City, Omaha, Des Moines, Denver, Cheyenne, North Platte, Wichita, Oklahoma City, Little Rock, Memphis, Nashville, Atlanta, Birmingham, Montgomery, Jackson, Mobile, New Orleans, Jacksonville, Savannah, Charleston, Raleigh, Tampa, Miami, Dallas, Fort Worth, Houston, San Antonio, Austin, Albuquerque, Laredo, Brownsville

Matamoros, Monterrey, Torreón, Tampico, Veracruz, MEXICO CITY, Puebla, Guadalajara, CIUDAD ...

Havana, La Habana, Santiago de Cuba, Nassau, Kingston, Port-au-Prince, Santo Domingo, San Juan

Managua, San José, San Salvador, Guatemala, Belmopan

CARACAS, Maracaibo, Barquisimeto, Barcelona, Valencia, Ciudad Bolívar, Ciudad Guayana

BOGOTÁ, Medellín, Cali, Cartagena, Barranquilla, Cúcuta, Bucaramanga, Buenaventura

QUITO, Guayaquil, Cuenca, Esmeraldas, Tumaco

LIMA, Iquitos, Chiclayo, Trujillo

Georgetown, Paramaribo, Cayenne

Belém, Manaus, São Luís, Teresina, Fortaleza, Natal, João Pessoa, Recife, Maceió, Aracaju, Salvador, Campina Grande

Rivers:
Mississippi, Missouri, Ohio, Red, Brazos, Colorado, Pecos, Rio Grande, Bravo del Norte, Arkansas, Platte, South Platte, Wabash, Cumberland

Amazon, Negro, Orinoco, Madeira, Tocantins, São Francisco, Xingu, Tapajós, Purus, Juruá, Putumayo, Napo, Marañón, Ucayali, Japurá, Caquetá, Meta, Apure, Guaviare, Branco, Essequibo, Oyapock

GALAPAGOS ISLANDS (Ec.)

ARCHIPIÉLAGO DE COLÓN (Ec.)

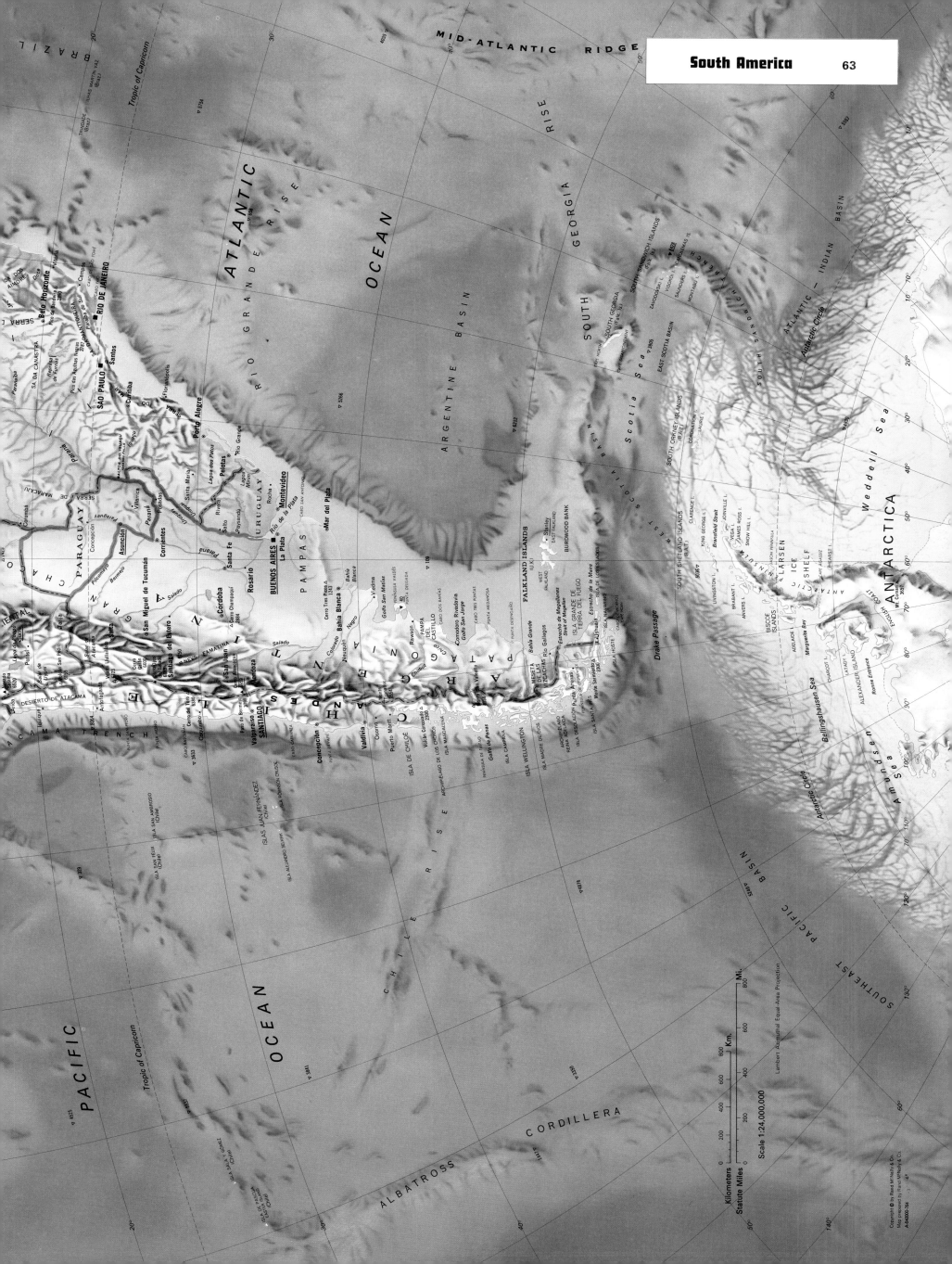

Kilometers
Statute Miles

Scale 1:12,000,000

One centimeter represents 120 kilometers.
One inch represents approximately 190 miles.
Miller Oblated Stereographic Projection

Kilometers
Statute Miles

0   100   200   300   Km.
0   100   200   300   Mi.

Scale 1:6,000,000

One centimeter represents 60 kilometers.
One inch represents approximately 95 miles.
Lambert Conformal Conic Projection

The annexation of Latvia and Estonia in 1940 by the Soviet Union has never been officially recognized by the United States Government

Copyright © by Rand McNally & Co.
Map compiled by Esselte Map Service AB, Stockholm.
Map produced by Rand McNally & Co.
A-554400-264

Kilometers
Statute Miles

Scale 1:3,000,000

One centimeter represents 30 kilometers.
One inch represents approximately 47 miles.
Conic Projection, Two Standard Parallels

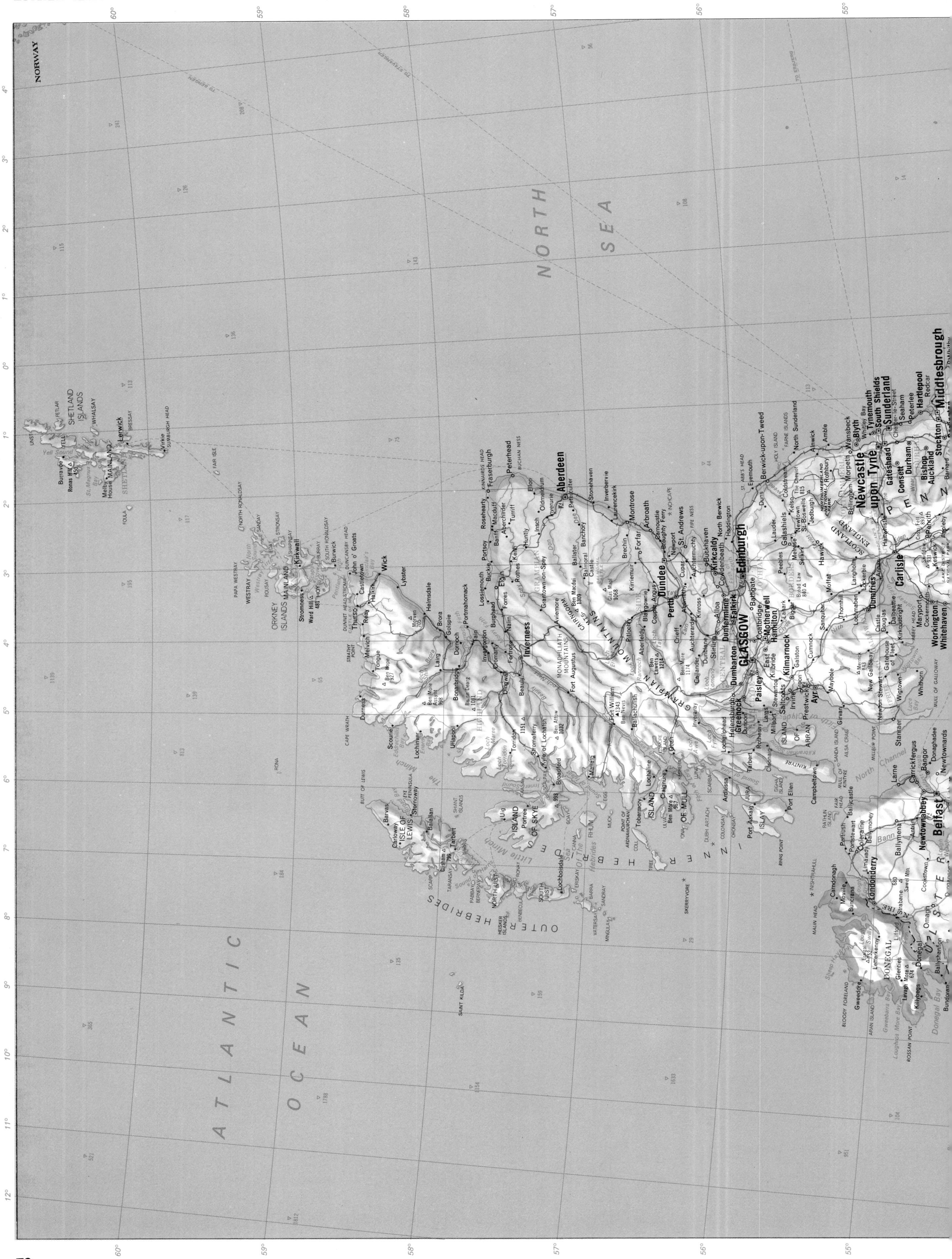

NORWAY

NORTH SEA

ATLANTIC OCEAN

SHETLAND ISLANDS

Lerwick

ORKNEY ISLANDS

Kirkwall
Stromness

Wick
Thurso

Inverness

GRAMPIAN MOUNTAINS

Aberdeen
Peterhead
Fraserburgh

Dundee
Perth

GLASGOW
Edinburgh
Paisley
Falkirk
Motherwell
Hamilton
Kilmarnock
Ayr
Dumbarton
Greenock

ISLE OF LEWIS
OUTER HEBRIDES
ISLE OF SKYE
ISLAND OF MULL
ISLAY
NORTH UIST
SOUTH UIST
BARRA

The Minch
Little Minch

SANT KILDA

ENGLAND
SCOTLAND

PENNINE

Newcastle upon Tyne
Sunderland
South Shields
Gateshead
Tynemouth
Blyth
Middlesbrough
Hartlepool
Stockton
Bishop Auckland
Durham
Consett
Carlisle
Dumfries
Workington
Whitehaven

Belfast
ULSTER
Londonderry
Newtownabbey
Ballymena
Coleraine
Bangor
DONEGAL

NORTH CHANNEL

71

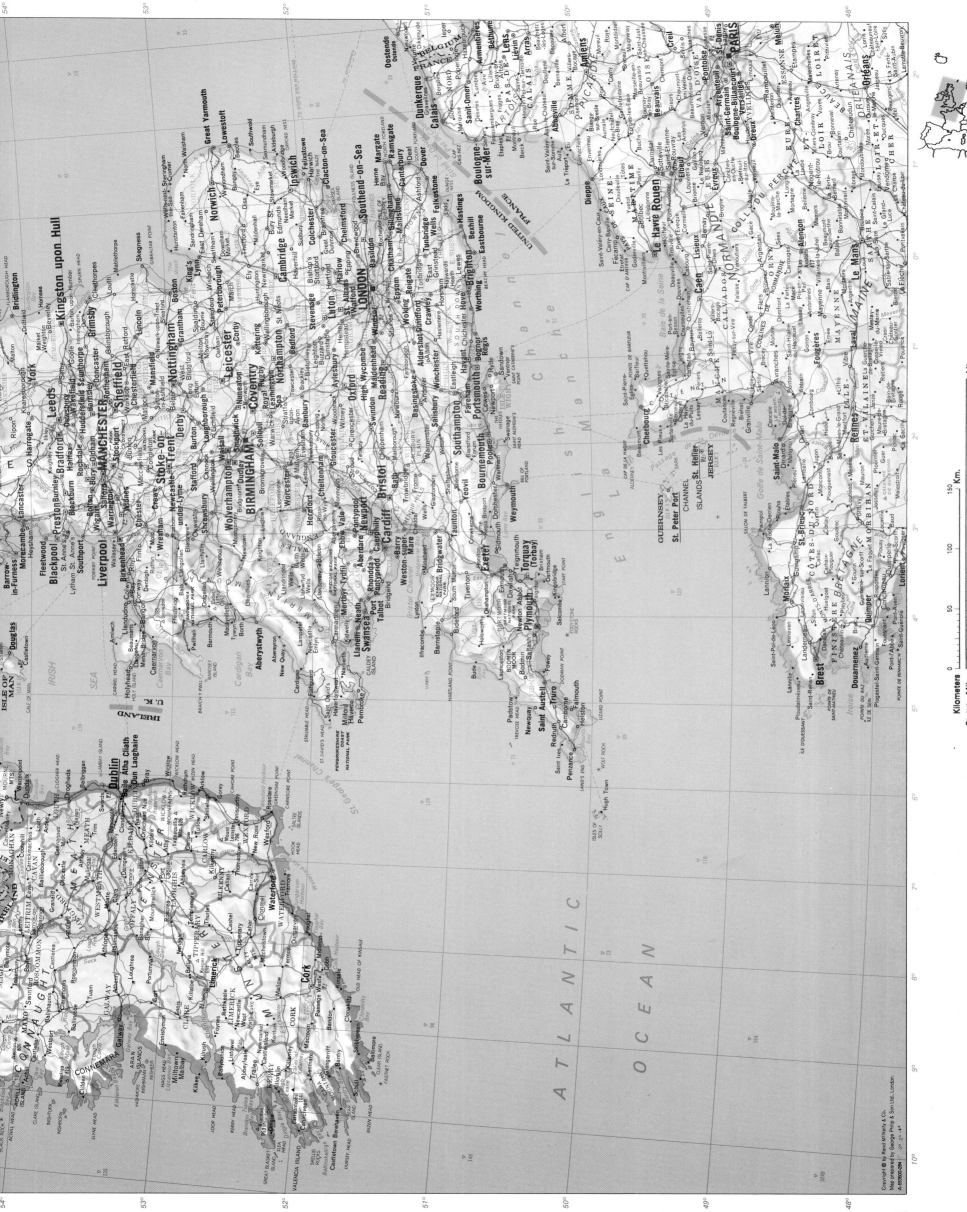

Kilometers
Statute Miles

Mi.

Km.

Scale 1:3,000,000

One centimeter represents 30 kilometers.
One inch represents approximately 47 miles.

Conic Projection, Two Standard Parallels

Copyright by Rand McNally & Co.
Map prepared by George Philip & Son, Ltd., London

A-55500004

71

Kilometers
Statute Miles

0 50 100 150 Km.
0   50   100   150 Mi.

Scale 1:3,000,000

One centimeter represents 30 kilometers.
One inch represents approximately 47 miles.
Conic Projection, Two Standard Parallels.

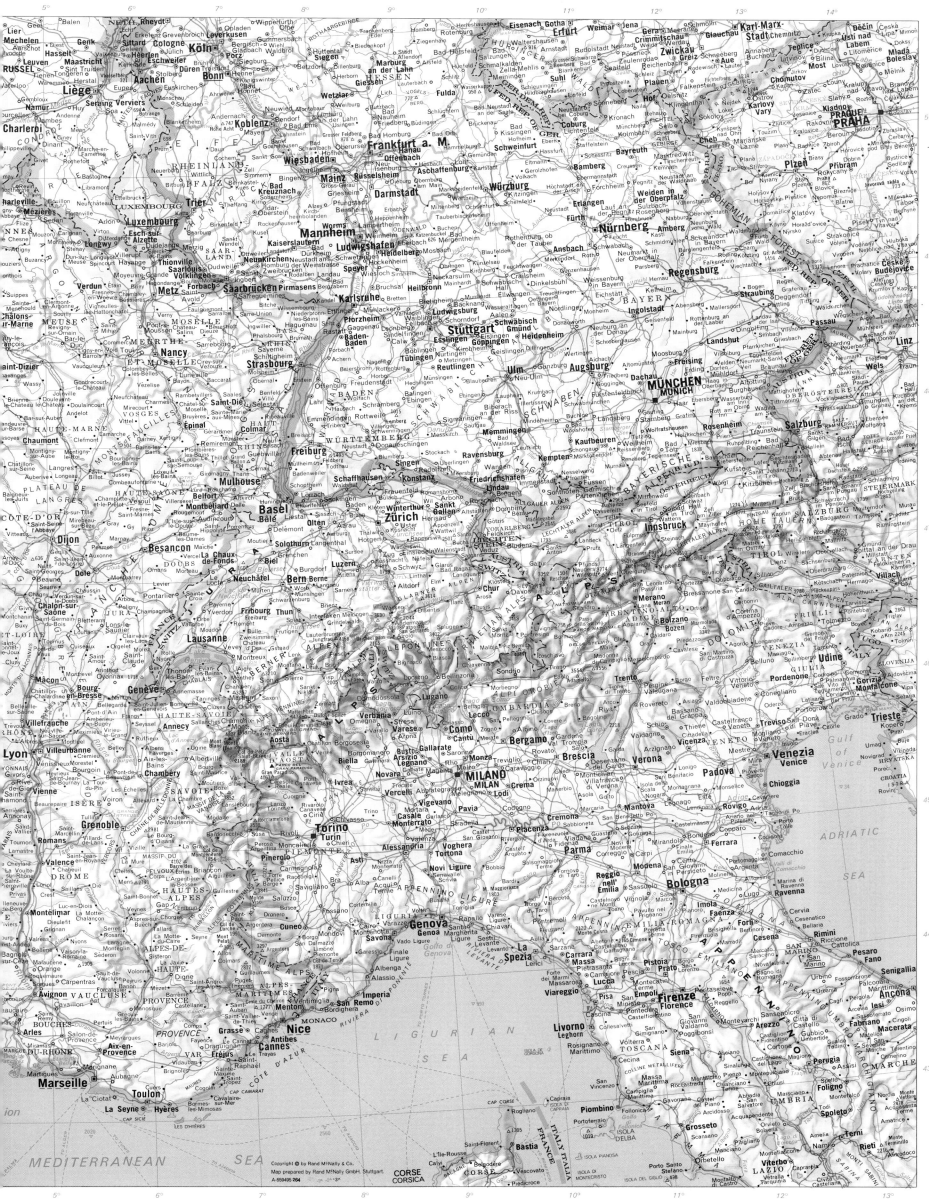

Kilometers
Statute Miles

Km.
Mi.

Scale 1:3,000,000
One centimeter represents 30 kilometers.
One inch represents approximately 47 miles.
Lambert Conformal Conic Projection

Spain and Portugal

MEDITERRANEAN SEA

ISLAS BALEARES
BALEARIC ISLANDS

MENORCA
MINORCA
Ciudadela
Mahón

MALLORCA
MAJORCA
Palma

BALEARES

Golfe
du Lion

Golfo de
Valencia

Toulouse
Montpellier
Marseille
Nice

Zaragoza
BARCELONA
Valencia
Murcia
Cartagena

ALGER
ALGIERS
Oran
(Ouahran)

ATLAS MOUNTAINS
ATLAS TELLIEN

ALGERIA
ALGÉRIE

Kilometers
Statute Miles

Scale 1:3,000,000

One centimeter represents 30 kilometers.
One inch represents approximately 47 miles.

Conic Projection, Two Standard Parallels

ADRIATIC SEA
LIGURIAN SEA
Gulf of Venice
MILANO MILAN
Torino Turin
Genova Genoa
Venezia Venice
Firenze Florence
Bologna
Trieste
Ljubljana
Zagreb
WIEN VIENNA
BUDAPEST
Bratislava
MÜNCHEN MUNICH
Zürich
Basel
Bern
Innsbruck
Salzburg
Graz
Rijeka
Split
Sarajevo
Mostar
Dubrovnik
Ancona
Pescara
Livorno Leghorn
Pisa
La Spezia
Nice
Cannes
Bastia
CORSE CORSICA
Ajaccio
ISOLA D'ELBA
Zadar
Šibenik
Pula
Padova
Verona
Brescia
Bergamo
Parma
Modena
Ravenna
Rimini
Perugia
Terni
Civitavecchia
Grosseto
Siena
ITALY ITALIA
FRANCE

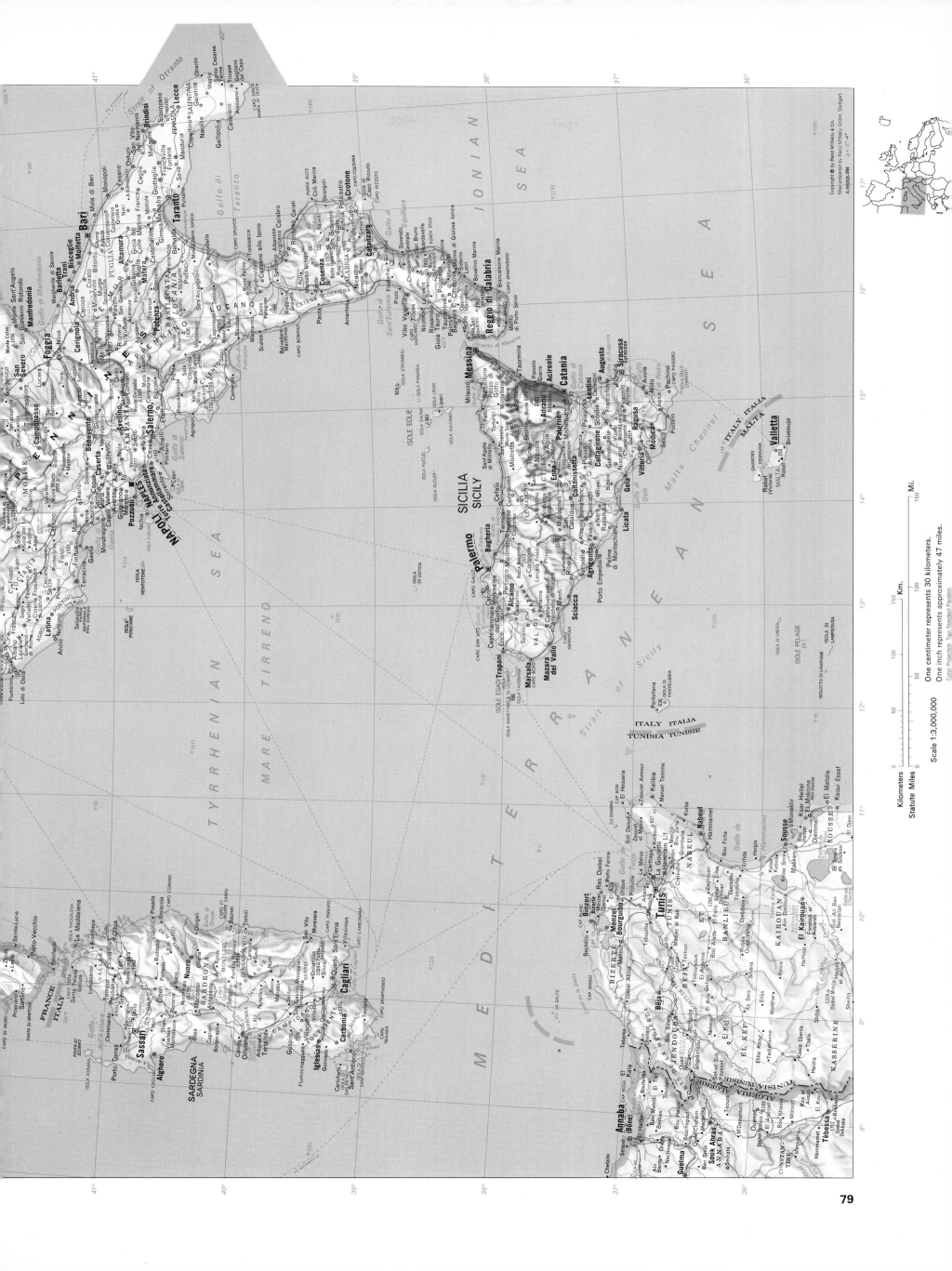

Kilometers

Mi.

Statute Miles

Scale 1:3,000,000

One centimeter represents 30 kilometers.
One inch represents approximately 47 miles.

Conic Projection, Two Standard Parallels

BLACK   SEA

Mouths of the Danube

CARPATHIAN   MOUNTAINS

ROMÂNIA

Kišin'ov
Kishinev
Benderŷ
Tiraspol
Orgejev
Dubossary
Kotovsk

Černovcy
Suceava
Botoşani
IAŞI
Iaşi
Bacău
Galaţi
GALAŢI
Brăila
BRĂILA
Tecuci
Focşani
Buzău
BUZĂU

Baia-Mare
Satu Mare
Cluj
Turda
Dej
Bistriţa
Târgu Mureş
Mediaş
Sibiu
Braşov
Sighişoara
Alba-Iulia
Petroşani
Deva
Hunedoara
Lugoj
Timişoara
Arad
Oradea

BUCUREŞTI
BUCHAREST
Ploieşti
Târgovişte
Piteşti
Craiova
Târgu-Jiu

Constanţa
CONSTANŢA
Medgidia
Tulcea
Varna
Burgas

Ruse
Pleven
Sofija
Sofia
Vraca
Veliko Tárnovo
Gabrovo
Stara Zagora
Sliven
Novi Pazar
Razgrad
Tŭrgovište

BULGARIA

YUGOSLAVIA
Beograd
Belgrade
Novi Sad
Subotica
Smederevo
Pančevo
Kikinda
Niš
Kragujevac
Kruševac
Čačak
Valjevo
Užice
Kosovska Mitrovica
Priština
Prizren
Sarajevo
Tuzla
Zenica

HUNGARY
MAGYARORSZÁG
BUDAPEST
Miskolc
Debrecen
Szeged
Szolnok
Kecskemét
Nyíregyháza
Békéscsaba
Hódmezővásárhely
Eger
Pécs
Győr
Székesfehérvár
Tatabánya

ČESKOSLOVENSKO
Košice
Užhorod
Mukačevo

ODESSA
UKRAINSKAJA S.S.R.

80

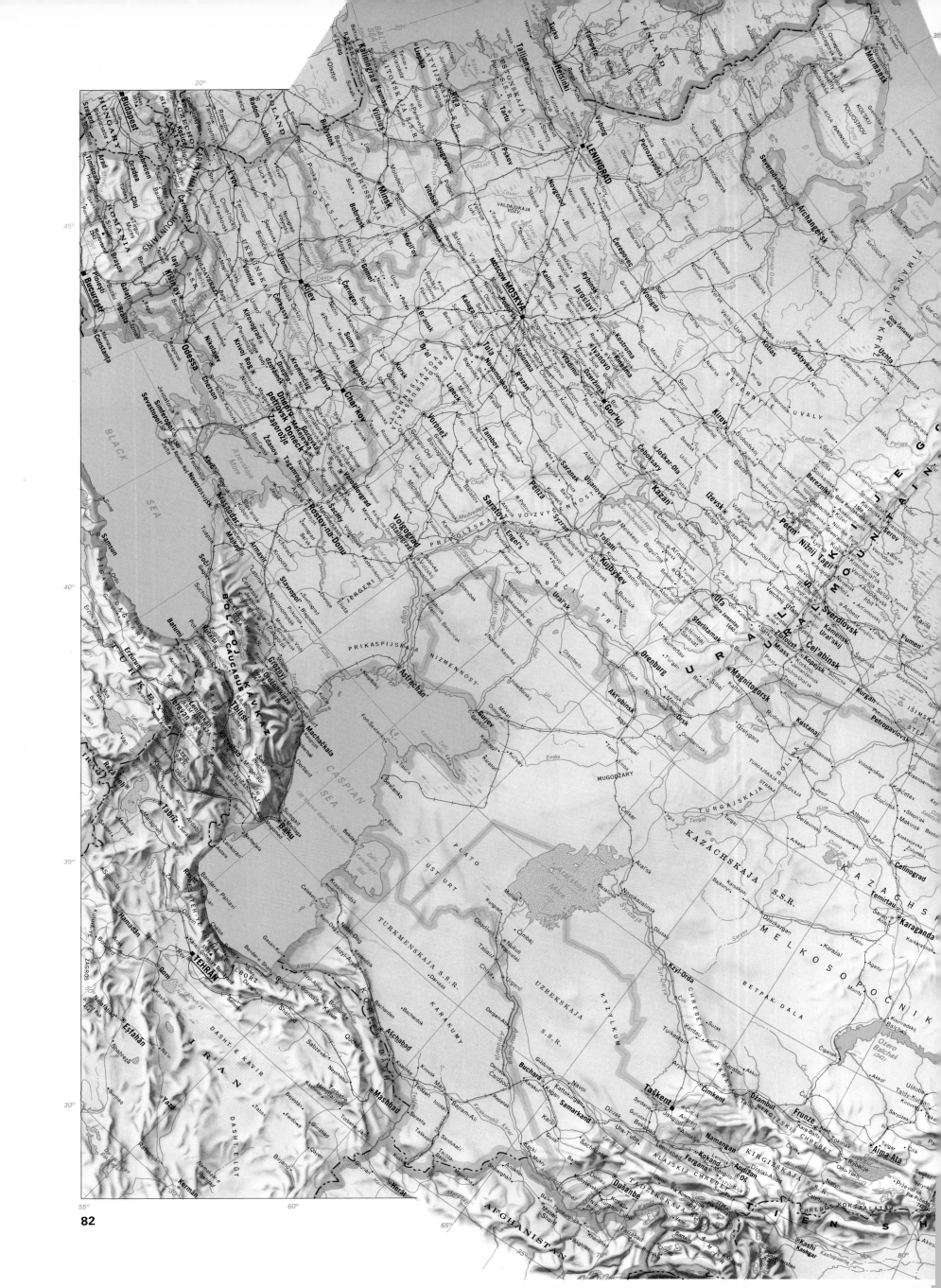

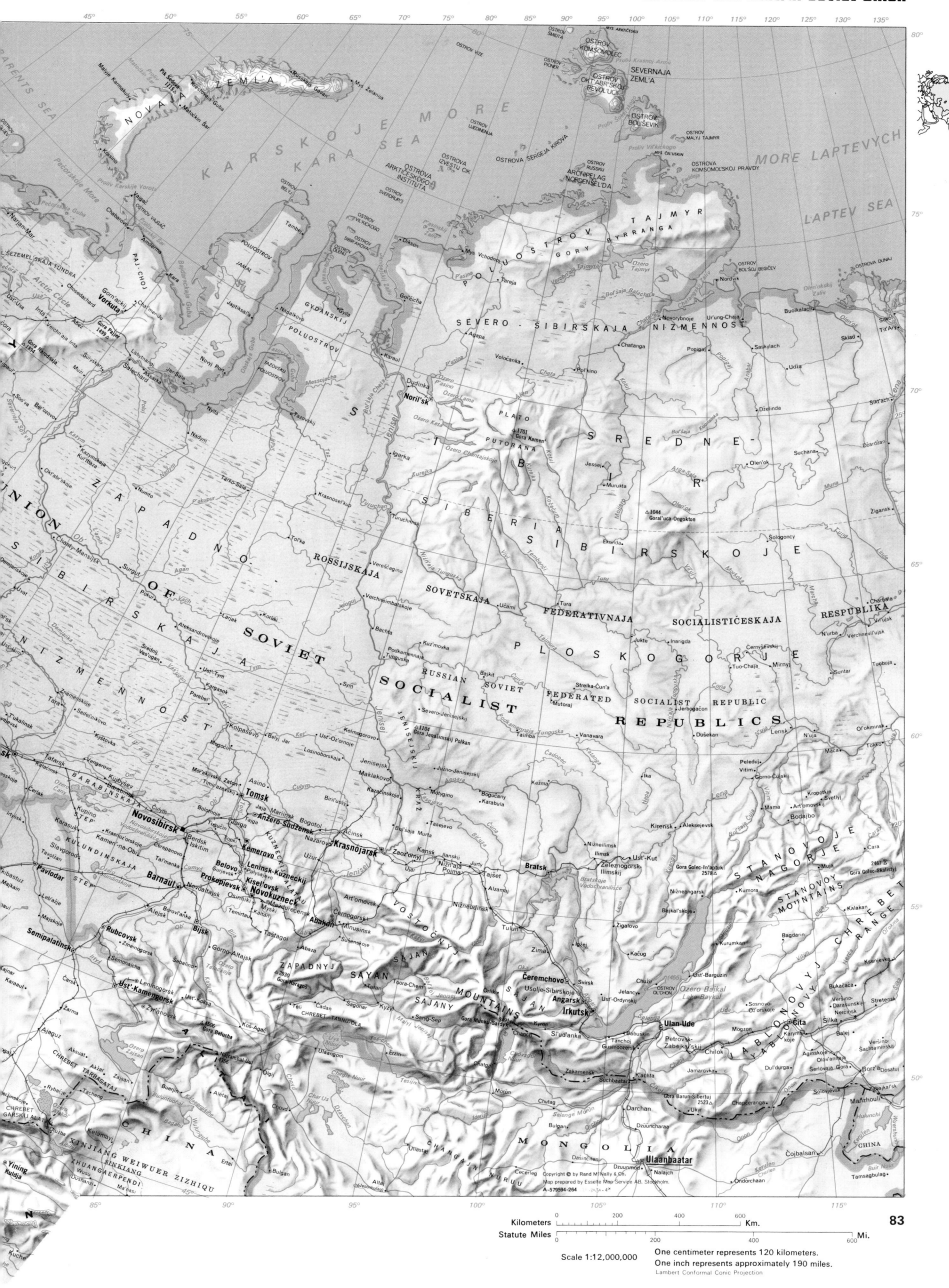

Kilometers

Statute Miles

Scale 1:12,000,000

One centimeter represents 120 kilometers.
One inch represents approximately 190 miles.

Lambert Conformal Conic Projection

Copyright © by Rand McNally & Co.
Map prepared by Esselte Map Service AB, Stockholm.
A-579594-264

Kilometers

Statute Miles

Scale 1:12,000,000

One centimeter represents 120 kilometers.
One inch represents approximately 190 miles.

Lambert Conformal Conic Projection

The annexation of Lithuania, Latvia, and Estonia in 1940 by the Soviet Union has never been officially recognized by the United States Government.

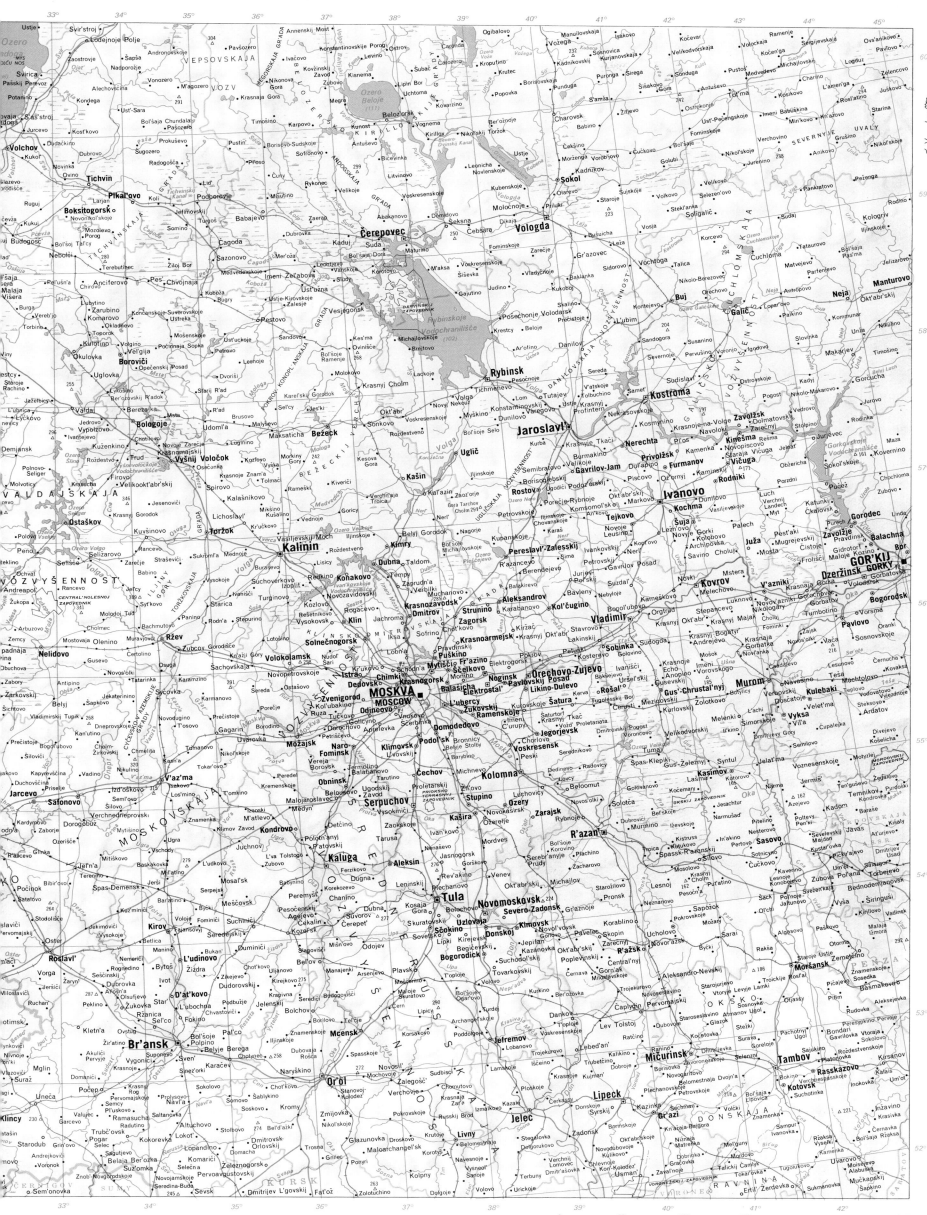

Kilometers | 0 | 50 | 100 | 150 Km.

Statute Miles | 0 | 50 | 100 | 150 Mi.

Scale 1:3,000,000

One centimeter represents 30 kilometers.
One inch represents approximately 47 miles.

Lambert Conformal Conic Projection

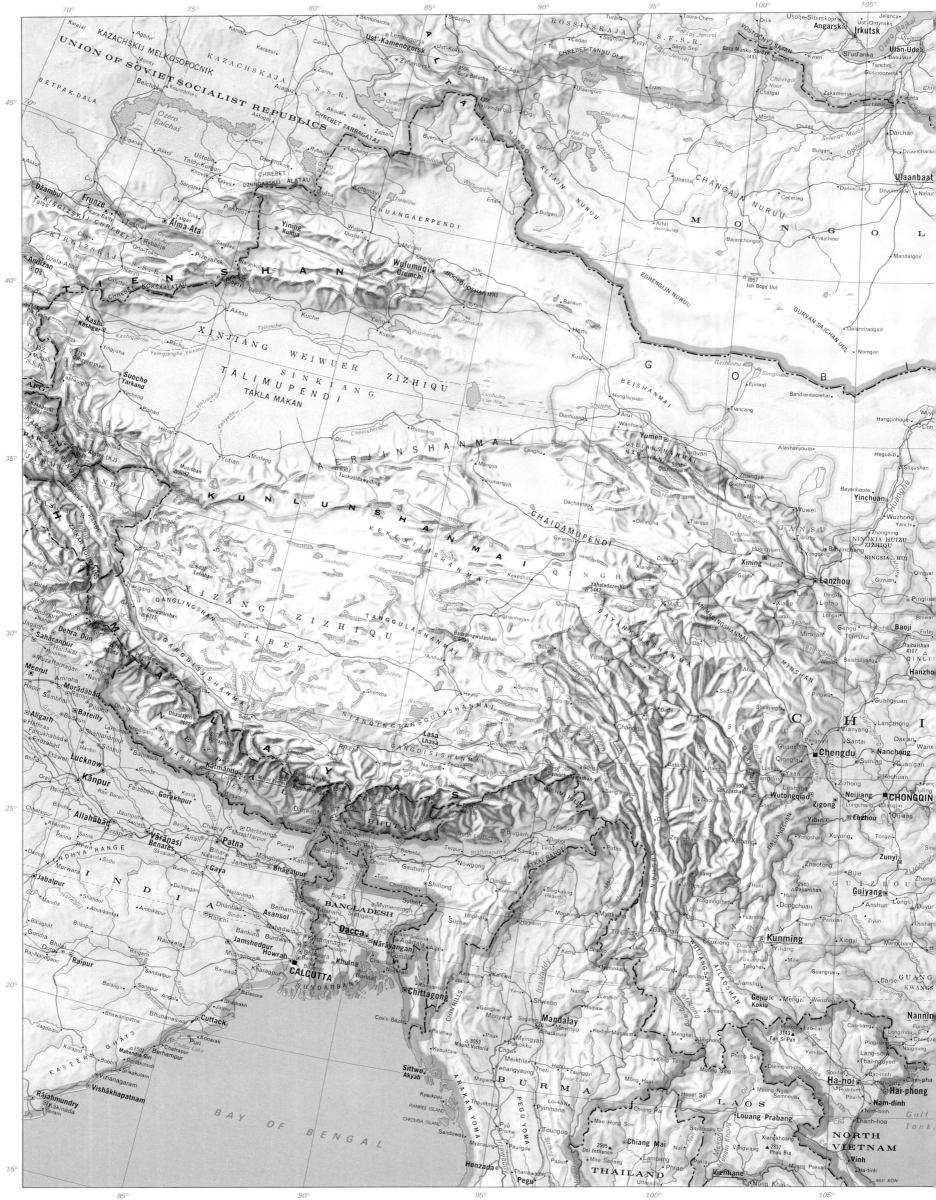

Kilometers

Statute Miles

Scale 1:12,000,000

One centimeter represents 120 kilometers.
One inch represents approximately 190 miles.
Lambert Conformal Conic Projection

Copyright © by Rand McNally & Co.
Map prepared by Esselte Map Service AB, Stockholm
A-569700-264

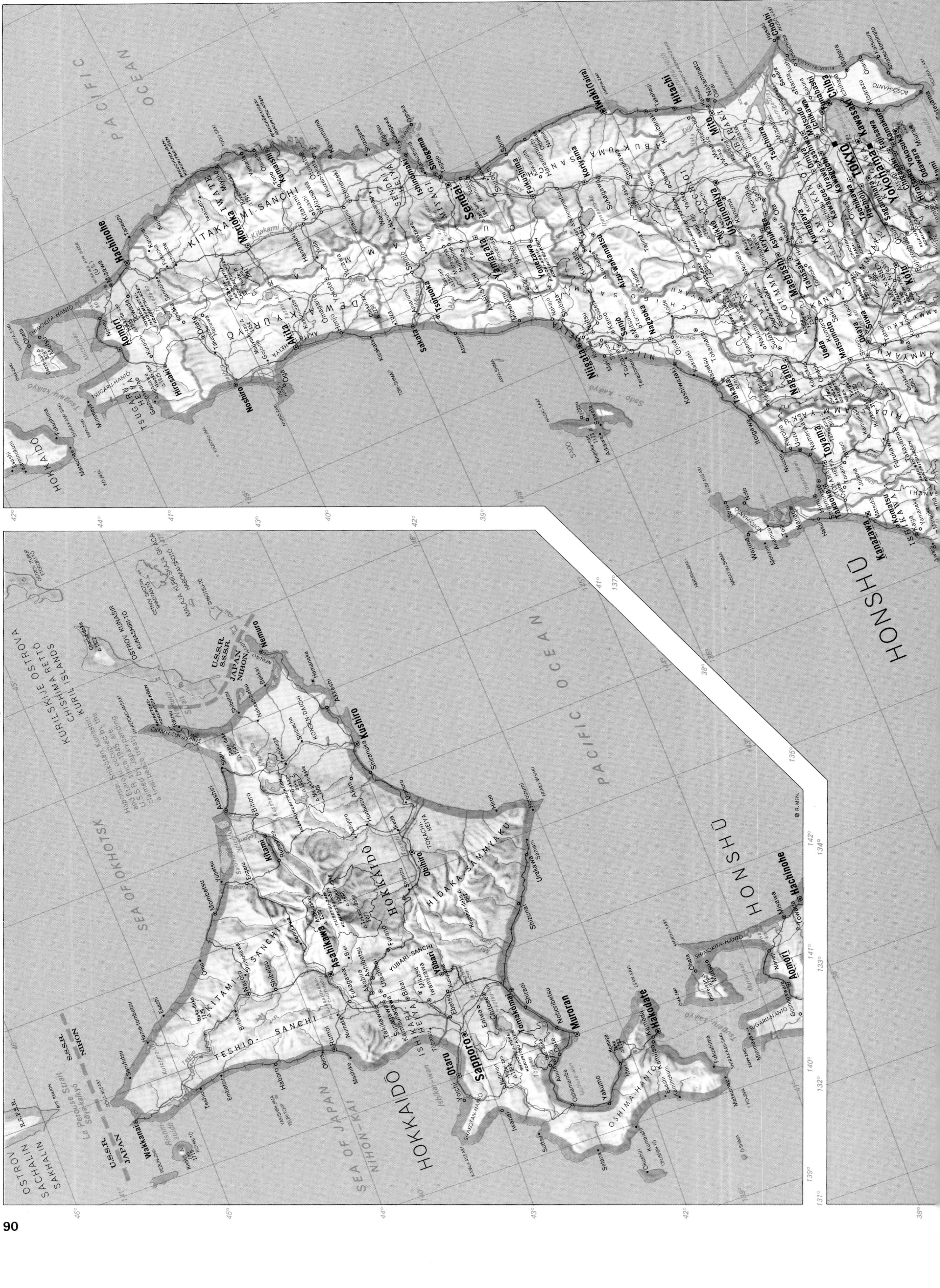

PACIFIC OCEAN

HOKKAIDO

SHIMOKITA-HANTO
TSUGARU-HANTO

Hachinohe
Aomori
Hirosaki
Noshiro
Akita
MORIOKA
Morioka
KITAKAMI SANCHI
KITAKAMI
OU SANCHI
DEWA
Sakata
Tsuruoka
Yamagata
Sendai
MIYAGI
SENDAI
Iwaki (Taira)
ABUKUMA SANCHI
Hitachi
Mito
IBARAKI
Utsunomiya
Nikko
Koriyama
Aizuwakamatsu
Fukushima

Niigata
NIIGATA
Nagaoka
Sado - Kaikyo
SADO

Choshi
BOSO-HANTO
Chiba
TOKYO
Kawasaki
Yokohama
SAITAMA
KANTO
GUMMA
Maebashi
Takasaki
Kofu
Ueda
Matsumoto
Nagano
Toyama
Kanazawa
ISHIKAWA
Komatsu
HIDA SAMMYAKU
KISO SAMMYAKU

HONSHŪ

SEA OF OKHOTSK

OSTROV SACHALIN SAKHALIN
OSTROV
U.S.S.R.

KURIL'SKIJE OSTROVA
CHISHIMA RETTO
KURIL ISLANDS

OSTROV KUNAŠIR
KUNASHIR-TO

U.S.S.R. S.S.H.
JAPAN NIHON
Nemuro
Nemuro Strait

La Perouse Strait
Soya-Kaikyo
Wakkanai
U.S.S.R.
JAPAN
NIHON
S.S.H.

Kushiro
SHIRETOKO-HANTO
KONSEN DAICHI
NEMURO-HANTO

Asahikawa
Kitami
KITAMI SANCHI
HOKKAIDO
Obihiro
HIDAKA SAMMYAKU
TOKACHI HEIYA

TESHIO SANCHI

ISHIKARI HEIYA
YUBARI SANCHI
Yubari

Sapporo
Otaru
ISHIKARI-WAN
Muroran
Tomakomai
OSHIMA-HANTO
Hakodate

SEA OF JAPAN
NIHON-KAI

HOKKAIDO

HONSHŪ
TSUGARU-HANTO
TSUGARU-KAIKYO
SHIMOKITA-HANTO
Aomori
Hachinohe

PACIFIC OCEAN

R. MTN.

Hidaka Shikotan, Kunashri, occupied by the
U.S.S.R. since 1945 are
and Etorofu, Shikotan, Kunashiri
claimed by Japan pending
a final peace settlement

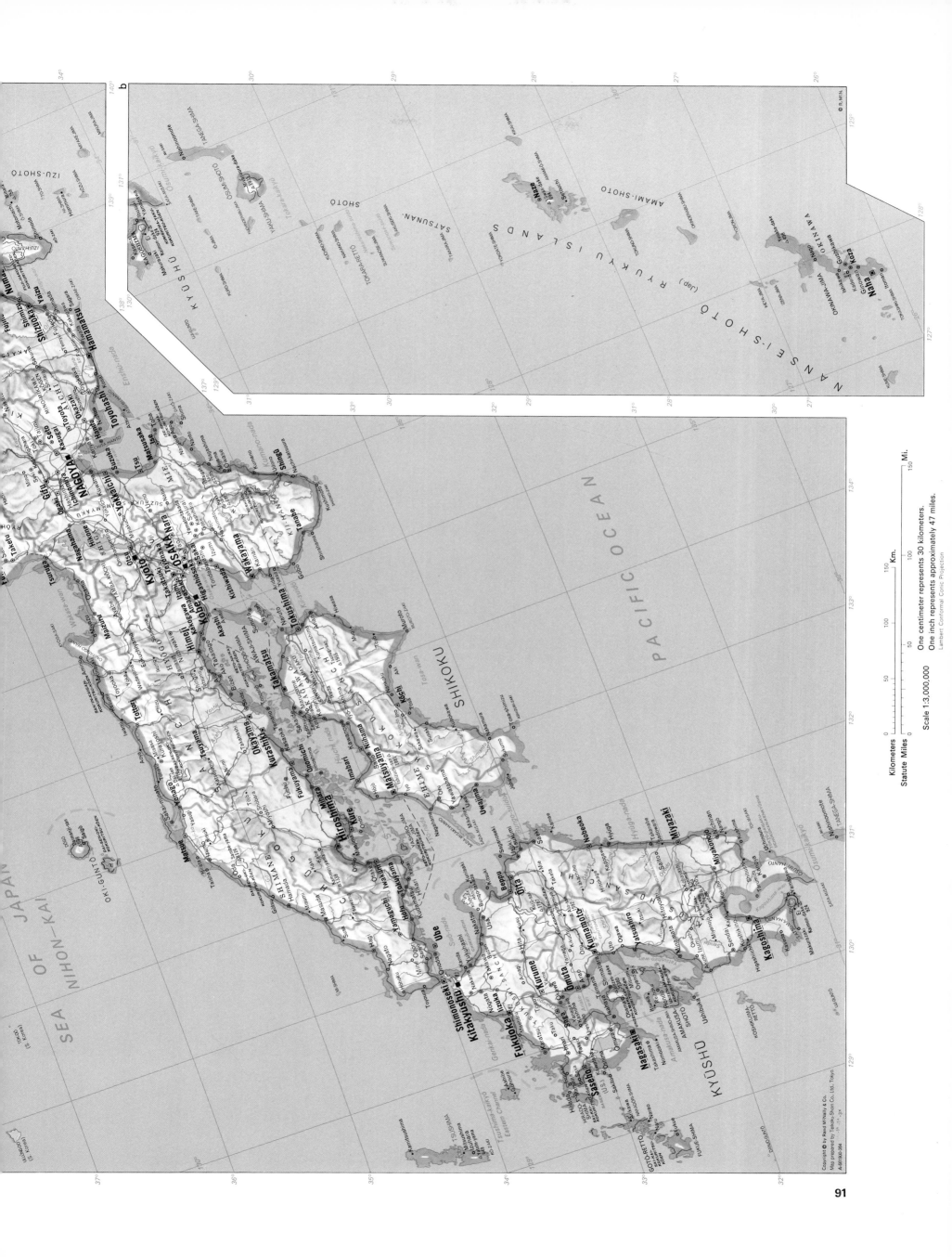

SEA OF JAPAN

NIHON-KAI

PACIFIC OCEAN

KYUSHU

SHIKOKU

NANSEI-SHOTO   RYUKYU ISLANDS (Jap.)

AMAMI-SHOTO

OSUMI-SHOTO

TOKARA-RETTO

SATSUNAN-SHOTO

OKINAWA-JIMA

Naha   Koza
Ginowa

IZU-SHOTO

NAGOYA
Gifu
Hamamatsu
Toyohashi
Okazaki
Yokkaichi
Shizuoka

KYOTO
OSAKA
Kobe
Nara
Wakayama
Himeji
Otsu
Maizuru
Tottori
Matsue

Toyama

Kurashiki
Okayama
Onomichi
Fukuyama
Takamatsu
Tokushima
Kure
Hiroshima
Iwakuni
Yamaguchi
Tokuyama
Ube
Shimonoseki
Kitakyushu
Fukuoka
Iizuka

Takmatsu
Matsuyama
Imabari
Niihama
Kochi
Uwajima

Oita
Beppu
Kumamoto
Nobeoka
Miyazaki
Kumamoto
Yatsushiro
Kurume
Omuta
Saga
Nagasaki
Sasebo

Kagoshima
Miyakonojo

KII-HANTO
Tsu
Matsusaka
Shingu
Tanabe

OKI-GUNTO

TSUSHIMA
GOTO-RETTO
FUKUE-SHIMA

AKIYOSHI
TOKYO
(S. Korea)
ULLUNG-DO
(S. Korea)

Scale 1:3,000,000

Kilometers
Statute Miles

One centimeter represents 30 kilometers.
One inch represents approximately 47 miles.
Lambert Conformal Conic Projection

Copyright © by Rand McNally & Co.
Map prepared by Teikoku-Shoin Co., Ltd. Tokyo.
A-SP/90/364

91

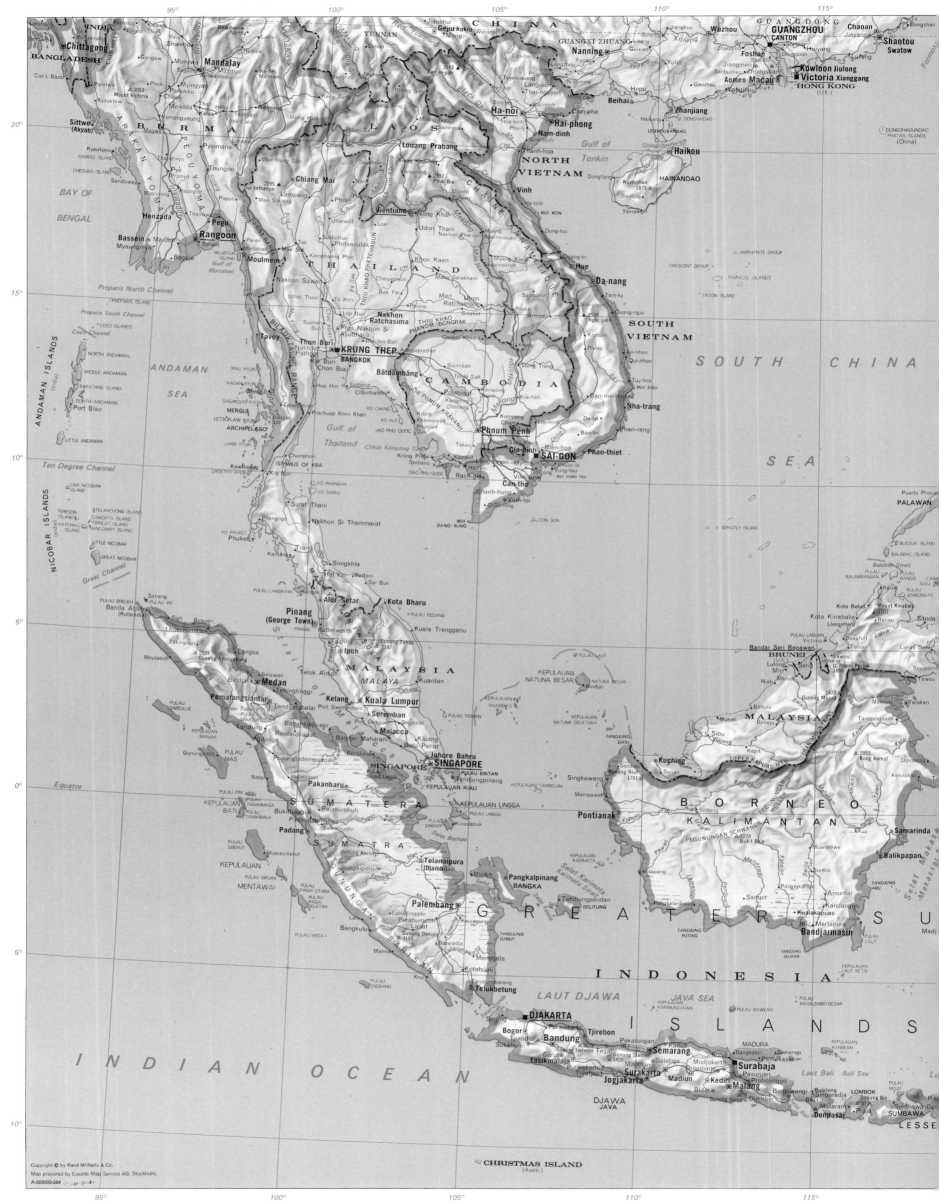

Kilometers
Statute Miles

0   200   400   Km.
0   200   400   Mi.

Scale 1:12,000,000

One centimeter represents 120 kilometers.
One inch represents approximately 190 miles.

Lambert Conformal Conic Projection

Mi.
300

Km.
300
200
100
0

Kilometers

Statute Miles

One centimeter represents 60 kilometers.
One inch represents approximately 95 miles.

Scale 1:6,000,000

Lambert Conformal Conic Projection

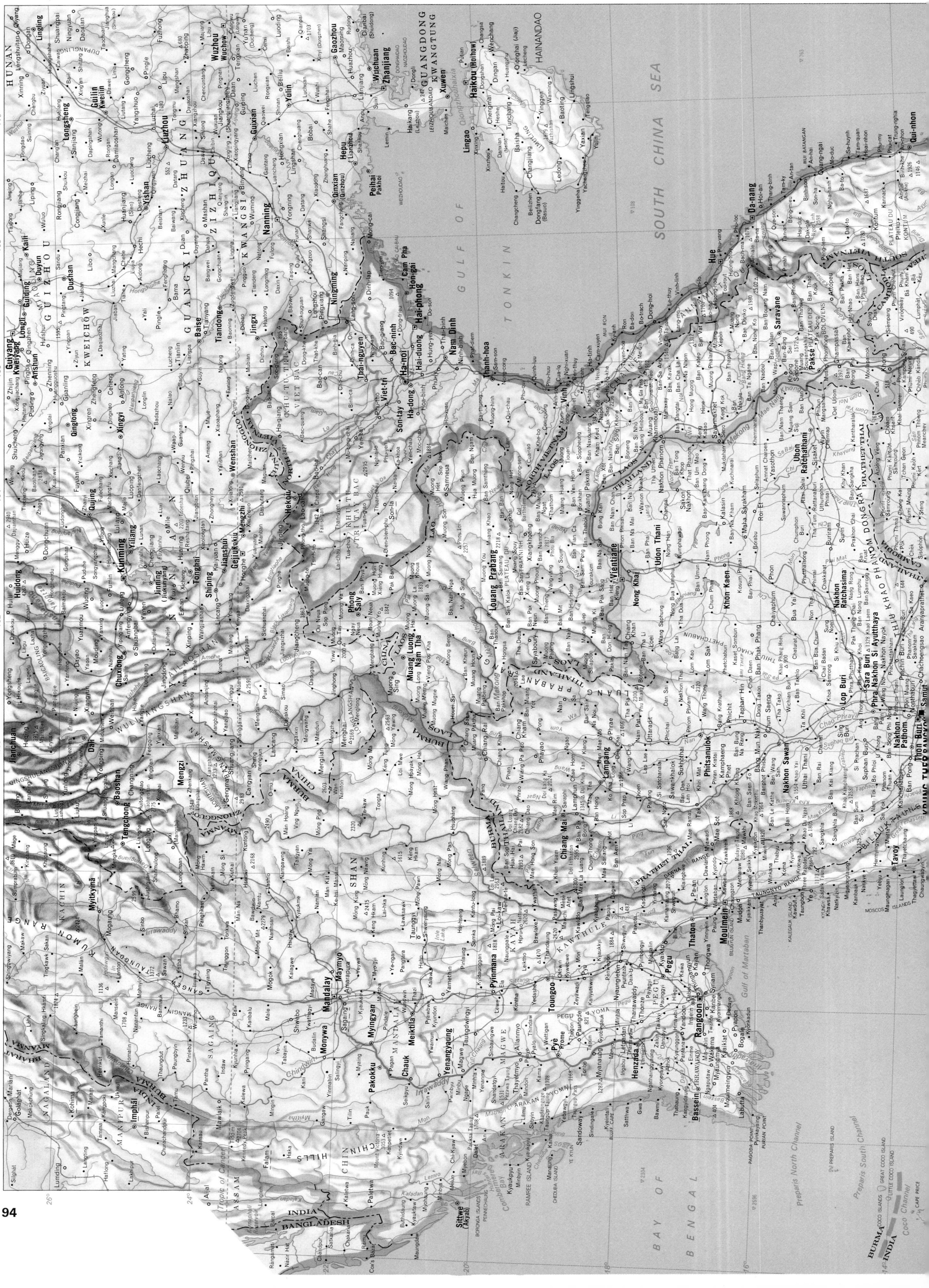

SOUTH CHINA SEA

GULF OF TONKIN

BAY OF BENGAL

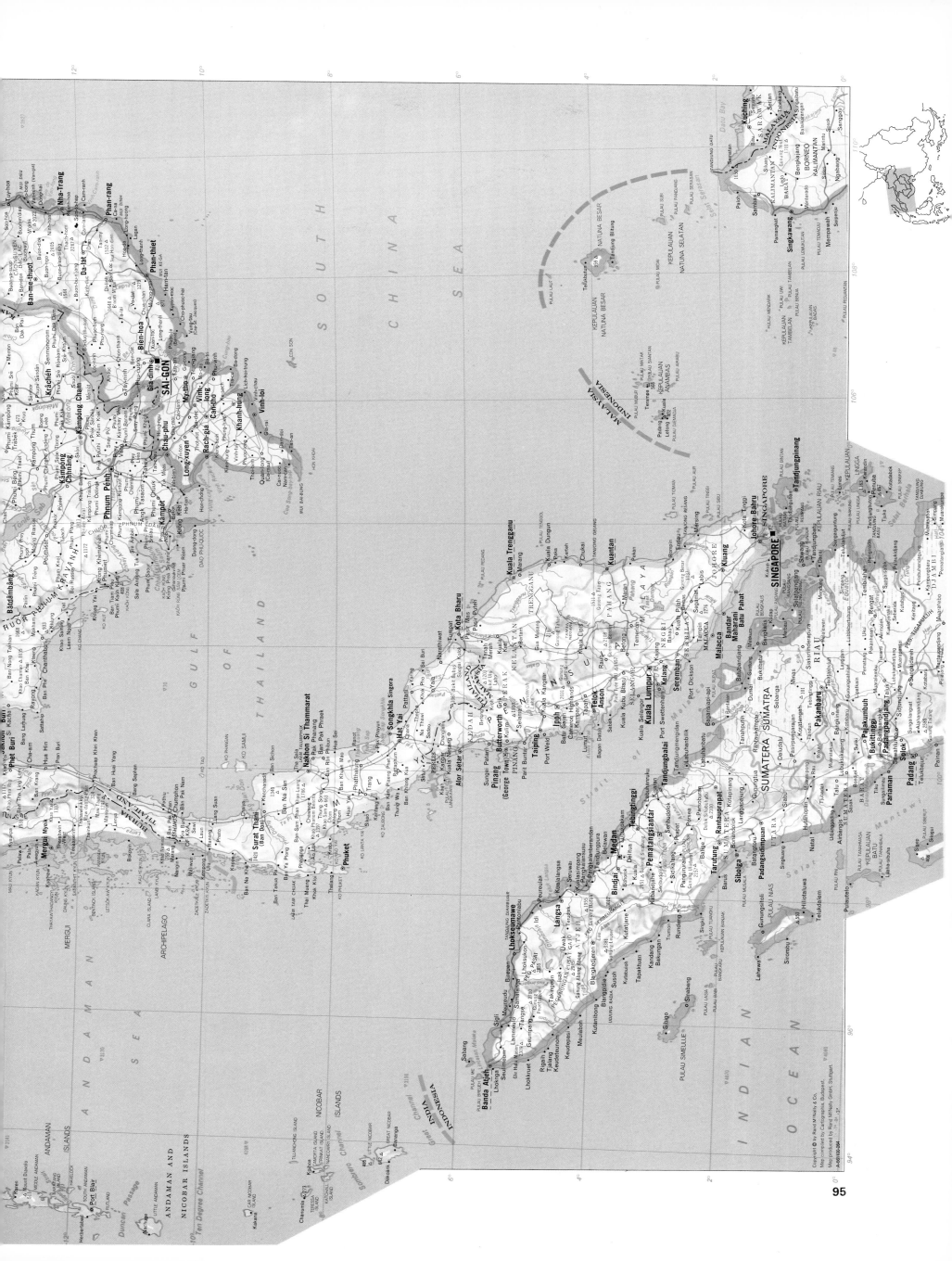

95

Philippines

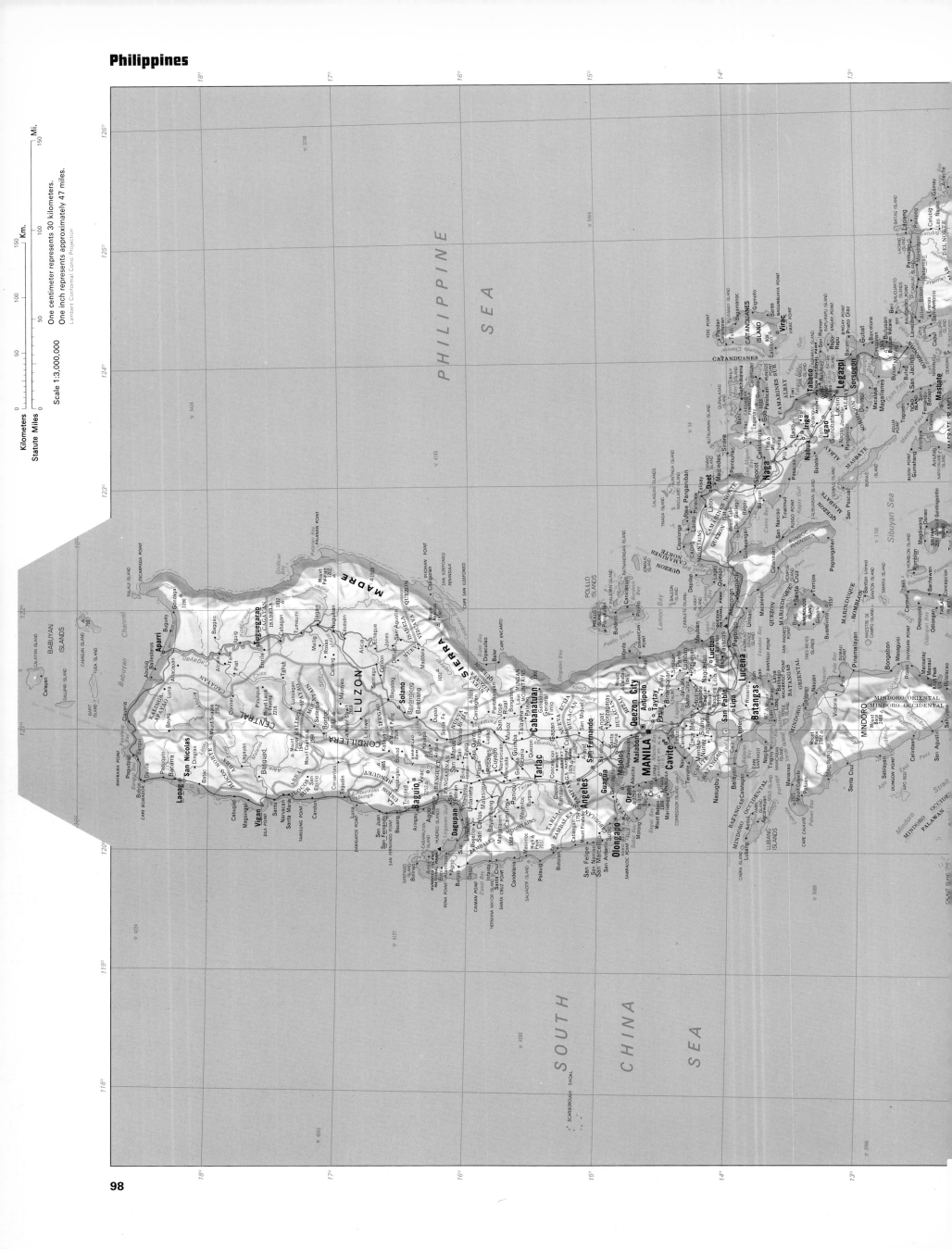

Scale 1:3,000,000

One centimeter represents 30 kilometers.
One inch represents approximately 47 miles.

Lambert Conformal Conic Projection

Kilometers
Statute Miles

PHILIPPINE SEA

SOUTH CHINA SEA

Sibuyan Sea

BABUYAN ISLANDS

Aparri

Laoag
Vigan
San Nicolas
Baguio
Dagupan
Angeles
Olongapo
Tarlac
Cabanatuan
San Fernando
MANILA
Quezon City
Cavite
Malolos
Batangas
Lucena
San Pablo
Lipa

LUZON

SIERRA MADRE

CORDILLERA CENTRAL

MINDORO
MINDORO ORIENTAL
MINDORO OCCIDENTAL

Naga
Daet
Iriga
Nabua
Ligao
Tabaco
Legazpi
Sorsogon
CATANDUANES
Virac
MASBATE
Masbate

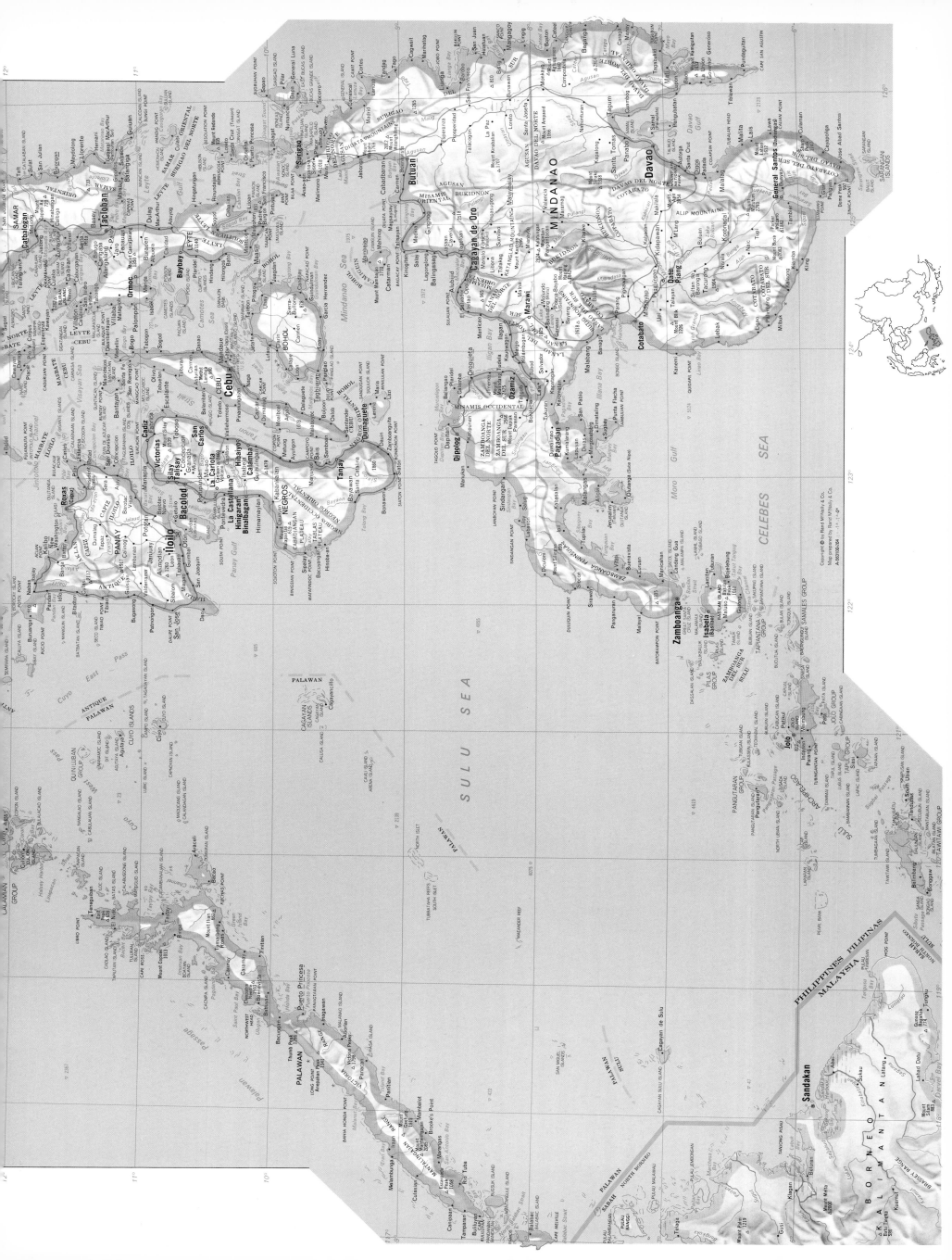

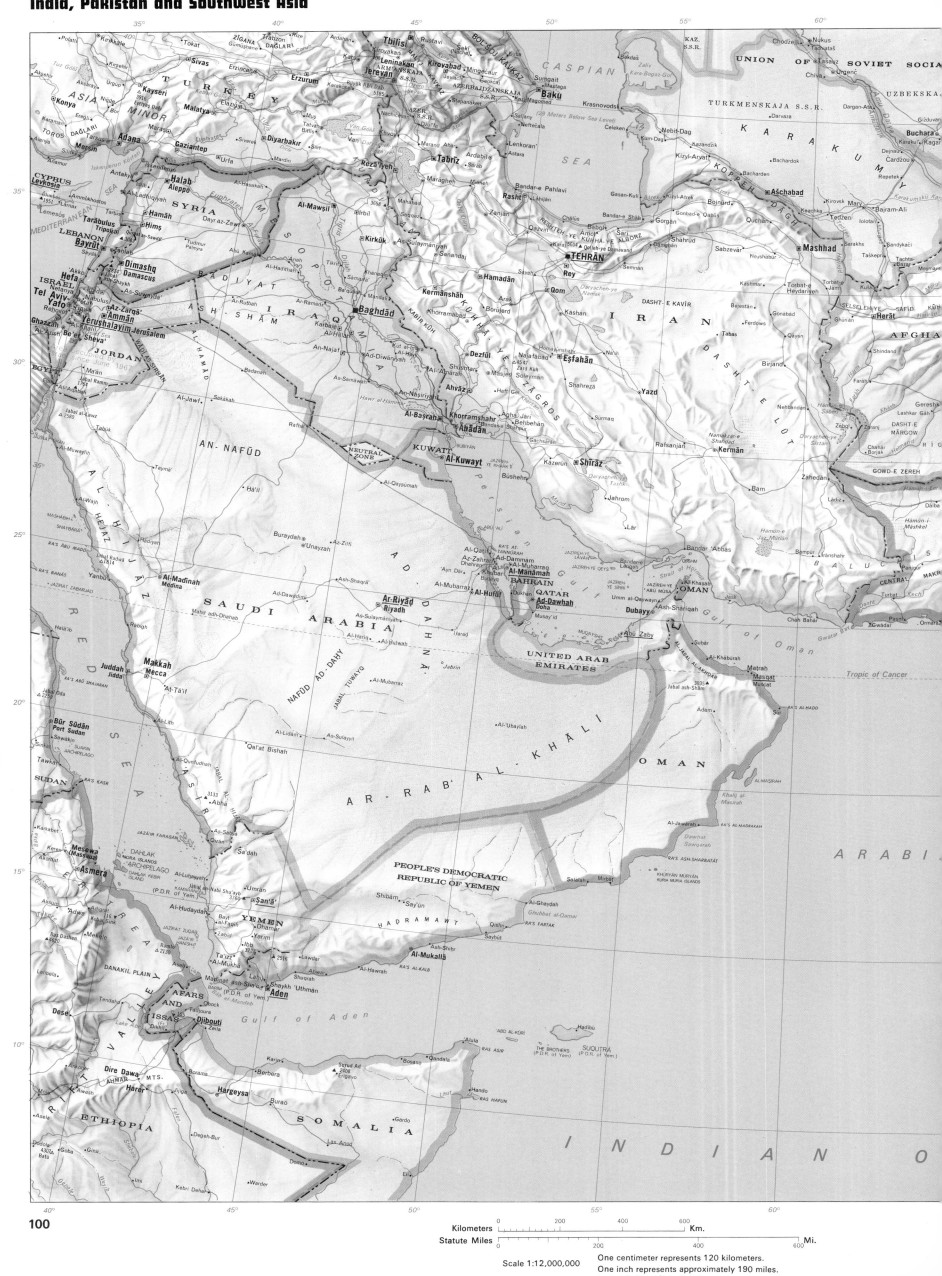

Kilometers 0 | 200 | 400 | 600 Km.

Statute Miles 0 | 200 | 400 | 600 Mi.

Scale 1:12,000,000

One centimeter represents 120 kilometers.
One inch represents approximately 190 miles.

Lambert Conformal Conic Projection

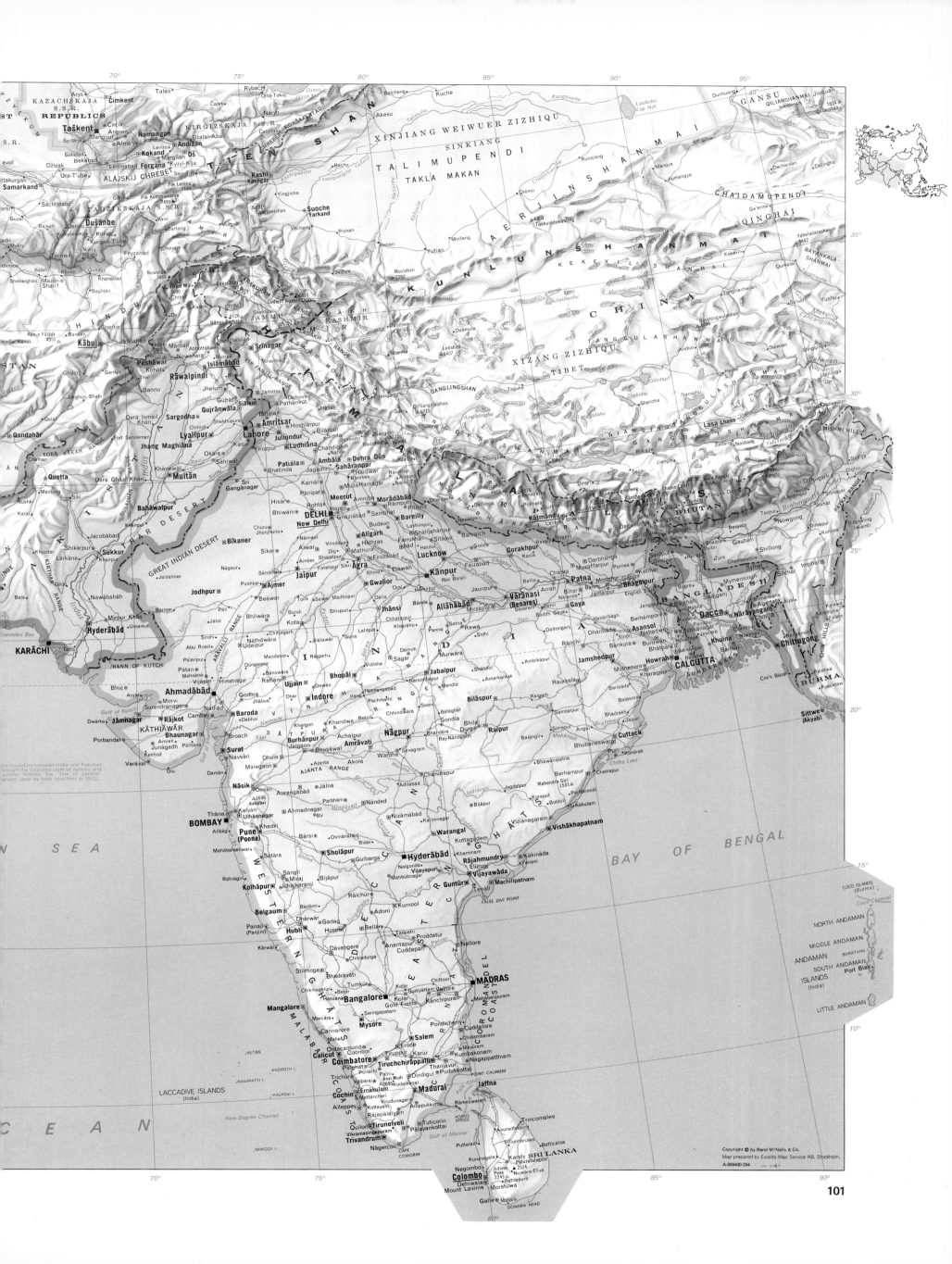

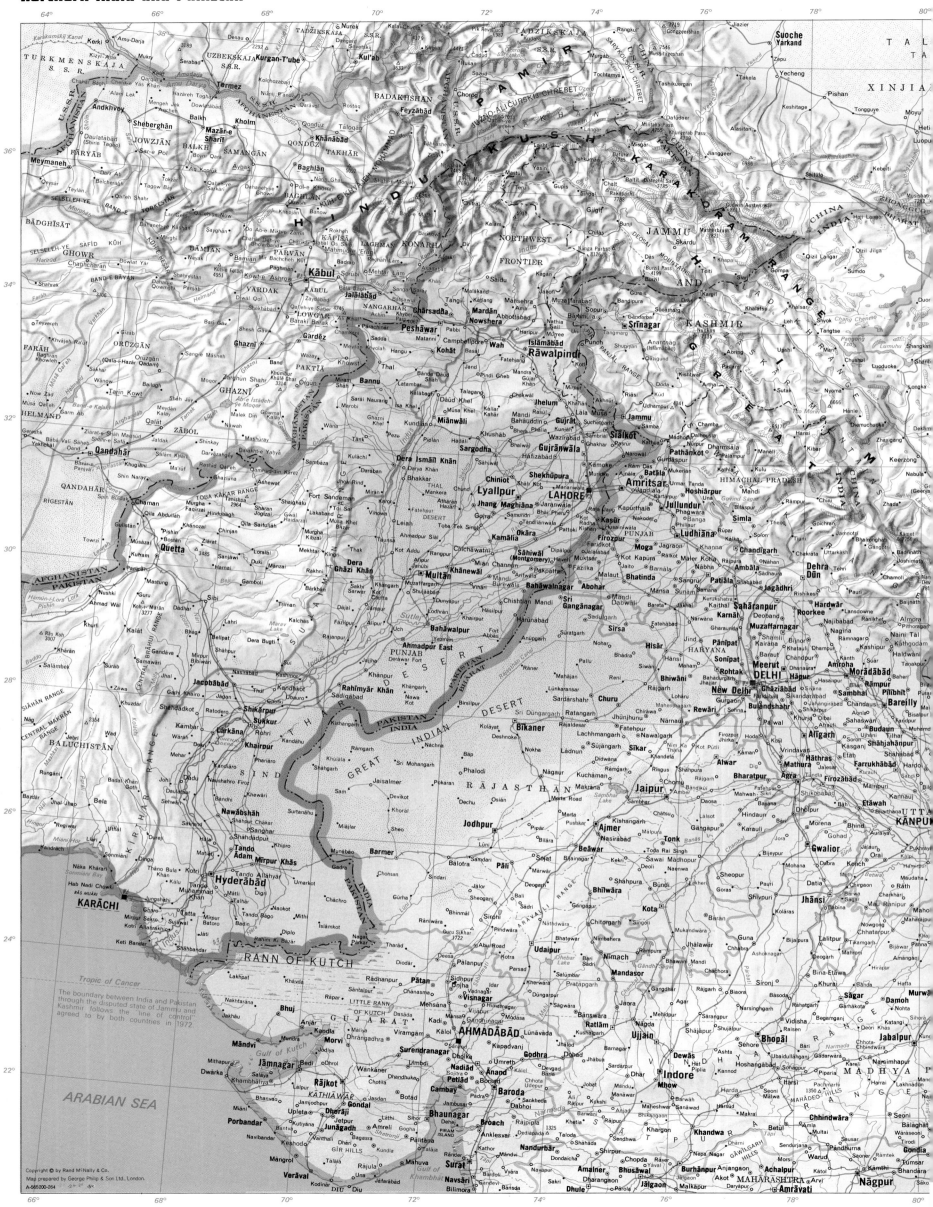

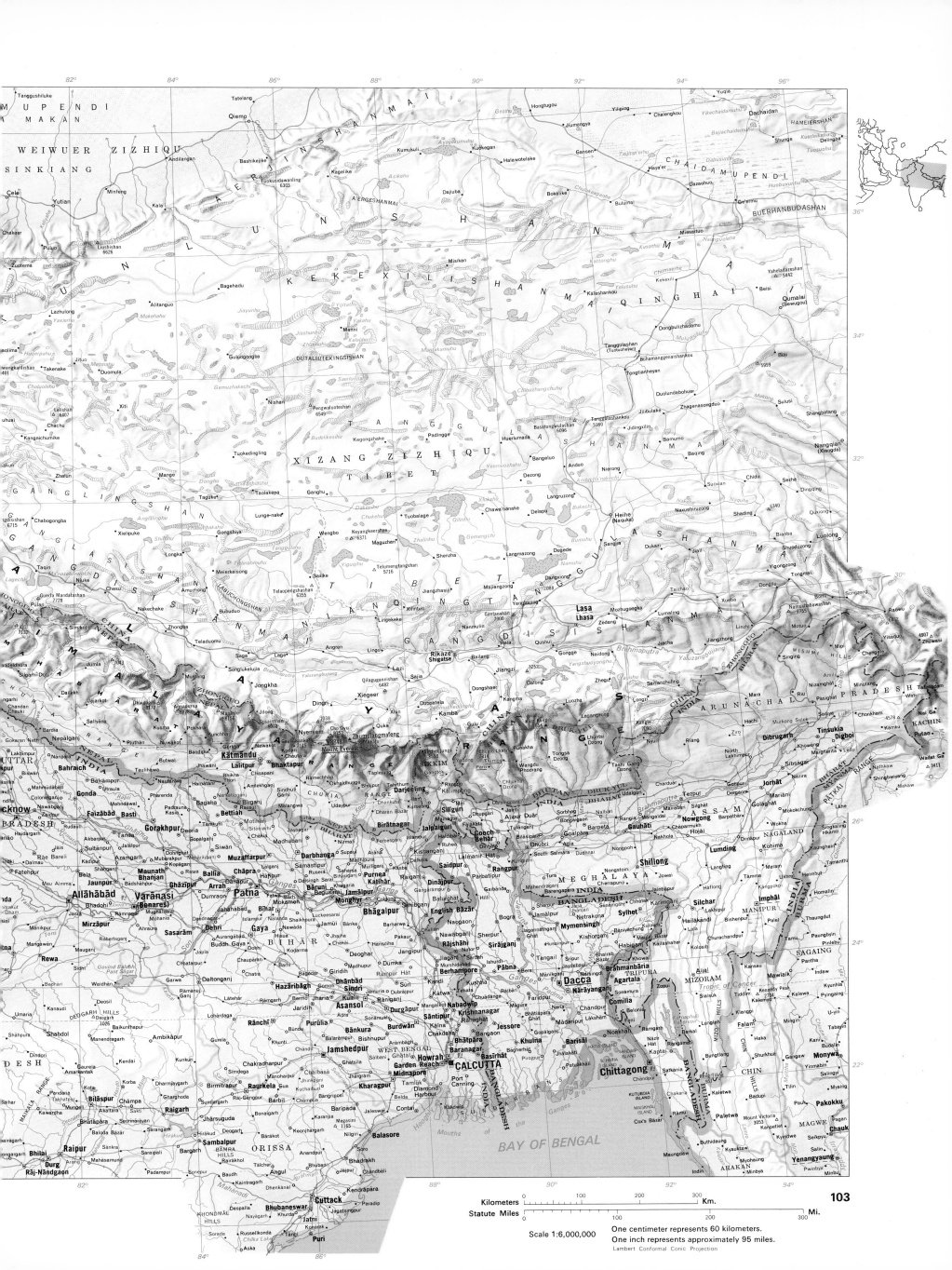

Kilometers

Statute Miles

Scale 1:6,000,000

One centimeter represents 60 kilometers.
One inch represents approximately 95 miles.

Lambert Conformal Conic Projection

ANKARA
Kırıkkale
Keskin
Polatlı
Haymana
Bālā
Yozgat
Tokat
Sivas
Erzincan
Erzurum
Kars
Kirovabad
Jerevan
ARM'ANSKAIA S.S.R.
AZERBAIJANSKAJA S.S.R.
Stepanakert
Nachičevan' A.S.S.R.

Konya
Ereğli
Karaman
Aksaray
Kayseri
Niğde
Malatya
Elâzığ
Diyarbakır
Van
Tabrīz
REZĀ'ĪYEH
ĀZARBĀIJĀN-E KHĀVARĪ
Mīāneh
Zanjān
GĪLĀN

Adana
Mersin
Tarsus
İçel
TOROS DAĞLARI
Ceyhan
Osmaniye
Gaziantep
Urfa
Mardin
Nusaybin
Al-Qāmishlī
Dahūk
Al-'Amādiyah
Mahābād
KORDESTĀN
As-Sulaymānīyah
Sanandaj
Hamadān
KERMĀNSHĀHĀN
Kermānshāh

ANTAKYA
Antioch
Halab Aleppo
İskenderun
CYPRUS KIPROS
Levkosía Nicosia
Lemesós Limassol
Famagusta
Al-Lādhiqīyah Latakia
Idlib
Ar-Raqqah
Tall 'Afar
Al-Mawṣil Mosul
Irbil
Kirkūk

MEDITERRANEAN SEA
Ḥamāh
Ḥimṣ Homs
Ṭarābulus Tripoli
LEBANON AL-LUBNĀN
Beirut Bayrūt
Dayr az-Zawr
Abū Kamāl
Al-Qā'im
Ānah
Tikrīt
Sāmarrā'

Dimashq Damascus
SYRIA AS-SURĪYAH
Ba'labakk
'Akko Acre
Ḥefa Haifa
ISRAEL YISRA'EL
PALESTINE
TEL AVIV-YAFO
Area occupied by Israel since June 1967
Yerushālayim Jerusalem
'Ammān
AL-URDUNN JORDAN
Az-Zarqā'
As-Suwaydā'
BĀDIYAT ASH-SHĀM
IRAQ AL-'IRĀQ
Ar-Ramādī
Al-Fallūjah
Al-Kāẓimīyah
BAGHDĀD
Karbalā'
Al-Ḥillah
An-Najaf
Ad-Dīwānīyah
Al-Kūt
Al-'Amārah

Dumyāṭ
Būr Sa'īd Port Said
Ghazzah Gaza
As-Suways Suez
Suez Canal
EGYPT
SINAI PENINSULA
JABAL AL-'AJMAH
Al-'Aqabah
Gulf of Aqaba
AL-URDUNN JORDAN
SAUDI ARABIA AL'ARABĪYAH AS-SA'ŪDĪYAH
Al-Jawf
AN-NAFŪD
NEUTRAL ZONE
KUWAIT AL-KUWAYT
Al-Kuwayt

RED SEA
AL-BAḤR AL-AḤMAR
AL-ḤIJĀZ
Yanbu
Al-Madīnah Medina
JABAL SHAMMAR
Ḥā'il
Burạydah
'Unayzah
Ar-Riyāḍ Riyadh
AD-DAHNĀ
AS-SUMMĀN

Tropic of Cancer
EGYPT MISR
SUDAN AS-SŪDĀN
Administrative Boundary
Area administered by Sudan

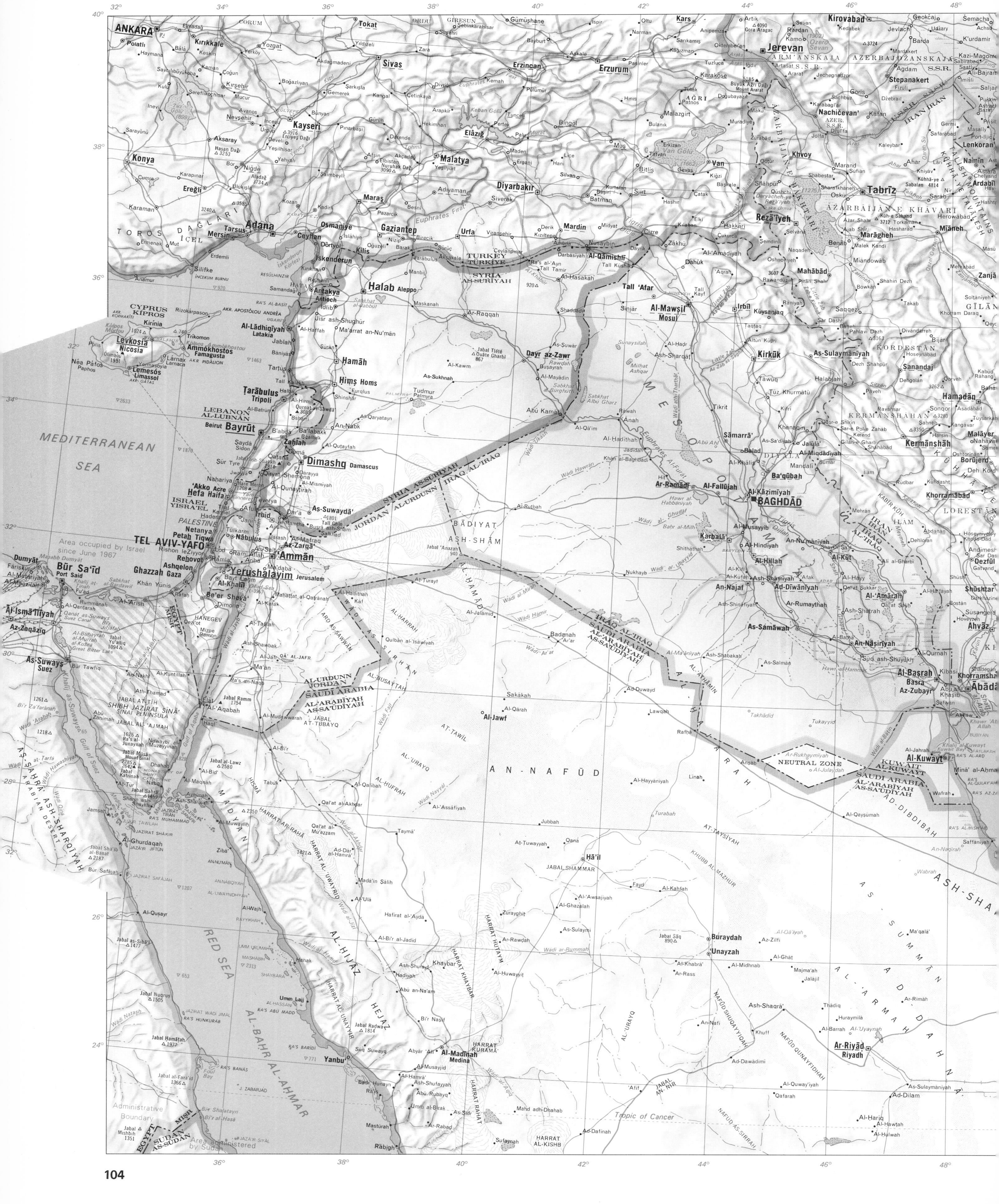

Kilometers 0   100   200   300 Km.

Statute Miles 0   100   200   300 Mi.

Scale 1:6,000,000

One centimeter represents 60 kilometers.
One inch represents approximately 95 miles.

Lambert Conformal Conic Projection

Western North Africa

MEDITERRANEAN SEA

ITALY

GREECE

TURKEY

CYPRUS

ALGERIA

TUNISIA

LIBYA

EGYPT

TARABULUS
TRIPOLITANIA

FAZZAN FEZZAN

BARQAH
CYRENAICA

AS-SAHRĀ
AL-GHARBĪYAH
WESTERN
DESERT

GRAND ERG ORIENTAL

PLATEAU DU TADEMAIT

PLATEAU DU TINRHERT

TASSILI N'AJJER

AHAGGAR

TASSILI DU HAGGAR

SARĪR TIBASTI

SARĪR NERASTRO

TIBESTI

S A H A R A

Tropic of Cancer

LIBYAN DESERT
AS-SAHRĀ AL-LĪBĪYAH

Lake
Nasser

NIGER

AÏR

GRAND ERG DE BILMA

BODÉLE

CHAD

ENNEDI

DÉPRESSION DU MOURDI

S U D A N

SUDAN

NIGERIA

Lake Chad
Lac Tchad

N'djamena
(Fort-Lamy)

MANDARA MOUNTAINS

ADAMAWA

CAMEROON

CENTRAL AFRICAN

REPUBLIC

CHAÎNE DES MONGOS

Bight of Benin

Lagos

Gulf
of
Guinea

Bight of Biafra

SAO TOME AND
PRINCIPE

MACÍAS NGUEMA BIYOGO
EQUAT. GUINEA

EQUAT.
GUINEA

GABON

CONGO

Yaoundé

ZAIRE

107

Kilometers

Km.

Statute Miles

Mi.

Scale 1:12,000,000

One centimeter represents 120 kilometers.
One inch represents approximately 190 miles.
Miller Oblated Stereographic Projection

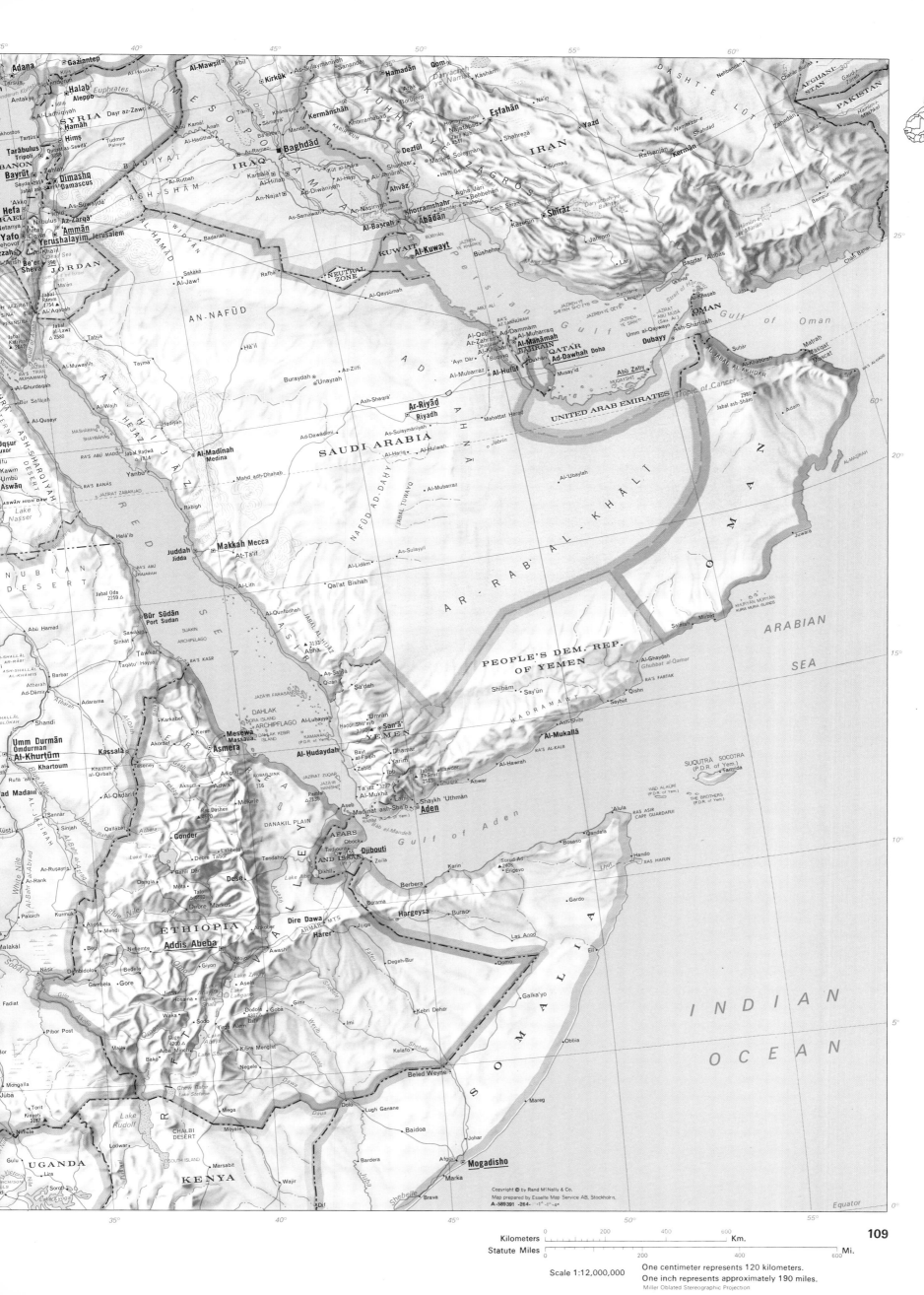

Kilometers ⊢───┼───┼───┼───┼───┼───┼ Km.
0   200   400   600

Statute Miles ⊢───┼───┼───┼───┼───┼───┼ Mi.
0   200   400   600

Copyright © by Rand McNally & Co.
Map prepared by Esselte Map Service AB, Stockholm.
A-589391 -264- -1⁰ -1⁰ -4⁰

Scale 1:12,000,000

One centimeter represents 120 kilometers.
One inch represents approximately 190 miles.
Miller Oblated Stereographic Projection

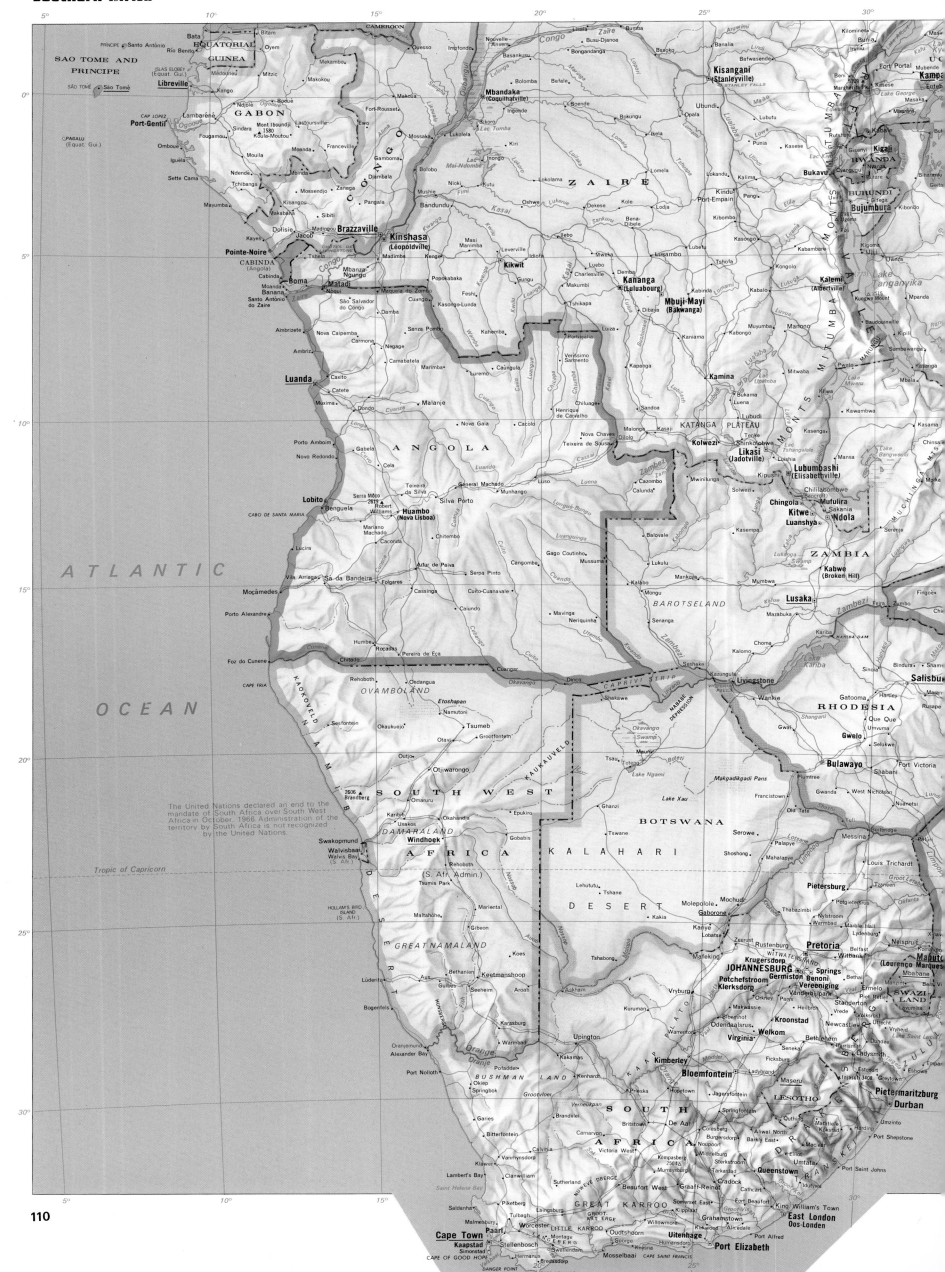

The United Nations declared an end to the
mandate of South Africa over South West
Africa in October, 1966. Administration of the
territory by South Africa is not recognized
by the United Nations.

INDIAN OCEAN

Equator

SOMALIA

KENYA
Nairobi

TANZANIA

SERENGETI PLAIN

MASAI STEPPE

Mombasa

Zanzibar

Dar-es-Salaam

MALAWI

Zomba
Blantyre

MOZAMBIQUE

Beira

SEYCHELLES

Victoria
MAHÉ ISLAND

AMIRANTE ISLANDS (Sey.)
ÎLE DESROCHES (Sey.)
PLATTE ISLAND (Sey.)

ALPHONSE ISLAND (Sey.)
COETIVY ISLAND (Sey.)

ALDABRA ISLANDS (Sey.)
PROVIDENCE ISLAND (Sey.)
COSMOLEDO GROUP (Sey.)
SAINT PIERRE ISLAND (Sey.)
CERF ISLAND (Sey.)
ASSUMPTION ISLAND (Sey.)
ASTOVE ISLAND (Sey.)
FARQUHAR GROUP (Sey.)

AGALEGA ISLANDS (Mauritius)

ÎLES GLORIEUSES (Mad.)
COMORO ISLANDS
Moroni
GRANDE COMORE
Mutsamudu ANJOUAN
Fomboni MOHELI
MAYOTTE (Fr.)
Dzaoudzi
BANC DU GEYSER
CAP D'AMBRE
CAP SAINT-SÉBASTIEN
Diégo-Suarez
NOSY MITSIO
NOSSI-BÉ
Hell-Ville
Ambilobe Vohémar
MASSIF DU TSARATANANA
NOSY LAVA
Analalava Bealanana
Doany Sambava
Antalaha
ÎLE SAINTE-MARIE
Majunga
Port-Bergé
Mampikony
Mandritsara
CAP EST
Maroantsetra
CAP SAINT-ANDRÉ
Soalala
Marovoay
Tsaratanana
Andriamena
Fénérive
ÎLE CHESTERFIELD
Maevatanana
ÎLE JUAN DE NOVA (Fr.)
Besalampy
Ankazobe
Ambatondrazaka
Tamatave
Morafenobe
MADAGASCAR
Maintirano
Ankavandra
Tsiroanomandidy
Tananarive
Brickaville
ÎLES BARREN
Belo
Miandrivazo
Ambatolampy
Vatomandry
ANKARATRA
Antsirabe
Morondava
Mahabo
Malaimbandy
Ambositra
Mahanoro
Mandabe
Nosy Varika
Manja
Mananjary
Morombe
Fianarantsoa
Beroroha
Ambalavao
PIC BOBY
Manakara
Ankazoabo
Tuléar
Betroka
Farafangana
Vangaindrano
Midongy Sud
Betioky
Bekily
Androka
Ampanihy
Tsihombe
Ambovombe
Fort-Dauphin
CAP SAINTE-MARIE

Port Louis
Curepipe
Mahébourg
MAURITIUS
Le Port
Saint-Denis
Saint-Paul
REUNION (Fr.)
Saint-Pierre
MASCARENE ISLANDS

TROMELIN (Fr.)

Mozambique Channel

Tropic of Capricorn

INDIAN OCEAN

Rhodesia unilaterally declared its independence from the United Kingdom on November 11, 1965.

BASSAS DA INDIA (Fr.)
ÎLE EUROPA (Fr.)
CAP SAINT-VINCENT

Copyright © by Rand McNally & Co.
Map prepared by Esselte Map Service AB, Stockholm.
A-589200-264

111

Kilometers |0 200 400 600| Km.
Statute Miles |0 200 400 600| Mi.

Scale 1:12,000,000
One centimeter represents 120 kilometers.
One inch represents approximately 190 miles.
Miller Oblated Stereographic Projection

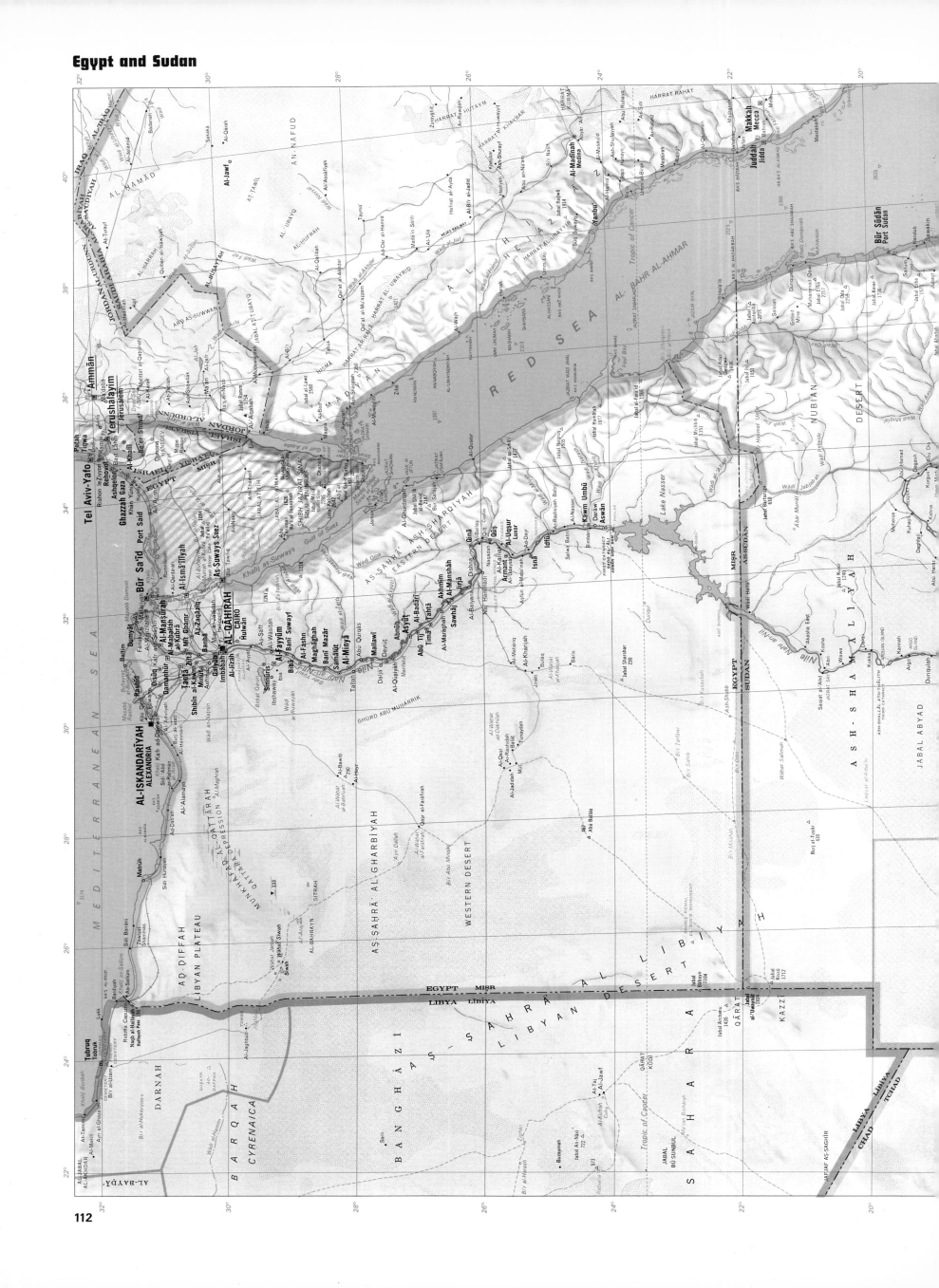

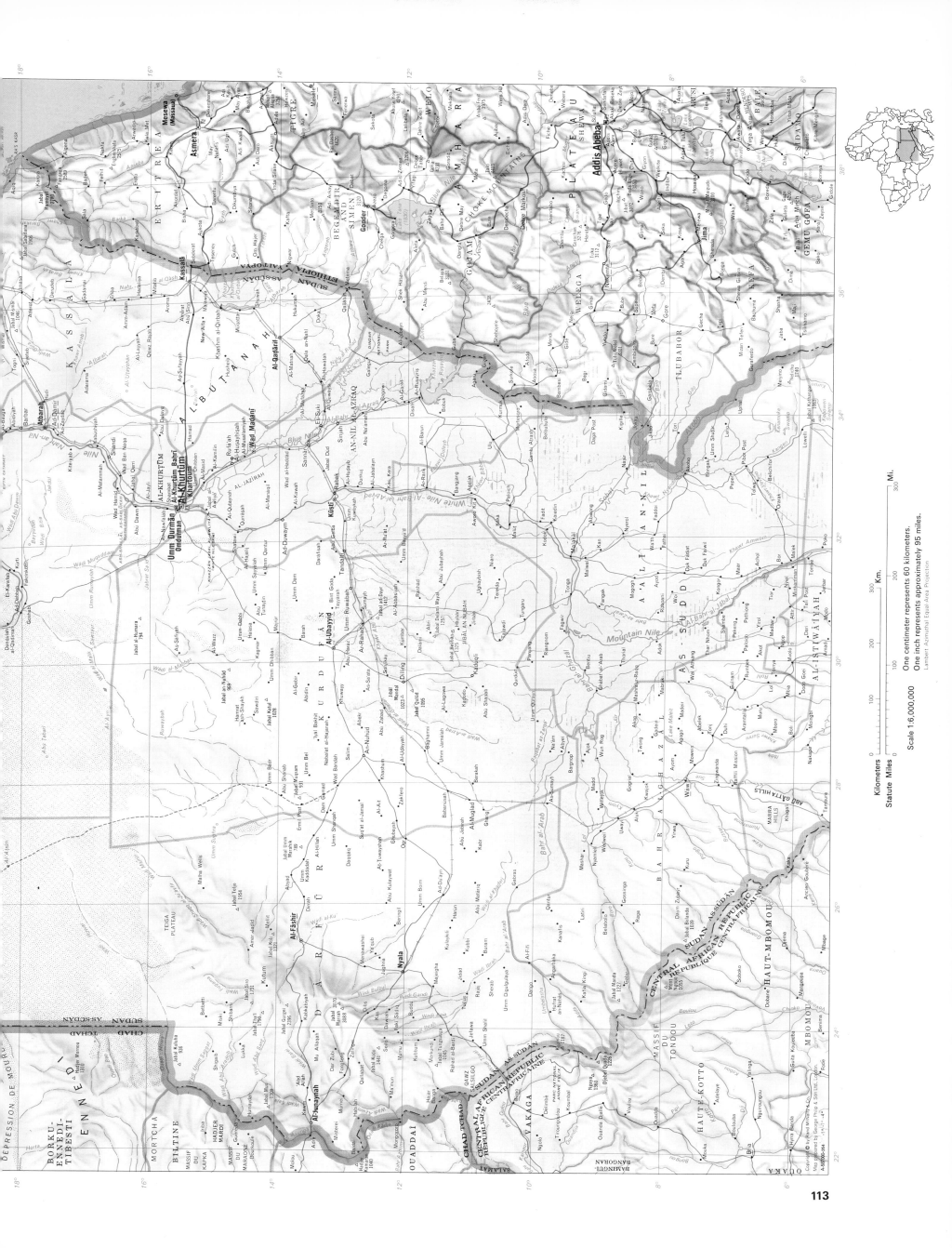

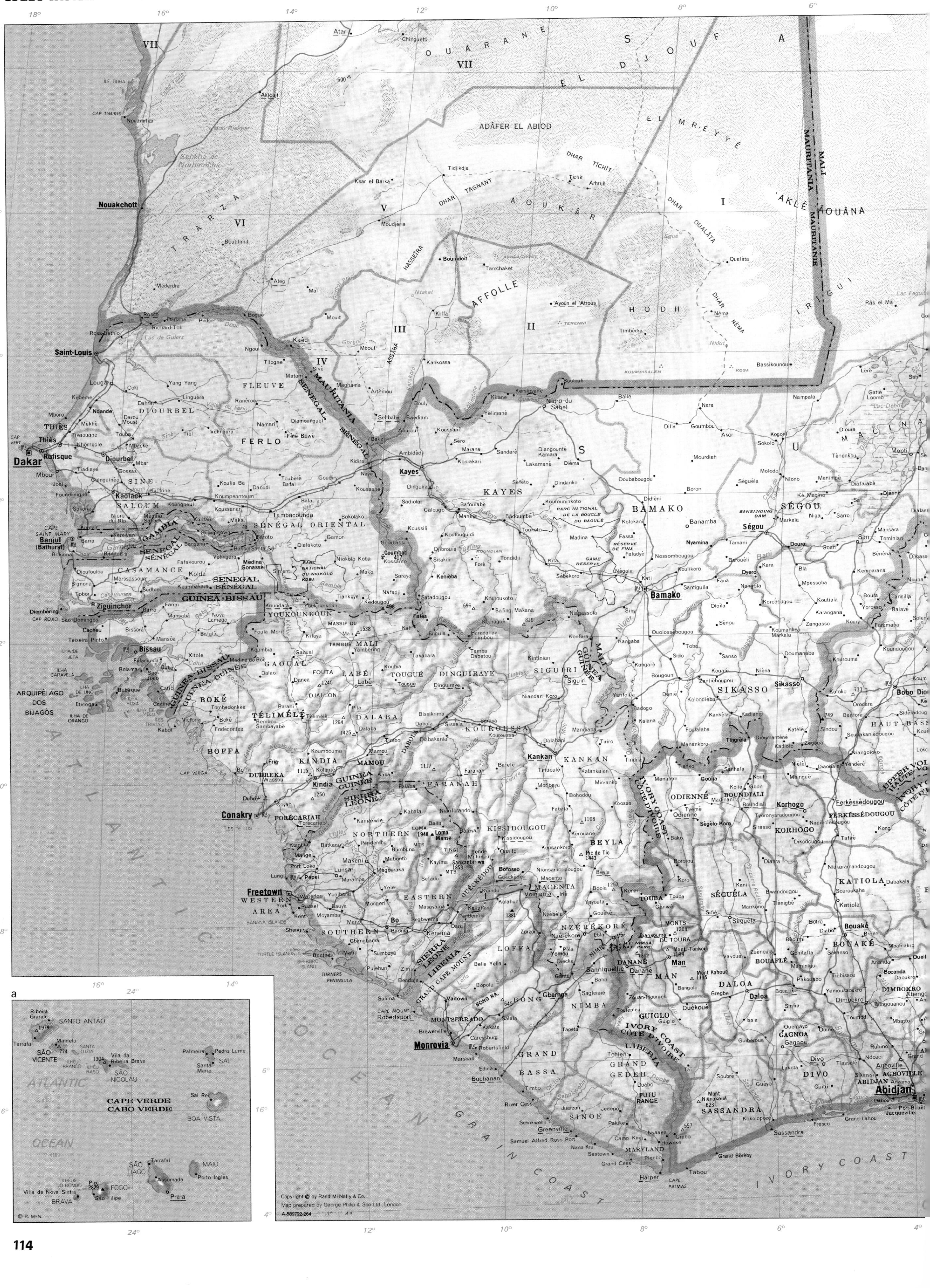

MAURITANIA
MAURITANIE
MALI
SENEGAL
SÉNÉGAL
GAMBIA
GUINEA-BISSAU
GUINEA
GUINÉE
SIERRA LEONE
LIBERIA
IVORY COAST
CÔTE D'IVOIRE
UPPER VOLTA
HAUTE-VOLTA
Nouakchott
Saint-Louis
Dakar
Thiès
Rufisque
Kaolack
Banjul (Bathurst)
Ziguinchor
Bissau
Conakry
Freetown
Monrovia
Bamako
Abidjan
Kayes
Ségou
Sikasso
Bouaké
Kankan
Kindia
Labé
Atar
Akjoujt
Chinguetti
Tidjikdja
Kiffa
Kaédi
Rosso
Aleg
Boutilimit
Néma
Nioro du Sahel
Tambacounda
Kolda
Bafatá
Boké
Fria
Mamou
Faranah
Kissidougou
Macenta
Nzérékoré
Bo
Kenema
Makeni
Buchanan
Greenville
Harper
Robertsport
Odienné
Korhogo
Man
Daloa
Gagnoa
Divo
Sassandra
Katiola
Bobo Dioulasso
Mopti
TRARZA
BRAKNA
AOUKÂR
HODH
AFFOLLÉ
ADÂFER EL ABIOD
EL DJOUF
OUARANE
EL MREYYÉ
FLEUVE
DIOURBEL
SINE-SALOUM
CASAMANCE
SÉNÉGAL ORIENTAL
FERLO
KAYES
BAMAKO
SÉGOU
SIKASSO
FOUTA DJALLON
ARQUIPÉLAGO DOS BIJAGÓS
CAP VERT
CAP ROXO
CAPE VERGA
ILES DE LOS
BANANA ISLANDS
TURTLE ISLANDS
SHERBRO ISLAND
CAPE MOUNT
CAPE PALMAS
ATLANTIC OCEAN
GRAIN COAST
IVORY COAST
Niger
Sénégal
Gambie
Bani
Lac de Guiers
Sebkha de Ndrhamcha
PARC NATIONAL DE LA BOUCLE DU BAOULÉ
PARC NATIONAL DU NIOKOLO KOBA
18°
16°
14°
12°
10°
8°
6°
4°
20°
a
CAPE VERDE
CABO VERDE
SANTO ANTÃO
SÃO VICENTE
SANTA LUZIA
SÃO NICOLAU
SAL
BOA VISTA
MAIO
SÃO TIAGO
FOGO
BRAVA
Ribeira Grande
Tarrafal
Mindelo
Vila da Ribeira Brava
Palmeira
Pedra Lume
Santa Maria
Sal Rei
Porto Inglês
Praia
Assomada
São Filipe
Villa de Nova Sintra
ATLANTIC
OCEAN
24°
© R.M.N.
Copyright © by Rand McNally & Co.
Map prepared by George Philip & Son Ltd., London.
A-569792-264

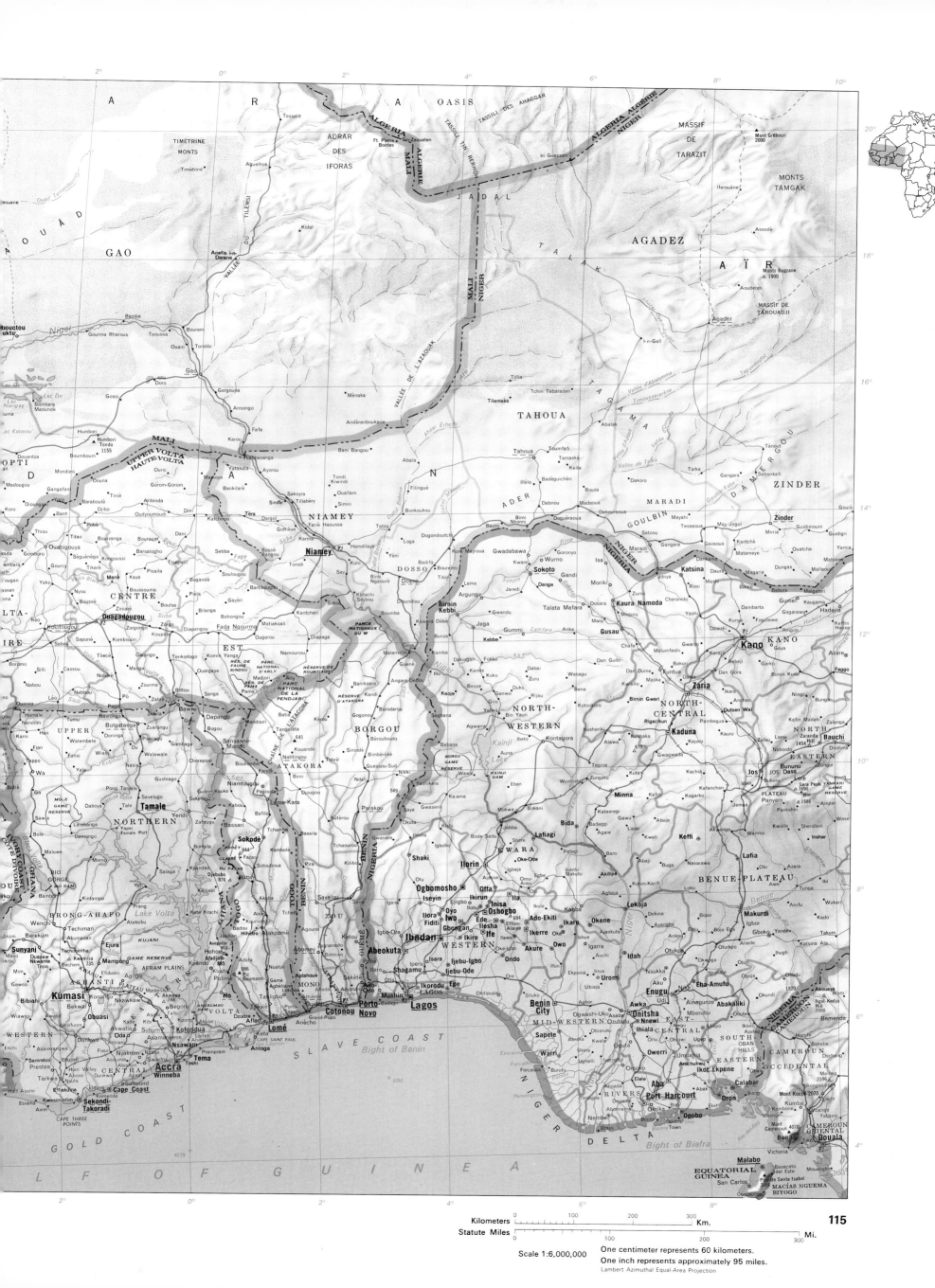

Kilometers 0 100 200 300 Km.

Statute Miles 0 100 200 300 Mi.

Scale 1:6,000,000   One centimeter represents 60 kilometers.
One inch represents approximately 95 miles.
Lambert Azimuthal Equal-Area Projection

Southern Africa and Madagascar

The United Nations declared an end to the mandate of South Africa over South West Africa in October, 1966. Administration of the territory by South Africa is not recognized by the United Nations.

Copyright © by Rand McNally & Co.
Map prepared by George Philip & Son Ltd., London.
A-589292-264

116

Kilometers 0 100 200 300 Km.
Statute Miles 0 100 200 300 Mi.
Scale 1:6,000,000
One centimeter represents 60 kilometers.
One inch represents approximately 95 miles.
Lambert Azimuthal Equal-Area Projection

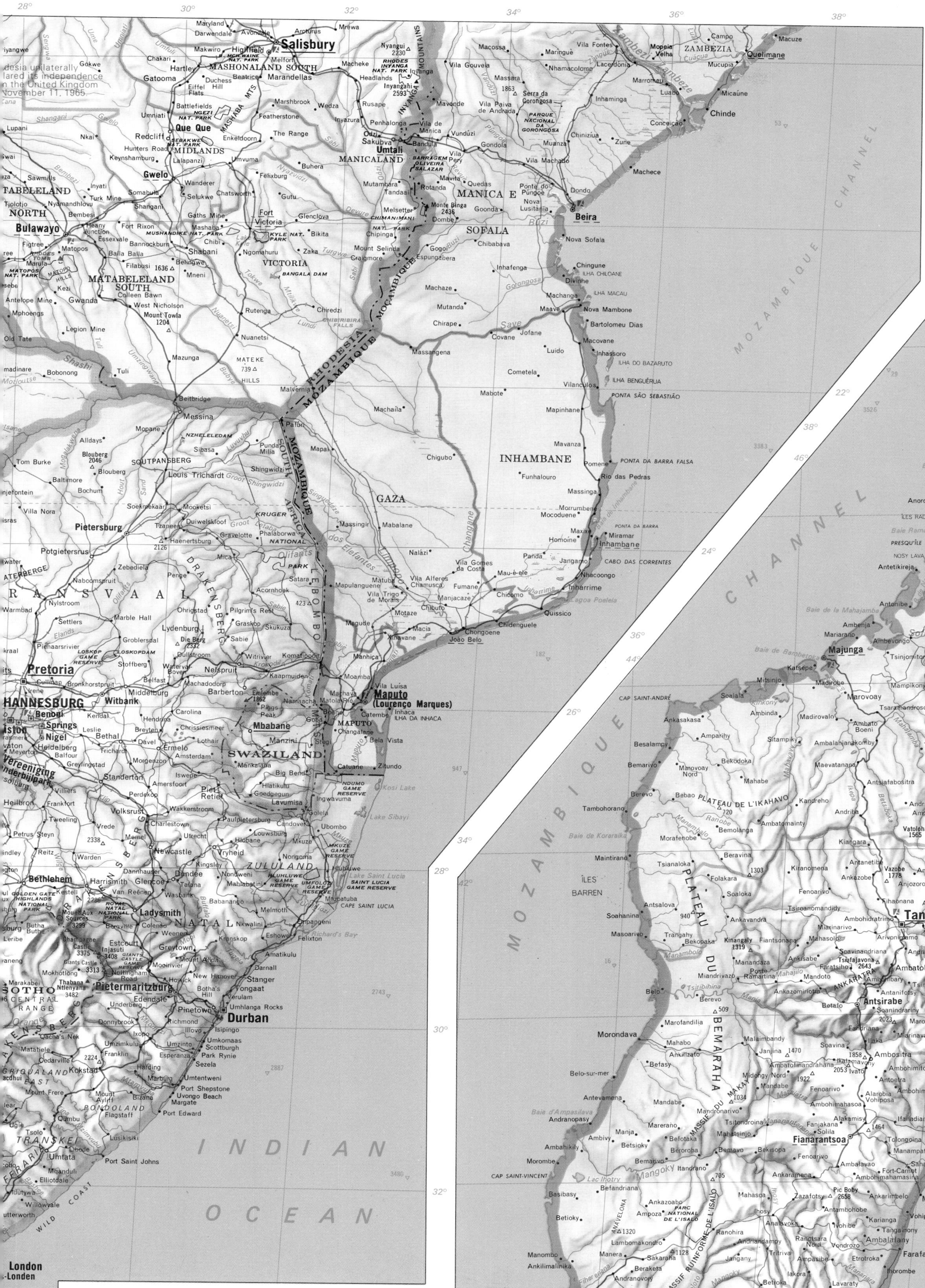

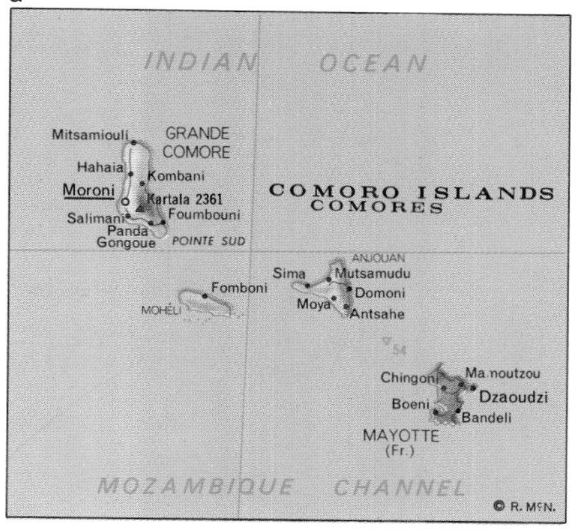

INDIAN OCEAN

COMORO ISLANDS
COMORES

MOZAMBIQUE CHANNEL

MADAGASCAR
MADAGASIKARA

INDIAN OCEAN

MOZAMBIQUE CHANNEL

SWAZILAND

RHODESIA
*desia unilaterally
*lared its independence
*in the United Kingdom
*November 11, 1965.

MOÇAMBIQUE

ZAMBEZIA

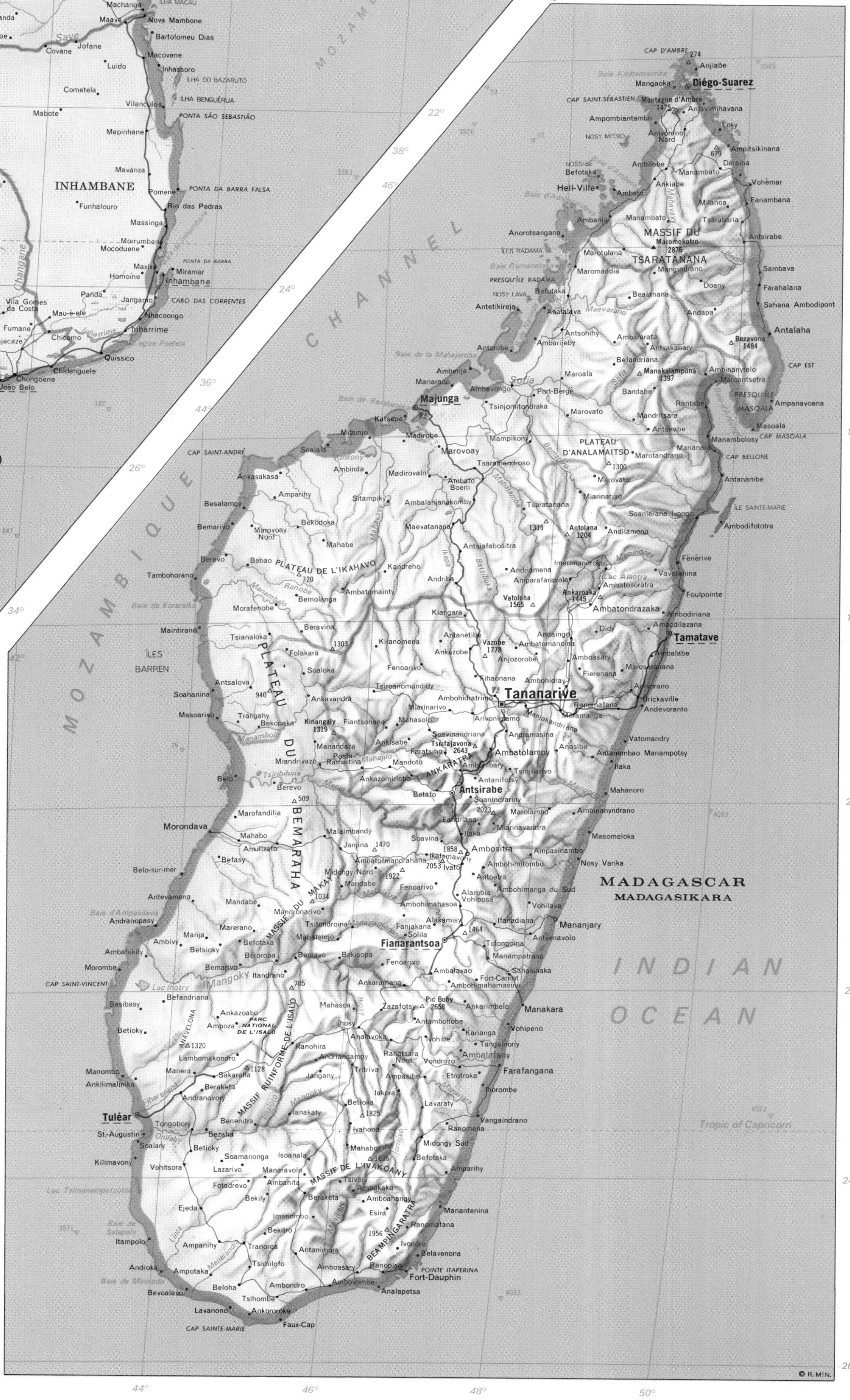

MANICA E SOFALA

INHAMBANE

GAZA

NATAL

ZULULAND

TRANSVAAL

MAURITIUS

RÉUNION

MASCARENE ISLANDS

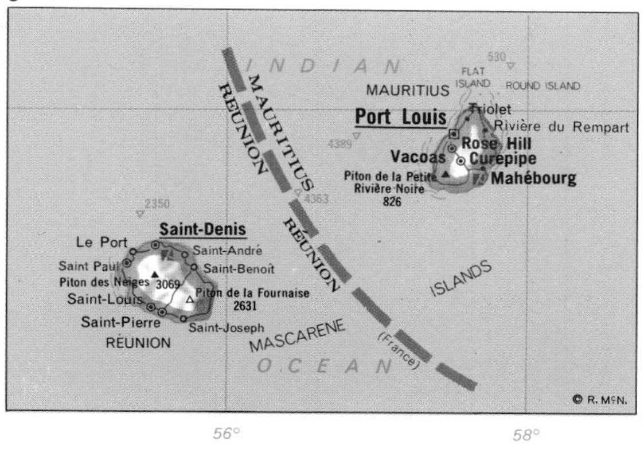

INDIAN OCEAN

Tropic of Capricorn

MAYOTTE (Fr.)

Australia

INDONESIA

DJAWA   JAVA

Tasikmalaja   Jogjakarta   Surakarta   Madiun   Kediri   Malang   Djember   Banjuwangi   Singaradja   Mataram Sumbawa Besar   SUMBAWA

Tjilatjap   Blitar   Gunung Semeru   Denpasar   LOMBOK   Waikabubak   SUMBA   Waingapu   FLORES   LESSER   SUNDA   ISLANDS

BALI   Baing   PULAU ROTI   Kupang   (Port. Timor)   Ocussi   PORTUGUESE TIMOR

Laut Sawu   PULAU SEMAU   Soe   TIMOR   Portuguese Timor has been occupied by Indonesia

SAWU

INDIAN   OCEAN

Timor   Sea

Arafura Sea

ASHMORE REEF   CARTIER ISLAND (Austl.)   HIBERNIA REEF

SANDY ISLET (Austl.)   SCOTT REEF   BROWSE ISLAND   BONAPARTE ARCHIPELAGO   CAPE LONDONDERRY   POINT BLAZE   Rum Jungle   Darwin

MELVILLE ISLAND   BATHURST ISLAND   CAPE CROKER   COBURG PENINSULA

Beagle Gulf   Van Diemen Gulf   Pine Creek   Katherine   ARNHEM LAND

ROWLEY SHOALS   LYNHER REEF   ADELE ISLANDS   BEAGLE BANK   BUCCANEER ARCHIPELAGO   Yampi Sound   CAPE LEVEQUE   Derby   KIMBERLEY PLATEAU   York Sound   Admiralty Gulf   Wyndham   Kununurra   Victoria River Downs   Daly Waters

KING LEOPOLD RANGES   936▲   Mount Ord   Fitzroy Crossing   Hains Creek   DURACK RANGE   Wave Hill   Newcastle Waters   Powell Cr

CAPE LATOUCHE TREVILLE   Broome   Fitzroy   Gordon Downs   NORTHERN

La Grange   EIGHTY MILE BEACH   TANAMI   TANAMI DESERT   Gregory Lake   TERRITORY

Port Hedland   De Grey   GREAT SANDY DESERT   Lake White (Dry)   Barrow

MONTE BELLO ISLANDS   DAMPIER   Dampier   Roebourne   Marble Bar   THROSSELL RANGE   Lake Dora (Dry)   Lake Auld (Dry)   Lake Mackay (Dry Salt Lake)   Mount Leisler   Mount Zie   1510   MACDONNE

BARROW ISLAND   Nullagine   Lake Macdonald (Dry)   Sp

MUIRON ISLANDS   Onslow   HAMERSLEY RANGE   Mount Brockman   1114▲   1227▲   Wittenoom   ROBERTSON RANGE   Lake Disappointment (Dry Salt Lake)   1006   Lake Amadeus (Dry)

NORTH WEST CAPE   Mount Bruce   WESTERN   GIBSON DESERT   RAWLINSON RANGE   Mount Olga   1069▲   Ayers Rock   867

POINT CLOATES   BARLEE RANGE   1106▲   Mount Augustus   ▲910   Mount Essendon   A U S T   MUSGRAVE RANGES   ▲1440   Mount Woodroffe

CAPE CUVIER   Lake McLeod   Ashburton   BARROW RANGE   Mount Aloysius ▲987

Tropic of Capricorn   Geographe Channel   Gascoyne   Lake Carnegie (Dry)   Lake Gillen (Dry)

BERNIER ISLAND   Carnarvon   Peak Hill   ROBINSON RANGES

DORRE ISLAND   Shark Bay   Wooramel   Lake Wells (Dry)

Naturaliste Channel   Meekatharra   Wiluna

DIRK HARTOG ISLAND   Nannine   AUSTRALIA   Lake Yeo (Dry)   GREAT VICTORIA DESERT

STEEP POINT   Cue   Lake Austin (Dry)   Agnew   Lake Carey (Dry Salt Lake)   Lake Maurice (Dry)   SOU

Sandstone   Mount Reddiffe ▲576   Laverton   Maralinga   Qoldea

Boogardie   Mount Magnet   Malcolm   Leonora   Lake Raeside (Dry)   Lake Minigwal (Dry)

HOUTMAN ROCKS   Northampton   Yalgoo   Lake Ballard (Dry)

Geraldton   Mullewa   Lake Barlee (Dry Salt Lake)   Kanowna

Dongara   Three Springs   Lake Moore (Dry)   Kalgoorlie   Coolgardie   Boulder   Zanthus   Rawlinna   Haig   NULLARBOR   PLAIN   Forrest   Deakin

GREEN HEAD   Dalwallinu   Bonnie Rock   Eucla   CAPE ADIEU   SAINT PETER ISLA

Moora   Bencubbin   Southern Cross   Lake Lefroy (Dry)   RED POINT ROCK

GEOGRAPHE   Muchea   Northam   Kellerberrin   Bullfinch   Lake Cowan (Dry Salt Lake)   Eyre

Perth   York   Beverley   Merredin   Norseman   Lake Dundas (Dry)   POINT CULVER

Fremantle   DARLING RANGE   Brookton   Hyden   The Johnston Lakes (Dry)

Pinjarra   Narrogin   Newdegate

Bunbury   Wagin   INDIAN   OCE

Geographe Bay   Collie   Nyabing   Ravensthorpe   Hopetoun   Esperance   CAPE ARID   SALISBURY ISLAND   Great Australian Bight   INVES

CAPE NATURALISTE   Busselton   Bridgetown   Katanning   Gnowangerup   CAPE KNOB   ARCHIPELAGO OF THE RECHERCHE

Augusta   Manjimup   STIRLING RANGE   HOOD POINT

CAPE LEEUWIN   Pemberton   Mount Barker   CAPE LE GRAND

POINT D'ENTRECASTEAUX   Denmark   Albany   CAPE VANCOUVER

TORBAY HEAD   George Sound

Cora Sea

135°   140°   145°   150°   155°

BOIGU
SAIBAI ISLAND
WARRIOR REEFS
BANKS ISLAND
PRINCE OF WALES ISLAND
Endeavour Strait
Daru
Gulf of Papua
Port Moresby
Rigo
PAPUA
NEW GUINEA
NEW GUINEA
Kokoda
Gona
Popondetta
Wanigela
OWEN STANLEY RANGE
Abau
Esa-Ala
Samarai
D'ENTRECASTEAUX ISLANDS
Losulai
Kulumadau
TROBRIAND ISLANDS
WOODLARK ISLAND
LOUISIADE ARCHIPELAGO
MISIMA ISLAND
TAGULA ISLAND
ROSSEL ISLAND
LONG REEF

VELLA LAVELLA
GANDOGGA
CHOISEUL
KOLOMBANGARA
BIZO
RENDOVA
NEW GEORGIA
VANGUNU
RUSSELL ISLANDS
BRITISH SOLOMON
ISLANDS
NGGELA GROUP
SANTA ISABEL
Tulaghi
GUADALCANAL
Honiara
Mt. Popomanasiu 2331

CAPE WESSEL
WESSEL ISLANDS
CROCODILE ISLAND
THE ENGLISH COMPANY'S ISLANDS
CAPE ARNHEM
CAPE GREY
CAPE YORK
CAPE GRENVILLE
GREAT
BARRIER
REEF
Solomon Sea

GROOTE EYLANDT
CAPE BEATRICE
DUIFKEN POINT
Weipa
Albatross Bay
YORK
Iron Range
Aurukun Mission
COEN
Archer Bay
CAPE KEER-WEER
PENINSULA
Gulf of Carpentaria
BORROLOOLA
SIR EDWARD PELLEW GROUP
MARIA ISLAND
VANDERLIN ISLAND
Limmen Bight
Coleman
Musgrave
Laura
Cooktown
OSPREY REEF
BOUGAINVILLE REEF
C o r a l   S e a
RENNELL ISLAND
INDISPENSABLE REEFS

BARKLY TABLELAND
MORNINGTON ISLAND
WELLESLEY ISLANDS
BENTINCK ISLAND
Burketown
Normanton
Mitchell
Chillago
Mareeba
Atherton
Cairns
Battle
Frere 1611
Innisfail
Ravenshoe
HOLMES REEFS
WILLIS ISLETS (Austl.)
CORINGA ISLETS (Austl.)
DIAMOND ISLETS (Austl.)
TREGOSSE ISLETS (Austl.)
LIHOU REEFS
MELLISH REEF
15°

Ranken Store
Avon Downs
Camooweal
Dobbyn
Croydon
Einasleigh
Forsayth
GREGORY RANGE
HINCHINBROOK ISLAND
Ingham
Halifax Bay
GREAT
BARRIER
Tennant Creek
Mount Isa
Cloncurry
Richmond
Hughenden
SELWYN RANGE
Duchess
Dajarra
Selwyn
Winton
Boulia
Charters Towers
Pentland
Bowen
Home Hill
Ayr
CAPE CLEVELAND
Townsville
Proserpine
Collinsville
WHITSUNDAY I.
CUMBERLAND IS.
FLINDERS REEFS
ABINGTON REEF
MALAY REEF
MARION REEF
ÎLES CHESTERFIELD (N. Cal.)
ÎLES DE SABLE (N. Cal.)
20°

SIMPSON DESERT
A L I A
Birdsville
GREAT ARTESIAN
Longreach
Ilfracombe
Barcaldine
Aramac
Blair Athol
Clermont
Netherdale
DENHAM RANGE
Mackay
Sarina
CAPE PALMERSTON
NORTHUMBERLAND ISLANDS
SWAIN REEFS
TOWNSHEND ISLAND
WRECK REEFS
KENN REEFS
SAUMAREZ REEF
CAYE DE L'OBSERVATOIRE (N. Cal.)
BELLONA REEFS
BIRD ISLET (Austl.)

QUEENSLAND
Windorah
Yaraka
Blackall
Alpha
Emerald
Springsure
Theodore
Monto
Gladstone
Biloela
Morgan
Rockhampton
Yeppoon
CAPITAL GROUP
CURTIS
BUNKER GROUP
CATO ISLAND
Tropic of Capricorn

BASIN
Eromanga
Adavale
GREY RANGE
Quilpie
Charleville
Augathella
Mitchell
Roma
Injune
Taroom
Childers
Gayndah
Bundaberg
Maryborough
SANDY CAPE
FRASER ISLAND
P A C I F I C
25°

AUSTRALIA
Warrina
Oodnadatta
Lake Eyre (North) (Dry Salt Lake)
Lake Eyre (South)
Marree
STURT DESERT
Thargomindah
Cunnamulla
Saint George
Dirranbandi
Mungindi
Goondiwindi
Wyandra
Wondai
Murgon
Kingaroy
Nanango
1143△
Mount Kiangarow
Dalby
Kingoy
Gympie
Nambour
Toowoomba
Ipswich
Brisbane
Southport
MORETON ISLAND
NORTH STRADBROKE ISLAND
O C E A N

Milparinka
Tibooburra
MAIN BARRIER RANGE
Wilcannia
Bourke
Walgett
Moree
Warialda
Inverell
Tenterfield
Casino
Lismore
Ballina
Stanthorpe
Warwick
CAPE BYRON
Murwillumbah
Glen Innes
Grafton
Maclean
Coffs Harbour
MIDDLETON REEF
ELIZABETH REEF
30°

Copley
Lake Torrens
Lake Frome (Dry Salt Lake)
FLINDERS RANGES
Saint Mary Peak 1165
Hawker
NOBBY RANGE
Broken Hill
Menindee
NEW SOUTH WALES
Cobar
Nyngan
Narrabri
Coonamble
Gunnedah
Tamworth
The Round Mountain 1615△
Armidale
SMOKY CAPE
Kempsey
Port Macquarie
SUGARLOAF POINT
LORD HOWE ISLAND (N.S.W.)
BALLS PYRAMID (N.S.W.)

Quorn
Peterborough
Jamestown
Burra
Ivanhoe
Roto
Wilcannia
Hillston
Condobolin
Wellington
Dubbo
Mudgee
Muswellbrook
Singleton
Maitland
Cessnock
Newcastle
Woy Woy

Whyalla
Iron Knob
Port Augusta
Kadina
Burra
Renmark
Lake Cargelligo
Forbes
Parkes
Orange
Bathurst
Lithgow
Katoomba
Penrith
SYDNEY
Campbelltown
EYRE PENINSULA
Cleve
Cowell
Wallaroo
Port Pirie
Gladstone
Balaklava
Loxton
Mildura
West Wyalong
Griffith
Leeton
Cootamundra
Young
Yass
Goulburn
Bowral
Wollongong
Shellharbour
Nowra

Port Lincoln
CAPE CATASTROPHE
Cummins
Port Neill
Elliston
Moonta
Gawler
Elizabeth
Adelaide
Murray Bridge
Pinnaroo
Ouyen
Swan Hill
Deniliquin
Narrandera
Junee
Wagga Wagga
Gundagai
Tumut
Canberra
Queanbeyan
Jervis Bay
30°

KANGAROO ISLAND
CAPE SPENCER
Victor Harbour
Encounter Bay
Meningie
Tailem Bend
Bordertown
Kerang
Echuca
Shepparton
Benalla
Wangaratta
Albury
RIVERINA
Cootamundra
Batlow
Cooma
Mount Kosciusko 2230
Bombala
35°

Kingston
CAPE JAFFA
Naracoorte
Penola
Millicent
Mount Gambier
Horsham
Stawell
Ararat
Maryborough
Castlemaine
Bendigo
Seymour
Whittlesea
VICTORIA
GREAT DIVIDING RANGE
Mount Buller
Sale
Bairnsdale
Orbost
CAPE HOWE

Hamilton
Portland
Port Fairy
Warrnambool
Colac
Ballarat
Geelong
MELBOURNE
Traralgon
Morwell
NINETY MILE BEACH
CAPE EVERARD
T a s m a n

CAPE NELSON
CAPE OTWAY
PHILLIP I.
WILSONS PROMONTORY
SOUTH EAST POINT
S e a

KING ISLAND
Bass Strait
KENT GROUP
FLINDERS ISLAND
FURNEAUX GROUP
CAPE BARREN ISLAND

HUNTER ISLAND
CAPE GRIM
Smithton
Burnie
Devonport
SANDY CAPE
Ulverstone
Beaconsfield
Scottsdale
Launceston
Saint Marys
FREYCINET PENINSULA

Zeehan
Mount Ossa 1617△
Queenstown
Strahan
CAPE SORELL
TASMANIA
New Norfolk
Huonville
Geeveston
Hobart
MARIA ISLAND
CAPE PILLAR
LOW ROCKY POINT
SOUTH WEST CAPE
SOUTH EAST CAPE
SOUTH BRUNY
40°

135°   140°   145°   150°   155°   160°   165°

119

Kilometers | 0   200   400   600   Km.
Statute Miles | 0   200   400   600   Mi.

Scale 1:12,000,000

One centimeter represents 120 kilometers.
One inch represents approximately 190 miles.
Lambert Conformal Conic Projection

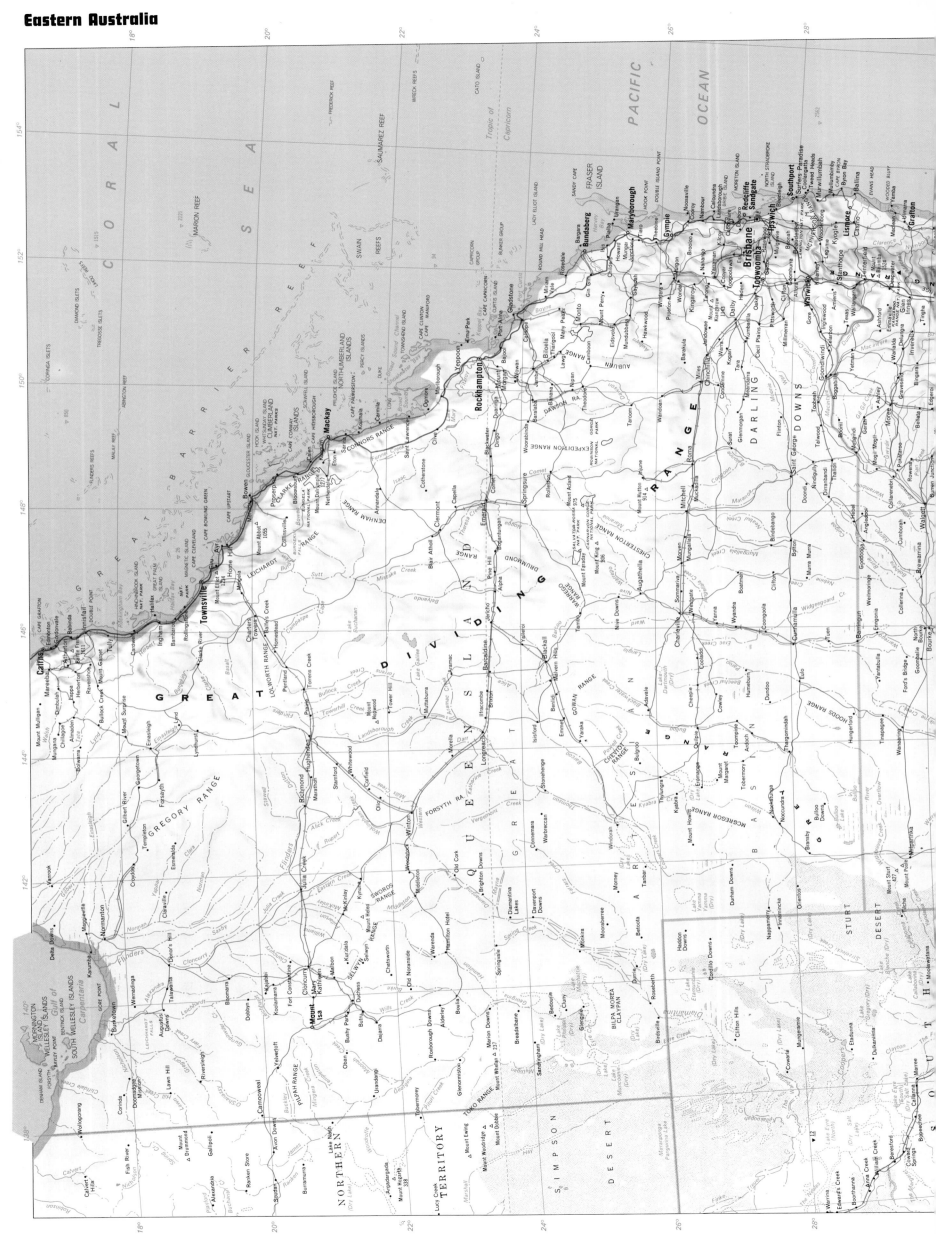

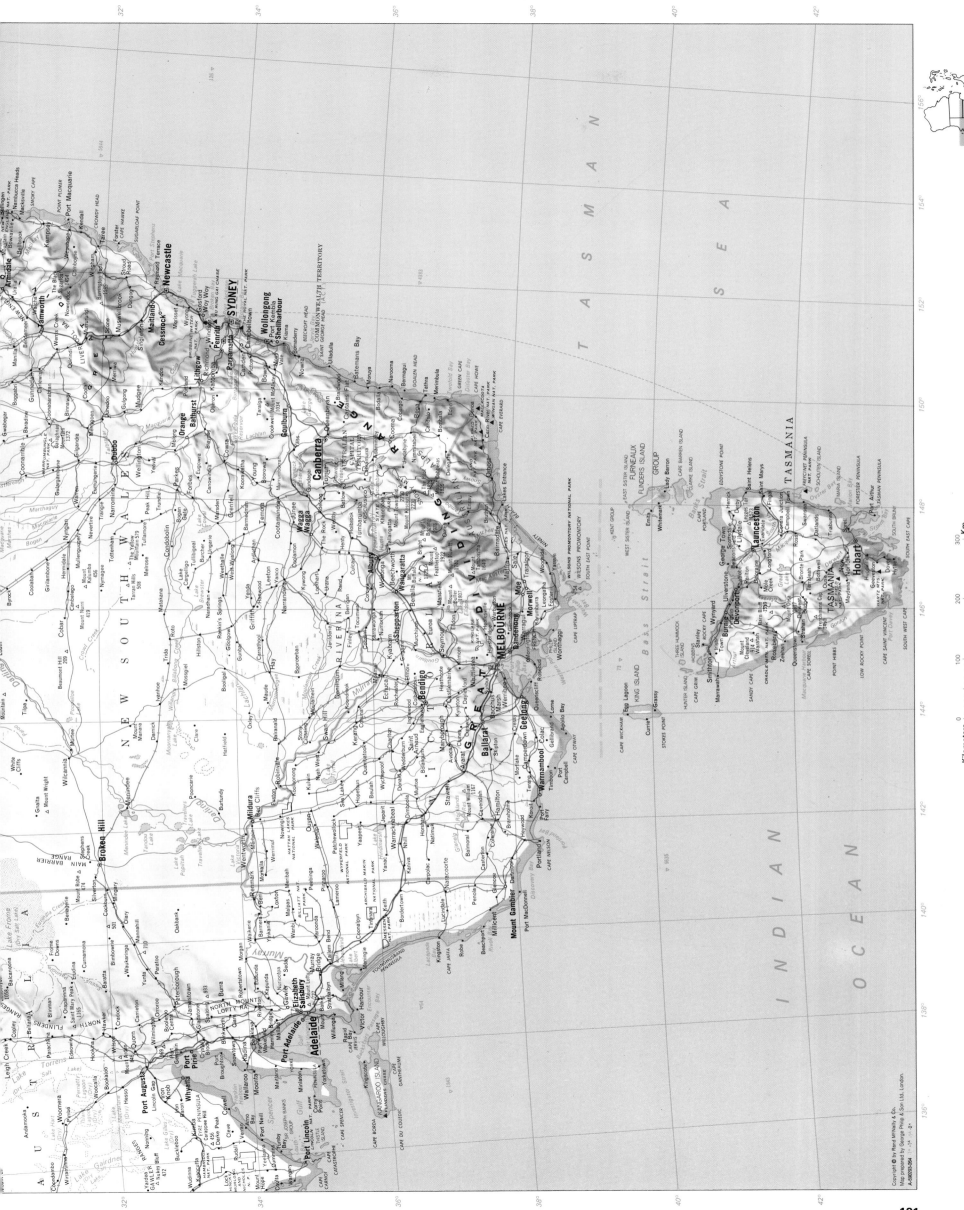

Kilometers
Statute Miles

Km.
Mi.

Scale 1:6,000,000

One centimeter represents 60 kilometers.
One inch represents approximately 95 miles.

Lambert Conformal Conic Projection

INDIAN OCEAN

GREAT SANDY DESERT

WESTERN

GIBSON DESERT

AUSTRALIA

Tropic of Capricorn

Perth
Fremantle

Geraldton

Bunbury

Kalgoorlie

Albany

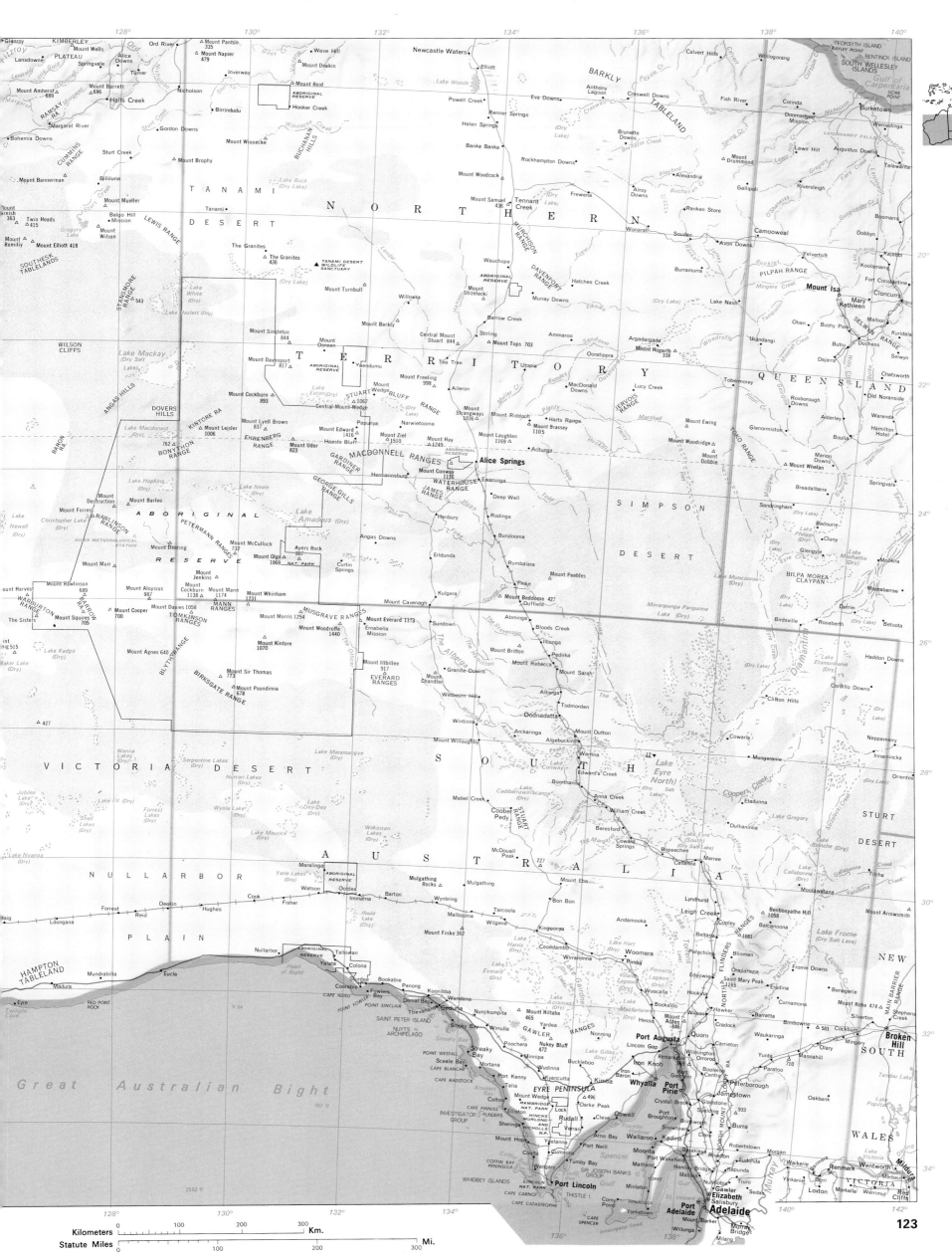

KIMBERLEY
PLATEAU
Gienroy
Lansdowne
Springvale
Mount Wells
Ord River
Alice
Downs
Mount Panton
335
Mount Napier
479
Mount Deakin
Wave Hill
Newcastle Waters
Elliott
Lake Woods
BARKLY
Anthony Lagoon
Calvert Hills
Wollogorang
FORSYTH ISLAND
BAYLEY POINT
BENTINCK ISLAND
SOUTH WELLESLEY
ISLANDS
GORE POINT
Gulf of
Carpentaria

Mount Amherst
689
Mount Barrett
696
Halls Creek
Nicholson
Turner
Inverway
Mount Reid
ABORIGINAL
RESERVE
Hooker Creek
Powell Creek
Eva Downs
Creswell Downs
Fish River
Corinda
Burketown
Doomadgee
Mission
Wernadinga

Margaret River
Bohemia Downs
CUMMINS
RANGE
Mount Bannerman
Sturt Creek
Gordon Downs
Birrindudu
Mount Brophy
Mount Winnecke
Winnecke Creek
BUCHANAN
HILLS
Renner Springs
Helen Springs
Banka Banka
Brunette
Downs
Brunette Creek
Alroy
Downs
Alexandria
TABLELAND
Gallipoli
Augustus Downs
Gregory
Lawn Hill
Riversleigh
Talawanta

Mount
363
Twin Heads
415
Balgo Hill
Mission
Mount Wilson
Mount Elliott 418
LEWIS RANGE
TANAMI
Tanami
DESERT
NORTHERN
Rockhampton Downs
Mount Woodcock
Mount Samuel
436
Tennant Creek
Frewena
Ranken Store
Wonarah
Soudan
Avon Downs
Camooweal
Dobbyn
Boomarra
PILPAH RANGE
Mount Isa
Mary
Kathleen
Cloncurry

SOUTHESK
TABLELANDS
STANSMORE RANGE
543
Lake White
(Dry)
The Granites
The Granites
436
TANAMI DESERT
WILDLIFE
SANCTUARY
Wauchope
MURCHISON RANGE
DAVENPORT RANGE
Hatches Creek
Burramurra
Oban
Bushy Park
Butru
Ucandangi
Koolamarra
Duchess
Selwyn
Malbon
Kuridala
SELWYN RANGE
Chatsworth

WILSON
CLIFFS
Lake Mackay
(Dry Salt
Lake)
Mount Singleton
844
Mount Turnbull
Willowra
Murray Downs
Mount Barkly
Central Mount
Stuart 844
Barrow Creek
Stirling
Mount Tops 703
Ammaroo
Ooratippa
Argadargada
Mount Hogarth
338
Tobermorey
Roxborough
Downs
Old Noranside
Alderley
Glenormiston
Boulia
Warenda
Hamilton
Hotel

ANGAS HILLS
DOVERS
HILLS
Lake
Hazlett (Dry)
Mount Davenport
817
ABORIGINAL
RESERVE
Yuendumu
TERRITORY
Mount
Wedge
Tea Tree
Mount Freeling
998
Aileron
Utopia
MacDonald
Downs
Lucy Creek
JERVOIS
RANGE
Marshall
Mount Ewing
Breadalbane
Sandringham
(Dry Lake)
Bedourie
Cluny
Glengyle

BARON
RA.
Lake Macdonald
(Dry)
762
KINTORE RA.
Mount Leisler
1006
Mount Lyell Brown
837
EHRENBERG
RANGE
Mount Edward
1416
Papunya
Mount Udor
823
Narwietooma
Haasts Bluff
Mount Ziel
1510
Mount Hay
1249
ABORIGINAL
RESERVE
Aritunga
Mount Strangways
1035
Mount Riddoch
Harts Range
Mount Brassey
1105
Mount Laughlen
1169
Mount Woodridge
Mount
Dobbie
Mount Whelan
Marion
Downs
TOKO RANGE
Lake
Machattie
(Dry)
Monkira

BONYTHON RANGE
GARDINER
RANGE
GEORGE GILLS
RANGE
Hermannsburg
MACDONNELL RANGES
Mount Conway
1136
Alice Springs
Ewaninga
WATERHOUSE
RANGE
JAMES
RANGE
Deep Well
Todd
SIMPSON
DESERT
Lake
Caroline
(Dry)

Lake Hopkins
(Dry)
Lake Neale
(Dry)
Mount
Destruction
Mount Barlee
PETERMANN RANGES
GILES METEOROLOGICAL
STATION
Mount Deering
RESERVE
Mount McCulloch
732
Lake Amadeus (Dry)
Ayers Rock
867
Mount Olga
1069
NAT. PARK
Angas Downs
Henbury
Rodinga
Bundooma
Finke
Mount Peebles
Mirranponga Pangunna
Lake (Dry)
Birdsville
Durrie
Roseberth
BILPA MOREA
CLAYPAN
Moorabberee

Lake
Newell
(Dry)
Mount Forrest
Christopher Lake
(Dry)
RAWLINSON
RANGE
Mount Muir
Mount Jenkins
Mount Mann
1231
Curtin
Springs
Erldunda
Kulgera
Rumbarara
Mount Cavenagh
Mount Beddome 427
Duffield
Abminga
Mount Muncoona
(Dry)
Lake
Etamunbanie
(Dry)
Haddon Downs

Mount Harvest
Mount Rawlinson
689
WARBURTON
RANGES
BARON RA.
Mount Squires
705
Mount Aloysius
987
Mount
Cockburn
1138
Mount Cooper
700
Mount Davies 1058
TOMKINSON
RANGES
Mount Mann
1174
MANN
RANGES
Mount Morris 1254
Mount Woodroffe
1440
Ernabella
Mission
MUSGRAVE RANGES
Mount Everard 1173
Sundown
Bloods Creek
Ilbunga
Pedirka
Mount Britton
Mount Rebecca
Todmorden
Clifton Hills
Cordillo Downs
(Dry Lake)

The Sisters
Baker Lake
(Dry)
Lake Kadgo
(Dry)
Mount Agnes 640
BLYTH RANGE
BIRKSGATE RANGE
Mount Sir Thomas
773
Mount Poondinna
678
Mount Kintore
1070
Mount Illbillee
917
EVERARD
RANGES
Welbourn Hill
Mount
Chandler
Granite Downs
Mount Sarah
Alberga
Arckaringa
Mount Dutton
Cowarie
Nappamerry
Innamincka
Orientos

427
Wanna
Lakes
(Dry)
Lake Nyanga
(Dry)
Serpentine Lakes
(Dry)
Lake Maurice
(Dry)
Wilkinson
Lakes
(Dry)
Wintinna
Oodnadatta
Mount Willoughby
Algebuckina
Warina
Mount
12
Lake
Eyre
North
Salt
Etadunna
Lake Gregory
(Dry)
Dulkaninna
Kopperamanna
STURT
DESERT

VICTORIA
Jubilee
Lake
(Dry)
Lake Ell (Dry)
DESERT
Forrest
Lakes
(Dry)
Lake Dey-Dey
(Dry)
SOUTH
Boorthanna
Anna Creek
William Creek
Cowans
Springs
Bopeechee
Marree
Lake
Callabonna
(Dry)
Gollaburra
Ticha
Moolawatana

NULLARBOR
Shell
Lakes
(Dry)
Wyola Lake
(Dry)
Lake Maurice
(Dry)
Mabel Creek
Coober
Pedy
STUART
RANGE
Cadibarrawirracanna
AUSTRALIA
Edward's Creek
Mungeranie
Lake
Blanche
(Dry)
Mount Arrowsmith

PLAIN
Loongana
Maralinga
Ooldea
Watson
ABORIGINAL
RESERVE
Yarle Lakes
(Dry)
Barton
Mulgathing
Rocks
Mulgathing
Mount Eba
Lyndhurst
Benbonyathe Hill
1058
Copley
Balcanoona
FLINDERS
Leigh Creek
Lake Frome
(Dry Salt Lake)

HAMPTON
TABLELAND
Forrest
Deakin
Reid
Hughes
Cook
Fisher
Immarna
Wynbring
Tarcoola
Wilgena
Kingoonya
Andamooka
Woomera
Pimba
Beltana
Parachilna
Blinman
1081
Blinman
RANGES
NEW

Mundrabilla
Madura
Eucla
RED POINT
ROCK
Nullarbor
ABORIGINAL
RESERVE
Tallowan
Colona
Malbooma
Wirraminna
Coondambo
Lake
Gairdner
(Dry)
Lake Torrens
(Dry Salt Lake)
Edeowie
Orapahanna
Saint Mary Peak
1165
Hookina
Wilson
Hawker
Erudina
Benagerie
Mount Robe 474
Stephens
Creek
MAIN BARRIER RANGE

Great   Australian   Bight
Twilight
Cove
HEAD
OF
BIGHT
Yalata
Sturdee
Bookabie
Penong
Fowlers
Bay
Koonibba
Wandana
Yardea
CAPE ADIEU
POINT FOWLER
POINT SINCLAIR
Denial Bay
Smoky Bay
Wirrulla
Nonning
Mount Hesso
Hessa
Mount Aden
846
Cradock
Carrieton
Orroroo
Johnburgh
Waukaringa
Silverton
Bimbowrie
501
Cockburn
Olary
Mannahill
710
Paratoo
Broken
Hill
SOUTH

SAINT PETER ISLAND
NUYTS
ARCHIPELAGO
Ceduna
Thevenard
Nunjikompita
Poochera
Mount Hiltaba
465
Minnipa
Wudinna
Kyancutta
Buckleboo
Kimba
GAWLER
RANGES
Iron Knob
Whyalla
Lincoln Gap
Port Augusta
Wilmington
Quorn
Jamestown
Peterborough
Yunta
Yarrabah
WALES

POINT WESTALL
Streaky Bay
Sceale Bay
CAPE BLANCHE
Mortana
Wirrulla
Poochera
Minnipa
Darke Peak
496
Cleve
Arno Bay
Cowell
Port Broughton
Snowtown
Balaklava
Gladstone
Burra
Robertstown
Morgan
Euddha
Waikerie
Barmera
Renmark
Wentworth
Mildura

POINT WESTALL
CAPE RADSTOCK
Anxious
Bay
Talia
Elliston
Sheringa
Mount Wedge
HINCKS
MURLONG AND
NICHOLLS N.P.
Lock
Rudall
Yerran
Ungarra
Wangary
Verran
Cummins
EYRE PENINSULA
Tumby Bay
Port Neill
Arno Bay
Wallaroo
Moonta
Maitland
Port Wakefield
Owen
Riverton
Eudunda
Truro
VICTORIA
Loxton
Morkalla
Werrimul
RED
CLIFFS

INVESTIGATOR
GROUP
FLINDERS
Mount Hope
COFFIN BAY
PENINSULA
Coulta
CAPE CATASTROPHE
Port Lincoln
LINCOLN
NAT. PARK
THISTLE I.
Yeelanna
Edillilie
Cummins
SIR JOSEPH BANKS
GROUP
Spencer
Gulf
CAPE CARNOT
CAPE SPENCER
Stansbury
Minlaton
Yorketown
Edithburgh
Gawler
Salisbury
Elizabeth
Port
Adelaide
Adelaide
Willunga
Barker
Murray
Bridge
Milang

WHIDBEY ISLANDS
2562
CAPE CATASTROPHE
497
Investigator Strait
Milang

123

Kilometers
0 100 200 300 Km.
Statute Miles
0 100 200 300 Mi.

Scale 1:6,000,000

One centimeter represents 60 kilometers.
One inch represents approximately 95 miles.

Lambert Conformal Conic Projection

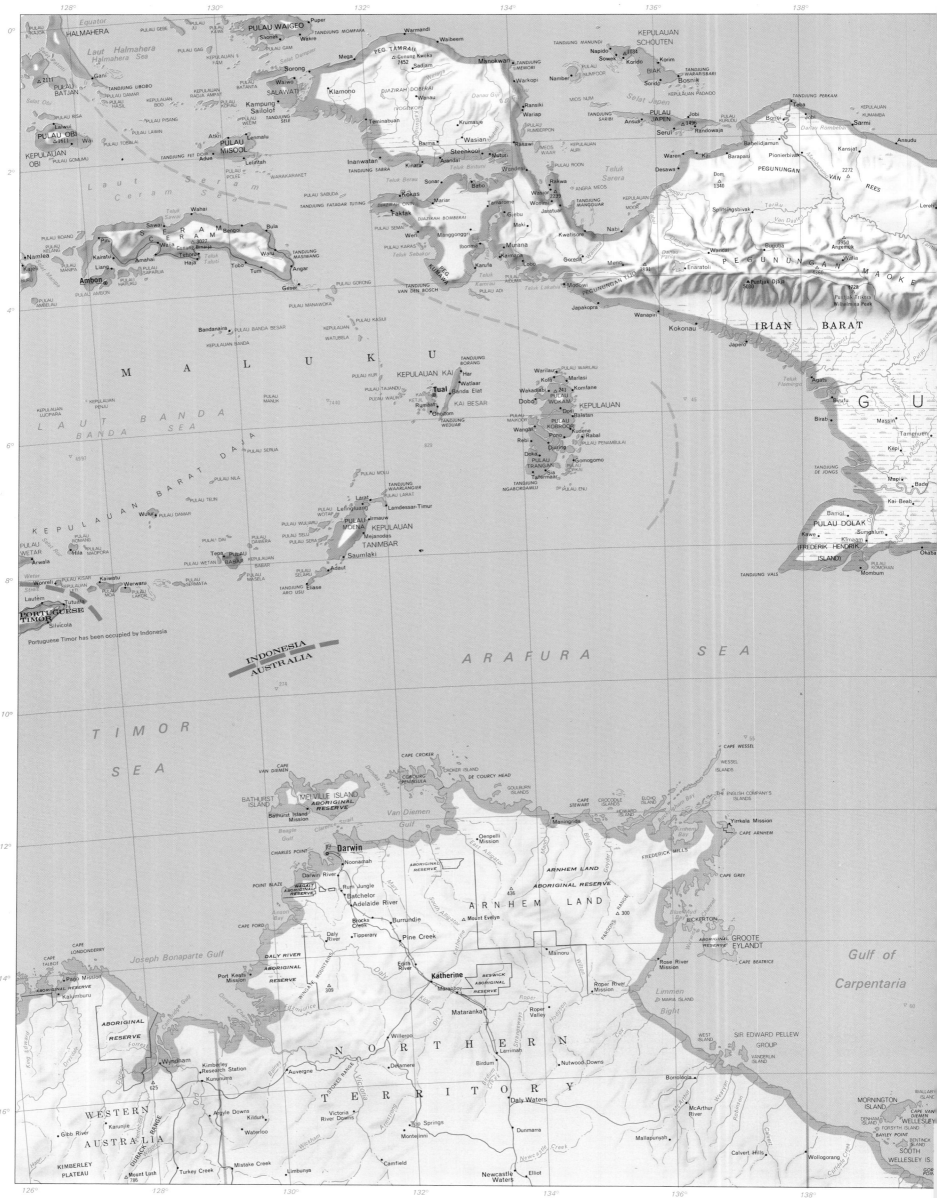

PACIFIC OCEAN

INDONESIA
PAPUA NEW GUINEA

BISMARCK ARCHIPELAGO

MANUS

ADMIRALTY ISLANDS

NEW IRELAND

SAINT MATTHIAS GROUP

BISMARCK SEA

NEW HANOVER

Kavieng

NEW IRELAND

N E W

G U I N E A

WEST SEPIK

EAST SEPIK

WESTERN HIGHLANDS

MADANG

Wewak

Madang

Mount Wilhelm 4694

SEPIK WAGHI DIVIDE

CHIMBU

EASTERN HIGHLANDS

SOUTHERN HIGHLANDS

GREAT PAPUAN PLATEAU

WESTERN

GULF

MOROBE

Lae

HUON PENINSULA

Finschhafen

WEST NEW BRITAIN

NEW BRITAIN

Rabaul

Kokopo

EAST NEW BRITAIN

WHITEMAN RANGE

SOLOMON SEA

Gulf of Papua

NORTHERN

Popondetta

OWEN STANLEY RANGE

CENTRAL

Port Moresby

MILNE BAY

LOUISIADE ARCHIPELAGO

TROBRIAND ISLANDS

D'ENTRECASTEAUX ISLANDS

WOODLARK ISLAND

Torres Strait

PAPUA NEW GUINEA
AUSTRALIA

CAPE YORK PENINSULA

Thursday Island

GREAT BARRIER REEF

QUEENSLAND

CORAL SEA

Cooktown

Cairns

Scale 1:6,000,000

Kilometers
0   100   200   300   Km.

Statute Miles
0   100   200   300   Mi.

One centimeter represents 60 kilometers.
One inch represents approximately 95 miles.
Lambert Conformal Conic Projection

125

Copyright © by Rand McNally & Co.
Map prepared by George Philip & Son Ltd., London.
A-593000-264

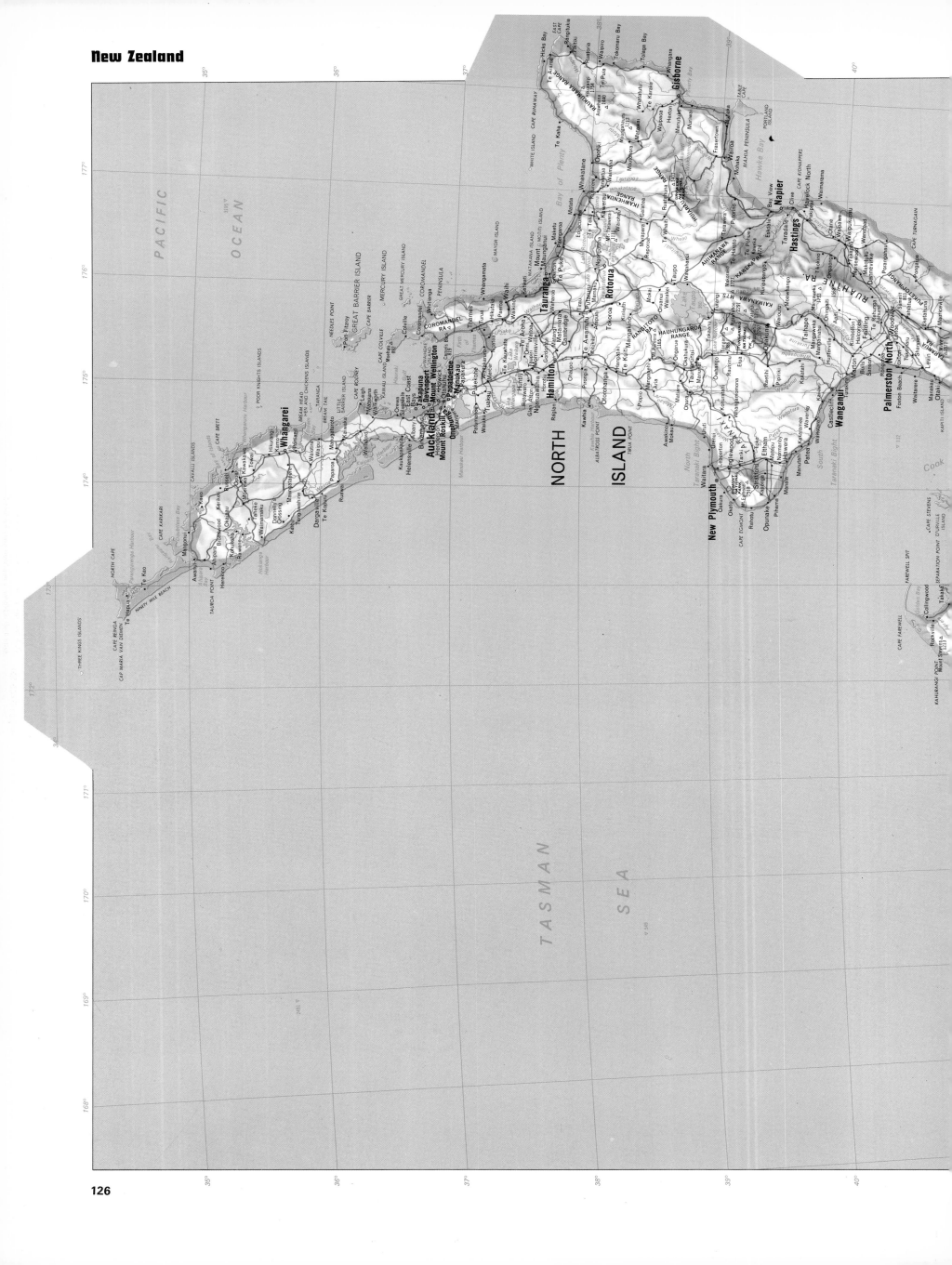

PACIFIC

OCEAN

TASMAN

SEA

NORTH

ISLAND

Auckland

Whangarei

Hamilton

Tauranga

Rotorua

Gisborne

Napier

Hastings

New Plymouth

Palmerston North

Wanganui

Mount Wellington

Devonport

Takapuna

Mount Roskill

Manukau

Papatoetoe

Cook

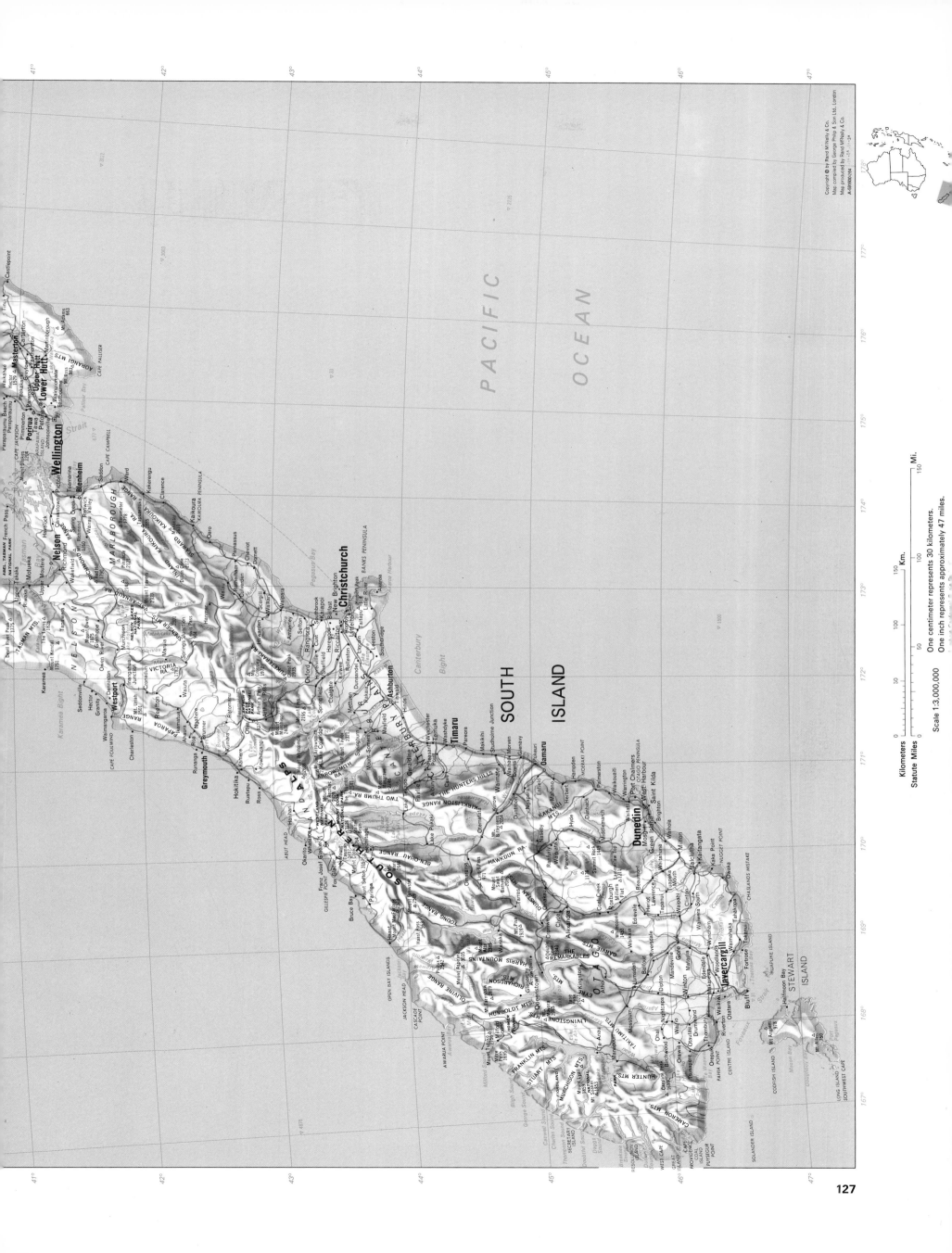

PACIFIC

OCEAN

SOUTH

ISLAND

STEWART
ISLAND

Wellington

Christchurch

Dunedin

Invercargill

Nelson

Blenheim

Greymouth

Westport

Timaru

Oamaru

Masterton
Upper Hutt
Lower Hutt
Porirua

Copyright © by Rand McNally & Co.
Map compiled by George Philip & Son Ltd., London
Map produced by Rand McNally & Co.
A-5PR00-064

Kilometers
Statute Miles

0   50   100   150   Km.
0   50   100   150   Mi.

Scale 1:3,000,000

One centimeter represents 30 kilometers.
One inch represents approximately 47 miles.

ATLANTIC OCEAN

CARIBBEAN SEA

WEST INDIES

GREATER ANTILLES

LESSER ANTILLES

BERMUDA (U.K.)
Hamilton

Tropic of Cancer

KENTUCKY
WEST VIRGINIA
VIRGINIA
Lynchburg
Roanoke Petersburg
Norfolk
Newport News
Portsmouth
Danville
Durham
Raleigh
Greensboro
Winston-Salem
Salisbury
Goldsboro
Knoxville
Asheville
Charlotte
CAROLINA
NORTH CAROLINA
Gastonia
Greenville
Spartanburg
Anderson
Columbia
SOUTH CAROLINA
Florence
CAPE HATTERAS
CAPE LOOKOUT
CAPE FEAR
Wilmington
Fayetteville
Augusta
Aiken
Charleston
Beaufort
Savannah
GEORGIA
Macon
Columbus
Americus
Albany
Dothan
Valdosta
Waycross
Brunswick
Jacksonville
Saint Augustine
FLORIDA
Palatka
Daytona Beach
Orlando
CAPE CANAVERAL
Sanford
Tampa
St. Petersburg
Clearwater
Lakeland
Sarasota
Vero Beach
Fort Pierce
West Palm Beach
Fort Lauderdale
Hollywood
Miami Beach
Miami
Fort Myers
CAPE SABLE
Key West
The Everglades
FLORIDA KEYS
Lake Okeechobee

Straits of Florida

BAHAMAS
Nassau
NEW PROVIDENCE
GRAND BAHAMA
Freeport
GREAT ABACO
ELEUTHERA
CAT ISLAND
ANDROS ISLAND
Exuma Sound
GREAT EXUMA
LONG ISLAND
SAN SALVADOR WATLING ISLAND
RUM CAY
CROOKED ISLAND
ACKLINS ISLAND
LITTLE INAGUA
GREAT INAGUA
MAYAGUANA ISLAND
CAICOS ISLANDS
TURKS AND CAICOS ISLANDS (U.K.)
Grand Turk
TURKS ISLANDS

La Habana Havana
Marianao
Matanzas
Cárdenas
Artemisa
Colón
Sagua la Grande
Caibarién
Placetas
Pinar del Río
CUBA
Güines
Santa Clara
Cienfuegos
Sancti Spíritus
Trinidad
Ciego de Ávila
Morón
CAYO COCO
CAYO ROMANO
Nueva Gerona
ISLA DE PINOS
CAYO LARGO
Nuevitas
Camagüey
Victoria de las Tunas
Banes
Santa Cruz del Sur
Holguín
Manzanillo
Bayamo
Palma Soriano
Guantánamo
SIERRA MAESTRA
Pico Turquino 2005
Santiago de Cuba

CABO SAN ANTONIO
CABO CORRIENTES

CAYMAN IS. (U.K.)
LITTLE CAYMAN
CAYMAN BRAC
GRAND CAYMAN
Georgetown

JAMAICA
Montego Bay
Savanna-la-Mar
Port Antonio
Mt. Denham 2256
Blue Mountain Peak 2256
Spanish Town
Kingston
MORANT CAYS (Jam.)

SWAN ISLANDS (Hond.)

HAITI
Cap-Haïtien
Môle St-Nicolas
Gonaïves
Saint-Marc
Port-au-Prince
Jérémie
Les Cayes
ÎLE DE LA TORTUE
ÎLE DE LA GONÂVE
Pic La Selle 2674
HISPANIOLA
ISLA BEATA

DOMINICAN REPUBLIC
Montecristi
Puerto Plata
San Francisco de Macorís
Sánchez
Santiago
La Vega
San Pedro de Macorís
Santo Domingo
San Juan
Barahona

PUERTO RICO (U.S.)
Arecibo
San Juan
Caguas
Mayagüez
Ponce
ISLA DE MONA
MONA PASSAGE
Windward Passage

VIRGIN ISLANDS
ST. THOMAS (U.S.)
Charlotte Amalie
ST. CROIX (U.S.)
ISLA DE VIEQUES (P.R.)
ANGUILLA (U.K.)
SAINT MARTIN (Guad. and Neth. Ant.)
SAINT-BARTHÉLEMY (Guad.)
BARBUDA (U.K.)
SAINT CHRISTOPHER
NEVIS
Basseterre
ANTIGUA
St. Johns
MONTSERRAT (U.K.)
Plymouth
GUADELOUPE (Fr.)
Basse-Terre
Pointe-à-Pitre
MARIE-GALANTE
DOMINICA
Roseau

LEEWARD IS.
WINDWARD IS.

MARTINIQUE (Fr.)
Fort-de-France
SAINT LUCIA
Castries
SAINT VINCENT
Kingstown
GRENADINE IS.
BARBADOS
Bridgetown
GRENADA
St. George's
TOBAGO
Scarborough
TRINIDAD AND TOBAGO
Port of Spain
TRINIDAD
ISLA DE MARGARITA (Ven.)
La Asunción
Porlamar
LA BLANQUILLA (Ven.)

NETHERLANDS ANTILLES
Oranjestad
ARUBA
CURAÇAO
Willemstad
BONAIRE
Kralendijk
LAS AVES (Ven.)
LOS ROQUES (Ven.)
LA ORCHILA (Ven.)
PUNTA GALLINAS
PENÍNSULA DE LA GUAJIRA
Punto Fijo
PENÍNSULA DE PARAGUANÁ
Coro
Puerto Cumarebo

ISLA DE PROVIDENCIA (Col.)
San Andrés
ISLA DE SAN ANDRÉS (Col.)
CORN ISLANDS (Nic.)
Bluefields
Puerto Cabezas
CAYOS MISKITOS
ISLA DEL MAÍZ
CABO GRACIAS A DIOS

CORDILLERA ISABELIA
Cerro Piu 1800
NICARAGUA
Matagalpa
Boaco
Managua
Masaya
Jinotepe
Granada
ISLA DE OMETEPE
Liberia
COSTA RICA
Puntarenas
Volcán Irazú 3432
San José
Cartago
Limón
PENÍNSULA DE NICOYA
Volcán de Chiriquí 3475
Puerto Cortés
PENÍNSULA DE OSA
Bocas del Toro
David
PUNTA MARIATO
ISLA DE COIBA
Santiago
Chitré
Las Tablas
PENÍNSULA DE AZUERO
Portobelo
Colón (Pan.)
CANAL ZONE (U.S.)
Panamá
La Chorrera
ISLA DEL REY
La Palma
Gulf of Panamá
PUERTA ARMUELLES
Golfo de Chiriquí

ISLA DEL COCO (C.R.)
ISLA DE MALPELO (Col.)

Santa Marta
Ciénaga
Barranquilla
Soledad
Sabanalarga
Cartagena
Calamar
Magangué
Mompós
Sincelejo
Lorica
Montería
Turbo
Apartadó
Puerto Berrío
Quibdó
Medellín
Itagüí
Pereira
Manizales
Cartago
Armenia
Ibagué
Girardot
Buga
Palmira
Tuluá
Buenaventura
Cali
Popayán
Neiva
COLOMBIA
Valledupar
Riohacha
Uribia
Ciudad Ojeda
CABO CORRIENTES
CORDILLERA

Maracaibo
Cabimas
Altagracia
Lago de Maracaibo
Ocaña
Cúcuta
Pamplona
Bucaramanga
Barrancabermeja
SIERRA DE PERIJÁ
Mérida
San Cristóbal
SIERRA NEVADA DE MÉRIDA
CORDILLERA DE MÉRIDA
Barinas
Valera
Arauca
Tame
Puerto Páez

VENEZUELA
Puerto Cabello
Maiquetía
La Guaira
Valencia
Maracay
Caracas
Barcelona
Barquisimeto
San Felipe
San Carlos
Guanare
Puerto de Nutrias
San Fernando de Apure
San Juan de los Morros
Aragua de Barcelona
Valle de la Pascua
El Tigre
Calabozo
Cumaná
Puerto La Cruz
Maturín
Guanta
Carúpano
Güiria
San Fernando
Cantaura
Ciudad Bolívar
Ciudad Guayana
Upata
Guasipati
Tumeremo
Cerro Bolívar 802
Cerro Yaví
LA GRAN SABANA
SIERRA DE GUAMPÍ 2441
Puerto Ayacucho
Cerro Marahuaca 2579
San Fernando de Atabapo
Maroa
San Carlos de Río Negro
AUYÁN TEPUI 2500
Mount Roraima 2772
PAKARAIMA MOUNTAINS
SIERRA PARIMA
GUYANA

Orinoco

LLANOS

BRAZIL
Boa Vista
San José del Guaviare
San Martín
Villavicencio
San Felipe

Kilometers | 0 | 200 | 400 | 600 Km.
Statute Miles | 0 | 200 | 400 | 600 Mi.

Scale 1:12,000,000

One centimeter represents 120 kilometers.
One inch represents approximately 190 miles.

Oblique Conic Conformal Projection

Mexico

PACIFIC

OCEAN

130

Kilometers | 0 | 100 | 200 | 300 | Km.

Statute Miles | 0 | 100 | 200 | 300 | Mi.

Scale 1:6,000,000

One centimeter represents 60 kilometers.
One inch represents approximately 95 miles.

Lambert Conformal Conic Projection

Caribbean Region

GULF OF MEXICO

UNITED STATES

FLORIDA

West Palm Beach
Palm Beach
Lake Worth
Belle Glade
Delray Beach
Boca Raton
Pompano Beach
Fort Lauderdale
Hollywood
Hialeah
MIAMI
Miami Beach
Coral Gables
Naples
Homestead
Key Largo

Fort Myers
Sanibel Island
Calosahatchee
Lake Okeechobee

The Everglades
Everglades National Park

Cape Sable
Florida Bay
Key West
Dry Tortugas
Marquesas Keys

FLORIDA KEYS
Straits of Florida

West End
Freeport
GRAND BAHAMA
LITTLE ABACO ISLAND
Marsh Harbour
GREAT ABACO
Cherokee Sound
Dunmore Town
BRIDGE POINT
MORES ISLAND
Cockburn Town
ELEUTHERA
Governors Harbour
ELEUTHERA
Arthurs Town
CAT ISLAND

BAHAMA

Nassau
NEW PROVIDENCE
Rock Sound
Kemps Bay
ANDROS ISLAND
Andros Town
Adelaide
Nicolls Town

Northwest Providence Channel
BERRY ISLANDS
NORTHEAST
POINT

BIMINI ISLANDS
Bimini
Alice Town

Tongue of the Ocean
MANGROVE CAY

The Bight
Old Bight
COLUMBUS POINT
SAN SALVADOR (WATLING)

LONG ISLAND
Deadmans Cay
Clarence Town
SOUTH POINT

RUM CAY
CAPE SANTA MARIA

CROOKED ISLAND

EXUMA SOUND

GREAT EXUMA
GEORGE TOWN

JUMENTOS CAYS
RAGGED ISLAND
SALINA POINT

LA HABANA
HAVANA
Marianao
Guanabacoa
Matanzas
Cárdenas
Jovellanos
Guira
Güines
Union de Reyes
San Antonio de los Baños
La Esperanza
Candelaria
Artemisa
Los Palacios
Consolación del Sur
La Isabela
San Cristóbal

Colón
Santa Isabel de las Lajas
Quemado de Güines
Sagua la Grande
Calabazar
Camajuani
Zulueta
Placetas
Yaguajay
Morón

Santa Clara
Cienfuegos
Palmira

Pico San Juan
1135

Pinar del Río
Minas de Matahambre
Mantua
Guane

Nueva Gerona
Santa Fé
ISLA DE PINOS
ISLE OF PINES

Trinidad
Sancti-Spíritus
Tunas de Zaza
Golfo de Ana María

Ciego de Ávila
Florida
Minas
Jatibonico
Júcaro

Camagüey
Martí
Vertientes
Puerto Padre
Chaparra
Gibara

CUBA

Esmeralda
CAYO GUAJABA
CAYO SABINAL
Nuevitas
Puerto Manatí

Holguín
Banes
Antilla
Cueto

SIERRA DEL CRISTAL
San Germán
Alto Cedro
Sagua de Tánamo
Baracoa

Victoria de las Tunas
Bayamo
Manzanillo
Palma Soriano
Niquero
Portillo
Campechuela
Jiguaní

Santiago de Cuba
Guantánamo
Caimanera

SIERRA MAESTRA
CABO CRUZ

W E S T   I N D I E S

GREAT BAHAMA BANK

Nicholas Channel
SNAP POINT

CAY SAL
CAY SAL BANK
ANGUILLA CAYS

Old Bahama Channel

GREATER

CAYMAN ISLANDS (U.K.)
Georgetown
GRAND CAYMAN
LITTLE CAYMAN
CAYMAN BRAC

MISTERIOSA BANK

ROSARIO BANK

SWAN ISLANDS (Hond.)

LIGHTHOUSE REEF

GLOVER REEF

THUNDER KNOLL

ROSALIND BANK

YUCATAN CHANNEL

YUCATÁN PENINSULA
YUCATÁN
MÉXICO
X-CAN
MÉXICO
QUINTANA ROO
Chemax
Tulum
ISLA DE COZUMEL
Cozumel

PUNTA FRANCESCA
CABO CATOCHE
Isla Contoy
Isla Mujeres
PUNTA CANCÚN
Cancún
Puerto Juárez
Kantunilkín
Puerto Morelos

Bahía de la Ascensión
Bahía del Espíritu Santo
BANCO CHINCHORRO

Golfo de Guanahacabibes
CABO SAN ANTONIO
Ensenada de Corrientes
CABO CORRIENTES
Ensenada de la Siguanea
PENÍNSULA DE ZAPATA

Golfo de Batabanó
PUNTA GORDA
Gerona
CAYOS DE SAN FELIPE

JARDINES DE LA REINA

CAYOS DE LAS DOCE LEGUAS
LABERINTO DE LAS DOCE LEGUAS

Golfo de Guacanayabo

Gulf of Honduras
ISLAS DE LA BAHÍA
Utila
ISLA DE UTILA
Roatán
ISLA DE ROATÁN
Guanaja
ISLA DE GUANAJA
CABO DE HONDURAS

HONDURAS
Trujillo
La Ceiba
El Triunfo
Pico Bonito
2435
Tocoa
Olanchito
Yoro
Salamá
Guanpata
Catacamas
San Ignacio
Juticalpa
CORDILLERA DE AGALTA
Guaimaca
2256

Tegucigalpa
Yuscarán
Danlí
Guinope
El Paraíso
Cedros
Talanga

Minas de Oro
San Juan

NICARAGUA
CORDILLERA ISABELIA
Cerro Kilambé
1750
Somoto
Condega
Estelí
San Rafael del Norte
Jinotega
Yalí
Cerro Piu
1800
Matagalpa
San Cristóbal
1745
Sébaco
Ciudad Darío
Boaco

Palacagüina
Ocotal
Mogotón
2107

León
Chinandega
Corinto
Volcán Momotombo
1191
El Sauce
La Paz Centro
Nagarote

MANAGUA
Masaya
GRANADA
Diriamba
Jinotepe
Volcán Concepción
1610
Nandaime
Rivas
Santa María
Jesús María

San Juan del Sur
CABO SANTA ELENA
PENÍNSULA DE NICOYA

COSTA RICA
Liberia
Santa Cruz
Bagaces
Cañas
Nicoya
Cerro Azul
2018

San Ramón
Puntarenas
SAN JOSÉ
Heredia
Alajuela
Cartago
Volcán Irazú
3432
Volcán Turrialba
3328
Volcán Barba
2906
La Fortuna
Venecia
Puerto Viejo
Guápiles
Siquirres
Limón

CORDILLERA DE GUANACASTE
Volcán Miravalles
2028

CORDILLERA CENTRAL
CORDILLERA DE TALAMANCA

PACIFIC OCEAN

Bocay
San Ramón
Waspán
Bilwascarma
RÍO COCO
CABO GRACIAS A DIOS
Puerto Cabezas
Yablis
Waunta
Prinzapolca
RÍO GRANDE
Río Grande
Santo Domingo
La Cruz
Tungla
Siuna
Bonanza
Bocana
Huahua
MOSQUITO COAST
COSTA DE MOSQUITOS

Laguna Caratasca
PUNTA PATUCA
BRUS LAGUNA
Brus Laguna
CABO CAMARÓN
Paya
RÍO PATUCA

CAYOS MISKITOS
PUNTA GORDA

ARRECIFE DE LA MEDIA LUNA

QUITA SUEÑO BANK (Col.)

SERRANA BANK (Col.)

SERRANILLA BANK (Col.)

RONCADOR BANK (Col.)

ISLA DE PROVIDENCIA
SAN ANDRÉS Y PROVIDENCIA (Col.)
ISLA DE SAN ANDRÉS
San Andrés
CAYOS DE ALBUQUERQUE

CORN ISLANDS (Nic.)

Tipitapa
La Libertad
Villa Sandino
Rama
Muelle de los Bueyes
El Bluff
Bluefields
Acoyapa
Juigalpa
Santo Tomás
SIERRA DE AMERRIQUE

LAGO DE NICARAGUA
ISLA DE OMETEPE
La Flor
Punta Gorda

San Carlos
El Castillo
Laguna de Perlas
Bahía de San Juan del Norte
RÍO SAN JUAN
San Juan del Norte
Colorado

PANAMA
CANAL ZONE (U.S.)
Colón
Portobelo
Panama
Bocas del Toro
Almirante
Changuinola
Chiriquí Grande
Nombre de Dios
Golfo de San Blas
CORDILLERA DE SAN BLAS
ISTHMUS OF PANAMA
PENÍNSULA VALIENTE
Golfo de los Mosquitos
Palmas Bellas
Río Indio
Mandinga
Ailigandí
Mulatupo

PUNTA MONA

CARIBBEAN

Montego Bay
Falmouth
Ocho Rios
Port Maria
Port Antonio
WEST POINT
Saint Ann's Bay
Savanna-la-Mar
Mount Denham
905
Mandeville
Spanish Town
Kingston
Port Morant
May Pen
Blue Mountain Peak
MORANT POINT
JAMAICA
PORTLAND POINT
Portland Bight
Morant Bay
MORANT CAYS

NAVASSA ISLAND (U.S.)

Windward Passage

Jérémie

COLOMBIA

Santa Marta
PUNTA FARO
Ciénaga
Barranquilla
Puerto Colombia
Soledad
Sabanalarga
ATLÁNTICO
BOLÍVAR
Cartagena
Turbaco
Arjona
Calamar
El Carmen de Bolívar
ISLAS DE ROSARIO
ISLAS DE SAN BERNARDO
San Onofre
San Juan Nepomuceno
Plato
Magangué
Mompós
MAGDALENA
CÓRDOBA
SUCRE
Sincelejo
Corozal
Sampués
Chinú
Ciénaga de Zapatosa
RÍO MAGDALENA

Kilometers

Statute Miles

133

Scale 1:6,000,000

One centimeter represents 60 kilometers.
One inch represents approximately 95 miles.

Lambert Conformal Conic Projection

Kilometers

Statute Miles

Scale 1:12,000,000

One centimeter represents 120 kilometers.
One inch represents approximately 190 miles.
Oblique Conic Conformal Projection

BARBADOS
Bridgetown

TOBAGO

Morawhanna

Spring Gardens
Parika
Charity
Georgetown
Hyde Park
Bartica
Rosignol
New Amsterdam
Mackenzie
Nieuw Nickerie
Rockstone
Wismar
Skeldon
Totness
Kwakoegron
Brokopondo

GUYANA
Prof. Dr. Ir. W.J. Van Blommestein Meer
Julianatop
1280
1230mtop

SURINAM

Paramaribo
Nieuw Amsterdam
Meerzorg
Paranam
Albina
Saint-Laurent-du-Maroni
Saint-Elie
Regina
Saül
830
Saint-Georges

FRENCH GUIANA
Cayenne
ÎLE DU DIABLE
Oiapoque

ACARAI MOUNTAINS
Lethem

WILHELMINA GEBERGTE
ORANJE GEBERGTE

TUMUC - HUMAC MOUNTAINS

Cunani
Calçoene

Serra do Navio

CABO ORANGE

ATLANTIC OCEAN

Amapá
ILHA DE MARACÁ

Macapá
Mazagão
ILHA BAILIQUE
ILHA CURUÁ
ILHA JANAUCU
ILHA CAVIANA
ILHA MEXIANA

CABO MAGUARINHO

Equator 0°

Oriximiná
Alenquer
Óbidos
Monte Alegre
Porto de Móz
Gurupá
ILHA DA LAGUNA
ILHA GRANDE DO GURUPÁ

ILHA DE MARAJÓ
ILHA DOS MACACOS

Breves
Portel
Curralinho
Cametá

Belém
Abaetetuba

Marapanim
Bragança
Carutapera
Camiranga
Cururupu

Alcântara

Maués
Parintins
Faro
Santarém

Itacoatiara
Borba

Itaituba
Altamira
Tucuruí

SERRA DO CACHIMBO

SERRA DOS CARAJÁS

Marabá
São João do Araguaia
Araguatins

Imperatriz

Pinheiro
São Bento
Rosário
Viana
Monção
Bacabal
Pedreiras

São Luís
Tutóia
Itapecuru-Mirim
Codó
Caxias

Parnaíba
Camocim
Acaraú

Sobral
Marangaupe
Parangaba

Fortaleza

Brejo
Barras
União
Campo Maior

Teresina

Crateús

Quixadá
Baturité
Ipu
Pedro II

Russas
Areia Branca
Macau

Aracati

Mossoró
Angicos
Lajes

CABO DE SÃO ROQUE

ATOL DAS ROCAS

ILHA FERNANDO DE NORONHA (Brazil)

Colinas
Mirador
Amarante
Floriano
Picos
Oeiras

Iguatu
Icó
Caicó
Currais Novos
Nova Cruz

Natal

Gradaús
Conceição do Araguaia
Araguacema
Miracema do Norte
Tocantínia

Carolina
Riachão
Balsas

Loreto
Benedito Leite

São Raimundo Nonato

Crato
Juazeiro do Norte
Cajàzeiras
Sousa
Patos

Campina Grande
Itabaiana
Guarabira
Alagoa Grande
Sapé

Rio Tinto
Cabedelo
João Pessoa

SERRA DO NORTE

SERRA DOS APIACÁS

SERRA FORMOSA

SERRA DO TOMBADOR

SERRA DOS CAIABIS

B R A Z I L
ILHA DO BANANAL

Pium
Cristalândia
Pôrto Nacional
Gurupi
Natividade
Dianópolis

Pedro Afonso
Tocantína
Alto Parnaíba
Santa Filomena
Gilbués

Paranaguá

Parnaguá

Remanso
Petrolina
Juazeiro

Paulistana

CHAPADA DAS MANGABEIRAS
SERRA DA TABATINGA

Cabrobó
Garanhuns

Sertânia
Arcoverde
Palmares

Flores
Nazaré da Mata
Limoeiro
Caruaru

Olinda
Recife
Jaboatão
Cabo

Barreiros
Pôrto de Pedras

União dos Palmares
Palmeira dos Indios

Rio Largo
Maceió

Diamantino
Rosário Oeste

PLANALTO DO MATO GROSSO

Cuiabá
Barão de Melgaço
Cáceres
Rondonópolis

Taguatinga
Arraias
São Domingos
Posse
Cavalcante

Paranã

Barreiras

Bom Jesus da Lapa
Paramirim
Pico das Almas 1850

Correntina
Carinhanha
Guanambi

SERRA DO ESPINHAÇO

Senhor do Bonfim
Jacobina
Morro do Chapéu

Itaberaba

Feira de Santana
Santo Antônio de Jesus
Cachoeira
Maragogipe
Nazaré
Valença

Salvador

Lençóis
Mucugê

Jeremoabo
Tucano
Propriá
Penedo

Aracaju
São Cristóvão
Estância

Alagoinhas
Inhambupe

ILHA DE TINHARÉ

Jequié
Ipiaú

Corumbá
Porto Esperança

Pôrto Suárez
Puerto Suárez

Aquidauana
Miranda
Nioaque

Campo Grande
Três Lagoas

Coxim
Rio Verde
Jataí
Mineiros

Itumbiara
Tupaciguara
Catalão
Araguari
Uberlândia

Uberaba
Araxá
SA. DA CANASTRA

Anápolis
Goiânia
Silvânia
Luziânia

Brasília

PLANALTO CENTRAL

Pirenópolis
Itaberaí
Goiás
Iporá
Alto Araguaia

SERRA CAIAPÓ

Pires do Rio
Campo Alegre de Goiás

Morrinhos

São Francisco
Januária

Monte Azul
Grão Mogol
Araçuaí
Minas Novas

Pedra Azul
Almenara

Canavieiras
Belmonte
Pôrto Seguro

Prado
Alcobaça
Caravelas

Vitória da Conquista
Ibicaraí
Itapetinga
Itabuna
Ilhéus

Montes Claros
Pirapora
Diamantina
Curvelo
Corinto
Peçanha

Nanuque
ILHA CAÇUMBA

AIMORÉS

Governador Valadares
Caratinga
Colatina

São Mateus

Aracruz

Vitória
Vila Velha

Paracatu
Patos de Minas
Patrocínio
Sete Lagoas
Pará de Minas
Divinópolis

Belo Horizonte
Itabira

Mariana
Ouro Prêto
Conselheiro Lafaiete
Barbacena

Cachoeiro de Itapemirim
Itapemirim

Campos
SÃO TOMÉ

Campo Grande
Presidente Prudente

São José do Rio Prêto
Votuporanga
Barretos
Franca
Passos
Poços de Caldas

Araraquara
São Carlos

Araçatuba
Andradina
Lins
Marília
Bauru
Piracicaba
Botucatu
Avaré
Sorocaba
Itapetininga

Campinas
Jundiaí

SÃO PAULO
São Vicente
Santos

Ribeirão Prêto

Juiz de Fora
Barra Mansa
Volta Redonda
Petrópolis
Niterói

RIO DE JANEIRO

CABO FRIO

Tropic of Capricorn
ILHA DE SÃO SEBASTIÃO

URUGUAY
GUAY

Pôrto Murtinho
Bela Vista
Puerto Sastre
Puerto Casado

ATLANTIC

OCEAN

NETHERLANDS **ANTILLES**
NEDERLANDSE **ANTILLEN**

CURAÇAO   BONAIRE

Willemstad   Kralendijk

68° 66° 64° 62° 60° 58° 56°

CARRIACOU
GRENADINE
ISLANDS

Victoria
Saint George's
GRENADA

TOBAGO   Speyside
Scarborough

GALERA POINT   **TRINIDAD**

Port of Spain   AND

TRINIDAD   **TOBAGO**

San Fernando

CARACAS

Maracaibo

Barquisimeto

Valencia

GUÁRICO

ANZOÁTEGUI

MONAGAS

DELTA   DEL

AMACURO

NORTH WEST

MAZARUNI

POTARO

Georgetown

New Amsterdam

EAST

BERBICE

WEST BERBICE

ESSEQUIBO
ISLANDS

APURE

San Fernando
de Apure

Ciudad Guayana

Ciudad
Bolívar

BOLÍVAR

VENEZUELA
COLOMBIA

LA GRAN
SABANA

PAKARAIMA   MOUNTAINS

Mount Roraima

COLOMBIA
VENEZUELA

AMAZONAS

SIERRA
PARIMA

RUPUNUNI

KANUKU
MOUNTAINS

NICKERIE

WILHELMINA
GEB.

SURINAM

GUYANA   SURINAME

KAYSER
GEBERGTE

SARAMACCA

Boa Vista

VENEZUELA
BRAZIL

BRAZIL
GUYANA

KAMOA
MOUNTAINS

ACARAI   MOUNTAINS

RORAIMA

AMAZONAS

Equator

PARÁ

Manaus

PARÁ

Kilometers   0   100   200   300   Km.

Statute Miles   0   100   200   300   Mi.

Scale 1:6,000,000

One centimeter represents 60 kilometers.
One inch represents approximately 95 miles.

Oblique Conic Conformal Projection

Kilometers

0   100   200   300   Km.

Statute Miles

0   100   200   300   Mi.

Scale 1:6,000,000

One centimeter represents 60 kilometers.
One inch represents approximately 95 miles.
Oblique Conic Conformal Projection

Kilometers

Statute Miles

Scale 1:12,000 000

One centimeter represents 120 kilometers.
One inch represents approximately 190 miles.

Lambert Conformal Conic Projection

143

Kilometers

Statute Miles

One centimeter represents 120 kilometers.
One inch represents approximately 190 miles.

Scale 1:12,000,000

Albers Conical Equal-Area Projection

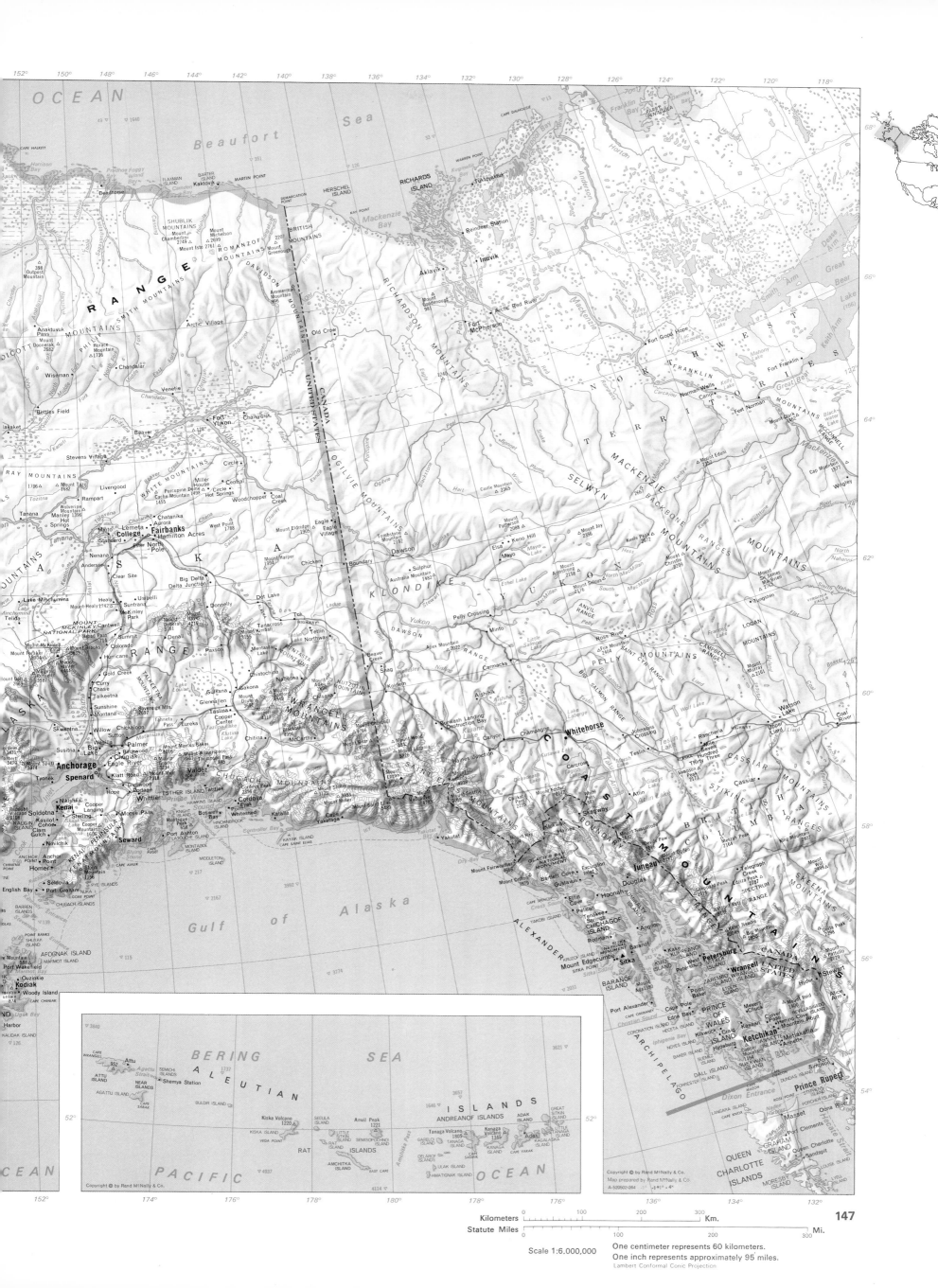

OCEAN

Beaufort   Sea

RANGE

BRITISH

OCEAN

BERING   SEA

ALEUTIAN   ISLANDS

ANDREANOF ISLANDS

RAT   ISLANDS

PACIFIC   OCEAN

Gulf   of   Alaska

NORTHWEST   TERRITORIES

Anchorage

Fairbanks

Whitehorse

Juneau

Ketchikan

Prince Rupert

QUEEN
CHARLOTTE
ISLANDS

Kilometers
0   100   200   300   Km.

Statute Miles
0   100   200   300   Mi.

Scale 1:6,000,000
One centimeter represents 60 kilometers.
One inch represents approximately 95 miles.
Lambert Conformal Conic Projection

Copyright © by Rand McNally & Co.
Map prepared by Rand McNally & Co.
A-520502-264

Kilometers 0 50 100 150 Km.

Statute Miles 0 50 100 150 Mi.

Scale 1:3,000,000

One centimeter represents 30 kilometers.
One inch represents approximately 47 miles.
Lambert Conformal Conic Projection

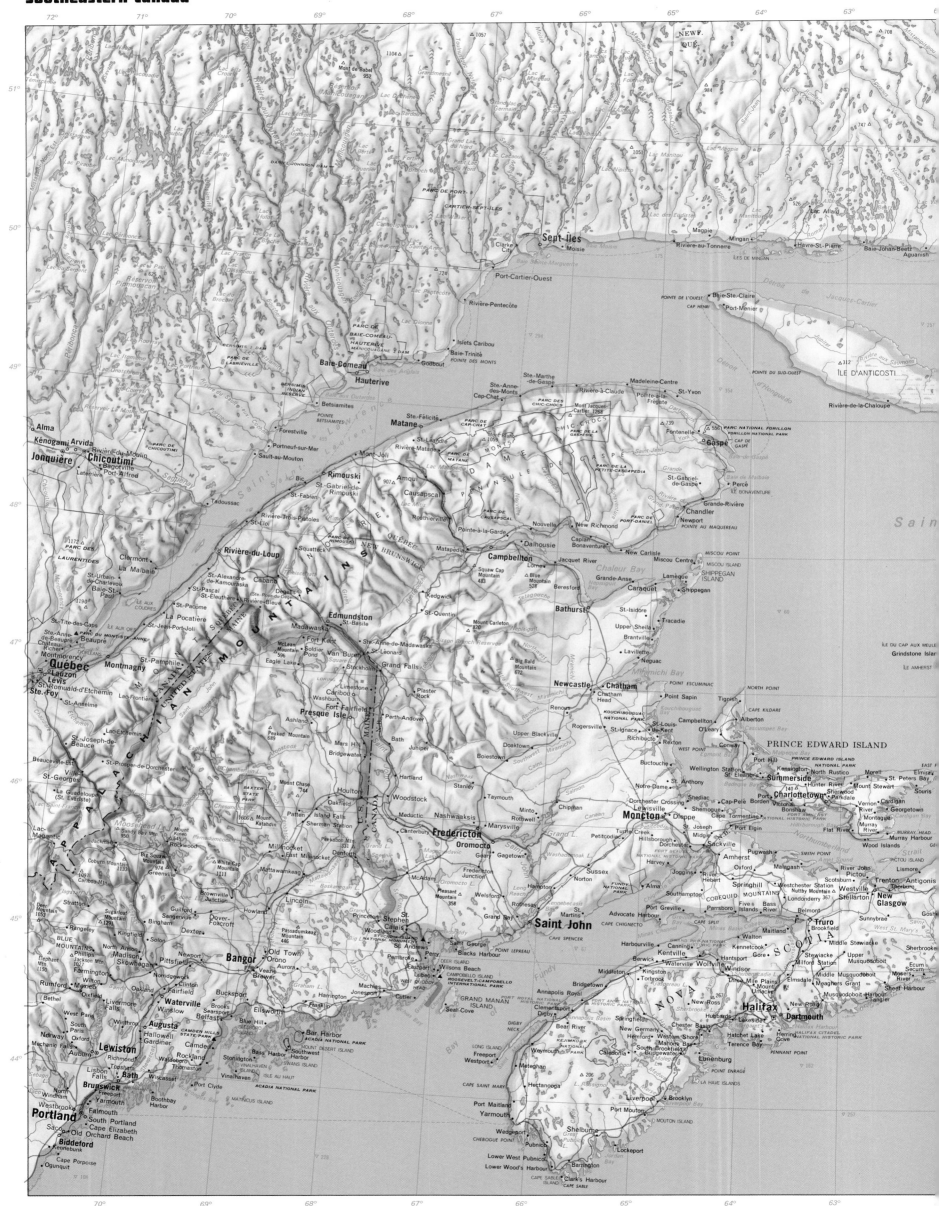

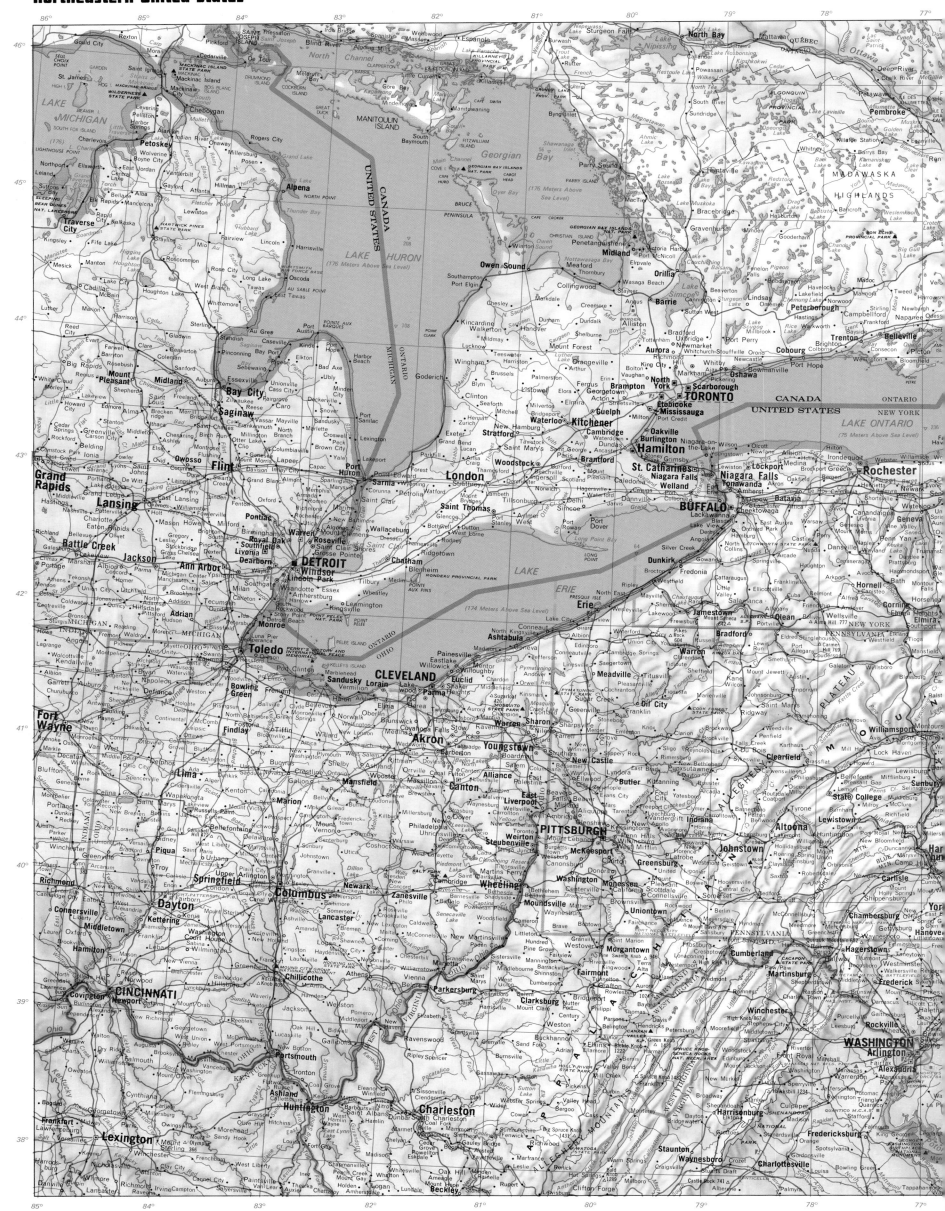

Kilometers
Statute Miles

One centimeter represents 30 kilometers.
One inch represents approximately 47 miles.

Scale 1:3,000,000

Albers Conical Equal-Area Projection

Copyright © by Rand McNally & Co.
Map prepared by Rand McNally & Co.
A-590506-264

Kilometers |0 50 100 150 | Km.
Statute Miles |0 50 100 150 | Mi.

Scale 1:3,000,000

One centimeter represents 30 kilometers.
One inch represents approximately 47 miles.

Albers Conical Equal-Area Projection

Southeastern United States

Kilometers 0 50 100 150 Km.
Statute Miles 0 50 100 150 Mi.

Scale 1:3,000,000

One centimeter represents 30 kilometers.
One inch represents approximately 47 miles.
Albers Conical Equal-Area Projection

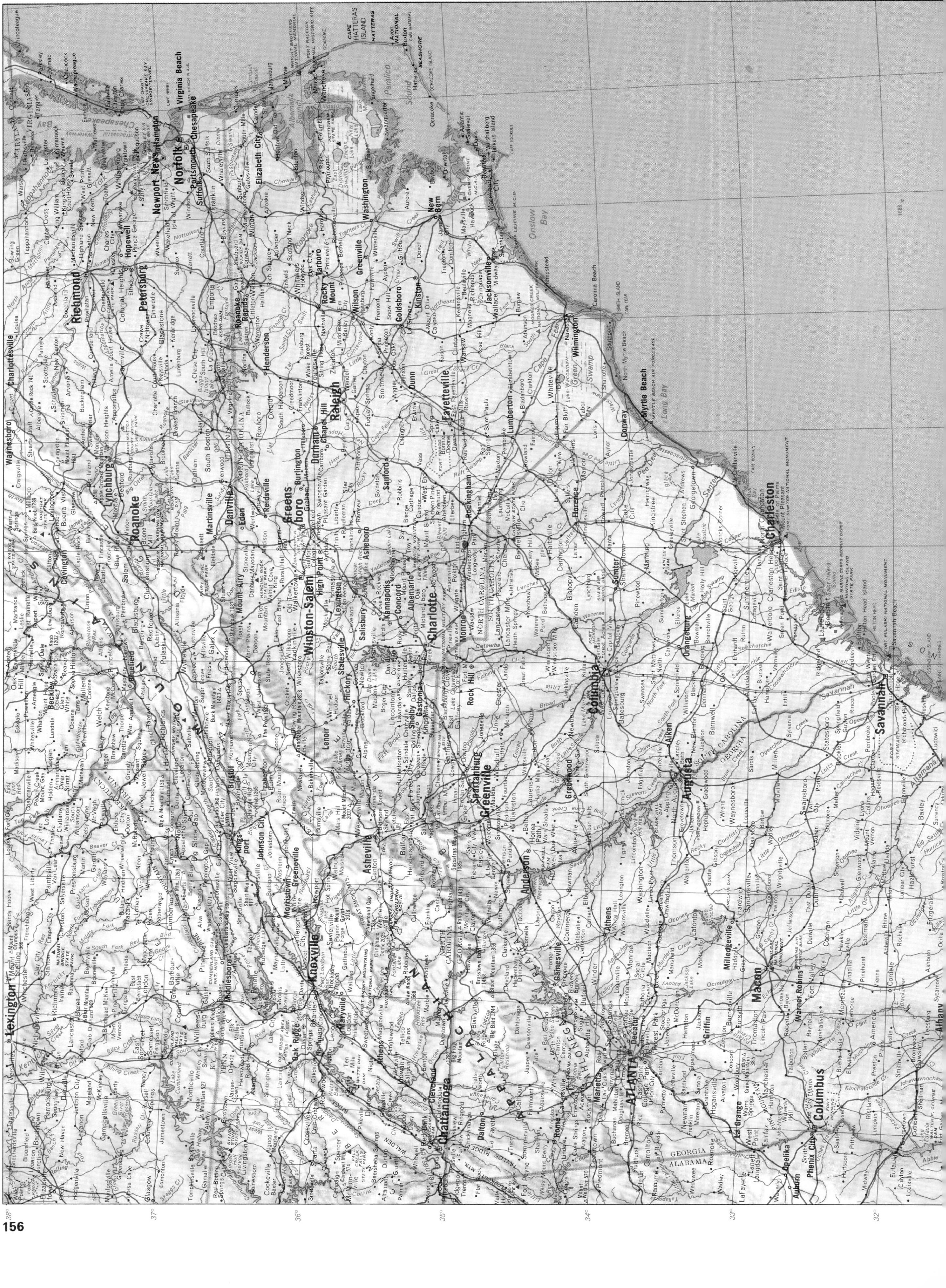

ATLANTIC

OCEAN

GULF OF

MEXICO

Tallahassee

GEORGIA

FLORIDA

Jacksonville

St. Augustine

Ormond Beach
Daytona Beach
New Smyrna Beach

Gainesville

Orlando
Winter Park

CAPE CANAVERAL
Merritt Island
Cocoa Beach
Melbourne

JOHN F. KENNEDY
SPACE CENTER

Titusville

Sanford

Ocala

**Lake
Land**

Winter Haven

Vero Beach

Fort Pierce

Tampa
Plant City

St. Petersburg
Clearwater
Dunedin

Sarasota

Bradenton

Fort Myers

Lake
Okeechobee

North Palm Beach
Riviera Beach
West Palm Beach
Palm Beach
Lake Worth
Boynton Beach
Delray Beach
Boca Raton
Deerfield Beach
Oakland Park
Pompano Beach
Fort Lauderdale
Hollywood
Hialeah
MIAMI
Miami Beach
Coral Gables
South Miami

EVERGLADES
NATIONAL
PARK

FLORIDA KEYS

**Key
West**

FLORIDA STRAITS

GREAT
ABACO
LITTLE ABACO
ISLAND

GRAND BAHAMA

Freeport

Northwest Providence Channel

BERRY
ISLANDS

BIMINI
ISLANDS

ANDROS
ISLAND

Nassau
NEW PROVIDENCE

ELEUTHERA

UNITED STATES
BAHAMAS

DRY TORTUGAS

157

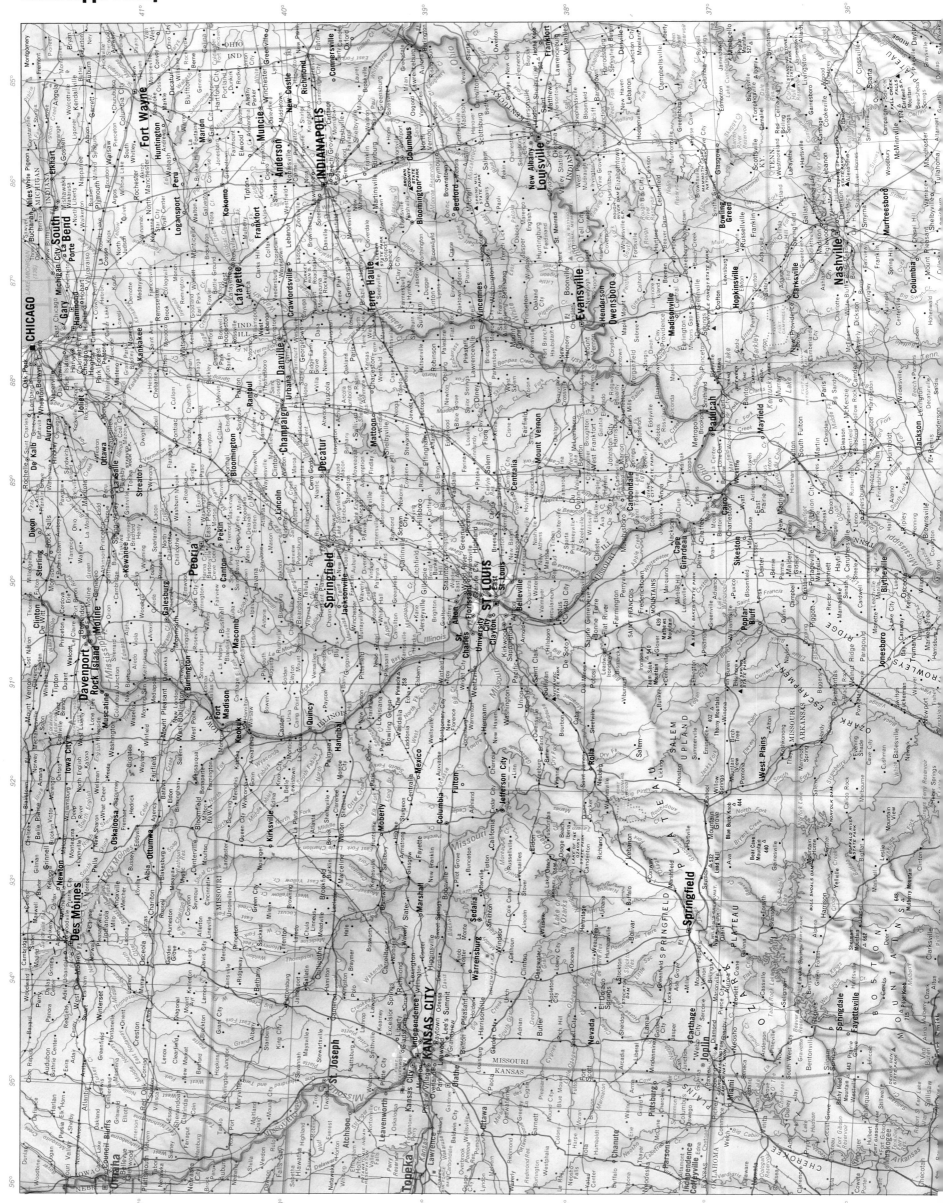

Kilometers

Statute Miles

One centimeter represents 30 kilometers.
One inch represents approximately 47 miles.
Scale 1:3,000,000
Albers Conical Equal-Area Projection

Copyright © by Rand McNally & Co.
Made/Printed in U.S.A. by Rand McNally & Co.
A-93139 204

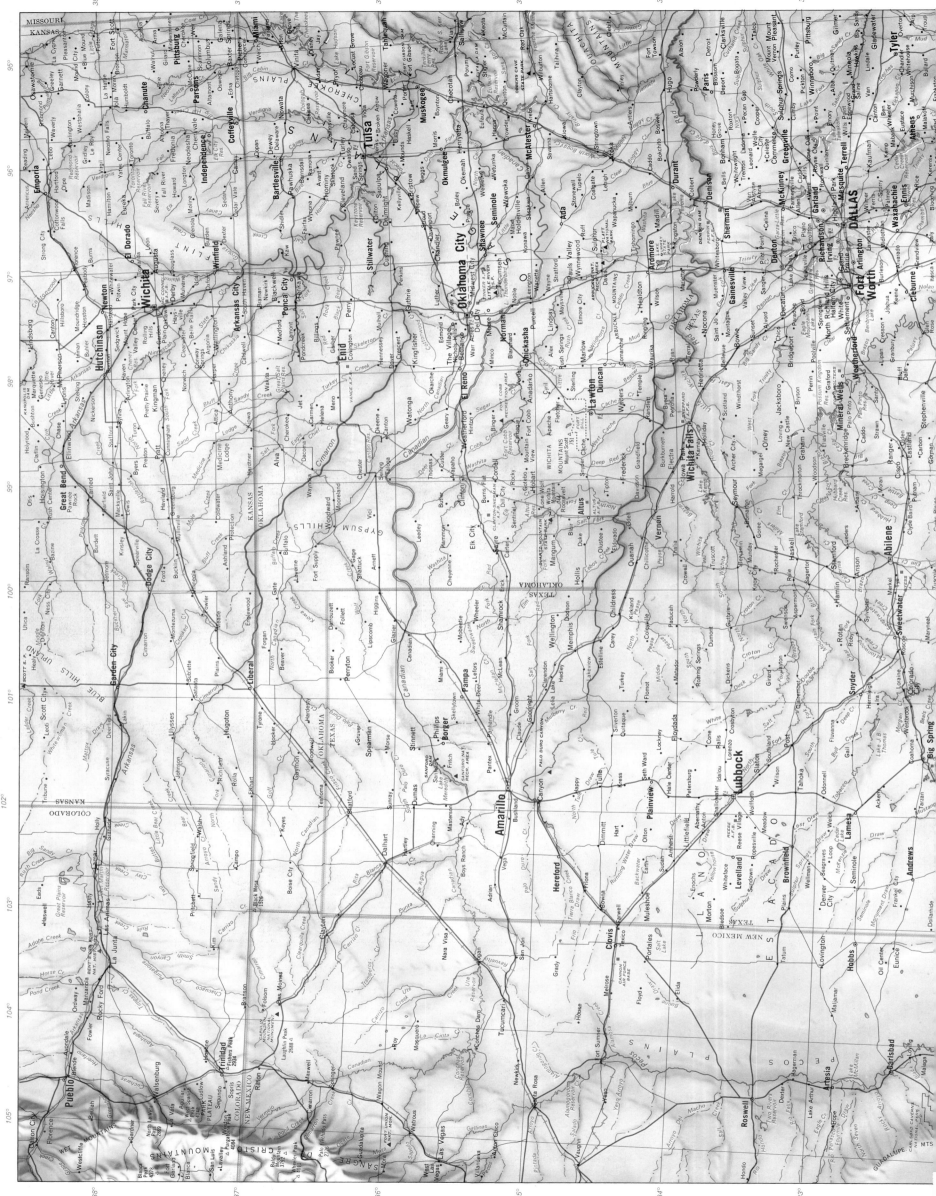

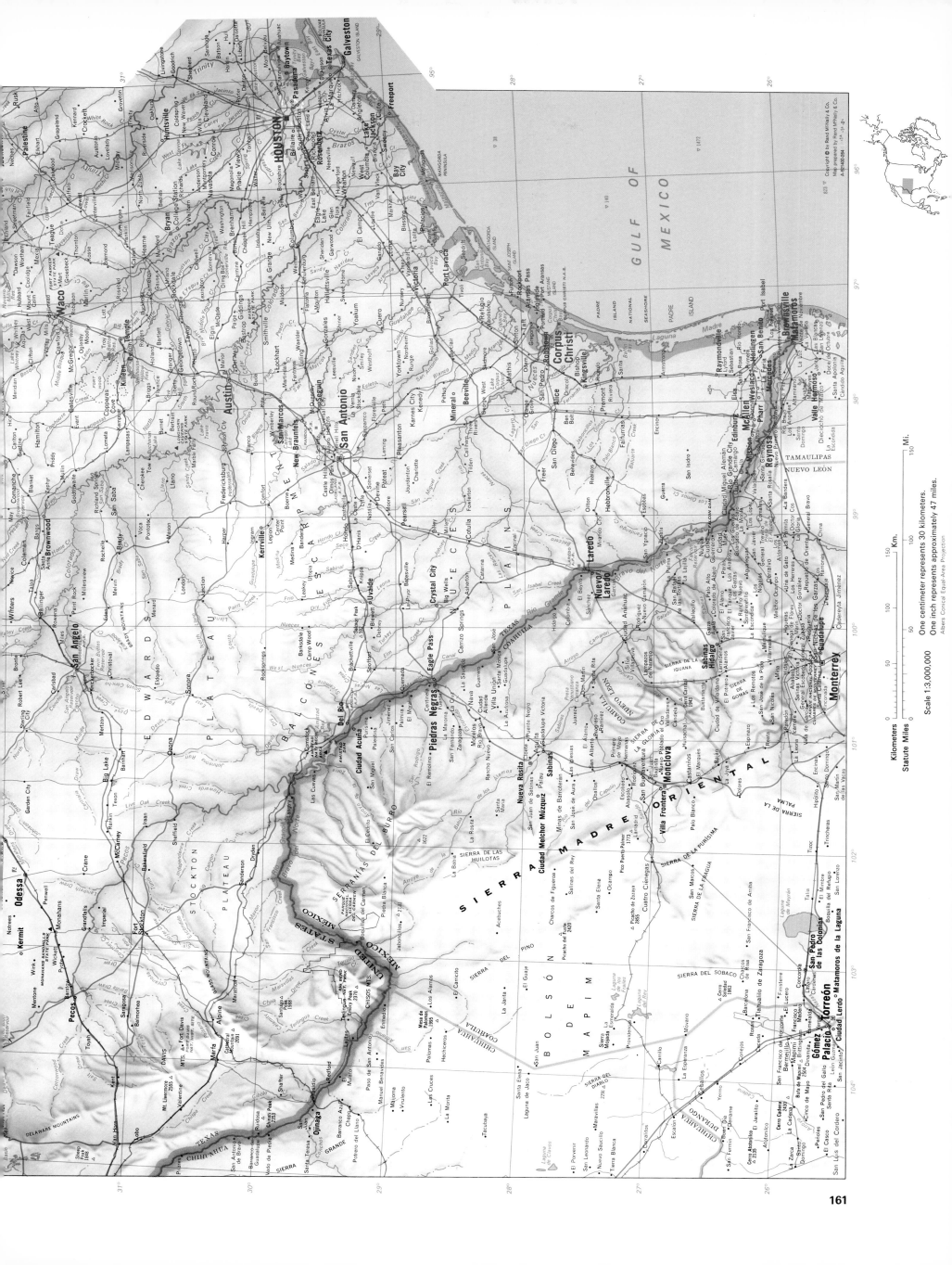

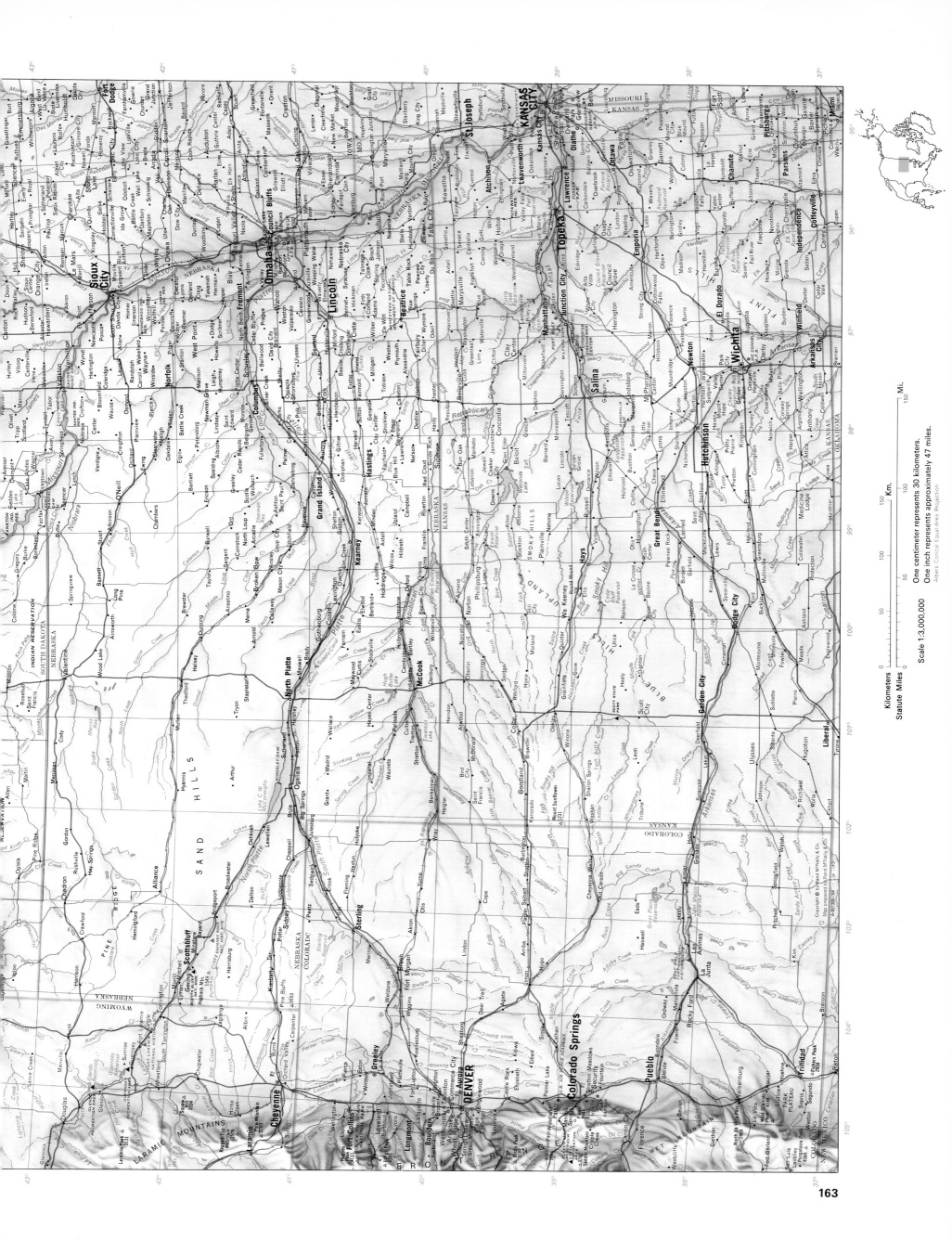

One centimeter represents 30 kilometers.
One inch represents approximately 47 miles.

Scale 1:3,000,000

Albers Conical Equal-Area Projection

Kilometers

Statute Miles

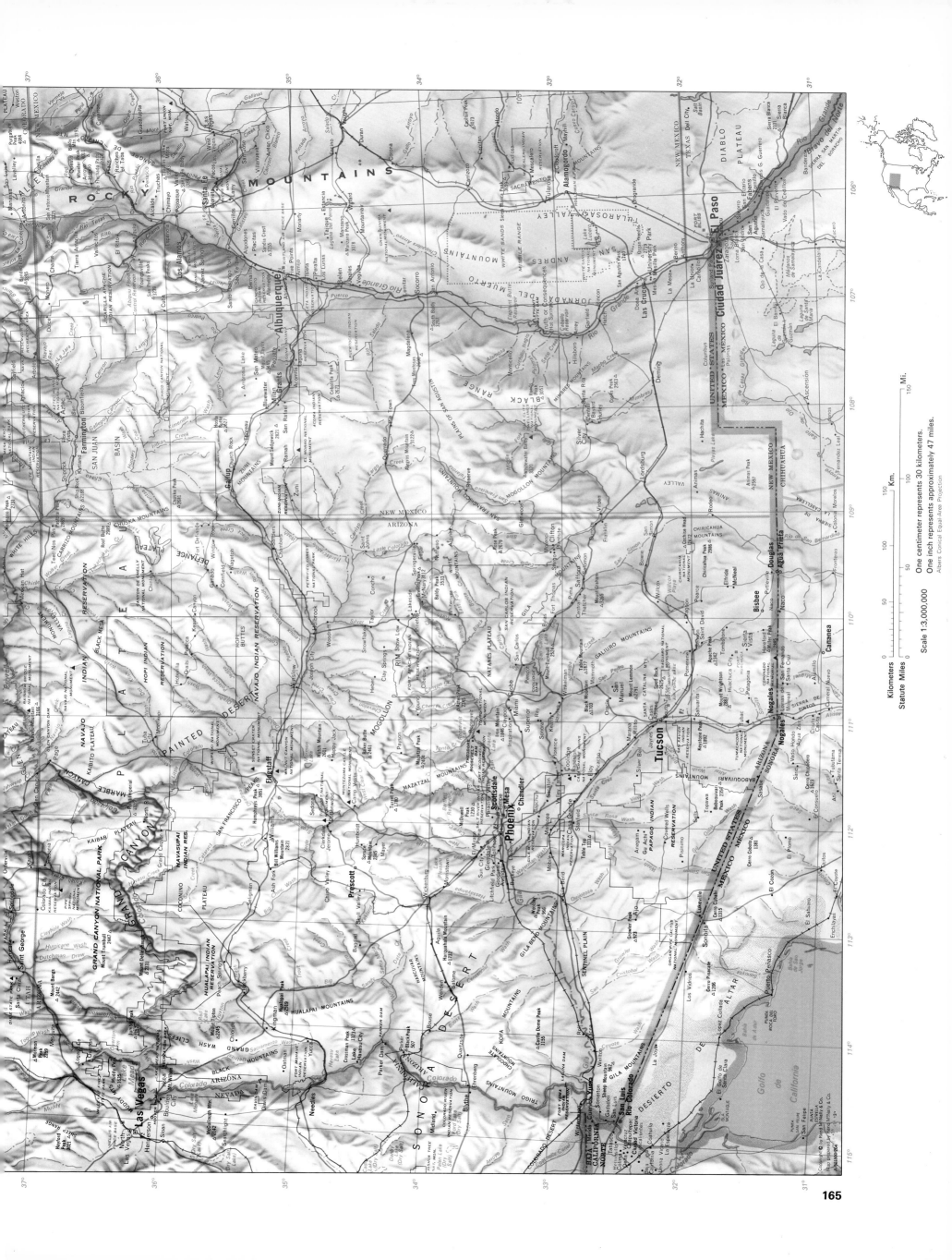

Kilometers

Statute Miles

Scale 1:3,000,000

One centimeter represents 30 kilometers.
One inch represents approximately 47 miles.

Albers Conical Equal-Area Projection

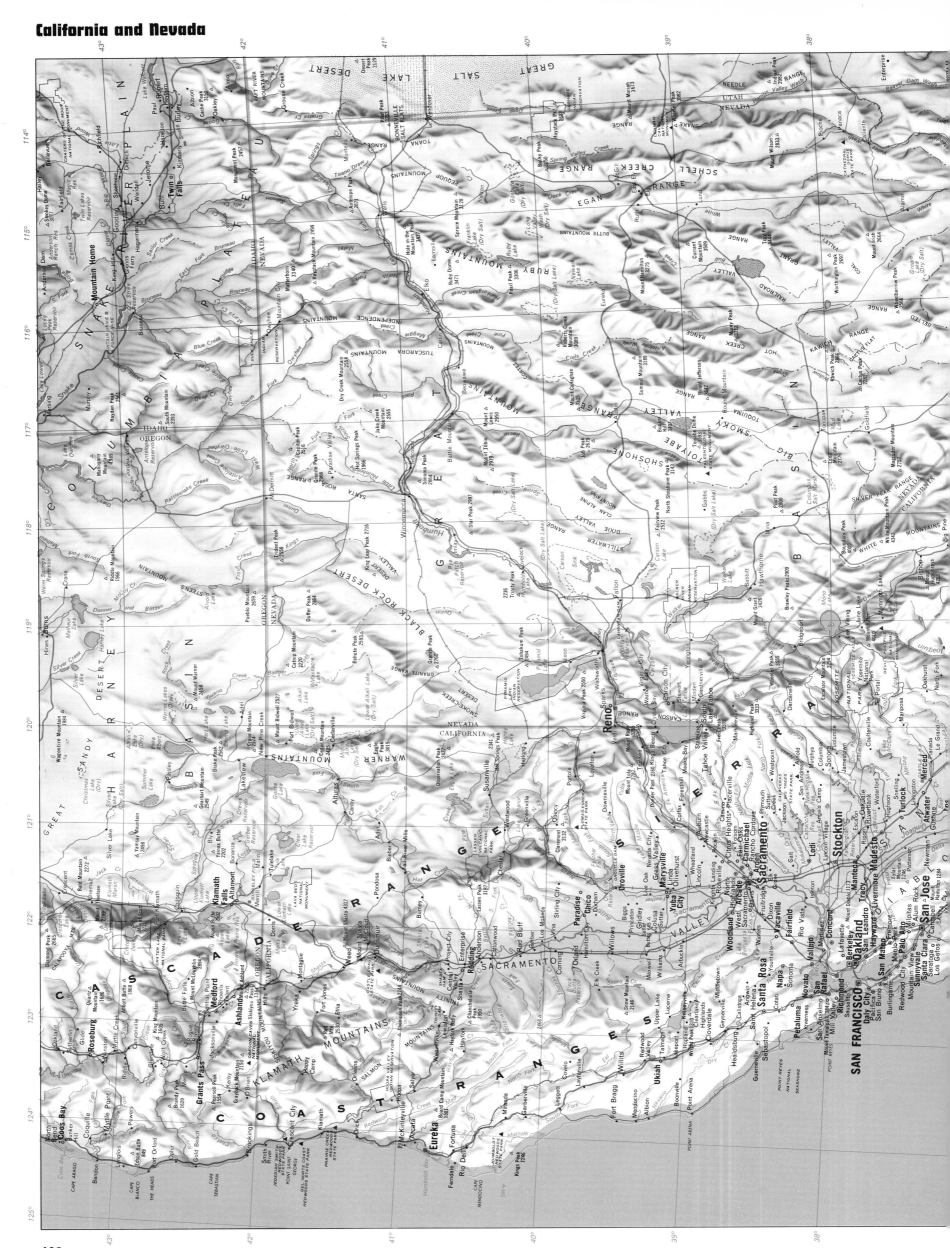

Hawaii

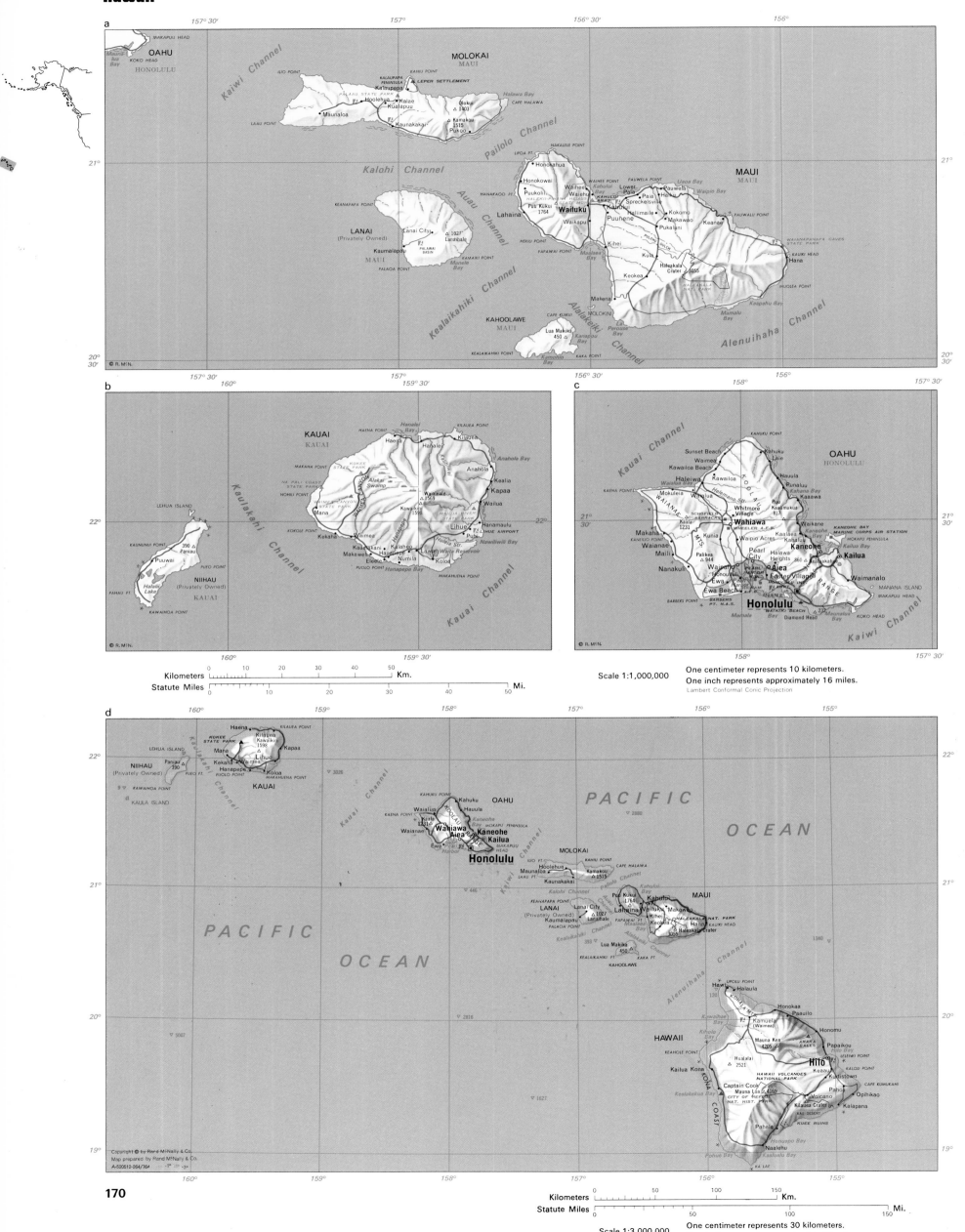

a

OAHU
HONOLULU

MOLOKAI
MAUI

MAKAPUU HEAD
Makapuu Bay
Mauna loa
KOKO HEAD

Kaiwi Channel
ILIO POINT
KALAUPAPA PENINSULA
Kalaupapa
KAHIU POINT
LEPER SETTLEMENT
Hoolehua
Kualapuu
Kalae
Maunaloa
Kaunakakai
Pukoo
Olokui △1403
Kamakou △1515
LAAU POINT
Halawa Bay
CAPE HALAWA
PALAAU STATE PARK

Pailolo Channel
LIPOA PT.
NAKALELE POINT
Honokahua
Honokowai
Kapalua
Kahakuloa
Waihee
Waiehu
Wailuku
Waikapu
Puu Kukui △1764
HALEAKALA—PUU NIANIAU
PAUWELA POINT
Uaoa Bay
Waipio Bay
Lower
Paia
Spreckelsville
Kahului
Kahului Bay
Puunene
Waihee Point
WAIHEE POINT
Kokomo
Makawao
Pukalani
Keanae
MAUI
MAUI
PAUWALU POINT
WAIANAPANAPA CAVES STATE PARK
Hana
Lahaina
Kihei
Kula
Keokea
Haleakala Crater △3055
HALEAKALA NAT. PARK
KAUIKI HEAD
Kaapahu Bay
HEKILI POINT
PAPAWAI POINT
Maalaea Bay
Makena
Makena
MOLOKINI
La Perouse Bay
Mamalu Bay
MUOLEA POINT

Kalohi Channel
Auau Channel

LANAI
(Privately Owned)
Lanai City △1027
Lanaihale
Kaumalapau
PALAWAI BASIN
MAUI
KAMAIKI POINT
PALAOA POINT
Manele Bay
KEANAPAPA POINT

KAHOOLAWE
MAUI
CAPE KUIKUI
Lua Makika 450 △
Kanapou Bay
KAKA POINT
KEALAIKAHIKI POINT
Kamohio Bay

Kealaikahiki Channel
Alalakeiki Channel
Alenuihaha Channel

R. McN.

b

KAUAI
KAUAI

LEHUA ISLAND
Hanalei Bay
Hanalei
HAENA POINT
Haena
KILAUEA POINT
Kilauea
Anahola Bay
NA PALI COAST STATE PARK
KOKEE STATE PARK
Alakai Swamp
WAIMEA CANYON
Waialeale △1569
Anahola
Kealia
Kapaa
Wailua
Mana
Kekaha
Waimea
Makaweli
Eleele
Hanapepe
Numila
Koloa
Kawaikini △1598
WAILUA RIVER STATE PARK
Hanamaulu
Lihue
Puhi
LIHUE AIRPORT
Nawiliwili Bay
Lawai
Waita Reservoir
NIIHAU
(Privately Owned)
KAUAI
Halalii Lake
Puuwai
Paniau △390
KAUNUINII POINT
PUEO POINT
PAHAU PT.
KAWAIHOA POINT
MAKAHUENA POINT
PUOLO POINT
Hanapepe Bay
NOHILI POINT
KOKOLE POINT

Kaulakahi Channel
Kauai Channel

R. McN.

c

OAHU
HONOLULU

KAHUKU POINT
Sunset Beach
Waimea
Kawailoa Beach
Kawailoa
Haleiwa
Mokuleia
Waialua
Kahuku
Laie
Hauula
Punaluu
Kahana Bay
Kaaawa
KAENA POINT
KOOLAU RANGE
WAIANAE MTS.
Waipio
Schofield Barracks
Wheeler A.F.B.
Wahiawa
Whitmore Village
Puu Kaumakua △817
Waikane
KANEOHE BAY MARINE CORPS AIR STATION
MOKAPU PENINSULA
Kailua Bay
Makaha
Kaala △1231
Kunia
Waipio Acres
Kahaluu
Kaneohe
Kailua
Waianae
Maili
Nanakuli
Palikea △944
Halawa Heights
Pearl City
Aiea
Foster Village
Honolulu
Ewa
Ewa Beach
Waipahu
Waimanalo
MANANA ISLAND
MAKAPUU HEAD
KOKO HEAD
BARBERS POINT
BARBERS PT. N.A.S.
WAIKIKI BEACH
Diamond Head
HONOLULU
Mamala Bay
Maunalua Bay

Kauai Channel
Kaiwi Channel

R. McN.

Scale 1:1,000,000

One centimeter represents 10 kilometers.
One inch represents approximately 16 miles.
Lambert Conformal Conic Projection

Kilometers 0 10 20 30 40 50 Km.
Statute Miles 0 10 20 30 40 50 Mi.

d

NIIHAU
(Privately Owned)
LEHUA ISLAND
Paniau △390
KAWAIHOA POINT
KAULA ISLAND

KAUAI
Haena
Mana
Kekaha
Hanapepe
KOKEE STATE PARK
Kilauea
Kawaikini △1598
Lihue
Waimea
Koloa
KILAUEA POINT
Kapaa
PUEO PT.
MAKAHUENA POINT
Kaulakahi Channel

OAHU
HONOLULU
Kahuku
Hauula
Waialua
Kaala △1231
Wahiawa
Aiea
Kaneohe
Kailua
Waianae
Ewa
Honolulu
KAENA POINT
MOKAPU PENINSULA
Kaneohe Bay
MAKAPUU HEAD
Pearl Harbor

PACIFIC OCEAN

PACIFIC OCEAN

MOLOKAI
Hoolehua
Maunaloa
Kaunakakai
ILIO POINT
LAAU POINT
Kamakou △1515
KAHIU POINT
CAPE HALAWA
Kalohi Channel
Pailolo Channel
Kaiwi Channel

LANAI
(Privately Owned)
Lanai City △1027
Lanaihale
Kaumalapau
KEANAPAPA POINT
PAPAWAI PT.
Maalaea Bay
Lua Makika 450 △
KAHOOLAWE
KEALAIKAHIKI POINT
KAKA PT.

MAUI
Lahaina
Wailuku
Kahului
Puu Kukui △1764
Makawao
Kihei
Keokea
Hana
Haleakala Crater △3055
HALEAKALA NAT. PARK
KAUIKI HEAD
Alenuihaha Channel

HAWAII
Hawi
Halaula
Honokaa
Paauilo
Kamuela (Waimea)
Honomu
Mauna Kea △4205
Papaikou
AKAKA FALLS
Hualalai △2521
Hilo
Kailua Kona
Captain Cook
Mauna Loa △4169
CITY OF REFUGE NAT. HIST. PARK
HAWAII VOLCANOES NATIONAL PARK
Kilauea Crater △
Volcano
Pahoa
Opihikao
Kalapana
KUEE RUINS
Pahala
Naalehu
KONA COAST
KOHALA MTS.
UPOLU POINT
KEAHOLE POINT
Kawaihae Bay
Hilo Bay
LELEIWI POINT
CAPE KUMUKAHI
KALAE POINT
Honuapo Bay
Pohue Bay
KA LAE

PACIFIC OCEAN

Scale 1:3,000,000

One centimeter represents 30 kilometers.
One inch represents approximately 47 miles.
Lambert Conformal Conic Projection

Kilometers 0 50 100 150 Km.
Statute Miles 0 50 100 150 Mi.

Legend to City Maps

Inhabited Localities

The symbol represents the number of inhabitants within the locality

- · 0—10,000
- ○ 10,000—25,000
- ◉ 25,000—100,000
- ⊡ 100,000—250,000
- ▣ 250,000—1,000,000
- ■ >1,000,000

The size of type indicates the relative economic and political importance of the locality

Écommoy	**Rouen**
Trouville	
Lisieux	**PARIS**
■	

Hollywood — Section of a City,
Westminster — Neighborhood
Northland ■
Center — Major Shopping Center

Urban Area (area of continuous industrial, commercial, and residential development)

Major Industrial Area

Wooded Area

Local Park or Recreational Area

Transportation

Road

PASSAIC EXPWY. (I-80) — Primary

BERLINER RING — Secondary

— Tertiary

Railway

CANADIAN NATIONAL — Primary

— Secondary

— Rapid Transit

Airport

LONDON (HEATHROW) AIRPORT

Rail or Air Terminal

SÜD BAHNHOF

REICHS-BRÜCKE — Bridge

GREAT ST. BERNARD TUNNEL — Tunnel

Houston Ship Channel — Shipping Channel

Canal du Midi — Navigable Canal

TO MALMÖ — Ferry

Miscellaneous Cultural Features

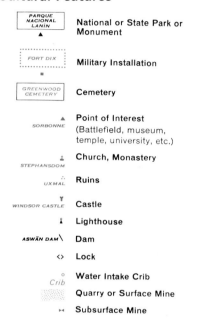

PARQUE NACIONAL LANÍN ▲	National or State Park or Monument
FORT DIX ■	Military Installation
GREENWOOD CEMETERY	Cemetery
▲ SORBONNE	Point of Interest (Battlefield, museum, temple, university, etc.)
⌘ STEPHANSDOM	Church, Monastery
∴ UXMAL	Ruins
� WINDSOR CASTLE	Castle
⚑	Lighthouse
ASWĀN DAM \	Dam
<>	Lock
○ Crib	Water Intake Crib
	Quarry or Surface Mine
⋈	Subsurface Mine

Political Boundaries

International (First-order political unit)

—·—·— Demarcated, Undemarcated, and Administrative

— — — — Demarcation Line

Internal

State, Province, etc. (Second-order political unit)

County, Oblast, etc. (Third-order political unit)

- - - - - Okrug, Kreis, etc. (Fourth-order political unit)

-------- City or Municipality (may appear in combination with another boundary symbol)

Capitals of Political Units

BUDAPEST	Independent Nation
Recife	State, Province, etc.
White Plains	County, Oblast, etc.
Iserlohn	Okrug, Kreis, etc.

Hydrographic Features

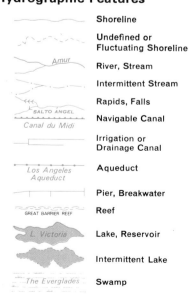

Shoreline

Undefined or Fluctuating Shoreline

Amur — River, Stream

Intermittent Stream

Rapids, Falls

SALTO ANGEL — Navigable Canal

Canal du Midi

Irrigation or Drainage Canal

Los Angeles Aqueduct — Aqueduct

Pier, Breakwater

GREAT BARRIER REEF — Reef

L. Victoria — Lake, Reservoir

Intermittent Lake

The Everglades — Swamp

Topographic Features

Mt. Kenya 5199 △ — Elevation Above Sea Level

Elevations are given in meters

⋆ Rock

A N D E S — Mountain Range, Plateau,
KUNLUNSHANMAI — Valley, etc.

BAFFIN ISLAND — Island

POLUOSTROV KAMČATKA — Peninsula, Cape, Point, etc.
CABO DE HORNOS

Paris

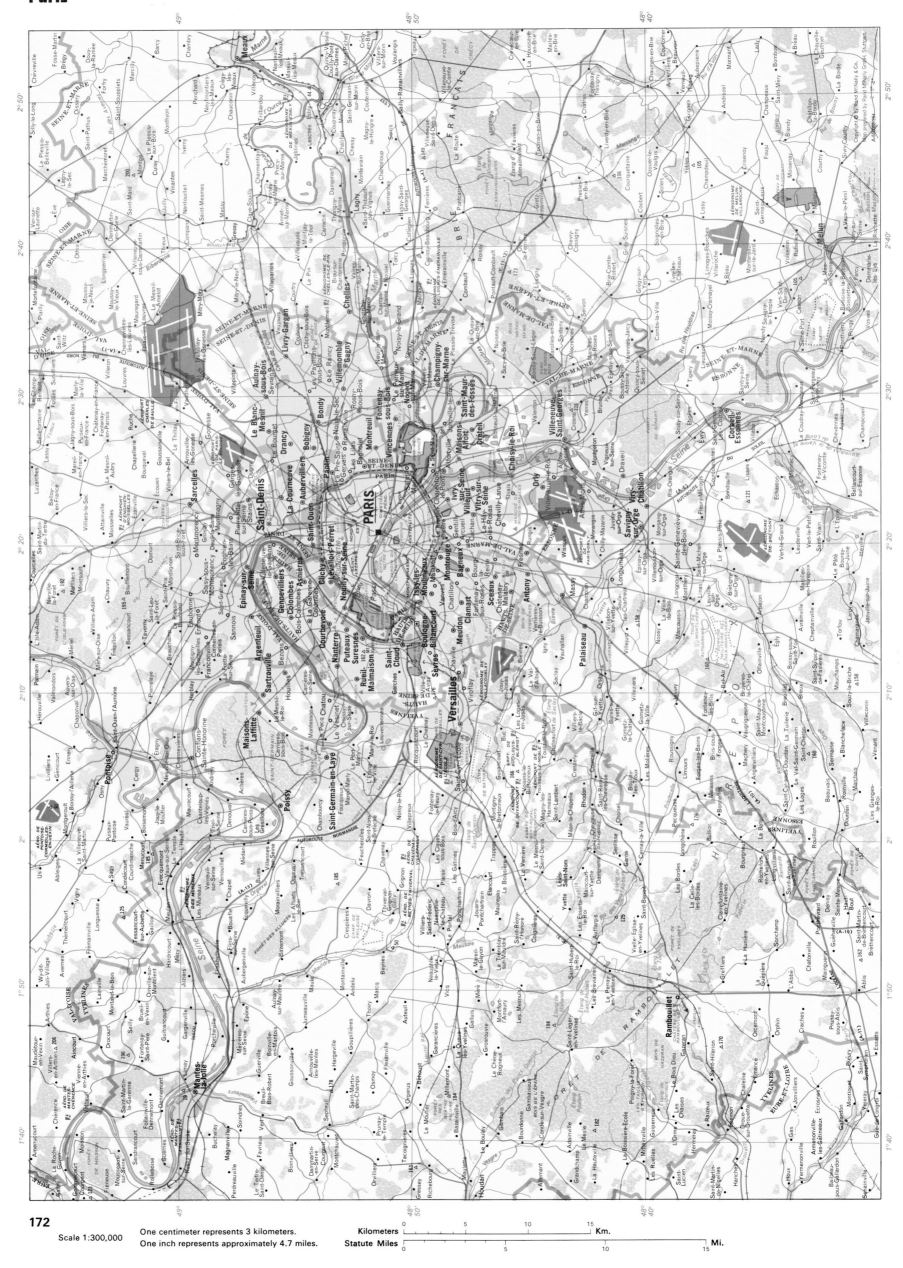

Scale 1:300,000

One centimeter represents 3 kilometers.
One inch represents approximately 4.7 miles.

Kilometers
0   5   10   15   Km.

Statute Miles
0   5   10   15   Mi.

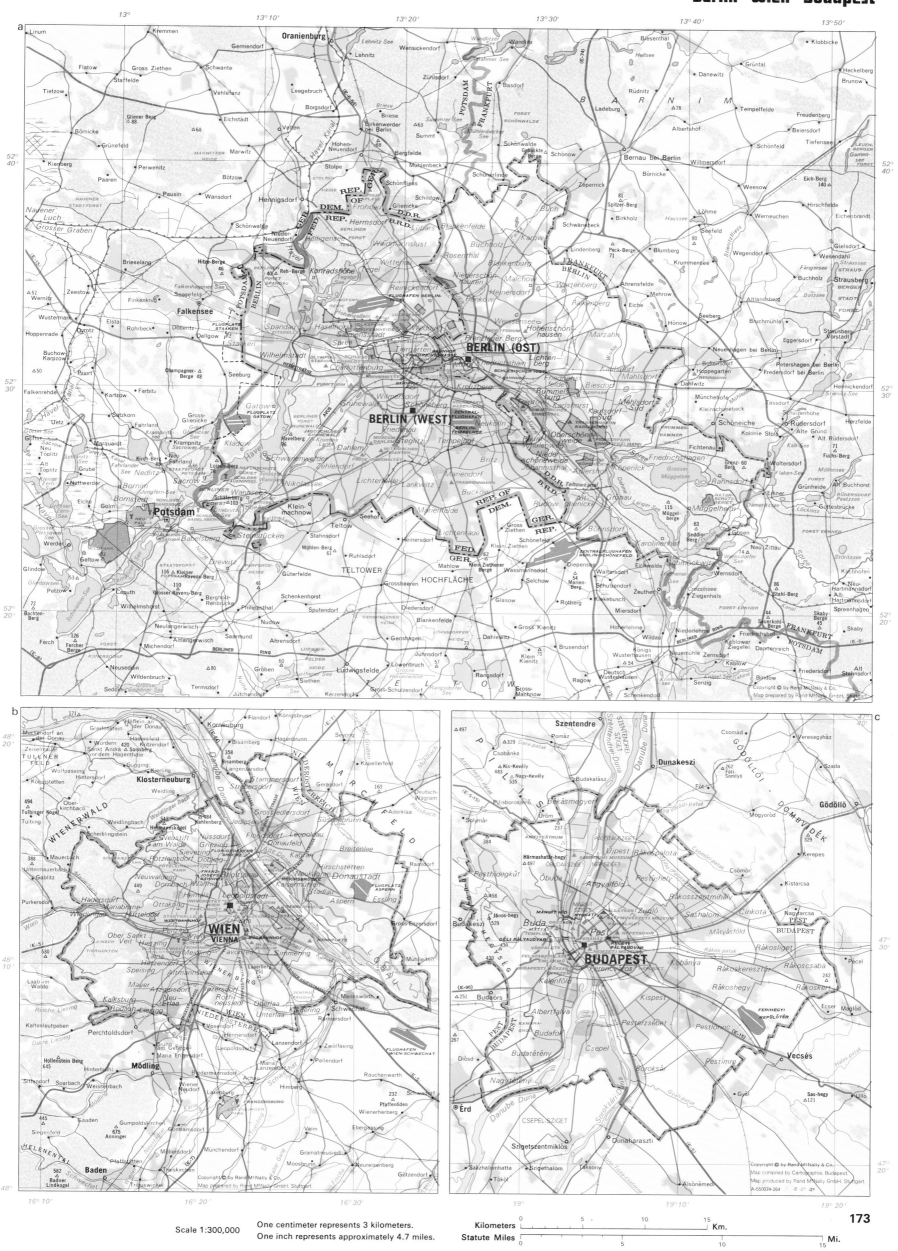

Scale 1:300,000

One centimeter represents 3 kilometers.
One inch represents approximately 4.7 miles.

Kilometers

Statute Miles

173

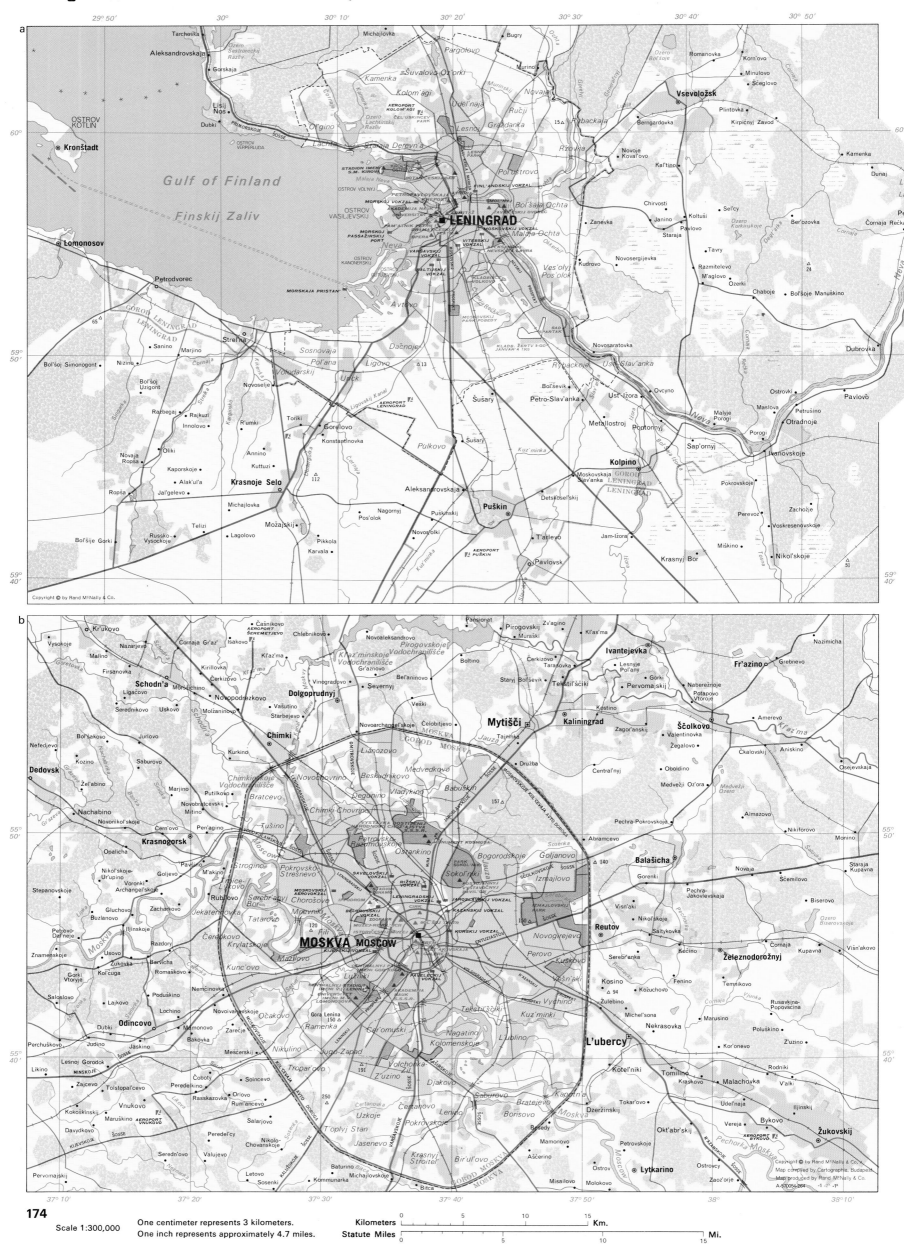

Scale 1:300,000

One centimeter represents 3 kilometers.
One inch represents approximately 4.7 miles.

Scale 1:300,000
One centimeter represents 3 kilometers.
One inch represents approximately 4.7 miles.

Kilometers
Statute Miles

London

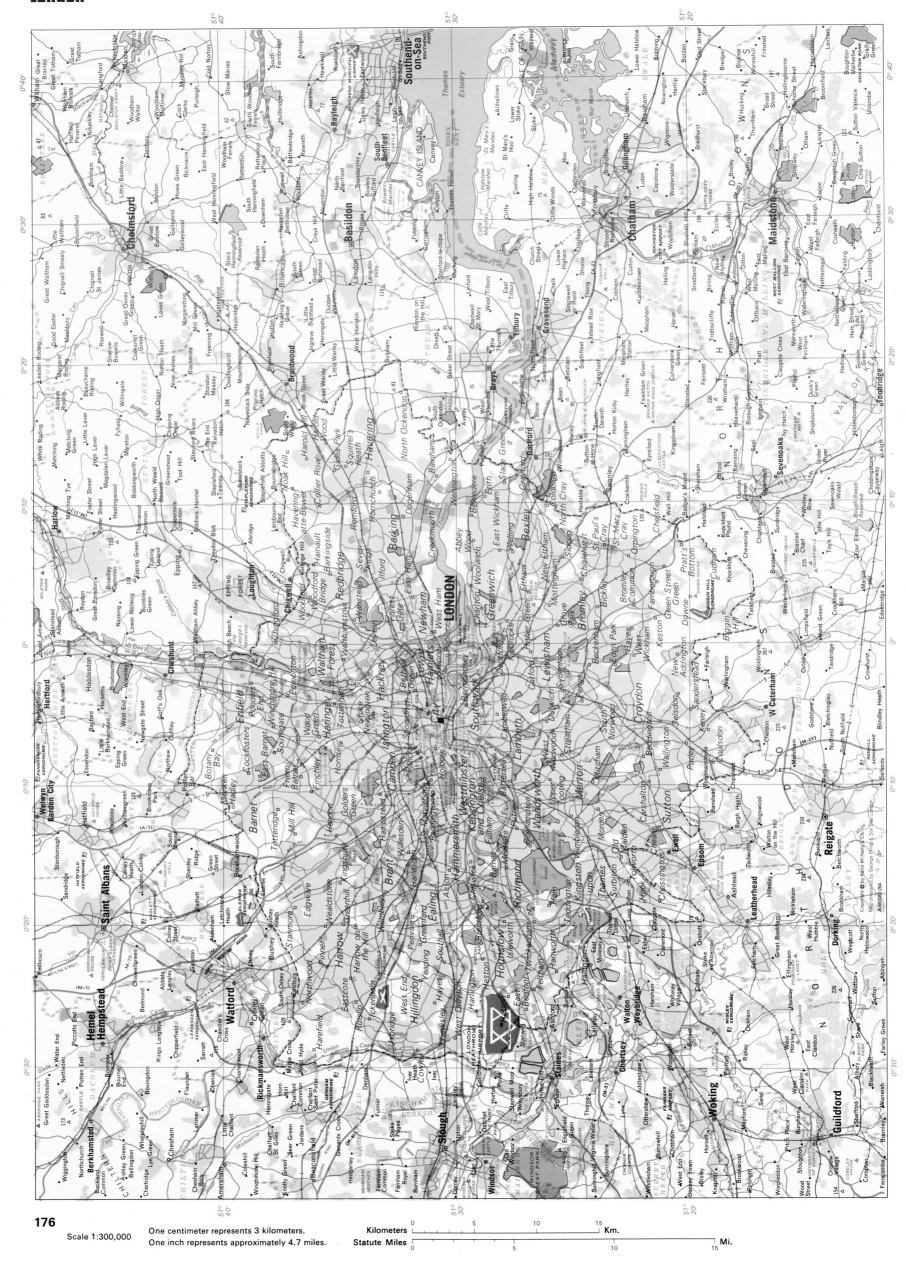

Scale 1:300,000

One centimeter represents 3 kilometers.
One inch represents approximately 4.7 miles.

Kilometers

Statute Miles

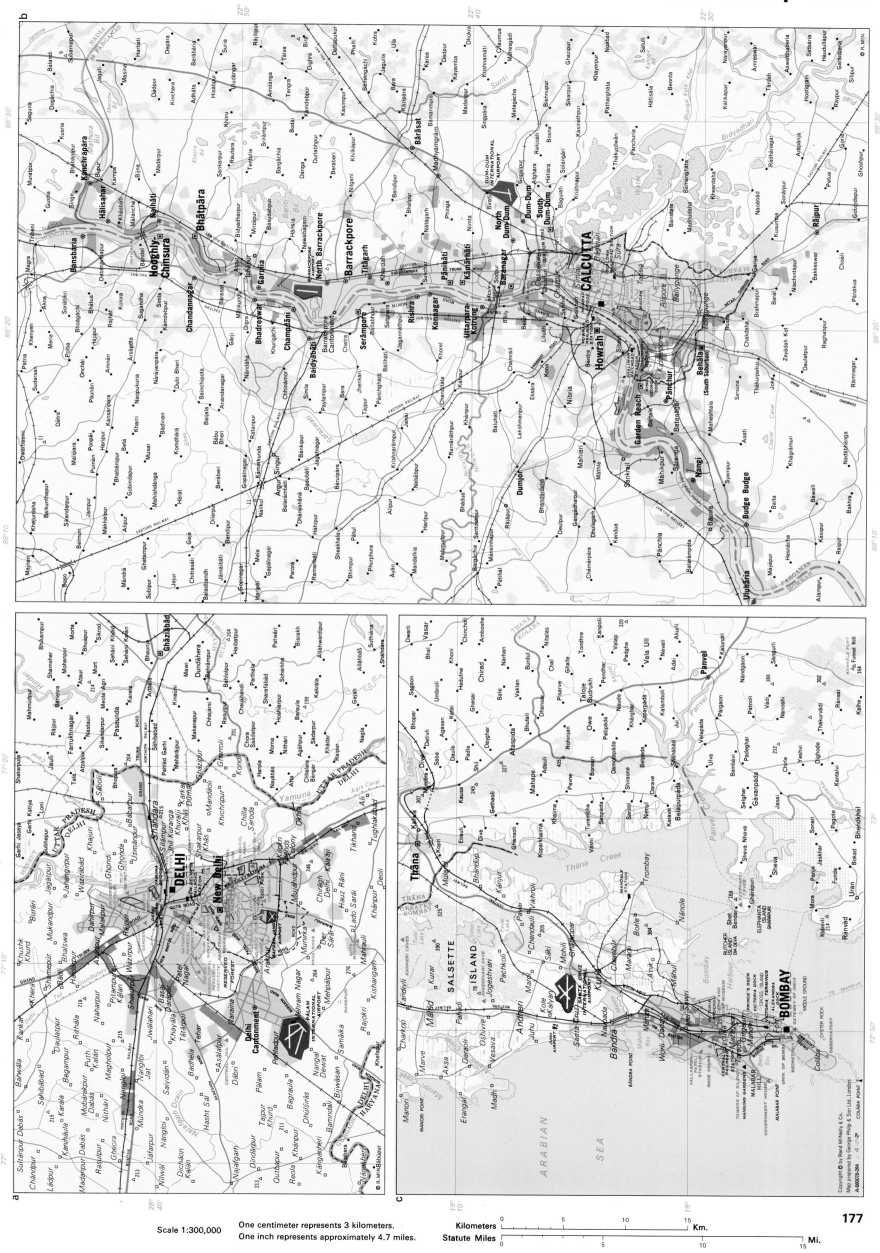

177

Scale 1:300,000

One centimeter represents 3 kilometers.
One inch represents approximately 4.7 miles.

Kilometers

Statute Miles

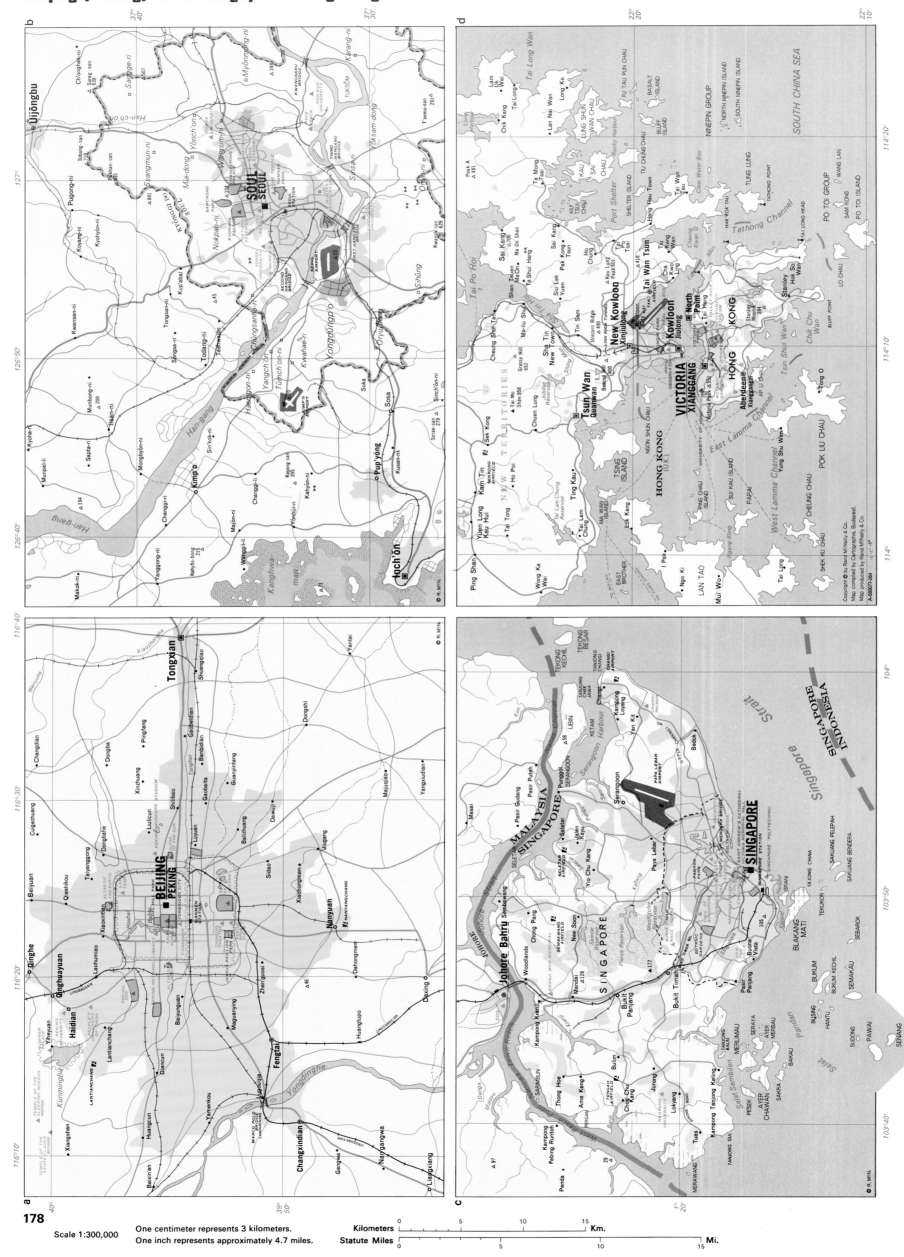

Scale 1:300,000
One centimeter represents 3 kilometers.
One inch represents approximately 4.7 miles.

Kilometers
Statute Miles

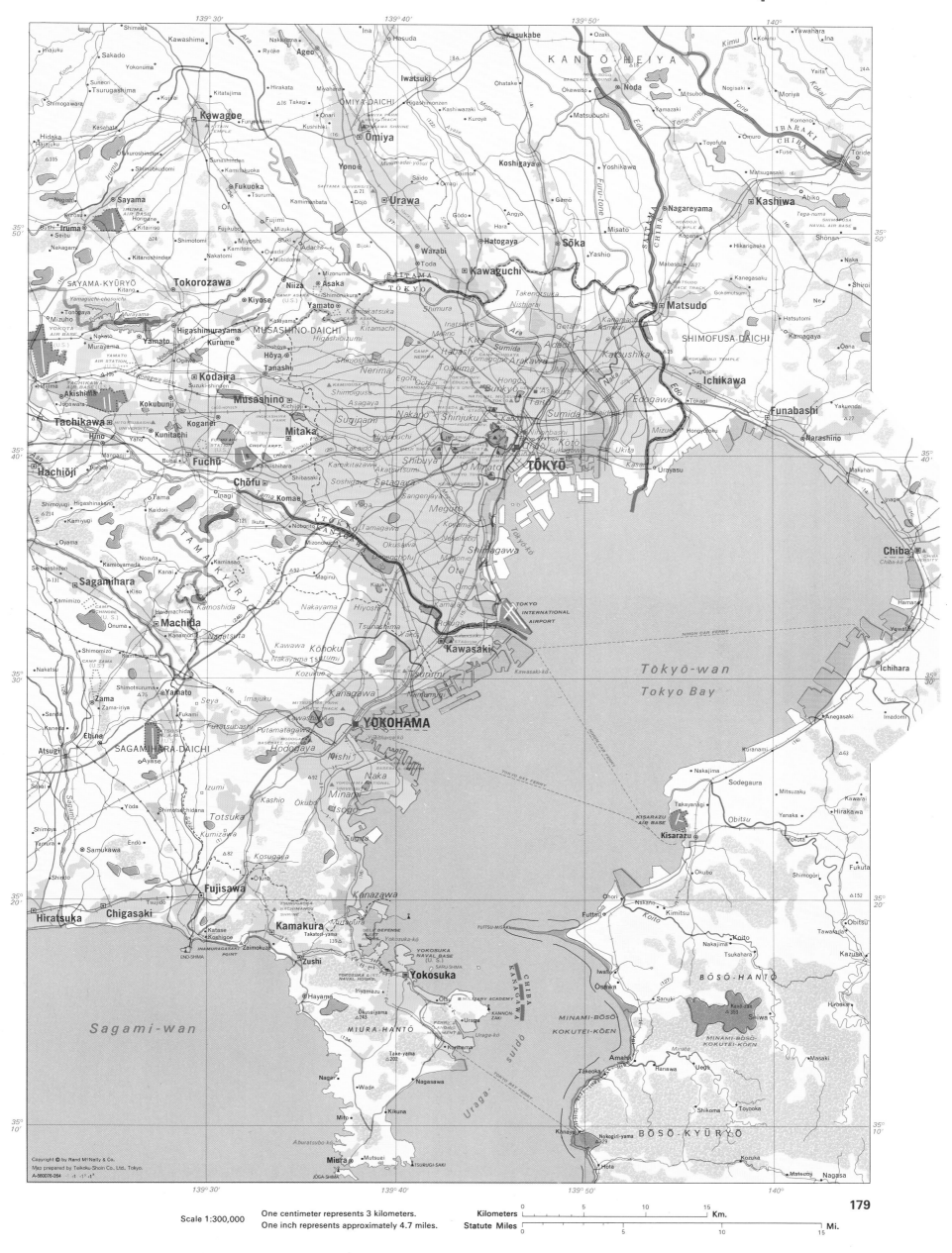

Tōkyō—Yokohama

Scale 1:300,000
One centimeter represents 3 kilometers.
One inch represents approximately 4.7 miles.

Kilometers
Statute Miles

Copyright © by Rand McNally & Co.
Map prepared by Teikoku-Shoin Co. Ltd. Tokyo.
A-560076-264

Krung Thep (Bangkok) · Sai-gon · Djakarta · Shanghai · Taipei · Manila

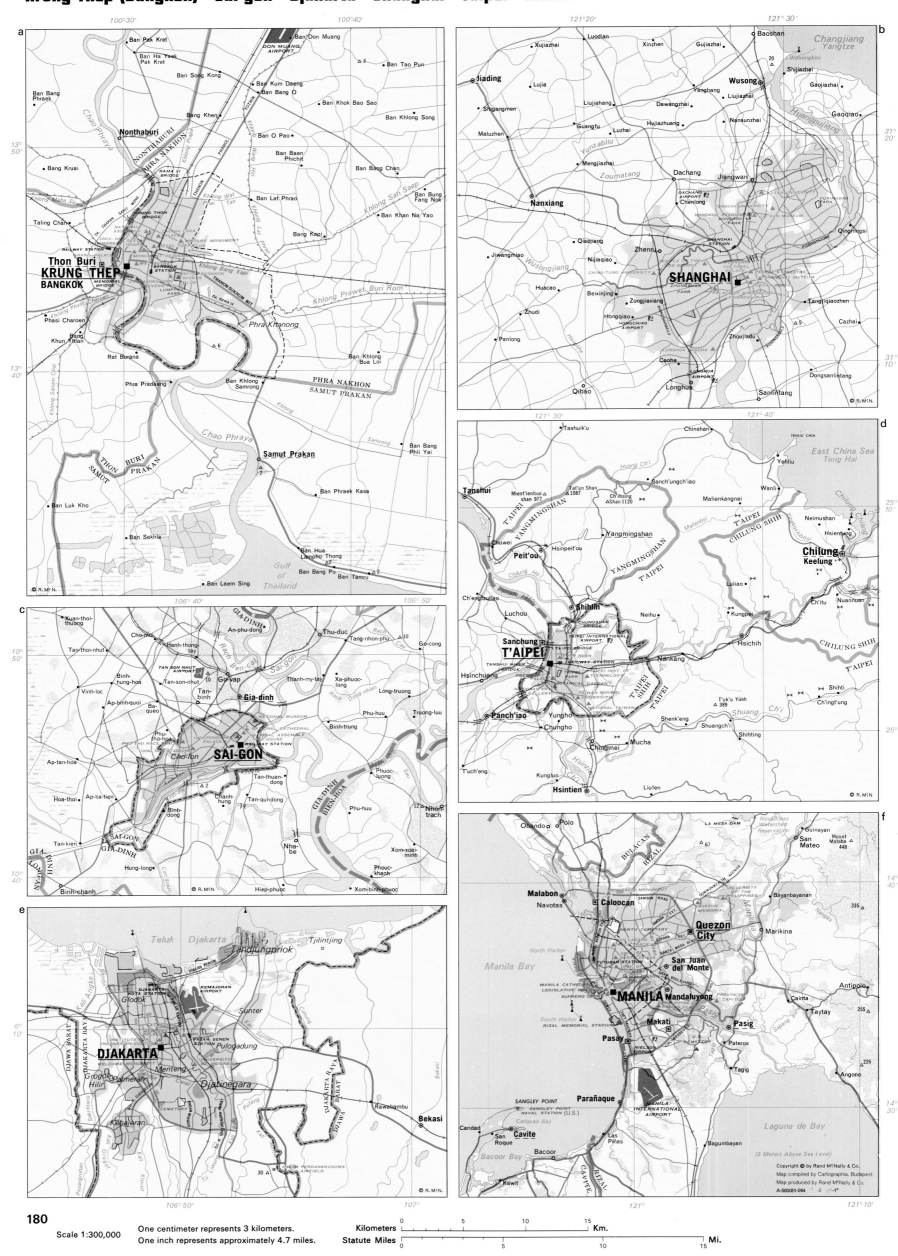

Scale 1:300,000

One centimeter represents 3 kilometers.
One inch represents approximately 4.7 miles.

Kilometers 0   5   10   15 Km.

Statute Miles 0   5   10   15 Mi.

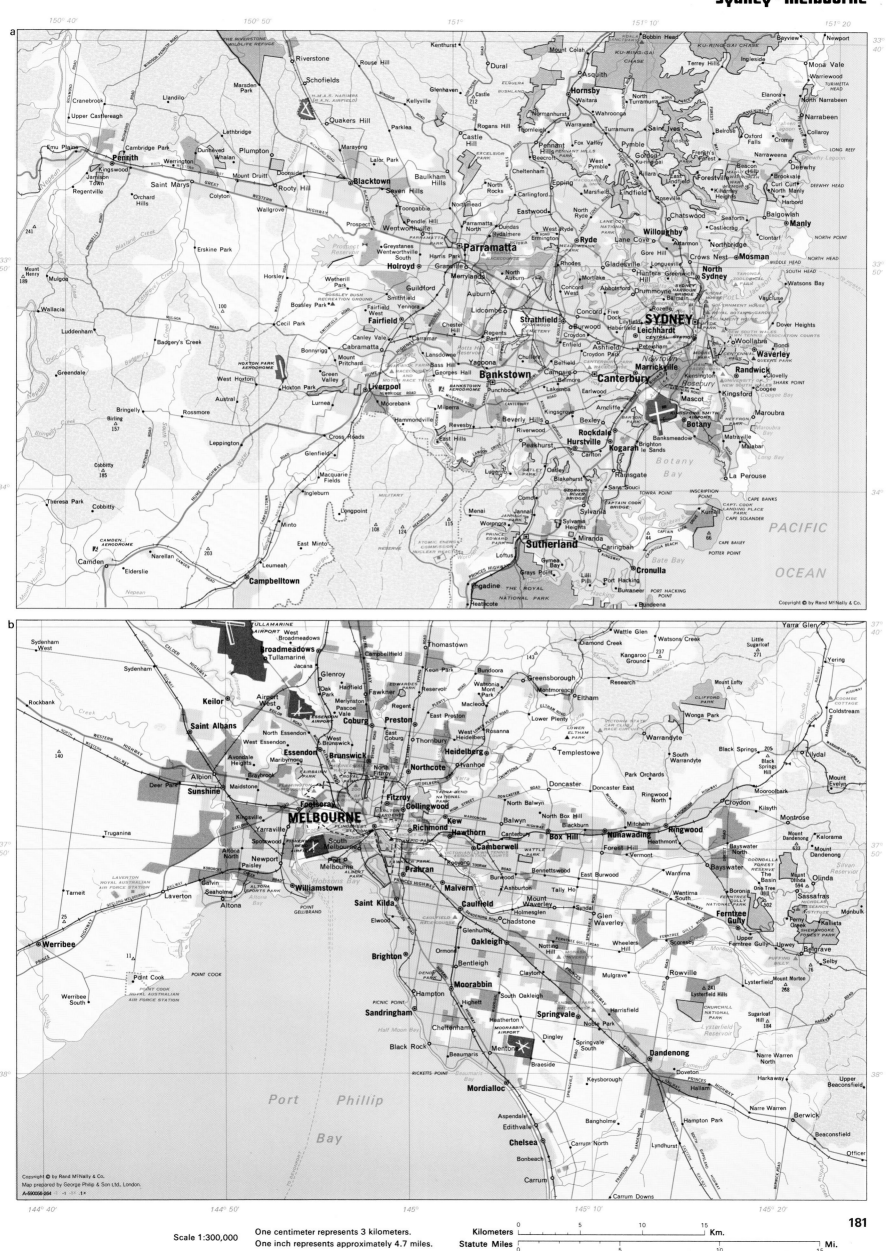

181

Scale 1:300,000   One centimeter represents 3 kilometers.
One inch represents approximately 4.7 miles.

Kilometers
Statute Miles

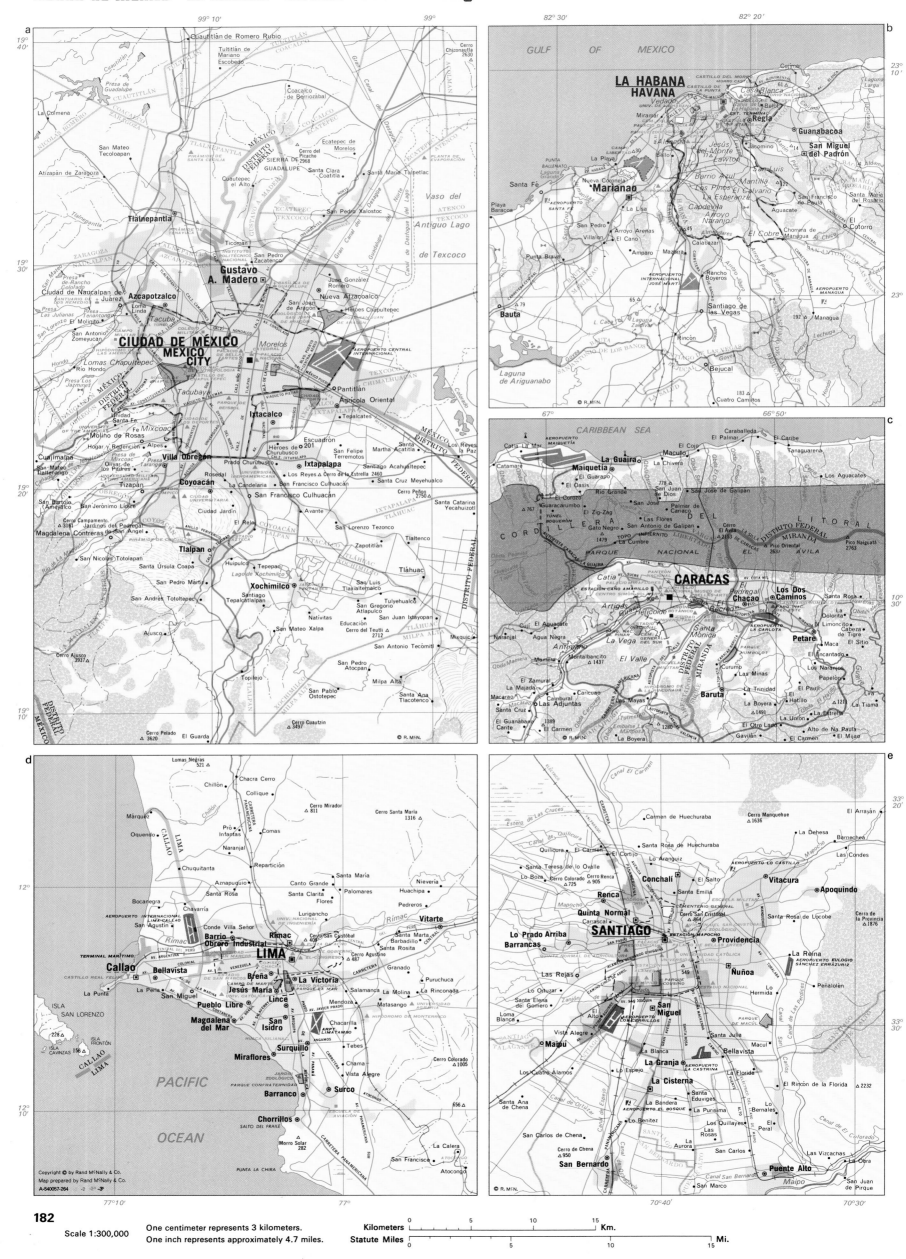

Scale 1:300,000

One centimeter represents 3 kilometers.
One inch represents approximately 4.7 miles.

Kilometers 0 5 10 15 Km.

Statute Miles 0 5 10 15 Mi.

Copyright © by Rand McNally & Co.
Map prepared by Rand McNally & Co.

A-540057-264

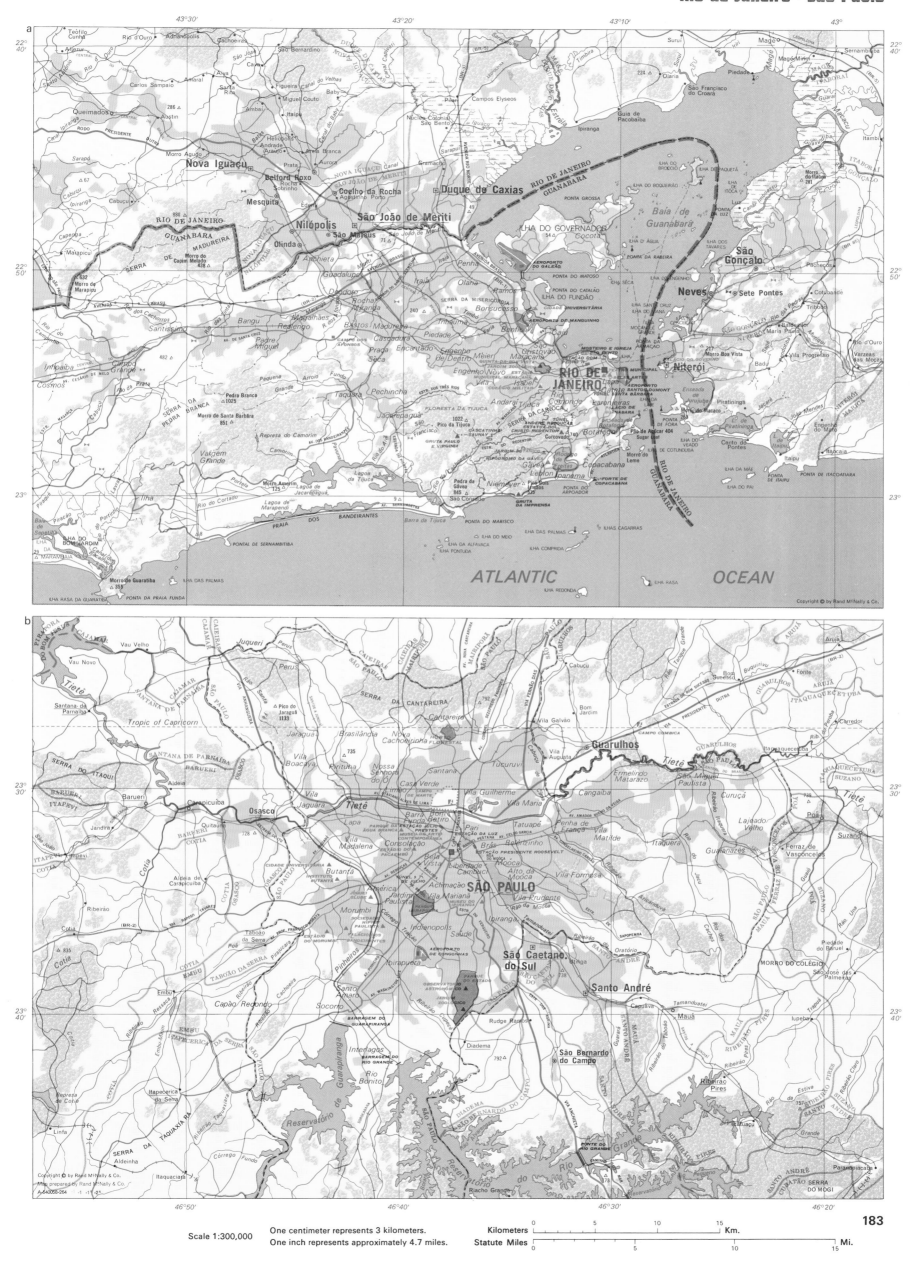

a

b

Scale 1:300,000

One centimeter represents 3 kilometers.
One inch represents approximately 4.7 miles.

Kilometers 0 5 10 15 Km.

Statute Miles 0 5 10 15 Mi.

Montréal · Toronto

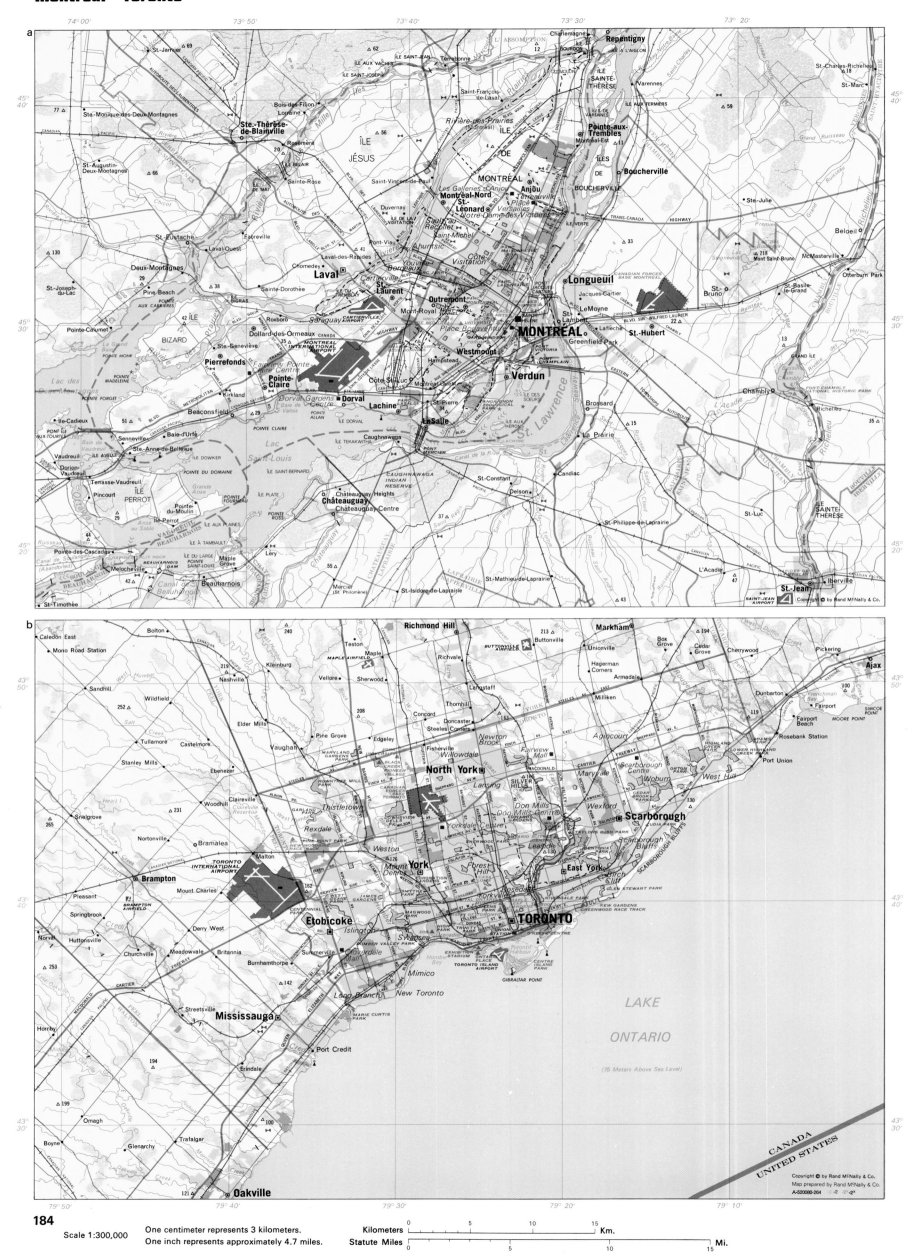

Scale 1:300,000

One centimeter represents 3 kilometers.
One inch represents approximately 4.7 miles.

Kilometers
Statute Miles

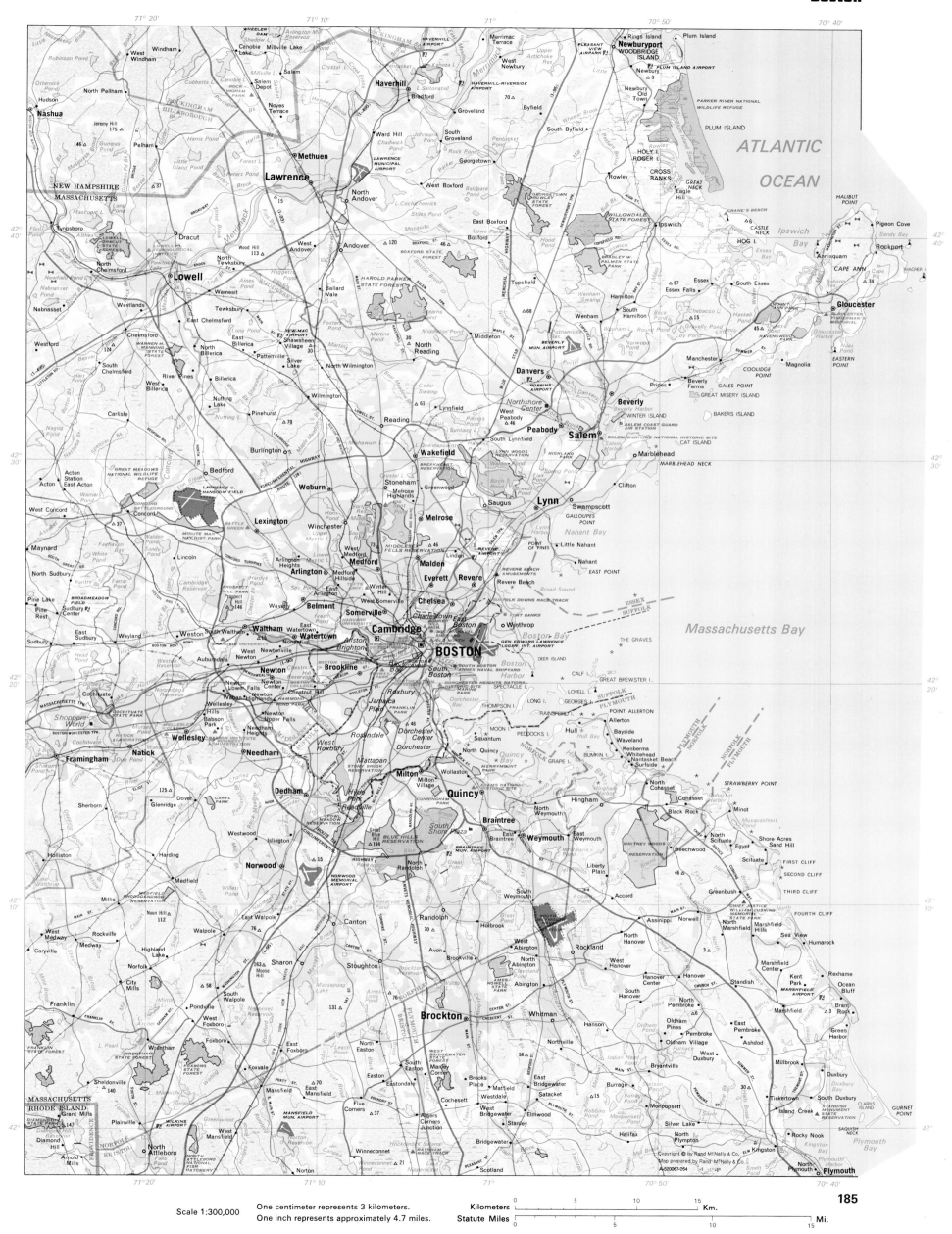

ATLANTIC
OCEAN

Massachusetts Bay

Scale 1:300,000

One centimeter represents 3 kilometers.
One inch represents approximately 4.7 miles.

Kilometers

Statute Miles

Scale 1:300,000

One centimeter represents 3 kilometers.
One inch represents approximately 4.7 miles.

Kilometers

Statute Miles

Philadelphia

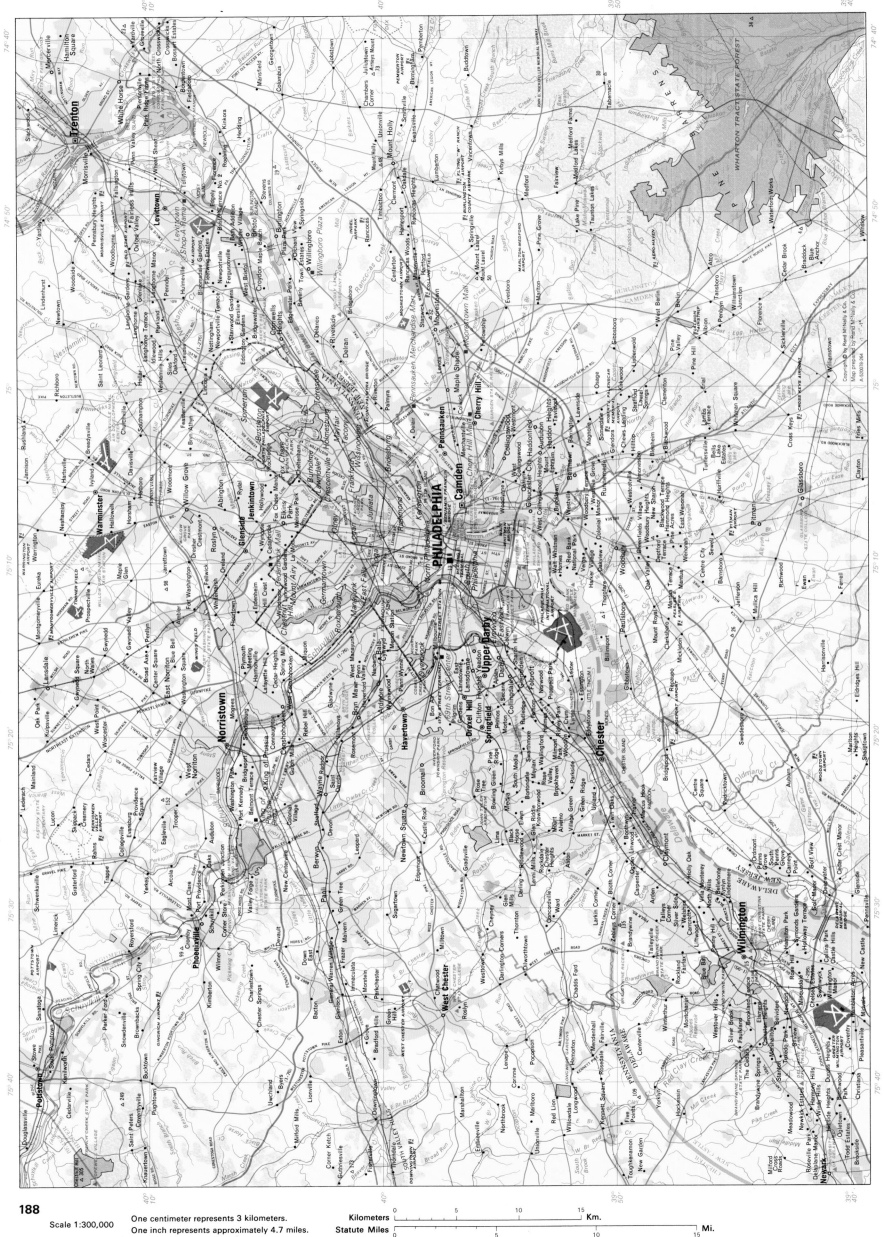

Scale 1:300,000

One centimeter represents 3 kilometers.
One inch represents approximately 4.7 miles.

Kilometers | 0 . . . 5 . . . 10 . . . 15 . . . Km.

Statute Miles | 0 . . . 5 . . . 10 . . . 15 . . . Mi.

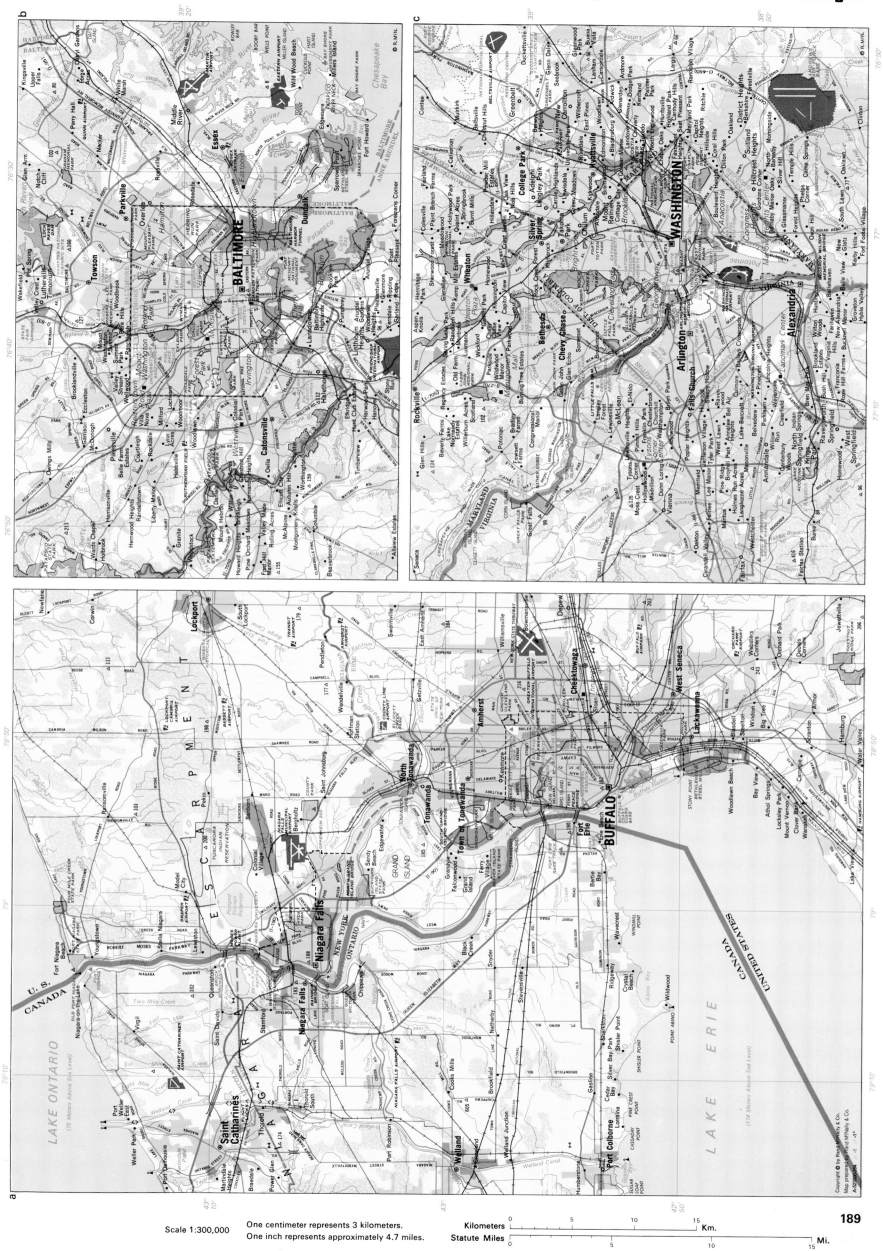

Scale 1:300,000

One centimeter represents 3 kilometers.
One inch represents approximately 4.7 miles.

Kilometers

0   5   10   15   Km.

Statute Miles

0   5   10   15   Mi.

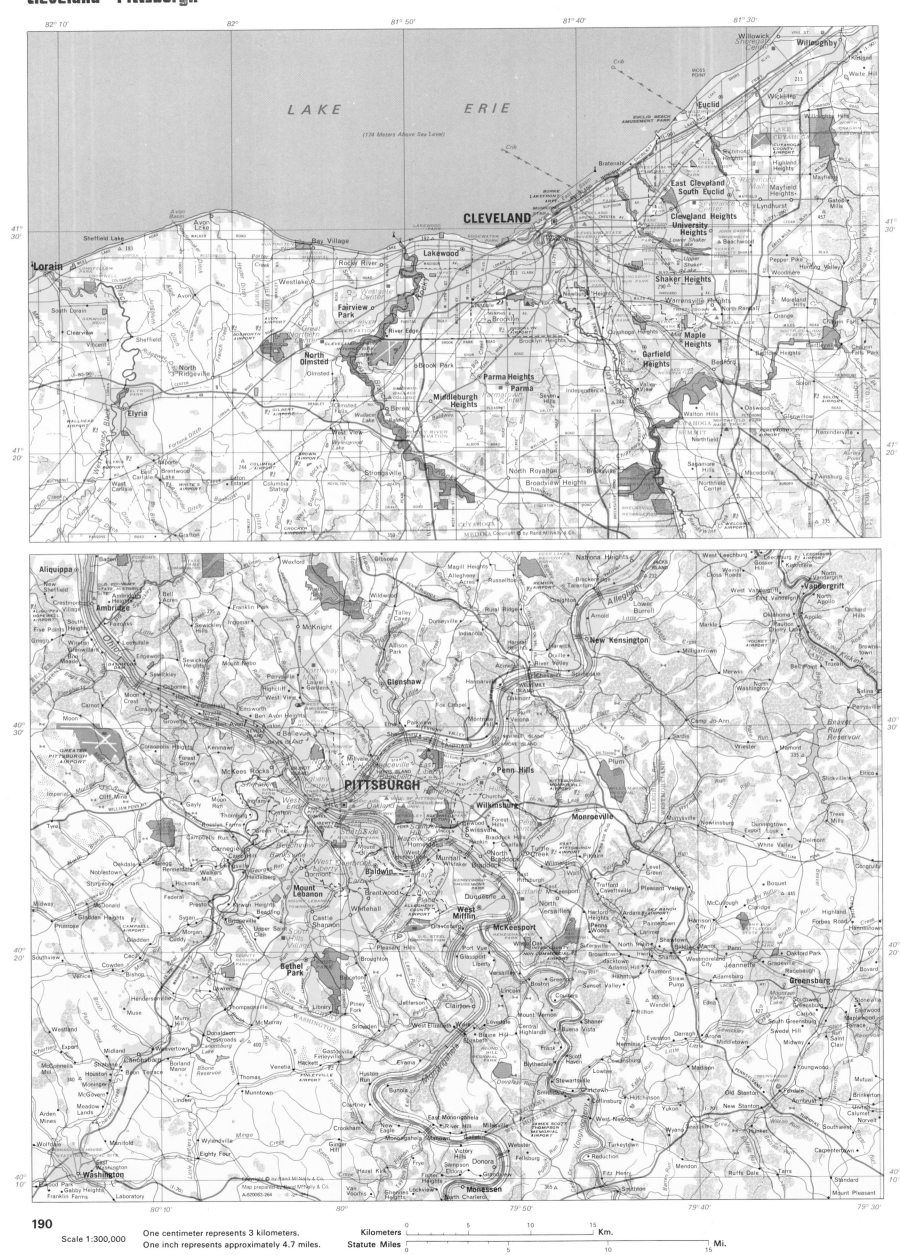

190

Scale 1:300,000

One centimeter represents 3 kilometers.
One inch represents approximately 4.7 miles.

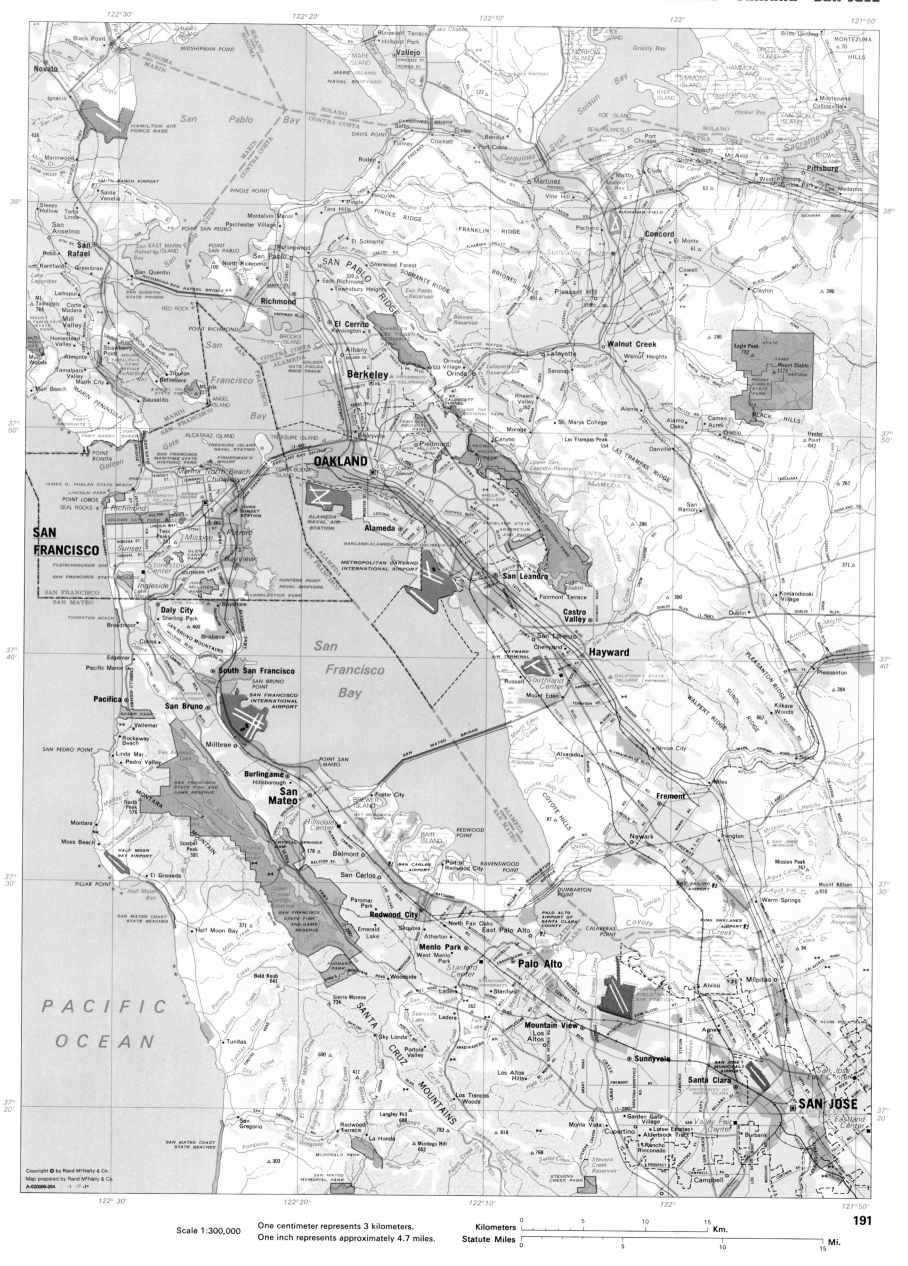

191

Scale 1:300,000

One centimeter represents 3 kilometers.
One inch represents approximately 4.7 miles.

Kilometers 0 5 10 15 Km.

Statute Miles 0 5 10 15 Mi.

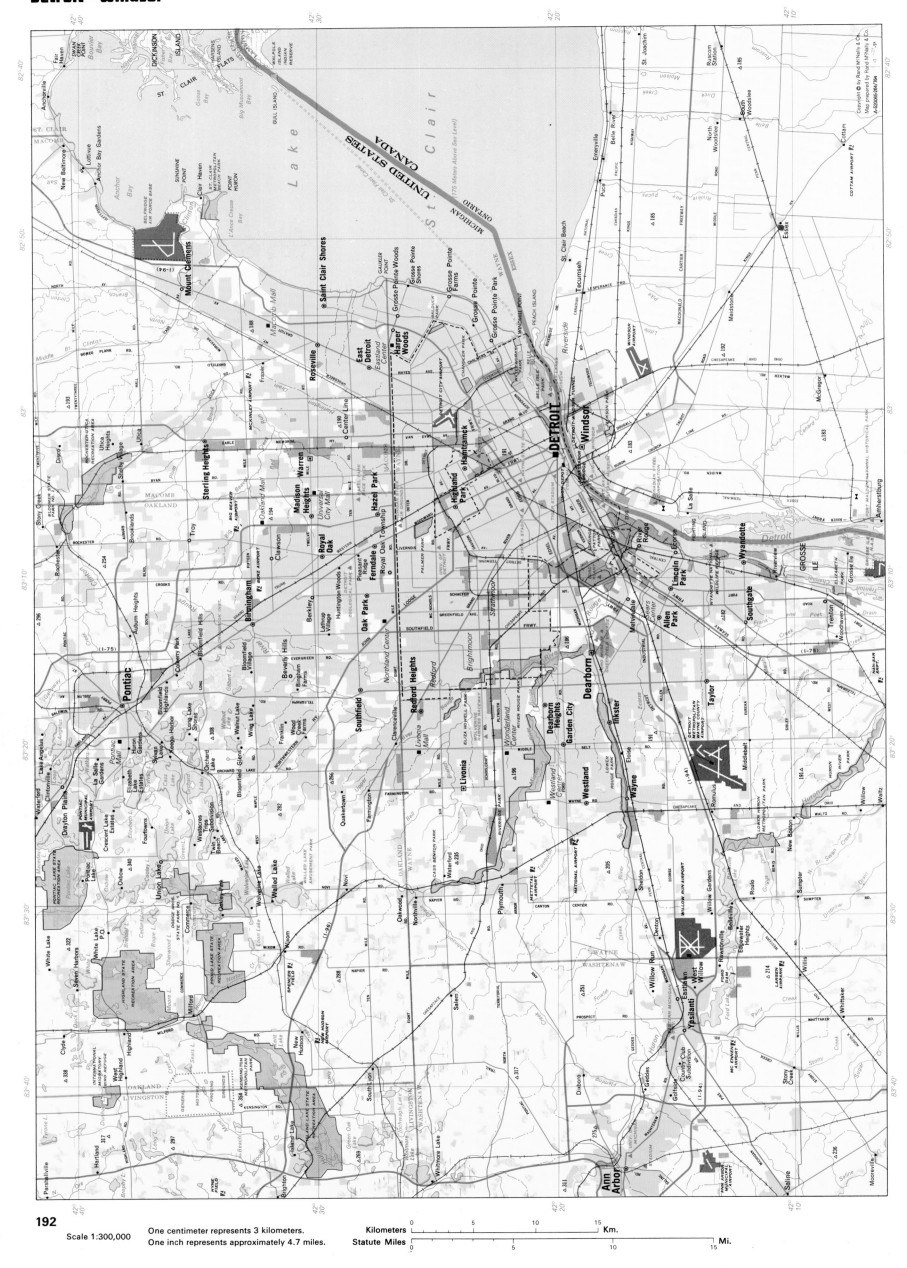

Scale 1:300,000

One centimeter represents 3 kilometers.
One inch represents approximately 4.7 miles.

Kilometers 0   5   10   15   Km.

Statute Miles 0   5   10   15   Mi.

LAKE

MICHIGAN

(176 Meters Above Sea Level)

ILLINOIS
INDIANA

Scale 1:300,000
One centimeter represents 3 kilometers.
One inch represents approximately 4.7 miles.

Kilometers
Statute Miles

193

Los Angeles

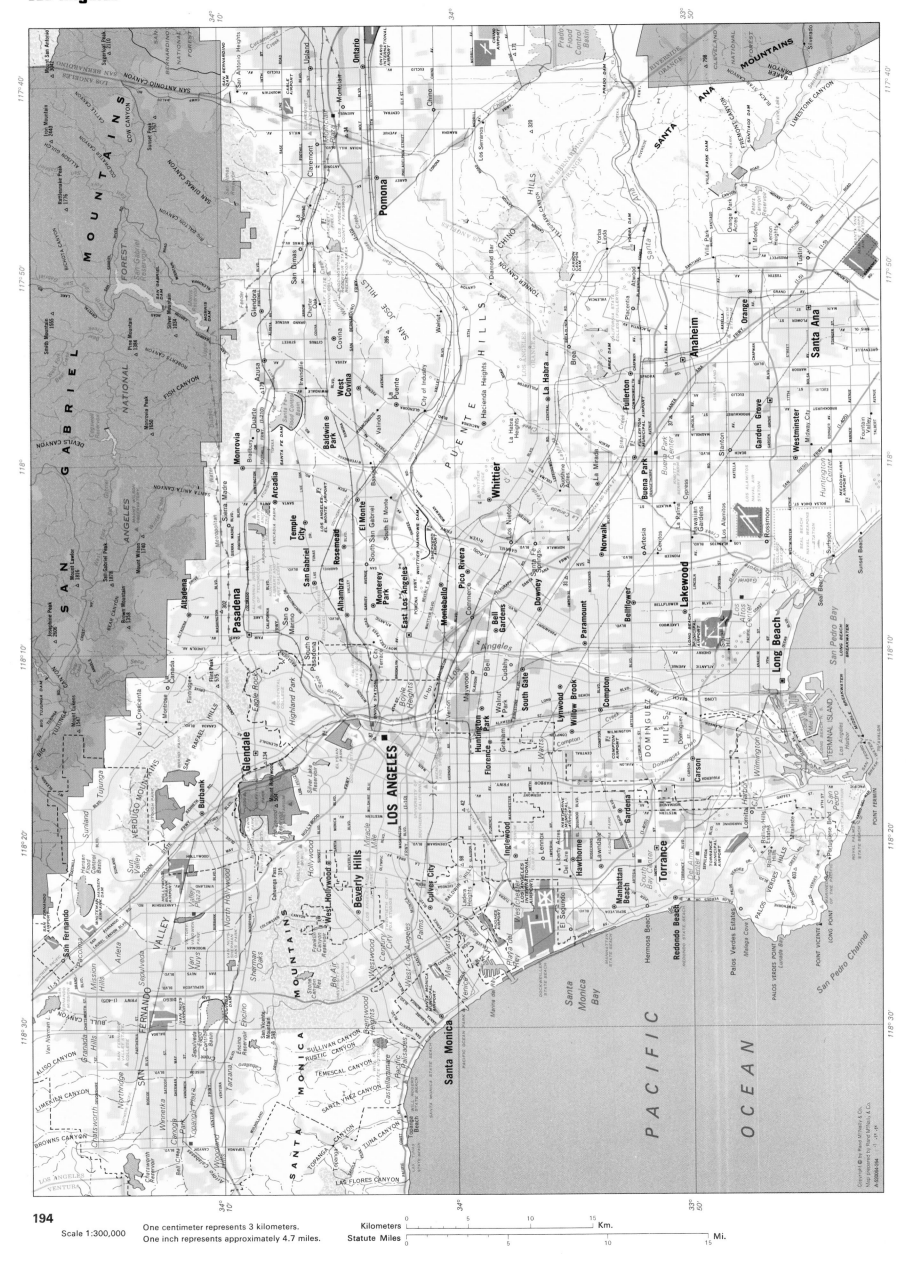

Scale 1:300,000

One centimeter represents 3 kilometers.
One inch represents approximately 4.7 miles.

Kilometers

Km.

Statute Miles

Mi.

Acknowledgments

Chief Editorial Consultants and Advisers

B. W. Atkinson, Ph.D., B.Sc.,
Dept. of Geography, Queen Mary College, University of London
Prof. K. F. Bowden, D.Sc., S.Inst.P.,
Professor of Oceanography, University of Liverpool
Graham Chedd, B.A.,
Life Science Editor, *New Scientist*
Miss A. Coleman, M.A.,
Reader in Geography, King's College, University of London
R. Dearnley, Ph.D., B.Sc., F.G.S.,
Principal Geologist, Institute of Geological Sciences, London
Prof. A. N. Duckham, C.B.E., F.I.Biol.,
Professor Emeritus, Dept. of Agriculture, University of Reading
F. W. Dunning, B.Sc., F.G.S.,
Curator, Geological Museum, London
David Fishlock,
Science Editor, *Financial Times*
Ken Gatland, F.R.A.S., F.B.I.S.,
Aerospace Consultant, Vice President, British Interplanetary Society

Arch C. Gerlach, Ph.D.,
lately Chief Geographer, U.S. Geological Survey
Prof. G. Melvyn Howe, Ph.D., M.Sc., F.R.G.S., F.R.Met.Soc.,
Professor of Geography, University of Strathclyde
Prof. Emrys Jones, Ph.D., M.Sc., F.R.G.S.,
Professor of Geography, London School of Economics
Patrick Moore, O.B.E., F.R.A.S.
A. Mountjoy, M.C., M.A., F.R.G.S.,
Reader in Geography, Bedford College, University of London
National Aeronautics and Space Administration
Prof. Sir Alan S. Parkes, C.B.E., Ph.D., D.Sc., Sc.D., F.R.S.,
Chairman, The Galton Foundation, London
Brian Stafford,
Industrial Consultant
Margaret Walters, Ph.D., B.Sc.,
formerly of Chester Beatty Research Institute, London

General Acknowledgments

A great many people and institutions have given advice and assistance during the preparation of this book. The publishers wish to extend their thanks to them all, and in particular to the following :

Air Pollution Research Unit (M.R.C.), London. Bedford College, London. British Antarctic Survey. British Leyland, Coventry. British Museum of Natural History. Brookhaven National Laboratory, U.S.A. California Academy of Sciences. Chevron Oil (U.K.) Ltd. Cranfield Institute of Technology. The *Daily Telegraph.* Deep Sea Venture Inc. (U.S.A.). Directors of Overseas Surveys (U.K.). *The Economist.* The Economist Intelligence Unit, London. Embassies and Cultural Offices of Australia, Canada, Denmark, Finland, India, Japan, Netherlands, New Zealand, Pakistan, South Africa, U.A.R., U.S.A., U.S.S.R. Environmental Science Services Administration (U.S.A.). Fairey Surveys Ltd., Maidenhead. The *Financial Times.* Food and Agricultural Organization (U.N.). The Galton Foundation, London. *Geographical Magazine.* Geological Survey and Museum, London. The Hale Observatories (Mt. Wilson and Palomar, U.S.A.). The Harvard Center for Population Studies, U.S.A. Huntings Surveys Ltd., London. Imperial Chemical Industries, London. Institute of Psychiatry, London. Laboratory of Human Mechanics (M.R.C.), London. The Laboratory of Molecular Evolution, Miami, U.S.A. London School of Economics. The London School of Hygiene and Tropical Medicine. Lowestoft Seal Research Unit. Marine Biological Association of the United Kingdom. Medical Research Council, London. Meteorological Office, London. Ministries of H.M. Government. Monks Wood Experimental Station, England. Nature Conservancy. National Aeronautics and Space Administration (U.S.A.). National Coal Board. The National Institute of Oceanography, Surrey. *New Scientist and Science Journal.* The *Observer.* The Ordnance Survey of Great Britain. Pilkington Bros. Ltd., London. Queen Mary College, London. Royal Aircraft Establishment, Farnborough. The Royal Astronomical Society, London. Royal Institute of Netherlands Architects. The Royal Society for the Protection of Birds, London. The Science Museum, London. *Scientific American.* Shell Petroleum Co., London. Short Bros., Belfast. The Soil Association, Suffolk. The Stockholm Peace Research Institute. Survival Service Commission of the International Union for the Conservation of Nature. Unilever, London. Union for the Conservation of Nature. United Kingdom Atomic Energy Authority. United States Department of the Interior. United States Geological Survey. Universities of Cambridge, Liverpool, Newcastle upon Tyne, Oxford, Reading, Sheffield, Strathclyde. The Water Research Association. The White Fish Authority (U.K.). World Health Organization (U.N.). *Weather* Magazine. The Zoological Society of London.

Illustrators

Section symbols throughout by Jim Bulman.
8–9 Diagram, Colin Rose (time clock) 10–11 Diagram 13 Diagram 14–15 Diagram 16–17 Diagram, Sheilagh Noble (line drawing) 18–19 Diagram 20–21 Diagram 22–23 Diagram 24 David Fryer & Centrum (map), Richard Lewis 25 David Fryer & Centrum (map), Centrum (clouds), Eric Jewel, Colin Rose 28 Colin Rose, Richard Lewis 29 Colin Rose, Richard Lewis 30–31 David Fryer 32

Diagram 33 David Fryer 34 David Fryer & Centrum (map), Richard Lewis, David Cook (line drawings) 35 Malcolm Topp, David Cook, Richard Lewis 36-37 David Fryer (map), Centrum (diagrams), David Cook 38–39 David Fryer (maps) Centrum (diagrams) 40–41 David Fryer & Centrum (maps), David Cook 42–43 David Fryer 44–45 Diagram, Colin Rose (maps) 46–47 Colin Rose (time scale) Roy Coombs/Artist Partners.

Photographers

1–5 John Moyes 6–7 The Hale Observatories (Mt. Wilson and Palomar) 10 The Hale Observatories (Mt. Wilson and Palomar) 12 N.A.S.A. 13 N.A.S.A., H. Brinton, W. Zunti 16 Solarfilma (Iceland) 17 Gerald Warhurst/Associated Press 25 Ken Pillsbury, Ken Pillsbury, Ken Pillsbury, M. J. Bramwell/N.H.P.A., Ken Pillsbury, Ken Pillsbury, Ken Pillsbury, M. J. Bramwell/N.H.P.A., Ken Pillsbury, J. Allan Cash, Picturepoint Ltd., Frank Lane, Ken Pillsbury 26–27 Fairey Surveys Ltd. 28 A. Loftas 31 N.E.R.C.

Copyright ; reproduced by permission of the Director of the Institute of Geological Sciences 32 Picturepoint Ltd., 33 National Coal Board, Peter Keen, Shell International Petroleum Co., U.K.A.E.A. 36 Picturepoint Ltd. 38 Picturepoint Ltd. 41 The Mansell Collection, Spectrum Colour Library 42 Picturepoint Ltd., Spectrum Colour Library, remainder Picturepoint Ltd. 44 *Daily Telegraph*, The Mansell Collection 45 Tom Kay.

Cartography

All maps in the sections The Great Cities of the Earth 171–194 ; The Face of the Earth 50–63 ; and Systematic Atlas of the Earth 64-170 by Rand McNally and Company. World Political Information Table, Largest Metropolitan Areas of the World and Geographical Index also by Rand McNally and Company.

World Political Information Table

This table lists all countries and dependencies in the world, U.S. States, Canadian provinces, and other important regions and political subdivisions. Besides specifying the form of government for all political areas, the table classifies them into six groups according to their political status. Units labeled **A** are independent sovereign nations. Units labeled **B** are independent as regards internal affairs, but for purposes of foreign affairs they are under the protection of another country. Areas under military government are also labeled **B.** Units labeled **C** are colonies, overseas territories, dependencies, etc., of other countries. Together the **A, B,** and **C** areas comprise practically the entire inhabited area of the world. The areas labeled **D** are physically separate units, such as groups of islands, which are *not* separate countries, but form part of a nation or dependency. Units labeled **E** are States, provinces, Soviet Republics, or similar major administrative subdivisions of important countries. Units in the table with no letter designation are regions or other areas that do not constitute separate political units by themselves.

Region or Political Division	Area in sq. miles	Estimated Population 1/1/76▲	Pop. per sq. mi.	Form of Government and Ruling Power	Capital; Largest City (unless same)	Predominant Languages
Afars & Issas (French Somaliland)	8,900	110,000	12	Overseas Territory (French)........C	Djibouti	Somali, French
Afghanistan†	250,000	19,530,000	78	Republic........A	Kābul	Pushtu (Afghan), Persian
Africa	11,706,727	418,600,000	36		........; Al-Qāhirah (Cairo)	
Alabama	51,609	3,579,000	69	State (U.S.)........E	Montgomery; Birmingham	
Alaska	586,412	340,000	0.6	State (U.S.)........E	Juneau; Anchorage	English, Indian, Eskimo
Albania†	11,100	2,520,000	227	People's Republic........A	Tiranë	Albanian
Alberta	255,285	1,780,000	6.9	Province (Canada)........E	Edmonton	English
Algeria†	919,595	17,045,000	19	Republic........A	Alger (Algiers)	Arabic, French
American Samoa	76	28,000	368	Unincorporated Territory (U.S.)........C	Pago Pago	Polynesian, English
Andaman & Nicobar Is.	3,202	140,000	44	Territory (India)........D	Port Blair	Andaman, Nicobar Malay
Andorra	175	26,000	149	Principality........A	Andorra	Catalan
Angola†	481,353	6,090,000	13	Republic........A	Luanda	Bantu languages
Anguilla	35	8,900	254	Colony (U.K.)........C	The Valley; South Hill	English
Antarctica	5,100,000					
Antigua (incl. Barbuda)	171	72,000	421	Associated State (U.K.)........B	St. Johns	English
Arabian Peninsula	1,142,050	18,685,000	16		........; Ar-Riyāḍ (Riyadh)	Arabic
Argentina†	1,072,162	25,550,000	24	Federal Republic........A	Buenos Aires	Spanish
Arizona	113,909	2,223,000	19.5	State (U.S.)........E	Phoenix	
Arkansas	53,104	2,073,000	39	State (U.S.)........E	Little Rock	
Arm'anskaja (Armenia) S.S.R.	11,500	2,785,000	242	Soviet Socialist Republic (U.S.S.R.)........E	Jerevan	Armenian
Aruba	69	63,000	913	Division of Netherlands Antilles (Neth.)........D	Oranjestad	Dutch, Spanish, English, Papiamento
Ascension I.	34	1,000	29	Dependency of St. Helena (U.K.)........D	Georgetown	English
Asia	17,085,000	2,359,200,000	138		........; Tōkyō	
Australia†	2,967,909	13,645,000	4.6	Monarchy (Federal)........A	Canberra; Sydney	English
Australian Capital Territory	939	190,000	202	Federal Territory (Australia)........E	Canberra	English
Austria†	32,374	7,745,000	239	Federal Republic........A	Wien (Vienna)	German
Azerbajdžanskaja (Azerbaidzhan) S.S.R.	33,450	5,620,000	168	Soviet Socialist Republic (U.S.S.R.)........E	Baku	Turkic languages, Russian, Armenian
Azores Is.	905	280,000	309	Part of Portugal (3 Districts)........D	........; Ponta Delgada	Portuguese
Baden-Württemberg	13,803	9,320,000	675	State (Germany, Federal Republic of)........E	Stuttgart	German
Bahamas†	5,380	205,000	38	Parliamentary State........A	Nassau	English
Bahrain†	240	260,000	1,083	Sheikdom........A	Al-Manāmah	Arabic
Balearic Is.	1,936	575,000	297	Part of Spain (Baleares Province)........D	Palma	Catalan
Baltic Republics	67,150	7,280,000	108	Union of Soviet Socialist Republics	........; Rīga	Lithuanian, Latvian, Estonian, Russian
Bangladesh†	55,126	77,650,000	1,408	Republic........A	Dacca	Bengali
Barbados†	166	245,000	1,476	Parliamentary State........A	Bridgetown	English
Basutoland, see Lesotho						
Bayern (Bavaria)	27,239	10,950,000	402	State (Germany, Federal Republic of)........E	München (Munich)	German
Bechuanaland, see Botswana						
Belgium†	11,781	9,865,000	837	Monarchy........A	Bruxelles (Brussels)	Flemish, French
Belize	8,867	145,000	16	Colony (U.K.)........C	Belmopan; Belize	English, Spanish, Indian languages
Belorusskaja (Byelorussia) S.S.R.†	80,150	9,430,000	118	Soviet Socialist Republic (U.S.S.R.)........E	Minsk	Byelorussian, Polish
Benelux	28,549	23,895,000	837		Bruxelles (Brussels)	Dutch, Flemish, French, Luxembourgeois
Benin (Dahomey)†	43,484	3,180,000	73	Republic........A	Porto Novo; Cotonou	Native languages, French
Berlin, West	185	2,070,000	11,189	State (Germany, Federal Republic of)........E	Berlin (West)	German
Bermuda	21	55,000	2,619	Colony (U.K.)........C	Hamilton	English
Bhutan†	18,200	1,185,000	65	Monarchy (Indian protection)........B	Paro and Thimbu	Tibetan dialects
Bismarck Archipelago	18,965	290,000	15	Part of Papua New Guinea........D	........; Rabaul	Malay-Polynesian and Papuan languages
Bolivia†	424,164	5,715,000	13	Republic........A	Sucre and La Paz; La Paz	Spanish, Quechua, Aymará, Guaraní
Borneo, Indonesian (Kalimantan)	208,286	5,765,000	28	Part of Indonesia........D	........; Bandjarmasin	Bahasa Indonesia (Indonesian)
Botswana (Bechuanaland)†	231,805	685,000	2.9	Republic........A	Gaborone; Serowe	Bechuana, other Bantu languages
Brazil†	3,286,487	108,640,000	33	Federal Republic........A	Brasília; São Paulo	Portuguese
Bremen	156	735,000	4,712	State (Germany, Federal Republic of)........E	Bremen	German
British Antarctic Territory (excl. Antarctic mainland)	2,040	Winter pop. 80		Colony (U.K.)........C	Stanley, Falkland Islands	
British Columbia	366,255	2,475,000	6.8	Province (Canada)........E	Victoria; Vancouver	English
British Guiana, see Guyana						
British Honduras, see Belize						
British Indian Ocean Territory	18	1,800	100	Colony (U.K.)........C	Victoria, Seychelles	Creole, English, French
Brunei	2,226	155,000	70	Sultanate (U.K. protection)........B	Bandar Seri Begawan	Malay-Polynesian languages
Bulgaria†	42,823	8,765,000	205	People's Republic........A	Sofia (Sofia)	Bulgarian
Burma†	261,790	31,415,000	120	Federal Republic........A	Rangoon	Burmese, English
Burundi (Urundi)†	10,747	3,805,000	354	Republic........A	Bujumbura	Bantu and Hamitic languages
California	158,693	21,066,000	134	State (U.S.)........E	Sacramento; Los Angeles	
Cambodia†	69,898	8,215,000	118	Republic........A	Phnum Pénh	Cambodian (Khmer), French
Cameroon†	183,569	6,450,000	35	Federal Republic........A	Yaoundé; Douala	Native languages, French
Canada†	3,851,809	22,975,000	5.9	Monarchy (Federal)........A	Ottawa; Montréal	English, French
Canal Zone	553	46,000	83	Under U.S. Jurisdiction........C	Balboa Heights; Balboa	Spanish, English
Canary Is.	2,808	1,280,000	456	Part of Spain (2 Provinces)........D	........; Las Palmas de Gran Canaria	Spanish
Canton & Enderbury	27			U.K.-U.S. Administration........C	Canton Island	Malay-Polynesian languages, English
Cape Verde†	1,557	300,000	192	Republic........A	Paria; Mindelo	Portuguese
Caroline Is.	463	75,000	162	Part of U.S. Pacific Is. Trust Ter. (4 Districts)...D		Malay-Polynesian languages
Cayman Is.	100	13,000	130	Colony (U.K.)........C	Georgetown	English
Celebes (Sulawesi)	72,987	9,545,000	131	Part of Indonesia........D	........; Makasar	Malay-Polynesian languages
Central African Republic†	240,535	2,700,000	11	Republic........A	Bangui	Bantu languages, French
Central America	202,063	19,303,000	96		........; Guatemala	Spanish, Indian languages
Central Asia, Soviet	493,950	22,640,000	46	Union of Soviet Socialist Republics	........; Taškent	Uzbek, Russian, Kirghiz, Turkoman, Tadzhik
Ceylon, see Sri Lanka						
Chad†	495,800	2,700,000	5.4	Republic........A	Ndjamena	Hamitic languages, Arabic, French
Channel Is. (Guernsey, Jersey, etc.)	75	130,000	1,733		........; St. Helier	English, French
Chile†	292,258	10,685,000	37	Republic........A	Santiago	Spanish
China (excl. Taiwan)†	3,691,500	845,300,000	229	People's Republic........A	Beijing (Peking); Shanghai	Chinese, Mongolian, Turkish, Tungus
China (Nationalist), see Taiwan						
Christmas I. (Indian Ocean)	52	3,200	67	External Territory (Australia)........C		Chinese, Malay, English
Cocos (Keeling) Is.	5	700	120	External Territory (Australia)........C		Malay, English

† Member of the United Nations (1976).
▲ Estimates for U.S. are 1/1/75.

Region or Political Division	Area in sq. miles	Estimated Population 1/1/76▲	Pop. per sq. mi.	Form of Government and Ruling Power	Capital; Largest City (unless same)	Predominant Languages
Colombia†	439,737	21,960,000	50	Republic...............................A	Bogotá	Spanish
Colorado	104,247	2,552,000	24	State (U.S.)..........................E	Denver	
Commonwealth of Nations	10,713,229	969,423,000	83		London	
Comoro Is.†	694	329,000	474	Republic...............................A	Moroni	Malagasy, French
Congo†	132,000	1,360,000	10	Republic...............................A	Brazzaville	Bantu languages, French
Congo, The, see Zaire						
Connecticut	5,009	3,074,000	614	State (U.S.)..........................E	Hartford	
Cook Is.	93	18,000	194	Self-governing Territory, (New Zealand).......C	Avarua	Malay-Polynesian languages
Corsica	3,352	220,000	66	Part of France (Corse Department).............D	Ajaccio; Bastia	French, Italian
Costa Rica†	19,600	1,990,000	101	Republic...............................A	San José	Spanish
Cuba†	44,218	9,340,000	211	Republic...............................A	La Habana (Havana)	Spanish
Curaçao	173	155,000	896	Division of Netherlands Antilles (Neth.).......D	Willemstad	Dutch, Spanish, English, Papiamento
Cyprus†	3,572	625,000	175	Republic...............................A	Levkósía (Nicosia)	Greek, Turkish, English
Czechoslovakia†	49,373	14,875,000	301	People's Republic.....................A	Praha (Prague)	Czech, Slovak
Dahomey, see Benin						
Delaware	2,057	584,000	284	State (U.S.)..........................E	Dover; Wilmington	
Denmark†	16,629	5,100,000	307	Monarchy..............................A	København (Copenhagen)	Danish
Denmark and Possessions	857,169	5,188,000	6		København (Copenhagen)	Danish, Faeroese, Greenlandic
District of Columbia	67	715,000	10,672	District (U.S.)........................E	Washington	
Dominica	290	76,000	262	Associated State (U.K.)...............B	Roseau	English, French
Dominican Republic†	18,816	4,760,000	253	Republic...............................A	Santo Domingo	Spanish
Ecuador†	109,483	6,615,000	60	Republic...............................A	Quito; Guayaquil	Spanish, Quechua
Egypt†	386,661	38,045,000	98	Republic‡‡.............................A	Al-Qāhirah (Cairo)	Arabic
Ellice Is., see Tuvalu						
El Salvador†	8,260	4,152,000	503	Republic...............................A	San Salvador	Spanish
England (excl. Monmouthshire)	50,332	46,515,000	924	United Kingdom........................	........; London	English
England & Wales	58,348	49,280,000	845	Administrative division of United Kingdom......E	London	English, Welsh
Equatorial Guinea†	10,830	315,000	29	Republic...............................A	Malabo	Bantu languages, Spanish
Estonskaja (S.S.R.)	17,400	1,455,000	84	Soviet Socialist Republic (U.S.S.R.)..........E	Tallinn	Estonian, Russian
Ethiopia†	471,778	28,265,000	60	Monarchy..............................A	Addis Abeba	Amharic and other Semitic languages, English, various Hamitic languages
Eurasia	20,910,000	3,008,800,000	144		........; Tōkyō	
Europe	3,825,000	649,600,000	170		........; London	
Faeroe Is.	540	40,000	74	Self-governing Territory (Denmark).............B	Tórshavn	Danish, Faeroese
Falkland Is. (excl. Deps)	4,618	2,000	0.4	Colony (U.K.).........................C	Stanley	English
Fernando Poo, see Macías Nguema Biyogo						
Fiji†	7,055	570,000	81	Monarchy (Federal)...................A	Suva	Malaya-Polynesian languages, English, Hindi
Finland†	130,120	4,710,000	141	Republic...............................A	Helsinki (Helsingfors)	Finnish, Swedish
Florida	58,560	8,286,000	123	State (U.S.)..........................E	Tallahassee; Miami	
France†	211,207	52,930,000	251	Republic...............................A	Paris	French
France and Possessions	238,881	54,686,000	229		Paris	
Franklin	549,253	9,000	0.02	District of Northwest Territories, Canada.......E	........; Cambridge Bay	English, Eskimo, Indian
French Gulana	35,100	64,000	1.8	Overseas Department (France)................C	Cayenne	French
French Polynesia	1,550	126,000	81	Overseas Territory (France)................C	Papeete	Malayo-Polynesian languages, French
French Somaliland, see Afars & Issas						
French Southern & Antarctic Ter. (excl. Adélie Coast)	2,918	200	0.07	Overseas Territory (France)................C		French
French West Indies	1,112	735,000	661		........; Fort-de-France	French
Gabon†	103,347	530,000	5.1	Republic...............................A	Libreville	Bantu languages, French
Galápagos Is. (Colon, Archipélago de)	3,075	4,200	1.3	Province (Ecuador)....................D	Puerto Baquerizo Moreno	Spanish
Gambia†	4,361	530,000	122	Republic...............................A	Banjul	Mandingo, Fula, English
Georgia	58,876	4,949,000	84	State (U.S.)..........................E	Atlanta	
Germany (Entire)	137,727	80,015,000	581		........; Essen	German
German Democratic Republic†	41,768	17,365,000	416	People's Republic.....................A	Ost-Berlin	German
Germany, Federal Republic of (incl. West Berlin)†	95,968	62,650,000	653	Federal Republic......................A	Bonn; Essen	German
Ghana†	92,100	9,990,000	108	Republic...............................A	Accra	Twi, Fanti, Ewe-Fon, English
Gibraltar	2	33,000	16,500	Colony (U.K.).........................C	Gibraltar	Spanish, English
Gilbert Islands	331	54,000	163	Colony (U.K.).........................C	Bairiki	Malayo-Polynesian languages
Great Britain & Northern Ireland, see United Kingdom						
Greece†	50,944	9,010,000	177	Republic...............................A	Athínai (Athens)	Greek
Greenland	840,000	48,000	0.06	Overseas Territory (Denmark)................C	Godthåb	Greenlandic, Danish, Eskimo
Grenada†	133	110,000	827	Parliamentary State..................A	Saint George's	English
Gruzinskaja (Georgia) S.S.R.	26,900	4,955,000	184	Soviet Socialist Republic (U.S.S.R.)..........E	Tbilisi	Georgic, Armenian, Russian
Guadeloupe (incl. Dependencies)	687	360,000	524	Overseas Department (France)................C	Basse-Terre; Pointe-à-Pitre	French
Guam	212	112,000	528	Unincorporated Territory (U.S.)................C	Agana	English, Chamorro
Guatemala†	42,042	5,920,000	141	Republic...............................A	Guatemala	Spanish, Indian languages
Guernsey (incl. Dependencies)	30	55,000	1,834	Bailiwick (U.K.)......................C	St. Peter Port	English, French
Guinea†	94,964	4,460,000	47	Republic...............................A	Conakry	Native languages, French
Guinea-Bissau†	13,948	535,000	38	Republic...............................A	Bissau	Native languages, Portuguese
Guyana†	83,000	795,000	9.6	Republic...............................A	Georgetown	English
Haiti†	10,714	4,620,000	431	Republic...............................A	Port-au-Prince	Creole, French
Hamburg	288	1,765,000	6,128	State (Germany, Federal Republic of)..........E	Hamburg	German
Hawaii	6,450	854,000	132	State (U.S.)..........................E	Honolulu	English, Japanese, Hawaiian
Hessen (Hesse)	8,150	5,630,000	690	State (Germany, Federal Republic of)..........E	Wiesbaden; Frankfurt am Main	German
Hispaniola	29,530	9,380,000	318		........; Santo Domingo	French, Spanish
Holland, see Netherlands						
Honduras†	43,277	3,150,000	73	Republic...............................A	Tegucigalpa	Spanish
Hong Kong	403	4,385,000	10,880	Colony (U.K.).........................C	Victoria (Xianggang)	Chinese, English
Hungary†	35,920	10,510,000	293	People's Republic.....................A	Budapest	Hungarian
Iceland†	39,800	220,000	5.5	Republic...............................A	Reykjavík	Icelandic
Idaho	83,557	746,000	8.9	State (U.S.)..........................E	Boise (Boise City)	
Illinois	56,400	11,225,000	199	State (U.S.)..........................E	Springfield; Chicago	
India (incl. part of Kashmir)†	1,269,210	604,000,000	476	Republic...............................A	New Delhi; Calcutta	Hindi and other Indo-Aryan languages, Dravidian languages, English
Indiana	36,291	5,342,000	147	State (U.S.)..........................E	Indianapolis	
Indonesia (incl. West Irian)†	735,271	133,160,000	181	Republic...............................A	Djakarta	Bahasa Indonesia (Indonesian), Chinese, English
Iowa	56,290	2,862,000	51	State (U.S.)..........................E	Des Moines	
Iran (Persia)†	636,300	33,365,000	52	Monarchy..............................A	Tehrān	Persian, Turkish dialects, Kurdish
Iraq†	167,925	11,300,000	67	Republic...............................A	Baghdād	Arabic, Kurdish
Ireland†	27,137	3,165,000	117	Republic...............................A	Dublin (Baile Átha Cliath)	English, Irish
Isle of Man	227	62,000	273	Possession (U.K.).....................C	Douglas	English
Israel†	8,019	3,480,000	434	Republic‡‡.............................A	Yerushalayim; Tel Aviv-Yafo	Hebrew, Arabic
Italy†	116,304	56,060,000	482	Republic...............................A	Roma (Rome)	Italian
Ivory Coast†	124,504	6,795,000	55	Republic...............................A	Abidjan	French, native languages

† Member of the United Nations (1976).
‡‡ Areas for Egypt, Israel, Jordan and Syria do not reflect de facto changes which took place during 1967.
▲ Estimates for U.S. are 1/1/75.

World Political Information Table (Continued)

Region or Political Division	Area in sq. miles	Estimated Population 1/1/76▲	Pop. per sq. mi.	Form of Government and Ruling Power	Capital; Largest City (unless same)	Predominant Languages
Jamaica†	4,232	2,035,000	481	Parliamentary State..........A	Kingston	English
Japan†	143,751	111,680,000	777	Monarchy..........A	Tōkyō	Japanese
Java (Djawa) (incl. Madura)	51,033	85,140,000	1,668	Part of Indonesia (5 Provinces)..........D	........; Djakarta	Bahasa Indonesia (Indonesian), Chinese, English
Jersey	45	75,000	1,667	Bailiwick (U.K.)..........C	St. Helier	English, French
Jordan†	37,738	3,430,000	91	Monarchy‡‡..........A	'Ammān	Arabic
Kansas	82,264	2,258,000	27	State (U.S.)..........E	Topeka; Wichita	
Kashmir, Jammu &	86,024	6,400,000	74	In dispute (India & Pakistan)........	Srīnagar	Kashmiri, Punjabi
Kazachskaja (Kazakh) S.S.R.	1,048,300	14,180,000	14	Soviet Socialist Republic (U.S.S.R.)..........E	Alma-Ata	Turkic languages, Russian
Keewatin	228,160	4,000	0.02	District of Northwest Territories, Canada..........E	........; Baker Lake	English, Eskimo, Indian
Kentucky	40,395	3,380,000	84	State (U.S.)..........E	Frankfort; Louisville	....
Kenya†	224,960	13,550,000	60	Republic..........A	Nairobi	Swahili and other Bantu languages, English
Kerguélen	2,700	90	0.03	Part of French Southern & Antarctic Ter. (Fr.)..D	....	French
Kirgizskaja (Kirghiz) S.S.R.	76,650	3,270,000	43	Soviet Socialist Republic (U.S.S.R.)..........E	Frunze	Turkic languages, Persian
Korea (Entire)‡	85,052	50,325,000	592		........; Sŏul (Seoul)	Korean
Korea, North	46,540	16,035,000	345	People's Republic..........A	P'yŏngyang	Korean
Korea, South	38,025	34,290,000	902	Republic..........A	Sŏul (Seoul)	Korean
Kuwait†	6,880	1,005,000	146	Shiekdom..........A	Al-Kuwayt	Arabic
Labrador	112,826	35,000	0.3	Part of Newfoundland Province, Canada..........D	........; Labrador City	English, Eskimo
Laos†	91,429	3,375,000	37	Republic..........A	Vientiane	Lao, French
Latin America	7,924,731	321,716,000	41		........; São Paulo	
Latvijskaja (Latvia) S.S.R.	24,600	2,505,000	102	Soviet Socialist Republic (U.S.S.R.)..........E	Rīga	Latvian, Russian
Lebanon†	4,015	3,485,000	868	Republic..........A	Bayrūt (Beirut)	Arabic, French, English
Lesotho (Basutoland)†	11,720	1,050,000	90	Monarchy..........A	Maseru	Kaffir, other Bantu languages
Liberia†	43,000	1,730,000	40	Republic..........A	Monrovia	Native languages, English
Libya†	679,362	2,495,000	3.7	Republic..........A	Tarābulus	Arabic
Liechtenstein	62	24,000	387	Principality..........A	Vaduz	German
Litovskaja (Lithuania) S.S.R.	25,150	3,320,000	132	Soviet Socialist Republic (U.S.S.R.)..........E	Vilnius	Lithuanian, Polish, Russian
Louisiana	48,523	3,816,000	79	State (U.S.)..........E	Baton Rouge; New Orleans	
Luxembourg†	998	335,000	336	Grand Duchy..........A	Luxembourg	Luxembourgeois, French
Macau	6	275,000	45,833	Overseas Province (Portugal)..........C	Macau	Chinese, Portuguese
Macías Nguema Biyogo	785	86,000	110	Part of Equatorial Guinea..........D	Santa Isabel	Bantu languages, Spanish
Mackenzie	527,490	27,000	0.05	District of Northwest Territories, Canada..........E	........; Yellowknife	English, Eskimo, Indian
Madagascar (Malagasy Republic)†	226,658	9,025,000	40	Republic..........A	Tananarive	French, Malagasy
Madeira Is.	308	255,000	828	Part of Portugal (Funchal District)..........D	Funchal	Portuguese
Maine	33,215	1,026,000	31	State (U.S.)..........E	Augusta; Portland	....
Malawi (Nyasaland)†	45,747	5,070,000	111	Republic..........A	Lilongwe; Blantyre	Bantu languages
Malaya	50,700	10,155,000	200	Part of Malaysia..........D	Kuala Lumpur	Malay, Chinese, English
Malaysia†	128,430	12,180,000	95	Constitutional Monarchy..........A	Kuala Lumpur	Malay, Chinese, English
Maldives†	115	139,000	1,209	Republic..........A	Male	Arabic
Mali†	478,655	5,810,000	12	Republic..........A	Bamako	Native languages, French, Arabic
Malta†	122	325,000	2,663	Republic..........A	Valletta	English, Maltese
Manitoba	251,000	1,025,000	4.1	Province (Canada)..........E	Winnipeg	English
Mariana Is. (excl. Guam)	184	15,000	82	District of U.S. Pacific Is. Trust Ter...........D	Saipan	Malay-Polynesian languages
Maritime Provinces (excl. Newfoundland)	51,963	1,630,000	31	Canada........	........; Halifax	English
Marshall Is.	70	25,000	357	District of U.S. Pacific Is. Trust Ter..........D	Majuro	Malay-Polynesian languages
Martinique	425	375,000	882	Overseas Department (France)..........C	Fort-de-France	French
Maryland	10,577	4,112,000	389	State (U.S.)..........E	Annapolis; Baltimore	
Massachusetts	8,257	5,845,000	705	State (U.S.)..........E	Boston	
Mauritania†	397,950	1,340,000	3.4	Republic..........A	Nouakchott	Arabic, French
Mauritius (incl. Dependencies)†	789	890,000	1,128	Parliamentary State..........A	Port Louis	Indo-Aryan languages, French, Creole, English
Mayotte†	144	26,000	181	Overseas Territory (France)..........C	Dzaoudzi	French
Mexico†	761,604	61,040,000	80	Federal Republic..........A	Ciudad de México (Mexico City)	Spanish
Michigan	58,216	9,102,000	156	State (U.S.)..........E	Lansing; Detroit	....
Middle America	1,054,731	107,460,000	102		........; Ciudad de México (Mexico City)	
Midway Is.	2	2,100	1,050	Possession (U.S.)..........C		English
Minnesota	84,068	3,934,000	47	State (U.S.)..........E	St. Paul; Minneapolis	
Mississippi	47,716	2,324,000	49	State (U.S.)..........E	Jackson	
Missouri	69,686	4,762,000	68	State (U.S.)..........E	Jefferson City; St. Louis	
Moldavskaja (Moldavia) S.S.R.	13,000	3,835,000	295	Soviet Socialist Republic (U.S.S.R.)..........E	Kišin'ov (Kishinev)	Moldavian, Russian, Ukrainian
Monaco	0.6	23,000	38,334	Principality..........A	Monaco	French, Italian
Mongolia†	604,200	1,460,000	2.4	People's Republic..........A	Ulaanbaatar (Ulan Bator)	Mongolian
Montana	147,138	724,000	4.9	State (U.S.)..........E	Helena; Billings	
Montserrat	39	13,000	334	Colony (U.K.)..........C	Plymouth	English
Morocco†	172,415	17,785,000	103	Monarchy..........A	Rabat; Casablanca	Arabic, Berber, French
Mozambique†	302,329	9,380,000	31	Republic..........A	Maputo (Lourenço Marques)	Bantu Languages, Portuguese
Nauru	8	7,200	900	Republic..........A		Malay-Polynesian languages, Chinese, English
Nebraska	77,227	1,525,000	20	State (U.S.)..........E	Lincoln; Omaha	
Nepal†	54,362	12,705,000	234	Monarchy..........A	Kātmāndu	Nepali, Tibeto-Burman languages
Netherlands†	15,770	13,695,000	868	Monarchy..........A	Amsterdam and s'-Gravenhage (The Hague); Amsterdam	Dutch
Netherlands and Possessions	16,141	13,930,000	863		Amsterdam and s'-Gravenhage; Amsterdam	
Netherlands Antilles	371	235,000	633	Self-governing Territory (Netherlands)..........C	Willemstad	Dutch, Spanish, English, Papiamento
Netherlands Guiana, see Surinam	....					
Nevada	110,540	602,000	5.4	State (U.S.)..........E	Carson City; Las Vegas	
New Brunswick	28,354	680,000	24	Province (Canada)..........E	Fredericton; Saint John	English, French
New Caledonia (incl. Deps.)	7,358	138,000	19	Overseas Territory (France)..........C	Nouméa	Malay-Polynesian languages, French
New England	66,608	12,155,000	182	United States..........E	........; Boston	English
Newfoundland	156,185	555,000	3.5	Province (Canada)..........E	St. John's	English
Newfoundland (excl. Labrador)	43,359	520,000	12		........; St. John's	English
New Hampshire	9,304	804,000	86	State (U.S.)..........E	Concord; Manchester	
New Hebrides	5,700	96,000	17	Condominium (France-U.K.)..........C	Vila	Malay-Polynesian languages, French
New Jersey	7,836	7,276,000	929	State (U.S.)..........E	Trenton; Newark	....
New Mexico	121,666	1,133,000	9.3	State (U.S.)..........E	Santa Fe; Albuquerque	
New South Wales	309,433	4,860,000	16	State (Australia)..........E	Sydney	English
New York	49,576	18,222,000	368	State (U.S.)..........E	Albany; New York	
New Zealand†	103,736	3,120,000	30	Monarchy..........A	Wellington; Auckland	English
Nicaragua†	50,200	2,185,000	44	Republic..........A	Managua	Spanish
Niedersachsen (Lower Saxony)	18,299	7,325,000	400	State (Germany, Federal Republic of)..........E	Hannover	German
Niger†	489,200	4,715,000	9.6	Republic..........A	Niamey	Hausa, Arabic, French
Nigeria†	356,669	75,080,000	211	Republic..........A	Lagos	Hausa, Ibo, Yoruba, English
Niue	100	3,500	35	Island Territory (New Zealand)..........C	Alofi	Malay-Polynesian languages, English
Nordrhein-Westfalen (North Rhine Westphalia)	13,145	17,400,000	1,324	State (Germany, Federal Republic of)..........E	Düsseldorf; Köln	German
Norfolk Island	14	2,200	157	External Territory (Australia)..........C	Kingston	English

† Member of the United Nations (1976).
‡ Includes 487 sq. miles of demilitarized zone, not included in North or South Korea figures.
‡‡ Areas for Egypt, Israel, Jordan and Syria do not reflect de facto changes which took place during 1967.
▲ Estimates for U.S. are 1/1/75.

198

World Political Information Table (Continued)

Region or Political Division	Area in sq. miles	Estimated Population 1/1/76▲	Pop. per sq. mi.	Form of Government and Ruling Power	Capital; Largest City (unless same)	Predominant Languages
North America............	9,420,000	345,100,000	37		........; New York	....
North Borneo, see Sabah..........						
North Carolina...............	52,586	5,377,000	102	State (U.S.)...............................E	Raleigh; Charlotte	....
North Dakota................	70,665	634,000	8.9	State (U.S.)...............................E	Bismarck; Fargo	....
Northern Ireland.............	5,463	1,545,000	283	Administrative division of United Kingdom.....E	Belfast	English
Northern Rhodesia, see Zambia....						
Northern Territory...............	520,280	110,000	0.2	Territory (Australia)..........................E	Darwin	English, Aboriginal languages
North Polar Regions.............						
Northwest Territories.............	1,304,903	40,000	0.03	Territory (Canada).....................E	Yellowknife	English, Eskimo, Indian
Norway†.....................	125,181	4,040,000	32	Monarchy...............................A	Oslo	Norwegian (Riksmål and Landsmål)
Nova Scotia.................	21,425	830,000	39	Province (Canada).....................E	Halifax	English
Nyasaland, see Malawi........						
Oceania (incl. Australia)..........	3,295,000	21,300,000	6.5		........; Sydney	....
Ohio........................	41,222	10,735,000	260	State (U.S.)...............................E	Columbus; Cleveland	
Oklahoma...................	69,919	2,673,000	38	State (U.S.)...............................E	Oklahoma City	
Oman†......................	82,030	770,000	9.4	Sultanate...............................A	Masqaṭ; Maṭraḥ	Arabic
Ontario.....................	412,582	8,290,000	20	Province (Canada).....................E	Toronto	English
Oregon.....................	96,981	2,252,000	23	State (U.S.)...............................E	Salem; Portland	
Orkney Is...................	376	17,800	47	Part of Scotland, U.K..................D	Kirkwall	English
Pacific Islands Trust Territory......	717	115,000	160	Trust Territory (U.S.).................E	Saipan	Malay-Polynesian languages, English
Pakistan (incl. part of Kashmir)†...	345,753	72,000,000	208	Federal Republic........................A	Islāmābād; Karāchī	Urdu, English
Palestine (Gaza Strip).............	146	330,000	2,260	Military Government (Egypt)‡‡..........B	Ghazzah (Gaza)	Arabic
Panama†....................	29,209	1,485,000	51	Republic...............................A	Panamá	Spanish
Papua New Guinea†..........	178,260	700,000	3.9	Republic...............................A	Port Moresby	Papuan and Negrito languages, English
Paraguay†...................	157,048	2,755,000	18	Republic...............................A	Asunción	Spanish, Guaraní
Pennsylvania................	45,333	11,821,000	261	State (U.S.)...............................E	Harrisburg; Philadelphia	
Persia, see Iran..............						
Peru†.......................	496,224	16,080,000	32	Republic...............................A	Lima	Spanish, Quechua
Philippines†.................	116,000	43,300,000	373	Republic...............................A	Quezon City; Manila	Tagalog and other Malay-Polynesian languages, English
Pitcairn (excl. Dependencies).......	2	100	50	Colony (U.K.).........................C	Adamstown	English
Poland†.....................	120,725	34,175,000	283	People's Republic......................A	Warszawa (Warsaw)	Polish
Portugal†...................	35,553	9,110,000	256	Republic...............................A	Lisboa (Lisbon)	Portuguese
Portugal and Possessions...........	41,332	10,147,000	245		Lisboa (Lisbon)	
Portuguese Guinea, see Guinea-Bissau...........						
Portuguese Timor.................	5,763	680,000	118	Overseas Province (Portugal)................C	Dili	Malay, Papuan languages, Portuguese
Prairie Provinces..............	757,985	3,730,000	4.9	Canada	........; Winnipeg	English
Prince Edward Island..........	2,184	120,000	55	Province (Canada).....................E	Charlottetown	English
Puerto Rico.................	3,435	3,150,000	917	Commonwealth (U.S.)..................C	San Juan	Spanish, English
Qatar†......................	4,247	280,000	66	Shiekdom...............................A	Ad-Dawḥah (Doha)	Arabic
Quebec.....................	594,860	6,235,000	10	Province (Canada).....................E	Québec; Montréal	French, English
Queensland.................	667,000	2,005,000	3.0	State (Australia).........................E	Brisbane	English
Reunion....................	969	510,000	526	Overseas Department (France)............C	St. Denis	French
Rheinland-Pfalz (Rhineland-Palatinate)..............	7,657	3,735,000	488	State (Germany, Federal Republic of)..........E	Mainz; Ludwigshafen	German
Rhode Island................	1,214	933,000	768	State (U.S.)...............................E	Providence	
Rhodesia...................	150,804	6,405,000	42	Self-governing Colony (U.K.)*..................C	Salisbury	Bantu languages, English
Rio Muni, see Equatorial Guinea....						
Rodrigues...................	42	28,000	667	Dependency of Mauritius (U.K.)...............D	Port Mathurin	English, French
Romania†...................	91,699	21,220,000	231	People's Republic......................A	Bucureşti (Bucharest)	Romanian, Hungarian
Rossijskaja Sovetskaja Federativnaja Socialističeskaja Respublika...........	6,592,850	135,375,000	21	Soviet Federated Socialist Republic (U.S.S.R.)..E	Moskva (Moscow)	Russian, Finno-Ugric languages, various Turkic, Iranian, and Mongol languages
Rossijskaja S.F.S.R. in Europe.....	1,527,350	99,625,000	65	Union of Soviet Socialist Republics...............	........; Moskva (Moscow)	Russian, Finno-Ugric languages
Rwanda†....................	10,169	4,235,000	416	Republic...............................A	Kigali	Bantu and Hamitic languages
Saarland (Saar)................	992	1,120,000	1,129	State (Germany, Federal Republic of)..........E	Saarbrücken	German
Sabah (North Borneo)..........	29,388	855,000	29	Administrative division of Malaysia............E	Kota Kinabalu; Sandakan	Malay, Chinese
St. Helena (incl. Dependencies)....	162	6,800	42	Colony (U.K.).........................C	Jamestown	English
St. Kitts-Nevis................	103	56,000	544	Associated State (U.K.)......................B	Basseterre	English
St. Lucia...................	238	113,000	475	Associated State (U.K.)......................B	Castries	English
St. Pierre & Miquelon..........	93	6,000	65	Overseas Territory (France)................C	St. Pierre	French
St. Vincent..................	150	120,000	800	Associated State (U.K.)......................B	Kingstown	English
Samoa (Entire)..............	1,173	188,000	160		........; Apia	Malay-Polynesian languages, English
San Marino.................	24	21,000	875	Republic...............................A	San Marino	Italian
Sao Tome & Principe†..............	372	82,000	220	Overseas Province (Portugal)................C	São Tomé	Bantu languages, Portuguese
Sarawak....................	48,342	1,170,000	24	Administrative division of Malaysia............E	Kuching	Malay, Chinese, English
Sardinia....................	9,301	1,555,000	167	Part of Italy (4 Provinces)................D	........; Cagliari	Italian
Saskatchewan...............	251,700	925,000	3.7	Province (Canada).....................E	Regina	English
Saudi Arabia†................	830,000	9,105,000	11	Monarchy...............................A	Ar-Riyāḍ (Riyadh)	Arabic
Scandinavia (incl. Finland and Iceland).....................	509,899	22,303,000	44		........; København (Copenhagen)	Swedish, Danish, Norwegian, Finnish, Icelandic
Schleswig-Holstein..............	6,046	2,600,000	430	State (Germany, Federal Republic of)..........E	Kiel	German
Scotland...................	30,414	5,235,000	172	Administrative division of United Kingdom.....E	Edinburgh; Glasgow	English
Senegal†....................	75,750	4,480,000	59	Republic...............................A	Dakar	Wolof, Poular French
Seychelles..................	156	61,000	421	Republic...............................A	Victoria	French, Creole, English
Shetland Is..................	550	19,000	35	Part of Scotland, U.K..................D	Lerwick	English
Siam, see Thailand..........						
Sicily......................	9,926	4,860,000	490	Part of Italy (Sicilia Autonomous Region).......D	Palermo	Italian
Sierra Leone†................	27,699	2,545,000	92	Republic...............................A	Freetown	Temme, Mende, English
Singapore†..................	224	2,330,000	10,401	Republic...............................A	Singapore	Chinese, Malay, English
Solomon Is. (Papua New Guinea)...	4,100	120,000	30	Part of Papua New Guinea................D	Sohano; Kieta	Malay-Polynesian languages
Solomon Is., British...........	10,983	195,000	18	Protectorate (U.K.)....................C	Honiara	Malay-Polynesian languages
Somalia†....................	246,201	3,205,000	13	Republic...............................A	Mogadisho	Somali
South Africa (incl. Walvis Bay)†....	471,879	25,815,000	55	Federal Republic........................A	Pretoria and Cape Town; Johannesburg	English, Afrikaans, Bantu languages
South America................	6,870,000	214,200,000	31		........; São Paulo	
South Australia..............	380,070	1,240,000	3.3	State (Australia).........................E	Adelaide	English
South Carolina..............	31,055	2,746,000	88	State (U.S.)...............................E	Columbia	
South Dakota...............	77,047	679,000	8.8	State (U.S.)...............................E	Pierre; Sioux Falls	
Southern Rhodesia, see Rhodesia...						
Southern Yemen, see Yemen, People's Democratic Republic of..						
South Georgia...............	1,450	20	0.01	Dependency of Falkland Is. (U.K.)..............D	Grytviken	English, Norwegian

† Member of the United Nations (1976).
* Rhodesia unilaterally declared its independence from the United Kingdom on November 11, 1965.
‡‡ Areas for Egypt, Israel, Jordan and Syria do not reflect de facto changes which took place during 1967.
▲ Estimates for U.S. are 1/1/75.

World Political Information Table (Continued)

Region or Political Division	Area in sq. miles	Estimated Population 1/1/76▲	Pop. per sq. mi.	Form of Government and Ruling Power	Capital; Largest City (unless same)	Predominant Languages
South Polar Regions...........	....	....	....			
South West Africa (excl. Walvis Bay)...	317,827	870,000	2.7	Under South African Administration**.........C	Windhoek	Bantu languages, Hottentot, Bushman, Afrikaans, English
Spain†....................	194,885	35,765,000	184	Monarchy....................A	Madrid	Spanish, Catalan, Galician, Basque
Spain and Possessions...........	194,897	36,125,000	185		Madrid	....
Spanish Possessions in North Africa................	12	119,000	9,916	Five Possessions (no central government) (Spain)................C	........; Melilla	Spanish, Arabic, Berber
Spitsbergen, see Svalbard.........						
Sri Lanka (Ceylon)†..........	25,332	14,250,000	562	Republic..................A	Colombo	Sinhalese, Tamil, English
Sudan†.................	967,499	14,790,000	15	Republic..................A	Al-Khurṭūm (Khartoum)	Arabic, native languages, English
Sumatra (Sumatera).........	182,860	23,285,000	127	Part of Indonesia (6 Provinces)................D	........; Medan	Bahasa Indonesia, English, Chinese
Surinam (Neth. Guiana)†.........	63,037	430,000	6.8	Republic..................A	Paramaribo	Dutch, Indo-Aryan languages
Svalbard (Spitsbergen) and Jan Mayen..............	24,102	Winter pop. 3,000		Dependency (Norway)..............C	Longyearbyen	Norwegian, Russian
Swaziland†................	6,705	500,000	75	Monarchy..................A	Mbabane	Swazi and other Bantu languages, English
Sweden†.................	173,732	8,190,000	47	Monarchy..................A	Stockholm	Swedish
Switzerland...............	15,941	6,410,000	402	Federal Republic..................A	Bern (Berne); Zürich	German, French, Italian
Syria†.................	71,498	7,460,000	104	Republic‡‡..................A	Dimashq (Damascus)	Arabic
Tadžikskaja (Tadzhik) S.S.R.......	55,250	3,345,000	61	Soviet Socialist Republic (U.S.S.R.)...........E	Dušanbe	Tadzhik, Turkic languages, Russian
Taiwan (Formosa) (Nationalist China)........	13,885	16,305,000	1,174	Republic..................A	T'aipei	Chinese
Tanganyika, see Tanzania.........	....	....	....			
Tanzania (Tanganyika & Zanzibar)†............	364,900	15,330,000	42	Republic..................A	Dar es Salaam	Swahili and other Bantu languages, English
Tasmania................	26,383	410,000	16	State (Australia)..................E	Hobart	English
Tennessee...............	42,244	4,136,000	98	State (U.S.)..................E	Nashville; Memphis	....
Texas.................	267,339	12,179,000	46	State (U.S.)..................E	Austin; Houston	....
Thailand (Siam)†............	198,500	42,860,000	216	Monarchy..................A	Krung Thep (Bangkok)	Thai, Chinese
Tibet (Xizang Zizhiqu).........	471,700	1,520,000	3.2	Autonomous Region (China)..................E	Lasa (Lhasa)	Tibetan
Togo†.................	21,600	2,240,000	104	Republic..................A	Lomé	Native languages, French
Tokelau (Union) Is...........	4	1,600	400	Island Territory (New Zealand)................C	........; Fakaofu	Malay-Polynesian languages
Tonga.................	270	100,000	370	Monarchy..................A	Nukualofa	Malay-Polynesian languages, English
Transcaucasia...........	71,850	13,360,000	186	Union of Soviet Socialist Republics...............A	........; Tbilisi	
Trinidad & Tobago†.........	1,980	1,095,000	553	Parliamentary State..................A	Port of Spain	English, Spanish
Tristan da Cunha...........	40	300	7.5	Dependency of St. Helena (U.K.)..............D	Edinburgh	English
Trucial States, see United Arab Emirates................	....	....	....			
Tunisia†................	63,170	5,905,000	93	Republic..................A	Tunis	Arabic, French
Turkey†................	301,382	39,675,000	132	Republic..................A	Ankara; İstanbul	Turkish
Turkey in Europe...........	9,121	3,425,000	376	Turkey..................E	........; İstanbul	Turkish
Turkmenskaja (Turkmen) S.S.R....	188,450	2,480,000	13	Soviet Socialist Republic (U.S.S.R.)...........E	Aschabad	Turkic languages, Russian
Turks & Caicos Is...........	166	6,000	36	Colony (U.K.)................C	Grand Turk	English
Tuvalu (Ellice Is.)...................	9.5	5,700	600	Colony (U.K.)................C	Funafuti	Malayo-Polynesian languages
Uganda†................	91,134	11,705,000	128	Republic..................A	Kampala	Bantu languages
Ukrainskaja (Ukraine) S.S.R.†....	233,100	49,420,000	212	Soviet Socialist Republic (U.S.S.R.)...........E	Kijev (Kiev)	Ukrainian, Russian
Union of Soviet Socialist Republics (Soviet Union)†.........	8,649,500	255,520,000	30	Federal Soviet Republics....................A	Moskva (Moscow)	Russian and other Slavic languages, various Finno-Ugric, Turkic and Mongol languages, Caucasian languages, Persian
Union of Soviet Socialist Republics in Europe..............	1,920,750	169,590,000	88	Union of Soviet Socialist Republics...............	........; Moskva (Moscow)	Russian, Ruthenian, various Finno-Ugric and Caucasian languages
United Arab Emirates (Trucial States)†...............	32,278	225,000	6.9	Self-governing Union..................A	Abū Ẓaby	Arabic
United Kingdom of Great Britain & Northern Ireland†................	94,227	57,605,000	611	Monarchy..................A	London	English, Welsh, Gaelic
United Kingdom & Possessions.....	288,049	68,280,000	237		London	....
United States†.................	*3,675,545	214,580,000	58	Federal Republic..................A	Washington; New York	English
United States and Possessions.....	3,680,713	218,135,000	59		Washington; New York	English, Spanish
Upper Volta†.................	105,800	6,115,000	58	Republic..................A	Ouagadougou	Voltaic and Mande languages, French
Uruguay†.................	68,536	2,780,000	41	Republic..................A	Montevideo	Spanish
Utah.................	84,916	1,184,000	14	State (U.S.)..................E	Salt Lake City	
Uzbekskaja (Uzbek) S.S.R.........	173,600	13,545,000	78	Soviet Socialist Republic (U.S.S.R.)...........E	Taškent	Turkic languages, Sart, Russian
Vatican City (Holy See)............	0.2	1,000	5,000	Ecclesiastical State..................A	Città del Vaticano (Vatican City)	Italian, Latin
Venezuela†.................	352,144	12,185,000	35	Federal Republic..................A	Caracas	Spanish
Vermont.................	9,609	473,000	49	State (U.S.)..................E	Montpelier; Burlington	
Victoria.................	87,884	3,710,000	42	State (Australia)..................E	Melbourne	English
Vietnam (Entire)*.................	128,402	46,430,000	362		........; Sai-gon	Annamese, Chinese
Vietnam, North*.................	61,294	25,165,000	411	People's Republic..................A	Ha-noi	Annamese, Chinese
Vietnam, South*.................	67,108	21,265,000	317	Republic..................A	Sai-gon	Annamese, Chinese
Virginia.................	40,817	5,000,000	123	State (U.S.)..................E	Richmond; Norfolk	
Virgin Is., British.................	59	10,000	170	Colony (U.K.)................C	Road Town	English
Virgin Is. of the U.S.................	133	99,000	744	Unincorporated Territory (U.S.)................C	Charlotte Amalie	English
Wake I.................	3	1,700	567	Possession (U.S.)................C		English
Wales (incl. Monmouthshire).......	8,016	2,765,000	345	United Kingdom..................C	Cardiff	English, Welsh
Wallis & Futuna.................	77	9,000	92	Overseas Territory (France)................C	Mata-Utu	Malay-Polynesian languages
Washington.................	68,192	3,447,000	51	State (U.S.)..................E	Olympia; Seattle	
Western Australia.................	975,920	1,120,000	1.1	State (Australia)..................E	Perth	English
Western Sahara.................	102,700	122,000	1.2	Administered by Morocco and Mauritania................C	El Aaiún	Arabic
Western Samoa.................	1,097	160,000	146	Constitutional Monarchy..................A	Apia	Malay-Polynesian languages, English
West Indies.................	92,041	27,117,000	295		........; La Habana (Havana)	....
West Virginia.................	24,181	1,792,000	74	State (U.S.)..................E	Charleston	
White Russia, see Belorusskaja.....						
Wisconsin.................	56,154	4,576,000	81	State (U.S.)..................E	Madison; Milwaukee	
World.................	57,280,000	4,008,000,000	70		........; Tōkyō	
Wyoming.................	97,914	348,000	3.6	State (U.S.)..................E	Cheyenne	
Yemen†.................	75,300	5,310,000	71	Republic..................A	San'ā'	Arabic
Yemen, People's Democratic Republic of,†.................	111,075	1,730,000	16	People's Republic..................A	Aden	Arabic, English
Yugoslavia†.................	87,183	21,465,000	246	Socialist Federal Republic..................A	Beograd (Belgrade)	Serbo-Croatian-Slovenian, Macedonian
Yukon.................	207,076	20,000	0.09	Territory (Canada)................C	Whitehorse	English, Eskimo, Indian
Zaire (Congo, The)†.................	905,567	25,205,000	28	Republic..................A	Kinshasa	Bantu languages, French
Zambia (Northern Rhodesia)†.................	290,586	4,960,000	17	Republic..................A	Lusaka	Bantu languages, English
Zanzibar.................	950	425,000	447	Part of Tanzania................D	........; Zanzibar	Arabic, English

† Member of the United Nations (1976).
‡‡ Areas for Egypt, Israel, Jordan and Syria do not reflect de facto changes which took place during 1967.
▲ Estimates for U.S. are 1/1/75.

** The United Nations declared an end to the mandate of South Africa over South West Africa in October 1966. Administration of the territory by South Africa is not recognized by the United Nations.
* In 1976 North and South Vietnam decided on reunification with Ha-noi as the capital.

Largest Metropolitan Areas of the World, 1975

This table lists the major metropolitan areas of the world according to their estimated population on January 1, 1975. For convenience in reference, the areas are grouped by major region, and the number of areas in each region and size group is given.

There are 24 areas with more than 5,000,000 population each; these are listed in rank order of estimated population, with the world rank given in parentheses following the name. For example, New York's 1975 rank is second. Below the 5,000,000 level, the metropolitan areas are listed alphabetically within region, not in order of size.

For ease of comparison, each metropolitan area has been defined by Rand McNally & Company according to consistent rules. A metropolitan area includes a central city, neighboring communities linked to it by continuous built-up areas, and more distant communities if the bulk of their population is supported by commuters to the central city. Some metropolitan areas have more than one central city, for example Tōkyō-Yokohama or Detroit-Windsor.

POPULATION CLASSIFICATION	UNITED STATES and CANADA	LATIN AMERICA	EUROPE (excl. U.S.S.R.)	U.S.S.R.	ASIA	AFRICA–OCEANIA
Over 15,000,000 (2)	New York (2)				Tōkyō–Yokohama (1)	
10,000,000–15,000,000 (4)		Ciudad de México (Mexico City) (4)	London (6)	Moskva (Moscow) (5)	Ōsaka–Kōbe–Kyōto (3)	
5,000,000–10,000,000 (18)	Los Angeles (11) Chicago (16) Philadelphia (21)	São Paulo (8) Buenos Aires (9) Rio de Janeiro (13)	Paris (10) Essen–Dortmund–Duisburg (The Ruhr) (19)	Leningrad (24)	Calcutta (7) Shanghai (12) Bombay (15) Sŏul (Seoul) (17) Djakarta (18) Manila (20) Delhi (22) Beijing (Peking) (23)	Al-Qāhirah (Cairo) (14)
3,000,000–5,000,000 (23)	Boston Detroit–Windsor San Francisco–Oakland–San Jose Washington	Bogotá Lima Santiago	Barcelona Berlin İstanbul Madrid Milano (Milan) Roma (Rome)		Chongqing (Chungking) Karāchi Krung Thep (Bangkok) Madras Nagoya Shenyang (Mukden) T'aipei (Taipei) Tehrān Tianjin (Tientsin) Victoria	
2,000,000–3,000,000 (33)	Cleveland Dallas–Fort Worth Houston Miami–Fort Lauderdale Montréal Pittsburgh St. Louis Toronto	Caracas Recife	Athínai (Athens) Birmingham Bruxelles (Brussel) (Brussels) Budapest Hamburg Katowice–Bytom–Gliwice Manchester	Kijev (Kiev)	Ahmādābād Baghdād Guangzhou (Canton) Haerbin (Harbin) Hyderābād Lahore Pusan Rangoon Sai–gon (Saigon) Singapore Wuhan	Alexandria Johannesburg Melbourne Sydney
1,500,000–2,000,000 (45)	Atlanta Baltimore Buffalo Minneapolis–St. Paul San Diego–Tijuana Seattle–Tacoma	Belo Horizonte Guadalajara La Habana (Havana) Medellín Monterrey Montevideo Pôrto Alegre	Amsterdam Bucureşti (Bucharest) Frankfurt am Main Glasgow København (Copenhagen) Köln (Cologne) Leeds–Bradford Lisboa (Lisbon) Liverpool München (Munich) Napoli (Naples) Stuttgart Torino (Turin) Warszawa (Warsaw) Wien (Vienna)	Baku Char'kov (Kharkov) Doneck (Donetsk) Gor'kij (Gorki) Taškent (Tashkent)	Ankara Bangalore Chengdu (Chengtu) Colombo Dacca Nanjing (Nanking) Surabaja Taiyuan Xi'an (Sian)	Alger (Algiers) Casablanca Kinshasa
1,000,000–1,500,000 (66)	Cincinnati Denver Hartford Indianapolis Kansas City Milwaukee New Orleans Phoenix Portland Vancouver	Fortaleza Guatemala Salvador San Juan	Antwerpen (Anvers) (Antwerp) Beograd (Belgrade) Düsseldorf Lille Lyon Mannheim Marseille Newcastle–Sunderland Praha (Prague) Rotterdam Sofija (Sofia) Stockholm Valencia	Čel'abinsk (Chelyabinsk) Dnepropetrovsk Jerevan (Yerevan) Kujbyšev (Kuybyshev) Minsk Novosibirsk Odessa Perm Rostov-na-Donu Saratov Sverdlovsk Tbilisi Volgograd	Anshan Bandung Bayrūt (Beirut) Changchun (Hsinking) Dimashq (Damascus) Fukuoka Fushun Hiroshima–Kure Jinan (Tsinan) Kānpur Kaohsiung Kitakyūshū Kunming Lüda (Dairen) Nāgpur Pune P'yŏngyang Qingdao (Tsingtao) Sapporo Taegu Tel Aviv–Yafo Zhengzhou (Chengchow)	Addis Abeba (Addis Ababa) Cape Town Durban Lagos
Total by Region (191)	32	20	44	21	62	12

Introduction to the Index

The Index includes in a single alphabetical list some 34,000 names appearing on the maps. Each name is followed by a page reference and by the location of the feature on the map. The map location is designated by latitude and longitude coordinates. If a page contains several maps, a lowercase letter identifies the inset map. The page reference for two-page maps is always to the left hand page.

Most map features are indexed to the largest-scale map on which they appear. Countries, mountain ranges, and other extensive features are generally indexed to the map that shows them in their entirety.

The features indexed are of three types: *point, areal,* and *linear.* For *point* features (for example, cities, mountain peaks, dams), latitude and longitude coordinates give the location of the point on the map. For *areal* features (countries, mountain ranges, etc.), the coordinates generally indicate the approximate center of the feature. For *linear* features (rivers, canals, aqueducts), the coordinates locate a terminating point—for example, the mouth of a river, or the point at which a feature reaches the map margin.

NAME FORMS Names in the Index, as on the maps, are generally in the local language and insofar as possible are spelled according to official practice. Diacritical marks are included, except that those used to indicate tone, as in Vietnamese, are usually not shown. Most features that extend beyond the boundaries of one country have no single official name, and these are usually named in English. Many conventional English names and former names are cross referenced to the primary map name. All cross references are indicated by the symbol→. A name that appears in a shortened version on the map due to space limitations is given in full in the Index, with the portion that is omitted on the map enclosed in brackets, for example, Acapulco [de Juárez].

TRANSLITERATION For names in languages not written in the Roman alphabet, the locally official transliteration system has been used where one exists. Thus, names in the Soviet Union and Bulgaria have been transliterated according to the systems adopted by the academies of science of these countries. Similarly, the transliteration for mainland Chinese names follows the Pinyin system, which has been officially adopted in mainland China. For languages with no one locally accepted transliteration system, notably Arabic, transliteration in general follows closely a system adopted by the United States Board on Geographic Names.

ALPHABETIZATION Names are alphabetized in the order of the letters of the English alphabet. Spanish *ll* and *ch*, for example, are not treated as distinct letters. Furthermore, diacritical marks are disregarded in alphabetization—German or Scandinavian *a* or *ö* are treated as *a* or *o*.

The names of physical features may appear inverted, since they are always alphabetized under the proper, not the generic, part of the name, thus: "Gibraltar, Strait of ⋃." Otherwise every entry, whether consisting of one word or more, is alphabetized as a single continuous entity. "Lakeland," for example, appears after "La Crosse" and before "La Salle." Names beginning with articles (Le Havre, Den Helder, Al-Qāhirah, As-Suways) are not inverted. Names beginning "Mc" are alphabetized as though spelled "Mac," and names beginning "St." and "Sainte" as though spelled "Saint."

In the case of identical names, towns are listed first, then political divisions, then physical features. Entries that are completely identical (including symbols, discussed below) are distinguished by abbreviations of their official country names and are sequenced alphabetically by country name. The many duplicate names in Canada, the United Kingdom, and the United States are further distinguished by abbreviations of the names of their primary subdivisions. (See list of abbreviations on pages 202 and 203).

ABBREVIATION AND CAPITALIZATION Abbreviation and styling have been standardized for all languages. A period is used after every abbreviation even when this may not be the local practice. The abbreviation "St." is used only for "Saint." "Sankt" and other forms of the term are spelled out.

All names are written with an initial capital letter except for a few Dutch names, such as 's-Gravenhage. Capitalization of noninitial words in a name generally follows local practice.

SYMBOL The symbols that appear in the Index graphically represent the broad categories of the features named, for example, ʌ for mountain (Everest, Mount ʌ). Superior numbers following some symbols in the Index indicate finer distinctions, for example, ʌ^1 for volcano (Fuji-san ʌ^1). A complete list of the symbols and those with superior numbers is given on page 203.

LIST OF ABBREVIATIONS

	LOCAL NAME	ENGLISH
Afg.	Afghānestān	Afghanistan
Afr.	—	Africa
A./I.	Afars et Issas	Afars and Issas
Ala., U.S.	Alabama	Alabama
Alaska, U.S.	Alaska	Alaska
Alg.	Algérie	Algeria
Alta., Can.	Alberta	Alberta
Am. Sam.	American Samoa	American Samoa
And.	Andorra	Andorra
Ang.	Angola	Angola
Anguilla	Anguilla	Anguilla
Ant.	—	Antarctica
Antig.	Antigua	Antigua
Arc. O.	—	Arctic Ocean
Arg.	Argentina	Argentina
Ariz., U.S.	Arizona	Arizona
Ark., U.S.	Arkansas	Arkansas
Ar. Sa.	Al-'Arabīyah as-Sa'ūdīyah	Saudi Arabia
As.	—	Asia
Atl. O.	—	Atlantic Ocean
Austl.	Australia	Australia
Ba.	Bahamas	Bahamas
Baḥr.	Al-Baḥrayn	Bahrain
Barb.	Barbados	Barbados
B.A.T.	British Antarctic Territory	British Antarctic Territory
B.C., Can.	British Columbia	British Columbia
Bdi.	Burundi	Burundi
Bel.	Belgique België	Belgium
Belize	Belize	Belize
Benin	Benin	Benin
Ber.	Bermuda	Bermuda
Ber. S.	—	Bering Sea
Bhārat	Bhārat	India
B.I.O.T.	British Indian Ocean Territory	British Indian Ocean Territory
Blg.	Bâlgarija	Bulgaria
Bngl.	Bangladesh	Bangladesh
Bol.	Bolivia	Bolivia
Bots.	Botswana	Botswana
Bra.	Brasil	Brazil
B.R.D.	Bundesrepublik Deutschland	Federal Republic of Germany
Br. Sol. Is.	British Solomon Islands	British Solomon Islands
Bru.	Brunei	Brunei
Br. Vir. Is.	British Virgin Islands	British Virgin Islands
Calif., U.S.	California	California
Cam.	Cameroun	Cameroon
Can.	Canada	Canada
Can./End.	Canton and Enderbury	Canton and Enderbury
Carib. S.	—	Caribbean Sea
Cay. Is.	Cayman Islands	Cayman Islands
Centraf.	République centrafricaine	Central African Republic
Česko.	Československo	Czechoslovakia
Chile	Chile	Chile
Christ. I.	Christmas Island	Christmas Island
C. Iv.	Côte d'Ivoire	Ivory Coast
C.M.I.K.	Chosŏn Minjujuŭi In'min Konghwaguk	North Korea
Cocos Is.	Cocos (Keeling) Islands	Cocos (Keeling) Islands
Col.	Colombia	Colombia
Colo., U.S.	Colorado	Colorado
Comores	Comores	Comoro Islands
Congo	Congo	Congo
Conn., U.S.	Connecticut	Connecticut
Cook Is.	Cook Islands	Cook Islands
C.R.	Costa Rica	Costa Rica
Cuba	Cuba	Cuba
C.V.	Cabo Verde	Cape Verde
C.Z.	Canal Zone	Canal Zone
Dan.	Danmark	Denmark
D.C., U.S.	District of Columbia	District of Columbia
D.D.R.	Deutsche Demokratische Republik	German Democratic Republic
Del., U.S.	Delaware	Delaware
Den.	Danmark	Denmark
Dom.	Dominica	Dominica
D.Y.	Druk-Yul	Bhutan
Ec.	Ecuador	Ecuador
Eire	Eire	Ireland
Ellás	Ellás	Greece
El Sal.	El Salvador	El Salvador
Eng., U.K.	England	England
Esp.	España	Spain
Eur.	—	Europe
Falk. Is.	Falkland Islands	Falkland Islands (Islas Malvinas)
Fiji	Fiji	Fiji
Fla., U.S.	Florida	Florida
Før.	Føroyar	Faeroe Islands
Fr.	France	France
Ga., U.S.	Georgia	Georgia
Gabon	Gabon	Gabon
Gam.	Gambia	Gambia
Gaza	—	Gaza Strip
Ghana	Ghana	Ghana
Gib.	Gibraltar	Gibraltar
Gilb. Is.	Gilbert Islands	Gilbert Islands
Gren.	Grenada	Grenada
Grn.	Grønland	Greenland
Guad.	Guadeloupe	Guadeloupe
Guam	Guam	Guam
Guat.	Guatemala	Guatemala
Guer.	Guernsey	Guernsey
Gui.-B.	Guinea-Bissau	Guinea-Bissau
Gui. Ecu.	Guinea Ecuatorial	Equatorial Guinea
Guinée	Guinée	Guinea
Guy.	Guyana	Guyana
Guy. fr.	Guyane française	French Guiana
Haï.	Haïti	Haiti
Haw., U.S.	Hawaii	Hawaii
H.K.	Hong Kong	Hong Kong
Hond.	Honduras	Honduras
H. Vol.	Haute-Volta	Upper Volta
Idaho, U.S.	Idaho	Idaho
I.I.A.	Ittiḥād al-Imārāt al-'Arabīyah	United Arab Emirates
Ill., U.S.	Illinois	Illinois
Ind., U.S.	Indiana	Indiana
Ind. O.	—	Indian Ocean
Indon.	Indonesia	Indonesia
I. of Man	Isle of Man	Isle of Man
Iowa, U.S.	Iowa	Iowa
Īrān	Īrān	Iran
'Irāq	Al-'Irāq	Iraq
Ísland	Ísland	Iceland
It.	Italia	Italy
Jam.	Jamaica	Jamaica
Jersey	Jersey	Jersey
Jugo.	Jugoslavija	Yugoslavia
Kam.	Kampuchea	Cambodia
Kans., U.S.	Kansas	Kansas
Kenya	Kenya	Kenya
Kípros	Kípros Kıbrıs	Cyprus
Kuwayt	Al-Kuwayt	Kuwait
Ky., U.S.	Kentucky	Kentucky
La., U.S.	Louisiana	Louisiana
Lao	Lao	Laos
Leso.	Lesotho	Lesotho
Liber.	Liberia	Liberia
Lībiyā	Lībiyā	Libya
Liech.	Liechtenstein	Liechtenstein
Lubnān	Al-Lubnān	Lebanon
Lux.	Luxembourg	Luxembourg
Macau	Macau	Macau
Madag.	Madagasikara	Madagascar
Magreb	Al-Magreb	Morocco
Magy.	Magyarország	Hungary
Maine, U.S.	Maine	Maine
Malawi	Malawi	Malawi
Malay.	Malaysia	Malaysia
Mald.	Maldives	Maldives
Mali	Mali	Mali
Malta	Malta	Malta
Man., Can.	Manitoba	Manitoba
Mart.	Martinique	Martinique
Mass., U.S.	Massachusetts	Massachusetts
Maur.	Mauritanie	Mauritania
Maus.	Mauritius	Mauritius
Md., U.S.	Maryland	Maryland
Medit. S.	—	Mediterranean Sea
Méx.	México	Mexico
Mich., U.S.	Michigan	Michigan
Mid. Is.	Midway Islands	Midway Islands
Minn., U.S.	Minnesota	Minnesota
Miṣr	Miṣr	Egypt
Miss., U.S.	Mississippi	Mississippi
Mo., U.S.	Missouri	Missouri
Moç.	Moçambique	Mozambique
Monaco	Monaco	Monaco
Mong.	Mongol Ard Uls	Mongolia
Mont., U.S.	Montana	Montana
Monts.	Montserrat	Montserrat
Mya.	Myanma	Burma
N.A.	—	North America
Nauru	Nauru	Nauru
N.B., Can.	New Brunswick	New Brunswick
N.C., U.S.	North Carolina	North Carolina
N. Cal.	Nouvelle-Calédonie	New Caledonia
N. Dak., U.S.	North Dakota	North Dakota
Nebr., U.S.	Nebraska	Nebraska
Ned.	Nederland	Netherlands
Ned. Ant.	Nederlandse Antillen	Netherlands Antilles
Nepāl	Nepāl	Nepal
Nev., U.S.	Nevada	Nevada
Newf., Can.	Newfoundland	Newfoundland
N.H., U.S.	New Hampshire	New Hampshire
N. Heb.	New Hebrides Nouvelles-Hébrides	New Hebrides
Nic.	Nicaragua	Nicaragua
Nig.	Nigeria	Nigeria
Niger	Niger	Niger
Nihon	Nihon	Japan
N. Ire., U.K.	Northern Ireland	Northern Ireland
Niue	Niue	Niue
N.J., U.S.	New Jersey	New Jersey
N. Mex., U.S.	New Mexico	New Mexico
Nor.	Norge	Norway
Norf. I.	Norfolk Island	Norfolk Island
N.S., Can.	Nova Scotia	Nova Scotia
N.W. Ter., Can.	Northwest Territories	Northwest Territories
N.Y., U.S.	New York	New York
N.Z.	New Zealand	New Zealand
Oc.	—	Oceania
Ohio, U.S.	Ohio	Ohio
Okla., U.S.	Oklahoma	Oklahoma
Ont., Can.	Ontario	Ontario
Oreg., U.S.	Oregon	Oregon
Öst.	Österreich	Austria
Pa., U.S.	Pennsylvania	Pennsylvania
Pac. O.	—	Pacific Ocean
Pāk.	Pākistān	Pakistan
Pan.	Panamá	Panama
Pap. N. Gui.	Papua New Guinea	Papua New Guinea
Para.	Paraguay	Paraguay
P.E.I., Can.	Prince Edward Island	Prince Edward Island
Perú	Perú	Peru
Pil.	Pilipinas	Philippines
Pit.	Pitcairn	Pitcairn
P.I.T.T.	Pacific Islands Trust Territory	Pacific Islands Trust Territory
Pol.	Polska	Poland
Poly. fr.	Polynésie française	French Polynesia
Port.	Portugal	Portugal
P.R.	Puerto Rico	Puerto Rico
P.S.N.Á.	Plazas de Soberanía en el Norte de África	Spanish North Africa
Qaṭar	Qaṭar	Qatar
Que., Can.	Québec	Quebec
Rep. Dom.	República Dominicana	Dominican Republic
Réu.	Réunion	Reunion
Rh.	Rhodesia	Rhodesia
R.I., U.S.	Rhode Island	Rhode Island
Rom.	România	Romania
Rw.	Rwanda	Rwanda
S.A.	—	South America
S. Afr.	South Africa Suid-Afrika	South Africa
Sask., Can.	Saskatchewan	Saskatchewan
S.C., U.S.	South Carolina	South Carolina
S. Ch. S.	—	South China Sea
Schw.	Schweiz; Suisse; Svizzera	Switzerland
Scot., U.K.	Scotland	Scotland
S. Dak., U.S.	South Dakota	South Dakota
Sén.	Sénégal	Senegal
Sey.	Seychelles	Seychelles
Shq.	Shqipëri	Albania
Sing.	Singapore	Singapore
S.L.	Sierra Leone	Sierra Leone
S. Lan.	Sri Lanka	Sri Lanka
S. Mar.	San Marino	San Marino
Som.	Somaliya	Somalia
Sp.	España	Spain
S.S.R.	Sovetskaja Socialističeskaja Respublika	Soviet Socialist Republic
S.S.S.R.	Sojuz Sovetskich Socialističeskich Respublik	Union of Soviet Socialist Republics
St. Hel.	St. Helena	St. Helena
St. K.-N.	St. Kitts-Nevis	St. Kitts-Nevis
St. Luc.	St. Lucia	St. Lucia
S. Tom./P.	São Tomé e Príncipe	Sao Tome and Principe
St. P./M.	St.-Pierre-et-Miquelon	St. Pierre and Miquelon
St. Vin.	St. Vincent	St. Vincent
Sūd.	As-Sūdān	Sudan
Suomi	Suomi	Finland
Sur.	Suriname	Surinam
Sūriy.	As-Sūrīyah	Syria
Sval.	Svalbard og Jan Mayen	Svalbard and Jan Mayen
Sve.	Sverige	Sweden
S.W. Afr.	South West Africa	South West Africa
Swaz.	Swaziland	Swaziland
T.a.a.f.	Terres australes et antarctiques françaises	French Southern and Antarctic Territories
Taehan	Taehan-Min'guk	South Korea
T'aiwan	T'aiwan	Taiwan
Tan.	Tanzania	Tanzania
Tchad	Tchad	Chad
T./C. Is.	Turks and Caicos Islands	Turks and Caicos Islands
Tenn., U.S.	Tennessee	Tennessee
Tex., U.S.	Texas	Texas
Thai.	Prathet Thai	Thailand
Timor	Timor	Portuguese Timor
Togo	Togo	Togo
Tok. Is.	Tokelau Islands	Tokelau Islands
Tonga	Tonga	Tonga
Trin.	Trinidad and Tobago	Trinidad and Tobago
Tun.	Tunisie	Tunisia
Tür.	Türkiye	Turkey
Tuvalu	Tuvalu	Tuvalu
Ug.	Uganda	Uganda
U.K.	United Kingdom	United Kingdom
'Umān	'Umān	Oman
Ur.	Uruguay	Uruguay
Urd.	Al-Urdunn	Jordan
U.S.	United States	United States

LIST OF ABBREVIATIONS CON'T.

	LOCAL NAME	ENGLISH
U.S.S.R.	Sojuz Sovetskich Socialističeskich Respublik	Union of Soviet Socialist Republics
Utah, U.S.	Utah	Utah
Va., U.S.	Virginia	Virginia
Vat.	Città del Vaticano	Vatican City
Ven.	Venezuela	Venezuela
Viet. N.	Viet-nam Dan-chu Cong-hoa	North Vietnam
Viet. S.	Viet-nam Cong-hoa	South Vietnam
Vir. Is., U.S.	Virgin Islands	Virgin Islands (U.S.)
Vt., U.S.	Vermont	Vermont
Wake I.	Wake Island	Wake Island
Wales, U.K.	Wales	Wales
Wal./F.	Wallis et Futuna	Wallis and Futuna
Wash., U.S.	Washington	Washington
Wis., U.S.	Wisconsin	Wisconsin
W. Sah.	Western Sahara	Western Sahara
W. Sam.	Western Samoa	Western Samoa
W. Va., U.S.	West Virginia	West Virginia
Wyo., U.S.	Wyoming	Wyoming
Yai.	Yaitopya	Ethiopia
Yaman	Al-Yaman	Yemen
Yam. S.	Al-Yaman ash-Sha'bīyah	People's Democratic Republic of Yemen
Yis.	Yisra'el	Israel
Yukon, Can.	Yukon	Yukon
Zaïre	Zaïre	Zaire
Zam.	Zambia	Zambia
Zhg.	Zhongguo	China

KEY TO SYMBOLS

∧ **Mountain**
∧[1] Volcano
∧[2] Hill
⩓ **Mountains**
⩓[1] Plateau
⩓[2] Hills
)(**Pass**
V **Valley, Canyon**
≚ **Plain**
≚[1] Basin
≚[2] Delta
≻ **Cape**
≻[1] Peninsula
≻[2] Spit, Sand Bar
I **Island**
I[1] Atoll
I[2] Rock
II **Islands**
II[1] Rocks
• **Other Topographic Features**
•[1] Continent
•[2] Coast, Beach
•[3] Isthmus
•[4] Cliff
•[5] Cave, Caves
•[6] Crater
•[7] Depression
•[8] Dunes
•[9] Lava Flow
≏ **River**
≏[1] River Channel
≋ **Canal**
≋[1] Aqueduct
↳ **Waterfall, Rapids**
⩊ **Strait**
C **Bay, Gulf**
C[1] Estuary
C[2] Fjord
C[3] Bight
⊜ **Lake, Lakes**
⊜[1] Reservoir
≣ **Swamp**
⊓ **Ice Features, Glacier**
⊤ **Other Hydrographic Features**
⊤[1] Ocean
⊤[2] Sea
⊤[3] Anchorage
⊤[4] Oasis, Well, Spring
✧ **Submarine Features**
✧[1] Depression
✧[2] Reef, Shoal
✧[3] Mountain, Mountains
✧[4] Slope, Shelf
□ **Political Unit**
□[1] Independent Nation
□[2] Dependency
□[3] State, Canton, Republic
□[4] Province, Region, Oblast
□[5] Department, District, Prefecture
□[6] County
□[7] City, Municipality
□[8] Miscellaneous
□[9] Historical
♁ **Cultural Institution**
♁[1] Religious Institution
♁[2] Educational Institution
♁[3] Scientific, Industrial Facility
⊥ **Historical Site**
♠ **Recreational Site**
⊠ **Airport**
■ **Military Installation**
⊸ **Miscellaneous**
⊸[1] Region
⊸[2] Desert
⊸[3] Forest, Moor
⊸[4] Reserve, Reservation
⊸[5] Transportation
⊸[6] Dam
⊸[7] Mine, Quarry
⊸[8] Neighborhood
⊸[9] Shopping Center

Index

Name	Page	Lat ° ′	Long ° ′
A			
Aachen	72	50.47 N	6.05 E
Aaiun → El Aaiún	106	27.09 N	13.12 W
Aalen	72	48.50 N	10.05 E
Aalst (Alost)	74	50.56 N	4.02 E
Äänekoski	68	62.36 N	25.44 E
Aarau	74	47.23 N	8.03 E
Aarburg	74	47.19 N	7.54 E
Aare ≏	74	47.37 N	8.13 E
Aarschot	72	50.59 N	4.50 E
Aba, Nig.	114	5.06 N	7.21 E
Aba, Zhg.	88	33.06 N	101.59 E
Abacaxis ≏	138	3.54 S	58.47 W
Ābādān	104	30.20 N	48.16 E
Abaetetuba	134	18.02 S	45.12 W
Abagaqi	88	43.41 N	114.40 E
Abaí	140	25.58 S	55.57 W
Abaj	82	49.38 N	72.52 E
Abakaliki	114	6.21 N	8.06 E
Abakan	84	53.43 N	91.26 E
Abakan ≏	84	53.43 N	91.30 E
Abancay	134	13.35 S	72.55 W
Abashiri	90a	44.01 N	144.17 E
Abasolo	130	20.27 N	101.32 W
Abaya, Lake ⊜	108	6.20 N	37.55 E
Abayita, Lake ⊜	108	7.37 N	38.35 E
Abaza	84	52.39 N	90.06 E
Abbasanta	78	40.08 N	8.50 E
Abbeville, Fr.	74	50.06 N	1.50 E
Abbeville, La., U.S.	158	29.58 N	92.08 W
Abbeville, S.C., U.S.	156	34.11 N	82.23 W
Abbeyfeale	70	52.24 N	9.18 W
Abbey Head ≻	70	54.46 N	3.58 W
Abbeyleix	70	52.55 N	7.20 W
Abbiategrasso	78	45.24 N	8.54 E
Abbot, Mount ∧	120	20.03 S	147.45 E
Abbottābād	102	34.09 N	73.13 E
'Abd al-Kūrī I	100	12.12 N	52.15 E
'Abd Allāh, Khawr ⩊	104	29.50 N	48.20 E
Abdulino	82	53.42 N	53.40 E
Abe, Lake ⊜	108	11.06 N	41.50 E
Abéché	108	13.49 N	20.49 E
Abéjar	76	41.48 N	2.47 W
Abengourou	114	6.44 N	3.29 W
Abenójar	76	38.53 N	4.21 W
Åbenrå	68	55.02 N	9.26 E
Abensberg	72	48.49 N	11.51 E
Abeokuta	114	7.10 N	3.26 E
Aberavon → Port Talbot	70	51.36 N	3.47 W
Aberayron	70	52.15 N	4.15 W
Aberchirder	70	57.33 N	2.38 W
Abercorn → Mbala	110	8.50 S	31.22 E
Aberdare	70	51.43 N	3.27 W
Aberdeen, Scot., U.K.	70	57.10 N	2.04 W
Aberdeen, Md., U.S.	152	39.30 N	76.10 W
Aberdeen, Miss., U.S.	158	33.49 N	88.33 W
Aberdeen, N.C., U.S.	156	35.08 N	79.26 W
Aberdeen, S. Dak., U.S.	162	45.28 N	98.29 W
Aberdeen, Wash., U.S.	166	46.59 N	123.50 W
Aberdeen Lake ⊜	142	64.27 N	99.00 W
Aberfeldy	70	56.37 N	3.54 W
Abergavenny	70	51.50 N	3.00 W
Abernathy	160	33.50 N	101.51 W
Abernethy	70	56.20 N	3.19 W
Aberystwyth	70	52.25 N	4.05 W
Abetone	78	44.08 N	10.40 E
Abez'	66	66.32 N	61.42 E
Abhā	100	18.13 N	42.30 E
Abidjan	114	5.19 N	4.02 W
Abilene, Kans., U.S.	162	38.55 N	97.13 W
Abilene, Tex., U.S.	160	32.27 N	99.44 W
Abingdon, Ill., U.S.	154	40.48 N	90.24 W
Abingdon, Va., U.S.	156	36.43 N	81.59 W
Abington Reef ✧[2]	120	18.00 S	149.36 E
Āb-i-Panja (P'andž) ≏	82	37.06 N	68.20 E
Abisko	66	68.20 N	18.51 E
Abisko Nationalpark ♠	66	68.20 N	18.30 E
Abitau ≏	142	59.53 N	109.03 W
Abitibi ≏	154	51.03 N	80.55 W
Abitibi, Lake ⊜	154	48.42 N	79.45 W
Ablis	74	48.31 N	1.50 E
Abnūb	112	27.16 N	31.09 E
Åbo → Turku	68	60.27 N	22.17 E
Abohar	102	30.09 N	74.11 E
Abomey	114	7.11 N	1.59 E
Abong Abong, Gunung ∧	94	4.15 N	96.47 E
Abong Mbang	106	3.59 N	13.10 E
Abony	72	47.11 N	20.01 E
Aborigen, Pik ∧	84	61.59 N	149.19 E
Abou Deïa	108	11.27 N	19.17 E
Abramovskaja	66	65.11 N	51.43 E
Abra Pampa	140	22.43 S	65.42 W
Abruzzi □[4]	78	42.20 N	13.45 E
Absaroka Range ⩓	166	44.45 N	109.50 W
Absecon	152	39.26 N	74.30 W
Abtenau	72	47.33 N	13.21 E
Abū 'Alī I	104	27.20 N	49.33 E
Abū Ḥamad	112	19.32 N	33.19 E
Abū Kamāl	104	34.27 N	40.55 E
Abū Madd, Ra's ≻	104	24.50 N	37.07 E
Abū Mūsā, Jazīreh-ye I	104	25.52 N	55.03 E
Abunã	134	9.42 S	65.23 W
Abuná ≏	134	9.41 S	65.23 W
Abu Road	100	24.29 N	72.47 E
Abū Shajarah, Ra's ≻	112	21.04 N	37.14 E
Abū Ẓaby	104	24.28 N	54.22 E
Åbybro	68	57.09 N	9.45 E
Acajutla	128	13.36 N	89.50 W
Acámbaro	130	20.02 N	100.44 W
Acaponeta	130	22.30 N	105.22 W
Acapulco [de Juárez]	130	16.51 N	99.55 W
Acarai Mountains ⩓	138	1.50 N	57.40 W
Acaraú	134	2.53 S	40.07 W
Acarigua	138	9.33 N	69.12 W
Acatlán [de Osorio]	130	18.12 N	98.03 W
Acay, Nevado de ∧	140	24.22 S	66.10 W
Acayucan	130	17.57 N	94.55 W
Accomac	156	37.43 N	75.40 W
Accoville	156	37.46 N	81.50 W
Accra	114	5.33 N	0.13 W
Acerra	78	40.57 N	14.22 E
Achacachi	134	16.03 S	68.43 W
Achalpur	102	21.16 N	77.31 E
Acheng	88	45.32 N	126.59 E
Achern	72	48.37 N	8.04 E
Achill	70	53.56 N	9.54 W
Achtuba ≏	64	46.42 N	48.00 E
Achtubinsk	82	48.17 N	46.10 E
Achtyrka	82	50.19 N	34.55 E
Ačinsk	84	56.17 N	90.30 E
Acireale	78	37.37 N	15.10 E
Ačisaj	82	43.35 N	68.53 E
Ackerman	158	33.19 N	89.10 W
Acklins Island I	132	22.25 N	74.00 W
Acomita	164	35.03 N	107.35 W
Aconcagua, Cerro ∧	140	32.39 S	70.00 W
Acquapendente	78	42.44 N	11.52 E
Acqui Terme	78	44.41 N	8.28 E
Acre → 'Akko	104	32.55 N	35.05 E
Acre ≏	134	8.45 S	67.22 W
Acri	78	39.29 N	16.23 E
Acton	154	43.37 N	80.02 W
Acton Vale	152	45.39 N	72.34 W
Actopan	130	20.16 N	98.56 W
Acworth	156	34.04 N	84.41 W
Ada, Jugo.	80	45.48 N	20.08 E
Ada, Minn., U.S.	162	47.18 N	96.31 W
Ada, Ohio, U.S.	152	40.46 N	83.49 W
Ada, Okla., U.S.	160	34.46 N	96.41 W
Adair	158	36.26 N	95.16 W
Adair, Cape ≻	142	71.24 N	71.13 W
Adairsville	156	34.22 N	84.56 W
Adak, S.S.S.R.	66	66.30 N	59.38 E
Adak, Alaska, U.S.	146	51.54 N	176.35 W
Adak Island I	146	51.45 N	176.40 W
Ādam	100	22.24 N	57.32 E
Adam, Mount ∧	136	51.34 S	60.04 W
Adamawa ⩓	106	7.00 N	12.00 E
Adamów	72	51.45 N	22.17 E
Adams, Mass., U.S.	152	42.37 N	73.07 W
Adams, Nebr., U.S.	162	40.28 N	96.31 W
Adams, N. Dak., U.S.	162	48.25 N	98.05 W
Adams, N.Y., U.S.	152	43.49 N	76.01 W
Adams, Mount ∧	166	46.12 N	121.28 W
Adams Bridge ✧[2]	100	9.04 N	79.37 E
Adams Lake ⊜	148	51.13 N	119.33 W
Adams Peak ∧	100	6.48 N	80.30 E
Adana	104	37.01 N	35.18 E
Adanero	76	40.56 N	4.36 W
Adapazarı	64	40.46 N	30.24 E
Adarama	112	17.05 N	34.54 E
Adavale	120	25.55 S	144.36 E
Ad-Dabbah	112	18.03 N	30.57 E
Ad-Dahnā' ⊸[2]	104	24.30 N	48.10 E
Ad-Dāmir	108	17.35 N	33.58 E
Ad-Dammām	104	26.26 N	50.07 E
Ad-Dawādimī	100	24.28 N	44.18 E
Ad-Dawḥah (Doha)	104	25.17 N	51.32 E
Aḍ-Ḍiffah (Libyan Plateau) ⩓[1]	112	30.30 N	25.30 E
Addis Ababa → Addis Abeba	108	9.00 N	38.50 E
Addis Abeba	108	9.00 N	38.50 E
Addison	154	41.59 N	84.21 W
Ad-Dīwānīyah	104	31.59 N	44.56 E
Ad-Duwaym	112	14.00 N	32.19 E
Adel, Ga., U.S.	156	31.08 N	83.25 W
Adel, Iowa, U.S.	154	41.37 N	94.01 W
Adel, Oreg., U.S.	166	42.11 N	119.54 W
Adelaide	120	34.55 S	138.35 E
Adelaide Peninsula ≻[1]	142	68.09 N	97.45 W
Adelaide River	124	13.15 S	131.06 E
Adèle Island I	118	15.32 S	123.09 E
Aden	100	12.45 N	45.12 E
Aden, Gulf of C	100	12.30 N	48.00 E
Ader ⩓[1]	114	14.10 N	5.05 E
Adi, Pulau I	124	4.18 S	133.26 E
Adieu, Cape ≻	122	31.59 S	132.09 E
Adigrat	108	14.18 N	39.31 E
Ādilābād	100	19.40 N	78.32 E
Adimi	84	47.20 N	138.56 E
Adin	168	41.12 N	120.57 W
Adirondack Mountains ⩓	152	44.00 N	74.00 W
Admiralty Gulf C	118	14.20 S	125.50 E
Admiralty Inlet C	142	73.00 N	86.00 W
Admiralty Island I, N.W. Ter., Can.	142	69.30 N	101.00 W
Admiralty Island I, Alaska, U.S.	146	57.50 N	134.30 W
Ado-Ekiti	114	7.38 N	5.12 E
Adonara, Pulau I	96	8.20 S	123.10 E
Ādoni	100	15.38 N	77.17 E
Adra	76	36.44 N	3.01 W
Adrano	78	37.40 N	14.50 E
Adrar	106	27.54 N	0.17 W
Adrar ⊸[1]	106	20.30 N	13.30 W
Adria	78	45.03 N	12.03 E
Adrian, Mich., U.S.	152	41.54 N	84.02 W
Adrian, Minn., U.S.	162	43.38 N	95.56 W
Adrian, Mo., U.S.	158	38.24 N	94.21 W
Adrian, Oreg., U.S.	166	43.44 N	117.04 W
Adrian, W. Va., U.S.	152	38.54 N	80.17 W
Adrianople → Edirne	80	41.40 N	26.34 E
Adriatic Sea ⊤[2]	64	42.30 N	16.00 E
Adwa	108	14.10 N	38.55 E
Adyča ≏	84	68.13 N	134.41 E
Adz'vavom	66	66.36 N	59.12 E
Aegean Sea ⊤[2]	80	38.30 N	25.00 E
A'erjinshanmai ⩓	102	37.30 N	86.30 E
Aershan	88	47.11 N	119.57 E
Afanasjevo	66	58.52 N	53.12 E
Afándou	80	36.17 N	28.10 E
Afars and Issas □[2]	108	11.30 N	43.00 E
Affton	158	38.33 N	90.20 W
Afghanistan □[1]	100	33.00 N	65.00 E
Afikpo	114	5.53 N	7.56 E
Åfjord	68	63.58 N	10.12 E
Afonicha	66	68.13 N	53.17 E
Afton, Iowa, U.S.	158	41.02 N	94.12 W
Afton, N.Y., U.S.	152	42.14 N	75.32 W
Afton, Okla., U.S.	158	36.42 N	94.58 W
Aga	68	60.18 N	6.36 E
Agadez	114	16.58 N	7.59 E
Agadir	106	30.26 N	9.36 W
Agadyr'	82	48.17 N	72.53 E
Agalega Islands II	110	10.24 S	56.37 E
Agan ≏	84	61.23 N	74.35 E
Agana	92	13.28 N	144.45 E
Agapa	84	71.27 N	89.15 E
Agartala	102	23.49 N	91.16 E
Agboville	114	5.56 N	4.13 W
Agde	74	43.19 N	3.28 E
Agege	114	6.37 N	3.20 E
Agen	74	44.12 N	0.37 E
Agency	158	41.00 N	92.18 W
Āghā Jārī	104	30.42 N	49.50 E
Aginskoje	84	55.15 N	94.55 E
Agira	78	37.39 N	14.32 E
Agnew	122	28.01 S	120.30 E
Agnone	78	41.48 N	14.22 E
Agordat → Akordat	108	15.35 N	37.54 E
Āgra	102	27.11 N	78.01 E
Agram → Zagreb	78	45.48 N	15.58 E
Ágreda	76	41.51 N	1.56 W
Agrigento	78	37.18 N	13.35 E
Agrihan I	92	18.46 N	145.40 E
Agrínion	80	38.37 N	21.24 E
Aguachica	138	8.19 N	73.38 W
Aguada de Pasajeros	132	22.23 N	80.51 W
Aguadas	138	5.37 N	75.27 W
Aguadilla	132	18.26 N	67.09 W
Aguadulce	138	8.15 N	80.32 W
Aguanus ≏	150	50.13 N	62.05 W
Agua Prieta	130	31.18 N	109.34 W
Aguarico ≏	138	0.59 S	75.11 W
Aguascalientes	130	21.53 N	102.18 W
Agu Bay C	142	70.18 N	86.30 W
Agudos	140	22.28 S	49.00 W
Águeda ≏	76	41.02 N	6.56 W
Aguijan I	92	14.51 N	145.34 E
Aguila	164	33.56 N	113.11 W
Águilas	76	37.24 N	1.35 W
Agulhas, Cape ≻	116	34.52 S	20.00 E
Agulhas Negras, Pico das ∧	136	22.23 S	44.38 W
Agusan ≏	98	9.00 N	125.30 E
Agustín Codazzi	138	10.02 N	73.14 W
Ahaggar ⩓	106	23.00 N	6.30 E
Ahaggar, Tassili du ⩓[1]	106	21.00 N	6.00 E
Aha Hills ⩓[2]	116	19.45 S	21.10 E
Ahar	104	38.28 N	47.04 E
Ahaus	72	52.04 N	7.00 E
Ahipara Bay C	126	35.10 S	173.08 E
Ahklun Mountains ⩓	146	59.15 N	161.00 W
Ahlen	72	51.46 N	7.53 E
Ahmadābād	102	23.02 N	72.37 E
Ahmadnagar	100	19.05 N	74.45 E
Ahmadpur East	102	29.09 N	71.16 E
Ahmar Mountains ⩓	108	9.15 N	41.00 E
Ahoskie	156	36.17 N	76.59 W
Ahrensburg	72	53.40 N	10.14 E
Ahrweiler	72	50.32 N	7.05 E
Ähtäri	68	62.34 N	24.06 E
Ahuacatlán	130	21.03 N	104.29 W
Ahun	74	46.05 N	2.05 E
Ahvāz	104	31.19 N	48.42 E
Ahvenanmaa □[4]	68	60.15 N	20.00 E
Ahvenanmaa (Åland) II	68	60.15 N	20.00 E
Aḥwar	100	13.31 N	46.42 E
Aibihu ⊜	88	44.55 N	82.55 E
Aichach	72	48.28 N	11.08 E
Aiea	170c	21.23 N	157.56 W
Aigen im Mühlkreis	72	48.39 N	13.58 E
Aigle	74	46.19 N	6.58 E
Aigre	74	45.54 N	0.01 E
Aigueperse	74	46.01 N	3.12 E
Aigues-Mortes	74	43.34 N	4.11 E
Aiguilles	74	44.47 N	6.52 E
Aigurande	74	46.26 N	1.50 E
Aihun	88	50.13 N	127.33 E
Aijal	102	23.44 N	92.43 E
Aiken	156	33.34 N	81.43 W
Ailaoshan ⩓	94	24.08 N	101.25 E
Aim	84	58.50 N	134.12 E
Aimorés	134	19.30 S	41.04 W
Ain □[5]	74	46.10 N	5.20 E
Ainsworth	162	42.33 N	99.52 W
Aïr ⩓	114	18.00 N	8.30 E
Aires	70	50.38 N	2.24 E
Aire-sur-l'Adour	74	43.42 N	0.16 W
Air Force Island I	142	67.55 N	74.10 W
Airolo	74	46.32 N	8.37 E
Airvault	74	46.50 N	0.08 W
Aishihik Lake ⊜	146	61.25 N	137.06 W
Aisne □[5]	74	49.30 N	3.30 E
Aïssa, Djebel ∧	106	32.51 N	0.30 W
Aitape	124	3.08 S	142.21 E
Aitkin	154	46.32 N	93.43 W
Aiud	80	46.19 N	23.44 E
Aix-en-Provence	74	43.32 N	5.26 E
Aix-la-Chapelle → Aachen	72	50.47 N	6.05 E
Aíyion	80	38.15 N	22.05 E
Aizpute	86	56.43 N	21.38 E
Aizu-wakamatsu	90	37.30 N	139.56 E
Ajaccio	78	41.55 N	8.44 E
Ajaguz	84	47.56 N	80.23 E
Ajan	84	56.27 N	138.10 E
Ajan ≏	84	70.10 N	95.50 E
Ajanta	100	20.30 N	75.48 E
Ajanta Range ⩓	100	20.30 N	76.00 E
Ajax	154	43.51 N	79.02 W
Ajdābiyah	108	30.48 N	20.14 E
Ajjer, Tassili n' ⩓[1]	106	25.10 N	8.00 E
Ajka	72	47.07 N	17.34 E
Ajlune	166	46.31 N	122.26 W
Ajmer	102	26.27 N	74.38 E
Ajo	164	32.22 N	112.52 W
Ajon, Ostrov I	84	69.50 N	168.40 E
Ajtos	80	42.42 N	27.15 E
Aju, Kepulauan II	92	0.28 N	131.03 E
Akademii, Zaliv C	84	54.15 N	138.05 E
'Akasha East	112	21.05 N	30.43 E
Akashi	90	34.38 N	134.59 E
Akershus □[6]	68	60.00 N	11.10 E
Akesu	88	41.10 N	80.20 E
Aketi	108	2.44 N	23.46 E
Akharnai	80	38.05 N	23.44 E
Akhisar	80	38.55 N	27.51 E
Akiachak	146	60.55 N	161.27 W
Akimiski Island I	142	53.00 N	81.20 W
Akita	90	39.43 N	140.07 E
Akjoujt	114	19.45 N	14.23 W
Akkerman → Belgorod-Dnestrovskij	82	46.12 N	30.20 E
'Akko (Acre)	104	32.55 N	35.05 E
Akkol', S.S.S.R.	82	43.25 N	70.47 E
Akkol', S.S.S.R.	82	45.02 N	75.40 E
Aklavik	146	68.12 N	135.00 W
'Aklé 'Âduâna ⊸[1]	114	18.00 N	5.30 W
Akobo ≏	112	7.48 N	33.03 E
Akola	100	20.42 N	77.00 E
Akordat	108	15.35 N	37.54 E
Akpatok Island I	142	60.25 N	68.00 W
Akranes	66a	64.18 N	22.02 W
Åkrehamn	68	59.16 N	5.11 E
Akron, Colo., U.S.	162	40.10 N	103.13 W
Akron, Ind., U.S.	158	41.02 N	86.01 W
Akron, Iowa, U.S.	162	42.49 N	96.33 W
Akron, N.Y., U.S.	152	43.01 N	78.30 W
Akron, Ohio, U.S.	152	41.05 N	81.31 W
Akron, Pa., U.S.	152	40.09 N	76.12 W
Aksaray	100	38.23 N	34.03 E
Aksarka	84	66.36 N	67.46 E
Akşehir	100	38.21 N	31.25 E
Aksuat	84	47.48 N	82.50 E
Aksum	108	14.08 N	38.48 E
Aktogaj	84	46.57 N	79.40 E
Akt'ubinsk	82	50.17 N	57.10 E
Akure	114	7.15 N	5.12 E
Akureyri	66a	65.44 N	18.08 W
Akžar	84	47.35 N	83.42 E
Ål	68	60.38 N	8.34 E
Alabama □[3]	144	32.50 N	87.00 W
Alabaster	158	33.15 N	86.49 W
Alachua	156	29.47 N	82.30 W
Alagir	82	43.03 N	44.14 E
Alagoa Grande	134	7.03 S	35.38 W
Alagoinhas	134	12.07 S	38.26 W
Alajärvi	68	63.00 N	23.49 E
Alajõe	66	59.01 N	27.26 E
Alajskij Chrebet ⩓	82	39.45 N	72.00 E
Alajuela	132	10.01 N	84.13 W
Alakol', Ozero ⊜	84	46.10 N	81.45 E
Al-'Alamayn	112	30.49 N	28.57 E
Alamagan I	92	17.36 N	145.50 E
Al-'Amārah	104	31.50 N	47.09 E
Alameda, Calif., U.S.	168	37.46 N	122.16 W
Alameda, N. Mex., U.S.	164	35.11 N	106.37 W
Alamein → Al-'Alamayn	108	30.49 N	28.57 E
Alamo	158	35.47 N	89.07 W
Alamogordo	164	32.54 N	105.57 W
Alamogordo Reservoir ⊜[1]	160	34.38 N	104.25 W
Alamo Heights	160	29.28 N	98.28 W
Alamosa	164	37.28 N	105.52 W
Aland Sea ⊤[2]	68	60.00 N	19.30 E
Alanya	100	36.33 N	32.01 E
Alaotra, Lac ⊜	117b	17.30 S	48.30 E
Alapaha ≏	156	30.26 N	83.06 W
Alapajevsk	82	57.52 N	61.42 E
Al-'Aqabah	104	29.31 N	35.00 E
Alarcón, Embalse de ⊜[1]	76	39.36 N	2.10 W
Al-'Arīsh	112	31.08 N	33.48 E
Alashanyouqi	88	40.02 N	103.33 E
Alaska □[3]	146	62.00 N	153.00 W
Alaska, Gulf of C	146	58.00 N	146.00 W
Alaska Peninsula ≻[1]	146	57.00 N	158.00 W
Alaska Range ⩓	146	62.30 N	150.00 W
Alassio	78	44.00 N	8.10 E
Alastaro	68	60.56 N	22.55 E
Alatri	78	41.43 N	13.21 E
Al-'Aṭrūn	112	18.11 N	26.36 E
Alatyr'	66	54.51 N	46.36 E
Alausí	138	2.12 S	78.50 W
Alavieska	68	64.10 N	24.18 E
Alavus	68	62.35 N	23.37 E
Alazeja ≏	84	70.51 N	153.34 E
Al-'Azīzīyah	108	32.32 N	13.01 E
Alba, It.	78	44.42 N	8.02 E
Alba, Mich., U.S.	154	44.59 N	84.58 W
Albacete	76	38.59 N	1.51 W
Ålbæk	68	57.36 N	10.25 E
Alba-Iulia	80	46.04 N	23.35 E
Alban	74	43.54 N	2.28 E
Albanel, Lac ⊜	142	50.55 N	73.12 W
Albania □[1]	64	41.00 N	20.00 E
Albano Laziale	78	41.44 N	12.39 E
Albany, Austl.	122	35.02 S	117.53 E
Albany, Ga., U.S.	156	31.35 N	84.10 W
Albany, Ind., U.S.	158	40.18 N	85.14 W
Albany, Ky., U.S.	158	36.42 N	85.08 W
Albany, Minn., U.S.	154	45.38 N	94.34 W
Albany, N.Y., U.S.	152	42.39 N	73.45 W
Albany, Oreg., U.S.	166	44.38 N	123.06 W
Albany, Wis., U.S.	154	42.43 N	89.26 W
Albany ≏	142	52.17 N	81.31 W
Albardón	140	31.26 S	68.30 W
Al-Baṣrah (Basra)	104	30.30 N	47.47 E
Albatross Bay C	124	12.45 S	141.43 E
Al-Bawīṭī	112	28.21 N	28.52 E
Albemarle	156	35.21 N	80.12 W
Albemarle Sound ⩊	156	36.03 N	76.12 W
Albenga	78	44.03 N	8.13 E
Albens	74	45.47 N	5.57 E
Alberene	156	37.53 N	78.37 W
Albert	74	50.00 N	2.39 E
Albert, Lake ⊜	110	1.40 N	31.00 E
Alberta □[4]	142	54.00 N	113.00 W
Albert City	162	42.47 N	94.57 W
Albert Edward Bay C	142	69.32 N	103.00 W
Al'bertin	86	53.05 N	25.23 E
Albertirsa	72	47.15 N	19.38 E
Albert Lea	154	43.39 N	93.22 W
Alberton	150	46.49 N	64.04 W
Albertville, Fr.	74	45.41 N	6.23 E
Albertville, Ala., U.S.	158	34.16 N	86.12 W
Albertville → Kalemi, Zaïre	110	5.56 S	29.12 E
Albi	74	43.56 N	2.09 E
Albia	154	41.02 N	92.48 W
Albina	134	5.30 N	54.03 W
Albino	78	45.46 N	9.47 E
Albion, Calif., U.S.	168	39.13 N	123.46 W
Albion, Mich., U.S.	154	42.15 N	84.45 W
Albion, Nebr., U.S.	162	41.42 N	98.00 W
Albion, N.Y., U.S.	152	43.15 N	78.12 W
Albion, Pa., U.S.	152	41.53 N	80.22 W
Alborán, Isla de I	76	35.58 N	3.02 W
Ålborg	68	57.03 N	9.56 E
Alborz, Reshteh-ye Kūhhā-ye ⩓	104	36.00 N	53.00 E
Ālbū Gharz, Sabkhat ⊜	104	34.45 N	41.15 E
Al-Buḥayrah al-Murrah al-Kubrā ⊜	112	30.20 N	32.23 E
Albuñol	76	36.47 N	3.12 W
Albuquerque	164	35.05 N	106.40 W
Alburg	152	44.59 N	73.18 W
Albury	120	36.05 S	146.55 E
Alcalá de Guadaira	76	37.20 N	5.50 W
Alcalá de Henares	76	40.29 N	3.22 W
Alcalde	164	36.05 N	106.03 W
Alcamo	78	37.59 N	12.58 E
Alcanar	76	40.33 N	0.29 E
Alcañiz	76	41.03 N	0.08 W
Alcântara	134	2.24 S	44.24 W
Alcantarilla	76	37.58 N	1.13 W
Alcázar de San Juan	76	39.24 N	3.12 W
Alcester	162	43.01 N	96.38 W
Alcira	76	39.09 N	0.26 W
Alcoa	156	35.48 N	83.59 W
Alcobaça	134	17.30 S	39.13 W
Alcorn College	158	31.52 N	91.09 W
Alcoy	76	38.42 N	0.28 W
Aldabra Islands I[1]	110	9.25 S	46.22 E
Aldama	130	28.51 N	105.54 W
Aldan	84	58.37 N	125.24 E
Aldan ≏	84	63.28 N	129.35 E
Aldanskoje Nagorje ⩓[1]	84	57.00 N	127.00 E
Aldeburgh	70	52.09 N	1.35 E
Alderney I	70	49.43 N	2.12 W
Aldershot	70	51.15 N	0.47 W
Alderson	156	37.43 N	80.39 W
Aledo	154	41.12 N	90.45 W
Aleg	114	17.03 N	13.55 W
Alegrete	140	29.46 S	55.46 W
Alejandro Selkirk, Isla (Isla Más Afuera) I	136	33.45 S	80.46 W
Alejsk	84	52.58 N	82.45 E
Aleknagik	146	59.17 N	158.38 W
Aleksandrija	82	48.40 N	33.07 E
Aleksandro-Nevskij	86	53.28 N	40.13 E
Aleksandrov	86	56.24 N	38.43 E
Aleksandrov Gaj	82	50.09 N	48.34 E
Aleksandrovsk	82	48.35 N	39.12 E
Aleksandrovskoje	84	60.26 N	77.50 E
Aleksandrovsk-Sachalinskij	84	50.54 N	142.10 E
Aleksejevka, S.S.S.R.	82	51.59 N	70.59 E
Aleksejevka, S.S.S.R.	82	50.37 N	38.42 E
Aleksejevsk	84	57.50 N	108.23 E
Aleksin	86	54.31 N	37.05 E
Aleksinac	80	43.32 N	21.43 E
Alemania	140	25.35 S	65.40 W
Alençon	74	48.26 N	0.05 E
Alenquer	134	1.56 S	54.46 W
Alentejo □[9]	76	38.00 N	8.00 W
Aleppo → Ḥalab	104	36.12 N	37.10 E
Aléria	78	42.05 N	9.30 E
Alert Bay	148	50.35 N	126.55 W
Alès	74	44.08 N	4.05 E
Alessandria	78	44.54 N	8.37 E
Alessano	78	39.53 N	18.20 E
Ålesund	68	62.28 N	6.09 E
Aletai	88	47.52 N	88.07 E
Aleutian Islands II	146	52.00 N	176.00 W
Aleutka	84	45.57 N	150.10 E
Alevina, Mys ≻	84	58.50 N	151.20 E
Alex	160	34.55 N	97.47 W
Alexander Archipelago II	146	56.30 N	134.00 W
Alexander Bay	116	28.40 S	16.30 E
Alexander City	158	32.56 N	85.57 W
Alexandra	126	45.20 S	169.23 E
Alexandra ≏	120	18.14 S	139.54 E
Alexandra Falls ↳	142	60.29 N	116.18 W
Alexandretta → İskenderun	104	36.37 N	36.07 E
Alexandria, Ont., Can.	152	45.19 N	74.38 W
Alexandria → Al-Iskandarīyah, Miṣr	112	31.12 N	29.54 E
Alexandria, Rom.	80	43.58 N	25.20 E
Alexandria, Ind., U.S.	158	40.16 N	85.41 W
Alexandria, Ky., U.S.	152	38.58 N	84.23 W
Alexandria, La., U.S.	158	31.18 N	92.27 W
Alexandria, Minn., U.S.	162	45.53 N	95.22 W
Alexandria, Va., U.S.	152	38.48 N	77.03 W
Alexandria Bay	152	44.20 N	75.55 W
Alexandrina, Lake ⊜	120	35.26 S	139.10 E
Alexandroúpolis	80	40.50 N	25.52 E
Alexis	154	41.04 N	90.33 W
Alfaro	138	2.12 S	79.50 W
Al-Fāshir	112	13.38 N	25.21 E
Al-Fayyūm	112	29.19 N	30.50 E
Alfeld	72	51.59 N	9.50 E
Alfenas	140	21.26 S	45.57 W
Alfred, Ont., Can.	152	45.34 N	74.53 W
Alfred, N.Y., U.S.	152	42.15 N	77.47 W
Alfred and Marie Range ⩓	122	24.40 S	125.40 E
Alga	82	49.46 N	57.20 E
Ålgård	68	58.46 N	5.51 E
Algarve □[9]	76	37.10 N	8.15 W
Algeciras	76	36.08 N	5.30 W
Algemesí	76	39.11 N	0.26 W
Alger (Algiers)	106	36.47 N	3.03 E
Algeria □[1]	106	28.00 N	3.00 E
Al-Ghayḍah	100	16.12 N	52.15 E
Alghero	78	40.34 N	8.19 E
Al-Ghurdaqah	112	27.14 N	33.50 E
Algiers → Alger	106	36.47 N	3.03 E
Alginet	76	39.16 N	0.28 W
Algodones	164	35.23 N	106.29 W
Algoma	154	44.36 N	87.27 W
Algona, Iowa, U.S.	154	43.04 N	94.14 W
Algonac	154	42.37 N	82.32 W
Algonquin	154	42.10 N	88.18 W
Algood	158	36.12 N	85.27 W
Algorta, Esp.	76	43.22 N	3.01 W
Algorta, Ur.	140	32.25 S	57.23 W

Symbols in the index entries are identified on page 203.

Name	Page	Lat	Long
Al-Hadīthah	104	34.07 N	42.23 E
Al-Hajarah ←1	104	30.00 N	44.00 E
Al-Hamād ☲	104	32.00 N	39.30 E
Al-Harīq	104	23.37 N	46.31 E
Al-Harūj al-Aswad ↗2	108	27.00 N	17.10 E
Al-Hasakah	104	36.29 N	40.45 E
Alhaurin el Grande	76	36.38 N	4.41 W
Al-Hawrah	100	13.49 N	47.37 E
Al-Hayy	100	32.10 N	46.03 E
Al-Hijāz ←1	104	24.30 N	38.30 E
Al-Hillah	104	32.29 N	44.25 E
Al Hoceima	106	35.15 N	3.55 W
Al Hoceima, Baie d' C	76	35.20 N	3.50 W
Al-Hudaydah	100	14.48 N	42.57 E
Al-Hufūf	100	25.22 N	49.34 E
Al-Hulwah	100	23.27 N	46.47 E
Aliaga	76	40.40 N	0.42 W
Aliaksin, Cape ↘	146	55.30 N	160.43 W
Alibāg	100	18.39 N	72.53 E
Alibunar	80	45.05 N	20.58 E
Alicante	76	38.21 N	0.29 W
Alice	160	27.45 N	98.04 W
Alicedale	116	33.19 S	26.05 E
Alice Springs	122	23.42 S	133.53 E
Aliceville	158	33.08 N	88.09 W
Aligarh	102	27.54 N	78.05 E
Alikovo	66	55.45 N	46.45 E
Alīma ≈	110	1.36 S	16.36 E
Alingsås	68	57.56 N	12.31 E
Aliquippa	152	40.37 N	80.15 W
Al-'Irq	108	29.02 N	21.33 E
Al-Iskandarīyah (Alexandria)	112	31.12 N	29.54 E
Al-Ismā'īlīyah	112	30.35 N	32.16 E
Aliwal North	116	30.45 S	26.45 E
Al-Jabal al-Akhḍar ↗1	104	23.15 N	57.20 E
Al-Jaghbūb	112	29.45 N	24.31 E
Al-Jawārah	100	18.55 N	57.17 E
Al-Jawf, Ar. Sa.	104	29.50 N	39.52 E
Al-Jawf, Libya	112	24.11 N	23.19 E
Al-Jazīrah ←1	112	14.25 N	33.00 E
Aljezur	76	37.19 N	8.48 W
Al-Jilf al-Kabīr, Hadabat ↗1	108	23.27 N	26.00 E
Al-Jīzah	112	30.01 N	31.13 E
Al-Julaydah ☲4	112	29.03 N	45.38 E
Al-Junaynah	112	13.27 N	22.27 E
Aljustrel	76	37.52 N	8.10 W
Al-Kāẓimīyah	104	33.22 N	44.20 E
Al-Khābūrah	100	23.59 N	57.08 E
Al-Khalīl	104	31.32 N	35.06 E
Al-Khandaq	112	18.36 N	30.34 E
Al-Kharijah	112	25.26 N	30.33 E
Al-Khaṣab	100	26.12 N	56.15 E
Al-Khubar	104	26.17 N	50.12 E
Al-Khums	108	32.39 N	14.16 E
Al-Khurṭūm (Khartoum)	112	15.36 N	32.32 E
Al-Khurṭūm Baḥrī	112	15.38 N	32.33 E
Alkmaar	72	52.37 N	4.44 E
Al-Kufrah ←1	108	24.20 N	23.15 E
Al-Kūt	104	32.25 N	45.49 E
Al-Kuwayt	104	29.20 N	47.59 E
Allach-Jun'	84	61.08 N	138.03 E
Al-Lādhiqīyah (Latakia)	104	35.31 N	35.47 E
Allahābād	102	25.27 N	81.51 E
Allanche	74	45.14 N	2.56 E
Al-'Ubaylah	100	21.59 N	50.57 E
Allardt	158	36.23 N	84.53 W
Allegan	152	42.32 N	85.51 W
Allegany	152	42.06 N	78.30 W
Allegheny ≈	152	40.27 N	80.00 W
Allegheny Mountains ↗1	152	38.00 N	80.00 W
Allegheny Plateau ↗1	152	41.30 N	78.00 W
Allegheny Reservoir @1	152	42.00 N	78.56 W
Allen, Okla., U.S.	160	34.53 N	96.25 W
Allen, S. Dak., U.S.	162	43.17 N	101.55 W
Allen, Mount ∧	146	62.14 N	142.13 W
Allendale	158	33.06 N	81.18 W
Allende	130	25.17 N	100.01 W
Allendorf	72	51.02 N	8.38 E
Allenstein → Olsztyn	72	53.48 N	20.29 E
Allentown	152	40.36 N	75.29 W
Allentsteig	72	48.42 N	15.20 E
Alleppey	100	9.30 N	76.20 E
Aller ≈	72	52.57 N	9.11 E
Allerton	154	40.42 N	93.22 W
Allevard	74	45.24 N	6.04 E
Allgäuer Alpen ↗	74	47.20 N	10.15 E
Alliance, Nebr., U.S.	162	42.06 N	102.52 W
Alliance, Ohio, U.S.	152	40.55 N	81.06 W
Al-Lidām	100	20.29 N	44.50 E
Allier ☐5	74	46.25 N	3.00 E
Allinge	68	55.16 N	14.49 E
Allison	156	42.45 N	92.48 W
Allisonia	156	36.60 N	80.44 W
Alliston	154	44.09 N	79.52 W
Al-Līth	100	20.09 N	40.16 E
Alloa	70	56.07 N	3.49 W
Allora	120	28.02 S	151.59 E
Allos	74	44.14 N	6.38 E
Allott, Mount ∧2	122	26.06 S	124.46 E
Allouez	154	44.28 N	88.01 W
Al-Luḥayyah	100	15.42 N	42.42 E
Allumette Lake @	154	45.53 N	77.13 W
Alma, Qué., Can.	150	48.33 N	71.39 W
Alma, Ark., U.S.	158	35.29 N	94.13 W
Alma, Ga., U.S.	158	31.33 N	82.28 W
Alma, Kans., U.S.	162	39.01 N	96.17 W
Alma, Mich., U.S.	152	43.22 N	84.39 W
Alma, Nebr., U.S.	162	40.06 N	99.22 W
Alma-Ata	82	43.15 N	76.57 E
Almada	76	38.41 N	9.09 W
Almadén	76	38.46 N	4.50 W
Al-Madīnah (Medina)	104	24.28 N	39.36 E
Al-Maḥallah al-Kubrā	112	30.58 N	31.10 E
Almalyk	82	40.50 N	69.35 E
Al-Manāmah	104	26.13 N	50.35 E
Almansa	76	38.52 N	1.05 W
Al-Manṣūrah	112	31.03 N	31.23 E
Al-Marj	108	32.30 N	20.54 E
Almas, Pico das ∧	134	13.33 S	41.56 W
Al-Maṣīrah I	100	20.25 N	58.50 E
Al-Mawṣil (Mosul)	104	36.20 N	43.08 E
Almeida	76	40.43 N	6.54 W
Almeirim	76	39.12 N	8.38 W
Almelo	72	52.21 N	6.39 E
Almenar	76	41.48 N	2.34 W
Almenara	134	16.11 S	40.42 W
Almendralejo	76	38.41 N	6.24 W
Almería	76	36.50 N	2.27 W
Al'metjevsk	66	54.53 N	52.20 E
Al-Minyā	112	28.06 N	30.45 E
Almira	154	47.43 N	118.56 W
Almirante	138	9.17 N	82.23 W
Almodôvar	76	37.31 N	8.04 W
Almont	152	42.55 N	83.03 W
Almonte, Ont., Can.	154	45.14 N	76.12 W
Almonte, Esp.	76	37.15 N	6.31 W
Almora	102	29.36 N	79.41 E
Al-Mubarraz	104	25.55 N	49.36 E
Al-Muglad	112	11.02 N	27.44 E
Al-Mukallā	100	14.32 N	49.08 E
Al-Mukhā	100	13.19 N	43.15 E
Al-Muwaylih	112	27.41 N	35.27 E
Alnwick	70	55.25 N	1.42 W
Alor, Pulau I	96	8.15 S	124.45 E
Alor Setar	96	6.07 N	100.22 E
Alost → Aalst	74	50.56 N	4.02 E
Aloysius, Mount ∧	122	26.00 S	128.34 E
Alpaugh	168	35.53 N	119.29 W
Alpena, Mich., U.S.	152	45.04 N	83.26 W
Alpena, S. Dak., U.S.	162	44.11 N	98.22 W
Alpes-de-Haute-Provence ☐5	74	44.10 N	6.40 E
Alpes Maritimes ☐5	74	44.00 N	7.10 E
Alpha	120	23.39 S	146.38 E
Alpharetta	156	34.04 N	84.18 W
Alphonse Island I	110	7.00 S	52.45 E
Alpiarça	76	39.15 N	8.35 W
Alpine, Ariz., U.S.	164	33.51 N	109.09 W
Alpine, Tex., U.S.	160	30.22 N	103.40 W
Alps ↗	64	46.25 N	10.00 E
Al-Qādarif	112	14.02 N	35.24 E
Al-Qāhirah (Cairo)	112	30.03 N	31.15 E
Al-Qāmishlī	104	37.02 N	41.14 E
Al-Qaryah ash-Sharqīyah	108	30.24 N	13.36 E
Al-Qash (Gash) ≈	108	16.48 N	35.51 E
Al-Qaṣr	112	25.42 N	28.53 E
Al-Qaṭif	104	26.33 N	50.00 E
Al-Qaṭrūn	108	24.56 N	14.38 E
Al-Qaṭṭārah, Munkhafad ⚊7	108	30.00 N	27.30 E
Al-Qayṣūmah	100	28.16 N	46.03 E
Al-Quds → Yerushalayim	104	31.46 N	35.14 E
Al-Qunfudhah	100	19.08 N	41.05 E
Al-Quṣayr	112	26.06 N	34.17 E
Alsace ☐9	74	48.30 N	7.30 E
Alsek ≈	146	59.10 N	138.10 W
Alsfeld	72	50.45 N	9.16 E
Alsunga	66	56.59 N	21.34 E
Alta	162	42.40 N	95.18 W
Alta Gracia, Arg.	138	31.40 S	64.26 W
Altagracia, Ven.	138	10.43 N	71.32 W
Altagracia de Orituco	138	9.52 N	66.23 W
Altai ≈	88	48.00 N	90.00 E
Altai (Jesönbulag)	88	46.25 N	96.20 E
Altamaha ≈	156	31.19 N	81.17 W
Altamira, Bra.	134	3.12 S	52.12 W
Altamira, Chile	140	25.47 S	69.51 W
Altamont, Kans., U.S.	162	37.12 N	95.18 W
Altamont, Oreg., U.S.	166	42.12 N	121.44 W
Altamont, Tenn., U.S.	158	35.26 N	85.43 W
Altamura	78	40.50 N	16.33 E
Altata	130	24.38 N	107.55 W
Altavista	156	37.06 N	79.17 W
Altdorf	74	46.53 N	8.39 E
Altenburg	72	53.42 N	13.14 E
Alter do Chão	76	39.12 N	7.40 W
Altheimer	158	34.19 N	91.51 W
Althofen	72	46.54 N	14.27 E
Altiplano ↗1	134	18.00 S	68.00 W
Altkirch	74	47.37 N	7.15 E
Altmark ☐9	72	52.40 N	11.20 E
Altmünster	72	47.54 N	13.46 E
Alto, Eng., U.K.	70	51.09 N	0.59 W
Alton, Ill., U.S.	158	38.54 N	90.10 W
Alton, Iowa, U.S.	162	42.59 N	96.01 W
Alton, N.H., U.S.	152	43.27 N	71.13 W
Altona	162	49.06 N	97.33 W
Altoona, Iowa, U.S.	154	41.39 N	93.28 W
Altoona, Pa., U.S.	152	40.30 N	78.24 W
Altoona, Wis., U.S.	154	44.48 N	91.26 W
Alto Río Senguerr	136	45.02 S	70.50 W
Altötting	72	48.13 N	12.40 E
Altstätten, Öst.	78	47.28 N	9.30 E
Altstätten, Schw.	74	47.23 N	9.33 E
Alturas	168	41.29 N	120.32 W
Altus, Ark., U.S.	158	35.27 N	93.45 W
Altus, Okla., U.S.	160	34.38 N	99.20 W
Al-Ubayyiḍ	112	13.11 N	30.13 E
Al-Uqayyah	112	12.03 N	28.17 E
Alūksne	86	57.25 N	27.03 E
'Alula	100	11.58 N	50.48 E
Alum Rock	168	37.23 N	121.50 W
Alunda	68	60.04 N	18.05 E
Al-'Uqaylah	108	30.16 N	19.12 E
Al-Uqṣur (Luxor)	112	25.41 N	32.39 E
Alva	160	36.48 N	98.40 W
Alvaiázere	76	39.49 N	8.23 W
Alvarado, Méx.	130	18.46 N	95.46 W
Alvarado, Tex., U.S.	160	32.24 N	97.13 W
Alvdal	68	62.07 N	10.39 E
Alvear	140	29.06 S	56.30 W
Alverca	76	38.54 N	9.02 W
Alvesta	68	56.54 N	14.33 E
Alvin	160	29.25 N	95.15 W
Alvito	76	38.15 N	7.59 W
Älvsborgs Län ☐6	68	58.00 N	12.30 E
Al-Wāḥāt ad-Dākhilah ⚊4	112	25.30 N	29.05 E
Al-Wāḥāt al-Baḥrīyah ⚊4	112	28.15 N	28.57 E
Al-Wāḥāt al-Farāfirah ⚊4	112	27.15 N	28.10 E
Al-Wāḥāt al-Khārijah ⚊4	112	25.20 N	30.35 E
Al-Wajh	112	26.15 N	36.26 E
Alwar	102	27.34 N	76.36 E
Alytus	86	54.24 N	24.03 E
Alzamay	84	55.33 N	98.39 E
Alzey	72	49.45 N	8.07 E
Amacuro ≈	138	8.32 N	60.28 W
Amadeus, Lake @	122	24.50 S	130.45 E
Amadi	112	5.31 N	30.20 E
Amadjuak Lake @	142	65.00 N	71.00 W
Amagansett	152	40.58 N	72.08 W
Amagasaki	90	34.43 N	135.25 E
Amahai	124	3.20 S	128.55 E
Amak Island I	146	55.25 N	163.07 W
Amalfi, It.	78	40.38 N	14.36 E
Amaliás	80	37.49 N	21.23 E
Amalner	102	21.03 N	75.04 E
Amambai	134	23.05 S	55.13 W
Amambaí, Serra de ↗	138	23.10 S	55.30 W
Amami-Ō-shima I	91b	28.15 N	129.20 E
Amapá	134	2.03 N	50.48 W
Amarante	76	41.16 N	8.05 W
Amarapura	94	21.54 N	96.03 E
Amareleja	76	38.12 N	7.14 W
Amares	76	41.38 N	8.21 W
Amargosa	134	13.02 S	39.36 W
Amargosa Range ↗	168	36.30 N	116.48 W
Amarillo	160	35.13 N	101.49 W
Amarkantak	100	22.40 N	81.45 E
Amasa	154	46.14 N	88.27 W
Amazon (Solimões) (Amazonas) ≈	134	0.05 S	50.00 W
Amazonas ☐3	138	3.00 S	62.00 W
Amazonas ☐8	138	4.20 S	78.00 W
Ambāla	102	30.23 N	76.46 E
Ambalavao	117b	21.50 S	46.56 E
Ambalema	138	4.47 N	74.46 W
Ambarčik	84	69.39 N	162.20 E
Ambarnyj	66	65.56 N	33.43 E
Ambato	138	1.15 S	78.37 W
Ambatolampy	117b	19.23 S	47.25 E
Ambatondrazaka	117b	17.50 S	48.25 E
Amber	100	3.51 S	127.12 E
Amberg	72	49.27 N	11.52 E
Ambérieu-en-Bugey	74	45.57 N	5.21 E
Ambert	74	45.33 N	3.45 E
Ambikāpur	102	23.08 N	83.11 E
Ambilobe	117b	13.12 S	49.04 E
Amble	70	55.20 N	1.34 W
Ambositra	117b	20.31 S	47.15 E
Amboy	168	34.33 N	115.45 W
Ambridge	152	40.36 N	80.14 W
Ambriz	110	7.50 S	13.06 E
Ambunti	124	4.14 S	142.50 E
Amderma	82	69.45 N	61.39 E
Ameagle	156	37.57 N	81.25 W
Ameca	130	20.33 N	104.02 W
Amecameca [de Juárez]	130	19.07 N	98.46 W
Amelia	78	42.33 N	12.25 E
American Falls	166	42.47 N	112.51 W
American Falls Reservoir @1	166	43.00 N	113.00 W
American Fork	164	40.23 N	111.48 W
Americus	156	32.04 N	84.14 W
Amersfoort	72	52.09 N	5.24 E
Amery	154	45.19 N	92.22 W
Ames	154	42.02 N	93.37 W
Amesbury	152	42.51 N	70.56 W
Amfissa	80	38.31 N	22.24 E
Amga	84	60.53 N	132.00 E
Amga ≈	84	62.38 N	134.32 E
Amgun' ≈	84	52.56 N	139.40 E
Amherst, N.S., Can.	150	45.49 N	64.14 W
Amherst, Mass., U.S.	152	42.23 N	72.31 W
Amherst, N.Y., U.S.	152	42.58 N	78.48 W
Amherst, Ohio, U.S.	152	41.24 N	82.14 W
Amherst, Tex., U.S.	160	34.01 N	102.25 W
Amherst, Va., U.S.	156	37.35 N	79.03 W
Amherstburg	152	42.06 N	83.06 W
Amherstdale	156	37.47 N	81.49 W
Amherstview	154	44.13 N	76.38 W
Amiens	74	49.54 N	2.18 E
Amirante Islands II	110	6.00 S	53.10 E
Amistad Reservoir @1	160	29.34 N	101.15 W
Amite	158	30.44 N	90.30 W
Amite, East Fork ≈	158	30.58 N	90.51 W
Amity, Ark., U.S.	158	34.16 N	93.28 W
Amity, Oreg., U.S.	166	45.07 N	123.12 W
Āmli	68	58.47 N	8.30 E
Amlwch	70	53.25 N	4.20 W
'Ammān	104	31.57 N	35.56 E
Ammaroo	122	21.45 S	135.15 E
Ammerān ≈	68	63.09 N	16.13 E
Ammokhostos (Famagusta)	104	35.07 N	33.57 E
Ammon	166	43.30 N	111.57 W
Amne Machin Shan → Animaqingshanmai	88	34.24 N	100.10 E
Amo ≈	104	26.16 N	89.36 E
Åmol	104	36.23 N	52.20 E
Amorgós I	80	36.50 N	25.59 E
Amory	158	33.59 N	88.29 W
Amos	148	48.35 N	78.07 W
Åmot, Nor.	68	59.35 N	8.00 E
Åmot, Nor.	68	59.54 N	9.54 E
Amoy → Xiamen	88	24.28 N	118.07 E
Ampanihy	117b	24.42 S	44.45 E
Amphitrite Group II	92	17.00 N	112.25 E
Amposta	76	40.43 N	0.35 E
Amqui	150	48.28 N	67.26 W
Amrāvati	102	20.56 N	77.45 E
Amreli	102	21.37 N	71.14 E
Amritsar	102	31.35 N	74.53 E
Amroha	102	28.54 N	78.28 E
Amsterdam, Ned.	72	52.22 N	4.54 E
Amsterdam, N.Y., U.S.	152	42.57 N	74.11 W
Amstetten	72	48.07 N	14.52 E
Am Timan	108	11.02 N	20.17 E
Amu Darya (Amudarja) ≈	82	43.40 N	59.01 E
Amundsen Gulf C	142	71.00 N	124.00 W
Amuntai	96	2.26 S	115.15 E
Amur (Heilongjiang) ≈	84	52.56 N	141.10 E
Anabar ≈	84	73.08 N	113.36 E
Anaco	138	9.27 N	64.28 W
Anaconda	166	46.08 N	112.57 W
Anacortes	166	48.30 N	122.37 W
Anadarko	160	35.04 N	98.14 W
Anadyr' ≈	84	64.55 N	177.29 E
Anadyr' ≈	146	65.59 N	176.09 E
Anadyrskij Zaliv C	146	64.00 N	179.00 W
Anadyrskoje Ploskogorje ↗1	146	67.00 N	174.00 E
Anagni	78	41.44 N	13.09 E
'Ānah	104	34.28 N	41.56 E
Anaheim	168	33.51 N	117.57 W
Anahola	169a	22.09 N	159.19 W
Anahuac	160	29.46 N	94.41 W
Ānai Mudi ∧	100	10.10 N	77.04 E
Anajás, Ilha I	134	0.20 S	50.30 W
Anaklava	117b	14.38 S	47.45 E
Anambas, Kepulauan II	96	3.00 N	106.00 E
Anamosa	154	42.06 N	91.17 W
Anamur	104	36.06 N	32.50 E
Anand	102	22.34 N	72.56 E
Anantnāg (Islāmābād)	102	33.44 N	75.10 E
Anápolis	134	16.20 S	48.58 W
Anatahan I	92	16.22 N	145.40 E
Añatuya	140	28.30 S	62.50 W
Anauá ≈	138	0.58 N	61.21 W
Anavilhanas, Arquipélago das II	138	2.42 S	60.45 W
Anawalt	156	37.15 N	81.26 W
'Anazah, Jabal ∧	104	32.12 N	39.18 E
Anbanjing	88	23.57 N	100.55 E
Ancenis	74	47.22 N	1.11 W
Anch'ing → Anqing	88	30.31 N	117.02 E
Anchorage	146	61.13 N	149.53 W
Anchor Point	146	59.46 N	151.52 W
Ancón de Sardinas, Bahia de C	138	1.30 N	79.00 W
Ancud	136	41.52 S	73.50 W
Ancud, Golfo de C	136	42.05 S	73.00 W
Ancy-le-Franc	74	47.46 N	4.10 E
Anda	88	46.24 N	125.19 E
Andalgalá	140	27.36 S	66.20 W
Andalsnes	68	62.33 N	7.42 E
Andalucia ☐9	76	37.36 N	4.30 W
Andalusia	158	31.18 N	86.29 W
Andaman Islands II	94	12.30 N	92.45 E
Andaman Sea ▼2	94	10.00 N	95.00 E
Andamooka	120	30.27 S	137.12 E
Andelot	74	48.15 N	5.18 E
Andenne	72	50.29 N	5.06 E
Anderlecht	72	50.50 N	4.18 E
Andernach	72	50.26 N	7.24 E
Anderson, Ala., U.S.	158	34.55 N	87.16 W
Anderson, Calif., U.S.	168	40.27 N	122.18 W
Anderson, Ind., U.S.	152	40.06 N	85.41 W
Anderson, Mo., U.S.	158	36.39 N	94.26 W
Anderson, S.C., U.S.	156	34.31 N	82.39 W
Anderson ≈	142	69.42 N	129.00 W
Andes ↗	134	20.00 S	67.00 W
Andhīkhāra ≈	80	40.50 N	27.07 E
Andhímákhia	80	36.48 N	27.07 E
Andhra ☐9	100	15.00 N	79.00 E
Andikíthira I	80	35.52 N	23.18 E
Andimeshk	104	32.26 N	48.21 E
Andižan	82	40.45 N	72.22 E
Andkhvoy	102	36.56 N	65.08 E
Andong, Taehan	88	36.35 N	128.44 E
Andong, Zhg.	88	41.08 N	124.20 E
Andorra	76	42.30 N	1.31 E
Andorra ☐1	76	42.30 N	1.30 E
Andover, Eng., U.K.	70	51.13 N	1.28 W
Andover, Mass., U.S.	152	42.39 N	71.08 W
Andover, N.Y., U.S.	152	42.09 N	77.48 W
Andover, Ohio, U.S.	152	41.36 N	80.34 W
Andøya I	66	69.08 N	15.54 E
Andradina	134	20.54 S	51.23 W
Andrew Gordon Bay C	142	64.58 N	75.30 W
Andrews, Ind., U.S.	152	40.52 N	85.36 W
Andrews, S.C., U.S.	156	33.27 N	79.34 W
Andrews, Tex., U.S.	160	32.19 N	102.32 W
Andria	78	41.13 N	16.18 E
Andriamena	117b	17.26 S	47.30 E
Androka	117b	25.02 S	44.05 E
Åndros I	80	37.45 N	24.42 E
Androscoggin ≈	152	43.55 N	69.55 W
Andros Island I	132	24.25 N	78.00 W
Androth Island I	100	10.49 N	73.40 E
Andrychów	72	49.52 N	19.21 E
Andújar	76	38.03 N	4.04 W
Anduo	88	32.18 N	91.04 E
Anduze	74	44.03 N	3.59 E
Anécho	114	6.14 N	1.36 E
Anegada I	132	18.45 N	64.20 W
Anegada Passage ⋓	132	18.15 N	63.45 W
Anegam	164	32.23 N	112.02 W
Aneta	162	47.41 N	97.59 W
Aneto, Pico de ∧	76	42.38 N	0.40 E
Angamos, Punta ↘	140	23.01 S	70.32 W
Ang'angxi	88	47.09 N	123.48 E
Angara ≈	84	58.06 N	93.00 E
Angarsk	84	52.34 N	103.54 E
Angas Downs	122	24.49 S	132.14 E
Angas Hills ↗2	122	22.55 S	128.00 E
Ángel, Salto (Angel Falls) ⌐	138	5.57 N	62.30 W
Ángel de la Guarda, Isla I	130	29.20 N	113.25 W
Angeles	96	15.09 N	120.35 E
Angel Falls → Ángel, Salto ↳	138	5.57 N	62.30 W
Ångelholm	68	56.15 N	12.51 E
Angellala Creek ≈	120	26.40 S	146.08 E
Angels Camp	168	38.04 N	120.32 W
Ångermanälven ≈	66	62.48 N	17.56 E
Ångermanland ☐9	68	63.30 N	18.05 E
Angermünde	72	53.01 N	14.00 E
Angers	74	47.28 N	0.33 W
Angerville	74	48.19 N	2.00 E
Angicos	134	5.40 S	36.36 W
Angijak Island I	142	65.40 N	62.15 W
Angikuni Lake @	142	62.13 N	99.50 W
Angiola	168	35.26 N	119.29 W
Angkor 1	94	13.26 N	103.52 E
Angleton	160	29.10 N	95.26 W
Anglin ≈	74	46.42 N	0.52 E
Angmagssalik	142	65.36 N	37.41 W
Angoche, Ilha I	117b	16.20 S	39.50 E
Angol	136	37.48 S	72.43 W
Angola, Ind., U.S.	158	41.38 N	85.00 W
Angola, N.Y., U.S.	152	42.38 N	79.02 W
Angola ☐1	110	12.30 S	18.30 E
Angoon	146	57.30 N	134.35 W
Angoram	124	4.04 S	144.04 E
Angoulême	74	45.39 N	0.09 E
Angoumois ☐9	74	45.30 N	0.05 W
Angra do Heroísmo	106a	38.40 N	27.13 W
Anguang	88	45.29 N	123.47 E
Anguilla ☐2	132	18.15 N	63.05 W
Angul	102	20.51 N	85.06 E
Angwin	168	38.34 N	122.26 W
Anholt I	68	56.42 N	11.34 E
Aniak	146	61.35 N	159.31 W
Animaqingshanmai ↗	88	34.20 N	100.10 E
Animas	164	31.57 N	108.48 W
Animas ≈	164	36.43 N	108.13 W
Aniva, Zaliv C	84	46.16 N	142.48 E
Anjār	102	23.08 N	70.01 E
Anjou ☐9	74	47.20 N	0.30 W
Anjouan I	117a	12.15 S	44.25 E
Anju	88	39.36 N	125.40 E
Anjudin	66	60.45 N	58.12 E
Ankang	88	32.40 N	109.01 E
Ankara	104	39.56 N	32.52 E
Ankaratra ↗	117b	19.25 S	47.12 E
Ankazoabo	117b	22.18 S	44.31 E
Ankazobe	117b	18.21 S	47.07 E
Ankeny	154	41.44 N	93.36 W
Anking → Anqing	88	30.31 N	117.02 E
Anklam	72	53.51 N	13.41 E
Ankober	112	9.30 N	39.44 E
Anmoore	156	39.11 N	80.16 W
Anna	158	37.27 N	89.15 W
Annaba (Bône)	106	36.54 N	7.46 E
Annaberg-Buchholz	72	50.35 N	13.00 E
An-Nafūd ⚊2	104	28.30 N	41.00 E
An-Najaf	104	31.59 N	44.20 E
Annan	70	54.59 N	3.16 W
Annandale, Austl.	120	31.34 S	116.48 E
Annandale, Va., U.S.	152	38.50 N	77.13 W
Annapolis	152	38.59 N	76.30 W
Ann Arbor	152	42.18 N	83.45 W
An-Nāṣirīyah	104	31.02 N	46.16 E
Annecy	74	45.54 N	6.07 E
Annemasse	74	46.12 N	6.15 E
Annenkov Island I	136	54.29 S	37.05 W
Annenskij Most	66	60.45 N	37.10 E
Annette	146	55.03 N	131.34 W
An-nhon	94	13.53 N	109.06 E
Anniston	158	33.39 N	85.49 W
Annobón I	110	1.25 S	5.36 E
Annonay	74	45.14 N	4.40 E
Annot	74	43.58 N	6.40 E
Annotto Bay	132	18.16 N	76.46 W
Annville	152	40.19 N	76.30 W
Anoka	154	45.11 N	93.23 W
Anopino	86	55.42 N	40.40 E
Anori	138	3.47 S	61.38 W
Anqing	88	30.31 N	117.02 E
Ansager	68	55.42 N	8.45 E
Ansbach	72	49.17 N	10.34 E
Anserma	138	5.13 N	75.47 W
Anshan	88	41.08 N	122.59 E
Anson	160	32.45 N	99.53 W
Anson Bay C	124	13.20 S	130.06 E
Ansongo	114	15.40 N	0.30 E
Ansonville	154	48.45 N	80.41 W
Ansted	156	38.08 N	81.06 W
Antakya (Antioch)	104	36.14 N	36.07 E
Antalya	104	36.53 N	30.42 E
Antalya, Gulf of → Antalya Körfezi C	64	36.30 N	31.00 E
Antalya Körfezi C	104	36.30 N	31.00 E
Antelope Peak ∧	164	32.41 N	114.58 W
Antequera	76	37.01 N	4.33 W
Anthony, Kans., U.S.	160	37.09 N	98.01 W
Anthony, Tex., U.S.	164	31.59 N	106.36 W
Antholong Lagoon C	117b	17.59 S	135.32 E
Anti Atlas ↗	106	30.00 N	8.30 W
Anticosti, Île d'I	150	49.30 N	63.00 W
Antigonish	150	45.37 N	61.53 W
Antigua ☐1	132	17.03 N	61.48 W
Antilla	132	20.50 N	75.45 W
Antioch	168	38.00 N	121.48 W
Antioch → Antakya, Tür.	104	36.14 N	36.07 E
Antioquia	138	6.33 N	75.50 W
Antioquia ☐5	138	7.00 N	75.30 W
Antlers	160	34.14 N	95.37 W
Antofagasta	140	23.39 S	70.24 W
Antofagasta ☐4	140	23.30 S	69.00 W
Antofagasta, Salar de ⚊	140	23.30 S	67.45 W
Anton Chico	164	35.12 N	105.09 W
Antoing, Baie d' C	117b	15.45 S	48.43 W
Antonina	134	25.26 S	48.42 W
Antonino Enes	117b	16.14 S	39.58 E
Antopol'	86	52.12 N	24.47 E
Antrain	74	48.28 N	1.29 W
Antrim	70	54.43 N	6.13 W
Antsirabe	117b	19.51 S	47.02 E
Antsiranana	117b	12.16 S	49.17 E
Antsohihy	117b	14.53 S	47.59 E
Antwerp → Antwerpen, Bel.	72	51.13 N	4.25 E
Antwerp, Ohio, U.S.	152	41.11 N	84.45 W
Antwerpen (Anvers)	72	51.13 N	4.25 E
An'ujsk	84	68.18 N	161.38 E
An'uiskij Chrebet ↗	84	67.30 N	166.00 E
Anuradhapura	100	8.21 N	80.23 E
Anvers → Antwerpen	72	51.13 N	4.25 E
Anvik	146	62.40 N	160.12 W
Anxi	88	40.32 N	95.51 E
Anyang	88	36.06 N	114.21 E
Anzero-Sudžensk	84	56.07 N	86.00 E
Anzin	74	50.22 N	3.30 E
Anzio	78	41.27 N	12.37 E
Anžu, Ostrova II	84	75.30 N	143.00 E
Aoga-shima I	88	32.28 N	139.46 E
Aomori	90	40.49 N	140.45 E
Aosta	78	45.44 N	7.20 E
Aouk, Bahr ≈	108	8.51 N	18.53 E
Aoukâr ←1	114	18.00 N	9.30 W
Aoulef	106	26.58 N	1.05 E
Aozou	108	21.49 N	17.25 E
Apache	160	34.54 N	98.22 W
Apalachee Bay C	156	30.00 N	84.13 W
Apalachicola	156	29.44 N	84.59 W
Apalachicola ≈	156	29.44 N	84.59 W
Apaporis ≈	138	1.23 S	69.25 W
Aparri	96	18.22 N	121.38 E
Apaseo el Grande	130	20.33 N	100.41 W
Apatin	80	45.40 N	18.59 E
Apatity	66	67.34 N	33.18 E
Apeldoorn	72	52.13 N	5.58 E
Apen	72	53.14 N	7.48 E
Apennines → Appennino ↗	78	43.00 N	13.00 E
Apex	156	35.44 N	78.51 W
Apiacás, Serra dos ↗1	134	10.15 S	57.15 W
Apizaco	130	19.25 N	98.09 W
Apo, Mount ∧	98	7.00 N	125.16 E
Apolakkiá	80	36.06 N	27.50 E
Apolda	72	51.01 N	11.31 E
Apollo	152	40.35 N	79.34 W
Apolo	134	14.43 S	68.31 W
Aporé ≈	134	19.27 S	50.57 W
Apostle Islands II	154	46.50 N	90.30 W
Apóstoles	140	27.55 S	55.45 W
Apostolovo	86	47.39 N	33.44 E
Appalachia	156	36.54 N	82.47 W
Appalachian Mountains ↗	144	41.00 N	77.00 W
Appenweier	72	48.32 N	7.58 E
Appenzell	74	47.20 N	9.25 E
Apple → Appleton	152	44.16 N	88.25 W
Appleton, Minn., U.S.	154	45.12 N	96.01 W
Appleton City	154	38.11 N	94.02 W
Apt	74	43.53 N	5.24 E
Apucarana	134	23.33 S	51.29 W
Apure ☐3	138	7.10 N	68.50 W
Apure ≈	138	7.37 N	66.25 W
Apurímac ≈	134	12.17 S	73.56 W
Aqaba, Gulf of C	104	29.00 N	34.40 E
Aquidauana	134	20.28 S	55.48 W
Arab	158	34.19 N	86.29 W
'Arab, Bahr al- ≈	108	9.02 N	29.28 E
'Arab, Shatt al- ≈	104	29.57 N	48.34 E
Arabian Sea ▼2	100	15.00 N	65.00 E
Aracá ≈	138	0.25 S	62.55 W
Aracaju	134	10.55 S	37.04 W
Aracati	134	4.34 S	37.46 W
Aracruz	134	19.49 S	40.16 W
Araçuaí	134	16.52 S	42.04 W
Arad	80	46.11 N	21.20 E
Arafura Sea ▼2	124	9.00 S	133.00 E
Aragarças	134	15.55 S	52.15 W
Aragats, gora ∧	104	40.32 N	44.11 E
Aragón ☐3	76	41.25 N	0.40 W
Aragón ≈	76	42.13 N	1.44 W
Aragua ☐3	138	10.00 N	67.10 W
Araguacema	134	8.50 S	49.34 W
Aragua de Barcelona	138	9.28 N	64.49 W
Araguaia ≈	134	5.21 S	48.41 W
Araguaiana	134	15.44 S	51.49 W
Araguari	134	18.38 S	48.11 W
Araguatins	134	5.38 S	48.07 W
Arak, Alg.	106	25.18 N	3.45 E
Arāk, Īrān	104	34.05 N	49.41 E
Arakan Yoma ↗	94	19.00 N	94.40 E
Aral'sk	82	46.48 N	61.40 E
Aral'skoje More → Aral Sea ▼2	82	45.00 N	60.00 E
Aramac	120	22.58 S	145.14 E
Aramac Creek ≈	120	22.55 S	145.18 E
Aranda de Duero	76	41.41 N	3.41 W
Aranđelovac	80	44.19 N	20.56 E
Aranjuez	76	40.02 N	3.36 W
Arapawa Pass	124	6.15 S	143.15 E
Arapiraca	134	9.45 S	36.39 W
Arapongas	134	23.25 S	51.25 W
Araquari	134	26.23 S	48.46 W
'Ar'ar, Wādī ≈	104	31.23 N	42.02 E
Ararangua	134	28.56 S	49.29 W
Araraquara	134	21.47 S	48.10 W
Araras, Serra das ↗2	134	18.20 S	53.00 W
Ararat, Austl.	120	37.17 S	142.56 E
Ararat, Mount → Büyük Ağrı Dağı ∧	104	39.42 N	44.18 E
Araras (Araks) ≈	104	39.47 N	48.10 E
Arātos	80	40.59 N	25.33 E
Arauca	138	7.05 N	70.45 W
Arauca ≈	138	7.24 N	66.35 W
Arauco	140	37.15 S	73.19 W
Arauquita	138	7.02 N	71.26 W
Aravalli Range ↗	102	25.00 N	73.30 E
Arba Minch	112	6.02 N	37.40 E
Arboga	68	59.24 N	15.50 E
Arbois	74	46.54 N	5.46 E
Arborea	78	39.46 N	8.35 E
Arbroath	70	56.34 N	2.35 W
Arbuckle	168	39.01 N	122.03 W
Arbuckle Mountains ↗	160	34.25 N	97.20 W
Arcos de la Frontera	76	36.45 N	5.48 W
Arcoverde	134	8.25 S	37.04 W
Arctic Bay	142	73.02 N	85.11 W
Arctic Ocean ▼1	146	71.00 N	153.00 E
Arctic Red	146	67.27 N	133.46 W
Arctic Village	146	68.08 N	145.19 W
Arda ≈	80	41.39 N	26.29 E
Ardabil	104	38.15 N	48.18 E
Ardahan	104	41.07 N	42.42 E
Årdalstangen	68	61.14 N	7.43 E
Ardèche ☐5	74	44.40 N	4.20 E
Ardee	70	53.52 N	6.33 W
Arden	168	38.36 N	121.23 W
Arden, Mount ∧	120	32.09 S	137.59 E
Ardennes ☐5	74	49.40 N	4.40 E
Ardennes ←1	72	50.10 N	5.45 E
Ardila ≈	76	38.12 N	7.28 W
Ardlethan	120	34.21 S	146.54 E
Ardlussa	70	56.02 N	5.47 W
Ardmore, Okla., U.S.	160	34.10 N	97.08 W
Ardmore, Pa., U.S.	152	40.01 N	75.18 W
Ardoch	168	53.24 N	103.4 W
Arecibo	132	18.28 N	66.43 W
Areia Branca	134	4.56 S	37.07 W
Arena de la Ventana, Punta ↘	130	24.04 N	109.52 W
Arendal	68	58.27 N	8.48 E
Arequipa	134	16.24 S	71.33 W
Arezzo	78	43.25 N	11.53 E
Argadargada	120	21.40 S	136.40 E
Arganda	76	40.18 N	3.26 W
Arga-Sala ≈	84	68.30 N	112.12 E
Argelès-Gazost	74	43.01 N	0.06 E
Argelès-sur-Mer	74	42.33 N	3.01 E
Argenta	78	44.37 N	11.50 E
Argentan	74	48.45 N	0.01 W
Argentat	74	45.06 N	1.56 E
Argentina ☐1	136	34.00 S	64.00 W
Argentino, Lago @	136	50.13 S	73.00 W
Argenton-Château	74	46.59 N	0.27 W
Argenton-sur-Creuse	74	46.35 N	1.31 E
Argentré	74	48.05 N	0.39 W
Argeş ☐4	80	45.00 N	24.45 E
Arghandāb ≈	102	31.27 N	64.23 E
Argolís ☐5	80	37.40 N	22.50 E
Argonne ←1	74	49.30 N	5.00 E
Árgos, Ellás	80	37.39 N	22.44 E
Argos, Ind., U.S.	158	41.14 N	86.15 W
Argostólion	80	38.10 N	20.30 E
Argun' (Ergu'nahe) ≈	84	53.20 N	121.28 E
Argyle Downs	124	16.17 S	128.47 E
Århus	68	56.09 N	10.13 E
Ariano Irpino	78	41.09 N	15.05 E
Arica, Chile	134	18.29 S	70.20 W
Arica, Col.	138	2.08 S	71.47 W
Arid, Cape ↘	122	34.00 S	123.09 E
Ariège ☐5	74	42.55 N	1.30 E
Arilje	80	43.45 N	20.06 E
Arima	132	10.38 N	61.17 W
Arinos ≈	134	10.25 S	58.20 W
Arinthod	74	46.23 N	5.34 E
Ario de Rosales	130	19.12 N	101.43 W
Ariogala	86	55.16 N	23.30 E
Aripuanã ≈	134	5.07 S	60.24 W
Ariquemes	134	9.56 S	63.04 W
Arizaro, Salar de ⚊	140	24.42 S	67.45 W
Arizgoiti	76	43.01 N	2.24 W
Arizona	140	35.49 S	65.20 W
Arizona ☐3	164	34.00 N	112.00 W
Arjäng	68	59.23 N	12.08 E
Arjona	76	37.56 N	4.03 W
Arka	84	60.08 N	142.12 E
Arkadelphia	158	34.07 N	93.04 W
Arkalyk	82	50.15 N	66.50 E
Arkansas ☐3	144	34.50 N	93.40 W
Arkansas ≈	144	33.48 N	91.04 W
Arkansas, Salt Fork ≈	160	36.36 N	97.03 W
Arkansas City, Ark., U.S.	158	33.36 N	91.12 W
Arkansas City, Kans., U.S.	160	37.04 N	97.02 W
Arklow	70	52.48 N	6.09 W
Arktičeskij, Mys ↘	84	81.15 N	95.45 E
Arktičeskogo Instituta, Ostrova II	66	75.20 N	81.55 E
Arkul'	66	57.17 N	50.03 E
Arles	74	43.40 N	4.38 E
Arlington, Fla., U.S.	156	30.20 N	81.36 W
Arlington, Kans., U.S.	160	37.54 N	98.11 W
Arlington, Minn., U.S.	154	44.36 N	94.05 W
Arlington, Ohio, U.S.	152	40.54 N	83.39 W
Arlington, S. Dak., U.S.	162	44.22 N	97.08 W
Arlington, Tenn., U.S.	158	35.18 N	89.40 W
Arlington, Tex., U.S.	160	32.44 N	97.07 W
Arlington, Va., U.S.	152	38.52 N	77.05 W
Arlington, Wash., U.S.	166	48.12 N	122.08 W
Arlington Heights	154	42.05 N	87.59 W
Arma	160	37.32 N	94.42 W
Armada	152	42.51 N	82.53 W
Armadale	122	32.09 S	116.00 E
Armagh	70	54.21 N	6.39 W
Armagnac ☐9	74	43.40 N	0.10 E
Armant	112	25.37 N	32.32 E
Armavir	62	45.00 N	41.08 E
Armenian Soviet Socialist Republic → Arm'anskaja Sovetskaja Socialističeskaja Respublika ☐3	82	40.00 N	45.00 E
Armenis	80	45.12 N	22.19 E
Armentières	74	50.41 N	2.53 E
Armeria ≈	130	18.45 N	103.51 W
Armidale	120	30.31 S	151.39 E
Armilla	164	36.54 N	106.00 W
Armona	168	36.19 N	119.42 W
Armour	162	43.19 N	98.21 W
Armstrong, B.C., Can.	148	50.27 N	119.12 W
Armstrong, Iowa, U.S.	154	43.24 N	94.28 W
Armstrong, Mount ∧	146	63.12 N	133.16 W
Armstrong Station	148	50.18 N	89.02 W
Arnaud ≈	142	60.00 N	69.46 W
Arnay-le-Duc	74	47.08 N	4.29 E
Årnes	68	60.09 N	11.28 E
Arnett	160	36.08 N	99.46 W
Arnhem	72	51.59 N	5.55 E
Arnhem, Cape ↘	124	12.21 S	136.21 E
Arnhem Bay C	124	12.20 S	136.12 E
Arnhem Land ←1	124	13.10 S	134.30 E
Arnissa	80	40.48 N	21.51 E
Arno ≈	78	43.41 N	10.17 E
Arnold, Calif., U.S.	168	38.15 N	120.21 W
Arnold, Mo., U.S.	162	38.26 N	90.23 W
Arnold, Nebr., U.S.	162	41.25 N	100.12 W
Arnoldstein	72	46.33 N	13.43 E
Arnolds Park	154	43.22 N	95.08 W
Arnon ≈	74	47.13 N	2.27 E
Arnøya I	66	70.09 N	20.40 E
Arnprior	154	45.26 N	76.21 W
Arnsberg	72	51.24 N	8.03 E
Arnstadt	72	50.50 N	10.57 E
Aroab	116	26.47 S	19.40 E
Arolsen	72	51.23 N	9.01 E
Aroostook ≈	150	46.48 N	67.45 W
Ar-Rab' al-Khālī ⚊2	100	20.00 N	51.00 E
Arpajon	74	48.35 N	2.15 E
Ar-Rahad	112	12.43 N	30.39 E
Ar-Ramādī	104	33.25 N	43.17 E
Ar-Rank	112	11.45 N	32.48 E
Arras	74	50.17 N	2.47 E

Name	Page	Lat	Long
Arrecife	106	28.57 N	13.32 W
Arrecifes	140	34.05 S	60.05 W
Arriaga	130	16.14 N	93.54 W
Arriba	162	39.17 N	103.17 W
Ar-Riyāḍ (Riyadh)	104	24.38 N	46.43 E
Arronches	76	39.07 N	7.17 W
Arrowsmith, Mount ⋀	120	30.09 S	141.50 E
Arrowsmith Bay C	142	68.00 N	95.15 W
Arroyo de la Luz	76	39.29 N	6.35 W
Arroyo Grande	168	35.07 N	120.34 W
Arroyo Hondo	164	36.32 N	105.40 W
Ar-Ruṣayriş	108	11.51 N	34.23 E
Ar-Ruṭbah	100	33.02 N	40.17 E
Ārs	68	56.48 N	9.32 E
Arsenjev	84	44.10 N	133.15 E
Ars-on-Rē	74	46.12 N	1.31 W
Ārta	80	39.09 N	20.59 E
Artemisa	132	22.49 N	82.46 W
Artenay	74	48.05 N	1.53 E
Artesia, Colo., U.S.	162	40.15 N	109.01 W
Artesia, N. Mex., U.S.	160	32.51 N	104.24 W
Artesian	162	44.00 N	97.55 W
Arthabaska	152	46.02 N	71.55 W
Arthur, Ont., Can.	154	43.50 N	80.32 W
Arthur, Ill., U.S.	158	39.43 N	88.28 W
Arthur Fiord C²	142	76.33 N	93.11 W
Artigas	140	30.24 S	56.28 W
Artillery Lake ⊜	142	63.09 N	107.52 W
Artois ☐⁹	74	50.30 N	2.30 E
Art'om	84	54.21 N	132.13 E
Art'omovsk	84	54.21 N	93.26 E
Art'omovskij, S.S.S.R.	82	57.21 N	61.54 E
Art'omovskij, S.S.S.R.	84	54.21 N	93.26 E
Artur de Paiva	110	14.28 S	16.20 E
Artyk	84	64.12 N	145.06 E
Aru, Kepulauan II	124	6.00 S	134.30 E
Aru, Tandjung ⊁	96	2.10 S	116.34 E
Arua	108	3.01 N	30.55 E
Aruánã (Luangwa) ⋩	110	14.52 S	51.05 W
Aruba I	110	15.36 S	30.25 E
Aruba I	132	12.30 N	69.58 W
Aruppukkottai	100	9.31 N	78.07 E
Arusha	110	3.22 S	36.41 E
Aruwimi ⋩	110	1.13 N	23.36 E
Arvada	164	39.50 N	105.05 W
Arvaicheer	88	46.15 N	102.45 E
Arvida	150	48.25 N	71.11 W
Arvika	68	59.39 N	12.36 E
Arvin	168	35.12 N	118.50 W
Arvonia	156	37.41 N	78.20 W
Arys	82	42.26 N	68.48 E
Arzachena	78	41.05 N	9.22 E
Arzamas	66	55.23 N	43.50 E
Arzignano	78	45.31 N	11.20 E
Aš, Česko.	72	50.10 N	12.10 E
Ås, Nor.	68	59.40 N	10.48 E
Aša	82	55.00 N	57.16 E
Asahikawa	90a	43.46 N	142.22 E
Asansol	100	23.41 N	86.59 E
Asbest	82	57.00 N	61.30 E
Asbestos	152	45.46 N	71.57 W
Asbury Park	152	40.13 N	74.01 W
Āschanbad	84	37.57 N	58.23 E
Aschach an der Donau	72	48.22 N	14.02 E
Aschaffenburg	72	49.59 N	9.09 E
Aschersleben	72	51.45 N	11.27 E
Ascoli Piceno	78	42.51 N	13.34 E
Ascona	74	46.09 N	8.46 E
Aseb	108	13.00 N	42.45 E
Åseda	68	57.10 N	15.20 E
Asela	108	7.59 N	39.08 E
Åsen	68	63.36 N	11.03 E
Asenovgrad	80	42.01 N	24.52 E
Åsgårdstrand	68	59.21 N	10.28 E
Ashburn	156	31.43 N	83.39 W
Ashburton	126	43.54 S	171.45 E
Ashburton ⋩	118	21.40 S	114.56 E
Ashburton Downs	122	23.24 S	117.04 E
Ash Creek ⋩	148	41.05 N	121.08 W
Ashcroft	148	50.43 N	121.17 W
Ashdown	158	33.41 N	94.08 W
Asheboro	156	35.42 N	79.49 W
Asheville	156	35.34 N	82.33 W
Asheweig ⋩	142	54.17 N	87.12 W
Ashford, Austl.	120	29.20 S	151.06 E
Ashford, Eng., U.K.	70	51.26 N	0.27 E
Ashford, Ala., U.S.	158	31.11 N	85.14 W
Ash Fork	164	35.13 N	112.29 W
Ashikaga	90	36.20 N	139.27 E
Ashland, Kans., U.S.	162	37.11 N	99.46 W
Ashland, Ky., U.S.	156	38.28 N	82.38 W
Ashland, Maine, U.S.	150	46.38 N	68.24 W
Ashland, Nebr., U.S.	162	41.03 N	96.22 W
Ashland, N.H., U.S.	152	43.42 N	71.38 W
Ashland, Ohio, U.S.	152	40.52 N	82.19 W
Ashland, Oreg., U.S.	166	42.12 N	122.42 W
Ashland, Pa., U.S.	152	40.46 N	76.21 W
Ashland, Va., U.S.	156	37.45 N	77.29 W
Ashland, Wis., U.S.	154	46.35 N	90.53 W
Ashland City	156	36.16 N	87.04 W
Ashmore Reef ⋪²	118	12.14 S	123.05 E
Ash-Shallāl al-Khāmis (Fifth Cataract) ⌣	112	18.23 N	33.47 E
Ash-Shallāl ar-Rābi' (Fourth Cataract) ⌣	112	18.47 N	32.03 E
Ash-Shallāl as-Sablūkah (Sixth Cataract) ⌣	112	16.20 N	32.42 E
Ash-Shallāl ath-Thālith (Third Cataract) ⌣	112	19.49 N	30.19 E
Ash-Shaqrā'	100	25.15 N	45.15 E
Ash-Shiḥr	100	14.44 N	49.35 E
Ashtabula	152	41.52 N	80.48 W
Ashton, Idaho, U.S.	166	44.04 N	111.27 W
Ashton, Ill., U.S.	158	41.52 N	89.13 W
Ashuanipi Lake ⊜	142	52.35 N	66.10 W
Ashville, Ala., U.S.	158	33.50 N	86.15 W
Ashville, Ohio, U.S.	152	39.43 N	82.57 W
Ashwaubenon	154	44.29 N	88.03 W
Asia, Kepulauan II	92	1.03 N	131.18 E
Asia Minor ⊁¹	64	39.00 N	32.00 E
Asilah	106	35.32 N	6.00 W
Asino	84	57.00 N	86.09 E
'Asīr ⊁¹	100	19.00 N	42.00 E
'Asīr, Ras ⊁	108	11.50 N	51.16 E
Askam	116	26.59 S	30.47 E
Askim	68	59.35 N	11.10 E
Askvoll	68	61.21 N	5.04 E
Asmera	108	15.20 N	38.53 E
Asola	78	45.13 N	10.24 E
Asosa	108	10.03 N	34.32 E
Asotin	166	46.20 N	117.03 W
Aspang Markt	72	47.33 N	16.06 E
Aspe	76	38.21 N	0.46 W
Aspen	164	39.11 N	106.49 W
Aspiring, Mount ⋀	126	44.23 S	168.44 E
Aspres-sur-Buēch	74	44.31 N	5.45 E
Aş-Şabyā	100	17.09 N	42.37 E
Assad, Buḥayrat al- ⊜	104	36.00 N	38.00 E
Aş-Şaḥrā' Al-Gharbīyah (Western Desert) ⛶²	108	27.00 N	27.00 E
Aş-Şaḥrā' al-Lībīyah (Libyan Desert) ⛶²	108	24.00 N	25.00 E
Aş-Şaḥrā' Ash-Sharqīyah (Eastern Desert) ⛶²	108	28.00 N	32.00 E
As-Sallūm	112	31.34 N	25.09 E
As-Samāwah	100	31.18 N	45.17 E
Assateague Island I	152	38.05 N	75.10 W
Asse	72	50.55 N	4.12 E
Assen	72	52.59 N	6.34 E
Assiniboia	142	49.38 N	105.59 W
Assiniboine ⋩	142	49.53 N	97.08 W
Assiniboine, Mount ⋀	148	50.52 N	115.39 W
Assis	140	22.40 S	50.25 W
Assisi	78	43.04 N	12.37 E
As-Sulaymānīyah, Ar. Sa.	100	24.09 N	46.19 E
As-Sulaymānīyah, 'Irāq	104	35.33 N	45.26 E
As-Sulayyil	100	20.27 N	45.34 E
Assumption	158	39.31 N	89.03 W
Assumption Island I	110	9.45 S	46.30 E
As-Suwaydā'	104	32.42 N	36.34 E
As-Suways (Suez)	112	29.58 N	32.33 E
Astaffort	74	44.04 N	0.40 E
Astara	100	38.29 N	48.52 E
Asti	78	44.54 N	8.12 E
Astipálaia	80	36.30 N	26.20 E
Astorga	76	42.27 N	6.03 W
Astoria	166	46.11 N	123.50 W
Astove Island I	110	10.06 S	47.45 E
Astrachan'	64	46.21 N	48.03 E
Asunción	140	25.16 S	57.40 W
Asunción, Wādi V	112	13.21 N	22.17 E
Aswān	112	24.05 N	32.53 E
Asyūt	112	27.11 N	31.11 E
Aszód	72	47.39 N	19.31 E
Atacama ☐⁴	140	27.30 S	70.00 W
Atacama, Desierto de ⛶²	140	22.30 S	69.15 W
Atacama, Puna de ⋀¹	140	25.00 S	68.00 W
Atacama, Salar de ⊜	140	23.30 S	68.15 W
Ataco	138	3.35 N	75.23 W
Atakpamé	114	7.32 N	1.08 E
Atami	90	35.05 N	139.04 E
Atar	114	20.31 N	13.03 W
Atascadero	168	35.29 N	120.40 W
Atasu	82	48.42 N	71.38 E
Atauro, Ilha de	96	8.15 S	125.33 E
Aṭbara ('Aṭbarah) ⋩	112	17.40 N	33.56 E
'Aṭbarah (Atbara) ⋩	112	17.40 N	33.56 E
Atbasar	82	51.48 N	68.20 E
Atchison	162	39.34 N	95.07 W
Ath	74	50.38 N	3.47 E
Athabasca	148	54.43 N	113.17 W
Athabasca ⋩	148	58.40 N	110.50 W
Athabasca, Lake ⊜	142	59.07 N	110.00 W
Athena	166	45.49 N	118.30 W
Athenry	70	53.18 N	8.45 W
Athens, Ont., Can.	152	44.38 N	75.57 W
Athens → Athínai, Ellás	80	37.58 N	23.43 E
Athens, Ala., U.S.	158	34.48 N	86.58 W
Athens, Ga., U.S.	156	33.57 N	83.23 W
Athens, Mich., U.S.	154	42.05 N	85.14 W
Athens, N.Y., U.S.	152	42.16 N	73.49 W
Athens, Ohio, U.S.	152	39.20 N	82.06 W
Athens, Pa., U.S.	152	41.57 N	76.31 W
Athens, Tenn., U.S.	156	35.27 N	84.36 W
Athens, Tex., U.S.	158	32.12 N	95.51 W
Atherton	120	17.16 S	145.29 E
Athínai (Athens)	80	37.58 N	23.43 E
Athol	70	53.25 N	7.56 W
Áthos ⋀	80	40.09 N	24.19 E
Athy	70	53.00 N	7.00 W
Atikokan	154	48.45 N	91.37 W
Atikonak Lake ⊜	142	52.40 N	64.30 W
Atka	84	60.50 N	151.48 E
Atkarsk	82	51.52 N	45.00 E
Atkinson	162	42.32 N	98.58 W
Atlanta, Ga., U.S.	156	33.45 N	84.23 W
Atlanta, Ill., U.S.	158	40.16 N	89.14 W
Atlanta, Mich., U.S.	154	45.00 N	84.09 W
Atlanta, Tex., U.S.	158	33.07 N	94.10 W
Atlantic	162	41.24 N	95.01 W
Atlantic City	152	39.22 N	74.26 W
Atlántico ☐⁵	138	10.45 N	75.00 W
Atlantic Ocean ⊽¹	54	5.00 N	25.00 W
Atlántida	140	34.46 S	55.45 W
Atlas Mountains ⋀	106	33.00 N	2.00 W
Atlasova, Ostrov I	84	50.53 N	155.27 E
Atlas Saharien ⋀	106	33.25 N	1.20 E
Atlas Tellien ⋀	106	36.00 N	3.00 E
Atlin	146	59.35 N	133.42 W
Atlin Lake ⊜	142	59.26 N	133.45 W
Atmore	158	31.02 N	87.29 W
Atnosen	68	61.44 N	10.49 E
Atoka	160	34.23 N	96.08 W
Atotonilco el Alto	130	20.33 N	102.31 W
Atoyac de Alvarez	130	17.12 N	100.26 W
Atrā	68	59.59 N	8.45 E
Atrato ⋩	138	8.17 N	76.58 W
Atrek (Atrak) ⋩	104	37.35 N	53.57 E
Atri	78	42.35 N	13.58 E
Atrisco	164	34.59 N	106.41 W
Aṭ-Ṭā'if	100	21.16 N	40.24 E
Attalla	158	34.01 N	86.05 W
Attawapiskat	142	52.55 N	82.26 W
Attawapiskat ⋩	142	52.57 N	82.18 W
Attawapiskat Lake ⊜	142	52.18 N	87.54 W
Attendorn	72	51.07 N	7.54 E
Attersee ⊜	72	47.55 N	13.33 E
Attica, Ind., U.S.	158	40.17 N	87.15 W
Attica, N.Y., U.S.	152	42.52 N	78.17 W
Attigny	74	49.29 N	4.35 E
Attleboro	152	41.56 N	71.17 W
Attopeu	94	14.48 N	106.50 E
Attur	100	11.36 N	78.36 E
Atuel ⋩	140	36.17 S	66.50 W
Atwater	168	37.21 N	120.36 W
Atwood	162	39.48 N	101.03 W
Auasberg ⋀	116	22.45 S	17.22 E
Aubagne	74	43.17 N	5.34 E
Aube ☐⁵	74	48.34 N	3.43 E
Aube ⋩	74	48.34 N	3.43 E
Aubenas	74	44.37 N	4.23 E
Aubigny-sur-Nère	74	47.29 N	2.26 E
Aubin	74	44.32 N	2.14 E
Aubry Lake ⊜	146	67.23 N	126.30 W
Auburn, Ala., U.S.	158	32.36 N	85.29 W
Auburn, Calif., U.S.	168	38.53 N	121.04 W
Auburn, Ill., U.S.	158	39.36 N	89.45 W
Auburn, Ind., U.S.	158	41.22 N	85.04 W
Auburn, Ky., U.S.	156	36.52 N	86.43 W
Auburn, Maine, U.S.	152	44.06 N	70.14 W
Auburn, Mass., U.S.	152	42.12 N	71.50 W
Auburn, Nebr., U.S.	162	40.23 N	95.51 W
Auburn, N.Y., U.S.	152	42.55 N	76.34 W
Auburn, Wash., U.S.	166	47.18 N	122.13 W
Auburn Heights	152	42.41 N	83.15 W
Auburn Range ⋀	120	25.10 S	150.58 E
Aubusson	74	45.57 N	2.11 E
Auch	74	43.39 N	0.35 E
Auchterarder	70	56.18 N	3.43 W
Auchtermuchty	70	56.18 N	3.14 W
Auckland	126	36.55 S	174.45 E
Aude ☐⁵	74	43.07 N	2.28 E
Aude ⋩	74	43.13 N	3.14 E
Audenge	74	44.41 N	1.01 W
Audierne	74	48.01 N	4.32 W
Audincourt	74	47.29 N	6.50 E
Audubon	162	41.43 N	94.55 W
Auerbach	72	50.30 N	12.24 E
Augathella	120	25.48 S	146.35 E
Au Gres	154	44.03 N	83.42 W
Augsburg	72	48.22 N	10.54 E
Augusta, Austl.	122	34.19 S	115.09 E
Augusta, Ark., U.S.	158	35.17 N	91.22 W
Augusta, Ga., U.S.	156	33.28 N	81.57 W
Augusta, Maine, U.S.	152	44.19 N	69.47 W
Augusta, Wis., U.S.	154	44.41 N	91.07 W
Augustów	72	53.51 N	22.59 E
Augustowski, Kanał ⋨	72	53.54 N	23.26 E
Augustus, Mount ⋀	122	24.20 S	116.50 E
Aulanko	68	61.02 N	24.27 E
Auld, Lake ⊜	122	22.32 S	123.44 E
Aulestad	68	61.13 N	10.17 E
Aulitvik Island I	142	69.32 N	67.50 W
Aulnay	74	46.02 N	0.22 W
Ault	164	40.35 N	104.44 W
Aumale	74	49.46 N	1.45 E
Aumont-Aubrac	74	44.43 N	3.17 E
Auneau	74	48.27 N	1.46 E
Auning	68	56.26 N	10.23 E
Auob ⋩	116	26.25 S	20.35 E
Aura	68	60.36 N	22.34 E
Aurangābād	100	19.53 N	75.20 E
Auray	74	47.40 N	2.59 W
Aurdal	68	60.56 N	9.24 E
Aure	68	63.16 N	8.32 E
Aure ⋩	124	7.05 S	145.19 E
Aurich	72	53.28 N	7.29 E
Aurillac	74	44.56 N	2.26 E
Aurland	68	60.54 N	7.11 E
Aurlandsvangen	68	60.54 N	7.11 E
Auronzo di Cadore	78	46.33 N	12.26 E
Aurora, Ont., Can.	154	44.00 N	79.28 W
Aurora, Colo., U.S.	164	39.44 N	104.52 W
Aurora, Ill., U.S.	154	42.46 N	88.19 W
Aurora, Minn., U.S.	154	47.31 N	92.14 W
Aurora, Mo., U.S.	158	36.58 N	93.43 W
Aurora, Nebr., U.S.	162	40.52 N	98.00 W
Aurora, N.Y., U.S.	152	42.46 N	76.42 W
Aurora, Ohio, U.S.	152	41.19 N	81.21 W
Aurora, Utah, U.S.	164	38.55 N	111.56 W
Aurora, W. Va., U.S.	152	39.19 N	79.33 W
Aurukun Mission	124	13.19 S	141.45 E
Aus	116	26.40 S	16.15 E
Au Sable Forks	152	44.26 N	73.41 W
Ausangate, Nevado ⋀	134	13.47 S	71.13 W
Auschwitz → Oświęcim	72	50.03 N	19.12 E
Aussig → Ústí nad Labem	72	50.40 N	14.02 E
Aust-Agder ☐⁶	68	58.50 N	8.00 E
Austin, Ind., U.S.	158	38.45 N	85.48 W
Austin, Minn., U.S.	154	43.40 N	92.59 W
Austin, Nev., U.S.	164	39.30 N	117.04 W
Austin, Pa., U.S.	152	41.38 N	78.05 W
Austin, Tex., U.S.	160	30.16 N	97.45 W
Austin, Lake ⊜	122	27.40 S	118.00 E
Austin Channel ⋓	142	75.35 N	103.25 W
Austintown	152	41.06 N	80.46 W
Austinville	156	36.51 N	80.55 W
Australia ☐¹	118	25.00 S	135.00 E
Australian Alps ⋀	120	37.00 S	148.00 E
Australian Capital Territory ☐⁸	118	35.30 S	149.00 E
Austria ☐¹	64	47.20 N	13.20 E
Autlán de Navarro	130	19.46 N	104.22 W
Autun	74	46.57 N	4.18 E
Auvergne ⛶⁹	74	45.25 N	3.00 E
Auvergne ⛶⁹	74	45.20 N	3.00 E
Auxerre	74	47.48 N	3.34 E
Auxi-le-Château	74	50.14 N	2.07 E
Auxonne	74	47.12 N	5.23 E
Auzances	74	46.02 N	2.30 E
Ava	158	36.57 N	92.40 W
Avaldsnes	68	59.21 N	5.16 E
Avallon	74	47.29 N	3.54 E
Avalon	168	33.49 N	118.16 W
Avant	160	36.29 N	96.04 W
Avaré	140	23.05 S	48.55 W
Avegadje	114	7.14 N	0.38 E
Aveiro	76	40.38 N	8.39 W
Avellaneda	140	34.40 S	58.20 W
Avellino	78	40.54 N	14.47 E
Aversa	78	40.58 N	14.12 E
Avery, Idaho, U.S.	166	47.15 N	115.49 W
Avery, Tex., U.S.	158	33.33 N	94.47 W
Aves, Islas de II	138	12.00 N	67.30 W
Avesnes	74	50.07 N	3.56 E
Avesta	68	60.09 N	16.12 E
Aveyron ☐⁵	74	44.15 N	2.40 E
Aveyron ⋩	74	44.05 N	1.16 E
Avezzano	78	42.02 N	13.25 E
Aviemore	70	57.12 N	3.50 W
Avigliano	78	40.44 N	15.44 E
Avignon	74	43.57 N	4.49 E
Ávila	76	40.39 N	4.42 W
Avilés	76	43.33 N	5.55 W
Aviz	76	39.04 N	7.53 W
Avoca, Iowa, U.S.	162	41.29 N	95.20 W
Avoca, N.Y., U.S.	152	42.25 N	77.25 W
Avola	78	36.54 N	15.09 E
Avon ☐⁶	70	51.30 N	2.40 W
Avon ⋩	70	52.25 N	1.31 W
Avondale, Ariz., U.S.	164	33.26 N	112.21 W
Avondale, Colo., U.S.	164	38.14 N	104.21 W
Avon Downs	120	20.05 S	137.30 E
Avon Lake	152	41.30 N	82.01 W
Avonmore	152	40.31 N	79.28 W
Avon Park	156	27.35 N	81.30 W
Avranches	74	48.41 N	1.22 W
Awash	108	8.59 N	40.10 E
Awash ⋩	112	11.45 N	41.05 E
Awaso	114	6.14 N	2.16 W
Awbārī	106	26.35 N	12.46 E
Awjilah	108	29.07 N	21.15 E
Awka	114	6.12 N	7.05 E
Axat	74	42.48 N	2.14 E
Axiós (Vardar) ⋩	80	40.31 N	22.43 E
Ax-les-Thermes	74	42.43 N	1.50 E
Ayacucho, Arg.	140	37.09 S	58.29 W
Ayacucho, Perú	134	13.07 S	74.13 W
Ayamonte	76	37.13 N	7.24 W
Ayapel	138	8.19 N	75.09 W
Ayaviri	134	14.52 S	70.35 W
Ayden	156	35.28 N	77.25 W
Ayer	152	42.34 N	71.35 W
Ayers Rock ⋀	122	25.23 S	131.05 E
Ayía Paraskeví	80	39.15 N	26.16 E
Ayiássos	80	39.05 N	26.23 E
Áyion Óros ☐⁸	80	40.15 N	24.15 E
Áyios Nikólaos	80	35.11 N	25.43 E
Aylesbury	70	51.48 N	0.49 W
Aylmer East	152	45.23 N	72.22 W
Aylmer Lake ⊜	142	64.05 N	108.30 W
Aylmer West	154	42.46 N	80.59 W
'Ayn Dār	100	25.59 N	49.23 E
'Ayoûn el 'Atroûs	114	16.40 N	9.37 W
Ayr, Austl.	120	19.35 S	147.24 E
Ayr, Ont., Can.	154	43.17 N	80.27 W
Ayr, Scot., U.K.	70	55.28 N	4.38 W
Ayre, Point of ⊁	70	54.26 N	4.22 W
Azalea Park	156	28.33 N	81.18 W
Azambuja	76	39.04 N	8.52 W
Azaouad ⛶²	114	18.00 N	3.00 W
Azaouak, Vallée de l' V	114	15.30 N	3.18 E
Azar V	114	16.02 N	4.04 E
Azare	114	11.40 N	10.11 E
Azay-le-Rideau	74	47.16 N	0.28 E
Azerbaijan Soviet Socialist Republic → Azerbajdžanskaja Sovetskaja Socialističeskaja Respublika ☐³	64	40.30 N	47.30 E
Azores → Açores II	106	38.30 N	28.00 W
Azov → Azov	64	47.07 N	39.25 E
Azov, Sea of → Azovskoje More ⋫²	64	46.00 N	36.00 E
Azovskoje More ⋫²	64	46.00 N	36.00 E
Aztec	164	36.49 N	107.59 W
Azua	132	18.27 N	70.44 W
Azuaga	76	38.16 N	5.41 W
Azuero, Península de ⊁¹	132	7.40 N	80.30 W
Azul	140	36.45 S	59.50 W
Azul, Cordillera ⋀	134	9.00 S	76.00 W
'Azūm, Wādi (Bahr 'Azūm) ⋩	112	12.00 N	21.40 E
Azur, Côte d' ⊁²	74	43.30 N	7.00 E
Az-Zaqāzīq	112	30.35 N	31.31 E
Az-Zarqā'	104	32.05 N	36.06 E
Az-Zāwiyah	112	32.45 N	12.44 E
Az-Zilfī	100	26.18 N	44.48 E
Az-Zubayr	104	30.23 N	47.43 E

B

Name	Page	Lat	Long
Ba ⋩	94	13.05 N	109.18 E
Baarn	72	52.13 N	5.16 E
Babaeski	80	41.26 N	27.06 E
Babahoyo	138	1.49 S	79.31 W
Babajevo	66	59.23 N	35.56 E
Babar, Kepulauan II	124	7.50 S	129.45 E
Babar, Pulau I	124	7.55 S	129.45 E
Babbitt, Minn., U.S.	154	47.43 N	91.57 W
Babbitt, Nev., U.S.	168	38.39 N	118.37 W
Babelthuap I	92	7.30 N	134.36 E
Babina Greda	80	45.07 N	18.33 E
Babinda	120	17.20 S	145.55 E
Babine Lake ⊜	148	54.45 N	126.00 W
Babo	124	2.33 S	133.25 E
Bābol	104	36.34 N	52.42 E
Babuškin	84	51.41 N	105.54 E
Babuyan Island I	98	19.32 N	121.57 E
Babuyan Islands II	98	19.10 N	121.40 E
Babylon	104	32.33 N	44.25 E
Bacabal	134	4.14 S	44.47 W
Bacău	80	46.34 N	26.55 E
Bacău ☐⁴	80	46.30 N	26.45 E
Baccarat	74	48.27 N	6.45 E
Bacchus Marsh	120	37.41 S	144.27 E
Bachardok	82	38.26 N	57.25 E
Bacha	84	62.28 N	89.00 E
Bachu	88	39.50 N	78.20 E
Back ⋩	142	67.15 N	95.15 W
Bačka Palanka	80	45.15 N	19.24 E
Bačka Topola	80	45.49 N	19.38 E
Backnang	72	48.56 N	9.25 E
Bac-lieu (Vinh-loi)	94	9.17 N	105.43 E
Bacolod	98	10.40 N	122.57 E
Bad Axe	154	43.48 N	83.00 W
Bad Bergzabern	72	49.06 N	8.00 E
Bad Blankenburg	72	50.41 N	11.16 E
Bad Bramstedt	72	53.55 N	9.53 E
Bad Doberan	72	54.06 N	11.53 E
Bad Dürkheim	72	49.28 N	8.10 E
Bad Dürrenberg	72	51.18 N	12.04 E
Bad Ems	72	50.20 N	7.43 E
Baden, Öst.	72	48.00 N	16.14 E
Baden, Schw.	74	47.28 N	8.18 E
Baden-Baden	72	48.46 N	8.14 E
Badenweiler	72	47.48 N	7.40 E
Baden-Württemberg ☐³	72	48.30 N	9.00 E
Bad Freienwalde	72	52.47 N	14.01 E
Badgastein	72	47.07 N	13.08 E
Badger Creek ⋩	168	40.28 N	119.31 W
Bad Hall	72	48.02 N	14.13 E
Bad Harzburg	72	51.53 N	10.33 E
Bad Hersfeld	72	50.52 N	9.42 E
Bad Homburg [vor der Höhe]	72	50.13 N	8.37 E
Bad Honnef	72	50.39 N	7.13 E
Bad Ischl	72	47.43 N	13.37 E
Bad Kissingen	72	50.12 N	10.04 E
Bad Kreuznach	72	49.52 N	7.51 E
Badlands ⛶²	162	46.45 N	103.30 W
Bad Langensalza	72	51.06 N	10.38 E
Bad Lauterberg	72	51.38 N	10.28 E
Bad Leonfelden	72	48.33 N	14.19 E
Bad Liebenwerda	72	51.31 N	13.23 E
Bad Mergentheim	72	49.30 N	9.46 E
Bad Muskau	72	51.32 N	14.43 E
Bad Nauheim	72	50.22 N	8.44 E
Bad Neustadt an der Saale	72	50.19 N	10.13 E
Bad Oeynhausen	72	52.12 N	8.48 E
Bad Oldesloe	72	53.48 N	10.22 E
Bad Orb	72	50.14 N	9.20 E
Bad Pyrmont	72	51.59 N	9.15 E
Bad Reichenhall	72	47.43 N	12.53 E
Bad Salzuflen	72	52.05 N	8.44 E
Bad Salzungen	72	50.48 N	10.13 E
Bad Sankt Leonhard im Lavanttal	72	46.58 N	14.48 E
Bad Schwartau	72	53.55 N	10.42 E
Bad Segeberg	72	53.56 N	10.17 E
Bad Tölz	72	47.46 N	11.34 E
Bad Waldsee	72	47.55 N	9.45 E
Bad Wörishofen	72	48.00 N	10.36 E
Baena	76	37.37 N	4.19 W
Bafatá	114	12.10 N	14.40 W
Baffin Bay C	142	73.00 N	66.00 W
Baffin Island I	142	68.00 N	70.00 W
Bafing ⋩	114	13.49 N	10.50 W
Bafoussam	114	5.28 N	10.25 E
Bafwasende	110	1.05 N	27.16 E
Bagamoyo	110	6.26 S	38.54 E
Baganga	98	7.34 N	126.33 E
Bagansiapi-api	96	2.09 N	100.48 E
Bagdad → Baghdād, 'Irāq	104	33.21 N	44.25 E
Bagdad, Ariz., U.S.	164	34.34 N	113.11 W
Bagé	140	31.20 S	54.06 W
Bagenkop	68	54.45 N	10.41 E
Baggs	166	41.02 N	107.39 W
Baghdād	104	33.21 N	44.25 E
Baghlān	104	36.13 N	68.46 E
Bagn	68	60.49 N	9.34 E
Bagnara Cálabra	78	38.17 N	15.49 E
Bagnères-de-Bigorre	74	43.04 N	0.09 E
Bagnols-sur-Cèze	74	44.10 N	4.37 E
Bago	98	16.25 N	120.36 E
Bagrationovsk	86	54.26 N	20.38 E
Baguio	98	16.25 N	120.36 E
Bagzane, Monts ⋀	114	17.43 N	8.45 E
Bahamas ☐¹	132	24.15 N	76.00 W
Baharampur	100	24.06 N	88.15 E
Bahawalnagar	102	29.59 N	73.16 E
Bahawalpur	102	29.24 N	71.41 E
Bahia → Salvador	134	12.59 S	38.31 W
Bahía, Islas de la II	132	16.20 N	86.30 W
Bahía Blanca	140	38.43 S	62.16 W
Bahia de Caráquez	138	0.36 S	80.25 W
Bahraich	100	27.36 N	81.36 E
Bahrain ☐¹	104	26.00 N	50.30 E
Baía-Mare	80	47.40 N	23.35 E
Bai-bung, Mui ⊁	94	8.36 N	104.43 E
Baicheng, Zhg.	88	45.38 N	122.46 E
Baidoa	108	3.04 N	43.48 E
Baiersbronn	72	48.30 N	8.22 E
Baie-Comeau	150	49.13 N	68.10 W
Baie-Saint-Paul	150	47.27 N	70.30 W
Baie Verte	150	49.56 N	56.11 W
Baigneux-les-Juifs	74	47.36 N	4.38 E
Baile Átha Cliath → Dublin	70	53.20 N	6.15 W
Bailén	76	38.06 N	3.46 W
Băileşti	80	44.02 N	23.21 E
Bailique, Ilha I	134	1.02 N	49.58 W
Bailleul	74	50.44 N	2.44 E
Baillie ⋩	142	65.10 N	104.24 W
Baillieborough	70	53.55 N	6.58 W
Baillie Islands II	142	70.33 N	128.10 W
Baillie-Hamilton Island I	142	75.53 N	94.35 W
Bailongjiang ⋩	88	32.18 N	105.42 E
Bainbridge, Ga., U.S.	156	30.54 N	84.34 W
Bainbridge, Ohio, U.S.	152	39.14 N	83.16 W
Baing	96	10.14 S	120.34 E
Bains-les-Bains	74	48.00 N	6.16 E
Bainville	162	48.08 N	104.13 W
Baird Peninsula ⊁¹	142	69.00 N	75.15 W
Bairnsdale	120	37.50 S	147.38 E
Bais	74	48.15 N	0.22 W
Baise ⋩	94	23.57 N	106.26 E
Baishuijiang	88	33.29 N	106.01 E
Baiyinchang	88	36.47 N	104.07 E
Baiyunebo	88	41.58 N	110.02 E
Baja	72	46.11 N	18.57 E
Baja California ⊁¹	130	27.30 N	113.00 W
Baja California Norte ☐³	168	30.00 N	115.00 W
Bajanaul	82	50.47 N	75.42 E
Bajanchongor	88	46.10 N	100.45 E
Bajānsenye	72	46.48 N	16.23 E
Bajkal, Ozero (Lake Baykal) ⊜	84	53.00 N	107.40 E
Bajkal'skoje	84	55.21 N	109.12 E
Bajkit	84	61.41 N	96.25 E
Bajkonyr	82	47.50 N	66.03 E
Bajmak	82	52.36 N	58.19 E
Bajos de Haina	132	18.25 N	70.01 W
Bajram-Ali	104	37.37 N	62.10 E
Baker, La., U.S.	158	30.35 N	91.10 W
Baker, Mont., U.S.	162	46.22 N	104.17 W
Baker, Oreg., U.S.	166	44.47 N	117.50 W
Baker, Mount ⋀	166	48.47 N	121.49 W
Baker Island I	128	0.13 N	176.28 W
Bakersfield, Calif., U.S.	168	35.23 N	119.01 W
Bakersfield, Tex., U.S.	160	30.53 N	102.12 W
Bakhtegān, Daryācheh-ye ⊜	104	29.20 N	54.05 E
Bakel	114	14.54 N	12.27 W
Bakoye ⋩	114	13.49 N	10.50 W
Baku	104	40.23 N	49.51 E
Bala	70	52.54 N	3.35 W
Balabac Island I	98	7.55 N	117.00 E
Balabac Strait ⋓	98	7.35 N	117.00 E
Ba'labakk (Baalbek)	104	34.00 N	36.12 E
Bałachna	66	56.30 N	43.36 E
Balad'ok ⋩	84	53.41 N	133.07 E
Balagne ⛶¹	78	42.33 N	8.50 E
Balakovo	64	52.02 N	47.47 E
Balambangan, Pulau I	98	7.15 N	116.57 E
Balāngīr	100	20.43 N	83.30 E
Balašicha	66	55.49 N	37.58 E
Balašov	64	51.33 N	43.10 E
Balassagyarmat	72	48.05 N	19.18 E
Balaton ⊜	72	46.50 N	17.45 E
Balboa Heights	138	8.57 N	79.34 W
Balbriggan	70	53.37 N	6.11 W
Balcarce	140	37.52 S	58.15 W
Balch Springs	160	32.43 N	96.37 W
Balchaš	82	46.49 N	74.59 E
Balchaš, Ozero ⊜	82	46.00 N	74.00 E
Bald Knob	158	35.19 N	91.34 W
Bald Mountain ⋀	164	43.16 N	121.21 W
Baldock Lake ⊜	142	56.33 N	97.57 W
Baldwin, Mich., U.S.	154	43.54 N	85.51 W
Baldwin, Wis., U.S.	154	44.58 N	92.22 W
Baldwin, N. Dak., U.S.	162	47.02 N	100.45 W
Baldwin Peninsula ⊁¹	146	66.48 N	162.15 W
Baldwinsville	152	43.09 N	76.19 W
Baldwyn	158	34.31 N	88.38 W
Baldy Peak ⋀	164	33.55 N	109.35 W
Baleares, Islas (Balearic Islands) II	64	39.30 N	3.00 E
Baleares ☐⁴	76	39.30 N	3.00 E
Balen	74	51.10 N	5.09 E
Balestrand	68	61.12 N	6.32 E
Balfe's Creek	120	20.12 S	145.55 E
Balfour	116	26.40 S	28.35 E
Bali, Selat ⋓	96	8.18 S	114.25 E
Bali, Laut (Bali Sea) ⋫²	96	7.45 S	115.30 E
Balikesir	104	39.39 N	27.53 E
Balikpapan	96	1.17 S	116.50 E
Balimo	124	8.03 S	142.56 E
Balingen	72	48.16 N	8.51 E
Balintang Channel ⋓	98	19.49 N	121.40 E
Balkan Mountains → Stara Planina ⋀	80	43.15 N	25.00 E
Balkh	102	36.46 N	66.54 E
Balkhash → Balchaš	82	46.49 N	74.59 E
Balladonia	122	32.27 S	123.51 E
Ballarat	120	37.34 S	143.52 E
Ballard, Lake ⊜	122	29.27 S	120.55 E
Ballater	70	57.03 N	3.03 W
Ballia	100	25.45 N	84.10 E
Ballina, Austl.	120	28.52 S	153.33 E
Ballina, Eire	70	54.07 N	9.09 W
Ballinasloe	70	53.20 N	8.13 W
Ballinger	160	31.44 N	99.57 W
Balls Pyramid I	118	31.45 S	159.15 E
Ballston Spa	152	43.00 N	73.51 W
Ballville	152	41.20 N	83.09 W
Ballybunnion	70	52.31 N	9.40 W
Ballycastle	70	55.12 N	6.15 W
Ballyhaunis	70	53.46 N	8.46 W
Ballymena	70	54.52 N	6.17 W
Ballymoney	70	55.04 N	6.31 W
Ballymote	70	54.06 N	8.31 W
Ballyshannon	70	54.30 N	8.11 W
Balmaceda	136	45.55 S	71.41 W
Balmoral	70	57.20 N	3.15 W
Balogoje	66	57.54 N	34.02 E
Balonne ⋩	120	28.47 S	147.56 E
Balovale	110	13.33 S	23.06 E
Balraald	122	33.20 S	142.10 E
Balsas ⋩, Bra.	134	7.14 S	44.33 W
Balsas ⋩, Méx.	130	17.55 N	102.10 W
Balta	82	47.55 N	29.37 E
Baltasar Brum	140	30.44 S	57.19 W
Baltic Sea ⋫²	68	57.00 N	19.00 E
Baltijsk	86	54.39 N	19.55 E
Baltijskaja Kosa ⊁²	72	54.25 N	19.35 E
Baltimore, Eire	70	51.29 N	9.22 W
Baltimore, Md., U.S.	152	39.17 N	76.37 W
Baltimore, Ohio, U.S.	152	39.51 N	82.36 W
Baluchistan ☐⁹	104	28.00 N	63.00 E
Balvi	86	57.08 N	27.17 E
Balygyčan	84	63.56 N	154.12 E
Balzar	138	1.22 S	79.54 W
Bam	104	29.06 N	58.21 E
Bamaga	124	10.52 S	142.24 E
Bamako	114	12.39 N	8.00 W
Bamba	114	17.02 N	1.24 W
Bambari	108	5.45 N	20.40 E
Bamberg, B.R.D.	72	49.53 N	10.53 E
Bamberg, S.C., U.S.	156	33.17 N	81.02 W
Bamboo Springs	122	22.04 S	119.38 E
Bamenda	114	5.56 N	10.10 E
Bāmiān	102	34.50 N	67.50 E
Bamingui	108	8.33 N	19.05 E
Bampūr	104	27.12 N	60.27 E
Banagher	70	53.11 N	7.59 W
Banalia	110	1.33 N	25.20 E
Banana	110	6.01 S	12.24 E
Bananal, Ilha do I	134	11.30 S	50.15 W
Banas ⋩	102	25.54 N	76.45 E
Banās, Ra's ⊁	112	23.54 N	35.48 E
Banat ⛶⁹	80	45.20 N	20.40 E
Banbridge	70	54.21 N	6.16 W
Banbury	70	52.04 N	1.20 W
Banchory	70	57.30 N	2.30 W
Bancroft, Ont., Can.	154	45.03 N	77.51 W
Bancroft, Idaho, U.S.	166	42.43 N	111.53 W
Bancroft → Chililabombwe, Zam.	110	12.18 S	27.43 E
Bānda	100	25.29 N	80.20 E
Banda, Kepulauan II	124	4.34 S	129.55 E
Banda, Laut (Banda Sea) ⋫²	124	5.00 S	128.00 E
Banda Atjeh (Kutaradja)	94	5.34 N	95.20 E
Bandama ⋩	114	5.10 N	5.00 W
Bandama Blanc ⋩	114	6.54 N	5.31 W
Bandama Rouge ⋩	114	6.54 N	5.31 W
Bandar → Machilipatnam	100	16.11 N	81.08 E
Bandar 'Abbās	104	27.11 N	56.17 E
Bandar-e Lengeh	104	26.33 N	54.53 E
Bandar-e Pahlavi	104	37.28 N	49.27 E
Bandar-e Shāhpūr	104	30.26 N	49.05 E
Bandar Maharani	96	2.02 N	102.34 E
Bandar Seri Begawan	96	4.56 N	114.55 E
Bandeira, Pico da ⋀	134	20.26 S	41.47 W
Bandera, Arg.	140	28.53 S	62.16 W
Bandera, Tex., U.S.	160	29.44 N	99.04 W
Bandirma	104	40.20 N	27.58 E
Bandon, Eire	70	51.45 N	8.45 W
Bandon, Oreg., U.S.	166	43.07 N	124.25 W
Bandundu	110	3.18 S	17.20 E
Bandung	96	6.54 S	107.36 E
Banes	132	20.58 N	75.43 W
Banff, Alta., Can.	148	51.10 N	115.34 W
Banff, Scot., U.K.	70	57.40 N	2.31 W
Bangalore	100	12.59 N	77.35 E
Bangassou	108	4.44 N	22.49 E
Bangeta, Mount ⋀	124	6.11 S	147.05 E
Banghāzī	108	32.07 N	20.04 E
Bangka, Selat ⋓	96	2.30 S	105.45 E
Bangka, Pulau I	96	2.00 S	106.00 E
Bangkok → Krung Thep	94	13.45 N	100.31 E
Bangladesh ☐¹	100	24.00 N	90.00 E
Bangor, Wales, U.K.	70	53.13 N	4.08 W
Bangor, Maine, U.S.	152	44.48 N	68.46 W
Bangor, Mich., U.S.	154	42.18 N	86.07 W
Bangor, Pa., U.S.	152	40.52 N	75.12 W
Bangued	98	17.36 N	120.37 E
Bangui	108	4.22 N	18.35 E
Bangweulu, Lake ⊜	110	11.05 S	29.45 E
Bani	132	18.17 N	70.20 W
Bani ⋩	114	14.30 N	4.12 W
Bani Suwayf	112	29.05 N	31.05 E
Banja Luka	78	44.46 N	17.11 E
Banjarmasin	96	3.20 S	114.35 E
Banjul	114	13.28 N	16.39 W
Banjuwangi	96	8.12 S	114.21 E
Banks Island I, B.C., Can.	148	53.25 N	130.10 W
Banks Island I, N.W. Ter., Can.	142	73.15 N	121.30 W
Banks Strait ⋓	120	40.40 S	148.07 E
Bankura	100	23.15 N	87.04 E
Ban-me-thuot	94	12.40 N	108.03 E
Banning	168	33.56 N	116.52 W
Banningville → Bandundu	110	3.18 S	17.20 E
Bannu	102	32.59 N	70.36 E
Baños	138	1.24 S	78.25 W
Banská Bystrica	72	48.44 N	19.09 E
Banská Štiavnica	72	48.27 N	18.55 E
Banswara	102	23.33 N	74.27 E
Bantry	70	51.41 N	9.27 W
Baode	88	39.06 N	111.11 E
Baoding	88	38.52 N	115.29 E
Baoji	88	34.22 N	107.14 E
Baoqing	88	46.20 N	132.11 E
Baoshan	94	25.09 N	99.09 E
Baoulé ⋩	114	13.46 N	10.56 W
Baoying	88	33.16 N	119.21 E
Bapaume	74	50.06 N	2.51 E
Bapchule	164	33.08 N	111.50 W
Ba'qūbah	104	33.45 N	44.38 E
Baquedano	140	23.20 S	69.51 W
Bar	80	42.05 N	19.06 E
Barabai	96	2.35 S	115.23 E
Barabinsk	84	55.21 N	78.20 E
Barabinskaja Step' ⛶¹	82	55.00 N	79.00 E
Baraboo	154	43.28 N	89.44 W
Baracoa	132	20.21 N	74.30 W
Baradero	140	33.48 S	59.30 W
Baraga	154	46.46 N	88.29 W
Barahona	132	18.13 N	71.06 W
Baraka, Khawr (Barka) ⋩	112	18.13 N	37.35 E

Name	Page	Lat	Long
Barat Daja, Kepulauan II	124	7.25 S	128.00 E
Barbacena	134	21.14 S	43.46 W
Barbacoas	138	1.41 N	78.09 W
Barbados □1	128	13.10 N	59.32 W
Barbar	112	18.01 N	33.59 E
Barbas, Cabo ⌐	106	22.18 N	16.41 W
Barbastro	76	42.02 N	0.08 E
Barberton	152	41.01 N	81.36 W
Barbezieux	74	45.28 N	0.09 W
Barboursville	152	38.24 N	82.18 W
Barbourville	156	36.52 N	83.53 W
Barby	72	51.58 N	11.53 E
Barcaldine	120	23.33 S	145.17 E
Barce → Al-Marj	108	32.30 N	20.54 E
Barcellona Pozzo di Gotto	78	38.09 N	15.13 E
Barcelona, Esp.	76	41.23 N	2.11 E
Barcelona, Méx.	130	26.12 N	103.25 W
Barcelona, Ven.	138	10.08 N	64.42 W
Barcelos, Bra.	138	0.58 S	62.57 W
Barcelos, Port.	76	41.32 N	8.37 W
Barcin	72	52.52 N	17.57 E
Barcoo ≃	120	25.30 S	142.50 E
Barcs	72	45.58 N	17.28 E
Barczewo	72	53.50 N	20.42 E
Bardaï	108	21.22 N	16.59 E
Bardejov	72	49.18 N	21.16 E
Bárdenas Reales ⌐1	76	42.10 N	1.25 W
Bardera	108	2.21 N	42.20 E
Bardi	74	44.38 N	9.44 E
Bardiyah	112	31.46 N	25.06 E
Bardonecchia	78	45.05 N	6.42 E
Bardsey Island I	70	52.45 N	4.45 W
Bardstown	158	37.49 N	85.28 W
Bardwell	158	36.52 N	89.01 W
Bareilly	102	28.21 N	79.25 E
Barentin	74	49.33 N	0.57 E
Barents Sea (Barenc'ovo More) ⊤2	66	69.00 N	40.00 E
Barfleur	74	49.40 N	1.15 W
Barguzin ≃	84	53.27 N	109.00 E
Bar Harbor	152	44.23 N	68.13 W
Bari	78	41.07 N	16.52 E
Barim I	100	12.40 N	43.25 E
Barima ≃	138	8.33 N	60.25 W
Barinas	138	8.38 N	70.12 W
Barinas □3	138	8.10 N	69.50 W
Baring, Cape ⌐	142	70.05 N	117.20 W
Baring Channel U	142	73.48 N	98.50 W
Baripāda	102	21.56 N	86.43 E
Bariri	134	22.04 S	48.44 W
Bārīs	112	24.40 N	30.36 E
Barisāl	102	22.42 N	90.22 E
Barisan, Pegunungan ⌐	96	3.00 S	102.15 E
Barjac	74	44.18 N	4.21 E
Barjols	74	43.33 N	6.00 E
Barka (Khawr Baraka) ≃	112	18.13 N	37.35 E
Barkley, Lake ⊖1	158	36.40 N	87.55 W
Barkley Sound U	148	48.53 N	125.20 W
Barkly East	116	30.58 S	27.33 E
Barkly Tableland ⌐1	122	19.00 S	138.00 E
Barlee, Lake ⊖	122	29.10 S	119.30 E
Barlee Range ⌐	122	23.35 S	116.00 E
Barletta	78	41.19 N	16.17 E
Barmer	102	25.45 N	71.23 E
Barmouth	70	52.43 N	4.03 W
Barnard Castle	70	54.33 N	1.55 E
Barnaul	84	53.22 N	83.45 E
Barn Bluff ∧	166	41.43 N	145.56 E
Barnegat	152	39.45 N	74.13 W
Barnesboro	152	40.40 N	78.47 W
Barnesville, Ga., U.S.	156	33.03 N	84.09 W
Barnesville, Minn., U.S.	162	46.39 N	96.25 W
Barnesville, Ohio, U.S.	152	39.59 N	81.11 W
Barneville-Carteret	74	49.23 N	1.47 W
Barnsdall	160	36.34 N	96.10 W
Barnsley	70	53.34 N	1.28 W
Barnstable	152	41.42 N	70.18 W
Barnstaple	70	51.05 N	4.04 W
Barnwell	156	33.15 N	81.23 W
Baro ≃	108	8.26 N	33.13 E
Baroda	102	22.18 N	73.12 E
Barotseland □9	110	16.00 S	24.00 E
Barpeta	102	26.19 N	91.00 E
Barqah (Cyrenaica) ⌐1	108	31.00 N	22.30 E
Barquisimeto	138	10.04 N	69.19 W
Barra	134	11.05 S	43.10 W
Barra, Ponta da ⌐	116	23.45 S	35.30 E
Barraba	120	30.22 S	150.36 E
Barra do Corda	134	5.30 S	45.15 W
Barra Falsa, Ponta da ⌐	116	22.55 S	35.37 E
Barrafranca	78	37.23 N	14.13 E
Barra Mansa	134	22.32 S	44.11 W
Barranca	138	4.50 S	76.40 W
Barrancabermeja	138	7.03 N	73.52 W
Barrancas	138	8.42 N	62.11 W
Barrancos	76	38.08 N	6.59 W
Barranco do Velho	76	37.14 N	7.56 W
Barranqueras	140	27.29 S	58.56 W
Barranquilla	138	10.59 N	74.48 W
Barras	134	4.15 S	42.18 W
Barre, Mass., U.S.	152	42.25 N	72.06 W
Barre, Vt., U.S.	152	44.12 N	72.30 W
Barreiras	134	12.08 S	45.00 W
Barreiro	76	38.40 N	9.04 W
Barren ≃	134	8.49 S	35.12 E
Barrême	74	43.57 N	6.22 E
Barren, Îles II	117b	18.25 S	43.40 E
Barren Islands II	146	58.55 N	152.15 W
Barretos	134	20.33 S	48.33 W
Barrett, Mount ∧	122	16.42 S	125.56 E
Barrie	154	44.24 N	79.40 W
Barringun	120	29.01 S	145.43 E
Barron	154	45.24 N	91.51 W
Barrow	146	71.17 N	156.47 W
Barrow, Point ⌐	146	71.23 N	156.30 W
Barrow Creek	122	21.33 S	133.53 E
Barrow-in-Furness	70	54.07 N	3.14 W
Barrow Island I	122	20.48 S	115.23 E
Barrow Range ⌐	122	26.04 S	127.28 E
Barrow Strait U	142	74.21 N	94.10 W
Barru	96	4.25 S	119.37 E
Barry	70	51.24 N	3.18 W
Barrys Bay	154	45.29 N	77.41 W
Barsi	100	18.15 N	75.42 E
Barsinghausen	72	52.18 N	9.27 E
Barstow	168	34.54 N	117.01 W
Bar-sur-Aube	74	48.14 N	4.43 E
Bar-sur-Seine	74	48.07 N	4.22 E
Bartang ≃	82	38.05 N	71.51 E
Barth	72	54.22 N	12.43 E
Bartholomew, Bayou ≃	158	32.43 N	92.04 W
Bartica	138	6.24 N	58.37 W
Bartle Frere ∧	120	17.23 S	145.49 E
Bartlesville	160	36.45 N	95.59 W
Bartolomeu Dias	116	21.10 S	35.09 E
Barton	152	44.45 N	72.11 W
Barton-upon-Humber	70	53.41 N	0.27 W
Bartonville	154	40.39 N	89.39 W
Bartoszyce	72	54.16 N	20.49 E
Bartow	156	27.53 N	81.50 W
Bāruni	102	25.29 N	85.59 E
Barun-Šibertuj, Gora ∧	84	49.42 N	109.59 E
Baruun Urt	88	46.40 N	113.12 E
Barvas	70	58.22 N	6.32 W
Barwon ≃	120	30.00 S	148.05 E
Baryš	66	53.39 N	47.08 E
Basankusu	110	1.14 N	19.48 E
Basatongwulashan ∧	102	33.05 N	91.30 E
Basco	94	20.27 N	121.58 E
Bascuñán, Cabo ⌐	140	28.51 S	71.30 W
Basel (Bâle)	74	47.33 N	7.35 E
Basey	92	11.17 N	125.04 E
Bashi Channel U	92	22.00 N	121.00 E
Basilan	92	6.42 N	121.58 E
Basilan Island I	98	6.35 N	122.02 E
Basildon	70	51.35 N	0.25 E
Basilicata □4	78	40.30 N	16.10 E
Basilio	140	31.53 S	53.01 W
Basin	166	44.23 N	108.02 W
Basingstoke	70	51.15 N	1.05 W
Baskatong, Réservoir ⊖1	154	46.48 N	75.50 W
Bašmakovo	86	53.12 N	43.02 E
Basoko	110	1.14 N	23.36 E
Basra → Al-Başrah	104	30.30 N	47.47 E
Bas-Rhin □5	74	48.35 N	7.40 E
Bassano del Grappa	78	45.46 N	11.44 E
Bassar	114	9.15 N	0.47 E
Bassas da India ⌐2	94	16.47 N	94.44 E
Basse-Pyrénées □5	74	43.15 N	0.50 W
Basse-Terre, Guad.	132	16.00 N	61.44 W
Basseterre, St. K.-N.	132	17.18 N	62.43 W
Bassett, Nebr., U.S.	162	42.35 N	99.32 W
Bassett, Va., U.S.	156	36.46 N	79.59 W
Bass Strait U	120	39.20 S	145.30 E
Basswood Lake ⊖	154	48.06 N	91.40 W
Bastelica	78	42.00 N	9.02 E
Basti	102	26.48 N	82.43 E
Bastia	74	42.42 N	9.27 E
Bastian	156	37.09 N	81.09 W
Bastogne	72	50.00 N	5.43 E
Bastrop, La., U.S.	158	32.47 N	91.55 W
Bastrop, Tex., U.S.	160	30.07 N	97.19 W
Bastuträsk	68	64.46 N	20.02 E
Bata	110	1.51 N	9.45 E
Batabanó, Golfo de C	132	22.15 N	82.30 W
Batagaj	84	67.38 N	134.38 E
Batagaj-Alyta	84	67.48 N	130.25 E
Batai Kandao)(	102	33.23 N	70.19 E
Batajsk	64	47.10 N	39.44 E
Batala	102	31.49 N	75.12 E
Batalha	76	39.39 N	8.50 W
Batang	88	30.02 N	99.02 E
Batangas	92	13.45 N	121.03 E
Batan Island I	98	13.15 N	124.00 E
Batan Islands II	92	20.35 N	121.55 E
Batanta, Pulau I	124	0.50 S	130.40 E
Bātāszék	72	46.12 N	18.44 E
Batavia, Ill., U.S.	154	41.51 N	88.19 W
Batavia, Iowa, U.S.	154	41.00 N	92.10 W
Batavia, N.Y., U.S.	152	43.00 N	78.11 W
Batchelor	124	13.04 S	131.01 E
Bätdâmbâng	94	13.06 N	103.12 E
Batemans Bay	120	35.43 S	150.11 E
Batesburg	156	33.54 N	81.33 W
Batesville, Ark., U.S.	158	35.46 N	91.39 W
Batesville, Ind., U.S.	158	39.18 N	85.13 W
Batesville, Miss., U.S.	158	34.18 N	89.56 W
Bath, Eng., U.K.	70	51.23 N	2.22 W
Bath, Maine, U.S.	152	43.55 N	69.49 W
Bath, N.Y., U.S.	152	42.20 N	77.19 W
Bath, S.C., U.S.	156	33.31 N	81.51 W
Bathgate, Scot., U.K.	70	55.55 N	3.39 W
Bathgate, N. Dak., U.S.	162	48.53 N	97.29 W
Bathurst, Austl.	120	33.25 S	149.35 E
Bathurst, N.B., Can.	150	47.36 N	65.39 W
Bathurst → Banjul, Gam.	114	13.28 N	16.39 W
Bathurst, Cape ⌐	142	70.35 N	128.00 W
Bathurst Inlet	142	66.50 N	108.01 W
Bathurst Inlet C	142	68.10 N	108.50 W
Bathurst Island I, Austl.	124	11.37 S	130.23 E
Bathurst Island I, N.W. Ter., Can.	142	76.00 N	100.30 W
Bātin, Wādī al- V	104	30.30 N	47.00 E
Batjan, Pulau I	124	0.35 S	127.30 E
Batlow	120	35.31 S	148.09 E
Baton ≃	138	3.30 N	6.11 E
Baton Rouge	158	30.23 N	91.11 W
Batouri	106	4.26 N	14.22 E
Batson	160	30.15 N	94.37 W
Batticaloa	100	7.43 N	81.42 E
Battipaglia	78	40.37 N	14.59 E
Battle ≃	142	52.42 N	108.15 W
Battle Creek, Iowa, U.S.	162	42.19 N	95.36 W
Battle Creek, Mich., U.S.	154	42.19 N	85.11 W
Battle Ground	158	40.31 N	86.50 W
Battle Harbour	142	52.16 N	55.35 W
Battle Mountain	168	40.38 N	116.56 W
Battonya	72	46.17 N	21.01 E
Batu ∧	108	6.55 N	39.46 E
Batu, Kepulauan II	96	0.18 S	98.28 E
Batu Pahat	96	1.50 N	102.56 E
Baturadja	96	4.08 S	104.10 E
Baturité	134	4.20 S	38.53 W
Bau	96	1.25 N	110.09 E
Bauchi	114	10.19 N	9.50 E
Baud	74	47.52 N	3.01 W
Baudette	154	48.42 N	94.36 W
Baudouinville	110	7.04 S	29.46 E
Baugé	74	47.33 N	0.06 W
Bauld, Cape ⌐	142	51.38 N	55.25 W
Baume-les-Dames	74	47.21 N	6.22 E
Bauru	134	22.19 S	49.04 W
Bauska	86	56.24 N	24.14 E
Bautzen	72	51.11 N	14.26 E
Bauxite	158	34.33 N	92.30 W
Bavaria → Bayern □3	72	49.00 N	11.30 E
Bawean, Pulau I	96	5.46 S	112.40 E
Baxley	156	31.46 N	82.21 W
Baxter, Minn., U.S.	154	46.20 N	94.16 W
Baxter, Tenn., U.S.	158	36.09 N	85.38 W
Baxter Springs	158	37.02 N	94.44 W
Bay, Laguna de ⊖	92	14.23 N	121.15 E
Bayamo	132	20.23 N	76.39 W
Bayamón	132	18.24 N	66.09 W
Bayankalashanmai ∧	88	33.48 N	98.10 E
Bayard, Nebr., U.S.	162	41.45 N	103.20 W
Bayard, N. Mex., U.S.	164	32.46 N	108.08 W
Bayard, W. Va., U.S.	152	39.16 N	79.22 W
Bay City, Mich., U.S.	154	43.36 N	83.53 W
Bay City, Oreg., U.S.	166	45.31 N	123.53 W
Bay City, Tex., U.S.	160	28.59 N	95.58 W
Bayern □3	72	49.00 N	11.30 E
Bayeux	74	49.16 N	0.42 W
Bayfield, Colo., U.S.	164	37.14 N	107.36 W
Bayfield, Wis., U.S.	154	46.49 N	90.49 W
Bay Minette	158	30.53 N	87.47 W
Bayon	74	48.29 N	6.19 E
Bayonne, Fr.	74	43.29 N	1.29 W
Bayonne, N.J., U.S.	152	40.40 N	74.07 W
Bayou La Batre	158	30.24 N	88.14 W
Bayport	154	45.01 N	92.47 W
Bayreuth	72	49.56 N	11.35 E
Bayrischzell	72	47.40 N	12.01 E
Bay Roberts	150	47.36 N	53.16 W
Bayrūt (Beirut)	104	33.53 N	35.30 E
Bay Saint Louis	158	30.19 N	89.20 W
Bay Shore	152	40.43 N	73.15 W
Bayt al-Faqih	100	14.32 N	43.20 E
Bayt Laḥm	104	31.43 N	35.12 E
Baytown	160	29.44 N	94.58 W
Baza	76	37.29 N	2.46 W
Bazaruto, Ilha do I	116	21.40 S	35.28 E
Bazas	74	44.26 N	0.13 W
Bazège	114	14.26 N	13.17 E
Beach Haven	152	39.34 N	74.14 W
Beacon, Austl.	122	30.26 S	117.51 E
Beacon, N.Y., U.S.	152	41.30 N	73.58 W
Beaconsfield	120	41.12 S	146.48 E
Beagle Bank ⌐4	118	15.00 S	123.08 E
Beagle Gulf C	124	12.00 S	130.15 E
Bealanana	117b	14.33 S	48.44 E
Bear ≃	164	41.30 N	112.08 W
Bear Bay C	142	75.47 N	87.00 W
Bear Creek ≃	160	37.45 N	101.23 W
Bearden	158	33.43 N	92.37 W
Beardmore	142	49.36 N	87.57 W
Beardstown	158	40.01 N	90.26 W
Bear Lake ⊖	164	42.00 N	111.20 W
Bearn ⌐1	74	43.20 N	0.45 W
Bear Tooth Pass)(	166	44.58 N	109.28 W
Beartooth Range ⌐	166	45.00 N	109.30 W
Beasain	76	43.03 N	2.11 W
Beata, Isla I	132	17.34 N	71.31 W
Beatrice, Ala., U.S.	158	31.38 N	87.19 W
Beatrice, Nebr., U.S.	162	40.16 N	96.44 W
Beatrice, Cape ⌐	124	14.15 S	136.59 E
Beatton ≃	148	56.10 N	120.25 W
Beattyville	156	37.35 N	83.42 W
Beaucaire	74	43.48 N	4.38 E
Beauce ⌐1	74	48.22 N	1.50 E
Beauceville-Est	152	46.12 N	70.46 W
Beaudesert	120	27.59 S	153.00 E
Beaufort, Malay.	96	5.22 N	115.38 E
Beaufort, N.C., U.S.	156	34.43 N	76.40 W
Beaufort, S.C., U.S.	156	32.26 N	80.40 W
Beaufort Sea ⊤2	142	73.00 N	140.00 W
Beaufort West	116	32.18 S	22.36 E
Beaugency	74	47.47 N	1.38 E
Beauharnois	152	45.19 N	73.52 W
Beauly	70	57.29 N	4.29 W
Beaumaris	70	53.16 N	4.05 W
Beaumetz-lès-Loges	74	50.14 N	2.39 E
Beaumont, Fr.	74	48.13 N	0.08 E
Beaumont, Fr.	74	42.42 N	9.27 E
Beaumont, Calif., U.S.	168	33.56 N	116.58 W
Beaumont, Miss., U.S.	158	31.11 N	88.55 W
Beaumont, Tex., U.S.	158	30.05 N	94.06 W
Beaumont Hill ∧2	120	31.33 S	145.13 E
Beaumont-sur-Oise	74	49.08 N	2.17 E
Beaumont-sur-Sarthe	74	48.13 N	0.08 E
Beaune	74	47.02 N	4.50 E
Beaune-la-Rolande	74	48.04 N	2.26 E
Beaupré	150	47.03 N	70.54 W
Beaurepaire	74	45.20 N	5.03 E
Beausejour	142	50.04 N	96.33 W
Beauvais	74	49.26 N	2.05 E
Beauvoir-sur-Mer	74	46.55 N	2.02 W
Beauvoir-sur-Niort	74	46.11 N	0.28 W
Beaver, Alaska, U.S.	146	66.22 N	147.24 W
Beaver, Okla., U.S.	160	36.49 N	100.31 W
Beaver, Pa., U.S.	152	40.42 N	80.18 W
Beaver, Utah, U.S.	164	38.17 N	112.38 W
Beaver, W. Va., U.S.	156	37.45 N	81.09 W
Beaver ≃, Can.	142	54.30 N	107.45 W
Beaver ≃, Can.	142	59.43 N	124.16 W
Beaver Creek ≃, U.S.	162	40.04 N	99.20 W
Beaver Creek ≃, U.S.	162	43.25 N	103.59 W
Beaver Creek, Ky., U.S.	158	37.24 N	86.52 W
Beaver Dam, Wis., U.S.	154	43.28 N	88.50 W
Beaver Dam Wash ≃	164	36.54 N	114.55 W
Beaver Falls	152	40.46 N	80.19 W
Beaverhead Mountains ⌐	166	45.00 N	113.20 W
Beaver Mountains ⌐	146	62.54 N	156.58 W
Beaverton, Ont., Can.	154	44.26 N	79.09 W
Beaverton, Oreg., U.S.	166	45.29 N	122.48 W
Beāwar	102	26.06 N	74.19 E
Bécancour ≃	152	46.22 N	72.27 W
Beccles	70	52.28 N	1.34 E
Bečej	80	45.37 N	20.03 E
Beckley	156	37.46 N	81.11 W
Beckum	72	51.45 N	8.02 E
Beckville	158	32.14 N	94.27 W
Bedale	70	54.17 N	1.35 W
Bédarieux	74	43.37 N	3.09 E
Bedburg	72	51.00 N	6.34 E
Bedelé	108	8.33 N	36.23 E
Bedford, Qué., Can.	152	45.07 N	72.59 W
Bedford, Eng., U.K.	70	52.08 N	0.29 W
Bedford, Ind., U.S.	158	38.52 N	86.29 W
Bedford, Pa., U.S.	152	40.01 N	78.30 W
Bedford, Va., U.S.	156	37.20 N	79.31 W
Bedford, Cape ⌐	120	15.14 S	145.21 E
Bedworth	70	52.28 N	1.29 W
Beebe	158	35.04 N	91.53 W
Beechal Creek ≃	120	27.24 S	145.13 E
Beech Grove	158	39.43 N	86.03 W
Beechworth	120	36.22 S	146.41 E
Beecroft Head ⌐	120	35.01 S	150.51 E
Beelitz	72	52.14 N	12.58 E
Beenleigh	120	27.43 S	153.12 E
Bee Ridge	156	27.16 N	82.31 W
Beersheba → Be'er Sheva', Isr.	104	31.14 N	34.47 E
Beersheba Springs	158	35.28 N	85.39 W
Be'er Sheva'	104	31.14 N	34.47 E
Beeville	160	28.24 N	97.45 W
Befale	110	0.26 N	20.58 E
Befandriana	117b	15.16 S	48.32 E
Bega	120	36.40 S	149.50 E
Bega (Begej) ≃	80	45.13 N	20.19 E
Begej (Bega) ≃	80	45.13 N	20.19 E
Beggs	160	35.45 N	96.04 W
Begi	108	9.16 N	34.32 E
Behbehān	104	30.35 N	50.14 E
Beian	88	48.14 N	126.29 E
Beida → Zāwiyat al-Bayḍā', Libya	108	32.46 N	21.43 E
Beihai (Pakhoi)	94	21.29 N	109.05 E
Beijing (Peking)	88	39.55 N	116.25 E
Beijing Shih □7	88	40.15 N	116.28 E
Beipiaojiang ≃	88	38.20 N	106.00 E
Beira	116	19.49 S	34.52 E
Beira Baixa □9	76	39.58 N	7.30 W
Beira Litoral □9	76	40.15 N	8.25 W
Beirut → Bayrūt, Leb.	104	33.53 N	35.30 E
Beishannmai ∧	88	41.12 N	97.05 E
Beitbridge	116	22.13 S	30.00 E
Béja, Port.	76	38.01 N	7.52 W
Béja, Tun.	78	36.44 N	9.11 E
Bejaïa	106	36.45 N	5.05 E
Béjar	76	40.23 N	5.46 W
Bejestān	104	34.31 N	58.10 E
Bekabad	82	40.13 N	69.14 E
Bekdaš	82	41.34 N	52.32 E
Békés	72	46.46 N	21.08 E
Békéscsaba	72	46.41 N	21.06 E
Bela	102	26.12 N	81.00 E
Bela Crkva	80	44.54 N	21.26 E
Belaga	96	2.42 N	113.47 E
Bel Air	152	39.32 N	76.21 W
Belaja ≃	66	56.00 N	54.32 E
Belaja Cerkov'	64	49.49 N	30.07 E
Belaja Cholunica	66	58.50 N	50.52 E
Belajan ≃	96	0.14 S	116.26 E
Bela Vista, Bra.	140	22.06 S	56.31 W
Bela Vista, Moç.	116	26.20 S	32.40 E
Belawan	96	3.47 N	98.41 E
Belcher Islands II	142	56.20 N	79.30 W
Belding	154	43.05 N	85.13 W
Belebej	66	54.07 N	54.07 E
Beled Weyne	108	4.44 N	45.12 E
Belém, Bra.	134	1.27 S	48.29 W
Belén, Para.	140	27.40 S	57.06 W
Belén, N. Mex., U.S.	164	34.40 N	106.46 W
Belfast, N. Ire., U.K.	70	54.35 N	5.55 W
Belfast, Maine, U.S.	152	44.25 N	69.00 W
Belfort	74	47.38 N	6.52 E
Belgaum	100	15.52 N	74.30 E
Belgioioso	78	45.09 N	9.19 E
Belgorod	64	50.36 N	36.35 E
Belgorod-Dnestrovskij	82	46.12 N	30.20 E
Belgrade → Beograd, Jugo.	80	44.50 N	20.30 E
Belgrade, Mont., U.S.	166	45.47 N	111.11 W
Belhaven	156	35.33 N	76.37 W
Beli Drim ≃	80	42.06 N	20.25 E
Beli Manastir	80	45.46 N	18.36 E
Belin	74	44.30 N	0.47 W
Belington	152	39.01 N	79.56 W
Belitung I	96	2.50 S	107.55 E
Belize □2	128	17.30 N	88.12 W
Belize □2	128	17.15 N	88.45 W
Belkofski	146	55.05 N	162.02 W
Bel'kovskij, Ostrov I	84	75.32 N	135.44 E
Bella Bella	148	52.09 N	128.07 W
Bellac	74	46.07 N	1.02 E
Bella Coola	148	52.22 N	126.46 W
Bellaire, Mich., U.S.	154	44.59 N	85.13 W
Bellaire, Ohio, U.S.	152	40.02 N	80.45 W
Bellaire, Tex., U.S.	160	29.43 N	95.03 W
Bellamy	158	32.22 N	88.08 W
Bellary	100	15.09 N	76.56 E
Bella Unión	140	30.15 S	57.35 W
Bella Vista, Arg.	140	28.30 S	59.00 W
Bella Vista, Arg.	140	27.02 S	65.19 W
Bellavista, Perú	138	4.54 S	80.42 W
Belle, Mo., U.S.	158	38.17 N	91.43 W
Belle, W. Va., U.S.	156	38.14 N	81.32 W
Bellefontaine	152	40.22 N	83.46 W
Bellefonte	152	40.55 N	77.46 W
Belle Fourche	162	44.40 N	103.51 W
Belle Fourche ≃	162	44.26 N	102.19 W
Bellegarde	74	46.06 N	5.49 E
Belle Glade	156	26.41 N	80.40 W
Belle-Île I	74	47.20 N	3.10 W
Belle Isle I	142	51.55 N	55.20 W
Belle Isle, Strait of U	142	51.35 N	56.30 W
Belle Plaine, Iowa, U.S.	154	41.54 N	92.17 W
Belle Plaine, Minn., U.S.	154	44.37 N	93.46 W
Belle River	152	42.18 N	82.43 W
Belleville, Ont., Can.	154	44.10 N	77.23 W
Belleville, Ill., U.S.	158	38.31 N	90.00 W
Belleville, Kans., U.S.	162	39.49 N	97.38 W
Belleville-sur-Saône	74	46.06 N	4.45 E
Bellevue, Idaho, U.S.	166	43.28 N	114.16 W
Bellevue, Iowa, U.S.	154	42.15 N	90.26 W
Bellevue, Mich., U.S.	154	42.12 N	83.29 W
Bellevue, Nebr., U.S.	162	41.09 N	95.54 W
Bellevue, Ohio, U.S.	152	41.17 N	82.50 W
Bellevue, Wash., U.S.	166	47.37 N	122.12 W
Belley	74	45.46 N	5.41 E
Bellin	142	60.01 N	70.01 W
Bellingham, Eng., U.K.	70	55.09 N	2.16 W
Bellingham, Wash., U.S.	166	48.45 N	122.29 W
Bellinzona	74	46.11 N	9.02 E
Bell Island Hot Springs	148	55.56 N	131.34 W
Bellmead	160	31.35 N	97.06 W
Bello	138	6.20 N	75.33 W
Bello Horizonte → Belo Horizonte, Bra.	134	19.55 S	43.56 W
Bellot Strait U	142	71.58 N	94.45 W
Bellows Falls	152	43.08 N	72.26 W
Bell Peninsula ⌐1	142	63.50 N	82.00 W
Bells	160	33.37 N	96.25 W
Bellville, Ohio, U.S.	152	40.37 N	82.31 W
Bellville, Tex., U.S.	160	29.57 N	96.16 W
Bellwood	152	40.36 N	78.20 W
Belly ≃	148	49.52 N	112.02 W
Belmond	154	42.51 N	93.37 W
Belmont, Ohio, U.S.	152	40.02 N	80.55 W
Belmont, Miss., U.S.	158	34.31 N	88.13 W
Belmont, N.H., U.S.	152	43.27 N	71.29 W
Belmont, N.Y., U.S.	152	42.13 N	78.02 W
Belmonte, Bra.	134	15.51 S	38.54 W
Belmonte, Port.	76	40.21 N	7.21 W
Belmopan	130	17.15 N	88.46 W
Belmullet	70	54.14 N	10.00 W
Belo	117b	19.42 S	44.32 E
Belogorsk, S.S.S.R.	88	50.57 N	128.25 E
Belogorsk, S.S.S.R.	64	45.03 N	34.36 E
Belo Horizonte	134	19.55 S	43.56 W
Beloit, Kans., U.S.	162	39.27 N	98.06 W
Beloit, Wis., U.S.	154	42.30 N	89.02 W
Beloje, Ozero ⊖	66	60.11 N	37.37 E
Beloje More (White Sea) ⊤2	66	65.30 N	38.00 E
Belomorsk	66	64.32 N	34.48 E
Beloomut	66	54.57 N	39.22 E
Belorečensk	64	44.46 N	39.52 E
Belorusskaja Sovetskaja Socialističeskaja Respublika □3	86	53.50 N	28.00 E
Belovo	84	54.25 N	86.18 E
Beloz'orsk	66	60.02 N	37.48 E
Belpre	152	39.16 N	81.34 W
Belt	166	47.23 N	110.55 W
Belton, Mo., U.S.	158	38.49 N	94.32 W
Belton, S.C., U.S.	156	34.31 N	82.30 W
Belton, Tex., U.S.	160	31.03 N	97.27 W
Belucha, Gora ∧	84	49.48 N	86.40 E
Belvedere Marittimo	78	39.37 N	15.52 E
Belvès	74	44.47 N	1.00 E
Belvidere, Ill., U.S.	154	42.15 N	88.50 W
Belvidere, N.J., U.S.	152	40.49 N	75.04 W
Belvis de la Jara	76	39.45 N	4.57 W
Belyando ≃	120	21.38 S	146.50 E
Belyj, Ostrov I	84	73.10 N	70.45 E
Belyj Jar	84	58.26 N	85.57 E
Belzig	72	52.08 N	12.35 E
Belzoni	158	33.10 N	90.29 W
Bemidji	154	47.28 N	94.53 W
Bena-Dibele	110	4.00 S	22.50 E
Benagerie	120	31.25 S	140.24 E
Benares → Vārānasi, India	102	25.20 N	83.00 E
Benavente, Esp.	76	42.00 N	5.41 W
Benavente, Port.	76	38.59 N	8.48 W
Benavides	160	27.36 N	98.25 W
Bencubbin	122	30.48 S	117.52 E
Bend	166	44.03 N	121.19 W
Bendel □3	106	6.00 N	6.00 E
Bendemeer	120	30.53 S	151.10 E
Bender Beyla	108	9.30 N	50.48 E
Bendery	64	46.49 N	29.29 E
Bendigo	120	36.46 S	144.17 E
Benē Beraq	104	32.05 N	34.50 E
Benedito Leite	134	7.13 S	44.34 W
Bénévent-l'Abbaye	74	46.07 N	1.36 E
Benevento	78	41.08 N	14.45 E
Benfeld	74	48.22 N	7.36 E
Bengal, Bay of C	100	15.00 N	90.00 E
Bengbu	88	32.57 N	117.21 E
Benghazi → Banghāzī, Libya	108	32.07 N	20.04 E
Bengkalis	96	1.28 N	102.07 E
Bengkulu	96	3.48 S	102.16 E
Benguela	110	12.35 S	13.25 E
Benguéra, Ilha I	116	21.53 S	35.28 E
Beni	138	10.23 S	65.24 W
Beni ≃	138	10.23 S	65.24 W
Béni Abbès	106	30.08 N	2.10 W
Beni-Mellal	106	32.22 N	6.29 W
Benin □1	106	9.30 N	2.15 E
Benin, Bight of C3	106	5.30 N	3.00 E
Benin City	114	6.19 N	5.41 E
Benisa	76	38.34 N	0.03 E
Benjamin	160	33.35 N	99.48 W
Benjamin Constant	138	4.22 S	70.02 W
Benkelman	162	40.03 N	101.32 W
Ben Lomond ∧	120	41.33 S	147.40 E
Bennetta, Ostrov I	84	76.21 N	148.56 E
Bennettsville	156	34.37 N	79.41 W
Bennington, Kans., U.S.	162	39.02 N	97.36 W
Bennington, Vt., U.S.	152	42.53 N	73.12 W
Benoni	116	26.19 S	28.27 E
Bénoué (Benue) ≃	106	7.48 N	6.46 E
Bensheim	72	49.41 N	8.37 E
Benson, Ariz., U.S.	164	31.58 N	110.18 W
Benson, Minn., U.S.	162	45.19 N	95.36 W
Benson, N.C., U.S.	156	35.23 N	78.33 W
Bentinck Island I	124	17.04 S	139.30 E
Benton, Ark., U.S.	158	34.34 N	92.35 W
Benton, Ill., U.S.	158	38.00 N	88.55 W
Benton, Pa., U.S.	152	41.12 N	76.23 W
Benton City	166	46.16 N	119.29 W
Benton Harbor	154	42.06 N	86.27 W
Bentonville	158	36.22 N	94.13 W
Benue (Bénoué) ≃	106	7.48 N	6.46 E
Benxi	88	41.18 N	123.45 E
Beograd (Belgrade)	80	44.50 N	20.30 E
Beppu	90	33.17 N	131.30 E
Berat	80	40.42 N	19.57 E
Berau, Teluk C	124	2.30 S	132.30 E
Berber	108	18.01 N	33.59 E
Berbérati	108	4.16 N	15.47 E
Berbice ≃	138	6.20 N	57.32 W
Berchtesgaden	72	47.38 N	13.01 E
Berck	74	50.24 N	1.34 E
Berd'ansk	64	46.45 N	36.47 E
Berdičev	64	49.54 N	28.36 E
Berdigest'ach	84	62.06 N	126.40 E
Berdsk	84	54.47 N	83.02 E
Berea	156	37.34 N	84.17 W
Berens ≃	142	52.21 N	97.02 W
Berens River	142	52.21 N	97.02 W
Beresford, Austl.	120	29.14 S	136.40 E
Beresford, N.B., Can.	150	47.42 N	65.42 W
Beresford, S. Dak., U.S.	162	43.05 N	96.47 W
Berettau (Berettyó) ≃	72	46.59 N	21.07 E
Berettyó (Berettau) ≃	72	46.59 N	21.07 E
Berettyóújfalu	72	47.14 N	21.32 E
Berezina ≃	64	52.33 N	30.14 E
Berezniki	66	59.24 N	56.46 E
Berga	76	42.06 N	1.51 E
Bergamo	78	45.41 N	9.43 E
Bergen → Mons, Bel.	72	50.27 N	3.56 E
Bergen, B.R.D.	72	52.53 N	10.58 E
Bergen, Ned.	72	52.40 N	4.41 E
Bergen, Nor.	68	60.23 N	5.20 E
Bergen [auf Rügen]	72	54.25 N	13.26 E
Bergen op Zoom	72	51.30 N	4.17 E
Bergerac	74	44.51 N	0.29 E
Bergheim	72	50.55 N	6.38 E
Bergisch Gladbach	72	50.59 N	7.07 E
Bergslagen ⌐1	68	59.55 N	15.00 E
Berguent	106	34.03 N	2.02 W
Berhala, Selat U	96	0.48 S	104.25 E
Berhampur	100	24.06 N	88.15 E
Beringa, Ostrov I	84	55.00 N	165.15 E
Beringovskij	84	63.03 N	179.19 E
Bering Sea ⊤2	146	60.00 N	170.00 W
Bering Strait U	146	65.30 N	169.00 W
Berino	164	32.04 N	106.37 W
Berkåk	68	62.50 N	10.00 E
Berkeley	168	37.57 N	122.16 W
Berkshire □6	70	51.30 N	1.20 W
Berlaimont	74	50.12 N	3.49 E
Berlin, Md., U.S.	152	38.20 N	75.13 W
Berlin, N.H., U.S.	152	44.28 N	71.10 W
Berlin, N.J., U.S.	152	39.48 N	74.57 W
Berlin, Wis., U.S.	154	43.58 N	88.56 W
Berlin □5	72	52.30 N	13.20 E
Berlin,east → Ost-Berlin	72	52.30 N	13.25 E
Berlin,west → West-Berlin	72	52.30 N	13.20 E
Berlinguet Inlet C	142	71.10 N	85.35 W
Berlin Lake ⊖1	152	41.00 N	81.00 W
Bermejo ≃, Arg.	140	32.13 S	62.33 W
Bermejo ≃, Arg.	140	26.51 S	58.23 W
Bermejo, Paso de)(	140	32.50 S	70.05 W
Bermen, Lac ⊖	150	53.35 N	68.55 W
Bermuda □2	128	32.20 N	64.45 W
Bern (Berne)	74	46.57 N	7.26 E
Bernalda	78	40.24 N	16.41 E
Bernau bei Berlin	72	52.40 N	13.35 E
Bernay	74	49.06 N	0.36 E
Bernburg	72	51.48 N	11.44 E
Berne → Bern, Switz.	74	46.57 N	7.26 E
Berner Alpen ⌐	74	46.25 N	7.30 E
Bernie	158	36.40 N	89.58 W
Bernier Bay C	142	71.08 N	88.10 W
Bernier Island I	122	24.52 S	113.08 E
Bernina, Piz ∧	74	46.23 N	9.54 E
Bernkastel-Kues	72	49.55 N	7.04 E
Bersenbrück	72	52.33 N	7.57 E
Beroroha	117b	21.41 S	45.10 E
Beroun	72	49.58 N	14.04 E
Beroza	86	52.32 N	24.59 E
Ber'ozovka	66	59.25 N	56.52 E
Ber'ozovo	84	63.56 N	65.03 E
Berrechid	106	33.16 N	7.35 W
Berri	120	34.17 S	140.35 E
Berrigan	120	35.39 S	145.49 E
Berry ⌐9	74	46.50 N	2.00 E
Berry Islands II	132	25.35 N	77.50 W
Berryville, Ark., U.S.	158	36.21 N	93.34 W
Berryville, Va., U.S.	152	39.09 N	77.59 W
Berthold	162	48.19 N	101.44 W
Berthoud	164	40.18 N	105.04 W
Bertincourt	74	50.05 N	2.58 E
Bertinoro	78	44.09 N	12.08 E
Bertoua	106	4.35 N	13.41 E
Bertrand	162	40.31 N	99.38 W
Berwick, N.S., Can.	150	45.03 N	64.44 W
Berwick, Maine, U.S.	152	43.16 N	70.51 W
Berwick, Pa., U.S.	152	41.03 N	76.14 W
Berwick-upon-Tweed	70	55.46 N	2.00 W
Berwyn	154	41.50 N	87.47 W
Besalampy	117b	16.45 S	44.30 E
Besançon	74	47.15 N	6.02 E
Beskid Mountains ⌐	72	49.40 N	20.00 E
Beslan	64	43.12 N	44.33 E
Bessarabia □9	64	47.00 N	28.30 E
Bessemer, Ala., U.S.	158	33.24 N	86.58 W
Bessemer, Mich., U.S.	154	46.28 N	90.03 W
Bessemer, Pa., U.S.	152	40.58 N	80.29 W
Bessemer City	156	35.17 N	81.17 W
Bessèges	74	44.18 N	4.08 E
Best	72	51.30 N	5.24 E
Bestah	84	61.39 N	129.25 E
Bétaré Oya	106	5.36 N	14.05 E
Betanzos	76	43.17 N	8.13 W
Bétérou	114	9.12 N	2.16 E
Bethal	116	26.27 S	29.28 E
Bethany, Mo., U.S.	158	40.15 N	94.01 W
Bethany, Okla., U.S.	160	35.31 N	97.38 W
Bethel, Alaska, U.S.	146	60.48 N	161.46 W
Bethel, Conn., U.S.	152	41.22 N	73.25 W
Bethel, Ohio, U.S.	152	38.58 N	84.05 W
Bethel Springs	158	35.14 N	88.36 W
Bethesda, Md., U.S.	152	38.59 N	77.06 W
Bethesda, Ohio, U.S.	152	40.01 N	81.04 W
Bethlehem, S. Afr.	116	28.15 S	28.15 E
Bethlehem, Pa., U.S.	152	40.37 N	75.25 W
Bethlehem, W. Va., U.S.	152	40.02 N	80.40 W
Bethlehem → Bayt Laḥm, Urd.	104	31.43 N	35.12 E
Béthune, Fr.	74	50.32 N	2.38 E
Bethune, S.C., U.S.	156	34.25 N	80.21 W
Betioky	117b	23.42 S	44.22 E
Betoota	120	25.42 S	140.44 E
Betpak-Dala ⌐1	82	46.00 N	70.00 E
Betroka	117b	23.16 S	46.06 E
Betsiamites ≃	150	48.56 N	68.38 W
Betsiboka ≃	117b	16.03 S	46.36 E
Bette ∧	108	22.00 N	19.12 E
Bettendorf	154	41.32 N	90.30 W
Bettiah	102	26.48 N	84.30 E
Bettles Field	146	66.55 N	151.30 W
Betwa ≃	102	25.55 N	80.12 E
Betzdorf	72	50.47 N	7.53 E
Beulah, Colo., U.S.	164	38.05 N	104.59 W
Beulah, N. Dak., U.S.	162	47.16 N	101.47 W
Bevensen	72	53.05 N	10.34 E
Beverley, Austl.	122	32.06 S	116.56 E
Beverley, Eng., U.K.	70	53.52 N	0.26 W
Beverly, Mass., U.S.	152	42.33 N	70.53 W
Beverly, Ohio, U.S.	152	39.33 N	81.38 W
Beverly Hills	168	34.04 N	118.26 W
Beverly Lake ⊖	142	64.36 N	100.30 W
Beverungen	72	51.39 N	9.22 E
Beverwijk	72	52.28 N	4.40 E
Bexhill	70	50.50 N	0.29 E
Bexley	152	39.58 N	82.56 W
Beyşehir Gölü ⊖	64	37.40 N	31.30 E
Bezau	72	47.23 N	9.54 E
Bežeck	86	57.47 N	36.42 E
Béziers	74	43.21 N	3.15 E
Bhadrakh	102	21.04 N	86.30 E
Bhadravati	100	13.52 N	75.43 E
Bhāgalpur	102	25.15 N	87.00 E
Bhaktapur	102	27.40 N	85.26 E
Bhandāra	102	21.10 N	79.39 E
Bharatpur	102	27.13 N	77.29 E
Bhatinda	102	30.12 N	74.57 E
Bhātpāra	102	22.52 N	88.24 E
Bhaunagar	102	21.46 N	72.09 E
Bhāwanipatna	100	19.55 N	83.10 E
Bhilai	102	21.13 N	81.26 E
Bhilwāra	102	25.21 N	74.38 E
Bhima ≃	100	16.25 N	77.17 E
Bhind	102	26.35 N	78.48 E
Bhiwāni	102	28.47 N	76.08 E
Bhopāl	102	23.16 N	77.24 E
Bhubaneswar	102	20.14 N	85.50 E
Bhuj	102	23.15 N	69.40 E
Bhusāwal	102	21.03 N	75.46 E
Bhutan □1	102	27.30 N	90.30 E
Bia, Phou ∧	94	18.59 N	103.10 E
Biafra, Bight of C3	106	4.00 N	8.00 E
Biak	124	1.10 S	136.05 E
Biała	72	50.24 N	17.40 E
Biała Podlaska	72	52.02 N	23.06 E
Biała Rawska	72	51.49 N	20.29 E
Białogard	72	54.01 N	15.59 E
Białystok	72	53.09 N	23.09 E
Bianco, Monte (Mont Blanc) ∧	74	45.50 N	6.52 E
Biaro, Pulau I	96	2.05 N	125.20 E
Biarritz	74	43.29 N	1.34 W
Biasca	74	46.22 N	8.58 E
Bibai	90a	43.19 N	141.52 E
Bibb City	156	32.30 N	84.58 W
Biberach an der Riss	72	48.06 N	9.48 E
Bic	150	48.22 N	68.42 W
Bickerton Island I	124	13.45 S	136.12 E
Bicknell, Ind., U.S.	158	38.47 N	87.18 W
Bicknell, Utah, U.S.	164	38.20 N	111.33 W
Bicske	72	47.29 N	18.37 E
Bida	114	9.05 N	6.01 E
Biddeford	152	43.29 N	70.27 W
Bideford	70	51.01 N	4.13 W
Biedenkopf	72	50.55 N	8.32 E
Biel [bienne]	74	47.10 N	7.12 E
Bielefeld	72	52.01 N	8.31 E
Bieler Lake ⊖	142	70.17 N	73.00 W
Bielersee ⊖	74	47.05 N	7.10 E
Biella	78	45.34 N	8.03 E
Bielsko-Biała	72	49.49 N	19.02 E
Bielsk Podlaski	72	52.47 N	23.12 E
Bien-hoa	94	10.59 N	106.49 E
Bienville, Lac ⊖	142	55.05 N	72.40 W
Bietigheim	72	48.58 N	9.07 E
Big Bear Lake	168	34.15 N	116.53 W
Big Blue ≃	162	39.11 N	96.33 W
Big Cabin Creek ≃	160	36.12 N	95.15 W
Big Creek	168	37.12 N	119.09 W
Big Creek, East Fork ≃	158	40.16 N	94.00 W
Bigelow Bight C3	152	43.05 N	70.30 W
Big Escambia Creek ≃	156	31.00 N	87.14 W
Biggar, Sask., Can.	142	52.04 N	108.00 W
Biggar, Scot., U.K.	70	55.38 N	3.32 W
Biggs	166	39.25 N	121.43 W
Bighorn ≃	166	46.09 N	107.28 W
Big Horn Basin ⌐1	166	44.15 N	108.10 W
Bighorn Mountains ⌐	166	44.00 N	107.30 W
Big Island I	142	62.43 N	70.43 W
Big Koniuji Island I	146	55.06 N	159.30 W
Big Lake	160	31.12 N	101.28 W
Big Piney	166	42.32 N	110.06 W
Big Quill Lake ⊖	142	51.55 N	104.22 W
Big Rapids	154	43.41 N	85.29 W
Big Sand Lake ⊖	142	57.45 N	99.42 W
Big Sandy ≃, Tenn., U.S.	158	36.16 N	88.05 W
Big Sandy, Levisa Fork ≃	156	37.48 N	82.36 W
Big Sandy, Rolling Fork ≃	156	37.24 N	82.36 W
Big Sandy, Tug Fork ≃	156	38.06 N	82.36 W
Big Sandy ≃, Ariz., U.S.	164	34.19 N	113.31 W
Big Sheep Mountain ∧	166	47.03 N	105.43 W
Big Sioux ≃	162	42.30 N	96.25 W
Big Spring	160	32.15 N	101.28 W
Big Stone City	162	45.18 N	96.28 W
Big Stone Gap	156	36.52 N	82.47 W
Big Timber	166	45.50 N	109.57 W
Big Trout Lake ⊖	142	53.45 N	90.00 W
Big Wells	160	28.34 N	99.34 W
Bihać	78	44.49 N	15.52 E
Bihār	102	25.11 N	85.31 E
Bihār □3	102	25.00 N	86.00 E
Biharamulo	110	2.38 S	31.20 E
Bihor □5	80	47.00 N	22.15 E
Bijagós, Arquipélago dos II	114	11.25 N	16.20 W
Bijāpur, Bhārat	100	16.50 N	75.42 E
Bijāpur, Bhārat	100	18.50 N	80.49 E
Bijeljina	80	44.45 N	19.13 E
Bijelo Polje	80	43.02 N	19.45 E
Bijie	88	27.18 N	105.17 E
Bijsk	84	...	
Bikaner	102	28.01 N	73.18 E

Symbols in the index entries are identified on page 203.

Name	Page	Lat	Long
Bikin	84	46.48 N	134.16 E
Bikin ≃	84	46.51 N	134.02 E
Bikoro	110	0.45 S	18.07 E
Bilāspur	102	22.05 N	82.09 E
Bilauktaung Range ⋏	94	13.00 N	99.00 E
Bilbao	76	43.15 N	2.58 W
Bili ≃	108	4.09 N	22.29 E
Bilma	72	50.35 N	13.45 E
Biliran Island I	98	11.35 N	124.30 E
Billings, Mont., U.S.	166	45.47 N	118.27 W
Billings, Okla., U.S.	160	36.32 N	97.27 W
Billom	74	45.44 N	3.21 E
Biloela	120	24.24 S	150.30 E
Biloxi	158	30.24 N	88.53 W
Biltmore Forest	156	35.32 N	82.32 W
Bilugyun Island I	94	16.24 N	97.32 E
Binche	72	50.24 N	4.10 E
Bindjai	94	3.36 N	98.30 E
Binga, Monte ⋏	116	19.45 S	33.04 E
Bingara	120	29.52 S	150.34 E
Bingen	72	48.07 N	9.16 E
Bingham	152	45.03 N	69.53 W
Binghamton	152	42.08 N	75.54 W
Binhai	88	34.03 N	119.51 E
Binongko, Pulau I	96	5.57 S	124.02 E
Bintan, Pulau I	96	1.05 N	104.30 E
Bintulu	92	3.13 N	113.04 E
Binxian	88	35.00 N	108.08 E
Binzert (Bizerte)	106	37.17 N	9.52 E
Bío-Bío □4	140	37.45 S	72.00 W
Bío-Bío ≃	140	36.49 S	73.10 W
Bir	100	18.59 N	75.46 E
Birao	108	10.17 N	22.47 E
Birātnagar	102	26.29 N	87.17 E
Birch	142	58.30 N	112.15 W
Birch Mountains ⋏2	142	57.30 N	112.30 W
Birch Run	154	43.15 N	83.48 W
Birchwood	154	45.40 N	91.33 W
Bird Island	162	44.46 N	94.54 W
Bird Island I	136	54.00 S	38.05 W
Bird Islet I	118	22.10 S	155.28 E
Birdum	120	25.54 S	139.22 E
Bireuen	124	15.39 S	133.13 E
Birganj	102	27.00 N	84.52 E
Biril'ussy	84	57.07 N	90.32 E
Birjand	104	32.53 N	59.13 E
Birkeland	68	58.20 N	8.14 E
Birkenfeld	72	49.39 N	7.10 E
Birkenhead, N.Z.	126	36.49 S	174.44 E
Birkenhead, Eng., U.K.	70	53.24 N	3.02 W
Birkerød	68	55.50 N	12.26 E
Birkfeld	72	47.21 N	15.42 E
Birlad	80	46.14 N	27.40 E
Birmingham, Eng., U.K.	70	52.30 N	1.50 W
Birmingham, Iowa, U.S.	154	40.53 N	91.57 W
Birmingham, Mich., U.S.	154	42.33 N	83.15 W
Bir Mogrein	106	25.14 N	11.35 W
Birni Kebbi	114	12.32 N	4.12 E
Birni Nkonni	114	13.48 N	5.15 E
Birobidžan	84	48.48 N	132.57 E
Birr	70	53.05 N	7.54 W
Birrie ≃	120	29.43 S	146.37 E
Birrindudu	122	18.22 S	129.27 E
Bi'r Safājah	112	26.44 N	33.56 E
Birsk	82	55.25 N	55.32 E
Bir'usa ≃	84	57.34 N	95.24 E
Birža	86	56.12 N	24.45 E
Birzebbuġa	78	35.49 N	14.32 E
Bisa, Pulau I	96	1.15 S	127.28 E
Bisbee	164	31.27 N	109.55 W
Biscarrosse	74	44.24 N	1.10 W
Biscay, Bay of C	74	44.00 N	4.00 W
Bisceglie	78	41.14 N	16.31 E
Bischofsburg → Biskupiec	72	53.52 N	20.27 E
Bischofshofen	72	47.25 N	13.13 E
Bischofswerda	72	51.07 N	14.10 E
Biscoe	156	35.22 N	79.47 W
Bišhārah, Maʿtan ⊤4	112	22.58 N	22.23 E
Bishop, Calif., U.S.	168	37.22 N	118.24 W
Bishop, Tex., U.S.	160	27.35 N	97.48 W
Bishop Auckland	70	54.40 N	1.40 W
Bishop's Falls	150	49.01 N	55.30 W
Bishop's Stortford	70	51.53 N	0.09 E
Biskra	106	34.51 N	5.44 E
Bislig	92	8.13 N	126.19 E
Bismarck, Mo., U.S.	158	37.46 N	90.38 W
Bismarck, N. Dak., U.S.	162	46.48 N	100.47 W
Bismarck Range ⋏	124	5.30 S	144.45 E
Bismo	68	61.53 N	8.16 E
Bissau	114	11.51 N	15.35 W
Bisset	142	51.02 N	95.40 W
Bistcho Lake ⊜	142	59.40 N	118.40 W
Bistineau, Lake ⊜1	158	32.25 N	93.22 W
Bistrita	80	47.08 N	24.30 E
Bistrita-Năsăud □4	80	47.15 N	24.30 E
Bisztynek	72	54.06 N	20.55 E
Bitam	110	2.05 N	11.29 E
Bitburg	72	49.58 N	6.31 E
Bitche	72	49.03 N	7.26 E
Bitlis	104	38.22 N	42.06 E
Bitonto	78	41.06 N	16.42 E
Bitterfeld	72	51.37 N	12.20 E
Bitterfontein	116	31.00 S	18.32 E
Bitterroot Range ⋏	166	46.00 N	114.25 W
Bitti	78	40.29 N	9.23 E
Bitung	96	1.27 N	125.11 E
Biwa-ko ⊜	90	35.15 N	136.05 E
Bixby	160	35.57 N	95.53 W
Bjala Slatina	80	43.28 N	23.56 E
Bjelaja → Belaja ≃	82	56.00 N	54.32 E
Bjelovar	78	45.54 N	16.51 E
Bjørkelangen	68	59.53 N	11.34 E
Björköby	68	63.21 N	21.19 E
Black (Lixianjiang) (Da) ≃, As.	94	21.15 N	105.20 E
Black ≃, Ala., U.S.	158	35.38 N	91.19 W
Black ≃, Alaska, U.S.	146	66.58 N	144.50 W
Blackall	120	24.25 S	145.28 E
Blackburn	70	53.45 N	2.29 W
Black Butte ⋏	166	44.54 N	111.51 W
Black Buttes ⋏	166	41.33 N	108.42 W
Black Cypress Bayou ≃	158	32.42 N	93.55 W
Black Duck ≃	142	56.51 N	89.02 W
Black Eagle	166	47.31 N	111.17 W
Blackfoot	166	43.11 N	112.20 W
Black Forest → Schwarzwald ⋏	72	48.00 N	8.15 E
Black Hills ⋏	162	44.00 N	104.00 W
Black Lake ⊜	146	59.12 N	105.20 W
Black Mesa ⋏	164	36.35 N	110.20 W
Blackmore, Mount ⋏	166	45.27 N	111.01 W
Black Mountain	156	35.37 N	82.19 W
Black Mountain ⋏	168	44.45 N	107.22 W
Black Mountains ⋏	164	35.30 N	114.30 W
Blackpool	70	53.50 N	3.03 W
Black Range ⋏	164	33.10 N	107.50 W
Black River	154	44.01 N	75.48 W
Black River Falls	154	44.18 N	90.51 W
Black Rock ⋏	112	14.00 N	24.30 E
Black Rock Desert ⋍2	168	41.10 N	119.00 W
Blacksburg, S.C., U.S.	156	35.07 N	81.31 W
Blacksburg, Va., U.S.	156	37.14 N	80.25 W
Black Sea ⊤2	64	43.00 N	35.00 E
Blacks Fork ≃	164	41.24 N	109.38 W
Blacks Harbour	150	45.03 N	66.49 W
Blackshear	156	31.18 N	82.14 W
Blackstone	156	37.04 N	78.00 W
Blackville	156	33.22 N	81.16 W
Black Volta (Volta Noire) ≃	114	8.41 N	1.33 W
Blackwater ≃	158	34.00 N	87.02 W
Blackwater Creek ≃	120	25.56 S	144.30 E
Blackwater Lake ⊜	146	64.00 N	123.05 W
Blackwell, Okla., U.S.	160	36.48 N	97.17 W
Blackwell, Tex., U.S.	160	32.05 N	100.19 W
Blagodarnoje	82	45.06 N	43.27 E
Blagoevgrad	80	42.01 N	23.06 E
Blagoveščensk	84	50.17 N	127.32 E
Blain	74	47.29 N	1.46 W
Blaine, Minn., U.S.	154	45.11 N	93.14 W
Blair, Nebr., U.S.	162	41.33 N	96.08 W
Blair, Wis., U.S.	154	44.18 N	91.14 W
Blair Athol	120	22.42 S	147.33 E
Blairgowrie	70	56.36 N	3.21 W
Blairmore	148	49.36 N	114.26 W
Blairsville	156	34.52 N	79.16 W
Blakely	156	31.23 N	84.56 W
Blanc, Cap ⊁	106	20.46 N	17.03 W
Blanc, Mont (Monte Bianco) ⋏	74	45.50 N	6.52 E
Blanca, Bahia C	140	38.55 S	62.10 W
Blanca, Cordillera ⋏	134	9.00 S	77.30 W
Blanca Peak ⋏	164	37.35 N	105.29 W
Blanchard	160	35.08 N	97.39 W
Blanchard ≃	152	41.02 N	84.18 W
Blanche, Lake ⊜, Austl.	120	29.15 S	139.39 E
Blanche, Lake ⊜, Austl.	122	22.25 S	123.17 E
Blanchester	152	39.17 N	83.55 W
Blanco	160	30.06 N	98.25 W
Blanco, Cape ⊁	166	42.50 N	124.34 W
Bland	156	37.06 N	81.07 W
Blandford Forum	70	50.52 N	2.11 W
Blanding	164	37.37 N	109.29 W
Blandinsville	154	40.33 N	90.52 W
Blanes	76	41.41 N	2.48 E
Blangy-sur-Bresle	74	49.56 N	1.38 E
Blankenberge	72	51.19 N	3.08 E
Blankenburg	72	51.48 N	10.58 E
Blankenheim	72	50.26 N	6.39 E
Blankenfort	74	44.53 N	0.39 W
Blansko	72	49.22 N	16.39 E
Blantyre	110	15.47 S	35.00 E
Blasdell	152	42.47 N	78.49 W
Blaubeuren	72	48.24 N	9.47 E
Blaufelden	72	49.18 N	9.58 E
Blaye-et-Sainte-Luce	74	45.08 N	0.39 W
Blaze, Point ⊁	124	12.56 S	130.12 E
Bleiburg	72	46.35 N	14.48 E
Blekinge I	68	56.20 N	15.05 E
Blekinge Län □6	68	56.20 N	15.20 E
Blenheim, Ont., Can.	152	42.20 N	82.00 W
Blenheim, N.Z.	126	41.31 S	173.57 E
Bléré	74	47.20 N	1.00 E
Bletchley	70	52.00 N	0.46 W
Bletterans	74	46.45 N	5.27 E
Bleus, Monts ⋏, Afr.	108	1.30 N	30.30 E
Bleus, Monts ⋏, Zaïre	110	4.31 S	21.02 E
Blida	106	36.28 N	2.50 E
Blind River	148	46.10 N	82.58 W
Blissfield	154	41.50 N	83.52 W
Blitar	96	8.06 S	112.09 E
Block Island I	152	41.10 N	71.34 W
Bloemfontein	116	29.12 S	26.07 E
Bloemhof	116	27.38 S	25.32 E
Blois	74	47.35 N	1.20 E
Blönduós	66a	65.39 N	20.15 W
Bloods Creek	122	26.28 S	135.17 E
Bloodvein ≃	142	51.45 N	96.44 W
Bloomer	154	45.07 N	91.29 W
Bloomfield, Ind., U.S.	158	39.01 N	86.56 W
Bloomfield, Iowa, U.S.	154	40.45 N	92.25 W
Bloomfield, Mo., U.S.	158	36.53 N	89.56 W
Bloomfield, Nebr., U.S.	162	42.36 N	97.39 W
Bloomfield, N. Mex., U.S.	164	36.43 N	107.59 W
Bloomfield, Vt., U.S.	152	44.55 N	71.38 W
Blooming Prairie	154	43.52 N	93.03 W
Bloomington, Ill., U.S.	158	40.29 N	88.60 W
Bloomington, Ind., U.S.	158	39.10 N	86.32 W
Bloomington, Minn., U.S.	154	44.50 N	93.17 W
Bloomington, Wis., U.S.	154	42.53 N	90.55 W
Bloomsburg	152	41.00 N	76.27 W
Bloomville	152	41.03 N	83.00 W
Blora	96	6.57 S	111.25 E
Blossburg	152	41.41 N	77.04 W
Blouberg ⋏	116	23.01 S	28.59 E
Blountstown	156	30.27 N	85.03 W
Blowering Reservoir ⊜1	120	35.30 S	148.15 E
Bludenz	72	47.09 N	9.49 E
Bluecreek	148	48.19 N	117.49 W
Blue Earth	154	43.38 N	94.06 W
Bluefield, Va., U.S.	156	37.15 N	81.13 W
Bluefield, W. Va., U.S.	156	37.16 N	81.13 W
Bluefields	132	12.00 N	83.45 W
Blue Hill	152	44.25 N	68.36 W
Blue Hill Bay C	152	44.15 N	68.30 W
Blue Island	154	41.40 N	87.41 W
Blue Mound	158	40.05 N	95.00 W
Blue Mountain Peak ⋏	132	18.03 N	76.35 W
Blue Mountains ⋏	166	44.35 N	118.25 W
Blue Mud Bay C	124	13.26 S	135.56 E
Blue Nile (Al-Baḥr al-Azraq) (Abay) ≃	112	15.38 N	32.31 E
Bluenose Lake ⊜	146	68.30 N	119.35 W
Blue Rapids	162	39.41 N	96.39 W
Blue Ridge, Ga., U.S.	156	34.52 N	84.20 W
Blue Ridge, Tex., U.S.	160	33.18 N	96.24 W
Blue Ridge ⋏	144	37.00 N	82.00 W
Bluestone ≃	156	37.34 N	80.59 W
Bluestone Reservoir ⊜1	156	37.30 N	80.50 W
Bluewater	164	35.15 N	107.59 W
Bluff	126	46.36 S	168.20 E
Bluff Creek ≃	160	36.58 N	97.20 W
Bluff Knoll ⋏	122	34.23 S	118.20 E
Bluff Park	158	33.24 N	86.47 W
Bluff Point ⊁	122	27.50 S	114.06 E
Bluffton, Ind., U.S.	158	40.44 N	85.11 W
Bluffton, Ohio, U.S.	152	40.53 N	83.54 W
Blumberg	72	47.50 N	8.31 E
Blumenau	140	26.56 S	49.03 W
Bly	166	42.24 N	121.02 W
Blyth ≃	124	12.04 S	134.35 E
Blyth ≃	120	12.04 S	134.35 E
Blythe	168	33.37 N	114.36 W
Blytheville	158	35.56 N	89.55 W
Blyth Range ⋏	122	26.50 S	129.00 E
Bø, No. ⊁	68	59.25 N	9.04 E
Bo, S.L.	114	7.56 N	11.21 W
Boaco	132	12.28 N	85.43 W
Boardman	152	41.02 N	80.40 W
Boa Nova	138	14.22 S	40.10 W
Boa Vista	134a	16.05 N	22.50 W
Boaz	158	34.12 N	86.10 W
Bobbili	100	18.35 N	83.22 E
Bobbio	78	44.46 N	9.23 E
Bobcaygeon	152	44.33 N	78.33 W
Böblingen	72	48.41 N	9.01 E
Bobo Dioulasso	114	11.12 N	4.18 W
Bobolice	72	53.57 N	16.36 E
Bobr ≃	72	52.04 N	15.04 E
Bobrujsk	86	53.09 N	29.14 E
Boby, Pic ⋏	117b	22.12 S	46.55 E
Bôca de Quadra ⋃	148	55.08 N	130.50 W
Bôca do Acre	134	8.45 S	67.23 W
Bocas del Toro	138	9.22 N	82.14 W
Bochnia	72	49.58 N	20.26 E
Bocholt	72	51.50 N	6.36 E
Bochum	72	51.29 N	7.13 E
Bocognano	74	42.05 N	9.03 E
Boda	108	4.19 N	17.28 E
Bodajbo	84	57.51 N	114.10 E
Bodallin	122	31.22 S	118.52 E
Boddington	122	32.48 S	116.28 E
Bodele ⋍1	108	16.30 N	16.30 E
Boden	68	65.50 N	21.42 E
Bodensee ⊜	74	47.35 N	9.25 E
Bodmin	74	50.29 N	4.43 W
Bodø	66	67.17 N	14.23 E
Bodrog ≃	80	48.07 N	21.25 E
Bodrum	108	37.02 N	27.26 E
Boende	110	0.13 S	20.52 E
Boën-sur-Lignon	74	45.44 N	3.59 E
Boerne	160	29.47 N	98.44 W
Bogan ≃	120	32.45 S	148.08 E
Bogalusa	158	30.47 N	89.52 W
Bogan ≃	120	32.45 S	148.08 E
Bogeduoshanmai ⋏	88	43.30 N	89.45 E
Bogen	72	48.55 N	12.43 E
Bogenfels	116	27.23 S	15.22 E
Bogense	68	55.34 N	10.06 E
Boger City	156	35.29 N	81.13 W
Boggabri	120	30.42 S	150.02 E
Bognor Regis	70	50.47 N	0.41 W
Bogo	92	11.03 N	124.00 E
Bogol'ubovo	86	56.13 N	40.31 E
Bogong, Mount ⋏	120	36.44 S	147.19 E
Bogor	96	6.35 S	106.47 E
Bogorodsk	86	56.06 N	43.31 E
Bogotá	138	4.36 N	74.05 W
Bogotol	84	56.12 N	89.33 E
Bogra	102	24.51 N	89.22 E
Boguchany	84	58.23 N	97.29 E
Boguslav	86	49.33 N	30.53 E
Bogue Chitto ≃	158	30.35 N	89.49 W
Bohai C	88	38.30 N	120.00 E
Bohain-en-Vermandois	74	49.59 S	3.27 E
Bohemian Forest ⋏	72	49.15 N	12.45 E
Bohol I	98	9.50 N	124.10 E
Bohuslän □9	68	58.15 N	11.50 E
Boiano	78	41.29 N	14.29 E
Boigu I	124	9.16 S	142.12 E
Boiling Springs	156	35.16 N	81.40 W
Bois, Lac des ⊜	146	66.40 N	125.15 W
Bois de Sioux ≃	162	46.16 N	96.36 W
Bois du Roi ⋏	74	47.00 N	4.02 E
Boise	166	43.37 N	116.13 W
Boissevain	162	49.14 N	100.03 W
Boizenburg	72	53.22 N	10.43 E
Bojador, Cabo ⊁	106	26.08 N	14.30 W
Bojeador, Cape ⊁	98	18.30 N	120.34 E
Bojnūrd	104	37.28 N	57.19 E
Boké	114	10.56 N	14.18 W
Bokelu	88	48.46 N	121.57 E
Bokhara ≃	120	29.55 S	146.42 E
Boksburg	116	26.12 S	28.14 E
Boksitogorsk	86	59.28 N	33.51 E
Bokungu	110	0.41 S	22.19 E
Bolama	114	11.35 N	15.28 W
Bolbec	74	49.34 N	0.29 E
Bolchov	86	53.27 N	36.01 E
Bolesławiec	72	51.16 N	15.34 E
Boley	160	35.29 N	96.29 W
Bolgart	122	31.16 S	116.30 E
Bolgatanga	114	10.46 N	0.52 W
Boli	88	45.46 N	130.35 E
Bolívar, Arg.	140	36.14 S	61.07 W
Bolívar, Col.	138	5.50 N	76.01 W
Bolívar, Mo., U.S.	158	37.37 N	93.25 W
Bolívar, N.Y., U.S.	152	42.04 N	78.14 W
Bolívar, Tenn., U.S.	158	35.16 N	88.59 W
Bolívar □4	138	6.20 N	63.30 W
Bolívar □4	138	1.15 S	79.05 W
Bolívar □5	138	9.00 N	74.40 W
Bolívar, Cerro ⋏	138	7.28 N	63.25 W
Bolívar, Pico (La Columna) ⋏	138	8.30 N	71.02 W
Bolivia □1	134	17.00 S	65.00 W
Bollnäs	68	61.21 N	16.25 E
Bollullos par del Condado	76	37.20 N	6.32 W
Bolobo	110	2.10 S	16.14 E
Bolochovo	86	54.05 N	37.50 E
Bologna	78	44.29 N	11.20 E
Bologoje	86	57.54 N	34.02 E
Bolomba	110	0.29 N	19.12 E
Bolotnoje	84	55.41 N	84.23 E
Bol'šaja Balachn'a ≃	84	73.37 N	107.05 E
Bol'šaja Cheta ≃	84	69.33 N	84.15 E
Bol'šaja Čuja ≃	84	58.56 N	112.13 E
Bol'šaja Ižora	86	59.56 N	29.34 E
Bol'šaja Kuonamka ≃	84	70.45 N	113.24 E
Bol'šaja Murta	84	56.55 N	93.07 E
Bol'šaja Višera	86	58.55 N	32.08 E
Bolsena	78	42.39 N	11.59 E
Bol'šereck	84	52.25 N	156.24 E
Bol'ševik, Ostrov I	84	62.44 N	147.30 E
Bol'šoj An'uj ≃	84	68.30 N	160.49 E
Bol'šoj Begičev, Ostrov I	84	74.20 N	112.30 E
Bol'šoj Jenisej ≃	84	51.43 N	94.26 E
Bol'šoj Kavkaz ⋏	64	43.30 N	45.00 E
Bol'šoj L'achovskij, Ostrov I	84	73.35 N	142.00 E
Bol'šoj Uzen' ≃	82	48.50 N	49.40 E
Bolsward	72	53.03 N	5.31 E
Bolton, Austl.	120	28.05 S	147.15 E
Bolton, Ont., Can.	152	43.53 N	79.44 W
Bolton, Eng., U.K.	70	53.35 N	2.26 W
Bolton, Miss., U.S.	158	32.21 N	90.28 W
Bóly	72	45.58 N	18.32 E
Bolzano (Bozen)	78	46.31 N	11.22 E
Boma	110	5.51 S	13.03 E
Bomaderry	120	34.51 S	150.36 E
Bombala	120	36.54 S	149.14 E
Bombarral	76	39.16 N	9.09 W
Bombay	100	18.58 N	72.50 E
Bom Despacho	134	19.43 S	45.15 W
Bom Jesus da Lapa	134	13.15 S	43.25 W
Bomnak	84	54.46 N	128.51 E
Bomokandi ≃	108	3.39 N	26.08 E
Bomu (Mbomou) ≃	108	4.08 N	22.26 E
Bon, Cap ⊁	106	37.05 N	11.03 E
Bon Air	156	37.32 N	77.34 W
Bonaire I	132	12.10 N	68.15 W
Bonanza	160	40.00 N	109.11 W
Bonaparte ≃	146	66.30 N	72.03 W
Bonaparte Archipelago II	122	14.17 S	125.18 E
Bonarbridge	70	57.53 N	4.21 W
Bonarcado	78	40.04 N	8.38 E
Bonavista Bay C	150	48.44 N	53.07 W
Bonavista Bay C	150	48.45 N	53.20 W
Bondeno	78	44.53 N	11.25 E
Bondo	108	3.49 N	23.40 E
Bondoukou	114	8.02 N	2.48 W
Bône → Annaba	106	36.54 N	7.46 E
Bone, Teluk C	96	4.00 S	120.40 E
Bongandanga	110	1.30 N	21.03 E
Bongor	108	10.17 N	15.22 E
Bonham	160	33.35 N	96.11 W
Bonifacio	78	41.23 N	9.10 E
Bonifacio, Strait of ⋃	78	41.20 N	9.15 E
Bonifay	156	30.48 N	85.40 W
Bonners Ferry	166	48.41 N	116.18 W
Bonnétable	74	48.11 N	0.26 E
Bonne Terre	158	37.55 N	90.33 W
Bonnet Plume ≃	146	65.55 N	134.58 W
Bonneville	74	46.05 N	6.25 E
Bonneville Salt Flats ⋍	168	40.45 N	113.52 W
Bonnie Doone	156	35.05 N	78.58 W
Bonnie Rock	122	30.32 S	118.21 E
Bonny	114	4.27 N	7.10 E
Bonnyrigg	70	55.52 N	3.06 W
Bonorva	78	40.25 N	8.46 E
Bonsecours ⋏	74	49.59 N	5.30 E
Bonthain → Bantaeng	96	5.32 S	119.56 E
Bonthe	114	7.32 N	12.30 W
Bontoc	98	17.06 N	120.58 E
Bonython Range ⋏	122	23.51 S	129.00 E
Boogardie	122	28.02 S	117.47 E
Bookaloo	120	31.55 S	137.22 E
Book Cliffs ⬤4	164	39.20 N	109.00 W
Booker	160	36.27 N	100.32 W
Boolaloo	122	22.35 S	115.51 E
Boom	72	51.05 N	4.22 E
Boomarra	120	19.33 S	140.20 E
Boonah	120	28.00 S	152.41 E
Boone, Iowa, U.S.	154	42.04 N	93.53 W
Boone, N.C., U.S.	156	36.13 N	81.41 W
Booneville, Ark., U.S.	158	35.08 N	93.55 W
Booneville, Miss., U.S.	158	34.39 N	88.34 W
Boonville, Calif., U.S.	168	39.00 N	123.22 W
Boonville, Ind., U.S.	158	38.03 N	87.16 W
Boonville, Mo., U.S.	158	38.58 N	92.44 W
Boonville, N.Y., U.S.	152	43.29 N	75.20 W
Boorindal	120	30.21 S	146.08 E
Boorthanna	120	28.38 S	135.54 E
Boothbay Harbor	152	43.51 N	69.38 W
Boothia, Gulf of C	146	71.00 N	91.00 W
Boothia Peninsula ⊁1	142	70.30 N	95.00 W
Bootle	70	53.28 N	3.00 W
Boopeechee	120	29.36 S	137.23 E
Boquerón □5	140	21.30 S	60.00 W
Boquete	138	8.46 N	82.27 W
Bor, Jugo.	80	44.05 N	22.07 E
Bor, S.S.S.R.	86	56.22 N	44.05 E
Bor, Súd.	112	6.12 N	31.33 E
Bor, Tür.	104	37.54 N	34.34 E
Borah Peak ⋏	166	44.08 N	113.48 W
Borama	108	9.58 N	43.07 E
Borås	68	57.43 N	12.55 E
Borba, Bra.	138	4.24 S	59.35 W
Borba, Port.	76	38.48 N	7.27 W
Borda, Cape ⊁	120	35.45 S	136.34 E
Bordeaux	74	44.50 N	0.34 W
Borden Peninsula ⊁1	142	73.00 N	83.00 W
Borders Region □4	70	55.37 N	3.15 W
Bordertown	120	36.19 S	140.47 E
Bordeyri	66a	65.12 N	21.09 W
Bordighera	78	43.46 N	7.39 E
Bordj Bou Arreridj	76	36.04 N	4.46 E
Borðj (Porvoo)	68a	60.24 N	25.40 E
Borgarnes	66a	64.35 N	21.53 W
Borger	160	35.39 N	101.24 W
Borghorst	72	52.07 N	7.23 E
Borgne, Lake C	158	30.05 N	89.40 W
Borgomanero	78	45.42 N	8.28 E
Borgosesia	78	45.43 N	8.16 E
Borgsă ≃	84	51.23 N	42.06 E
Borisov	86	54.15 N	28.30 E
Borisoglebsk	82	51.23 N	42.06 E
Borisoglebskij	86	57.16 N	39.09 E
Borisov	86	54.15 N	28.30 E
Borken	72	51.51 N	6.51 E
Borković	86	55.40 N	28.20 E
Borlänge	68	60.29 N	15.25 E
Bormes-les-Mimosas	74	43.09 N	6.20 E
Bormio	78	46.28 N	10.22 E
Borna	72	51.19 N	13.11 E
Borneo (Kalimantan) I	96	0.30 N	114.00 E
Bornholm I	68	55.10 N	15.00 E
Boro ≃	112	8.52 N	26.11 E
Borogoncy	84	62.42 N	131.08 E
Boron	168	34.60 N	117.39 W
Borovichi	86	58.24 N	33.55 E
Borovl'anka	84	52.38 N	84.29 E
Borovoj	66	59.55 N	51.38 E
Borovsk	86	55.12 N	36.30 E
Borroloola	124	16.04 S	136.17 E
Borșa	80	47.39 N	24.40 E
Borščovočnyj Chrebet ⋏	84	52.00 N	117.00 E
Borsod-Abaúj-Zemplén □4	72	48.15 N	21.00 E
Bort-les-Orgues	74	45.24 N	2.30 E
Borüjerd	104	33.54 N	48.46 E
Borz'a	84	50.38 N	116.38 E
Bosa	78	40.18 N	8.30 E
Bosanska Dubica	78	45.09 N	16.49 E
Bosanska Gradiška	78	45.09 N	17.15 E
Bosanski Novi	78	45.03 N	16.23 E
Bosanski Šamac	80	45.03 N	18.28 E
Bosaso	108	11.13 N	49.08 E
Bosavi, Mount ⋏	124	6.35 S	142.50 E
Bosbokstrand	116	30.00 S	17.00 E
Bosham	70	50.49 N	0.52 W
Bositenghu ⊜	88	42.00 N	87.00 E
Bosna ≃	80	45.04 N	18.29 E
Bosna i Hercegovina (Bosnia-Hercegovina) □3	80	44.15 N	17.50 E
Bosnik	124	1.10 S	136.14 E
Bosporus → İstanbul Boğazı ⋃	80	41.00 N	29.00 E
Bossangoa	108	6.29 N	17.27 E
Bossembélé	108	5.16 N	17.39 E
Bossier City	158	32.31 N	93.43 W
Bosso, Dallol V	114	12.25 S	2.50 E
Bossut, Cape ⊁	122	18.43 S	121.38 E
Boston, Eng., U.K.	70	52.59 N	0.01 W
Boston, Mass., U.S.	152	42.21 N	71.04 W
Boston Mountains ⋏	158	35.50 N	93.20 W
Boswell, Ind., U.S.	158	40.31 N	87.23 W
Boswell, Okla., U.S.	158	34.02 N	95.52 W
Boswell, Pa., U.S.	152	40.10 N	79.02 W
Botany Bay C	120	34.00 S	151.12 E
Boteti ≃	116	20.08 S	23.23 E
Bothnia, Gulf of C	68	63.00 N	20.00 E
Boticas	76	41.41 N	7.40 W
Botkins	152	40.28 N	84.11 W
Botna ≃	80	46.49 N	29.29 E
Botoşani	80	47.45 N	26.40 E
Botoşani □4	80	47.45 N	26.45 E
Botswana □1	110	22.00 S	24.00 E
Bottenhavet (Selkämeri) C	68	62.00 N	20.00 E
Bottenviken (Perämeri) C	68	65.00 N	23.00 E
Bottineau	162	48.50 N	100.27 W
Bottrop	72	51.31 N	6.55 E
Botucatu	140	22.52 S	48.26 W
Botwood	150	49.09 N	55.21 W
Bouaflé	114	6.59 N	5.45 W
Bouaké	114	7.41 N	5.02 W
Bouar	108	5.57 N	15.36 E
Bouarfa	106	32.32 N	1.42 W
Bouches-du-Rhône □5	76	43.30 N	5.00 E
Bougainville Reef ⊸2	124	15.30 S	147.06 E
Bougaroun, Cap ⊁	76	37.05 N	6.28 E
Bouillon	72	49.48 N	5.04 E
Boukol-Moselle □5	74	49.11 N	6.30 E
Boulder, Colo., U.S.	164	40.01 N	105.17 W
Boulder, Mont., U.S.	166	46.14 N	112.07 W
Boulder City	168	35.58 N	114.50 W
Boulia	120	22.54 S	139.54 E
Boulogne-Billancourt	74	48.50 N	2.15 E
Boulogne-sur-Gesse	74	43.18 N	0.39 E
Boulogne-sur-Mer	74	50.43 N	1.37 E
Bouloire	74	47.58 N	0.33 E
Bouna	114	9.16 N	3.00 W
Boundary Peak ⋏	168	37.51 N	118.21 W
Boundary Ranges ⋏	146	58.00 N	132.00 W
Bountiful	166	40.53 N	111.53 W
Bourbon-Lancy	74	46.38 N	3.46 E
Bourbonnais □9	74	46.30 N	3.30 E
Bourbonne-les-Bains	74	47.57 N	5.45 E
Bourem	114	16.58 N	0.22 W
Bourganeuf	74	45.57 N	1.46 E
Bourg-en-Bresse	74	46.12 N	5.13 E
Bourges	74	47.05 N	2.24 E
Bourget	152	45.26 N	75.09 W
Bourgneuf-en-Retz	74	47.02 N	1.57 W
Bourgoin	74	45.35 N	5.17 E
Bourg-Saint-Andéol	74	44.22 N	4.39 E
Bourg-Saint-Maurice	74	45.37 N	6.46 E
Bourgueil	74	47.17 N	0.10 E
Bourke	120	30.05 S	145.56 E
Bourne	70	52.46 N	0.23 W
Bournemouth	70	50.43 N	1.54 W
Bou-Saâda	106	35.13 N	4.11 E
Bouse	164	33.56 N	114.00 W
Boussac	74	46.21 N	2.13 E
Bousso	108	10.29 N	16.43 E
Boussu	72	50.26 N	3.48 E
Boutilimit	114	17.33 N	14.42 W
Bøvågen	68	60.40 N	4.58 E
Bøverdal	68	61.43 N	8.21 E
Bovey	154	47.17 N	93.25 W
Bovill	166	46.51 N	116.24 W
Bovina	160	34.31 N	102.53 W
Bow ≃	148	49.56 N	111.42 W
Bowdon	156	33.32 N	85.15 W
Bowen	120	20.01 S	148.15 E
Bowie, Ariz., U.S.	164	32.19 N	109.29 W
Bowie, Md., U.S.	152	39.00 N	76.47 W
Bowie, Tex., U.S.	160	33.34 N	97.51 W
Bowling Green, Ky., U.S.	156	27.38 N	81.50 W
Bowling Green, Mo., U.S.	158	37.00 N	86.27 W
Bowling Green, Ohio, U.S.	158	39.20 N	91.12 W
Bowling Green, Va., U.S.	156	38.03 N	77.21 W
Bowling Green, Cape ⊁	120	19.19 S	145.25 E
Bowman	162	46.11 N	103.24 W
Bowman Bay C	142	65.30 N	73.40 W
Bowman-Haley Reservoir ⊜1	162	46.00 N	103.20 W
Bowral	120	34.28 S	150.25 E
Bowron ≃	148	54.03 N	121.50 W
Bowutu Mountains ⋏	124	7.47 S	147.15 E
Box Elder	162	44.18 N	110.01 W
Box Elder Creek ≃	162	45.59 N	103.57 W
Boxian	88	33.53 N	115.45 E
Boxtel	72	51.35 N	5.20 E
Boyacá □5	138	5.30 N	73.30 W
Boyce	158	31.23 N	92.40 W
Boyd	160	33.05 N	97.34 W
Boyertown	152	40.20 N	75.38 W
Boyle, Eire	70	53.58 N	8.18 W
Boyle, Miss., U.S.	158	33.42 N	90.44 W
Boylston	158	32.26 N	86.17 W
Boyne ≃	120	23.56 S	151.21 E
Boyne City	154	45.13 N	85.01 W
Boynton	160	35.39 N	95.39 W
Boynton Beach	156	26.32 N	80.03 W
Boysen Reservoir ⊜1	166	43.19 N	108.11 W
Boyup Brook	122	33.50 S	116.24 E
Bozeman	166	45.40 N	111.02 W
Bozen → Bolzano	78	46.31 N	11.22 E
Bozhen	88	38.07 N	116.32 E
Bozoum	108	6.19 N	16.23 E
Bra	78	44.42 N	7.51 E
Bracciano	78	42.06 N	12.10 E
Bracebridge	154	45.02 N	79.19 W
Brach	106	27.32 N	14.16 E
Bracieux	74	47.33 N	1.33 E
Brackettville	160	29.19 N	100.24 W
Brackley	70	52.02 N	1.09 W
Bradano ≃	78	40.23 N	16.51 E
Bradenton	156	27.29 N	82.34 W
Bradford, Ont., Can.	154	44.07 N	79.34 W
Bradford, Eng., U.K.	70	53.48 N	1.45 W
Bradford, Ark., U.S.	158	35.25 N	91.27 W
Bradford, Ohio, U.S.	152	40.07 N	84.26 W
Bradford, Tenn., U.S.	158	36.05 N	88.51 W
Bradford, Vt., U.S.	152	43.59 N	72.09 W
Bradley, Ark., U.S.	158	33.06 N	93.39 W
Bradley, Fla., U.S.	156	27.48 N	81.59 W
Bradley, Ill., U.S.	154	41.09 N	87.52 W
Bradwell ≃	70	51.44 N	0.54 E
Braedstrup	68	55.58 N	9.37 E
Braeside	152	45.28 N	76.24 W
Braga	76	41.33 N	8.26 W
Bragado	140	35.10 S	60.30 W
Bragança, Bra.	134	1.03 S	46.46 W
Bragança, Port.	76	41.49 N	6.45 W
Bragança Paulista	140	22.57 S	46.34 W
Brahmanbaria	102	23.59 N	91.07 E
Brahmani ≃	102	20.39 N	86.46 E
Brahmaputra (Yaluzangbujiang) ≃	102	24.02 N	90.59 E
Braich y Pwll ⊁	70	52.48 N	4.36 W
Braidwood, Austl.	120	35.27 S	149.48 E
Braidwood, Ill., U.S.	154	41.15 N	88.12 W
Brăila	80	45.16 N	27.58 E
Brăila □4	80	45.15 N	27.40 E
Braine-l'Alleud	72	50.41 N	4.22 E
Braine-le-Comte	72	50.37 N	4.08 E
Brainerd	154	46.21 N	94.12 W
Braintree	70	51.53 N	0.32 E
Brakpan	116	26.13 S	28.20 E
Brålanda	68	58.33 N	12.22 E
Braman	160	36.55 N	97.20 W
Bramsche	72	52.25 N	7.58 E
Branchville	156	33.15 N	80.49 W
Branco ≃	138	1.24 S	61.51 W
Brandberg ⋏	116	21.10 S	14.33 E
Brandbu	68	60.26 N	10.30 E
Brandenburg □9	72	52.15 N	12.30 E
Brand-Erbisdorf	72	50.52 N	13.20 E
Brandon, Man., Can.	162	49.50 N	99.57 W
Brandon, Miss., U.S.	158	32.16 N	89.59 W
Brandon, Vt., U.S.	152	43.47 N	73.05 W
Brandvlei	116	30.25 S	20.30 E
Brandýs nad Labem	72	50.10 N	14.40 E
Braniewo	72	54.24 N	19.50 E
Bransby	120	28.14 S	142.04 E
Brańsk, Pol.	72	52.45 N	22.50 E
Br'ansk, S.S.S.R.	86	53.15 N	34.22 E
Branson	158	36.38 N	93.13 W
Brantford	154	43.08 N	80.16 W
Brantley	158	31.35 N	86.15 W
Brantôme	74	45.22 N	0.39 E
Branxholme	120	37.51 S	141.47 E
Bras d'Or Lake C	150	45.52 N	60.50 W
Brasiléia	134	11.00 S	68.44 W
Brasília	134	15.47 S	47.55 W
Braşov	80	45.39 N	25.37 E
Braşov □4	80	45.50 N	25.15 E
Bratislava	72	48.09 N	17.07 E
Bratsk	84	56.05 N	101.48 E
Bratskoje Vodochranilišče ⊜1	84	56.10 N	102.10 E
Brattleboro	152	42.51 N	72.34 W
Brattvåg	68	62.36 N	6.27 E
Braunau [am Inn]	72	48.15 N	13.02 E
Braunlage	72	51.44 N	10.37 E
Braunschweig	72	52.16 N	10.31 E
Brava I	114a	14.52 N	24.43 W
Bråviken C	68	58.38 N	16.32 E
Bravo del Norte (Rio Grande) ≃	160	25.57 N	97.09 W
Brawley	168	32.59 N	115.31 W
Bray, Bel.	72	50.18 N	4.24 E
Bray, Eire	70	53.12 N	6.06 W
Bray Island I	142	69.20 N	77.00 W
Brazeau ≃	148	52.55 N	115.14 W
Brazil	154	39.31 N	87.07 W
Brazil □1	134	10.00 S	55.00 W
Brazos ≃	160	28.53 N	95.23 W
Brazzaville	110	4.16 S	15.17 E
Brčko	80	44.52 N	18.49 E
Breadalbane	120	23.49 S	139.35 E
Breaux Bridge	158	30.16 N	91.54 W
Brécey	74	48.44 N	1.10 W
Brechin	70	56.44 N	2.40 W
Breckenridge, Colo., U.S.	164	39.29 N	106.03 W
Breckenridge, Mich., U.S.	154	43.24 N	84.29 W
Breckenridge, Minn., U.S.	162	46.16 N	96.35 W
Breckenridge, Tex., U.S.	160	32.45 N	98.54 W
Břeclav	72	48.46 N	16.53 E
Brecon	70	51.57 N	3.24 W
Brecon Beacons National Park ♦	70	51.52 N	3.25 W
Breda	72	51.35 N	4.46 E
Bredasdorp	116	34.32 S	20.02 E
Bredstedt	72	54.37 N	8.59 E
Brée ≃	116	34.38 S	20.50 E
Breese	158	38.36 N	89.32 W
Breeza	120	14.50 S	144.07 E
Bregenz	72	47.30 N	9.46 E
Breguzzo	78	46.00 N	10.42 E
Bréhal	74	48.54 N	1.31 W
Breiðafjörður C	66a	65.15 N	23.15 W
Breil-sur-Roya	74	43.56 N	7.30 E
Breisach	72	48.01 N	7.40 E
Brejo	134	3.41 S	42.47 W
Brekken	68	62.39 N	11.53 E
Brekstad	68	63.41 N	9.41 E
Bremen, B.R.D.	72	53.04 N	8.49 E
Bremen, Ga., U.S.	156	33.43 N	85.09 W
Bremen, Ind., U.S.	158	41.27 N	86.09 W
Bremerhaven	72	53.33 N	8.34 E
Bremerton	166	47.34 N	122.38 W
Bremervörde	72	53.29 N	9.08 E
Bremond	160	31.10 N	96.41 W
Brenne ⬤1	74	46.45 N	1.10 E
Brenner Pass)(	72	47.00 N	11.30 E
Brent, Ala., U.S.	158	32.56 N	87.10 W
Brent, Fla., U.S.	158	30.27 N	87.15 W
Brentwood, Eng., U.K.	70	51.38 N	0.18 E
Brentwood, N.Y., U.S.	152	40.47 N	73.14 W
Brescia	78	45.33 N	10.15 E
Breslau → Wrocław	72	51.06 N	17.00 E
Bresnahan, Mount ⋏	122	23.50 S	117.55 E
Bressanone	78	46.43 N	11.39 E
Bresse ⬤1	74	46.30 N	5.15 E
Bressuire	74	46.51 N	0.30 W
Brest, Fr.	74	48.24 N	4.29 W
Brest, S.S.S.R.	72	52.06 N	23.42 E
Bretagne □9	74	48.00 N	3.00 W
Bretenoux	74	44.55 N	1.50 E
Breteuil	74	49.39 N	1.28 E
Breteuil-sur-Iton	74	48.50 N	0.55 E
Bretten	72	49.02 N	8.42 E
Breueh, Pulau I	94	5.41 N	95.05 E
Brevard	156	35.09 N	82.44 W
Breves	134	1.40 S	50.29 W
Brevik	68	59.04 N	9.42 E
Brevoort Island I	142	63.30 N	64.10 W
Brewarrina	120	29.57 S	146.52 E
Brewer	152	44.48 N	68.46 W
Brewster, Kans., U.S.	162	39.22 N	101.23 W
Brewster, Ohio, U.S.	152	40.43 N	81.36 W
Brewster, Wash., U.S.	166	48.06 N	119.47 W
Brewster, Lake ⊜	120	33.28 S	146.00 E
Brewton	158	31.06 N	87.04 W
Brežice	78	45.54 N	15.36 E
Brezno	72	48.50 N	19.38 E
Bria	108	6.32 N	21.59 E
Briançon	74	44.54 N	6.39 E
Briare	74	47.38 N	2.44 E
Brickaville	117b	18.49 S	49.04 E
Bricquebec	74	49.28 N	1.38 W
Bridge City	158	30.01 N	93.51 W
Bridgend	70	51.31 N	3.35 W
Bridgeport, Ala., U.S.	158	34.57 N	85.43 W
Bridgeport, Conn., U.S.	152	41.11 N	73.11 W
Bridgeport, Mich., U.S.	154	43.21 N	83.53 W
Bridgeport, Nebr., U.S.	162	41.40 N	103.06 W
Bridgeport, Tex., U.S.	160	33.13 N	97.45 W
Bridgeport, W. Va., U.S.	152	39.17 N	80.15 W
Bridger	166	45.18 N	108.55 W
Bridgeton, Mo., U.S.	158	39.26 N	75.14 W
Bridgeton, N.J., U.S.	152	39.25 N	75.14 W
Bridgetown, Austl.	122	33.57 S	116.08 E
Bridgetown, Barb.	132	13.06 N	59.37 W
Bridgeville	152	38.45 N	75.36 W
Bridgewater, N.S., Can.	150	44.23 N	64.31 W
Bridgewater, Mass., U.S.	152	41.59 N	70.58 W
Bridgewater, Va., U.S.	152	38.23 N	78.58 W
Bridgnorth	70	52.33 N	2.25 W
Bridgton	152	44.03 N	70.42 W
Bridgwater	70	51.08 N	3.00 W
Bridlington	70	54.05 N	0.12 W
Bridport	70	50.44 N	2.46 W
Brie □9	74	48.40 N	3.10 E
Brie-Comte-Robert	74	48.42 N	2.37 E
Brienne-le-Château	74	48.24 N	4.32 E
Brienz	74	46.45 N	8.02 E
Brienzer See ⊜	74	46.43 N	7.58 E
Briey	74	49.15 N	5.56 E
Brig	74	46.19 N	7.59 E
Brigham City	166	41.31 N	112.01 W
Brighouse	70	53.42 N	1.47 W
Brighton, Ont., Can.	154	44.02 N	77.44 W
Brighton, Eng., U.K.	70	50.50 N	0.08 W
Brighton, Colo., U.S.	164	39.59 N	104.49 W
Brighton, Iowa, U.S.	154	41.10 N	91.49 W
Brighton, Mich., U.S.	154	42.32 N	83.47 W
Brighton Downs	120	23.22 S	141.34 E
Brignoles	74	43.24 N	6.04 E
Brilon	72	51.24 N	8.34 E
Brindisi	78	40.38 N	17.56 E
Brinkley	158	34.53 N	91.12 W
Brionne	74	49.12 N	0.43 E
Brioude	74	45.18 N	3.23 E
Brisbane	120	27.28 S	153.02 E
Bristol, Eng., U.K.	70	51.27 N	2.35 W
Bristol, Conn., U.S.	152	41.40 N	72.57 W
Bristol, N.H., U.S.	152	43.36 N	71.45 W
Bristol, Pa., U.S.	152	40.06 N	74.51 W
Bristol, R.I., U.S.	152	41.41 N	71.16 W
Bristol, Tenn., U.S.	156	36.36 N	82.11 W
Bristol, Vt., U.S.	152	44.08 N	73.05 W
Bristol Channel ⋃	70	51.20 N	4.00 W
Bristow	160	35.50 N	96.23 W
British Columbia □4	146	54.00 N	125.00 W
British Honduras → Belize □2	128	17.15 N	88.45 W
British Indian Ocean Territory □2	110	7.00 S	72.00 E
British Mountains ⋏	146	69.00 N	140.20 W
British Solomon Islands → Solomon Islands □1	118	8.00 S	159.00 E
Britstown	116	30.37 S	23.30 E
Britt	154	43.05 N	93.48 W
Britton	162	45.47 N	97.45 W
Brive-la-Gaillarde	74	45.10 N	1.32 E
Briviesca	76	42.33 N	3.19 W
Brno	72	49.12 N	16.37 E
Broad ≃	156	34.01 N	81.04 W
Broad Arrow	122	30.27 S	121.17 E
Broadback ≃	142	51.21 N	78.52 W
Broadford	70	57.14 N	5.54 W
Broad Sound ⋃	120	22.10 S	149.45 E
Broad Sound Channel ⋃	120	22.05 S	150.22 E
Broadway	156	38.37 N	78.48 W
Brochet	142	57.53 N	101.40 W
Brocken, Mount ⋏	122	26.02 S	118.16 E
Brockport	152	43.13 N	77.56 W
Brocks Creek	124	13.28 S	131.25 E
Brockville	152	44.35 N	75.41 W

Name	Page	Lat °′	Long °′
Brockway	152	41.15 N	78.47 W
Brocton	152	42.23 N	79.27 W
Brodeur Peninsula ≻[1]	142	73.00 N	88.00 W
Brodhead	154	42.37 N	89.22 W
Brodick	70	55.35 N	5.09 W
Brodnax	156	36.42 N	78.02 W
Brodnica	72	53.16 N	19.23 E
Brogan	166	44.15 N	117.31 W
Broglie	74	49.01 N	0.32 E
Broken Arrow	160	36.03 N	95.48 W
Broken Bay C	120	33.34 S	151.18 E
Broken Bow, Nebr., U.S.	162	41.24 N	99.38 W
Broken Bow, Okla., U.S.	158	34.02 N	94.44 W
Broken Hill, Austl.	120	31.57 S	141.27 E
Broken Hill → Kabwe, Zam.	110	14.27 S	28.27 E
Brokopondo	134	5.03 N	54.59 W
Bromptonville	152	45.28 N	71.57 W
Bromsgrove	70	52.20 N	2.03 W
Bronlund Peak ∧	142	57.26 N	126.38 W
Bronnicy	86	55.25 N	38.16 E
Bronson, Fla., U.S.	156	29.27 N	82.38 W
Bronson, Kans., U.S.	162	37.54 N	95.04 W
Bronson, Mich., U.S.	154	41.52 N	85.12 W
Bronte, It.	78	37.48 N	14.50 E
Bronte, Tex., U.S.	160	31.53 N	100.18 W
Brook	158	40.52 N	87.22 W
Brookeland	158	31.09 N	94.00 W
Brookfield, Mo., U.S.	158	39.47 N	93.04 W
Brookfield, Wis., U.S.	154	43.04 N	88.09 W
Brookhaven	158	31.35 N	90.26 W
Brookings, Oreg., U.S.	166	42.03 N	124.17 W
Brookings, S. Dak., U.S.	162	44.19 N	96.48 W
Brooklyn	154	41.44 N	92.27 W
Brooklyn Center	154	45.05 N	93.20 W
Brookneal	156	37.03 N	78.57 W
Brooks	148	50.35 N	111.53 W
Brooks, Mount ∧	146	63.11 N	150.40 W
Brookshire	160	29.47 N	95.57 W
Brooks Mountain ∧	146	65.33 N	167.09 W
Brooks Range ⩘	146	68.00 N	154.00 W
Brookston	158	40.36 N	86.52 W
Brooksville, Fla., U.S.	156	28.33 N	82.23 W
Brooksville, Miss., U.S.	158	33.14 N	88.35 W
Brookton	122	32.22 S	117.01 E
Brookville, Ind., U.S.	158	39.25 N	85.01 W
Brookville, Pa., U.S.	152	41.09 N	79.05 W
Broome	122	17.58 S	122.14 E
Broomfield	164	39.56 N	105.04 W
Broons	74	48.19 N	2.16 W
Brora	70	58.01 N	3.51 W
Brossac	74	45.20 N	0.03 W
Brou	74	48.13 N	1.11 E
Broughton Island I	142	67.35 N	63.50 W
Broughty Ferry	70	56.28 N	2.53 W
Broussard	158	30.09 N	91.58 W
Brovst	68	57.06 N	9.32 E
Brown City	154	43.13 N	82.59 W
Brown Deer	154	43.10 N	87.59 W
Browne Bay C	142	73.08 N	97.30 W
Brownfield	160	33.11 N	102.16 W
Browning	166	48.34 N	113.01 W
Brown Lake ⊜	142	65.55 N	91.15 W
Brownlee	166	44.50 N	116.55 W
Brownlee Reservoir ⊜[1]	166	44.40 N	117.05 W
Brownsburg, Qué., Can.	152	45.41 N	74.25 W
Brownsburg, Ind., U.S.	158	39.51 N	86.24 W
Brownstown	158	38.53 N	86.03 W
Browns Valley	162	45.36 N	96.50 W
Brownsville, La., U.S.	158	32.30 N	92.10 W
Brownsville, Oreg., U.S.	166	44.24 N	122.59 W
Brownsville, Pa., U.S.	152	40.01 N	79.53 W
Brownsville, Tenn., U.S.	158	35.36 N	89.15 W
Brownsville, Tex., U.S.	160	25.54 N	97.30 W
Brownville	158	33.24 N	87.52 W
Brownville Junction	152	45.21 N	69.03 W
Brownwood	160	31.43 N	98.59 W
Browse Island I	118	14.07 S	123.33 E
Bruay-en-Artois	74	50.29 N	2.33 E
Bruce, Miss., U.S.	158	33.59 N	89.21 W
Bruce, S. Dak., U.S.	162	44.26 N	96.54 W
Bruce, Mount ∧	122	22.36 S	118.08 E
Bruce Rock	122	31.53 S	118.09 E
Bruchsal	72	49.07 N	8.35 E
Bruck [an der Grossglocknerstrasse]	72	47.17 N	12.49 E
Bruck an der Leitha	72	47.57 N	16.44 E
Bruck an der Mur	72	47.25 N	15.16 E
Brückenau	72	50.18 N	9.47 E
Bruges → Brugge	72	51.13 N	3.14 E
Brugg	74	47.29 N	8.12 E
Brugge	72	51.13 N	3.14 E
Brühl	72	50.48 N	6.54 E
Brule ≃	154	45.57 N	88.12 W
Brûlé, Lac ⊜	142	52.17 N	63.52 W
Brumath	74	48.44 N	7.43 E
Brumby Creek ≃	122	24.09 S	118.39 E
Brummen	72	52.05 N	6.09 E
Brumunddal	68	60.53 N	10.56 E
Brundidge	158	31.43 N	85.49 W
Bruneau	166	42.53 N	115.48 W
Bruneau ≃	166	42.57 N	115.58 W
Brunei → Bandar Seri Begawan	96	4.56 N	114.55 E
Brunei □[1]	92	4.30 N	114.40 E
Brunei Bay C	96	5.05 N	115.18 E
Brunette Creek ≃	122	18.47 S	135.41 E
Brunette Downs	122	18.38 S	135.57 E
Brunkeberg	68	59.26 N	8.29 E
Brunn am Gebirge	72	48.07 N	16.17 E
Brunner	126	42.26 S	171.19 E
Brunsbüttel	72	53.54 N	9.08 E
Brunson	156	32.56 N	81.11 W
Brunswick → Braunschweig, B.R.D.	72	52.16 N	10.31 E
Brunswick, Ga., U.S.	156	31.10 N	81.29 W
Brunswick, Maine, U.S.	152	43.55 N	69.58 W
Brunswick, Md., U.S.	152	39.19 N	77.37 W
Brunswick, Mo., U.S.	158	39.26 N	93.08 W
Brunswick, Ohio, U.S.	152	41.14 N	81.50 W
Brunswick, Península de ≻[1]	136	53.25 S	71.25 W
Brunswick Junction	122	33.15 S	115.51 E
Bruntál	72	49.59 N	17.28 E
Brush	162	40.15 N	103.37 W
Brusque	140	27.06 S	48.56 W
Brussels → Bruxelles	74	50.50 N	4.20 E
Bruthen	120	37.43 S	147.48 E
Bruxelles (Brussel)	72	50.50 N	4.20 E
Bruyères	74	48.12 N	6.43 E
Bryan, Ohio, U.S.	154	41.28 N	84.33 W
Bryan, Tex., U.S.	160	30.40 N	96.22 W
Bryansk → Br'ansk	86	53.15 N	34.22 E
Bryant	162	44.35 N	97.28 W
Bryne	68	58.44 N	5.39 E
Bryson	160	33.10 N	98.23 W
Brzeg	72	50.52 N	17.27 E
Brzesko	72	49.59 N	20.36 E
Brzeziny	72	51.48 N	19.46 E
Bua Yai	92	15.34 N	102.24 E
Buayan	92	6.06 N	125.15 E
Bubaque	114	11.17 N	15.50 W
Būbiyān I	104	29.47 N	48.10 E
Bublitz → Bobolice	72	53.57 N	16.36 E
Bubus, Bukit ∧	94	6.12 N	101.06 E
Bucaramanga	138	7.08 N	73.09 W
Buccaneer Archipelago II	118	16.17 S	123.20 E
Buccino	78	40.37 N	15.23 E
Buchanan, Liber.	114	5.57 N	10.02 W
Buchanan, Mich., U.S.	154	41.50 N	86.22 W
Buchanan, Va., U.S.	156	37.32 N	79.41 W
Buchanan, Lake ⊜, Austl.	120	21.28 S	145.52 E
Buchanan, Lake ⊜, Austl.	122	25.33 S	123.02 E
Buchan Gulf C	142	71.47 N	74.16 W
Buchans	150	48.49 N	56.52 W
Buchara	104	39.48 N	64.25 E
Bucharest → București	80	44.26 N	26.06 E
Buchen	72	49.32 N	9.17 E
Buchholz	72	53.20 N	9.52 E
Buchloe	72	48.02 N	10.44 E
Buchs	74	47.10 N	9.28 E
Buchy	74	49.35 N	1.22 E
Bückeburg	72	52.16 N	9.02 E
Buckeye	164	33.22 N	112.35 W
Buckeye Lake	152	39.56 N	82.29 W
Buckeye Lake ⊜[1]	152	39.55 N	82.30 W
Buckhannon	152	38.59 N	80.14 W
Buckhaven	70	56.11 N	3.03 W
Buckholts	160	30.52 N	97.08 W
Buckie	70	57.40 N	2.58 W
Buckingham	152	45.35 N	75.25 W
Buckingham Bay C	124	12.10 S	135.46 E
Buckinghamshire □[6]	70	51.45 N	0.48 W
Buckland	146	66.16 N	161.20 W
Buckley	166	47.10 N	122.02 W
Buckley ≃	120	20.22 S	137.57 E
Buckow	72	52.34 N	14.04 E
Bucksport	152	44.34 N	68.48 W
Buctouche	150	46.28 N	64.43 W
București	80	44.26 N	26.06 E
Bucyrus	152	40.48 N	82.58 W
Bud	68	62.55 N	6.55 E
Budapest	72	47.30 N	19.05 E
Budaun	102	28.03 N	79.07 E
Buddh Gaya	100	24.42 N	84.59 E
Bude, Eng., U.K.	70	50.50 N	4.33 W
Bude, Miss., U.S.	158	31.28 N	90.51 W
Büdingen	72	50.17 N	9.07 E
Búđir	66a	64.56 N	13.58 W
Budogošč'	86	59.17 N	32.27 E
Buea	106	4.09 N	9.14 E
Buena Esperanza	140	34.46 S	65.16 W
Buenaventura, Méx.	130	29.51 N	107.29 W
Buena Vista, Bol.	134	17.27 S	63.40 W
Buena Vista, Colo., U.S.	164	38.50 N	106.08 W
Buena Vista, Ga., U.S.	156	32.19 N	84.31 W
Buena Vista, Va., U.S.	156	37.44 N	79.21 W
Buendia, Embalse de ⊜[1]	76	40.25 N	2.43 W
Buenos Aires	140	34.36 S	58.27 W
Buenos Aires □[4]	140	36.00 S	60.00 W
Buerjin	88	47.43 N	86.53 E
Buffalo, Kans., U.S.	162	37.42 N	95.42 W
Buffalo, Minn., U.S.	154	45.10 N	93.53 W
Buffalo, Mo., U.S.	158	37.39 N	93.06 W
Buffalo, N.Y., U.S.	152	42.54 N	78.53 W
Buffalo, Ohio, U.S.	152	39.55 N	81.31 W
Buffalo, S.C., U.S.	156	34.43 N	81.41 W
Buffalo, S. Dak., U.S.	162	45.35 N	103.33 W
Buffalo, Tex., U.S.	160	31.28 N	96.04 W
Buffalo, Wyo., U.S.	166	44.21 N	106.42 W
Buffalo ≃	142	60.55 N	115.00 W
Buffalo, Mount ∧	120	36.47 S	146.47 E
Buffalo Center	154	43.23 N	93.57 W
Buffalo Creek ≃	162	45.57 N	102.56 W
Buffalo Lake ⊜	142	60.10 N	115.30 W
Buford	156	34.07 N	84.00 W
Bug ≃	64	52.31 N	21.05 E
Buga	138	3.54 N	76.17 W
Buganga	110	0.03 S	31.59 E
Bugeat	74	45.35 N	1.59 E
Buggs Island Lake ⊜[1]	156	36.35 N	78.28 W
Bugojno	78	44.03 N	17.27 E
Bugsuk Island I	98	8.15 N	117.18 E
Bugul'ma	66	54.33 N	52.48 E
Buguruslan	64	53.39 N	52.26 E
Buhl, Idaho, U.S.	166	42.36 N	114.46 W
Buhl, Minn., U.S.	154	47.30 N	92.47 W
Buhler	162	38.08 N	97.46 W
Buhuși	80	46.43 N	26.41 E
Builth Wells	70	52.09 N	3.24 W
Buinsk	66	55.12 N	47.03 E
Buir Nuur ⊜	88	47.48 N	117.42 E
Buj	86	58.30 N	41.30 E
Bujalance	76	37.54 N	4.22 W
Bujnaksk	82	42.49 N	47.07 E
Bujumbura	110	3.23 S	29.22 E
Bukačača	84	52.59 N	116.55 E
Bukama	110	9.12 S	25.51 E
Bukavu	110	2.30 S	28.52 E
Bukittinggi	96	0.19 S	100.22 E
Bukoba	110	1.20 S	31.49 E
Bukovina □[9]	80	48.00 N	25.30 E
Bula	124	3.06 S	130.30 E
Bülach	74	47.31 N	8.32 E
Bulan	92	12.40 N	123.52 E
Bulandshahr	102	28.24 N	77.51 E
Bulawayo	116	20.09 S	28.36 E
Buleleng	92	8.06 S	115.05 E
Bulgan, Mong.	88	48.52 N	103.34 E
Bulgan, Mong.	88	46.53 N	91.05 E
Bulgaria □[1]	64	43.00 N	25.00 E
Bulkley ≃	148	55.13 N	127.40 W
Bullabulling	122	31.01 S	120.32 E
Bullas	76	38.03 N	1.40 W
Bulle	74	46.37 N	7.04 E
Buller, Mount ∧	120	37.09 S	146.26 E
Bullfinch	122	30.59 S	119.06 E
Bullock Creek	120	17.43 S	144.31 E
Bulloo ≃	120	28.43 S	142.30 E
Bull Shoals Lake ⊜[1]	158	36.30 N	92.50 W
Bulukumba	92	5.33 S	120.11 E
Buluntuohai ⊜	88	47.15 N	87.20 E
Bulyee	122	32.22 S	117.31 E
Bumba	110	2.11 N	22.28 E
Bumpus, Mount ∧[2]	142	69.33 N	112.40 W
Bunbury	122	33.19 S	115.38 E
Buncrana	70	55.08 N	7.27 W
Bundaberg	120	24.52 S	152.21 E
Bundarra ≃	120	29.54 S	150.59 E
Bünde	72	52.12 N	8.35 E
Bundey ≃	122	21.46 S	135.37 E
Būndi	102	25.27 N	75.39 E
Bundooma	122	24.54 S	134.16 E
Bundoran	70	54.28 N	8.17 W
Bungay	70	52.28 N	1.26 E
Bungo-suidō ⩌	90	33.00 N	132.13 E
Bunia	110	1.34 N	30.15 E
Bunker Group II	120	23.48 S	152.20 E
Bunker Hill	166	43.21 N	124.12 W
Bunkie	158	30.57 N	92.11 W
Bunnell	156	29.28 N	81.15 W
Buntine	122	29.59 S	116.34 E
Buntok	92	1.42 S	114.48 E
Buolkalach	84	72.56 N	119.50 E
Buor-Chaja, Guba C	84	71.30 N	131.00 E
Buor-Chaja, Mys ≻	84	71.56 N	132.40 E
Buqayq	100	25.26 N	49.40 E
Bura	110	1.06 S	39.57 E
Burakin	122	30.31 S	117.10 E
Burao	108	9.30 N	45.30 E
Buras	158	29.21 N	89.32 W
Buraydah	104	26.20 N	43.59 E
Burbank	168	34.12 N	118.18 W
Burcher	120	33.32 S	147.18 E
Burdekin ≃	120	19.39 S	147.30 E
Burdekin Falls ↳	120	20.39 S	147.09 E
Burden	162	37.19 N	96.45 W
Burdur	108	37.43 N	30.17 E
Burdwān	102	23.15 N	87.51 E
Bureinskij Chrebet ⩘	84	50.35 N	133.35 E
Bureja ≃	84	49.25 N	129.35 E
Büren	72	51.33 N	8.33 E
Burford	154	43.06 N	80.26 W
Burg	72	50.42 N	8.19 E
Burgas	80	42.30 N	27.28 E
Burg [auf Fehmarn]	72	54.26 N	11.12 E
Burg [bei Magdeburg]	72	52.16 N	11.51 E
Burgdorf, B.R.D.	72	52.27 N	10.00 E
Burgdorf, Schw.	74	47.04 N	7.37 E
Burgenland □[3]	72	47.30 N	16.20 E
Burgeo	150	47.37 N	57.37 W
Burgersdorp	116	31.00 S	26.20 E
Burgettstown	152	40.23 N	80.23 W
Burghausen	72	48.09 N	12.49 E
Burghead	70	57.42 N	3.30 W
Burglengenfeld	72	49.13 N	12.03 E
Burgos	76	42.21 N	3.42 W
Burgos □[4]	76	42.20 N	3.40 W
Burgstädt	72	50.55 N	12.49 E
Burgsteinfurt	72	52.08 N	7.20 E
Burhānpur	102	21.18 N	76.14 E
Burias Island I	98	12.55 N	123.05 E
Burien	166	47.27 N	122.21 W
Burin	150	47.02 N	55.10 W
Burjasot	76	39.31 N	0.25 W
Burkburnett	160	34.06 N	98.34 W
Burke	162	43.11 N	99.18 W
Burke ≃	120	23.12 S	139.33 E
Burkesville	158	36.48 N	85.22 W
Burketown	120	17.44 S	139.22 E
Burleson	160	32.33 N	97.19 W
Burley	166	42.32 N	113.48 W
Burlingame, Calif., U.S.	168	37.35 N	122.22 W
Burlingame, Kans., U.S.	162	38.45 N	95.50 W
Burlington, Ont., Can.	154	43.19 N	79.47 W
Burlington, Colo., U.S.	162	39.18 N	102.16 W
Burlington, Iowa, U.S.	154	40.49 N	91.14 W
Burlington, Kans., U.S.	162	38.12 N	95.45 W
Burlington, N.J., U.S.	152	40.04 N	74.49 W
Burlington, N.C., U.S.	156	36.04 N	79.26 W
Burlington, Vt., U.S.	152	44.29 N	73.13 W
Burlington, Wash., U.S.	166	48.28 N	122.20 W
Burlington, Wis., U.S.	154	42.41 N	88.17 W
Burlington Junction	158	40.27 N	95.04 W
Burma □[1]	92	22.00 N	98.00 E
Burnaby	148	49.15 N	122.57 W
Burnet	160	30.46 N	98.14 W
Burnett ≃	120	24.46 S	152.25 E
Burnett Bay C	142	73.53 N	124.00 W
Burney	168	40.53 N	121.40 W
Burnham	152	40.38 N	77.34 W
Burnie	120	41.04 S	145.54 E
Burnley	70	53.48 N	2.14 W
Burns	166	43.35 N	119.03 W
Burns Flat	160	35.21 N	99.10 W
Burnside ≃	142	66.51 N	108.04 W
Burns Lake	148	54.14 N	125.46 W
Burnsville	156	35.55 N	82.18 W
Burntwood ≃	142	56.08 N	96.30 W
Burra	120	33.40 S	138.56 E
Burragorang, Lake ⊜	120	33.58 S	150.25 E
Burramurra	120	20.30 S	137.20 E
Burravoe	70	60.32 N	1.28 W
Burriana	76	39.53 N	0.05 W
Burrinjuck Reservoir ⊜[1]	120	35.00 S	148.45 E
Burrton	162	38.02 N	97.41 W
Burruyacú	140	26.30 S	64.45 W
Bursa	80	40.11 N	29.04 E
Būr Sa'īd (Port Said)	112	31.16 N	32.18 E
Būr Sūdān (Port Sudan)	112	19.37 N	37.14 E
Burton upon Trent	70	52.49 N	1.36 W
Burtundy	120	33.44 S	142.16 E
Buru I	96	3.24 S	126.40 E
Burundi □[1]	110	3.15 S	30.00 E
Burwell	162	41.47 N	99.08 W
Burwick	70	58.44 N	2.57 W
Bury	70	53.36 N	2.17 W
Bury Saint Edmunds	70	52.15 N	0.43 E
Busalla	78	44.34 N	8.57 E
Busca	78	44.31 N	7.29 E
Būshehr	104	28.59 N	50.50 E
Bushimaie ≃	110	6.02 S	23.45 E
Bushnell, Fla., U.S.	156	28.40 N	82.07 W
Bushnell, Ill., U.S.	154	40.33 N	90.30 W
Bushy Head Mountain ∧	158	36.02 N	94.35 W
Buskerud □[6]	68	60.25 N	9.12 E
Busko Zdrój	72	50.28 N	20.44 E
Busselton	122	33.39 S	115.20 E
Bussey	154	41.12 N	92.53 W
Bussum	72	52.16 N	5.10 E
Busto Arsizio	78	45.37 N	8.51 E
Busuanga Island I	98	12.05 N	120.05 E
Busu-Djanoa	110	1.43 N	21.23 E
Büsum	72	54.08 N	8.51 E
Buta	108	2.48 N	24.44 E
Butare	110	2.36 S	29.44 E
Butehaqi	88	48.02 N	122.43 E
Bute Inlet C	148	50.37 N	124.53 W
Butera	78	37.11 N	14.11 E
Butere	110	0.13 N	34.30 E
Butler, Ala., U.S.	158	32.05 N	88.13 W
Butler, Ga., U.S.	156	32.34 N	84.14 W
Butler, Ind., U.S.	158	41.26 N	84.52 W
Butler, Mo., U.S.	158	38.16 N	94.20 W
Butler, Ohio, U.S.	152	40.35 N	82.26 W
Butler, Pa., U.S.	152	40.52 N	79.54 W
Bütow → Bytów	72	54.11 N	17.30 E
Butru	120	21.30 S	139.43 E
Butte	166	46.00 N	112.32 W
Butte City	166	43.36 N	113.15 W
Butte Falls	166	42.33 N	122.34 W
Butterworth, Malay.	96	5.24 N	100.24 E
Butterworth, S. Afr.	116	32.23 S	28.04 E
Button Islands II	142	60.35 N	64.45 W
Buttonwillow	168	35.24 N	119.28 W
Butuan	92	8.57 N	125.33 E
Butung, Pulau I	96	5.00 S	122.55 E
Buturlino	66	55.34 N	44.55 E
Butzbach	72	50.26 N	8.40 E
Bützow	72	53.50 N	11.59 E
Buxtehude	72	53.28 N	9.41 E
Buxton, Eng., U.K.	70	53.15 N	1.55 W
Buxton, N. Dak., U.S.	162	47.36 N	97.06 W
Buxy	74	46.43 N	4.41 E
Büyük Ağrı Dağı (Mount Ararat) ∧	104	39.42 N	44.18 E
Buzançais	74	46.53 N	1.25 E
Buzancy	74	49.25 N	4.57 E
Buzău	80	45.09 N	26.49 E
Buzău □[4]	80	47.40 N	23.00 E
Búzi ≃	116	19.50 S	34.43 E
Buzuluk	64	52.47 N	52.15 E
Byam Channel ⩌	142	75.20 N	105.20 W
Byam Martin Channel ⩌	142	75.45 N	104.00 W
Byam Martin Island I	142	75.15 N	104.00 W
Bychov	86	53.32 N	30.12 E
Bydgoszcz	72	53.08 N	18.00 E
Byelorussian Soviet Socialist Republic → Belorusskaja Socialističeskaja Respublika □[3]	72	53.30 N	28.00 E
Byers	160	34.04 N	98.11 W
Byesville	152	39.58 N	81.32 W
Bygdin	68	61.20 N	8.48 E
Byglandsfjord	68	58.41 N	7.48 E
Bykle	68	59.21 N	7.20 E
Bylas	164	33.08 N	110.07 W
Bylot Island I	142	73.13 N	78.34 W
Byrdstown	158	36.34 N	85.08 W
Byron, Ga., U.S.	156	32.39 N	83.46 W
Byron, Wyo., U.S.	166	44.48 N	108.30 W
Byron, Cape ≻	120	28.39 S	153.38 E
Byron, Isla I	136	47.45 S	75.11 W
Byron Bay	120	28.39 S	153.37 E
Byrranga, Gory ⩘	84	75.00 N	104.00 E
Bystrzyca Kłodzka	72	50.18 N	16.38 E
Bytantaj ≃	84	68.46 N	134.20 E
Bytom (Beuthen)	72	50.22 N	18.54 E
Bytoš'	86	53.50 N	34.06 E
Bytów	72	54.11 N	17.30 E
Byxelkrok	68	57.20 N	17.00 E

C

Name	Page	Lat °′	Long °′
Ca ≃	94	18.46 N	105.47 E
Caacupé	140	25.23 S	57.09 W
Caaguazú □[5]	140	25.00 S	55.45 W
Caazapá	140	26.09 S	56.24 W
Caazapá □[5]	140	26.10 S	56.00 W
Cabaiguán	132	22.05 N	79.30 W
Cabanatuan	92	15.29 N	120.58 E
Cabano	150	47.41 N	68.53 W
Cabedelo	134	6.58 S	34.50 W
Cabeza del Buey	76	38.43 N	5.13 W
Cabimas	138	10.23 N	71.28 W
Cabinda	110	5.33 S	12.12 E
Cabinda □[5]	110	5.00 S	12.30 E
Cables	122	27.59 S	123.23 E
Cabo	134	8.17 S	35.02 W
Cabo Blanco	136	47.15 S	65.45 W
Cabonga, Réservoir ⊜[1]	154	47.20 N	76.35 W
Cabool	158	37.07 N	92.06 W
Caboolture	120	27.05 S	152.57 E
Caborca	130	30.37 N	112.06 W
Cabot	158	34.58 N	92.01 W
Cabot Strait ⩌	150	47.20 N	59.30 W
Cabourg	74	49.17 N	0.08 W
Cabra	76	37.28 N	4.27 W
Cabramurra	120	35.58 S	148.23 E
Cabrera I	76	39.09 N	2.56 E
Cabrobó	134	8.31 S	39.19 W
Caçador	140	26.47 S	51.00 W
Čačak	80	43.53 N	20.21 E
Caçapava	140	23.06 S	45.42 W
Caccamo	78	37.56 N	13.40 E
Cáceres, Bra.	134	16.04 S	57.41 W
Cáceres, Esp.	76	39.29 N	6.22 W
Cachimbo, Serra do ⩘	134	8.30 S	55.50 W
Cachoeira	134	12.36 S	38.58 W
Cachoeira do Sul	140	30.02 S	52.54 W
Cachoeiro de Itapemirim	134	20.51 S	41.06 W
Cacólo	110	10.07 S	19.17 E
Caconda	110	13.43 S	15.06 E
Caçumba, Ilha I	134	17.46 S	39.17 W
Čadan	84	51.17 N	91.35 E
Caddo	160	34.07 N	96.16 W
Caddo Lake ⊜[1]	158	32.42 N	94.01 W
Caddo Mills	160	33.04 N	96.14 W
Cadereyta Jiménez	130	25.36 N	100.00 W
Cader Idris ∧	70	52.42 N	3.54 W
Cadillac, Fr.	74	44.38 N	0.19 W
Cadillac, Mich., U.S.	154	44.15 N	85.24 W
Cádiz, Esp.	76	36.32 N	6.18 W
Cadiz, Ohio, U.S.	152	40.16 N	81.00 W
Cádiz, Golfo de C	76	36.50 N	7.10 W
Čadobec ≃	84	58.40 N	98.50 E
Caen	74	49.11 N	0.21 W
Caernarvon	70	53.08 N	4.16 W
Caernarvon Bay C	70	53.05 N	4.30 W
Caerphilly	70	51.35 N	3.14 W
Caeté	134	19.54 S	43.40 W
Caetité	134	14.04 S	42.29 W
Cafayate	140	26.06 S	65.57 W
Cagayan de Oro	92	8.29 N	124.39 E
Cagayan Islands II	98	9.40 N	121.25 E
Cagayan Sulu Island I	98	7.00 N	118.28 E
Čagda	84	58.45 N	130.37 E
Cagli	78	43.33 N	12.39 E
Cagliari	78	39.13 N	9.06 E
Cagnes	74	43.40 N	7.09 E
Čagoda	86	59.10 N	35.17 E
Cagoyan ≃	92	18.25 N	121.40 E
Caguas	132	18.14 N	66.02 W
Caher	70	52.21 N	7.56 W
Cahirciveen	70	51.57 N	10.13 W
Cahors	74	44.27 N	1.26 E
Caia ≃	76	38.50 N	7.05 W
Caiabis, Serra dos ⩘[1]	134	11.30 S	56.30 W
Caiapó, Serra ⩘	134	17.00 S	52.00 W
Caibarién	132	22.31 N	79.28 W
Caicara	138	7.37 N	66.10 W
Caicedonia	138	4.20 N	75.50 W
Caicó	134	6.27 S	37.06 W
Caicos Islands II	132	21.50 N	71.50 W
Caicos Passage ⩌	132	22.15 N	72.40 W
Caimanera	132	19.59 N	75.09 W
Cairns	120	16.55 S	145.46 E
Cairo → Al-Qāhirah, Miṣr	112	30.03 N	31.15 E
Cairo, Ga., U.S.	156	30.53 N	84.12 W
Cairo, Ill., U.S.	158	37.00 N	89.11 W
Cairo, W. Va., U.S.	152	39.13 N	81.09 W
Cairo Montenotte	78	44.24 N	8.16 E
Caiundo	110	15.46 S	17.28 E
Cajamarca	134	7.10 S	78.31 W
Cajarc	74	44.29 N	1.50 E
Cajàzeiras	134	6.54 S	38.34 W
Čajek	82	41.56 N	74.30 E
Čajkovskij	66	56.40 N	54.10 E
Čakovec	78	46.23 N	16.26 E
Calabar	114	4.57 N	8.19 E
Calabozo	138	8.56 N	67.26 W
Calabria □[4]	78	39.00 N	16.30 E
Calacuccia	78	42.20 N	9.03 E
Calafate	136	50.20 S	72.16 W
Calahorra	76	42.18 N	1.58 W
Calais, Fr.	74	50.57 N	1.50 E
Calais, Maine, U.S.	152	45.11 N	67.17 W
Calais, Pas de (Strait of Dover ⩌	70	51.00 N	1.30 E
Calama	140	22.28 S	68.56 W
Calamian Group II	98	12.00 N	120.10 E
Calapan	92	13.25 N	121.11 E
Călărași	80	44.11 N	27.20 E
Calarcá	138	4.31 N	75.38 W
Calatayud	76	41.21 N	1.38 W
Calau	72	51.45 N	13.56 E
Calayan Island I	98	19.20 N	121.25 E
Calbayog	92	12.04 N	124.36 E
Calbe	72	51.54 N	11.46 E
Calçoene	134	2.30 N	50.57 W
Calcutta	102	22.32 N	88.22 E
Caldaro	78	46.25 N	11.14 E
Caldas	138	6.05 N	75.38 W
Caldas □[5]	138	5.15 N	75.30 W
Caldas da Rainha	76	39.24 N	9.08 W
Caldera	140	27.04 S	70.50 W
Caldey Island I	70	51.38 N	4.41 W
Caldwell, Idaho, U.S.	166	43.40 N	116.41 W
Caldwell, Kans., U.S.	162	37.02 N	97.37 W
Caldwell, Ohio, U.S.	152	39.45 N	81.31 W
Caldwell, Tex., U.S.	160	30.32 N	96.42 W
Caledon ≃	116	30.31 S	26.05 E
Caledonia, Ont., Can.	154	43.04 N	79.56 W
Caledonia, Minn., U.S.	154	43.38 N	91.29 W
Caledonia, N.Y., U.S.	152	42.58 N	77.51 W
Caledonia, Ohio, U.S.	152	40.38 N	82.58 W
Calella	76	41.37 N	2.40 E
Calera	158	33.06 N	86.45 W
Calexico	168	32.40 N	115.30 W
Calf of Man I	70	54.03 N	4.48 W
Calgary	148	51.03 N	114.05 W
Calhan	162	39.02 N	104.18 W
Calhoun	156	34.30 N	84.57 W
Calhoun City	158	33.51 N	89.19 W
Calhoun Falls	156	34.06 N	82.36 W
Cali	138	3.27 N	76.31 W
Calico Rock	158	36.07 N	92.09 W
Calicut	100	11.15 N	75.46 E
Caliente	168	37.37 N	114.31 W
California, Mo., U.S.	158	38.38 N	92.34 W
California, Pa., U.S.	152	40.04 N	79.53 W
California □[3]	144	37.30 N	119.30 W
California, Golfo de C	130	28.00 N	112.00 W
Calimere, Point ≻	100	10.18 N	79.52 E
Calipatria	168	33.08 N	115.31 W
Calistoga	168	38.35 N	122.35 W
Calitri	78	40.54 N	15.27 E
Callabonna, Lake ⊜	120	29.45 S	140.04 E
Callac	74	48.24 N	3.26 W
Callahan	156	30.34 N	81.49 W
Callan	70	52.33 N	7.23 W
Callander	70	56.15 N	4.14 W
Callanna	120	29.38 S	137.55 E
Callao	134	12.02 S	77.05 W
Callosa de Segura	76	38.08 N	0.52 W
Čalna	66	61.55 N	34.01 E
Caloundra	120	26.48 S	153.09 E
Calpe	76	38.39 N	0.03 E
Caltagirone	78	37.14 N	14.31 E
Caltanissetta	78	37.29 N	14.04 E
Calumet	154	47.14 N	88.27 W
Calumet City	158	41.37 N	87.31 W
Calunda	110	12.06 S	23.23 E
Calvados □[5]	74	49.10 N	0.30 W
Calvert	160	30.59 N	96.40 W
Calvert ≃	124	16.17 S	137.44 E
Calvi	74	42.34 N	8.45 E
Calvillo	130	21.51 N	102.43 W
Calvin	162	48.51 N	98.56 W
Calvinia	116	31.25 S	19.45 E
Calw	72	48.43 N	8.44 E
Calwa	168	36.42 N	119.46 W
Camabatela	110	8.11 S	15.22 E
Camagüey	132	21.23 N	77.55 W
Camaiore	78	43.56 N	10.18 E
Camaná	134	16.36 S	72.40 W
Camanche	154	41.47 N	90.15 W
Camaquã	140	30.51 S	51.49 W
Camará	138	3.55 S	62.44 W
Camarès	74	43.49 N	2.53 E
Camargue ←[1]	74	43.34 N	4.34 E
Camarones	136	44.45 S	65.40 W
Camas	76	37.24 N	6.02 W
Ca-mau → Quan-long	94	9.11 N	105.08 E
Cambay	102	22.18 N	72.37 E
Cambodia □[1]	92	13.00 N	105.00 E
Camboon	120	25.03 S	150.26 E
Camborne	70	50.12 N	5.19 W
Cambrai	74	50.10 N	3.14 E
Cambria	168	35.34 N	121.05 W
Cambrian Mountains ⩘	70	52.35 N	3.35 W
Cambridge, Ont., Can.	154	43.22 N	80.19 W
Cambridge, N.Z.	126	37.53 S	175.28 E
Cambridge, Eng., U.K.	70	52.13 N	0.08 E
Cambridge, Idaho, U.S.	166	44.34 N	116.41 W
Cambridge, Ill., U.S.	154	41.18 N	90.12 W
Cambridge, Iowa, U.S.	154	41.54 N	93.32 W
Cambridge, Md., U.S.	152	38.34 N	76.04 W
Cambridge, Mass., U.S.	152	42.22 N	71.06 W
Cambridge, Minn., U.S.	154	45.31 N	93.14 W
Cambridge, Nebr., U.S.	162	40.17 N	100.10 W
Cambridge, N.Y., U.S.	152	43.02 N	73.23 W
Cambridge, Ohio, U.S.	152	40.02 N	81.35 W
Cambridge Bay	142	69.03 N	105.05 W
Cambridge City	158	39.49 N	85.10 W
Cambridge Fiord C[2]	142	71.20 N	74.44 W
Cambridge Gulf C	124	14.55 S	128.15 E
Cambridgeshire □[6]	70	52.20 N	0.05 E
Cambridge Springs	152	41.48 N	80.04 W
Camden, Austl.	120	34.03 S	150.42 E
Camden, Ark., U.S.	158	33.35 N	92.50 W
Camden, Del., U.S.	152	39.07 N	75.33 W
Camden, Maine, U.S.	152	44.12 N	69.04 W
Camden, N.J., U.S.	144	39.57 N	75.07 W
Camden, N.Y., U.S.	152	43.02 N	75.45 W
Camden, Ohio, U.S.	152	39.38 N	84.39 W
Camden, S.C., U.S.	156	34.16 N	80.36 W
Camden, Tenn., U.S.	158	36.04 N	88.06 W
Cameron, La., U.S.	158	29.48 N	93.19 W
Cameron, Mo., U.S.	158	39.44 N	94.14 W
Cameron, S.C., U.S.	156	33.33 N	80.43 W
Cameron, Tex., U.S.	160	30.51 N	96.59 W
Cameron, W. Va., U.S.	152	39.50 N	80.34 W
Cameron Hills ⩘[2]	142	59.48 N	118.00 W
Cameroon □[1]	108	6.00 N	12.00 E
Camerota	78	40.02 N	15.23 E
Cameroun, Mont ∧	114	4.12 N	9.11 E
Cametá	134	2.15 S	49.30 W
Camiguin Island I	98	18.54 N	121.55 E
Camilla	156	31.14 N	84.12 W
Caminha	76	41.52 N	8.50 W
Camino	168	38.44 N	120.41 W
Camiranga	134	1.48 S	46.17 W
Camiri	134	20.03 S	63.31 W
Camocim	134	2.54 S	40.50 W
Camooweal	120	19.55 S	138.07 E
Camorta Island I	94	8.08 N	93.30 E
Campana	140	34.10 S	58.57 W
Campana, Isla I	136	48.25 S	75.20 W
Campanario	76	38.52 N	5.37 W
Campania □[4]	78	41.00 N	14.30 E
Campbell	168	37.17 N	121.57 W
Campbellford	154	44.18 N	77.48 W
Campbell River	148	50.01 N	125.15 W
Campbellsville	158	37.21 N	85.20 W
Campbellton, N.B., Can.	150	48.00 N	66.40 W
Campbellton, Newf., Can.	150	49.17 N	54.56 W
Campbelltown, Austl.	120	34.04 S	150.49 E
Campbell Town, Austl.	120	41.56 S	147.29 E
Campbeltown	70	55.26 N	5.36 W
Campeche	130	19.51 N	90.32 W
Campeche, Bahía de C	130	20.00 N	94.00 W
Camperdown	120	38.14 S	143.09 E
Cam-pha	94	21.07 N	107.19 E
Camp Hill	152	40.14 N	76.55 W
Campina Grande	134	7.13 S	35.53 W
Campinas	140	22.54 S	47.05 W
Campo	162	37.06 N	102.35 W
Campoalegre	138	2.41 N	75.20 W
Campo Alegre de Goiás	134	22.54 S	47.05 W
Campobasso	78	41.34 N	14.39 E
Campo Belo	134	20.53 S	45.16 W
Campo de Criptana	76	39.24 N	3.07 W
Campo Gallo	140	26.35 S	62.50 W
Campo Grande	134	20.27 S	54.37 W
Campo Maior, Bra.	134	4.49 S	42.10 W
Campo Maior, Port.	76	39.01 N	7.04 W
Campo Mourão	140	24.03 S	52.22 W
Campos	136	21.45 S	41.18 W
Camps-en-Amiénois	70	49.52 N	1.58 E
Campti	158	31.54 N	93.07 W
Camp Verde	164	34.34 N	111.51 W
Camrose	148	53.01 N	112.50 W
Camsell ≃	142	65.40 N	118.07 W
Canaan, Conn., U.S.	152	42.02 N	73.20 W
Canaan, Vt., U.S.	152	45.00 N	71.32 W
Canada □[1]	142	60.00 N	95.00 W
Cañada de Gómez	140	32.49 S	61.25 W
Cañada Honda	140	32.00 S	68.33 W
Canadian	160	35.55 N	100.23 W
Canadian ≃	160	35.27 N	95.03 W
Canajoharie	152	42.54 N	74.35 W
Çanakkale	80	40.09 N	26.24 E
Çanakkale Boğazı (Dardanelles) ⩌	80	40.15 N	26.25 E
Canal Fulton	152	40.54 N	81.36 W
Canal Point	156	26.52 N	80.38 W
Canal Winchester	152	39.51 N	82.48 W
Canal Zone □[2]	128	9.10 N	79.48 W
Canandaigua	152	42.54 N	77.17 W
Cananea	130	30.57 N	110.18 W
Cañar □[4]	138	2.30 S	79.00 W
Canarias, Islas (Canary Islands II	106	28.00 N	15.30 W
Canary Islands → Canarias, Islas II	106	28.00 N	15.30 W
Canastota	152	43.10 N	75.45 W
Canastra, Serra da ⩘[2]	134	20.00 S	46.20 W
Canatlán	130	24.31 N	104.47 W
Canaveral, Cape ≻	156	28.27 N	80.32 W
Canavieiras	134	15.39 S	38.57 W
Canberra	120	35.17 S	149.08 E
Canby, Calif., U.S.	168	41.27 N	120.52 W
Canby, Minn., U.S.	162	44.43 N	96.16 W
Canby, Oreg., U.S.	166	45.16 N	122.42 W
Cancale	74	48.11 N	1.51 W
Cancon	74	44.32 N	0.38 E
Candé	74	47.34 N	1.02 W
Candeias	134	12.40 S	38.33 W
Candle	146	65.55 N	161.56 W
Candor	152	42.14 N	76.21 W
Cane Creek ≃	158	36.29 N	90.28 W
Canelli	78	44.43 N	8.17 E
Canelones	140	34.32 S	56.17 W
Cañete	76	40.03 N	1.35 W
Caney	162	37.01 N	95.56 W
Caney ≃	160	36.20 N	95.42 W
Caney Creek ≃	160	36.50 N	95.58 W
Cangombe	110	14.24 S	19.59 E
Canguçu	140	31.24 S	52.41 W
Cangzhou	88	38.19 N	116.51 E
Caniapiscau ≃	142	57.40 N	69.30 W
Caniapiscau, Lac ⊜	142	54.10 N	69.55 W
Canicattì	78	37.21 N	13.51 E
Canisteo	152	42.16 N	77.36 W
Cañitas	130	23.36 N	102.43 W
Cannanore	100	11.58 N	75.21 E
Cannelton	158	37.55 N	86.45 W
Cannes	74	43.33 N	7.01 E
Cannington	154	44.21 N	79.02 W
Cannock	70	52.42 N	2.09 W
Cannon Beach	166	45.55 N	123.57 W
Cannon Falls	154	44.31 N	92.54 W
Cann River	120	37.34 S	149.10 E
Canoas ≃	140	27.36 S	51.25 W
Canon City	164	38.27 N	105.14 W
Canonsburg	152	40.16 N	80.11 W
Canora	142	51.37 N	102.26 W
Canosa [di Puglia]	78	41.13 N	16.04 E
Canova	162	43.53 N	97.30 W
Canova Beach	156	28.08 N	80.34 W
Canowindra	120	33.34 S	148.38 E
Canso	150	45.20 N	61.00 W
Cantábrica, Cordillera ⩘	76	43.00 N	5.00 W
Cantal □[5]	74	45.05 N	2.45 E
Cantal ⩘	74	45.10 N	2.40 E
Cantanhede	76	40.21 N	8.36 W
Cantaura	138	9.19 N	64.21 W
Canterbury	70	51.17 N	1.05 E
Canterbury Bight C[3]	126	44.20 S	172.00 E
Can-tho	94	10.02 N	105.47 E
Canton, Ga., U.S.	156	34.14 N	84.29 W
Canton, Ill., U.S.	154	40.33 N	90.02 W
Canton, Kans., U.S.	162	38.23 N	97.26 W
Canton, Miss., U.S.	158	32.37 N	90.02 W
Canton, N.C., U.S.	156	35.32 N	82.50 W
Canton, N.Y., U.S.	152	44.36 N	75.10 W
Canton, Ohio, U.S.	152	40.48 N	81.22 W
Canton, Pa., U.S.	152	41.39 N	76.51 W
Canton, S. Dak., U.S.	162	43.18 N	96.35 W
Canton, Tex., U.S.	160	32.33 N	95.52 W
Canton → Guangzhou, Zhg.	88	23.06 N	113.16 E
Cantonment	158	30.38 N	87.19 W
Cantù	78	45.44 N	9.08 E
Cantwell	146	63.23 N	148.57 W
Cañuelas	140	35.03 S	58.44 W
Canutama	134	6.32 S	64.20 W
Čany, Ozero ⊜	84	54.50 N	77.30 E
Cany-Barville	74	49.47 N	0.38 E
Canyon	160	34.59 N	101.55 W
Canyon City	166	44.23 N	118.57 W
Canyonville	166	42.56 N	123.17 W
Cao-bang	88	22.40 N	106.15 E
Capac	154	43.01 N	82.56 W
Čapajevsk	66	52.58 N	49.41 E
Capanaparo ≃	138	7.01 N	67.07 W
Capanema	140	25.40 S	53.48 W
Capão Bonito	140	24.01 S	48.20 W
Cap-Chat	150	49.06 N	66.42 W
Cape ≃	120	20.49 S	146.51 E
Cape Barren Island I	120	40.25 S	148.12 E
Cape Breton Island I	150	46.00 N	60.30 W
Cape Canaveral	156	28.24 N	80.37 W
Cape Coast	114	5.05 N	1.15 W
Cape Dorset	142	64.14 N	76.32 W
Cape Elizabeth	152	43.34 N	70.12 W
Cape Girardeau	158	37.19 N	89.32 W
Cape May	152	38.56 N	74.55 W
Cape May Court House	152	39.05 N	74.50 W
Cape Pole	146	55.58 N	133.48 W
Cape Romanzof	146	61.49 N	165.56 W
Capesterre	132	16.03 N	61.34 W
Cape Town (Kaapstad)	116	33.55 S	18.22 E
Cape Verde □[1]	106	16.00 N	24.00 W
Cape Verde Islands → Cape Verde □[1]	106a	16.00 N	24.00 W
Cape Yakataga	146	60.04 N	142.26 W
Cape York Peninsula ≻[1]	124	14.00 S	142.30 E
Cap-Haïtien	132	19.45 N	72.15 W
Capim ≃	134	1.40 S	47.47 W
Capitan	164	33.35 N	105.35 W
Capitola	168	36.59 N	121.57 W
Capitol Peak ∧	168	41.50 N	117.18 W
Capitol View	156	33.57 N	80.56 W
Cap-Pelé	150	46.13 N	64.18 W
Capreol	154	46.43 N	80.56 W
Capri, Isola di I	78	40.33 N	14.13 E
Capricorn, Cape ≻	120	23.30 S	151.13 E
Capricorn Group II	120	23.28 S	152.00 E
Caprivi Strip □[9]	110	17.59 S	23.00 E
Captains Flat	120	35.35 S	149.27 E
Captieux	74	44.18 N	0.16 W
Capua	78	41.06 N	14.12 E
Caquetá □[8]	138	1.00 N	74.00 W
Caquetá (Japurá) ≃	138	3.08 S	64.46 W
Čara	84	56.54 N	118.12 E
Čara ≃	84	60.22 N	120.50 E
Carabobo □[3]	138	10.10 N	68.05 W
Caracal	80	44.07 N	24.21 E
Caracaraí	138	1.50 N	61.08 W
Caracas	138	10.30 N	66.56 W
Caraghnan Mountain ∧	120	31.20 S	149.03 E
Carajás, Serra dos ⩘	134	6.00 S	51.20 W
Carangola	134	20.44 S	42.04 W
Caransebeș	80	45.25 N	22.13 E
Carappee Hill ∧[2]	120	33.26 S	136.16 E
Caraquet	150	47.48 N	64.57 W
Caraș-Severin □[4]	80	45.00 N	22.00 E
Caratasca, Laguna de C	132	15.20 N	83.50 W
Caratinga	134	19.47 S	42.08 W
Carauari	138	4.52 S	66.54 W
Caravaca	76	38.06 N	1.51 W
Caravaggio	78	45.30 N	9.38 E
Caravelas	134	17.45 S	39.15 W
Caràzinho	140	28.18 S	52.48 W
Carballino	76	42.26 N	8.04 W
Carberry	162	49.52 N	99.20 W
Carbon-Blanc	74	44.53 N	0.31 W
Carbondale, Colo., U.S.	164	39.24 N	107.13 W
Carbondale, Ill., U.S.	158	37.44 N	89.13 W
Carbondale, Pa., U.S.	152	41.35 N	75.30 W
Carbonear	150	47.45 N	53.13 W
Carbonia	78	39.11 N	8.32 E
Carcagente	76	39.08 N	0.27 W
Carcajou ≃	146	65.37 N	128.43 W
Carcassonne	74	43.13 N	2.21 E
Carchi □[4]	138	0.45 N	78.00 W
Carcross	146	60.10 N	134.42 W
Cárdenas, Cuba	132	23.05 N	81.10 W
Cárdenas, Méx.	130	22.00 N	99.40 W
Cardiel, Lago ⊜	136	48.55 S	71.10 W
Cardiff	70	51.29 N	3.13 W
Cardigan	70	52.06 N	4.40 W
Cardigan Bay C	70	52.30 N	4.20 W
Cardinal	152	44.47 N	75.23 W
Cardington	152	40.30 N	82.53 W
Cardston	148	49.12 N	113.18 W
Cardwell	120	18.16 S	146.02 E
Cardwell Mountain ∧	158	35.41 N	85.41 W
Čardžou	104	39.06 N	63.34 E
Carei	80	47.42 N	22.28 E
Carencro	158	30.19 N	92.03 W

Symbols in the index entries are identified on page 203.

Name	Page	Lat	Long
Carentan	74	49.18 N	1.14 W
Cares	76	43.19 N	4.49 W
Caretta	156	37.20 N	81.41 W
Carey	152	40.57 N	83.23 W
Carey, Lake ◉	122	29.05 S	122.15 E
Carhaix-Plouguer	74	48.17 N	3.35 W
Cariati	78	39.30 N	16.56 E
Caribbean Sea ▼²	128	15.00 N	73.00 W
Cariboo Mountains ⋀	148	53.00 N	121.00 W
Caribou	150	46.52 N	68.01 W
Caribou ≃	142	59.20 N	94.44 W
Caribou Mountains ⋀	142	59.12 N	115.40 W
Carignan	74	49.38 N	5.10 E
Carinhanha	134	14.18 S	43.47 W
Carini	78	38.08 N	13.11 E
Caripito	138	10.08 N	63.06 W
Carleton	154	42.04 N	83.23 W
Carleton, Mount ⋀	150	47.23 N	66.53 W
Carleton Place	154	45.08 N	76.09 W
Carletonville	116	26.23 S	27.22 E
Carlin	168	40.43 N	116.07 W
Carlinville	158	39.17 N	89.53 W
Carlisle, Eng., U.K.	70	54.54 N	2.25 W
Carlisle, Ark., U.S.	158	34.47 N	91.45 W
Carlisle, Iowa, U.S.	154	41.30 N	93.29 W
Carlisle, Pa., U.S.	152	40.12 N	77.12 W
Carl Junction	158	37.11 N	94.34 W
Carlos Casares	140	35.37 S	61.22 W
Carlow	70	52.50 N	6.55 W
Carlow □⁶	70	52.50 N	7.00 W
Carloway	70	58.17 N	6.48 W
Carlsbad → Karlovy Vary, Česko.	72	50.11 N	12.52 E
Carlsbad, Calif., U.S.	168	33.10 N	117.21 W
Carlsbad, N. Mex., U.S.	160	32.25 N	104.14 W
Carlsbad, Tex., U.S.	160	31.36 N	100.38 W
Carlton	166	45.18 N	123.11 W
Carlyle	158	38.37 N	89.22 W
Carmacks	146	62.05 N	136.18 W
Carmagnola	78	44.51 N	7.43 E
Carman	162	49.32 N	98.00 W
Carmarthen	70	51.52 N	4.19 W
Carmaux	74	44.03 N	2.09 E
Carmel, Calif., U.S.	168	36.33 N	121.55 W
Carmel, Ind., U.S.	158	39.59 N	86.08 W
Carmel Head ➤	70	53.24 N	4.34 W
Carmelo	140	34.00 S	58.17 W
Carmel Valley	168	36.29 N	121.43 W
Carmel Woods	168	36.34 N	121.54 W
Carmen, Isla I	130	25.55 N	111.10 W
Carmen de Patagones	136	40.48 S	63.00 W
Carmer Hill ⋀²	152	41.54 N	77.58 W
Carmichael	168	38.38 N	121.19 W
Carmona, Ang.	110	7.37 S	15.03 E
Carmona, Esp.	76	37.28 N	5.38 W
Carnarvon, Austl.	122	24.53 S	113.40 E
Carnarvon, S. Afr.	116	30.56 S	22.08 E
Carnatic ⋆¹	100	12.30 N	78.15 E
Carndonagh	70	55.15 N	7.15 W
Carnegie	160	35.06 N	98.36 W
Carnegie, Lake ◉	122	26.10 S	122.30 E
Carniche, Alpi ⋀	78	46.40 N	13.00 E
Car Nicobar Island I	94	9.10 N	92.47 E
Carnoustie	70	56.30 N	2.44 W
Carnwath ≃	146	68.26 N	128.50 W
Caro	154	43.29 N	83.24 W
Carol City	156	25.56 N	80.16 W
Carolina	134	7.20 S	47.28 W
Carolina Beach	156	34.02 N	77.54 W
Caroline Islands II	92	8.00 N	147.00 E
Caroni ≃	138	8.21 N	62.43 W
Carora	138	10.11 N	70.05 W
Carpathian Mountains → Karpaty ⋀	64	48.00 N	24.00 E
Carpentaria, Gulf of C	124	14.00 S	139.00 E
Carpenter	162	41.03 N	104.22 W
Carpentersville	154	42.07 N	88.17 W
Carpentras	74	44.03 N	5.03 E
Carpi	78	44.47 N	10.53 E
Carpinteria	168	34.24 N	119.31 W
Carpolac	120	36.44 S	141.19 E
Carquefou	74	47.18 N	1.30 W
Carr	162	40.53 N	104.53 W
Carrara	78	44.05 N	10.06 E
Carrauntoohill ⋀	70	52.00 N	9.45 W
Carrboro	156	35.54 N	79.04 W
Carreria	140	21.59 S	58.35 W
Carreta, Punta ➤	134	14.12 S	76.17 W
Carrickfergus	70	54.43 N	5.49 W
Carrickmacross	70	53.58 N	6.43 W
Carrick-on-Shannon	70	53.57 N	8.05 W
Carrick-on-Suir	70	52.21 N	7.25 W
Carriere	158	30.37 N	89.39 W
Carriers Mills	158	37.41 N	88.38 W
Carrington	162	47.26 N	99.07 W
Carrión de los Condes	76	42.20 N	4.36 W
Carrizal Bajo	140	28.05 S	71.10 W
Carrizo Creek ≃, U.S.	160	36.55 N	103.55 W
Carrizo Creek ≃, U.S.	164	34.36 N	109.26 W
Carrizo Mountains ⋀	164	36.40 N	109.20 W
Carrizo Springs	160	28.31 N	99.52 W
Carrizozo	160	33.38 N	105.53 W
Carroll	162	42.04 N	94.52 W
Carrollton, Ala., U.S.	156	33.16 N	88.05 W
Carrollton, Ga., U.S.	156	33.35 N	85.05 W
Carrollton, Ill., U.S.	158	39.18 N	90.24 W
Carrollton, Ky., U.S.	158	38.41 N	85.11 W
Carrollton, Mich., U.S.	154	43.27 N	83.54 W
Carrollton, Mo., U.S.	158	39.22 N	93.30 W
Carrollton, Ohio, U.S.	152	40.34 N	81.05 W
Carrollton, Tex., U.S.	160	32.57 N	96.54 W
Carrot ≃	142	53.50 N	101.17 W
Carrouges	74	48.34 N	0.09 W
Carryville	156	36.44 N	85.18 W
Caršk	88	49.35 N	121.05 E
Carson	166	45.44 N	121.49 W
Carson, East Fork ≃	168	39.00 N	119.49 W
Carson City, Mich., U.S.	154	43.11 N	84.51 W
Carson City, Nev., U.S.	168	39.10 N	119.46 W
Carson Sink ◉	168	39.45 N	118.30 W
Carstensz-Toppen → Djaja, Puntjak ⋀	124	4.05 S	137.11 E
Cartagena, Col.	138	10.25 N	75.32 W
Cartagena, Esp.	76	37.36 N	0.59 W
Cartago, Col.	138	4.45 N	75.55 W
Cartago, C.R.	132	9.52 N	83.55 W
Cartaxo	76	39.09 N	8.47 W
Carter	162	44.04 N	95.54 W
Cartersville	156	34.10 N	84.48 W
Carterton	126	41.02 S	175.32 E
Carterville	158	37.46 N	89.05 W
Carthage, Tun.	106	36.51 N	10.21 E
Carthage, Ill., U.S.	154	40.25 N	91.08 W
Carthage, Ind., U.S.	158	39.44 N	85.34 W
Carthage, Miss., U.S.	158	32.44 N	89.32 W
Carthage, Mo., U.S.	158	37.11 N	94.19 W
Carthage, N.Y., U.S.	152	43.59 N	75.36 W
Carthage, Tenn., U.S.	156	36.15 N	85.57 W
Carthage, Tex., U.S.	160	32.09 N	94.20 W
Carter Island I	118	12.32 S	123.32 E
Cartwright	142	53.42 N	57.01 W
Caruaru	134	8.17 S	35.58 W
Carúpano	138	10.40 N	63.14 W
Carutapera	134	1.13 S	46.01 W
Caruthersville	158	36.11 N	89.39 W
Carvin	74	50.29 N	2.58 E
Carvoeiro	138	1.24 S	61.59 W
Cary	156	35.47 N	78.46 W
Caryville	156	30.46 N	85.49 W
Casablanca (Dar-el-Beida)	106	33.39 N	7.35 W
Casa Branca	134	21.46 S	47.04 W
Casa Grande	164	32.53 N	111.45 W
Casale Monferrato	78	45.08 N	8.27 E
Casanare □⁸	138	5.45 N	72.00 W
Casanare ≃	138	6.02 N	69.51 W
Casarano	78	40.00 N	18.10 E
Casas Adobes	164	32.19 N	110.59 W
Casas Ibañez	76	39.17 N	1.28 W
Casasimarro	76	39.22 N	2.02 W
Casavieja	76	40.17 N	4.46 W
Cascade, Idaho, U.S.	166	44.31 N	116.02 W
Cascade, Mont., U.S.	166	47.16 N	111.42 W
Cascade, Wis., U.S.	154	43.40 N	88.00 W
Cascade Locks	166	45.40 N	121.54 W
Cascade Range ⋀	144	49.00 N	120.00 W
Cascais	76	38.42 N	9.25 W
Cascavel	140	24.57 S	53.28 W
Cascina	78	43.41 N	10.33 E
Caserta	78	41.04 N	14.20 E
Casey, Ill., U.S.	158	39.18 N	87.59 W
Casey, Iowa, U.S.	154	41.31 N	94.32 W
Cashel	70	52.31 N	7.53 W
Cashmere	166	47.31 N	120.28 W
Cashmere Downs	122	28.58 S	119.35 E
Casilda	140	33.03 S	61.10 W
Casino	120	28.52 S	153.03 E
Casiquiare, Brazo ≃	138	2.01 N	67.07 W
Casper	162	42.51 N	106.19 W
Caspian	154	46.03 N	88.38 W
Caspian Sea ▼²	82	42.00 N	50.30 E
Cass ≃	152	38.24 N	79.55 W
Casselman	152	45.19 N	75.05 W
Cassiar	146	59.16 N	129.40 W
Cassiar Mountains ⋀	142	59.00 N	129.00 W
Cassinga	110	15.08 S	16.05 E
Cassino	78	41.30 N	13.49 E
Cass Lake	154	47.23 N	94.36 W
Cassopolis	154	41.55 N	86.01 W
Cassville	158	36.41 N	93.52 W
Castalia	152	41.24 N	82.48 W
Castanheira de Pêra	76	40.00 N	8.13 W
Castanhal	134	1.18 S	47.55 W
Castaños	160	26.47 N	101.25 W
Castelbuono	78	37.56 N	14.06 E
Castelfiorentino	78	43.46 N	10.58 E
Castelfranco Veneto	78	45.40 N	11.55 E
Casteljaloux	74	44.19 N	0.05 E
Castellammare del Golfo	78	38.01 N	12.53 E
Castellammare [di Stabia]	78	40.42 N	14.29 E
Castellane	74	43.51 N	6.31 E
Castellaneta	78	40.37 N	16.57 E
Castellón □⁴	76	40.10 N	0.10 W
Castellón de la Plana	76	39.59 N	0.02 W
Castelmassa	78	45.01 N	11.18 E
Castelmoron-sur-Lot	74	44.24 N	0.30 E
Castelnau-Montratier	74	44.16 N	1.21 E
Castelnaudary	74	43.19 N	1.57 E
Castelo Branco	76	39.49 N	7.30 W
Castelsarrasin	74	44.02 N	1.06 E
Castelvetrano	78	37.41 N	12.47 E
Castets	74	43.53 N	1.09 W
Castile	152	42.38 N	78.03 W
Castilla	134	5.12 S	80.38 W
Castilla la Nueva □⁹	76	40.00 N	3.45 W
Castilla la Vieja □⁹	76	41.30 N	4.00 W
Castillo, Pampa del ⋈	136	45.58 S	68.24 W
Castillon-la-Bataille	74	44.51 N	0.02 W
Castillos	140	34.12 S	53.50 W
Castlebar	70	53.52 N	9.17 W
Castleblayney	70	54.07 N	6.44 W
Castlecliff	126	39.57 S	174.59 E
Castle Dale	164	39.13 N	111.01 W
Castle Douglas	70	54.57 N	3.56 W
Castle Hills	160	29.32 N	98.31 W
Castleisland	70	52.14 N	9.27 W
Castlemaine	120	37.04 S	144.13 E
Castle Mountain ⋀	146	63.32 N	135.25 W
Castlerea	70	53.46 N	8.29 W
Castlereagh ≃	120	30.12 S	147.32 E
Castle Rock	162	39.22 N	104.51 W
Castleton	152	43.37 N	73.11 W
Castletown, I. of Man	70	54.04 N	4.40 W
Castletown, Scot., U.K.	70	58.35 N	3.23 W
Castletown Berehaven	70	51.39 N	9.55 W
Castres	74	43.36 N	2.15 E
Castro, Bra.	140	24.47 S	50.00 W
Castro, Chile	136	42.29 S	73.46 W
Castro del Rio	76	37.41 N	4.28 W
Castro Marim	76	37.13 N	7.26 W
Castro Verde	76	37.42 N	8.05 W
Castroville, Calif., U.S.	168	36.46 N	121.45 W
Castroville, Tex., U.S.	160	29.21 N	98.53 W
Castuera	76	38.43 N	5.33 W
Catacaos	134	5.15 S	80.42 W
Catalão	134	18.10 S	47.57 W
Catalina	140	25.13 S	69.43 W
Catamarca □⁹	140	28.30 S	65.45 W
Catamarca	140	28.30 S	65.45 W
Catanduanes Island I	98	13.45 N	124.15 E
Catanduva	134	21.08 S	48.58 W
Catania	78	37.30 N	15.06 E
Catanzaro	78	38.54 N	16.36 E
Catarroja	76	39.24 N	0.24 W
Catastrophe, Cape ➤	120	34.59 S	136.00 E
Catawba ≃	156	34.30 N	80.54 W
Catawba, Lake ◉¹	156	34.25 N	80.58 W
Catbalogan	92	11.47 N	124.53 E
Catete	110	9.06 S	13.43 E
Cathcart	110	31.18 S	27.09 E
Cathedral City	168	33.47 N	116.28 W
Cathlamet	166	46.12 N	123.23 W
Catlettsburg	156	38.23 N	82.36 W
Catlin	158	40.16 N	87.42 W
Catoche, Cabo ➤	130	21.36 N	87.07 W
Cato Island I	118	23.15 S	155.32 E
Catonsville	152	39.16 N	76.44 W
Catril	140	38.35 S	63.24 W
Catrimani	138	0.28 N	61.44 W
Catskill	152	42.13 N	73.52 W
Catskill Mountains ⋀	152	42.10 N	74.30 W
Cattaraugus	152	42.20 N	78.52 W
Cattolica	78	43.58 N	12.44 E
Catus	74	44.34 N	1.20 E
Čatyrtaš	84	41.15 N	76.26 E
Caudry	74	50.08 N	3.25 E
Caulonia	78	38.23 N	16.25 E
Čaunskaja Guba C	86	69.20 N	170.00 E
Cauquenes	140	35.58 S	72.21 W
Caura ≃	138	7.38 N	64.53 W
Causapscal	150	48.22 N	67.14 W
Caussade	74	44.10 N	1.32 E
Causy	86	53.48 N	30.58 E
Cauterets	74	42.52 N	0.07 W
Cautín □⁴	136	38.50 S	72.20 W
Cauvery ≃	100	11.10 N	79.51 E
Caux, Pays de ⋆¹	74	49.40 N	0.40 E
Cava [de' Tirreni]	78	40.42 N	14.42 E
Cavaillon	74	43.50 N	5.02 E
Cavalaire-sur-Mer	74	43.10 N	6.32 E
Cavalcante	134	13.48 S	47.28 W
Cavalese	78	46.17 N	11.27 E
Cavalier	162	48.48 N	97.37 W
Cavalla (Cavally) ≃	114	4.22 N	7.32 W
Cavan	70	54.00 N	7.21 W
Cavan □⁶	70	53.55 N	7.30 W
Čavan'ga	66	66.06 N	37.47 E
Cavarzere	78	45.08 N	12.05 E
Cave City	158	37.08 N	85.58 W
Cavendish	120	37.31 S	142.02 E
Cave Springs	156	34.07 N	85.20 W
Caviana, Ilha I	134	0.10 N	50.10 W
Cavite	92	14.29 N	120.55 E
Caxias	134	4.50 S	43.21 W
Caxias do Sul	140	29.10 S	51.11 W
Caxito	110	8.33 S	13.36 E
Cayambe	138	0.03 N	78.08 W
Cayambe ⋀¹	138	0.02 N	77.59 W
Cayce	156	33.59 N	81.04 W
Cayenne	134	4.56 N	52.20 W
Caylus	74	44.14 N	1.46 E
Cayman Brac I	132	19.43 N	79.49 W
Cayman Islands □²	132	19.30 N	80.40 W
Cay Sal Bank ⋆⁴	128	23.45 N	80.00 W
Cayucos	168	35.27 N	120.54 W
Cayuga, Ont., Can.	154	42.56 N	79.51 W
Cayuga, Tex., U.S.	160	31.57 N	95.57 W
Cayuga Lake ◉	152	42.45 N	76.45 W
Cazenovia	152	42.56 N	75.51 W
Cazères	74	43.13 N	1.05 E
Cazombo	110	11.54 S	22.52 E
Cchinvali	82	42.13 N	43.56 E
Ceanannus Mór	70	53.44 N	6.53 W
Ceará-Mirim	134	5.38 S	35.26 W
Čeboksary	66	56.09 N	47.15 E
Cebollar	140	29.06 S	66.34 W
Cebu	98	10.18 N	123.54 E
Cebu I	98	10.15 N	123.40 E
Ceccano	78	41.34 N	13.20 E
Cecerleg	88	47.30 N	101.28 E
Čechov	86	55.09 N	37.27 E
Cecil Rhodes, Mount ⋀	122	25.26 S	121.26 E
Cecina	78	43.17 N	10.31 E
Čečorsk	86	52.55 N	30.55 E
Cedarburg	154	43.17 N	87.59 W
Cedar City, Mo., U.S.	158	38.36 N	92.11 W
Cedar City, Utah, U.S.	164	37.41 N	113.04 W
Cedar Creek ≃	162	47.17 N	101.21 W
Cedaredge	164	38.54 N	107.56 W
Cedar Falls	154	42.32 N	92.27 W
Cedar Grove, W. Va., U.S.	156	38.13 N	81.26 W
Cedar Grove, Wis., U.S.	154	43.33 N	87.45 W
Cedar Hills	166	45.30 N	122.48 W
Cedar Key	156	29.08 N	83.02 W
Cedar Lake	158	41.22 N	87.26 W
Cedar Lake ◉¹	142	53.10 N	100.00 W
Cedar Rapids	154	41.59 N	91.40 W
Cedar Springs	154	43.13 N	85.33 W
Cedar Vale	158	37.06 N	96.30 W
Cedarville, Calif., U.S.	168	41.32 N	120.10 W
Cedarville, N.J., U.S.	152	39.20 N	75.12 W
Cedillo, Embalse de ⋈¹	76	39.40 N	7.25 E
Cedros, Isla I	130	28.10 N	115.15 W
Ceduna	122	32.07 S	133.40 E
Cefalù	78	38.02 N	14.01 E
Çegdomyn	84	51.07 N	133.05 E
Céglād	72	47.10 N	19.48 E
Ceglie Messapico	78	40.39 N	17.31 E
Cehegín	76	38.06 N	1.48 W
Cekalin	86	54.06 N	36.15 E
Cela	110	11.25 S	15.07 E
Celano	78	42.05 N	13.33 E
Celaya	130	20.31 N	100.37 W
Celebes → Sulawesi I	96	2.00 S	121.00 E
Celebes Sea ▼²	96	3.00 N	122.00 E
Celeken	104	39.26 N	53.07 E
Celeste	160	33.18 N	96.12 W
Celina, Ohio, U.S.	152	40.33 N	84.34 W
Celina, Tenn., U.S.	156	36.33 N	85.30 W
Celina, Tex., U.S.	160	33.19 N	96.47 W
Celinograd	84	51.10 N	71.30 E
Celje	78	46.14 N	15.16 E
Celkar	82	47.50 N	59.36 E
Celldömölk	72	47.16 N	17.09 E
Celle	72	52.37 N	10.05 E
Celorico da Beira	76	40.38 N	7.23 W
Cel'uskin, Mys ➤	84	77.45 N	104.20 E
Cemerno	78	43.11 N	18.37 E
Centennial Mountains ⋀	166	44.35 N	111.55 W
Center, Colo., U.S.	164	37.45 N	106.06 W
Center, N. Dak., U.S.	162	47.07 N	101.18 W
Center, Tex., U.S.	158	31.48 N	94.11 W
Center Moriches	152	40.48 N	72.48 W
Center Point, Ala., U.S.	156	33.38 N	86.41 W
Center Point, Iowa, U.S.	154	42.11 N	91.46 W
Centerville, Ind., U.S.	158	39.49 N	85.00 W
Centerville, Iowa, U.S.	154	40.43 N	92.52 W
Centerville, Pa., U.S.	152	41.44 N	79.46 W
Centerville, Tenn., U.S.	156	35.47 N	87.28 W
Centerville, Utah, U.S.	166	40.55 N	111.52 W
Cento	78	44.43 N	11.17 E
Central, N. Mex., U.S.	164	32.46 N	108.09 W
Central, S.C., U.S.	156	34.43 N	82.47 W
Central, Cordillera ⋀, Bol.	134	18.30 S	64.55 W
Central, Cordillera ⋀, Col.	138	5.00 N	75.00 W
Central, Cordillera ⋀, Perú	134	8.00 S	77.00 W
Central, Massif ⋀	74	45.00 N	3.10 E
Central, Planalto ⋀¹	134	18.00 S	47.00 W
Central, Sistema ⋀	76	40.30 N	5.00 W
Central African Republic □¹	108	7.00 N	21.00 E
Central City, Ill., U.S.	158	41.14 N	88.16 W
Central City, Iowa, U.S.	154	42.12 N	91.31 W
Central City, Ky., U.S.	158	37.18 N	87.07 W
Central City, Nebr., U.S.	162	41.07 N	98.00 W
Central City, Pa., U.S.	152	40.06 N	78.48 W
Central Heights	164	33.25 N	110.48 W
Centralia, Ill., U.S.	158	38.31 N	89.08 W
Centralia, Mo., U.S.	158	39.13 N	92.08 W
Centralia, Wash., U.S.	166	46.43 N	122.58 W
Central Lake	154	45.04 N	85.16 W
Central Makrān Range ⋀	102	26.40 N	64.30 E
Central Point	166	42.23 N	122.55 W
Central Region □⁴	70	56.15 N	4.00 W
Central Valley	152	41.25 N	74.07 W
Centre	74	47.00 N	2.05 E
Centreville, Ala., U.S.	156	32.57 N	87.08 W
Centreville, Mich., U.S.	158	41.55 N	85.32 W
Century	156	30.58 N	87.16 W
Černyševskij	84	63.00 N	112.15 E
Cervalvo, Isla I	130	24.17 N	109.52 W
Cerrillos	130	35.26 N	106.08 W
Cerritos	130	22.26 N	100.17 W
Cerro Azul	134	21.12 N	97.44 W
Cerro de Pasco	134	10.41 S	76.16 W
Čerski	84	68.45 N	161.45 E
Čerskogo, Chrebet ⋀	84	52.00 N	114.00 E
Červen'	86	53.42 N	28.26 E
Červen Brjag	80	43.16 N	24.06 E
Cerveteri	78	41.40 N	12.06 E
Cervia	78	44.15 N	12.22 E
Cervione	74	42.20 N	9.31 E
Červonograd	82	50.24 N	24.14 E
Cesena	78	44.08 N	12.15 E
Cesenatico	78	44.12 N	12.24 E
Cēsis	66	57.18 N	25.15 E
Česká Socialistická Republika □³	72	49.40 N	15.10 E
Česká Třebová	72	49.54 N	16.27 E
České Budějovice	72	48.59 N	14.28 E
Český Těšín	72	49.45 N	18.37 E
Československá Guba C	84	70.30 N	151.21 E
Cestos ≃	114	5.40 N	9.10 W
Cetinje	80	42.23 N	18.55 E
Četlasskij Kamen', Gora ⋀²	66	64.22 N	50.45 E
Ceuta	106	35.53 N	5.19 W
Ceva	78	44.23 N	8.02 E
Cévennes ⋆¹	74	44.00 N	3.30 E
Ceylon → Sri Lanka □¹	100	7.00 N	81.00 E
Chabanais	74	45.52 N	0.43 E
Chabarovsk	84	48.27 N	135.06 E
Chabeuil	74	44.54 N	5.01 E
Chablais ⋆¹	74	46.18 N	6.39 E
Chablis	74	47.49 N	3.48 E
Chacabuco	140	34.38 S	60.29 W
Chachani, Nevado ⋀	134	16.12 S	71.32 W
Chachapoyas	134	6.10 S	77.50 W
Chacon, Cape ➤	146	54.42 N	132.00 W
Chaco □⁴	140	26.25 S	60.30 W
Chad □¹	108	15.00 N	19.00 E
Chad, Lake (Lac Tchad) ◉	108	13.20 N	14.00 E
Chadbourn	156	34.19 N	78.50 W
Chadileuvú ≃	140	37.46 S	66.00 W
Chadron	162	42.49 N	102.59 W
Chāgai Hills ⋀²	104	29.30 N	64.15 E
Chagny	74	46.55 N	4.45 E
Chāh Bahār	104	25.18 N	60.37 E
Chaidamupendi ⋆¹	88	37.00 N	95.00 E
Chaillé-les-Marais	74	46.24 N	1.01 W
Chaîne Annamitique ⋀	94	17.00 N	106.00 E
Chaîne des Mongos ⋀	108	8.40 N	22.25 E
Chaiyaphum	94	15.48 N	102.02 E
Chake Chake	110	5.15 S	39.46 E
Chalais	74	45.16 N	0.02 E
Chalbi Desert ⋆²	108	3.00 N	37.20 E
Chaleur Bay C	150	48.00 N	65.45 W
Chalkyitsik	146	66.39 N	143.43 W
Challans	74	46.51 N	1.53 W
Challis	166	44.30 N	114.13 W
Chalmer-Ju	66	67.58 N	64.50 E
Chalmette	158	29.56 N	89.58 W
Châlonnes-sur-Loire	74	47.21 N	0.46 W
Châlons-sur-Marne	74	48.57 N	4.22 E
Chalon-sur-Saône	74	46.47 N	4.51 E
Chalosse ⋆¹	74	43.45 N	0.30 W
Châlus, Fr.	74	45.39 N	0.59 E
Chālūs, Īrān	104	36.38 N	51.26 E
Cham	72	49.13 N	12.41 E
Chama	164	36.54 N	106.35 W
Chama, Río ≃	164	36.03 N	106.05 W
Chamba	102	32.34 N	76.08 E
Chambal ≃	102	26.30 N	79.15 E
Chamberlain	162	43.49 N	99.20 W
Chambers	164	35.11 N	109.26 W
Chambersburg	152	39.56 N	77.39 W
Chambéry	74	45.34 N	5.56 E
Chamblee	156	33.54 N	84.18 W
Chambly, Qué., Can.	152	45.27 N	73.17 W
Chambon-sur-Voueize	74	46.11 N	2.25 E
Chamical (Gobernador Gordillo)	140	30.22 S	66.19 W
Chamonix-Mont-Blanc	74	45.55 N	6.52 E
Champagne □⁹	74	49.00 N	4.30 E
Champagne Castle ⋀	116	29.06 S	29.20 E
Champagnole	74	46.45 N	5.55 E
Champaign	158	40.07 N	88.14 W
Champaqui, Cerro ⋀	140	31.58 S	64.56 W
Champdeniers	74	46.29 N	0.25 W
Champdoré, Lac ◉	142	55.55 N	65.49 W
Champerico	130	14.18 N	91.55 W
Champéry	74	46.10 N	6.52 E
Champion	152	44.59 N	75.45 W
Champlain	152	44.59 N	73.26 W
Champlain, Lake ◉	152	44.45 N	73.15 W
Champlitte-et-le-Prélot	74	47.37 N	5.31 E
Champotón	130	19.21 N	90.43 W
Chamusca	76	39.21 N	8.29 W
Chañaral	140	26.21 S	70.37 W
Chanch	88	51.30 N	100.40 E
Chanchiang → Zhanjiang	88	21.16 N	110.28 E
Chandalar ≃	146	66.36 N	145.48 W
Chandalar, Middle Fork ≃	146	67.10 N	148.19 W
Chandīgarh	102	30.44 N	76.55 E
Chandler, Qué., Can.	150	48.21 N	64.41 W
Chandler, Ariz., U.S.	164	33.18 N	111.50 W
Chandler, Ind., U.S.	158	38.02 N	87.22 W
Chandler ≃	146	68.15 N	152.43 W
Chāndpur	102	23.13 N	90.39 E
Chandrapur	100	19.57 N	79.18 E
Chandydža	84	62.40 N	135.36 E
Chang, Ko I	94	12.05 N	102.20 E
Changane ≃	116	24.43 S	33.32 E
Changbaishan ⋀	88	42.05 N	128.00 E
Changchow → Zhangzhou	88	24.33 N	117.39 E
Changchun	88	43.53 N	125.19 E
Changde	88	29.02 N	111.35 E
Changjiang (Yangtze) ≃	88	31.48 N	121.10 E
Changli	88	39.41 N	119.11 E
Changsha	88	28.12 N	113.00 E
Changzhi	88	36.11 N	113.06 E
Changzhou	88	31.47 N	119.57 E
Chantilly	74	49.12 N	2.28 E
Chantonnay	74	46.41 N	1.03 W
Chantrey Inlet C	142	67.48 N	96.20 W
Chanty-Mansijsk	84	61.00 N	69.06 E
Chanute	162	37.41 N	95.27 W
Chaoan	88	23.41 N	116.38 E
Chaohu	88	31.36 N	117.53 E
Chao Phraya ≃	94	13.32 N	100.36 E
Chaoyang	88	41.35 N	120.26 E
Chao'yang	88	41.35 N	128.08 E
Chapala	130	20.18 N	103.12 W
Chapala, Lago de ◉	130	20.15 N	103.00 W
Chaparral	138	3.43 N	75.28 W
Chapčeranga	84	49.42 N	112.24 E
Chapel Hill, N.C., U.S.	156	35.55 N	79.04 W
Chapel Hill, Tenn., U.S.	156	35.38 N	86.41 W
Chapin	158	39.46 N	90.24 W
Chapleau	154	47.50 N	83.24 W
Chapman	162	38.58 N	97.01 W
Chapman, Cape ➤	142	69.12 N	88.59 W
Chapmanville	156	37.58 N	82.01 W
Chappell	162	41.06 N	102.28 W
Chappell Hill	160	30.09 N	96.16 W
Chāpra	102	25.46 N	84.45 E
Chapulhuacán	130	21.09 N	98.54 W
Chapultepec ⋀	130	23.27 N	103.04 W
Charadai	140	27.43 S	59.55 W
Charbala	84	64.07 N	120.19 E
Char'kov	64	50.00 N	36.15 E
Charleroi	72	50.25 N	4.26 E
Charles, Peak ⋀	122	32.52 S	121.11 E
Charles City	154	43.03 N	92.40 W
Charles Island I	142	62.40 N	74.15 W
Charles Point ➤	124	12.23 S	130.36 E
Charleston, Ark., U.S.	158	35.18 N	94.02 W
Charleston, Ill., U.S.	158	39.30 N	88.10 W
Charleston, Miss., U.S.	158	34.00 N	90.04 W
Charleston, Mo., U.S.	158	36.55 N	89.21 W
Charleston, S.C., U.S.	156	32.48 N	79.57 W
Charleston, W. Va., U.S.	152	38.21 N	81.38 W
Charlestown, Ind., U.S.	158	38.27 N	85.40 W
Charlestown, N.H., U.S.	152	43.14 N	72.26 W
Charlesville	110	5.27 S	20.58 E
Charlevoix	154	45.19 N	85.16 W
Charlieu	74	46.10 N	4.10 E
Charlotte, Mich., U.S.	154	42.36 N	84.50 W
Charlotte, N.C., U.S.	156	35.13 N	80.50 W
Charlotte, Tenn., U.S.	156	36.11 N	87.24 W
Charlotte Amalie	132	18.21 N	64.56 W
Charlottesville	152	38.01 N	78.29 W
Charlottetown	150	46.14 N	63.08 W
Charlton Island I	142	52.00 N	79.30 W
Charmes	74	48.22 N	6.17 E
Charolles	74	46.26 N	4.17 E
Charost	74	47.01 N	2.07 E
Charroux	74	46.09 N	0.24 E
Charsadda	102	34.09 N	71.44 E
Charter Oak	162	42.04 N	95.35 W
Charters Towers	120	20.05 S	146.16 E
Chartres	74	48.27 N	1.30 E
Chascomús	140	35.35 S	58.00 W
Chase	162	38.21 N	98.21 W
Chase City	156	36.48 N	78.28 W
Chaska	154	44.48 N	93.35 W
Chatanbulag	88	43.11 N	109.10 E
Chatanga	84	71.58 N	102.30 E
Chatangskij Zaliv C	84	73.30 N	109.00 E
Chatanika ≃	146	65.07 N	149.18 W
Chateaubriant	74	47.43 N	1.23 W
Château-Chinon	74	47.04 N	3.56 E
Château-d'Oex	74	46.28 N	7.08 E
Château-du-Loir	74	47.42 N	0.25 E
Châteaudun	74	48.05 N	1.20 E
Châteaugay	152	44.56 N	74.05 W
Château-Gontier	74	47.50 N	0.42 W
Château-la-Vallière	74	47.33 N	0.19 E
Châteaulin	74	48.12 N	4.05 W
Châteaumeillant	74	46.34 N	2.12 E
Châteauneuf-de-Randon	74	44.38 N	3.40 E
Châteauneuf-en-Thymerais	74	48.35 N	1.14 E
Châteauneuf-sur-Charente	74	45.36 N	0.03 W
Châteauneuf-sur-Loire	74	47.52 N	2.14 E
Châteauneuf-sur-Sarthe	74	47.41 N	0.30 W
Château-Renault	74	47.35 N	0.55 E
Château-Richer	152	46.58 N	71.02 W
Château-Salins	74	48.49 N	6.30 E
Château-Thierry	74	49.03 N	3.24 E
Châtelguyon	74	45.55 N	3.04 E
Châtellerault	74	46.49 N	0.33 E
Châtel-sur-Moselle	74	48.19 N	6.24 E
Châtenois	74	48.17 N	5.50 E
Chatgal	88	50.26 N	100.07 E
Chatham, N.B., Can.	150	47.02 N	65.28 W
Chatham, Ont., Can.	154	42.24 N	82.11 W
Chatham, Eng., U.K.	70	51.23 N	0.32 E
Chatham, Ill., U.S.	158	39.40 N	89.42 W
Chatham, N.Y., U.S.	152	42.21 N	73.35 W
Chatham Islands II	118	44.00 S	176.30 W
Chatham Strait ⧵	146	57.30 N	134.45 W
Châtillon-Coligny	74	47.49 N	2.51 E
Châtillon-en-Bazois	74	47.03 N	3.39 E
Châtillon-sur-Indre	74	46.59 N	1.10 E
Châtillon-sur-Seine	74	47.51 N	4.33 E
Chatom	158	31.28 N	88.15 W
Chatrapur	100	19.21 N	85.01 E
Chatsworth	158	40.45 N	88.17 W
Chattahoochee	156	30.42 N	84.50 W
Chattahoochee ≃	156	30.52 N	84.57 W
Chattanooga	156	35.02 N	85.18 W
Chattaroy	156	37.42 N	82.17 W
Chaudes-Aigues	74	44.51 N	3.00 E
Chau-phu	94	10.42 N	105.07 E
Chaumont	74	48.07 N	5.08 E
Chaumont-en-Vexin	74	49.16 N	1.53 E
Chauny	74	49.37 N	3.13 E
Chaussin	74	46.58 N	5.23 E
Chavanges	74	48.31 N	4.34 E
Chaves	76	41.44 N	7.28 W
Cheb	72	50.01 N	12.25 E
Chebanse	158	41.00 N	87.54 W
Cheboygan	154	45.38 N	84.28 W
Chech, Erg ⋆²	106	25.00 N	2.15 W
Cheddar	70	51.17 N	2.46 W
Cheduba Island I	94	18.48 N	93.38 E
Cheektowaga	152	42.55 N	78.46 W
Chef-Boutonne	74	46.07 N	0.04 W
Chehalis	166	46.39 N	122.58 W
Cheju	88	33.31 N	126.32 E
Cheju-do I	88	33.20 N	126.30 E
Chelan	166	47.50 N	120.01 W
Chelia, Djebel ⋀	106	35.19 N	6.20 E
Chełm	72	51.10 N	23.28 E
Chelmsford, Ont., Can.	154	46.35 N	81.12 W
Chelmsford, Eng., U.K.	70	51.44 N	0.28 E
Chełmża	72	53.12 N	18.37 E
Chelsea, Mich., U.S.	154	42.19 N	84.01 W
Chelsea, Okla., U.S.	160	36.32 N	95.26 W
Chelsea, Vt., U.S.	152	43.59 N	72.27 W
Cheltenham	70	51.54 N	2.04 W
Chemainus	148	48.55 N	123.43 W
Chemillé	74	47.13 N	0.44 W
Chemnitz → Karl-Marx-Stadt	72	50.50 N	12.55 E
Chemult	166	43.13 N	121.47 W
Chenab ≃	102	29.23 N	71.02 E
Chenachane	106	26.00 N	4.15 E
Chenango Bridge	152	42.10 N	75.53 W
Cheney	166	47.29 N	117.34 W
Chengde	88	40.58 N	117.53 E
Chengdu	88	30.39 N	104.04 E
Chengshanjiao ➤	88	37.23 N	122.39 E
Chengtu → Chengdu	88	30.39 N	104.04 E
Chenoa	154	40.45 N	88.43 W
Chepen	134	7.15 S	79.25 W
Chepes	140	31.21 S	66.40 W
Cher □⁵	74	47.05 N	2.30 E
Cher ≃	74	47.21 N	0.29 E
Cheraw	156	34.42 N	79.53 W
Cherbourg	74	49.39 N	1.39 W
Cheremchovo → Čeremchovo	84	53.09 N	103.05 E
Chergui, Chott ech ◉	106	34.21 N	0.30 E
Cheribon → Tjirebon	96	6.44 S	108.34 E
Cheriton	156	37.17 N	75.58 W
Cherkassy → Čerkassy	64	49.26 N	32.04 E
Chernigov → Černigov	64	51.30 N	31.18 E
Cherokee, Iowa, U.S.	162	42.45 N	95.33 W
Cherokee, Kans., U.S.	158	37.21 N	94.49 W
Cherokee, Okla., U.S.	160	36.45 N	98.21 W
Cherokee Plains ⋈	158	37.00 N	95.15 W
Cherrabun	122	18.29 S	125.19 E
Cherry Hill	152	39.55 N	75.01 W
Cherryvale	158	37.15 N	95.33 W
Cherryville	156	35.23 N	81.23 W
Cherson	64	46.38 N	32.35 E
Chesaning	154	43.11 N	84.07 W
Chesapeake	156	36.43 N	76.15 W
Chesapeake Bay C	144	38.40 N	76.25 W
Chesapeake City	152	39.32 N	75.49 W
Cheshire, Conn., U.S.	152	41.30 N	72.54 W
Cheshire □⁶	70	53.23 N	2.30 W
Chester, Eng., U.K.	70	53.12 N	2.54 W
Chester, Calif., U.S.	168	40.19 N	121.14 W
Chester, Ill., U.S.	158	37.55 N	89.49 W
Chester, Mont., U.S.	166	48.30 N	110.58 W
Chester, Okla., U.S.	160	36.13 N	98.55 W
Chester, Pa., U.S.	152	39.51 N	75.21 W
Chester, S.C., U.S.	156	34.43 N	81.12 W
Chester, Vt., U.S.	152	43.16 N	72.36 W
Chester, Va., U.S.	156	37.21 N	77.27 W
Chesterfield, Eng., U.K.	70	53.15 N	1.25 W
Chesterfield, S.C., U.S.	156	34.44 N	80.05 W
Chesterfield, Îles II	118	19.52 S	158.00 E
Chesterfield Inlet C	142	63.25 N	90.45 W
Chesterhill	152	39.29 N	81.52 W
Chester-le-Street	70	54.52 N	1.34 W
Chesterton	158	41.36 N	87.04 W
Chesterton Range ⋀	120	25.30 S	147.27 E
Chestertown	152	39.13 N	76.04 W
Cheta ≃	84	71.54 N	102.06 E
Chetopa	158	37.02 N	95.05 W
Chetumal Bay C	130	18.35 N	88.07 W
Cheviot	126	42.49 S	173.16 E
Cheviot Range ⋀	120	25.20 S	143.40 E
Chew Bahir (Lake Stefanie) ◉	108	4.40 N	36.50 E
Cheyenne	162	41.08 N	104.49 W
Cheyenne ≃	162	44.40 N	101.15 W
Cheyenne Wells	162	38.49 N	102.21 W
Cheyne Bay C	122	34.35 S	118.50 E
Chezhou	88	33.43 N	120.45 E
Chhāk Kâmpóng Saôm C	94	10.50 N	103.32 E
Chhindwāra	102	22.04 N	78.56 E
Chi ≃	94	15.13 N	104.45 E
Chiai	88	23.29 N	120.27 E
Chiamussu → Jiamusi	88	46.50 N	130.21 E
Chiang Mai	94	18.46 N	98.58 E
Chiang Rai	94	19.54 N	99.50 E
Chiapa de Corzo	130	16.42 N	93.00 W
Chiari	78	45.32 N	9.56 E
Chiasso	78	45.50 N	9.02 E
Chiavari	78	44.19 N	9.19 E
Chiavenna	78	46.19 N	9.24 E
Chibia	110	15.11 S	13.42 E
Chibougamau	150	49.55 N	74.22 W
Chibuto	116	24.44 S	33.33 E
Chicago	154	41.53 N	87.38 W
Chicago Heights	154	41.30 N	87.38 W
Chicapa ≃	110	6.26 S	20.47 E
Chichagof Island I	146	57.30 N	135.30 W
Chichester	70	50.50 N	0.48 W
Chickaloon	146	61.48 N	148.28 W
Chickamauga	156	34.52 N	85.17 W
Chickasaw	156	30.45 N	88.05 W
Chiclana de la Frontera	76	36.25 N	6.08 W
Chiclayo	134	6.46 S	79.50 W
Chico ≃, Arg.	136	49.56 S	68.32 W
Chico ≃, Arg.	136	43.48 S	66.25 W
Chicoana	140	25.06 S	65.32 W
Chicomo	116	24.31 S	34.18 E
Chicopee	152	42.10 N	72.36 W
Chicoutimi	150	48.26 N	71.04 W
Chidambaram	100	11.24 N	79.42 E
Chidley, Cape ➤	142	60.23 N	64.26 W
Chiefland	156	29.28 N	82.51 W
Chiemsee ◉	72	47.54 N	12.29 E
Chieri	78	45.01 N	7.49 E
Chiese ≃	78	45.08 N	10.25 E
Chieti	78	42.21 N	14.10 E
Chifeng	88	42.17 N	118.56 E
Chignecto Bay C	150	45.33 N	64.45 W
Chignik	146	56.18 N	158.24 W
Chignik Lake	146	56.20 N	158.46 W
Chihli, Gulf of → Bohai C	88	38.30 N	120.00 E
Chihuahua	130	28.38 N	106.05 W
Chikaskia ≃	160	36.36 N	97.18 W
Chilakalūrupet	100	16.05 N	80.10 E
Chilapa de Alvarez	130	17.36 N	99.10 W
Chilcotin ≃	148	51.44 N	122.23 W
Childers	120	25.14 S	152.17 E
Childersburg	156	33.17 N	86.21 W
Chile □¹	136	30.00 S	71.00 W
Chile Chico	136	46.33 S	71.44 W
Chilecito, Arg.	140	29.10 S	67.30 W
Chilecito, Arg.	140	29.06 S	67.34 W
Chilete	134	7.14 S	78.51 W
Chilia, Braţul ≃¹	80	45.18 N	29.40 E
Chililabombwe (Bancroft)	110	12.18 S	27.43 E
Chilka Lake ◉	100	19.46 N	85.20 E
Chillagoe	120	17.09 S	144.32 E
Chillán	140	36.36 S	72.07 W
Chillicothe, Ill., U.S.	154	40.55 N	89.29 W
Chillicothe, Mo., U.S.	158	39.48 N	93.33 W
Chillicothe, Ohio, U.S.	152	39.20 N	82.59 W
Chillicothe, Tex., U.S.	160	34.15 N	99.31 W

Symbols in the index entries are identified on page 203.

Name	Page	Lat °′	Long °′
Chilliwack	148	49.10 N	121.57 W
Chillon ⊥	74	46.25 N	6.56 E
Chiloé, Isla de I	136	42.30 S	73.55 W
Chilok	84	51.21 N	110.28 E
Chilok ≃	84	51.19 N	106.59 E
Chiloquin	166	42.35 N	121.52 W
Chilpancingo [de los Bravos]	130	17.33 N	99.30 W
Chilton	154	44.02 N	88.10 W
Chiluage	110	9.30 S	21.47 E
Chilung	88	25.08 N	121.44 E
Chilwa, Lake ⊜	110	15.12 S	35.50 E
Chimayo	164	36.00 N	105.56 W
Chimborazo ☐[4]	138	2.00 S	78.40 W
Chimborazo ∧[1]	138	1.28 S	78.48 W
Chimbote	134	9.05 S	78.36 W
Chimkent → Čimkent	82	42.18 N	69.36 E
Chimki	86	55.54 N	37.26 E
China ☐[1]	88	35.00 N	105.00 E
China Lake ⊜	168	35.46 N	117.39 W
Chinandega	132	12.37 N	87.09 W
Chincha, Islas de II	134	13.39 S	76.24 W
Chincha Alta	134	13.27 S	76.08 W
Chinchaga ≃	142	58.50 N	118.20 W
Chinchilla	120	26.45 S	150.38 E
Chinchiná	138	4.58 N	75.36 W
Chinchón	76	40.08 N	3.25 W
Chinchorro, Banco ≈[4]	130	18.35 N	87.20 W
Chinde	116	18.37 S	36.24 E
Chindwin ≃	94	21.26 N	95.15 E
Chingola	110	12.32 S	27.52 E
Chinguetti	114	20.27 N	12.22 W
Chinhae	88	35.09 N	128.40 E
Chin Hills ⋀[2]	94	22.30 N	93.30 E
Chiniot	102	31.43 N	72.59 E
Chinju	88	35.11 N	128.05 E
Chinkiang → Zhenjiang	88	32.13 N	119.26 E
Chinko ≃	112	4.50 N	23.53 E
Chinle	164	36.09 N	109.33 W
Chinle Creek ≃	164	37.12 N	109.43 W
Chino	168	34.01 N	117.42 W
Chinon	74	47.10 N	0.15 E
Chinook	166	48.35 N	109.14 W
Chino Valley	164	34.45 N	112.27 W
Chinsali	110	10.34 S	32.03 E
Chinú	138	9.06 N	75.24 W
Chioggia	78	45.13 N	12.17 E
Chios → Khíos	80	38.22 N	26.08 E
Chipata	110	13.39 S	32.40 E
Chipley	158	30.47 N	85.32 W
Chipman	150	46.11 N	65.53 W
Chippenham	70	51.28 N	2.07 W
Chippewa ≃	154	44.25 N	92.10 W
Chippewa Falls	154	44.56 N	91.24 W
Chipping Norton	70	51.56 N	1.32 W
Chiquimula	130	14.48 N	89.33 W
Chiquinquirá	138	5.37 N	73.50 W
Chira ≃	138	4.54 S	81.08 W
Chirfa	106	20.57 N	12.21 E
Chirgis Nuur ⊜	88	49.12 N	93.24 E
Chiricahua Peak ∧	164	31.52 N	109.20 W
Chirikof Island I	146	55.50 N	155.35 W
Chiriquí, Golfo de C	138	8.00 N	82.20 W
Chiriquí, Volcán de (Volcán Barú ∧[1]	138	8.48 N	82.33 W
Chiromo	110	16.33 S	35.08 E
Chirripó, Cerro ∧	132	9.29 N	83.29 W
Chisholm, Maine, U.S.	152	44.29 N	70.12 W
Chisholm, Minn., U.S.	154	47.29 N	92.53 W
Chislaviči	86	54.11 N	32.10 E
Chist'akovo → Torez	64	48.01 N	38.37 E
Chistochina	146	62.34 N	144.40 W
Chitado	116	17.20 S	13.54 E
Chitembo	110	13.34 S	16.40 E
Chitina	146	61.31 N	144.27 W
Chitipa	110	9.43 S	33.15 E
Chitorgarh	102	24.53 N	74.38 E
Chitradurga	100	14.14 N	76.24 E
Chitrāl	100	35.51 N	71.47 E
Chitré	138	7.58 N	80.26 W
Chittagong	102	22.20 N	91.50 E
Chittoor	100	13.14 N	79.07 E
Chiumbe ≃	110	7.00 S	21.12 E
Chiusi	78	43.01 N	11.57 E
Chiuta, Lake ⊜	110	14.55 S	35.50 E
Chiva	82	41.24 N	60.22 E
Chivacoa	138	10.10 N	68.54 W
Chivasso	78	45.11 N	7.53 E
Chivilcoy	140	34.52 S	60.02 W
Chixoy (Negro) ≃	130	16.05 N	90.26 W
Chkalov → Orenburg	64	51.54 N	55.06 E
Chloride	164	35.25 N	114.19 W
Chmel'nickij	64	49.25 N	27.00 E
Chŏâm Khsant	92	14.13 N	104.56 E
Chobe (Linyanti) ≃	116	17.50 S	25.05 E
Chochis, Cerro ∧	134	18.10 S	59.53 W
Chocó ☐[5]	138	6.00 N	77.00 W
Chocolate Mountains ⋀	164	33.25 N	114.10 W
Chocope	134	7.47 S	79.12 W
Chodecz	72	52.24 N	19.01 E
Chodžejli	100	42.48 N	59.25 E
Chodzież	72	52.59 N	16.56 E
Choele-Choel	140	39.15 S	65.30 W
Choiseul I	118	7.00 S	157.00 E
Chojnice	72	53.42 N	17.34 E
Chojnów	72	51.17 N	15.56 E
Cholet	74	47.04 N	0.53 W
Cholm	86	57.09 N	31.11 E
Cholmsk	84	47.03 N	142.03 E
Cholo	110	16.10 S	35.10 E
Choluj	86	56.34 N	41.53 E
Cholula [de Rivadabia]	130	19.04 N	98.18 W
Choluteca	132	13.18 N	87.12 W
Choluteca ≃	132	13.05 N	87.20 W
Choma	110	16.48 S	26.59 E
Chomo Lhāri ∧	102	27.50 N	89.15 E
Chomutov	72	50.28 N	13.26 E
Ch'ŏnan	88	36.48 N	127.09 E
Chon Buri	94	13.22 N	100.59 E
Chone	138	0.41 S	80.06 W
Ch'ŏngjin	88	41.47 N	129.50 E
Ch'ŏngju	88	36.39 N	127.31 E
Chongqing	88	29.39 N	106.34 E
Chongzuo	88	22.21 N	107.26 E
Chŏnju	88	35.49 N	127.08 E
Chonos, Archipiélago de los II	136	45.00 S	74.00 W
Chonuu	84	66.27 N	143.06 E
Cho Oyu ∧	102	28.06 N	86.39 E
Chop'or ≃	64	49.36 N	42.19 E
Chor ≃	84	47.48 N	134.43 E
Chorges	74	44.33 N	6.17 E
Chorlovo	86	55.20 N	38.49 E
Chorog	102	37.31 N	71.33 E
Ch'ŏrwŏn	88	38.16 N	127.12 E
Chosedachard	66	67.02 N	59.22 E
Chosen	156	26.42 N	80.41 W
Chōshi	90	35.44 N	140.50 E
Chos Malal	140	37.20 S	70.15 W
Choszczno	72	53.10 N	15.26 E
Choteau	166	47.49 N	112.11 W
Chouteau	160	36.11 N	95.21 W
Chovd	88	48.01 N	91.39 E
Chovd ≃	88	48.06 N	92.11 E
Chövsgöl Nuur ⊜	88	51.00 N	100.30 E
Chowchilla	168	37.07 N	120.16 W
Christanshåb	142	68.50 N	51.12 W
Christchurch, N.Z.	126	43.42 S	172.38 E
Christchurch, Eng., U.K.	70	50.44 N	1.45 W
Christian, Cape ≻	142	70.31 N	68.18 W
Christiansburg	156	37.08 N	80.24 W
Christiansfeld	68	55.21 N	9.29 E
Christiansted	132	17.45 N	64.42 W
Christie Bay C	142	62.32 N	111.10 W
Christina ≃	148	56.40 N	111.03 W
Christmas Creek	122	18.53 S	125.55 E
Christmas Island ☐[2]	92	10.30 S	105.40 E
Christopher	158	37.58 N	89.03 W
Chroma ≃	84	71.36 N	144.49 E
Chromtau	82	50.17 N	58.27 E
Chrudim	72	49.57 N	15.48 E
Chrzanów	72	50.09 N	19.24 E
Chu ≃	92	19.53 N	105.45 E
Chubbuck	166	42.55 N	112.28 W
Chubut ≃	136	43.20 S	65.05 W
Chugach Islands II	146	59.06 N	151.42 W
Chugach Mountains ⋀	146	61.00 N	145.00 W
Chugiak	146	61.25 N	149.30 W
Chugwater	164	41.46 N	104.49 W
Chukchi Sea ▼[2]	146	69.00 N	171.00 W
Chula Vista	168	32.39 N	117.05 W
Chulucanas	134	5.06 S	80.10 W
Chumbicha	140	28.50 S	66.18 W
Chumphon	94	10.32 N	99.13 E
Ch'unch'ŏn	88	37.52 N	127.43 E
Ch'ungju	88	36.58 N	127.58 E
Chungking → Chongqing	88	29.39 N	106.34 E
Chuŏr Phnum Krâvanh ⋀	94	12.00 N	103.15 E
Chuquicamata	140	22.19 S	68.56 W
Chur	74	46.51 N	9.32 E
Churchill	142	58.46 N	94.10 W
Churchill ≃, Can.	142	58.47 N	94.12 W
Churchill ≃, Newf., Can.	142	53.30 N	60.10 W
Churchill, Cape ≻	142	58.46 N	93.12 W
Churchill Falls ᒪ	142	53.35 N	64.27 W
Churchill Lake ⊜	142	55.55 N	108.20 W
Church Point	158	30.24 N	92.13 W
Church Rock	164	35.46 N	108.35 W
Churu	102	28.18 N	74.57 E
Chuska Mountains ⋀	164	36.15 N	108.50 W
Chutag	88	49.23 N	102.43 E
Chuxiong	88	25.02 N	101.30 E
Chužir	84	53.11 N	107.20 E
Chvojnaja	86	58.54 N	34.32 E
Chyrov	72	49.33 N	22.49 E
Cibecue	164	34.03 N	110.29 W
Cicero, Ill., U.S.	158	41.51 N	87.45 W
Cicero, Ind., U.S.	158	40.08 N	86.01 W
Ciechanów	72	52.53 N	20.38 E
Ciechocinek	72	52.52 N	18.49 E
Ciego de Avila	132	21.51 N	78.46 W
Ciénaga	138	11.01 N	74.15 W
Ciénaga de Oro	138	8.53 N	75.37 W
Cienfuegos	132	22.09 N	80.27 W
Cieszyn	72	49.45 N	18.38 E
Cieza	76	38.14 N	1.25 W
Čiganak	82	51.47 N	43.18 E
Cigüela ≃	76	39.08 N	3.44 W
Čiili	82	44.10 N	66.45 E
Čikoj ≃	84	51.02 N	106.39 E
Čilik	82	43.36 N	78.15 E
Cimarron, Kans., U.S.	162	37.48 N	100.21 W
Cimarron, N. Mex., U.S.	164	36.31 N	104.55 W
Cimarron ≃	160	36.10 N	96.17 W
Cimarron, North Fork ≃	162	37.25 N	101.13 W
Čimbaj	82	42.57 N	59.47 E
Čimkent	82	42.18 N	69.36 E
Ciml'anskoje Vodochranilišče ⊜[1]	64	48.00 N	43.00 E
Cîmpina	80	45.08 N	25.44 E
Cîmpulung	80	45.16 N	25.03 E
Cîmpulung Moldovenesc	80	47.31 N	25.34 E
Cincinnati, Iowa, U.S.	154	40.38 N	92.56 W
Cincinnati, Ohio, U.S.	152	39.06 N	84.31 W
Ciney	72	50.18 N	5.06 E
Cingoli	78	43.22 N	13.13 E
Cintalapa [de Figueroa]	130	16.44 N	93.43 W
Cinto, Monte ∧	78	42.23 N	8.56 E
Cipa ≃	84	55.23 N	115.55 E
Cipolletti	140	38.56 S	67.59 W
Čirčik	82	41.29 N	69.35 E
Circle	166	47.25 N	105.35 W
Circleville, Ohio, U.S.	152	39.36 N	82.57 W
Circleville, Utah, U.S.	164	38.10 N	112.16 W
Cirencester	70	51.44 N	1.59 W
Cirey-sur-Vezouze	74	48.35 N	6.57 E
Ciriè	78	45.14 N	7.36 E
Čirpan	80	42.12 N	25.20 E
Cisco	160	32.23 N	98.59 W
Cissna Park	154	40.34 N	87.54 W
Čistoje	86	56.32 N	43.02 E
Čistopol'	66	55.21 N	50.37 E
Čita	84	52.03 N	113.30 E
Citlaltépetl, Volcán ∧[1]	130	19.01 N	97.16 W
Citrus Heights	168	38.42 N	121.17 W
Cittadella	78	45.39 N	11.47 E
Città di Castello	78	43.27 N	12.14 E
Cittanova	78	38.21 N	16.05 E
City View	156	34.51 N	82.26 W
Ciudad Acuña	130	29.18 N	100.55 W
Ciudad Allende	130	28.20 N	100.51 W
Ciudad Altamirano	130	18.20 N	100.40 W
Ciudad Anáhuac	130	27.14 N	100.09 W
Ciudad Bolívar	138	8.08 N	63.33 W
Ciudad Camargo, Méx.	130	27.40 N	105.10 W
Ciudad Camargo, Méx.	130	26.19 N	98.50 W
Ciudad Chetumal	130	18.30 N	88.18 W
Ciudad de Guayana → Ciudad Guayana	138	8.22 N	62.40 W
Ciudad del Carmen	130	18.38 N	91.50 W
Ciudad de México (Mexico City)	130	19.24 N	99.09 W
Ciudad de Valles	130	21.59 N	99.01 W
Ciudad de Villaldama	130	26.30 N	100.26 W
Ciudadela	76	40.02 N	3.50 E
Ciudad Guayana	138	8.22 N	62.40 W
Ciudad Guerrero	130	28.33 N	107.30 W
Ciudad Guzmán	130	19.41 N	103.29 W
Ciudad Hidalgo	130	19.41 N	100.34 W
Ciudad Ixtepec	130	16.34 N	95.06 W
Ciudad Jiménez	130	27.08 N	104.55 W
Ciudad Juárez	130	31.44 N	106.29 W
Ciudad Lerdo	160	25.32 N	103.32 W
Ciudad Madero	130	22.16 N	97.50 W
Ciudad Mante	130	22.44 N	98.57 W
Ciudad Melchor Múzquiz	130	27.53 N	101.31 W
Ciudad Miguel Alemán	130	26.23 N	99.01 W
Ciudad Obregón	130	27.29 N	109.56 W
Ciudad Ojeda (Lagunillas)	138	10.12 N	71.19 W
Ciudad Real	76	38.59 N	3.56 W
Ciudad Rodrigo	76	40.36 N	6.32 W
Ciudad Trujillo → Santo Domingo	132	18.28 N	69.54 W
Ciudad Victoria	130	23.44 N	99.08 W
Civil'sk	66	55.53 N	47.29 E
Civitanova Marche	78	43.18 N	13.44 E
Civitavecchia	78	42.06 N	11.48 E
Civray	74	46.09 N	0.18 E
Clacton-on-Sea	70	51.48 N	1.09 E
Claire, Lake ⊜	142	58.30 N	112.00 W
Clairton	152	40.18 N	79.53 W
Clairvaux-les-Lacs	74	46.34 N	5.45 E
Clamecy	74	47.27 N	3.31 E
Clanton	158	32.50 N	86.38 W
Clanwilliam	116	32.11 S	18.54 E
Claonaig	70	55.46 N	5.22 W
Clara	70	53.20 N	7.36 W
Clara ≃	120	18.30 S	141.18 E
Clara City	162	44.57 N	95.22 W
Claraville	120	18.40 S	141.43 E
Clare, Austl.	120	33.50 S	138.36 E
Clare, Mich., U.S.	154	43.49 N	84.46 W
Clare ☐[6]	70	52.50 N	9.00 W
Claremont, Calif., U.S.	168	34.06 N	117.43 W
Claremont, N.H., U.S.	152	43.23 N	72.20 W
Claremore	160	36.19 N	95.36 W
Claremorris	70	53.44 N	9.00 W
Clarence, Iowa, U.S.	154	41.53 N	91.04 W
Clarence, Mo., U.S.	158	39.44 N	92.16 W
Clarence ≃	120	29.25 S	153.22 E
Clarence Strait ⋓	124	12.00 S	131.00 E
Clarendon	158	34.42 N	91.18 W
Clarenville	150	48.10 N	53.58 W
Claresholm	148	50.02 N	113.35 W
Clarinda	162	40.44 N	95.02 W
Clarion, Iowa, U.S.	154	42.44 N	93.44 W
Clarion, Pa., U.S.	152	41.13 N	79.24 W
Clark, Lake ⊜	146	60.15 N	154.15 W
Clarkdale	164	34.46 N	112.03 W
Clarke ≃	120	19.12 S	145.30 E
Clarke Island I	120	40.33 S	148.10 E
Clarke Range ⋀	120	20.50 S	148.33 E
Clarkfield	162	44.48 N	95.48 W
Clark Fork	148	48.08 N	116.11 W
Clark Fork ≃	166	48.09 N	116.15 W
Clark Hill Reservoir ⊜[1]	156	33.50 N	82.20 W
Clarksburg	152	39.17 N	80.21 W
Clarksdale	158	34.12 N	90.34 W
Clarks Hill	158	40.15 N	86.43 W
Clarks Point	146	58.51 N	158.30 W
Clarks Summit	152	41.30 N	75.42 W
Clarksville, Ark., U.S.	158	35.28 N	93.28 W
Clarksville, Ga., U.S.	156	34.37 N	83.31 W
Clarksville, Ind., U.S.	158	38.17 N	85.45 W
Clarksville, Tenn., U.S.	158	36.32 N	87.21 W
Clarksville, Tex., U.S.	160	33.37 N	95.03 W
Clarkton	158	36.27 N	89.58 W
Claro ≃	134	19.08 S	50.40 W
Clatskanie	166	46.06 N	123.12 W
Claude	160	35.07 N	101.22 W
Clausthal-Zellerfeld	72	51.48 N	10.20 E
Claxton	156	32.10 N	81.55 W
Clay	158	37.29 N	87.49 W
Clay Center	162	39.23 N	97.08 W
Clay City	158	38.41 N	88.21 W
Claymont	152	39.48 N	75.28 W
Claypool	164	33.25 N	110.51 W
Clayton, Ala., U.S.	158	31.53 N	85.27 W
Clayton, Del., U.S.	152	39.17 N	75.38 W
Clayton, Ga., U.S.	156	34.53 N	83.23 W
Clayton, Mo., U.S.	158	38.39 N	90.20 W
Clayton, N. Mex., U.S.	160	36.27 N	103.11 W
Clayton, N.C., U.S.	156	35.39 N	78.28 W
Clayton, N.Y., U.S.	152	44.14 N	76.05 W
Clayton, Okla., U.S.	160	34.35 N	95.21 W
Clayton ≃	120	29.06 S	138.05 E
Clearbrook	162	47.42 N	95.26 W
Clearfield, Pa., U.S.	152	41.02 N	78.27 W
Clearfield, Utah, U.S.	166	41.07 N	112.01 W
Clear Lake	154	43.08 N	93.23 W
Clearlake Highlands	168	38.57 N	122.38 W
Clearquilla Creek ≃	160	36.36 N	102.52 W
Clearwater, Fla., U.S.	156	27.58 N	82.48 W
Clearwater, Kans., U.S.	162	37.30 N	97.30 W
Clearwater ≃	142	56.44 N	111.25 W
Clearwater Mountains ⋀	166	46.00 N	115.30 W
Clebit	160	34.21 N	94.52 W
Cleburne	160	32.21 N	97.23 W
Cleethorpes	70	53.34 N	0.02 W
Clefmont	74	48.06 N	5.31 E
Clelles	74	44.50 N	5.37 E
Clemson	156	34.41 N	82.50 W
Clerke Rocks II[1]	136	55.01 S	34.41 W
Clermont, Austl.	120	22.49 S	147.39 E
Clermont, Qué., Can.	150	47.41 N	70.14 W
Clermont, Fr.	74	49.23 N	2.24 E
Clermont, Fla., U.S.	156	28.33 N	81.46 W
Clermont-en-Argonne	74	49.06 N	5.04 E
Clermont-Ferrand	74	45.47 N	3.05 E
Cles	78	46.22 N	11.02 E
Cleveland, Miss., U.S.	158	33.45 N	90.50 W
Cleveland, Ohio, U.S.	152	41.30 N	81.41 W
Cleveland, Okla., U.S.	160	36.19 N	96.28 W
Cleveland, Tenn., U.S.	158	35.10 N	84.53 W
Cleveland, Tex., U.S.	160	30.21 N	95.05 W
Cleveland, Cape ≻	120	19.11 S	147.01 E
Cleveland, Mount ∧	120	41.25 S	145.23 E
Cleveland Heights	152	41.30 N	81.34 W
Clewiston	156	26.45 N	80.56 W
Clifden	70	53.29 N	10.01 W
Cliffdale Creek ≃	120	16.56 S	138.48 E
Clifton, Ariz., U.S.	164	33.03 N	109.18 W
Clifton, Tex., U.S.	160	31.47 N	97.35 W
Clifton Forge	156	37.49 N	79.49 W
Climax, Colo., U.S.	164	39.22 N	106.11 W
Climax, Mich., U.S.	154	42.14 N	85.20 W
Clinch ≃	156	35.53 N	84.29 W
Clinchco	156	37.10 N	82.22 W
Clingmans Dome ∧	156	35.35 N	83.30 W
Clint	164	31.35 N	106.14 W
Clinton, B.C., Can.	148	51.05 N	121.35 W
Clinton, Ont., Can.	154	43.37 N	81.32 W
Clinton, Conn., U.S.	152	41.17 N	72.32 W
Clinton, Ill., U.S.	158	40.09 N	88.57 W
Clinton, Ind., U.S.	158	39.40 N	87.24 W
Clinton, Iowa, U.S.	154	41.51 N	90.12 W
Clinton, Ky., U.S.	158	36.40 N	89.02 W
Clinton, La., U.S.	158	30.52 N	91.01 W
Clinton, Mass., U.S.	152	42.25 N	71.41 W
Clinton, Mich., U.S.	154	42.04 N	83.58 W
Clinton, Miss., U.S.	158	32.20 N	90.20 W
Clinton, Mo., U.S.	158	38.22 N	93.46 W
Clinton, N.C., U.S.	156	35.00 N	78.20 W
Clinton, Okla., U.S.	160	35.31 N	98.59 W
Clinton, S.C., U.S.	156	34.29 N	81.53 W
Clinton, Tenn., U.S.	156	36.06 N	84.08 W
Clinton, Wis., U.S.	154	42.34 N	88.52 W
Clinton, Cape ≻	120	22.32 S	150.47 E
Clinton-Colden Lake ⊜	142	63.58 N	107.27 W
Clintonville	154	44.37 N	88.46 W
Clintwood	156	37.09 N	82.27 W
Clio, Ala., U.S.	158	31.43 N	85.36 W
Clio, Mich., U.S.	154	43.11 N	83.44 W
Clipperton I[1]	128	10.17 N	109.13 W
Clisson	74	47.05 N	1.17 W
Cloates, Point ≻	122	22.43 S	113.40 E
Clodomira	140	27.35 S	64.10 W
Clonakilty	70	51.37 N	8.54 W
Cloncurry	120	20.42 S	140.30 E
Cloncurry ≃	120	18.37 S	140.40 E
Clondalkin	70	53.19 N	6.24 W
Clonmel	70	52.21 N	7.42 W
Cloppenburg	72	52.50 N	8.02 E
Cloquet	154	46.43 N	92.28 W
Clorinda	140	25.20 S	57.40 W
Cloudcroft	164	32.58 N	105.45 W
Cloud Peak ∧	166	44.25 N	107.10 W
Clover	156	35.07 N	81.14 W
Cloverdale, Ala., U.S.	158	34.56 N	87.46 W
Cloverdale, Calif., U.S.	168	38.48 N	123.01 W
Clover Pass	146	55.28 N	131.47 W
Cloverport	158	37.50 N	86.38 W
Clovis, Calif., U.S.	168	36.49 N	119.42 W
Clovis, N. Mex., U.S.	160	34.24 N	103.12 W
Cluj	80	46.47 N	23.36 E
Cluj ☐[4]	80	46.45 N	23.45 E
Clunes	120	37.18 S	143.47 E
Cluny	74	46.26 N	4.39 E
Cluses	74	46.04 N	6.36 E
Clusone	78	45.53 N	9.57 E
Clute, Tex., U.S.	158	29.01 N	95.24 W
Clute, Tex., U.S.	160	29.01 N	95.24 W
Clutha ≃	126	46.20 S	169.49 E
Clwyd ☐[6]	70	53.05 N	3.20 W
Clyde, N.W. Ter., Can.	142	70.25 N	68.30 W
Clyde, Kans., U.S.	162	39.36 N	97.24 W
Clyde, N.Y., U.S.	152	43.05 N	76.52 W
Clyde, Ohio, U.S.	152	41.18 N	82.59 W
Clyde, Tex., U.S.	160	32.24 N	99.30 W
Clyde Park	166	45.53 N	110.36 W
Clymer	152	40.40 N	79.01 W
Coachella	168	33.41 N	116.10 W
Coahoma	160	32.18 N	101.18 W
Coal ≃	146	59.39 N	126.57 W
Coal City	154	41.17 N	88.17 W
Coalcomán de Matamoros	130	18.47 N	103.09 W
Coaldale	148	49.43 N	112.37 W
Coal Fire Creek ≃	158	33.15 N	88.18 W
Coalgate	160	34.32 N	96.13 W
Coal Grove	152	38.30 N	82.39 W
Coalinga	168	36.09 N	120.21 W
Coalport	152	40.45 N	78.32 W
Coalville	166	40.55 N	111.24 W
Coamo	132	18.05 N	66.22 W
Coari	138	4.05 S	63.08 W
Coari ≃	138	4.30 S	63.33 W
Coast Mountains ⋀	142	55.00 N	129.00 W
Coast Ranges ⋀	144	41.00 N	123.30 W
Coatbridge	70	55.52 N	4.01 W
Coatesville	152	39.59 N	75.49 W
Coaticook	152	45.08 N	71.48 W
Coats Island I	142	62.30 N	83.00 W
Coatzacoalcos	130	18.09 N	94.25 W
Cobalt	154	47.24 N	79.41 W
Cobán	128	15.29 N	90.19 W
Cobar	120	31.30 S	145.49 E
Cobberas, Mount ∧	120	36.52 S	148.10 E
Cobden	158	37.32 N	89.15 W
Cobh	70	51.51 N	8.17 W
Cobham ≃	142	53.15 N	93.58 W
Cobija	134	11.02 S	68.44 W
Cobleskill	152	42.41 N	74.29 W
Cobourg	154	43.58 N	78.10 W
Cobourg Peninsula ≻[1]	124	11.20 S	132.15 E
Cobram	120	35.55 S	145.39 E
Cóbuè	110	12.04 S	34.50 E
Coburg	72	50.15 N	10.58 E
Coburg Island I	142	76.00 N	79.25 W
Cocentaina	76	38.45 N	0.26 W
Cochabamba	134	17.24 S	66.09 W
Cochem	72	50.11 N	7.09 E
Cochin	100	9.58 N	76.15 E
Cochran	156	32.23 N	83.21 W
Cochrane	142	49.04 N	81.01 W
Cochrane ≃	142	57.52 N	101.38 W
Cochrane, Lago (Lago Puyerredón ⊜	136	47.20 S	72.00 W
Cochranton	152	41.31 N	80.03 W
Cockburn, Mount ∧	122	22.46 S	130.36 E
Cockermouth	70	54.40 N	3.21 W
Coco ≃	132	15.00 N	83.08 W
Coco, Isla del I	128	5.32 N	87.04 W
Cocoa	156	28.21 N	80.44 W
Cocoa Beach	156	28.19 N	80.36 W
Coco Channel ⋓	94	13.45 N	93.00 E
Coco Islands II	94	14.05 N	93.18 E
Cocula	130	20.23 N	103.50 W
Cod, Cape ≻	152	41.42 N	70.15 W
Codajás	138	3.50 S	62.05 W
Cod Island I	142	57.45 N	61.50 W
Codó	134	4.29 S	43.53 W
Codogno	78	45.09 N	9.42 E
Cody	166	44.32 N	109.03 W
Coeburn	156	36.57 N	82.28 W
Coen	124	13.56 S	143.12 E
Coetivy Island I	110	7.08 S	56.16 E
Coeur d'Alene	166	47.41 N	116.46 W
Coeur d'Alene ≃	166	47.45 N	116.00 W
Coffeeville	158	33.59 N	89.40 W
Coffeyville	162	37.02 N	95.37 W
Coffin Bay C	122	34.27 S	135.19 E
Coffin Bay Peninsula ≻[1]	122	34.32 S	135.15 E
Coffs Harbour	120	30.18 S	153.08 E
Cognac	64	45.42 N	0.20 W
Cogolin	74	43.15 N	6.32 E
Cohoe	146	60.23 N	151.18 W
Cohoes	152	42.46 N	73.42 W
Cohuna	120	35.49 S	144.13 E
Coiba, Isla de I	138	7.23 N	81.48 W
Coig (Coyle) ≃	136	51.00 S	69.10 W
Coimbatore	100	11.00 N	76.57 E
Coimbra	76	40.12 N	8.25 W
Coin	76	36.40 N	4.45 W
Coipasa, Salar de ≚	134	19.26 S	68.09 W
Čojbalsan	88	48.34 N	114.50 E
Cojedes ☐[3]	138	9.20 N	68.20 W
Cokato	154	45.05 N	94.11 W
Cokeville	166	42.05 N	110.57 W
Čokurdach	84	70.38 N	147.55 E
Colac	120	38.20 S	143.35 E
Colares	76	38.48 N	9.27 W
Colatina	134	19.32 S	40.37 W
Colbert	160	33.51 N	96.30 W
Colborne	154	44.00 N	77.53 W
Colby	162	39.24 N	101.03 W
Colchagua ☐[4]	140	34.30 S	71.15 W
Colchester, Eng., U.K.	70	51.54 N	0.54 E
Colchester, Conn., U.S.	152	41.34 N	72.20 W
Colchester, Ill., U.S.	154	40.25 N	90.48 W
Cold Bay	146	55.11 N	162.30 W
Cold Spring, Minn., U.S.	154	45.27 N	94.26 W
Cold Spring, N.Y., U.S.	152	41.25 N	73.57 W
Coldstream	70	55.39 N	2.15 W
Coldwater, Kans., U.S.	162	37.16 N	99.19 W
Coldwater, Mich., U.S.	154	41.57 N	84.60 W
Coldwater, Miss., U.S.	158	34.41 N	89.59 W
Coldwater, Ohio, U.S.	152	40.29 N	84.38 W
Colebrook	152	44.54 N	71.30 W
Cole Camp	158	38.28 N	93.12 W
Coleman, Fla., U.S.	156	28.48 N	82.04 W
Coleman, Mich., U.S.	154	43.46 N	84.35 W
Coleman, Tex., U.S.	160	31.50 N	99.26 W
Coleman ≃	124	15.06 S	141.38 E
Coleraine, Austl.	120	37.36 S	141.42 E
Coleraine, N. Ire., U.K.	70	55.08 N	6.40 W
Coleraine, Minn., U.S.	154	47.17 N	93.27 W
Coleridge	162	42.30 N	97.13 W
Colesberg	116	30.45 S	25.05 E
Coleto Creek ≃	160	28.41 N	97.01 W
Colfax, Calif., U.S.	168	39.06 N	120.57 W
Colfax, Ill., U.S.	154	40.34 N	88.37 W
Colfax, Iowa, U.S.	154	41.41 N	93.14 W
Colfax, La., U.S.	158	31.31 N	92.42 W
Colfax, Wash., U.S.	166	46.53 N	117.22 W
Colfax, Wis., U.S.	154	45.00 N	91.44 W
Colhué Huapi, Lago ⊜	136	45.30 S	68.48 W
Colico	78	46.08 N	9.22 E
Colima	130	19.14 N	103.43 W
Colinas	134	14.12 S	48.03 W
Coll I	70	56.40 N	6.35 W
Collarenebri	120	29.33 S	148.35 E
College	146	64.51 N	147.47 W
Collegedale	158	35.04 N	85.03 W
College Heights	158	33.35 N	91.49 W
College Park	156	33.39 N	84.27 W
College Place	166	46.03 N	118.23 W
College Station	160	30.37 N	96.21 W
Collegeville, Ind., U.S.	158	40.56 N	87.09 W
Collegeville, Minn., U.S.	154	45.36 N	94.22 W
Collerina	120	29.41 S	146.38 E
Colleyville	160	32.53 N	97.09 W
Collie	122	33.21 S	116.09 E
Collier Bay C	118	16.10 S	124.15 E
Collier Range ⋀	122	24.43 S	119.12 E
Collierville	158	35.03 N	89.40 W
Collingwood	154	44.29 N	80.13 W
Collins	158	31.39 N	89.33 W
Collins Bay	154	44.15 N	76.36 W
Collinsville, Austl.	120	20.34 S	147.51 E
Collinsville, Okla., U.S.	160	36.22 N	95.51 W
Collinwood	158	35.10 N	87.44 W
Collipulli	140	37.57 S	72.26 W
Collooney	70	54.11 N	8.29 W
Colman	162	43.59 N	96.49 W
Colmar	74	48.05 N	7.22 E
Colmars	74	41.11 N	6.38 E
Colnett, Cabo ≻	130	31.00 N	116.20 W
Colo ≃	120	33.26 S	150.53 E
Cologne → Köln	72	50.56 N	6.59 E
Coloma	154	42.11 N	86.19 W
Colomb-Béchar → Béchar	106	31.37 N	2.13 W
Colombey-les-Belles	74	48.32 N	5.54 E
Colombia ☐[1]	134	4.00 N	72.00 W
Colombo	100	6.56 N	79.51 E
Colón, Arg.	140	32.15 S	58.10 W
Colón, Arg.	140	33.55 S	61.05 W
Colón, Cuba	132	22.43 N	80.54 W
Colón, Pan.	138	9.22 N	79.54 W
Colon, Mich., U.S.	154	41.57 N	85.19 W
Colón, Archipiélago de → Galapagos Islands II	138a	0.30 S	90.30 W
Colonia Anáhuac	130	28.25 N	106.40 W
Colonia del Sacramento	140	34.28 S	57.51 W
Colonia Dora	140	28.40 S	63.00 W
Colonia Las Heras	136	46.33 S	68.57 W
Colonial Heights	156	37.15 N	77.25 W
Colorado ☐[3]	144	39.30 N	105.30 W
Colorado ≃, Arg.	140	39.50 S	62.08 W
Colorado ≃, N.A.	144	31.45 N	114.40 W
Colorado City, Ariz., U.S.	164	36.58 N	112.58 W
Colorado City, Tex., U.S.	160	32.24 N	100.52 W
Colorado Desert ⊸[2]	168	33.15 N	115.15 W
Colorado Plateau ⋀[1]	164	36.30 N	108.00 W
Colorado Springs	164	38.50 N	104.49 W
Colotlán	130	22.06 N	103.16 W
Colquechaca	134	18.40 S	66.01 W
Colquitt	156	31.10 N	84.44 W
Colton, Austl.	122	33.29 S	134.56 E
Colton, Calif., U.S.	168	34.04 N	117.20 W
Colton, S. Dak., U.S.	162	43.47 N	96.56 W
Columbia, Ill., U.S.	158	38.27 N	90.12 W
Columbia, Ky., U.S.	158	37.06 N	85.18 W
Columbia, La., U.S.	158	32.06 N	92.05 W
Columbia, Miss., U.S.	158	31.15 N	89.56 W
Columbia, Mo., U.S.	158	38.57 N	92.20 W
Columbia, Pa., U.S.	152	40.02 N	76.30 W
Columbia, S.C., U.S.	156	34.00 N	81.03 W
Columbia, Tenn., U.S.	158	35.37 N	87.02 W
Columbia ≃	142	46.15 N	124.05 W
Columbia, Mount ∧	148	52.09 N	117.25 W
Columbia City	158	41.10 N	85.29 W
Columbia Falls	166	48.23 N	114.11 W
Columbiana, Ala., U.S.	158	33.11 N	86.36 W
Columbiana, Ohio, U.S.	152	40.53 N	80.42 W
Columbia Plateau ⋀[1]	166	44.00 N	117.30 W
Columbus, Ga., U.S.	156	32.29 N	84.59 W
Columbus, Ind., U.S.	158	39.13 N	85.55 W
Columbus, Kans., U.S.	162	37.10 N	94.50 W
Columbus, Miss., U.S.	158	33.30 N	88.25 W
Columbus, Mont., U.S.	166	45.38 N	109.15 W
Columbus, Nebr., U.S.	162	41.25 N	97.22 W
Columbus, N. Mex., U.S.	164	31.50 N	107.38 W
Columbus, N. Dak., U.S.	162	48.54 N	102.47 W
Columbus, Ohio, U.S.	152	39.57 N	83.00 W
Columbus, Tex., U.S.	160	29.42 N	96.33 W
Columbus, Wis., U.S.	154	43.21 N	89.01 W
Columbus Grove	152	40.55 N	84.04 W
Columbus Junction	154	41.17 N	91.22 W
Colusa	168	39.13 N	122.01 W
Colville	148	48.33 N	117.54 W
Colville Lake ⊜	146	67.10 N	126.00 W
Colwyn Bay	70	53.18 N	3.43 W
Comacchio	78	44.42 N	12.11 E
Comalcalco	130	18.16 N	93.13 W
Comanche, Okla., U.S.	160	34.22 N	97.58 W
Comanche, Tex., U.S.	160	31.54 N	98.36 W
Comandante Fontana	140	25.20 S	59.41 W
Comayagua	130	14.25 N	87.37 W
Combarbalá	140	31.11 S	71.02 W
Combeaufontaine	74	47.43 N	5.53 E
Combourg	74	48.25 N	1.45 W
Comboyne	120	31.36 S	152.29 E
Combronde	74	45.59 N	3.05 E
Comfort	160	29.58 N	98.49 W
Comfort, Cape ≻	142	65.08 N	83.21 W
Comilla	102	23.28 N	91.10 E
Comiso	78	36.56 N	14.37 E
Comitán [de Domínguez]	130	16.15 N	92.08 W
Commentry	74	46.17 N	2.44 E
Commerce, Ga., U.S.	156	34.12 N	83.28 W
Commerce, Okla., U.S.	160	36.56 N	94.53 W
Commerce, Tex., U.S.	160	33.15 N	95.54 W
Commerce City	164	39.49 N	104.55 W
Commercy	74	48.45 N	5.35 E
Comminges ⊸[1]	74	43.15 N	0.45 E
Committee Bay C	142	68.30 N	86.30 W
Commoron Creek ≃	120	28.22 S	150.08 E
Como, It.	78	45.47 N	9.05 E
Como, Miss., U.S.	158	34.31 N	90.03 W
Comodoro Rivadavia	136	45.50 S	67.30 W
Comorin, Cape ≻	100	8.06 N	77.33 E
Comoro Islands ☐[1]	110	12.10 S	44.15 E
Comox	148	49.40 N	124.55 W
Compiègne	74	49.25 N	2.50 E
Compostela	130	21.15 N	104.53 W
Comprida, Ilha I	140	24.50 S	47.42 W
Compton	168	33.54 N	118.13 W
Comstock	160	29.41 N	101.11 W
Comstock Park	154	43.02 N	85.40 W
Čona ≃	84	62.54 N	111.06 E
Conakry	114	9.31 N	13.43 W
Conasauga ≃	156	34.33 N	84.55 W
Concarneau	74	47.52 N	3.55 W
Conceição do Araguaia	134	8.15 S	49.17 W
Concepción, Arg.	140	27.20 S	65.36 W
Concepción, Bol.	134	16.15 S	62.04 W
Concepción, Chile	140	36.50 S	73.03 W
Concepción, Pan.	138	8.31 N	82.38 W
Concepción, Para.	140	23.25 S	57.17 W
Concepción ☐[4]	140	37.00 S	72.30 W
Concepción ☐[5]	140	23.00 S	57.00 W
Concepción, Laguna ⊜	134	17.29 S	61.25 W
Concepcion del Oro	130	24.38 N	101.25 W
Concepción del Uruguay	140	32.30 S	58.14 W
Conception Bay C, Newf., Can.	150	47.45 N	53.00 W
Conception Bay C, S.W. Afr.	116	23.53 S	14.28 E
Conchas Dam	160	35.22 N	104.11 W
Conches, Fr.	74	48.58 N	0.56 E
Conches, Fr.	74	48.51 N	2.43 E
Conchos ≃	130	29.32 N	104.25 W
Conconully	148	48.34 N	119.45 W
Concord, Calif., U.S.	168	37.59 N	122.02 W
Concord, Mich., U.S.	154	42.10 N	84.38 W
Concord, N.H., U.S.	152	43.12 N	71.32 W
Concord, N.C., U.S.	156	35.25 N	80.35 W
Concordia, Arg.	140	31.24 S	58.02 W
Concórdia, Bra.	138	4.35 S	66.35 W
Concordia, Kans., U.S.	162	39.34 N	97.39 W
Concordia, Mo., U.S.	158	38.59 N	93.34 W
Condat-en-Féniers	74	45.21 N	2.46 E
Condé, Fr.	74	48.51 N	0.33 W
Conde, S. Dak., U.S.	162	45.09 N	98.06 W
Condobolin	120	33.05 S	147.09 E
Condom	74	43.58 N	0.22 E
Condon	166	45.14 N	120.11 W
Condoto	138	5.06 N	76.37 W
Condroz ☐[9]	74	50.25 N	5.00 E
Conecuh ≃	158	30.58 N	87.14 W
Conegliano	78	45.53 N	12.18 E
Confluence	152	39.49 N	79.21 W
Confolens	74	46.01 N	0.41 E
Confuso ≃	140	25.09 S	57.34 W
Congleton	70	53.10 N	2.13 W
Congo ☐[1]	110	1.00 S	15.00 E
Congo (Zaire) (Zaïre) ≃	110	6.04 S	12.24 E
Conjeeveram → Kānchipuram	100	12.50 N	79.43 E
Conjuror Bay C	142	65.45 N	118.07 W
Connaught ☐[9]	70	53.45 N	9.00 W
Conneaut	152	41.57 N	80.34 W
Conneautville	152	41.36 N	80.18 W
Connecticut ☐[3]	152	41.45 N	72.45 W
Connecticut ≃	152	41.17 N	72.21 W
Connell	166	46.40 N	118.52 W
Connellsville	152	40.01 N	79.35 W
Connersville	158	39.39 N	85.08 W
Conn Lake ⊜	142	70.34 N	73.30 W
Connors Range ⋀	120	21.40 S	149.10 E
Conover	156	35.42 N	81.12 W
Conrad, Iowa, U.S.	154	42.14 N	92.52 W
Conrad, Mont., U.S.	166	48.10 N	111.57 W
Conroe	160	30.19 N	95.27 W
Conselheiro Lafaiete	134	20.40 S	43.48 W
Consett	70	54.51 N	1.49 W
Con Son II	94	8.43 N	106.36 E
Constance, Lake → Bodensee ⊜	74	47.35 N	9.25 E
Constanța	80	44.11 N	28.39 E
Constanța ☐[4]	80	44.20 N	28.20 E
Constantina	76	37.52 N	5.37 W
Constantine, Alg.	106	36.22 N	6.37 E
Constantine, Mich., U.S.	154	41.50 N	85.40 W
Constantinople → İstanbul	80	41.01 N	28.58 E
Constânzia	76	39.28 N	8.20 W
Constitución	140	35.20 S	72.25 W
Consuegra	76	39.28 N	3.36 W
Contes	74	43.49 N	7.19 E
Continental	152	41.06 N	84.16 W
Contres	74	47.25 N	1.26 E
Contwoyto Lake ⊜	142	65.42 N	110.50 W
Conty	74	49.44 N	2.09 E
Conversano	78	40.58 N	17.08 E
Converse	158	40.35 N	85.52 W
Convoy	152	40.55 N	84.42 W
Conway, Wales, U.K.	70	53.17 N	3.50 W
Conway, Ark., U.S.	158	35.05 N	92.26 W
Conway, N.H., U.S.	152	43.59 N	71.07 W
Conway, S.C., U.S.	156	33.50 N	79.03 W
Conway, Mount ∧	122	23.45 S	133.25 E
Conway Springs	162	37.24 N	97.39 W
Conyers	156	33.40 N	84.01 W
Cooa ≃	158	32.30 N	86.16 W
Coober Pedy	122	29.01 S	134.43 E
Cooch Behār	102	26.19 N	89.26 E
Coogoon ≃	120	27.19 S	148.50 E
Cook	122	30.37 S	130.25 E
Cook, Cape ≻	148	50.08 N	127.55 W
Cook, Mount ∧	126	43.36 S	170.08 E
Cooke, Mount ∧	122	32.25 S	116.18 E
Cookeville	158	36.10 N	85.31 W
Cook Inlet C	146	60.30 N	152.00 W
Cookstown	70	54.39 N	6.45 W
Cook Strait ⋓	126	41.14 S	174.30 E
Cooktown	124	15.28 S	145.15 E
Coolah	120	31.50 S	149.42 E
Coolamon	120	34.49 S	147.12 E
Coolangatta	120	28.10 S	153.32 E
Coolawanyah	122	21.47 S	117.48 E
Cooleemee	156	35.49 N	80.33 W
Coolgardie	122	30.57 S	121.10 E
Coolidge, Ariz., U.S.	164	32.59 N	111.31 W
Coolidge, Tex., U.S.	160	31.45 N	96.39 W
Coolidge, Mount ∧	162	43.44 N	103.29 W
Cooma	120	36.14 S	149.08 E
Coonabarabran	120	31.16 S	149.17 E
Coonamble	120	30.57 S	148.23 E
Coongoola	120	27.39 S	145.54 E
Coonoor	100	11.21 N	76.49 E
Coon Rapids	154	45.09 N	93.18 W
Coon Valley	154	43.42 N	91.01 W
Cooper	160	33.23 N	95.35 W
Cooper, Mount ∧	122	26.11 S	127.56 E
Cooper Landing	146	61.57 N	145.18 W
Cooper Mountain ∧	146	60.23 N	149.51 W
Coopers Creek ≃	120	28.29 S	137.46 E
Cooperstown	152	42.42 N	74.56 W
Coopersville	154	40.31 N	75.23 W
Cooroy	120	26.25 S	152.55 E
Coos Bay	166	43.22 N	124.13 W
Cootamundra	120	34.39 S	148.02 E
Cootehill	70	54.04 N	7.05 W
Copan	160	36.54 N	95.56 W
Copenhagen → København	68	55.40 N	12.35 E
Copertino	78	40.16 N	18.03 E
Copiapó	140	27.22 S	70.20 W
Copley	120	30.32 S	138.25 E
Copparo	78	44.54 N	11.49 E
Copper ≃	146	60.30 N	144.50 W
Copperas Cove	160	31.08 N	97.54 W
Coppermine	142	67.50 N	115.05 W
Coppermine ≃	142	67.49 N	115.04 W
Copulhué, Paso de)(	140	37.35 S	71.08 W
Coquilhatville → Mbandaka	110	0.04 N	18.16 E
Coquille	166	43.11 N	124.11 W
Coquimbo	140	29.58 S	71.21 W
Coquimbo ☐[4]	140	31.00 S	71.00 W
Corabia	80	43.46 N	24.30 E
Coral Gables	156	25.45 N	80.16 W
Coral Harbour	142	64.08 N	83.10 W
Coral Sea ▼[2]	118	20.00 S	158.00 E
Coralville	154	41.40 N	91.35 W
Coralville Lake ⊜[1]	154	41.47 N	91.48 W
Coram	166	48.36 N	114.02 W
Corato	78	41.09 N	16.25 E
Corbeil-Essonnes	74	48.36 N	2.29 E
Corbigny	74	47.15 N	3.40 E
Corbin	156	36.57 N	84.05 W
Corby	70	52.29 N	0.40 W
Corcoran	168	36.06 N	119.33 W
Corcovado, Golfo C	136	43.30 S	73.20 W
Corcovado, Volcán ∧[1]	136	43.12 S	72.48 W
Cordele	156	31.58 N	83.47 W
Cordell	160	35.17 N	98.59 W
Cordillera ☐[5]	140	25.15 S	57.00 W
Cordillo Downs	120	26.43 S	140.38 E
Córdoba, Arg.	140	31.25 S	64.10 W
Córdoba, Esp.	76	37.53 N	4.46 W
Córdoba, Méx.	130	18.53 N	96.56 W
Córdoba ☐[4]	140	32.00 S	64.00 W
Córdoba ☐[5]	138	8.20 N	75.40 W
Cordova, Ala., U.S.	158	33.46 N	87.11 W
Cordova, Alaska, U.S.	146	60.33 N	145.46 W
Corfu → Kérkira	80	39.36 N	19.56 E
Coria del Río	76	37.16 N	6.03 W
Corigliano Calabro	78	39.36 N	16.31 E
Corinda	120	18.04 S	138.54 E
Coringa Islets II	120	16.58 S	149.58 E
Corinna	152	44.55 N	69.16 W
Corinne	166	41.35 N	112.07 W
Corinth → Kórinthos, Ellás	80	37.56 N	22.56 E
Corinth, Miss., U.S.	158	34.56 N	88.31 W
Corinth, N.Y., U.S.	152	43.15 N	73.49 W
Corinth, Gulf of → Korinthiakós Kólpos C	80	38.19 N	22.04 E
Corinto	134	18.21 S	44.27 W
Corixa Grande ≃	134	17.31 S	57.52 W
Cork	70	51.54 N	8.28 W
Cork ☐[6]	70	52.00 N	8.30 W
Corlay	74	48.19 N	3.03 W
Corleone	78	37.49 N	13.18 E
Çorlu	80	41.09 N	27.48 E
Cormeilles	74	49.15 N	0.23 E
Cornelia	156	34.31 N	83.32 W
Cornelius	156	35.29 N	80.52 W
Cornelius Grinnell Bay C	142	63.20 N	64.50 W
Corner Brook	150	48.57 N	57.57 W
Corning, Ark., U.S.	158	36.24 N	90.35 W
Corning, Calif., U.S.	168	39.56 N	122.11 W
Corning, Iowa, U.S.	162	40.59 N	94.44 W
Corning, N.Y., U.S.	152	42.09 N	77.04 W
Corning, Ohio, U.S.	152	39.36 N	82.05 W
Corn Islands II	132	12.15 N	83.00 W
Corno Grande ∧	78	42.28 N	13.34 E
Cornucopia	166	45.00 N	117.12 W
Cornwall	152	45.02 N	74.44 W
Cornwall ☐[6]	70	50.30 N	4.40 W
Cornwallis Island I	142	75.15 N	94.30 W
Coro	138	11.25 N	69.41 W
Corocoro	134	17.12 S	68.29 W
Corocoro Island I	138	8.30 N	60.10 W
Coroico	134	16.10 S	67.50 W
Coromandel Coast ⏏[2]	100	13.30 N	80.30 E
Coromandel Peninsula ≻[1]	126	37.00 S	175.40 E
Corona, Calif., U.S.	168	33.52 N	117.34 W

Symbols in the index entries are identified on page 203.

Name	Page	Lat	Long
Corona, N. Mex., U.S.	164	34.15 N	105.36 W
Coronado	168	32.41 N	117.11 W
Coronation Gulf C	142	68.25 N	110.00 W
Coronel	140	37.01 S	73.08 W
Coronel Dorrego	140	38.45 S	61.17 W
Coronel Fabriciano	134	19.31 S	42.38 W
Coronel Oviedo	140	25.25 S	56.27 W
Coronel Pringles	140	38.00 S	61.20 W
Coronel Suárez	140	37.25 S	61.56 W
Coropuna, Nevado ∧	134	15.30 S	72.41 W
Corowa	120	36.02 S	146.23 E
Corozal, Belize	130	18.24 N	88.24 W
Corozal, Col.	138	9.19 N	75.18 W
Corps	74	44.49 N	5.57 E
Corpus Christi	160	27.48 N	97.24 W
Corral	136	39.52 S	73.26 W
Correggio	78	44.46 N	10.47 E
Corrente ≃	134	13.08 S	43.28 W
Corrèze □5	74	45.20 N	1.50 E
Corrientes	140	27.30 S	58.50 W
Corrientes □4	140	29.00 S	58.00 W
Corrientes ≃	138	3.43 S	74.35 W
Corrientes, Cabo ➤, Cuba	132	21.45 N	84.31 W
Corrientes, Cabo ➤, Méx.	130	20.25 N	105.42 W
Corry	152	41.56 N	73.39 W
Corse □5	78	42.00 N	9.00 E
Corse, Cap ➤	78	42.40 N	9.05 E
Corsica I	74	43.00 N	9.25 E
Corsica → Corse □5	78	42.00 N	9.00 E
Corsicana	160	32.06 N	96.28 W
Cort Adelaer, Kap ➤	142	62.00 N	42.00 W
Cortazar	130	20.29 N	100.56 W
Corte	78	42.18 N	9.08 E
Cortegana	76	37.55 N	6.49 W
Cortez	164	37.21 N	108.35 W
Cortina d'Ampezzo	78	46.32 N	12.08 E
Cortland, N.Y., U.S.	152	42.36 N	76.11 W
Cortland, Ohio, U.S.	152	41.20 N	80.44 W
Cortona	78	43.16 N	11.59 E
Corubal (Koliba) ≃	114	11.57 N	15.06 W
Coruche	76	38.57 N	8.31 W
Çoruh ≃	82	41.36 N	41.35 E
Çorum	64	40.33 N	34.58 E
Corumbá	134	19.01 S	57.39 W
Corumbá ≃	134	18.19 S	48.55 W
Coruna, Ont., Can.	152	42.53 N	82.26 W
Corunna, Mich., U.S.	154	42.59 N	84.07 W
Corunna Downs	122	21.28 S	119.51 E
Coruripe	134	10.08 S	36.10 W
Corvallis, Mont., U.S.	166	46.19 N	114.07 W
Corvallis, Oreg., U.S.	166	44.34 N	123.16 W
Corydon, Ind., U.S.	158	38.13 N	86.07 W
Corydon, Iowa, U.S.	154	40.45 N	93.19 W
Cosenza	78	39.17 N	16.15 E
Coshocton	152	40.16 N	81.51 W
Cosmoledo Group II	110	9.43 S	47.35 E
Cosne-sur-Loire	74	47.24 N	2.55 E
Cossatot ≃	158	33.48 N	94.09 W
Cossé-la-Vivien	70	47.57 N	0.55 W
Costa Mesa	168	33.39 N	117.55 W
Costa Rica □1	128	10.00 N	84.00 W
Costermansville → Bukavu	110	2.30 S	28.52 E
Costilla	164	36.59 N	105.32 W
Costilla Creek ≃	164	36.59 N	105.43 W
Coswig	72	51.53 N	12.26 E
Cotabambas	134	13.45 S	72.20 W
Cotabato	98	7.14 N	124.15 E
Cotati	168	38.20 N	122.42 W
Côte-d'Or □5	74	47.30 N	4.50 E
Cotentin ➤1	74	49.30 N	1.30 W
Côtes-du-Nord □5	74	48.25 N	2.40 W
Cotherstone	120	22.37 S	148.14 E
Cotija de la Paz	130	19.49 N	102.43 W
Cotonou	106	6.21 N	2.26 E
Cotopaxi □4	138	0.55 S	78.55 W
Cotopaxi ∧1	138	0.40 S	78.26 W
Cottage Grove	166	43.48 N	123.03 W
Cottageville	152	32.56 N	80.29 W
Cottbus	72	51.45 N	14.19 E
Cottbus □5	72	51.45 N	14.00 E
Cottiennes, Alpes (Alpi Cozie) ∧	78	44.45 N	7.00 E
Cottondale, Ala., U.S.	158	33.11 N	87.27 W
Cottondale, Fla., U.S.	156	30.48 N	85.23 W
Cotton Plant	158	35.00 N	91.15 W
Cottonport	158	30.59 N	92.03 W
Cotton Valley	158	32.49 N	93.25 W
Cottonwood, Ariz., U.S.	164	34.45 N	112.01 W
Cottonwood, Calif., U.S.	168	40.23 N	122.17 W
Cottonwood, Idaho, U.S.	166	46.03 N	116.21 W
Cottonwood, Minn., U.S.	162	44.37 N	95.41 W
Coudersport	152	41.46 N	78.01 W
Couhé	74	46.18 N	0.11 E
Coulee City	166	47.37 N	119.17 W
Coulee Dam	166	47.58 N	118.59 W
Coulommiers	74	48.49 N	3.05 E
Coulterville	168	37.43 N	120.12 W
Council	166	44.44 N	116.26 W
Council Bluffs	162	41.16 N	95.52 W
Council Grove	162	38.40 N	96.29 W
Country Homes	166	47.45 N	117.24 W
Coupar Angus	70	56.33 N	3.17 W
Courantyne (Corantijn) ≃	138	5.55 N	57.05 W
Courcelles	72	50.28 N	4.22 E
Courchevel	74	45.25 N	6.38 E
Courçon	74	46.15 N	0.49 W
Courseulles	74	49.20 N	0.27 W
Courson-les-Carrières	74	47.36 N	3.30 E
Courtalain	74	48.05 N	1.09 E
Courtenay	148	49.41 N	125.00 W
Courtland	156	36.43 N	77.04 W
Courtrai → Kortrijk	72	50.50 N	3.16 E
Coushatta	158	32.00 N	93.21 W
Coutances	74	49.03 N	1.26 W
Coutras	74	45.02 N	0.08 W
Couture, Lac ⊜	142	60.07 N	75.20 W
Covasna □4	80	46.00 N	26.00 E
Cove	166	45.18 N	117.49 W
Covelo	168	39.48 N	123.15 W
Coventry	70	52.25 N	1.30 W
Covert	154	42.17 N	86.16 W
Covilhã	76	40.17 N	7.30 W
Covington, Ind., U.S.	158	40.09 N	87.24 W
Covington, Ky., U.S.	152	39.05 N	84.30 W
Covington, La., U.S.	158	30.29 N	90.06 W
Covington, Ohio, U.S.	152	40.07 N	84.21 W
Covington, Okla., U.S.	158	36.18 N	97.35 W
Covington, Tenn., U.S.	158	35.34 N	89.38 W
Covington, Va., U.S.	156	37.47 N	79.59 W
Cowal, Lake ⊜	120	33.35 S	147.25 E
Cowan	158	35.10 N	86.01 W
Cowan, Lake ⊜	122	31.50 S	121.50 E
Cowansville	152	45.12 N	72.45 W
Coward	156	33.58 N	79.45 W
Coward Springs	120	29.24 S	136.49 E
Cowdenbeath	70	56.07 N	3.21 W
Cowell	120	33.41 S	136.55 E
Cowes	70	50.45 N	1.18 W
Coweta	160	35.57 N	95.39 W
Cowley, Austl.	120	17.41 S	145.49 E
Cowley, Wyo., U.S.	166	44.53 N	108.28 W
Cowra	120	33.50 S	148.41 E
Coxsackie	152	42.21 N	73.48 W
Cox's Bāzār	100	21.26 N	91.59 E
Coyhaique	136	45.34 S	72.04 W
Coyuca de Catalán	130	18.20 N	100.39 W
Cozad	162	40.52 N	99.59 W
Cozes	74	45.35 N	0.50 W
Cozie, Alpi (Alpes Cottiennes) ∧	78	44.45 N	7.00 E
Cozumel, Isla de I	130	20.25 N	86.55 W
Cradock	116	32.08 S	25.36 E
Craig, Alaska, U.S.	148	55.29 N	133.09 W
Craig, Colo., U.S.	164	40.31 N	107.33 W
Craigmont	166	46.15 N	116.28 W
Craignure	70	56.28 N	5.42 W
Craigsville	152	40.47 N	85.06 W
Crailsheim	72	49.08 N	10.04 E
Craiova	80	44.19 N	23.48 E
Cranbrook, Austl.	122	34.18 S	117.32 E
Cranbrook, B.C., Can.	148	49.31 N	115.46 W
Crandon	154	45.34 N	88.54 W
Crane	160	31.24 N	102.21 W
Cranston	152	41.47 N	71.26 W
Craon	74	47.51 N	0.57 W
Craonne	74	49.27 N	3.47 E
Craponne	74	45.20 N	3.51 E
Crasna (Kraszna) ≃	80	48.09 N	22.20 E
Crater Lake ⊜	166	42.56 N	122.06 W
Cratéus	134	5.10 S	40.40 W
Crato	134	7.14 S	39.23 W
Crauford, Cape ➤	134	73.43 N	84.50 W
Crawford, Nebr., U.S.	162	42.41 N	103.25 W
Crawford, Tex., U.S.	160	31.32 N	97.27 W
Crawfordsville	158	40.02 N	86.54 W
Crawley	70	51.07 N	0.12 W
Crécy-en-Brie	74	48.51 N	2.55 E
Crécy-en-Ponthieu	74	50.15 N	1.53 E
Cree ≃	142	59.00 N	105.47 W
Creede	164	37.51 N	106.56 W
Cree Lake ⊜	142	57.30 N	106.50 W
Creighton	162	42.28 N	97.54 W
Creighton Mine	154	46.28 N	81.11 W
Creil	74	49.16 N	2.29 E
Crema	78	45.22 N	9.41 E
Crémieu	74	45.43 N	5.15 E
Cremona	78	45.07 N	10.02 E
Crenshaw	158	34.30 N	90.12 W
Crépy-en-Valois	74	49.14 N	2.54 E
Cresaptown	152	39.36 N	78.50 W
Crescent	166	43.29 N	121.41 W
Crescent City	168	41.45 N	124.12 W
Crescent Group II	92	16.31 N	111.38 E
Crescent Lake ⊜	156	43.22 N	92.07 W
Cresco	154	43.22 N	92.07 W
Cresson, Pa., U.S.	152	40.28 N	78.35 W
Cresson, Tex., U.S.	160	32.32 N	97.37 W
Crest	74	44.44 N	5.02 E
Crested Butte	164	38.52 N	106.59 W
Crestline, Calif., U.S.	168	34.14 N	117.17 W
Crestline, Ohio, U.S.	152	40.47 N	82.44 W
Creston, B.C., Can.	148	49.06 N	116.31 W
Creston, Iowa, U.S.	154	41.04 N	94.22 W
Crestview	158	30.46 N	86.34 W
Creswell Bay C	142	72.35 N	93.25 W
Creswell Downs	122	17.57 S	135.55 E
Creswick	120	37.26 S	143.54 E
Crete, Ill., U.S.	154	41.27 N	87.38 W
Crete, Nebr., U.S.	162	40.38 N	96.58 W
Crete → Kríti I	80	35.29 N	24.42 E
Creuse ≃	74	47.00 N	0.34 E
Creuse □5	74	46.05 N	2.00 E
Crève Coeur	154	40.39 N	89.35 W
Crevillente	76	38.15 N	0.48 W
Crewe, Eng., U.K.	70	53.05 N	2.27 W
Crewe, Va., U.S.	156	37.05 N	78.08 W
Crewkerne	70	50.53 N	2.48 W
Criciúma	140	28.40 S	49.23 W
Crieff	70	56.23 N	3.52 W
Crikvenica	78	45.11 N	14.42 E
Crimea → Krymskij Poluostrov ➤1	64	45.00 N	34.00 E
Crimmitschau	72	50.49 N	12.23 E
Cripple Creek	164	38.45 N	105.11 W
Crisfield	152	37.59 N	75.51 W
Cristalândia	134	10.36 S	49.11 W
Cristóbal	138	9.20 N	79.55 W
Cristóbal Colón, Pico ∧	138	10.50 N	73.45 W
Crişu Alb ≃	80	46.42 N	21.17 E
Crişu Negru ≃	80	46.42 N	21.16 E
Crişu Repede (Sebes Körös) ≃	80	46.55 N	20.59 E
Crna Gora □3	80	42.30 N	19.18 E
Črnomelj	78	45.34 N	15.11 E
Croatia → Hrvatska □3	78	45.10 N	15.30 E
Crockett	160	31.19 N	95.28 W
Crocodile Islands II	124	11.43 S	135.08 E
Crocus Hill → The Valley	132	18.13 N	63.04 W
Croix, Lac la ⊜	154	48.21 N	92.05 W
Croker, Cape ➤	124	10.58 S	132.35 E
Croker Island I	124	11.12 S	132.32 E
Cromarty	70	57.41 N	4.02 W
Cromer	70	52.56 N	1.18 E
Crooked Creek	146	61.52 N	158.08 W
Crooked Creek ≃	152	30.50 N	100.06 W
Crooked Island I	132	22.45 N	74.12 W
Crooked Lake ⊜	162	39.46 N	82.06 W
Crookston	162	47.46 N	96.37 W
Crooksville	152	39.46 N	82.06 W
Crookwell	120	34.27 S	149.28 E
Crosby, Minn., U.S.	154	46.28 N	93.57 W
Crosby, Miss., U.S.	158	31.17 N	91.04 W
Crosby, N. Dak., U.S.	162	48.54 N	103.18 W
Cross ≃	114	4.42 N	8.21 E
Cross City	156	29.39 N	83.07 W
Crossett	158	33.08 N	91.58 W
Cross Lake ⊜	142	54.45 N	97.30 W
Cross Plains	160	32.07 N	99.10 W
Cross Sound ⹁	146	58.10 N	136.30 W
Crossville	158	35.58 N	85.02 W
Croswell	154	43.16 N	82.37 W
Crothersville	158	38.48 N	85.50 W
Crotone	78	39.05 N	17.07 E
Crow Agency	166	45.36 N	107.27 W
Crow Creek ≃	162	40.23 N	104.29 W
Crowdy Head ➤	120	31.51 S	152.45 E
Crowell	160	33.59 N	99.43 W
Crowley	158	30.13 N	92.22 W
Crowleys Ridge ∧	158	35.45 N	90.45 W
Crown Point	158	41.25 N	87.22 W
Crown Prince Frederick Island I	142	70.02 N	86.50 W
Crownest Pass)(	148	49.39 N	114.45 W
Croydon	120	18.12 S	142.14 E
Crozet	74	46.19 N	5.57 E
Crozon	74	48.15 N	4.29 W
Cruz, Cabo ➤	132	19.51 N	77.44 W
Cruz Alta	140	28.39 S	53.36 W
Cruz del Eje	140	30.44 S	64.48 W
Cruzeiro do Sul	134	7.38 S	72.36 W
Crystal	162	28.41 N	99.50 W
Crystal Beach	152	42.52 N	79.04 W
Crystal City, Mo., U.S.	158	38.13 N	90.23 W
Crystal City, Tex., U.S.	160	28.41 N	99.50 W
Crystal Falls	154	46.05 N	88.20 W
Crystal Lake	154	42.14 N	88.20 W
Crystal River	156	28.54 N	82.36 W
Crystal Springs	158	31.59 N	90.21 W
Csongrád	72	46.43 N	20.09 E
Csongrád □6	72	46.25 N	20.15 E
Csorna	72	47.37 N	17.16 E
Csurgó	72	46.16 N	17.06 E
Ču ≃	82	45.00 N	67.44 E
Cuando (Kwando) ≃	110	18.27 S	23.32 E
Cuangar	110	17.34 S	18.39 E
Cuango ≃	110	6.17 S	16.41 E
Cuango (Kwango) ≃	110	3.14 S	17.22 E
Cuanza ≃	110	9.19 S	13.08 E
Cuauhtémoc	130	28.25 N	106.52 W
Cuautitlán [de Romero Rubio]	130	19.41 N	99.11 W
Cuautla	130	18.48 N	98.57 W
Cuba, Port.	76	38.10 N	7.53 W
Cuba, Ill., U.S.	154	40.30 N	90.12 W
Cuba, Kans., U.S.	162	39.48 N	97.27 W
Cuba, Mo., U.S.	158	38.04 N	91.24 W
Cuba, N. Mex., U.S.	164	36.01 N	107.04 W
Cuba, N.Y., U.S.	152	42.13 N	78.17 W
Cuba □1	128	21.30 N	80.00 W
Cubango (Okavango) ≃	110	18.50 S	22.25 E
Čuchloma	86	58.45 N	42.41 E
Čučkovo	86	54.17 N	41.26 E
Cúcuta	138	7.54 N	72.31 W
Cudahy	154	42.57 N	87.52 W
Cuddalore	100	11.45 N	79.46 E
Cuddapah	100	14.29 N	78.50 E
Čudovo	86	59.07 N	31.41 E
Čudskoje Ozero (Peipsi Järv) ⊜	86	58.45 N	27.30 E
Cue	122	27.25 S	117.54 E
Cuenca, Ec.	138	2.53 S	78.59 W
Cuenca, Esp.	76	40.04 N	2.08 W
Cuencamé [de Ceniceros]	130	24.53 N	103.42 W
Cuerámaro	130	20.37 N	101.43 W
Cuernavaca	130	18.55 N	99.15 W
Cuero	160	29.06 N	97.18 W
Cuers	74	43.14 N	6.04 E
Cuervos	130	32.38 N	114.52 W
Cufra → Al-Kufrah ✦1	108	24.20 N	23.15 E
Cugir	80	45.50 N	23.22 E
Cuglieri	78	40.11 N	8.34 E
Cuiabá	134	15.35 S	56.05 W
Cuiabá ≃	134	17.05 S	56.36 W
Cuiari	138	1.30 N	68.11 W
Cuilo (Kwilu) ≃	110	3.22 S	17.22 E
Cuiseaux	74	46.30 N	5.24 E
Cuito ≃	116	18.01 S	20.48 E
Cuito-Cuanavale	110	15.10 S	19.10 E
Cuitzeo, Lago de ⊜	130	19.55 N	101.05 W
Čukotskij, Mys ➤	146	64.14 N	173.10 W
Čukotskij Poluostrov ➤1	146	66.00 N	175.00 W
Culbertson	166	48.09 N	104.31 W
Culcairn	120	35.40 S	147.03 E
Culgoa ≃	120	29.56 S	146.20 E
Culiacán	130	24.48 N	107.24 W
Culion Island I	98	11.50 N	120.00 E
Cullen	158	32.58 N	93.27 W
Cullera	76	39.10 N	0.15 W
Cullman	158	34.11 N	86.51 W
Cullowhee	156	35.19 N	83.10 W
Čul'man	84	56.52 N	124.52 E
Culpeper	152	38.28 N	77.53 W
Culuene ≃	134	12.56 S	52.51 W
Culver	166	44.32 N	121.13 W
Culver, Point ➤	122	32.54 S	124.43 E
Cumaná	138	10.28 N	64.10 W
Cumbal, Volcán de ∧1	138	0.57 N	77.52 W
Cumberland, B.C., Can.	148	49.37 N	125.01 W
Cumberland, Ky., U.S.	156	36.59 N	82.59 W
Cumberland, Md., U.S.	152	39.39 N	78.46 W
Cumberland ≃	158	37.09 N	88.25 W
Cumberland, Lake ⊜1	158	36.57 N	84.55 W
Cumberland City	158	36.23 N	87.38 W
Cumberland Gap)(	156	36.36 N	83.41 W
Cumberland Islands II	120	20.40 S	149.09 E
Cumberland Peninsula ➤1	142	66.50 N	64.00 W
Cumberland Plateau ∧1	144	36.00 N	85.00 W
Cumberland Sound ⹁	142	65.10 N	65.30 W
Cumbria □6	70	54.30 N	3.00 W
Cumby	160	33.08 N	95.50 W
Čumikan	84	54.42 N	135.19 E
Cuminapanema ≃	134	1.09 S	54.54 W
Cumming	156	34.13 N	84.08 W
Cummins	120	34.16 S	135.44 E
Cummins Range ∧	122	19.05 S	127.10 E
Cumnock	70	55.27 N	4.16 W
Čumyš ≃	84	53.31 N	83.10 E
Cun'a ≃, S.S.S.R.	84	61.36 N	96.30 E
Čuna ≃, S.S.S.R.	84	57.47 N	95.26 E
Cunani	134	2.52 N	51.06 W
Cunco	136	38.55 S	72.02 W
Cunderdin	122	31.39 S	117.15 E
Cundinamarca □5	138	5.00 N	74.00 W
Cunene ≃	110	17.20 S	11.50 E
Cuneo	78	44.23 N	7.32 E
Cunnamulla	120	28.04 S	145.41 E
Cupa	86	66.16 N	33.00 E
Curaçao I	132	12.11 N	69.00 W
Curacautin	140	38.26 S	71.53 W
Curanilahue	140	37.28 S	73.21 W
Čurapča	84	62.00 N	132.24 E
Curaray ≃	138	2.20 S	74.05 W
Curepipe	117c	20.19 S	57.31 E
Curicó	140	34.59 S	71.14 W
Curitiba	140	25.25 S	49.15 W
Curitibanos	140	27.18 S	50.36 W
Curlewis	120	31.07 S	150.16 E
Curnamona	120	31.39 S	139.32 E
Currais Novos	134	6.15 S	36.31 W
Curralinho	134	1.48 S	49.47 W
Currant Mountain ∧	168	38.55 N	115.25 W
Currie	168	39.56 N	114.45 W
Curtea-de-Argeş	80	45.08 N	24.41 E
Curtis	162	40.38 N	100.31 W
Curtis Island ⟋3	120	24.00 S	151.50 E
Curtis Lake ⊜	154	66.38 N	89.02 W
Curuá, Ilha I	134	5.23 S	54.22 W
Curuá ≃	134	0.35 N	50.00 W
Curug ≃	80	45.17 N	20.04 E
Curupira, Serra de ∧	138	1.25 N	64.58 W
Cururupu	134	1.50 S	44.52 W
Curuzú-Cuatiá	140	29.50 S	58.05 W
Curvelo	134	18.45 S	44.25 W
Cushing, Okla., U.S.	160	35.59 N	96.46 W
Cushing, Tex., U.S.	160	31.48 N	94.50 W
Cusick	166	48.20 N	117.16 W
Čusovoj	64	58.17 N	57.49 E
Cut Bank	166	48.38 N	112.20 W
Cut Bank Creek ≃	166	48.35 N	112.25 W
Cuthbert	156	31.46 N	84.48 W
Cutler	168	36.31 N	119.17 W
Cutlerville	154	42.51 N	85.40 W
Cutral-Có	140	38.58 S	69.15 W
Cutro	78	39.02 N	16.59 E
Cuttack	100	20.30 N	85.50 E
Cuvier, Cape ➤	122	23.14 S	113.22 E
Cuvo ≃	110	10.50 S	13.10 E
Cuxhaven	72	53.52 N	8.42 E
Cuyahoga Falls	152	41.08 N	81.29 W
Cuyo Islands II	98	10.53 N	121.00 E
Cuyuni ≃	138	6.23 N	58.41 W
Cuzco	134	13.31 S	71.59 W
Cyangugu	110	2.29 S	28.54 E
Cynthiana	152	38.23 N	84.18 W
Cyprus □1	64	35.00 N	33.00 E
Cyrenaica → Barqah ✦1	108	31.00 N	22.30 E
Cyrus Field Bay C	142	62.50 N	64.55 W
Czarna Woda ≃	72	53.51 N	18.06 E
Czechoslovakia □1	64	49.30 N	17.00 E
Czechowice-Dziedzice	72	49.54 N	19.00 E
Częstochowa	72	50.49 N	19.06 E
Człuchów	72	53.41 N	17.21 E
D			
Dabashan ∧	88	31.55 N	109.05 E
Dabhoi	102	22.11 N	73.26 E
Dabieshan ∧	88	31.00 N	115.40 E
Dabney	160	29.10 N	100.03 W
Dabola	114	10.45 N	11.07 W
Dacca	102	23.43 N	90.25 E
Dachaidan	88	37.53 N	95.07 E
Dachau	72	48.15 N	11.27 E
Dade City	156	28.22 N	82.12 W
Dadeville	158	32.50 N	85.46 W
Dādu	102	26.44 N	67.47 E
Daerhanmaoming'-anqi	88	41.42 N	110.23 E
Daet	92	14.07 N	122.57 E
Dagana	114	16.31 N	15.30 W
Dagash	108	19.22 N	33.24 E
Dagu	88	38.59 N	117.40 E
Dagupan	98	16.03 N	120.20 E
Dahlak Archipelago II	108	15.45 N	40.30 E
Dahlonega	156	34.32 N	83.59 W
Dahlonega Plateau ∧1	156	34.30 N	84.20 W
Dahme	72	51.52 N	13.25 E
Dahomey → Benin □1	106	9.30 N	2.15 E
Dahra	108	29.34 N	17.50 E
Dahy, Nafūd ad- ✦8	84	22.20 N	45.35 E
Daimiel	76	39.04 N	3.37 W
Daingean	70	53.18 N	7.17 W
Daingerfield	158	33.02 N	94.44 W
Daireaux	140	36.37 S	61.45 W
Dairen → Lüda	88	38.53 N	121.35 E
Daisetsu	90a	43.30 N	142.57 E
Daisy	156	35.15 N	85.11 W
Dajarra	120	21.42 S	139.31 E
Dajiangshan ∧	88	30.09 N	104.38 E
Dakar	114	14.40 N	17.26 W
Dak-gle	92	15.12 N	107.48 E
Dakota City	162	42.25 N	96.25 W
Đakovica	80	42.23 N	20.25 E
Dalälven ≃	68	60.38 N	17.27 E
Dalandzadgad	88	43.35 N	104.25 E
Dalarna □9	68	61.01 N	14.04 E
Da-lat	94	11.56 N	108.25 E
Dālbandin	100	28.53 N	64.25 E
Dalbeattie	70	54.56 N	3.49 W
Dalby, Austl.	120	27.11 S	151.16 E
Dalby, Sve.	68	55.40 N	13.21 E
Dale, Nor.	68	60.35 N	5.49 E
Dale, Nor.	68	61.22 N	5.25 E
Dale Creek ≃	164	40.54 N	105.22 W
Dale Hollow Lake ⊜1	156	36.36 N	85.19 W
Daleville	158	40.07 N	85.33 W
Dalgety Downs	122	25.17 S	116.11 E
Dalhart	160	36.04 N	102.31 W
Dalhousie, Bhārat	102	32.32 N	75.59 E
Dalhousie, N.B., Can.	150	48.04 N	66.23 W
Dalhousie, Cape ➤	146	70.14 N	129.42 W
Dali	94	25.38 N	100.09 E
Daliangshan ∧	88	28.00 N	103.00 E
Dallas, N.C., U.S.	156	35.19 N	81.11 W
Dallas, Oreg., U.S.	166	44.55 N	123.19 W
Dallas, Pa., U.S.	152	41.20 N	75.58 W
Dallas, Tex., U.S.	160	32.47 N	96.48 W
Dallas Center	154	41.41 N	93.58 W
Dalli Rājhara	102	20.35 N	81.05 E
Dalmacija □9	78	43.00 N	17.00 E
Dalmatia → Dalmacija □9	78	43.00 N	17.00 E
Daloa	114	6.53 N	6.27 W
Dalrymple, Mount ∧	120	21.02 S	148.38 E
Dalsland □9	68	58.30 N	12.50 E
Dalton, Ga., U.S.	156	34.47 N	84.58 W
Dalton, Mass., U.S.	152	42.29 N	73.09 W
Daltongarj	102	24.03 N	84.04 E
Dalton Gardens	166	47.43 N	116.46 W
Daluin Island I	98	19.05 N	121.13 E
Dalvík	66a	65.59 N	18.32 W
Dalwallinu	122	30.17 S	116.40 E
Daly Bay C	142	64.00 N	89.40 W
Daly City	168	37.42 N	122.29 W
Daly Lake ⊜	142	56.32 N	105.39 W
Daly River	124	13.45 S	130.42 E
Daly Waters	124	16.15 S	133.22 E
Damān	100	20.25 N	72.50 E
Damanhūr	108	31.02 N	30.28 E
Damar, Pulau I	96	7.09 S	128.40 E
Damaraland □9	116	22.34 S	17.06 E
Damascus → Dimashq, Sūrīy.	104	33.30 N	36.18 E
Damascus, Md., U.S.	152	39.17 N	77.12 W
Dāmāvand, Qolleh-ye ∧	104	35.56 N	52.08 E
Damba	110	6.41 S	15.08 E
Dāmghān	104	36.10 N	54.22 E
Damietta → Dumyāt	108	31.25 N	31.48 E
Dammartin-en-Goële	74	49.03 N	2.41 E
Dāmodar ≃	102	22.17 N	88.05 E
Damoh	102	23.50 N	79.27 E
Dampier	122	20.39 S	116.45 E
Dampier, Selat ⹁	96	0.40 S	130.40 E
Dampier Archipelago II	122	20.35 S	116.35 E
Dampier Land ➤1	122	17.30 S	122.55 E
Dampier Strait ⹁	124	5.36 S	148.12 E
Da-nang	94	16.04 N	108.13 E
Danbury, Conn., U.S.	152	41.23 N	73.27 W
Danbury, Tex., U.S.	160	29.14 N	95.21 W
Dandaragan	122	30.40 S	115.42 E
Dandenong	120	37.59 S	145.12 E
Danger Point ➤	116	34.40 S	19.17 E
Dania	156	26.03 N	80.09 W
Danielson	152	41.48 N	71.53 W
Danilov	86	58.12 N	40.12 E
Dankov	86	53.15 N	39.08 E
Dannemora	152	44.43 N	73.43 W
Dannenberg	72	53.06 N	11.05 E
Dannevirke	126	40.12 S	176.06 E
Dansville	152	42.33 N	77.42 W
Danube, Mouths of the ≃1	64	45.20 N	29.40 E
Danville, Qué., Can.	152	45.47 N	72.01 W
Danville, Ill., U.S.	158	40.08 N	87.37 W
Danville, Ind., U.S.	158	39.46 N	86.32 W
Danville, Ky., U.S.	158	37.39 N	84.46 W
Danville, Pa., U.S.	152	40.57 N	76.36 W
Danville, Va., U.S.	156	36.35 N	79.24 W
Danville, Vt., U.S.	152	44.25 N	72.08 W
Danxian	94	19.31 N	109.34 E
Danzig → Gdańsk	72	54.23 N	18.40 E
Daochengxian	94	29.03 N	100.18 E
Daoulas	74	48.22 N	4.15 W
Dapango	114	10.52 N	0.12 E
Darabani	80	48.11 N	26.35 E
Daraj	108	30.10 N	10.28 E
Darbhanga	102	26.10 N	85.54 E
Darby, Pa., U.S.	152	39.54 N	75.15 W
Dardanelle, Ark., U.S.	158	35.13 N	93.09 W
Dardanelle, Calif., U.S.	168	38.20 N	119.50 W
Dardanelles → Çanakkale Boğazı ⹁	80	40.15 N	26.25 E
Dar-el-Beida	106	33.39 N	7.35 W
Dar-es-Salaam	110	6.48 S	39.17 E
Dargan-Ata	84	40.29 N	62.10 E
Dargaville	126	35.56 S	173.52 E
Dari	88	33.45 N	99.54 E
Darien	156	31.22 N	81.26 W
Darien, Serrania del ∧	138	8.20 N	77.22 W
Dariganga	88	45.21 N	113.38 E
Darjeeling	102	27.02 N	88.16 E
Darling ≃	120	34.07 S	141.55 E
Darling Downs ✦1	120	27.30 S	150.30 E
Darling Range ∧	122	32.00 S	116.30 E
Darlington, Eng., U.K.	70	54.31 N	1.34 W
Darlington, S.C., U.S.	156	34.18 N	79.52 W
Darlington, Wis., U.S.	154	42.41 N	90.07 W
Darłowo	72	54.26 N	16.23 E
Darnah	108	32.46 N	22.39 E
Darnétal	74	49.27 N	1.09 E
Darney	74	48.05 N	6.03 E
Darnley Bay C	146	69.30 N	123.30 W
Daroca	76	41.07 N	1.25 W
Darrah, Mount ∧	148	49.28 N	114.35 W
Darrouzett	160	36.27 N	100.20 W
Dartmouth, Eng., U.K.	70	50.21 N	3.35 W
Dartmouth, Lake ⊜	120	26.04 S	145.18 E
Daru	124	9.04 S	143.12 E
Daruvar	78	45.36 N	17.13 E
Darvaza	82	40.11 N	58.24 E
Darwin	124	12.28 S	130.50 E
Darwin River	124	12.49 S	130.58 E
Dasht ≃	100	25.10 N	61.40 E
Dašinčilen	88	47.51 N	104.03 E
Dassow	72	53.50 N	10.59 E
Datia	102	25.41 N	78.28 E
D'at'kovo	86	53.36 N	34.20 E
Datong	88	40.05 N	113.18 E
Datu, Tanjung ➤	96	2.06 N	109.39 E
Datu Piang	98	7.01 N	124.29 E
Daugai	72	54.22 N	24.20 E
Daugava (Zapadnaja Dvina) ≃	86	57.04 N	24.03 E
Daugavpils	86	55.53 N	26.32 E
Daule	138	1.50 S	79.56 W
Daule ≃	138	2.10 S	79.52 W
Daun	72	50.11 N	6.50 E
Dauphin	142	51.09 N	100.03 W
Dauphiné □9	74	44.50 N	6.00 E
Dauphin Lake ⊜	142	51.17 N	99.48 W
Dāvangere	100	14.28 N	75.55 E
Davao	98	7.04 N	125.36 E
Davao Gulf C	98	6.40 N	125.55 E
Davenport, Fla., U.S.	156	28.10 N	81.36 W
Davenport, Iowa, U.S.	154	41.32 N	90.41 W
Davenport, Wash., U.S.	166	47.39 N	118.09 W
Davenport, Mount ∧	122	22.23 S	130.51 E
Davenport Range ∧	124	20.45 S	134.28 E
Davey, Port C	120	43.19 S	145.55 E
David	138	8.27 N	82.27 W
David City	162	41.15 N	97.08 W
Davidson	156	35.30 N	80.51 W
Davies, Mount ∧	122	26.14 S	129.16 E
Davis, Calif., U.S.	168	38.33 N	121.44 W
Davis, Okla., U.S.	160	34.30 N	97.07 W
Davis ≃	164	36.15 N	114.34 W
Davis Dam	164	35.11 N	114.35 W
Davis Mountains ∧	160	30.35 N	104.06 W
Davison	154	43.02 N	83.31 W
Davis Strait ⹁	142	67.00 N	57.00 W
Davlekanovo	82	54.13 N	55.03 E
Davos	74	46.48 N	9.50 E
Dawa (Daua) ≃	108	4.11 N	42.06 E
Dawna Range ∧	94	16.50 N	98.15 E
Dawson, Yukon, Can.	146	64.04 N	139.25 W
Dawson, Ga., U.S.	156	31.46 N	84.26 W
Dawson, Minn., U.S.	162	44.55 N	96.03 W
Dawson, Tex., U.S.	160	31.54 N	96.43 W
Dawson ≃	120	23.38 S	149.46 E
Dawson Creek	148	55.46 N	120.14 W
Dawson, Isla I	136	54.00 S	70.40 W
Dawson Inlet C	142	61.50 N	93.25 W
Dawson Range ∧, Austl.	120	24.20 S	149.45 E
Dawson Range ∧, Yukon, Can.	146	62.40 N	139.00 W
Dawson Springs	158	37.10 N	87.41 W
Dax	74	43.43 N	1.03 W
Daxian	88	31.18 N	107.30 E
Daya	106	30.06 N	114.57 E
Daye	88	30.06 N	114.57 E
Daylesford	120	37.21 S	144.09 E
Dayr az-Zawr	104	35.20 N	40.09 E
Dayrūt	108	27.33 N	30.49 E
Dayton, Ohio, U.S.	152	39.45 N	84.15 W
Dayton, Tenn., U.S.	156	35.30 N	85.00 W
Dayton, Tex., U.S.	160	30.03 N	94.53 W
Dayton, Wash., U.S.	166	46.19 N	117.58 W
Dayton, Wyo., U.S.	166	44.53 N	107.16 W
Daytona Beach	156	29.12 N	81.00 W
Dayu	88	25.24 N	114.22 E
Dayville	166	44.28 N	119.32 W
De Aar	116	30.39 S	24.00 E
Dead Sea ⊜	104	31.30 N	35.30 E
Deadwood	162	44.22 N	103.43 W
Deakin	122	30.46 S	129.06 E
Deal	70	51.14 N	1.24 E
Dean Channel ⹁	148	52.33 N	127.13 W
Deán Funes	140	30.26 S	64.20 W
Dease ≃	146	59.54 N	128.30 W
Dease Arm C	146	66.52 N	119.37 W
Dease Strait ⹁	142	68.40 N	108.00 W
Death Valley V	168	36.30 N	117.00 W
Deauville	74	49.22 N	0.04 E
Debar	80	41.31 N	20.32 E
Dębica	72	50.04 N	21.24 E
De Bilt	72	52.06 N	5.11 E
Deblin	72	51.35 N	21.50 E
Debno	72	52.45 N	14.42 E
Debre Markos	108	10.20 N	37.43 E
Debre Tabor	108	11.50 N	38.02 E
Debrecen	72	47.32 N	21.38 E
Debrzno	72	53.32 N	17.14 E
Decatur, Ala., U.S.	158	34.36 N	86.58 W
Decatur, Ga., U.S.	156	33.46 N	84.17 W
Decatur, Ill., U.S.	158	39.50 N	88.57 W
Decatur, Ind., U.S.	158	40.49 N	84.55 W
Decatur, Mich., U.S.	154	42.06 N	85.58 W
Decatur, Miss., U.S.	158	32.26 N	89.06 W
Decatur, Tex., U.S.	160	33.14 N	97.35 W
Decaturville	158	35.35 N	88.06 W
Decazeville	74	44.34 N	2.15 E
Decherd	158	35.12 N	86.05 W
Děčín	72	50.48 N	14.13 E
Decize	74	46.50 N	3.27 E
Deckerville	154	43.31 N	82.44 W
Decorah	154	43.18 N	91.48 W
De Courcy Head ➤	124	14.49 S	129.24 E
Dej	80	47.09 N	23.52 E
Dedovsk	86	55.52 N	37.07 E
Deep Creek ≃	164	41.44 N	113.00 W
Deep River, Ont., Can.	152	46.06 N	77.30 W
Deep River, Conn., U.S.	152	41.23 N	72.26 W
Deerfield, Ill., U.S.	154	42.10 N	87.50 W
Deerfield, Kans., U.S.	162	37.59 N	101.08 W
Deerfield Beach	156	26.19 N	80.06 W
Deer Lake	150	49.10 N	57.26 W
Deer Lodge	166	46.24 N	112.44 W
Deer Park	166	47.57 N	117.28 W
Deerpass Bay C	142	65.56 N	122.25 W
Deer Trail	162	39.37 N	104.02 W
Defiance	152	41.17 N	84.21 W
De Funiak Springs	158	30.43 N	86.07 W
Dege	88	31.50 N	98.40 E
Degeh-Bur	108	8.14 N	43.35 E
Dégelis (Saint-Rose-du-Dégelis)	150	47.33 N	68.39 W
Deggendorf	72	48.51 N	12.59 E
De Graff	152	40.19 N	83.55 W
De Grey ≃	122	20.10 S	119.12 E
Degtjarsk	82	56.42 N	60.06 E
Dehiwala-Mount Lavinia	100	6.51 N	79.52 E
Dehra Dún	102	30.19 N	78.02 E
Dehri	102	24.54 N	84.11 E
Dehui	88	44.34 N	125.43 E
Deinze	72	50.59 N	3.32 E
Dej	80	47.09 N	23.52 E
Dejnau	82	39.15 N	63.11 E
De Kalb, Ill., U.S.	154	41.55 N	88.45 W
De Kalb, Miss., U.S.	158	32.46 N	88.39 W
De Kalb, Tex., U.S.	158	33.31 N	94.37 W
Dekese	110	3.27 S	21.24 E
De Land	156	29.02 N	81.18 W
Delano, Calif., U.S.	168	35.46 N	119.15 W
Delano, Minn., U.S.	154	45.02 N	93.47 W
Delaware, Ohio, U.S.	152	40.18 N	83.04 W
Delaware, Okla., U.S.	160	36.47 N	95.38 W
Delaware □3	144	39.10 N	75.30 W
Delaware, West Branch ≃	152	41.56 N	75.17 W
Delaware Bay C	152	39.05 N	75.15 W
Delaware City	152	39.34 N	75.36 W
Del City	160	35.27 N	97.27 W
Delegate	120	37.03 S	148.58 E
Delémont	74	47.22 N	7.21 E
De Leon	160	32.07 N	98.32 W
Delft	72	52.00 N	4.21 E
Delfzijl	72	53.19 N	6.46 E
Delgado, Cabo ➤	110	10.40 S	40.35 E
Delhi, Bhārat	102	28.40 N	77.13 E
Delhi, Ont., Can.	152	42.51 N	80.30 W
Delhi, La., U.S.	158	32.27 N	91.30 W
Delhi, N.Y., U.S.	152	42.17 N	74.55 W
Delicias	130	28.13 N	105.28 W
Delingha	88	37.14 N	97.11 E
Delitzsch	72	51.31 N	12.20 E
Delle	74	47.30 N	7.00 E
Del Mar, Calif., U.S.	168	32.58 N	117.16 W
Delmar, Del., U.S.	152	38.27 N	75.34 W
Delmenhorst	72	53.03 N	8.37 E
Delmont	152	40.24 N	79.34 W
Del Norte	164	37.41 N	106.21 W
De-Longa, Ostrova II	84	76.30 N	153.00 E
Deloraine	120	41.31 S	146.39 E
Delorme, Lac ⊜	150	54.31 N	69.52 W
Delphi	158	40.35 N	86.40 W
Delphos, Kans., U.S.	162	39.16 N	97.46 W
Delphos, Ohio, U.S.	152	40.50 N	84.20 W
Delray Beach	156	26.28 N	80.04 W
Del Rio	160	29.22 N	100.54 W
Delta, Colo., U.S.	164	38.44 N	108.04 W
Delta, Ohio, U.S.	152	41.34 N	84.00 W
Delta, Utah, U.S.	164	39.21 N	112.35 W
Delta Amacuro □8	138	8.30 N	61.30 W
Delta Downs	120	17.00 S	141.18 E
Delta Junction	146	64.02 N	145.44 W
Delta Peak ∧	146	56.39 N	129.34 W
Del Valle	160	30.12 N	97.40 W
Demarcation Point ➤	146	69.41 N	141.15 W
Demba	110	5.30 S	22.16 E
Dembidolo	108	8.30 N	34.48 E
Deming	164	32.16 N	107.45 W
Demini ≃	138	0.46 S	62.56 W
Demjanka ≃	84	59.34 N	69.17 E
Demjansk	86	57.38 N	32.28 E
Demjanskoje	84	59.36 N	69.18 E
Demopolis	158	32.31 N	87.50 W
Demorest	156	34.34 N	83.33 W
Dempo, Gunung ∧	96	4.02 S	103.09 E
Denain	74	50.20 N	3.23 E
Denau	82	38.16 N	67.54 E
Denbigh	70	53.11 N	3.25 W
Dendermonde	72	51.02 N	4.07 E
Denham, Mount ∧	132	18.13 N	77.32 W
Denham Island I	120	16.43 S	139.09 E
Denham Range ∧	120	21.55 S	147.46 E
Denham Sound ⹁	122	25.55 S	113.32 E
Denham Springs	158	30.29 N	90.57 W
Denia	76	38.51 N	0.07 E
Deniliquin	120	35.32 S	144.58 E
Denison, Iowa, U.S.	154	42.01 N	95.21 W
Denison, Tex., U.S.	160	33.45 N	96.32 W
Denisovka	82	52.26 N	61.45 E
Denizli	64	37.46 N	29.06 E
Denmark, Austl.	122	34.57 S	117.21 E
Denmark, S.C., U.S.	156	33.19 N	81.08 W
Denmark □1	66	56.00 N	10.00 E
Denmark Strait ⹁	66a	67.00 N	25.00 W
Dennis Port	152	41.39 N	70.08 W
Dennison	152	40.23 N	81.20 W
Denton, Md., U.S.	152	38.53 N	75.49 W
Denton, Mont., U.S.	166	47.19 N	109.57 W
Denton, Tex., U.S.	160	33.13 N	97.08 W
D'Entrecasteaux, Point ➤	122	34.50 S	116.00 E
D'Entrecasteaux Islands II	124	9.30 S	150.40 E
Denver, Colo., U.S.	162	39.43 N	105.01 W
Denver, Iowa, U.S.	154	42.40 N	92.20 W
Denver, Pa., U.S.	152	40.14 N	76.08 W
Denver City	160	32.58 N	102.50 W
Deoali	100	19.56 N	73.50 E
De Pere	154	44.27 N	88.03 W
Depew, N.Y., U.S.	152	42.54 N	78.41 W
Depew, Okla., U.S.	160	35.48 N	96.30 W
Deposit	152	42.03 N	75.25 W
Depue	154	41.19 N	89.17 W
Dera Ghāzi Khān	102	30.03 N	70.38 E
Dera Ismāīl Khān	102	31.50 N	70.54 E
Derby, Austl.	122	17.18 S	123.38 E
Derby, Eng., U.K.	70	52.55 N	1.29 W
Derby, Conn., U.S.	152	41.19 N	73.05 W
Derby, Kans., U.S.	162	37.33 N	97.16 W
Derby, N.Y., U.S.	152	42.41 N	78.58 W
Derbyshire □6	70	53.00 N	1.33 W
Derecske	72	47.21 N	21.34 E
Derry	152	40.20 N	79.18 W
Derval	74	47.40 N	1.40 W
Derventa	78	44.59 N	17.55 E
Derwent ≃	70	53.45 N	0.57 W
Des Allemands	158	29.49 N	90.28 W
Desaguadero ≃, Arg.	140	34.13 S	66.47 W
Desaguadero ≃, Bol.	134	18.24 S	67.05 W
Deschambault Lake ⊜	142	54.40 N	103.35 W
Deschutes ≃, Oreg.	166	45.38 N	120.54 W
Dese	108	11.05 N	39.41 E

Name	Page	Lat	Long
Deseado ≃	136	47.45 S	65.50 W
Desengaño, Punta ➤	136	49.15 S	67.35 W
Desenzano del Garda	78	45.28 N	10.32 E
Deshler, Nebr., U.S.	162	40.08 N	97.44 W
Deshler, Ohio, U.S.	152	41.12 N	83.54 W
Des Lacs ≃	162	48.17 N	101.25 W
De Smet, Lake ⊜[1]	166	44.29 N	106.45 W
Des Moines	154	41.35 N	93.37 W
Des Moines ≃	154	40.22 N	91.26 W
Des Moines, East Fork ≃	162	42.41 N	94.12 W
Des Moines, West Fork ≃	162	42.41 N	94.12 W
Desna ≃	82	50.33 N	30.32 E
Desolación, Isla ꟷ	136	53.00 S	74.10 W
Désolation, Cap de la → Disappointment, Cape ➤	136	54.53 S	36.07 W
De Soto, Ill., U.S.	158	37.49 N	89.14 W
De Soto, Kans., U.S.	162	38.59 N	94.58 W
De Soto, Mo., U.S.	158	38.08 N	90.33 W
Des Plaines ≃	154	42.02 N	87.41 W
Dessau	72	51.50 N	12.14 E
Destin	158	30.24 N	86.30 W
Destruction Bay	146	61.15 N	138.48 W
Desvres	74	50.40 N	1.50 E
Detčino	86	54.49 N	36.19 E
Detmold	72	51.56 N	8.52 E
De Tour	154	46.00 N	83.53 W
Detroit, Mich., U.S.	154	42.20 N	83.03 W
Detroit, Oreg., U.S.	166	44.44 N	122.09 W
Detroit, Tex., U.S.	158	33.40 N	95.16 W
Detroit ≃	154	42.06 N	83.08 W
Detroit Beach	154	41.55 N	83.20 W
Detroit Lakes	162	46.49 N	95.51 W
Deurne	72	51.28 N	5.47 E
Deutschlandsberg	72	46.49 N	15.13 E
Deux-Sèvres □[5]	74	46.30 N	0.20 W
Deva	80	45.53 N	22.55 E
Dévaványa	72	47.02 N	20.58 E
Devecser	72	47.06 N	17.26 E
Deventer	72	52.15 N	6.10 E
Devil's Island → Diable, Île du ꟷ	134	5.18 N	52.35 W
Devils Lake	162	48.07 N	98.59 W
Devils Paw ⋀	146	58.44 N	133.50 W
Devon	70	50.45 N	3.50 W
Devon Island ꟷ	142	75.00 N	87.00 W
Devonport, Austl.	120	41.11 S	146.21 E
Devonport, N.Z.	126	36.49 S	174.48 E
Dewas	102	22.58 N	76.04 E
Dewey	162	36.48 N	95.56 W
Deweyville	158	30.18 N	93.45 W
De Witt, Ark., U.S.	158	34.18 N	91.20 W
De Witt, Iowa, U.S.	154	41.49 N	90.33 W
De Witt, Mich., U.S.	154	42.51 N	84.34 W
De Witt, N.Y., U.S.	152	42.50 N	76.04 W
Dewsbury	70	53.42 N	1.37 W
Dexter, Maine, U.S.	152	45.01 N	69.18 W
Dexter, Mich., U.S.	154	42.20 N	83.53 W
Dexter, Mo., U.S.	158	36.48 N	89.57 W
Dexter, N. Mex., U.S.	164	33.12 N	104.22 W
Dexterity Fiord C[2]	142	71.11 N	73.03 W
Deyang	88	31.08 N	104.23 E
Dezful	104	32.23 N	48.24 E
Dezhou	88	37.27 N	116.18 E
Dežneva, Mys ➤	146	66.06 N	169.45 W
Dhamār	100	14.46 N	44.23 E
Dhānbād	102	23.48 N	86.27 E
Dhangarhi	102	28.41 N	80.36 E
D'hanis	160	29.20 N	99.17 W
Dhār	102	22.36 N	75.18 E
Dhārwār	100	15.28 N	75.01 E
Dhaulāgiri ⋀	102	28.42 N	83.30 E
Dhodhekánisos ꟷꟷ	80	36.10 N	27.00 E
Dhorāji	102	21.44 N	70.27 E
Dhubri	102	26.01 N	89.59 E
Diable, Île du ꟷ	134	5.18 N	52.35 W
Diaka ꟷ[1]	114	15.13 N	4.14 W
Diamante	140	32.05 S	60.35 W
Diamante ≃	140	34.31 S	66.56 W
Diamantina	134	18.15 S	43.36 W
Diamantina ≃	120	26.45 S	139.10 E
Diamantino	134	14.25 S	56.27 W
Diamond Head ⋀[6]	170a	21.16 N	157.49 W
Diamond Islets ꟷꟷ	120	17.25 S	150.58 E
Diamond Lake ⊜	166	43.10 N	122.09 W
Diana, Baie C	142	60.50 N	69.50 W
Dianchi ⊜	94	24.50 N	102.42 E
Dianópolis	134	11.38 S	46.50 W
Dibaya	110	6.30 S	22.57 E
D'Iberville	158	30.26 N	88.54 W
Diboll	158	31.11 N	94.47 W
Dibrugarh	102	27.29 N	94.54 E
Dickens	160	33.37 N	100.50 W
Dickinson, N. Dak., U.S.	162	46.53 N	102.47 W
Dickinson, Tex., U.S.	160	29.28 N	95.03 W
Dickson	158	36.05 N	87.23 W
Didibran	81	51.58 N	139.20 E
Die	74	44.45 N	5.22 E
Dieburg	72	49.54 N	8.50 E
Dieciocho de Marzo	160	25.58 N	97.50 W
Diego de Almagro, Isla ꟷ	136	51.25 S	75.10 W
Diego Ramírez, Islas ꟷꟷ	136	56.30 S	68.44 W
Diégo-Suarez	117b	12.16 S	49.17 E
Dien-bien-phu	88	21.23 N	103.01 E
Diepholz	72	52.35 N	8.21 E
Dieppe, N.B., Can.	150	46.06 N	64.45 W
Dieppe, Fr.	70	49.56 N	1.05 E
Dierks	158	34.07 N	94.01 W
Diest	72	50.59 N	5.03 E
Dietrich	166	42.55 N	114.16 W
Dieu, Mui ➤	94	12.53 N	109.28 E
Dieulefit	74	44.31 N	5.04 E
Dieuze	74	48.49 N	6.43 E
Dif	108	1.00 N	41.00 E
Differdange	72	49.32 N	5.52 E
Dig	102	27.28 N	77.20 E
Digboi	102	27.23 N	95.38 E
Digby	152	44.37 N	65.46 W
Digges Islands ꟷꟷ	142	62.35 N	77.50 W
Dighton	162	38.29 N	100.28 W
Digne	74	44.06 N	6.14 E
Digoin	74	46.29 N	3.59 E
Digul ≃	124	7.07 S	138.42 E
Dijon	74	47.19 N	5.01 E
Dikhil	100	11.06 N	42.22 E
Diksmuide (Dixmude)	74	51.02 N	2.52 E
Dikson	84	73.30 N	80.35 E
Dikwa	106	12.02 N	13.56 E
Dili	96	8.33 S	125.35 E
Dill City	160	35.17 N	99.08 W
Dillenburg	72	50.44 N	8.17 E
Dilley	160	28.40 N	99.10 W
Dillingen [An Der Donau]	72	48.34 N	10.29 E
Dillingham	146	59.03 N	158.29 W
Dillon, Colo., U.S.	164	39.37 N	106.04 W
Dillon, Mont., U.S.	166	45.13 N	112.38 W
Dillon, S.C., U.S.	156	34.25 N	79.22 W
Dilolo	110	10.42 S	22.20 E
Dilworth	162	46.53 N	96.42 W
Dimāpur	102	25.54 N	93.45 E
Dimashq (Damascus)	104	33.30 N	36.18 E
Dimbokro	114	6.39 N	4.42 W
Dîmbovița □[4]	80	45.00 N	25.30 E
Dîmbovița ≃	80	44.14 N	26.13 E
Dime Box	160	30.21 N	96.50 W
Dimitrovgrad, Blg.	80	42.03 N	25.36 E
Dimitrovgrad, S.S.S.R.	66	54.14 N	49.39 E
Dimitrovo ⋀	80	42.36 N	23.06 E
Dimmitt	160	34.33 N	102.19 W
Dimona	112	31.04 N	35.02 E
Dinagat Island ꟷ	98	10.10 N	125.35 E
Dinājpur	102	25.38 N	88.38 E
Dinan	74	48.27 N	2.02 W
Dinant	72	50.16 N	4.55 E
Dinara ⋀	78	44.03 N	16.35 E
Dinard	74	48.38 N	2.04 W
Dinaric Alps → Dinara ⋀	78	43.50 N	16.35 E
Dindar, Nahr ad- (Dinder ≃)	112	14.06 N	33.40 E
Dinder (Nahr ad-Dindar) ≃	112	14.06 N	33.40 E
Dindigul	100	10.21 N	77.58 E
Dingolfing	72	48.38 N	12.31 E
Dingqing	102	31.32 N	95.27 E
Dingo	120	23.38 S	149.20 E
Dingwall	70	57.35 N	4.29 W
Dingxi	88	35.38 N	104.29 E
Dingxian	88	38.32 N	114.59 E
Dinkelsbühl	72	49.04 N	10.19 E
Dinsmore	156	30.26 N	81.46 W
Dinuba	168	36.32 N	119.23 W
Diois □[9]	74	44.40 N	5.20 E
Diomede	146	65.47 N	169.00 W
Diourbel	114	14.40 N	16.15 W
Dipolog	92	8.36 N	123.20 E
Dippoldiswalde	72	50.54 N	13.40 E
Dir	100	35.12 N	71.53 E
Dire Dawa	108	9.37 N	41.52 E
Diriamba	132	11.53 N	86.15 W
Dirico	116	17.58 S	20.47 E
Dirk Hartog Island ꟷ	122	25.48 S	113.00 E
Dirranbandi	120	28.35 S	148.14 E
Disappointment, Cape ➤, Falk. Is.	136	54.53 S	36.07 W
Disappointment, Cape ➤, Wash., U.S.	166	46.18 N	124.03 W
Disappointment, Lake ⊜	122	23.30 S	122.50 E
Disaster Bay C	120	37.17 S	150.00 E
Discovery Bay C	120	38.12 S	141.07 E
Disentis	76	46.42 N	8.51 E
Dishman	166	47.40 N	117.17 W
Disko ꟷ	142	69.50 N	53.30 W
Disko Bugt C	142	69.15 N	52.00 W
Dismal Lakes ⊜	142	67.26 N	117.07 W
Dismal Swamp ⫩	156	36.30 N	76.30 W
Disney	160	36.29 N	95.01 W
Disraeli	152	45.54 N	71.21 W
District Columbia □[3]	144	38.54 N	77.01 W
Distrito Federal □[5]	134	10.30 N	66.55 W
Disūq	112	31.08 N	30.39 E
Diu	102	20.42 N	70.59 E
Divilican Bay C	98	17.23 N	122.20 E
Divinópolis	134	20.09 S	44.54 W
Divisor, Serra do ⋀[1]	134	8.20 S	73.30 W
Divnoje	82	45.55 N	43.22 E
Dixfield	152	44.32 N	70.27 W
Dixon, Calif., U.S.	168	38.27 N	121.49 W
Dixon, Ill., U.S.	154	41.50 N	89.29 W
Dixon, Mo., U.S.	158	37.59 N	92.06 W
Dixon Entrance ⫩	146	54.25 N	132.30 W
Diyālā (Sīrwān) ≃	104	33.14 N	44.31 E
Diyarbakir	104	37.55 N	40.14 E
Dja ≃	106	2.02 N	15.12 E
Djado	106	21.00 N	12.20 E
Djailolo → Djaja, Puntjak ➤	124	1.05 S	137.30 E
Djajapura (Sukarnapura)	124	2.32 S	140.42 E
Djakarta	96	6.10 S	106.48 E
Djambala	110	2.33 S	14.45 E
Djambi → Telanaipura	96	1.36 S	103.37 E
Djawa ꟷ	96	7.30 S	110.00 E
Djawa, Laut (Java Sea) ⫘[2]	96	5.00 S	110.00 E
Djedi, Oued ⩘	106	34.28 N	6.05 E
Djember	96	8.10 S	113.42 E
Djénné	114	13.54 N	4.33 W
Djerba, Île de ꟷ	106	33.48 N	10.54 E
Djerem ≃	106	5.20 N	13.24 E
Djerid, Chott ⧉	106	33.42 N	8.26 E
Djibouti	100	11.36 N	43.09 E
Djidjelli	106	36.48 N	5.46 E
Djombang	96	7.33 S	112.14 E
Djougou	114	9.42 N	1.40 E
Djursholm	68	59.24 N	18.05 E
Dmitrija Lapteva, Proliv ⫩	84	73.00 N	142.00 E
Dmitrov	86	56.21 N	37.31 E
Dnepr ≃	64	46.30 N	32.18 E
Dneprodzeržinsk	64	48.30 N	34.37 E
Dnepropetrovsk	64	48.27 N	34.59 E
Dneprovskoje	64	55.40 N	33.55 E
Dnestr ≃	64	46.18 N	30.17 E
Dnieper → Dnepr ≃	64	46.30 N	32.18 E
Dniester → Dnestr ≃	82	46.18 N	30.17 E
Dno	86	57.50 N	29.59 E
Doany	117b	14.22 S	49.31 E
Doba	108	8.39 N	16.51 E
Dobbiaco	78	46.44 N	12.14 E
Dobbie, Mount ⋀	120	23.19 S	137.39 E
Dobbyn	120	19.48 S	140.00 E
Dobele	86	56.37 N	23.16 E
Döbeln	72	51.07 N	13.07 E
Doberai, Djazirah (Vogelkop) ➤[1]	124	1.30 S	132.30 E
Dobo	124	5.46 S	134.13 E
Doboj	80	44.44 N	18.06 E
Dobr'anka	82	58.27 N	56.25 E
Dobruš	86	52.25 N	31.19 E
Doce ≃	134	19.37 S	39.49 W
Dodecanese → Dhodhekánisos	80	36.10 N	27.00 E
Dodge Center	154	44.02 N	92.51 W
Dodge City	162	37.45 N	100.01 W
Dodgeville	154	42.57 N	90.08 W
Dodoma	108	7.02 N	39.07 E
Dodson	162	6.11 S	35.45 E
Doerun	156	31.19 N	83.55 W
Doetinchem	72	51.58 N	6.17 E
Dogondoutchi	114	13.38 N	4.02 E
Doiran, Lake ⊜	80	41.13 N	22.44 E
Dokka	68	60.50 N	10.05 E
Doksÿcy	86	54.54 N	27.46 E
Dolak, Pulau ꟷ	124	7.50 S	138.30 E
Dolbeau	142	48.53 N	72.14 W
Dol-de-Bretagne	74	48.33 N	1.45 W
Dole	74	47.06 N	5.30 E
Dolgellau	70	52.44 N	3.53 W
Dolgeville	152	43.06 N	74.46 W
Dolinsk	84	47.21 N	142.48 E
Dolisie	110	4.12 S	12.41 E
Dolj □[4]	80	44.15 N	23.45 E
Dolo	108	4.13 N	42.08 E
Dolomites → Dolomiti ⋀	78	46.25 N	11.50 E
Dolores, Arg.	140	36.19 S	57.40 W
Dolores, Colo., U.S.	164	37.28 N	108.30 W
Dolores, Ur.	140	33.33 S	58.13 W
Dolores Hidalgo	130	21.10 N	100.56 W
Dolphin and Union Strait ⫩	142	69.05 N	114.45 W
Dombarovskij	82	50.46 N	59.32 E
Dombås	68	62.05 N	9.08 E
Dombrád	72	48.14 N	21.56 E
Domeyko, Cordillera ⋀	140	24.30 S	69.00 W
Dominica □[1]	132	15.30 N	61.20 W
Dominica Channel ⫩	132	15.10 N	61.15 W
Dominican Republic □[1]	128	19.00 N	70.40 W
Dominion	150	46.14 N	60.01 W
Dominion, Cape ➤	142	66.13 N	74.28 W
Domo	108	7.54 N	46.52 E
Domodedovo	86	55.26 N	37.46 E
Domodossola	78	46.07 N	8.17 E
Dom Pedrito	140	30.59 S	54.40 W
Dompierre-sur-Besbre	74	46.31 N	3.41 E
Domuyo, Volcán ⋀[1]	140	36.37 S	70.28 W
Don ≃	64	47.04 N	39.18 E
Donaghadee	70	54.39 N	5.33 W
Donald	120	36.22 S	143.00 E
Donaldsonville	158	30.06 N	90.59 W
Donalsonville	156	31.03 N	84.53 W
Donaueschingen	72	47.57 N	8.29 E
Donauwörth	72	48.43 N	10.46 E
Don Benito	76	38.57 N	5.52 W
Doncaster	70	53.32 N	1.07 W
Dondo, Ang.	110	9.38 S	14.25 E
Dondo, Moç.	116	19.36 S	34.44 E
Dondra Head ➤	100	5.55 N	80.35 E
Doneck	64	48.00 N	37.48 E
Donegal	70	54.39 N	8.07 W
Donegal □[6]	70	54.50 N	8.00 W
Donegal Bay C	70	54.30 N	8.30 W
Donelson	158	36.10 N	86.40 W
Donetsk → Doneck	64	48.00 N	37.48 E
Donga	114	8.19 N	9.58 E
Dongara	122	29.15 S	114.56 E
Dongchuan	94	26.10 N	103.01 E
Dongen	72	51.37 N	4.56 E
Dongfang (Basuo)	94	19.05 N	108.39 E
Donggala	96	0.40 S	119.44 E
Donghai	88	34.34 N	119.11 E
Donghaidao ꟷ	94	21.02 N	110.25 E
Dong-hoi	94	17.29 N	106.36 E
Dongjiang ≃	88	23.02 N	113.32 E
Dong-nai ≃	94	10.45 N	106.48 E
Dongola → Dunqulah	112	19.10 N	30.29 E
Dongshaqundao (Pratas Islands) ꟷꟷ	88	20.42 N	116.43 E
Dongtinghu ⊜	88	29.20 N	112.54 E
Dongyang	88	29.16 N	120.14 E
Donie	160	31.30 N	96.14 W
Doniphan	158	36.37 N	90.50 W
Donji Vakuf	78	44.09 N	17.25 E
Donner Pass ✕	168	39.19 N	120.20 W
Donnybrook	122	33.35 S	115.49 E
Donora	152	40.10 N	79.52 W
Donskoj	86	53.58 N	38.20 E
Doomadgee Mission	120	17.56 S	138.49 E
Doornik → Tournai	74	50.36 N	3.23 E
Dora	158	33.44 N	87.05 W
Dora, Lake ⊜	122	22.05 S	122.55 E
Doraville	156	33.54 N	84.17 W
Dorchester, Cape ➤	142	65.29 N	77.30 W
Dordogne □[5]	74	45.10 N	0.45 E
Dordogne ≃	74	45.02 N	0.35 W
Dordrecht	72	51.49 N	4.40 E
Doré Lake ⊜	142	54.46 N	107.17 W
Dores do Indaiá	134	19.27 S	45.36 W
Dorfen	72	48.17 N	12.08 E
Dori	114	14.02 N	0.02 W
Dormans	74	49.04 N	3.38 E
Dornbirn	72	47.25 N	9.44 E
Dornoch	70	57.52 N	4.02 W
Dorochovo	86	55.32 N	36.23 E
Dorogobuž	86	54.55 N	33.18 E
Dorohoi	80	47.57 N	26.24 E
Dorre Island ꟷ	120	25.09 S	113.07 E
Dorrigo	120	30.21 S	152.43 E
Dorris	168	41.58 N	121.55 W
Dorset □[6]	70	50.47 N	2.20 W
Dortmund	72	51.31 N	7.28 E
Doruma	108	4.44 N	27.42 E
Dosatuj	84	50.23 N	118.38 E
Dos Bahias, Cabo ➤	136	44.55 S	65.32 W
Dosčatoje	86	55.23 N	42.07 E
Dos Hermanas	76	37.17 N	5.55 W
Dos Palos	168	36.59 N	120.37 W
Dossor	82	47.32 N	53.01 E
Dothan	158	31.13 N	85.24 W
Dotnuva	86	55.21 N	23.54 E
Douala	106	4.03 N	9.42 E
Douarnenez	74	48.06 N	4.20 W
Double Island Point ➤	120	25.56 S	153.11 E
Double Point ➤	120	17.39 S	146.09 E
Doubs □[5]	74	47.10 N	6.20 E
Doubs ≃	74	46.53 N	5.01 E
Doudeville	74	49.43 N	0.48 E
Douentza	114	15.00 N	2.57 W
Douglas, I. of Man	70	54.09 N	4.28 W
Douglas, Alaska, U.S.	146	58.16 N	134.24 W
Douglas, Ariz., U.S.	164	31.21 N	109.33 W
Douglas, Ga., U.S.	156	31.30 N	82.51 W
Douglas, N. Dak., U.S.	162	47.51 N	101.30 W
Douglas, Wyo., U.S.	166	42.45 N	105.24 W
Douglas, Cape ➤	146	58.52 N	153.18 W
Douglas, Mount ⋀	146	58.52 N	153.33 W
Douglas Channel ⫩	148	53.30 N	129.12 W
Douglass	162	37.31 N	96.59 W
Douglasville	156	33.45 N	84.45 W
Doulaincourt	74	48.19 N	5.12 E
Doulevant-le-Château	74	48.23 N	4.55 E
Doullens	74	50.09 N	2.21 E
Doumé	106	4.14 N	13.27 E
Dourada, Serra ⋀[1]	134	13.10 S	48.45 W
Dourados	140	22.13 S	54.48 W
Dourdan	74	48.32 N	2.01 E
Douro (Duero) ≃	76	41.08 N	8.40 W
Douvres	74	49.17 N	0.23 W
Dove Creek	164	37.46 N	108.54 W
Dover, Austl.	120	43.18 S	147.01 E
Dover, Eng., U.K.	70	51.08 N	1.19 E
Dover, Del., U.S.	152	39.10 N	75.32 W
Dover, Idaho, U.S.	166	48.15 N	116.36 W
Dover, N.H., U.S.	152	43.12 N	70.56 W
Dover, N.J., U.S.	152	40.53 N	74.34 W
Dover, Ohio, U.S.	152	40.31 N	81.29 W
Dover, Okla., U.S.	160	35.59 N	97.55 W
Dover, Strait of (Pas de Calais) ⫩	70	51.00 N	1.30 E
Dover-Foxcroft	152	45.11 N	69.13 W
Dovre	68	62.05 N	9.15 E
Dowagiac	154	41.59 N	86.06 W
Downers Grove	154	41.48 N	88.01 W
Downey	166	42.26 N	112.07 W
Downham Market	70	52.36 N	0.23 E
Downieville	168	39.34 N	120.49 W
Downingtown	152	40.00 N	75.42 W
Downpatrick	70	54.20 N	5.43 W
Doylestown, Ohio, U.S.	152	40.58 N	81.42 W
Doylestown, Pa., U.S.	152	40.19 N	75.08 W
Doyline	158	32.31 N	93.25 W
Dra, Hamada du ⫟[2]	106	28.43 N	6.00 W
Drâa, Oued ⩘	106	28.40 N	11.09 W
Drac ≃	74	45.13 N	5.42 E
Dracut	152	42.40 N	71.18 W
Drăgănești	80	44.10 N	24.16 E
Dragerton	164	39.33 N	110.26 W
Dragignan	74	43.32 N	6.28 E
Dragonera	76	...	...
Draguignan	74	43.32 N	6.28 E
Drahičyn	72	52.11 N	25.09 E
Drake	162	47.55 N	100.22 W
Drakensberg ⋀	116	27.00 S	30.00 E
Dráma	80	41.09 N	24.09 E
Drammen	68	59.44 N	10.15 E
Drau (Drava) (Dráva) ≃	78	45.33 N	18.55 E
Drava (Drau) (Dráva) ≃	78	45.33 N	18.55 E
Drawno	72	53.13 N	15.45 E
Drayton	162	48.34 N	97.10 W
Drayton Valley	148	53.13 N	114.59 W
Dresden, Ont., Can.	152	42.35 N	82.11 W
Dresden, D.D.R.	72	51.03 N	13.44 E
Dresden, Ohio, U.S.	152	40.07 N	82.01 W
Dresden, Tenn., U.S.	158	36.18 N	88.42 W
Dresden □[5]	72	51.10 N	14.00 E
Dreux	74	48.44 N	1.22 E
Driffield	70	54.00 N	0.27 E
Driggs	166	43.44 N	111.14 W
Drina ≃	80	44.53 N	19.21 E
Driscoll	160	27.40 N	97.45 W
Drøbak	68	59.39 N	10.39 E
Drobeta-Turnu-Severin	80	44.38 N	22.39 E
Drogheda	70	53.43 N	6.21 W
Drogobyč	82	49.21 N	23.30 E
Drohiczyn	72	52.24 N	22.41 E
Droichead Átha → Drogheda	70	53.43 N	6.21 W
Droichead Nua	70	53.11 N	6.48 W
Drôme □[5]	74	44.35 N	5.10 E
Drummond, Mont., U.S.	166	46.40 N	113.09 W
Drummond, Wis., U.S.	154	46.20 N	91.15 W
Drummond, Mount ⋀	120	18.47 S	137.30 E
Drummond Range ⋀	120	23.30 S	147.15 E
Drummondville	152	45.53 N	72.29 W
Druskininkai	86	54.01 N	23.58 E
Družba	84	45.15 N	82.28 E
Družina	84	68.14 N	145.18 E
Dry Bay C	146	59.08 N	138.25 W
Dry Cimarron ≃	160	36.52 N	102.59 W
Dry Creek Mountain ⋀	168	41.22 N	116.22 W
Dryden, Ont., Can.	142	49.47 N	92.50 W
Dryden, N.Y., U.S.	152	42.29 N	76.18 W
Drysdale ≃	124	13.59 S	126.51 E
Dschang	106	5.27 N	10.04 E
Duarte, Pico ⋀	132	19.00 N	71.00 W
Dubach	158	32.42 N	92.39 W
Dubai → Dubayy	104	25.18 N	55.18 E
Dubawnt ≃	142	64.33 N	100.06 W
Dubawnt Lake ⊜	142	63.08 N	101.30 W
Dubayy	104	25.18 N	55.18 E
Dubbo	120	32.15 S	148.36 E
Dublin (Baile Átha Cliath), Éire	70	53.20 N	6.15 W
Dublin, Ga., U.S.	156	32.32 N	82.54 W
Dublin, Tex., U.S.	160	32.05 N	98.21 W
Dublin □[6]	70	53.20 N	6.15 W
Dubna	86	56.44 N	37.10 E
Dubois, Idaho, U.S.	166	44.10 N	112.14 W
Du Bois, Pa., U.S.	152	41.07 N	78.46 W
Dubréka	114	9.48 N	13.31 W
Dubrovka, S.S.S.R.	86	53.42 N	33.10 E
Dubrovka, S.S.S.R.	86	59.51 N	30.56 E
Dubrovnik	80	42.38 N	18.07 E
Dubrovno	86	54.35 N	30.41 E
Dubuque	154	42.30 N	90.41 W
Duchesne	164	40.10 N	110.24 W
Duchess	120	21.22 S	139.52 E
Ducktown	156	35.03 N	84.23 W
Du Couedic, Cape ➤	120	36.04 S	136.42 E
Dudelange	72	49.28 N	6.05 E
Duderstadt	72	51.30 N	10.15 E
Dudinka	84	69.25 N	86.15 E
Dudley	70	52.30 N	2.05 W
Dudweiler	72	49.17 N	7.02 E
Due West	156	34.20 N	82.23 W
Duffield	156	36.43 N	82.47 W
Dufourspitze ⋀	76	45.57 N	7.52 E
Dufur	166	45.27 N	121.08 W
Dugger	154	39.04 N	87.16 W
Dugi Otok ꟷ	78	44.00 N	15.04 E
Du Gué ≃	142	57.21 N	70.45 W
Duifken Point ➤	124	12.33 S	141.38 E
Duisburg	72	51.25 N	6.46 E
Duitama	138	5.50 N	73.02 W
Duk Fadiat	108	7.45 N	31.25 E
Duke Islands ꟷꟷ	120	21.58 S	150.09 E
Duke of York Bay C	142	65.25 N	84.50 W
Dukhān	104	25.25 N	50.48 E
Dulce	164	36.56 N	107.00 W
Dulce ≃	140	30.32 S	62.33 W
Dul'durga	84	50.41 N	113.36 E
Dulgalach ≃	84	67.44 N	133.12 E
Dulkaninna	120	29.01 S	138.27 E
Dülmen	72	51.51 N	7.16 E
Duluth, Ga., U.S.	156	34.00 N	84.09 W
Duluth, Minn., U.S.	154	46.47 N	92.06 W
Dumaguete	98	9.18 N	123.18 E
Dumaran Island ꟷ	98	10.33 N	119.50 E
Dumaresq ≃	120	28.40 S	150.28 E
Dumas, Ark., U.S.	158	33.52 N	91.29 W
Dumas, Tex., U.S.	160	35.52 N	101.58 W
Dumbarton	70	55.57 N	4.35 W
Dumfries	70	55.04 N	3.37 W
Dumfries and Galloway Region □[4]	70	55.00 N	4.00 W
Dümmer ⊜[7]	72	52.30 N	8.20 E
Dunaföldvár	72	46.48 N	18.57 E
Dunaj, Ostrova ꟷꟷ	84	73.52 N	124.27 E
Dunakeszi	72	47.38 N	19.08 E
Dunaújváros	72	46.58 N	18.57 E
Dunbar	120	16.03 S	142.23 E
Dunblane	70	56.12 N	3.58 W
Duncan, B.C., Can.	148	48.47 N	123.42 W
Duncan, Ariz., U.S.	164	32.43 N	109.06 W
Duncan, Okla., U.S.	160	34.30 N	97.57 W
Duncannon	152	40.24 N	77.02 W
Dundalk	70	54.01 N	6.25 W
Dundas	152	43.16 N	79.58 W
Dundas Peninsula ➤[1]	142	74.50 N	111.30 W
Dundas Strait ⫩	124	11.20 S	131.35 E
Dundee, S. Afr.	116	28.07 S	30.42 E
Dundee, Scot., U.K.	70	56.28 N	3.00 W
Dundee, Fla., U.S.	156	28.01 N	81.37 W
Dundee, Mich., U.S.	154	41.57 N	83.39 W
Dundee, Ohio, U.S.	152	40.36 N	81.37 W
Dunedin, N.Z.	126	45.53 S	170.30 E
Dunedin, Fla., U.S.	156	28.00 N	82.47 W
Dunedoo	120	32.01 S	149.24 E
Dungannon	70	54.31 N	6.46 W
Dungarpur	102	23.50 N	73.43 E
Dungarvan	70	52.05 N	7.37 W
Dungun	96	4.45 N	103.25 E
Dunhua	88	43.22 N	128.13 E
Dunhuang	88	40.12 N	94.41 E
Dunkerque	74	51.03 N	2.22 E
Dunkirk → Dunkerque, Fr.	74	51.03 N	2.22 E
Dunkirk, Ind., U.S.	154	40.23 N	85.13 W
Dunkirk, N.Y., U.S.	152	42.29 N	79.20 W
Dunkirk, Ohio, U.S.	152	40.48 N	83.39 W
Dunkwa	114	5.58 N	1.47 W
Dún Laoghaire	70	53.17 N	6.08 W
Dunlap, Iowa, U.S.	162	41.51 N	95.36 W
Dunlap, Tenn., U.S.	156	35.22 N	85.23 W
Dunleary → Dún Laoghaire	70	53.17 N	6.08 W
Dun-le-Palestel	74	46.18 N	1.40 E
Dunmarra	124	16.42 S	133.25 E
Dunmore	152	41.25 N	75.38 W
Dunn	156	35.18 N	78.36 W
Dunnellon	156	29.03 N	82.28 W
Dunning	162	41.49 N	100.06 W
Dunnville	152	42.54 N	79.37 W
Dunolly	120	36.52 S	143.44 E
Dunoon	70	55.57 N	4.56 W
Dunqulah	112	19.10 N	30.29 E
Duns	70	55.47 N	2.20 W
Dunseith	162	48.49 N	100.03 W
Dunsmuir	168	41.12 N	122.16 W
Dunstable	70	51.53 N	0.32 W
Dun-sur-Auron	74	46.53 N	2.34 E
Dun-sur-Meuse	74	49.23 N	5.11 E
Dunville	150	47.16 N	53.54 W
Duomaer	88	34.15 N	79.45 E
Duolun	88	42.11 N	116.28 E
Du Page ≃	154	41.25 N	88.14 W
Dupont	156	32.47 N	80.03 W
Dupuy, Cape ➤	122	20.41 S	115.27 E
Dupuyer	166	48.11 N	112.30 W
Duque de York, Isla ꟷ	136	50.37 S	75.25 W
DuQuoin	158	38.01 N	89.14 W
Durack Range ⋀	118	17.00 S	128.00 E
Durand, Mich., U.S.	154	42.55 N	83.59 W
Durand, Wis., U.S.	154	44.38 N	91.58 W
Durango, Esp.	76	43.10 N	2.37 W
Durango, Méx.	130	24.02 N	104.40 W
Durango, Colo., U.S.	164	37.16 N	107.53 W
Durant, Iowa, U.S.	154	41.36 N	90.54 W
Durant, Miss., U.S.	158	33.04 N	89.51 W
Durant, Okla., U.S.	160	34.00 N	96.23 W
Duras	74	44.41 N	0.11 E
Durazno	140	33.22 S	56.31 W
Durban	116	29.55 S	30.56 E
Durdevac	78	46.03 N	17.04 E
Düren	72	50.48 N	6.28 E
Durg	102	21.11 N	81.17 E
Durgāpur	102	23.29 N	87.20 E
Durham, Ont., Can.	154	44.10 N	80.49 W
Durham, Eng., U.K.	70	54.47 N	1.34 W
Durham, Calif., U.S.	168	39.39 N	121.48 W
Durham, N.H., U.S.	152	43.08 N	70.56 W
Durham, N.C., U.S.	156	36.00 N	78.54 W
Durham □[6]	70	54.45 N	1.45 W
Durham Heights ⋀	142	71.08 N	122.56 W
Durmitor ⋀	80	43.08 N	19.01 E
Durness	70	58.33 N	4.45 W
Dürnkrut	72	48.28 N	16.51 E
Dürres	80	41.19 N	19.26 E
Dusänbe	82	38.35 N	68.48 E
Dushan	94	25.53 N	107.30 E
Dushanzi	88	44.20 N	84.51 E
Düsseldorf	72	51.12 N	6.47 E
Dutch John	164	40.55 N	109.24 W
Dutchman Draw ⩘	164	37.00 N	113.29 W
Dutton	166	47.51 N	111.43 W
Dutton ≃	120	20.45 S	143.12 E
Duyun	94	26.12 N	107.31 E
Dvoriši	66	58.12 N	35.13 E
Dvuch Cirkoje, Gora ⋀	84	67.35 N	168.07 E
Dvůr Králové [nad Labem]	72	50.26 N	15.48 E
Dwārka	102	22.14 N	68.58 E
Dwight	154	41.05 N	88.26 W
Dyer	158	36.04 N	88.59 W
Dyer, Cape ➤	142	66.37 N	61.18 W
Dyersburg	158	36.02 N	89.23 W
Dyersville	154	42.29 N	91.08 W
Dyfed □[6]	70	52.00 N	4.30 W
Dyje (Thaya) ≃	72	48.37 N	16.56 E
Dyrnesvägen	68	63.26 N	7.51 E
Dzalal-Abad	82	40.56 N	73.00 E
Dzambejty	82	50.16 N	52.35 E
Dzambul	82	42.54 N	71.22 E
Dzankoj	64	45.43 N	34.24 E
Dzanybek	82	49.25 N	46.51 E
Dzardzan	84	68.43 N	124.02 E
Dzaudzhikau → Ordžonikidze	64	43.03 N	44.40 E
Dzavchan ≃	88	48.54 N	93.23 E
Dželinda	84	70.08 N	114.00 E
Dzeržinsk	86	56.15 N	43.24 E
Dzeržinskoje	84	56.50 N	95.07 E
Dzetygara	82	52.11 N	61.12 E
Dzezkazgan	82	47.47 N	67.46 E
Dzierżoniów (Reichenbach)	72	50.44 N	16.39 E
Dzizak	82	40.06 N	67.50 E
Džugdžur, Chrebet ⋀	84	58.00 N	136.00 E
Džul'fa	84	38.56 N	45.38 E
Džungarskij Alatau, Chrebet ⋀	82	45.00 N	80.00 E
Džusaly	82	45.28 N	64.05 E
Dzüüncharaa	88	48.52 N	106.28 E
Dzuunmod	88	47.45 N	106.58 E
E			
Eads	162	38.29 N	102.47 W
Eagar	164	34.06 N	109.17 W
Eagle, Alaska, U.S.	146	64.47 N	141.12 W
Eagle, Colo., U.S.	164	39.39 N	106.50 W
Eagle ≃	142	53.35 N	57.25 W
Eagle Grove	154	42.40 N	93.54 W
Eagle Lake, Maine, U.S.	152	47.03 N	68.36 W
Eagle Lake, Tex., U.S.	160	29.35 N	96.20 W
Eagle Pass	160	28.42 N	100.30 W
Eagle River	154	45.55 N	89.15 W
Eaglehawk	120	36.43 S	144.15 E
Earaheedy	122	25.34 S	121.39 E
Earle	158	35.16 N	90.28 W
Earlimart	168	35.53 N	119.16 W
Earlington	158	37.16 N	87.30 W
Early	162	42.28 N	95.09 W
Easley	156	34.49 N	82.36 W
East Alton	158	38.53 N	90.06 W
East Angus	152	45.29 N	71.40 W
East Aurora	152	42.46 N	78.36 W
East Bank	152	38.12 N	81.26 W
East Berbice □[5]	138	5.00 N	57.58 W
East Berlin → Ost-Berlin	72	52.30 N	13.25 E
East Brady	152	40.59 N	79.36 W
East Brewton	158	31.05 N	87.03 W
East Chicago	154	41.38 N	87.27 W
East China Sea ⫘[2]	88	30.00 N	126.00 E
East Dennis	152	41.45 N	70.10 W
East Demerara □[5]	138	6.30 N	58.00 W
East Dereham	70	52.41 N	0.56 E
East Dublin	156	32.33 N	82.54 W
East Ely	168	39.15 N	114.53 W
Eastern Creek ≃	120	20.41 S	141.30 E
Eastern Desert → Aş-Şaḥrā'ash-Sharqīyah ⫟	112	28.00 N	32.00 E
Eastern Ghāts ⋀	100	14.00 N	78.50 E
Eastern Sayans → Vostočnyj Sajan ⋀	84	53.00 N	97.00 E
East Falkland ꟷ	136	51.45 S	58.50 W
East Fayetteville	156	35.04 N	78.51 W
East Flat Rock	156	35.17 N	82.26 W
East Frisian Islands → Ostfriesische Inseln ꟷꟷ	72	53.44 N	7.25 E
East Gaffney	156	35.04 N	81.38 W
East Glacier Park	166	48.27 N	113.13 W
East Grand Rapids	154	42.56 N	85.37 W
East Grand Forks	162	47.55 N	97.01 W
East Greenwich	152	41.39 N	71.27 W
East Hampton	152	41.00 N	72.11 W
East Helena	166	46.35 N	111.56 W
East Jordan	154	45.09 N	85.07 W
East Kilbride	70	55.46 N	4.10 W
East Lansing	154	42.44 N	84.29 W
East Liverpool	152	40.37 N	80.34 W
Eastleigh	70	50.58 N	1.22 W
East London (Oos-Londen)	116	33.00 S	27.55 E
East Longmeadow	152	42.03 N	72.30 W
East Machias	152	44.44 N	67.22 W
Eastmain	142	52.15 N	78.30 W
Eastmain ≃	142	52.15 N	78.30 W
Eastman	156	32.12 N	83.10 W
East Millcreek	164	40.43 N	111.47 W
East Millinocket	152	45.37 N	68.35 W
East Moline	154	41.31 N	90.25 W
East Naples	156	26.08 N	81.46 W
Easton, Md., U.S.	152	38.46 N	76.04 W
Easton, Pa., U.S.	152	40.42 N	75.12 W
Eastover	156	33.52 N	80.41 W
East Palatka	156	29.39 N	81.36 W
East Palestine	152	40.50 N	80.33 W
East Peoria	154	40.40 N	89.34 W
East Point	156	33.40 N	84.27 W
Eastport	152	44.54 N	67.00 W
East Prairie	158	36.47 N	89.23 W
East Retford	70	53.19 N	0.56 W
East Rockingham	156	34.55 N	79.45 W
East Saint Louis	158	38.37 N	90.09 W
East Somerset	156	37.06 N	84.35 W
East Spencer	156	35.41 N	80.26 W
East Stroudsburg	152	41.00 N	75.11 W
East Tawas	154	44.17 N	83.29 W
East Troy	154	42.47 N	88.24 W
East Walker ≃	168	38.53 N	119.10 W
East Wilmington	156	34.13 N	77.53 W
Eaton, Colo., U.S.	164	40.32 N	104.42 W
Eaton, Ohio, U.S.	152	39.45 N	84.38 W
Eaton Rapids	154	42.36 N	84.39 W
Eatonton	156	33.20 N	83.23 W
Eau Claire	154	44.49 N	91.31 W
Eau-Claire, Lac à l' ⊜	142	56.10 N	74.25 W
Eauripik ꟷ[1]	92	6.42 N	143.03 E
Eauze	74	43.52 N	0.06 E
Ebano	130	22.13 N	98.22 W
Ebbw Vale	70	51.47 N	3.12 W
Ebensburg	152	40.29 N	78.44 W
Ebensee	72	47.48 N	13.46 E
Eberbach	72	49.28 N	8.59 E
Ebermannstadt	72	49.23 N	11.13 E
Ebern	72	50.05 N	10.47 E
Ebersbach	72	51.00 N	14.35 E
Ebersberg	72	48.05 N	11.58 E
Eberstein	72	46.48 N	14.34 E
Eberswalde	72	52.50 N	13.49 E
Ebingen	72	48.13 N	9.01 E
Eboli	78	40.37 N	15.04 E
Ebolowa	106	2.54 N	11.09 E
Ebro ≃	76	40.43 N	0.54 E
Ebro, Embalse del ⊜[1]	76	43.00 N	3.58 W
Echt	72	51.06 N	5.52 E
Echuca	120	36.08 S	144.46 E
Eckernförde	72	54.28 N	9.50 E
Eckert	164	38.51 N	107.58 W
Eclipse Sound ⫩	142	72.38 N	79.00 W
Écommoy	74	47.50 N	0.16 E
Écouen	74	49.01 N	2.23 E
Ecuador □[1]	134	2.00 S	77.30 W
Ed	68	58.55 N	11.55 E
Edam	72	52.31 N	5.03 E
Eddystone Point ➤	120	40.59 S	148.21 E
Eddystone Rocks ꟷꟷ[1]	70	50.12 N	4.15 W
Eddyville, Iowa, U.S.	154	41.09 N	92.38 W
Eddyville, Ky., U.S.	158	37.03 N	88.04 W
Ede, Ned.	72	52.03 N	5.40 E
Ede, Nig.	114	7.44 N	4.27 E
Edéa	106	3.48 N	10.08 E
Edehon Lake ⊜	142	60.25 N	97.15 W
Edelény	72	48.18 N	20.44 E
Eden, Austl.	120	37.04 S	149.54 E
Eden, N.C., U.S.	156	36.29 N	79.51 W
Edenderry	70	53.21 N	7.03 W
Edenton	156	36.03 N	76.36 W
Edeowie	120	31.27 S	138.27 E
Edgar	154	40.22 N	97.58 W
Edgar Ranges ⋀	118	18.43 S	123.25 E
Edgefield	156	33.47 N	81.56 W
Edgemont	162	43.17 N	103.50 W
Edgerton, Minn., U.S.	162	43.53 N	96.08 W
Edgerton, Wis., U.S.	154	42.50 N	89.04 W
Edgewater, Ala., U.S.	158	33.32 N	86.57 W
Edgewater, Fla., U.S.	156	29.00 N	80.54 W
Edgewood	166	47.48 N	122.22 W
Edhessa	80	40.48 N	22.03 E
Edina, Minn., U.S.	154	44.54 N	93.20 W
Edina, Mo., U.S.	158	40.10 N	92.10 W
Edinboro	152	41.52 N	80.08 W
Edinburg, Ill., U.S.	154	39.39 N	89.23 W
Edinburg, Ind., U.S.	154	39.21 N	85.58 W
Edinburg, Tex., U.S.	160	26.18 N	98.10 W
Edinburg, Va., U.S.	152	38.49 N	78.34 W
Edinburgh	70	55.57 N	3.13 W
Edirne	80	41.40 N	26.34 E
Edison	152	40.31 N	74.22 W
Edith River	124	14.11 S	132.02 E
Edmonds	166	47.48 N	122.22 W
Edmonton, Austl.	120	17.01 S	145.45 E
Edmonton, Alta., Can.	148	53.33 N	113.28 W
Edmore	162	48.25 N	98.27 W
Edmundston	150	47.22 N	68.20 W
Edna, Kans., U.S.	162	37.04 N	95.22 W
Edna, Tex., U.S.	160	28.59 N	96.39 W
Edolo	78	46.11 N	10.20 E
Edremit	80	39.36 N	27.01 E
Edrengijn Nuruu ⋀	88	44.55 N	97.45 E
Edson	148	53.35 N	116.26 W
Eduardo Castex	140	35.55 S	64.20 W
Edward, Lake ⊜	110	0.25 S	29.30 E
Edward, Mount ⋀	120	22.53 S	135.10 E
Edwards	168	34.55 N	117.56 W
Edwards Plateau ⋀[1]	160	31.20 N	101.00 W
Edwardsville	158	38.48 N	89.57 W
Eek	146	60.12 N	162.15 W
Eel ≃	168	40.40 N	124.20 W
Eergu'nahe (Argun') ≃	84	53.20 N	121.28 E
Eferding	72	48.18 N	14.01 E
Effingham, Ill., U.S.	154	39.07 N	88.32 W
Effingham, Kans., U.S.	162	39.31 N	95.24 W
Ega ≃	76	42.19 N	1.55 W
Egadi, Isole ꟷꟷ	78	37.56 N	12.16 E
Egede og Rothes Fjord C[2]	142	66.00 N	38.00 W
Egedesminde	142	68.42 N	52.45 W
Egegik	146	58.13 N	157.22 W
Eger	72	47.54 N	20.23 E
Eggenburg	72	48.39 N	15.50 E
Egg Harbor City	152	39.31 N	74.38 W
Eggiwil	76	46.52 N	7.47 E
Egilsstaðir	66a	65.16 N	14.24 W
Egletons	74	45.24 N	2.03 E
Eğridir Gölü ⊜	64	38.02 N	30.53 E
Egtved	68	55.37 N	9.18 E
Egvekinot	84	66.19 N	179.10 W
Eha-Amufu	114	6.40 N	7.46 E
Ehingen	72	48.17 N	9.43 E
Ehrenberg Range ⋀	122	23.18 S	130.20 E
Éibar	76	43.11 N	2.28 W
Eibiswald	72	46.41 N	15.15 E
Eidfjord	68	60.28 N	7.05 E
Eidsvåg, Nor.	68	62.47 N	8.03 E
Eidsvoll	68	60.20 N	11.16 E
Eighty Mile Beach ⫽[2]	122	19.45 S	121.00 E
Eil	108	7.58 N	49.49 E
Eildon	120	37.14 S	145.56 E

Symbols in the index entries are identified on page 203.

Name	Page	Lat	Long
Eilenburg	72	51.27 N	12.37 E
Eil Malk I	92	7.09 N	134.22 E
Eina	68	60.38 N	10.36 E
Einasleigh	120	18.31 S	144.05 E
Einasleigh ≈	120	17.30 S	142.17 E
Einbeck	72	51.49 N	9.52 E
Eindhoven	72	51.26 N	5.28 E
Einsiedeln	74	47.08 N	8.45 E
Eire → Ireland □1	64	53.00 N	8.00 W
Eirunepé	134	6.40 S	69.52 W
Eisenach	72	50.59 N	10.19 E
Eisenberg	72	50.58 N	11.53 E
Eisenerz	72	47.33 N	14.53 E
Eisenhüttenstadt	72	52.10 N	14.39 E
Eisenkappel	80	46.29 N	14.36 E
Eisenstadt	72	47.51 N	16.32 E
Eisfeld	72	50.26 N	10.54 E
Eisleben	72	51.31 N	11.32 E
Eislingen	72	48.42 N	9.42 E
Eitorf	72	50.46 N	7.26 E
Ejea de los Caballeros	76	42.08 N	1.08 W
Ejinaqi	88	41.50 N	100.50 E
Ejutla de Crespo	130	16.34 N	96.44 W
Ekalaka	162	45.53 N	104.33 W
Ekaterinodar → Krasnodar	64	45.02 N	39.00 E
Ekenäs (Taamisaari)	68	59.58 N	23.26 E
Ekeren	72	51.17 N	4.25 E
Ekiatapskij Chrebet ⋏	146	69.00 N	177.00 E
Ekibastuz	84	51.40 N	75.22 E
Ekimčan	84	53.04 N	132.58 E
Ekonda	84	65.47 N	105.17 E
Ekwan ≈	142	53.14 N	82.13 W
Ekwok	146	59.22 N	157.30 W
El- → Ad-, Al-, An-, Ar-, As-, Az-			
El Aaiún	106	27.09 N	13.12 W
El Alamein → Al-'Alamayn	112	30.49 N	28.57 E
El Arahal	76	37.16 N	5.33 W
El Asnam	106	36.10 N	1.20 E
Elat	104	29.33 N	34.57 E
Elat, Gulf of → 'Aqaba, Gulf of C	104	29.00 N	34.40 E
Elâziğ	104	38.41 N	39.14 E
Elba	158	31.25 N	86.04 W
Elba, Isola d' I	78	42.46 N	10.17 E
El Banco	132	9.00 N	73.58 W
Elbasan	80	41.06 N	20.05 E
Elbe (Labe) ≈	72	53.50 N	9.00 E
Elbert	72	39.13 N	104.32 W
Elbert, Mount ⋏	164	39.07 N	106.27 W
Elberta	158	30.25 N	87.42 W
Elberton	156	34.07 N	82.52 W
Elbeuf	74	49.17 N	1.00 E
Elbing → Elblag	72	54.10 N	19.25 E
Elblag (Elbing)	72	54.10 N	19.25 E
Elbow Lake	162	45.59 N	95.58 W
El'brus, Gora ⋏	64	43.21 N	42.26 E
Elbrus → El'brus, Gora ⋏	64	43.21 N	42.26 E
Elburz Mountains → Alborz, Reshteh-ye Kühhä-ye ⋏	104	36.00 N	53.00 E
El Cajon	168	32.48 N	116.58 W
El Campo	160	29.12 N	96.16 W
El Capitan ⋏	166	46.01 N	114.23 W
El Carmen, Arg.	140	34.24 S	65.15 W
El Carmen, Col.	138	8.30 N	73.27 W
El Carmen de Bolívar	138	9.43 N	75.08 W
El Centro	168	32.48 N	115.34 W
El Cerrito	138	3.42 N	76.19 W
El Cesar □5	138	9.00 N	73.40 W
Elda	76	38.15 N	0.47 W
El'dikan	84	60.48 N	135.11 E
El Djouf ⇌2	106	20.30 N	8.00 W
Eldon	158	38.21 N	92.35 W
Eldora	154	42.19 N	93.06 W
Eldorado, Arg.	140	26.26 S	54.40 W
Eldorado, Méx.	130	24.17 N	107.21 W
El Dorado, Ark., U.S.	158	33.13 N	92.40 W
Eldorado, Ill., U.S.	158	37.49 N	88.26 W
El Dorado, Kans., U.S.	162	37.49 N	96.52 W
Eldorado, Tex., U.S.	160	30.52 N	100.36 W
El Dorado Springs	158	37.52 N	94.01 W
Eldoret	110	0.31 N	35.17 E
Electra	160	34.02 N	98.55 W
Elefantes, Rio dos (Olifants) ≈	116	24.10 S	32.40 E
Eleja	86	56.26 N	23.42 E
Elektrogorsk	86	55.53 N	38.47 E
Elektrostal'	86	55.47 N	38.28 E
El Encanto	138	1.37 S	73.14 W
Elephant Butte Reservoir @1	164	33.19 N	107.10 W
El Eulma	106	36.08 N	5.40 E
Eleuthera I	132	25.15 N	76.20 W
Eleva	154	44.35 N	91.28 W
Elevsis	80	38.02 N	23.32 E
Eleven Point ≈	158	36.25 N	90.46 W
El Ferrol del Caudillo	76	43.29 N	8.14 W
Elfrida	164	31.41 N	109.41 W
El Fuerte	130	26.25 N	108.39 W
El Galpón	140	25.24 S	64.39 W
Elgin, Scot., U.K.	70	57.39 N	3.20 W
Elgin, Ill., U.S.	154	42.02 N	88.17 W
Elgin, Nebr., U.S.	162	41.59 N	98.05 W
Elgin, Oreg., U.S.	166	45.34 N	117.55 W
Elgin, Tex., U.S.	160	30.21 N	97.22 W
El Goléa	106	30.35 N	2.50 E
El Hank ⇌4	106	24.30 N	7.00 W
Elhovo	80	42.10 N	26.34 E
Elida	160	33.57 N	103.39 W
Elila ≈	110	2.45 S	25.53 E
Elim	146	64.37 N	162.15 W
Elinghu ❂	88	34.50 N	97.35 E
Eliot	152	43.09 N	70.48 W
Élisabethville → Lubumbashi	110	11.40 S	27.28 E
Elisenvaara	86	61.25 N	29.46 E
Elista	64	46.16 N	44.14 E
Elizabeth, Austl.	120	34.43 S	138.40 E
Elizabeth, Colo., U.S.	164	39.22 N	104.36 W
Elizabeth, Ill., U.S.	154	42.19 N	90.13 W
Elizabeth, La., U.S.	158	30.52 N	92.48 W
Elizabeth, N.J., U.S.	152	40.39 N	74.11 W
Elizabeth City	156	36.18 N	76.14 W
Elizabeth Reef I1	118	29.56 S	159.04 E
Elizabethton	156	36.21 N	82.13 W
Elizabethtown, Ill., U.S.	158	37.27 N	88.18 W
Elizabethtown, Ky., U.S.	156	37.42 N	85.52 W
Elizabethtown, Pa., U.S.	152	40.09 N	76.36 W
El-Jadida	106	33.16 N	8.30 W
Elk, Pol.	72	53.50 N	22.22 E
Elk, Wyo., U.S.	166	43.41 N	110.25 W
El Kairouan	106	35.41 N	10.07 E
El Kasserine	106	35.11 N	8.48 E
Elk City	160	35.25 N	99.25 W
Elk Creek	168	39.36 N	122.32 W
El Kef	106	36.11 N	8.43 E
Elk Grove	168	38.25 N	121.22 W
Elkhart, Ind., U.S.	154	41.41 N	85.58 W
Elkhart, Kans., U.S.	162	37.00 N	101.54 W
Elkhart, Tex., U.S.	160	31.38 N	95.35 W
Elk Horn, Iowa, U.S.	162	41.36 N	95.03 W
Elkhorn, Wis., U.S.	154	42.40 N	88.33 W
Elkhorn City	156	37.18 N	82.21 W
Elkin	156	36.16 N	80.51 W
Elkins	156	38.55 N	79.51 W
Elkland	152	41.59 N	77.31 W
Elk Mountain	162	41.40 N	106.25 W
Elko	166	40.50 N	115.46 W
Elk Point	162	42.41 N	96.41 W
Elk Rapids	154	44.54 N	85.25 W
Elk River	154	45.18 N	93.35 W
Elkton, Ky., U.S.	158	36.49 N	87.09 W
Elkton, Md., U.S.	152	39.36 N	75.50 W
Elkton, Mich., U.S.	154	43.49 N	83.11 W
Elkville	158	37.55 N	89.14 W
Ellavalla	122	25.05 S	114.22 E
Elleker	122	35.00 S	117.43 E
Ellendale	162	46.00 N	98.32 W
Ellensburg	166	47.00 N	120.32 W
Ellenville	152	41.43 N	74.24 W
Ellesmere	70	52.54 N	2.54 W
Ellettsville	158	39.14 N	86.37 W
Ellice ≈	142	68.02 N	103.26 W
Ellichpur → Achalpur	102	21.16 N	77.31 E
Ellicott City	152	39.16 N	76.48 W
Ellicottville	152	42.17 N	78.40 W
Ellijay	156	34.42 N	84.28 W
Ellinwood	162	38.21 N	98.35 W
Elliot	116	31.18 S	27.50 E
Elliot, Mount ⋏	120	19.29 S	146.58 E
Elliot Lake	142	46.23 N	82.39 W
Elliott	122	17.33 S	133.32 E
Ellis	162	38.56 N	99.34 W
Elliston, Austl.	122	33.39 S	134.55 E
Elliston, Mont., U.S.	166	46.33 N	112.26 W
Ellisville	158	31.36 N	89.12 W
Ellon	70	57.22 N	2.05 W
Ellore → Elūru	100	16.42 N	81.06 E
Ellsworth, Kans., U.S.	162	38.44 N	98.14 W
Ellsworth, Maine, U.S.	152	44.33 N	68.26 W
Ellwangen	72	48.57 N	10.07 E
Ellwood City	152	40.50 N	80.17 W
Elm	74	46.55 N	9.11 E
Elma	166	47.00 N	123.25 W
Elm Creek	162	40.43 N	99.22 W
Elmer	152	39.36 N	75.10 W
Elmhurst	154	41.53 N	87.56 W
Elmira, Ont., Can.	154	43.36 N	80.33 W
Elmira, N.Y., U.S.	152	42.06 N	76.49 W
Elmira Heights	152	42.08 N	76.49 W
El Mirage	164	33.36 N	112.19 W
El Moknine	106	35.38 N	10.54 E
El Molinillo	76	39.28 N	4.13 W
Elmore, Austl.	122	36.30 S	144.37 E
Elmore, Minn., U.S.	154	43.30 N	94.05 W
Elmore, Ohio, U.S.	154	41.29 N	83.18 W
El Mreyyé ⇌1	114	19.30 N	7.00 W
Elmshorn	72	53.45 N	9.39 E
Elmsta	68	59.58 N	18.48 E
Elmwood	154	40.47 N	89.58 W
Elne	74	42.36 N	2.58 E
El Nevado, Cerro ⋏	138	3.59 N	74.04 W
Elobey, Islas II	110	0.59 N	9.30 E
Eloise	158	28.00 N	81.44 W
Elora	158	35.01 N	86.21 W
El Oro □4	130	3.30 S	79.50 W
El Oued	106	33.20 N	6.58 E
Eloy	164	32.45 N	111.33 W
El Paso, Ill., U.S.	154	40.44 N	89.01 W
El Paso, Tex., U.S.	164	31.45 N	106.29 W
El Portal	168	37.41 N	119.47 W
El Potro, Cerro ⋏	140	28.24 S	69.39 W
El Progreso	130	15.21 N	87.49 W
El Puerto de Santa María	76	36.36 N	6.13 W
El Reno	160	35.32 N	97.57 W
El Rio	168	34.14 N	119.10 W
Elsa, Yukon, Can.	146	63.55 N	135.28 W
Elsa, Tex., U.S.	160	26.18 N	97.59 W
El Salto	130	23.47 N	105.22 W
El Salvador □1	128	13.50 N	88.55 W
Elsberry	158	39.10 N	90.47 W
Elsie	154	43.05 N	84.23 W
Elsinore → Helsingør, Dan.	68	56.02 N	12.37 E
Elsinore, Calif., U.S.	168	33.40 N	117.20 W
Elsinore, Utah, U.S.	164	38.41 N	112.09 W
Elspe	72	51.09 N	8.04 E
Elsterwerda	72	51.28 N	13.31 E
Eltham	126	39.26 S	174.18 E
Eltmann	72	49.58 N	10.40 E
El Tigre	138	8.55 N	64.15 W
El Tocuyo	138	9.47 N	69.48 W
El Toro	138	29.27 S	71.15 W
Elton	158	30.29 N	92.42 W
El Turbio	136	51.41 S	72.05 W
Elūru	100	16.42 N	81.06 E
Elvas	76	38.53 N	7.10 W
Elverum	68	60.53 N	11.34 E
El Viejo	138	12.38 N	87.11 W
El Vigia	138	8.38 N	71.39 W
Elwood, Ind., U.S.	158	40.17 N	85.50 W
Elwood, Kans., U.S.	162	39.45 N	94.52 W
Ely, Eng., U.K.	70	52.24 N	0.16 E
Ely, Minn., U.S.	154	47.54 N	91.51 W
Ely, Nev., U.S.	166	39.15 N	114.53 W
Elyria	154	41.22 N	82.06 W
Emba	82	48.50 N	58.08 E
Emba ≈	82	46.38 N	53.14 E
Embarcación	140	23.15 S	64.10 W
Embira ≈	134	7.19 S	70.15 W
Embreeville	156	36.11 N	82.28 W
Embrun	74	44.34 N	6.30 E
Emden	72	53.22 N	7.12 E
Emerald	120	23.32 S	148.10 E
Emery, S. Dak., U.S.	162	43.36 N	97.37 W
Emery, Utah, U.S.	164	38.55 N	111.15 W
Emilia-Romagna □4	78	44.35 N	11.00 E
Emin	88	46.29 N	83.38 E
Eminence	158	37.09 N	91.21 W
Emlenton	152	41.11 N	79.43 W
Emmaus	152	40.32 N	75.30 W
Emmaville	122	29.26 S	151.36 E
Emmeloord	72	52.47 N	5.46 E
Emmen	72	52.47 N	6.55 E
Emmendingen	72	48.07 N	7.50 E
Emmerich	72	51.50 N	6.15 E
Emmetsburg	162	43.07 N	94.41 W
Emmett	166	43.52 N	116.30 W
Emmonak	146	62.46 N	164.30 W
Emory	160	32.52 N	95.46 W
Emory University	156	33.48 N	84.19 W
Empalme	130	27.58 N	110.51 W
Empangeni	116	28.50 S	31.48 E
Empedrado	140	27.55 S	58.45 W
Empire	164	39.23 N	114.17 W
Empoli	78	43.43 N	10.57 E
Emporia, Kans., U.S.	162	38.24 N	96.11 W
Emporia, Va., U.S.	156	36.41 N	77.32 W
Emporium	152	41.30 N	78.14 W
Emsdetten	72	52.10 N	7.31 E
En (Inn) ≈	72	48.35 N	13.28 E
Encampment	164	41.18 N	106.47 W
Encarnación	140	27.20 S	55.54 W
Encinal	160	28.02 N	99.21 W
Encinitas	168	33.03 N	117.17 W
Encino	160	34.39 N	105.28 W
Encounter Bay C	122	35.35 S	138.44 E
Ende	96	8.50 S	121.39 E
Endeavour Strait ⋃	124	10.50 S	142.15 E
Endicott, N.Y., U.S.	152	42.06 N	76.03 W
Endicott, Wash., U.S.	166	46.56 N	117.41 W
Enfield, N.H., U.S.	152	43.38 N	72.09 W
Enfield, N.C., U.S.	156	36.11 N	77.47 W
Engano, Pulau I	96	5.24 S	102.16 E
Engan	68	63.09 N	8.32 E
England □8	66	52.30 N	1.30 W
Englefield, Cape ⋗	142	69.50 N	85.39 W
Englehart	154	47.49 N	79.52 W
Englewood, Colo., U.S.	164	39.39 N	104.59 W
Englewood, Fla., U.S.	158	26.58 N	82.21 W
Englewood, Kans., U.S.	160	37.02 N	100.01 W
English ≈	142	50.12 N	95.00 W
English, N.A.	152	45.13 N	73.50 W
English Bay	146	59.22 N	151.55 W
English Bazar	102	25.00 N	88.09 E
English Channel (La Manche) ⋃	70	50.20 N	1.00 W
Enid	160	36.19 N	97.48 W
Enkhuizen	72	52.42 N	5.17 E
Enköping	68	59.38 N	17.04 E
Enmelen	146	65.01 N	175.54 W
Enna	78	37.34 N	14.17 E
Ennadai Lake ❂	142	60.53 N	101.15 W
Ennedi ⇘1	112	17.15 N	22.00 E
Ennis, Eire	70	52.50 N	8.59 W
Ennis, Mont., U.S.	166	45.21 N	111.44 W
Ennis, Tex., U.S.	160	32.20 N	96.38 W
Enniscorthy	70	52.30 N	6.34 W
Enniskillen	70	54.21 N	7.38 W
Ennistymon	70	52.57 N	9.13 W
Enns	72	48.13 N	14.29 E
Eno	68	62.48 N	30.09 E
Enon	152	39.53 N	83.56 W
Enosburg Falls	152	44.55 N	72.48 W
Enschede	72	52.12 N	6.53 E
Ensenada, Arg.	140	34.51 S	57.55 W
Ensenada, Méx.	130	31.52 N	116.37 W
Enshi	88	30.17 N	109.19 E
Entebbe	110	0.04 N	32.28 E
Enterprise, Ala., U.S.	158	31.19 N	85.51 W
Enterprise, Calif., U.S.	168	40.32 N	121.22 W
Enterprise, Oreg., U.S.	166	45.25 N	117.17 W
Enterprise, Utah, U.S.	164	37.34 N	113.43 W
Entraygues	74	44.39 N	2.34 E
Entre-Rios	110	14.57 S	37.20 E
Entre Rios □4	140	32.00 S	59.20 W
Entroncamento	76	39.28 N	8.28 W
Enugu	114	6.27 N	7.27 E
Enumclaw	166	47.12 N	121.59 W
Enurmino	146	66.57 N	171.49 W
Envalira, Port d')(	76	42.33 N	1.45 E
Envermeu	74	49.54 N	1.16 E
Envigado	138	6.10 N	75.35 W
Eo ≈	76	43.28 N	7.03 W
Eolie, Isole II	78	38.30 N	15.00 E
Epe	114	6.37 N	3.59 E
Épernay	74	49.03 N	3.57 E
Ephraim	164	39.22 N	111.35 W
Ephrata, Pa., U.S.	152	40.11 N	76.10 W
Ephrata, Wash., U.S.	166	47.19 N	119.33 W
Épinal	74	48.11 N	6.27 E
Epping, Eng., U.K.	70	51.43 N	0.07 E
Epping, N.H., U.S.	152	43.02 N	71.04 W
Epsom	70	51.20 N	0.16 W
Épuisay	74	47.54 N	0.56 E
Epukiro	116	21.41 S	19.08 E
Epukiro ≈	116	20.45 S	21.05 E
Equality	158	37.44 N	88.20 W
Equatorial Guinea □1	106	2.00 N	9.00 E
Eradu	122	28.41 S	115.02 E
Erath	158	29.58 N	92.02 W
Erba	78	45.48 N	9.15 E
Erciyeş Dağı ⋏	104	38.32 N	35.28 E
Érd	72	47.23 N	18.56 E
Erdene	88	44.40 N	111.05 E
Erding	72	48.18 N	11.54 E
Erechim	140	27.38 S	52.17 W
Ereğli	104	37.31 N	34.04 E
Erfoud	106	31.28 N	4.10 W
Erfurt	72	51.20 N	11.01 E
Erfurt □5	72	51.20 N	10.50 E
Erges (Erjas) ≈	76	39.40 N	7.01 W
Erhai ❂	94	25.48 N	100.11 E
Erice	78	38.02 N	12.36 E
Ericeira	76	38.59 N	9.25 W
Erichsen Lake ❂	142	70.38 N	80.21 W
Erick	160	35.12 N	99.52 W
Erie, Kans., U.S.	162	37.34 N	95.15 W
Erie, Pa., U.S.	152	42.08 N	80.04 W
Erie, Lake ❂	154	42.15 N	81.00 W
Erigavo	108	10.35 N	47.20 E
Erimo-misaki ⋗	90a	41.55 N	143.15 E
Eritrea □9	108	15.20 N	39.00 E
Erivan → Jerevan	104	40.11 N	44.30 E
Erjas (Erges) ≈	76	39.40 N	7.01 W
Erkelenz	72	51.05 N	6.19 E
Erkner	72	52.25 N	13.45 E
Erlangen	72	49.36 N	11.01 E
Erldunda	122	25.14 S	133.12 E
Erlian	88	43.46 N	112.05 E
Erlistoun	122	28.20 S	122.08 E
Ermelo	116	26.34 S	29.59 E
Ermoúpolis	80	37.26 N	24.56 E
Ernabella Mission	122	26.17 S	132.07 E
Ernakulam	100	9.59 N	76.17 E
Ernée	74	48.18 N	0.56 W
Erode	100	11.21 N	77.43 E
Eromanga	120	26.40 S	143.16 E
Errol	152	44.47 N	71.08 W
Errol Heights	166	45.29 N	122.33 W
Erskine Inlet ⋃	142	76.15 N	102.20 W
Erstein	74	48.25 N	7.40 E
Ertai	88	46.07 N	90.06 E
Ertil'	86	51.50 N	40.49 E
Erudina	122	31.28 S	139.23 E
Ervy-le-Châtel	74	48.02 N	3.55 E
Erwin, N.C., U.S.	156	35.20 N	78.41 W
Erwin, Tenn., U.S.	156	36.09 N	82.25 W
Erzgebirge (Krušné hory) ⋏	72	50.30 N	13.10 E
Erzincan	104	39.44 N	39.29 E
Erzin	104	36.36 N	36.12 E
Erzurum	104	39.55 N	41.17 E
Esbjerg	68	55.28 N	8.27 E
Esca ≈	76	42.35 N	1.04 W
Escalante	164	37.46 N	111.36 W
Escalón	130	26.45 N	104.20 W
Escanaba	154	45.44 N	87.04 W
Escanaba ≈	154	45.47 N	87.04 W
Escarpada Point ⋗	98	18.31 N	122.13 E
Escatawpa ≈	158	30.25 N	88.35 W
Escaut (Schelde) ≈	72	51.22 N	4.15 E
Esch-sur-Alzette	72	49.30 N	5.59 E
Eschwege	72	51.11 N	10.04 E
Eschweiler	72	50.49 N	6.16 E
Escondido	168	33.07 N	117.05 W
Escuinapa [de Hidalgo]	130	22.51 N	105.48 W
Escuintla	130	14.18 N	90.47 W
Escurial, Serra do ⋏	134	10.04 S	41.05 W
Eşfahān (Isfahan)	104	32.40 N	51.38 E
Esk ≈	70	54.58 N	3.04 W
Eskdale	122	37.34 S	146.27 E
Eskilstrup	68	54.51 N	11.54 E
Eskilstuna	68	59.22 N	16.30 E
Eskimo Lakes ❂	146	69.15 N	132.17 W
Eskimo Point	142	61.07 N	94.03 W
Eskişehir	104	39.46 N	30.32 E
Eslöv	68	55.50 N	13.20 E
Esmeralda	136	48.55 S	75.25 W
Esmeralda, Isla I	136	48.55 S	75.25 W
Esmeraldas	138	0.59 N	79.42 W
Esmeraldas □4	138	0.40 N	79.30 W
Espalion	74	44.31 N	2.46 E
Espanola, Ont., Can.	154	46.15 N	81.46 W
Espanola, N. Mex., U.S.	164	36.00 N	106.02 W
Espelkamp	72	52.22 N	8.36 E
Esperance	122	33.51 S	121.53 E
Esperance Bay C	122	33.51 S	121.53 E
Esperanza, Arg.	140	31.30 S	60.56 W
Esperanza, Méx.	130	27.35 N	109.56 W
Espevær	68	59.35 N	5.09 E
Espinal	138	4.09 N	74.53 W
Espinho, Serra do ⋏	134	17.30 S	43.30 W
Espírito Santo □3	134	20.00 S	40.45 W
Espíritu Santo, Isla del I	130	24.30 N	110.20 W
Espita	130	21.01 N	88.19 W
Espoo (Esbo)	68	60.13 N	24.40 E
Esposende	76	41.32 N	8.47 W
Espungabera	110	20.29 S	32.48 E
Esquel	136	42.55 S	71.20 W
Esquimalt	148	48.26 N	123.24 W
Esquina	140	30.00 S	59.30 W
Essaouira	106	31.30 N	9.47 W
Essen	72	51.28 N	7.01 E
Essendon, Mount ⋏	122	24.59 S	120.28 E
Essequibo	138	7.00 N	59.00 W
Essequibo ≈	138	6.50 N	58.30 W
Essequibo Islands □5	138	6.55 N	58.55 W
Essex, Ont., Can.	154	42.10 N	82.49 W
Essex, Iowa, U.S.	162	40.50 N	95.18 W
Essex, Md., U.S.	152	39.18 N	76.29 W
Essex □6	70	51.48 N	0.40 E
Essex Junction	152	44.29 N	73.07 W
Essexville	154	43.37 N	83.50 W
Essonne □5	74	48.45 N	2.20 E
Essonne ≈	74	48.30 N	2.24 E
Essoyes	74	48.04 N	4.32 E
Est, Cap ⋗	117b	15.16 S	50.29 E
Est, Pointe de l' ⋗	150	49.08 N	61.41 W
Estacada	166	45.17 N	122.20 W
Estacado, Llano ≈	160	33.30 N	102.40 W
Estância, Bra.	134	11.16 S	37.26 W
Estancia, N. Mex., U.S.	164	34.45 N	106.04 W
Estarreja	76	40.45 N	8.34 W
Estats, Pique d' ⋏	76	42.40 N	1.24 E
Estcourt	116	29.01 S	29.52 E
Este	78	45.14 N	11.39 E
Esteli	132	13.05 N	86.23 W
Estella	76	42.40 N	2.02 W
Estelline, S. Dak., U.S.	162	44.35 N	96.54 W
Estelline, Tex., U.S.	160	34.33 N	100.26 W
Estonian Soviet Socialist Republic → Estonskaja Sovetskaja Socialističeskaja Respublika □3	82	59.00 N	26.00 E
Estonskaja Sovetskaja Socialističeskaja Respublika □3	82	59.00 N	26.00 E
Estremadura □9	76	39.15 N	9.10 W
Estremoz	76	38.51 N	7.35 W
Estrondo, Serra do ⋏	134	9.00 S	48.45 W
Esztergom	72	47.48 N	18.45 E
Étables	74	48.38 N	2.50 W
Etadunna	122	28.43 S	138.38 E
Etain	74	49.13 N	5.38 E
Étampes	74	48.26 N	2.09 E
Étaples	74	50.31 N	1.39 E
Eten	134	6.55 S	79.50 W
Ethan	162	43.33 N	97.59 W
Ethel	166	46.33 N	122.54 W
Ethel Creek	122	22.54 S	120.09 E
Ethiopia □1	108	8.00 N	38.00 E
Ethridge	166	48.34 N	112.08 W
Etna ≈	74	48.24 N	5.10 E
Etna, Calif., U.S.	166	41.27 N	122.54 W
Etna, Wyo., U.S.	166	43.02 N	111.00 W
Etna, Monte ⋏1	78	37.46 N	15.00 E
Etoshapan ⇌	116	18.45 S	16.15 E
Etowah	156	35.20 N	84.32 W
Étréchy	74	48.30 N	2.12 E
Étretat	74	49.42 N	0.12 E
Ettelbruck	72	49.51 N	6.05 E
Etten-Leur	72	51.34 N	4.38 E
Ettlingen	72	48.56 N	8.24 E
Ettrick	156	37.14 N	77.25 W
Etzatlán	130	20.46 N	104.05 W
Eu	74	50.03 N	1.25 E
Eucla	122	31.43 S	128.52 E
Euclid	152	41.33 N	81.32 W
Eudora, Ark., U.S.	158	33.07 N	91.16 W
Eudora, Kans., U.S.	162	38.57 N	95.06 W
Eudunda	122	34.11 S	139.04 E
Eufaula, Ala., U.S.	158	31.54 N	85.09 W
Eufaula, Okla., U.S.	160	35.17 N	95.35 W
Eufaula Lake ❂1	160	35.17 N	95.31 W
Eugene	166	44.02 N	123.05 W
Eugenia, Punta ⋗	130	27.50 N	115.03 W
Eugowra	122	33.26 S	148.23 E
Eunice, La., U.S.	158	30.30 N	92.25 W
Eunice, N. Mex., U.S.	160	32.26 N	103.09 W
Eupen	72	50.38 N	6.02 E
Euphrates (Firat) (Al-Furāt) ≈	104	31.00 N	47.25 E
Eupora	158	33.32 N	89.16 W
Eure □5	74	49.10 N	1.00 E
Eure ≈	74	49.18 N	1.12 E
Eure-et-Loir □5	74	48.25 N	1.30 E
Eureka, Calif., U.S.	166	40.47 N	124.09 W
Eureka, Ill., U.S.	154	40.43 N	89.16 W
Eureka, Kans., U.S.	162	37.49 N	96.17 W
Eureka, Mont., U.S.	166	48.53 N	115.03 W
Eureka, Utah, U.S.	164	39.57 N	112.07 W
Eureka Springs	158	36.24 N	93.44 W
Europa, Île I	110	22.20 S	40.22 E
Europa Point ⋗	76	36.06 N	5.21 W
Euskirchen	72	50.39 N	6.47 E
Eustis	158	28.51 N	81.41 W
Eutaw	158	32.50 N	87.53 W
Eutin	72	54.08 N	10.37 E
Eutsuk Lake ❂	148	53.20 N	126.44 W
Evacuation Creek ≈	164	39.58 N	109.09 W
Evans, Lac ❂	142	50.55 N	77.00 W
Evans City	152	40.46 N	80.03 W
Evans Head ⋗	122	29.07 S	153.26 E
Evans Strait ⋃	142	63.15 N	82.00 W
Evanston, Ill., U.S.	154	42.02 N	87.41 W
Evanston, Wyo., U.S.	166	41.16 N	110.58 W
Evansville, Ind., U.S.	158	37.58 N	87.35 W
Evansville, Wyo., U.S.	166	42.51 N	106.16 W
Evart	154	43.54 N	85.08 W
Eveleth	154	47.27 N	92.32 W
Evensk	84	61.57 N	159.14 E
Everard, Cape ⋗	122	37.48 S	149.17 E
Everard, Lake ❂	122	31.25 S	135.05 E
Everard, Mount ⋏	122	26.16 S	132.04 E
Everard Ranges ⋏	122	27.05 S	132.28 E
Everest, Mount (Zhumulangmafeng (Qomolangma Feng)) ⋏	102	27.59 N	86.56 E
Everett, Pa., U.S.	152	40.01 N	78.23 W
Everett, Wash., U.S.	166	47.59 N	122.12 W
Everett Mountains ⋏	142	62.45 N	67.12 W
Evergem	72	51.06 N	3.42 E
Evergreen, Ala., U.S.	158	31.26 N	86.57 W
Evergreen, Calif., U.S.	168	37.20 N	121.46 W
Evergreen Park	154	41.43 N	87.42 W
Everly	162	43.10 N	95.20 W
Evesham	70	52.06 N	1.56 W
Évian-les-Bains	74	46.23 N	6.35 E
Evje	68	58.36 N	7.51 E
Évora	76	38.34 N	7.54 W
Évreux	74	49.01 N	1.09 E
Évron	74	48.10 N	0.24 W
Évry	74	48.38 N	2.27 E
Évvoia I	80	38.34 N	23.50 E
Évvoia □5	80	38.30 N	24.00 E
Ewa Beach	170c	21.20 N	158.02 W
Ewab → Kai, Kepulauan II	124	5.35 S	132.45 E
Ewarton	132	18.11 N	77.05 W
Ewing	162	42.15 N	98.21 W
Ewing, Mount ⋏	122	31.50 S	121.16 E
Ewo	110	0.53 S	14.49 E
Excelsior Springs	158	39.20 N	94.13 W
Exeter, Ont., Can.	154	43.21 N	81.29 W
Exeter, Eng., U.K.	70	50.43 N	3.31 W
Exeter, Calif., U.S.	168	36.18 N	119.09 W
Exeter, N.H., U.S.	152	42.59 N	70.57 W
Exeter Sound ⋃	142	66.14 N	62.00 W
Exira	162	41.35 N	94.52 W
Exmore	156	37.32 N	75.50 W
Exmoor	70	51.10 N	3.45 W
Exmouth	70	50.37 N	3.25 W
Exmouth Gulf C	122	22.00 S	114.20 E
Experiment	156	33.16 N	84.17 W
Exuma Sound ⋃	132	24.00 N	76.00 W
Eyasi, Lake ❂	110	3.40 S	35.05 E
Eydehavn	68	58.31 N	8.53 E
Eye	70	52.19 N	1.09 E
Eyemouth	70	55.52 N	2.06 W
Eymet	74	44.40 N	0.24 E
Eymoutiers	74	45.44 N	1.44 E
Eyrarbakki	66a	63.52 N	21.05 W
Eyre	122	32.15 S	126.18 E
Eyre (North), Lake ❂, Austl.	120	29.30 S	137.20 E
Eyre (South), Lake ❂, Austl.	120	29.30 S	137.10 E
Eyre Creek ≈	120	26.40 S	139.00 E
Eyre Peninsula ⋗1	122	34.00 S	135.45 E

F

Name	Page	Lat	Long
Fabens	164	31.30 N	106.10 W
Fåberg	68	61.10 N	10.24 E
Faber Lake ❂	142	63.56 N	117.15 W
Fabriano	78	43.20 N	12.54 E
Facatativá	138	4.49 N	74.22 W
Fada	114	17.14 N	21.33 E
Fada Ngourma	114	12.04 N	0.21 E
Fadd	72	46.28 N	18.50 E
Faddeja, Zaliv C	84	76.40 N	107.20 E
Faddejevskij, Ostrov I	84	75.30 N	144.00 E
Faenza	78	44.17 N	11.53 E
Faeroe Islands □2	64	62.00 N	7.00 W
Fafe	76	41.27 N	8.10 W
Fafen ≈	108	6.07 N	44.20 E
Făgăraş	80	45.51 N	24.58 E
Fagernes	68	60.59 N	9.15 E
Fagersta	68	60.00 N	15.47 E
Faguibine, Lac ❂	114	16.45 N	3.54 W
Fairbanks	146	64.50 N	147.43 W
Fairburn	156	33.34 N	84.35 W
Fairbury, Nebr., U.S.	162	40.08 N	97.11 W
Fairbury, Ill., U.S.	154	40.44 N	88.30 W
Fairfax, Okla., U.S.	160	36.34 N	96.42 W
Fairfax, S.C., U.S.	156	32.58 N	81.14 W
Fairfax, Va., U.S.	152	38.51 N	77.18 W
Fairfield, Calif., U.S.	168	38.15 N	122.03 W
Fairfield, Ill., U.S.	158	38.22 N	88.21 W
Fairfield, Iowa, U.S.	154	40.56 N	91.57 W
Fairfield, Maine, U.S.	152	44.35 N	69.36 W
Fairfield, Mont., U.S.	166	47.37 N	111.59 W
Fairfield, Ohio, U.S.	152	39.20 N	84.33 W
Fairfield, Tex., U.S.	160	31.44 N	96.10 W
Fairgrove	154	43.31 N	83.33 W
Fairhaven, Mass., U.S.	152	41.39 N	70.54 W
Fairhope	158	30.31 N	87.54 W
Fair Isle I	70	59.30 N	1.40 W
Fairland	156	36.45 N	94.51 W
Fairlie	126	44.06 S	170.50 E
Fairmont, Minn., U.S.	154	43.38 N	94.27 W
Fairmont, Nebr., U.S.	162	40.38 N	97.35 W
Fairmont, W. Va., U.S.	152	39.29 N	80.08 W
Fairmount, Ind., U.S.	158	40.25 N	85.39 W
Fairmount, N. Dak., U.S.	162	46.03 N	96.36 W
Fair Ness ⋗	142	63.24 N	72.05 W
Fair Oaks, Calif., U.S.	168	38.39 N	121.16 W
Fair Oaks, Ga., U.S.	156	33.55 N	84.32 W
Fair Plain	154	42.05 N	86.28 W
Fairport	152	43.06 N	77.27 W
Fairport Harbor	152	41.45 N	81.17 W
Fairview, Alta., Can.	148	56.04 N	118.23 W
Fairview, Mich., U.S.	154	44.43 N	84.03 W
Fairview, Mont., U.S.	162	47.51 N	104.03 W
Fairview, Okla., U.S.	160	36.16 N	98.29 W
Fairview, Pa., U.S.	152	42.02 N	80.15 W
Fairview, Tenn., U.S.	158	35.59 N	87.07 W
Fairview, Utah, U.S.	164	39.38 N	111.26 W
Fairview Park	154	41.26 N	81.51 W
Fairweather, Cape ⋗	136	51.36 S	68.53 W
Fairweather, Mount ⋏	146	58.54 N	137.32 W
Fais I	92	9.46 N	140.31 E
Faith	162	45.01 N	102.02 W
Faizābād	102	26.47 N	82.08 E
Fajardo	132	18.20 N	65.39 W
Fakenham	70	52.50 N	0.51 E
Faku	88	42.30 N	123.18 E
Falaise	74	48.54 N	0.12 W
Falam	94	22.55 N	93.43 E
Falcón □3	138	11.00 N	69.50 W
Falconara Marittima	78	43.37 N	13.24 E
Falcon Reservoir ❂1	160	26.37 N	99.11 W
Falémé ≈	114	14.46 N	12.14 W
Falfurrias	160	27.14 N	98.09 W
Falkenberg, Sve.	68	56.54 N	12.28 E
Falkenberg, D.D.R.	72	51.35 N	13.14 E
Falkensee	72	52.34 N	13.05 E
Falkenstein	72	50.29 N	12.22 E
Falkirk	70	56.00 N	3.48 W
Falkland Islands (Islas Malvinas) □2	136	51.45 S	59.00 W
Falkland Sound ⋃	136	51.45 S	59.25 W
Fallbrook	168	33.23 N	117.15 W
Fallersleben	72	52.25 N	10.43 E
Fall River, Mass., U.S.	152	41.43 N	71.08 W
Fall River, Wis., U.S.	154	43.23 N	89.03 W
Fall River Mills	168	41.00 N	121.25 W
Falls City, Nebr., U.S.	162	40.03 N	95.36 W
Falls City, Oreg., U.S.	166	44.52 N	123.26 W
Fallon	166	39.28 N	118.46 W
Falmouth, Eng., U.K.	70	50.08 N	5.04 W
Falmouth, Ky., U.S.	152	38.40 N	84.19 W
Falmouth, Maine, U.S.	152	43.44 N	70.15 W
False Divi Point ⋗	100	15.45 N	80.47 E
Fălticeni	80	47.28 N	26.18 E
Falun	68	60.36 N	15.38 E
Famagusta → Ammóhostos	104	35.07 N	33.57 E
Famatina, Nevado de ⋏	140	29.00 S	67.51 W
Famenne □9	72	50.10 N	5.15 E
Fangak	108	9.04 N	30.53 E
Fang	94	19.55 N	99.15 E
Fanling	94	22.30 N	114.08 E
Fannrem	68	63.16 N	9.50 E
Fano	78	43.50 N	13.01 E
Fan-si-pan ⋏	94	22.15 N	103.46 E
Faraday, Mount ⋏	120	24.55 S	147.17 E
Farafangana	117b	22.49 S	47.50 E
Farah	102	32.22 N	62.07 E
Farallon de Medinilla I	92	16.01 N	146.04 E
Farallon de Pajaros I	92	20.32 N	144.54 E
Faranah	114	10.02 N	10.44 W
Faraulep I1	92	8.36 N	144.33 E
Fareham	70	50.51 N	1.10 W
Farewell, Cape ⋗	126	40.30 S	172.41 E
Fargo	162	46.52 N	96.48 W
Faribault	154	44.18 N	93.16 W
Faribault, Lac ❂	142	59.00 N	72.00 W
Faridpur	102	23.39 N	89.46 E
Farley	154	42.27 N	91.00 W
Farmer City	158	40.15 N	88.38 W
Farmersville	158	33.10 N	96.22 W
Farmerville	158	32.47 N	92.24 W
Farmington, Ill., U.S.	154	40.42 N	90.00 W
Farmington, Maine, U.S.	152	44.40 N	70.09 W
Farmington, Minn., U.S.	154	44.38 N	93.08 W
Farmington, Mo., U.S.	158	37.47 N	90.25 W
Farmington, N.H., U.S.	152	43.24 N	71.04 W
Farmington, N. Mex., U.S.	164	36.44 N	108.12 W
Farmington, Utah, U.S.	166	40.59 N	111.53 W
Farmville, N.C., U.S.	156	35.36 N	77.35 W
Farmville, Va., U.S.	156	37.18 N	78.24 W
Farnborough	70	51.17 N	0.46 W
Farnham	70	51.13 N	0.49 W
Faro, Bra.	134	2.11 S	56.44 W
Faro, Port.	76	37.01 N	7.56 W
Fårön I	68	57.56 N	19.08 E
Farquhar Group II	112	10.10 S	51.10 E
Farrars Creek ≈	120	25.35 S	140.43 E
Farrell	152	41.13 N	80.30 W
Farrukhābād	102	27.24 N	79.34 E
Farsund	68	58.05 N	6.48 E
Fartak, Ra's ⋗	100	15.38 N	52.15 E
Farvel, Kap ⋗	144	59.45 N	43.54 W
Farwell	160	34.23 N	103.02 W
Fasano	78	40.50 N	17.22 E
Fatehpur Sikri	102	27.06 N	77.40 E
Fátima	76	39.37 N	8.39 W
Fat'ož	86	52.07 N	35.52 E
Faulkton	162	45.02 N	99.08 W
Fauquembergues	74	50.36 N	2.05 E
Fauske	66	67.15 N	15.24 E
Fåvang	68	61.27 N	10.11 E
Favara	78	37.19 N	13.40 E
Faverges	74	45.45 N	6.18 E
Fawn ≈	142	55.22 N	88.20 W
Faxaflói C	66a	64.24 N	23.00 W
Faxälven ≈	68	63.15 N	17.13 E
Fayence	74	43.37 N	6.41 E
Fayette, Ala., U.S.	158	33.42 N	87.50 W
Fayette, Iowa, U.S.	154	42.51 N	91.48 W
Fayette, Miss., U.S.	158	31.42 N	91.04 W
Fayette, Mo., U.S.	158	39.09 N	92.41 W
Fayetteville, Ark., U.S.	158	36.04 N	94.10 W
Fayetteville, Ga., U.S.	156	33.27 N	84.27 W
Fayetteville, N.C., U.S.	156	35.03 N	78.53 W
Fayetteville, Tenn., U.S.	158	35.09 N	86.35 W
Fayetteville, W. Va., U.S.	156	38.03 N	81.06 W
Fayl-Billot	74	47.47 N	5.36 E
Fazzān (Fezzan) ⇌1	108	26.00 N	14.00 E
Fdérik	106	22.41 N	12.43 W
Fear, Cape ⋗	156	33.50 N	77.58 W
Feathertop, Mount ⋏	122	36.54 S	147.08 E
Fécamp	74	49.45 N	0.22 E
Fedala → Mohammedia	106	33.44 N	7.24 W
Federal	140	30.55 S	58.45 W
Federalsburg	152	38.41 N	75.47 W
Fedjadj, Chott el ⋍	106	33.55 N	9.10 E
Fedje	68	60.47 N	4.43 E
Fehérgyarmat	72	47.58 N	22.32 E
Fehmarn Belt ⋃	72	54.35 N	11.15 E
Feia, Lagoa C	134	22.00 S	41.20 W
Feijó	134	8.09 S	70.21 W
Feilding	126	40.13 S	175.34 E
Feira	110	15.37 S	30.25 E
Feira de Santana	134	12.15 S	38.57 W
Fejér □6	72	47.10 N	18.35 E
Feldbach	72	46.57 N	15.54 E
Feldkirch	72	47.14 N	9.36 E
Feldkirchen in Kärnten	72	46.43 N	14.05 E
Felipe Carrillo Puerto	130	19.35 N	88.03 W
Felix, Cape ⋗	142	69.54 N	97.50 W
Felixstowe	70	51.58 N	1.20 E
Fellbach	72	48.48 N	9.16 E
Felletin	74	45.53 N	2.10 E
Fellsmere	156	27.46 N	80.36 W
Feltre	78	46.01 N	11.54 E
Femundsenden	68	61.55 N	11.55 E
Fénérive	117b	17.22 S	49.25 E
Fengcheng	88	40.28 N	124.04 E
Fengdu	94	29.54 N	107.41 E
Fengfeng	88	36.28 N	114.14 E
Fengjie	94	31.02 N	109.32 E
Fengyang	88	32.52 N	117.18 E
Fengzhen	88	40.24 N	113.09 E
Fenhe ≈	88	35.36 N	110.42 E
Fenton	154	42.47 N	83.42 W
Fenyang	88	37.19 N	111.41 E
Feodosija	64	45.02 N	35.23 E
Ferdinand	158	38.14 N	86.52 W
Ferdows	104	34.00 N	58.09 E
Fère-Champenoise	74	48.45 N	3.59 E
Fère-en-Tardenois	74	49.12 N	3.31 E
Fergana	82	40.23 N	71.46 E
Fergus	154	43.42 N	80.22 W
Fergus Falls	162	46.16 N	96.04 W
Ferlach	72	46.31 N	14.18 E
Ferlo, Vallée du ≈	114	15.42 N	15.30 W
Fermo	78	43.09 N	13.43 E
Fermoy	70	52.08 N	8.16 W
Fernandina de Noronha, Ilha I	134	3.51 S	32.25 W
Fernandópolis	134	20.16 S	50.14 W
Fernando Poo → Macías Nguema Biyogo I	106	3.30 N	8.40 E
Ferndale, Calif., U.S.	168	40.35 N	124.16 W
Ferndale, Mich., U.S.	154	42.27 N	83.08 W
Ferndale, Wash., U.S.	166	48.51 N	122.36 W
Fernie	148	49.30 N	115.03 W
Fern Park	156	28.39 N	81.20 W
Ferrara	78	44.50 N	11.35 E
Ferreira do Alentejo	76	38.03 N	8.07 W
Ferreñafe	134	6.38 S	79.48 W
Ferriday	158	31.37 N	91.33 W
Ferrières	74	48.05 N	2.47 E
Ferron	164	39.05 N	111.08 W
Ferrysburg	154	43.05 N	86.13 W
Fès	106	34.05 N	4.57 W
Feshi	110	6.07 S	18.10 E
Fessenden	162	47.39 N	99.38 W
Festus	158	38.13 N	90.24 W
Fetesti	80	44.23 N	27.50 E
Fethiye	104	36.37 N	29.07 E
Fetisovo	82	43.02 N	52.38 E
Fetsund	68	59.56 N	11.03 E
Feuchtwangen	72	49.10 N	10.20 E
Feuilles, Baie aux C	142	58.55 N	69.20 W
Feuilles, Rivière aux ≈	142	58.47 N	70.04 W
Feurs	74	45.45 N	4.14 E
Fevik	68	58.24 N	8.42 E
Feyzābād, Afg.	102	37.06 N	70.34 E
Fez → Fès	106	34.05 N	4.57 W
Ffestiniog	70	52.58 N	3.55 W
Fianarantsoa	117b	21.26 S	47.05 E
Ficksburg	116	28.53 S	27.53 E
Fidenza	78	44.52 N	10.03 E
Fieri	80	40.43 N	19.34 E
Fife □6	70	56.13 N	3.02 W
Fifield	154	45.52 N	90.26 W
Figeac	74	44.36 N	2.02 E
Figueira da Foz	76	40.09 N	8.52 W

Name	Page	Lat	Long
Figuig	106	32.10 N	1.15 W
Filey	70	54.12 N	0.17 W
Filipstad	68	59.43 N	14.10 E
Fillmore, Calif., U.S.	168	34.24 N	118.55 W
Fillmore, Utah, U.S.	164	38.58 N	112.20 W
Fimi ≃	110	3.01 S	16.58 E
Finale Ligure	78	44.10 N	8.20 E
Fincastle	156	37.30 N	79.53 W
Findlay, Ill., U.S.	158	39.31 N	88.45 W
Findlay, Ohio, U.S.	152	41.02 N	83.39 W
Fingal	120	41.39 S	147.58 E
Fingoè	110	15.12 S	31.50 E
Finistère □5	74	48.20 N	4.00 W
Finisterre, Cabo de ➤	76	42.53 N	9.16 W
Finke	122	25.34 S	134.35 E
Finke □1	122	27.00 S	136.10 E
Finland □1	64	64.00 N	26.00 E
Finland, Gulf of (Suomenlahti) (Finski Zaliv) C	68	60.00 N	27.00 E
Finlay ≃	142	57.00 N	125.05 W
Finley, Austl.	120	35.39 S	145.35 E
Finley, Okla., U.S.	160	34.20 N	95.30 W
Finn ≃	70	54.50 N	7.29 W
Finnie Bay C	142	65.13 N	77.30 W
Finnmark □6	66	70.00 N	25.00 E
Finse	68	60.36 N	7.30 E
Finspång	68	58.43 N	15.47 E
Finsterwalde	72	51.38 N	13.42 E
Finucane Island I	122	20.18 S	118.34 E
Fiora ≃	78	42.20 N	11.34 E
Fircrest	166	47.14 N	123.31 W
Firebaugh	168	36.52 N	120.27 W
Firenze (Florence)	78	43.46 N	11.15 E
Firmat	140	33.25 S	61.30 W
Firminy	74	45.23 N	4.18 E
Firovo	86	57.29 N	33.40 E
Firozābād	102	27.09 N	78.25 E
Firozpur	102	30.55 N	74.36 E
Firth ≃	116	69.32 N	139.22 W
Fish ≃	116	28.07 S	17.45 E
Fisher	158	40.19 N	88.21 W
Fisher Strait ⊔	142	63.15 N	83.30 W
Fishguard	70	51.59 N	4.59 W
Fismes	74	49.18 N	3.41 E
Fitchburg	152	42.35 N	71.48 W
Fitzgerald	156	31.43 N	83.15 W
Fitz Roy	136	47.00 S	67.15 W
Fitzroy ≃, Austl.	122	23.32 S	150.52 E
Fitzroy ≃, Austl.	122	17.31 S	123.35 E
Fitzroy, Monte (Cerro Chaltel) ∧	136	49.17 S	73.05 W
Fitzroy Crossing	122	18.11 S	125.35 E
Fiumicino	78	41.46 N	12.14 E
Five Points	168	36.04 N	106.41 W
Fizi	110	4.18 S	28.57 E
Fjerritslev	68	57.05 N	9.16 E
Flagler Beach	156	29.29 N	81.07 W
Flagstaff	164	35.12 N	111.39 W
Flåm	68	60.50 N	7.07 E
Fläming ✦1	72	52.00 N	12.30 E
Flaming Gorge Reservoir @1	164	41.15 N	109.30 W
Flandreau	162	44.03 N	96.36 W
Flat ≃	146	61.33 S	125.18 W
Flatey	66a	65.19 N	23.07 W
Flathead ≃	148	48.40 N	114.20 W
Flathead, South Fork ≃	148	48.23 N	114.04 W
Flathead Lake @	166	47.52 N	114.08 W
Flatow → Złotów	72	53.22 N	17.02 E
Flat River	158	37.51 N	90.31 W
Flat Rock, Ala., U.S.	158	34.46 N	85.42 W
Flat Rock, Mich., U.S.	152	42.06 N	83.18 W
Flattery, Cape ➤	166	48.23 N	124.43 W
Flatwoods	152	38.31 N	82.43 W
Flaxville	148	48.49 N	105.10 W
Fleetwood, Eng., U.K.	70	53.56 N	3.01 W
Fleetwood, Pa., U.S.	152	40.27 N	75.49 W
Flekkefjord	68	58.17 N	6.41 E
Flemingsburg	152	38.25 N	83.44 W
Flensburg	72	54.47 N	9.26 E
Fleurance	74	43.50 N	0.40 E
Fleury-sur-Andelle	74	49.22 N	1.21 E
Flinders ≃	120	17.36 S	140.36 E
Flinders Bay C	122	34.23 S	115.19 E
Flinders Island I	120	40.00 S	148.00 E
Flinders Reefs ✦2	120	17.37 S	148.31 E
Flin Flon	142	54.46 N	101.53 W
Flint, Wales, U.K.	70	53.15 N	3.07 W
Flint, Mich., U.S.	154	43.01 N	83.41 W
Flint ≃	156	30.52 N	84.38 W
Flint Lake @	142	69.10 N	74.20 W
Flintville	158	34.59 N	86.25 W
Flisa	68	60.34 N	12.06 E
Flize	74	49.42 N	4.46 E
Flomaton	158	31.00 N	87.16 W
Flora, Ill., U.S.	158	38.40 N	88.29 W
Flora, Ind., U.S.	158	40.33 N	86.31 W
Florac	74	44.19 N	3.36 E
Florala	158	31.00 N	86.20 W
Floral Park	152	45.57 N	112.26 W
Florence → Firenze, It.	78	43.46 N	11.15 E
Florence, Ala., U.S.	158	34.49 N	87.40 W
Florence, Kans., U.S.	162	38.14 N	96.55 W
Florence, Colo., U.S.	164	38.23 N	105.08 W
Florence, Oreg., U.S.	166	43.58 N	124.07 W
Florence, S.C., U.S.	156	34.12 N	79.46 W
Florencia	138	1.36 N	75.36 W
Florenville	74	49.42 N	5.18 E
Flores I	96	8.30 S	121.00 E
Flores, Laut ≃2	96	8.00 S	120.00 E
Flores da Cunha	140	29.02 S	51.11 W
Flores Sea → Flores, Laut ≃2	96	8.00 S	120.00 E
Floriano	134	6.47 S	43.01 W
Florianópolis	140	27.35 S	48.34 W
Florida, Col.	138	3.21 N	76.15 W
Florida, Ur.	140	34.06 S	56.13 W
Florida □8	156	28.00 N	82.00 W
Florida, Straits of ⊔	132	24.00 N	81.00 W
Floridablanca	138	7.04 N	73.06 W
Florida City	156	25.27 N	80.29 W
Florida Keys II	156	24.45 N	81.00 W
Floridia	78	37.04 N	15.10 E
Flórina	80	40.47 N	21.24 E
Florissant	158	38.47 N	90.20 W
Flora ≃	68	61.36 N	5.00 E
Florvåg	68	60.25 N	5.14 E
Floyd ≃	156	36.55 N	80.19 W
Floydada	160	33.59 N	101.20 W
Flushing → Vlissingen, Ned.	72	51.26 N	3.35 E
Flushing, Mich., U.S.	154	43.03 N	83.51 W
Flushing, Ohio, U.S.	152	40.09 N	81.04 W
Fluvanna	160	32.53 N	101.09 W
Fly ≃	124	7.45 S	141.45 E
Flying Fish Cove	96	10.25 S	105.43 E
Foča	80	43.31 N	18.46 E
Focșani	84	45.41 N	27.11 E
Foggia	78	41.27 N	15.34 E
Fogo I	114a	14.55 N	24.25 W
Fogo Island I	150	49.40 N	54.13 W
Fohnsdorf	72	47.13 N	14.41 E
Foix	74	42.58 N	1.36 E
Foix ✦1	74	43.00 N	1.40 E
Fokino	86	53.27 N	34.22 E
Foley, Ala., U.S.	158	30.25 N	87.41 W
Foley, Minn., U.S.	154	45.40 N	93.55 W
Foley Island I	142	68.35 N	75.10 W
Folgares	110	14.54 S	15.08 E
Foligno	78	42.57 N	12.42 E
Folkestone	70	51.05 N	1.11 E
Folkston	156	30.50 N	82.00 W
Follebu	68	61.14 N	10.17 E
Follett	160	36.26 N	100.08 W
Follonica	78	42.55 N	10.45 E
Follonica, Golfo di C	78	42.54 N	10.43 E
Folsom	168	38.41 N	121.10 W
Fonda, Iowa, U.S.	154	42.34 N	94.51 W
Fonda, N.Y., U.S.	152	42.57 N	74.22 W
Fond du Lac, Sask., Can.	142	59.19 N	107.10 W
Fond du Lac, Wis., U.S.	154	43.47 N	88.27 W
Fond du Lac ≃	142	59.17 N	106.00 W
Fondi	78	41.21 N	13.25 E
Fonni	78	40.07 N	9.15 E
Fonseca, Golfo de C	128	13.08 N	87.40 W
Fontainebleau	74	48.24 N	2.42 E
Fontana	168	34.06 N	117.26 W
Fontas ≃	142	58.20 N	121.50 W
Fonte Boa	138	2.32 S	66.01 W
Fontenay-le-Comte	74	46.28 N	0.48 W
Fontur ➤	66a	66.23 N	14.30 W
Foochow → Fuzhou	88	26.06 N	119.17 E
Foraker, Mount ∧	146	62.56 N	151.26 W
Forbach, B.R.D.	72	48.41 N	8.21 E
Forbach, Fr.	74	49.11 N	6.54 E
Forbes	120	33.23 S	148.01 E
Forchheim	72	49.43 N	11.04 E
Ford	162	37.38 N	99.45 W
Ford City, Calif., U.S.	168	35.09 N	119.27 W
Ford City, Pa., U.S.	152	40.46 N	79.32 W
Førde, Nor.	68	59.36 N	5.29 E
Førde, Nor.	68	61.27 N	5.52 E
Fordyce	158	33.49 N	92.25 W
Forel, Mont ∧	142	67.00 N	37.00 W
Foreman	158	33.43 N	94.24 W
Forest, Ont., Can.	154	43.06 N	82.00 W
Forest, Miss., U.S.	158	32.22 N	89.28 W
Forest, Ohio, U.S.	152	40.48 N	83.31 W
Forest Acres	156	34.01 N	104.42 W
Forest City, Iowa, U.S.	154	43.16 N	93.39 W
Forest City, N.C., U.S.	156	35.20 N	81.52 W
Forest City, Pa., U.S.	152	41.39 N	75.28 W
Foresthill	168	39.01 N	120.49 W
Forestier Peninsula ➤1	120	42.57 S	147.55 E
Forest Lake	154	45.17 N	92.59 W
Forest Park	156	33.37 N	84.22 W
Forestville	150	48.45 N	69.06 W
Forfar	70	56.38 N	2.54 W
Forges-les-Eaux	70	49.37 N	1.33 E
Forlì	78	44.13 N	12.03 E
Forman	162	46.07 N	97.38 W
Formentera I	76	38.42 N	1.28 E
Formentera	76	39.39 N	1.44 E
Formia	78	41.15 N	13.37 E
Formiga	140	20.27 S	45.25 W
Formosa, Arg.	140	26.10 S	58.11 W
Formosa, Bra.	134	15.32 S	47.20 W
Formosa □4	140	25.00 S	60.00 W
Formosa → Taiwan I	88	23.30 N	121.00 E
Formosa, Serra ✦1	134	12.00 S	55.00 W
Formosa Strait ⊔	88	24.00 N	119.00 E
Forney	160	32.45 N	96.28 W
Fornos	86	57.37 N	30.35 E
Forrest, Austl.	122	30.51 S	128.06 E
Forrest, Ill., U.S.	158	40.45 N	88.25 W
Forrest City	158	35.01 N	90.47 W
Forrester Island I	146	54.48 N	133.32 W
Forsan	160	32.07 N	101.22 W
Forsayth	120	18.35 S	143.36 E
Forsbacka	68	60.37 N	16.53 E
Forsby	68	60.30 N	25.56 E
Forssa	68	60.49 N	23.38 E
Forst	72	51.44 N	14.39 E
Forster	120	32.11 S	152.31 E
Forsyth, Ga., U.S.	156	33.02 N	83.56 W
Forsyth, Mont., U.S.	166	46.16 N	106.41 W
Forsyth Island I	126	40.50 S	173.56 E
Forsyth Range ∧	120	22.45 S	143.15 E
Fort Albany	142	52.15 N	81.37 W
Fortaleza	134	3.43 S	38.30 W
Fort-Archambault → Sarh	108	9.09 N	18.23 E
Fort Assiniboine	148	54.20 N	114.46 W
Fort Atkinson	154	42.55 N	88.50 W
Fort Augustus	70	57.09 N	4.41 W
Fort Beaufort	116	32.46 S	26.40 E
Fort Benton	166	47.49 N	110.40 W
Fort Bidwell	168	41.52 N	120.09 W
Fort Bragg	168	39.26 N	123.48 W
Fort Branch	158	38.15 N	87.35 W
Fort-Chimo	142	58.06 N	68.25 W
Fort Chipewyan	142	58.42 N	111.08 W
Fort Cobb	160	35.06 N	98.26 W
Fort Collins	164	40.35 N	105.04 W
Fort-Dauphin	117b	25.02 S	47.00 E
Fort Davis	160	30.35 N	103.54 W
Fort Defiance	164	35.45 N	109.05 W
Fort Deposit	158	31.59 N	86.35 W
Fort Dodge	154	42.29 N	94.10 W
Fort Edward	152	43.16 N	73.35 W
Fort Erie	154	42.54 N	78.56 W
Fortescue ≃	122	21.00 S	116.06 E
Fortezza	78	46.47 N	11.37 E
Fort Fairfield	150	46.46 N	67.50 W
Fort Fitzgerald	142	59.53 N	111.37 W
Fort Frances	154	48.36 N	93.24 W
Fort Franklin	146	65.11 N	123.46 W
Fort Gaines	156	31.37 N	85.03 W
Fort Gay	152	38.07 N	82.36 W
Fort-George	142	53.50 N	79.00 W
Fort Gibson	160	35.48 N	95.15 W
Fort Good Hope	146	66.15 N	128.38 W
Forth, Firth of C1	70	56.05 N	2.55 W
Fortín Coronel Eugenio Garay	134	20.31 S	62.08 W
Fort Kent	150	47.15 N	68.36 W
Fort-Klamath	166	42.42 N	122.00 W
Fort-Lamy → Ndjamena	108	12.07 N	15.03 E
Fort Laramie	164	42.13 N	104.31 W
Fort Lauderdale	156	26.07 N	80.08 W
Fort Liard	142	60.15 N	123.28 W
Fort Loramie	152	40.21 N	84.22 W
Fort Lupton	164	40.05 N	104.49 W
Fort Macleod	148	49.43 N	113.25 W
Fort Madison	154	40.37 N	91.27 W
Fort McMurray	142	56.44 N	111.23 W
Fort McPherson	146	67.27 N	134.53 W
Fort Meade	156	27.45 N	81.48 W
Fort Mill	156	35.01 N	80.57 W
Fort Morgan	164	40.15 N	103.48 W
Fort Myers	156	26.37 N	81.52 W
Fort Myers Beach	156	26.27 N	81.57 W
Fort Nelson	142	58.49 N	122.39 W
Fort Nelson ≃	142	59.30 N	124.00 W
Fort Norman	146	64.54 N	125.34 W
Fort Payne	158	34.26 N	85.43 W
Fort Peck Reservoir @1	166	48.01 N	106.27 W
Fort Pierce	156	27.27 N	80.20 W
Fort Plain	152	42.56 N	74.38 W
Fort Portal	110	0.40 N	30.17 E
Fort Providence	142	61.21 N	117.39 W
Fort Qu'Appelle	142	50.46 N	103.48 W
Fort Recovery	152	40.24 N	84.46 W
Fort Reliance	142	62.42 N	109.10 W
Fort Resolution	142	61.10 N	113.40 W
Fortrose	70	57.34 N	4.08 W
Fort Rosebery → Mansa	110	11.12 S	28.53 E
Fort-Rousset	110	0.29 S	15.55 E
Fort Saint James	148	54.26 N	124.15 W
Fort Saint John	142	56.15 N	120.51 W
Fort Sandeman	102	31.20 N	69.27 E
Fort Scott	162	37.50 N	94.42 W
Fort-Ševčenko	82	44.31 N	50.16 E
Fort Severn	142	56.00 N	87.38 W
Fort Simpson	142	61.52 N	121.23 W
Fort Smith, N.W. Ter., Can.	142	60.00 N	111.53 W
Fort Smith, Ark., U.S.	158	35.23 N	94.25 W
Fort Stockton	160	30.53 N	102.53 W
Fort Sumner	160	34.28 N	104.15 W
Fort Thomas	164	33.02 N	109.58 W
Fortuna	168	40.36 N	124.09 W
Fortuna Ledge (Marshall)	146	61.53 N	162.05 W
Fortune	150	47.04 N	55.50 W
Fortune Bay C	150	47.25 N	55.25 W
Fort Valley	156	32.33 N	83.53 W
Fort Vermilion	142	58.24 N	116.00 W
Fort Victoria	116	20.05 S	30.50 E
Fortville	158	39.56 N	85.51 W
Fort Walton Beach	158	30.25 N	86.36 W
Fort Washakie	166	43.00 N	108.53 W
Fort Wayne	154	41.04 N	85.09 W
Fort William	70	56.49 N	5.07 W
Fort Williams → Thunder Bay	154	48.23 N	89.15 W
Fort Worth	160	32.45 N	97.20 W
Fort Yukon	146	66.34 N	145.17 W
Foshan	88	23.03 N	113.09 E
Fosnavåg	68	62.21 N	5.39 E
Fossano	78	44.33 N	7.43 E
Fossil	166	45.00 N	120.13 W
Fossil Downs	122	18.08 S	125.38 E
Foster	158	38.39 N	84.14 W
Foster, Mount ∧	146	55.47 N	105.49 W
Foster Village	170c	21.22 N	157.56 W
Fostoria	152	41.09 N	83.25 W
Fouesnant	74	47.54 N	4.01 W
Fougamou	110	1.13 S	10.36 E
Fougères	74	48.21 N	1.12 W
Foumban	108	5.43 N	10.55 E
Foumbouni	117a	11.50 S	43.30 E
Fountain	164	38.41 N	104.42 W
Fountain Green	164	39.38 N	111.38 E
Fountain Inn	156	34.42 N	82.12 W
Fountain Place	158	30.31 N	91.09 W
Four Corners	166	44.56 N	123.02 W
Fourmies	74	50.00 N	4.03 E
Four Oaks	156	35.27 N	78.26 W
Fours	74	46.49 N	3.43 E
Fouta Djallon ✦1	114	11.30 N	12.30 W
Fowey	70	50.20 N	4.38 W
Fowler, Calif., U.S.	168	36.38 N	119.41 W
Fowler, Colo., U.S.	164	38.08 N	104.01 W
Fowler, Ind., U.S.	158	40.37 N	87.19 W
Fowler, Point ➤	122	32.02 S	132.29 E
Fowlers Bay	122	31.59 S	132.27 E
Fowlerville	154	42.40 N	84.04 W
Fox ≃	158	40.18 N	91.30 W
Foxe Basin C	142	68.25 N	77.00 W
Foxe Channel ⊔	142	64.30 N	80.00 W
Foxen @	68	59.23 N	11.52 E
Foxe Peninsula ➤1	142	65.00 N	76.00 W
Fox Lake, Ill., U.S.	154	42.25 N	88.09 W
Fox Lake, Wis., U.S.	154	43.34 N	88.55 W
Foxpark	164	41.05 N	106.09 W
Foyle, Lough C	70	55.07 N	7.08 W
Foynes	70	52.37 N	9.06 W
Foz do Cunene	110	17.16 S	11.50 E
Foz do Iguaçu	140	25.33 S	54.35 W
Foz Giraldo	76	40.00 N	7.43 W
Framingham	152	42.17 N	71.25 W
Frampol	72	50.41 N	22.40 E
Franca	134	20.32 S	47.24 W
Francavilla Fontana	78	40.31 N	17.35 E
Frances Lake	146	61.25 N	129.30 W
Franceville	110	1.38 S	13.35 E
Franche-Comté □9	74	47.00 N	6.00 E
Francis Case, Lake @1	162	43.15 N	99.00 W
Francisco I. Madero	116	25.45 N	103.21 W
Francistown	116	21.11 S	27.32 E
Francofonte	78	37.13 N	14.53 E
François Lake @	148	54.00 N	125.40 W
Frangy	74	46.01 N	5.56 E
Frankenberg	72	50.54 N	13.01 E
Frankenberg-Eder	72	51.03 N	8.48 E
Frankenmuth	154	43.20 N	83.44 W
Frankfort, Kans., U.S.	162	39.42 N	96.25 W
Frankfort, Ky., U.S.	144	38.12 N	84.52 W
Frankfort, Ky., U.S.	158	38.12 N	84.52 W
Frankfort, Mich., U.S.	154	44.38 N	86.14 W
Frankfort, N.Y., U.S.	152	43.02 N	75.04 W
Frankfurt □5	72	52.20 N	14.00 E
Frankfurt am Main	72	50.07 N	8.40 E
Frankfurt an der Oder	72	52.20 N	14.33 E
Frankland ≃	122	34.58 S	116.49 E
Franklin, Idaho, U.S.	166	42.59 N	111.48 W
Franklin, Ind., U.S.	158	39.29 N	86.03 W
Franklin, Ky., U.S.	158	36.43 N	86.35 W
Franklin, La., U.S.	158	29.48 N	91.30 W
Franklin, Mass., U.S.	152	42.05 N	71.24 W
Franklin, Nebr., U.S.	162	40.06 N	98.57 W
Franklin, N.H., U.S.	152	43.27 N	71.39 W
Franklin, N.J., U.S.	152	41.07 N	74.35 W
Franklin, N.C., U.S.	156	35.11 N	83.23 W
Franklin, Pa., U.S.	152	41.24 N	79.50 W
Franklin, Tenn., U.S.	158	35.55 N	86.52 W
Franklin, Va., U.S.	156	36.41 N	76.55 W
Franklin, W. Va., U.S.	152	38.39 N	79.20 W
Franklin □5	142	72.00 N	96.00 W
Franklin Bay C	146	69.45 N	126.00 W
Franklin Harbour C	120	33.42 S	136.56 E
Franklin Lake @	168	40.24 N	115.10 W
Franklin Mountains ∧	142	63.15 N	123.30 W
Franklin Strait ⊔	142	72.00 N	96.00 W
Franklinton, La., U.S.	158	30.51 N	90.09 W
Franklinton, N.C., U.S.	156	36.06 N	78.27 W
Franklinville	152	42.20 N	78.28 W
Franks Peak ∧	166	43.58 N	109.20 W
Frankston	158	31.39 N	89.09 W
Frascati	78	41.49 N	12.41 E
Fraser ≃, B.C., Can.	148	49.09 N	123.12 W
Fraser ≃, Newf., Can.	142	56.35 N	61.55 W
Fraser, Mount ∧	122	25.06 S	118.23 E
Fraserburgh	70	57.42 N	2.00 W
Fraser Island I	120	25.15 S	153.10 E
Fraser Plateau ✦1	148	51.30 N	122.00 W
Frauenfeld	74	47.34 N	8.54 E
Fray Bentos	140	33.08 S	58.18 W
Frazee	154	46.44 N	95.42 W
Frederic	166	48.03 N	106.02 W
Frederick, Md., U.S.	152	39.25 N	77.25 W
Frederick, Okla., U.S.	160	34.23 N	99.01 W
Frederick Hills ✦2	124	12.41 S	136.00 E
Frederick Reef ✦2	120	20.58 S	154.23 E
Fredericksburg, Tex., U.S.	160	30.17 N	98.52 W
Fredericksburg, Va., U.S.	152	38.18 N	77.29 W
Fredericktown	158	37.33 N	90.18 W
Fredericton	150	45.58 N	66.39 W
Frederikshåb	142	62.00 N	49.43 W
Frederikshavn	68	57.26 N	10.32 E
Frederikssund	68	55.50 N	12.04 E
Fredonia, Ariz., U.S.	164	36.57 N	112.32 W
Fredonia, Kans., U.S.	162	37.32 N	95.49 W
Fredonia, N.Y., U.S.	152	42.26 N	79.19 W
Fredonia, N. Dak., U.S.	162	46.19 N	99.06 W
Fredrikstad	68	59.13 N	10.57 E
Freeburg	158	38.26 N	89.55 W
Freehold	152	40.15 N	74.16 W
Freeland, Mich., U.S.	154	43.32 N	84.07 W
Freeland, Pa., U.S.	152	41.01 N	75.54 W
Freeling, Mount ∧	122	22.35 S	133.06 E
Freels, Cape ➤	150	49.16 N	53.29 W
Freeport, Fla., U.S.	158	30.30 N	86.08 W
Freeport, Ill., U.S.	154	42.17 N	89.36 W
Freeport, Maine, U.S.	152	43.51 N	70.06 W
Freeport, N.Y., U.S.	152	40.39 N	73.35 W
Freeport, Pa., U.S.	152	40.40 N	79.41 W
Freeport, Tex., U.S.	160	28.58 N	95.22 W
Freer	160	27.53 N	98.37 W
Freetown	114	8.30 N	13.15 W
Fregenal de la Sierra	76	38.10 N	6.39 W
Freiberg	72	50.54 N	13.20 E
Freiburg → Świebodzice, Pol.	72	50.52 N	16.19 E
Freiburg → Fribourg, Schw.	74	46.48 N	7.09 E
Freiburg (im Breisgau)	72	47.59 N	7.51 E
Freireina	140	28.30 S	71.06 W
Freising	72	48.23 N	11.44 E
Freistadt	72	48.31 N	14.31 E
Freital	72	51.00 N	13.39 E
Fréjus	74	43.26 N	6.44 E
Fremont, Calif., U.S.	168	37.34 N	122.01 W
Fremont, Ind., U.S.	158	41.44 N	84.56 W
Fremont, Mich., U.S.	154	43.28 N	85.57 W
Fremont, Nebr., U.S.	162	41.26 N	96.30 W
Fremont, Ohio, U.S.	152	41.21 N	83.07 W
Fremont Island I	164	41.09 N	112.20 W
Fremont ≃	164	38.24 N	110.07 W
French Creek ≃	152	41.24 N	79.50 W
Frenchman Creek ≃, N.A.	148	48.24 N	107.05 W
Frenchman Creek ≃, U.S.	162	40.13 N	100.50 W
Frenchmans Cap ∧	120	42.16 S	145.50 E
Fresco ≃	114	5.39 S	51.59 W
Freshfield, Mount ∧	148	51.44 N	116.57 W
Fresne-Saint-Mamès	74	47.33 N	5.52 E
Fresnes-en-Woëvre	74	49.08 N	5.39 E
Fresnillo	130	23.10 N	102.53 W
Fresno	168	36.44 N	119.45 W
Freudenstadt	72	48.28 N	8.25 E
Frewena	122	19.25 S	135.25 E
Freycinet Peninsula ➤1	122	42.03 S	79.10 W
Fría, Cape ➤	110	18.30 S	12.01 E
Friars Point	158	34.22 N	90.38 W
Frias	140	28.40 S	65.10 W
Fribourg (Freiburg)	74	46.48 N	7.09 E
Friday Harbor	166	48.32 N	123.01 W
Friedberg, B.R.D.	72	50.20 N	8.45 E
Friedberg, B.R.D.	72	48.21 N	10.58 E
Friedberg, Öst.	72	47.27 N	16.03 E
Friedland	72	53.40 N	13.33 E
Friedrichshafen	72	47.39 N	9.28 E
Friedrichsort	72	54.24 N	10.11 E
Friedrichstadt	72	54.22 N	9.05 E
Friend	162	40.38 N	97.17 W
Friendship, N.Y., U.S.	152	42.12 N	78.08 W
Friendship, Wis., U.S.	154	43.58 N	89.49 W
Friendship Shoal ✦2	96	5.58 N	112.38 E
Friesland □9	72	53.00 N	5.40 E
Frio, Cabo ➤	136	22.53 S	42.00 W
Frio ≃	160	28.26 N	98.11 W
Frio Draw V	160	34.50 N	102.19 W
Friona	160	34.38 N	102.43 W
Frisco City	158	31.26 N	87.24 W
Frisco Creek ≃	160	36.34 N	101.24 W
Frisian Islands II	72	53.35 N	6.40 E
Fristad	68	57.50 N	13.01 E
Fritch	160	35.38 N	101.36 W
Friuli-Venezia-Giulia □4	78	46.00 N	13.00 E
Frobisher, Proliv ⊔	84	45.30 N	149.10 E
Frobisher Bay C	142	62.30 N	66.00 W
Frobisher Lake @	142	56.25 N	108.20 W
Frohnleiten	72	47.16 N	15.20 E
Froid	148	48.20 N	104.30 W
Frolovo	82	49.48 N	43.40 E
Frombork	72	54.22 N	19.41 E
Frome	70	51.14 N	2.20 W
Frome ≃	120	29.48 S	137.59 E
Frome, Lake @	120	30.48 S	139.48 E
Frontera	130	18.32 N	92.38 W
Frontier	166	41.49 N	110.32 W
Front Range ∧	164	40.00 N	105.50 W
Front Royal	152	38.55 N	78.11 W
Frosinone	78	41.38 N	13.19 E
Frostburg	152	39.39 N	78.56 W
Frostproof	156	27.44 N	81.32 W
Frøya I	68	63.43 N	8.42 E
Fruges	74	50.31 N	2.08 E
Fruita	164	39.09 N	108.44 W
Fruitdale	158	31.19 N	88.24 W
Fruitland	166	38.19 N	75.37 W
Fruitridge	168	38.31 N	121.27 W
Fruitvale	148	38.31 N	121.27 W
Frunze	82	42.54 N	74.36 E
Frydek-Mistek	72	49.41 N	18.22 E
Fryeburg	152	44.01 N	70.59 W
Fuchunjiang ≃	88	30.10 N	120.20 E
Fuensalida	76	40.04 N	4.12 W
Fuentesaúco	76	41.14 N	5.30 W
Fuerte ≃	130	25.50 N	109.25 W
Fuerteventura I	114	28.20 N	14.00 W
Fufeng	88	34.20 N	107.51 E
Fuga Island I	98	18.53 N	121.22 E
Fuji ∧	90	35.09 N	138.39 E
Fuji, Mount → Fuji-san ∧1	90	35.22 N	138.44 E
Fujian □4	88	26.00 N	118.00 E
Fujin	88	47.14 N	132.01 E
Fujinomiya	90	35.12 N	138.38 E
Fuji-san (Fujiyama) ∧1	90	35.22 N	138.44 E
Fujisawa	90	35.21 N	139.29 E
Fukui	90	36.04 N	136.13 E
Fukuoka	90	33.35 N	130.24 E
Fukushima	90	37.45 N	140.28 E
Fukuyama	90	34.29 N	133.22 E
Füláji	88	34.38 N	67.32 E
Fulda, B.R.D.	72	50.33 N	9.41 E
Fulda, Minn., U.S.	154	43.52 N	95.36 W
Fuling	88	29.42 N	107.21 E
Fullerton, Calif., U.S.	162	33.52 N	117.55 W
Fullerton, Nebr., U.S.	162	41.22 N	97.58 W
Fulton, Ill., U.S.	154	41.51 N	90.10 W
Fulton, Ky., U.S.	158	36.30 N	88.53 W
Fulton, Miss., U.S.	158	34.16 N	88.24 W
Fulton, Mo., U.S.	158	38.50 N	91.57 W
Fulton, N.Y., U.S.	152	43.19 N	76.25 W
Fulton, Ohio, U.S.	152	40.28 N	82.50 W
Fulton, Tex., U.S.	160	28.04 N	97.02 W
Fumay	74	49.59 N	4.42 E
Fumel	74	44.29 N	0.57 E
Funabashi	90	35.42 N	139.59 E
Funan	88	32.32 N	107.59 E
Funchal	114	32.38 N	16.54 W
Fundão	76	40.08 N	7.30 W
Fundy, Bay of C	150	45.00 N	66.00 W
Funhalouro	116	23.03 S	34.25 E
Funing	88	33.48 N	119.48 E
Funnel Creek ≃	120	21.28 S	148.25 E
Fuquay Springs	156	35.35 N	78.48 W
Furancungo	110	14.55 S	33.37 E
Furmanov	86	57.15 N	41.07 E
Furnas, Reprêsa de @1	140	20.40 S	46.19 W
Furneaux Group II	120	40.10 S	148.05 E
Furnes → Veurne	72	51.04 N	2.40 E
Fürstenfeld	72	47.03 N	16.05 E
Fürstenfeldbruck	72	48.11 N	11.15 E
Fürstenwalde	72	52.21 N	14.04 E
Fürth	72	49.28 N	10.59 E
Furth im Wald	72	49.18 N	12.51 E
Fury and Hecla Strait ⊔	142	69.56 N	84.00 W
Fusagasugá	138	4.21 N	74.22 W
Fuse → Higashiōsaka	90	34.39 N	135.35 E
Fushun	88	41.52 N	123.53 E
Füssen	72	47.34 N	10.42 E
Fuxian, Zhg.	88	39.37 N	122.01 E
Fuxian, Zhg.	88	36.02 N	109.13 E
Fuxianhu @	94	24.30 N	102.55 E
Fuxinshi	88	42.01 N	121.46 E
Fuyang	88	32.52 N	115.42 E
Fuyu	88	45.10 N	124.50 E
Fuzhou, Zhg.	88	26.06 N	119.17 E
Fuzhou, Zhg.	88	28.01 N	116.20 E
Fyn I	66	55.20 N	10.30 E

G

Name	Page	Lat	Long
Gabas ≃	74	43.46 N	0.42 W
Gabbs	168	38.52 N	117.55 W
Gabela	110	10.48 S	14.20 E
Gaberones → Gaborone	116	24.45 S	25.55 E
Gabès	106	33.53 N	10.07 E
Gabès, Golfe de C	106	34.00 N	10.25 E
Gabon □1	110	1.00 S	11.45 E
Gaborone	116	24.45 S	25.55 E
Gabriel Strait ⊔	142	61.45 N	65.30 W
Gabrovo	80	42.52 N	25.19 E
Gach Sārān	100	30.12 N	50.47 E
Gadag	100	15.25 N	75.38 E
Gadsden	158	34.02 N	86.00 W
Gaeta	78	41.12 N	13.35 E
Gaferut I	92	9.14 N	145.23 E
Gaffney	156	35.05 N	81.39 W
Gafsa	106	34.25 N	8.48 E
Gagarin	86	55.33 N	35.00 E
Gaggenau	72	48.48 N	8.19 E
Gagino	86	55.14 N	45.02 E
Gagnoa	114	6.08 N	5.56 W
Gagnon	142	51.53 N	68.10 W
Gago Coutinho	110	14.08 S	21.25 E
Gagra	82	43.20 N	40.15 E
Gaillac	74	43.54 N	1.55 E
Gaillefontaine	74	49.39 N	1.37 E
Gaillon	74	49.10 N	1.20 E
Gainesville, Fla., U.S.	156	29.40 N	82.20 W
Gainesville, Ga., U.S.	156	34.18 N	83.50 W
Gainesville, Tex., U.S.	160	33.37 N	97.08 W
Gainsborough	70	53.24 N	0.46 W
Gairdner, Lake @	120	31.35 S	136.00 E
Gaithersburg	152	39.08 N	77.11 W
Gajny	66	60.18 N	54.15 E
Gakugsa	88	36.14 N	36.26 E
Galán, Cerro ∧	140	25.55 S	66.52 W
Galana ≃	110	3.09 S	40.08 E
Galapagos Islands II	138a	0.30 S	90.30 W
Galashiels	70	55.37 N	2.49 W
Galați	80	45.26 N	28.03 E
Galați □4	80	45.45 N	27.45 E
Galatina	78	40.10 N	18.10 E
Galax	156	36.40 N	80.56 W
Galela	92	1.50 N	127.50 E
Galena, Austl.	122	27.50 S	114.41 E
Galena, Alaska, U.S.	146	64.44 N	156.57 W
Galena, Ill., U.S.	154	42.25 N	90.26 W
Galena, Kans., U.S.	162	37.04 N	94.38 W
Galena Park	160	29.44 N	95.14 W
Galera, Punta ➤	138	0.49 N	80.03 W
Galera Point ➤	132	10.49 N	60.55 W
Galesburg, Ill., U.S.	154	40.57 N	90.22 W
Galesburg, Mich., U.S.	154	42.17 N	85.25 W
Galeton	152	41.44 N	77.39 W
Galič	86	58.23 N	42.21 E
Galicia □9, Esp.	76	43.00 N	8.00 W
Galicia □9, Eur.	72	50.00 N	21.00 E
Galilee, Lake @	120	22.21 S	145.48 E
Galion	152	40.44 N	82.47 W
Galka'yo	108	6.49 N	47.23 E
Gallarate	78	45.40 N	8.47 E
Gallatin, Mo., U.S.	158	39.55 N	93.58 W
Gallatin, Tenn., U.S.	158	36.24 N	86.27 W
Gallatin ≃	166	45.56 N	111.29 W
Galle	100	6.02 N	80.13 E
Galliate	78	45.29 N	8.42 E
Gallinas, Punta ➤	138	12.28 N	71.40 W
Gallipoli, It.	78	40.03 N	17.58 E
Gallipoli → Gelibolu, Tür.	80	40.24 N	26.40 E
Gallipolis	152	38.48 N	82.12 W
Gällivare	68	67.07 N	20.45 E
Gallup	164	35.31 N	108.44 W
Gallur	76	41.52 N	1.19 W
Galston	122	27.33 S	152.17 E
Galt	168	38.15 N	121.18 W
Galty Mountains ∧	70	52.22 N	8.10 W
Galveston	160	29.18 N	94.48 W
Galveston Bay C	160	29.36 N	94.50 W
Gálvez	140	32.02 S	61.15 W
Galway	70	53.16 N	9.03 W
Galway □6	70	53.20 N	9.00 W
Gamaches	74	49.59 N	1.33 E
Gamarra	138	8.20 N	73.45 W
Gambell	146	63.46 N	171.46 W
Gambia □1	114	13.28 N	16.34 W
Gambia (Gambie) ≃	114	13.28 N	16.34 W
Gamboma	110	1.53 S	15.51 E
Gamboula	108	4.08 N	15.09 E
Gamleby	68	57.54 N	16.24 E
Gamla Uppsala	68	59.54 N	17.38 E
Gammelstad ✦1	68	65.35 N	22.02 E
Ganado, Ariz., U.S.	164	35.43 N	109.33 W
Ganado, Tex., U.S.	160	29.02 N	96.31 W
Gananoque	152	44.20 N	76.10 W
Gand → Gent	72	51.03 N	3.43 E
Gandak ≃	102	25.39 N	85.13 E
Gander	150	48.57 N	54.37 W
Ganderkesee	72	53.02 N	8.32 E
Gandesa	76	41.03 N	0.26 E
Gandhinagar	102	23.13 N	72.41 E
Ganges (Ganga) (Padma) ≃	102	23.22 N	90.32 E
Ganges, Mouths of the ≃1	102	22.00 N	89.00 E
Gangi	78	37.48 N	14.13 E
Ganglingshan ∧	88	34.20 N	99.02 E
Gangtok	102	27.20 N	88.37 E
Gangu	88	34.38 N	105.27 E
Gannat	74	46.06 N	3.12 E
Gannett Peak ∧	166	43.11 N	109.39 W
Gänserndorf	72	48.20 N	16.43 E
Gansu □4	88	37.00 N	103.00 E
Ganteaume, Cape ➤	122	36.05 S	137.27 E
Ganzhou	88	25.54 N	114.57 E
Gao	114	16.16 N	0.03 W
Gaoyouhu @	88	32.50 N	119.15 E
Garber	160	36.26 N	97.35 W
Garberville	168	40.06 N	123.48 W
Garça	140	22.14 S	49.37 W
García de Sola, Embalse de @1	76	39.15 N	5.05 W
Gard □5	74	44.00 N	4.10 E
Garda	78	45.34 N	10.42 E
Garda, Lago di @	78	45.40 N	10.41 E
Gardelegen	72	52.31 N	11.23 E
Garden City, Ga., U.S.	156	32.06 N	81.09 W
Garden City, Kans., U.S.	162	37.58 N	100.53 W
Gardendale	158	33.39 N	86.49 W
Garden Grove	168	33.46 N	117.57 W
Garden Reach	102	22.33 N	88.17 E
Gardermoen	68	60.13 N	11.06 E
Gardez	102	33.37 N	69.07 E
Gardiner, Maine, U.S.	152	44.14 N	69.46 W
Gardiner, Mont., U.S.	166	45.02 N	110.42 W
Gardiner, Oreg., U.S.	166	43.44 N	124.07 W
Gardiner Range ∧	122	23.50 S	131.46 E
Garner, Iowa, U.S.	154	43.06 N	93.36 W
Gardner, Mass., U.S.	152	42.34 N	71.60 W
Garner, N.C., U.S.	156	35.43 N	78.37 W
Gardo	108	9.30 N	49.03 E
Gardone Val Trompia	78	45.41 N	10.11 E
Garešnica	78	45.35 N	16.56 E
Garfield, Kans., U.S.	162	38.05 N	99.14 W
Garfield, N. Mex., U.S.	164	32.46 N	107.16 W
Garfield, Wash., U.S.	166	47.01 N	117.09 W
Garfield Mountain ∧	166	44.31 N	112.38 W
Garibaldi	166	45.34 N	123.55 W
Garies	116	30.30 S	18.00 E
Garissa	110	0.28 S	39.38 E
Garland, Tex., U.S.	160	32.54 N	96.39 W
Garland, Utah, U.S.	166	41.45 N	112.10 W
Garlasco	78	45.11 N	8.55 E
Garlin	74	43.34 N	0.15 W
Garm	82	39.02 N	70.22 E
Garmisch-Partenkirchen	72	47.29 N	11.05 E
Garner, Iowa, U.S.	154	43.06 N	93.36 W
Garner, N.C., U.S.	156	35.43 N	78.37 W
Garnet Bay C	142	65.17 N	75.15 W
Garnett	162	38.17 N	95.14 W
Garonne ≃	74	45.02 N	0.36 W
Garoua	106	9.18 N	13.24 E
Garrel	72	52.57 N	8.01 E
Garrison	162	47.40 N	101.25 W
Garrovillas	76	39.43 N	6.33 W
Garry Bay C	142	68.55 N	85.05 W
Garry Lake @	142	66.00 N	100.00 W
Garsen	110	2.16 S	40.07 E
Garut	96	46.34 N	80.52 W
Gary	154	41.36 N	87.20 W
Garzón	138	2.12 N	75.38 W
Gasan-Kuli	82	37.27 N	53.59 E
Gas City	158	40.29 N	85.37 W
Gascoyne ≃	122	24.52 S	113.37 E
Gascoyne, Mount ∧	122	24.58 S	116.38 E
Gash (Nahr al-Qāsh) ≃	112	16.48 N	35.51 E
Gashaka	106	7.21 N	11.27 E
Gashunhu @	88	42.22 N	100.34 E
Gaspé	150	48.50 N	64.29 W
Gaston	156	36.30 N	78.00 W
Gaston, Lake @1	156	36.35 N	78.00 W
Gastonia	156	35.16 N	81.11 W
Gastre	136	42.17 S	69.15 W
Gästrikland □9	68	60.30 N	16.27 E
Gatčina	86	59.34 N	30.08 E
Gateshead	70	54.58 N	1.37 W
Gatehouse of Fleet	70	54.53 N	4.11 W
Gatesville	160	31.26 N	97.45 W
Gatineau	152	45.29 N	75.38 W
Gatineau ≃	152	45.27 N	75.40 W
Gatooma	116	18.21 S	29.55 E
Gattinara	78	45.37 N	8.22 E
Gatton	122	27.33 S	152.17 E
Gaud-i-Zirreh ≃	108	29.50 N	62.00 E
Gauer Lake @	142	57.00 N	97.50 W
Gauhāti	102	26.11 N	91.44 E
Gauri Sankar ∧	102	28.06 N	86.21 E
Gausta ∧	68	59.50 N	8.35 E
Gauting	72	48.04 N	11.23 E
Gavá	76	41.18 N	2.01 E
Gävle	68	60.40 N	17.10 E
Gävleborgs Län □6	68	61.30 N	16.15 E
Gavrilov-Jam	86	57.18 N	39.57 E
Gavrilov-Posad	86	56.34 N	40.08 E
Gawler	120	34.37 S	138.44 E
Gawler Ranges ∧	122	32.30 S	136.00 E
Gaya	102	24.47 N	85.00 E
Gaylord, Mich., U.S.	154	45.02 N	84.40 W
Gaylord, Minn., U.S.	154	44.33 N	94.13 W
Gaziantep	104	37.05 N	37.22 E
Gbarnga	114	7.00 N	9.29 W
Gbongan	114	7.29 N	4.21 E
Gdańsk (Danzig)	72	54.23 N	18.40 E
Gdov	86	58.44 N	27.48 E
Gdynia	72	54.32 N	18.33 E
Gebe, Pulau I	124	0.05 S	129.20 E
Gebo	166	43.46 N	108.13 W
Gebweiler → Guebwiller	74	47.55 N	7.12 E
Gedser	68	54.35 N	11.57 E
Geel	72	51.10 N	5.00 E
Geelong	120	38.08 S	144.21 E
Geelvink Channel ⊔	122	28.30 S	114.10 E
Geer ≃	72	51.10 N	5.33 E
Ge'ermu	88	36.23 N	94.50 E
Geesthacht	72	53.26 N	10.22 E
Geeveston	120	43.10 S	146.55 E
Geikie ≃	122	18.08 S	125.43 E
Geilo	68	60.31 N	8.12 E
Geiranger	68	62.06 N	7.12 E
Geisenfeld	72	48.41 N	11.37 E
Geislingen	72	48.37 N	9.50 E
Geithain	72	51.03 N	12.41 E
Gejiu (Kokiu)	94	23.22 N	103.06 E
Gela	78	37.04 N	14.15 E
Gelai ∧1	110	2.33 S	36.05 E
Geldern	72	51.31 N	6.20 E
Geleen	72	50.58 N	5.52 E
Gelendžik	82	44.34 N	38.00 E
Gelibolu	80	40.24 N	26.40 E
Gelsenkirchen	72	51.31 N	7.07 E
Gembloux	72	50.34 N	4.41 E
Gemena	108	3.15 N	19.46 E
Gemert	72	51.33 N	5.41 E
Gemlik	80	40.26 N	29.09 E
Gemona del Friuli	78	46.16 N	13.09 E
Gemünden	72	50.03 N	9.42 E
Genalē (Jubba) ≃	108	0.15 S	42.38 E
Gençay	74	46.23 N	0.23 E
General Acha	140	37.20 S	64.36 W
General Alvear	140	34.58 S	67.42 W
General Conesa	136	40.06 S	64.29 W
General Guido	140	36.40 S	57.45 W
General Juan Madariaga	140	37.00 S	57.10 W
General La Madrid	140	37.15 S	61.16 W
General Levalle	140	34.00 S	63.55 W
General Machado	110	12.03 S	17.30 E
General Paz	140	35.32 S	58.18 W
General Pico	140	35.40 S	63.44 W
General Pinedo	140	27.19 S	61.20 W
General Roca	136	39.02 S	67.35 W
General San Martín	140	34.35 S	58.32 W
General Villegas	140	35.02 S	63.01 W
Genesee ≃	152	43.16 N	77.36 W
Geneseo, Ill., U.S.	154	41.27 N	90.09 W
Geneseo, N.Y., U.S.	152	42.48 N	77.49 W
Geneva → Genève, Schw.	74	46.12 N	6.09 E
Geneva, Ala., U.S.	158	31.02 N	85.52 W
Geneva, Nebr., U.S.	162	40.31 N	97.36 W
Geneva, N.Y., U.S.	152	42.52 N	76.58 W
Geneva, Ohio, U.S.	152	41.48 N	80.57 W
Genève (Geneva)	74	46.12 N	6.09 E
Genhe	88	50.16 N	121.27 E
Genk	72	50.58 N	5.30 E
Genlis	74	47.14 N	5.13 E

Symbols in the index entries are identified on page 203.

Name	Page	Lat °′	Long °′
Gennes	74	47.20 N	0.14 W
Genoa → Genova, It.	78	44.25 N	8.57 E
Genoa, Ill., U.S.	154	42.06 N	88.42 W
Genoa, Nebr., U.S.	162	41.27 N	97.44 W
Genoa, Ohio, U.S.	152	41.31 N	83.22 W
Genova (Genoa)	78	44.25 N	8.57 E
Genrijetty, Ostrov I	84	77.06 N	156.30 E
Gent (Gand)	72	51.03 N	3.43 E
Genthin	72	52.24 N	12.09 E
Gentioux	74	45.47 N	1.59 E
Geographe Bay C	122	33.35 S	115.15 E
Geographe Channel ⊔	122	24.40 S	113.20 E
Geokčaj	104	40.39 N	47.44 E
George, S. Afr.	116	33.58 S	22.24 E
George, Iowa, U.S.	162	43.21 N	96.00 W
George ≃	142	58.49 N	66.10 W
George, Lake ⊜, Austl.	120	35.05 S	149.25 E
George, Lake ⊜, N.A.	154	46.28 N	84.10 W
George, Lake ⊜, Ug.	110	0.00 N	30.12 E
George Town, Austl.	120	41.06 S	146.50 E
Georgetown, Ont., Can.	154	43.39 N	79.55 W
Georgetown, P.E.I., Can.	150	46.11 N	62.32 W
Georgetown, Cay. Is.	132	19.18 N	81.23 W
Georgetown, Guy.	138	6.48 N	58.10 W
George Town → Pinang, Malay.	96	5.24 N	100.19 E
Georgetown, Del., U.S.	152	38.42 N	75.23 W
Georgetown, Idaho, U.S.	166	42.29 N	111.22 W
Georgetown, Ill., U.S.	158	39.59 N	87.38 W
Georgetown, Ky., U.S.	152	38.13 N	84.33 W
Georgetown, Ohio, U.S.	152	38.52 N	83.54 W
Georgetown, S.C., U.S.	156	33.23 N	79.17 W
Georgetown, Tex., U.S.	160	30.38 N	97.41 W
George West	160	28.20 N	98.07 W
Georgia □3	144	32.50 N	83.15 W
Georgia, Strait of ⊔	148	49.20 N	124.00 W
Georgiana	158	31.33 N	86.44 W
Georgian Bay C	154	45.15 N	80.50 W
Georgian Soviet Socialist Republic → Gruzinskaja Sovetskaja Socialističeskaja Respublika □3	82	42.00 N	44.00 E
Georgijevsk	82	44.09 N	43.28 E
Georgina ≃	120	23.30 S	139.47 E
Georgiu-Dež (Liski)	64	50.59 N	39.30 E
Gera	72	50.52 N	12.04 E
Gera □5	72	51.08 N	10.56 E
Geraardsbergen	74	50.46 N	3.52 E
Geral, Serra ⏏4	140	26.30 S	50.30 W
Geral de Goiás, Serra ⏏4	134	13.00 S	46.15 W
Geraldine, N.Z.	126	44.05 S	171.14 E
Geraldine, Mont., U.S.	166	47.36 N	110.16 W
Geral do Paranã, Serra ⋀2	134	14.45 S	47.30 W
Geraldton, Austl.	122	28.46 S	114.36 E
Geraldton, Ont., Can.	142	49.44 N	86.57 W
Gérardmer	74	48.04 N	6.53 E
Gerber	168	40.03 N	122.09 W
Gerdine, Mount ∧	146	61.35 N	152.26 W
Gereshk	102	31.48 N	64.34 E
Gering	162	41.50 N	103.40 W
German Democratic Republic (East Germany) □1	64	52.00 N	12.30 E
Germantown, Tenn., U.S.	158	35.05 N	89.49 W
Germantown, Wis., U.S.	154	43.14 N	88.06 W
Germany, Federal Republic of (West Germany) □1	64	51.00 N	9.00 E
Germiston	116	26.15 S	28.05 E
Gerolzhofen	72	49.54 N	10.21 E
Gerona	76	41.59 N	2.49 E
Gers □5	74	43.40 N	0.30 E
Geseke	72	51.38 N	8.31 E
Geser	124	3.53 S	130.54 E
Geta	68	60.23 N	19.50 E
Getafe	76	40.18 N	3.43 W
Gettysburg	152	39.50 N	77.14 W
Gévora ≃	76	38.53 N	6.57 W
Gex	74	46.20 N	6.04 E
Geyser, Banc du ✧2	110	12.25 S	46.25 E
Geyserville	168	38.42 N	122.54 W
Ghāghra ≃	102	25.47 N	84.37 E
Ghana □1	106	8.00 N	2.00 W
Ghanzi	116	21.38 S	21.45 E
Ghardaïa	106	32.31 N	3.37 E
Gharyān	108	32.10 N	13.01 E
Ghāt	108	24.58 N	10.11 E
Ghawdex I	78	36.03 N	14.15 E
Ghazāl, Baḥr al- ≃	112	9.31 N	30.25 E
Ghazal, Bahr el ≃	108	13.01 N	15.28 E
Ghāziābād	102	28.40 N	77.26 E
Ghāzīpur	102	25.35 N	83.34 E
Ghaznī	102	33.33 N	68.26 E
Ghazzah (Gaza)	104	31.30 N	34.28 E
Ghedi	78	45.24 N	10.16 E
Ghent → Gent	72	51.03 N	3.43 E
Gheorghe Gheorghiu-Dej	80	46.14 N	26.22 E
Gheorgheni	80	46.43 N	25.36 E
Ghisonaccia	78	42.00 N	9.25 E
Ghudāmis	108	30.08 N	9.30 E
Ghūrīān	104	34.21 N	61.30 E
Gia-dinh	94	10.49 N	106.42 E
Giant's Castle ∧	116	29.20 S	29.30 E
Giarre	78	37.43 N	15.11 E
Gibbon	162	40.45 N	98.51 W
Gibb River	124	15.39 S	126.38 E
Gibeon	116	25.09 S	17.43 E
Gibraltar	76	36.09 N	5.21 W
Gibraltar □2	64	36.11 N	5.22 W
Gibraltar, Strait of ⊔	64	35.57 N	5.36 W
Gibsland	158	32.33 N	93.03 W
Gibson	122	33.39 S	121.48 E
Gibsonburg	152	41.23 N	83.19 W
Gibson City	154	40.28 N	88.22 W
Gibson Desert ⇀2	122	24.30 S	126.00 E
Gibsons	148	49.24 N	123.30 W
Giddings	160	30.11 N	96.56 W
Gideon	158	36.27 N	89.55 W
Gidgee	122	27.16 S	119.22 E
Gidrotorf	86	56.28 N	43.33 E
Gien	74	47.42 N	2.38 E
Giessen	72	50.35 N	8.40 E
Gifford	156	27.41 N	80.25 W
Gifford ≃	142	70.21 N	83.05 W
Gifford Creek	122	24.05 S	116.11 E
Gifford Fjord C2	142	69.57 N	81.55 W
Gifhorn	72	52.29 N	10.33 E
Gifu	90	35.25 N	136.45 E
Gila ≃	164	32.43 N	114.33 W
Gila Bend	164	32.57 N	112.43 W
Gila Bend Mountains ⋀	164	33.10 N	113.10 W
Gila Mountains ⋀	164	33.05 N	109.50 W
Gilbert	154	47.29 N	92.28 W
Gilbert ≃	120	16.35 S	141.15 E
Gilbués	134	9.50 S	45.21 W
Gildford	166	48.34 N	110.18 W
Giles Creek ≃	122	23.52 S	134.44 E
Giles Meteorological Station	122	25.02 S	128.18 E
Gilgai	122	31.15 S	119.56 E
Gilgandra	120	31.42 S	148.39 E
Gil Gil Creek ≃	120	30.19 S	148.42 E
Gilgit	102	35.55 N	74.18 E
Gilgit ≃	102	35.44 N	74.38 E
Gillam	142	56.21 N	94.43 W
Gilleleje	68	56.07 N	12.19 E
Gillen, Lake ⊜	122	26.11 S	124.38 E
Gilles, Lake ⊜	120	32.50 S	136.45 E
Gillespie	158	39.07 N	89.49 W
Gillett	158	34.07 N	91.22 W
Gillette	162	44.18 N	105.30 W
Gillian, Lake ⊜	142	69.32 N	75.23 W
Gillingham	70	51.24 N	0.33 E
Gilman, Ill., U.S.	154	40.46 N	87.60 W
Gilman, Mont., U.S.	148	47.31 N	112.21 W
Gilmer	160	32.44 N	94.57 W
Gilo ≃	108	8.10 N	33.15 E
Gilroy	168	37.00 N	121.43 W
Gil'uj ≃	84	53.58 N	127.30 E
Giluwe, Mount ∧	124	6.05 S	143.50 E
Gimli	142	50.38 N	96.59 W
Gimont	74	43.38 N	0.53 E
Gin Gin	120	25.00 S	151.58 E
Ginir	108	7.07 N	40.46 E
Ginosa	78	40.34 N	16.46 E
Gioia del Colle	78	40.48 N	16.56 E
Gioia Tauro	78	38.26 N	15.54 E
Girard, Kans., U.S.	162	37.31 N	94.51 W
Girard, Ohio, U.S.	152	41.10 N	80.42 W
Girard, Pa., U.S.	152	42.00 N	80.19 W
Girardot	138	4.18 N	74.48 W
Girdwood	146	60.57 N	149.10 W
Girgarre	120	36.24 S	144.59 E
Giromagny	74	47.45 N	6.50 E
Gironde □5	74	44.45 N	0.35 W
Gironde C1	74	45.20 N	0.45 W
Giru	120	19.31 S	147.06 E
Girvan	70	55.15 N	4.51 W
Girvas	66	62.30 N	33.40 E
Girwa ≃	102	28.17 N	81.07 E
Gisborne	126	38.40 S	178.02 E
Gisenyi	110	1.42 S	29.15 E
Gisors	74	49.17 N	1.47 E
Gitega	110	3.26 S	29.56 E
Giugliano [in Campania]	78	40.56 N	14.12 E
Giulianova	78	42.45 N	13.57 E
Giurgiu	80	43.53 N	25.57 E
Givet	74	50.08 N	4.50 E
Givors	74	45.35 N	4.46 E
Givry	74	46.47 N	4.45 E
Giyon	108	8.30 N	38.00 E
Giza → Al-Jīzah	112	30.01 N	31.13 E
Gižduvan	104	40.06 N	64.41 E
Gižiga	84	62.03 N	160.30 E
Gižiginskaja Guba C	84	61.30 N	158.00 E
Gizo	118	8.07 S	156.52 E
Giżycko	72	54.03 N	21.47 E
Gjirokastër	80	40.05 N	20.10 E
Gjoa Haven	142	68.38 N	95.57 W
Gjøvik	68	60.48 N	10.42 E
Glace Bay	150	46.12 N	59.57 W
Glacier Bay C	146	58.40 N	136.00 W
Gladbach → Mönchengladbach	72	51.12 N	6.28 E
Gladbeck	72	51.34 N	6.59 E
Glade Spring	156	36.47 N	81.47 W
Gladewater	160	32.33 N	94.56 W
Gladstone, Austl.	120	23.51 S	151.16 E
Gladstone, Austl.	120	33.17 S	138.22 E
Gladstone, Mich., U.S.	154	45.50 N	87.03 W
Gladstone, Mo., U.S.	158	39.13 N	94.34 W
Gladwin	154	43.59 N	84.29 W
Glåma ≃	68	59.12 N	10.57 E
Glamsbjerg	68	55.16 N	10.07 E
Glan ⊜	68	58.37 N	15.58 E
Glarner Alpen ⋀	74	46.55 N	9.00 E
Glarus	74	47.02 N	9.04 E
Glasco	162	39.22 N	97.50 W
Glasgow, Scot., U.K.	70	55.53 N	4.15 W
Glasgow, Ky., U.S.	158	37.00 N	85.55 W
Glasgow, Mo., U.S.	158	39.14 N	92.50 W
Glasgow, Mont., U.S.	166	48.12 N	106.38 W
Glasgow, Va., U.S.	156	37.38 N	79.27 W
Glassboro	152	49.32 N	99.15 W
Glastonbury	70	51.06 N	2.43 W
Glauchau	72	50.49 N	12.32 E
Glazier	160	36.01 N	100.16 W
Glazov	66	58.09 N	52.40 E
Glazunovka	86	52.30 N	36.19 E
Gleason	158	36.13 N	88.37 W
Gleisdorf	72	47.06 N	15.44 E
Gleiwitz → Gliwice	72	50.17 N	18.40 E
Glen Burnie	152	39.10 N	76.37 W
Glen Canyon V	164	37.10 N	110.50 W
Glencoe, Austl.	120	37.42 S	140.37 E
Glencoe, Ala., U.S.	158	33.57 N	85.56 W
Glencoe, Ill., U.S.	154	42.08 N	87.45 W
Glencoe, Minn., U.S.	154	44.46 N	94.09 W
Glen Cove	152	40.52 N	73.37 W
Glendale, Ariz., U.S.	164	33.32 N	112.11 W
Glendale, Calif., U.S.	168	34.10 N	118.17 W
Glendale, Oreg., U.S.	166	42.44 N	123.26 W
Glendale, Wis., U.S.	154	43.07 N	87.57 W
Glendive	162	47.06 N	104.43 W
Glendo	164	42.30 N	105.02 W
Glen Flora	160	29.21 N	96.12 W
Glengarriff	70	51.45 N	9.33 W
Glengarry Range ⋀	122	26.13 S	118.59 E
Glen Lyon	152	41.10 N	76.05 W
Glenmora	158	30.59 N	92.35 W
Glenmorgan	120	27.15 S	149.41 E
Glennallen	146	62.07 N	145.33 W
Glenns Ferry	166	42.57 N	115.18 W
Glennville	156	31.56 N	81.56 W
Glenoma	166	46.31 N	122.09 W
Glenormiston	120	22.55 S	138.48 E
Glenreagh	120	30.03 S	152.59 E
Glen Rose	160	32.14 N	97.45 W
Glenroy, Austl.	122	21.46 S	114.49 E
Glenroy, Austl.	122	17.22 S	126.06 E
Glens Falls	152	43.19 N	73.39 W
Glenshaw	152	40.31 N	79.57 W
Glenties	70	54.47 N	8.17 W
Glenville	152	38.56 N	80.50 W
Glenwood, Iowa, U.S.	162	41.03 N	95.45 W
Glenwood, Minn., U.S.	162	45.39 N	95.23 W
Glenwood, Oreg., U.S.	166	45.39 N	123.16 W
Glenwood, Utah, U.S.	164	38.46 N	111.59 W
Glenwood, Va., U.S.	156	36.35 N	79.22 W
Glenwood City	154	45.04 N	92.10 W
Glenwood Springs	164	39.33 N	107.19 W
Glidden, Iowa, U.S.	162	42.04 N	94.44 W
Glidden, Wis., U.S.	154	46.09 N	90.34 W
Glide	166	43.18 N	123.06 W
Glittertinden ∧	68	61.39 N	8.33 E
Gliwice (Gleiwitz)	72	50.17 N	18.40 E
Globe	164	33.24 N	110.47 W
Gloggnitz	72	47.40 N	15.57 E
Głogów	72	51.40 N	16.05 E
Glorieta	164	35.35 N	105.46 W
Glorieuses, Îles II	110	11.30 S	47.20 E
Gloster	158	31.12 N	91.01 W
Gloucester, Austl.	120	31.59 S	151.58 E
Gloucester, Eng., U.K.	70	51.53 N	2.14 W
Gloucester, Mass., U.S.	152	42.41 N	70.39 W
Gloucester Island I	120	20.01 S	148.27 E
Gloucestershire □6	70	51.47 N	2.15 W
Glouster	152	39.30 N	82.05 W
Gloversville	152	43.03 N	74.20 W
Glovertown	150	48.41 N	54.02 W
Gloverville	156	33.32 N	81.50 W
Głowno	72	51.58 N	19.44 E
Głuchołazy	72	50.20 N	17.22 E
Glücksburg	72	54.50 N	9.33 E
Glückstadt	72	53.47 N	9.25 E
Gmünd	72	48.47 N	15.00 E
Gmunden	72	47.55 N	13.48 E
Gnalta	120	31.03 S	142.20 E
Gnarp	68	62.03 N	17.16 E
Gniew	72	53.51 N	18.49 E
Gniewkowo	72	52.54 N	18.25 E
Gniezno	72	52.31 N	17.37 E
Gnjilane	80	42.28 N	21.29 E
Gnoien	72	53.58 N	12.42 E
Gnowangerup	122	33.56 S	117.59 E
Goalen Head ≻	120	36.40 S	150.05 E
Goālpāra	102	26.11 N	90.37 E
Goba	108	7.02 N	40.00 E
Gobabis	116	22.30 S	18.58 E
Gobernador Gregores	136	48.46 S	70.15 W
Gobernador Ingeniero Valentín Virasoro	140	28.02 S	56.00 W
Gobi ⇀2	88	43.00 N	105.00 E
Gobles	154	42.21 N	85.53 W
Goce Delčev	80	41.34 N	23.44 E
Goch	72	51.41 N	6.10 E
Godāvari ≃	100	16.37 N	82.18 E
Goderich	154	43.45 N	81.43 W
Goderville	74	49.39 N	0.22 E
Godfrey	158	38.57 N	90.11 W
Godhavn	142	69.15 N	53.33 W
Godhra	102	22.45 N	73.38 E
Gödöllő	72	47.36 N	19.22 E
Godoy Cruz	140	32.55 S	68.50 W
Gods ≃	142	56.22 N	92.51 W
Gods Lake ⊜	142	54.45 N	94.00 W
Gods Mercy, Bay of C	142	63.30 N	86.10 W
Godthåb	142	64.11 N	51.44 W
Godwin Austen (K2) ∧	102	35.53 N	76.30 E
Goéland, Lac au ⊜	142	49.47 N	76.48 W
Goélands, Lac aux ⊜	142	55.27 N	64.17 W
Goes	72	51.30 N	3.54 E
Goffstown	152	43.01 N	71.36 W
Gogebic Range ⋀2	154	46.45 N	89.25 W
Göggingen	72	48.20 N	10.52 E
Goiana	134	7.33 S	34.59 W
Goiânia	134	16.40 S	49.16 W
Goiás	134	15.56 S	50.08 W
Góis	76	40.09 N	8.07 W
Goito	78	45.15 N	10.40 E
Gol	68	60.42 N	8.57 E
Gol'čicha	84	71.43 N	83.36 E
Golconda	158	37.22 N	88.29 W
Gołdap	72	54.19 N	22.19 E
Gold Beach	166	42.25 N	124.25 W
Gold Coast → Southport	120	27.58 S	153.25 E
Gold Coast ⏏2	114	5.10 N	1.00 W
Gold Coast ⏏2, Ghana	114	5.20 N	0.45 W
Golden, B.C., Can.	148	51.18 N	116.58 W
Golden, Colo., U.S.	164	39.46 N	105.13 W
Golden Hinde ∧	148	49.40 N	125.45 W
Golden Meadow	158	29.23 N	90.16 W
Goldfield	168	37.42 N	117.14 W
Goldpan Peak ∧	146	61.12 N	153.22 W
Goldsboro	156	35.23 N	77.59 W
Goldsmith	160	31.59 N	102.40 W
Goldthwaite	160	31.27 N	98.34 W
Golec-In'aptuk, Gora ∧	84	56.22 N	110.11 E
Golec-Skalistyj, Gora ∧	84	56.24 N	119.12 E
Goleniów	72	53.36 N	14.50 E
Goleta	168	34.27 N	119.50 W
Golfito	138	8.38 N	83.11 W
Golo ≃	74	42.31 N	9.32 E
Golovin	146	64.33 N	163.02 W
Golspie	70	57.58 N	3.58 W
Golyšmanovo	82	56.23 N	68.23 E
Goma	110	1.41 S	29.14 E
Gomati ≃	102	25.32 N	83.10 E
Gombe ≃	110	4.38 S	31.40 E
Gomel'	86	52.25 N	31.00 E
Gomera I	106	28.06 N	17.08 W
Gómez Palacio	130	25.34 N	103.30 W
Gonābād	100	34.20 N	58.42 E
Gonaïves	132	19.30 N	72.40 W
Gonam	84	57.21 N	131.12 E
Gonam ≃	84	57.21 N	131.14 E
Gonâve, Île de la I	132	18.45 N	73.00 W
Gonbad-e Qābūs	104	37.17 N	55.17 E
Gonda	102	27.08 N	81.56 E
Gondal	102	21.58 N	70.48 E
Gonder	108	12.40 N	37.30 E
Gondia	102	21.27 N	80.12 E
Gondomar	76	41.09 N	8.32 W
Gondrecourt-le-Château	74	48.31 N	5.30 E
Gonesse	70	48.59 N	2.27 E
Gongbujiangda	88	30.01 N	93.08 E
Gonggashan ∧	88	29.35 N	101.51 E
Gonggeershan ∧	102	38.37 N	75.20 E
Gongola ≃	106	9.30 N	12.04 E
Gongxian	88	34.48 N	113.03 E
Gonzales, Calif., U.S.	168	36.31 N	121.32 W
Gonzales, La., U.S.	158	30.14 N	90.55 W
Gonzales, Tex., U.S.	160	29.30 N	97.27 W
González Chaves	140	38.02 S	60.05 W
Goode, Mount ∧	146	61.20 N	148.02 W
Good Hope, Cape of ≻	116	34.24 S	18.30 E
Good Hope Mountain ∧	148	51.09 N	124.10 W
Gooding	166	42.56 N	114.43 W
Goodland, Ind., U.S.	158	40.46 N	87.18 W
Goodland, Kans., U.S.	162	39.21 N	101.43 W
Goodlettsville	158	36.19 N	86.43 W
Goodman, Miss., U.S.	158	32.58 N	89.55 W
Goodman, Wis., U.S.	154	45.38 N	88.21 W
Goodnews Bay	146	59.07 N	161.35 W
Goodnight	160	35.02 N	101.11 W
Goodrich, N. Dak., U.S.	162	47.28 N	100.08 W
Goodrich, Tex., U.S.	160	30.36 N	94.57 W
Goodview	154	44.04 N	91.41 W
Goodwater	158	33.04 N	86.03 W
Goodwell	160	36.36 N	101.38 W
Goodyear	164	33.26 N	112.21 W
Goole	70	53.42 N	0.52 W
Goolgowi	120	33.59 S	145.42 E
Goombalie	120	29.59 S	145.23 E
Goondiwindi	120	28.32 S	150.19 E
Goose Bay	142	53.20 N	60.25 W
Goose Creek ≃	166	42.33 N	113.46 W
Goose Lake ⊜	168	41.57 N	120.25 W
Göppingen	72	48.42 N	9.40 E
Góra	72	51.40 N	16.33 E
Gorakhpur	102	26.45 N	83.22 E
Gorbatov	86	56.08 N	43.04 E
Gorbatovka	86	56.15 N	43.45 E
Gorčucha	86	57.43 N	43.43 E
Gorda, Punta ≻	132	22.24 N	82.10 W
Gordil	108	9.44 N	21.35 E
Gordo	158	33.19 N	87.54 W
Gordon, Ga., U.S.	156	32.53 N	83.20 W
Gordon, Nebr., U.S.	162	42.48 N	102.12 W
Gordon ≃	120	42.25 S	145.31 E
Gordon Downs	122	18.44 S	128.35 E
Gordonvale	120	17.05 S	145.47 E
Gore, N.Z.	126	46.06 S	168.56 E
Gore, Yai.	108	8.08 N	35.33 E
Goree	160	33.28 N	99.31 W
Gore Point ≻	120	17.38 S	139.56 E
Goreville	158	37.33 N	88.58 W
Gorey	70	52.40 N	6.18 W
Gorgān	104	36.50 N	54.29 E
Gorham, Maine, U.S.	152	43.41 N	70.26 W
Gorham, N.H., U.S.	152	44.23 N	71.10 W
Gori	64	41.58 N	44.07 E
Goricy	66	57.09 N	36.44 E
Gorinchem	72	51.50 N	5.00 E
Gorizia	78	45.57 N	13.38 E
Gorj □4	80	45.00 N	23.20 E
Gorki, S.S.S.R.	86	54.17 N	30.59 E
Gorki → Gor'kij, S.S.S.R.	86	56.20 N	44.00 E
Gor'kij (Gorky)	86	56.20 N	44.00 E
Gor'kovskoje Vodochranilišče ⊜1	66	57.00 N	43.10 E
Gorky → Gor'kij	86	56.20 N	44.00 E
Gorlice	72	49.40 N	21.10 E
Görlitz	72	53.24 N	13.54 E
Gorlovka	64	48.18 N	38.03 E
Gorman	160	32.12 N	98.41 W
Gorn'ackij	66	67.32 N	64.03 E
Gorn'ak	86	53.36 N	39.29 E
Gorna Orjahovica	80	43.07 N	25.41 E
Gornji Milanovac	80	44.01 N	20.27 E
Gorno-Altajsk	84	51.58 N	85.58 E
Gorno-Čujskij	84	59.12 N	112.25 E
Gornozavodsk	84	46.34 N	141.49 E
Gorochovec	86	56.12 N	42.40 E
Gorodec	86	56.38 N	43.30 E
Gorodeja	86	53.19 N	26.32 E
Gorodenka	80	48.41 N	25.29 E
Gorodišče	86	53.19 N	26.00 E
Gorodok	86	55.28 N	29.59 E
Goroka	124	6.05 S	145.25 E
Gorontalo	96	0.33 N	123.03 E
Gorron	70	48.25 N	0.49 W
Gort	70	53.04 N	8.50 W
Gosford	120	33.26 S	151.21 E
Goshen, Calif., U.S.	168	36.21 N	119.25 W
Goshen, Ind., U.S.	158	41.35 N	85.50 W
Goshen, N.Y., U.S.	152	41.24 N	74.20 W
Goslar	72	51.54 N	10.25 E
Gostivar	80	41.47 N	20.54 E
Gostyń	72	51.53 N	17.00 E
Gostynin	72	52.26 N	19.29 E
Gotebo	160	35.04 N	98.53 W
Göteborg (Gothenburg)	68	57.43 N	11.58 E
Göteborgs Och Bohus län □6	68	58.30 N	11.30 E
Gotha	72	50.57 N	10.41 E
Gothenburg → Göteborg, Sve.	68	57.43 N	11.58 E
Gothenburg, Nebr., U.S.	162	40.56 N	100.09 W
Gotland I	68	57.30 N	18.33 E
Gotlands Län □6	68	57.30 N	18.30 E
Gotō-rettō II	90	32.50 N	129.00 E
Gotska Sandön I	68	58.23 N	19.16 E
Göttingen	72	51.32 N	9.55 E
Gottwaldov	72	49.13 N	17.41 E
Götzis	72	47.20 N	9.38 E
Gouala ≃	114	10.14 N	8.38 W
Gouarec	74	48.13 N	3.11 W
Gouda	72	52.01 N	4.43 E
Gouin, Réservoir ⊜1	142	48.38 N	74.54 W
Goulburn	120	34.45 S	149.43 E
Goulburn Islands II	124	11.33 S	133.26 E
Gould	158	33.59 N	91.34 W
Goulds	156	25.33 N	80.23 W
Goundam	114	16.25 N	3.40 W
Gourdon	74	44.44 N	1.23 E
Gouré	114	13.58 N	10.18 E
Gourin	74	48.08 N	3.36 W
Gournay-en-Bray	74	49.29 N	1.44 E
Gouverneur	152	44.20 N	75.28 W
Gove	162	38.58 N	100.29 W
Governador Valadares	134	18.51 S	41.56 W
Gowanda	152	42.28 N	78.56 W
Gowan Range ⋀	120	25.00 S	145.00 E
Gowmal (Gumal) ≃	102	31.56 N	70.22 E
Goya	140	29.10 S	59.20 W
Graaff-Reinet	116	32.14 S	24.32 E
Grabow	72	53.16 N	11.34 E
Gračanica	80	44.42 N	18.19 E
Grace	166	42.35 N	111.44 W
Graceville, Fla., U.S.	156	30.58 N	85.31 W
Graceville, Minn., U.S.	162	45.34 N	96.26 W
Gracias a Dios, Cabo ≻	132	15.00 N	83.08 W
Gradačac	80	44.53 N	18.26 E
Gradaús	134	7.43 S	51.11 W
Gradaús, Serra dos ⋀1	134	8.00 S	50.45 W
Grado, Esp.	76	43.23 N	6.04 W
Grado, It.	78	45.40 N	13.23 E
Grafenau	72	48.52 N	13.25 E
Gräfenhainichen	72	51.44 N	12.27 E
Grafing [Bei München]	72	48.02 N	11.59 E
Graford	160	32.56 N	98.14 W
Grafton, Austl.	120	29.41 S	152.56 E
Grafton, Ill., U.S.	158	38.58 N	90.26 W
Grafton, N. Dak., U.S.	162	48.25 N	97.25 W
Grafton, Ohio, U.S.	152	41.16 N	82.04 W
Grafton, W. Va., U.S.	152	39.20 N	80.01 W
Grafton, Wis., U.S.	154	43.19 N	87.56 W
Grafton, Cape ≻	120	16.52 S	145.55 E
Graham, N.C., U.S.	156	36.05 N	79.25 W
Graham, Tex., U.S.	160	33.06 N	98.35 W
Graham Island I	148	53.40 N	132.30 W
Graham Moore, Cape ≻	142	72.52 N	76.04 W
Graham Moore Bay C	142	75.26 N	101.25 W
Grahamstown	116	33.19 S	26.31 E
Grain Coast ⏏2	114	5.00 N	9.00 W
Grainfield	162	39.07 N	100.28 W
Grajaú	134	5.49 S	46.08 W
Grajaú ≃	134	3.41 S	44.48 W
Grajewo	72	53.39 N	22.27 E
Gram	68	55.17 N	9.04 E
Gramat	74	44.47 N	1.43 E
Grambling	158	32.32 N	92.43 W
Grammichele	78	37.13 N	14.38 E
Grampian Region □4	70	57.15 N	2.45 W
Granada, Esp.	76	37.13 N	3.41 W
Granada, Nic.	132	11.56 N	85.57 W
Granada, Colo., U.S.	162	38.04 N	102.19 W
Granard	70	53.47 N	7.30 W
Granbury	160	32.27 N	97.47 W
Granby, Qué., Can.	152	45.24 N	72.44 W
Granby, Colo., U.S.	164	40.05 N	105.56 W
Granby, Mo., U.S.	158	36.55 N	94.15 W
Gran Canaria I	106	28.00 N	15.36 W
Gran Chaco ≚	136	23.00 S	60.00 W
Grand ≃	158	39.23 N	93.06 W
Grand, East Fork ≃	158	40.12 N	94.21 W
Grand, North Fork ≃	162	45.47 N	102.16 W
Grand Bahama I	132	26.40 N	78.20 W
Grand Bank	150	47.06 N	55.46 W
Grand-Bassam	114	5.12 N	3.44 W
Grand Bay	158	30.29 N	88.21 W
Grand Blanc	154	42.56 N	83.38 W
Grand Canyon	164	36.03 N	112.09 W
Grand Canyon V	164	36.10 N	112.45 W
Grand Cayman I	132	19.20 N	81.15 W
Grand Cess	114	4.36 N	8.10 W
Grand-Couronne	74	49.21 N	1.00 E
Grande ≃, Bol.	134	15.51 S	64.39 W
Grande ≃, Bra.	134	11.05 S	43.09 W
Grande ≃, Bra.	134	19.52 S	50.20 W
Grande, Bahía C	136	50.45 S	68.45 W
Grande, Boca ≃1	138	8.38 N	60.30 W
Grande, Ilha I	136	23.09 S	44.14 W
Grande, Rio (Bravo (Del Norte ≃	144	25.57 N	97.09 W
Grande Comore I	117a	11.35 S	43.20 E
Grande de Tarija ≃	136	22.53 S	64.21 W
Grande do Gurupá, Ilha I	134	1.00 S	51.30 W
Grande-Prairie, Alta., Can.	142	32.45 N	96.59 W
Grande-Prairie, Alta., Can.	148	55.10 N	118.48 W
Grand Erg de Bilma ⇀2	106	18.30 N	14.00 E
Grand Erg Occidental ⇀2	106	30.30 N	0.30 E
Grand Erg Oriental ⇀2	106	30.30 N	7.00 E
Grande Ronde ≃	166	46.05 N	116.59 W
Grandes, Salinas ≚	140	29.37 S	64.56 W
Grand Falls, N.B., Can.	150	47.03 N	67.44 W
Grand Falls, Newf., Can.	150	48.56 N	55.40 W
Grandfalls, Tex., U.S.	160	31.20 N	102.51 W
Grand Forks, B.C., Can.	148	49.02 N	118.27 W
Grand Forks, N. Dak., U.S.	162	47.55 N	97.03 W
Grand-Fougeray	74	47.44 N	1.44 W
Grand Haven	154	43.04 N	86.13 W
Grand Hers ≃	74	43.47 N	1.20 E
Grandin, Lac ⊜	142	63.59 N	119.00 W
Grand Island	162	40.55 N	98.21 W
Grand Isle	158	29.14 N	90.00 W
Grand Junction, Colo., U.S.	164	39.05 N	108.33 W
Grand Junction, Iowa, U.S.	162	42.02 N	94.14 W
Grand Lake ⊜	150	45.43 N	67.50 W
Grand Ledge	154	42.45 N	84.45 W
Grand Manan Channel ⊔	150	44.45 N	66.52 W
Grand Marais	154	47.45 N	90.20 W
Grand'Mère	142	46.37 N	72.41 W
Grândola	76	38.10 N	8.34 W
Grand Prairie	160	32.45 N	96.59 W
Grand Rapids, Man., Can.	142	53.08 N	99.20 W
Grand Rapids, Mich., U.S.	154	42.58 N	85.40 W
Grand Rapids, Minn., U.S.	154	47.14 N	93.31 W
Grandrieu	74	44.47 N	3.38 E
Grand Rivière de la Baleine ≃	142	55.16 N	77.47 W
Grand-Saint-Bernard, Col du)(	74	45.50 N	7.10 E
Grand-Saint-Bernard, Tunnel du ⇀5	74	45.50 N	7.10 E
Grand Saline	160	32.41 N	95.43 W
Grand Teton ∧	164	43.44 N	110.48 W
Grand Tower	158	37.38 N	89.30 W
Grand Traverse Bay C	154	45.02 N	85.30 W
Grand Turk	132	21.28 N	71.08 W
Grand Valley	164	39.27 N	108.03 W
Grandview, Man., Can.	142	51.10 N	100.45 W
Grandview, Mo., U.S.	158	38.53 N	94.32 W
Grandview, Ohio, U.S.	152	39.31 N	81.05 W
Grandview, Wash., U.S.	166	46.15 N	119.54 W
Grand Wash Cliffs ⏏4	164	36.30 N	113.40 W
Granger	166	41.35 N	109.58 W
Grangeville	166	45.56 N	116.07 W
Granite City	158	38.42 N	90.09 W
Granite Falls, Minn., U.S.	162	44.49 N	95.33 W
Granite Falls, N.C., U.S.	156	35.48 N	81.26 W
Granite Peak ∧	166	45.10 N	109.48 W
Graniteville	156	33.34 N	81.48 W
Granki	66	54.51 N	31.27 E
Gränna	68	58.01 N	14.28 E
Granollers	76	41.37 N	2.18 E
Gransee	72	53.00 N	13.09 E
Grant	162	40.50 N	101.56 W
Grant City	158	40.29 N	94.25 W
Grantham	70	52.55 N	0.39 W
Grantown-on-Spey	70	57.20 N	3.58 W
Grant Park	154	41.14 N	87.39 W
Grant Point ≻1	142	68.19 N	98.53 W
Grant Range ⋀	168	38.25 N	115.30 W
Grants	164	35.09 N	107.52 W
Grants Pass	166	42.26 N	123.19 W
Grant-Suttie Bay C	142	69.47 N	77.15 W
Grantsville, Utah, U.S.	164	40.36 N	112.28 W
Grantsville, W. Va., U.S.	152	38.55 N	81.06 W
Grantville	156	33.14 N	84.50 W
Granville, Fr.	74	48.50 N	1.36 W
Granville, N. Dak., U.S.	162	48.16 N	100.47 W
Granville, N.Y., U.S.	152	43.24 N	73.16 W
Granville, Ohio, U.S.	152	40.04 N	82.31 W
Granville, W. Va., U.S.	152	39.39 N	79.59 W
Granville Lake ⊜	142	56.18 N	100.30 W
Granvin	68	60.33 N	6.43 E
Grão Mogol	134	16.34 S	42.54 W
Gras, Lac de ⊜	142	64.30 N	110.30 W
Grass ≃	142	56.03 N	96.33 W
Grasse	74	43.40 N	6.55 E
Grass Lake	154	49.49 N	111.43 W
Grassrange	166	47.01 N	108.48 W
Grass Valley	168	39.13 N	121.04 W
Grassy	120	40.03 S	144.04 E
Gråsten	68	54.55 N	9.36 E
Gravatá	134	8.12 S	35.34 W
Gravelbourg	142	49.53 N	106.34 W
Gravelines	74	50.59 N	2.07 E
Gravell Point ≻	142	67.10 N	76.43 W
Gravenhurst	154	44.55 N	79.22 W
Gravette	158	36.26 N	94.27 W
Gravina in Puglia	78	40.49 N	16.25 E
Gray, Fr.	74	47.27 N	5.35 E
Gray, Ga., U.S.	156	33.01 N	83.32 W
Gray, Maine, U.S.	152	43.53 N	70.20 W
Grayling, Alaska, U.S.	146	62.57 N	160.03 W
Grayling, Mich., U.S.	154	44.40 N	84.43 W
Grayson, Ala., U.S.	158	34.15 N	87.24 W
Grayson, Ky., U.S.	152	38.20 N	82.57 W
Grays Peak ∧	164	39.37 N	105.45 W
Graysville	158	35.27 N	85.05 W
Grayville	158	38.16 N	87.59 W
Graz	72	47.05 N	15.27 E
Grazalema	76	36.46 N	5.22 W
Gr'azi	86	52.29 N	39.57 E
Gr'aznoje	86	54.02 N	39.07 E
Gr'azovec	86	58.53 N	40.14 E
Greåker	68	59.16 N	11.02 E
Great Abaco I	132	26.25 N	77.10 W
Great Artesian Basin ≚1	120	25.00 S	143.00 E
Great Australian Bight C3	122	35.00 S	135.00 E
Great Bahama Bank ✧4	132	23.15 N	78.00 W
Great Barrier Reef ✧2	118	18.00 S	145.50 E
Great Barrington	152	42.12 N	73.22 W
Great Basin ≚1	144	40.00 N	117.00 W
Great Bear Lake ⊜	146	66.00 N	120.00 W
Great Bend	162	38.22 N	98.46 W
Great Bitter Lake → Al-Buḥayrah al-Murrah al-Kubrā ⊜	112	30.20 N	32.23 E
Great Channel ⊔	94	6.25 N	94.20 E
Great Dividing Range ⋀	118	25.00 S	147.00 E
Great Dunmow	70	51.53 N	0.22 E
Greater Antilles II	132	20.00 N	74.00 W
Greater Sunda Islands II	92	2.00 S	110.00 E
Great Exuma I	132	23.30 N	75.50 W
Great Falls, Mont., U.S.	166	47.30 N	111.17 W
Great Falls, S.C., U.S.	156	34.34 N	80.54 W
Great Himalaya Range ⋀	102	29.00 N	83.00 E
Great Inagua I	132	21.02 N	73.20 W
Great Indian Desert (Thar Desert) ⇀2	102	28.00 N	72.00 E
Great Malvern	70	52.07 N	2.19 W
Great Namaland □9	110	25.00 S	17.00 E
Great Nicobar I	94	7.00 N	93.50 E
Great North East Channel ⊔	124	9.30 S	143.25 E
Great Palm Island I	120	18.43 S	146.37 E
Great Plain of the Koukdjuak ≚	142	66.00 N	73.00 W
Great Ruaha ≃	110	7.56 S	37.52 E
Great Saint Bernard Pass → Grand-Saint-Bernard, Col du)(	78	45.50 N	7.10 E
Great Salt Lake ⊜	164	41.10 N	112.30 W
Great Salt Lake Desert ⇀2	164	40.40 N	113.30 W
Great Sandy Desert ⇀2, Austl.	122	21.30 S	125.00 E
Great Sandy Desert ⇀2, Oreg., U.S.	166	43.35 N	120.15 W
Great Scarcies (Kolenté) ≃	114	8.55 N	13.08 W
Great Slave Lake ⊜	142	61.30 N	114.00 W
Great Smoky Mountains ⋀	156	35.35 N	83.30 W
Great Victoria Desert ⇀2	122	28.30 S	127.45 E
Great Yarmouth	70	52.37 N	1.44 E
Great Zab (Büyükzap) (Az-Zāb al-Kabīr) ≃	104	36.00 N	43.21 E
Gréboun, Mont ∧	114	20.00 N	8.35 E
Greece	152	43.14 N	77.38 W
Greece □1	64	39.00 N	22.00 E
Greeley, Colo., U.S.	164	40.25 N	104.42 W
Greeley, Kans., U.S.	162	38.22 N	95.08 W
Greeleyville	156	33.35 N	79.58 W
Green ≃	164	38.11 N	109.53 W
Greenacres	166	47.39 N	117.06 W
Green Bay	154	44.30 N	88.01 W
Green Bay C	154	45.00 N	87.30 W
Greenbrier	158	36.27 N	86.49 W
Green Cape ≻	120	37.15 S	150.03 E
Greencastle, Ind., U.S.	158	39.38 N	86.52 W
Greencastle, Pa., U.S.	152	39.47 N	77.44 W
Green Cove Springs	156	30.00 N	81.41 W
Greendale	158	39.07 N	84.52 W
Greene, Iowa, U.S.	154	42.54 N	92.48 W
Greene, N.Y., U.S.	152	42.20 N	75.46 W
Greenfield, Calif., U.S.	168	36.19 N	121.15 W
Greenfield, Iowa, U.S.	162	41.18 N	94.28 W
Greenfield, Mass., U.S.	152	42.36 N	72.36 W
Greenfield, Mo., U.S.	158	37.25 N	93.51 W
Greenfield, Ohio, U.S.	152	39.21 N	83.23 W
Greenfield, Tenn., U.S.	158	36.09 N	88.48 W
Green Forest	158	36.20 N	93.26 W
Green Head ≻	122	30.05 S	114.58 E
Green Island	126	45.54 S	170.26 E
Greenland □2	142	70.00 N	40.00 W
Greenland Sea ≂2	66a	77.00 N	1.00 W
Greenleaf	162	39.44 N	96.59 W
Green Mountains ⋀	152	43.45 N	72.45 W
Greenock	70	55.57 N	4.45 W
Green Pond	156	32.44 N	80.37 W
Greenport	152	41.06 N	72.22 W
Green River, Utah, U.S.	164	38.59 N	110.10 W
Green River, Wyo., U.S.	164	41.32 N	109.28 W
Greensboro, Ala., U.S.	158	32.42 N	87.36 W
Greensboro, Fla., U.S.	156	30.34 N	84.45 W
Greensboro, Ga., U.S.	156	33.35 N	83.11 W
Greensboro, N.C., U.S.	156	36.04 N	79.47 W
Greensburg, Ind., U.S.	158	39.20 N	85.29 W
Greensburg, Kans., U.S.	162	37.36 N	99.18 W
Greensburg, Ky., U.S.	158	37.16 N	85.30 W
Green Springs	152	41.15 N	83.03 W
Greenup, Ill., U.S.	158	39.15 N	88.10 W
Greenup, Ky., U.S.	152	38.34 N	82.50 W
Greenville, Liber.	114	5.01 N	9.03 W
Greenville, Ala., U.S.	158	31.50 N	86.38 W
Greenville, Calif., U.S.	168	40.08 N	120.57 W
Greenville, Fla., U.S.	156	30.28 N	83.38 W
Greenville, Ill., U.S.	158	38.53 N	89.25 W
Greenville, Ky., U.S.	158	37.12 N	87.11 W
Greenville, Maine, U.S.	152	45.28 N	69.35 W
Greenville, Mich., U.S.	154	43.11 N	85.15 W
Greenville, Miss., U.S.	158	33.25 N	91.05 W
Greenville, N.H., U.S.	152	42.46 N	71.49 W
Greenville, N.C., U.S.	156	35.37 N	77.23 W
Greenville, Ohio, U.S.	152	40.06 N	84.38 W
Greenville, Pa., U.S.	152	41.24 N	80.23 W
Greenville, S.C., U.S.	156	34.51 N	82.23 W
Greenville, Tex., U.S.	160	33.08 N	96.07 W
Greenwich, Conn., U.S.	152	41.01 N	73.38 W
Greenwich, N.Y., U.S.	152	43.05 N	73.30 W
Greenwich, Ohio, U.S.	152	41.02 N	82.31 W
Greenwood, Ark., U.S.	158	35.13 N	94.15 W
Greenwood, Ind., U.S.	158	39.37 N	86.07 W
Greenwood, Miss., U.S.	158	33.31 N	90.11 W
Greenwood, S.C., U.S.	156	34.12 N	82.10 W
Greer	156	34.56 N	82.14 W
Gregory	160	27.55 N	97.17 W
Gregory ≃	120	17.53 S	139.17 E
Gregory, Lake ⊜, Austl.	120	28.55 S	139.00 E
Gregory, Lake ⊜, Austl.	122	25.38 S	119.58 E
Gregory Lake ⊜	122	20.10 S	127.20 E
Gregory Range ⋀	120	19.00 S	143.05 E
Greifswald	72	54.05 N	13.23 E
Grein	72	48.14 N	14.51 E
Greiz	72	50.39 N	12.12 E
Grem'ačinsk	82	58.34 N	57.51 E
Gremicha	66	68.03 N	39.27 E
Grenå	68	56.25 N	10.53 E
Grenada	158	33.47 N	89.55 W
Grenada □1	128	12.07 N	61.40 W
Grenada Reservoir ⊜1	158	33.50 N	89.40 W
Grenadine Islands II	132	12.40 N	61.15 W
Grenchen	74	47.11 N	7.24 E
Grenfell	120	33.54 S	148.10 E
Grenoble	74	45.10 N	5.43 E
Grenville, Cape ≻	124	11.58 S	143.14 E
Gréoux-les-Bains	74	43.45 N	5.53 E
Gresham	166	45.30 N	122.26 W
Gresham Park	156	33.42 N	84.19 W
Gresik	96	7.09 S	112.38 E
Gresten	72	48.00 N	15.02 E
Gretna, La., U.S.	158	29.55 N	90.03 W
Gretna, Va., U.S.	156	36.57 N	79.22 W
Greven	72	52.05 N	7.36 E
Grevená	80	40.05 N	21.25 E
Grevenbroich	72	51.05 N	6.35 E
Grevesmühlen	72	53.51 N	11.10 E
Grey, Cape ≻	124	13.00 S	136.40 E
Greybull	166	44.30 N	108.03 W
Grey Islands II	150	50.50 N	55.37 W
Greylock, Mount ∧	152	42.38 N	73.10 W
Greymouth	126	42.27 S	171.12 E
Grey Range ⋀	120	27.00 S	143.35 E
Greytown	116	29.07 S	30.30 E
Grez-en-Bouére	70	47.53 N	0.31 W
Gribanovskij	82	51.27 N	41.58 E
Gridley	168	39.22 N	121.42 W
Griesbach	72	48.28 N	13.11 E
Griesheim	72	49.50 N	8.34 E
Griffin	156	33.15 N	84.16 W
Griffith	120	34.17 S	146.03 E
Griffith Island I	142	74.35 N	95.30 W
Griggsville	158	39.42 N	90.43 W
Grignan	74	44.25 N	4.54 E
Grignols	74	44.23 N	0.03 W
Grijalva ≃	130	18.36 N	92.39 W
Grim, Cape ≻	120	40.41 S	144.41 E
Grimma	72	51.14 N	12.43 E
Grimmen	72	54.07 N	13.02 E
Grimsby, Ont., Can.	154	43.12 N	79.34 W
Grimsby, Eng., U.K.	70	53.35 N	0.05 W
Grimselpass)(	74	46.34 N	8.21 E
Grímsey I	66a	66.34 N	18.00 W
Grimshaw	148	56.11 N	117.36 W
Grímsstaðir	66a	65.40 N	16.01 W
Grimstad	68	58.20 N	8.36 E
Grindavík	66a	63.52 N	22.27 W
Grindelwald	74	46.37 N	8.02 E
Grinnell	154	41.45 N	92.43 W
Grinnell Peninsula ≻1	142	76.40 N	95.00 W
Grip	68	63.14 N	7.37 E
Griswold	162	41.14 N	95.08 W
Grizzly Bear Mountain ∧	142	65.22 N	121.00 W
Grizzly Mountain ∧	166	44.26 N	120.57 W
Grodków	72	50.43 N	17.22 E
Grodno	86	53.41 N	23.50 E
Grodno □4	66	54.45 N	26.00 E
Grodzisk Mazowiecki	72	52.07 N	20.37 E
Groesbeck	160	31.31 N	96.32 W
Groix	74	47.38 N	3.28 W
Grójec	72	51.52 N	20.52 E
Gronau	72	52.13 N	7.00 E
Grong	66	64.28 N	12.18 E
Groningen	72	53.13 N	6.33 E
Groot ≃	116	33.45 S	24.36 E
Groote Eylandt I	124	14.00 S	136.40 E
Grootfontein	116	19.32 S	18.05 E
Groot-Karasberge ⋀	116	27.20 S	18.40 E
Groot-Kei ≃	116	32.41 S	28.22 E
Groot Laagte ≃	116	20.37 S	21.37 E
Groot Letaba ≃	116	23.58 S	31.50 E
Groot Shingwidzi (Singuédeze) ≃	116	23.53 S	32.17 E
Groot-Swartberge ⋀	116	32.22 S	22.20 E
Groot-Vis ≃	116	33.30 S	27.08 E
Grootvloer ⊜	116	30.00 S	20.40 E
Gros Morne ∧	150	49.36 N	57.48 W
Grossenhain	72	51.17 N	13.31 E
Grosse Pointe	154	42.24 N	82.55 W
Grosseto	78	42.46 N	11.08 E
Gross-Gerau	72	49.55 N	8.29 E
Grossglockner ∧	72	47.04 N	12.42 E
Grossräschen	72	51.35 N	14.00 E

Symbols in the index entries are identified on page 203.

Name	Page	Lat	Long
Gross Wartenberg → Syców	72	51.19 N	17.43 E
Groswater Bay C	142	54.20 N	57.30 W
Groton, Conn., U.S.	152	41.19 N	72.12 W
Groton, N.Y., U.S.	152	42.35 N	76.22 W
Grottaglie	78	40.32 N	17.26 E
Grouard Mission	148	55.31 N	116.09 W
Groundhog ≃	154	49.43 N	81.58 W
Grove	160	36.36 N	94.46 W
Grove City, Ohio, U.S.	152	39.53 N	83.06 W
Grove City, Pa., U.S.	152	41.10 N	80.05 W
Groveland	156	28.34 N	81.51 W
Grover City	156	35.07 N	120.37 W
Groves	158	29.57 N	93.55 W
Groveton	158	31.42 N	71.31 W
Grovetown	156	33.27 N	82.12 W
Groznyj	64	43.20 N	45.42 E
Grudziadz	72	53.29 N	18.45 E
Gruetli	158	35.22 N	85.40 W
Grulla	158	26.16 N	98.39 W
Grums	72	59.21 N	13.06 E
Grünau [im Almtal]	72	47.51 N	13.57 E
Grünberg → Zielona Góra	72	51.56 N	15.31 E
Grundy	160	37.17 N	82.06 W
Grundy Center	154	42.22 N	92.47 W
Grušino	66	59.27 N	44.09 E
Gruver	160	36.16 N	101.24 W
Gruzinskaja Sovetskaja Socialističeskaja Respublika □3	82	42.00 N	44.00 E
Grybów	72	49.38 N	20.56 E
Gryfice	72	53.56 N	15.12 E
Gstaad	74	46.28 N	7.17 E
Guacanayabo, Golfo de C	132	20.30 N	77.35 W
Guacara	138	10.14 N	67.53 W
Gu Achi	164	32.20 N	112.02 W
Guadalajara, Esp.	76	40.38 N	3.10 W
Guadalajara, Méx.	130	20.40 N	103.20 W
Guadalcanal I	118	9.32 S	160.12 E
Guadalén ≃	76	38.05 N	3.32 W
Guadalén, Embalse de @1	76	38.25 N	3.15 W
Guadalmena ≃	76	38.19 N	2.56 W
Guadalquivir ≃	76	36.47 N	6.22 W
Guadalupe, Méx.	130	25.41 N	100.15 W
Guadalupe, Méx.	130	22.45 N	102.31 W
Guadalupe, Calif., U.S.	156	34.58 N	120.34 W
Guadalupe, Isla de I	144	29.00 N	118.16 W
Guadalupe Mountains ⋏	160	32.20 N	105.00 W
Guadalupe Peak ⋏	160	31.50 N	104.52 W
Guadalupe Victoria	130	24.27 N	104.07 W
Guadalupita	164	36.08 N	105.14 W
Guadeloupe □2	128	16.15 N	61.35 W
Guadeloupe Passage	132	16.40 N	61.50 W
Guadiana ≃	76	37.14 N	7.22 W
Guadix	76	37.18 N	3.08 W
Guafo, Isla I	140	43.35 S	74.50 W
Guainía □5	138	2.30 N	69.00 W
Guainía ≃	138	2.01 N	67.07 W
Guairá ≃	140	25.45 S	56.30 W
Guairá, Salto del (Salto das Sete Quedas) ⌐	140	24.02 S	54.16 W
Guajará Mirim	134	10.48 S	65.22 W
Guajabo Tadino	78	43.14 N	12.47 E
Gualeguay	140	33.10 S	59.20 W
Gualeguaychú	140	33.00 S	58.30 W
Gualicho, Salina ≃	136	40.25 S	65.20 W
Guam □2	22	13.28 N	144.47 E
Guamini	140	37.02 S	62.26 W
Guampi, Sierra de ⋏	138	6.00 N	65.35 W
Guamúchil	130	25.28 N	108.06 W
Guanabacoa	132	23.07 N	82.18 W
Guanajay	132	22.55 N	82.42 W
Guanare	138	9.03 N	69.45 W
Guandacol	140	29.30 S	68.35 W
Guane	132	22.12 N	84.05 W
Guang'an	88	30.28 N	106.39 E
Guangdong □4	88	23.00 N	113.00 E
Guanghua	88	32.25 N	111.36 E
Guangnan	88	24.10 N	105.06 E
Guangxi Zhuang Zizhiqu □4	88	24.00 N	109.00 E
Guangyuan	88	32.23 N	105.58 E
Guangzhou (Canton)	88	23.06 N	113.16 E
Guantánamo	132	20.08 N	75.12 W
Guanxian	88	30.59 N	103.40 E
Guapi	138	2.36 N	77.54 W
Guaporé (Iténez) ≃	134	11.55 S	65.04 W
Guaqui	134	16.35 S	68.51 W
Guarabira	134	6.51 S	35.29 W
Guarapuava	140	25.23 S	51.27 W
Guarda	76	40.32 N	7.16 W
Guardafui, Cape → Asir, Ras >	108	11.48 N	51.22 E
Guardavalle	78	38.30 N	16.30 E
Guardiagrele	78	42.11 N	14.13 E
Guardo	76	42.47 N	4.50 W
Guareim (Quaraí) ≃	140	30.12 S	57.36 W
Guárico □3	138	8.40 N	66.35 W
Guasave	130	25.34 N	108.27 W
Guasdualito	138	7.15 N	70.44 W
Guasipati	138	7.28 N	61.54 W
Guastalla	78	44.55 N	10.39 E
Guatemala	128	14.38 N	90.31 W
Guatemala □1	128	15.30 N	90.15 W
Guatire	138	10.28 N	66.32 W
Guaviare ≃	138	4.03 N	67.44 W
Guaxupé	140	21.18 S	46.42 W
Guayama	132	17.59 N	66.07 W
Guayana → Ciudad Guayana	138	8.22 N	62.40 W
Guayaquil	138	2.10 S	79.50 W
Guayaquil, Golfo de C	138	3.00 S	80.30 W
Guaymallén	140	32.54 S	68.47 W
Guaymas	130	27.56 N	110.54 W
Gubacha	64	58.52 N	57.36 E
Gubbio	78	43.21 N	12.35 E
Gubin	72	51.56 N	14.45 E
Gubkin	64	51.18 N	37.32 E
Guchengzi	88	43.20 N	100.39 E
Guchermes	88	43.20 N	46.08 E
Gudhjem	72	55.13 N	14.59 E
Gudiyattam	100	12.57 N	78.53 E
Gudvangen	68	60.52 N	6.50 E
Guebwiller	74	47.55 N	7.12 E
Guelma	106	36.28 N	7.26 E
Guelph	154	43.33 N	80.15 W
Guémené-sur-Scorff	74	48.04 N	3.12 W
Guer	74	47.54 N	2.07 W
Güera	106	20.48 N	17.08 W
Guérande	74	47.20 N	2.26 W
Guéret	74	46.10 N	1.52 E
Guerneville	168	38.30 N	123.00 W
Guernsey □2	64	49.28 N	2.35 W
Guernsey I	64	49.28 N	2.35 W
Gueydan	158	30.02 N	92.30 W
Guga	158	52.43 N	137.35 E
Guge ⋏	108	6.10 N	37.26 E
Guguan I	92	17.19 N	145.51 E
Guibes	110	26.35 N	16.42 E
Guichen	74	47.58 N	1.48 W
Guide	88	36.03 N	101.28 E
Guildford	88	51.14 N	0.35 W
Guilford	152	45.14 N	69.29 W
Guilford College	152	36.05 N	79.53 W
Guilin (Kweilin)	88	25.11 N	110.09 E
Guillaume-Delisle, Lac @	142	56.15 N	76.17 W
Guillaumes	74	44.05 N	6.51 E
Guillestre	74	44.40 N	6.39 E
Guilvinec	74	47.47 N	4.17 W
Guimarães	76	41.27 N	8.18 W
Guimaras Island I	98	10.35 N	122.37 E
Guin	158	33.58 N	87.55 W
Guinea □1	106	10.00 N	10.00 W
Guinea, Gulf > C	106	2.00 N	2.30 E
Guinea-Bissau □1	106	12.00 N	15.00 W
Güines, Cuba	132	22.50 N	82.02 W
Güines, Fr.	74	50.52 N	1.52 E
Guingamp	74	48.33 N	3.11 W
Guiping	94	23.23 N	110.09 E
Güira de Melena	132	22.48 N	82.30 W
Guiratinga	134	16.21 S	53.45 W
Güiria	138	10.34 N	62.18 W
Güitres	74	45.03 N	0.11 W
Guiuan	92	11.02 N	125.44 E
Guixian	94	23.06 N	109.39 E
Guiyang (Kweiyang)	94	26.35 N	106.43 E
Guizhou □4	94	27.00 N	107.00 E
Gujrānwāla	102	32.26 N	74.33 E
Gujrāt	102	32.34 N	74.05 E
Gulbarga	100	17.20 N	76.50 E
Gulfport, Fla., U.S.	156	27.44 N	82.43 W
Gulfport, Miss., U.S.	158	30.22 N	89.06 W
Gulgong	120	32.20 N	149.32 E
Gulistan	82	40.30 N	68.46 E
Gull Lake	142	50.08 N	108.27 W
Gulšvik	68	60.23 N	9.35 E
Gulu	108	2.47 N	32.18 E
Gumal (Gowmal) ≃	102	31.56 N	70.22 E
Gumbinnen → Gusev	86	54.36 N	22.12 E
Gummersbach	72	51.02 N	7.34 E
Gümüşhane	104	40.27 N	39.29 E
Guna	102	24.39 N	77.19 E
Gundagai	120	35.04 S	148.07 E
Gungu	110	5.44 S	19.19 E
Gunisao ≃	142	53.54 N	97.58 W
Gunnar	142	59.23 N	108.53 W
Gunnedah	120	30.59 S	150.15 E
Gunnison, Colo., U.S.	164	38.33 N	106.56 W
Gunnison, Utah, U.S.	164	39.09 N	111.49 W
Gunnison ≃	164	39.03 N	108.35 W
Guntersville	158	34.21 N	86.18 W
Guntramsdorf	72	48.03 N	16.19 E
Güntür	100	16.18 N	80.27 E
Gunungsitoli	94	1.17 N	97.37 E
Gunyidi	122	30.08 S	116.04 E
Günzburg	72	48.27 N	10.16 E
Gunzenhausen	72	49.07 N	10.45 E
Gurara ≃	114	8.21 N	6.41 E
Gurdon	158	33.55 N	93.09 W
Gurgéia ≃	134	6.42 S	43.24 W
Gurjev	64	47.07 N	51.56 E
Gurjevsk, S.S.S.R.	86	54.17 N	85.56 E
Gurjevsk, S.S.S.R.	86	54.47 N	20.38 E
Gurkha	100	28.00 N	84.37 E
Gurupá	134	1.25 S	51.39 W
Gurupi	134	11.43 S	49.04 W
Gurupi ≃	134	1.13 S	46.06 W
Gurupi, Serra do ⋏	134	5.00 S	47.30 W
Gurvan Sajchan Uul ⋏	88	43.30 N	103.30 E
Gusau	114	12.12 N	6.40 E
Gus`-Chrustal`nyj	86	55.37 N	40.40 E
Gusev	86	54.36 N	22.12 E
Gusinoozersk	84	51.17 N	106.30 E
Guspini	78	39.32 N	8.38 E
Güssing	72	47.04 N	16.20 E
Gustav Holm, Kap >	146	66.00 N	34.00 W
Gustavus	146	58.25 N	135.44 W
Gustine, Calif., U.S.	168	37.15 N	121.00 W
Gustine, Tex., U.S.	160	31.51 N	98.24 W
Güstrow	72	53.48 N	12.10 E
Gütersloh	72	51.54 N	8.23 E
Guthrie, Ky., U.S.	158	36.39 N	87.10 W
Guthrie, Okla., U.S.	160	35.53 N	97.25 W
Guthrie, Tex., U.S.	160	33.37 N	100.19 W
Guthrie Center	154	41.40 N	94.30 W
Gutian	88	26.36 N	118.46 E
Gutiérrez Zamora	130	20.27 N	97.05 W
Guttenberg	154	42.47 N	91.06 W
Guyana □1	134	5.00 N	59.00 W
Guyenne □9	74	44.30 N	1.00 E
Guymon	160	36.41 N	101.29 W
Guyot, Mount ⋏	156	35.42 N	83.15 W
Guyra	120	30.14 S	151.40 E
Guyuan	88	35.58 N	106.45 E
Guzar	82	38.37 N	66.15 E
Gvardejsk [Tapiau]	86	54.39 N	21.05 E
Gwädär	100	25.07 N	62.19 E
Gwai	116	19.15 S	27.42 E
Gwalia	122	28.55 S	121.20 E
Gwalior	102	26.13 N	78.10 E
Gwanda	116	20.57 S	29.01 E
Gwätär Bay C	100	25.04 N	61.36 E
Gweedore	70	55.03 N	8.14 W
Gwelo	116	19.27 S	29.49 E
Gwent □6	70	51.43 N	2.57 W
Gwinn	154	46.17 N	87.26 W
Gwynedd □6	70	53.00 N	4.00 W
Gyda	84	70.52 N	78.30 E
Gydanskaja Guba C	84	70.52 N	76.30 E
Gydanskij Poluostrov ▲1	84	70.50 N	79.00 E
Gyldenløves Fjord C2	146	64.30 N	41.30 W
Gy [les-Nonains]	74	47.24 N	5.49 E
Gympie	120	26.11 S	152.40 E
Gyoma	72	46.56 N	20.50 E
Gyömä	72	47.47 N	19.56 E
Gyöngyös	72	47.47 N	19.56 E
Györ	72	47.42 N	17.38 E
Györ-Sopron □6	72	47.35 N	17.15 E
Gypsum	164	39.38 N	106.57 W
Gypsum Creek ≃	164	38.17 N	118.13 W
Gypsum Point >	142	61.53 N	114.35 W
Gyula	72	46.39 N	21.17 E

H

Name	Page	Lat	Long
Haag in Oberbayern	72	48.10 N	12.11 E
Haag Stadt	78	48.07 N	14.34 E
Haaksbergen	72	52.09 N	6.44 E
Haapajärvi	68	63.45 N	25.20 E
Haapamäki	68	62.15 N	24.28 E
Haapsalu	86	58.56 N	23.33 E
Haar	72	48.06 N	11.44 E
Haarlem	72	52.23 N	4.38 E
Haast	126	43.52 S	169.03 E
Habomai-shoto II	88	43.30 N	146.10 E
Hachijō-jima I	88	33.05 N	139.48 E
Hachinohe	90	40.30 N	141.29 E
Hackensack	152	40.53 N	74.03 W
Hackettstown	152	40.51 N	74.50 W
Hackleburg	158	34.17 N	87.50 W
Hadd, Ra's al- >	100	22.32 N	59.48 E
Haddington	70	55.58 N	2.47 W
Hadejia	114	12.50 N	10.51 E
Haderslev	68	55.15 N	9.30 E
Hadibū	100	12.38 N	54.02 E
Hadley Bay C	142	72.30 N	107.45 W
Hadlock	168	48.02 N	122.46 W
Hadramawt ▲1	100	15.00 N	50.00 E
Hadsten	68	56.20 N	10.03 E
Hadur Shu'ayb ⋏	100	15.18 N	43.59 E
Haeju	88	38.02 N	125.42 E
Haenam	88	34.35 N	126.36 E
Hafnarfjörður	66a	64.03 N	21.56 W
Haft Gel	100	31.27 N	49.27 E
Hafun, Ras >	108	10.25 N	51.26 E
Hagemeister I	146	58.39 N	160.54 W
Hagen	72	51.21 N	7.28 E
Hagenow	72	53.25 N	11.11 E
Hagerman	160	33.07 N	104.20 W
Hagerstown, Ind., U.S.	158	39.55 N	85.10 W
Hagerstown, Md., U.S.	152	39.39 N	77.43 W
Hagersville	154	42.58 N	80.03 W
Hagetmau	74	43.40 N	0.35 W
Hagi, Mount ⋏	148	43.40 N	110.09 E
Hagondange	74	49.16 N	6.11 E
Hague	162	46.02 N	99.59 W
Haguenau	74	48.49 N	7.47 E
Hahira	156	30.57 N	83.22 W
Haicheng	88	40.52 N	122.45 E
Haifa → Hefa	104	32.50 N	35.00 E
Haig	122	30.31 S	126.05 E
Haig, Mount ⋏	148	49.17 N	114.29 W
Haikang (Leizhou)	94	20.56 N	110.04 E
Haikou	94	20.06 N	110.21 E
Hā'il	104	27.33 N	41.42 E
Hailar	88	49.12 N	119.42 E
Hailaerhe ≃	88	49.35 N	117.55 E
Hailey	166	43.31 N	114.19 W
Haileybury	154	47.27 N	79.38 W
Hailun	88	47.28 N	126.58 E
Hailuoto	68	65.00 N	24.43 E
Haimen	88	28.41 N	121.27 E
Hainandao I	88	19.00 N	109.30 E
Hainburg an der Donau	72	48.09 N	16.57 E
Haines, Alaska, U.S.	146	59.15 N	135.25 W
Haines, Oreg., U.S.	166	44.55 N	117.56 W
Haines City	156	28.07 N	81.37 W
Haines Junction	146	60.45 N	137.30 W
Hainfeld	72	48.02 N	15.46 E
Hai-phong	94	20.52 N	106.41 E
Hajdú-Bihar □6	72	47.25 N	21.30 E
Hajdúböszörmény	72	47.41 N	21.30 E
Hajdúdorog	72	47.51 N	21.26 E
Hajdúnánás	72	47.51 N	21.26 E
Hajdúszoboszló	72	47.27 N	21.24 E
Hajnówka	72	52.45 N	23.36 E
Hakodate	90a	41.45 N	140.43 E
Halab (Aleppo)	104	36.12 N	37.10 E
Halabi	88	38.15 N	97.40 E
Halā'ib	112	22.13 N	36.38 E
Halawa Heights	170c	21.23 N	157.55 W
Halberstadt	72	51.54 N	11.02 E
Halden	68	59.09 N	11.23 E
Haldensleben	72	52.18 N	11.26 E
Hale Center	160	34.04 N	101.51 W
Haleiwa	170c	21.35 N	158.07 W
Halethorpe	152	39.15 N	76.41 W
Haleyville	158	34.14 N	87.37 W
Halfway	166	44.53 N	117.07 W
Halfway ≃	142	56.10 N	121.35 W
Halifax, Austl.	120	18.35 S	146.18 E
Halifax, N.S., Can.	150	44.39 N	63.36 W
Halifax, Eng., U.K.	70	53.44 N	1.52 W
Halifax Bay C	120	18.50 S	146.30 E
Halkirk	70	58.30 N	3.30 W
Halland □9	68	57.00 N	12.40 E
Hallandale	156	25.59 N	80.09 W
Hallands Län □6	68	56.45 N	13.00 E
Halla-san ⋏	88	33.22 N	126.32 E
Halle, Bel.	72	50.44 N	4.13 E
Halle, D.D.R.	72	51.29 N	11.58 E
Halle □5	72	51.30 N	11.45 E
Hällefors	68	59.47 N	14.30 E
Hallein	72	47.41 N	13.06 E
Hallen	68	63.11 N	14.05 E
Hallettsville	160	29.27 N	96.56 W
Hall Lake	142	68.41 N	82.17 W
Hallock	142	48.47 N	96.57 W
Hall Peninsula >1	142	63.30 N	66.00 W
Halls	158	35.53 N	89.24 W
Hallsberg	68	59.04 N	15.07 E
Halls Creek	122	18.13 S	127.40 E
Hallstadt	72	49.57 N	10.54 E
Hallstahammar	68	59.37 N	16.13 E
Hallstatt	72	47.33 N	13.39 E
Hallsville	158	32.30 N	94.34 W
Halluin	74	50.47 N	3.08 E
Halmahera I	124	1.00 N	128.00 E
Halmahera, Laut (Halmahera Sea) ⁓2	124	1.00 S	129.00 E
Halmstad	68	56.39 N	12.50 E
Halsey	166	44.23 N	123.07 W
Hälsingborg → Helsingborg	68	56.03 N	12.42 E
Hälsingland □9	68	61.30 N	17.00 E
Halstead	162	38.00 N	97.30 W
Haltern	72	51.46 N	7.10 E
Halti[tunturi] ⋏	66	69.18 N	21.16 E
Haltom City	160	32.48 N	97.16 W
Haltwhistle	70	54.58 N	2.27 W
Hamada	90	34.53 N	132.05 E
Hamadän	104	34.48 N	48.30 E
Hamäh	104	35.08 N	36.45 E
Hamamatsu	90	34.42 N	137.44 E
Hamar	68	60.48 N	11.06 E
Hamburg, B.R.D.	72	53.33 N	9.59 E
Hamburg, Ark., U.S.	158	33.14 N	91.48 W
Hamburg, N.J., U.S.	152	41.09 N	74.35 W
Hamburg, N.Y., U.S.	152	42.43 N	78.50 W
Hamburg, Pa., U.S.	152	40.34 N	75.59 W
Hamden, Conn., U.S.	152	41.21 N	72.56 W
Hamden, Ohio, U.S.	158	39.10 N	82.32 W
Hameen läänl □4	68	61.00 N	24.20 E
Hämeenlinna	68	61.00 N	24.27 E
Hamelin Pool	122	26.26 S	114.11 E
Hameln	72	52.06 N	9.21 E
Hamersley Range ⋏	122	21.53 S	116.46 E
Hamhüng	88	39.54 N	127.32 E
Hami	88	42.47 N	93.32 E
Hamilton, Austl.	120	37.45 S	142.02 E
Hamilton, Ber.	22	32.17 N	64.46 W
Hamilton, Ont., Can.	154	43.15 N	79.51 W
Hamilton, N.Z.	126	37.47 S	175.17 E
Hamilton, Scot., U.K.	70	55.47 N	4.03 W
Hamilton, Ala., U.S.	158	34.08 N	87.59 W
Hamilton, Ill., U.S.	154	40.24 N	91.21 W
Hamilton, Mo., U.S.	162	39.45 N	94.01 W
Hamilton, Mont., U.S.	166	46.15 N	114.09 W
Hamilton, N.Y., U.S.	152	42.49 N	75.33 W
Hamilton, Ohio, U.S.	152	39.23 N	84.33 W
Hamilton, Tex., U.S.	160	31.42 N	98.07 W
Hamilton, Wash., U.S.	168	48.31 N	122.51 W
Hamilton Acres	146	64.51 N	147.40 W
Hamilton Dome	166	43.46 N	108.34 W
Hamilton Inlet C	142	54.20 N	57.30 W
Hamina	68	60.34 N	27.12 E
Hamirpur	102	25.57 N	80.09 E
Hamlet	156	34.53 N	79.41 W
Hamlin, Tex., U.S.	160	32.53 N	100.08 W
Hamlin, W. Va., U.S.	152	38.17 N	82.06 W
Hamlin Valley Wash V	164	38.53 N	114.01 W
Hammamet	106	36.24 N	10.37 E
Hammamet, Hawr al- ≃	104	30.50 N	47.10 E
Hammel	68	56.15 N	9.52 E
Hammelburg	72	50.07 N	9.53 E
Hammerfest	66	70.40 N	23.42 E
Hammond, Ind., U.S.	158	41.36 N	87.30 W
Hammond, La., U.S.	158	30.30 N	90.27 W
Hammond Bay C	154	45.30 N	84.00 W
Hammondsport	152	42.24 N	77.13 W
Hamoyet, Jabal ⋏	112	17.33 N	38.02 E
Hampden	126	44.45 S	80.50 E
Hampshire □6	70	51.03 N	1.20 W
Hampton, N.B., Can.	150	45.32 N	65.51 W
Hampton, Ark., U.S.	158	33.32 N	92.28 W
Hampton, Iowa, U.S.	154	42.45 N	93.12 W
Hampton, N.H., U.S.	152	42.56 N	70.50 W
Hampton, S.C., U.S.	156	32.52 N	81.06 W
Hampton, Va., U.S.	156	37.02 N	76.21 W
Hampton Bays	152	40.53 N	72.31 W
Handen	68	59.10 N	18.08 E
Handlová	72	48.44 N	18.46 E
Hando	108	10.37 N	51.08 E
Handsboro	158	30.25 N	89.02 W
Haney	148	49.13 N	122.36 W
Hanford	168	36.20 N	119.39 W
Hangchow → Hangzhou	88	30.15 N	120.10 E
Hanging Woman Creek ≃	166	45.19 N	106.31 W
Hanjinghouqi	88	40.41 N	106.59 E
Hangjinqi	88	39.59 N	108.57 E
Hangö	88	59.50 N	22.57 E
Hangzhou	88	30.15 N	120.10 E
Hanish, Jazā'ir II	100	13.45 N	42.45 E
Hanjiang	88	25.30 N	119.06 E
Hankasalmi	68	62.23 N	26.26 E
Hanke	68	59.12 N	10.47 E
Hanko → Hangö	88	59.50 N	22.57 E
Hanley	70	53.01 N	2.11 W
Hanmer	126	46.30 N	80.56 W
Hanna, Alta., Can.	148	51.38 N	111.54 W
Hanna, Wyo., U.S.	166	41.52 N	106.34 W
Hannah Bay C	142	51.05 N	79.45 W
Hannibal	158	39.42 N	91.22 W
Hannover	64	52.24 N	9.44 E
Ha-noi	94	21.02 N	105.51 E
Hanover, Ont., Can.	154	44.09 N	81.02 W
Hanover, Ind., U.S.	158	38.43 N	85.28 W
Hanover, Kans., U.S.	162	39.54 N	96.53 W
Hanover, N.H., U.S.	152	43.42 N	72.18 W
Hanover, Pa., U.S.	152	39.48 N	76.59 W
Hanshui ≃	88	30.35 N	114.17 E
Hanstholm	68	57.07 N	8.36 E
Hantzsch ≃	142	67.32 N	72.25 W
Hanwood	120	34.20 S	146.03 E
Hanzhong	88	32.59 N	107.11 E
Haparanda	68	65.50 N	24.10 E
Happy Camp	166	41.48 N	123.22 W
Happy Jack	164	34.45 N	111.17 W
Hapur	102	28.43 N	77.47 E
Harad	100	24.08 N	49.05 E
Harash, Bi'r al- ≃4	112	25.30 N	22.12 E
Harbin → Haerbin	88	45.45 N	126.41 E
Harbor	166	42.03 N	124.17 W
Harbor Beach	154	43.51 N	82.39 W
Harbor Springs	154	45.26 N	85.00 W
Harbour Breton	150	47.29 N	55.48 W
Harbour Grace	150	47.42 N	53.13 W
Härby	68	55.13 N	10.07 E
Hardangerfjorden C2	68	60.10 N	6.00 E
Hardenberg	72	52.34 N	6.37 E
Harderwijk	72	52.21 N	5.36 E
Hardin, Ill., U.S.	158	39.09 N	90.37 W
Hardin, Mont., U.S.	166	45.44 N	107.37 W
Harding, Lake @1	146	64.50 N	149.00 W
Hardisty	148	52.40 N	111.18 W
Hardisty Lake @	142	64.30 N	117.45 W
Hardoi	102	27.25 N	80.07 E
Hardwar → Haridvar	102	29.58 N	78.10 E
Hardwick, Ga., U.S.	156	33.09 N	83.13 W
Hardwick, Vt., U.S.	152	44.30 N	72.22 W
Hardy	158	36.19 N	91.29 W
Hardy Bay C	142	75.02 N	115.16 W
Hare Bay C	150	51.18 N	55.50 W
Hareid	68	62.22 N	6.02 E
Hare Indian ≃	142	66.18 N	128.38 W
Hareøen I	146	70.26 N	54.30 W
Harer	108	9.18 N	42.08 E
Hargeysa	108	9.30 N	44.03 E
Harghita □4	72	46.35 N	25.30 E
Harhorin	88	47.12 N	102.50 E
Harırūd ≃, As.	104	34.20 N	62.10 E
Harirud (Tedžen) ≃, As.	104	37.24 N	60.38 E
Harjavalta	68	61.19 N	22.08 E
Härjedalen □9	68	62.23 N	13.00 E
Harlan, Iowa, U.S.	162	41.39 N	95.19 W
Harlan, Ky., U.S.	156	36.51 N	83.19 W
Harlem, Fla., U.S.	156	26.44 N	80.58 W
Harlingen, Ned.	72	53.10 N	5.24 E
Harlingen, Tex., U.S.	160	26.11 N	97.42 W
Harlow	70	51.47 N	0.08 E
Harlowton	166	46.26 N	109.50 W
Harman	152	38.55 N	79.32 W
Harmony, Ind., U.S.	158	39.32 N	87.04 W
Harmony, Minn., U.S.	154	43.33 N	92.01 W
Haro	76	42.35 N	2.51 W
Harney Peak ⋏	162	43.52 N	103.32 W
Härnösand	68	62.38 N	17.56 E
Harper, Liber.	114	4.25 N	7.43 W
Harper, Kans., U.S.	162	37.17 N	98.01 W
Harper, Mount ⋏	146	64.14 N	143.50 W
Harricana ≃	142	51.15 N	79.45 W
Harriman	156	35.56 N	84.33 W
Harrington	156	38.55 N	75.35 W
Harris Islands II	142	56.34 N	78.58 W
Harrisburg, Ill., U.S.	158	37.44 N	88.32 W
Harrisburg, Ark., U.S.	158	35.34 N	90.43 W
Harrisburg, Oreg., U.S.	166	44.16 N	123.10 W
Harrisburg, Pa., U.S.	152	40.16 N	76.52 W
Harrismith, S. Afr.	116	28.16 S	29.08 E
Harrison, Ark., U.S.	158	36.14 N	93.06 W
Harrison, Mich., U.S.	154	44.01 N	84.48 W
Harrison, Cape >	142	54.55 N	57.55 W
Harrisonburg	152	38.26 N	78.52 W
Harrisonville	162	38.39 N	94.21 W
Harrisville, Mich., U.S.	154	44.39 N	83.17 W
Harrisville, W. Va., U.S.	152	39.12 N	81.03 W
Harrodsburg	158	37.46 N	84.51 W
Harrogate	70	54.00 N	1.33 W
Harstad	66	68.46 N	16.30 E
Hart, Mich., U.S.	154	43.42 N	86.22 W
Hart, Tex., U.S.	160	34.23 N	102.07 W
Hart, Lake ≃	120	31.08 S	136.24 E
Hartberg	72	47.17 N	15.59 E
Hartford, Ala., U.S.	156	31.06 N	85.42 W
Hartford, Conn., U.S.	152	41.46 N	72.41 W
Hartford, Ky., U.S.	158	37.27 N	86.55 W
Hartford, Mich., U.S.	154	42.12 N	86.10 W
Hartford, S. Dak., U.S.	162	43.37 N	96.57 W
Hartford, Wis., U.S.	154	43.19 N	88.22 W
Hartington	162	42.37 N	97.16 W
Hartland	150	46.18 N	67.31 W
Hartlepool	70	54.42 N	1.11 W
Hartley, Rh.	116	18.10 S	30.14 E
Hartley, Iowa, U.S.	162	43.11 N	95.29 W
Hartley, Tex., U.S.	160	35.53 N	102.24 W
Hartola	68	61.35 N	26.01 E
Hartselle	158	34.27 N	86.56 W
Hartshorne	160	34.51 N	95.33 W
Harts Range	122	23.00 S	134.55 E
Hartsville, S.C., U.S.	156	34.22 N	80.04 W
Hartsville, Tenn., U.S.	158	36.24 N	86.10 W
Hartwell	156	34.21 N	82.55 W
Hartwell Reservoir @1	156	34.30 N	82.55 W
Härüt ≃	100	31.35 N	61.18 E
Harvard, Ill., U.S.	154	42.25 N	88.37 W
Harvard, Nebr., U.S.	162	40.37 N	98.06 W
Harvey, Ill., U.S.	158	41.37 N	87.39 W
Harvey, N. Dak., U.S.	162	47.46 N	99.56 W
Harwich	70	51.57 N	1.17 E
Harwick	152	40.33 N	79.48 W
Haryana □3	102	29.00 N	76.00 E
Harz ⋏	72	51.40 N	10.40 E
Hasa, Jabal al- ⋏	104	30.24 N	36.00 E
Hasköy	80	41.57 N	25.07 E
Haskell, Okla., U.S.	160	35.49 N	95.40 W
Haskell, Tex., U.S.	160	33.10 N	99.44 W
Haskovo	80	41.56 N	25.33 E
Haslemere	70	51.06 N	0.43 W
Haslev	68	55.20 N	11.58 E
Hassan	100	13.00 N	76.06 E
Hasselt	72	50.56 N	5.20 E
Hassfurt	72	50.02 N	10.31 E
Hassi Messaoud	106	31.43 N	5.59 E
Hassi R'Mel	106	32.35 N	3.24 E
Hässleholm	68	56.09 N	13.46 E
Hastings, N.Z.	126	39.38 S	176.51 E
Hastings, Eng., U.K.	70	50.51 N	0.36 E
Hastings, Fla., U.S.	156	29.43 N	81.30 W
Hastings, Mich., U.S.	154	42.39 N	85.17 W
Hastings, Minn., U.S.	154	44.44 N	92.51 W
Hastings, Nebr., U.S.	162	40.35 N	98.23 W
Hatch	164	32.40 N	107.09 W
Hatchie ≃	158	35.36 N	89.53 W
Hat Creek ≃	166	43.16 N	103.36 W
Hatfield	162	43.26 N	104.54 W
Hāthras	102	27.36 N	78.03 E
Hatteras	156	35.13 N	75.42 W
Hatteras, Cape >	156	35.13 N	75.31 W
Hattiesburg	158	31.19 N	89.16 W
Hatvan	72	47.40 N	19.41 E
Hat Yai	94	7.01 N	100.27 E
Haubourdin	74	50.36 N	2.59 E
Haubstadt	158	38.12 N	87.34 W
Hauge	68	58.18 N	6.15 E
Haugesund	68	59.25 N	5.18 E
Haukeligrend	68	59.45 N	7.31 E
Haunstetten	72	48.17 N	10.54 E
Hausach	72	48.17 N	8.10 E
Haut Atlas ⋏	106	31.30 N	6.00 W
Haute-Garonne □5	74	43.25 N	1.30 E
Haute-Loire □5	74	45.05 N	3.50 E
Haute-Marne □5	74	48.05 N	5.10 E
Hauterive	150	49.12 N	68.16 W
Hautes-Alpes □5	74	44.40 N	6.30 E
Haute-Saône □5	74	47.40 N	6.10 E
Haute-Savoie □5	74	46.00 N	6.20 E
Hautes-Pyrénées □5	74	43.00 N	0.10 E
Hautes Fagnes ⋏	72	50.30 N	6.05 E
Haute-Vienne □5	74	45.50 N	1.15 E
Hautmont	74	50.15 N	3.56 E
Haut-Rhin □5	74	48.00 N	7.13 E
Hauts-de-Seine □5	74	48.50 N	2.11 E
Hauula	170c	21.37 N	157.55 W
Havana → La Habana, Cuba	132	23.08 N	82.22 W
Havana, Fla., U.S.	156	30.37 N	84.25 W
Havana, Ill., U.S.	158	40.18 N	90.04 W
Havana, N. Dak., U.S.	162	45.57 N	97.37 W
Havant	70	50.51 N	0.29 W
Havasu Lake @1	164	34.30 N	114.20 W
Havdrup	68	55.33 N	12.08 E
Havelberg	72	52.50 N	12.04 E
Havelock	156	34.52 N	76.54 W
Havelock North	126	39.40 S	176.53 E
Haven	162	37.54 N	97.47 W
Haverfordwest	70	51.49 N	4.58 W
Haverhill, Eng., U.K.	70	52.05 N	0.26 E
Haverhill, Mass., U.S.	152	42.46 N	71.04 W
Haverstraw	152	41.12 N	73.58 W
Havířov	72	49.48 N	18.25 E
Havlíčkův Brod	72	49.36 N	15.35 E
Havre	166	48.33 N	109.41 W
Havre-de-Grace	152	39.32 N	76.05 W
Havre-Saint-Pierre	150	50.14 N	63.36 W
Hawaii □3	170d	20.00 N	157.45 W
Hawaii I	170d	19.30 N	155.30 W
Hawarden	72	43.00 N	96.29 W
Hawera	126	39.35 S	174.17 E
Hawick	70	55.25 N	2.47 W
Hawke, Cape >	150	53.02 N	55.50 W
Hawke Bay C	126	39.20 S	177.30 E
Hawker	120	31.53 S	138.25 E
Hawkesbury	154	45.36 N	74.37 W
Hawkins	160	32.35 N	95.12 W
Hawkinsville	156	32.17 N	83.28 W
Hawley, Minn., U.S.	162	46.53 N	96.19 W
Hawley, Pa., U.S.	152	41.28 N	75.11 W
Hawthorne, Fla., U.S.	156	29.36 N	82.05 W
Hawthorne, Nev., U.S.	168	38.31 N	118.38 W
Hay	120	34.30 S	144.51 E
Hay ≃, Austl.	120	24.56 S	138.00 E
Hay ≃, Can.	142	60.50 N	115.44 W
Hay, Cape >	142	60.52 N	115.44 W
Hay, Mount ⋏, Austl.	122	23.25 S	133.05 E
Hay, Mount ⋏, N.A.	146	59.15 N	137.37 W
Hayange	74	49.20 N	6.03 E
Hayden, Ariz., U.S.	164	33.00 N	110.47 W
Hayden, Colo., U.S.	164	40.30 N	107.16 W
Hayes ≃, Man., Can.	142	57.03 N	92.09 W
Hayes ≃, N.W. Ter., Can.	142	67.18 N	95.02 W
Hayes, Mount ⋏	146	63.37 N	146.43 W
Hayesville	156	35.03 N	83.49 W
Hayfork	166	40.33 N	123.11 W
Haynesville	158	32.58 N	93.08 W
Hayrabolu	80	41.12 N	27.06 E
Hay River	142	60.51 N	115.40 W
Hays, Kans., U.S.	162	38.53 N	99.20 W
Hays, Mont., U.S.	166	48.03 N	108.43 W
Haysville	162	37.34 N	97.21 W
Hayti, Mo., U.S.	158	36.14 N	89.45 W
Hayti, S. Dak., U.S.	162	44.40 N	97.12 W
Hayward, Calif., U.S.	168	37.40 N	122.05 W
Hayward, Wis., U.S.	154	46.01 N	91.28 W
Haywards Heath	70	51.00 N	0.06 W
Hazard	156	37.15 N	83.12 W
Hazārībāgh	102	23.59 N	85.21 E
Hazebrouck	74	50.43 N	2.32 E
Hazelton, B.C., Can.	148	55.15 N	127.40 W
Hazelton, N. Dak., U.S.	162	46.28 N	100.17 W
Hazen	162	47.18 N	101.38 W
Hazlehurst, Ga., U.S.	156	31.52 N	82.36 W
Hazlehurst, Miss., U.S.	158	31.52 N	90.24 W
Hazleton	152	40.57 N	75.59 W
Headland	156	31.21 N	85.21 W
Headley	168	40.31 N	122.38 W
Healdsburg	168	38.36 N	122.52 W
Healdton	160	34.14 N	97.29 W
Healesville	120	37.40 S	145.31 E
Healy	146	63.51 N	148.58 W
Hearne	160	30.53 N	96.35 W
Hearst	142	49.41 N	83.40 W
Heath Springs	156	34.35 N	80.40 W
Heavener	160	34.53 N	94.36 W
Hebbronville	160	27.18 N	98.41 W
Hebei □4	88	39.00 N	116.00 E
Heber	164	40.30 N	111.25 W
Heber Springs	158	35.29 N	92.01 W
Hebi	88	35.53 N	114.11 E
Hebrides II	64	57.00 N	6.30 W
Hebron, Ill., U.S.	154	42.28 N	88.26 W
Hebron, N. Dak., U.S.	162	46.54 N	102.02 W
Hebron → Al-Khalil, Urd.	104	31.32 N	35.06 E
Hecate Strait ⋓	148	53.00 N	131.00 W
Hechi	94	24.43 N	108.02 E
Hechingen	72	48.21 N	8.58 E
Hechuan	88	30.00 N	106.16 E
Hecla	162	45.53 N	98.09 W
Hede, Sve.	68	62.25 N	13.30 E
Hedemora	68	60.17 N	15.59 E
Hedmark □6	68	61.20 N	11.30 E
Heeg	72	52.58 N	5.33 E
Heerde	72	52.23 N	6.02 E
Heerenveen	72	52.57 N	5.55 E
Heerlen	72	50.54 N	5.59 E
Hefa (Haifa)	104	32.50 N	35.00 E
Hefei	88	31.51 N	117.17 E
Heflin	158	33.39 N	85.35 W
Hegang	88	47.24 N	130.17 E
Hegra	68	63.28 N	11.01 E
Heguaizi	88	39.39 N	106.41 E
Heho	92	20.43 N	96.49 E
Heide	72	54.12 N	9.06 E
Heidelberg, B.R.D.	72	49.25 N	8.43 E
Heidelberg, Miss., U.S.	158	31.53 N	88.59 W
Heidenheim	72	48.41 N	10.44 E
Heidenreichstein	72	48.52 N	15.07 E
Heihe (Naquka)	102	31.34 N	92.00 E
Heilbron	116	27.16 S	27.58 E
Heilbronn	72	49.08 N	9.13 E
Heiligenblut	72	47.02 N	12.50 E
Heiligenhafen	72	54.22 N	10.58 E
Heiligenstadt	72	51.23 N	10.09 E
Heilongjiang □4	88	48.00 N	128.00 E
Heilongjiang (Amur) ≃	88	52.56 N	141.10 E
Heinävesi	68	62.26 N	28.36 E
Heinola	68	61.13 N	26.02 E
Hejaz → Al-Hijāz ←1	104	24.30 N	38.30 E
Hekla ⋏1	66a	64.00 N	19.39 W
Hekou	94	22.38 N	103.56 E
Hel	72	54.37 N	18.48 E
Helagsfjället ⋏	68	62.55 N	12.27 E
Helbra	72	51.33 N	11.29 E
Helen, Mount ⋏	120	21.34 S	141.13 E
Helena, Ark., U.S.	158	34.32 N	90.35 W
Helena, Mont., U.S.	166	46.36 N	112.01 W
Helena, Okla., U.S.	160	36.33 N	98.16 W
Helen Island I	92	2.58 N	131.49 E
Helensburgh	70	56.01 N	4.44 W
Helen Springs	122	18.26 S	133.52 E
Helensville	126	36.41 S	174.27 E
Helenwood	156	36.26 N	84.32 W
Hell-Ville	117b	13.25 S	48.16 E
Hellin	76	38.31 N	1.41 W
Hells Canyon V	166	45.20 N	116.45 W
Helmand ≃	104	31.12 N	61.34 E
Helmond	72	51.29 N	5.40 E
Helmsdale	70	58.07 N	3.40 W
Helmstedt	72	52.13 N	11.00 E
Helper	164	39.41 N	110.51 W
Helsingborg	68	56.03 N	12.42 E
Helsingfors → Helsinki	68	60.10 N	24.58 E
Helsingør (Elsinore)	68	56.02 N	12.37 E
Helsinki (Helsingfors)	68	60.10 N	24.58 E
Helston	70	50.05 N	5.16 W
Hemau	72	49.03 N	11.47 E
Hemel Hempstead	70	51.46 N	0.28 W
Hemet	168	33.45 N	116.58 W
Hemingford	162	42.19 N	103.04 W
Hemingway	156	33.45 N	79.27 W
Hemphill	160	31.20 N	93.51 W
Hempstead	160	30.06 N	96.05 W
Hemse	68	57.14 N	18.22 E
Hemsedal	68	60.52 N	8.34 E
Henan □4	88	34.00 N	114.00 E
Henderson, N.Z.	126	36.53 S	174.38 E
Henderson, Ky., U.S.	158	37.50 N	87.35 W
Henderson, N.C., U.S.	156	36.20 N	78.25 W
Henderson, Tenn., U.S.	158	35.27 N	88.38 W
Henderson, Tex., U.S.	160	32.09 N	94.48 W
Hendersonville	156	35.19 N	82.28 W
Henefer	164	41.01 N	111.30 W
Hengelo	72	52.15 N	6.45 E
Hengshan, Zhg.	88	37.56 N	109.53 E
Hengshan, Zhg.	88	27.15 N	112.51 E
Hengyang	88	26.53 N	112.36 E
Hennebont	74	47.48 N	3.17 W
Hennef	72	50.46 N	7.16 E
Hennessey	160	36.06 N	97.54 W
Hennigsdorf	72	52.38 N	13.12 E
Henniker	152	43.11 N	71.49 W
Henrietta, N.Y., U.S.	152	43.03 N	77.37 W
Henrietta, Tex., U.S.	160	33.49 N	98.12 W
Henrietta Maria, Cape >	142	55.09 N	82.20 W
Henrique de Carvalho	110	9.39 S	20.24 E
Henry, Ill., U.S.	158	41.07 N	89.21 W
Henry, S. Dak., U.S.	162	44.53 N	97.28 W
Henry ≃	122	22.40 S	115.40 E
Henry, Mount ⋏, Austl.	122	28.22 S	120.00 E
Henry, Mount ⋏, Mont., U.S.	166	48.53 N	115.31 W
Henry, Point >	152	34.29 S	119.23 E
Henryetta	160	35.26 N	95.58 W
Henry Kater, Cape >	142	69.05 N	66.44 W
Henrys Fork ≃	166	44.00 N	109.30 W
Henty	120	35.33 S	147.02 E
Henzada	92	17.38 N	95.28 E
Heppenheim	72	49.38 N	8.38 E
Hepu (Lianzhou)	94	21.39 N	109.11 E
Herät	104	34.20 N	62.12 E
Herät □5	104	34.00 N	62.00 E
Herbertingen	72	48.03 N	9.26 E
Herborn	72	50.41 N	8.17 E
Herceg-Novi	80	42.27 N	18.32 E
Herculaneum	158	38.16 N	90.23 W
Hereford, Eng., U.K.	70	52.04 N	2.43 W
Hereford, Ariz., U.S.	164	31.26 N	110.06 W
Hereford, Tex., U.S.	160	34.49 N	102.24 W
Hereford and Worcester □6	70	52.10 N	2.30 W
Herford	72	52.07 N	8.40 E
Herington	162	38.40 N	96.57 W
Herkimer	152	43.01 N	74.59 W
Herlen ≃	88	48.48 N	117.00 E
Hermagor	72	46.38 N	13.22 E
Herman	162	45.48 N	96.08 W
Hermann	158	38.42 N	91.26 W
Hermannsburg	122	23.57 S	132.45 E
Hermansverk	68	61.11 N	6.51 E
Hermiston	166	45.50 N	119.17 W
Hermosa Beach	168	33.51 N	118.24 W
Hermosillo	130	29.04 N	110.58 W
Hernád (Hornád) ≃	72	47.56 N	21.08 E
Hernando	158	34.49 N	89.59 W
Herne	72	51.32 N	7.13 E
Herne Bay	70	51.23 N	1.08 E
Herning	68	56.08 N	8.59 E
Hervey Bay C	120	25.00 S	153.00 E
Heves □6	72	47.50 N	20.15 E
Heves	72	47.36 N	20.17 E
Hexian	88	24.25 N	111.43 E
Heywood	120	36.38 S	144.17 E
Hialeah	156	25.49 N	80.17 W
Hiawatha	162	39.51 N	95.32 W
Hibbing	154	47.25 N	92.56 W

Name	Page	Lat °′	Long °′
Hibbs, Point ≻	120	42.38 S	145.15 E
Hibernia Reef ✧2	118	12.00 S	123.23 E
Hickman	158	36.34 N	89.11 W
Hickory	156	35.44 N	81.21 W
Hicksville	152	41.18 N	84.46 W
Hico	160	31.59 N	98.02 W
Hidalgo	130	24.15 N	99.26 W
Hidalgo del Parral	130	26.56 N	105.40 W
Hieflau	72	47.36 N	14.44 E
Hierro I	106	27.45 N	18.00 W
Higashiōsaka	90	34.39 N	135.35 E
Higginsville	158	39.04 N	93.43 W
Highland, Calif., U.S.	168	34.08 N	117.12 W
Highland, Ill., U.S.	158	38.44 N	89.41 W
Highland, Ind., U.S.	158	41.33 N	87.27 W
Highland, N.Y., U.S.	152	41.43 N	73.58 W
Highland Park, Ill., U.S.	154	42.11 N	87.48 W
Highland Park, Mich., U.S.	154	42.24 N	83.06 W
Highland Park, Tex., U.S.	160	32.50 N	96.48 W
Highland Region □4	70	57.40 N	5.00 W
Highlands, N.J., U.S.	152	40.24 N	73.59 W
Highlands, Tex., U.S.	160	29.49 N	95.04 W
Highland Springs	156	37.33 N	77.20 W
High Plains ≚	144	38.30 N	103.00 W
High Point	156	35.58 N	80.01 W
High Prairie	148	55.26 N	116.29 W
High River	148	50.35 N	113.52 W
High Springs	156	29.50 N	82.36 W
Hightstown	152	40.16 N	74.31 W
Highwood, Ill., U.S.	154	42.13 N	87.48 W
Highwood, Mont., U.S.	166	47.35 N	110.47 W
High Wycombe	70	51.38 N	0.46 W
Hiiumaa I	86	58.52 N	22.40 E
Ḥijāz, Jabal al- ⋀	100	19.45 N	41.55 E
Hildburghausen	72	50.25 N	10.44 E
Hilden	72	51.10 N	6.56 E
Hildesheim	72	52.09 N	9.57 E
Hill City	162	39.22 N	99.51 W
Hillcrest Center	168	35.23 N	118.57 W
Hilliard	156	30.41 N	81.55 W
Hill Island Lake ⊜	142	60.29 N	109.50 W
Hillsboro, Ill., U.S.	158	39.09 N	89.29 W
Hillsboro, Kans., U.S.	162	38.21 N	97.12 W
Hillsboro, N.H., U.S.	152	43.07 N	71.54 W
Hillsboro, N. Dak., U.S.	162	47.26 N	97.03 W
Hillsboro, Ohio, U.S.	152	39.12 N	83.37 W
Hillsboro, Oreg., U.S.	166	45.31 N	122.59 W
Hillsboro, Tex., U.S.	160	32.01 N	97.08 W
Hillsborough, Cape ≻	120	20.54 S	149.03 E
Hillsdale	154	41.55 N	84.38 W
Hillston	120	33.29 S	145.32 E
Hilo	170d	19.43 N	155.05 W
Hilo Bay C	170d	19.44 N	155.05 W
Hiltaba, Mount ∧	122	32.09 S	135.03 E
Hilton	152	43.17 N	77.48 W
Hilton Head Island	156	32.13 N	80.45 W
Hilton Head Island I	156	32.12 N	80.45 W
Hilts	168	41.59 N	122.37 W
Hilversum	72	52.14 N	5.10 E
Himalayas ⋀	102	28.00 N	84.00 E
Himanka	68	64.04 N	23.39 E
Himatnagar	100	23.36 N	72.58 E
Himeji	90	34.49 N	134.42 E
Ḥimṣ (Homs)	104	34.44 N	36.43 E
Hinche	132	19.09 N	72.01 W
Hinchinbrook Entrance ⩊	146	60.25 N	146.50 W
Hinchinbrook Island I, Austl.	120	18.23 S	146.17 E
Hinchinbrook Island I, Alaska, U.S.	146	60.22 N	146.30 W
Hindmarsh, Lake ⊜	120	36.03 S	141.55 E
Hindu Kush ⋀	102	36.00 N	71.30 E
Hinesville	156	31.51 N	81.36 W
Hingham	152	42.14 N	70.53 W
Hingol ≃	102	25.23 N	65.28 E
Hinnerjoki	68	61.00 N	22.00 E
Hinnøya I	66	68.30 N	16.00 E
Hinojosa del Duque	76	38.30 N	5.09 W
Hinsdale, Mont., U.S.	166	48.24 N	107.05 W
Hinsdale, N.H., U.S.	152	42.47 N	72.29 W
Hinterrhein ≃	74	46.32 N	9.12 E
Hinton, Alta., Can.	148	53.25 N	117.34 W
Hinton, Okla., U.S.	160	35.28 N	98.21 W
Hinton, W. Va., U.S.	156	37.41 N	80.53 W
Hirara	88	24.48 N	125.17 E
Hiratsuka	90	35.19 N	139.21 E
Hirosaki	90	40.35 N	140.28 E
Hiroshima	90	34.24 N	132.27 E
Hirson	74	49.55 N	4.05 E
Hirtshals	68	57.35 N	9.58 E
Hisār	102	29.10 N	75.43 E
Hispaniola I	132	19.00 N	71.00 W
Hitachi	90	36.36 N	140.39 E
Hitchcock	160	29.21 N	95.01 W
Hitra I	68	63.33 N	8.45 E
Hittarp	68	56.06 N	12.38 E
Hiwassee ≃	156	35.19 N	84.47 W
Hixson	156	35.09 N	85.14 W
Hjelmelandsvågen	68	59.14 N	6.11 E
Hjørring	68	57.28 N	9.59 E
Hlohovec	72	48.25 N	17.47 E
Ho	114	6.35 N	0.30 E
Hoa-binh	94	20.50 N	105.20 E
Hoare Bay C	142	65.20 N	62.30 W
Hobart, Austl.	120	42.53 S	147.19 E
Hobart, Ind., U.S.	158	41.32 N	87.15 W
Hobart, Okla., U.S.	160	35.01 N	99.06 W
Hobbs	160	32.42 N	103.08 W
Hobe Sound	156	27.04 N	80.08 W
Hoboken, Bel.	72	51.10 N	4.21 E
Hoboken, N.J., U.S.	152	40.45 N	74.03 W
Hobro	68	56.38 N	9.48 E
Hobson	166	47.00 N	109.52 W
Höchstadt an der Aisch	72	49.42 N	10.44 E
Hockenheim	72	49.19 N	8.33 E
Hodeida → Al-Ḥudaydah	100	14.48 N	42.57 E
Hodgenville	158	37.34 N	85.44 W
Hódmezővásárhely	72	46.25 N	20.20 E
Hodna, Chott el ⊜	106	35.25 N	4.45 E
Hodonín	72	48.51 N	17.08 E
Hoek van Holland	72	51.59 N	4.09 E
Hof, B.R.D.	72	50.18 N	11.55 E
Hof, Ísland	66a	64.34 N	14.39 W
Hofgeismar	72	51.30 N	9.22 E
Hofheim in Unterfranken	72	50.08 N	10.31 E
Höfn	66a	64.17 N	15.10 W
Hofors	68	60.33 N	16.17 E
Hofsjökull ⛉	66a	64.48 N	18.50 W
Hōfu	90	34.03 N	131.34 E
Hofuf → Al-Hufūf	104	25.22 N	49.34 E
Hogansville	156	33.11 N	84.55 W
Hogarth, Mount ∧2	120	21.48 S	136.58 E
Hogback Mountain ∧	156	35.10 N	82.17 W
Hoggar → Ahaggar ⋀	106	23.00 N	6.30 E
Hohenau an der March	72	48.36 N	16.55 E
Hohenlimburg	72	51.21 N	7.35 E
Hohen Neuendorf	72	52.40 N	13.16 E
Hohenthurn	72	46.33 N	13.40 E
Hohenwald	158	35.33 N	87.33 W
Hohoe	114	7.09 N	0.28 E
Hoisington	162	38.31 N	98.47 W
Hojāi	102	26.00 N	92.51 E
Højer	68	54.58 N	8.43 E
Hökensås ⋀2	68	58.11 N	14.08 E
Hokes Bluff	158	34.00 N	85.52 W
Hokitika	126	42.43 S	170.58 E
Hokkaidō I	90a	44.00 N	143.00 E
Hokksund	68	59.47 N	9.59 E
Holbæk	68	55.43 N	11.43 E
Holbrook, Austl.	120	35.44 S	147.19 E
Holbrook, Ariz., U.S.	164	34.54 N	110.10 W
Holden	158	38.43 N	94.01 W
Holdenville	160	35.05 N	96.24 W
Holder	156	28.58 N	82.25 W
Holdrege	162	40.26 N	99.22 W
Holgate	152	41.15 N	84.08 W
Holguín	132	20.53 N	76.15 W
Hollabrunn	72	48.34 N	16.05 E
Holladay	164	40.40 N	111.49 W
Hollam's Bird Island I	116	24.45 S	14.34 E
Holland	154	42.47 N	86.07 W
Holland → Netherlands □1	64	52.15 N	5.30 E
Hollandale	158	33.10 N	90.58 W
Hollandia → Djajapura	124	2.32 S	140.42 E
Holleton	122	31.57 S	119.02 E
Holley	152	43.14 N	78.02 W
Hollis	160	34.41 N	99.55 W
Hollister	168	36.51 N	121.24 W
Holly	162	38.03 N	102.07 W
Holly Hill	156	29.14 N	81.02 W
Holly Springs	158	34.41 N	89.26 W
Hollywood	156	26.00 N	80.09 W
Holman Island	142	70.43 N	117.43 W
Hólmavík	66a	65.43 N	21.43 W
Holmen	68	60.40 N	10.22 E
Holmenkollen	68	59.58 N	10.40 E
Holmes Creek ≃	158	30.30 N	85.47 W
Holmes Reefs ✧2	124	16.27 S	148.00 E
Holmestrand	68	59.29 N	10.18 E
Holmsbu	68	59.33 N	10.27 E
Holmsund	68	63.42 N	20.21 E
Holstebro	68	56.21 N	8.38 E
Holsteinsborg	142	66.55 N	53.40 W
Holston, North Fork ≃	156	36.33 N	82.36 W
Holsworthy	70	50.49 N	4.21 W
Holt, Ala., U.S.	158	33.15 N	87.29 W
Holt, Mich., U.S.	154	42.39 N	84.31 W
Holton	162	39.28 N	95.44 W
Holtville	168	32.49 N	115.23 W
Holy Cross	146	62.12 N	159.47 W
Holyhead	70	53.19 N	4.38 W
Holy Island I, Eng., U.K.	70	55.41 N	1.48 W
Holy Island I, Wales, U.K.	70	53.18 N	4.37 W
Holyoke, Colo., U.S.	162	40.35 N	102.18 W
Holyoke, Mass., U.S.	152	42.12 N	72.37 W
Holyrood	162	38.35 N	98.25 W
Holzkirchen	72	47.52 N	11.42 E
Holzminden	72	51.50 N	9.27 E
Homalin	88	24.52 N	94.55 E
Homāyūnshahr	104	32.41 N	51.31 E
Homberg	72	51.28 N	6.43 E
Hombori Tondo ∧	114	15.16 N	1.40 W
Hombre Muerto, Salar de ≚	140	25.20 S	67.05 W
Homburg, B.R.D.	72	49.19 N	7.20 E
Homburg → Bad Homburg vor der Höhe, B.R.D.	72	50.13 N	8.37 E
Home Bay C	142	68.45 N	67.10 W
Home Hill	120	19.40 S	147.25 E
Homer, Alaska, U.S.	146	59.39 N	151.33 W
Homer, La., U.S.	158	32.48 N	93.04 W
Homer, Mich., U.S.	154	42.09 N	84.49 W
Homer, N.Y., U.S.	152	42.38 N	76.11 W
Homer City	152	40.32 N	79.10 W
Homerville	156	31.02 N	82.45 W
Homestead	156	25.29 N	80.29 W
Homewood	158	33.29 N	86.48 W
Hominy	160	36.25 N	96.24 W
Hommersåk	68	58.58 N	5.42 E
Homs → Al-Khums	108	32.39 N	14.16 E
Honan → Henan □4	88	34.00 N	114.00 E
Honda	138	5.12 N	74.45 W
Hondo, N. Mex., U.S.	164	33.23 N	105.16 W
Hondo, Tex., U.S.	160	29.21 N	99.09 W
Hondo ≃	130	18.29 N	88.19 W
Honduras □1	128	15.00 N	86.30 W
Honduras, Gulf of C	128	16.10 N	87.50 W
Honea Path	156	34.27 N	82.24 W
Hønefoss	68	60.10 N	10.18 E
Honesdale	152	41.34 N	75.16 W
Honfleur	74	49.25 N	0.14 E
Høng	68	55.31 N	11.18 E
Hon-gai	94	20.57 N	107.05 E
Hongdong	88	36.19 N	111.39 E
Honghu	88	29.48 N	113.27 E
Hongjiang	88	27.00 N	109.51 E
Hong Kong → Victoria	88	22.17 N	114.09 E
Hong Kong □2	88	22.15 N	114.10 E
Hongliuyuan	88	41.04 N	95.26 E
Hongshuihe ≃	94	23.24 N	110.12 E
Honguedo, Détroit d' ⩊	150	49.15 N	64.00 W
Hongzehu ⊜	88	33.16 N	118.34 E
Honiara	118	9.27 S	159.57 E
Honiton	70	50.48 N	3.13 W
Honolulu	170c	21.19 N	157.52 W
Honouliuli	170c	21.22 N	158.02 W
Honshū I	90	36.00 N	138.00 E
Hood ≃	142	67.26 N	108.53 W
Hood, Mount ∧	166	45.23 N	121.41 W
Hood Point ≻	122	34.23 S	119.34 E
Hood River	166	45.43 N	121.31 W
Hoods Range ⋀	120	28.35 S	144.30 E
Hoogeveen	72	52.43 N	6.29 E
Hoogezand	72	53.09 N	6.47 E
Hooker Creek	122	18.20 S	130.40 E
Hookina	120	31.45 S	138.20 E
Hook Island I	120	20.08 S	148.55 E
Hook Point ≻	120	25.48 S	153.05 E
Hooks	158	33.28 N	94.15 W
Hoolehua	170a	21.10 N	157.06 W
Hoonah	146	58.07 N	135.26 W
Hoopa	168	41.03 N	123.40 W
Hooper Bay	146	61.31 N	166.06 W
Hoopeston	154	40.28 N	87.40 W
Hoorn	72	52.38 N	5.04 E
Hoosick Falls	152	42.54 N	73.21 W
Hope, B.C., Can.	148	49.23 N	121.26 W
Hope, Ark., U.S.	158	33.40 N	93.36 W
Hope, Ind., U.S.	158	39.18 N	85.46 W
Hopedale	142	55.28 N	60.13 W
Hopelchén	130	19.46 N	89.51 W
Hope Mills	156	34.59 N	78.57 W
Hopes Advance, Baie C	142	59.25 N	69.40 W
Hopes Advance, Cap ≻	142	61.04 N	69.34 W
Hopetoun, Austl.	120	35.44 S	142.22 E
Hopetoun, Austl.	122	33.57 S	120.07 E
Hopetown	116	29.34 S	24.03 E
Hopewell	156	37.18 N	77.17 W
Hopewell Islands II	142	58.25 N	78.00 W
Hopkinsville	158	36.52 N	87.29 W
Hopland	168	38.58 N	123.07 W
Hopwood, Mount ∧	120	21.49 S	144.26 E
Hoquiam	166	46.59 N	123.53 W
Horb	72	48.26 N	8.41 E
Hordaland □6	68	60.15 N	6.30 E
Horgen	74	47.15 N	8.36 E
Horicon	154	43.27 N	88.38 W
Hormuz, Strait of ⩊	104	26.34 N	56.15 E
Horn	72	48.40 N	15.40 E
Horn ≻	66a	66.28 N	22.28 W
Horn ≃	142	61.30 N	118.01 W
Horn, Cape → Hornos, Cabo de ≻	136	56.00 S	67.16 W
Hornád (Hernád) ≃	72	47.56 N	21.08 E
Hornaday ≃	146	69.22 N	123.50 W
Hornafjörður C	66a	64.17 N	15.16 W
Hornavan ⊜	66	66.10 N	17.30 E
Hornbeak	158	36.20 N	89.18 W
Hornby Bay C	142	66.35 N	117.50 W
Horncastle	70	53.13 N	0.07 W
Hornell	152	42.19 N	77.40 W
Hornepayne	142	49.13 N	84.47 W
Hornindal	68	61.58 N	6.31 E
Horn Island I	124	10.37 S	142.17 E
Hornos, Cabo de (Cape Horn) ≻	136	56.00 S	67.16 W
Horn Plateau ⋀1	142	62.15 N	119.15 W
Hornsea	70	53.55 N	0.10 W
Hornslet	68	56.19 N	10.20 E
Horqueta	140	23.24 S	56.53 W
Horse Cave	158	37.11 N	85.54 W
Horse Creek	164	41.25 N	105.11 W
Horseheads	152	42.10 N	76.50 W
Horse Islands II	150	50.13 N	55.45 W
Horsens	68	55.52 N	9.52 E
Horsham, Austl.	120	36.43 S	142.13 E
Horsham, Eng., U.K.	70	51.04 N	0.21 W
Hørsholm	68	55.53 N	12.30 E
Horten	68	59.25 N	10.30 E
Hortobágy □9	72	47.35 N	21.00 E
Horton	162	39.40 N	95.32 W
Horton ≃	146	70.00 N	126.53 W
Horton Lake ⊜	142	67.30 N	122.28 W
Hortonville	154	44.20 N	88.38 W
Hosaina	108	7.38 N	37.52 E
Hösbach	72	50.00 N	9.12 E
Hoséré Batandji ∧	106	8.20 N	13.15 E
Hosford	156	30.23 N	84.48 W
Hoshangābād	102	22.45 N	77.44 E
Hoshiārpur	102	31.32 N	75.54 E
Hospet	100	15.16 N	76.24 E
Hospitalet	76	41.22 N	2.08 E
Hossegor	74	43.40 N	1.27 W
Hoste, Isla I	136	55.10 S	69.00 W
Hotchkiss	164	38.48 N	107.43 W
Hotevilla	164	35.56 N	110.41 W
Hotham Inlet C	146	66.45 N	162.00 W
Hoting	68	64.07 N	16.10 E
Hot Springs, Mont., U.S.	166	47.37 N	114.40 W
Hot Springs → Truth Or Consequences, N. Mex., U.S.	164	33.08 N	107.15 W
Hot Springs, S. Dak., U.S.	162	43.26 N	103.29 W
Hot Springs National Park	158	34.30 N	93.03 W
Hottah Lake ⊜	142	65.04 N	118.29 W
Houdan	74	48.47 N	1.36 E
Houeillès	74	44.12 N	0.02 E
Houei Sai	92	20.18 N	100.26 E
Houghton, Mich., U.S.	154	47.06 N	88.34 W
Houghton, N.Y., U.S.	152	42.25 N	78.10 W
Houghton Lake	154	44.18 N	84.45 W
Houlton	152	46.08 N	67.51 W
Houma, La., U.S.	158	29.36 N	90.43 W
Houma, Zhg.	88	35.40 N	111.29 E
Housatonic	152	42.16 N	73.22 W
Houston, Minn., U.S.	154	43.45 N	91.34 W
Houston, Miss., U.S.	158	33.54 N	89.00 W
Houston, Mo., U.S.	158	37.22 N	91.58 W
Houston, Tex., U.S.	160	29.46 N	95.22 W
Houtman Rocks II1	118	28.35 S	113.45 E
Hove	70	50.49 N	0.10 W
Hovmantorp	68	56.47 N	15.08 E
Howa, Ouadi (Wādī Howar) ∟	112	17.30 N	27.08 E
Howar, Wādī (Ouadi Howa) ∟	112	17.30 N	27.08 E
Howard, Austl.	120	25.19 S	152.34 E
Howard, Pa., U.S.	152	41.01 N	77.40 W
Howard, Wis., U.S.	154	44.33 N	88.04 W
Howard City	154	43.24 N	85.28 W
Howard Island I	124	12.10 S	135.24 E
Howard Lake	154	45.04 N	94.04 W
Howe	158	41.43 N	85.25 W
Howe, Cape ≻	120	37.31 S	149.59 E
Howell	154	42.36 N	83.55 W
Howick	126	36.54 S	174.56 E
Howitt, Mount ∧	120	37.10 S	146.40 E
Howland	152	45.14 N	68.40 W
Howrah	102	22.35 N	88.20 E
Howse Peak ∧	148	51.49 N	116.41 W
Hoxie, Ark., U.S.	158	36.03 N	90.58 W
Hoxie, Kans., U.S.	162	39.21 N	100.26 W
Höxter	72	51.46 N	9.23 E
Høyanger	68	61.13 N	6.05 E
Hoyerswerda	72	51.26 N	14.14 E
Hoyt Lakes	154	47.31 N	92.08 W
Hradec Králové	72	50.12 N	15.50 E
Hranice	72	49.33 N	17.44 E
Hronov	72	50.29 N	16.12 E
Hrubieszów	72	50.49 N	23.55 E
Hrvatska (Croatia) □3	78	45.10 N	15.30 E
Hsian → X1'an	88	34.15 N	108.52 E
Hsinchu	88	24.48 N	120.58 E
Hsinkao Shan ∧	88	23.28 N	120.57 E
Hsipaw	92	22.37 N	97.18 E
Huacho	134	11.07 S	77.37 W
Huachuca City	164	31.34 N	110.21 W
Huadian	88	42.58 N	126.43 E
Huagaruancha, Cerro ∧	134	10.32 S	75.56 W
Hua Hin	94	12.34 N	99.58 E
Huaian	88	33.32 N	119.10 E
Huaide	88	43.32 N	124.50 E
Huaihe ≃	88	32.58 N	118.17 E
Huailai	88	40.23 N	115.33 E
Huainan	88	32.40 N	117.00 E
Huaiyang	88	33.44 N	114.53 E
Huaiyin	88	33.35 N	119.02 E
Huajuapan de León	130	17.48 N	97.46 W
Hualfín	140	27.15 S	66.50 W
Hualien	88	23.58 N	121.36 E
Huallaga ≃	134	5.07 S	75.30 W
Huallanca	134	8.50 S	77.50 W
Huamachuco	134	7.50 S	78.05 W
Huambo	110	12.44 S	15.47 E
Huancavelica	134	12.46 S	75.02 W
Huancayo	134	12.04 S	75.14 W
Huanchaca	134	20.20 S	66.39 W
Huangchuan	88	32.09 N	115.03 E
Huanggang	88	30.27 N	114.52 E
Huanghe ≃	88	37.32 N	118.19 E
Huangling	88	35.41 N	109.09 E
Huangshi	88	30.13 N	115.05 E
Huangyuan	88	36.42 N	101.25 E
Huánuco	134	9.55 S	76.14 W
Huanuni	134	18.16 S	66.51 W
Huaral	134	11.32 S	77.13 W
Huaraz	134	9.32 S	77.32 W
Huasaga ≃	138	3.42 S	76.26 W
Huascarán, Nevado ∧	134	9.07 S	77.37 W
Huasco	140	28.28 S	71.14 W
Huatabampo	130	26.50 N	109.38 W
Huauchinango	130	20.11 N	98.03 W
Huaxian	88	23.22 N	113.12 E
Hubbard	160	31.51 N	96.48 W
Hubbell	154	47.11 N	88.26 W
Hubei □4	88	31.00 N	112.00 E
Hubli	100	15.20 N	75.08 E
Huddersfield	70	53.39 N	1.47 W
Huddinge	68	59.14 N	17.59 E
Hudiksvall	68	61.44 N	17.07 E
Hudson, Fla., U.S.	156	28.22 N	82.42 W
Hudson, Mass., U.S.	152	42.24 N	71.35 W
Hudson, Mich., U.S.	154	41.51 N	84.21 W
Hudson, N.H., U.S.	152	42.46 N	71.26 W
Hudson, N.C., U.S.	156	35.51 N	81.30 W
Hudson, N.Y., U.S.	152	42.15 N	73.47 W
Hudson, Ohio, U.S.	152	41.15 N	81.26 W
Hudson, Wis., U.S.	154	44.53 N	92.45 W
Hudson, Wyo., U.S.	166	42.54 N	108.35 W
Hudson ≃	152	40.42 N	74.02 W
Hudson Bay	142	52.52 N	102.25 W
Hudson Bay C	142	60.00 N	86.00 W
Hudson Falls	152	43.18 N	73.35 W
Hudson Strait ⩊	142	62.30 N	72.00 W
Hudsonville	154	42.52 N	85.52 W
Hue	94	16.28 N	107.36 E
Huehuetenango	130	15.20 N	91.28 W
Huelgoat	74	48.22 N	3.45 W
Huelva	76	37.16 N	6.57 W
Huerva ≃	76	41.39 N	0.52 W
Huesca	76	42.08 N	0.25 W
Huesca □4	76	42.05 N	0.00
Huetamo de Núñez	130	18.35 N	100.53 W
Huete	76	40.08 N	2.41 W
Hueytown	158	33.27 N	86.59 W
Hughenden	120	20.51 S	144.12 E
Hughes	146	66.03 N	154.16 W
Hughes Springs	158	33.05 N	94.38 W
Hughesville	152	41.14 N	76.44 W
Hughson	168	37.36 N	120.52 W
Hugh Town	70	49.55 N	6.17 W
Hugo, Colo., U.S.	162	39.08 N	103.28 W
Hugo, Okla., U.S.	160	34.01 N	95.31 W
Hugoton	162	37.11 N	101.21 W
Huhehaote	88	40.51 N	111.40 E
Hŭich'ŏn	88	40.10 N	126.17 E
Huila □5	138	2.30 N	75.45 W
Huila, Nevado del ∧	138	3.00 N	76.00 W
Huili	94	26.43 N	102.10 E
Huimin	88	37.29 N	117.29 E
Huinan	88	42.40 N	126.00 E
Huitzuco [de los Figueroa]	130	18.18 N	99.21 W
Huixtla	130	15.09 N	92.28 W
Huiyang	88	23.05 N	114.24 E
Huize	94	26.27 N	103.09 E
Ḥukayyim, Bi'r al- ⍑4	112	31.36 N	23.29 E
Hulan	88	46.00 N	126.38 E
Hulbert	158	35.56 N	95.09 W
Hulett	162	44.41 N	104.36 W
Hull, Qué., Can.	152	45.26 N	75.43 W
Hull → Kingston upon Hull, Eng., U.K.	70	53.45 N	0.20 W
Hull, Tex., U.S.	160	30.09 N	94.39 W
Hulunchi ⊜	88	49.01 N	117.32 E
Ḥulwān	112	29.51 N	31.20 E
Huma	88	51.43 N	126.38 E
Humacao	132	18.09 N	65.50 W
Humaerhe ≃	84	51.40 N	126.44 E
Humahuaca	140	23.12 S	65.25 W
Humaitá, Bra.	134	7.31 S	63.02 W
Humaitá, Para.	140	27.03 S	58.33 W
Humansdorp	116	34.02 S	26.46 E
Humbe	110	16.40 S	14.55 E
Humbe, Serra do ⋀	110	12.13 S	15.25 E
Humberside □6	70	53.50 N	0.30 W
Humboldt, Sask., Can.	142	52.12 N	105.07 W
Humboldt, Ariz., U.S.	164	34.30 N	112.14 W
Humboldt, Iowa, U.S.	154	42.44 N	94.13 W
Humboldt, Kans., U.S.	162	37.49 N	95.26 W
Humboldt, Nebr., U.S.	162	40.10 N	95.57 W
Humboldt, Tenn., U.S.	158	35.49 N	88.55 W
Humboldt ≃	168	40.02 N	118.31 W
Humboldt Salt Marsh ☷	168	39.50 N	117.55 W
Hume	168	36.47 N	118.55 W
Hume, Lake ⊜1	120	36.06 S	147.05 E
Humeburn	120	27.24 S	145.14 E
Humenné	72	48.56 N	21.55 E
Humeston	154	40.52 N	93.30 W
Humphrey	158	34.25 N	91.42 W
Humphreys, Mount ∧	168	37.17 N	118.40 W
Humphreys Peak ∧	164	35.20 N	111.40 W
Humppila	68	60.56 N	23.22 E
Hunan □4	88	28.00 N	111.00 E
Hunchun	88	42.54 N	130.22 E
Hundested	68	55.58 N	11.52 E
Hundorp	68	61.33 N	9.45 E
Hundred	152	39.41 N	80.28 W
Hunedoara	80	45.45 N	22.54 E
Hunedoara □4	80	45.45 N	23.00 E
Hünfeld	72	50.40 N	9.46 E
Hungary □1	64	47.00 N	20.00 E
Hungerford	160	29.24 N	96.05 W
Hŭngnam	88	39.50 N	127.38 E
Hungry Horse	148	48.23 N	114.04 W
Huningue	74	47.36 N	7.35 E
Hunjiang	88	41.56 N	126.29 E
Hunsberge ⋀	116	27.45 S	17.12 E
Hunstanton	70	52.57 N	0.30 E
Hunter Island I	120	40.32 S	144.45 E
Hunters	148	48.07 N	118.12 W
Huntingburg	158	38.18 N	86.57 W
Huntingdon, Qué., Can.	152	45.05 N	74.10 W
Huntingdon, Eng., U.K.	70	52.20 N	0.12 W
Huntingdon, Pa., U.S.	152	40.29 N	78.01 W
Huntingdon, Tenn., U.S.	158	36.00 N	88.26 W
Huntington, Ind., U.S.	158	40.53 N	85.30 W
Huntington, N.Y., U.S.	152	40.51 N	73.25 W
Huntington, Oreg., U.S.	166	44.21 N	117.16 W
Huntington, Tex., U.S.	158	31.17 N	94.34 W
Huntington, W. Va., U.S.	152	38.25 N	82.26 W
Huntington Beach	168	33.39 N	117.60 W
Huntley	166	45.54 N	108.19 W
Huntly, N.Z.	126	37.33 S	175.10 E
Huntly, Scot., U.K.	70	57.27 N	2.47 W
Huntsville, Ont., Can.	154	45.20 N	79.13 W
Huntsville, Ala., U.S.	158	34.44 N	86.35 W
Huntsville, Mo., U.S.	158	39.26 N	92.33 W
Huntsville, Tenn., U.S.	156	36.25 N	84.29 W
Huntsville, Tex., U.S.	160	30.43 N	95.33 W
Hunucmá	130	21.01 N	89.52 W
Hunyani ≃	110	15.37 S	30.39 E
Hunyuan	88	39.48 N	113.41 E
Huonville	120	43.01 S	147.02 E
Hupeh → Hubei □4	88	31.00 N	112.00 E
Hurao	88	45.46 N	132.59 E
Hurd, Cape ≻	154	45.13 N	81.44 W
Huriel	74	46.23 N	2.29 E
Hurley, N. Mex., U.S.	164	32.42 N	108.08 W
Hurley, Wis., U.S.	154	46.28 N	90.08 W
Huron, Calif., U.S.	168	36.12 N	120.06 W
Huron, Ohio, U.S.	152	41.24 N	82.33 W
Huron, S. Dak., U.S.	162	44.22 N	98.13 W
Huron, Lake ⊜	154	44.30 N	82.15 W
Hurricane, Utah, U.S.	164	37.11 N	113.17 W
Hurricane, W. Va., U.S.	152	38.26 N	82.01 W
Hurstbridge	120	37.38 S	145.12 E
Hürth	72	50.52 N	6.51 E
Hurtsboro	158	32.14 N	85.25 W
Húsavík	66a	66.04 N	17.18 W
Huşi	80	46.40 N	28.04 E
Huskerville	162	40.52 N	96.47 W
Huskvarna	68	57.48 N	14.16 E
Huslia	146	65.42 N	156.25 W
Husum	72	54.28 N	9.03 E
Hutanopan	92	0.41 N	99.42 E
Hutchinson, Kans., U.S.	162	38.05 N	97.56 W
Hutchinson, Minn., U.S.	154	44.54 N	94.22 W
Hutte Sauvage, Lac de la ⊜	142	56.15 N	64.45 W
Hutto	160	30.33 N	97.33 W
Hutton, Mount ∧	120	25.51 S	148.20 E
Huy	72	50.31 N	5.14 E
Huzhou	88	30.52 N	120.06 E
Hvannadalshnúkur ∧	66a	64.01 N	16.41 W
Hveragerði	66a	64.03 N	21.10 W
Hvittingfoss	68	59.29 N	10.01 E
Hwang Ho → Huanghe ≃	88	37.32 N	118.19 E
Hyannis	152	41.39 N	70.17 W
Hyattville	166	44.15 N	107.36 W
Hydaburg	146	55.12 N	132.49 W
Hyden	122	32.27 S	118.53 E
Hyde Park, Guy.	138	6.30 N	58.16 W
Hyde Park, N.Y., U.S.	152	41.47 N	73.56 W
Hyde Park, Vt., U.S.	152	44.36 N	72.37 W
Hyderābād, Bhārat	100	17.23 N	78.29 E
Hyderābād, Pāk.	102	25.22 N	68.22 E
Hyères	74	43.07 N	6.07 E
Hyères, Îles d' II	76	43.00 N	6.20 E
Hyesan	88	41.23 N	128.12 E
Hyland ≃	146	59.50 N	128.10 W
Hylestad	68	59.05 N	7.32 E
Hyndman	152	39.49 N	78.44 W
Hyndman Peak ∧	166	43.50 N	114.10 W
Hyrum	166	41.38 N	111.51 W
Hyrynsalmi	68	64.40 N	28.32 E
Hysham	166	46.18 N	107.14 W
Hyvinkää	68	60.38 N	24.52 E
I			
Iaco (Yaco) ≃	134	9.03 S	68.34 W
Ialomiţa □4	80	44.30 N	27.20 E
Iaoxing'anling-shanmai ≃	88	50.00 N	126.25 E
Iaşi	80	47.10 N	27.35 E
Iaşi □4	80	47.15 N	27.15 E
Iatt, Lake ⊜1	158	31.35 N	92.40 W
Ibadan	114	7.17 N	3.30 E
Ibagué	138	4.27 N	75.14 W
Ibarra	138	0.21 N	78.07 W
Ibb	100	14.01 N	44.10 E
Ibbenbüren	72	52.16 N	7.43 E
Iberville	152	45.18 N	73.14 W
Iberville, Lac d' ⊜	142	55.55 N	73.15 W
Iberville, Mont d' ∧	142	58.53 N	63.43 W
Ibiá	134	19.29 S	46.32 W
Ibicaraí	134	14.51 S	39.36 W
Ibicuí ≃	140	29.25 S	56.47 W
Ibitinga	140	21.45 S	48.49 W
Ibiza	76	38.54 N	1.26 E
Ibiza I	76	39.00 N	1.25 E
Ibo	110	12.20 S	40.35 E
Iboundji, Mont ∧	110	1.08 S	11.48 E
Ica	134	14.04 S	75.42 W
Ica ≃, Perú	134	14.53 S	75.33 W
Içá (Putumayo) ≃, S.A.	138	3.07 S	67.58 W
Içana	138	0.21 N	67.19 W
Içana (Isana) ≃	138	0.26 N	67.19 W
Iceland □1	64	65.00 N	18.00 W
Ichalkaranji	100	16.41 N	74.28 E
Ichang → Yichang	88	30.42 N	111.11 E
Ich Bogd Uul ⋀	88	44.55 N	100.20 E
Ichikawa	90	35.44 N	139.55 E
Ichilo ≃	134	15.57 S	64.42 W
Ichinomiya	90	35.18 N	136.48 E
Icó	134	6.24 S	38.51 W
Icoraci	134	1.18 S	48.28 W
Icy Bay C	146	60.00 N	141.15 W
Ida	154	41.55 N	83.34 W
Ida, Mount ∧	122	29.14 S	120.25 E
Idabel	158	33.54 N	94.50 W
Ida Grove	162	42.21 N	95.28 W
Idaho □3	144	45.00 N	115.00 W
Idaho City	166	43.50 N	115.50 W
Idaho Falls	166	43.30 N	112.02 W
Idaho Springs	164	39.45 N	105.31 W
Idalou	160	33.40 N	101.41 W
Idanha-a-Nova	76	39.55 N	7.14 W
Idar-Oberstein	72	49.42 N	7.19 E
Iderijn ≃	88	49.16 N	100.41 E
Idfū	112	24.58 N	32.52 E
Ídhi Óros ∧	80	35.18 N	24.43 E
Idi	94	4.55 N	97.47 E
Idiofa	110	5.02 S	19.36 E
Idlib	104	35.55 N	36.38 E
Idrica	86	56.21 N	28.53 E
Idrija	78	46.00 N	14.01 E
Idutywa	116	32.02 S	28.16 E
Idyllwild	168	33.45 N	116.43 W
Ieper	72	50.51 N	2.53 E
Iesi	78	43.31 N	13.14 E
Ifalik I1	92	7.15 N	144.27 E
Ife	114	7.30 N	4.30 E
Iferouâne	114	19.04 N	8.24 E
Ifni □9	106	29.00 N	10.00 W
Iforas, Adrar des ⋀	114	20.00 N	2.00 E
Igal	72	46.31 N	17.55 E
Igarka	84	67.28 N	86.35 E
Igatimí	140	24.05 S	55.30 W
Iglesias	78	39.19 N	8.32 E
Igloolik	142	69.24 N	81.49 W
Iguaçu ≃	140	25.36 S	54.36 W
Iguaçu, Saltos do (Iguassu Falls) ∨	136	25.41 S	54.26 W
Iguala	130	18.21 N	99.32 W
Igualada	76	41.35 N	1.38 E
Iguape	140	24.43 S	47.33 W
Iguassu Falls → Iguaçu, Saltos do ∟	136	25.41 S	54.26 W
Iguatu	134	6.22 S	39.18 W
Iguéla	110	1.55 S	9.19 E
Iguidi, Erg ⚍8	106	26.35 N	5.40 W
Igžej	84	53.59 N	103.10 E
Iheya-shima I	91b	27.00 N	127.56 E
Ihiala	114	5.51 N	6.51 E
Ihosy ≃	117b	21.58 S	43.38 E
Ii	68	65.19 N	25.22 E
Iida	90	35.31 N	137.50 E
Iisalmi	68	63.34 N	27.11 E
Iittala	68	61.04 N	24.10 E
Iizuka	90	33.38 N	130.41 E
Ijebu-Igbo	114	6.56 N	4.01 E
Ijebu-Ode	114	6.50 N	3.56 E
Ijill, Kediet ∧	106	22.38 N	12.33 W
IJmuiden	72	52.27 N	4.36 E
IJsselmeer (Zuiderzee) ⍑2	72	52.45 N	5.25 E
Ijuí	140	28.23 S	53.55 W
Ika	84	59.18 N	106.12 E
Ikaalinen	68	61.46 N	23.03 E
Ikare	114	7.32 N	5.45 E
Ikaría I	80	37.41 N	26.20 E
Ikast	68	56.08 N	9.10 E
Ikela	110	1.11 S	23.16 E
Ikerre	114	7.31 N	5.14 E
Ikire	114	7.23 N	4.12 E
Ikirun	114	7.55 N	4.41 E
Ikorodu	114	6.37 N	3.31 E
Ikot Ekpene	114	5.12 N	7.40 E
Ikša	86	56.10 N	37.31 E
Ila	114	8.01 N	4.55 E
Ilagan	92	17.09 N	121.53 E
Ilan	88	24.45 N	121.44 E
Ilanskij	84	56.14 N	96.03 E
Ilanz	74	46.46 N	9.12 E
Iława	72	53.37 N	19.33 E
Ilbenge	84	62.49 N	124.24 E
Île-à-la-Crosse	142	55.27 N	107.53 W
Île-à-la-Crosse, Lac ⊜	142	55.40 N	107.45 W
Ilebo	110	4.19 S	20.35 E
Île-de-France □9	74	49.00 N	2.20 E
Île Desroches I	110	5.41 S	53.41 E
Ilek ≃	82	51.30 N	53.20 E
Ilesha	114	7.38 N	4.45 E
Ileza	66	60.43 N	43.54 E
Ilfov □4	80	44.30 N	26.00 E
Ilfracombe, Austl.	120	23.30 S	144.30 E
Ilfracombe, Eng., U.K.	70	51.13 N	4.08 W
Ilhabela	140	23.47 S	45.21 W
Ílhavo	76	40.36 N	8.40 W
Ilhéus	134	14.49 S	39.02 W
Ili	82	43.53 N	77.12 E
Ili ≃	88	45.24 N	74.02 E
Ilia □5	80	37.50 N	21.30 E
Iliamna	146	59.45 N	154.54 W
Iliamna Lake ⊜	146	59.30 N	155.00 W
Iligan	92	8.14 N	124.14 E
Ilimsk	84	56.46 N	103.52 E
Ilion	152	43.01 N	75.02 W
Il'jinskij	84	47.58 N	142.12 E
Ilkley	70	53.55 N	1.50 W
Illampu, Nevado ∧	134	15.50 S	68.34 W
Illapel	140	31.38 S	71.10 W
Illbillee, Mount ∧	122	27.02 S	132.30 E
Ille-et-Vilaine □5	74	48.10 N	1.30 W
Illéla	114	14.28 N	5.15 E
Illertissen	72	48.13 N	10.06 E
Illescas	76	40.07 N	3.50 W
Illiers	74	48.18 N	1.15 E
Illimani, Nevado ∧	134	16.39 S	67.48 W
Illinois □3	144	40.00 N	89.00 W
Illinois ≃, U.S.	158	35.30 N	95.06 W
Illinois ≃, Ill., U.S.	154	38.58 N	90.27 W
Illinois Peak ∧	166	47.02 N	115.04 W
Illizi	106	26.29 N	8.28 E
Il'men', Ozero ⊜	86	58.17 N	31.20 E
Ilmenau	72	50.41 N	10.55 E
Ilo	134	17.38 S	71.20 W
Iloilo	92	10.43 N	122.33 E
Ilomantsi	68	62.40 N	30.55 E
Ilorin	114	8.30 N	4.32 E
Il'pyrskij	84	59.56 N	164.10 E
Ilwaki	92	7.56 S	126.26 E
Imabari	90	34.03 N	133.00 E
Iman	84	45.55 N	133.43 E
Imandra, Ozero ⊜	66	67.30 N	33.00 E
Imatra	68	61.10 N	28.46 E
Imbābah	112	30.04 N	31.13 E
Imbabura □4	138	0.22 N	78.25 W
Imbituba	140	28.14 S	48.40 W
Imeni Kirova	84	46.27 N	77.13 E
Imeni Vorovskogo	86	55.43 N	41.06 E
Imeni Žel'abova	86	58.57 N	36.36 E
Imi	108	6.28 N	42.18 E
Imlay	168	40.39 N	118.09 W
Imlay City	154	43.02 N	83.05 W
Immenstadt	72	47.33 N	10.13 E
Immingham Dock	70	53.37 N	0.12 W
Immokalee	156	26.25 N	81.25 W
Imola	78	44.21 N	11.42 E
Imotski	78	43.27 N	17.13 E
Imperatriz	134	5.32 S	47.29 W
Imperia	78	43.53 N	8.03 E
Imperial, Calif., U.S.	168	32.51 N	115.34 W
Imperial, Nebr., U.S.	162	40.31 N	101.39 W
Imperial, Tex., U.S.	160	31.16 N	102.41 W
Imperial Beach	168	32.35 N	117.08 W
Impfondo	110	1.37 N	18.04 E
Imphāl	102	24.49 N	93.57 E
Imst	72	47.14 N	10.44 E
In'a	84	59.24 N	144.48 E
In'a ≃	84	59.23 N	144.54 E
In Aménas	106	28.05 N	9.30 E
Inanwatan	124	2.01 S	132.07 E
Inari	64	68.54 N	27.10 E
Inari ⊜	66	69.00 N	28.00 E
Inarigda	84	63.14 N	107.27 E
Inca	76	39.43 N	2.54 E
Inca de Oro	140	26.45 S	69.54 W
Inch'ŏn	88	37.28 N	126.38 E
Incomati (Komati) ≃	116	25.46 S	32.43 E
Incy	66	65.48 N	40.26 E
Indalsälven ≃	68	62.31 N	17.27 E
Independence, Calif., U.S.	168	36.48 N	118.12 W
Independence, Iowa, U.S.	154	42.28 N	91.54 W
Independence, Kans., U.S.	162	37.13 N	95.42 W
Independence, La., U.S.	158	30.38 N	90.30 W
Independence, Mo., U.S.	158	39.05 N	94.24 W
Independence, Oreg., U.S.	166	44.51 N	123.11 W
Independence, Wis., U.S.	154	44.21 N	91.25 W
Inderborskij	82	48.33 N	51.44 E
India □1	100	20.00 N	77.00 E
Indialantic	156	28.05 N	80.34 W
Indiana	152	40.37 N	79.09 W
Indiana □3	144	40.00 N	86.15 W
Indianapolis	158	39.46 N	86.09 W
Indian Creek ≃	162	44.39 N	103.19 W
Indian Head	142	50.32 N	103.40 W
Indian Ocean ⍑1	100	15.00 N	65.00 E
Indianola, Iowa, U.S.	154	41.22 N	93.34 W
Indianola, Miss., U.S.	158	33.27 N	90.39 W
Indian Springs	168	36.34 N	115.40 W
Indiantown	156	27.01 N	80.28 W
Indigirka ≃	84	70.48 N	148.54 E
Indio	168	33.43 N	116.13 W
Indispensable Reefs ✧2	118	12.40 S	160.25 E
Indonesia □1	92	5.00 S	120.00 E
Indore	102	22.43 N	75.50 E
Indragiri ≃	96	0.22 S	103.26 E
Indrāvati ≃	100	18.43 N	80.17 E
Indre □5	74	46.45 N	1.30 E
Indre-et-Loire □5	74	47.15 N	0.45 E
Indus ≃	102	24.20 N	67.47 E
Industry	160	29.58 N	96.30 W
Inez	160	28.54 N	96.47 W
Infiernillo, Presa del ⊜1	130	18.35 N	101.45 W
I-n-Gall	114	16.47 N	6.56 E
Ingelheim	72	49.59 N	8.05 E
Ingende	110	0.15 S	18.57 E
Ingeniero Luiggi	140	35.25 S	64.29 W
Ingersoll	154	43.02 N	80.53 W
Ingham	120	18.39 S	146.10 E
Ingleside	160	27.53 N	97.13 W
Inglewood, Austl.	120	28.25 S	151.05 E
Inglewood, N.Z.	126	39.09 S	174.12 E
Inglewood, Calif., U.S.	168	33.58 N	118.21 W
Inglewood, Tenn., U.S.	158	36.12 N	86.46 W
Ingolstadt	72	48.46 N	11.27 E
Ingomar	166	46.35 N	107.23 W
Ingram	160	30.04 N	99.14 W
In Guezzam	106	19.32 N	5.42 E
Ingwiller	74	48.52 N	7.29 E
Inhaca, Ilha da I	116	26.03 S	32.57 E
Inhambane	116	23.51 S	35.29 E
Inhambupe	134	11.47 S	38.21 W
Inhaminga	116	18.24 S	35.00 E
Inharrime	116	24.29 S	35.01 E
Inirida ≃	138	3.55 N	67.52 W
Injasuti ∧	116	29.09 S	29.23 E
Injune	120	25.51 S	148.34 E
Inland Sea → Seto-naikai ⍑2	90	34.20 N	133.30 E
Inle Lake ⊜	94	20.32 N	96.55 E
Inman	156	35.03 N	82.05 W
Inn (En) ≃	74	48.35 N	13.28 E
Innamincka	120	27.45 S	140.44 E
Inner Mongolia → Neimenggu Zizhiqu □4	88	43.00 N	115.00 E
Innisfail, Austl.	120	17.32 S	146.02 E
Innisfail, Alta., Can.	148	52.02 N	113.57 W
Innsbruck	72	47.16 N	11.24 E
Inola	160	36.09 N	95.31 W
Inongo	110	1.57 S	18.16 E
Inoucdjouac	142	58.27 N	78.06 W
Inowrocław	72	52.48 N	18.15 E
In Salah	106	27.12 N	2.28 E
Insar	66	53.52 N	44.21 E
Insch	70	57.21 N	2.37 W
Inspiration	164	33.25 N	110.53 W
Insterburg → Čern'achovsk	86	54.38 N	21.49 E
Inta	66	66.02 N	60.08 E
Interlaken	74	46.41 N	7.51 E
International Falls	154	48.36 N	93.25 W
Inthanon, Doi ∧	94	18.38 N	98.30 E
Intiyaco	140	28.40 S	60.05 W
Intracoastal Waterway ≖	156	33.40 N	79.00 W
Inuvik	146	68.25 N	133.30 W
Inveraray	70	56.13 N	5.05 W
Inverbervie	70	56.51 N	2.17 W
Invercargill	126	46.25 S	168.27 E
Inverell	120	29.47 S	151.07 E
Invergordon	70	57.42 N	4.10 W
Inverness, N.S., Can.	150	46.14 N	61.18 W
Inverness, Scot., U.K.	70	57.27 N	4.15 W
Inverness, Fla., U.S.	156	28.51 N	82.20 W
Inverness, Miss., U.S.	158	33.21 N	90.35 W
Inverurie	70	57.17 N	2.23 W
Investigator Group II	122	33.45 S	134.30 E
Investigator Strait ⩊	120	35.25 S	137.10 E
Inyangani ∧	116	18.20 S	32.50 E
Inza	66	53.51 N	46.21 E
Ioánnina	80	39.40 N	20.50 E
Iola	162	37.55 N	95.24 W
Iolotan'	104	37.18 N	62.21 E
Ione, Calif., U.S.	168	38.21 N	120.56 W
Ione, Wash., U.S.	148	48.45 N	117.25 W
Ionia	154	42.59 N	85.04 W

Symbols in the index entries are identified on page 203.

Name	Page	Lat	Long
Ionian Islands → Iónioi Nisoi II	80	38.30 N	20.30 E
Ionian Sea ⊤²	64	39.00 N	19.00 E
Iónioi Nisoi II	80	38.30 N	20.30 E
Iony, Ostrov I	84	56.26 N	143.25 E
Iowa □³	144	42.15 N	93.15 W
Iowa City	154	41.40 N	91.32 W
Iowa Falls	154	42.31 N	93.16 W
Iowa Park	160	33.57 N	98.40 W
Ipameri	134	17.43 S	48.09 W
Ipel'(Ipoly) ≈	72	47.49 N	18.52 E
Ipiales	138	0.50 N	77.37 W
Ipiaú	134	14.08 S	39.44 W
Ipoh	96	4.35 N	101.04 E
Ipoly (Ipel') ≈	72	47.49 N	18.52 E
Iporá	134	16.28 S	51.07 W
Ipswich, Austl.	120	27.36 S	152.46 E
Ipswich, Eng., U.K.	70	52.04 N	1.10 E
Ipswich, Mass., U.S.	152	42.41 N	70.50 W
Ipu	134	4.20 S	40.42 W
Iquique	134	20.13 S	70.10 W
Iquitos	138	3.50 S	73.15 W
Iráklion	80	35.20 N	25.09 E
Iran (Īrān) □¹	100	32.00 N	53.00 E
Iran Mountains ↗	96	2.05 N	114.55 E
Īrānshahr	100	27.13 N	60.41 E
Irapuato	130	20.41 N	101.28 W
Iraq □¹	100	33.00 N	44.00 E
Irati	140	25.27 S	50.39 W
Irazú, Volcán ∧¹	132	9.59 N	83.51 W
Irbid	104	32.33 N	35.51 E
Irbil	94	36.11 N	44.01 E
Irbit	84	57.41 N	63.03 E
Irdning	72	47.33 N	14.01 E
Ireland □¹	64	53.00 N	8.00 W
Irene	162	43.05 N	97.10 W
Ireng (Maú) ≈	138	3.33 N	59.51 W
Irgiz	82	48.37 N	61.16 E
Iri	88	35.56 N	126.57 E
Iriga	92	13.25 N	123.25 E
Irīgui ✦¹	114	16.43 N	5.30 W
Iringa	110	7.46 S	35.42 E
Iriomote-jima I	88	24.20 N	123.50 E
Iriri ≈	134	3.52 S	52.37 W
Irish Sea ⊤²	70	53.30 S	5.20 W
Irkutsk	84	52.16 N	104.20 E
Iron City	158	35.01 N	87.35 W
Irondale	158	33.32 N	86.42 W
Irondequoit	152	43.12 N	77.36 W
Iron Gate V	80	44.41 N	22.31 E
Iron Gate Reservoir ⊜¹	80	44.30 N	22.00 E
Iron Knob	120	32.44 S	137.08 E
Iron Mountain	154	45.49 N	88.04 W
Iron Mountains ↗	156	36.30 N	81.50 W
Iron Range	120	12.42 S	143.18 E
Iron River, Mich., U.S.	154	46.05 N	88.39 W
Iron River, Wis., U.S.	154	46.34 N	91.24 W
Ironton, Mo., U.S.	158	37.36 N	90.38 W
Ironton, Ohio, U.S.	152	38.31 N	82.40 W
Ironwood	154	46.27 N	90.10 W
Iroquois	162	44.22 N	97.51 W
Iroquois ≈	152	41.05 N	87.49 W
Iroquois Falls	142	48.46 N	80.41 W
Irrawaddy ≈	94	15.50 N	95.06 E
Irtyš ≈	84	61.04 N	68.52 E
Irtyšsk	84	53.21 N	75.27 E
Irumu	110	1.27 N	29.52 E
Irún	76	43.21 N	1.47 W
Irurzun	76	42.55 N	1.50 W
Irvine, Scot., U.K.	70	55.37 N	4.40 W
Irvine, Ky., U.S.	156	37.42 N	83.58 W
Irvinestown	70	54.29 N	7.38 W
Irving	160	32.49 N	96.56 W
Irvington	158	37.53 N	86.17 W
Isaac ≈	120	22.52 S	149.20 E
Isabela (Basilan)	92	6.42 N	121.58 E
Isabela, Cordillera ↗	132	13.45 N	85.15 W
Ísafjörður	66a	66.08 N	23.13 W
Isana (Içana) ≈	138	0.26 N	67.19 W
Isar ≈	72	48.49 N	12.58 E
Ischia	78	40.44 N	13.57 E
Ischia, Isola d' I	78	40.43 N	13.54 E
Ise	90	34.29 N	136.42 E
Isère □⁵	74	45.10 N	5.50 E
Iserlohn	72	51.22 N	7.41 E
Isernia	78	41.36 N	14.14 E
Iset' ≈	82	56.36 N	66.24 E
Iseyin	114	7.58 N	3.36 E
Isfahan → Eşfahān	104	32.40 N	51.38 E
Ishigaki-shima I	88	24.24 N	124.12 E
Ishikari ≈	90a	43.15 N	141.23 E
Ishinomaki	90	38.25 N	141.18 E
Ishpeming	154	46.29 N	87.40 W
Isigny	74	49.19 N	1.06 W
Isil'-Kul'	82	54.55 N	71.16 E
Išim	82	56.09 N	69.27 E
Išim ≈	82	57.45 N	71.12 E
Išimbaj	82	53.28 N	56.02 E
Išimskaja Step' ≃	82	55.00 N	70.00 E
Isiolo	110	0.21 N	37.35 E
Isiro	108	2.47 N	27.37 E
Isisford	120	24.16 S	144.26 E
Iskenderun	104	36.37 N	36.07 E
Iskenderun Körfezi C	104	36.30 N	35.40 E
Iskitim	84	54.38 N	83.18 E
Iskut ≈	146	56.42 N	131.45 W
Isla ≈	70	56.31 N	3.20 W
Islāmābād	100	33.42 N	73.10 E
Island Falls	152	46.00 N	68.16 W
Island Lake	142	53.47 N	94.25 W
Island Park	166	44.24 N	111.19 W
Island Pond	152	44.48 N	71.53 W
Islands, Bay of C	126	35.15 S	174.15 E
Isla Vista	168	34.25 N	119.53 W
Islay I	70	55.46 N	6.10 W
Isle of Hope	156	31.58 N	81.05 W
Isle of Man □²	64	54.15 N	4.30 W
Isle of Palms	156	32.47 N	79.48 W
Isle of Wight □⁶	70	50.40 N	1.20 W
Isleta	164	34.55 N	106.42 W
Ismailia → Al-Ismā'īlīyah	112	30.35 N	32.16 E
Ismaning	72	48.14 N	11.41 E
Isnā	112	25.18 N	32.33 E
Isna	72	43.41 N	13.22 E
Isojoki	68	62.07 N	21.58 E
Isokyrö	68	63.00 N	22.19 E
isparta	64	37.46 N	30.33 E
Israel □¹	100	31.30 N	35.00 E
Issigeac	74	44.44 N	0.36 E
Issoire	74	45.33 N	3.15 E
Issoudun	74	46.57 N	1.59 E
Is-sur-Tille	74	47.31 N	5.06 E
Issyk-Kul', Ozero	82	42.25 N	77.15 E
İstanbul	64	41.01 N	28.58 E
İstanbul □³	64	41.01 N	28.58 E
İstanbul Boğazı (Bosporus) Ü	80	41.06 N	29.04 E
Isto, Mount ∧	146	69.12 N	143.48 W
Istra	78	55.55 N	36.52 E
Itá	134	25.29 S	57.21 W
Itabaiana, Bra.	134	7.20 S	35.20 W
Itabaiana, Bra.	134	10.41 S	37.26 W
Itaberaí	134	16.02 S	49.48 W
Itabira	134	19.37 S	43.13 W
Itabuna	134	14.48 S	39.16 W
Itacoatiara	138	3.08 S	58.25 W
Itaguí	134	6.10 N	75.36 W
Itaituba	134	4.17 S	55.59 W
Itajaí	140	26.53 S	48.39 W
Itajubá	134	22.26 S	45.27 W
Italy (Italia) □¹	64	42.50 N	12.50 E
Itami	90	34.46 N	135.25 E
Itapecuru-Mirim	134	3.24 S	44.20 W
Itapemirim	134	21.01 S	40.50 W
Itaperuna	134	21.12 S	41.54 W
Itapetinga	134	15.15 S	40.15 W
Itapetininga	134	23.36 S	48.03 W
Itapeva	134	23.58 S	48.52 W
Itapicuru ≈, Bra.	134	2.52 S	44.12 W
Itapicuru ≈, Bra.	134	11.47 S	37.32 W
Itapúa □⁵	140	26.50 S	55.50 W
Itaquari	134	20.20 S	40.22 W
Itaqui	134	29.08 S	56.33 W
Itararé	134	24.07 S	49.20 W
Itārsi	102	22.37 N	77.46 E
Itaúna	134	20.04 S	44.34 W
Itbayat Island I	92	20.45 N	121.50 E
Itchen Lake ⊜	142	65.33 N	112.50 W
Ithaca, Mich., U.S.	154	43.18 N	84.36 W
Ithaca, N.Y., U.S.	152	42.27 N	76.30 W
Itháki I	80	38.24 N	20.42 E
Ita Bena	158	33.30 N	90.20 W
Itu	138	23.16 S	47.19 W
Ituango	138	7.04 N	75.45 W
Ituí ≈	138	4.38 S	70.19 W
Ituiutaba	134	18.58 S	49.28 W
Itumbiara	134	18.25 S	49.13 W
Ituri ≈	108	1.40 N	27.01 E
Iturup, Ostrov (Etorofu-tō) I	90a	44.54 N	147.30 E
Ituxi ≈	134	7.18 S	64.51 W
Itzehoe	72	53.55 N	9.31 E
Iuka	158	34.49 N	88.11 W
Iul'tin	146	67.50 N	178.48 W
Ivaí ≈	140	23.18 S	53.42 W
Ivalo	68	68.42 N	27.30 E
Ivangorod	86	59.24 N	28.10 E
Ivangrad	82	42.50 N	19.52 E
Ivanhoe, Austl.	120	32.54 S	144.18 E
Ivanhoe, Calif., U.S.	168	36.23 N	119.13 W
Ivano	86	54.40 N	37.57 E
Ivano-Frankovsk	86	48.55 N	24.43 E
Ivanovo	86	57.00 N	40.59 E
Ivdel'	82	60.42 N	60.24 E
Ivnja	86	51.03 N	36.07 E
Ivory Coast □¹	106	8.00 N	5.00 W
Ivrea	78	45.28 N	7.52 E
Ivujivik	142	62.24 N	77.55 W
Ivywild	162	39.49 N	104.51 W
Iwaki (Taira)	90	37.03 N	140.55 E
Iwakuni	90	34.09 N	132.11 E
Iwamizawa	90a	43.12 N	141.46 E
Iwo	114	7.38 N	4.11 E
Ixmiquilpan	130	20.29 N	99.14 W
Ixtlán del Río	130	21.02 N	104.22 W
Izberbaš	82	42.33 N	47.52 E
Izbica	72	54.42 N	17.26 E
Izd'oškovo	86	55.08 N	33.37 E
Izegem	72	50.55 N	3.12 E
Iževsk	86	56.51 N	53.14 E
Ižma ≈	66	65.19 N	52.54 E
Izmail	64	45.21 N	28.50 E
İzmir	64	38.25 N	27.09 E
İzmit (Kocaeli)	64	40.46 N	29.55 E
Iznajan, Embalse de ⊜¹	76	37.15 N	4.30 W
Izoplit	86	56.30 N	36.12 E
Izozog, Bañados de ⊜¹	134	18.48 S	62.10 W
Izsák	72	46.48 N	19.22 E
Izúcar de Matamoros	130	18.36 N	98.28 W
Izu'm	82	49.12 N	37.19 E
Izumo	90	35.22 N	132.46 E
Izu-shotō II	90	34.30 N	139.30 E
Izvestij CIK, Ostrova II	84	75.55 N	82.30 E
Jalutorovsk	82	56.40 N	66.18 E
Jamaica □¹	128	18.15 N	77.30 W
Jamaica Channel Ü	128	18.00 N	75.30 W
Jamal, Poluostrov ⊁¹	84	70.00 N	70.00 E
Jamalo-Neneckij Nacional'nyj Okrug □⁸	66	66.30 N	64.00 E
Jamálpur	102	25.18 N	86.30 E
Jamame	110	0.04 N	42.46 E
Jamantau, Gora ∧	82	54.15 N	58.06 E
Jamarovka	84	50.38 N	110.16 E
Jambes	72	50.26 N	4.52 E
Jambol	64	42.29 N	26.30 E
Jamdena, Pulau I	124	7.36 S	131.25 E
James ≈	162	42.52 N	97.18 W
James Bay C	142	53.30 N	80.30 W
James City	156	35.05 N	77.02 W
James Price Point ⊁	122	17.30 S	122.08 E
James Range ↗	122	24.06 S	132.30 E
James Ross, Cape ⊁	122	74.40 N	114.25 W
James Ross Strait Ü	142	69.40 N	95.30 W
Jamestown, Austl.	120	33.12 S	138.36 E
Jamestown, N. Dak., U.S.	162	46.54 N	98.42 W
Jamestown, N.Y., U.S.	152	42.06 N	79.14 W
Jamestown, Ohio, U.S.	152	39.39 N	83.44 W
Jamestown, Tenn., U.S.	158	36.26 N	84.57 W
Jamiltepec	130	16.17 N	97.49 W
Jamm	86	58.26 N	28.03 E
Jammu	100	32.42 N	74.52 E
Jammu and Kashmir □²	100	35.00 N	76.00 E
Jämnagar	102	22.28 N	70.04 E
Jamnotri	100	31.01 N	78.28 E
Jämsä	68	61.52 N	25.12 E
Jamshedpur	102	22.48 N	86.11 E
Jämtland □⁶	68	63.00 N	14.40 E
Jämtlands Län □⁶	68	63.00 N	14.40 E
Jamuna ≈	102	23.51 N	89.45 E
Jana ≈	84	71.31 N	136.32 E
Janaúca, Ilha I	134	4.00 S	50.10 W
Janesville, Minn., U.S.	154	44.07 N	93.42 W
Janesville, Wis., U.S.	154	42.41 N	89.01 W
Jangarej	86	68.46 N	61.25 E
Jangīyul'	102	41.07 N	69.03 E
Jangipur	102	24.28 N	88.03 E
Jánoshalma	72	46.18 N	19.20 E
Jánosháza	72	47.08 N	17.10 E
Janovičí	86	55.17 N	30.42 E
Jánoshida	72	47.23 N	20.10 E
Janskij	84	68.28 N	134.48 E
Janskij Zaliv C	84	71.50 N	136.00 E
Jantarnyj	86	54.52 N	19.57 E
Januária	134	15.29 S	44.22 W
Janzé	74	47.58 N	1.30 W
Japan □¹	86	40.00 N	135.00 E
Japan, Sea of ⊤²	86	40.00 N	135.00 E
Japen, Pulau I	124	1.45 S	136.15 E
Japtiksal'a	86	69.21 N	72.32 E
Japurá (Caquetá) ≈	138	3.08 S	64.46 W
Jaraguá do Sul	140	26.29 S	49.04 W
Jarama ≈	76	40.02 N	3.39 W
Jaransk	86	57.19 N	47.52 E
Jarbidge ≈	166	42.19 N	115.39 W
Jarcevo	86	55.03 N	32.41 E
Jardines de la Reina II	132	20.45 N	78.50 W
Jarega	86	63.27 N	53.26 E
Jarensk	86	62.11 N	49.02 E
Jargeau	74	47.52 N	2.07 E
Jari ≈	134	1.09 S	51.54 W
Jarmen	72	53.55 N	13.20 E
Jarnac	74	45.41 N	0.10 W
Jarocin	72	51.59 N	17.31 E
Jaromer	72	50.21 N	15.55 E
Jaroslavl'	86	57.37 N	39.52 E
Jar-Sale	84	66.50 N	70.50 E
Järvelä	68	60.52 N	25.17 E
Järvenpää	68	60.28 N	25.06 E
Jaša Tomić	80	45.27 N	20.51 E
Jäsk	100	25.38 N	57.46 E
Jasło	72	49.45 N	21.29 E
Jasnogorsk	86	54.29 N	37.42 E
Jasnyj	84	53.17 N	127.59 E
Jason Islands II	136	51.00 S	61.00 W
Jasonville	158	39.10 N	87.12 W
Jasper, Alta., Can.	148	52.53 N	118.05 W
Jasper, Ala., U.S.	158	33.50 N	87.16 W
Jasper, Fla., U.S.	156	30.31 N	82.57 W
Jasper, Ga., U.S.	156	34.28 N	84.26 W
Jasper, Ind., U.S.	158	38.23 N	86.56 W
Jasper, Tenn., U.S.	158	35.04 N	85.38 W
Jasper, Tex., U.S.	160	30.55 N	94.01 W
Jászapáti	72	47.30 N	20.10 E
Jászberény	72	47.30 N	19.55 E
Jat, Uad el V	106	26.15 N	13.03 W
Jatai	134	17.53 S	51.43 W
Játiva	76	38.59 N	0.31 W
Jatni	102	20.10 N	85.42 E
Jaú	134	22.18 S	48.33 W
Jauaperi ≈	138	1.26 S	61.35 W
Jauja	138	11.46 S	75.28 W
Jaunjelgava	86	56.37 N	25.05 E
Jaunpur	102	25.44 N	82.41 E
Java → Djawa I	96	7.30 S	110.00 E
Javari (Yavari) ≈	134	4.21 S	70.02 W
Javas	86	54.29 N	42.51 E
Java Sea → Djawa, Laut ⊤²	92	5.00 S	110.00 E
Jawor	72	51.03 N	16.11 E
Jay, Fla., U.S.	158	30.57 N	87.09 W
Jay, Okla., U.S.	160	36.25 N	94.48 W
Jayb, Wādī al- V	104	30.58 N	35.24 E
Jaz Mūriān, Hāmūn-e ⊜	100	27.20 N	58.55 E
Jeanerette	158	29.55 N	91.40 W
Jebba	114	9.08 N	4.49 E
Jedburgh	70	55.29 N	2.34 W
Jeddore Lake ⊜¹	150	48.03 N	55.55 W
Jędrzejów	72	50.39 N	20.18 E
Jefferson, Ga., U.S.	156	34.07 N	83.35 W
Jefferson, Iowa, U.S.	162	42.01 N	94.23 W
Jefferson, La., U.S.	158	29.58 N	90.09 W
Jefferson, Ohio, U.S.	152	41.44 N	80.46 W
Jefferson, S. Dak., U.S.	162	42.36 N	96.34 W
Jefferson, Tex., U.S.	160	32.45 N	94.21 W
Jefferson, Wis., U.S.	154	43.00 N	88.48 W
Jefferson, Mount ∧	166	44.40 N	121.47 W
Jefferson City, Mo., U.S.	162	38.34 N	92.10 W
Jefferson City, Tenn., U.S.	156	36.07 N	83.30 W
Jeffersonton	152	38.38 N	77.54 W
Jeffersontown	152	38.12 N	85.35 W
Jeffersonville, Ga., U.S.	156	32.41 N	83.34 W
Jeffersonville, Ind., U.S.	158	38.17 N	85.44 W
Jeffersonville, Ohio, U.S.	152	39.39 N	83.34 W
Jefremov	86	53.09 N	38.07 E
Jegorjevsk	86	55.23 N	39.02 E
Jejsk	86	46.42 N	38.16 E
Jeju → Cheju	88	33.31 N	126.32 E
Jekabpils	86	56.29 N	25.51 E
Jekaterinu, Proliv Ü	90a	43.55 N	145.45 E
Jekyll Island I	156	31.04 N	81.25 W
Jelabuga	66	55.47 N	52.04 E
Jelancy	84	52.49 N	106.25 E
Jelec	86	52.37 N	38.30 E
Jelenia Góra (Hirschberg)	72	50.55 N	15.46 E
Jelenski	86	53.33 N	34.16 E
Jelgava	86	56.39 N	23.42 E
Jelizavety, Mys ⊁	84	54.24 N	142.42 E
Jelizovo	84	53.24 N	158.27 E
Jellico	156	36.35 N	84.07 W
Jelling	68	55.45 N	9.26 E
Jel'n'a	86	54.35 N	33.11 E
Jeloguj ≈	84	63.13 N	87.45 E
Jemanželinsk	82	54.45 N	61.20 E
Jemca	84	63.04 N	40.20 E
Jemez Springs	164	35.46 N	106.42 W
Jena, D.D.R.	72	50.56 N	11.35 E
Jena, La., U.S.	158	31.41 N	92.08 W
Jenašimskij Polkan, Gora ∧	84	59.50 N	92.52 E
Jenbach	72	47.24 N	11.47 E
Jenisej ≈	84	71.50 N	82.40 E
Jenisejsk	84	58.27 N	92.10 E
Jenisejskij Kr'až □⁹	84	59.00 N	93.00 E
Jenisejskij Zaliv C	84	72.30 N	80.00 E
Jenkins, Mount ∧	122	25.36 S	129.41 E
Jenkintown	152	40.06 N	75.08 W
Jenks	160	36.01 N	95.58 W
Jennersdorf	72	46.57 N	16.08 E
Jennings, Fla., U.S.	156	30.36 N	83.06 W
Jennings, Kans., U.S.	162	39.41 N	100.18 W
Jennings, La., U.S.	158	30.13 N	92.39 W
Jensen Beach	156	27.15 N	80.14 W
Jens Munk Island I	142	69.42 N	79.30 W
Jeparit	120	36.09 S	141.59 E
Jequié	134	13.51 S	40.05 W
Jequitinhonha ≈	134	15.51 S	38.53 W
Jerada	106	34.17 N	2.13 W
Jerbogačon	84	61.16 N	108.00 E
Jérémie	132	18.39 N	74.08 W
Jeremoabo	134	10.04 S	38.21 W
Jerevan	104	40.11 N	44.30 E
Jerez de García Salinas	130	22.39 N	103.00 W
Jerez de la Frontera	76	36.41 N	6.08 W
Jerez de los Caballeros	76	38.19 N	6.46 W
Jergeni □²	64	47.00 N	44.00 E
Jericho → Arīhā	104	31.52 N	35.27 E
Jerilderie	120	35.22 S	145.44 E
Jermolino	86	55.12 N	36.36 E
Jerofej Pavlovič	84	53.58 N	121.01 E
Jerome	166	42.43 N	114.31 W
Jersey □²	64	49.15 N	2.10 W
Jersey City	152	40.44 N	74.02 W
Jersey Shore	152	41.12 N	77.16 W
Jerseyville	158	39.07 N	90.20 W
Jeršov	82	51.20 N	48.17 E
Jerusalem → Yerushalayim	104	31.46 N	35.14 E
Jervis Bay C	120	35.05 S	150.44 E
Jervis Range ↗	122	22.38 S	136.05 E
Jesenice	78	46.27 N	14.04 E
Jesi → Iesi	78	43.31 N	13.14 E
Jesil'	82	51.58 N	66.24 E
Jessej	84	68.29 N	102.10 E
Jesselton → Kota Kinabalu	96	5.58 N	116.04 E
Jessen	72	51.47 N	12.58 E
Jessentuki	64	44.03 N	42.51 E
Jessheim	68	60.09 N	11.11 E
Jessore	102	23.10 N	89.13 E
Jessup	152	41.28 N	75.34 W
Jesup	156	31.36 N	81.53 W
Jesús Carranza	130	17.26 N	95.02 W
Jesús María	140	31.00 S	64.06 W
Jeumont	74	50.18 N	4.06 E
Jever	72	53.34 N	7.54 E
Jevlach	104	40.36 N	47.09 E
Jevnaker	68	60.15 N	10.28 E
Jevpatorija	64	45.12 N	33.22 E
Jewell	162	39.40 N	98.10 W
Jewell Ridge	156	37.11 N	81.48 W
Jewett City	152	41.36 N	71.59 W
Jeziorany	72	53.58 N	20.46 E
Jhābua	102	22.46 N	74.35 E
Jhālāwār	102	24.36 N	76.09 E
Jhang Maghiāna	102	31.16 N	72.19 E
Jhānsi	102	25.26 N	78.35 E
Jhārsuguda	102	21.51 N	84.02 E
Jhelum	102	32.56 N	73.44 E
Jhelum ≈	102	31.12 N	72.08 E
Jhunjhunu	102	28.08 N	75.24 E
Jiali	88	30.47 N	93.24 E
Jialing Jiang ≈	88	30.02 N	106.18 E
Jiamusi	88	46.50 N	130.21 E
Ji'an	88	27.07 N	114.58 E
Jianchuan	88	26.34 N	99.53 E
Jiangda	88	31.27 N	98.15 E
Jiangjin	88	29.17 N	106.15 E
Jiangkou	88	23.31 N	110.17 E
Jiangmen	88	22.35 N	113.05 E
Jiangsu □⁴	88	33.00 N	120.00 E
Jiangxi □⁴	88	28.00 N	116.00 E
Jianou	88	27.03 N	118.19 E
Jiaohe	88	43.42 N	127.19 E
Jiaozuo	88	35.15 N	113.16 E
Jiashan	88	32.49 N	118.07 E
Jiashun Hu ⊜	102	35.13 N	86.05 E
Jiawang	88	34.26 N	117.27 E
Jiaxing	88	30.46 N	120.45 E
Jičín	72	50.26 N	15.21 E
Jidda → Juddah	100	21.30 N	39.12 E
Jieznas	86	54.36 N	24.10 E
Jiggalong Mission	122	23.25 S	120.47 E
Jihlava	72	49.24 N	15.36 E
Jihočeský Kraj □⁴	72	49.00 N	14.30 E
Jihomoravský Kraj □⁴	72	49.05 N	16.40 E
Jijiga	108	9.22 N	42.47 E
Jijona	76	38.32 N	0.30 W
Jilemutu	88	52.14 N	120.47 E
Jilib	110	0.28 N	42.50 E
Jilin	88	43.51 N	126.33 E
Jilin □⁴	88	44.00 N	126.00 E
Jima	108	7.36 N	36.52 E
Jimbolia	80	45.47 N	20.43 E
Jim Thorpe	152	40.52 N	75.45 W
Jinan (Tsinan)	88	36.40 N	116.57 E
Jincheng	88	35.30 N	112.50 E
Jindřichův Hradec	72	49.09 N	15.01 E
Jingdezhen	88	29.16 N	117.11 E
Jinggangshan	88	26.36 N	114.05 E
Jinghong	88	22.01 N	100.48 E
Jingshan	88	31.45 N	111.22 E
Jingxian	88	23.08 N	109.22 E
Jinhua	88	29.07 N	119.39 E
Jining, Nei., China	88	41.06 N	113.06 E
Jining, Zhg., China	88	35.25 N	116.35 E
Jinja	110	0.26 N	33.12 E
Jinning (Jiukuang)	88	24.41 N	102.36 E
Jinotega	132	13.06 N	86.00 W
Jinotepe	132	11.51 N	86.12 W
Jinshi	88	29.40 N	111.50 E
Jinxi	88	40.46 N	120.50 E
Jinxian	88	45.18 N	125.03 E
Jiparaná ≈	138	8.03 S	62.52 W
Jipijapa	138	1.20 S	80.35 W
Jiquilpan [de Juárez]	130	19.59 N	102.43 W
Jishou	88	28.18 N	109.43 E
Jitai	88	44.01 N	89.28 E
Jiujiang	88	29.44 N	116.00 E
Jiulianshan ↗	88	24.41 N	114.46 E
Jiuquan	88	39.44 N	98.30 E
Jixi	88	45.17 N	130.59 E
Jixian	88	40.02 N	117.24 E
Joaçaba	140	27.10 S	51.30 W
João Pessoa	134	7.07 S	34.53 W
Joaquín V. González	140	25.05 S	64.11 W
Job Peak ∧	168	39.35 N	118.14 W
Jobson (Vera)	140	29.30 S	60.10 W
Jódar	76	37.50 N	3.21 W
Jodhpur	102	26.17 N	73.02 E
Joensuu	68	62.36 N	29.46 E
Joffre, Mount ∧	148	50.32 N	115.13 W
Jõgeva	86	58.45 N	26.24 E
Jogjakarta	96	7.48 S	110.22 E
Johannesburg	116	26.15 S	28.00 E
Johanngeorgenstadt	72	50.26 N	12.43 E
Johar	108	2.48 N	45.33 E
John Day	166	44.25 N	118.57 W
John Day ≈	166	45.44 N	120.39 W
John o' Groats	70	58.38 N	3.05 W
Johnson, Kans., U.S.	162	37.34 N	101.45 W
Johnson, Vt., U.S.	152	44.38 N	72.41 W
Johnsonburg	152	41.29 N	78.41 W
Johnson City, N.Y., U.S.	152	42.07 N	75.57 W
Johnson City, Tenn., U.S.	156	36.19 N	82.21 W
Johnson City, Tex., U.S.	160	30.17 N	98.25 W
Johnston City	158	37.49 N	88.56 W
Johnstown, Colo., U.S.	164	40.20 N	104.54 W
Johnstown, N.Y., U.S.	152	43.00 N	74.22 W
Johnstown, Ohio, U.S.	152	40.09 N	82.41 W
Johnstown, Pa., U.S.	152	40.20 N	78.55 W
Johore Bahru	96	1.27 N	103.45 E
Joigny	74	47.59 N	3.24 E
Joinville	140	26.18 S	48.50 W
Joinville	74	48.27 N	5.08 E
Jokela	68	60.44 N	25.02 E
Jokioinen	68	60.49 N	23.28 E
Joliet, Ill., U.S.	154	41.32 N	88.05 W
Joliet, Mont., U.S.	166	45.29 N	108.58 W
Joliette	152	46.01 N	73.27 W
Jolo	98	6.03 N	121.00 E
Jolo Island I	98	6.00 N	121.10 E
Jonava	86	55.05 N	24.17 E
Jonesboro, Ark., U.S.	158	35.50 N	90.42 W
Jonesboro, Ga., U.S.	156	33.32 N	84.21 W
Jonesboro, Ind., U.S.	158	40.29 N	85.38 W
Jonesboro, La., U.S.	158	32.14 N	92.43 W
Jones Mill	158	34.27 N	92.50 W
Jonesport	152	44.32 N	67.36 W
Jones Sound Ü	142	76.00 N	85.00 W
Jonesville, La., U.S.	158	31.38 N	91.49 W
Jonesville, Mich., U.S.	154	41.59 N	84.40 W
Jonesville, N.C., U.S.	156	36.15 N	80.51 W
Jonesville, Va., U.S.	156	36.41 N	83.07 W
Jönköping	68	57.47 N	14.11 E
Jönköpings Län □⁶	68	57.30 N	14.30 E
Jonquière	152	48.24 N	71.15 W
Jonzac	74	45.27 N	0.26 W
Joplin	162	37.06 N	94.31 W
Jordan, Minn., U.S.	154	44.40 N	93.37 W
Jordan, Mont., U.S.	166	47.19 N	106.55 W
Jordan □¹	100	31.00 N	36.00 E
Jordan ≈	104	31.46 N	35.33 E
Jordan Creek ≈	166	42.52 N	117.38 W
Jordanów	72	49.40 N	19.50 E
Jordan Valley	166	42.58 N	117.03 W
Jordet	68	61.25 N	12.09 E
Jorhāt	102	26.45 N	94.13 E
Jørpeland	68	59.01 N	6.03 E
Jos	114	9.55 N	8.53 E
José Batlle y Ordóñez	140	33.28 S	55.07 W
José de San Martín	136	44.04 S	70.26 W
Joseph, Lac ⊜	142	52.45 N	65.15 W
Joseph Bonaparte Gulf C	124	14.15 S	128.30 E
Joseph City	164	34.57 N	110.20 W
Joshua Tree	168	34.08 N	116.19 W
Jostedalsbreen ⊠	68	61.40 N	7.00 E
Josselin	74	47.57 N	2.33 W
Joutsa	68	61.44 N	26.07 E
Joutseno	68	61.06 N	28.30 E
Juan Aldama	130	24.19 N	103.21 W
Juan de Fuca, Strait of Ü	148	48.18 N	124.00 W
Juan de Nova, Île I	110	17.03 S	42.45 E
Juan Fernández, Islas II	136	33.00 S	80.00 W
Juan José Castelli	140	25.37 S	60.57 W
Juan L. Lacaze	140	34.26 S	57.27 W
Juárez, Arg.	140	37.40 S	59.49 W
Juárez → Ciudad Juárez, Méx.	130	31.44 N	106.29 W
Juàzeiro	134	9.25 S	40.30 W
Juàzeiro do Norte	134	7.12 S	39.20 W
Jūbā	108	4.51 N	31.37 E
Juba ≈	108	0.12 N	42.40 E
Juby, Cap ⊁	106	27.58 N	12.55 W
Júcar ≈	76	39.09 N	0.14 W
Juchitán [de Zaragoza]	130	16.26 N	95.01 W
Juddah (Jidda)	100	21.30 N	39.12 E
Judenburg	72	47.10 N	14.40 E
Judith Gap	166	46.41 N	109.45 W
Judoma ≈	84	59.08 N	135.06 E
Judson	156	34.50 N	82.27 W
Judsonia	158	35.16 N	91.38 W
Jugon	74	48.25 N	2.19 W
Jugorskij Šar, Proliv Ü	82	69.45 N	60.35 E
Juigalpa	132	12.05 N	85.24 W
Juillac	74	45.19 N	1.19 E
Juiz de Fora	134	21.45 S	43.20 W
Jujuy → San Salvador de Jujuy	140	24.10 S	65.20 W
Jujuy □⁴	140	23.00 S	66.00 W
Jukagirskoje Ploskogorje ↗¹	84	66.00 N	155.00 E
Jukte	84	63.26 N	105.31 E
Julaca	134	20.55 S	66.44 W
Juliaca	138	15.30 S	70.08 W
Julian Alps ↗	78	46.20 N	14.05 E
Julianehåb	142	60.43 N	46.01 W
Jullundur	102	31.19 N	75.34 E
Jumbo	156	32.16 N	95.22 W
Jumentos Cays II	132	23.00 N	75.50 W
Jumet	72	50.26 N	4.25 E
Jumilla	76	38.29 N	1.19 W
Junàgadh	102	21.31 N	70.28 E
Junction, Tex., U.S.	160	30.29 N	99.46 W
Junction, Utah, U.S.	164	38.14 N	112.13 W
Junction City, Kans., U.S.	162	39.01 N	96.50 W
Junction City, Ky., U.S.	156	37.35 N	84.48 W
Junction City, Oreg., U.S.	166	44.13 N	123.12 W
Jundiaí	134	23.11 S	46.52 W
Juneau, Alaska, U.S.	146	58.18 N	134.25 W
Juneau, Wis., U.S.	154	43.24 N	88.42 W
Jungfrau ∧	74	46.32 N	7.58 E
Junín, Arg.	140	34.35 S	60.57 W
Junín, Lago de ⊜	138	11.00 S	76.05 W
Junín de los Andes	136	39.56 S	71.05 W
Juniville	74	49.24 N	4.23 E
Junsele	68	63.41 N	16.54 E
Juntura	166	43.45 N	118.04 W
Jupiter	156	26.56 N	80.05 W
Jupiter ≈	150	49.29 N	63.37 W
Jur ≈	108	8.45 N	29.15 E
Jura □⁵	74	46.45 N	5.45 E
Jura ↗	74	46.45 N	6.30 E
Jura I	70	56.00 N	5.50 W
Jurbarkas	86	55.05 N	22.46 E
Jūrmala	86	56.58 N	23.34 E
Jurty	84	56.07 N	99.00 E
Juruá ≈	138	2.37 S	65.44 W
Juruena ≈	134	7.20 S	58.03 W
Jur'uzan'	82	55.25 N	58.26 E
Jussey	74	47.49 N	5.54 E
Justo Daract	140	33.52 S	65.11 W
Jutland → Jylland ⊁¹	68	56.00 N	9.15 E
Juva	68	61.54 N	27.51 E
Juwara	108	18.55 N	57.17 E
Juža	86	56.35 N	42.01 E
Južno-Jenisejskij	84	58.48 N	94.39 E
Južno-Sachalinsk	84	46.58 N	142.42 E
Južno-Ural'sk	82	54.26 N	61.15 E
Južnyj, Mys ⊁	84	57.45 N	156.45 E
Južnyj Bug ≈	64	46.59 N	31.58 E
Jyväskylä	68	62.14 N	25.44 E

K

Name	Page	Lat	Long
K2 → Godwin Austen ∧	102	35.53 N	76.30 E
Kaachka	102	37.21 N	59.36 E
Kaalaea	170c	21.28 N	157.51 W
Kaap Plato ↗¹	116	28.30 S	23.57 E
Kaapstad → Cape Town	116	33.55 S	18.22 E
Kaavi	68	62.59 N	28.30 E
Kabaena, Pulau I	96	5.15 S	121.55 E
Kabale	110	1.15 S	30.00 E
Kabalo	110	6.03 S	26.55 E
Kabambare	110	4.42 S	27.43 E
Kabinda	110	6.08 S	24.29 E
Kabīr Kūh ↗	104	33.25 N	46.45 E
Kabompo ≈	110	14.10 S	23.11 E
Kabongo	110	7.19 S	25.35 E
Kābul	100	34.31 N	69.12 E
Kabwe (Broken Hill)	110	14.27 S	28.27 E
Kachemak Bay C	146	59.35 N	151.30 W
Kachovskoje Vodochranilišče ⊜¹	64	47.25 N	34.10 E
Kačug	84	53.58 N	105.52 E
Kadaňai (Kadaney) ≈	102	31.02 N	66.09 E
Kadaney (Kadaňai) ≈	102	31.02 N	66.09 E
Kadan Kyun I	94	12.30 N	98.22 E
Kade	114	6.06 N	0.50 W
Kadei ≈	108	3.31 N	16.05 E
Kadijevka	64	48.34 N	38.40 E
Kadina	120	33.58 S	137.43 E
Kadja, Ouadi (Wādī Kaja) V	112	12.02 N	22.28 E
Kadom	86	54.34 N	42.30 E
Kaduna	114	10.33 N	7.27 E
Kaduna ≈	114	8.45 N	5.45 E
Kadugli	112	11.01 N	29.43 E
Kadykčan	84	63.02 N	146.50 E
Kadžerom	66	64.41 N	55.54 E
Kaédi	106	16.09 N	13.30 W
Kaesŏng	88	37.59 N	126.33 E
Kafia Kingi	108	9.16 N	24.25 E
Kafu ≈	110	1.08 N	31.05 E
Kagami Island I	110	5.58 S	28.55 E
Kagera ≈	110	0.57 S	31.47 E
Kagoshima	90	31.36 N	130.33 E
Kahajan ≈	96	3.20 S	114.04 E
Kahama	110	3.50 S	32.36 E
Kahemba	110	7.17 S	19.00 E
Kahoka	154	40.25 N	91.43 W
Kahoku ≈	170c	21.41 N	157.57 W
Kahului	170a	20.54 N	156.28 W
Kai, Kepulauan II	124	5.35 S	132.45 E
Kaiapoi	126	43.23 S	172.39 E
Kai Besar I	124	5.35 S	133.00 E
Kaieteur Fall ⨽	138	5.10 N	59.28 W
Kaifeng	88	34.51 N	114.21 E
Kai Ketjil I	124	5.45 S	132.40 E
Kaikohe	126	35.25 S	173.48 E
Kaikoura	126	42.24 S	173.41 E
Kaili	88	26.34 N	107.58 E
Kailu	88	43.36 N	121.14 E
Kailua	170c	21.24 N	157.44 W
Kailua Kona	170d	19.39 N	155.59 W
Kaimakchalán ∧	80	40.58 N	21.48 E
Kaimana	124	3.39 S	133.45 E
Kaimanawa Mountains ↗	126	39.15 S	175.55 E
Kaiserslautern	72	49.14 N	7.46 E
Kaišiadorys	86	54.52 N	24.27 E
Kaitaia	126	35.07 S	173.15 E
Kaiwi Channel Ü	170a	21.15 N	157.30 W
Kajaani	68	64.14 N	27.41 E
Kajan ≈	96	2.55 N	117.35 E
Kajnar	82	49.12 N	77.25 E
Kajuagung	96	3.24 S	104.50 E
Kakamas	116	28.45 S	20.33 E
Kakamega	110	0.17 N	34.45 E
Kake	146	56.59 N	133.57 W
Kākināda	100	16.57 N	82.14 E
Kakisa Lake ⊜	142	60.56 N	117.40 W
Kakogawa	90	34.46 N	134.51 E
Kaktovik	146	70.08 N	143.37 W
Kalabahi	96	8.13 S	124.31 E
Kalabo	110	14.58 S	22.40 E
Kalač	64	50.25 N	41.01 E
Kalač-na-Donu	64	48.43 N	43.31 E
Kaladan ≈	94	20.09 N	92.57 E
Kalahari Desert ⊹²	116	24.00 S	21.30 E
Kalajoki	68	64.15 N	23.57 E
Kalakan	84	55.08 N	116.45 E
Kalámai	80	37.04 N	22.07 E
Kalamazoo	154	42.17 N	85.35 W
Kalamazoo ≈	154	42.40 N	86.10 W
Kalannie	122	30.22 S	117.07 E
Kalao, Pulau I	96	7.18 S	120.58 E
Kalaotoa, Pulau I	96	7.22 S	121.47 E
Kalašnikovo	86	57.17 N	35.13 E
Kalat	102	29.02 N	66.35 E
Kalaupapa	170b	21.12 N	156.59 W
Kal'azin	86	57.15 N	37.52 E
Kalb, Ra's al- ⊁	100	14.02 N	48.41 E
Kalemi (Albertville)	110	5.56 S	29.12 E
Kalevala	66	65.13 N	31.08 E
Kalewa	94	23.11 N	94.18 E
Kalgan → Zhangjiakou	88	40.50 N	114.53 E
Kalgoorlie	122	30.45 S	121.28 E
Kāli (Sārda) ≈	102	29.05 N	80.40 E
Kalima	110	2.34 S	26.37 E
Kalimantan → Borneo I	96	0.30 N	114.00 E
Kálimnos I	80	36.59 N	26.59 E
Kálimnos I	80	36.57 N	27.00 E
Kalinin	86	56.52 N	35.55 E
Kaliningrad, S.S.S.R.	86	54.43 N	20.30 E
Kaliningrad (Königsberg), S.S.S.R.	86	54.43 N	20.30 E
Kalinkovici	86	52.08 N	29.20 E
Kalinovka	64	49.29 N	28.31 E
Kalispell	166	48.12 N	114.19 W
Kalisz	72	51.46 N	18.05 E
Kalix ≈	68	65.50 N	23.11 E
Kalkaska	154	44.44 N	85.10 W
Kallinge	68	56.14 N	15.17 E
Kallsjön ⊜	68	63.35 N	13.00 E
Kalmar	68	56.40 N	16.22 E
Kalmar Län □⁶	68	57.05 N	16.10 E
Kalmarsund Ü	68	56.40 N	16.25 E
Kalmykovo	64	49.05 N	51.47 E
Kalomo	110	17.02 S	26.29 E
Kalona	154	41.29 N	91.43 W

Name	Page	Lat °′	Long °′
Kalpeni Island I	100	10.05 N	73.38 E
Kalskag	146	61.30 N	160.23 W
Kalsūbai ∧	100	19.36 N	73.43 E
Kaltag	146	64.20 N	158.44 W
Kaltan	84	53.30 N	87.17 E
Kaluga	86	54.31 N	36.16 E
Kalumba, Mount ∧	120	31.49 S	146.22 E
Kalumburu	124	14.18 S	126.39 E
Kałuszyn	72	52.13 N	21.49 E
Kalvåg	68	61.46 N	4.53 E
Kalvarija	86	54.21 N	23.14 E
Kälviä	68	63.52 N	23.26 E
Kalwang	72	47.26 N	14.46 E
Kalyān	100	19.15 N	73.08 E
Kama ≃	66	55.45 N	52.00 E
Kamaishi	90	39.16 N	141.53 E
Kamakura	90	35.19 N	139.33 E
Kamālia	102	30.44 N	72.39 E
Kamarān I	100	15.21 N	42.34 E
Kamarang ≃	138	5.53 N	60.35 W
Kamas	164	40.38 N	111.17 W
Kamay	160	33.51 N	98.48 W
Kambarka	82	56.17 N	54.12 E
Kamčatka ≃	84	56.15 N	162.30 E
Kamčatka, Poluostrov ≻[1]	84	56.00 N	160.00 E
Kamčatskij Zaliv C	84	55.35 N	162.21 E
Kamen', Gora ∧	84	69.06 N	94.48 E
Kamenec	86	52.24 N	23.49 E
Kamenec-Podol'skij	64	48.41 N	26.36 E
Kamenka	66	65.54 N	44.05 E
Kamen'-na-Obi	84	53.47 N	81.20 E
Kamennogorsk	66	60.58 N	29.07 E
Kamenskoje	84	62.30 N	166.12 E
Kamensk-Ural'skij	82	56.28 N	61.54 E
Kamenz	72	51.16 N	14.06 E
Kāmet ∧	102	30.54 N	79.37 E
Kamiah	166	46.14 N	116.02 W
Kamienna Góra	72	50.47 N	16.01 E
Kamieńsk	72	51.12 N	19.30 E
Kamilukuak Lake ⊜	142	62.22 N	101.40 W
Kamina	110	8.44 S	25.00 E
Kaminak Lake ⊜	142	62.10 N	95.00 W
Kaminskij	86	57.10 N	41.28 E
Kaminuriak Lake ⊜	142	63.00 N	95.40 W
Kamishak Bay C	146	59.15 N	153.45 W
Kamloops	148	50.40 N	120.20 W
Kampala	110	0.19 N	32.25 E
Kampar ≃	96	0.32 N	103.08 E
Kampen	72	52.33 N	5.54 E
Kamphaeng Phet	94	16.26 N	99.33 E
Kâmpóng Cham	94	12.00 N	105.27 E
Kâmpóng Chhnăng	94	12.15 N	104.40 E
Kâmpóng Thum	94	12.42 N	104.52 E
Kâmpôt	94	10.37 N	104.11 E
Kamrau, Teluk C	124	3.30 S	133.36 E
Kamsack	142	51.34 N	101.54 W
Kamskij	66	60.04 N	53.13 E
Kamskoje Ustje	66	55.13 N	49.16 E
Kamskoje Vodochranilišče ⊜[1]	66	58.52 N	56.15 E
Kamuela (Waimea)	170d	20.01 N	155.41 W
Kamyšin	64	50.06 N	45.24 E
Kamyšlov	82	56.52 N	62.43 E
Kan ≃	94	13.32 N	105.58 E
Kanaaupscow ≃	142	53.39 N	77.09 W
Kanab	164	37.03 N	112.32 W
Kanab Creek ≃	164	36.24 N	112.38 W
Kanairiktok ≃	142	55.05 N	60.20 W
Kananga (Luluabourg)	110	5.54 S	22.25 E
Kanarraville	164	37.32 N	113.11 W
Kanaš	66	55.31 N	47.30 E
Kanazawa	90	36.34 N	136.39 E
Kānchenjunga ∧	102	27.42 N	88.08 E
Kānchipuram	100	12.50 N	79.43 E
Kandagač	82	49.28 N	57.25 E
Kandalakša	66	67.09 N	32.21 E
Kandangan	96	2.47 S	115.16 E
Kandava	86	57.05 N	22.49 E
Kandel	72	49.05 N	8.11 E
Kandik ≃	146	65.24 N	142.34 W
Kandos	120	32.52 S	149.58 E
Kandy	100	7.18 N	80.38 E
Kane	152	41.40 N	78.49 W
Kaneohe	170c	21.25 N	157.48 W
Kangalassy	84	62.23 N	129.59 E
Kangar	96	6.26 N	100.12 E
Kangaroo Island I	120	35.50 S	137.06 E
Kangasniemi	68	61.59 N	26.38 E
Kangding	88	30.03 N	102.02 E
Kangean, Kepulauan II	96	6.55 S	115.30 E
Kanggye	88	40.58 N	126.34 E
Kangnŭng	88	37.45 N	128.54 E
Kango	110	0.09 N	10.08 E
Kangto ∧	102	27.52 N	92.30 E
Kaniama	110	7.31 S	24.11 E
Kanin, Poluostrov ≻[1]	66	68.00 N	45.00 E
Kanin Nos	66	68.39 N	43.14 E
Kanin Nos, Mys ≻	66	68.39 N	43.16 E
Kaniva	120	36.23 S	141.15 E
Kanjiža	80	46.04 N	20.04 E
Kankakee	154	41.07 N	87.52 W
Kankakee ≃	158	41.23 N	88.16 W
Kankan	114	10.23 N	9.18 W
Kankunskij	84	57.37 N	126.08 E
Kanmaw Kyun I	94	11.40 N	98.28 E
Kannapolis	156	35.30 N	80.37 W
Kannonkoski	68	62.58 N	25.15 E
Kannus	68	63.54 N	23.54 E
Kano	114	12.00 N	8.30 E
Kanopolis	162	38.43 N	98.09 W
Kanosh	164	38.48 N	112.26 W
Kanowna	122	30.36 S	121.36 E
Kânpur	102	26.28 N	80.21 E
Kansas	158	39.33 N	87.56 W
Kansas □3	144	38.45 N	98.15 W
Kansas City, Kans., U.S.	162	39.07 N	94.39 W
Kansas City, Mo., U.S.	158	39.05 N	94.35 W
Kansk	84	56.13 N	95.41 E
Kant	82	42.55 N	74.55 E
Kantang	92	7.23 N	99.32 E
Kantishna ≃	146	64.45 N	149.58 W
Kanturk	70	52.10 N	8.55 W
Kanye	116	24.59 S	25.19 E
Kaohsiung	88	22.38 N	120.17 E
Kaokoveld ⋀[1]	116	21.00 S	14.20 E
Kaolack	114	14.09 N	16.04 W
Kapaa	170b	22.05 N	159.19 W
Kapanga	110	8.21 S	22.35 E
Kapfenberg	72	47.26 N	15.18 E
Kapiskau ≃	142	52.47 N	81.55 W
Kapit	92	2.02 N	112.54 E
Kaplan	158	30.00 N	92.17 W
Kaposvár	72	46.22 N	17.47 E
Kapp	68	60.42 N	10.52 E
Kappeln	72	54.40 N	9.56 E
Kaprun	72	47.16 N	12.46 E
Kapsukas	86	54.33 N	23.21 E
Kapuas ≃	96	0.25 S	109.04 E
Kapunda	120	34.21 S	138.54 E
Kapuskasing	142	49.25 N	82.26 W
Kapuskasing ≃	142	49.49 N	82.00 W
Kapuvár	72	47.36 N	17.02 E
Kara	82	69.14 N	65.00 E
Kara ≃	114	10.01 N	0.25 E
Karaaul	84	48.57 N	79.15 E
Kara-Balty	82	42.50 N	73.52 E
Karabanovo	86	56.19 N	38.42 E
Karabaš	82	55.29 N	60.14 E
Kara-Bogaz-Gol, Zaliv C	82	41.00 N	53.15 E
Karabük	64	41.12 N	32.37 E
Karabula	84	58.08 N	97.23 E
Karačev	86	53.07 N	35.00 E
Karāchi	102	24.52 N	67.03 E
Karaganda	82	49.50 N	73.10 E
Karaginskij, Ostrov I	84	58.50 N	164.00 E
Karaginskij Zaliv C	84	58.50 N	164.00 E
Karagoš, Gora ∧	84	51.44 N	89.24 E
Karaj	104	35.48 N	50.59 E
Karakelong, Pulau I	92	4.15 N	126.48 E
Karakoram Range ⋀	102	35.30 N	77.00 E
Karakoro ≃	114	14.43 N	12.03 W
Karaköse	104	39.44 N	43.03 E
Karakul'	82	39.32 N	63.50 E
Karakumskij Kanal ≍	104	37.35 N	61.50 E
Karakumy ◆[2]	82	39.00 N	60.00 E
Karaman	104	37.11 N	33.14 E
Karasburg	116	28.00 S	18.43 E
Karasuk	84	53.44 N	78.02 E
Karatau	82	43.10 N	70.28 E
Karatau, Chrebet ⋀	82	43.50 N	68.30 E
Karaton	82	46.25 N	53.30 E
Karaul	84	70.06 N	83.08 E
Karawanken ⋀	78	46.30 N	14.25 E
Karažal	82	48.02 N	70.49 E
Karbalā'	104	32.36 N	44.02 E
Karcag	72	47.19 N	20.56 E
Kardhitsa	80	39.21 N	21.55 E
Kärdla	86	59.00 N	22.45 E
Kârdžali	80	41.39 N	25.22 E
Kargasok	84	59.07 N	80.53 E
Kargopol'	66	61.30 N	38.58 E
Karhula	68	60.31 N	26.57 E
Kariba	116	16.30 S	28.45 E
Kariba, Lake ⊜[1]	110	17.00 S	28.00 E
Karibib	116	21.58 S	15.51 E
Karimata, Kepulauan II	96	1.25 S	109.05 E
Karīmnagar	100	18.26 N	79.08 E
Karimundjawa, Kepulauan II	96	5.50 S	110.25 E
Karin	108	10.51 N	45.45 E
Karkabet	108	16.13 N	37.30 E
Karkaralinsk	82	49.23 N	75.21 E
Karkkila	68	60.32 N	24.11 E
Karkku	68	61.25 N	23.01 E
Karl-Marx-Stadt (Chemnitz)	72	50.50 N	12.55 E
Karl-Marx-Stadt □5	72	50.45 N	12.45 E
Karlovac	78	45.29 N	15.34 E
Karlovo	80	42.38 N	24.48 E
Karlovy Vary	72	50.11 N	12.52 E
Karlsbad → Karlovy Vary	72	50.11 N	12.52 E
Karlshamn	68	56.10 N	14.51 E
Karlskoga	68	59.20 N	14.31 E
Karlskrona	68	56.10 N	15.35 E
Karlsöarna II	68	57.17 N	17.58 E
Karlsruhe	72	49.03 N	8.24 E
Karlstad	68	59.22 N	13.30 E
Karlstadt	72	49.57 N	9.45 E
Karnack	158	32.40 N	94.10 W
Karnāl	102	29.41 N	76.59 E
Karnāli ≃	102	28.38 N	81.12 E
Karnes City	160	28.53 N	97.54 W
Karnobat	80	42.39 N	26.59 E
Kärnten □3	72	46.50 N	13.50 E
Karonga	110	9.56 S	33.56 E
Karonie	122	30.58 S	122.32 E
Kárpathos I	80	35.40 N	27.10 E
Karpenísion	80	38.55 N	21.40 E
Karpinsk	82	59.45 N	60.01 E
Karpogory	66	64.00 N	44.24 E
Karrats Isfjord C[2]	142	71.20 N	54.00 W
Karridale	122	34.13 S	115.05 E
Kars	104	40.36 N	43.05 E
Karsakpaj	82	47.49 N	66.41 E
Kārsava	86	56.47 N	27.40 E
Karši	104	38.53 N	65.48 E
Karskije Vorota, Proliv ⊔	82	70.30 N	58.00 E
Karskoje More (Kara Sea) ▾[2]	84	76.00 N	80.00 E
Karstula	68	62.52 N	24.47 E
Kartaly	82	53.03 N	60.40 E
Kartuzy	72	54.20 N	18.12 E
Karufa	124	3.50 S	133.26 E
Karunjie	124	16.18 S	127.12 E
Karunki	68	66.02 N	24.01 E
Karup	68	56.18 N	9.10 E
Karūr	100	10.57 N	78.05 E
Karviná	72	49.50 N	18.30 E
Kārwār	100	14.48 N	74.08 E
Karymskoje	84	51.37 N	114.21 E
Kasaan	146	55.32 N	132.24 W
Kasai (Cassai) ≃	110	3.06 S	16.57 E
Kasaji	110	10.22 S	23.27 E
Kasama	110	10.13 S	31.12 E
Kasanga	110	8.28 S	31.09 E
Kasba Lake ⊜	142	60.18 N	102.07 W
Kasempa	110	13.27 S	25.50 E
Kasenga	110	10.22 S	28.38 E
Kasese, Ug.	110	0.10 N	30.05 E
Kasese, Zaïre	110	1.38 S	27.07 E
Kāshān	104	33.59 N	51.29 E
Kashgar → Kashi	88	39.29 N	75.59 E
Kashi (Kashgar)	88	39.29 N	75.59 E
Kashigaerhe ≃	88	39.40 N	78.00 E
Kashiwa	90	35.52 N	139.59 E
Kāshmar	104	35.12 N	58.27 E
Kashunuk ≃	146	61.18 N	165.36 W
Kasia	100	26.44 N	83.54 E
Kasigluk	146	60.52 N	162.32 W
Kasimov	86	54.56 N	41.24 E
Kašin	86	57.21 N	37.37 E
Kašira	86	54.51 N	38.10 E
Kasiruta, Pulau I	92	0.25 S	127.12 E
Kaskattama ≃	142	57.03 N	90.07 W
Kasli	82	55.53 N	60.46 E
Kasongo	110	4.27 S	26.40 E
Kasongo-Lunda	110	6.28 S	16.49 E
Kásos I	80	35.22 N	26.56 E
Kaspijsk	82	42.52 N	47.38 E
Kaspijskij	82	45.22 N	47.24 E
Kasr, Ra's ≻	112	18.02 N	38.35 E
Kassalā	112	15.28 N	36.24 E
Kassel	72	51.19 N	9.29 E
Kasserine → El Kasserine	106	35.11 N	8.48 E
Kasson	154	44.03 N	92.45 W
Kastelholm	68	60.14 N	20.04 E
Kastl	72	49.22 N	11.42 E
Kastoría	80	40.31 N	21.15 E
Kasugai	90	35.14 N	136.58 E
Kasūr	102	31.07 N	74.27 E
Katahdin, Mount ∧	152	45.55 N	68.55 W
Katanga ≃	84	58.18 N	104.10 E
Katanga Plateau ⋀[1]	110	10.30 S	25.30 E
Katanning	122	33.42 S	117.33 E
Katchall Island I	94	7.57 N	93.22 E
Kateríni	80	40.16 N	22.30 E
Kates Needle ∧	146	57.03 N	132.03 W
Katha	88	24.11 N	96.21 E
Katherine	124	14.28 S	132.16 E
Kāthiāwār ≻[1]	102	22.00 N	71.00 E
Katihār	100	25.32 N	87.35 E
Katiola	114	8.08 N	5.06 W
Kātmāndu	102	27.43 N	85.19 E
Katoomba	120	33.42 S	150.18 E
Katowice	72	50.16 N	19.00 E
Katrīnah, Jabal ∧	112	28.31 N	33.57 E
Katrineholm	68	59.00 N	16.12 E
Katsina	114	13.00 N	7.32 E
Katsina Ala ≃	114	7.45 N	9.05 E
Kattakurgan	100	39.55 N	66.15 E
Kattegat ⊔	68	57.00 N	11.00 E
Katun' ≃	84	52.25 N	85.05 E
Katunki	86	56.50 N	43.14 E
Katwijk aan Zee	72	52.13 N	4.24 E
Kaufbeuren	72	47.53 N	10.37 E
Kaufman	160	32.35 N	96.19 W
Kauhajoki	68	62.26 N	22.11 E
Kauhava	68	63.06 N	23.05 E
Kaukauveld ⋀[1]	116	22.00 S	20.30 E
Kaumakani	170b	21.06 N	157.02 W
Kaunakakai	170a	21.06 N	157.01 W
Kaunas	86	54.54 N	23.54 E
Kaupanger	68	61.11 N	7.14 E
Kaura Namoda	114	12.35 N	6.35 E
Kausala	68	60.54 N	26.22 E
Kaustinen	68	63.32 N	23.42 E
Kauttua	68	61.06 N	22.10 E
Kavača	84	60.16 N	169.51 E
Kavajë	80	41.11 N	19.33 E
Kavalerovo	84	44.15 N	135.04 E
Kavála	80	40.56 N	24.25 E
Kavaratti Island I	100	10.34 N	72.39 E
Kavīr, Dasht-e ◆[2]	104	34.40 N	54.30 E
Kawagoe	90	35.55 N	139.29 E
Kawaguchi	90	35.48 N	139.43 E
Kawaihoa Point ≻	170b	21.47 N	160.12 W
Kawailoa Beach	170c	21.37 N	158.05 W
Kawambwa	110	9.47 S	29.05 E
Kawasaki	90	35.32 N	139.43 E
Kawerau	126	38.03 S	176.43 E
Kawich Peak ∧	168	37.58 N	116.27 W
Kawm Umbū	112	24.28 N	32.57 E
Kayak Island I	146	59.52 N	144.30 W
Kayangel Islands II	92	8.04 N	134.43 E
Kayes, Congo	110	4.25 S	11.41 E
Kayes, Mali	114	14.27 N	11.26 W
Kayseri	104	38.43 N	35.30 E
Kaysville	166	41.02 N	111.56 W
Kazachskaja Sovetskaja Socialističeskaja Res □3	84	48.00 N	68.00 E
Kazachskij Melkosopočnik ⋀[2]	82	49.00 N	72.00 E
Kažačinskoje	84	57.49 N	93.17 E
Kazačje	84	70.44 N	136.13 E
Kazakh Soviet Socialist Republic → Kazachskaja Sovetskaja Socialističeskaja Res □3	84	48.00 N	68.00 E
Kazalinsk	82	45.46 N	62.07 E
Kazan'	66	55.49 N	49.08 E
Kazan ≃	142	64.02 N	95.30 W
Kazandžik	104	39.16 N	55.32 E
Kazanlâk	80	42.38 N	25.21 E
Kazanovka	86	53.46 N	38.34 E
Kazbek, Gora ∧	82	42.42 N	44.31 E
Kāzerūn	104	29.37 N	51.38 E
Kažim	66	60.20 N	51.30 E
Kazi-Magomed	104	40.03 N	48.56 E
Kazimierza Wielka	72	50.16 N	20.30 E
Kazincbarcika	72	48.16 N	20.37 E
Kazinka	86	52.32 N	39.42 E
Kazlu Rūda	86	54.46 N	23.30 E
Kazungula	110	17.45 S	25.20 E
Kazym ≃	84	63.54 N	65.50 E
Kazymskaja Kul'tbaza	84	63.40 N	67.14 E
Kazyr ≃	84	53.47 N	92.53 E
Kéa I	80	37.34 N	24.22 E
Keaau	170d	19.37 N	155.02 W
Kealakekua Bay C	170d	19.28 N	155.56 W
Keams Canyon	164	35.49 N	110.12 W
Kearney	162	40.42 N	99.05 W
Kearns	164	40.39 N	111.59 W
Kearny	164	33.03 N	110.55 W
Keban Gölü ⊜[1]	104	38.50 N	39.15 E
Kebnekaise ∧	66	67.53 N	18.33 E
Kebri Dehar	108	6.47 N	44.17 E
Kecel	72	46.32 N	19.16 E
Kech ≃	104	26.00 N	62.44 E
Kechika ≃	146	59.36 N	127.05 W
Kecskemét	72	46.54 N	19.42 E
Kėdainiai	86	55.17 N	24.00 E
Kediri	96	7.49 S	112.01 E
Kedon	84	64.08 N	159.14 E
Kédougou	114	12.33 N	12.11 W
Kędzierzyn	72	50.20 N	18.12 E
Keele ≃	146	64.24 N	124.50 W
Keele Peak ∧	146	63.26 N	130.19 W
Keelung → Chilung	88	25.08 N	121.44 E
Keene, N.H., U.S.	152	42.56 N	72.17 W
Keene, Tex., U.S.	160	32.24 N	97.20 W
Keenesburg	164	40.07 N	104.31 W
Keer-weer, Cape ≻	124	13.58 S	141.30 E
Keeseville	152	44.30 N	73.29 W
Keetmanshoop	116	26.36 S	18.08 E
Keewatin, Ont., Can.	162	49.46 N	94.34 W
Keewatin, Minn., U.S.	154	47.24 N	93.05 W
Keewatin □5	142	65.00 N	95.00 W
Kefallinía □5	80	38.16 N	20.21 E
Kefallinía I	80	38.15 N	20.35 E
Keffi	114	8.51 N	7.52 E
Keflavík	66a	64.02 N	22.36 W
Keglo, Baie C	142	59.10 N	65.50 W
Keg River	142	57.48 N	117.52 W
Kehl	72	48.35 N	7.50 E
Ke-hsi Mānsām	92	21.56 N	97.50 E
Keighley	70	53.52 N	1.54 W
Keila	86	59.18 N	24.25 E
Keitele	68	63.11 N	26.22 E
Keith	70	57.32 N	2.57 W
Keith Arm C	146	65.20 N	122.15 W
Keizer	166	44.57 N	123.01 W
Kekaha	170b	21.58 N	159.43 W
Kekertaluk Island I	142	68.10 N	66.30 W
Kekeshili	88	35.11 N	93.35 E
Kekexili	100	35.11 N	93.35 E
Kekexilishanmai ⋀	102	35.20 N	90.00 E
Kelafo	108	5.40 N	44.20 E
Kelai ≃	96	2.10 N	117.29 E
Kelamayi	88	45.37 N	84.53 E
Kelang	96	3.02 N	101.28 E
Kelantan ≃	96	6.11 N	102.15 E
Kelasa, Selat ⊔	96	2.40 S	107.15 E
Kelheim	72	48.55 N	11.52 E
Keliyahe ≃	102	39.00 N	81.40 E
Kellerberrin	122	31.38 S	117.43 E
Keller Lake ⊜	142	64.00 N	121.30 W
Kellett, Cape ≻	142	71.59 N	125.34 W
Kellogg	166	47.32 N	116.07 W
Kelmė	86	55.38 N	22.56 E
Kélo	108	9.19 N	15.48 E
Kelolokan	92	1.08 N	117.54 E
Kelowna	148	49.53 N	119.29 W
Kelso, Scot., U.K.	70	55.36 N	2.25 W
Kelso, Wash., U.S.	166	46.09 N	122.54 W
Keltie Inlet C	142	64.28 N	73.28 W
Kem'	66	64.57 N	34.36 E
Kemano	148	53.34 N	127.56 W
Kemerovo	84	55.20 N	86.05 E
Kemi	68	65.49 N	24.32 E
Kemie	68	62.14 N	30.20 E
Kemijoki ≃	68	65.47 N	24.30 E
Kemmerer	164	41.48 N	110.32 W
Kemmuna I	78	36.00 N	14.20 E
Kemnath	72	49.52 N	11.54 E
Kempen	72	51.22 N	6.25 E
Kempsey	120	31.05 S	152.50 E
Kempt, Lac ⊜	142	47.25 N	74.22 W
Kempten [allgäu]	72	47.43 N	10.19 E
Kemptville	152	45.01 N	75.38 W
Kemul, Kong ∧	96	1.52 N	116.11 E
Kenadsa	106	31.48 N	2.26 W
Kenai	146	60.33 N	151.15 W
Kenai Peninsula ≻[1]	146	60.10 N	150.00 W
Kenbridge	156	36.58 N	78.08 W
Kendal	70	54.20 N	2.45 W
Kendall	156	25.41 N	80.19 W
Kendall, Cape ≻	142	63.36 N	87.09 W
Kendallville	158	41.27 N	85.16 W
Kendari	92	3.57 S	122.35 E
Kendrick	166	46.37 N	116.39 W
Kenedy	160	28.49 N	97.51 W
Kenema	114	7.52 N	11.12 W
Kenge	110	4.52 S	16.59 E
Kēng Tung	92	21.17 N	99.36 E
Kenhardt	116	29.19 S	21.12 E
Kenitra	106	34.16 N	6.40 W
Kenmare, Eire	70	51.53 N	9.35 W
Kenmare, N. Dak., U.S.	162	48.40 N	102.05 W
Kennebec ≃	152	44.00 N	69.50 W
Kennebunk	152	43.23 N	70.33 W
Kennedy	158	33.35 N	87.59 W
Kennedy, Cape → Canaveral, Cape ≻	156	28.27 N	80.32 W
Kennedy, Mount ∧	146	60.30 N	139.00 W
Kennedy Entrance ⊔	146	59.00 N	152.00 W
Kennedy Range ⋀	122	24.30 S	115.00 E
Kenner	158	29.59 N	90.15 W
Kennett	158	36.14 N	90.03 W
Kennett Square	152	39.51 N	75.43 W
Kennewick	166	46.12 N	119.07 W
Kenn Reefs ✧[2]	118	21.12 S	155.46 E
Kénogami	150	48.26 N	71.14 W
Kenogami ≃	142	51.06 N	84.28 W
Keno Hill	146	63.55 N	135.18 W
Kenora	162	49.47 N	94.29 W
Kenosha	154	42.35 N	87.49 W
Kenova	152	38.24 N	82.35 W
Kensington, P.E.I., Can.	150	46.26 N	63.38 W
Kensington, Kans., U.S.	162	39.46 N	99.02 W
Kensington Park	156	27.22 N	82.31 W
Kent	152	41.09 N	81.22 W
Kent □6	70	51.15 N	0.40 E
Kentau	82	43.36 N	68.36 E
Kent Bay C	142	69.59 N	96.02 W
Kent Group II	120	39.27 S	147.20 E
Kentland	158	40.46 N	87.27 W
Kenton, Ohio, U.S.	152	40.39 N	83.36 W
Kenton, Tenn., U.S.	158	36.12 N	89.01 W
Kent Peninsula ≻[1]	142	68.30 N	107.00 W
Kentucky □3	144	37.30 N	85.15 W
Kentucky Lake ⊜[1]	158	36.25 N	88.05 W
Kentville	150	45.05 N	64.30 W
Kentwood	158	30.56 N	90.31 W
Kenya □1	110	1.00 N	38.00 E
Kenya, Mount ∧	110	0.10 S	37.20 E
Kenyon	154	44.16 N	92.59 W
Keokuk	154	40.24 N	91.24 W
Keo Neua, Col de)(	94	18.23 N	105.09 E
Keosauqua	154	40.44 N	91.58 W
Keota	154	41.21 N	91.57 W
Kepi	124	6.34 S	139.20 E
Kępice	72	54.15 N	16.52 E
Kępno	72	51.17 N	17.59 E
Keppel Bay C	120	23.21 S	150.55 E
Kerang	120	35.44 S	143.55 E
Kerava	68	60.24 N	25.07 E
Kerč'	82	45.22 N	36.27 E
Kerčevskij	66	59.55 N	56.17 E
Keren	108	15.46 N	38.28 E
Kerga	66	62.39 N	46.00 E
Kericho	110	0.22 S	35.17 E
Kerimäki	68	61.55 N	29.17 E
Kerintji, Gunung ∧	96	1.42 S	101.16 E
Kerkenna, Îles II	106	34.44 N	11.12 E
Kerki, S.S.S.R.	66	63.43 N	54.05 E
Kerki, S.S.S.R.	104	37.50 N	65.12 E
Kérkira (Corfu)	80	39.36 N	19.56 E
Kérkira I	80	39.40 N	19.42 E
Kerkrade [-Holz]	72	50.52 N	6.04 E
Kermān, Īrān	104	30.17 N	57.05 E
Kerman, Calif., U.S.	168	36.43 N	120.04 W
Kermānshāh	104	34.19 N	47.04 E
Kermit	160	31.51 N	103.06 W
Kernersville	156	36.07 N	80.04 W
Kernville	168	35.43 N	118.26 W
Kerrobert	142	51.55 N	109.08 W
Kerr Reservoir ⊜[1]	156	36.35 N	70.28 W
Kerrville	160	30.03 N	99.08 W
Kerry □6	70	52.10 N	9.30 W
Kerulen (Cherlen) (Kelulunhe) ≃	88	48.48 N	117.00 E
Kesagami Lake ⊜	142	50.23 N	80.15 W
Keşan	80	40.51 N	26.37 E
Kesennuma	90	38.54 N	141.35 E
Keshod	102	21.18 N	70.15 E
Keski-Suomen lääni □4	68	62.30 N	25.30 E
Kestilä	68	64.21 N	26.17 E
Keszthely	72	46.46 N	17.15 E
Ket' ≃	84	58.55 N	81.32 E
Keta	114	5.55 N	1.00 E
Keta, Ozero ⊜	84	68.44 N	90.00 E
Ketapang	96	1.52 S	109.59 E
Ketchikan	146	55.21 N	131.35 W
Ketchum	166	43.41 N	114.22 W
Kete Krachi	114	7.46 N	0.03 W
Ketoj, Ostrov I	84	47.20 N	152.28 E
Kętrzyn (Rastenburg)	72	54.06 N	21.23 E
Kettering, Eng., U.K.	70	52.24 N	0.44 W
Kettering, Ohio, U.S.	152	39.41 N	84.10 W
Kettle ≃	148	48.42 N	118.07 W
Kettle Falls	166	48.36 N	118.03 W
Kevelaer	72	51.35 N	6.15 E
Kevin	166	48.45 N	111.58 W
Kew	132	21.54 N	72.02 W
Kewanee	154	41.14 N	89.56 W
Kewanna	158	41.01 N	86.25 W
Kewaunee	154	44.27 N	87.30 W
Keweenaw Point ≻	154	47.30 N	87.50 W
Keya Paha ≃	162	42.54 N	99.00 W
Keyes	160	36.49 N	102.15 W
Key Largo	156	25.04 N	80.28 W
Keystone Heights	156	29.47 N	82.01 W
Keysville	156	37.04 N	78.29 W
Key West	156	24.33 N	81.48 W
Kežma	84	58.59 N	101.09 E
Kežmarok	72	49.08 N	20.25 E
Khadki	100	18.34 N	73.52 E
Khairpur	102	27.32 N	68.46 E
Khajrāho	100	24.50 N	79.58 E
Khakhea	116	24.51 S	23.20 E
Khalkidhikí □9	80	40.25 N	23.27 E
Khalkis	80	38.28 N	23.36 E
Khambhāt, Gulf of C	102	21.00 N	72.30 E
Khammam	100	17.15 N	80.09 E
Khānābād	102	36.41 N	69.07 E
Khānaqīn	104	34.21 N	45.22 E
Khancoban	120	36.12 S	148.05 E
Khandwa	102	21.50 N	76.20 E
Khānewāl	102	30.18 N	71.56 E
Khanh-hung	94	9.36 N	105.58 E
Khaniá	80	35.31 N	24.02 E
Khānpur	102	28.39 N	70.39 E
Kharagpur	102	22.20 N	87.20 E
Khargon	102	21.49 N	75.36 E
Khārk, Jazīreh-ye I	104	29.15 N	50.20 E
Kharkov → Char'kov	64	50.00 N	36.15 E
Khartoum → Al-Khurṭūm	112	15.36 N	32.32 E
Khartoum North → Al-Khurṭūm Baḥrī	112	15.38 N	32.33 E
Khashm al-Qirbah	112	14.58 N	35.55 E
Khemis Miliana	106	36.16 N	2.13 E
Khersan ≃	104	31.33 N	50.22 E
Khíos	80	38.22 N	26.08 E
Khíos I	80	38.22 N	26.00 E
Kholm	102	36.42 N	67.41 E
Khong	94	14.07 N	105.51 E
Khon Kaen	94	16.26 N	102.50 E
Khorramābād	104	33.30 N	48.20 E
Khorramshahr	104	30.25 N	48.11 E
Khouribga	106	32.54 N	6.57 W
Khulna	102	22.48 N	89.33 E
Khunjerab Pass)(	102	36.52 N	75.27 E
Khūryān Mūryān II	100	17.30 N	56.00 E
Khuzdār	100	27.48 N	66.37 E
Khvoy	104	38.33 N	44.58 E
Khyber Pass)(	102	34.05 N	71.10 E
Kiama	120	34.41 S	150.51 E
Kiamba	92	5.59 N	124.37 E
Kiana	146	66.59 N	160.25 W
Kiangarow, Mount ∧	120	26.49 S	151.33 E
Kibangou	110	3.27 S	12.21 E
Kibombo	110	3.54 S	25.55 E
Kibondo	110	3.35 S	30.42 E
Kibre Mengist	108	5.52 N	39.00 E
Kičevo	80	41.31 N	20.57 E
Kichčik	84	53.24 N	156.03 E
Kickapoo ≃	154	43.05 N	90.53 W
Kicking Horse Pass)(	148	51.27 N	116.18 W
Kidal	114	18.26 N	1.24 E
Kidira	114	14.28 N	12.13 W
Kidwelly	70	51.45 N	4.18 W
Kiefersfelden	72	47.37 N	12.11 E
Kiel, B.R.D.	72	54.20 N	10.08 E
Kiel, Wis., U.S.	154	43.55 N	88.02 W
Kielce	72	50.52 N	20.37 E
Kiev → Kijev	64	50.26 N	30.31 E
Kiffa	114	16.37 N	11.24 W
Kifisiá	80	38.04 N	23.48 E
Kigali	110	1.57 S	30.04 E
Kigoma	110	4.52 S	29.38 E
Kihei	170a	20.47 N	156.28 W
Kihniö	68	62.12 N	23.11 E
Kii-suidō ⊔	90	33.55 N	134.55 E
Kijev	64	50.26 N	30.31 E
Kijevskoje Vodochranilišče ⊜[1]	64	51.00 N	30.00 E
Kikerino	86	59.28 N	29.35 E
Kikerk Lake ⊜	142	67.20 N	113.20 W
Kikinda	80	45.50 N	20.28 E
Kiklādhes II	80	37.30 N	25.00 E
Kikori	124	7.35 S	144.16 E
Kikori ≃	124	7.10 S	144.05 E
Kikwit	110	5.02 S	18.49 E
Kilauea	170b	22.13 N	159.25 W
Kilcoy	120	26.57 S	152.33 E
Kildare	70	53.10 N	6.55 W
Kildare □6	70	53.15 N	6.45 W
Kilgore	158	32.23 N	94.53 W
Kilian Island I	142	73.35 N	107.53 W
Kilimanjaro ∧	110	3.04 S	37.22 E
Kilindoni	110	7.55 S	39.39 E
Kilingi-Nõmme	86	58.09 N	24.58 E
Kilis	104	36.44 N	37.05 E
Kilkee	70	52.41 N	9.38 W
Kilkenny	70	52.39 N	7.15 W
Kilkenny □6	70	52.40 N	7.20 W
Kilkis	80	41.00 N	22.53 E
Killala	70	54.13 N	9.13 W
Killaloe	70	52.48 N	8.27 W
Killarney, Man., Can.	162	49.12 N	99.42 W
Killarney, Eire	70	52.03 N	9.30 W
Killbuck	152	40.30 N	81.59 W
Killeen	160	31.08 N	97.44 W
Killen	158	34.52 N	87.32 W
Killorglin	70	52.06 N	9.47 W
Killybegs	70	54.38 N	8.27 W
Kilmarnock	70	55.36 N	4.30 W
Kilombero ≃	110	8.31 S	37.22 E
Kilomines	110	1.48 N	30.14 E
Kilosa	110	6.50 S	36.59 E
Kilrush	70	52.39 N	9.30 W
Kiltān I	100	11.29 N	73.00 E
Kilwa	110	9.18 S	28.25 E
Kilwa Kisiwani	110	8.58 S	39.30 E
Kilwa Kivinje	110	8.45 S	39.24 E
Kim ≃	106	5.28 N	11.07 E
Kimba	120	33.09 S	136.25 E
Kimball	162	41.14 N	103.40 W
Kimberley, B.C., Can.	148	49.41 N	115.59 W
Kimberley, S. Afr.	116	28.43 S	24.46 E
Kimberley Downs	122	17.24 S	124.22 E
Kimberley Plateau ⋀[1]	118	17.00 S	127.00 E
Kimberley Research Station	124	15.39 S	128.43 E
Kimberly, Idaho, U.S.	166	42.32 N	114.22 W
Kimberly, Wis., U.S.	154	44.17 N	88.20 W
Kimch'aek	88	40.41 N	129.12 E
Kimch'ŏn	88	36.07 N	128.05 E
Kimovsk	86	53.58 N	38.32 E
Kimry	86	56.52 N	37.21 E
Kinabalu, Mount ∧	96	6.05 N	116.33 E
Kincaid	158	39.35 N	89.25 W
Kincardine	154	44.11 N	81.38 W
Kindberg	72	47.31 N	15.27 E
Kinde	154	43.56 N	83.00 W
Kinder	158	30.29 N	92.51 W
Kindersley	142	51.27 N	109.10 W
Kindia	114	10.04 N	12.51 W
Kindu-Port-Empain	110	2.57 S	25.56 E
Kinel'	66	53.14 N	50.39 E
Kinešma	86	57.26 N	42.09 E
King, Mount ∧	120	25.10 S	147.31 E
Kingaroy	120	26.33 S	151.50 E
King City, Ont., Can.	154	43.56 N	79.32 W
King City, Calif., U.S.	168	36.13 N	121.08 W
King City, Mo., U.S.	158	40.03 N	94.31 W
King Cove	146	55.04 N	162.19 W
Kingfield	152	44.57 N	70.09 W
Kingfisher	160	35.52 N	97.56 W
King George Islands II	142	57.20 N	78.25 W
King George Sound ⊔	122	35.03 S	117.57 E
Kingisepp	86	59.22 N	28.36 E
King Island I	120	39.50 S	144.00 E
King Leopold Ranges ⋀	118	17.30 S	125.45 E
Kingman, Ariz., U.S.	164	35.12 N	114.04 W
Kingman, Kans., U.S.	162	37.39 N	98.07 W
Kingoonya	122	30.54 S	135.18 E
King Salmon	146	58.14 N	157.24 W
Kings Beach	168	39.14 N	120.01 W
Kingsbridge	70	50.17 N	3.46 W
Kingsburg	168	36.31 N	119.33 W
Kingsford	154	45.48 N	88.04 W
Kingsland	156	30.48 N	81.41 W
Kingsley, Iowa, U.S.	162	42.35 N	95.58 W
Kingsley, Mich., U.S.	154	44.35 N	85.32 W
King's Lynn	70	52.45 N	0.24 E
Kings Mountain	156	35.15 N	81.20 W
King Sound ⊔	122	17.00 S	123.30 E
Kingsport	156	36.32 N	82.33 W
Kingston, Austl.	120	36.50 S	139.51 E
Kingston, N.S., Can.	150	44.59 N	64.57 W
Kingston, Ont., Can.	154	44.18 N	76.34 W
Kingston, Jam.	132	18.00 N	76.50 W
Kingston, Mass., U.S.	152	41.59 N	70.43 W
Kingston, N.Y., U.S.	152	41.56 N	74.00 W
Kingston, Okla., U.S.	160	34.00 N	96.43 W
Kingston, Pa., U.S.	152	41.16 N	75.54 W
Kingston, Tenn., U.S.	156	35.52 N	84.31 W
Kingston upon Hull	70	53.45 N	0.20 W
Kingstown	132	13.09 N	61.14 W
Kingstree	156	33.40 N	79.50 W
Kings Valley	166	44.42 N	123.26 W
Kingsville, Ont., Can.	154	42.02 N	82.45 W
Kingsville, Tex., U.S.	160	27.31 N	97.52 W
King William Island I	142	69.00 N	97.30 W
King William's Town	116	32.51 S	27.22 E
Kinkony, Lac ⊜	117b	16.08 S	45.50 E
Kinn	68	61.36 N	4.45 E
Kinna	68	57.30 N	12.41 E
Kinnaird	148	49.17 N	117.39 W
Kinnairds Head ≻	70	57.42 N	2.00 W
Kinnula	68	63.22 N	24.58 E
Kinross	70	56.13 N	3.27 W
Kinsale	70	51.42 N	8.32 W
Kinsarvik	68	60.23 N	6.43 E
Kinshasa (Léopoldville)	110	4.18 S	15.18 E
Kinsley	162	37.55 N	99.25 W
Kinston	156	35.16 N	77.35 W
Kintore Range ⋀	122	23.25 S	129.20 E
Kintyre ≻[1]	70	55.32 N	5.35 W
Kinyeti ∧	108	3.57 N	32.54 E
Kinzua	166	44.59 N	120.03 W
Kiowa, Kans., U.S.	162	37.01 N	98.29 W
Kiowa, Okla., U.S.	160	34.43 N	95.54 W
Kiowa Creek ≃	160	36.46 N	99.55 W
Kipawa, Lac ⊜	154	46.55 N	79.00 W
Kipembawe	110	7.39 S	33.24 E
Kipengere Range ⋀	110	9.10 S	34.15 E
Kipijevo	66	65.40 N	54.23 E
Kipili	110	7.26 S	30.36 E
Kipini	110	2.32 S	40.31 E
Kipnuk	146	59.56 N	164.03 W
Kipushi	110	11.46 N	27.14 E
Kirchbach in Steiermark	72	46.54 N	15.44 E
Kirchberg	72	49.12 N	9.58 E
Kirchdorf an der Krems	72	47.56 N	14.07 E
Kirchheim	72	48.10 N	10.30 E
Kirchheimbolanden	72	49.40 N	8.00 E
Kirchmöser	72	52.22 N	12.25 E
Kirchschlag in der Buckligen Welt	72	47.31 N	16.18 E
Kirejevsk	86	53.56 N	37.56 E
Kirenga ≃	84	57.47 N	108.07 E
Kirensk	84	57.46 N	108.08 E
Kirghiz Soviet Socialist Republic → Kirgizskaja Sovetskaja Socialističeskaja Respublika □3	82	41.30 N	75.00 E
Kirgizskaja Sovetskaja Socialističeskaja Respublika □3	82	41.30 N	75.00 E
Kirgizskij Chrebet ⋀	82	42.30 N	74.00 E
Kiri	110	1.27 S	19.00 E
Kırıkkale	104	39.50 N	33.31 E
Kirillov	86	59.52 N	38.23 E
Kirin O Jilin → □4	88	44.00 N	126.00 E
Kiriši	86	59.27 N	32.02 E
Kirkcaldy	70	56.07 N	3.10 W
Kirkcudbright	70	54.50 N	4.03 W
Kirkee → Khadki	100	18.34 N	73.52 E
Kirkenær	68	60.28 N	12.03 E
Kirkenes	66	69.40 N	30.03 E
Kirkjubæjarklaustur	66a	63.47 N	18.04 W
Kirkland, Ill., U.S.	154	42.06 N	88.51 W
Kirkland, Tex., U.S.	160	34.23 N	100.04 W
Kirkland, Wash., U.S.	166	47.41 N	122.12 W
Kirkland Lake	154	48.09 N	80.02 W
Kırklareli	80	41.44 N	27.12 E
Kirksville	158	40.12 N	92.35 W
Kirkūk	104	35.28 N	44.28 E
Kirkwall	70	58.59 N	2.58 W
Kirkwood, S. Afr.	116	33.24 S	25.26 E
Kirkwood, Mo., U.S.	158	38.35 N	90.24 W
Kirn	72	49.47 N	7.28 E
Kirov, S.S.S.R.	66	58.38 N	49.42 E
Kirov, S.S.S.R.	86	54.05 N	34.20 E
Kirovabad	104	40.40 N	46.22 E
Kirovakan	82	40.48 N	44.30 E
Kirovgrad	82	57.26 N	60.04 E
Kirovo-Čepeck	66	58.33 N	50.01 E
Kirovograd	64	48.30 N	32.18 E
Kirovograd □4	80	48.10 N	30.20 E
Kirovsk, S.S.S.R.	66	67.37 N	33.35 E
Kirovsk, S.S.S.R.	82	37.42 N	60.23 E
Kirovskij, S.S.S.R.	84	54.18 N	155.47 E
Kirovskij, S.S.S.R.	88	44.52 N	78.12 E
Kirriemuir	70	56.41 N	3.01 W
Kirs	66	59.21 N	52.14 E
Kirsanov	86	52.38 N	42.43 E
Kırşehir	104	39.09 N	34.10 E
Kīrthar Range ⋀	102	27.00 N	67.10 E
Kirtland	164	36.44 N	108.21 W
Kiruna	66	67.51 N	20.16 E
Kirwin	162	39.40 N	99.07 W
Kiryū	90	36.24 N	139.20 E
Kiržač	86	56.09 N	38.52 E
Kisangani (Stanleyville)	110	0.30 N	25.12 E
Kisar, Pulau I	96	8.05 S	127.10 E
Kisbér	72	47.30 N	18.02 E
Kisel'ovsk	84	54.00 N	86.39 E
Kishiwada	90	34.28 N	135.22 E
Kisii	110	0.41 S	34.46 E
Kišin'ov	64	47.00 N	28.50 E
Kiskőrös	72	46.38 N	19.17 E
Kiskunfélegyháza	72	46.43 N	19.52 E
Kiskunhalas	72	46.26 N	19.30 E
Kiskunmajsa	72	46.30 N	19.45 E
Kislovodsk	64	43.55 N	42.44 E
Kismayu	110	0.23 S	42.30 E
Kissidougou	114	9.11 N	10.06 W
Kissimmee	156	28.18 N	81.24 W
Kississing Lake ⊜	142	55.10 N	101.20 W
Kisújszállás	72	47.13 N	20.46 E
Kisumu	110	0.06 S	34.45 E
Kisvárda	72	48.13 N	22.05 E
Kita	114	13.03 N	9.29 W
Kita-daitō-jima I	88	25.57 N	131.18 E
Kitakyūshū	90	33.53 N	130.50 E
Kitale	110	1.01 N	35.00 E
Kitami	90a	43.48 N	143.54 E
Kit Carson	162	38.46 N	102.48 W
Kitchener	154	43.27 N	80.29 W
Kitee	68	62.06 N	30.09 E
Kíthira I	80	36.20 N	22.58 E
Kíthnos I	80	37.25 N	24.28 E
Kitimat	148	54.03 N	128.33 W
Kittanning	152	40.49 N	79.32 W
Kittery	152	43.05 N	70.45 W
Kittery Point	152	43.05 N	70.41 W
Kitui	110	1.22 S	38.01 E
Kitwe	110	12.49 S	28.13 E
Kitzbühel	72	47.27 N	12.23 E
Kitzingen	72	49.44 N	10.09 E
Kiujiang → Jiujiang	88	29.44 N	115.59 E
Kiuruvesi	68	63.39 N	26.37 E
Kiviõli	86	59.21 N	26.57 E
Kivu, Lac ⊜	110	2.00 S	29.10 E
Kizel	64	59.03 N	57.40 E
Kızıl ≃	104	41.44 N	35.58 E
Kiz'oma	66	61.08 N	44.50 E
Kizyl-Arvat	104	38.58 N	56.15 E
Kizyl-Atrek	100	37.36 N	54.46 E
Kjellerup	68	56.17 N	9.26 E
Kjustendil	80	42.17 N	22.41 E
Klabat, Gunung ∧	96	1.28 N	125.02 E
Kladanj	80	44.13 N	18.41 E
Kladno	72	50.08 N	14.05 E
Klagenfurt	72	46.38 N	14.18 E
Klagetoh	164	35.30 N	109.32 W
Klaipėda (Memel)	86	55.43 N	21.07 E
Klamath	168	41.32 N	124.02 W
Klamath ≃	168	41.33 N	124.04 W
Klamath Falls	166	42.13 N	121.46 W
Klamath Mountains ⋀	168	41.40 N	123.20 W
Klarälven (Trysilelva) ≃	68	59.23 N	13.32 E
Klatovy	72	49.24 N	13.18 E
Klawer	116	31.44 S	18.36 E
Klawock	146	55.33 N	133.06 W
Kleck	86	53.04 N	26.38 E
Klein	166	46.24 N	108.32 W
Klerksdorp	116	26.58 S	26.39 E
Kletn'a	86	53.23 N	33.12 E
Kleve	72	51.48 N	6.09 E
Kličev	86	53.29 N	29.21 E
Klimovsk	86	55.22 N	37.32 E
Klin	86	56.20 N	36.44 E
Klincy	86	52.47 N	32.14 E
Klingenthal	72	50.21 N	12.28 E
Klintehamn	68	57.24 N	18.12 E
Klipplaat	116	33.02 S	24.21 E
Kłobuck	72	50.55 N	18.57 E
Kłodzko	72	50.27 N	16.39 E
Kløfta	68	60.04 N	11.09 E
Klondike □9	146	63.30 N	139.00 W
Klosterneuburg	72	48.18 N	16.20 E
Klosters	74	46.54 N	9.53 E
Kloten	74	47.27 N	8.35 E
Klotz, Lac ⊜	142	60.32 N	73.40 W
Klötze	72	52.38 N	11.10 E
Klouto	114	6.57 N	0.34 E
Kluane Lake ⊜	146	61.15 N	138.40 W
Kluang	96	2.01 N	103.19 E
Kl'učevskaja Sopka, Vulkan ∧[1]	84	56.04 N	160.38 E
Kl'uči	84	56.18 N	160.51 E
Kluczbork	72	50.59 N	18.13 E
Klukwan	146	59.24 N	135.54 W
Knaben gruver	68	58.39 N	7.04 E
Knaresborough	70	54.00 N	1.27 W
Knee Lake ⊜	142	55.03 N	94.40 W
Kneža	80	43.30 N	24.05 E
Knighton	70	52.21 N	3.03 W
Knights Landing	168	38.48 N	121.43 W
Knightstown	158	39.48 N	85.32 W
Knin	78	44.02 N	16.12 E
Knippa	160	29.18 N	99.38 W
Knittelfeld	72	47.14 N	14.50 E
Knob, Cape ≻	122	34.32 S	119.16 E
Knobby Head ≻	122	29.40 S	114.58 E
Knob Noster	158	38.46 N	93.33 W
Knokke	72	51.21 N	3.17 E
Knox, Ind., U.S.	158	41.18 N	86.37 W

Symbols in the index entries are identified on page 203.

Name	Page	Lat	Long
Knox, Pa., U.S.	152	41.14 N	79.32 W
Knox, Cape ►	148	54.11 N	133.04 W
Knox City	160	33.25 N	99.49 W
Knoxville, Ill., U.S.	154	40.55 N	90.17 W
Knoxville, Iowa, U.S.	154	41.19 N	93.06 W
Knoxville, Tenn., U.S.	156	35.58 N	83.56 W
Knysna	116	34.02 S	23.02 E
Knyszyn	72	53.19 N	22.55 E
Kob'aj	83	63.34 N	126.30 E
Kobar Sink ≛[7]	108	14.00 N	40.30 E
Kōbe	90	34.41 N	135.10 E
København (Copenhagen)	68	55.40 N	12.35 E
Koblenz	72	50.21 N	7.35 E
Kobona	66	60.01 N	31.36 E
Koboža	66	58.49 N	35.01 E
Kobrin	86	52.13 N	24.21 E
Kobrinskoje	86	59.25 N	30.07 E
Kobroor, Pulau I	124	6.12 S	134.32 E
Kočani	80	41.55 N	22.25 E
Kočečum ≈	84	64.17 N	100.10 E
Kočevje	78	45.38 N	14.52 E
Kōchi	90	33.33 N	133.33 E
Koch Island I	142	69.38 N	78.15 W
Kochma	86	56.56 N	41.06 E
Kodaikānal	100	10.14 N	77.29 E
Kodari	100	27.56 N	85.56 E
Kodiak	146	57.48 N	152.23 W
Kodiak Island I	146	57.30 N	153.30 W
Kodok	112	9.53 N	32.07 E
Koforidua	114	6.03 N	0.17 W
Kōfu	90	35.39 N	138.35 E
Kogaluc ≈	142	59.40 N	77.35 W
Kogaluc, Baie C	142	59.20 N	77.50 W
Kogaluk ≈	142	56.12 N	61.44 W
Kogon	120	27.03 S	150.46 E
Køge	68	55.27 N	12.11 E
Køge Bugt C	142	65.00 N	40.30 W
Kohāt	102	33.35 N	71.26 E
Kohima	102	25.40 N	94.07 E
Kohtla-Järve	86	59.24 N	27.15 E
Koigorodok	66	60.26 N	50.58 E
Koindu	82	40.33 N	70.57 E
Kokčetav	82	53.17 N	69.25 E
Kokemäki	68	61.15 N	22.21 E
Kokkola (Gamlakarleby)	68	63.50 N	23.07 E
Kokomo, Haw., U.S.	170a	20.53 N	156.19 W
Kokomo, Ind., U.S.	154	40.29 N	86.08 W
Kokonau	124	4.43 S	136.26 E
Kokoreva	86	52.35 N	34.16 E
Koksaalatau, Chrebet ⋀	82	41.00 N	78.00 E
Koksoak ≈	142	58.32 N	68.10 W
Kokstad	116	30.32 S	29.29 E
Kola, Pulau I	92	5.30 S	134.35 E
Kolaka	96	4.03 S	121.36 E
Kolār	100	13.08 N	78.08 E
Kolār Gold Fields	100	12.55 N	78.17 E
Kolbio	110	1.10 S	41.15 E
Kolbotn	68	59.49 N	10.48 E
Kol'čugino	86	56.18 N	39.23 E
Kolda	114	12.53 N	14.57 W
Kolding	68	55.31 N	9.29 E
Kolenté (Great Scarcies) ≈	114	8.55 N	13.08 W
Kolgujev, Ostrov I	66	69.05 N	49.15 E
Kolhāpur	100	16.42 N	74.13 E
Kolho	68	62.08 N	24.31 E
Koliba (Corubal) ≈	114	11.57 N	15.06 W
Koliganek	146	59.48 N	157.25 W
Kolín	72	50.01 N	15.13 E
Kolmården ⋀[2]	68	58.40 N	16.35 E
Köln (Cologne)	72	50.56 N	6.59 E
Kolno	72	53.25 N	21.56 E
Koło	72	52.12 N	18.38 E
Koloa	170b	21.55 N	159.28 W
Kolobovo	86	56.47 N	41.21 E
Kołobrzeg	72	54.12 N	15.33 E
Kolodn'a	86	54.48 N	32.09 E
Kologriv	86	58.51 N	44.17 E
Kolombangara I	118	8.00 S	157.05 E
Kolomna	86	55.05 N	38.49 E
Kolomyja	84	48.32 N	25.04 E
Kolpaševo	84	58.20 N	82.50 E
Kolpino	86	59.45 N	30.36 E
Kolpny	86	52.15 N	37.02 E
Kol'skij Polvostrov (Kola Peninsula) ⋗[1]	66	67.30 N	37.00 E
Kolwezi	110	10.43 S	25.28 E
Kolyma ≈	84	69.30 N	161.00 E
Kolymskaja	84	68.44 N	158.44 E
Kolymskaja Nizmennost' ≊	84	68.30 N	154.00 E
Komádugu Gana ≈	106	13.05 N	12.24 E
Komádugu Yobe ≈	106	13.43 N	13.20 E
Komandorskije Ostrova II	84	55.00 N	167.00 E
Komárno	72	47.45 N	18.09 E
Komárom	72	47.44 N	18.08 E
Komárom ⬚[6]	72	47.40 N	18.15 E
Komati (Incomati) ≈	116	25.46 S	32.43 E
Komatsu	90	36.24 N	136.27 E
Komering ≈	96	2.59 S	104.50 E
Komló	72	46.12 N	18.16 E
Kommunarsk	64	48.30 N	38.47 E
Kommunizma, Pik ⋀	82	38.57 N	72.01 E
Komodo, Pulau I	96	8.36 S	119.30 E
Komoé ≈	114	5.12 N	3.44 W
Komotiní	80	41.07 N	25.24 E
Komsberg ⋀	116	31.45 S	21.32 E
Komsomolec, Ostrov I	84	80.30 N	95.00 E
Komsomolec, Zaliv C	64	45.30 N	52.45 E
Komsomol'sk	82	57.02 N	40.18 E
Komsomol'sk-na-Amure	84	50.35 N	137.02 E
Komsomol'skij Pravdy, Ostrova II	84	77.20 N	107.40 E
Konakovo	86	56.42 N	36.46 E
Konār ≈	102	34.26 N	70.32 E
Konawa	160	34.58 N	96.45 W
Konda ≈	84	61.20 N	63.48 E
Konda ≈	84	60.40 N	69.46 E
Kondagaon	100	19.36 N	81.40 E
Kondega	86	60.14 N	33.20 E
Kondinskoje	84	59.41 N	67.25 E
Kondoa	110	4.54 S	35.47 E
Kondopoga	66	62.12 N	34.17 E
Kondrovo	86	54.48 N	35.56 E
Konecbor	66	64.52 N	57.44 E
Kongolo	110	5.23 S	27.00 E
Kongquhe ≈	88	40.40 N	90.10 E
Kongsberg	68	59.39 N	9.39 E
Kongsvinger	68	60.12 N	12.00 E
Kongsvoll	68	62.18 N	9.37 E
Königsberg → Kaliningrad	86	54.43 N	20.30 E
Königswinter	72	50.41 N	7.11 E
Königs Wusterhausen	72	52.18 N	13.37 E
Konin	72	52.13 N	18.16 E
Konjic	80	43.39 N	17.57 E
Könkämäälv ≈	68	68.29 N	22.17 E
Konkouré ≈	114	9.58 N	13.42 W
Konoša	66	60.58 N	40.15 E
Konotop	64	51.14 N	33.12 E
Konpienga ≈	114	11.10 N	0.51 E
Konskie	72	51.12 N	20.26 E
Konstantinovka	64	48.32 N	37.43 E
Konstantinovskij	86	57.50 N	39.36 E
Konstanz	72	47.40 N	9.10 E
Kontagora	114	10.24 N	5.28 E
Kontiomäki	68	64.21 N	28.09 E
Kontum	94	14.21 N	108.00 E
Konya	104	37.52 N	32.31 E
Konz	72	49.42 N	6.34 E
Konza	110	1.45 S	37.07 E
Konžakovskij Kamen', Gora ⋀	82	59.38 N	59.08 E
Koocanusa, Lake ⊜[1]	148	49.00 N	115.10 W
Koolamarra	120	20.12 S	140.14 E
Koolau Range ⋀	170c	21.35 N	158.00 W
Kooloonong	120	34.53 S	143.09 E
Koondrook	120	35.39 S	144.08 E
Koorda	122	30.50 S	117.29 E
Kooskia	166	46.09 N	115.59 W
Kootenai (Kootenay) ≈	148	49.15 N	117.39 W
Kootenay (Kootenai) ≈	148	49.15 N	117.39 W
Kópavogur	66a	64.06 N	21.50 W
Kopejsk	82	55.07 N	61.37 E
Koper	78	45.33 N	13.44 E
Köping	68	59.31 N	16.00 E
Koppang	68	61.34 N	11.04 E
Kopparbergs Län ⬚[6]	68	61.00 N	14.30 E
Koppeh Dāgh ⋀	104	37.50 N	58.00 E
Koppera	68	63.24 N	11.51 E
Koprivnica	78	46.10 N	16.50 E
Kopys'	86	54.19 N	30.18 E
Korab ⋀	80	41.47 N	20.34 E
Korablino	86	53.55 N	40.01 E
Kor'akskoje Nagorje ⋀	84	62.30 N	172.00 E
Koraput	100	18.48 N	82.41 E
Korbach	72	51.16 N	8.52 E
Korçë	80	40.37 N	20.46 E
Korea, North ⬚[1]	88	40.00 N	127.00 E
Korea, South ⬚[1]	88	36.30 N	128.00 E
Korea Bay C	88	39.00 N	124.00 E
Korea Strait ⋃	88	34.00 N	129.00 E
Koreliči	86	53.34 N	26.08 E
Korf	84	60.19 N	165.50 E
Korfovskij	84	48.14 N	135.02 E
Korhogo	114	9.27 N	5.38 W
Kórinthos (Corinth)	80	37.56 N	22.56 E
Koriyama	90	37.24 N	140.23 E
Korkino	82	54.54 N	61.23 E
Korliki	84	61.31 N	82.22 E
Körmend	72	47.01 N	16.37 E
Korneuburg	72	48.21 N	16.20 E
Kornsjø	68	58.57 N	11.39 E
Korogwe	110	5.09 S	38.29 E
Koror	92	7.20 N	134.29 E
Korosten'	64	50.57 N	28.39 E
Koro Toro	108	16.05 N	18.30 E
Korpilahti	68	62.01 N	25.33 E
Korsakov	84	46.38 N	142.46 E
Korso	68	60.21 N	25.06 E
Korsør	68	55.20 N	11.09 E
Kortrijk (Courtrai)	74	50.50 N	3.16 E
Korumburra	120	38.26 S	145.49 E
Kos	80	36.50 N	27.10 E
Kosa	66	59.56 N	54.55 E
Koš-Agač	84	50.00 N	88.40 E
Kościan	72	52.06 N	16.38 E
Kościerzyna	72	54.08 N	18.00 E
Kosciusko	158	32.58 N	89.35 W
Kosciusko, Mount ⋀	120	36.27 S	148.16 E
Košice	72	48.43 N	21.15 E
Koski	68	60.39 N	23.09 E
Koslan	66	63.28 N	48.52 E
Kosovska Mitrovica	80	42.53 N	20.52 E
Kosse	160	31.18 N	96.38 W
Kostrzyn	72	52.37 N	14.39 E
Kost'ukoviči	86	53.20 N	32.03 E
Koszalin (Köslin)	72	54.12 N	16.09 E
Kőszeg	72	47.23 N	16.33 E
Kota	102	25.11 N	75.50 E
Kotabaru	96	3.14 S	116.13 E
Kota Bharu	96	6.07 N	102.15 E
Kotabumi	96	4.50 S	104.54 E
Kotadabok	92	0.30 S	104.33 E
Kota Kinabalu (Jesselton)	96	5.58 N	116.04 E
Kotamobagu	96	0.46 N	124.19 E
Kotcho Lake ⊜	142	59.05 N	121.10 W
Kotel'nič	66	58.18 N	48.20 E
Kotel'nikovo	64	47.38 N	43.09 E
Kotel'nyj, Ostrov I	84	75.45 N	138.44 E
Kotka	68	51.45 N	11.58 E
Kotlas	66	61.16 N	46.35 E
Kotovsk	86	52.36 N	41.32 E
Kötschach-[Mauthen]	72	46.40 N	13.00 E
Kötzting	72	49.11 N	12.52 E
Koudougou	114	12.15 N	2.22 W
Koukdjuak ≈	142	66.35 N	73.09 W
Koula-Moutou	110	1.08 S	12.29 E
Koulikoro	114	12.53 N	7.33 W
Koulountou ≈	114	13.15 N	13.37 W
Koumra	108	8.55 N	17.33 E
Kounda Ko ≈	114	13.05 N	11.24 W
Kounradskij	82	46.59 N	75.00 E
Kountze	158	30.22 N	94.19 W
Kouroussa	114	10.39 N	9.53 W
Koussi, Emi ⋀	108	19.50 N	18.33 E
Koutiala	106	12.23 S	5.28 W
Kouts	158	41.19 N	87.02 W
Kouvola	68	60.52 N	26.42 E
Kovarskas	86	55.26 N	24.55 E
Kovdor	66	67.34 N	30.22 E
Kovel'	64	51.13 N	24.41 E
Kovernino	86	57.07 N	43.49 E
Kovrov	66	56.22 N	41.18 E
Kovylkino	66	54.01 N	43.53 E
Kowalewo Pomorskie	72	53.10 N	18.53 E
Kowkcheh ≈	102	37.10 N	69.23 E
Kowloon (Jiulong)	88	22.18 N	114.10 E
Koyuk	146	64.56 N	161.08 W
Koyukuk	146	64.53 N	157.43 W
Koyukuk ≈	146	64.56 N	157.30 W
Kozáni	80	40.18 N	21.47 E
Kozel'sk	86	54.02 N	35.48 E
Kožle	72	50.20 N	18.08 E
Kozlovo	86	56.20 N	36.16 E
Koz'modemjansk	66	56.20 N	46.36 E
Kozlu	104	41.26 N	31.47 E
Kpandu	114	7.00 N	0.18 E
Kra, Isthmus of ⋅[3]	94	10.20 N	99.00 E
Kra Buri	94	10.24 N	98.47 E
Krachèh	94	12.29 N	106.01 E
Kragerø	68	58.52 N	9.25 E
Kragujevac	80	44.01 N	20.55 E
Kraków	72	50.03 N	19.58 E
Kraljevica	132	45.16 N	14.34 E
Kraljevo	80	43.43 N	20.41 E
Kralupy nad Vltavou	72	50.13 N	14.18 E
Kramatorsk	64	48.43 N	37.32 E
Kranj	78	46.15 N	14.21 E
Krasino	66	70.45 N	54.18 E
Krasneno	146	64.38 N	174.48 E
Krasnik Fabryczny	72	50.56 N	22.13 E
Krasnoarmejsk	86	56.08 N	38.08 E
Krasnoarmejskij	84	69.30 N	172.00 E
Krasnodar	64	45.02 N	39.00 E
Krasnogorsk, S.S.S.R.	86	48.24 N	142.06 E
Krasnogorsk, S.S.S.R.	86	55.50 N	37.20 E
Krasnoj Armii, Proliv ⋃	84	80.00 N	94.35 E
Krasnojarsk	84	56.01 N	92.50 E
Krasnoje, Ozero ⊜	84	64.30 N	174.24 E
Krasnoje Echo	86	55.48 N	40.42 E
Krasnoje-na-Volge	86	57.31 N	41.14 E
Krasnoje Selo	86	59.44 N	30.05 E
Krasnokamsk	64	58.04 N	55.48 E
Krasnoje	86	54.24 N	22.23 E
Krasnosel'kup	84	65.41 N	82.28 E
Krasnoslobodsk	86	48.42 N	44.34 E
Krasnoturjinsk	82	59.46 N	60.12 E
Krasnoufimsk	64	56.37 N	57.46 E
Krasnoural'sk	82	58.21 N	60.03 E
Krasnovišersk	66	60.23 N	56.59 E
Krasnovodsk	104	40.00 N	53.00 E
Krasnozavodsk	86	56.27 N	38.25 E
Krasnoznamensk	64	54.57 N	22.30 E
Krasnoznamenskij	82	51.03 N	69.30 E
Krasnoz'orskoje	84	54.02 N	79.14 E
Krasnyj Bogatyr'	86	56.02 N	41.08 E
Krasnyj Cholm	86	58.03 N	37.07 E
Krasnyj Tkač	86	55.28 N	39.05 E
Krasnyj Kut	66	50.57 N	46.58 E
Krasnystaw	72	50.59 N	23.10 E
Kraszna (Crasna) ≈	72	48.09 N	22.20 E
Kremenčug	64	49.04 N	33.25 E
Kremenčugskoje Vodochranilišče ⊜[1]	64	49.20 N	32.30 E
Kremmling	164	40.03 N	106.24 W
Krems an der Donau	72	48.25 N	15.36 E
Kremsmünster	72	48.03 N	14.08 E
Kreole	158	30.24 N	88.30 W
Kresta, Zaliv C	146	65.40 N	180.00 E
Krestcy	86	58.15 N	32.31 E
Krest-Major	84	67.37 N	144.45 E
Krestovaja Guba	82	74.07 N	55.33 E
Kretinga	86	55.53 N	21.13 E
Kribi	106	2.57 N	9.55 E
Kričov	86	53.42 N	31.43 E
Kriens	74	47.02 N	8.17 E
Krimml	72	47.13 N	12.11 E
Krishna ≈	100	15.43 N	80.55 E
Krishnanagar	102	23.24 N	88.30 E
Kristdala	68	57.24 N	16.11 E
Kristiansand	68	58.10 N	8.00 E
Kristianstad	68	56.02 N	14.08 E
Kristianstads Län ⬚[6]	68	56.15 N	14.00 E
Kristiansund	68	63.07 N	7.45 E
Kristinehamn	68	59.20 N	14.07 E
Kríti I	80	35.29 N	24.42 E
Kritikón Pélagos ⊤[2]	80	35.46 N	23.54 E
Kriva Palanka	80	42.12 N	22.20 E
Krivči	84	54.43 N	27.17 E
Krivoj Rog	64	47.55 N	33.21 E
Križevci	78	46.02 N	16.33 E
Krnov	72	50.05 N	17.41 E
Krobia	72	60.21 N	25.06 E
Krokodil ≈	116	25.26 S	31.58 E
Krokowa	72	54.48 N	18.11 E
Kroměříž	72	49.18 N	17.24 E
Kromy	86	52.42 N	35.46 E
Kronach	72	50.14 N	11.20 E
Krŏng Kêb	94	10.30 N	104.19 E
Krŏng Khémôreăh Phumĭnt	94	11.37 N	102.59 E
Kronobergs Län ⬚[6]	68	56.40 N	14.40 E
Kronockij Zaliv C	84	54.00 N	160.00 E
Kronoki	84	54.36 N	161.10 E
Kronštadt	86	59.59 N	29.45 E
Kroonstad	116	27.46 S	27.12 E
Kropotkin, S.S.S.R.	64	45.26 N	40.34 E
Kropotkin, S.S.S.R.	84	58.30 N	115.17 E
Krosno	72	49.42 N	21.46 E
Krotoszyn	72	51.42 N	17.26 E
Krotz Springs	158	30.32 N	91.45 W
Krugersdorp	116	26.05 S	27.35 E
Krui	96	5.11 S	103.58 E
Kr'ukovo	84	66.30 N	159.31 E
Krumbach [Schwaben]	72	48.14 N	10.22 E
Krŭng Thep (Bangkok)	94	13.45 N	100.31 E
Kruševac	80	43.35 N	21.20 E
Kruševo	80	41.22 N	21.14 E
Krušné hory (Erzgebirge) ⋀	72	50.30 N	13.15 E
Kruzenšterna, Proliv ⋃	84	48.30 N	153.50 E
Kruzof Island I	146	57.10 N	135.40 W
Krymskij Poluostrov ⋗	64	45.00 N	34.00 E
Krynica	72	49.25 N	20.56 E
Ksar-el-Kebir	106	35.01 N	5.54 W
Ksar-es-Souk	106	31.58 N	4.25 W
Ksenjevka	84	53.07 N	118.10 E
Ksenofontova	66	60.58 N	56.12 E
Kstovo	66	56.08 N	44.11 E
Kuala Kapuas	96	2.59 S	114.21 E
Kuala Lumpur	96	3.10 N	101.43 E
Kuala Terengganu	96	5.20 N	103.08 E
Kualapu	170a	21.09 N	157.01 W
Kuala Trengganu	96	5.20 N	103.09 E
Kuantan	96	3.50 N	103.20 E
Kuba	100	3.14 S	16.13 E
Kuban' ≈	64	45.20 N	37.30 E
Kubenskoje	66	59.26 N	39.40 E
Kučema	66	64.58 N	40.00 E
Kuche	88	41.43 N	82.54 E
Kuching	96	1.32 N	110.19 E
Kudat	96	6.53 N	116.48 E
Kudirkos Naumiestis	86	54.46 N	22.53 E
Kudus	96	6.48 S	110.50 E
Kudymkar	66	59.01 N	54.37 E
Kufstein	72	47.35 N	12.10 E
Kuhmo	68	64.08 N	29.31 E
Kuhmoinen	68	61.34 N	25.11 E
Kuiu Island I	146	57.45 N	134.10 W
Kujbyšev, S.S.S.R.	84	55.27 N	78.19 E
Kujbyšev, S.S.S.R.	66	53.12 N	50.09 E
Kujbyševskoje Vodochranilišče ⊜[1]	66	53.40 N	49.00 E
Kujū-san ⋀	90	33.05 N	131.15 E
Kukawa	106	12.56 N	13.35 E
Kukerin	122	33.11 S	118.07 E
Kukkola	68	65.59 N	24.33 E
Kukuj	84	60.48 N	90.04 E
Kula	80	45.36 N	19.32 E
Kul'ab	102	37.55 N	69.46 E
Kula Kangri ⋀	102	28.03 N	90.27 E
Kuldīga	86	56.58 N	21.59 E
Kuldja → Yining	88	43.55 N	81.14 E
Kulebaki	66	55.26 N	42.32 E
Kulgera	120	25.50 S	133.18 E
Kulju	68	61.23 N	23.46 E
Kulm	162	46.18 N	98.56 W
Kulmbach	72	50.06 N	11.27 E
Kuloj ≈	66	66.25 N	42.32 E
Kulotino	86	58.27 N	33.21 E
Kul'sary	64	46.59 N	54.01 E
Kulunda	84	52.35 N	78.57 E
Kulundinskaja Step' ≊	84	53.00 N	79.00 E
Kulundinskoje, Ozero ⊜	84	53.00 N	79.36 E
Kulunqi	88	42.44 N	121.40 E
Kuma ≈	64	44.56 N	47.00 E
Kumagaya	90	36.08 N	139.23 E
Kumamoto	90	32.48 N	130.43 E
Kumano	90	33.54 N	136.06 E
Kumanovo	80	42.08 N	21.43 E
Kumara	126	42.38 S	171.11 E
Kumasi	114	6.41 N	1.35 W
Kumba	106	4.38 N	9.25 E
Kumbakonam	100	10.58 N	79.23 E
Kum-Dag	104	39.16 N	54.35 E
Kumertau	82	52.46 N	55.47 E
Kume-shima I	91b	26.21 N	126.47 E
Kumla	68	59.08 N	15.08 E
Kumo	106	10.03 N	11.13 E
Kunashir, Ostrov (Kunashiri-tō) I	84	44.10 N	146.00 E
Kunda	86	59.29 N	26.32 E
Kundar ≈	102	31.56 N	69.19 E
Kundūz	82	37.45 N	68.51 E
Kungrad	82	43.06 N	58.54 E
Kungur	64	57.25 N	56.57 E
Kunhegyes	72	47.22 N	20.38 E
Kunia	170c	21.29 N	158.07 W
Kunlunshanmai ⋀	94	36.30 N	88.00 E
Kunming	94	25.05 N	102.40 E
Kunsan	88	35.58 N	126.41 E
Kunszentmárton	72	46.51 N	20.18 E
Kununurra	124	15.47 S	128.44 E
Künzelsau	72	49.16 N	9.41 E
Kuopio	68	62.54 N	27.41 E
Kuopion lääni ⬚[4]	68	63.00 N	27.30 E
Kuortane	68	62.48 N	23.30 E
Kupang	96	10.10 S	123.35 E
Kupansk	64	49.42 N	37.38 E
Kupino	84	54.22 N	77.18 E
Kupiškis	86	55.50 N	24.58 E
Kupreanof Island I	146	56.50 N	133.30 W
Kura ≈	64	39.24 N	49.24 E
Kurashiki	90	34.35 N	133.46 E
Kure	90	34.14 N	132.34 E
Kurejka ≈	84	66.30 N	87.12 E
Kurenalus	68	65.21 N	26.59 E
Kuressaare	86	58.15 N	22.28 E
Kurgan	82	55.26 N	65.18 E
Kurgan-T'ube	82	37.50 N	68.48 E
Kuria Muria Islands → Khūryān Mūryān II	100	17.30 N	56.00 E
Kuridala	120	21.17 S	140.30 E
Kurikka	68	62.37 N	22.25 E
Kuril Islands → Kuril'skije Ostrova II	84	46.10 N	152.00 E
Kuril'sk	84	45.14 N	147.53 E
Kuril'skije Ostrova (Kuril Islands) II	84	46.10 N	152.00 E
Kurlovskij	86	55.27 N	40.36 E
Kurmuk	112	10.33 N	34.17 E
Kurnool	100	15.50 N	78.03 E
Kurow	126	44.44 S	170.28 E
Kursk	64	51.42 N	36.12 E
Kurti	112	18.07 N	31.33 E
Kurtistown	170d	19.36 N	155.04 W
Kuru	68	61.52 N	23.44 E
Kurume	90	33.19 N	130.31 E
Kuruman	116	27.28 S	23.28 E
Kurunegala	100	7.29 N	80.22 E
Kusa	82	55.20 N	59.29 E
Kusawa Lake ⊜	146	60.20 N	136.15 W
Kusel	72	49.32 N	7.24 E
Kushiro	90a	42.58 N	144.23 E
Kushui	88	42.11 N	94.25 E
Kuška ≈	104	35.16 N	62.20 E
Kuskokwim ≈	146	60.17 N	162.27 W
Kuskokwim Mountains ⋀	146	62.30 N	156.00 W
Kušmurun	82	52.27 N	64.36 E
Küsnacht	74	47.19 N	8.35 E
Küssnacht	74	47.05 N	8.27 E
Kustanaj	82	53.10 N	63.35 E
Küstl	112	13.10 N	32.40 E
K'us'ur	84	70.39 N	127.15 E
Kusva	82	58.18 N	59.45 E
Kut, Ko I	94	11.40 N	102.35 E
Kütahya	104	39.25 N	29.59 E
Kutaisi	64	42.15 N	42.40 E
Kūt al-Imāra	104	32.25 N	45.49 E
Kutaradja → Banda Atjeh	94	5.34 N	95.20 E
Kutch, Gulf of C	102	22.36 N	69.30 E
Kutina	78	45.29 N	16.46 E
Kutná Hora	72	49.57 N	15.16 E
Kutno	72	52.15 N	19.23 E
Kutu	110	2.44 S	18.09 E
Kutztown	152	40.31 N	75.47 W
Kuusamo	68	65.58 N	29.11 E
Kuusankoski	68	60.54 N	26.38 E
Kuvandyk	82	51.28 N	57.21 E
Kuwait ⬚[1]	104	29.30 N	47.45 E
Kuwait → Al-Kuwayt	104	29.20 N	47.59 E
Kuz'movka	84	62.19 N	92.02 E
Kuzneck	66	53.07 N	46.36 E
Kuzneckij Alatau ⋀	84	54.45 N	88.00 E
Kuznecovka	84	56.24 N	88.33 E
Kwakoegron	134	5.12 N	55.22 W
Kwando (Cuando) ≈	110	18.27 S	23.32 E
Kwangchow → Guangzhou	88	23.06 N	113.16 E
Kwangju	88	35.09 N	126.54 E
Kwango (Cuango) ≈	110	3.14 S	17.23 E
Kweisui → Huhehaote	88	40.51 N	111.40 E
Kwenge ≈	110	4.50 S	18.42 E
Kwethluk	146	60.49 N	161.27 W
Kwidzyn	72	53.45 N	18.56 E
Kwigillingok	146	59.51 N	163.08 W
Kwilu (Cuilo) ≈	110	3.22 S	17.22 E
Kwinana	122	32.15 S	115.48 E
Kwoka ⋀	124	0.31 S	132.25 E
Kwobrup	122	33.44 S	118.17 E
Kyabra Creek ≈	120	25.36 S	142.55 E
Kyabram	120	36.19 S	145.03 E
Kyaukpyu	94	19.05 N	93.52 E
Kyaukse	94	21.36 N	96.08 E
Kybartai	86	54.39 N	22.45 E
Kyle	122	27.01 S	97.53 E
Kyle of Lochalsh	70	57.17 N	5.43 W
Kymi lääni ⬚[4]	68	61.00 N	28.00 E
Kyneton	120	37.15 S	144.27 E
Kyoga, Lake ⊜	110	1.30 N	33.00 E
Kyogle	120	28.37 S	152.59 E
Kyŏngju	88	35.50 N	129.13 E
Kyōto	90	35.00 N	135.45 E
Kyren	84	51.41 N	102.08 E
Kyritz	72	52.56 N	12.23 E
Kyrksæterøra	68	63.17 N	9.06 E
Kyrkslätt (Kirkkonummi)	68	60.07 N	24.26 E
Kyrö	68	60.42 N	22.45 E
Kýthira I	80	36.15 N	23.00 E
Kyūshū I	90	32.50 N	131.00 E
Kywong	120	34.59 S	146.44 E
Kyzyl	84	51.42 N	94.27 E
Kyzyl-Kija	82	40.16 N	72.08 E
Kyzylkum ⋅[2]	82	42.00 N	64.00 E
Kyzyl-Orda	82	44.48 N	65.28 E
Kzyltu	82	53.53 N	72.20 E

L

Name	Page	Lat	Long
Laa an der Thaya	72	48.43 N	16.23 E
La Albufera C	76	39.20 N	0.22 W
La Alcarria ⋀[1]	76	40.30 N	2.45 W
La Asunción	138	11.02 N	63.53 W
La Baie	152	48.21 N	70.53 W
La Bañeza	76	42.18 N	5.54 W
La Barca	130	20.17 N	102.33 W
La Bassée	74	50.32 N	2.48 E
La Baule	74	47.17 N	2.24 W
Labastide-Murat	74	44.39 N	1.34 E
La Belle	156	26.46 N	81.26 W
Laberge, Lake ⊜	146	61.11 N	135.12 W
Labin	78	45.05 N	14.07 E
La Bisbal	76	41.57 N	3.03 E
La Blanquilla I	138	11.51 N	64.37 W
Laboe	72	54.24 N	10.15 E
Labouchere, Mount ⋀	122	25.12 S	118.18 E
Laboulaye	140	34.05 S	63.25 W
Labrador ◄[1]	142	54.00 N	62.00 W
Labrador City	142	52.57 N	66.55 W
Labrador Sea ⊤[2]	142	57.00 N	53.00 W
Lábrea	134	7.16 S	64.47 W
La Brède	74	44.41 N	0.31 W
Labrit	74	44.07 N	0.33 W
Labuan, Pulau I	96	5.21 N	115.13 E
Labuha	92	0.37 S	127.29 E
Labytnangi	84	66.39 N	66.21 E
Lacanau	74	44.59 N	1.05 W
La Canourgue	74	44.26 N	3.13 E
Lacapelle-Marival	74	44.44 N	1.54 E
La Carlota	76	37.40 N	4.56 W
La Carolina	76	38.16 N	3.37 W
Laccadive Islands II	100	10.00 N	73.00 E
La Ceiba	132	15.47 N	86.50 W
Lacepede Bay C	120	36.45 S	139.45 E
Lac-Etchemin	152	46.24 N	70.30 W
La Chambre	74	45.22 N	6.18 E
La Chapelle-d'Angillon	74	47.22 N	2.26 E
La Charité-sur-Loire	74	47.11 N	3.01 E
La Chartre-sur-le-Loir	74	47.44 N	0.34 E
La Châtaigneraie	74	46.39 N	0.44 W
La Châtre	74	46.35 N	1.59 E
La Chaux-de-Fonds	74	47.06 N	6.50 E
Lachine	152	45.26 N	73.40 W
Lachlan ≈	120	34.21 S	143.57 E
La Chorrera, Col.	138	0.44 S	73.01 W
La Chorrera, Pan.	138	8.53 N	79.47 W
La Ciotat	74	43.10 N	5.36 E
Lackawanna	152	42.49 N	78.49 W
La Clayette	74	46.17 N	4.19 E
Lac-Mégantic	152	45.36 N	70.53 W
Lacombe	148	52.28 N	113.44 W
Lacon	154	41.02 N	89.24 W
Laconia	152	43.31 N	71.28 W
Lacoochee	156	28.28 N	82.10 W
La Coruña	76	43.22 N	8.23 W
La Coste	160	29.19 N	98.49 W
La Courtine	74	45.42 N	2.16 E
La Crescent	154	43.50 N	91.19 W
La Crosse, Ind., U.S.	158	41.19 N	86.53 W
La Crosse, Wash., U.S.	166	46.49 N	117.53 W
La Crosse, Wis., U.S.	154	43.48 N	91.15 W
La Cruz	162	1.35 N	76.58 W
La Cygne	162	38.21 N	94.46 W
Ladākh ⋀[1]	102	34.45 N	78.00 E
Ladākh Range ⋀	102	34.00 N	78.00 E
La Digue I	110	4.21 S	55.50 E
Lādīz	104	28.56 N	61.19 E
Ladoga, Lake → Ladožskoje Ozero ⊜	66	61.00 N	31.30 E
Ladonia	160	33.25 N	95.57 W
La Dorada	138	5.27 N	74.40 W
Ladožskoje Ozero (Lake Ladoga) ⊜	66	61.00 N	31.30 E
Ladue ≈	146	62.30 N	140.25 W
Laduškin	72	54.36 N	20.11 E
Ladva	66	61.21 N	34.34 E
Ladva-Vetka	66	61.21 N	34.27 E
Lady Ann Strait ⋃	142	75.30 N	79.50 W
Ladybrand	116	29.12 S	27.25 E
Lady Elliot Island I	120	24.07 S	152.42 E
Ladysmith, B.C., Can.	148	48.58 N	123.49 W
Ladysmith, S. Afr.	116	28.34 S	29.45 E
Ladysmith, Wis., U.S.	154	45.27 N	91.06 W
Lae	124	6.45 S	147.00 E
La Encantada, Cerro de ⋀	130	31.00 N	115.24 W
Lærdalsøyri	68	61.06 N	7.29 E
La Esmeralda	140	22.13 S	62.34 W
Læsø I	68	57.16 N	11.01 E
Lafayette, Ala., U.S.	158	32.54 N	85.24 W
Lafayette, Calif., U.S.	168	37.53 N	122.07 W
La Fayette, Ga., U.S.	158	34.42 N	85.17 W
La Fayette, Ind., U.S.	154	40.25 N	86.53 W
Lafayette, La., U.S.	158	30.13 N	92.01 W
Lafayette, Tenn., U.S.	156	36.31 N	86.01 W
La Fère	74	49.40 N	3.22 E
La Feria	160	26.09 N	97.49 W
La Ferté-Bernard	74	48.11 N	0.39 E
La Ferté-Gaucher	74	48.47 N	3.18 E
La Ferté-Saint-Aubin	74	47.43 N	1.56 E
La Ferté-Vidame	74	48.37 N	0.53 E
Lafia	114	8.29 N	8.31 E
La Flèche	74	47.42 N	0.05 W
La Follette	156	36.23 N	84.07 W
La Fregeneda	76	40.58 N	6.52 W
La Fuente de San Esteban	76	40.48 N	6.15 W
La Gacilly	74	47.46 N	2.08 W
Lagan ≈	68	56.35 N	12.56 E
Lågen ≈	68	61.08 N	10.25 E
Laghouat	106	33.48 N	2.52 E
Lagny	74	48.52 N	2.42 E
Lagos, Nig.	114	6.27 N	3.24 E
Lagos, Port.	76	37.06 N	8.40 W
La Grand'Combe	74	44.13 N	4.02 E
La Grande	166	45.19 N	118.05 W
La Grande ≈	142	53.50 N	79.00 W
La Grange, Austl.	122	18.41 S	121.45 E
Lagrange, Ind., U.S.	154	41.39 N	85.25 W
La Grange, Ga., U.S.	158	33.02 N	85.01 W
La Grange, Ky., U.S.	156	38.24 N	85.22 W
La Grange, Maine, U.S.	152	45.10 N	68.50 W
La Grange, N.C., U.S.	156	35.18 N	77.47 W
La Grange, Tex., U.S.	160	29.54 N	96.52 W
La Gran Sabana ≊	138	5.30 N	61.30 W
La Grave	74	45.03 N	6.18 E
La Guaira	138	10.36 N	66.56 W
La Guajira ⬚[1]	138	11.30 N	72.00 W
La Guajira, Península de ⋗	138	12.00 N	71.40 W
La Guerche-de-Bretagne	74	47.56 N	1.14 W
La Guerche-sur-l'Aubois	74	46.57 N	2.57 E
Laguiole	74	44.41 N	2.50 E
Laguna, Bra.	140	28.29 S	48.47 W
Laguna, N. Mex., U.S.	164	35.02 N	107.23 W
Laguna, Ilha da I	134	1.40 S	51.00 W
Laguna Beach	168	33.33 N	117.47 W
Lahad Datu	96	5.02 N	118.19 E
Lahaina	170a	20.52 N	156.41 W
La Harpe, Ill., U.S.	154	40.35 N	90.58 W
La Harpe, Kans., U.S.	162	37.55 N	95.18 W
Lahat	96	3.48 S	103.32 E
Lahijan	104	37.12 N	50.01 E
Lahnstein	72	50.18 N	7.38 E
Lahore	102	31.35 N	74.18 E
Lahr	72	48.20 N	7.52 E
Lahti	68	60.58 N	25.40 E
Laï	108	9.24 N	16.18 E
Laingsburg, S. Afr.	116	33.11 S	20.51 E
Laingsburg, Mich., U.S.	154	42.54 N	84.21 W
Lairg	70	58.01 N	4.25 W
Lais	96	3.32 S	102.03 E
Laissac	74	44.23 N	2.49 E
Laiwui	124	1.22 S	127.40 E
Laiyang	88	36.58 N	120.44 E
Laizhouwan C	88	37.16 N	119.30 E
La Jara	164	37.16 N	105.58 W
La Javie	74	44.10 N	6.21 E
Lajeado	140	29.27 S	51.58 W
Lajes	140	27.48 S	50.19 W
Lajitas	160	29.16 N	103.48 W
Lajosmizse	72	47.02 N	19.34 E
La Junta	162	37.59 N	103.33 W
Lake Alfred	156	28.05 N	81.44 W
Lake Arthur, La., U.S.	158	30.05 N	92.41 W
Lake Arthur, N. Mex., U.S.	160	33.00 N	104.22 W
Lake Butler	156	30.01 N	82.20 W
Lake Cargelligo	120	33.18 S	146.23 E
Lake Carmel	152	41.27 N	73.40 W
Lake Charles	158	30.13 N	93.12 W
Lake City, Fla., U.S.	156	30.11 N	82.38 W
Lake City, Mich., U.S.	154	44.20 N	85.13 W
Lake City, Pa., U.S.	152	42.01 N	80.21 W
Lake City, S.C., U.S.	156	33.52 N	79.45 W
Lake Cowichan	148	48.50 N	124.03 W
Lake Crystal	154	44.06 N	94.13 W
Lake Dallas	160	33.07 N	97.02 W
Lakefield, Ont., Can.	152	44.26 N	78.16 W
Lakefield, Minn., U.S.	154	43.41 N	95.10 W
Lake Forest, Fla., U.S.	156	30.24 N	81.41 W
Lake Forest, Ill., U.S.	154	42.15 N	87.50 W
Lake Geneva	154	42.36 N	88.26 W
Lake George	152	43.25 N	73.43 W
Lake Harbour	142	62.51 N	69.53 W
Lake Havasu City	164	34.27 N	114.22 W
Lake Helen	156	28.59 N	81.14 W
Lake Hopatcong	152	40.55 N	74.39 W
Lakehurst	152	40.01 N	74.19 W
Lake Jackson	160	29.02 N	95.27 W
Lakeland, Fla., U.S.	156	28.03 N	81.57 W
Lakeland, Ga., U.S.	156	31.02 N	83.04 W
Lake Mills, Iowa, U.S.	154	43.31 N	93.32 W
Lake Mills, Wis., U.S.	154	43.05 N	88.55 W
Lakemont	152	40.31 N	78.23 W
Lakemore	152	41.01 N	81.26 W
Lake Nash	120	21.00 S	137.55 E
Lake Odessa	154	42.47 N	85.08 W
Lake Oswego	166	45.26 N	122.39 W
Lake Park, Fla., U.S.	156	26.49 N	80.04 W
Lake Park, Iowa, U.S.	154	43.27 N	95.19 W
Lake Placid, Fla., U.S.	156	27.18 N	81.22 W
Lake Placid, N.Y., U.S.	152	44.17 N	73.59 W
Lakeport	168	39.03 N	122.55 W
Lake Providence	158	32.48 N	91.10 W
Lake Shore	154	42.54 N	84.41 W
Lakeside, N.S., Can.	150	44.38 N	63.41 W
Lakeside, Ariz., U.S.	164	34.09 N	109.58 W
Lakeside, Calif., U.S.	168	32.52 N	116.55 W
Lakeview, Ga., U.S.	156	34.59 N	85.16 W
Lake View, Iowa, U.S.	154	42.18 N	95.03 W
Lakeview, Mich., U.S.	154	43.27 N	85.17 W
Lakeview, Oreg., U.S.	166	42.11 N	120.21 W
Lakeview, Tex., U.S.	160	34.40 N	100.42 W
Lake Village	158	33.20 N	91.17 W
Lakeville	154	44.39 N	93.14 W
Lake Wales	156	27.54 N	81.35 W
Lakewood, Colo., U.S.	164	39.44 N	105.06 W
Lakewood, N.J., U.S.	152	40.06 N	74.13 W
Lakewood, Ohio, U.S.	152	41.29 N	81.48 W
Lakewood Park	156	27.26 N	80.23 W
La Libertad, Guat.	132	16.47 N	90.07 W
La Libertad, Méx.	130	29.55 N	112.43 W
La Ligua	140	32.27 S	71.14 W
Lalín	76	42.40 N	8.06 W
Lalinde	74	44.50 N	0.44 E
La Loche	142	56.29 N	109.27 W
La Loupe	74	48.28 N	1.01 E
La Louvière	72	50.28 N	4.11 E
Lama, Ozero ⊜	84	69.30 N	90.30 E
La Maddalena	78	41.13 N	9.24 E
La Madrid	140	27.40 S	65.15 W
La Manche (English Channel) ⋃	74	50.20 N	1.00 W
Lamandau ≈	96	2.42 S	111.34 E
Lamar, Colo., U.S.	162	38.05 N	102.37 W
Lamar, Mo., U.S.	162	37.30 N	94.16 W
Lamar, S.C., U.S.	156	34.10 N	80.04 W
La Mesa, Calif., U.S.	168	32.46 N	117.01 W
La Mesa, N. Mex., U.S.	160	32.07 N	106.42 W
Lamastre	74	44.59 N	4.35 E
La Marque	160	29.22 N	94.58 W
Lamas	134	6.25 S	76.30 W
Lamballe	74	48.28 N	2.31 W
Lambaréné	110	0.42 S	10.13 E
Lambay Island I	70	53.29 N	6.01 W
Lambayeque	134	6.42 S	79.55 W
Lambert	162	47.41 N	104.37 W
Lambert's Bay	116	32.05 S	18.18 E
Lamberton	154	44.14 N	95.16 W
Lambton, Cape ►	142	71.05 N	123.10 W
Lame Deer	162	45.37 N	106.40 W
Lamego	76	41.06 N	7.49 W
Lamesa	160	32.44 N	101.57 W
Lamia	80	38.54 N	22.26 E
L'amin ≈	84	61.18 N	71.48 E
La Moille	154	41.32 N	89.17 W
Lamon Bay C	98	14.33 N	121.50 E
Lamoni	154	40.37 N	93.56 W
Lamont	168	35.15 N	118.55 W
La Mothe-Achard	74	46.37 N	1.40 W
La Mothe-Saint-Héraye	74	46.21 N	0.07 W
La Motte-du-Caire	74	44.20 N	6.03 E
La Moure	162	46.21 N	98.18 W
Lampang	94	18.16 N	99.34 E
Lampasas	160	31.03 N	98.10 W
Lampazos de Naranjo	130	27.01 N	100.31 W
Lampedusa I	78	35.31 N	12.35 E
Lampertheim	72	49.35 N	8.28 E
Lamu	110	2.16 S	40.54 E
La Mure	74	44.54 N	5.47 E
Lamy	164	35.29 N	105.53 W
Lanark	70	55.41 N	3.46 W
Lanbi Kyun I	94	10.50 N	98.15 E
Lancaster, Eng., U.K.	70	54.03 N	2.48 W
Lancaster, Calif., U.S.	168	34.41 N	118.08 W
Lancaster, Ky., U.S.	156	37.37 N	84.35 W
Lancaster, N.H., U.S.	152	44.29 N	71.34 W
Lancaster, N.Y., U.S.	152	42.54 N	78.40 W
Lancaster, Ohio, U.S.	152	39.43 N	82.36 W
Lancaster, Pa., U.S.	152	40.02 N	76.18 W
Lancaster, S.C., U.S.	156	34.43 N	80.46 W
Lancaster, Wis., U.S.	154	42.51 N	90.43 W
Lancaster Mills	152	42.27 N	71.40 W
Lancaster Sound ⋃	142	74.13 N	84.00 W

Name	Page	Lat ° ′	Long ° ′
Lance Creek	164	43.02 N	104.39 W
Lanciano	78	42.14 N	14.23 E
Lancing	156	36.13 N	84.39 W
Łańcut	72	50.05 N	22.13 E
Landau	72	49.12 N	8.07 E
Landau an der Isar	72	48.40 N	12.43 E
Landeck	72	47.08 N	10.34 E
Lander	164	42.50 N	108.44 W
Landerneau	74	48.27 N	4.15 W
Landes □5	74	44.20 N	1.00 W
Landete	76	39.54 N	1.22 W
Landis	156	35.33 N	80.37 W
Landivisiau	74	48.31 N	4.04 W
Lando	156	34.43 N	81.01 W
Land O'lakes	154	46.10 N	89.13 W
Landor	122	25.09 S	116.54 E
Landösjön ⊜	68	63.35 N	14.04 E
Landquart	74	46.58 N	9.33 E
Landsberg [am Lech]	72	48.05 N	10.55 E
Landsberg an der Warthe → Gorzów Wielkopolski	72	52.44 N	15.15 E
Land's End ≻	70	50.03 N	5.44 W
Landshut	72	48.33 N	12.09 E
Landskrona	68	55.52 N	12.50 E
Landstuhl	72	49.25 N	7.34 E
Lanesboro	154	43.43 N	91.59 W
Lanett	158	32.57 N	85.12 W
Langano, Lake ⊜	108	7.35 N	38.48 E
Langchuhe (Sutlej) ≃	102	29.23 N	71.02 E
Langdale	158	32.44 N	85.11 W
Langdon	162	48.46 N	98.22 W
Langeac	74	45.06 N	3.30 E
Langeais	74	47.20 N	0.24 E
Langeberg ⋀	116	28.20 S	22.35 E
Längelmävesi ⊜	68	61.32 N	24.22 E
Langenfeld, B.R.D.	72	51.07 N	6.56 E
Langenfeld, Öst.	72	47.04 N	10.58 E
Langenhagen	72	52.27 N	9.44 E
Langenthal	74	47.13 N	7.47 E
Langesund	68	59.00 N	9.45 E
Langevåg	68	62.27 N	6.12 E
Langholm	70	55.09 N	3.00 W
Langjökull ⊼	66a	64.42 N	20.12 W
Langkawi, Pulau I	94	6.22 N	99.50 E
Langley, B.C., Can.	148	49.06 N	122.39 W
Langley, S.C., U.S.	156	33.31 N	81.50 W
Langlo ≃	120	26.26 S	146.05 E
Langlois	166	42.56 N	124.27 W
Långnäs	68	60.03 N	22.28 E
Langnau	74	46.57 N	7.47 E
Langogne	74	44.43 N	3.51 E
Langon	74	44.33 N	0.15 W
Langøya I	66	68.44 N	14.50 E
Langres	74	47.52 N	5.20 W
Langsa	94	4.28 N	97.58 E
Lang-son	94	21.50 N	106.44 E
Langtry	160	29.48 N	101.34 W
Languedoc □9	74	44.00 N	4.00 E
Langzhong	88	31.35 N	105.59 E
Länkipohja	68	61.44 N	24.48 E
Lannemezan	74	43.08 N	0.23 E
Lannilis	74	48.34 N	4.31 W
Lannion	74	48.44 N	3.28 W
L'Annonciation	152	46.25 N	74.52 W
Lansdale	152	40.15 N	75.17 W
Lansdowne	122	17.53 S	126.39 E
L'Anse	154	46.45 N	88.27 W
Lansing	152	42.43 N	84.34 W
Lanslebourg	74	45.17 N	6.52 E
Lantana	156	26.35 N	80.03 W
Lanusei	78	39.52 N	9.34 E
Lanxi	88	29.12 N	119.28 E
Lanzarote I	106	29.00 N	13.40 W
Lanzhou	88	36.03 N	103.41 E
Laoag	98	18.12 N	120.36 E
Laoang	92	12.34 N	125.00 E
Lao-cai	94	22.30 N	103.57 E
Laoighis □6	70	53.00 N	7.30 W
Laon	74	49.34 N	3.40 E
La Orchila I	138	11.48 N	66.09 W
La Oroya	134	11.32 S	75.54 W
Laos □1	92	18.00 N	105.00 E
Lapa	140	25.45 S	49.42 W
Lapalisse	74	46.15 N	3.38 E
La Palma	138	8.25 N	78.07 W
La Paloma	140	34.40 S	54.10 W
La Pampa □4	140	37.00 S	66.00 W
La Paragua	138	6.50 N	63.20 W
La Paz, Arg.	140	30.45 S	59.38 W
La Paz, Arg.	140	33.28 S	67.34 W
La Paz, Bol.	134	16.30 S	68.09 W
La Paz, Méx.	130	23.41 N	100.43 W
La Paz, Méx.	130	24.10 N	110.18 W
La Paz, Ur.	140	34.46 S	56.15 W
Lapeer	154	43.03 N	83.19 W
La Perouse Strait (Sōya-kaikyō) ⌣	90a	45.45 N	142.00 E
La Piedad [Cavadas]	130	20.21 N	102.00 W
La Pine	166	43.40 N	121.30 W
Lapin lääni □4	68	66.00 N	27.00 E
Lapinlahti	68	63.22 N	27.24 E
Lapland ⟵1	66	68.00 N	25.00 E
La Plata, Arg.	140	34.55 S	57.57 W
La Plata, Md., U.S.	152	38.32 N	76.59 W
La Plata, Mo., U.S.	158	40.02 N	92.29 W
La Plata ≃	164	36.54 N	108.15 W
La Pocatière	150	47.22 N	68.41 W
Laporte, Colo., U.S.	164	40.38 N	105.08 W
La Porte, Ind., U.S.	158	41.36 N	86.43 W
La Porte City	154	42.19 N	92.12 W
La Potherie, Lac ⊜	142	58.50 N	74.24 W
Lappa	120	17.22 S	144.53 E
Lappajärvi	68	63.12 N	23.38 E
Lappeenranta	68	61.04 N	28.11 E
Lappfjärd (Lapväärtti)	68	62.15 N	21.32 E
La Pryor	160	28.57 N	99.51 W
Laptev Sea → Laptevych, More ⫧2	84	76.00 N	126.00 E
Laptevych, More (Laptev Sea) ⫧2	84	76.00 N	126.00 E
Lapua	68	62.57 N	23.00 E
La Quiaca	140	22.05 S	65.36 W
L'Aquila	78	42.22 N	13.22 E
Lār	104	27.41 N	54.17 E
Lara □3	138	10.10 N	69.50 W
Larache	106	35.12 N	6.10 W
Laragne-Montéglin	74	44.19 N	5.49 E
Laramie	164	41.19 N	105.35 W
Laramie ≃	164	42.12 N	104.32 W
Laramie Mountains ⋀	164	42.00 N	105.40 W
Laramie Peak ∧	162	42.17 N	105.27 W
Larantuka	96	8.21 S	122.59 E
Larat, Pulau I	124	7.10 S	131.50 E
L'Arbresle	74	45.50 N	4.37 E
Larche, Col de)(	74	44.25 N	6.53 E
Larchwood	162	43.27 N	96.26 W
Laredo, Esp.	76	43.24 N	3.25 W
Laredo, Tex., U.S.	160	27.31 N	99.30 W
La Réole	74	44.35 N	0.02 W
Largeau	108	17.55 N	19.07 E
L'Argentière-la-Bessée	74	44.47 N	6.33 E
Largo	156	27.55 N	82.47 W
Largo, Cayo I	132	21.38 N	81.28 W
Largs	70	55.48 N	4.52 W
Lariang ≃	96	1.25 S	119.17 E
Larino	78	41.48 N	14.54 E
La Rioja	140	29.25 S	66.50 W
La Rioja □4	140	29.30 S	67.00 W
Lárisa	80	39.38 N	22.25 E
Larjak	84	61.16 N	80.15 E
Lārkāna	102	27.33 N	68.13 E
Larnaca → Lárnax	104	34.55 N	33.38 E
Lárnax (Larnaca)	104	34.55 N	33.38 E
Larne	70	54.51 N	5.49 W
Larned	162	38.11 N	99.06 W
La Roche-Bernard	74	47.31 N	2.18 W
La Roche-Derrien	70	48.45 N	3.16 W
La Rochefoucauld	74	45.45 N	0.23 E
La Rochelle	74	46.10 N	1.10 W
La Roche-sur-Yon	74	46.40 N	1.26 W
La Roda	76	39.13 N	2.09 W
La Romana	132	18.25 N	68.58 W
La Ronge	142	55.06 N	105.17 W
Laroquebrou	74	44.58 N	2.11 E
Larose	158	29.35 N	90.23 W
Larrey Point ≻	122	19.58 S	119.07 E
Larrimah	124	15.35 S	133.12 E
Larsen Bay	146	57.33 N	154.04 W
La Rubia	140	30.05 S	61.50 W
La Rue	152	40.35 N	83.23 W
Laruns	74	42.59 N	0.25 W
Larvik	68	59.04 N	10.00 E
Lasa (Lhasa)	102	29.40 N	91.09 E
La Salle, Colo., U.S.	164	40.21 N	104.42 W
La Salle, Ill., U.S.	154	41.20 N	89.06 W
Las Animas	162	38.04 N	103.13 W
Las Anod	108	8.26 N	47.24 E
La Sarre	154	48.48 N	79.12 W
Lascano	140	33.40 S	54.12 W
Las Casitas, Cerro ∧	130	23.32 N	109.59 W
Las Choapas	130	17.55 N	94.05 W
Las Cruces	164	32.23 N	106.29 W
La Selle, Pic ∧	132	18.22 N	72.00 W
La Serena	140	29.54 S	71.16 W
La Seyne	74	43.06 N	5.53 E
Las Flores	140	36.02 S	59.07 W
Las Heras	140	32.50 S	68.50 W
Lashio	92	22.56 N	97.45 E
Lashkar Gāh	100	31.35 N	64.21 E
Łasin	72	53.32 N	19.05 E
Las Lajas	140	38.30 S	70.23 W
Las Lomitas	140	24.43 S	60.35 W
Lašma	86	54.56 N	41.09 E
Las Minas, Cerro ∧	130	14.33 N	88.39 W
La Solana	76	38.56 N	3.14 W
Las Palmas	140	27.05 S	58.40 W
Las Palmas de Gran Canaria	106	28.06 N	15.24 W
La Spezia	78	44.07 N	9.50 E
Las Piedras	140	34.44 S	56.13 W
Las Piedras, Río de ≃	134	12.37 S	69.10 W
Las Plumas	136	43.40 S	67.15 W
Las Rosas	130	16.24 N	92.23 W
Lassay	74	48.26 N	0.30 W
Lassen Peak ∧1	168	40.29 N	121.31 W
Las Tablas	138	7.47 N	80.17 W
Las Termas	140	27.30 S	64.50 W
Last Mountain Lake ⊜	142	51.05 N	105.10 W
Las Tórtolas, Cerro ∧	140	29.56 S	69.54 W
Lastoursville	110	0.49 S	12.42 E
La Suze	74	47.54 N	0.02 E
Las Varillas	140	31.50 S	62.44 W
Las Vegas, Nev., U.S.	168	36.11 N	115.08 W
Las Vegas, N. Mex., U.S.	164	35.36 N	105.13 W
Latacunga	138	0.56 S	78.37 W
Latakia → Al-Lādhiqīyah	104	35.31 N	35.47 E
La Teste-de-Buch	74	44.38 N	1.09 W
Lathrop	158	39.33 N	94.20 W
Latina	78	41.28 N	12.52 E
Latisana	78	45.47 N	13.00 E
Latorica ≃	72	48.28 N	21.50 E
La Tortuga, Isla I	138	10.56 N	65.20 W
Latouche Treville, Cape ≻	122	18.27 S	121.49 E
La Tour-d'Auvergne	74	45.32 N	2.41 E
La Tour-du-Pin	74	45.34 N	5.27 E
Latowicz	72	52.02 N	21.48 E
La Tremblade	74	45.46 N	1.08 W
La Trimouille	74	46.28 N	1.02 E
Latrobe, Austl.	120	41.14 S	146.24 E
Latrobe, Pa., U.S.	152	40.19 N	79.23 W
La Tuque	142	47.26 N	72.47 W
Latvian Soviet Socialist Republic → Lalvijskaja Sovetskaja Socialističeskaja Respublika □3	64	57.00 N	25.00 E
Latvijskaja Sovetskaja Socialističeskaja Respublika □3	64	57.00 N	25.00 E
Lauchhammer	72	51.30 N	13.47 E
Lauder	70	55.43 N	2.45 W
Lauenburg	72	53.22 N	10.33 E
Lauf an der Pegnitz	72	49.30 N	11.17 E
Laufen	74	47.57 N	12.56 E
Laughlen, Mount ∧	122	23.23 S	134.23 E
Laukaa	68	62.25 N	25.57 E
Launceston, Austl.	120	41.26 S	147.08 E
Launceston, Eng., U.K.	70	50.38 N	4.21 W
La Unión, Chile	136	40.17 S	73.05 W
La Unión, El Sal.	128	13.20 N	87.51 W
La Unión, Esp.	76	37.37 N	0.52 W
La Union, N. Mex., U.S.	164	31.57 N	106.39 W
Laupheim	72	48.14 N	9.52 E
Laurel, Del., U.S.	152	38.33 N	75.34 W
Laurel, Fla., U.S.	156	27.08 N	82.27 W
Laurel, Ind., U.S.	158	39.30 N	85.11 W
Laurel, Md., U.S.	152	39.06 N	76.51 W
Laurel, Miss., U.S.	158	31.42 N	89.08 W
Laurel, Mont., U.S.	166	45.40 N	108.46 W
Laurel, Nebr., U.S.	162	42.26 N	97.06 W
Laureldale	152	40.23 N	75.55 W
Laurelville	152	39.28 N	82.44 W
Laurencekirk	70	56.50 N	2.29 W
Laurens	162	42.51 N	94.51 W
Lauria	78	40.02 N	15.50 E
Laurière	74	46.05 N	1.28 E
Laurinburg	156	34.47 N	79.27 W
Lauritsala	68	61.04 N	28.16 E
Laurium	154	47.14 N	88.26 W
Lausanne	74	46.31 N	6.38 E
Laut, Pulau I, Indon.	96	3.40 S	116.10 E
Laut, Pulau I, Indon.	96	4.43 N	107.59 E
Lauta	72	51.27 N	14.04 E
Lautaro	140	38.31 S	72.27 W
Lauterbach	72	50.38 N	9.24 E
Lauterbrunnen	74	46.36 N	7.55 E
Lauter [sachsen]	72	50.33 N	12.44 E
Laut Kecil, Kepulauan II	96	4.50 S	115.45 E
Lauzerte	74	44.15 N	1.08 E
Lauzon	150	46.50 N	71.10 W
Lauzun	74	44.38 N	0.28 E
Lava (Łyna) ≃	86	54.37 N	21.14 E
Lava, Nosy I	117b	14.33 S	47.36 E
Lava Hot Springs	166	42.37 N	112.01 W
Laval, Qué., Can.	152	45.33 N	73.44 W
Laval, Fr.	74	48.04 N	0.46 W
Lavapié, Punta ≻	140	37.09 S	73.35 W
Lávara	80	41.16 N	26.22 E
Lavardac	74	44.11 N	0.18 E
La Vega	132	19.13 N	70.31 W
Lavelanet	74	42.56 N	1.51 E
Lavello	78	41.03 N	15.48 E
La Vernia	160	29.21 N	98.07 W
Laverton	122	28.38 S	122.25 E
La Veta	164	37.31 N	105.00 W
Lavia	68	61.36 N	22.36 E
La Victoria	138	10.14 N	67.20 W
Lavik	68	61.06 N	5.30 E
Lavina	166	46.18 N	108.56 W
La Volla	168	32.51 N	117.16 W
Lavonia	156	34.26 N	83.06 W
La Voulte-sur-Rhône	74	44.48 N	4.47 E
Lavrentija	146	65.35 N	171.00 W
Lavumisa	110	27.20 S	31.55 E
Lawai	170b	21.55 N	159.31 W
Lawdar	100	13.53 N	45.52 E
Lawn	160	32.08 N	99.49 W
Lawn Hill	120	18.35 S	138.35 E
Lawrence, Ind., U.S.	158	39.50 N	86.02 W
Lawrence, Kans., U.S.	162	38.58 N	95.14 W
Lawrence, Mass., U.S.	144	42.42 N	71.09 W
Lawrence, Mass., U.S.	152	42.42 N	71.09 W
Lawrenceburg, Ind., U.S.	158	39.06 N	84.51 W
Lawrenceburg, Ky., U.S.	158	38.02 N	84.54 W
Lawrenceburg, Tenn., U.S.	158	35.15 N	87.20 W
Lawrenceville, Ill., U.S.	158	38.44 N	87.41 W
Lawrenceville, N.J., U.S.	152	40.18 N	74.44 W
Lawton, Mich., U.S.	154	42.10 N	85.50 W
Lawton, N. Dak., U.S.	162	48.18 N	98.22 W
Lawton, Okla., U.S.	160	34.37 N	98.25 W
Lawz, Jabal al- ∧	104	28.40 N	35.18 E
Layton	166	41.04 N	111.58 W
Laytonville	168	39.41 N	123.29 W
Lazarev	84	52.13 N	141.32 E
Lazdijai	86	54.14 N	23.31 E
Lazio □4	78	42.00 N	12.30 E
Leachville	158	35.56 N	90.15 W
Lead	162	44.21 N	103.46 W
Leader	142	50.53 N	109.31 W
Leadore	166	44.41 N	113.21 W
Leadville	164	39.15 N	106.20 W
Leadwood	158	37.52 N	90.36 W
League City	160	29.31 N	95.05 W
Leakesville	158	31.09 N	88.33 W
Leakey	160	29.44 N	99.46 W
Lealman	156	27.50 N	82.41 W
Leamington	154	42.03 N	82.36 W
Leatherwood	156	37.02 N	83.11 W
Leavenworth	162	39.19 N	94.55 W
Lebak	92	6.37 N	124.03 E
Lebanon, Ind., U.S.	158	40.03 N	86.28 W
Lebanon, Ky., U.S.	158	37.34 N	85.15 W
Lebanon, Mo., U.S.	158	37.41 N	92.40 W
Lebanon, N.H., U.S.	152	43.38 N	72.15 W
Lebanon, Ohio, U.S.	152	39.26 N	84.13 W
Lebanon, Oreg., U.S.	166	44.32 N	122.54 W
Lebanon, Pa., U.S.	152	40.20 N	76.25 W
Lebanon, Tenn., U.S.	158	36.12 N	86.18 W
Lebanon, Va., U.S.	156	36.54 N	82.05 W
Lebanon □1	100	33.50 N	35.50 E
Lebanon Junction	158	37.50 N	85.44 W
Leb'ažje, S.S.S.R.	66	57.25 N	49.32 E
Leb'ažje, S.S.S.R.	84	51.28 N	77.46 E
Lebec	168	34.50 N	118.52 W
Lebed'an'	86	53.01 N	39.09 E
Le Blanc	74	46.38 N	1.04 E
Lebomboberge ⋀	116	25.15 S	32.00 E
Lebombo Mountains ⋀2	116	25.15 S	32.00 E
Lębork	72	54.33 N	17.44 E
Lebos Creek ≃	160	34.25 N	99.35 W
Le Bourg-d'Oisans	74	45.03 N	6.02 E
Lebrija	76	36.55 N	6.04 W
Lebu	140	37.37 S	73.39 W
Le Bugue	74	44.55 N	0.56 E
Le Cannet	74	43.34 N	7.01 E
Le Cateau	74	50.06 N	3.33 E
Lecce	78	40.23 N	18.11 E
Lecco	78	45.51 N	9.23 E
Le Center	154	44.24 N	93.44 W
Lech ≃	72	48.44 N	10.56 E
Le-Château-d'Oléron	74	45.53 N	1.11 W
Le Châtelet	74	46.39 N	2.17 E
Le Chesne	74	49.31 N	4.46 E
Le Cheylard	74	44.45 N	4.25 E
Le Claire	154	41.36 N	90.21 W
Lecompte	158	31.05 N	92.24 W
Le Conquet	74	48.22 N	4.46 W
Le Creusot	74	46.48 N	4.26 E
Le Croisic	74	47.18 N	2.31 W
Łęczyca	72	52.04 N	19.13 E
Lëd'anaja, Gora ∧	84	61.53 N	171.09 W
Ledbury	70	52.02 N	2.25 W
Ledo	100	27.18 N	95.42 E
Le Donjon	74	46.21 N	3.48 E
Le Dorat	74	46.13 N	1.05 E
Ledu	88	36.32 N	102.25 E
Leduc	148	53.16 N	113.33 W
Lee	152	42.19 N	73.15 W
Leechburg	152	40.38 N	79.36 W
Leech Lake ⊜	154	47.09 N	94.23 W
Leeds, Eng., U.K.	70	53.50 N	1.35 W
Leeds, Ala., U.S.	158	33.33 N	86.33 W
Leer	72	53.14 N	7.26 E
Leesburg, Fla., U.S.	156	28.49 N	81.53 W
Leesburg, Va., U.S.	152	39.07 N	77.34 W
Lees Summit	158	38.55 N	94.23 W
Leesville, La., U.S.	158	31.08 N	93.16 W
Leesville, Tex., U.S.	160	29.24 N	97.45 W
Leeton	120	34.33 S	146.24 E
Leetonia	152	40.53 N	80.45 W
Leeuwarden	72	53.12 N	5.46 E
Leeuwin, Cape ≻	122	34.22 S	115.08 E
Lee Vining	168	37.58 N	119.07 W
Leeward Islands II	132	17.00 N	62.00 W
Le Faouët	70	48.02 N	3.29 W
Lefors	160	35.26 N	100.48 W
Lefroy, Lake ⊜	122	31.15 S	121.40 E
Legazpi	92	13.08 N	123.44 E
Légé	74	46.53 N	1.36 W
Legendre Island I	122	20.23 S	116.54 E
Legges Tor ∧	120	41.32 S	147.40 E
Leghorn → Livorno	78	43.33 N	10.19 E
Legion	160	30.01 N	99.07 W
Legionowo	72	52.25 N	20.56 E
Legnago	78	45.11 N	11.18 E
Legnano	78	45.36 N	8.54 E
Legnica (Liegnitz)	72	51.13 N	16.09 E
Le Grand	168	37.14 N	120.15 W
Le Grand-Lucé	74	47.52 N	0.28 E
Le Grau-du-Roi	74	43.32 N	4.08 E
Leh	100	34.10 N	77.35 E
Le Havre	74	49.30 N	0.08 E
Lehi	164	40.24 N	111.51 W
Lehigh Acres	156	26.36 N	81.39 W
Lehrte	72	52.22 N	9.59 E
Lehututu	116	23.58 S	21.51 E
Leibnitz	72	46.48 N	15.32 E
Leicester	70	52.38 N	1.05 W
Leicestershire □6	70	52.40 N	1.10 W
Leichhardt ≃	120	17.35 S	139.48 E
Leiden	72	52.09 N	4.30 E
Leie (Lys) ≃	74	51.03 N	3.43 E
Leigh Creek	120	30.28 S	138.25 E
Leighton	158	34.42 N	87.32 W
Leighton Buzzard	70	51.55 N	0.40 W
Leikanger	68	61.10 N	6.52 E
Leinster □9	70	53.05 N	7.00 W
Leipsic	152	41.06 N	83.59 W
Leipzig	72	51.19 N	12.20 E
Leipzig □5	72	51.15 N	12.45 E
Leiria	76	39.45 N	8.48 W
Leirvik	68	59.45 N	5.30 E
Leisler, Mount ∧	122	23.28 S	129.17 E
Leitchfield	158	37.29 N	86.18 W
Leitha (Lajta) ≃	72	47.54 N	17.17 E
Leitrim	70	54.00 N	8.04 W
Leitrim □6	70	54.20 N	8.20 W
Leizhoubandao ≻1	94	21.15 N	110.09 E
Leksvik	68	63.40 N	10.37 E
Leland, Ill., U.S.	154	41.37 N	88.48 W
Leland, Miss., U.S.	158	33.24 N	90.54 W
Leleque	136	42.24 S	71.04 W
Lelia Lake	160	34.54 N	100.46 W
Le Lion-d'Angers	74	47.38 N	0.43 W
Lelishan ∧	102	33.26 N	81.42 E
Le Locle	74	47.03 N	6.45 E
Le Lude	74	47.39 N	0.09 E
Le Maire, Estrecho de ⌣	136	54.50 S	65.00 W
Le Mans	74	48.00 N	0.12 E
Le Mars	162	42.47 N	96.10 W
Le Mayet-de-Montagne	74	46.05 N	3.40 E
Le Merlerault	74	48.42 N	0.18 E
Lemesós (Limassol)	104	34.40 N	33.02 E
Lemeta	146	64.52 N	147.44 W
Lemgo	72	52.02 N	8.54 E
Lemhi Pass)(	166	44.58 N	113.27 W
Lemieux Islands II	142	64.30 N	64.40 W
Lemitar	164	34.09 N	106.55 W
Lemmon	162	45.56 N	102.10 W
Le Monastier	74	45.56 N	4.00 E
Lemoncove	168	36.23 N	119.01 W
Lemon Grove	168	32.44 N	117.02 W
Lemont	152	40.49 N	77.49 W
Le Montet	74	46.25 N	3.03 E
Lemoore	168	36.18 N	119.47 W
Le Moule	132	16.20 N	61.21 W
Lempäälä	68	61.19 N	23.45 E
Lena	154	42.23 N	89.50 W
Lena ≃	84	72.25 N	126.40 E
Lencloître	74	46.49 N	0.20 E
Lençóis	134	12.34 S	41.23 W
Le Neubourg	70	49.09 N	0.55 E
Lenggries	72	47.41 N	11.34 E
Lenghu	88	38.30 N	93.15 E
Lenhovda	68	57.00 N	15.17 E
Lenina, Pik ∧	82	39.20 N	72.55 E
Leninabad	100	40.17 N	69.37 E
Leninakan	64	40.48 N	43.50 E
Leningrad	86	59.55 N	30.15 E
Leninogorsk, S.S.S.R.	66	54.36 N	52.30 E
Leninogorsk, S.S.S.R.	84	50.27 N	83.32 E
Leninsk	82	40.38 N	72.15 E
Leninskij	86	54.18 N	37.28 E
Leninsk-Kuzneckij	84	54.38 N	86.10 E
Leninskoje, S.S.S.R.	66	58.19 N	47.06 E
Leninskoje, S.S.S.R.	84	47.56 N	132.38 E
Lenk	74	46.28 N	7.27 E
Lenkoran'	104	38.45 N	48.50 E
Lennonville	122	27.58 S	117.50 E
Lennox	162	43.21 N	96.53 W
Lennox, Isla I	136	55.18 S	66.50 W
Lennoxville	152	45.22 N	71.51 W
Lenoir	156	35.55 N	81.32 W
Lenoir City	156	35.48 N	84.16 W
Lenox, Iowa, U.S.	162	40.53 N	94.34 W
Lenox, Mass., U.S.	152	42.22 N	73.17 W
Lenox, Tenn., U.S.	158	36.05 N	89.30 W
Lens	74	50.26 N	2.50 E
Lensk	84	61.00 N	114.50 E
Lenti	72	46.37 N	16.33 E
Lentini	78	37.17 N	15.00 E
Léo	114	11.06 N	2.06 W
Leoben	72	47.23 N	15.06 E
Leola	162	45.43 N	98.56 W
Leominster, Eng., U.K.	70	52.14 N	2.45 W
Leominster, Mass., U.S.	152	42.32 N	71.45 W
León, Esp.	76	42.36 N	5.34 W
Léon, Fr.	74	43.53 N	1.18 W
León, Méx.	128	21.07 N	101.40 W
León, Nic.	132	12.26 N	86.54 W
Leon, Iowa, U.S.	154	40.44 N	93.45 W
León □9	76	42.00 N	6.00 W
Leonberg	72	48.48 N	9.01 E
León [de los Aldamas]	130	21.07 N	101.40 W
Leonforte	78	37.39 N	14.24 E
Leongatha	120	38.29 S	145.57 E
Leonora	122	28.53 S	121.20 E
Leopoldina	136	21.32 S	42.38 W
Léopoldville → Kinshasa	110	4.18 S	15.18 E
Leoti	162	38.29 N	101.21 W
Le Palais	74	47.21 N	3.09 W
Lepanto	158	35.36 N	90.20 W
Lepe	76	37.15 N	7.12 W
Lepel'	86	54.53 N	28.42 E
Le Pellerin	74	47.12 N	1.45 W
L'Épiphanie	152	45.51 N	73.30 W
Le Pont-de-Beauvoisin	74	45.32 N	5.40 E
Lepontine, Alpi ⋀	74	46.25 N	8.40 E
Le Port	117c	20.55 S	55.18 E
Lepsy	82	46.15 N	78.55 E
Le Puy	74	45.02 N	3.53 E
Lequeitio	76	43.22 N	2.30 W
Léraba ≃	114	9.42 N	4.35 W
Lerici	78	44.04 N	9.55 E
Lérida	76	41.37 N	0.37 E
Le Roy, Kans., U.S.	162	38.05 N	95.38 W
Le Roy, N.Y., U.S.	152	42.59 N	77.59 W
Lerwick	70	60.09 N	1.09 W
Les Aix-d'Angillon	74	47.12 N	2.34 E
Les Andelys	74	49.15 N	1.25 E
Lesbos → Lésvos I	80	39.10 N	26.20 E
Les Cayes	132	18.12 N	73.45 W
Les Échelles	74	45.26 N	5.45 E
Le Sel	70	47.54 N	1.37 W
Les Essarts	74	46.46 N	1.14 W
Leshan	88	29.34 N	103.45 E
Les Herbiers	74	46.52 N	1.01 W
Lesjaskog	68	62.15 N	8.22 E
Lesko	72	49.29 N	22.21 E
Leskovac	80	42.59 N	21.57 E
Leslie	154	42.27 N	84.26 W
Lesneven	70	48.34 N	4.19 W
Lesnoj	86	54.11 N	40.27 E
Lesotho □1	110	29.30 S	28.30 E
Lesozavodsk	84	45.28 N	133.27 E
Lesozavodskij	66	66.44 N	32.49 E
Lesparre-Médoc	74	45.18 N	0.56 W
Les Pieux	74	49.31 N	1.48 W
Les Riceys	74	47.59 N	4.22 E
Les Sables-d'Olonne	74	46.30 N	1.47 W
Lessay	74	49.13 N	1.32 W
Lesser Antilles II	132	15.00 N	61.00 W
Lesser Khingan Mountains → Xiaoxiang'anling-shanmai ⋀	88	48.45 N	127.00 E
Lesser Slave Lake ⊜	148	55.25 N	115.30 W
Lesser Sunda Islands II	92	9.00 S	120.00 E
Lestijärvi	68	63.32 N	24.39 E
Le Sueur	154	44.27 N	93.54 W
Lešukonskoje	82	64.54 N	45.40 E
Les Vans	74	44.24 N	4.08 E
Lévos □5, Ellás	80	39.10 N	25.50 E
Lésvos I, Ellás	80	39.10 N	26.20 E
Leszno	72	51.51 N	16.35 E
Letcher	162	43.54 N	98.08 W
Letenye	72	46.26 N	16.43 E
Lethbridge	148	49.42 N	112.50 W
Lethem	138	3.20 N	59.50 W
Le Thillot	74	47.53 N	6.46 E
Leti, Kepulauan II	124	8.12 S	127.41 E
Leticia	138	4.09 S	69.57 W
Le Trayas	74	43.28 N	6.55 E
Le Tréport	74	50.04 N	1.22 E
Letsôk-aw Kyun I	94	11.37 N	98.15 E
Letterkenny	70	54.57 N	7.44 W
Leucadia	168	33.04 N	117.18 W
Leuk	74	46.19 N	7.38 E
Leuna	72	51.19 N	12.01 E
Leutkirch	72	47.49 N	10.01 E
Leuven	72	50.53 N	4.42 E
Levádhia	80	38.25 N	22.54 E
Levanger	68	63.45 N	11.18 E
Levanto	78	44.10 N	9.38 E
Levelland	160	33.35 N	102.23 W
Levelock	146	59.07 N	156.52 W
Leveque, Cape ≻	122	16.24 S	122.56 E
Leverkusen	72	51.03 N	6.59 E
Leverville	110	4.50 S	18.44 E
Levice	72	48.13 N	18.37 E
Levie	78	41.42 N	9.07 E
Levier	74	46.57 N	6.08 E
Levin	126	40.37 S	175.17 E
Lévis	150	46.48 N	71.11 W
Levittown	152	40.09 N	74.50 W
Levkás	80	38.50 N	20.41 E
Levkás I	80	38.39 N	20.27 E
Levkosia (Nicosia)	104	35.10 N	33.22 E
Levroux	74	46.59 N	1.37 E
Lev Tolstoj	86	53.13 N	39.27 E
Lewes, Eng., U.K.	70	50.52 N	0.01 E
Lewes, Del., U.S.	152	38.47 N	75.08 W
Lewis, Isle of I	70	58.10 N	6.40 W
Lewis and Clark Lake ⊜1	162	42.50 N	97.45 W
Lewisburg, Pa., U.S.	152	40.58 N	76.53 W
Lewisburg, Tenn., U.S.	158	35.27 N	86.48 W
Lewisburg, W. Va., U.S.	152	37.48 N	80.27 W
Lewisporte	150	49.15 N	55.03 W
Lewis Range ⋀	166	48.30 N	113.15 W
Lewis Run	152	41.52 N	78.40 W
Lewiston, Calif., U.S.	168	40.43 N	122.48 W
Lewiston, Idaho, U.S.	166	46.25 N	117.01 W
Lewiston, Maine, U.S.	152	44.06 N	70.13 W
Lewiston, Mich., U.S.	154	44.53 N	84.18 W
Lewiston, N.Y., U.S.	152	43.10 N	79.03 W
Lewiston, Utah, U.S.	164	41.58 N	111.51 W
Lewistown, Ill., U.S.	158	40.24 N	90.09 W
Lewistown, Mont., U.S.	166	47.04 N	109.26 W
Lewistown, Pa., U.S.	152	40.36 N	77.31 W
Lewisville, N.B., Can.	150	45.06 N	64.46 W
Lewisville, Ark., U.S.	158	33.22 N	93.35 W
Lewisville, Tex., U.S.	160	33.03 N	96.60 W
Lexington, Ill., U.S.	154	40.39 N	88.47 W
Lexington, Ky., U.S.	156	38.03 N	84.30 W
Lexington, Mass., U.S.	152	42.27 N	71.14 W
Lexington, Mich., U.S.	154	43.16 N	82.32 W
Lexington, Miss., U.S.	158	33.07 N	90.03 W
Lexington, Mo., U.S.	158	39.11 N	93.52 W
Lexington, Nebr., U.S.	162	40.47 N	99.45 W
Lexington, N.C., U.S.	156	35.49 N	80.15 W
Lexington, Oreg., U.S.	166	45.27 N	119.41 W
Lexington, Tenn., U.S.	158	35.39 N	88.24 W
Lexington, Va., U.S.	156	37.47 N	79.27 W
Lexington Park	152	38.16 N	76.27 W
Leyte I	98	10.55 N	124.50 E
Leyte Gulf C	98	10.40 N	125.25 E
L'gov	82	51.43 N	35.17 E
Lhasa → Lasa	102	29.40 N	91.09 E
Lhokseumawe	94	5.10 N	97.08 E
Lhut ≃	108	10.25 N	51.05 E
Lianxian	88	24.41 N	112.21 E
Lianyun'gang	88	34.44 N	119.30 E
Liaocheng	88	36.30 N	115.59 E
Liaodongbandao ≻1	88	40.00 N	122.20 E
Liaodongwan C	88	40.30 N	121.30 E
Liaohe ≃	88	40.40 N	122.09 E
Liaoning □4	88	41.00 N	123.00 E
Liaotung Peninsula → Liaodongbandao ≻1	88	40.00 N	122.20 E
Liaoyang	88	41.17 N	123.11 E
Liaoyuan	88	42.54 N	125.07 E
Liard ≃	142	61.52 N	121.18 W
Líbano	138	4.55 N	75.04 W
Libby	166	48.23 N	115.33 W
Libenge	108	3.39 N	18.38 E
Liberal	162	37.02 N	100.55 W
Liberec	72	50.46 N	15.03 E
Liberia	132	10.38 N	85.27 W
Liberia □1	106	6.00 N	10.00 W
Libertador General San Martín (Ledesma)	140	23.50 S	64.45 W
Liberty, Ky., U.S.	158	37.19 N	84.56 W
Liberty, Mo., U.S.	158	39.15 N	94.25 W
Liberty, N.C., U.S.	156	35.51 N	79.34 W
Liberty, N.Y., U.S.	152	41.48 N	74.45 W
Liberty, S.C., U.S.	156	34.48 N	82.42 W
Liberty, Tex., U.S.	160	30.03 N	94.47 W
Libertyville	154	42.17 N	87.57 W
Libourne	74	44.55 N	0.14 W
Libramont	72	49.55 N	5.23 E
Libreville	110	0.23 N	9.27 E
Libya □1	108	27.00 N	17.00 E
Libyan Desert → Aş-Şaḥrā' al-Lībīyah ⟵2	108	24.00 N	25.00 E
Licantén	140	34.59 S	72.00 W
Licata	78	37.05 N	13.56 E
Lich	72	50.33 N	8.50 E
Lichfield	70	52.42 N	1.48 W
Lichtenburg	116	26.08 S	26.08 E
Lichtenfels	72	50.09 N	11.04 E
Lichtenstein	72	50.45 N	12.37 E
Lickershamn	68	57.50 N	18.31 E
Licking ≃	152	39.06 N	84.30 W
Lida	86	53.53 N	25.18 E
Liddon Gulf C	142	75.03 N	113.00 W
Lidgerwood	162	46.05 N	97.09 W
Lidingö	68	59.22 N	18.08 E
Lidköping	68	58.30 N	13.10 E
Lidzbark	72	53.17 N	19.49 E
Lidzbark Warmiński	72	54.09 N	20.35 E
Liechtenstein □1	64	47.09 N	9.35 E
Liège	72	50.38 N	5.34 E
Lieksa	68	63.19 N	30.01 E
Lienz	72	46.50 N	12.47 E
Liepāja	86	56.31 N	21.01 E
Lier	72	51.08 N	4.34 E
Liestal	74	47.29 N	7.44 E
Liévin	74	50.25 N	2.46 E
Lièvre, Rivière du ≃	152	45.31 N	75.26 W
Liezen	72	47.35 N	14.15 E
Lifford	70	54.50 N	7.29 W
Liffré	74	48.13 N	1.30 W
Lighthouse Point	156	26.17 N	80.07 W
Lignières	74	46.45 N	2.11 E
Ligny-en-Barrois	74	48.41 N	5.20 E
Ligonha ≃	110	16.54 S	39.09 E
Ligonier, Ind., U.S.	158	41.28 N	85.35 W
Ligonier, Pa., U.S.	152	40.15 N	79.14 W
Ligueil	74	47.03 N	0.49 E
Liguria □4	78	44.30 N	8.50 E
Ligurian Sea ⫧2	78	43.30 N	9.00 E
Lihue	170b	21.59 N	159.22 W
Lijiang	88	26.57 N	100.15 E
Likasi (Jadotville)	110	10.59 S	26.44 E
Likino-Dulevo	86	55.43 N	38.58 E
Liknes	68	58.19 N	6.59 E
Likoma Island I	110	12.05 S	34.45 E
Likouala ≃	110	0.50 S	17.11 E
Lilbourn	158	36.35 N	89.37 W
L'Île-Bouchard	74	47.07 N	0.25 E
L'Île-Rousse	74	42.38 N	8.56 E
Lilienfeld	72	48.03 N	15.36 E
Lillby	68	63.28 N	23.00 E
Lille	74	50.38 N	3.04 E
Lillebonne	74	49.31 N	0.33 E
Lillehammer	68	61.08 N	10.30 E
Lillers	74	50.34 N	2.29 E
Lillesand	68	58.15 N	8.24 E
Lillestrøm	68	59.57 N	11.05 E
Lillooet	148	50.42 N	121.56 W
Lilongwe	110	13.59 S	33.44 E
Liloy	92	8.08 N	122.40 E
Lilydale	120	41.15 S	147.13 E
Lima, Perú	134	12.03 S	77.03 W
Lima, Mont., U.S.	166	44.38 N	112.36 W
Lima, Ohio, U.S.	152	40.46 N	84.06 W
Lima (Limia) ≃	76	41.41 N	8.50 W
Limanowa	72	49.43 N	20.26 E
Limassol → Lemesós	104	34.40 N	33.02 E
Limavady	70	55.03 N	6.57 W
Limay ≃	140	39.00 S	68.00 W
Limbang	92	4.45 N	115.00 E
Limbaži	86	57.31 N	24.42 E
Limburg an der Lahn	72	50.23 N	8.04 E
Limeira	140	22.34 S	47.24 W
Limerick	70	52.40 N	8.38 W
Limerick □6	70	52.30 N	9.00 W
Limestone, Austl.	122	21.11 S	119.50 E
Limestone, Maine, U.S.	150	46.55 N	67.50 W
Limfjorden ⌣	66	56.55 N	9.10 E
Limia (Lima) ≃	76	41.41 N	8.50 W
Liminka	68	64.49 N	25.24 E
Límnos I	80	39.54 N	25.21 E
Limoeiro	134	7.52 S	35.27 W
Limoges	74	45.50 N	1.16 E
Limogne	74	44.24 N	1.46 E
Limón, C.R.	132	10.00 N	83.02 W
Limon, Colo., U.S.	162	39.16 N	103.41 W
Limours	70	48.39 N	2.05 E
Limoux	74	43.04 N	2.14 E
Limpopo ≃	116	25.15 S	33.30 E
Linapacan Island I	98	11.18 N	119.47 E
Linares, Chile	140	35.51 S	71.36 W
Linares, Esp.	76	38.05 N	3.38 W
Linares, Méx.	130	24.52 N	99.34 W
Linares □4	140	36.00 S	71.20 W
Lincang	94	23.45 N	102.20 E
Linch	166	43.37 N	106.12 W
Lincoln, Arg.	140	34.55 S	61.30 W
Lincoln, Eng., U.K.	70	53.14 N	0.33 W
Lincoln, Calif., U.S.	168	38.54 N	121.17 W
Lincoln, Ill., U.S.	158	40.09 N	89.22 W
Lincoln, Kans., U.S.	162	39.02 N	98.09 W
Lincoln, Maine, U.S.	152	45.22 N	68.30 W
Lincoln, Mont., U.S.	166	46.58 N	112.41 W
Lincoln, Nebr., U.S.	162	40.48 N	96.42 W
Lincoln, N.H., U.S.	152	44.03 N	71.40 W
Lincoln City	166	44.59 N	123.59 W
Lincoln Gap	120	32.37 S	137.35 E
Lincoln Park, Ga., U.S.	156	32.52 N	84.19 W
Lincoln Park, Mich., U.S.	154	42.14 N	83.09 W
Lincolnshire □6	70	52.55 N	0.22 W
Lincolnton, Ga., U.S.	156	33.48 N	82.28 W
Lincolnton, N.C., U.S.	156	35.29 N	81.14 W
Lincoln Village	168	38.01 N	121.19 W
Linda	168	39.08 N	121.34 W
Lindale	156	34.11 N	85.11 W
Lindau	72	47.33 N	9.41 E
Linde ≃	84	64.57 N	124.36 E
Linden, Ala., U.S.	158	32.18 N	87.47 W
Linden, Mich., U.S.	154	42.49 N	83.47 W
Linden, Tenn., U.S.	158	35.37 N	87.50 W
Lindenows Fjord C2	142	60.45 N	43.30 W
Lindesnes ≻	68	58.00 N	7.02 E
Lindi	110	10.00 S	39.43 E
Lindi ≃	110	0.33 N	25.05 E
Lindlar	72	51.01 N	7.23 E
Lindsay, Ont., Can.	154	44.21 N	78.44 W
Lindsay, Calif., U.S.	168	36.12 N	119.05 W
Lindsay, Okla., U.S.	160	34.50 N	97.38 W
Lindsborg	162	38.35 N	97.40 W
Linesville	152	41.39 N	80.26 W
Lineville	158	33.19 N	85.45 W
Linfen	88	36.05 N	111.32 E
Lingao	94	20.00 N	109.40 E
Lingayen	92	16.01 N	120.14 E
Lingayen Gulf C	98	16.10 N	120.15 E
Lingen	72	52.31 N	7.19 E
Lingga, Kepulauan II	96	0.10 S	104.35 E
Lingga, Pulau I	96	0.12 S	104.35 E
Lingle	164	42.08 N	104.21 W
Lingling	94	26.11 N	111.29 E
Linguère	114	15.24 N	15.07 W
Linh, Ngoc ∧	94	15.05 N	108.00 E
Linhai	88	28.51 N	121.07 E
Linhe	88	40.51 N	107.30 E
Linjiang	88	41.49 N	126.54 E
Linköping	68	58.25 N	15.37 E
Linkou	88	45.15 N	130.16 E
Linkuva	86	56.05 N	23.59 E
Linlithgow	70	55.59 N	3.37 W
Linn, Kans., U.S.	162	39.41 N	97.05 W
Linn, Mo., U.S.	158	38.29 N	91.51 W
Linqing	88	36.53 N	115.41 E
Linru	88	34.11 N	112.49 E
Lins	140	21.40 S	49.45 W
Lintao	88	35.27 N	103.46 E
Linthal	74	46.55 N	9.00 E
Linton, Ind., U.S.	158	39.02 N	87.10 W
Linton, N. Dak., U.S.	162	46.16 N	100.14 W
Linxi	88	43.30 N	118.00 E
Linxia	88	35.34 N	103.08 E
Linyanti (Chobe) ≃	116	17.50 S	25.05 E
Linyi	88	35.04 N	118.22 E
Linz	72	48.18 N	14.18 E
Lion, Golfe du C	74	43.00 N	4.00 E
Liozno	86	55.02 N	30.48 E
Lipa	92	13.57 N	121.10 E
Lipeck	86	52.37 N	39.35 E
Lipki	86	53.58 N	37.42 E
Lipno	72	52.51 N	19.10 E
Lipoa Point ≻	170a	21.02 N	156.38 W
Lipova	80	46.05 N	21.40 E
Lippstadt	72	51.40 N	8.19 E
Liptovský Mikuláš	72	49.06 N	19.37 E
Liptrap, Cape ≻	120	38.54 S	145.55 E
Lira	108	2.15 N	32.54 E
Lisala	110	2.09 N	21.31 E
Lisboa (Lisbon)	76	38.43 N	9.08 W
Lisbon → Lisboa, Port.	76	38.43 N	9.08 W
Lisbon, Maine, U.S.	152	44.02 N	70.06 W
Lisbon, N.H., U.S.	152	44.13 N	71.55 W
Lisbon, N. Dak., U.S.	162	46.27 N	97.41 W
Lisbon, Ohio, U.S.	152	40.47 N	80.46 W
Lisbon Falls	152	44.03 N	70.03 W
Lisburn	70	54.31 N	6.03 W
Lisburne, Cape ≻	146	68.52 N	166.14 W
Lishui	88	28.27 N	119.54 E
Lishui ≃	88	29.24 N	112.01 E
Lisičansk	64	48.55 N	38.26 E
Lisieux	74	49.09 N	0.14 E
Liski → Georgiu-Dež	64	50.59 N	39.30 E
L'Isle Jourdain, Fr.	74	46.14 N	0.41 E
L'Isle-Jourdain, Fr.	74	43.37 N	1.05 E
L'Isle-sur-le-Doubs	74	47.27 N	6.35 E
Lismore	120	28.48 S	153.17 E
Listowel, Ont., Can.	154	43.44 N	80.57 W
Listowel, Eire	70	52.27 N	9.29 W
Lit	68	63.19 N	14.49 E
Litang, Zhg.	88	23.11 N	109.05 E
Litang, Zhg.	88	29.59 N	100.19 E
Litanghe ≃	88	28.04 N	101.30 E
Litchfield, Ill., U.S.	158	39.11 N	89.39 W
Litchfield, Mich., U.S.	154	42.03 N	84.46 W
Litchfield, Minn., U.S.	154	45.08 N	94.31 W
Litchfield Park	164	33.30 N	112.22 W
Lithgow	120	33.29 S	150.09 E
Lithonia	156	33.43 N	84.06 W
Lithuanian Soviet Socialist Republic → Litovskaja Sovetskaja Socialističeskaja Respublika □3	64	56.00 N	24.00 E
Lititz	152	40.09 N	76.18 W
Litoměřice	72	50.35 N	14.09 E
Litovko	84	49.15 N	135.11 E
Litovskaja Sovetskaja Socialističeskaja Respublik □3	64	56.00 N	24.00 E
Little ≃	158	33.37 N	93.52 W
Little, Mountain Fork ≃	158	33.57 N	94.34 W
Little Andaman I	94	10.45 N	92.30 E
Little Bear Creek ≃	160	37.43 N	101.43 W
Little Beaver Creek ≃, U.S.	162	46.17 N	103.56 W
Little Beaver Creek ≃, U.S.	162	39.49 N	101.03 W
Little Bighorn ≃	166	45.44 N	107.34 W
Little Black ≃	158	36.25 N	90.45 W
Little Blue ≃	162	39.41 N	96.40 W
Little Buffalo ≃	142	61.00 N	113.46 W
Little Cayman I	132	19.41 N	80.03 W
Little Cedar ≃	154	42.57 N	92.31 W
Little Chute	154	44.17 N	88.16 W
Little Colorado ≃	164	36.11 N	111.48 W
Little Current	154	45.58 N	81.56 W
Little Current ≃	142	50.57 N	84.36 W
Little Deschutes ≃	166	43.51 N	121.27 W
Little Diomede Island I	146	65.45 N	168.57 W
Little Falls	154	45.59 N	94.21 W
Littlefield	160	33.55 N	102.20 W
Little Inagua I	132	21.30 N	73.00 W
Little Karroo ⋀1	116	33.45 S	21.30 E
Little Mecatina ≃	142	50.28 N	59.35 W
Little Missouri ≃	162	47.30 N	102.25 W
Little Nicobar I	94	7.20 N	93.40 E
Little Osage ≃	158	38.02 N	94.14 W
Little Owyhee ≃	166	42.28 N	117.15 W
Little Powder ≃	162	45.28 N	105.20 W
Little Rock	158	34.44 N	92.15 W
Little Rock ≃	162	43.16 N	96.15 W
Little Scarcies ≃	114	8.51 N	13.09 W
Little Sioux ≃	162	41.49 N	96.04 W
Little Smoky ≃	148	55.42 N	117.38 W
Little Snake ≃	164	40.27 N	108.26 W
Littlestown	152	39.45 N	77.05 W
Little Tallapoosa ≃	156	33.18 N	85.34 W
Little Tennessee ≃	156	35.47 N	84.15 W
Littleton, Colo., U.S.	164	39.37 N	105.01 W
Littleton, N.H., U.S.	152	44.18 N	71.46 W

Symbols in the index entries are identified on page 203.

Name	Page	Lat	Long

Littleton, N.C., U.S. — 156 — 36.26 N — 77.54 W
Little Zab (Zāb-e Kūchek) (Az-Zāb as-Saghīr) ≃ — 104 — 35.12 N — 43.25 E
Litvinov — 72 — 50.37 N — 13.36 E
Liuan — 88 — 31.44 N — 116.31 E
Liucheng — 94 — 24.32 N — 109.21 E
Liuchonghe ≃ — 88 — 29.40 N — 107.25 E
Liuzhou — 94 — 24.22 N — 109.32 E
Līvāni — 86 — 56.22 N — 26.11 E
Livarot — 74 — 49.01 N — 0.09 E
Live Oak, Calif., U.S. — 168 — 39.17 N — 121.40 W
Live Oak, Fla., U.S. — 156 — 30.18 N — 82.59 W
Livermore, Calif., U.S. — 168 — 37.41 N — 121.46 W
Livermore, Ky., U.S. — 158 — 37.29 N — 87.08 W
Livermore Falls — 152 — 44.28 N — 70.11 W
Liverpool, N.S., Can. — 150 — 44.02 N — 64.43 W
Liverpool, Eng., U.K. — 70 — 53.25 N — 2.55 W
Liverpool, Cape ⊁ — 142 — 75.38 N — 78.06 W
Livingston, Guat. — 130 — 15.50 N — 88.45 W
Livingston, Ala., U.S. — 158 — 32.35 N — 88.11 W
Livingston, Calif., U.S. — 168 — 37.23 N — 120.43 W
Livingston, La., U.S. — 158 — 30.30 N — 90.45 W
Livingston, Mont., U.S. — 166 — 45.40 N — 110.34 W
Livingston, Tenn., U.S. — 158 — 36.23 N — 85.19 W
Livingston, Tex., U.S. — 160 — 30.43 N — 94.56 W
Livingston, Wis., U.S. — 154 — 42.54 N — 90.26 W
Livingstone — 110 — 17.50 S — 25.53 E
Livingstone, Chutes de ⌤ — 110 — 4.50 S — 14.30 E
Livingstone Falls → Livingstone, Chutes de ⌤ — 110 — 4.50 S — 14.30 E
Livingstonia — 110 — 10.36 S — 34.07 E
Livingston Manor — 152 — 41.54 N — 74.50 W
Livno — 78 — 43.50 N — 17.01 E
Livny — 86 — 52.25 N — 37.37 E
Livonia — 154 — 42.25 N — 83.23 W
Livorno (Leghorn) — 78 — 43.33 N — 10.19 E
Liwale — 110 — 9.46 S — 37.56 E
Lixi — 88 — 29.15 N — 114.46 E
Lijan — 88 — 59.51 N — 10.48 E
Ljubljana — 78 — 46.03 N — 14.31 E
Ljubuški — 78 — 43.12 N — 17.33 E
Ljungby — 68 — 56.50 N — 13.56 E
Ljungsbro — 68 — 58.31 N — 15.30 E
Ljusdal — 68 — 61.50 N — 16.05 E
Ljusnan ≃ — 68 — 61.12 N — 17.08 E
Llancanelo, Salina ≃ — 140 — 35.36 S — 69.11 W
Llandovery — 70 — 51.59 N — 3.48 W
Llandrindod Wells — 70 — 52.15 N — 3.23 W
Llandudno — 70 — 53.19 N — 3.49 W
Llanelli — 70 — 51.42 N — 4.10 W
Llanes — 76 — 43.25 N — 4.45 W
Llanfyllin — 70 — 52.46 N — 3.17 W
Llangefni — 70 — 53.16 N — 4.18 W
Llangollen — 70 — 52.58 N — 3.10 W
Llanidloes — 70 — 52.27 N — 3.32 W
Llano — 160 — 30.45 N — 98.41 W
Llano ≃ — 160 — 30.39 N — 98.25 W
Llano Estacado ≃¹ — 160 — 33.30 N — 102.40 W
Llanos ≃ — 138 — 5.00 N — 70.00 W
Llanwrtyd Wells — 70 — 52.07 N — 3.38 W
Lloydminster — 142 — 53.17 N — 110.00 W
Lluchmayor — 76 — 39.29 N — 2.54 E
Llullaillaco, Volcán ∧¹ — 140 — 24.43 S — 68.33 W
Loa — 164 — 38.24 N — 111.38 W
Loa ≃ — 140 — 21.26 S — 70.04 W
Loanda — 140 — 22.55 S — 53.10 W
Loange (Luangue) ≃ — 110 — 4.17 S — 20.02 E
Lobatse — 116 — 25.11 S — 25.40 E
Löbau — 72 — 51.05 N — 14.40 E
Lobaye ≃ — 108 — 3.41 N — 18.35 E
Lobenstein — 72 — 50.26 N — 11.38 E
Loberia — 140 — 38.07 S — 58.47 W
Lobito — 110 — 12.20 S — 13.34 E
Lobitos — 138 — 4.27 S — 81.15 W
Lobn'a — 86 — 56.01 N — 37.30 E
Lobo — 160 — 30.52 N — 104.48 W
Lobos — 140 — 35.10 S — 59.05 W
Lobos de Afuera, Islas II — 138 — 6.57 S — 80.42 W
Lobos de Tierra, Isla I — 138 — 6.27 S — 80.52 W
Lobstick Lake ⊜ — 142 — 54.00 N — 64.50 W
Locarno — 74 — 46.10 N — 8.48 E
Lochaline — 70 — 56.32 N — 5.47 W
Lochboisdale — 70 — 57.09 N — 7.19 W
Loches — 74 — 47.08 N — 1.00 E
Lochgilphead — 70 — 56.03 N — 5.26 W
Lochinver — 70 — 58.09 N — 5.15 W
Lochmaben — 70 — 55.08 N — 3.27 W
Lock — 120 — 33.34 S — 135.46 E
Lockerbie — 70 — 55.07 N — 3.22 W
Lockhart, Austl. — 120 — 35.14 S — 146.43 E
Lockhart, Tex., U.S. — 160 — 29.53 N — 97.41 W
Lock Haven — 152 — 41.08 N — 77.27 W
Lockney — 160 — 34.07 N — 101.27 W
Löcknitz — 72 — 53.27 N — 14.12 E
Lockport, Ill., U.S. — 154 — 41.36 N — 88.03 W
Lockport, La., U.S. — 158 — 29.39 N — 90.32 W
Lockport, N.Y., U.S. — 152 — 43.10 N — 78.42 W
Locminé — 70 — 47.53 N — 2.50 W
Loc-ninh — 92 — 11.50 N — 106.35 E
Locri — 78 — 38.14 N — 16.16 E
Locust Creek ≃ — 154 — 39.40 N — 93.17 W
Locust Grove — 160 — 36.12 N — 95.10 W
Lod (Lydda) — 104 — 31.58 N — 34.54 E
Lodejnoje Polje — 86 — 60.44 N — 33.30 E
Lodève — 74 — 43.43 N — 3.19 E
Lodge Creek ≃ — 166 — 48.58 N — 109.15 W
Lodge Grass — 166 — 45.19 N — 107.22 W
Lodgepole Creek ≃ — 162 — 41.20 N — 102.10 W
Lodi, It. — 78 — 45.19 N — 9.30 E
Lodi, Calif., U.S. — 168 — 38.08 N — 121.16 W
Lodi, Ohio, U.S. — 152 — 41.03 N — 82.01 W
Lodja — 110 — 3.29 S — 23.26 E
Lodwar — 108 — 3.07 N — 35.36 E
Łódź — 72 — 51.46 N — 19.30 E
Loen — 68 — 61.52 N — 6.52 E
Loeir — 72 — 48.35 N — 12.41 E
Loffa ≃ — 114 — 6.36 N — 11.08 W
Lofoten I — 68 — 68.30 N — 15.00 E
Lofthus — 68 — 60.20 N — 6.40 E
Lofty, Mount ∧ — 120 — 34.59 S — 138.42 E
Logan, Kans., U.S. — 162 — 39.40 N — 99.34 W
Logan, N.Mex., U.S. — 160 — 35.22 N — 103.25 W
Logan, Ohio, U.S. — 152 — 39.32 N — 82.25 W
Logan, Utah, U.S. — 164 — 41.44 N — 111.50 W
Logan ≃ — 152 — 37.51 N — 81.59 W
Logan, Mount ∧ — 146 — 60.34 N — 140.24 W
Logansport, Ind., U.S. — 158 — 40.45 N — 86.21 W
Logansport, La., U.S. — 158 — 31.58 N — 93.58 W
Logojsk — 86 — 54.12 N — 27.49 E
Logone ≃ — 106 — 12.06 N — 15.02 E
Logroño — 76 — 42.28 N — 2.27 W
Logroño □4 — 76 — 42.15 N — 2.20 W
Løgstør — 68 — 56.58 N — 9.15 E
Lohja — 68 — 60.15 N — 24.05 E
Lohne — 72 — 52.42 N — 8.12 E
Lohr — 72 — 50.00 N — 9.34 E
Loi-kaw — 94 — 19.41 N — 97.13 E
Loire □5 — 74 — 45.45 N — 4.15 E
Loire ≃ — 74 — 47.16 N — 2.11 W
Loire-Atlantique □5 — 74 — 47.25 N — 1.30 W
Loiret □5 — 74 — 47.55 N — 2.20 E
Loir-et-Cher □5 — 74 — 47.35 N — 1.20 E
Loitz — 72 — 53.58 N — 13.07 E
Loja, Ec. — 138 — 4.00 S — 79.13 W
Loja, Esp. — 76 — 37.10 N — 4.09 W
Lokandu — 110 — 2.31 S — 25.47 E
Løken — 68 — 59.48 N — 11.29 E
Lokeren — 72 — 51.06 N — 4.00 E
Løkken verk — 68 — 63.08 N — 9.42 E
Lokn'a — 86 — 56.50 N — 30.09 E
Lokolama — 110 — 2.34 S — 19.53 E
Loks Land I — 142 — 62.26 N — 64.38 W
Loliondo — 110 — 2.03 S — 35.37 E
Lolland I — 68 — 54.46 N — 11.30 E
Lolo Pass ✕ — 166 — 46.38 N — 114.35 W

Lom, Blg. — 80 — 43.49 N — 23.14 E
Lom, Nor. — 68 — 61.50 N — 8.33 E
Lom ≃ — 106 — 5.20 N — 13.24 E
Loma Mansa ∧ — 114 — 9.13 N — 11.07 W
Lomami ≃ — 110 — 0.46 N — 24.16 E
Lomas de Zamora — 140 — 34.46 S — 58.24 W
Lombard — 158 — 41.53 N — 88.01 W
Lombardia □4 — 78 — 45.40 N — 9.30 E
Lomblen, Pulau I — 96 — 8.25 S — 123.30 E
Lombok I — 96 — 8.45 S — 116.30 E
Lomé — 114 — 6.08 N — 1.13 E
Lomela — 110 — 2.18 S — 23.17 E
Lomela ≃ — 110 — 0.14 S — 20.42 E
Lomma — 160 — 31.13 N — 98.24 W
Lommel — 72 — 51.14 N — 5.18 E
Lomonosov — 86 — 59.55 N — 29.46 E
Lomonosovskij — 82 — 50.50 N — 66.28 E
Lompoc — 168 — 34.38 N — 120.27 W
Łomża — 72 — 53.11 N — 22.05 E
Lonaconing — 152 — 39.34 N — 78.59 W
Loncoche — 136 — 39.22 S — 72.38 W
Londinières — 74 — 49.50 N — 1.24 E
London, Ont., Can. — 154 — 42.59 N — 81.14 W
London, Eng., U.K. — 70 — 51.30 N — 0.10 W
London, Ky., U.S. — 158 — 37.08 N — 84.05 W
London, Ohio, U.S. — 152 — 39.53 N — 83.27 W
Londonderry — 160 — 30.41 N — 99.35 W
Londonderry, Cape ⊁ — 124 — 13.45 S — 126.55 E
Londonderry, Isla I — 136 — 55.03 S — 70.40 W
Londrina — 140 — 23.18 S — 51.09 W
Lone Mountain ∧ — 168 — 38.02 N — 117.29 W
Lone Oak, Ky., U.S. — 158 — 37.02 N — 88.40 W
Lone Oak, Tex., U.S. — 160 — 33.00 N — 95.57 W
Lone Rock — 154 — 43.11 N — 90.12 W
Lone Star — 158 — 32.55 N — 94.43 W
Lone Tree — 154 — 41.29 N — 91.26 W
Lonetree Creek ≃ — 164 — 40.25 N — 104.35 W
Longa ≃ — 110 — 10.15 S — 13.30 E
Longa, Proliv ⥾ — 84 — 70.20 N — 178.00 E
Long Bay C — 156 — 33.35 N — 78.45 W
Long Beach, Calif., U.S. — 168 — 33.46 N — 118.11 W
Long Beach, Miss., U.S. — 158 — 30.22 N — 89.07 W
Long Beach, N.Y., U.S. — 152 — 40.35 N — 73.41 W
Longboat Key I — 156 — 27.24 N — 82.39 W
Long Branch — 152 — 40.18 N — 74.00 W
Longchang — 94 — 29.21 N — 105.17 E
Long Creek — 166 — 44.43 N — 119.06 W
Long Creek ≃ — 166 — 49.07 N — 103.00 W
Long Eaton — 70 — 52.54 N — 1.15 W
Longford, Austl. — 120 — 38.10 S — 147.05 E
Longford, Eire — 70 — 53.44 N — 7.47 W
Longford □6 — 70 — 53.42 N — 7.45 W
Longhurst — 156 — 36.25 N — 78.58 W
Long Island I, Austl. — 120 — 22.09 S — 149.54 E
Long Island I, Ba. — 132 — 23.10 N — 75.10 W
Long Island I, N.W. Ter., Can. — 142 — 54.50 N — 79.20 W
Long Island I, N.Y., U.S. — 152 — 40.50 N — 73.00 W
Long Island Sound ⥾ — 152 — 41.05 N — 72.58 W
Longjiang — 88 — 47.19 N — 123.12 E
Longkou — 88 — 37.38 N — 120.18 E
Longli — 94 — 26.26 N — 106.58 E
Longmeadow — 152 — 42.03 N — 72.34 W
Longmont — 164 — 40.10 N — 105.06 W
Longnawan — 92 — 1.54 N — 114.53 E
Longny — 74 — 48.32 N — 0.45 E
Long Prairie — 154 — 45.59 N — 94.52 W
Longquan — 88 — 28.04 N — 119.07 E
Long Range Mountains ∧ — 150 — 49.20 N — 57.30 W
Longreach — 120 — 23.26 S — 144.15 E
Long Reef ÷² — 124 — 11.11 S — 151.40 E
Longsheng — 94 — 25.47 N — 110.01 E
Longué — 74 — 47.23 N — 0.06 W
Longueuil — 152 — 45.32 N — 73.30 W
Longuyon — 74 — 49.26 N — 5.36 E
Longview, N.C., U.S. — 156 — 35.44 N — 81.23 W
Longview, Tex., U.S. — 158 — 32.30 N — 94.44 W
Longview, Wash., U.S. — 166 — 46.08 N — 122.57 W
Longxi — 94 — 49.31 N — 5.46 E
Longxu — 88 — 34.56 N — 104.47 E
Long-xuyen — 92 — 10.23 N — 105.25 E
Longzhou — 94 — 22.22 N — 106.52 E
Lonigo — 78 — 45.23 N — 11.23 E
Löningen — 72 — 52.44 N — 7.46 E
Lonoke — 158 — 34.47 N — 91.54 W
Lons-le-Saunier — 74 — 46.40 N — 5.33 E
Loogootee — 158 — 38.41 N — 86.55 W
Lookout, Cape ⊁ — 156 — 34.35 N — 76.32 W
Lookout Mountain ∧ — 164 — 40.17 N — 104.22 W
Lookout Pass ✕ — 166 — 47.27 N — 115.42 W
Lookout Ridge ⋏ — 146 — 69.07 N — 158.36 W
Loongana — 122 — 30.57 S — 127.02 E
Loon op Zand — 72 — 51.38 N — 5.04 E
Lopatina, Gora ∧ — 84 — 50.52 N — 143.10 E
Lopatka, Mys ⊁ — 84 — 50.52 N — 156.40 E
Lop Buri — 92 — 14.48 N — 100.37 E
Lopez, Cap ⊁ — 110 — 0.37 S — 8.43 E
Loppi — 68 — 60.43 N — 24.27 E
Lora, Hāmūn-i- ≃ — 104 — 29.20 N — 64.50 E
Lora del Rio — 76 — 37.39 N — 5.32 W
Lorain — 152 — 41.28 N — 82.10 W
Loraine — 160 — 32.24 N — 100.43 W
Lorca — 76 — 37.40 N — 1.42 W
Lord Howe Island I — 118 — 31.33 S — 159.05 E
Lord Mayor Bay C — 142 — 69.44 N — 92.00 W
Lordsburg — 164 — 32.21 N — 108.43 W
Loreto, Bra. — 134 — 7.05 S — 45.09 W
Loreto, Méx. — 130 — 26.01 N — 111.21 W
Loreto □7 — 134 — 4.00 S — 74.00 W
Lorica — 138 — 9.14 N — 75.49 W
Lorient — 74 — 47.45 N — 3.22 W
Loriol-[du-Comtat] — 74 — 44.45 N — 4.49 E
Lormes — 74 — 47.17 N — 3.49 E
Lorne Glen — 120 — 26.14 S — 121.33 E
Lorne — 120 — 38.33 S — 143.59 E
Lörrach — 74 — 47.37 N — 7.40 E
Lorraine □9 — 74 — 49.00 N — 6.00 E
Lorris — 74 — 47.53 N — 2.31 E
Los — 68 — 61.44 N — 15.10 E
Los Alamos — 160 — 35.53 N — 106.19 W
Los Andes — 140 — 32.50 S — 70.37 W
Los Ángeles, Chile — 140 — 37.28 S — 72.21 W
Los Ángeles, Calif., U.S. — 168 — 34.03 N — 118.15 W
Los Banos — 168 — 37.04 N — 120.51 W
Los Blancos — 140 — 23.40 S — 62.36 W
Los Ebanos — 160 — 26.14 N — 98.34 W
Los Fresnos — 160 — 26.04 N — 97.29 W
Los Gatos — 168 — 37.14 N — 121.59 W
Losice — 72 — 52.14 N — 22.43 E
Losinoborskaja — 84 — 58.22 N — 89.28 E
Los Lagos — 136 — 39.51 S — 72.50 W
Los Lunas — 160 — 34.48 N — 106.44 W
Los Mochis — 130 — 25.45 N — 108.57 W
Los Molinos — 168 — 40.03 N — 122.06 W
Los Palacios y Villafranca — 76 — 37.10 N — 5.55 W
Los Pinos ≃ — 164 — 36.56 N — 107.36 W
Los Reyes [de Salgado] — 130 — 19.35 N — 102.29 W
Los Rios □4 — 138 — 1.30 S — 79.25 W
Los Roques, Islas II — 138 — 11.50 N — 66.45 W
Losser — 72 — 52.15 N — 7.00 E
Lossiemouth — 70 — 57.43 N — 3.18 W
Lost ≃ — 166 — 41.56 N — 121.30 W
Lost Hills — 168 — 35.37 N — 119.41 W
Lost Trail Pass ✕ — 166 — 45.42 N — 113.57 W
Los Vilos — 140 — 31.55 S — 71.31 W
Los Yébenes — 76 — 39.34 N — 3.53 W
Lot □5 — 74 — 44.35 N — 1.42 E
Lota — 140 — 37.05 S — 73.10 W
Løten — 68 — 60.49 N — 11.19 E
Lot-et-Garonne □5 — 74 — 44.20 N — 0.30 E

Lothair — 156 — 37.15 N — 83.10 W
Lothian Region □4 — 70 — 55.55 N — 3.00 W
Lotsane ≃ — 116 — 22.41 S — 28.11 E
Lott — 160 — 31.12 N — 97.02 W
Lotta ≃ — 68 — 68.36 N — 31.06 E
Lotung — 88 — 24.41 N — 121.46 E
Louang Prabang — 94 — 19.52 N — 102.08 E
Louchi — 66 — 66.04 N — 33.00 E
Loudéac — 70 — 48.10 N — 2.45 W
Loudon — 156 — 35.44 N — 84.20 W
Loudonville — 152 — 40.38 N — 82.14 W
Loudun — 74 — 47.01 N — 0.05 E
Loué — 70 — 48.00 N — 0.09 W
Louga — 114 — 15.37 N — 16.13 W
Loughborough — 70 — 52.47 N — 1.11 W
Loughrea — 70 — 53.12 N — 8.34 W
Louhans — 74 — 46.38 N — 5.13 E
Louisa, Ky., U.S. — 156 — 38.07 N — 82.36 W
Louisbourg — 150 — 45.55 N — 59.58 W
Louisburg, Kans., U.S. — 162 — 38.37 N — 94.41 W
Louisburg, N.C., U.S. — 156 — 36.06 N — 78.18 W
Louise — 160 — 29.06 N — 96.25 W
Louise, Lake ⊜ — 146 — 62.20 N — 146.30 W
Louisiade Archipelago II — 118 — 11.00 S — 153.00 E
Louisiana — 158 — 39.27 N — 91.03 W
Louisiana □3 — 158 — 31.15 N — 92.15 W
Louis Trichardt — 116 — 23.01 S — 29.43 E
Louisville, Ala., U.S. — 158 — 31.47 N — 85.33 W
Louisville, Colo., U.S. — 164 — 39.59 N — 105.08 W
Louisville, Ga., U.S. — 156 — 33.00 N — 82.24 W
Louisville, Ky., U.S. — 158 — 38.16 N — 85.45 W
Louisville, Miss., U.S. — 158 — 33.07 N — 89.03 W
Louisville, Nebr., U.S. — 162 — 41.00 N — 96.10 W
Louisville, Ohio, U.S. — 152 — 40.50 N — 81.16 W
Loulé — 76 — 37.08 N — 8.02 W
Louny — 72 — 50.21 N — 13.48 E
Loup City — 162 — 41.17 N — 98.58 W
Loup ≃ — 162 — 41.17 N — 98.23 W
Lourdes — 74 — 43.06 N — 0.03 W
Lourenço Marques → Maputo — 110 — 25.58 S — 32.35 E
Loures — 76 — 38.50 N — 9.10 W
Lourinhã — 76 — 39.14 N — 9.19 W
Lourosa — 76 — 40.19 N — 7.56 W
Lousã — 76 — 40.07 N — 8.15 W
Louth, Eire — 70 — 53.37 N — 6.53 W
Louth, Eng., U.K. — 70 — 53.22 N — 0.01 W
Louth □6 — 70 — 53.55 N — 6.30 W
Louth Bay C — 120 — 34.34 S — 136.02 E
Loutre, Bayou de ≃ — 158 — 32.41 N — 92.08 W
Louvain → Leuven — 72 — 50.53 N — 4.42 E
Louviers — 74 — 49.13 N — 1.10 E
Louvigné-du-Désert — 74 — 48.29 N — 1.08 W
Lovat' ≃ — 86 — 58.14 N — 31.28 E
Loveč — 80 — 43.08 N — 24.43 E
Lovelady — 158 — 31.08 N — 95.27 W
Loveland — 164 — 40.24 N — 105.05 W
Lovelock — 168 — 40.11 N — 118.28 W
Lovere — 78 — 45.49 N — 10.04 E
Loves Park — 154 — 42.19 N — 89.03 W
Loving, N.Mex., U.S. — 160 — 32.17 N — 104.06 W
Loving, Tex., U.S. — 160 — 33.16 N — 98.31 W
Lovington, Ill., U.S. — 158 — 39.43 N — 88.38 W
Lovington, N.Mex., U.S. — 160 — 32.57 N — 103.21 W
Low, Cape ⊁ — 142 — 63.07 N — 85.18 W
Lowa — 110 — 1.24 S — 25.51 E
Lowden — 154 — 41.52 N — 90.56 W
Lowell, Ind., U.S. — 158 — 41.18 N — 87.25 W
Lowell, Mass., U.S. — 152 — 42.39 N — 71.18 W
Lowell, Mich., U.S. — 154 — 42.56 N — 85.20 W
Löwenberg — 72 — 52.54 N — 13.08 E
Lower Alkali Lake ⊜ — 168 — 41.15 N — 120.02 W
Lower Hutt — 126 — 41.13 S — 174.55 E
Lower Kalskag — 146 — 61.31 N — 160.22 W
Lower Paia — 146a — 20.55 N — 156.23 W
Lower Post — 146 — 59.55 N — 128.30 W
Lower Red Lake ⊜ — 154 — 48.00 N — 94.50 W
Lower Sackville — 150 — 44.45 N — 63.40 W
Lower Trajan's Wall ⁺ — 80 — 45.40 N — 28.30 E
Lowestoft — 70 — 52.29 N — 1.45 E
Łowicz — 72 — 52.07 N — 19.56 E
Lowmoor — 156 — 37.47 N — 79.53 W
Lowrah (Pishin Lora) ≃ — 102 — 29.09 N — 64.55 E
Low Rocky Point ⊁ — 120 — 43.00 S — 145.30 E
Loxton — 120 — 34.27 S — 140.35 E
Loyalton — 168 — 39.41 N — 120.14 W
Lozère □5 — 74 — 44.30 N — 3.30 E
Loznica — 80 — 44.32 N — 19.13 E
Lua ≃ — 110 — 2.46 N — 18.26 E
Lualaba ≃ — 110 — 0.26 N — 25.20 E
Luama ≃ — 110 — 4.46 S — 26.53 E
Luanda — 110 — 8.48 S — 13.14 E
Luang Prabang → Louang Prabang — 94 — 19.52 N — 102.08 E
Luang Praban Range ⋏ — 94 — 18.30 N — 101.15 E
Luanginga ≃ — 110 — 15.11 S — 22.56 E
Luangwa (Aruângua) ≃, Afr. — 110 — 15.36 S — 30.25 E
Luangwa ≃, Zam. — 110 — 14.25 S — 30.25 E
Luanshya — 110 — 13.08 S — 28.24 E
Luapula ≃ — 110 — 9.26 S — 28.33 E
Luarca — 76 — 43.33 N — 6.32 W
Luau — 110 — 10.42 S — 22.12 E
Lubań, Pol. — 72 — 51.08 N — 15.18 E
L'uban', S.S.S.R. — 86 — 59.21 N — 31.11 E
Lubang Island I — 98 — 13.45 N — 120.10 E
Lubawa — 72 — 53.30 N — 19.45 E
Lübbenau — 72 — 51.52 N — 13.57 E
Lübben — 72 — 51.56 N — 13.53 E
Lubbock — 160 — 33.35 N — 101.51 W
Lübeck — 72 — 53.52 N — 10.40 E
Lübecker Bucht C — 72 — 54.00 N — 11.55 E
Lubefu — 110 — 4.43 S — 24.25 E
L'ubercy — 86 — 55.41 N — 37.53 E
Lubersac — 74 — 45.27 N — 1.24 E
L'ubilash ≃ — 110 — 6.02 S — 23.45 E
Lubin — 72 — 51.24 N — 16.13 E
Lublin — 72 — 51.15 N — 22.35 E
Lubliniec — 72 — 50.40 N — 18.41 E
Lubny — 86 — 50.01 N — 33.00 E
L'ubochna — 72 — 49.06 N — 19.11 E
Luboń — 72 — 52.23 N — 16.53 E
L'ubotin — 72 — 49.57 N — 35.57 E
Lübtheen — 72 — 53.18 N — 11.04 E
Lubudi — 110 — 9.57 S — 25.58 E
Lubudi ≃ — 110 — 9.13 S — 25.38 E
Lubuklinggau — 96 — 3.18 S — 102.52 E
Lubumbashi (Elisabethville) — 110 — 11.40 S — 27.28 E
Lubutu — 110 — 0.44 S — 26.35 E
Lübz — 72 — 53.27 N — 12.01 E
Lucania, Mount ∧ — 146 — 61.01 N — 140.28 W
L'uca-Ongokton, Gora ∧ — 84 — 65.45 N — 95.45 E
Lucca — 78 — 43.50 N — 10.29 E
Lucedale — 158 — 30.55 N — 88.35 W
Lucena, Esp. — 76 — 37.24 N — 4.29 W
Lucena, Pil. — 98 — 13.56 N — 121.37 E
Lucenay-l'Évêque — 74 — 47.05 N — 4.15 E
Lučenec — 72 — 48.20 N — 19.40 E
Lucera — 78 — 41.30 N — 15.20 E
Lucerne → Luzern, Schw. — 74 — 47.03 N — 8.18 E
Lucerne, Calif., U.S. — 168 — 39.06 N — 122.48 W
Lucindale — 120 — 36.59 S — 140.22 E
Lucira — 110 — 14.01 S — 12.31 E
Luck — 64 — 50.44 N — 25.20 E
Luckau — 72 — 51.51 N — 13.43 E
Luckenwalde — 72 — 52.05 N — 13.10 E
Lucknow, Ont., Can. — 152 — 43.58 N — 81.31 W
Lucknow — 102 — 26.51 N — 80.55 E
Luçon — 74 — 46.27 N — 1.10 W
Lüda (Dairen) — 88 — 38.53 N — 121.35 E
Lüdenscheid — 72 — 51.13 N — 7.38 E
Lüderitz — 116 — 26.38 S — 15.10 E
Ludhiāna — 102 — 30.54 N — 75.51 E
Lüdinghausen — 72 — 51.46 N — 7.26 E
Ludington — 154 — 43.57 N — 86.27 W
Ludlow, Eng., U.K. — 70 — 52.22 N — 2.43 W
Ludlow, Mass., U.S. — 152 — 42.10 N — 72.29 W
Ludlow, Vt., U.S. — 152 — 43.24 N — 72.42 W
Ludowici — 156 — 31.43 N — 81.45 W
Ludvika — 68 — 60.09 N — 15.11 E
Ludwigsburg — 72 — 48.54 N — 9.11 E
Ludwigsfelde — 72 — 52.17 N — 13.16 E
Ludwigshafen — 72 — 49.29 N — 8.26 E
Ludwigslust — 72 — 53.19 N — 11.30 E
Ludza — 86 — 56.33 N — 27.43 E
Luebo — 110 — 5.21 S — 21.25 E
Luena — 58 — 44 — 29.52 E
Lüeng ≃ — 94 — 25.07 N — 102.07 E
Lufira ≃ — 110 — 8.16 S — 26.27 E
Lufkin — 158 — 31.20 N — 94.44 W
Luga — 86 — 58.44 N — 29.52 E
Luga ≃ — 86 — 59.40 N — 28.18 E
Lugano — 74 — 46.01 N — 8.58 E
Lugano, Lago di ⊜ — 74 — 46.00 N — 9.00 E
Lugansk → Vorošilovgrad — 64 — 48.34 N — 39.20 E
Lugenda ≃ — 110 — 11.25 S — 38.33 E
Lugh Ganane — 108 — 3.56 N — 42.32 E
Lugo, Esp. — 76 — 43.00 N — 7.34 W
Lugo, It. — 78 — 44.25 N — 11.54 E
Lugoj — 80 — 45.41 N — 21.54 E
Luhanka — 68 — 61.47 N — 25.42 E
Luhit ≃ — 102 — 27.48 N — 95.28 E
Luik → Liège — 72 — 50.38 N — 5.34 E
Luilaka ≃ — 110 — 0.15 S — 20.12 E
Luimneach → Limerick — 70 — 52.40 N — 8.38 W
Luino — 74 — 46.00 N — 8.44 E
Luishia — 110 — 11.10 S — 27.02 E
Luiza — 110 — 7.12 S — 22.25 E
Luján, Arg. — 140 — 32.22 S — 65.56 W
Lukang — 88 — 24.04 N — 120.26 E

Lukenie ≃ — 110 — 2.44 S — 18.09 E
Luknovo — 86 — 56.02 N — 42.03 E
Lukojanov — 66 — 55.02 N — 44.30 E
Lukolela — 110 — 1.03 S — 17.12 E
Łuków — 72 — 51.56 N — 22.23 E
Lukuga ≃ — 110 — 5.40 S — 26.55 E
Lukula — 110 — 14.25 S — 23.12 E
Luleå — 68 — 65.34 N — 22.10 E
Lüleburgaz — 80 — 41.24 N — 27.21 E
Lüliangshan ⋏ — 88 — 37.25 N — 111.20 E
Luling — 160 — 29.41 N — 97.39 W
Lulonga ≃ — 110 — 0.42 N — 18.23 E
Lulua ≃ — 110 — 5.02 S — 21.07 E
Lumber ≃ — 156 — 34.12 N — 79.10 W
Lumber City — 156 — 31.56 N — 82.41 W
Lumberton, Miss., U.S. — 158 — 31.00 N — 89.27 W
Lumberton, N.C., U.S. — 156 — 34.37 N — 79.00 W
Lumbres — 74 — 50.42 N — 2.08 E
Lumpkin — 156 — 32.03 N — 84.48 W
Lumut, Tandjung ⊁ — 96 — 3.50 S — 105.57 E
Luna Pier — 154 — 41.48 N — 83.27 W
Lund — 68 — 55.42 N — 13.11 E
Lundazi — 110 — 12.19 S — 33.11 E
Lundi ≃ — 116 — 21.43 S — 32.34 E
Lüneburg — 72 — 53.15 N — 10.23 E
Lunel — 74 — 43.41 N — 4.08 E
Lünen — 72 — 51.36 N — 7.32 E
Lunenburg, N.S., Can. — 150 — 44.23 N — 64.19 W
Lunenburg, Va., U.S. — 156 — 36.58 N — 78.16 W
Lunéville — 74 — 48.36 N — 6.30 E
Lunga ≃ — 110 — 14.34 S — 26.25 E
Lungi — 114 — 8.38 N — 13.13 W
Lungué-Bungo ≃ — 110 — 14.19 S — 23.14 E
Lüni ≃ — 102 — 24.41 N — 71.15 E
Luninec — 86 — 52.15 N — 26.48 E
Luobubo (Lop Nor) ≃ — 88 — 40.20 N — 90.15 E
Luohe — 88 — 33.33 N — 114.01 E
Luolong — 88 — 34.42 N — 110.15 E
Luoyang — 88 — 34.41 N — 112.28 E
Lupeni — 80 — 45.21 N — 23.14 E
Luque — 76 — 37.33 N — 4.16 W
Luray — 156 — 38.40 N — 78.28 W
Lure — 74 — 47.41 N — 6.30 E
Luremo — 110 — 8.30 S — 17.50 E
Lurgan — 70 — 54.28 N — 6.20 W
Lurin — 138 — 12.17 S — 76.52 W
Lúrio — 110 — 13.35 S — 40.30 E
Lúrio ≃ — 110 — 13.35 S — 40.32 E
Lusaka — 110 — 15.25 S — 28.17 E
Lusambo — 110 — 4.58 S — 23.27 E
Lush, Mount ∧ — 120 — 17.02 S — 125.36 E
Lushan — 88 — 33.44 N — 112.53 E
Lushnje — 80 — 40.56 N — 19.42 E
Lushoto — 110 — 4.47 S — 38.17 E
Lüshun (Port Arthur) — 88 — 38.48 N — 121.13 E
Lusignan — 74 — 46.26 N — 0.07 E
Lusk — 162 — 42.45 N — 104.27 W
Lussac-les-Châteaux — 74 — 46.24 N — 0.43 E
Lustenau — 72 — 47.26 N — 9.39 E
Luster — 68 — 61.26 N — 7.24 E
Lūt, Dasht-e ⫶² — 104 — 33.00 N — 57.00 E
Lutcher — 158 — 30.02 N — 90.42 W
Luther — 160 — 35.40 N — 97.11 W
Luton — 70 — 51.53 N — 0.25 W
Lutong — 96 — 4.28 N — 114.00 E
Luttrell — 156 — 36.12 N — 83.44 W
Lutz — 156 — 28.09 N — 82.28 W
Lützow — 72 — 53.39 N — 11.11 E
Luverne, Ala., U.S. — 158 — 31.43 N — 86.16 W
La Verne, Iowa, U.S. — 154 — 43.23 N — 94.05 W
Luverne, Minn., U.S. — 154 — 43.39 N — 96.13 W
Luvua ≃ — 110 — 6.46 S — 27.00 E
Luwegu ≃ — 110 — 8.31 S — 37.23 E
Luwuk — 96 — 0.56 S — 122.47 E
Luxapalila Creek ≃ — 158 — 33.28 N — 88.26 W
Luxembourg — 74 — 49.45 N — 6.10 E
Luxembourg □1 — 74 — 49.45 N — 6.05 E
Luxembourg □4 — 74 — 49.58 N — 5.30 E
Luxeuil-les-Bains — 74 — 47.49 N — 6.23 E
Luxi (Mangshi) — 94 — 24.27 N — 98.34 E
Luza — 66 — 60.39 N — 47.10 E
Luzarches — 74 — 49.07 N — 2.25 E
Luzern (Lucerne) — 74 — 47.03 N — 8.18 E
Luzhou — 94 — 28.53 N — 105.24 E
Luziânia — 134 — 16.15 S — 47.56 W
Luzon I — 98 — 16.00 N — 121.00 E
Luzon Strait ⥾ — 92 — 20.30 N — 121.00 E
Luzy — 74 — 46.48 N — 3.58 E
L'vov — 64 — 49.50 N — 24.00 E
Lwówek — 72 — 52.28 N — 16.10 E
Lyallpur → Faisalābād — 102 — 31.25 N — 73.05 E
Lybster — 70 — 58.18 N — 3.18 W
Lyck → Ełk — 72 — 53.50 N — 22.22 E
Lydd — 70 — 50.57 N — 0.55 E
Lydda → Lod — 104 — 31.58 N — 34.54 E
Lydenburg — 116 — 25.10 S — 30.29 E
Lydia Mills — 156 — 34.21 N — 81.53 W
Lyell, Mount ∧ — 120 — 42.00 S — 145.34 E
Lyell Brown, Mount ∧ — 122 — 23.22 S — 130.24 E
Lykens — 152 — 40.34 N — 76.43 W
Lyles — 156 — 35.55 N — 87.19 W
Lyman, S.C., U.S. — 156 — 34.56 N — 82.09 W

Lyman, Wyo., U.S. — 166 — 41.20 N — 110.18 W
Lyme Regis — 70 — 50.44 N — 2.57 W
Łyna (Lava) ≃ — 86 — 54.37 N — 21.14 E
Lynchburg, Ohio, U.S. — 152 — 39.14 N — 83.48 W
Lynchburg, S.C., U.S. — 156 — 34.04 N — 80.04 W
Lynchburg, Va., U.S. — 156 — 37.24 N — 79.10 W
Lynches ≃ — 156 — 33.50 N — 79.22 W
Lynd — 86 — 18.56 S — 144.30 E
Lynden — 148 — 48.57 N — 122.27 W
Lyndhurst — 124 — 30.17 S — 138.21 E
Lyndon, Austl. — 122 — 23.37 S — 115.15 E
Lyndon, Kans., U.S. — 162 — 38.36 N — 95.34 W
Lyndon, Ky., U.S. — 158 — 38.16 N — 85.36 W
Lyndonville — 152 — 44.32 N — 72.01 W
Lyndora — 152 — 40.51 N — 79.55 W
Lyngdal — 68 — 58.08 N — 7.05 E
Lynger — 68 — 58.38 N — 9.12 E
Lynher Reef ÷² — 118 — 15.27 S — 121.55 E
Lynn — 152 — 42.28 N — 70.57 W
Lynndyl — 164 — 39.31 N — 112.22 W
Lynn Gardens — 156 — 36.35 N — 82.34 W
Lynn Haven — 156 — 30.15 N — 85.39 W
Lynn Lake — 142 — 56.51 N — 101.03 W
Lynton — 70 — 51.15 N — 3.50 W
Lynx Lake ⊜ — 142 — 62.25 N — 106.15 W
Lyon — 74 — 45.45 N — 4.51 E
Lyon Inlet C — 142 — 66.32 N — 83.53 W
Lyonnais, Monts du ⋏ — 74 — 45.40 N — 4.30 E
Lyons, Colo., U.S. — 164 — 40.13 N — 105.16 W
Lyons, Ga., U.S. — 156 — 32.12 N — 82.19 W
Lyons, Kans., U.S. — 162 — 38.21 N — 98.12 W
Lyons, Nebr., U.S. — 162 — 41.56 N — 96.28 W
Lyons, N.Y., U.S. — 152 — 43.04 N — 77.00 W
Lyons ≃ — 122 — 25.02 S — 115.09 E
Lys (Leie) ≃ — 74 — 50.39 N — 2.24 E
Lysaker — 68 — 59.54 N — 10.36 E
Lysekil — 68 — 58.16 N — 11.26 E
Lyskovo — 66 — 56.04 N — 45.02 E
Lys'va — 64 — 58.07 N — 57.47 E
Lytham Saint Anne's — 70 — 53.45 N — 2.57 W
Lyttelton — 126 — 43.35 S — 172.43 E

M

Ma ≃ — 94 — 19.47 N — 105.56 E
Ma'ān — 104 — 30.12 N — 35.44 E
Maaninka — 68 — 63.09 N — 27.18 E
Maanshan — 88 — 31.42 N — 118.30 E
Maas (Meuse) ≃ — 72 — 51.49 N — 5.01 E
Maaseik — 72 — 51.06 N — 5.48 E
Maastricht — 72 — 50.52 N — 5.43 E
Mababe Depression ⫶7 — 110 — 18.50 S — 24.15 E
Mablethorpe — 158 — 33.33 N — 89.05 W
Mableton — 156 — 33.21 N — 0.15 E
Mabton — 166 — 46.13 N — 120.00 W
Máca ≃ — 74 — 59.54 N — 117.35 E
Macacos, Ilha dos I — 134 — 1.20 S — 50.35 W
McAdam — 150 — 45.36 N — 67.20 W
McAdoo — 152 — 40.54 N — 76.01 W
Macaé — 134 — 22.23 S — 41.47 W
McAlester — 160 — 34.56 N — 95.46 W
Macalister ≃ — 120 — 38.02 S — 146.59 E
McAlister, Mount ∧ — 120 — 34.27 S — 149.46 E
McAllen — 160 — 26.12 N — 98.15 W
McAlmont — 158 — 34.49 N — 92.10 W
MacAlpine Lake ⊜ — 142 — 66.40 N — 103.15 W
Macão — 76 — 39.33 N — 7.59 W
Macao → Macau □2 — 88 — 22.10 N — 113.33 E
Macapá — 134 — 0.02 N — 51.03 W
Macará — 138 — 4.23 S — 79.57 W
McArthur — 152 — 39.15 N — 82.29 W
McArthur River — 124 — 16.27 S — 136.07 E
Macau, Bra. — 134 — 5.07 S — 36.38 W
Macau (Aomen) → Macau — 88 — 22.14 N — 113.35 E
Macau — 88 — 22.14 N — 113.35 E
Macau □2 — 88 — 22.10 N — 113.33 E
McBee — 156 — 34.28 N — 80.15 W
McBeth Fjord C² — 142 — 69.38 N — 68.30 W
McCall — 166 — 44.55 N — 116.06 W
McCamey — 160 — 31.08 N — 102.13 W
McCaysville — 156 — 34.59 N — 84.23 W
McClellanville — 156 — 33.05 N — 79.28 W
Macclenny — 156 — 30.18 N — 82.07 W
Macclesfield — 70 — 53.16 N — 2.07 W
McCloud — 168 — 41.15 N — 122.08 W
McClure — 152 — 40.42 N — 77.19 W
McColl — 156 — 34.40 N — 79.33 W
McComb, Miss., U.S. — 158 — 31.14 N — 90.27 W
McComb, Ohio, U.S. — 152 — 41.06 N — 83.48 W
McConald, Lake ⊜ — 148 — 48.35 N — 113.55 W
McConnellsburg — 152 — 39.56 N — 77.59 W
McConnelsville — 152 — 39.39 N — 81.51 W
McCook — 162 — 40.12 N — 100.38 W
McCrory — 158 — 35.15 N — 91.12 W
Mcculloch, Mount ∧ — 122 — 15.50 S — 129.52 E
McDavid — 156 — 30.52 N — 87.19 W
Macdonald, Lake ⊜ — 122 — 23.30 S — 129.02 E
Macdonnell Ranges ⋏ — 122 — 23.45 S — 133.20 E
McDonough — 156 — 33.27 N — 84.09 W
McDouall Peak — 124 — 29.51 S — 134.55 E
Macduff — 70 — 57.40 N — 2.29 W
Macedo de Cavaleiros — 76 — 41.32 N — 6.58 W
Macedonia → Makedonija □3 — 80 — 41.50 N — 22.00 E
Macedonia — 80 — 41.00 N — 23.00 E
Maceió — 134 — 9.40 S — 35.43 W
McElmo Creek ≃ — 164 — 37.13 N — 109.17 W
Macenta — 114 — 8.33 N — 9.29 W
Macerata — 78 — 43.18 N — 13.27 E
McFadden — 164 — 41.37 N — 106.07 W
McFarland, Calif., U.S. — 168 — 35.41 N — 119.14 W
McFarland, Wis., U.S. — 154 — 43.01 N — 89.17 W
MacFarlane ≃ — 142 — 59.12 N — 107.58 W
MacFarlane, Lake ⊜ — 124 — 31.55 S — 136.42 E
McGehee — 158 — 33.38 N — 91.24 W
McGill — 168 — 39.23 N — 114.47 W
Mcgraw — 152 — 42.36 N — 76.06 W
McGregor — 160 — 31.26 N — 97.24 W
McGregor Range ⋏ — 160 — 32.05 N — 106.15 W
Machačkala — 64 — 42.58 N — 47.30 E
Machado ≃ — 134 — 9.25 S — 61.50 W
Machala — 138 — 3.16 S — 79.58 W
Machattie, Lake ⊜ — 120 — 24.50 S — 139.48 E
Machecoul — 74 — 47.00 N — 1.49 W
Machias — 150 — 44.42 N — 67.27 W
Machilipatnam — 100 — 16.10 N — 81.08 E
Machupicchu — 138 — 13.07 S — 72.34 W
Mchinji — 110 — 13.48 S — 32.55 E
Macias Nguema Biyogo = Bioko I — 106 — 3.30 N — 8.40 E
Macintyre ≃ — 120 — 28.37 S — 150.47 E
Mackay, Austl. — 120 — 21.09 S — 149.11 E
Mackay, Idaho, U.S. — 166 — 43.54 N — 113.37 W
Mackay, Lake ⊜ — 122 — 22.30 S — 128.00 E
MacKay ≃ — 142 — 63.55 N — 110.25 W
McKeand ≃ — 142 — 69.18 N — 67.20 W
McKee — 156 — 37.26 N — 83.59 W
McKeesport — 152 — 40.21 N — 79.51 W
McKenna — 166 — 46.56 N — 122.33 W
McKenzie — 158 — 36.08 N — 88.31 W
Mackenzie □5 — 142 — 65.00 N — 115.00 W
Mackenzie ≃ — 146 — 69.15 N — 134.08 W
Mackenzie Bay C — 146 — 69.00 N — 137.30 W
Mackenzie Bridge — 166 — 44.05 N — 122.11 W
Mackenzie Mountains ⋏ — 146 — 64.00 N — 130.00 W
Mackinac, Straits of ⥾ — 154 — 45.49 N — 84.42 W
Mackinac Island I — 154 — 45.51 N — 84.37 W

Mackinac Island I — 154 — 45.51 N — 84.38 W
Mackinaw ≃ — 154 — 40.33 N — 89.44 W
Mackinaw City — 154 — 45.47 N — 84.44 W
Mc Kinley, Mount ∧ — 146 — 63.30 N — 151.00 W
McKinleyville — 168 — 40.57 N — 124.06 W
McKinney — 160 — 33.12 N — 96.37 W
Mackinnon Road — 110 — 3.44 S — 39.03 E
Macksville — 120 — 30.43 S — 152.55 E
McLean — 120 — 29.28 S — 153.13 E
McLean — 160 — 35.14 N — 100.36 W
McLeansboro — 158 — 38.06 N — 88.32 W
Maclear — 116 — 31.02 S — 28.27 E
McLennan — 142 — 55.42 N — 116.54 W
McLeod ≃ — 148 — 54.08 N — 115.42 W
McLeod, Lake ⊜ — 122 — 24.00 S — 113.35 E
McLeod Bay C — 142 — 62.53 N — 110.00 W
McLoughlin Bay C — 142 — 67.50 N — 99.00 W
McMillan ≃ — 142 — 62.50 N — 110.00 W
McMinnville, Oreg., U.S. — 166 — 45.13 N — 123.12 W
McMinnville, Tenn., U.S. — 158 — 35.41 N — 85.46 W
McNary — 164 — 34.04 N — 109.51 W
Macomb — 154 — 40.27 N — 90.40 W
Macomer — 78 — 40.16 N — 8.46 E
Mâcon, Fr. — 74 — 46.18 N — 4.50 E
Macon, Ga., U.S. — 156 — 32.50 N — 83.38 W
Macon, Ill., U.S. — 158 — 39.43 N — 89.00 W
Macon, Miss., U.S. — 158 — 33.07 N — 88.34 W
Macon, Mo., U.S. — 154 — 39.44 N — 92.28 W
Macon, Bayou ≃ — 158 — 31.55 N — 91.33 W
McPherson — 162 — 38.22 N — 97.40 W
Macquarie ≃, Austl. — 120 — 30.07 S — 147.24 E
Macquarie ≃, Austl. — 120 — 41.44 S — 147.08 E
Macquarie Harbour C — 120 — 42.19 S — 145.23 E
McRae — 156 — 32.04 N — 82.53 W
McRae, Mount ∧ — 122 — 22.17 S — 117.35 E
McRoberts — 156 — 37.12 N — 82.40 W
Macroom — 70 — 51.54 N — 8.57 W
Macuspana — 130 — 17.46 N — 92.36 W
Mada ≃ — 114 — 7.59 N — 7.55 E
Madagascar □1 — 111b — 19.00 S — 46.00 E
Madang — 124 — 5.15 S — 145.50 E
Madawaska — 150 — 47.21 N — 68.20 W
Madawaska ≃ — 152 — 45.27 N — 76.21 W
Maddaloni — 78 — 41.02 N — 14.23 E
Maddock — 162 — 47.58 N — 99.32 W
Madeira ≃ — 134 — 3.22 S — 58.45 W
Madeira, Arquipélago da (Madeira Islands) II — 106 — 32.40 N — 16.45 W
Mädelegabel ∧ — 74 — 47.18 N — 10.18 E
Madeleine, Îles de la II — 150 — 47.30 N — 61.45 W
Madelia — 154 — 44.03 N — 94.25 W
Madera, Méx. — 130 — 29.12 N — 108.07 W
Madera, Calif., U.S. — 168 — 36.57 N — 120.03 W
Madidi ≃ — 134 — 12.32 S — 66.52 W
Madill — 160 — 34.06 N — 96.46 W
Madimba — 110 — 4.58 S — 15.08 E
Madinat ash-Sha'b — 100 — 12.50 N — 44.56 E
Madingou — 110 — 4.09 S — 13.34 E
Madison, Ala., U.S. — 158 — 34.42 N — 86.45 W
Madison, Fla., U.S. — 156 — 30.28 N — 83.25 W
Madison, Ga., U.S. — 156 — 33.36 N — 83.28 W
Madison, Ind., U.S. — 158 — 38.44 N — 85.23 W
Madison, Maine, U.S. — 152 — 44.48 N — 69.53 W
Madison, Minn., U.S. — 154 — 45.01 N — 96.11 W
Madison, Nebr., U.S. — 162 — 41.50 N — 97.27 W
Madison, N.C., U.S. — 156 — 36.23 N — 79.58 W
Madison, S. Dak., U.S. — 162 — 44.00 N — 97.07 W
Madison, Wis., U.S. — 154 — 43.05 N — 89.22 W
Madison ≃ — 166 — 45.56 N — 111.30 W
Madison Heights — 152 — 37.25 N — 79.08 W
Madisonville, Ky., U.S. — 158 — 37.20 N — 87.30 W
Madisonville, La., U.S. — 158 — 30.24 N — 90.09 W
Madisonville, Tex., U.S. — 156 — 30.51 N — 84.22 W
Madiun — 96 — 30.57 S — 111.31 E
Madjene — 96 — 3.33 S — 118.57 E
Mado Gashi — 110 — 0.44 N — 39.10 E
Madras, Bhārat — 100 — 13.04 N — 80.16 E
Madras, Oreg., U.S. — 166 — 44.38 N — 121.08 W
Madre, Laguna C, Méx. — 130 — 25.00 N — 97.40 W
Madre, Laguna C, Tex., U.S. — 160 — 27.00 N — 97.35 W
Madre, Sierra ⋏ — 98 — 17.15 N — 122.00 E
Madre de Dios ≃ — 134 — 10.59 S — 66.08 W
Madre de Dios, Isla I — 136 — 50.15 S — 75.10 W
Madre del Sur, Sierra ⋏ — 130 — 17.00 N — 100.00 W
Madre Occidental, Sierra ⋏ — 130 — 25.00 N — 105.00 W
Madre Oriental, Sierra ⋏ — 130 — 22.00 N — 99.30 W
Madrid, Esp. — 76 — 40.24 N — 3.41 W
Madrid, Iowa, U.S. — 154 — 41.53 N — 93.49 W
Maduo — 88 — 34.53 N — 98.24 E
Madura — 120 — 31.55 S — 127.02 E
Madurai — 100 — 9.56 N — 78.08 E
Mae Hong Son — 94 — 19.16 N — 97.56 E
Mae Klong ≃ — 94 — 13.21 N — 100.00 E
Mae Sariang — 94 — 18.10 N — 97.56 E
Mae Sot — 94 — 16.41 N — 98.35 E
Maestra, Sierra ⋏ — 132 — 20.00 N — 76.45 W
Maevatanana — 111b — 16.56 S — 46.49 E
Mafeking — 116 — 25.53 S — 25.39 E
Mafia Island I — 110 — 7.50 S — 39.50 E
Mafra, Bra. — 140 — 26.07 S — 49.49 W
Mafra, Port. — 76 — 38.56 N — 9.20 W
Magadan — 84 — 59.34 N — 150.48 E
Magadi — 110 — 1.54 S — 36.17 E
Magallanes, Estrecho de (Strait of Magellan) ⥾ — 136 — 54.00 S — 71.00 W
Magangué — 138 — 9.14 N — 74.45 W
Magdalena, Bol. — 134 — 13.20 S — 64.08 W
Magdalena, Méx. — 130 — 30.38 N — 110.57 W
Magdalena ≃ — 138 — 11.06 N — 74.51 W
Magdalena, Isla I — 130 — 24.40 N — 112.15 W
Magdeburg — 72 — 52.07 N — 11.38 E
Magdeburg □5 — 72 — 52.15 N — 11.30 E
Magee — 158 — 31.52 N — 89.44 W
Magelang — 96 — 7.28 S — 110.13 E
Magenta — 78 — 45.28 N — 8.53 E
Maggiore, Lago ⊜ — 74 — 46.00 N — 8.39 E

Symbols in the index entries are identified on page 203.

Name	Page	Lat	Long
Mahābhārat Range ⋀	102	27.40 N	84.30 E
Mahabo	117b	20.23 S	44.40 E
Mahajamba, Baie de la C	117b	15.24 S	47.05 E
Mahakam ≃	96	0.35 S	117.17 E
Mahalapye	117b	23.05 S	26.51 E
Mahānadi ≃	100	20.19 N	86.45 E
Mahanoro	117b	19.54 S	48.48 E
Mahanoy City	152	40.49 N	76.08 W
Maha Sarakham	94	16.12 N	103.16 E
Mahaṭṭaṭ Haraḍ	108	24.08 N	49.05 E
Mahbūbnagar	100	16.44 N	77.59 E
Mahd adh-Dhahab	108	23.30 N	40.52 E
Mahe	100	11.42 N	75.32 E
Mahébourg	117c	20.24 S	57.42 E
Mahé Island I	100	4.40 S	55.28 E
Mahenge	110	8.41 S	36.43 E
Mahnomen	162	47.19 N	96.01 W
Mahón	76	39.53 N	4.15 E
Mahone Bay	150	44.27 N	64.23 W
Mahora	76	39.13 N	1.44 W
Mahtomedi	154	45.04 N	92.57 W
Maia	76	41.14 N	8.37 W
Maicao	138	11.23 N	72.13 W
Maîche	74	47.15 N	6.48 E
Maicurú ≃	134	2.14 S	54.17 W
Maiden	156	35.35 N	81.13 W
Maidenhead	70	51.32 N	0.44 W
Maidstone	70	51.17 N	0.32 E
Maiduguri	106	11.51 N	13.10 E
Maignelay	74	49.33 N	2.31 E
Maiko ≃	110	0.14 N	25.33 E
Maikoor, Pulau I	124	6.15 S	134.15 E
Maili	170c	21.25 N	158.11 W
Maïmèzais	74	46.22 N	0.44 W
Maimāna	82	35.55 N	64.47 E
Main Barrier Range ⋀	120	31.25 S	141.25 E
Mainburg	72	48.38 N	11.47 E
Mai-Ndombe, Lac ⊜	110	2.00 S	18.20 E
Maine □³	74	48.35 N	0.15 E
Maine ⊏⁹	144	45.15 N	69.15 W
Mainhardt	72	49.04 N	9.33 E
Mainland I	70	60.20 N	1.22 W
Mainoru	94	14.02 S	134.05 E
Maintenon	74	48.35 N	1.35 E
Maintirano	117b	18.03 S	44.01 E
Mainz	72	50.01 N	8.16 E
Maio I	114a	15.15 N	23.10 W
Maipo, Volcán ⋀¹	140	34.10 S	69.50 W
Maipú	140	36.52 S	57.54 W
Maiquetía	138	10.36 N	66.57 W
Mairland	120	34.22 S	137.40 E
Maitengwe ≃	117b	19.59 S	26.28 E
Maitland	120	32.44 S	151.33 E
Maizuru	90	35.27 N	135.20 E
Maja ≃	84	54.31 N	134.41 E
Maji	108	6.11 N	35.38 E
Majja	84	61.44 N	130.18 E
Majkain	84	51.27 N	75.52 E
Majkor	66	59.01 N	55.54 E
Majno-Pyl'gino	146	62.32 N	177.02 E
Majorca → Mallorca I	76	39.30 N	3.00 E
Majskij	84	52.18 N	129.38 E
Majskoje	84	50.55 N	78.15 E
Majunga	117b	15.43 S	46.19 E
Makabana	110	2.48 S	12.29 E
Makaha	170c	21.28 N	158.13 W
Makale	96	3.06 S	119.51 E
Makālu ⋀	100	27.54 N	87.06 E
Makarjev	66	57.52 N	43.48 E
Makarov, S.S.S.R.	84	48.38 N	142.48 E
Makarov, S.S.S.R.	88	50.28 N	29.49 E
Makarska	78	43.18 N	17.02 E
Makasar → Udjung Pandang ⋈	96	5.07 S	119.24 E
Makassar, Selat ⋈	96	2.00 S	117.30 E
Makassar Strait ⋈ → Makasar. Selat ⋈	96	2.00 S	117.30 E
Makat	82	47.39 N	53.19 E
Makauao	170a	20.52 N	156.19 W
Makedonija □³	80	41.50 N	22.00 E
Makejevka	64	48.02 N	37.58 E
Makeni	114	8.53 N	12.03 W
Makgadikgadi Pans ⟿	116	20.45 S	25.30 E
Makindu	110	2.17 S	37.49 E
Makinsk	82	52.37 N	70.26 E
M'akit	84	61.24 N	152.09 E
Makkah (Mecca)	108	21.27 N	39.49 E
Makkovik	144	55.00 N	59.10 W
Makó	72	46.13 N	20.29 E
Makokou	110	0.34 N	12.52 E
Makoua	110	0.01 N	15.39 E
M'aksa	66	58.54 N	38.12 E
Maksatiha	86	57.48 N	35.53 E
Makumbi	110	5.51 S	20.41 E
Makurdi	114	7.45 N	8.32 E
Makwassie	116	27.20 S	26.00 E
Malabang	96	7.36 N	124.04 E
Malabar Coast ⋆²	100	11.00 N	75.00 E
Malabo	106	3.45 N	8.47 E
Malacca, Strait of ⋈	96	2.11 N	102.16 E
Malacky	72	48.27 N	17.00 E
Malad ≃	166	41.35 N	112.07 W
Malad City	166	42.12 N	112.15 W
Málaga, Col.	138	6.42 N	72.44 W
Málaga, Esp.	76	36.43 N	4.25 W
Malagasy Republic → Madagascar □¹	110b	19.00 S	46.00 E
Malaimbandy	117b	20.20 S	45.36 E
Malaja Višera	86	58.51 N	32.14 E
Malakal	112	9.31 N	31.39 E
Malakoff	160	32.10 N	96.01 W
Malang	96	7.59 S	112.37 E
Malanje	110	9.32 S	16.20 E
Malanville	114	11.52 N	3.23 E
Mälaren ⊜	68	59.30 N	17.12 E
Malargüe	140	35.30 S	69.35 W
Malartic	148	48.08 N	78.08 W
Malaspina Glacier ⟿	146	59.50 N	140.30 W
Malatya	104	38.21 N	38.19 E
Malaucène	74	44.10 N	5.08 E
Malawi □¹	110	13.30 S	34.00 E
Malawi, Lake → Nyasa, Lake ⊜	110	12.00 S	34.30 E
Malaybalay	96	8.09 N	125.05 E
Malāyer	104	34.17 N	48.50 E
Malay Peninsula ⋋¹	94	6.00 N	102.00 E
Malay Reef ⋆²	120	17.55 S	149.18 E
Malaysia □¹	96	2.30 N	112.30 E
Malbork	72	54.02 N	19.01 E
Malchin	72	53.44 N	12.46 E
Malchow	72	53.28 N	12.25 E
Malcolm	122	28.56 S	121.30 E
Malcolm, Point ⊁	122	33.48 S	123.45 E
Maldegem	72	51.13 N	3.27 E
Malden	152	42.25 N	71.04 W
Maldon	70	51.45 N	0.40 E
Maldonado	140	34.54 S	54.57 W
Malé	78	46.21 N	10.55 E
Maléa, Ákra ⊁	80	36.26 N	23.12 E
Málegaon	100	20.26 N	74.32 E
Malen'ga	66	63.50 N	36.25 E
Malesherbes	74	48.18 N	2.25 E
Malha Wells	112	15.08 N	26.10 E
Malheur ≃	166	43.20 N	117.10 W
Malheur Lake ⊜	166	43.20 N	118.45 W
Mali □¹	106	17.00 N	4.00 W
Malik, Wādī al- V	112	18.02 N	30.58 E
Malik Siah, Kūh-i- ⋀	104	29.51 N	60.52 E
Mali Kyun I	94	13.06 N	98.16 E
Malin	88	50.46 N	29.15 E
Malindi	110	3.13 S	40.07 E
Malines → Mechelen	72	51.02 N	4.28 E
Malino, Bukit ⋀	96	0.45 N	120.47 E
Malka ≃	84	56.21 N	157.30 E
Malkara	80	40.53 N	26.54 E
Mallaig	70	57.00 N	5.50 W
Mallala	120	34.26 S	138.30 E
Mallapunyah	124	16.59 S	135.49 E
Mallawi	112	27.44 N	30.50 E
Malleco □⁴	140	38.10 S	72.20 W
Mallersdorf	72	48.47 N	12.16 E
Mallery Lake ⊜	142	64.05 N	98.25 W
Mallnitz	72	46.59 N	13.10 E
Mallorca I	76	39.30 N	3.00 E
Mallow	70	52.08 N	8.39 W
Malm	68	64.04 N	11.13 E
Malmberget	68	67.10 N	20.40 E
Malmédy	72	50.25 N	6.02 E
Malmesbury	116	33.28 S	18.44 E
Malmö	68	55.36 N	13.00 E
Malmöhus Län □⁶	68	55.45 N	13.30 E
Malmyž	66	56.31 N	50.41 E
Maloja	78	46.24 N	9.41 E
Malojaroslavec	86	55.01 N	36.28 E
Malone, Fla., U.S.	156	30.57 N	85.10 W
Malone, N.Y., U.S.	152	44.51 N	74.17 W
Malonga	110	10.24 S	23.10 E
Malošujka	66	63.45 N	37.22 E
Malott	166	48.17 N	119.42 W
Malòy	68	61.56 N	5.07 E
Malpas	70	53.01 N	2.46 W
Malpas, Presa de ⊜¹	130	17.10 N	93.40 W
Malpelo, Isla de I	134	3.59 N	81.35 W
Malta, Mont., U.S.	166	48.21 N	107.52 W
Malta, Ohio, U.S.	152	39.39 N	81.52 W
Malta □¹	78	35.50 N	14.35 E
Malta I	78	35.53 N	14.27 E
Malta Channel ⋈	78	36.20 N	15.00 E
Maltahöhe	116	24.50 S	17.00 E
Malton	70	54.08 N	0.48 W
Maluku (Moluccas) II	92	2.00 S	128.00 E
Maluku, Laut (Molucca Sea) ⊽²	92	0.30 S	125.00 E
Malvern, Ark., U.S.	158	34.22 N	92.49 W
Malvern, Iowa, U.S.	162	41.00 N	95.35 W
Malyj An'uj ≃	84	68.30 N	160.49 E
Malyj Jenisej ≃	84	51.43 N	94.26 E
Malyj Kavkaz ⋀	82	41.00 N	44.35 E
Malyj L'achovskij, Ostrov I	84	74.07 N	140.36 E
Malyj Tajmyr, Ostrov I	84	78.08 N	107.12 E
Mama	84	58.18 N	112.54 E
Mamberamo ≃	124	1.26 S	137.53 E
Mambéré ≃	108	3.31 N	16.03 E
Mamburao	92	13.13 N	120.35 E
Mamers	74	48.21 N	0.23 E
Mamfe	106	5.46 N	9.17 E
Mammoth	154	32.43 N	110.38 W
Mamoré ≃	134	10.23 S	65.23 W
Mamou, Guinée	114	10.23 N	12.05 W
Mamou, La., U.S.	158	30.38 N	92.25 W
Mampikony	117b	16.06 S	47.38 E
Man	114	7.24 N	7.33 W
Manabi □⁴	134	0.40 S	80.30 W
Manacapuru	138	3.18 S	60.37 W
Manacor	76	39.34 N	3.12 E
Manado	96	1.29 N	124.51 E
Managua	132	12.09 N	86.17 W
Managua, Lago de ⊜	132	12.20 N	86.20 W
Manakara	117b	22.08 S	48.01 E
Manali	100	32.15 N	77.10 E
Manam I	124	4.05 S	145.05 E
Manambolo ≃	117b	21.13 S	48.20 E
Manãs ≃	102	26.13 N	90.38 E
Manassa	162	37.11 N	105.56 W
Manasquan	152	40.07 N	74.03 W
Manassas	152	38.45 N	77.28 W
Manassas Park	152	38.47 N	77.28 W
Manati	132	18.26 N	66.29 W
Manaus	138	3.08 S	60.01 W
Mancha Real	76	37.47 N	3.37 W
Manche □⁵	74	49.00 N	1.10 W
Manchester, Eng., U.K.	70	53.30 N	2.15 W
Manchester, Conn., U.S.	152	41.47 N	72.31 W
Manchester, Ga., U.S.	156	32.51 N	84.37 W
Manchester, Iowa, U.S.	154	42.29 N	91.27 W
Manchester, Ky., U.S.	156	37.09 N	83.46 W
Manchester, Mass., U.S.	152	42.34 N	70.46 W
Manchester, Mich., U.S.	154	42.09 N	84.02 W
Manchester, N.H., U.S.	152	42.59 N	71.28 W
Manchester, Ohio, U.S.	152	38.41 N	83.36 W
Manchester, Tenn., U.S.	158	35.29 N	86.05 W
Manchouli → Manzhouli	88	49.35 N	117.22 E
Manchuria ⋆¹	88	47.00 N	125.00 E
Mancos	164	37.21 N	108.18 W
Mancos ≃	164	36.59 N	108.59 W
Manda	104	28.11 N	51.17 E
Mandabe	117b	21.03 S	44.55 E
Mandaguari	140	23.32 S	51.42 W
Mandal	68	58.02 N	7.27 E
Mandala, Puntjak ⋀	124	4.44 S	140.20 E
Mandalay	94	22.00 N	96.05 E
Mandalgovĭ	88	45.45 N	106.20 E
Mandali	104	33.45 N	45.32 E
Mandan	162	46.49 N	100.54 W
Mandara Mountains ⋀	106	10.45 N	13.40 E
Mandas	78	39.39 N	9.08 E
Mandasor	100	24.04 N	75.04 E
Mandeb, Bāb el- ⋈	108	12.40 N	43.20 E
Manderson	166	44.16 N	107.58 W
Mandeville, Jam.	132	18.02 N	77.30 W
Mandeville, La., U.S.	158	30.22 N	90.04 W
Mandimba	110	14.21 S	35.39 E
Mandioli, Pulau I	92	0.44 S	127.14 E
Mandla	100	22.36 N	80.23 E
Mandritsara	117b	15.50 S	48.49 E
Mandurah	122	32.32 S	115.43 E
Mandurah ≃	120	22.50 N	60.52 E
Manfalūṭ	112	27.19 N	30.58 E
Manfredonia	78	41.38 N	15.55 E
Mangabeiras, Chapada das ⋆²	134	10.00 S	46.30 W
Mangakino	126	38.22 S	175.47 E
Mangalia	80	43.50 N	28.35 E
Mangalore	100	12.52 N	74.52 E
Mangchang	88	25.08 N	107.31 E
Mangkalihat, Tandjung ⊁	96	1.02 N	118.59 E
Mangga	78	14.28 S	35.16 E
Mangoky ≃	117b	21.29 S	43.41 E
Mangole, Pulau I	96	1.53 S	125.50 E
Mangonui	126	34.59 S	173.32 E
Mangrol	100	21.07 N	70.07 E
Mangueira, Lagoa C	140	33.06 S	52.48 W
Mangum	160	34.53 N	99.30 W
Manhattan, Kans., U.S.	162	39.11 N	96.35 W
Manhattan, Mont., U.S.	166	45.52 N	111.20 W
Manhuaçu	138	20.15 S	42.02 W
Manhumirim	138	20.22 S	41.57 W
Mani	138	4.49 N	72.17 W
Manicoré	138	5.49 S	61.17 W
Manicouagan ≃	150	49.11 N	68.13 W
Manicouagan, Réservoir ⊜¹	150	51.30 N	68.19 W
Manila, Pil.	92	14.35 N	120.59 E
Manila, Utah, U.S.	164	40.59 N	109.43 W
Manila Bay C	92	14.35 N	120.45 E
Manila	124	6.29 N	165.23 E
Manipa, Selat ⋈	124	3.20 S	127.23 E
Manisa	104	38.36 N	27.26 E
Manistee	154	44.15 N	86.19 W
Manistee ≃	154	44.15 N	86.21 W
Manistique	154	45.57 N	86.15 W
Manistique Lake ⊜	154	46.15 N	85.45 W
Manito	158	40.25 N	89.47 W
Manitoba □⁴	142	54.00 N	97.00 W
Manitoba, Lake ⊜	142	51.00 N	98.45 W
Manitou Islands II	154	45.08 N	86.00 W
Manitou Springs	164	38.52 N	104.55 W
Manitowoc	154	44.06 N	87.40 W
Maniwaki	152	46.23 N	75.58 W
Manizales	138	5.05 N	75.32 W
Manja	117b	21.26 S	44.20 E
Manjacaze	116	24.44 S	33.53 E
Manjimup	122	34.14 S	116.09 E
Mānjra ≃	100	18.49 N	77.52 E
Mankato, Kans., U.S.	162	39.47 N	98.12 W
Mankato, Minn., U.S.	154	44.10 N	94.01 W
Mankoya	110	14.47 S	24.48 E
Mann, Mount ⋀	122	25.59 S	129.42 E
Mannahill	120	32.26 S	139.59 E
Mannar, Gulf of C	100	8.30 N	79.00 E
Mannheim	72	49.29 N	8.29 E
Manning, Iowa, U.S.	154	41.55 N	95.03 W
Manning, S.C., U.S.	156	33.42 N	80.13 W
Mannington	152	39.32 N	80.20 W
Mano ≃	114	6.56 N	11.31 W
Manokotak	146	58.40 N	159.09 W
Manokwari	124	0.52 S	134.05 E
Manono	110	7.18 S	27.25 E
Manorhamilton	70	54.18 N	8.10 W
Manosque	74	43.50 N	5.47 E
Manouane, Lac ⊜	150	50.41 N	70.45 W
Manresa	76	41.44 N	1.50 E
Mansel Island I	142	62.00 N	79.50 W
Mansfield, Austl.	120	37.03 S	146.05 E
Mansfield, Eng., U.K.	70	53.09 N	1.11 W
Mansfield, Ill., U.S.	158	40.13 N	88.31 W
Mansfield, La., U.S.	158	32.02 N	93.43 W
Mansfield, Mass., U.S.	152	42.02 N	71.13 W
Mansfield, Ohio, U.S.	152	40.45 N	82.30 W
Mansfield, Pa., U.S.	152	41.48 N	77.05 W
Mansfield, Tex., U.S.	160	32.34 N	97.09 W
Mansle	74	45.53 N	0.11 E
Manson, Iowa, U.S.	154	42.32 N	94.32 W
Manson, Wash., U.S.	166	47.58 N	120.09 W
Mansura	158	31.04 N	92.03 W
Manta	138	0.57 S	80.44 W
Manteca	168	37.48 N	121.13 W
Mantena	138	18.46 S	41.11 W
Manteno	154	41.14 N	88.12 W
Mantes-la-Jolie	74	48.59 N	1.43 E
Manti	164	39.16 N	111.38 W
Mantiqueira, Serra da ⋀	136	22.25 S	45.00 W
Manton	154	44.24 N	85.24 W
Mantova	78	45.09 N	10.48 E
Mänttä	68	62.02 N	24.38 E
Manturovo	66	58.20 N	44.46 E
Mäntyharju	68	61.25 N	26.53 E
Manu	124	2.16 S	70.55 W
Manui, Pulau I	96	3.35 S	123.08 E
Manukau	126	37.01 S	174.44 E
Manukau Harbour C	126	37.03 S	174.32 E
Manville	152	40.32 N	74.35 W
Many	158	31.34 N	93.29 W
Manyara, Lake ⊜	110	3.35 S	35.50 E
Manyč ≃	64	47.15 N	40.00 E
Manyoni	110	5.45 S	34.50 E
Manzanares	76	39.00 N	3.22 W
Manzanillo, Cuba	132	20.21 N	77.07 W
Manzanillo, Méx.	130	19.03 N	104.20 W
Manzanillo Bay C	132	19.45 N	71.45 W
Manzanola	162	38.06 N	103.52 W
Manzhouli	88	49.35 N	117.22 E
Manzini	116	26.30 S	31.25 E
Mao	106	14.07 N	15.19 E
Maoke, Pegunungan ⋀	124	4.00 S	138.00 E
Maoming	88	21.39 N	110.52 E
Maouri, Dallol V	114	12.05 N	3.32 E
Mapi ≃	124	7.07 S	139.23 E
Mapia, Kepulauan II	92	0.50 N	134.20 E
Maple Creek	142	49.55 N	109.27 W
Maple Lake	154	45.14 N	94.00 W
Mapleton, Iowa, U.S.	154	42.10 N	95.47 W
Mapleton, Minn., U.S.	154	43.55 N	93.57 W
Mapleton, Oreg., U.S.	166	44.02 N	123.52 W
Mapleton, Utah, U.S.	164	40.08 N	111.35 W
Maplewood	154	45.00 N	93.01 W
Mapuera ≃	138	1.05 S	57.02 W
Maputo	116	25.58 S	32.34 E
Maputo (Great Usutu) ≃	116	26.11 S	32.42 E
Maquela do Zombo	110	6.03 S	15.07 E
Maquoketa	154	42.04 N	90.40 W
Mar, Serra do ⋆⁴	140	25.00 S	48.00 W
Mara ≃	110	1.31 S	33.56 E
Maracá, Ilha de I	134	2.05 N	50.25 W
Maracaibo	138	10.40 N	71.37 W
Maracaibo, Lago de C	138	9.50 N	71.30 W
Maracaju, Serra de ⋀²	140	21.00 S	55.00 W
Maracay	138	10.15 N	67.36 W
Maradi	114	13.29 N	7.06 E
Marāgheh	104	37.23 N	46.13 E
Maragogipe	138	12.46 S	38.55 W
Marahuaca, Cerro ⋀	138	3.34 N	65.27 W
Marais des Cygnes ≃	162	38.02 N	94.14 W
Marajó, Baia de C	134	1.00 S	48.30 W
Marajó, Ilha de I	134	1.00 S	49.30 W
Maralal	110	1.06 N	36.42 E
Maralinga	122	30.13 S	131.35 E
Marampa	114	8.41 N	12.28 W
Maramureş □⁴	80	47.40 N	23.45 E
Maranalgo	122	29.23 S	117.48 E
Maranboy	124	14.33 S	132.45 E
Marand	104	38.26 N	45.46 E
Marandellas	116	18.11 S	31.36 E
Maranguape	138	3.53 S	38.40 W
Marano [di Napoli]	78	40.54 N	14.11 E
Marans	74	46.19 N	1.00 W
Marañón ≃	138	4.30 S	73.35 W
Maras	104	37.36 N	36.55 E
Marathon, Austl.	120	20.49 S	143.34 E
Marathon, Ont., Can.	148	48.40 N	86.25 W
Marathon, N.Y., U.S.	152	42.26 N	76.02 W
Marathon, Tex., U.S.	160	30.12 N	103.15 W
Marble ≃	154	46.19 N	93.18 W
Marble Bar	122	21.11 S	119.44 E
Marble Falls	160	30.34 N	98.16 W
Marble Hall	116	24.57 S	29.13 E
Marblehead	152	42.30 N	70.51 W
Marburg an der Lahn	72	50.49 N	8.46 E
Marcaria	78	45.07 N	10.32 E
Marceline	162	39.43 N	92.57 W
Marcellus	152	42.59 N	76.20 W
March	70	52.33 N	0.06 E
March (Morava) ≃	72	48.10 N	16.59 E
Marcha ≃	84	63.28 N	118.50 E
Marche □⁹	78	43.20 N	13.15 E
Marche-en-Famenne	72	50.13 N	5.21 E
Marchegg	72	48.17 N	16.55 E
Marche Real → Mancha Real	76	37.47 N	3.37 W
Marcigny	74	46.17 N	4.02 E
Marcillac-Vallon	74	44.29 N	2.28 E
Marcola	166	44.10 N	122.52 W
Marcos Juárez	140	32.42 S	62.05 W
Marcus	162	42.50 N	95.48 W
Marcus Baker, Mount ⋀	146	61.26 N	147.45 W
Mardān	102	34.12 N	72.02 E
Mar del Plata	140	38.01 S	57.35 W
Mardie	122	21.11 S	115.57 E
Marengo, Ill., U.S.	154	42.15 N	88.37 W
Marengo, Iowa, U.S.	154	41.48 N	92.04 W
Marennes	74	45.50 N	1.06 W
Mareuil-sur-Belle	74	45.28 N	0.28 E
Marfa	160	30.18 N	104.01 W
Margaret River	122	18.38 S	126.52 E
Margarita, Isla de I	138	11.00 N	64.00 W
Margate, Eng., U.K.	70	51.24 N	1.24 E
Margate, Fla., U.S.	156	26.18 N	80.12 W
Margate City	152	39.20 N	74.31 W
Margecany	72	48.54 N	21.01 E
Margherita Peak ⋀	110	0.22 N	29.51 E
Marghian	100	40.29 N	71.44 E
Märgow, Dasht-e ⋆²	104	30.45 N	63.10 E
Maria Elena	140	22.21 S	69.40 W
Maria Gail	72	46.36 N	13.52 E
Maria Island I, Austl.	122	14.52 S	135.40 E
Maria Islands II	92	16.00 N	145.30 E
Mariana	138	20.23 S	43.25 W
Marian Lake ⊜	142	63.00 N	116.10 W
Marianna, Ark., U.S.	158	34.46 N	90.46 W
Marianna, Fla., U.S.	156	30.47 N	85.14 W
Mariano Machado	110	13.02 S	14.40 E
Mariato, Punta ⊁	138	7.11 N	80.53 W
Mariazell	72	47.47 N	15.19 E
Maribo	68	54.46 N	11.31 E
Maribor	78	46.33 N	15.39 E
Marica (Évros) (Meriç) ≃	80	40.52 N	26.12 E
Marico ≃	116	24.12 S	26.52 E
Maricopa, Ariz., U.S.	154	33.04 N	112.03 W
Maricopa, Calif., U.S.	168	35.03 N	119.24 W
Maricourt (Wakeham Bay)	142	61.36 N	71.58 W
Marie-Galante I	132	15.56 N	61.16 W
Mariehamn	68	60.06 N	19.57 E
Mariel	132	23.00 N	82.45 W
Marienberg → Malbork	72	54.02 N	19.01 E
Mariental	116	24.36 S	17.59 E
Marienville	152	41.28 N	79.07 W
Mariestad	68	58.43 N	13.51 E
Marietta, Fla., U.S.	156	30.30 N	81.47 W
Marietta, Ga., U.S.	156	33.57 N	84.33 W
Marietta, Ohio, U.S.	152	39.25 N	81.27 W
Marietta, Okla., U.S.	160	33.56 N	97.07 W
Marieville	152	45.26 N	73.10 W
Mariga ≃	114	9.40 N	5.55 E
Marignane	74	43.25 N	5.13 E
Marília	140	22.13 S	49.56 W
Marín	76	42.23 N	8.42 W
Marina di Ravenna	78	44.29 N	12.17 E
Marinduque Island I	98	13.25 N	122.00 E
Marine City	154	42.43 N	82.30 W
Marinette	154	45.06 N	87.38 W
Maringá	140	23.25 S	51.55 W
Maringouin	158	30.29 N	91.31 W
Marinha Grande	76	39.45 N	8.56 W
Marino	78	41.46 N	12.39 E
Marinskij Posad	66	56.07 N	47.43 E
Marion, Ill., U.S.	158	37.44 N	88.56 W
Marion, Ind., U.S.	154	40.33 N	85.40 W
Marion, Iowa, U.S.	154	42.02 N	91.36 W
Marion, Kans., U.S.	162	38.21 N	97.01 W
Marion, Ky., U.S.	158	37.20 N	88.04 W
Marion, Mich., U.S.	154	44.06 N	85.09 W
Marion, N.C., U.S.	156	35.41 N	82.01 W
Marion, Ohio, U.S.	152	40.35 N	83.08 W
Marion, S. Dak., U.S.	162	43.25 N	97.16 W
Marion, Va., U.S.	156	36.50 N	81.31 W
Marion, Lake ⊜¹	156	33.30 N	80.25 W
Marion Bay C	120	22.48 S	147.55 E
Marion Junction	156	32.26 N	87.14 W
Marion Reef ⋆²	120	19.10 S	152.17 E
Marionville	158	37.00 N	93.38 W
Mariposa	168	37.29 N	119.58 W
Mariscal Estigarribia	140	22.02 S	60.38 W
Marissa	158	38.15 N	89.45 W
Maritime Alps ⋀	74	44.15 N	7.10 E
Marjina Gorka	86	53.31 N	28.09 E
Marka	108	1.47 N	44.52 E
Marked Tree	158	35.32 N	90.25 W
Market Weighton	70	53.52 N	0.40 W
Markham, Ont., Can.	154	43.52 N	79.16 W
Markham, Tex., U.S.	160	28.57 N	96.04 W
Markham Bay C	142	63.30 N	71.48 W
Markleeville	168	38.42 N	119.47 W
Markovo, S.S.S.R.	84	64.40 N	170.25 E
Markovo, S.S.S.R.	86	55.01 N	40.40 E
Marks, S.S.S.R.	64	51.43 N	46.44 E
Marks, Miss., U.S.	158	34.16 N	90.16 W
Marksville	158	31.08 N	92.04 W
Marktheidenfeld	72	49.50 N	9.36 E
Marktoberdorf	72	47.47 N	10.37 E
Marktredwitz	72	50.00 N	12.05 E
Marlboro, N.H., U.S.	152	42.54 N	72.12 W
Marlboro, N.J., U.S.	152	40.18 N	74.15 W
Marlborough, Austl.	120	22.49 S	149.53 E
Marlborough, Eng., U.K.	70	51.26 N	1.43 W
Marlborough, Mass., U.S.	152	42.21 N	71.33 W
Marle	74	49.44 N	3.46 E
Marlette	154	43.20 N	83.05 W
Marlin	160	31.18 N	96.53 W
Marlow	72	53.57 N	11.57 E
Marma ≃	68	61.16 N	16.52 E
Marmande	74	44.30 N	0.10 E
Marmara, Sea of → Marmara Denizi ⊽²		40.40 N	28.15 E
Marmara Denizi sea of (Marmara) ⊽²		40.40 N	28.15 E
Marmaton ≃	162	38.00 N	94.19 W
Marmelos, Rio dos ≃	138	6.08 S	61.46 W
Marmet	152	38.15 N	81.34 W
Marmolada ⋀	78	46.26 N	11.51 E
Marne □⁵	74	49.00 N	4.10 E
Marne ≃	74	48.49 N	2.24 E
Maroa, Ill., U.S.	158	40.02 N	88.57 W
Maroa, Ven.	138	2.43 N	67.33 W
Maroantsetra	117b	15.26 S	49.44 E
Maromokotro ⋀	117b	14.01 S	48.59 E
Maroni (Marowijne) ≃	134	5.45 N	53.58 W
Maros (Mureş) ≃	80	46.15 N	20.13 E
Maroua	106	10.36 N	14.20 E
Marovoay	117b	16.06 S	46.39 E
Marowijne (Maroni) ≃	134	5.45 N	53.58 W
Marshall, Ill., U.S.	158	39.23 N	87.42 W
Marshall, Mich., U.S.	154	42.16 N	84.58 W
Marshall, Minn., U.S.	162	44.27 N	95.47 W
Marshall, Mo., U.S.	162	39.07 N	93.12 W
Marshall, Tex., U.S.	158	32.33 N	94.23 W
Marshalltown	154	42.03 N	92.55 W
Marshallville	156	32.27 N	83.56 W
Marsh Creek ≃	166	42.47 N	112.14 W
Marshfield, Mo., U.S.	158	37.15 N	92.54 W
Marshfield, Wis., U.S.	154	44.40 N	90.10 W
Mars Hill	150	46.31 N	67.52 W
Marshville	156	34.59 N	80.26 W
Marshyhope Creek ≃	152	38.32 N	75.45 W
Marsing	166	43.33 N	116.48 W
Märsta	68	59.37 N	17.51 E
Mart	160	31.33 N	96.50 W
Martaban	94	16.30 N	97.37 E
Martaban, Gulf of C	94	16.30 N	97.00 E
Martapura	96	3.25 S	114.51 E
Martel	74	44.56 N	1.37 E
Marthaguy Creek ≃	120	30.16 S	147.35 E
Martha's Vineyard I	152	41.25 N	70.40 W
Martigny	74	46.06 N	7.04 E
Martigues	74	43.24 N	5.03 E
Martin, N. Dak., U.S.	162	47.50 N	100.07 W
Martin, Tenn., U.S.	158	36.21 N	88.51 W
Martina Franca	78	40.42 N	17.21 E
Martinborough	126	41.13 S	175.28 E
Martindale	160	29.50 N	97.51 W
Martinez	168	38.01 N	122.08 W
Martinez de la Torre	130	20.04 N	97.03 W
Martinique □²	128	14.40 N	61.00 W
Martinsberg	72	48.22 N	15.09 E
Martinsburg, Pa., U.S.	152	40.19 N	78.20 W
Martinsburg, W. Va., U.S.	152	39.27 N	77.58 W
Martins Ferry	152	40.06 N	80.44 W
Martinsville, Ind., U.S.	158	39.25 N	86.25 W
Martinsville, Va., U.S.	156	36.41 N	79.52 W
Marton	126	40.04 S	175.22 E
Martos	76	37.43 N	3.58 W
Martre, Lac la ⊜	142	63.15 N	116.55 W
Marudi	96	4.11 N	114.19 E
Marungu ⋀	110	7.42 S	30.00 E
Mary Dasht	104	29.50 N	52.40 E
Marvejols	74	44.33 N	3.18 E
Marvell	158	34.33 N	90.55 W
Mary ≃	120	25.38 S	152.43 E
Mary	82	37.36 N	61.50 E
Mary, Lake ⊜	154	46.15 N	94.05 W
Maryborough, Austl.	120	25.32 S	152.42 E
Maryborough, Austl.	120	37.03 S	143.45 E
Mary Kathleen	120	20.45 S	139.59 E
Maryland □³	144	39.00 N	76.45 W
Maryneal	160	32.14 N	100.27 W
Maryport	70	54.43 N	3.30 W
Marystown	144	47.10 N	55.09 W
Marysvale	164	38.27 N	112.11 W
Marysville, Calif., U.S.	168	39.09 N	121.35 W
Marysville, Kans., U.S.	162	39.51 N	96.39 W
Marysville, Mich., U.S.	154	42.54 N	82.29 W
Marysville, Ohio, U.S.	152	40.14 N	83.22 W
Marysville, Wash., U.S.	166	48.03 N	122.11 W
Maryville, Mo., U.S.	162	40.21 N	94.52 W
Maryville, Tenn., U.S.	156	35.45 N	83.58 W
Marzo, Cabo ⊁	138	6.50 N	77.42 W
Marzūq	106	25.55 N	13.55 E
Masai Steppe ⋀¹	110	4.45 S	37.00 E
Masaka	110	0.20 S	31.44 E
Masalembo-besar, Pulau I	96	5.34 S	114.26 E
Masan	88	35.11 N	128.32 E
Masasi	110	10.43 S	38.48 E
Masaya	132	11.58 N	86.06 W
Masbate	92	12.22 N	123.36 E
Masbate Island I	98	12.15 N	123.30 E
Mascara	106	35.45 N	0.01 E
Mascarene Islands II	117c	21.00 S	57.00 E
Mascot	156	36.04 N	83.44 W
Mascoutah	158	38.29 N	89.48 W
Masela, Pulau I	124	8.13 S	129.30 E
Maseru	116	29.28 S	27.30 E
Mashābih I	104	25.37 N	36.29 E
Mashhad	104	36.18 N	59.36 E
Mashkel (Māshkīd) ≃	104	28.02 N	63.25 E
Mashkel, Hāmūn-i- ⊜	104	28.15 N	63.00 E
Māshkīd (Mashkel) ≃	104	28.02 N	63.25 E
Masi-Manimba	110	4.46 S	17.53 E
Masindi	110	1.41 N	31.43 E
Maṣīrah, Khalīj al- C	108	20.10 N	58.15 E
Masjed Soleymān	104	31.58 N	49.18 E
Masku	110	6.01 N	34.32 E
Masoala, Presqu'île ⋋¹	117b	15.40 S	50.12 E
Mason, Mich., U.S.	154	42.35 N	84.26 W
Mason, Ohio, U.S.	152	39.21 N	84.18 W
Mason, Tex., U.S.	160	30.45 N	99.13 W
Mason, W. Va., U.S.	152	39.00 N	82.01 W
Mason City, Ill., U.S.	158	40.12 N	89.42 W
Mason City, Iowa, U.S.	154	43.09 N	93.12 W
Masontown	152	39.33 N	79.54 W
Masqat (Muscat)	108	23.37 N	58.35 E
Massa	78	44.01 N	10.09 E
Massachusetts □³	144	42.15 N	71.50 W
Massafra	78	40.35 N	17.07 E
Massa Marittima	78	43.03 N	10.53 E
Massapequa	152	40.40 N	73.28 W
Massarosa	78	43.52 N	10.20 E
Massawa → Mesewa	108	15.38 N	39.28 E
Massena	152	44.55 N	74.54 W
Massenya	106	11.24 N	16.10 E
Massiac	74	45.15 N	3.11 E
Massillon	152	40.47 N	81.31 W
Massive, Mount ⋀	164	39.12 N	106.28 W
Masson	152	45.33 N	75.25 W
Masterton	126	40.57 S	175.40 E
Mastic	152	40.48 N	72.51 W
Masuda	90	34.40 N	131.51 E
Masvingo	116	20.05 S	30.50 E
Matabeleland ⋆¹	116	19.00 S	28.00 E
Matadi	110	5.49 S	13.27 E
Matagalpa	132	12.53 N	85.57 W
Matagami	148	49.45 N	77.38 W
Matagorda Island I	160	28.12 N	96.25 W
Matale	100	7.28 N	80.37 E
Matam	114	15.39 N	13.15 W
Matamoros, Méx.	130	25.32 N	103.15 W
Matamoros, Méx.	130	25.53 N	97.30 W
Matamoros de la Laguna	130	25.32 N	103.15 W
Matandu ≃	110	8.45 S	39.19 E
Matane	150	48.51 N	67.32 W
Matanzas	132	23.03 N	81.35 W
Matapan, Cape → Taínaron, Ákra ⊁	80	36.23 N	22.29 E
Matapédia	150	48.00 N	66.58 W
Mataranka	124	14.56 S	133.07 E
Mataró	76	41.32 N	2.27 E
Matawan	152	40.24 N	74.14 W
Matehuala	130	23.39 N	100.39 W
Mateira	140	18.54 S	50.30 W
Mátészalka	72	47.57 N	22.19 E
Mateur	78	37.03 N	9.40 E
Mathis	160	28.05 N	97.49 W
Mato Grosso □³	140	16.00 S	56.00 W
Mato Grosso, Planalto do ⋀¹	134	15.30 S	56.00 W
Matopo Hills ⋀²	116	20.36 S	28.28 E
Matosinhos	76	41.11 N	8.42 W
Matoury	134	4.51 N	52.21 W
Maṭraḥ	104	23.38 N	58.34 E
Matrei in Osttirol	72	47.00 N	12.32 E
Matruh	112	31.21 N	27.14 E
Matsudo	90	35.47 N	139.54 E
Matsue	90	35.28 N	133.04 E
Matsumoto	90	36.14 N	137.58 E
Matsusaka	90	34.34 N	136.32 E
Matsu Shan I	88	26.09 N	119.56 E
Matsuyama	90	33.50 N	132.45 E
Mattancheri	100	9.58 N	76.14 E
Mattawa, Ont., Can.	148	46.19 N	78.42 W
Mattawa, Wash., U.S.	166	46.44 N	119.54 W
Mattawamkeag	152	45.31 N	68.21 W
Matterhorn ⋀	74	45.59 N	7.43 E
Mattersburg	72	47.44 N	16.24 E
Mattighofen	72	48.06 N	13.09 E
Mattoon	158	39.29 N	88.22 W
Mattydale	152	43.06 N	76.09 W
Maturín	138	9.45 N	63.11 W
Maú (Ireng) ≃	138	3.51 N	60.08 W
Maúa	110	13.51 S	37.10 E
Ma-ubin	94	16.44 N	95.39 E
Maud	158	35.08 N	96.47 W
Maud, Point ⊁	122	23.06 S	113.48 E
Maude	120	34.28 S	144.18 E
Maués	138	3.24 S	57.42 W
Maug Islands II	92	20.01 N	145.13 E
Maui I	170a	20.45 N	156.15 W
Mauldin	156	34.47 N	82.18 W
Mauléon	74	43.14 N	0.53 W
Maumee	152	41.34 N	83.39 W
Maumee ≃	152	41.42 N	83.28 W
Maumere	96	8.37 S	122.14 E
Maun	116	20.00 S	23.25 E
Maunath Bhanjan	102	25.57 N	83.33 E
Maunoir, Lac ⊜	146	67.30 N	125.00 W
Maure-de-Bretagne	74	47.54 N	1.59 W
Mauriac	74	45.13 N	2.20 E
Maurice, Lake ⊜	122	29.28 S	130.58 E
Mauritania □¹	106	20.00 N	12.00 W
Mauritius □¹	117c	20.17 S	57.33 E
Mauron	74	48.05 N	2.18 W
Maurs	74	44.43 N	2.11 E
Maury Channel ⋈	154	45.44 N	94.40 W
Mauston	154	43.48 N	90.05 W
Mautern	72	47.08 N	14.40 E
Mauterndorf	72	47.08 N	13.40 E
Mauvezin	74	43.44 N	0.53 E
Mauzé-sur-le-Mignon	74	46.12 N	0.40 W
Mavinga	110	15.50 S	20.21 E
Maw-daung Pass)(	94	11.47 N	99.39 E
Maw Taung ⋀	94	11.39 N	99.35 E
Maxcanú	130	20.35 N	89.59 W
Maxixe	116	23.51 S	35.21 E
Maxwell	168	39.17 N	122.11 W
Maxwell Bay C	142	74.35 N	89.00 W
Mayaguana I	132	22.23 N	73.00 W
Mayagüez	132	18.12 N	67.09 W
Maya Mountains ⋀	130	16.40 N	88.50 W
Maybole	70	55.21 N	4.41 W
Mayen	72	50.19 N	7.13 E
Mayenne	74	48.18 N	0.37 W
Mayenne □⁵	74	48.05 N	0.40 W
Mayenne ≃	74	47.30 N	0.33 W
Mayer	154	34.24 N	112.14 W
Mayfield, Ky., U.S.	158	36.44 N	88.38 W
Mayfield, Utah, U.S.	164	39.07 N	111.42 W
Mayfield Creek ≃	158	37.00 N	89.05 W
May Inlet C	142	76.15 N	100.45 W
Maymyo	94	22.02 N	96.28 E
Mayne ≃	120	23.34 S	141.18 E
Maynooth	156	36.15 N	83.48 W
Mayo, Yukon, Can.	146	63.35 N	135.54 W
Mayo, Fla., U.S.	156	30.03 N	83.10 W
Mayo, Md., U.S.	152	38.53 N	76.31 W
Mayodan	156	36.25 N	79.58 W
Mayon Volcano ⋀¹	98	13.15 N	123.42 E
Mayotte I	117b	12.50 S	45.10 E
May Pen	132	17.58 N	77.14 W
Mays Landing	152	39.27 N	74.44 W
Maysville, Ky., U.S.	152	38.38 N	83.46 W
Maysville, Mo., U.S.	162	39.53 N	94.21 W
Mayville, Mich., U.S.	154	43.20 N	83.21 W
Mayville, N. Dak., U.S.	162	47.30 N	97.19 W
Mayville, N.Y., U.S.	152	42.15 N	79.30 W
Mayville, Wis., U.S.	154	43.30 N	88.33 W
Maza	140	36.48 S	63.20 W
Mazabuka	110	15.51 S	27.46 E
Mazagan → El-Jadida	106	33.16 N	8.30 W
Mazamet	74	43.30 N	2.24 E
Mazán	138	3.30 S	73.00 W
Mazara del Vallo	78	37.39 N	12.36 E
Mazar-e Sharif	82	36.42 N	67.06 E
Mazaruni-Potaro □⁵	138	5.00 N	60.00 W
Mazatenango	130	14.32 N	91.30 W
Mazatlán	130	23.13 N	106.25 W
Mazoe ≃	116	16.32 S	33.25 E
Mazoe	116	17.30 S	30.58 E
Mbabane	116	26.18 S	31.06 E
Mbaïki	108	3.53 N	18.00 E
Mbala	110	8.50 S	31.22 E
Mbale	110	1.05 N	34.10 E
Mbalmayo	110	3.31 N	11.30 E
Mbamba Bay	110	11.17 S	34.46 E
Mbandaka (Coquilhatville)	110	0.04 N	18.16 E
Mbanza-Ngungu	110	5.15 S	14.52 E
Mbarara	110	0.36 S	30.39 E
Mbari ≃	108	4.34 N	22.43 E
Mbeya	110	8.54 S	33.27 E
Mbinda	110	2.11 S	12.51 E
Mbinga	110	10.56 S	35.03 E
Mbomou (Bomu) ≃	108	4.08 N	22.26 E
Mbuji-Mayi (Bakwanga)	110	6.09 S	23.38 E
M'Clintock Channel ⋈	142	71.00 N	101.00 W
M'Clure, Cape ⊁	146	74.35 N	121.08 W
M'Clure Strait ⋈	146	74.30 N	116.00 W
Mead, Lake ⊜¹	164	36.05 N	114.25 W
Meade	162	37.17 N	100.20 W
Meadow, Tex., U.S.	160	33.20 N	102.12 W
Meadow, Utah, U.S.	164	38.53 N	112.24 W
Meadow Valley Wash V	164	36.39 N	114.35 W
Meadville	152	41.38 N	80.09 W
Meaford	154	44.36 N	80.35 W
Méan	72	50.22 N	5.20 E
Meander River	142	59.02 N	117.42 W
Meath □⁶	70	53.35 N	6.40 W
Meaux	74	48.57 N	2.52 E
Mecca → Makkah	108	21.27 N	39.49 E
Mechanic Falls	150	44.07 N	70.24 W
Mechanicsburg, Ohio, U.S.	152	40.04 N	83.34 W
Mechanicsville	156	37.36 N	77.20 W
Mechanicville	152	42.54 N	73.41 W
Mechelen	72	51.02 N	4.28 E
Mechren'ga	66	61.46 N	40.57 E
Mecklenburg □⁹	72	53.30 N	13.00 E

Name	Page	Lat°′	Long°′
Mecklenburger Bucht C	72	54.20 N	11.40 E
Meda	76	40.58 N	7.16 W
Medan	94	3.35 N	98.40 E
Medanosa, Punta ≻	136	48.08 S	65.58 W
Medaryville	158	41.05 N	86.55 W
Mede	78	45.06 N	8.44 E
Médéa	76	36.12 N	2.50 E
Medellín	138	6.15 N	75.35 W
Medelpad □[9]	68	62.40 N	16.15 E
Médenine	106	32.21 N	10.30 E
Medford, Mass., U.S.	152	42.25 N	71.07 W
Medford, N.J., U.S.	152	39.54 N	74.49 W
Medford, Oreg., U.S.	166	42.19 N	122.52 W
Medford, Wis., U.S.	154	45.09 N	90.20 W
Medgidia	80	44.15 N	28.16 E
Media	152	39.54 N	75.23 W
Mediaș	80	46.10 N	24.21 E
Medical Lake	166	47.34 N	117.41 W
Medicina	78	44.28 N	11.38 E
Medicine Bow	164	41.54 N	106.12 W
Medicine Bow Mountains ⋀	164	41.10 N	106.25 W
Medicine Creek, East Fork ≃	158	40.06 N	93.22 W
Medicine Hat	142	50.03 N	110.40 W
Medicine Lake	162	48.30 N	104.30 W
Medicine Lodge	162	37.17 N	98.35 W
Medicine Lodge ≃	160	36.49 N	98.20 W
Medina → Al-Madīnah, Ar. Sa.	104	24.28 N	39.36 E
Medina, N.Y., U.S.	152	43.13 N	78.23 W
Medina, Ohio, U.S.	152	41.08 N	81.52 W
Medina, Tex., U.S.	160	29.48 N	99.15 W
Medina del Campo	76	41.18 N	4.55 W
Mediterranean Sea ▼[2]	64	36.00 N	15.00 E
Medjerda, Monts de la ⋀	78	36.35 N	8.15 E
Medjerda, Oued ≃	78	37.07 N	10.13 E
Mednogorsk	82	51.24 N	57.37 E
Mednyj, Ostrov I	84	54.45 N	167.35 E
Médoc ⬥[1]	74	45.20 N	1.00 W
Médouneu	110	0.57 N	10.47 E
Medvedica ≃	64	49.35 N	42.41 E
Medvežjegorsk	66	62.55 N	34.23 E
Medvežji Ostrova II	84	70.52 N	161.26 E
Medyn′	86	54.58 N	35.52 E
Meekatharra	122	26.36 S	118.29 E
Meeker	164	40.02 N	107.55 W
Meeks Bay	168	39.02 N	120.08 W
Meelpaeg Lake ⊜[1]	150	48.16 N	56.35 W
Meentheena	122	21.17 S	120.28 E
Meerane	72	50.51 N	12.28 E
Meersburg	72	47.41 N	9.16 E
Meerut	102	28.59 N	77.42 E
Meeteetse	166	44.09 N	108.52 W
Mega	108	4.07 N	38.16 E
Mega, Pulau I	96	3.55 S	100.55 E
Mégara	80	38.01 N	23.21 E
Megargel	160	33.27 N	98.56 W
Meghna ≃	100	22.50 N	90.50 E
Mehedinți □[4]	80	44.30 N	22.50 E
Meherrin ≃	156	36.26 N	76.57 W
Mehsāna	102	23.36 N	72.24 E
Mehun-sur-yèvre	74	47.09 N	2.13 E
Meigs	156	31.04 N	83.06 W
Meiktila	94	20.52 N	95.52 E
Meiners Oaks	168	34.30 N	119.17 W
Meiningen	72	50.34 N	10.25 E
Meiringen	74	46.43 N	8.12 E
Meissen	72	51.10 N	13.28 E
Meixian	88	24.21 N	116.08 E
Mejillones	140	23.06 S	70.27 W
Mekambo	110	1.01 N	13.56 E
Mekele	108	13.33 N	39.30 E
Mekerrhane, Sebkha ≃	106	26.19 N	1.20 E
Meknès	106	33.53 N	5.37 W
Mekong ≃	94	10.33 N	105.24 E
Mekoryuk	146	60.23 N	166.12 W
Mékrou ≃	114	12.24 N	2.49 E
Melawi ≃	96	0.05 S	111.29 E
Melbourne, Austl.	120	37.49 S	144.58 E
Melbourne, Fla., U.S.	156	28.05 N	80.37 W
Melbourne Island I	142	68.30 N	104.45 W
Melby House	70	60.18 N	1.39 W
Melcher	154	41.13 N	93.14 W
Meldorf	72	54.05 N	9.05 E
Melechovo	86	56.17 N	41.17 E
Melegnano	78	45.21 N	9.19 E
Melekess	82	54.14 N	49.39 E
Melenki	86	55.20 N	41.38 E
Meleuz	82	52.58 N	55.55 E
Mélèzes, Rivière aux ≃	142	57.40 N	69.29 W
Melfi, It.	78	40.59 N	15.40 E
Melfi, Tchad	108	11.04 N	17.56 E
Melfort	142	52.52 N	104.36 W
Melgaço	76	42.07 N	8.16 W
Melhus	68	63.17 N	10.16 E
Melilla	106	35.19 N	2.58 W
Melipilla	140	33.42 S	71.13 W
Melita	162	49.16 N	101.00 W
Melitopol′	64	46.50 N	35.22 E
Melk	72	48.14 N	15.20 E
Mellansel	68	63.26 N	18.19 E
Melle	74	46.13 N	0.09 W
Mellègue, Oued ≃	78	36.32 N	8.51 E
Mellen	154	46.20 N	90.40 W
Mellid	76	42.55 N	8.00 W
Mellish Reef I[1]	118	17.25 S	155.50 E
Mělník	72	50.20 N	14.29 E
Melo	140	32.22 S	54.11 W
Melrhir, Chott ⊜	106	34.20 N	6.20 E
Melrose, Austl.	122	27.56 S	121.19 E
Melrose, Scot., U.K.	70	55.36 N	2.44 W
Melrose, Minn., U.S.	162	45.40 N	94.49 W
Melsungen	72	51.08 N	9.32 E
Melton Mowbray	70	52.46 N	0.53 W
Melun	74	48.32 N	2.40 E
Melvich	70	58.33 N	3.55 W
Melville, Sask., Can.	142	50.55 N	102.48 W
Melville, La., U.S.	158	30.42 N	91.45 W
Melville, Lake ⊜	142	53.45 N	59.30 W
Melville Hills ⋀[2]	142	69.20 N	122.00 W
Melville Island I, Austl.	124	11.40 S	131.00 E
Melville Island I, N.W. Ter., Can.	142	75.15 N	110.00 W
Melville Peninsula ≻[1]	142	68.00 N	84.00 W
Melville Sound ⌣	142	68.05 N	107.30 W
Melvin, Ill., U.S.	154	40.34 N	88.15 W
Melvin, Tex., U.S.	160	31.13 N	99.35 W
Mélykút	72	46.13 N	19.24 E
Melzo	78	45.30 N	9.25 E
Memmingen	72	47.59 N	10.11 E
Mempawah	96	0.22 N	108.58 E
Memphis, Fla., U.S.	156	27.32 N	82.34 W
Memphis, Mo., U.S.	158	40.28 N	92.10 W
Memphis, Tenn., U.S.	158	35.08 N	90.03 W
Memphis, Tex., U.S.	160	34.44 N	100.32 W
Mena	158	34.35 N	94.15 W
Menai Bridge	70	53.14 N	4.10 W
Ménaka	114	15.55 N	2.24 E
Menasha	154	44.13 N	88.26 W
Mendawai ≃	96	3.17 S	113.21 E
Mende	74	44.30 N	3.30 E
Menden	72	51.26 N	7.47 E
Mendenhall	158	31.58 N	89.52 W
Mendi, Pap. N. Gui.	124	6.10 S	143.40 E
Mendi, Yai.	108	9.50 N	35.06 E
Mendocino	168	39.19 N	123.48 W
Mendocino, Cape ≻	168	40.25 N	124.25 W
Mendon	154	42.00 N	85.27 W
Mendota, Calif., U.S.	168	36.45 N	120.23 W
Mendota, Ill., U.S.	154	41.33 N	89.07 W
Mendoza	140	32.54 S	68.50 W
Mendoza □[4]	140	34.40 S	68.30 W
Ménéac	74	48.09 N	2.28 W
Mene Grande	138	9.49 N	70.56 W
Menén	74	50.48 N	3.07 E
Menfi	78	37.36 N	12.58 E
Mengcheng	88	33.17 N	116.33 E
Menggala	96	4.28 S	105.17 E
Menghai	94	22.00 N	100.26 E
Mengzhi	94	24.10 N	99.46 E
Mengzi	94	23.22 N	103.20 E
Menihek Lakes ⊜	142	54.00 N	66.35 W
Menindee	120	32.24 S	142.26 E
Menindee Lake ⊜	120	32.21 S	142.20 E
Menlo Park	168	37.28 N	122.13 W
Menno	162	43.14 N	97.34 W
Menominee	154	45.06 N	87.37 W
Menominee ≃	154	45.05 N	87.36 W
Menomonee Falls	154	43.11 N	88.07 W
Menomonie	154	44.53 N	91.55 W
Menorca I	76	40.00 N	4.00 E
Mens	74	44.49 N	5.45 E
Mentasta Mountains ⋀	146	62.40 N	143.07 W
Mentawai, Kepulauan II	96	2.00 S	99.30 E
Menton	74	43.47 N	7.30 E
Mentone	130	31.42 N	103.36 W
Mentor	152	41.40 N	81.20 W
Menzel Bourguiba	106	37.10 N	9.48 E
Menzelinsk	66	55.43 N	53.08 E
Menzies	122	29.41 S	121.02 E
Meoqui	130	28.17 N	105.29 W
Meppel	72	52.42 N	6.11 E
Meppen	72	52.41 N	7.17 E
Mer	74	47.42 N	1.30 E
Meråker	68	63.26 N	11.45 E
Merano (Meran)	78	46.40 N	11.09 E
Merate	78	45.42 N	9.25 E
Merauke	124	8.28 S	140.20 E
Mercāra	100	12.26 N	75.45 E
Merced	168	37.18 N	120.29 W
Mercedes, Arg.	140	34.40 S	59.25 W
Mercedes, Arg.	140	33.40 S	65.30 W
Mercedes, Arg.	140	29.10 S	58.02 W
Mercedes, Tex., U.S.	160	26.09 N	97.55 W
Mercedes, Ur.	140	33.16 S	58.01 W
Mercer, Pa., U.S.	152	41.14 N	80.15 W
Mercer, Wis., U.S.	154	46.10 N	90.04 W
Merchants Bay C	142	67.10 N	62.50 W
Mercy Bay C	142	74.05 N	119.00 W
Meredith	152	43.39 N	71.30 W
Merenkurkku (Norra Kvarken) ⌣	68	63.36 N	20.43 E
Mergui, Mya.	92	12.26 N	98.36 E
Mergui (Myeik), Mya.	94	12.26 N	98.36 E
Mergui Archipelago II	94	12.00 N	98.00 E
Meriç (Marica) (Évros) ≃	80	40.52 N	26.12 E
Mérida, Esp.	76	38.55 N	6.20 W
Mérida, Méx.	130	20.58 N	89.37 W
Mérida, Ven.	138	8.36 N	71.08 W
Mérida □[3]	138	8.30 N	71.10 W
Mérida, Cordillera de ⋀	138	8.40 N	71.00 W
Meriden	152	41.32 N	72.48 W
Meridian, Idaho, U.S.	166	43.37 N	116.24 W
Meridian, Miss., U.S.	158	32.22 N	88.42 W
Meridian, Tex., U.S.	160	31.55 N	97.39 W
Mérignac	74	44.50 N	0.42 W
Merimbula	120	36.53 S	149.54 E
Merín, Laguna (Lagoa Mirim C	140	32.45 S	52.50 W
Merino	162	40.29 N	103.21 W
Merir I	92	4.19 N	132.19 E
Merkel	160	32.28 N	100.01 W
Merkendorf	72	49.12 N	10.42 E
Merlo	140	32.21 S	65.02 W
Mernye	72	46.30 N	17.50 E
Merredin	122	31.29 S	118.16 E
Merrill, Mich., U.S.	154	43.25 N	84.20 W
Merrill, Oreg., U.S.	166	42.01 N	121.36 W
Merrill, Wis., U.S.	154	45.11 N	89.41 W
Merrillan	154	44.27 N	90.50 W
Merritt	148	50.07 N	120.47 W
Merritt Island	156	28.21 N	80.42 W
Merriwa	120	32.08 S	150.21 E
Merryville	158	30.45 N	93.33 W
Merseburg	72	51.21 N	11.59 E
Mersey ≃	120	41.10 S	146.22 E
Mersin	104	36.48 N	34.38 E
Merthyr Tydfil	70	51.46 N	3.23 W
Mértola	76	37.38 N	7.40 W
Mertzon	160	31.16 N	100.49 W
Méru, Fr.	74	49.14 N	2.08 E
Meru, Kenya	110	0.03 N	37.39 E
Meru ∧	110	3.14 S	36.45 E
Méry	74	48.30 N	3.53 E
Merzig	72	49.27 N	6.36 E
Mesa	164	33.25 N	111.50 W
Mesa ≃	76	41.15 N	1.48 W
Mesagne	78	40.33 N	17.49 E
Mescalero	164	33.09 N	105.46 W
Meschede	72	51.20 N	8.17 E
Meščovsk	86	54.19 N	35.17 E
Mesewa (Massaua)	108	15.38 N	39.28 E
Mesgouez, Lac ⊜	142	51.24 N	75.05 W
Mesick	154	44.24 N	85.43 W
Mesilla	164	32.16 N	106.48 W
Mesilla Park	164	32.17 N	106.46 W
Meslay-du-Maine	74	47.57 N	0.33 W
Mesocco	74	46.23 N	9.14 E
Mesolóngion	80	38.21 N	21.17 E
Mesopotamia ⬥[1]	104	34.00 N	44.00 E
Mesquite, Nev., U.S.	168	36.48 N	114.04 W
Mesquite, Tex., U.S.	160	32.46 N	96.36 W
Messalo ≃	110	11.40 S	40.26 E
Messina, It.	78	38.11 N	15.33 E
Messina, S. Afr.	116	22.23 S	30.00 E
Messina, Stretto di ⌣	78	38.15 N	15.35 E
Messíni	80	37.04 N	22.00 E
Messkirch	72	47.59 N	9.07 E
Messojacha ≃	84	67.52 N	77.27 E
Mestá	80	38.15 N	25.55 E
Mesta (Néstos) ≃	80	40.41 N	24.44 E
Mestre	78	45.29 N	12.15 E
Meta □[5]	138	3.30 N	73.00 W
Meta ≃	138	6.12 N	67.28 W
Metairie	158	29.59 N	90.09 W
Metaline Falls	148	48.52 N	117.22 W
Metamora	154	40.47 N	89.22 W
Metán	140	25.30 S	65.00 W
Methven	126	43.28 S	171.38 E
Metković	78	43.03 N	17.39 E
Metlakatla	146	55.08 N	131.35 W
Metropolis	158	37.09 N	88.44 W
Metter	156	32.24 N	82.03 W
Mettmann	72	51.15 N	6.58 E
Metz	74	49.08 N	6.10 E
Metzingen	72	48.32 N	9.17 E
Meulaboh	92	4.09 N	96.07 E
Meulan	74	49.01 N	1.54 E
Meurthe-et-Moselle □[5]	74	48.35 N	6.10 E
Meuse □[5]	74	49.00 N	5.30 E
Meuse (Maas) ≃	72	51.49 N	5.01 E
Meuselwitz	72	51.02 N	12.17 E
Mexia	160	31.41 N	96.29 W
Mexiana, Ilha I	134	0.02 S	49.35 W
Mexicali	130	32.40 N	115.29 W
Mexican Hat	164	37.09 N	109.52 W
Mexico, Maine, U.S.	152	44.34 N	70.33 W
Mexico, Mo., U.S.	158	39.10 N	91.53 W
Mexico, N.Y., U.S.	152	43.28 N	76.14 W
Mexico (México) □[1]	128	23.00 N	102.00 W
Mexico, Gulf of C	128	25.00 N	90.00 W
Mexico City → Ciudad de México	130	19.24 N	99.09 W
Meximieux	74	45.54 N	5.12 E
Meyersdale	152	39.45 N	79.05 W
Meyísti I	64	36.08 N	29.34 E
Meymac	74	45.32 N	2.09 E
Meymaneh	102	35.55 N	64.47 E
Meyrargues	74	43.38 N	5.32 E
Meyrueis	74	44.10 N	3.26 E
Meždurečensk	84	53.42 N	88.03 E
Mèze	74	43.25 N	3.36 E
Mézel	74	43.59 N	6.12 E
Mezen′	66	65.50 N	44.13 E
Mezen′ ≃	66	66.11 N	43.59 E
Mézières-en-Brenne	74	46.49 N	1.13 E
Mézin	74	44.03 N	0.16 E
Mezinovskij	86	55.30 N	40.21 E
Mezőberény	72	46.50 N	21.02 E
Mezőcsát	72	47.49 N	20.55 E
Mezőkovácsháza	72	46.25 N	20.46 E
Mezőkövesd	72	47.50 N	20.34 E
Mezőtúr	72	47.00 N	20.38 E
Mglin	86	53.04 N	32.51 E
M′goun, Irhil ∧	106	31.31 N	6.25 W
Mhow	102	22.33 N	75.46 E
Miahuatlán de Porfirio Díaz	130	16.20 N	96.36 W
Miami, Ariz., U.S.	164	33.24 N	110.52 W
Miami, Fla., U.S.	156	25.46 N	80.12 W
Miami, Okla., U.S.	160	36.53 N	94.53 W
Miami, Tex., U.S.	160	35.42 N	100.38 W
Miami Beach	156	25.47 N	80.08 W
Miami Springs	156	25.49 N	80.17 W
Miandrivazo	117b	19.31 S	45.28 E
Miāneh	104	37.26 N	47.42 E
Miangas, Pulau I	92	5.35 N	126.35 E
Miānwāli	102	32.35 N	71.33 E
Mianyang, Zhg.	88	30.23 N	113.25 E
Mianyang, Zhg.	88	31.30 N	104.49 E
Miaoli	88	23.45 N	120.15 E
Miass	82	54.59 N	60.06 E
Micanopy	156	29.30 N	82.17 W
Michajlovka	64	50.05 N	43.15 E
Michalovce	72	48.45 N	21.55 E
Michigan	162	48.07 N	98.07 W
Michigan □[3]	144	44.00 N	85.00 W
Michigan, Lake ⊜	154	44.00 N	87.00 W
Michigan Center	154	42.14 N	84.20 W
Michigan City	158	41.43 N	86.54 W
Michikamau Lake ⊜	142	54.00 N	64.00 W
Michipicoten Island I	154	47.45 N	85.45 W
Mičurinsk	86	52.54 N	40.30 E
Middalya	122	23.55 S	114.45 E
Middelburg, Ned.	72	51.30 N	3.37 E
Middelburg, S. Afr.	116	31.30 S	25.00 E
Middelharnis	72	51.45 N	4.11 E
Middle Andaman I	94	12.30 N	92.50 E
Middleboro	152	41.49 N	70.55 W
Middlebourne	152	39.30 N	80.54 W
Middleburg, N.Y., U.S.	152	42.36 N	74.20 W
Middleburg, Pa., U.S.	152	40.47 N	77.03 W
Middlebury	152	44.01 N	73.10 W
Middlefield	152	41.28 N	81.05 W
Middle Point	152	40.51 N	84.27 W
Middleport, N.Y., U.S.	152	43.13 N	78.29 W
Middleport, Ohio, U.S.	152	39.00 N	82.03 W
Middlesboro	156	36.36 N	83.43 W
Middlesbrough	70	54.35 N	1.14 W
Middle Swan	122	31.52 S	116.00 E
Middleton, N.S., Can.	150	44.57 N	65.04 W
Middleton, Tenn., U.S.	158	35.04 N	88.54 W
Middleton, Wis., U.S.	154	43.06 N	89.30 W
Middleton ≃	120	22.35 S	141.51 E
Middleton Island I	146	59.25 N	146.25 W
Middleton Reef I[1]	118	29.28 S	159.06 E
Middletown, Calif., U.S.	168	38.45 N	122.37 W
Middletown, Conn., U.S.	152	41.33 N	72.39 W
Middletown, Del., U.S.	152	39.25 N	75.47 W
Middletown, Ind., U.S.	158	40.03 N	85.32 W
Middletown, Ky., U.S.	158	38.15 N	85.32 W
Middletown, N.Y., U.S.	152	41.27 N	74.25 W
Middletown, Ohio, U.S.	152	39.29 N	84.25 W
Middletown, Pa., U.S.	152	40.12 N	76.44 W
Middletown, R.I., U.S.	152	41.32 N	71.17 W
Middleville	154	42.43 N	85.28 W
Mid Glamorgan □[6]	70	51.40 N	3.30 W
Midland, Ont., Can.	154	44.45 N	79.53 W
Midland, Mich., U.S.	154	43.37 N	84.14 W
Midland, Pa., U.S.	152	40.38 N	80.27 W
Midland, Tex., U.S.	160	32.00 N	102.05 W
Midleton	70	51.55 N	8.10 W
Midlothian	160	32.29 N	97.00 W
Midnapore	102	22.26 N	87.20 E
Midongy Sud	117b	23.35 S	47.01 E
Midvale, Idaho, U.S.	166	44.28 N	116.44 W
Midvale, Utah, U.S.	164	40.37 N	111.54 W
Midway, Ala., U.S.	158	32.05 N	85.31 W
Midway, Ky., U.S.	152	38.09 N	84.41 W
Midway, Tex., U.S.	160	31.02 N	95.45 W
Midway, Utah, U.S.	164	40.31 N	111.28 W
Midway Park	156	34.43 N	77.21 W
Midwest	166	43.25 N	106.16 W
Midwest City	160	35.27 N	97.24 W
Midžor (Midžur) ∧	80	43.23 N	22.42 E
Miechów	72	50.23 N	20.01 E
Międzychód	72	52.28 N	15.55 E
Międzyrzec Podlaski	72	52.00 N	22.47 E
Międzyrzecz	72	52.28 N	15.35 E
Miélan	74	43.26 N	0.19 E
Mielec	72	50.18 N	21.25 E
Mieres	76	43.15 N	5.46 W
Mifflinburg	152	40.55 N	77.03 W
Migennes	74	47.58 N	3.31 E
Miguel Alemán, Presa ⊜[1]	130	18.13 N	96.32 W
Miguel Auza	130	24.18 N	103.25 W
Mihajlovgrad	80	43.25 N	23.13 E
Mihara	90	34.24 N	133.05 E
Mikindani	110	10.17 S	40.07 E
Mikkeli	68	61.41 N	27.15 E
Mikkelin lääni □[4]	68	62.00 N	27.30 E
Mikkwa ≃	142	58.25 N	114.45 W
Mikolów	72	50.11 N	18.55 E
Mikumi	110	7.24 S	36.59 E
Mikun′	66	62.21 N	50.06 E
Milaca	154	45.45 N	93.39 W
Milagro, Arg.	140	31.00 S	66.00 W
Milagro, Ec.	138	2.07 S	79.36 W
Milan → Milano, It.	78	45.28 N	9.12 E
Milan, Ind., U.S.	158	39.07 N	85.08 W
Milan, Mich., U.S.	154	42.05 N	83.40 W
Milan, N. Mex., U.S.	164	35.09 N	107.54 W
Milan, Ohio, U.S.	152	41.18 N	82.36 W
Milan, Tenn., U.S.	158	35.55 N	88.46 W
Milano (Milan), It.	78	45.28 N	9.12 E
Milano, Tex., U.S.	160	30.43 N	96.52 W
Milazzo	78	38.14 N	15.15 E
Milbank	162	45.13 N	96.38 W
Mildenhall	70	52.21 N	0.30 E
Mildura	120	34.12 S	142.09 E
Mile	94	24.26 N	103.26 E
Miles, Austl.	120	26.40 S	150.11 E
Miles, Tex., U.S.	160	31.36 N	100.11 W
Miles City	166	46.25 N	105.51 W
Milford, Conn., U.S.	152	41.13 N	73.04 W
Milford, Del., U.S.	152	38.55 N	75.25 W
Milford, Ind., U.S.	158	41.25 N	85.51 W
Milford, Iowa, U.S.	162	43.20 N	95.09 W
Milford, Maine, U.S.	152	44.57 N	68.39 W
Milford, Mass., U.S.	152	42.08 N	71.32 W
Milford, Mich., U.S.	154	42.35 N	83.36 W
Milford, Nebr., U.S.	162	40.47 N	97.03 W
Milford, N.H., U.S.	152	42.50 N	71.39 W
Milford, N.J., U.S.	152	40.34 N	75.06 W
Milford, Pa., U.S.	152	41.19 N	74.48 W
Milford, Utah, U.S.	164	38.24 N	113.01 W
Milford Center	152	40.11 N	83.26 W
Milford Haven	70	51.40 N	5.02 W
Milicz	72	51.32 N	17.17 E
Milk ≃	166	48.05 N	106.15 W
Mil′kovo	84	54.43 N	158.37 E
Millard	162	41.13 N	96.07 W
Millau	74	44.06 N	3.05 E
Millbury	152	42.11 N	71.46 W
Mill City	166	44.45 N	122.29 W
Mill Creek	152	38.44 N	79.58 W
Milledgeville	156	33.04 N	83.14 W
Mille Lacs, Lac des ⊜	154	48.50 N	90.30 W
Mille Lacs Lake ⊜	154	46.15 N	93.40 W
Millen	156	32.48 N	81.57 W
Miller, Mo., U.S.	158	37.13 N	93.50 W
Miller, S. Dak., U.S.	162	44.31 N	98.59 W
Millerovo	82	48.55 N	40.25 E
Millersburg, Ohio, U.S.	152	40.33 N	81.55 W
Millersburg, Pa., U.S.	152	40.33 N	76.58 W
Millersport	152	39.54 N	82.32 W
Millersview	160	31.25 N	99.45 W
Millersville	152	40.00 N	76.22 W
Millerton	152	41.57 N	73.31 W
Millett	160	28.35 N	99.12 W
Millevaches, Plateau de ⋀[1]	74	45.30 N	2.10 E
Millicent	120	37.36 S	140.22 E
Milligan	158	30.45 N	86.38 W
Millington, Mich., U.S.	154	43.17 N	83.32 W
Millington, Tenn., U.S.	158	35.21 N	89.54 W
Millinocket	152	45.39 N	68.43 W
Mill Island I	142	64.00 N	78.00 W
Millmerran	120	27.52 S	151.16 E
Millport	70	55.46 N	4.55 W
Millry	158	31.33 N	88.19 W
Mills Lake ⊜	142	61.30 N	118.10 W
Millstatt	72	46.48 N	13.35 E
Millstream	122	21.35 S	117.04 E
Milltown	166	46.53 N	113.52 W
Milltown Malbay	70	52.52 N	9.23 W
Mill Valley	168	37.54 N	122.32 W
Millville	152	39.24 N	75.02 W
Millwood	152	39.04 N	78.02 W
Milne Bay C	124	10.22 S	150.30 E
Milo, Iowa, U.S.	154	41.17 N	93.27 W
Milo, Maine, U.S.	152	45.15 N	68.59 W
Milos I	80	36.41 N	24.15 E
Milparinka	120	29.44 S	141.53 E
Milpitas	168	37.26 N	121.54 W
Milroy	152	40.43 N	77.35 W
Miltenberg	72	49.42 N	9.15 E
Milton, N.Z.	126	46.07 S	169.58 E
Milton, Del., U.S.	152	38.47 N	75.19 W
Milton, Fla., U.S.	158	30.38 N	87.03 W
Milton, N. Dak., U.S.	162	48.38 N	98.03 W
Milton, Pa., U.S.	152	41.01 N	76.51 W
Milton, Vt., U.S.	152	44.38 N	73.07 W
Milton, W. Va., U.S.	152	38.26 N	82.08 W
Milton, Wis., U.S.	154	42.47 N	88.56 W
Milton-freewater	166	45.56 N	118.23 W
Miltonvale	162	39.21 N	97.27 W
Milwaukee	154	43.02 N	87.55 W
Milwaukie	166	45.27 N	122.38 W
Mimizan	74	44.12 N	1.14 W
Mims	156	28.40 N	80.51 W
Mina	168	38.24 N	118.07 W
Minahasa ≻[1]	96	1.00 N	124.35 E
Minami-Daitō-jima I	88	25.50 N	131.15 E
Minas	140	34.23 S	55.14 W
Minas Gerais □[3]	140	18.00 S	44.00 W
Minas Novas	134	17.15 S	42.36 W
Minatitlán	130	17.59 N	94.31 W
Mindanao I	98	7.30 N	125.00 E
Mindanao ≃	98	7.07 N	124.24 E
Mindanao Sea ▼[2]	98	9.10 N	124.20 E
Mindelheim	72	48.03 N	10.29 E
Mindelo	114a	16.53 N	25.00 W
Minden, B.R.D.	72	52.17 N	8.55 E
Minden, La., U.S.	158	32.37 N	93.17 W
Minden, Nebr., U.S.	162	40.30 N	98.57 W
Minden, Nev., U.S.	168	38.57 N	119.45 W
Minden City	154	43.40 N	82.47 W
Minderoo	122	22.00 S	115.02 E
Mindoro I	98	13.00 N	121.10 E
Mindoro Strait ⌣	98	12.30 N	120.30 E
Minehead	70	51.13 N	3.29 W
Mineiros	134	17.34 S	52.34 W
Mineola	160	32.40 N	95.29 W
Mineral′nyje Vody	82	44.12 N	43.08 E
Mineral Point	154	42.52 N	90.11 W
Mineral Wells	160	32.48 N	98.07 W
Minersville	152	40.41 N	76.16 W
Minerva	152	40.44 N	81.06 W
Minervino Murge	78	41.05 N	16.05 E
Mineville	152	44.05 N	73.31 W
Minfeng	88	37.05 N	82.40 E
Mingečaur	82	40.45 N	47.03 E
Mingela	120	19.53 S	146.38 E
Mingo Junction	152	40.19 N	80.37 W
Mingo Lake ⊜	142	64.35 N	72.10 W
Minho □[9]	76	41.40 N	8.30 W
Minho (Miño) ≃	76	41.52 N	8.51 W
Minicoy Island I	100	8.17 N	73.04 E
Minigwal, Lake ⊜	122	29.35 S	123.12 E
Minilya	122	23.51 S	113.58 E
Minjar	82	55.04 N	57.33 E
Minjiang ≃, Zhg.	88	28.54 N	105.28 E
Minjiang ≃, Zhg.	88	26.05 N	119.32 E
Minlaton	120	34.46 S	137.36 E
Minle	88	38.27 N	100.56 E
Minna	114	9.37 N	6.33 E
Minneapolis, Kans., U.S.	162	39.08 N	97.42 W
Minneapolis, Minn., U.S.	154	44.59 N	93.13 W
Minnechaduza Creek ≃	162	42.54 N	100.29 W
Minnedosa	142	50.14 N	99.51 W
Minnehaha	166	45.39 N	122.37 W
Minneola	162	37.26 N	100.01 W
Minneota	162	44.58 N	93.12 W
Minnesota □[3]	144	46.00 N	94.15 W
Minnesota ≃	154	44.54 N	93.10 W
Minnie Creek	122	24.02 S	115.42 E
Minnipa	122	32.51 S	135.09 E
Miño (Minho) ≃	76	41.52 N	8.51 W
Minong	154	46.06 N	91.49 W
Minonk	154	40.54 N	89.02 W
Minot	162	48.14 N	101.18 W
Minshan ⋀	88	33.15 N	103.15 E
Minsk	86	53.54 N	27.34 E
Minsk □[4]	66	54.30 N	28.00 E
Mińsk Mazowiecki	72	52.11 N	21.34 E
Minster	152	40.24 N	84.23 W
Mintaka Pass)(	102	36.58 N	74.54 E
Minto, N.B., Can.	150	46.05 N	66.05 W
Minto, Alaska, U.S.	146	64.53 N	149.11 W
Minto, Lac ⊜	142	51.00 N	73.37 W
Minto Inlet C	142	71.20 N	117.00 W
Minturn	164	39.35 N	106.26 W
Minturno	78	41.15 N	13.45 E
Minūf	112	30.28 N	30.56 E
Minusinsk	84	53.43 N	91.42 E
Minxian	88	34.22 N	104.08 E
Mio	154	44.39 N	84.08 W
Miory	86	55.37 N	27.38 E
Mir	86	53.27 N	26.28 E
Mira	78	45.26 N	12.08 E
Miracema do Norte	134	9.33 S	48.24 W
Mirador	134	6.22 S	44.22 W
Miraflores	138	5.12 N	73.12 W
Miraj	100	16.50 N	74.39 E
Miramar	140	38.16 S	57.52 W
Miramas	74	43.35 N	5.00 E
Mirambeau	74	45.23 N	0.34 W
Miramichi Bay C	150	47.08 N	65.08 W
Miranda □[3]	138	10.15 N	66.25 W
Miranda ≃	134	19.25 S	57.20 W
Miranda de Ebro	76	42.41 N	2.57 W
Miranda do Douro	76	41.30 N	6.16 W
Mirande	74	43.31 N	0.25 E
Mirandela	76	41.29 N	7.11 W
Mirandola	78	44.53 N	11.04 E
Mirbāṭ	100	17.00 N	54.45 E
Mirebeau-sur-Bèze	74	47.24 N	5.19 E
Mirecourt	74	48.18 N	6.08 E
Miri	96	4.23 N	113.59 E
Miriam Vale	120	24.20 S	151.34 E
Mirim, Lagoa (Laguna Merín C	140	32.45 S	52.50 W
Mirnyj, S.S.S.R.	66	53.30 N	50.18 E
Mirnyj, S.S.S.R.	84	62.33 N	113.53 E
Mirow	72	53.16 N	12.49 E
Mīrpur	100	33.11 N	73.47 E
Mīrpur Khās	102	25.32 N	69.00 E
Mirranponga Pangunna Lake ⊜	120	25.56 S	137.42 E
Mirzāpur	102	25.09 N	82.35 E
Misāḥah, Bi′r ▼[4]	112	22.12 N	27.57 E
Misantla	130	19.56 N	96.50 W
Mishan	88	45.33 N	131.52 E
Mishawaka	158	41.40 N	86.11 W
Mishicot	154	44.14 N	87.38 W
Mishmi Hills ⋀[2]	102	29.00 N	96.00 E
Misilmeri	78	38.01 N	13.27 E
Misima Island I	124	10.40 S	152.45 E
Misiones □[5]	140	27.00 S	57.00 W
Miskitos, Cayos II	132	14.23 N	82.46 W
Miskolc	72	48.06 N	20.47 E
Misool, Pulau I	124	1.52 S	130.10 E
Misrātah	108	32.23 N	15.06 E
Missinaibi ≃	154	50.44 N	81.29 W
Missinaibi Lake ⊜	154	48.23 N	83.40 W
Mission, Kans., U.S.	158	39.03 N	94.38 W
Mission, Tex., U.S.	160	26.13 N	98.20 W
Mission City	148	49.08 N	122.18 W
Mississinewa ≃	158	40.46 N	86.02 W
Mississippi □[3]	144	32.50 N	89.30 W
Mississippi ≃	144	29.00 N	89.15 W
Mississippi City	158	30.24 N	89.01 W
Mississippi Delta ≃[2]	158	29.10 N	89.15 W
Mississippi Sound ⌣	158	30.15 N	88.40 W
Missoula	166	46.52 N	114.01 W
Missouri □[3]	144	38.30 N	93.30 W
Missouri ≃	144	38.50 N	90.08 W
Missouri, Coteau du ⋀[2]	162	46.00 N	99.30 W
Missouri Valley	162	41.33 N	95.53 W
Mistake Creek	124	17.06 S	129.04 E
Mistassibi ≃	142	48.53 N	72.13 W
Mistassini, Lac ⊜	142	51.00 N	73.37 W
Mistelbach an der Zaya	72	48.34 N	16.35 E
Misterbianco	78	37.31 N	15.01 E
Misteriosa Bank ✧[4]	132	18.52 N	83.50 W
Misti, Volcán ∧[1]	134	16.17 S	71.24 W
Mistretta	78	37.56 N	14.22 E
Mita, Punta de ≻	130	20.47 N	105.33 W
Mitchell, Austl.	120	26.29 S	147.58 E
Mitchell, Ont., Can.	154	43.28 N	81.12 W
Mitchell, Ind., U.S.	158	38.44 N	86.28 W
Mitchell, Nebr., U.S.	162	41.57 N	103.48 W
Mitchell, S. Dak., U.S.	162	43.43 N	104.01 W
Mitchell ≃, Austl.	120	29.21 S	152.32 E
Mitchell ≃, Austl.	120	37.53 S	147.41 E
Mitchell, Mount ∧	156	35.46 N	82.16 W
Mitchell River Mission	124	15.28 S	141.44 E
Mitchellville	154	41.40 N	93.22 W
Mitchelstown	70	52.16 N	8.16 W
Mitilíni	80	39.06 N	26.32 E
Mito	90	36.22 N	140.28 E
Mitsio, Nosy I	117b	12.54 S	48.36 E
Mittenwald	72	47.27 N	11.15 E
Mittersill	72	47.16 N	12.29 E
Mittweida	72	50.59 N	12.59 E
Mitú	138	1.08 N	70.03 W
Mitumba, Monts ⋀	110	6.00 S	29.00 E
Mitwaba	110	8.38 S	27.20 E
Mitzic	110	0.47 N	11.34 E
Miyake-jima I	90	34.05 N	139.32 E
Miyako	90	39.38 N	141.57 E
Miyako-jima I	88	24.47 N	125.20 E
Miyakonojō	90	31.44 N	131.04 E
Miyazaki	90	31.54 N	131.26 E
Miyazu	90	35.32 N	135.11 E
Miyun	88	40.22 N	116.50 E
Mizdah	108	31.26 N	12.59 E
Mizen Head ≻	70	51.27 N	9.49 W
Mizque	134	17.56 S	65.19 W
Mjölby	68	58.19 N	15.08 E
Mjøndalen	68	59.45 N	10.01 E
Mjøsa ⊜	68	60.40 N	11.00 E
Mkalama	110	4.07 S	34.38 E
Mladá Boleslav	72	50.23 N	14.59 E
Mladenovac	80	44.26 N	20.42 E
Mlanje Peak → Sapitwa ∧	110	15.57 S	35.36 E
Mława	72	53.06 N	20.23 E
Mo	66	66.15 N	14.08 E
Mo ≃	114	8.45 N	11.36 W
Moa ≃	114	6.59 N	11.36 W
Moa, Pulau I	124	8.10 S	127.56 E
Moab	164	38.35 N	109.33 W
Moama	120	36.07 S	144.47 E
Moanda, Gabon	110	1.34 S	13.11 E
Moanda, Zaïre	110	5.56 S	12.21 E
Moate	70	53.24 N	7.58 W
Mobaye	108	4.19 N	21.11 E
Moberly	158	39.25 N	92.26 W
Mobile	158	30.42 N	88.05 W
Mobridge	162	45.32 N	100.26 W
Moca	132	19.24 N	70.31 W
Moçambique	110	15.06 S	40.50 E
Moçâmedes	110	15.10 S	12.09 E
Mocha → Al-Mukhā	100	13.19 N	43.15 E
Mocha, Isla I	140	38.22 S	73.56 W
Mochudi	116	24.28 S	26.05 E
Mocímboa da Praia	110	11.20 S	40.21 E
Mocksville	156	35.54 N	80.34 W
Môco, Serra ∧	110	12.28 S	15.10 E
Mocorito	130	25.29 N	107.55 W
Moctezuma	130	29.48 N	109.42 W
Mocuba	110	16.50 S	36.59 E
Modane	74	45.12 N	6.40 E
Modder ≃	116	29.02 S	24.37 E
Modena	78	44.40 N	10.55 E
Modesto	168	37.39 N	120.60 W
Modica	78	36.51 N	14.47 E
Modjokerto	92	7.28 S	112.26 E
Mödling	72	48.05 N	16.17 E
Modowi	124	4.05 S	134.39 E
Moe	120	38.10 S	146.15 E
Moei ≃	94	17.50 N	97.42 E
Moelv	68	60.56 N	10.42 E
Moengo	134	5.37 N	54.24 W
Moenkopi	164	36.07 N	111.13 W
Moers	72	51.27 N	6.37 E
Moffat	70	55.20 N	3.27 W
Moffit	162	46.41 N	100.18 W
Moga	102	30.48 N	75.10 E
Mogadisho	108	2.01 N	45.20 E
Mogador → Essaouira	106	31.30 N	9.47 W
Mogadouro	76	41.20 N	6.39 W
Mogaung	94	25.18 N	96.56 E
Mogi das Cruzes	140	23.31 S	46.11 W
Mogi-Guaçu ≃	140	20.53 S	48.10 W
Mogil′ov	86	53.54 N	30.21 E
Mogil′ov-Podol′skij	82	48.27 N	27.48 E
Mogincual	110	15.35 S	40.25 E
Mogliano Veneto	78	45.33 N	12.14 E
Mogoča	84	53.44 N	119.44 E
Mogočin	84	57.43 N	83.34 E
Mogotón, Cerro ∧	132	13.45 N	86.26 W
Moguer	76	37.16 N	6.50 W
Mogzon	84	51.45 N	111.58 E
Mohács	72	45.59 N	18.42 E
Mohammedia	106	33.44 N	7.24 W
Mohave, Lake ⊜[1]	168	35.25 N	114.38 W
Mohawk ≃	152	42.47 N	73.42 W
Mohe	88	53.29 N	122.19 E
Moheli I	117a	12.15 S	43.45 E
Moi	68	58.28 N	6.32 E
Moinești	80	46.28 N	26.29 E
Mointy	82	47.13 N	73.21 E
Mõisaküla	86	58.06 N	25.11 E
Moisdon	74	47.37 N	1.22 W
Moisie ≃	150	50.12 N	66.04 W
Moissac	74	44.06 N	1.05 E
Moita	76	38.39 N	8.59 W
Mojave	168	35.03 N	118.10 W
Mojave Desert ⬥[2]	168	35.00 N	117.00 W
Mojjero ≃	84	68.44 N	103.42 E
Mojo	108	8.38 N	39.07 E
Mojo, Pulau I	96	8.15 S	117.32 E
Mokp′o	88	34.48 N	126.22 E
Mokša ≃	86	54.44 N	41.53 E
Mokuleia	170c	21.35 N	158.09 W
Mol	72	51.11 N	5.06 E
Mola di Bari	78	41.04 N	17.05 E
Mold	70	53.10 N	3.08 W
Moldau → Vltava ≃	72	50.21 N	14.30 E
Moldavia □[9]	80	46.30 N	27.00 E
Moldavian Soviet Socialist Republic → Moldavskaja Sovetskaja Socialističeskaja Respublika □[3]	64	47.00 N	29.00 E
Moldavskaja Sovetskaja Socialističeskaja Respublika □[3]	64	47.00 N	29.00 E
Molde	68	62.44 N	7.11 E
Moldoveanu ∧	80	45.36 N	24.44 E
Molepolole	116	24.25 S	25.30 E
Molėtai	86	55.14 N	25.25 E
Molfetta	78	41.12 N	16.36 E
Molina de Segura	76	38.03 N	1.12 W
Moline, Ill., U.S.	154	41.30 N	90.31 W
Moline, Kans., U.S.	162	37.22 N	96.18 W
Molino	158	30.43 N	87.20 W
Molins de Rey	76	41.25 N	2.01 E
Molise □[4]	78	41.35 N	14.30 E
Molkom	68	59.36 N	13.43 E
Mollendo	134	17.02 S	72.01 W
Mölln	72	53.37 N	10.41 E
Mölndal	68	57.39 N	12.01 E
Moločnoje	86	59.17 N	39.41 E
Molodečno	86	54.19 N	26.49 E
Molong	120	33.06 S	148.52 E
Molopo ≃	116	28.30 S	20.13 E
Molotov → Perm′	64	58.00 N	56.15 E
Molsheim	74	48.32 N	7.29 E
Molson Lake ⊜	142	54.12 N	96.45 W
Molu, Pulau I	124	6.45 S	131.33 E
Moluccas → Maluku II	92	2.00 S	128.00 E
Molucca Sea → Maluku, Laut ▼[2]	92	0.30 S	125.00 E
Moma	110	16.44 S	39.14 E
Moma ≃	84	66.26 N	143.06 E
Mombasa	110	4.03 S	39.40 E
Mombetsu	90a	44.21 N	143.22 E
Momence	154	41.10 N	87.40 W
Mompós	138	9.14 N	74.26 W
Momskij Chrebet ⋀	84	66.00 N	146.00 E
Møn I	68	55.00 N	12.20 E
Mona, Canal de la ⌣	132	18.30 N	67.45 W
Mona, Isla I	132	18.05 N	67.53 W
Monaco	74	43.42 N	7.23 E
Monaco □[1]	64	43.45 N	7.25 E
Monagas □[3]	138	9.20 N	63.00 W
Monaghan	70	54.15 N	6.58 W
Monaghan □[6]	70	54.10 N	7.00 W
Monahans	160	31.36 N	102.54 W
Monashee Mountains ⋀	148	50.30 N	118.30 W
Monastir → Bitola	80	41.01 N	21.20 E
Monastyrščina	86	54.21 N	31.50 E
Moncalieri	78	45.00 N	7.41 E
Monção, Bra.	134	3.30 S	45.15 W
Monção, Port.	76	42.05 N	8.29 W
Mončegorsk	66	67.54 N	32.58 E
Mönchengladbach	72	51.12 N	6.28 E
Monchique	76	37.19 N	8.33 W
Moncks Corner	156	33.12 N	80.01 W
Monclova	130	26.54 N	101.25 W
Moncontour	74	48.21 N	2.39 W
Moncoutant	74	46.43 N	0.35 W
Moncton	150	46.06 N	64.47 W
Mondoubleau	74	47.59 N	0.54 E
Mondovì, It.	78	44.23 N	7.49 E
Mondovi, Wis., U.S.	154	44.34 N	91.40 W
Mondragone	78	41.07 N	13.53 E
Mondsee	72	47.52 N	13.21 E
Monessen	152	40.09 N	79.53 W
Monesterio	76	38.05 N	6.16 W
Monett	158	36.55 N	93.55 W
Monfalcone	78	45.49 N	13.32 E
Monflanquin	74	44.32 N	0.46 E
Monforte	76	39.03 N	7.26 W
Monforte de Lemos	76	42.31 N	7.30 W
Mongala ≃	108	1.53 N	19.46 E
Mongalla	108	5.12 N	31.46 E
Mong-cai	94	21.32 N	107.58 E
Monger, Lake ⊜	122	29.15 S	117.05 E
Möng Hsat	92	20.32 N	99.15 E
Monghyr	102	25.23 N	86.28 E
Mongo	108	12.11 N	18.42 E
Mongo ≃	114	9.34 N	12.11 W
Mongol Altajn Nuruu ⋀	88	47.00 N	92.00 E
Mongolia □[1]	88	46.00 N	105.00 E
Mongu	110	15.15 S	23.09 E
Monheim	72	48.50 N	10.51 E
Monico	154	45.35 N	89.09 W
Monida Pass)(	166	44.33 N	112.18 W
Monino	86	55.50 N	38.11 E
Monistrol-sur-Loire	74	45.17 N	4.10 E
Mońki	72	53.24 N	22.49 E
Monkira	120	24.49 S	140.34 E
Monmouth, Wales, U.K.	70	51.50 N	2.43 W
Monmouth, Ill., U.S.	154	40.55 N	90.39 W
Monmouth, Oreg., U.S.	166	44.51 N	123.14 W
Mono ≃	114	6.17 N	1.51 E
Mono Lake ⊜	168	38.00 N	119.00 W
Monon	158	40.52 N	86.53 W
Monona	154	43.04 N	89.20 W
Monongahela	152	40.11 N	79.56 W
Monopoli	78	40.57 N	17.19 E
Monor	72	47.21 N	19.27 E
Monreale	78	38.05 N	13.17 E
Monroe, Ga., U.S.	156	33.47 N	83.43 W
Monroe, La., U.S.	158	32.33 N	92.07 W
Monroe, Mich., U.S.	154	41.55 N	83.24 W
Monroe, N.C., U.S.	156	34.59 N	80.33 W
Monroe, N.Y., U.S.	152	41.20 N	74.11 W
Monroe, Va., U.S.	156	37.30 N	79.08 W
Monroe, Wash., U.S.	166	47.51 N	121.58 W
Monroe, Wis., U.S.	154	42.36 N	89.38 W
Monroe City, Ind., U.S.	158	38.37 N	87.21 W
Monroe City, Mo., U.S.	158	39.39 N	91.44 W
Monroeville, Ala., U.S.	158	31.31 N	87.20 W
Monroeville, Ohio, U.S.	152	41.15 N	82.42 W
Monrovia	114	6.18 N	10.47 W
Mons	72	50.27 N	3.56 E
Monschau	72	50.33 N	6.14 E
Monselice	78	45.14 N	11.45 E
Monson	152	45.17 N	69.30 W
Montabaur	72	50.26 N	7.50 E
Montagnana	78	45.14 N	11.28 E
Montagrier	74	45.16 N	0.29 E
Montagu	116	33.45 S	2.00 E
Montague, P.E.I., Can.	150	46.10 N	62.39 W
Montague, Calif., U.S.	168	41.44 N	122.32 W
Montague, Mich., U.S.	154	43.25 N	86.22 W
Montague Island I	146	60.00 N	147.30 W
Montaigu	74	46.59 N	1.19 W
Montaigut-en-Combraille	74	46.11 N	2.38 E
Montalcino	78	43.03 N	11.29 E
Montalegre	76	41.49 N	7.48 W
Montana	74	46.18 N	7.29 E
Montana □[3]	144	47.00 N	110.00 W
Montargil	76	39.05 N	8.10 W
Montargis	74	48.00 N	2.45 E
Montauban	74	44.01 N	1.21 E
Montbard	74	47.37 N	4.20 E
Montbarrey	74	47.01 N	5.39 E
Montbéliard	74	47.31 N	6.48 E
Mont Belvieu	160	29.51 N	94.54 W
Montbrison	74	45.36 N	4.03 E
Montbron	74	45.40 N	0.30 E
Montceau [-les-Mines]	74	46.40 N	4.22 E
Montchanin	74	46.45 N	4.27 E
Montclair, Calif., U.S.	168	34.06 N	117.41 W
Montclair, N.J., U.S.	152	40.49 N	74.13 W
Mont-de-Marsan	74	43.53 N	0.30 W
Montdidier	74	49.39 N	2.34 E
Monteagle	158	35.15 N	85.50 W
Monteagudo	134	19.49 S	63.59 W
Monte Alegre	134	2.01 S	54.04 W
Monte Bello Islands II	122	20.25 S	115.32 E

Symbols in the index entries are identified on page 203.

Name	Page	Lat °′	Long °′
Monte Caseros	140	30.15 S	57.38 W
Montecatini Terme	78	43.53 N	10.46 E
Montecito	168	34.26 N	119.39 W
Monte Comán	140	34.36 S	67.50 W
Montecristi	132	19.52 N	71.39 W
Monte Cristo, Cerro ∧	128	14.25 N	89.21 W
Montego Bay	132	18.30 N	77.55 W
Monte Lindo ≃	140	23.56 S	57.12 W
Montello	168	41.16 N	114.12 W
Montemorelos	130	25.12 N	99.49 W
Montemor-o-Novo	76	38.39 N	8.13 W
Montemor-o-Velho	76	40.10 N	8.41 W
Montendre	74	45.17 N	0.24 W
Montenegro	140	29.42 S	51.28 W
Montepuez	110	12.32 S	40.27 E
Montepulciano	78	43.05 N	11.47 E
Monte Quemado	140	25.50 S	62.50 W
Montereau-faut-Yonne	74	48.23 N	2.57 E
Monterey, Calif., U.S.	168	36.37 N	121.55 W
Monterey, Tenn., U.S.	158	36.09 N	85.16 W
Monterey, Va., U.S.	152	38.25 N	79.35 W
Monterey Bay C	168	36.45 N	121.55 W
Montería	138	8.46 N	75.53 W
Monteros	140	27.10 S	65.30 W
Monterotondo	78	42.03 N	12.37 E
Monterrey	130	25.40 N	100.19 W
Montesano, It.	78	40.16 N	15.43 E
Montesano, Wash., U.S.	166	46.59 N	123.36 W
Monte Sant'Angelo	78	41.42 N	15.57 E
Montesarchio	78	41.04 N	14.38 E
Montes Claros	134	16.43 S	43.52 W
Montevallo	158	33.06 N	86.52 W
Montevarchi	78	43.31 N	11.34 E
Montevideo, Minn., U.S.	162	44.57 N	95.43 W
Montevideo, Ur.	140	34.53 S	56.11 W
Monte Vista	164	37.35 N	106.09 W
Montezuma, Ga., U.S.	156	32.18 N	84.02 W
Montezuma, Iowa, U.S.	154	41.35 N	92.32 W
Montfaucon	74	45.10 N	4.18 E
Montfort, Fr.	74	48.08 N	1.58 W
Montfort, Wis., U.S.	154	42.58 N	90.26 W
Montgomery, Wales, U.K.	70	52.33 N	3.03 W
Montgomery, Ala., U.S.	158	32.23 N	86.18 W
Montgomery, Mich., U.S.	158	41.47 N	84.48 W
Montgomery, Minn., U.S.	154	44.26 N	93.35 W
Montgomery, Pa., U.S.	152	41.10 N	76.52 W
Montgomery, W. Va., U.S.	152	38.11 N	81.19 W
Montgomery City	158	38.59 N	91.30 W
Montguyon	74	45.13 N	0.11 W
Monthermé	74	49.53 N	4.44 E
Monthey	74	46.15 N	6.57 E
Monthois	74	49.19 N	4.43 E
Monticello, Ark., U.S.	158	33.38 N	91.47 W
Monticello, Fla., U.S.	156	30.33 N	83.52 W
Monticello, Ga., U.S.	156	33.18 N	83.40 W
Monticello, Ill., U.S.	158	40.01 N	88.34 W
Monticello, Iowa, U.S.	154	42.15 N	91.12 W
Monticello, Ky., U.S.	158	36.50 N	84.51 W
Monticello, Minn., U.S.	154	45.18 N	93.48 W
Monticello, Miss., U.S.	158	31.33 N	90.07 W
Monticello, N.Y., U.S.	152	41.39 N	74.42 W
Montichiari	78	45.25 N	10.23 E
Montignac	74	45.04 N	1.10 E
Montigny-le-Roi	74	48.00 N	5.30 E
Montigny-sur-Aube	74	47.57 N	4.46 E
Montijo, Esp.	76	38.55 N	6.37 W
Montijo, Port.	76	38.42 N	8.58 W
Montilla	76	37.35 N	4.38 W
Montivilliers	74	49.33 N	0.12 E
Mont-Joli	150	48.35 N	68.11 W
Mont-Laurier	142	46.33 N	75.30 W
Mont-Louis	74	42.31 N	2.07 E
Montluçon	74	46.21 N	2.36 E
Montluel	74	45.51 N	5.03 E
Montmagny	150	46.59 N	70.33 W
Montmédy	74	49.31 N	5.22 E
Montmirail	74	48.06 N	0.48 E
Montmoreau-Saint-Cybard	74	45.24 N	0.08 E
Montmorency	150	46.52 N	71.09 W
Montmorillon	74	46.26 N	0.52 E
Montmort	74	48.55 N	3.49 E
Monto	120	24.52 S	151.07 E
Montoro	76	38.01 N	4.23 W
Montour Falls	152	42.21 N	76.51 W
Montoursville	152	41.15 N	76.55 W
Montpelier, Idaho, U.S.	166	42.19 N	111.18 W
Montpelier, Ind., U.S.	152	40.33 N	85.17 W
Montpelier, Ohio, U.S.	152	41.35 N	84.36 W
Montpelier, Vt., U.S.	152	44.16 N	72.35 W
Montpellier	74	43.36 N	3.53 E
Montpon-Ménesterol	74	45.00 N	0.10 E
Montréal	152	45.31 N	73.34 W
Montreal ≃	154	46.44 N	90.25 W
Montreal Lake ⊜	142	54.20 N	105.40 W
Montrésor	74	47.09 N	1.12 E
Montreuil	74	50.28 N	1.46 E
Montreuil-Bellay	74	47.08 N	0.09 W
Montreux	74	46.26 N	6.55 E
Montrevel [-en-Bresse]	74	46.20 N	5.08 E
Montrichard	74	47.21 N	1.11 E
Montrose, Scot., U.K.	70	56.43 N	2.29 W
Montrose, Colo., U.S.	164	38.29 N	107.53 W
Montrose, Iowa, U.S.	154	40.31 N	91.25 W
Montrose, Mich., U.S.	154	43.11 N	83.54 W
Montross	152	38.06 N	76.50 W
Montserrat □²	128	16.45 N	62.12 W
Montsûrs	70	48.08 N	0.33 W
Montvale	156	37.23 N	79.43 W
Monument Draw V	160	32.26 N	102.10 W
Monument Valley V	164	36.50 N	110.20 W
Monywa	94	22.05 N	95.08 E
Monza	78	45.35 N	9.16 E
Moodie Island I	142	64.37 N	65.30 W
Moolawatana	120	29.55 S	139.43 E
Moonie ≃	120	29.19 S	148.43 E
Moonta	120	34.04 S	137.35 E
Moora	122	30.39 S	116.00 E
Moorarie	122	25.56 S	117.35 E
Moorcroft	162	44.16 N	104.57 W
Moore, Idaho, U.S.	166	43.44 N	113.22 W
Moore, Okla., U.S.	160	35.20 N	97.29 W
Moore, Lake ⊜	122	29.50 S	117.35 E
Moorefield	152	39.04 N	78.58 W
Moore Reservoir ⊜¹	152	44.25 N	71.50 W
Mooresville, Ind., U.S.	158	39.37 N	86.22 W
Mooresville, N.C., U.S.	156	35.35 N	80.48 W
Moorhead, Minn., U.S.	162	46.53 N	96.45 W
Moorhead, Miss., U.S.	158	33.27 N	90.30 W
Moornanyah Lake ⊜	120	33.02 S	143.58 E
Moosburg	72	48.29 N	11.57 E
Moosehead Lake ⊜	152	45.40 N	69.40 W
Moose Jaw	142	50.23 N	105.32 W
Moose Lake	154	46.26 N	92.45 W
Moose Pass	146	60.29 N	149.22 W
Moosomin	142	50.07 N	101.40 W
Moosonee	142	51.17 N	80.39 W
Mopti	114	14.30 N	4.12 W
Moquegua	134	17.20 S	70.55 W
Mór	72	47.23 N	18.12 E
Mora, Esp.	76	39.41 N	3.46 W
Mora, Port.	76	38.56 N	8.10 W
Mora, Minn., U.S.	154	45.53 N	93.18 W
Mora, N. Mex., U.S.	164	35.58 N	105.20 W
Morādābād	102	28.50 N	78.47 E
Mora de Rubielos	76	40.15 N	0.45 W
Morafenobe	117b	17.49 S	44.55 E
Mórahalom	72	46.13 N	19.54 E
Moraleda, Canal ⋓	136	44.30 S	73.30 W
Morant Bay	132	17.50 N	76.25 W
Morant Cays II	132	17.22 N	76.00 W
Mor'arovskij Zaton	84	56.45 N	84.41 E
Moratalla	76	38.12 N	1.53 W
Moratuwa	100	6.46 N	79.53 E
Morava □⁹	72	49.20 N	17.00 E
Morava (March) ≃	72	48.10 N	16.59 E
Moravia, Iowa, U.S.	154	40.53 N	92.49 W
Moravia, N.Y., U.S.	152	42.43 N	76.25 W
Morawhanna	138	8.17 N	59.44 W
Moray Firth C¹	70	57.50 N	3.30 W
Morbegno	78	46.08 N	9.34 E
Morbihan □⁵	74	47.55 N	2.50 W
Morcenx	74	44.02 N	0.55 W
Morden	162	49.11 N	98.05 W
Moreau ≃	162	45.18 N	100.43 W
Morecambe	70	54.04 N	2.53 W
Moree, Austl.	120	29.28 S	149.51 E
Morée, Fr.	74	47.54 N	1.14 E
Morehead	152	38.11 N	83.25 W
Morehead City	156	34.43 N	76.43 W
Morelia	130	19.42 N	101.07 W
Morena, Sierra ∧∧	76	38.00 N	5.00 W
Morenci	154	41.43 N	84.13 W
Møre og Romsdal □⁶	68	62.40 N	7.50 E
Moresby Island I	148	52.50 N	131.55 W
Morestel	74	45.40 N	5.28 E
Moreton Island I	120	27.10 S	153.25 E
Moreuil	74	49.46 N	2.29 E
Morez	74	46.31 N	6.02 E
Morgan City, Ala., U.S.	158	34.28 N	86.34 W
Morgan City, La., U.S.	158	29.42 N	91.12 W
Morganfield	158	37.41 N	87.55 W
Morgan Hill	168	37.08 N	121.39 W
Morganton	156	35.45 N	81.41 W
Morgantown, Ky., U.S.	158	37.14 N	86.41 W
Morgantown, Miss., U.S.	158	31.19 N	89.55 W
Morgantown, W. Va., U.S.	152	39.38 N	79.57 W
Morganza	158	30.44 N	91.36 W
Morghāb (Murgab) ≃	104	38.18 N	61.12 E
Moriah, Mount ∧	168	39.17 N	114.12 W
Moriarty	164	34.59 N	106.03 W
Moringen	72	51.42 N	9.52 E
Morioka	90	39.42 N	141.09 E
Morisset	120	33.06 S	151.29 E
Morkoka ≃	84	65.10 N	115.52 E
Morley	154	43.29 N	85.27 W
Morney	120	25.22 S	141.28 E
Mornington	120	38.13 S	145.03 E
Mornington, Isla I	136	49.45 S	75.20 W
Mornington Island I	120	16.33 S	139.24 E
Moro ≃	114	7.25 N	11.03 W
Morocco	158	40.57 N	87.27 W
Morocco □¹	106	32.00 N	5.00 W
Morogoro	110	6.49 S	37.40 E
Moro Gulf C	98	6.30 N	123.10 E
Moroleón	130	20.08 N	101.12 W
Morombe	117b	21.45 S	43.22 E
Morón, Cuba	132	22.06 N	78.38 W
Mörön, Mong.	88	49.38 N	100.10 E
Morona ≃	138	4.40 S	77.10 W
Morona-Santiago □⁴	138	2.30 S	78.00 W
Morondava	117b	20.17 S	44.17 E
Morón de Almazán	76	41.25 N	2.25 W
Morón de la Frontera	76	37.08 N	5.27 W
Moroni	117a	11.41 S	43.16 E
Morošečnoje	84	56.24 N	156.12 E
Morotai I	92	2.20 N	128.25 E
Morozovsk	82	48.22 N	41.50 E
Morpeth	70	55.10 N	1.41 W
Morrilton	158	35.09 N	92.45 W
Morrinhos	134	17.44 S	49.07 W
Morrinsville	126	37.39 S	175.32 E
Morris, Man., Can.	162	49.21 N	97.22 W
Morris, Ill., U.S.	154	41.22 N	88.26 W
Morris, Minn., U.S.	162	45.35 N	95.55 W
Morris, Okla., U.S.	160	35.36 N	95.51 W
Morris, Mount ∧	122	26.09 S	131.04 E
Morrisburg	152	44.54 N	75.11 W
Morrison	154	41.49 N	89.58 W
Morrisonville	158	39.25 N	89.27 W
Morristown, N.J., U.S.	152	40.48 N	74.29 W
Morristown, Tenn., U.S.	156	36.13 N	83.18 W
Morrisville, N.Y., U.S.	152	42.54 N	75.39 W
Morrisville, Pa., U.S.	152	40.13 N	74.47 W
Morrisville, Vt., U.S.	152	44.34 N	72.44 W
Morro, Punta ≻	140	27.07 S	70.57 W
Morro Bay	168	35.22 N	120.51 W
Morro do Chapéu	134	11.33 S	41.09 W
Morrumbene	116	23.39 S	35.20 E
Moršansk	86	53.26 N	41.49 E
Mortagne	74	48.31 N	0.33 E
Mortagne-sur-Sèvre	74	47.00 N	0.57 W
Mortain	74	48.39 N	0.56 W
Mortara	78	45.15 N	8.44 E
Morteau	74	47.04 N	6.37 E
Morteros	140	30.40 S	62.00 W
Mortes, Rio das ≃	134	11.45 S	50.44 W
Mortlake	120	38.05 S	142.48 E
Morton, Ill., U.S.	154	40.37 N	89.28 W
Morton, Miss., U.S.	158	32.21 N	89.40 W
Morton, Tex., U.S.	160	33.44 N	102.46 W
Mortons Gap	158	37.14 N	87.28 W
Moruya	120	35.55 S	150.05 E
Morven	120	26.25 S	147.07 E
Morvi	102	22.49 N	70.50 E
Morwell	120	38.14 S	146.24 E
Mosal'sk	86	54.29 N	34.59 E
Mosbach	72	49.21 N	9.08 E
Mosby	68	58.14 N	7.54 E
Moscow → Moskva, S.S.S.R.	86	55.45 N	37.35 E
Moscow, Idaho, U.S.	166	46.44 N	117.00 W
Mosel □⁵	72	50.22 N	7.36 E
Mosel (Moselle) ≃	74	50.22 N	7.36 E
Moselle □⁵	74	49.00 N	6.30 E
Moselle (Mosel) ≃	74	50.22 N	7.36 E
Moses Lake	166	47.08 N	119.17 W
Moses Point	146	64.42 N	162.03 W
Mosgiel	126	45.53 S	170.21 E
Mosheim	156	36.11 N	82.57 W
Moshi	110	3.21 S	37.20 E
Mosinee	154	44.47 N	89.43 W
Mosjøen	66	65.50 N	13.10 E
Moskva (Moscow)	86	55.45 N	37.35 E
Mosonmagyaróvár	72	47.51 N	17.17 E
Mosquera	138	2.30 N	78.29 W
Mosquero	160	35.47 N	103.58 W
Mosquitos, Golfo de los C	138	9.00 N	81.20 W
Moss	68	59.26 N	10.42 E
Mossaka	110	1.13 S	16.48 E
Mosselbaai	116	34.11 S	22.08 E
Mossendjo	110	2.57 S	12.44 E
Mossman	124	16.28 S	145.22 E
Mossoró	134	5.11 S	37.20 W
Moss Point	158	30.25 N	88.29 W
Moss Vale	120	34.33 S	150.22 E
Most	72	50.32 N	13.39 E
Mosta	86	56.32 N	42.10 E
Mostaganem	106	35.51 N	0.07 E
Mostar	78	43.20 N	17.49 E
Mostardas	140	31.06 S	50.57 W
Møsting, Kap ≻	142	64.00 N	41.00 W
Mostiska	72	49.48 N	23.09 E
Mosty	86	53.25 N	24.32 E
Mosul → Al-Mawṣil	104	36.20 N	43.08 E
Mota	108	11.02 N	37.52 E
Motagua ≃	128	15.44 N	88.14 W
Motala	68	58.33 N	15.03 E
Motril	76	36.45 N	3.31 W
Motru	80	44.50 N	23.00 E
Mottola	78	40.38 N	17.03 E
Motueka	126	41.07 S	173.00 E
Motygino	84	58.11 N	94.40 E
Motyklejka	84	59.26 N	148.38 E
Mouchoir Bank ✦⁴	132	20.55 N	70.45 W
Mouchoir Passage ⋓	132	21.15 N	71.00 W
Moudjéria	114	17.53 N	12.20 W
Moudon	74	46.40 N	6.48 E
Mouila	110	1.52 S	11.01 E
Moulamein	120	35.05 S	144.02 E
Moulamein Creek ≃	120	35.06 S	144.02 E
Moulay-Idriss	106	34.02 N	5.27 W
Moulins	74	46.34 N	3.20 E
Moulins-la-Marche	74	48.39 N	0.29 E
Moulmein	94	16.30 N	97.38 E
Moulouya, Oued ≃	106	35.05 N	2.25 W
Moulton	158	34.29 N	87.18 W
Moultrie	156	31.11 N	83.47 W
Mound City, Ill., U.S.	158	37.05 N	89.10 W
Mound City, Mo., U.S.	158	40.07 N	95.14 W
Moundou	108	8.34 N	16.05 E
Moundridge	162	38.12 N	97.31 W
Mounds	160	35.53 N	96.04 W
Moundsville	152	39.55 N	80.44 W
Mountain ≃	146	65.41 N	128.50 W
Mountainair	164	34.31 N	106.15 W
Mountain Brook	158	33.29 N	86.46 W
Mountain Creek	158	32.43 N	86.29 W
Mountain Grove	158	37.08 N	92.16 W
Mountain Home, Ark., U.S.	158	36.20 N	92.23 W
Mountain Home, Idaho, U.S.	166	43.08 N	115.41 W
Mountain Iron	154	47.32 N	92.37 W
Mountain Lake	162	43.57 N	94.56 W
Mountain Nile (Baḥr al-Jabal) ≃	112	9.30 N	30.30 E
Mountain Pine	158	34.34 N	93.10 W
Mountain Point	146	55.18 N	131.32 W
Mountain View, Calif., U.S.	168	37.23 N	122.04 W
Mountain View, Okla., U.S.	160	35.06 N	98.45 W
Mountain Village	146	62.05 N	163.44 W
Mount Airy	156	36.31 N	80.37 W
Mount Angel	166	45.04 N	122.48 W
Mount Ayr	162	40.43 N	94.14 W
Mount Barker, Austl.	120	35.04 S	138.52 E
Mount Barker, Austl.	122	34.38 S	117.40 E
Mount Berry	156	34.17 N	85.11 W
Mount Carmel, Ill., U.S.	158	38.25 N	87.46 W
Mount Carmel, Pa., U.S.	152	40.48 N	76.25 W
Mount Carroll	154	42.06 N	89.58 W
Mount Clemens	154	42.36 N	82.53 W
Mount Dora	156	28.48 N	81.38 W
Mount Edgecumbe	146	57.03 N	135.21 W
Mount Forest	154	43.59 N	80.44 W
Mount Gambier	120	37.50 S	140.46 E
Mount Garnet	120	17.41 S	145.07 E
Mount Gay	152	37.51 N	82.00 W
Mount Gilead, N.C., U.S.	156	35.10 N	79.56 W
Mount Gilead, Ohio, U.S.	152	40.33 N	82.50 W
Mount Hagen	124	5.50 S	144.15 E
Mount Holly	156	35.18 N	81.01 W
Mount Holly Springs	152	40.07 N	77.11 W
Mount Hope, Kans., U.S.	162	37.52 N	97.40 W
Mount Hope, W. Va., U.S.	152	37.54 N	81.10 W
Mount Horeb	154	43.00 N	89.44 W
Mount Isa	120	20.44 S	139.30 E
Mount Jackson	152	38.45 N	78.39 W
Mount Jewett	152	41.44 N	78.38 W
Mount Kisco	152	41.12 N	73.44 W
Mount Lebanon	152	40.23 N	80.03 W
Mount Magnet	122	28.04 S	117.49 E
Mount Manara	120	32.29 S	143.56 E
Mount Maunganui	126	37.38 S	176.11 E
Mountmellick	70	53.07 N	7.20 W
Mount Molloy	124	16.41 S	145.20 E
Mount Monger	122	30.59 S	121.53 E
Mount Morgan	120	23.39 S	150.23 E
Mount Morris, Ill., U.S.	154	42.03 N	89.26 W
Mount Morris, Mich., U.S.	154	43.07 N	83.42 W
Mount Morris, N.Y., U.S.	152	42.44 N	77.53 W
Mount Mulligan	120	16.51 S	144.52 E
Mount Olive, Ill., U.S.	158	39.04 N	89.43 W
Mount Olive, Miss., U.S.	158	31.46 N	89.39 W
Mount Olive, N.C., U.S.	156	35.12 N	78.04 W
Mount Perry	120	25.11 S	151.39 E
Mount Pleasant, Iowa, U.S.	154	40.58 N	91.33 W
Mount Pleasant, Mich., U.S.	154	43.35 N	84.47 W
Mount Pleasant, Pa., U.S.	152	40.09 N	79.33 W
Mount Pleasant, S.C., U.S.	156	32.47 N	79.52 W
Mount Pleasant, Tenn., U.S.	158	35.32 N	87.13 W
Mount Pleasant, Tex., U.S.	160	33.09 N	94.58 W
Mount Pocono	152	41.08 N	75.22 W
Mount Pulaski	158	40.01 N	89.17 W
Mount Rebecca	122	26.48 S	135.10 E
Mount Roskill	126	36.55 S	174.45 E
Mount Shasta	168	41.19 N	122.19 W
Mount Sterling, Ill., U.S.	158	39.59 N	90.45 W
Mount Sterling, Ky., U.S.	156	38.04 N	83.56 W
Mount Surprise	120	18.09 S	144.19 E
Mount Union	152	40.23 N	77.53 W
Mount Vernon, Austl.	122	24.13 S	118.14 E
Mount Vernon, Ala., U.S.	158	31.05 N	88.01 W
Mount Vernon, Ga., U.S.	156	32.11 N	82.36 W
Mount Vernon, Ill., U.S.	158	38.19 N	88.55 W
Mount Vernon, Ind., U.S.	158	37.56 N	87.54 W
Mount Vernon, Iowa, U.S.	154	41.55 N	91.23 W
Mount Vernon, Mo., U.S.	158	37.06 N	93.49 W
Mount Vernon, Ohio, U.S.	152	40.23 N	82.29 W
Mount Vernon, Wash., U.S.	166	48.25 N	122.20 W
Mount Victory	152	40.32 N	83.31 W
Mount Wedge	122	33.29 S	135.10 E
Mount Wellington	126	36.54 S	174.51 E
Moura, Bra.	138	1.27 S	61.38 W
Moura, Port.	76	38.08 N	7.27 W
Mourdi, Dépression du •⁷	112	18.10 N	23.00 E
Mouscron	74	50.44 N	3.13 E
Moussoro	108	13.39 N	16.29 E
Moutier	74	47.17 N	7.23 E
Moûtiers	74	45.29 N	6.32 E
Moutong	96	0.28 N	121.14 E
Mouzon	74	49.36 N	5.05 E
Moville, Eire	70	55.11 N	7.03 W
Moville, Iowa, U.S.	162	42.29 N	96.04 W
Moweaqua	158	39.38 N	89.01 W
Moxos, Llanos de ≚	134	15.00 S	65.00 W
Moyagee	122	27.45 S	117.54 E
Moyale	108	3.32 N	39.03 E
Moyamba	114	8.10 N	12.26 W
Moyen Atlas ∧∧	106	33.30 N	5.00 W
Moyeuvre-Grande	74	49.15 N	6.02 E
Moyie Springs	166	48.43 N	116.11 W
Moyobamba	134	6.02 S	76.58 W
Možajsk	86	55.30 N	36.01 E
Mozambique □¹	110	18.15 S	35.00 E
Mozambique Channel ⋓	110	19.00 S	41.00 E
Mozdok	82	43.44 N	44.38 E
Možga	66	56.23 N	52.17 E
Mozyr'	64	52.03 N	29.14 E
Mpanda	110	6.22 S	31.02 E
Mpika	110	11.54 S	31.26 E
Mpraeso	114	6.35 N	0.44 W
Mpwapwa	110	6.21 S	36.29 E
Mrągowo	72	53.52 N	21.19 E
Mstera	86	56.23 N	41.56 E
Mstislavl'	86	54.02 N	31.42 E
Mszczonów	72	51.58 N	20.31 E
Mtwara	110	10.16 S	40.11 E
Mu, Cerro ∧	138	9.29 N	73.07 W
Muang Khammouan	94	17.24 N	104.48 E
Muang Luong Nam Tha	94	20.57 N	101.25 E
Muang Pakxan	94	18.22 N	103.39 E
Muang Xépôn	92	16.41 N	106.14 E
Muarasiberut	92	1.36 S	99.11 E
Muaratewe	96	0.57 S	114.53 E
Mubende	110	0.35 N	31.23 E
Mucajaí ≃	138	2.25 N	60.52 W
Muchanovo	86	56.31 N	38.20 E
Mücheln	72	51.18 N	11.48 E
Muchinga Mountains ∧∧	110	12.00 S	31.45 E
Muchtolovo	86	55.27 N	43.13 E
Muckadilla	120	26.35 S	148.23 E
Mucugê	134	13.00 S	41.23 W
Mucuri ≃	134	18.05 S	39.34 W
Mud ≃	152	38.25 N	82.17 W
Mudanjiang	88	44.35 N	129.36 E
Mudanjiang ≃	88	46.22 N	129.33 E
Mud Creek ≃	162	43.17 N	96.15 W
Mudgee	120	32.36 S	149.35 E
Mufulira	110	12.33 S	28.14 E
Mu Gia, Deo (Mu Gia Pass))(	94	17.40 N	105.47 E
Muğla	80	37.12 N	28.22 E
Mugodžary ∧∧²	82	49.00 N	58.40 E
Mugron	74	43.45 N	0.45 W
Muḥammad, Ra's ≻	112	27.44 N	34.15 E
Mühlacker	72	48.57 N	8.50 E
Mühldorf	72	48.15 N	12.32 E
Mühlhausen	72	51.12 N	10.27 E
Muhola	68	63.20 N	25.05 E
Muhos	68	64.48 N	25.59 E
Muiron Islands II	122	21.35 S	114.20 E
Muja	84	56.24 N	115.39 E
Mujnak	82	43.48 N	59.02 E
Mukačevo	72	48.27 N	22.45 E
Mukah	92	2.54 N	112.02 E
Mukden → Shenyang	88	41.48 N	123.27 E
Mukry	100	37.36 N	65.44 E
Mukwonago	154	42.52 N	88.20 W
Mulanje	110	16.02 S	35.30 E
Mulberry, Fla., U.S.	156	27.54 N	81.59 W
Mulberry, Ind., U.S.	158	40.21 N	86.40 W
Mulchatna ≃	146	59.39 N	157.08 W
Mulchén	140	37.43 S	72.14 W
Mul'da	66	67.28 N	63.34 E
Muldoon	160	29.49 N	97.04 W
Muleshoe	160	34.13 N	102.43 W
Mulga Downs	122	22.08 S	118.26 E
Mulgowie	120	27.43 S	152.22 E
Mulgul	122	24.49 S	118.26 E
Mulhacén ∧	76	37.03 N	3.19 W
Mulhall	160	36.04 N	97.24 W
Mulhouse	74	47.45 N	7.20 E
Mull, Island of I	70	56.27 N	6.00 W
Mullan	166	47.28 N	115.48 W
Mullengudgery	120	31.41 S	147.26 E
Mullens	156	37.35 N	81.23 W
Muller, Pegunungan ∧∧	96	0.40 N	113.50 E
Mullewa	122	28.33 S	115.31 E
Müllheim	72	47.48 N	7.38 E
Mulligan ≃	120	25.00 S	138.30 E
Mullin	160	31.33 N	98.40 W
Mullingar	70	53.32 N	7.20 W
Mullins	156	34.12 N	79.15 W
Mullinville	162	37.35 N	99.29 W
Mullumbimby	120	28.33 S	153.30 E
Multān	102	30.11 N	71.29 E
Multia	68	62.25 N	24.47 E
Mulvane	162	37.29 N	97.14 W
Mulyah Mountain ∧	120	30.37 S	144.31 E
Mumbwa	110	14.59 S	27.04 E
Mumford	160	30.44 N	96.34 W
Mun ≃	94	15.19 N	105.31 E
Muna ≃	84	67.52 N	123.06 E
Muna, Pulau I	96	5.00 S	122.30 E
Münchberg	72	50.11 N	11.47 E
München (Munich)	72	48.08 N	11.34 E
München-Gladbach → Mönchengladbach	72	51.12 N	6.28 E
Muncie	158	40.11 N	85.23 W
Muncoonie, Lake ⊜	120	25.20 S	138.30 E
Muncy	152	41.12 N	76.47 W
Munday	160	33.27 N	99.38 W
Mundelein	154	42.16 N	88.00 W
Münden	72	51.25 N	9.39 E
Mundiwindi	122	23.52 S	120.09 E
Mundubbera	120	25.36 S	151.18 E
Munfordville	158	37.16 N	85.54 W
Mungallala	120	26.27 S	147.33 E
Mungbere	108	2.38 N	28.30 E
Mungindi	120	28.58 S	148.59 E
Munhango	110	12.12 S	18.42 E
Munich → München	72	48.08 N	11.34 E
Munising	154	46.25 N	86.40 W
Munku-Sardyk, Gora ∧	84	51.45 N	100.32 E
Münsingen, B.R.D.	72	48.25 N	9.29 E
Münsingen, Schw.	74	46.53 N	7.34 E
Münster, B.R.D.	72	51.57 N	7.37 E
Munster, B.R.D.	72	52.59 N	10.05 E
Munster, Fr.	74	48.03 N	7.08 E
Munster □⁹	70	52.25 N	8.20 W
Muntok	96	2.04 S	105.11 E
Muong Ngoi	92	20.43 N	102.41 E
Muong Sing	94	21.11 N	101.09 E
Muonio	64	67.57 N	23.42 E
Muoro	78	40.20 N	9.20 E
Muqayshiṭ I	104	24.12 N	53.42 E
Mur (Mura) ≃	72	46.18 N	16.53 E
Mura (Mur) ≃	72	46.18 N	16.53 E
Muraši	66	59.24 N	48.55 E
Murat	74	45.07 N	2.52 E
Murat ≃	104	38.39 N	39.50 E
Murau	72	47.07 N	14.10 E
Murča	76	41.24 N	7.27 W
Murchison, Austl.	120	36.37 S	145.14 E
Murchison, Tex., U.S.	160	32.17 N	95.45 W
Murchison ≃	122	26.01 S	117.06 E
Murchison, Mount ∧	122	26.46 S	116.25 E
Murchison Falls L	108	2.17 N	31.41 E
Murcia	76	37.59 N	1.07 W
Murcia □⁹	76	38.30 N	1.45 W
Mur-de-Barrez	74	44.51 N	2.39 E
Murdo	162	43.53 N	100.43 W
Mureck	72	46.42 N	15.46 E
Mureș □⁴	80	46.35 N	24.40 E
Mureș (Maros) ≃	80	46.15 N	20.13 E
Muret	74	43.28 N	1.21 E
Murfreesboro, Ark., U.S.	158	34.04 N	93.41 W
Murfreesboro, N.C., U.S.	156	36.27 N	77.06 W
Murfreesboro, Tenn., U.S.	158	35.51 N	86.23 W
Murgab	82	38.10 N	73.59 E
Murgab (Morghāb) ≃	104	38.18 N	61.12 E
Murgon	120	26.15 S	151.57 E
Murmansk	66	68.58 N	33.05 E
Murmino	86	54.36 N	40.03 E
Murnau	72	47.40 N	11.12 E
Murom	86	55.34 N	42.02 E
Muroran	90a	42.18 N	140.59 E
Murphy	156	35.05 N	84.01 W
Murphys	168	38.08 N	120.28 W
Murphysboro	158	37.46 N	89.20 W
Murray, Ky., U.S.	158	36.37 N	88.19 W
Murray, Utah, U.S.	164	40.40 N	111.53 W
Murray ≃, Austl.	120	35.22 S	139.22 E
Murray ≃, B.C., Can.	148	55.40 N	121.10 W
Murray, Lake ⊜	124	7.00 S	141.30 E
Murray Bridge	120	35.07 S	139.17 E
Murray Maxwell Bay C	142	70.00 N	80.00 W
Murraysburg	116	31.58 S	23.47 E
Murree	100	33.54 N	73.24 E
Murrhardt	72	48.59 N	9.34 E
Murrumbidgee ≃	120	34.43 S	143.12 E
Murrumburrah	120	34.33 S	148.21 E
Murrurundi	120	31.46 S	150.50 E
Murska Sobota	78	46.40 N	16.10 E
Murten	74	46.56 N	7.07 E
Murtoa	120	36.37 S	142.28 E
Murtosa	76	40.44 N	8.38 W
Murud, Gunong ∧	96	3.52 N	115.30 E
Murukta	84	67.46 N	102.01 E
Murwāra	102	23.51 N	80.24 E
Murwillumbah	120	28.19 S	153.24 E
Mürzzuschlag	72	47.36 N	15.41 E
Muş	104	38.44 N	41.30 E
Mūsā, Jabal ∧	112	28.32 N	33.59 E
Musay'īd	100	24.59 N	51.32 E
Muscat → Masqaṭ	104	23.37 N	58.35 E
Muscat and Oman → Oman □¹	100	22.00 N	58.00 E
Muscatine	154	41.25 N	91.03 W
Mus-Chaja, Gora ∧	84	62.35 N	140.50 E
Muscle Shoals	158	34.45 N	87.40 W
Muscongus Bay C	150	43.55 N	69.20 W
Musgrave	124	14.47 S	143.30 E
Musgrave Ranges ∧∧	122	26.10 S	131.50 E
Mushie	110	3.01 S	16.54 E
Mushin	114	6.32 N	3.22 E
Musi ≃	96	2.20 S	104.56 E
Musishan ∧	102	36.03 N	80.07 E
Muskegon	154	43.14 N	86.16 W
Muskegon Heights	154	43.12 N	86.12 W
Muskogee	160	35.45 N	95.22 W
Muskwa ≃	142	58.45 N	122.35 W
Musoma	110	1.30 S	33.48 E
Musselshell	166	46.31 N	108.06 W
Mussidan	74	45.02 N	0.22 E
Mussomeli	78	37.35 N	13.46 E
Mussuma	110	14.14 S	21.59 E
Mustla	86	58.14 N	25.52 E
Mustvee	86	58.51 N	26.56 E
Muswellbrook	120	32.16 S	150.53 E
Mutankiang → Mudanjiang	88	44.35 N	129.36 E
Mutoraj	84	61.20 N	100.30 E
Mutsamudu	117a	12.09 S	44.25 E
Mutsu	90	41.17 N	141.10 E
Muttaburra	120	22.36 S	144.33 E
Muxima	110	9.31 S	13.56 E
Muyumba	110	7.15 S	26.59 E
Muzaffarābād	102	34.22 N	73.28 E
Muzaffarnagar	102	29.28 N	77.41 E
Muzaffarpur	102	26.07 N	85.24 E
Muži	84	65.22 N	64.40 E
Muzillac	74	47.33 N	2.29 W
Mwadui	110	3.33 S	33.36 E
Mwanza	110	2.31 S	32.54 E
Mweka	110	4.51 S	21.34 E
Mweru, Lake ⊜	110	9.00 S	28.45 E
Mwinilunga	110	11.44 S	24.26 E
Myanaung	94	18.17 N	95.19 E
Myaungmya	94	16.36 N	94.56 E
Myerstown	152	40.22 N	76.19 W
Myingyan	94	21.28 N	95.23 E
Myitkyinā	94	25.23 N	97.24 E
Myjava	72	48.45 N	17.34 E
Myjeldino	66	61.46 N	54.48 E
Myla	66	65.25 N	50.48 E
Myllykoski	68	60.47 N	26.48 E
Myllymäki	68	62.32 N	24.17 E
Mymensingh	102	24.45 N	90.24 E
Myrtle Beach	156	33.42 N	78.52 W
Myrtle Creek	166	43.01 N	123.17 W
Myrtle Grove	158	30.25 N	87.18 W
Myrtle Point	166	43.04 N	124.08 W
Mysen	68	59.33 N	11.20 E
Mysia □⁹	80	39.15 N	28.00 E
Myski	84	53.42 N	87.48 E
Myškino	86	57.47 N	38.27 E
Myślenice	72	49.51 N	19.56 E
Mysłowice	72	50.15 N	19.07 E
Mysore	100	12.18 N	76.39 E
Mys Šmidta	146	68.56 N	179.26 W
Mystic, Conn., U.S.	152	41.21 N	71.58 W
Mystic, Iowa, U.S.	154	40.47 N	92.57 W
Mys Vchodnoj	84	73.53 N	86.43 E
Mysy	66	60.34 N	53.57 E
Mys Želanija	82	76.56 N	68.35 E
Myszków	72	50.36 N	19.20 E
My-tho	94	10.21 N	106.21 E
Mytišči	86	55.55 N	37.46 E
Mzimba	110	11.52 S	33.34 E
Mzuzu	110	11.27 S	33.55 E
N			
Naalehu	170d	19.04 N	155.35 W
Naantali	68	60.27 N	22.02 E
Naas	70	53.13 N	6.39 W
Nabadwīp	102	23.25 N	88.22 E
Nabburg	72	49.28 N	12.11 E
Naberežnyje Čelny	66	55.42 N	52.19 E
Nabesna	146	62.22 N	143.00 W
Nabeul	106	36.27 N	10.44 E
Nabire	124	3.22 S	135.26 E
Nabī Shu'ayb, Jabal an- ∧	100	15.18 N	43.59 E
Nābulus	104	32.13 N	35.16 E
Nacala-Velha	110	14.32 S	40.37 E
Nachičevan'	104	39.13 N	45.24 E
Nachingwea	110	10.23 S	38.46 E
Náchod	72	50.25 N	16.10 E
Nachodka	84	42.48 N	132.52 E
Nachvak Fiord C²	142	59.03 N	63.45 W
Nacka	68	59.18 N	18.10 E
Naco	164	31.20 N	109.57 W
Nacogdoches	158	31.36 N	94.39 W
Nacozari [de García]	130	30.24 N	109.39 W
Nadiād	102	22.42 N	72.52 E
Nădlac	80	46.10 N	20.45 E
Nador	106	35.12 N	2.55 W
Nadporožje	66	60.28 N	34.17 E
Nadvoicy	66	63.52 N	34.15 E
Nadym	84	65.35 N	72.42 E
Nadym ≃	84	66.12 N	72.00 E
Nærbø	68	58.40 N	5.39 E
Næstved	68	55.14 N	11.46 E
Näfels	74	47.06 N	9.04 E
Naga	92	13.38 N	123.11 E
Nagahama	90	35.23 N	136.16 E
Nagano	90	36.39 N	138.11 E
Nagaoka	90	37.27 N	138.51 E
Nāgappattinam	100	10.46 N	79.50 E
Nagarote	132	12.16 N	86.34 W
Nagasaki	90	32.48 N	129.55 E
Nāgaur	102	27.12 N	73.44 E
Nāgercoil	100	8.11 N	77.26 E
Nagold	72	48.33 N	8.43 E
Nagornyj	84	55.58 N	124.57 E
Nagorsk	66	59.18 N	50.48 E
Nagoya	90	35.10 N	136.55 E
Nāgpur	102	21.09 N	79.06 E
Nagua	132	19.23 N	69.50 W
Nagyatád	72	46.14 N	17.22 E
Nagybajom	72	46.23 N	17.31 E
Nagyecsed	72	47.42 N	22.19 E
Nagykanizsa	72	46.27 N	17.00 E
Nagykáta	72	47.25 N	19.45 E
Nagykőrös	72	47.02 N	19.43 E
Nagy-Milic ∧	72	48.35 N	21.28 E
Naha	91b	26.13 N	127.40 E
Nāhan	100	30.33 N	77.13 E
Nahang (Nihing) ≃	104	26.00 N	62.44 E
Nahe	88	48.28 N	124.52 E
Nahuel Huapi, Lago ⊜	136	41.00 S	71.32 W
Naicá	130	27.53 N	105.31 W
Naidong	88	29.14 N	31.46 E
Naila	72	50.19 N	11.42 E
Nain, Newf., Can.	142	56.32 N	61.41 W
Nā'īn, Īrān	100	32.52 N	53.05 E
Naini Tāl	102	29.23 N	79.27 E
Nairn	70	57.35 N	3.53 W
Nairobi	110	1.17 S	36.49 E
Naivasha	110	0.43 S	36.26 E
Najac	74	44.17 N	2.00 E
Najafābād	104	32.37 N	51.21 E
Nájera	76	42.25 N	2.44 W
Najin	88	42.15 N	130.18 E
Najramdal Uul ∧	88	49.10 N	87.52 W
Nakano-shima I	91b	29.49 N	129.52 E
Nakhon Pathom	94	13.49 N	100.06 E
Nakhon Phanom	94	17.22 N	104.46 E
Nakhon Ratchasima	94	14.57 N	102.09 E
Nakhon Sawan	94	15.42 N	100.06 E
Nakhon Si Thammarat	94	8.26 N	99.58 E
Nakina	142	50.10 N	86.42 W
Nakło nad Notecią	72	53.08 N	17.35 E
Naknek	146	58.44 N	157.02 W
Nakskov	68	54.50 N	11.09 E
Nakuru	110	0.17 S	36.04 E
Nalajch	88	47.45 N	107.13 E
Nālanda	100	17.03 N	79.16 E
Nal'čik	64	43.29 N	43.37 E
Nalgonda	100	17.03 N	79.16 E
Nālūt	108	31.52 N	10.59 E
Namak, Daryācheh-ye ⊜	104	34.45 N	51.36 E
Namakan Lake ⊜	154	48.27 N	92.35 W
Namakzār, Daryācheh-ye ⊜	104	34.00 N	60.30 E
Namangan	82	41.00 N	71.40 E
Namapa	110	13.43 S	39.50 E
Nambour	120	26.38 S	152.58 E
Nambucca Heads	120	30.39 S	153.00 E
Nam Dinh	94	20.25 N	106.10 E
Namhkam	88	23.50 N	97.41 E
Namib Desert ∻²	116	23.00 S	15.00 E
Namlea	124	3.18 S	127.06 E
Namoi ≃	120	30.00 S	148.07 E
Nampa	166	43.34 N	116.34 W
Namp'o	88	38.45 N	125.23 E
Nampula	110	15.07 S	39.15 E
Namsos	66	64.29 N	11.30 E
Namtu	92	23.05 N	97.24 E
Namu	148	51.49 N	127.52 W
Namuchabawashan ∧	102	29.38 N	95.04 E
Namuhu ⊜	102	30.42 N	90.30 E
Namur	72	50.28 N	4.52 E
Namutoni	116	18.49 S	16.55 E
Namysłów	72	51.05 N	17.42 E
Nan	94	18.48 N	100.46 E
Nan ≃	94	15.42 N	100.11 E
Nanaimo	148	49.10 N	123.56 W
Nanakuli	170c	21.23 N	158.09 W
Nanam	88	41.43 N	129.41 E
Nanango	120	26.40 S	152.00 E
Nanao	90	37.03 N	136.58 E
Nanchang	88	28.41 N	115.53 E
Nancheng	88	27.35 N	116.40 E
Nanchong	88	30.48 N	106.04 E
Nancowry Island I	94	7.59 N	93.32 E
Nancy	74	48.41 N	6.12 E
Nanda Devi ∧	102	30.23 N	79.59 E
Nānded	100	19.09 N	77.20 E
N'andoma	66	61.40 N	40.12 E
Nanduhe ≃	94	20.04 N	110.22 E
Nandurbār	102	21.22 N	74.15 E
Nānga Parbat ∧	102	35.15 N	74.36 E
Nanjing	88	32.03 N	118.47 E
Nanking → Nanjing	88	32.03 N	118.47 E
Nankou	88	40.14 N	116.07 E
Nanling ∧∧	88	25.00 N	112.00 E
Nannine	122	26.53 S	118.20 E
Nanning	94	22.48 N	108.20 E
Nanping	88	26.38 N	118.10 E
Nansa ≃	76	43.22 N	4.29 W
Nansei-shotō (Ryukyu Islands) II	91b	26.40 N	128.00 E
Nantais, Lac ⊜	142	60.59 N	74.00 W
Nantes	74	47.13 N	1.33 W
Nanteuil-le-Haudouin	74	49.08 N	2.48 E
Nanticoke	152	41.12 N	76.00 W
Nanticoke ≃	152	38.16 N	75.56 W
Nantong	88	32.02 N	120.53 E
Nantua	74	46.09 N	5.37 E
Nantucket	152	41.17 N	70.06 W
Nantucket Island I	152	41.16 N	70.03 W
Nanty Glo	152	40.28 N	78.50 W
Nanuque	134	17.50 S	40.21 W
Nanusa, Pulau-pulau II	92	4.42 N	127.06 E
Nanxiong	88	25.10 N	114.20 E
Nanyang	88	33.00 N	112.32 E
Nanyuki	110	0.01 N	37.04 E
Nao, Cabo de la ≻	76	38.44 N	0.14 E
Naococane, Lac ⊜	142	52.52 N	70.40 W
Naoetsu	90	37.11 N	138.15 E
Náousa	80	40.37 N	22.05 E
Napa	168	38.18 N	122.17 W
Napakiak	146	60.42 N	161.57 W
Napalkovo	84	70.03 N	73.47 E
Napanee	154	44.15 N	76.57 W
Napaskiak	146	60.42 N	161.54 W
Naperville	154	41.47 N	88.09 W
Napetipi ≃	150	51.21 N	58.08 W
Napier	126	39.29 S	176.54 E
Naples → Napoli, It.	78	40.51 N	14.17 E
Naples, Fla., U.S.	156	26.08 N	81.48 W
Naples, N.Y., U.S.	152	42.37 N	77.25 W
Napo □⁴	138	0.30 S	77.00 W
Napo ≃	138	3.20 S	72.40 W
Napoleon, N. Dak., U.S.	162	46.30 N	99.46 W
Napoleon, Ohio, U.S.	152	41.23 N	84.08 W
Napoleonville	158	29.57 N	91.01 W
Napoli (Naples)	78	40.51 N	14.17 E
Nappanee	158	41.27 N	86.00 W
Nara, Mali	114	15.10 N	7.17 W
Nara, Nihon	90	34.41 N	135.50 E
Naracoorte	120	36.58 S	140.44 E
Naradhan	120	33.37 S	146.19 E
Nārāyanganj	102	23.37 N	90.30 E
Narberth	70	51.48 N	4.45 W
Narbonne	74	43.11 N	3.00 E
Nardò	78	40.11 N	18.02 E
Naretha	122	31.00 S	124.50 E
Narew ≃	72	52.26 N	20.42 E
Narinda, Baie de C	117b	14.55 S	47.30 E
Narjan-Mar	66	67.39 N	53.00 E
Närke □⁹	68	59.06 N	15.03 E
Narmada ≃	102	21.38 N	72.36 E
Nārnaul	102	28.03 N	76.07 E
Narni	78	42.31 N	12.31 E
Naro	78	37.17 N	13.48 E
Narodnaja, Gora ∧	66	65.04 N	60.09 E
Naro-Fominsk	86	55.23 N	36.43 E
Narooma	120	36.14 S	150.08 E
Narrabri	120	30.19 S	149.47 E
Narran ≃	120	29.45 S	147.20 E
Narrandera	120	34.45 S	146.33 E
Narraway ≃	148	54.48 N	119.56 W
Narrogin	122	32.56 S	117.10 E
Narromine	120	32.14 S	148.15 E
Narrows	156	37.20 N	80.48 W
Narsimhapur	102	22.57 N	79.12 E
Narssaq	142	60.54 N	46.00 W
Narva	86	59.23 N	28.12 E
Narvik	66	68.26 N	17.25 E
Naryn	82	41.26 N	75.59 E
Naryn ≃	82	40.54 N	71.45 E
Narynkol	82	42.43 N	80.12 E
Naryškino	86	52.58 N	35.44 E
Nås	68	60.27 N	14.29 E
Nasbinals	74	44.40 N	3.03 E
Nashua, Mont., U.S.	166	48.08 N	106.22 W
Nashua, N.H., U.S.	152	42.46 N	71.27 W
Nashville, Ark., U.S.	158	33.57 N	93.51 W
Nashville, Ga., U.S.	156	31.12 N	83.15 W
Nashville, Ill., U.S.	158	38.21 N	89.23 W
Nashville, Mich., U.S.	154	42.36 N	85.05 W
Nashville, N.C., U.S.	156	35.58 N	77.58 W
Nashville, Tenn., U.S.	158	36.09 N	86.48 W
Nashwaaksis	150	45.59 N	66.39 W
Nashwauk	154	47.23 N	93.10 W
Nasielsk	72	52.36 N	20.48 E
Nāsik	100	19.59 N	73.47 E
Nāṣir	112	8.36 N	33.04 E
Naskaupi ≃	142	53.45 N	60.50 W
Nass ≃	148	55.00 N	129.50 W
Nassau, Ba.	132	25.05 N	77.21 W
Nassau, N.Y., U.S.	152	42.31 N	73.37 W
Nasser, Lake ⊜¹	112	22.40 N	32.00 E
Nassereith	72	47.19 N	10.50 E

Symbols in the index entries are identified on page 203.

Name	Page	Lat	Long
Nässjö	68	57.39 N	14.41 E
Nastapoca ≃	142	56.55 N	76.33 W
Nastapoka Islands II	142	57.00 N	76.50 W
Nasva	66	56.35 N	30.10 E
Nata, Bots.	116	20.12 S	26.12 E
Natá, Pan.	118	8.20 N	80.30 W
Natal, Bra.	134	5.47 S	35.13 W
Natal, Indon.	92	0.33 N	99.07 E
Natashquan ≃	142	50.06 N	61.49 W
Natchez	134	31.34 N	91.23 W
Natchitoches	100	31.46 N	93.05 W
Nâthdwâra	100	24.56 N	73.51 E
Natick	152	42.17 N	71.21 W
Natimuk	120	36.45 S	141.57 E
National City	168	32.40 N	117.06 W
Native Bay C	142	63.52 N	82.30 W
Natividade	134	11.43 S	47.47 W
Natron, Lake ⊜	110	2.25 S	36.00 E
Natuna Besar, ↡	94	4.00 N	108.15 E
Natuna Besar, Kepulauan II	96	4.40 N	108.00 E
Natuna Selatan, Kepulauan II	96	2.45 N	109.00 E
Naturaliste, Cape ↣	122	33.32 S	115.01 E
Naturaliste Channel ↵	122	25.25 S	113.00 E
Naturita	164	38.14 N	108.34 W
Naucelle	74	44.12 N	2.20 E
Nauders	72	46.53 N	10.30 E
Nauen	72	52.36 N	12.52 E
Naugatuck	152	41.30 N	73.04 W
Naujamiestis	86	55.44 N	23.10 E
Naumburg	72	51.09 N	11.48 E
Naustdal	68	61.31 N	5.43 E
Nautla	130	20.13 N	96.47 W
Navajo ≃	164	37.00 N	107.10 W
Navajo Mountain ∧	164	37.02 N	110.54 W
Navajo Reservoir ⊜[1]	164	36.55 N	107.30 W
Navan	70	53.39 N	6.41 W
Navarin, Mys ↣	146	62.16 N	179.10 E
Navarino, Isla I	136	55.05 S	67.40 W
Navarra	76	42.40 N	1.30 W
Navarre □[4]	152	40.43 N	81.32 W
Navasota	150	30.23 N	96.05 W
Navassa Island I	132	18.24 N	75.01 W
Navidad Bank ╼[4]	132	20.05 N	68.50 W
Navoi	82	40.15 N	65.15 E
Navojoa	130	27.06 N	109.26 W
Navolato	130	24.47 N	107.42 W
Návpaktos	80	38.23 N	21.50 E
Návplion	80	37.34 N	22.48 E
Navsāri	102	20.51 N	72.55 E
Nawābshāh	102	26.15 N	68.25 E
Nayoro	90a	44.21 N	142.28 E
Nazaré, Bra.	134	13.02 S	39.00 W
Nazaré, Port.	76	39.36 N	9.04 W
Nazare da Mata	134	7.44 S	35.14 W
Nazareth	152	40.44 N	75.19 W
Nazarovo	84	56.01 N	90.26 E
Nazas	130	25.14 N	104.08 W
Nazca	134	14.50 S	74.55 W
Naze	91b	28.23 N	129.30 E
N'azepetrovsk	82	56.03 N	59.36 E
Nazvjajevsk	82	55.34 N	71.21 E
Ndélé	108	8.24 N	20.39 E
Ndele	110	2.03 S	11.23 E
Ndjamena (Fort-Lamy)	108	12.07 N	15.03 E
Ndjolé	110	0.11 S	10.45 E
Ndola	110	12.58 S	28.38 E
Nea	68	63.13 N	11.02 E
Neamţ □[4]	80	47.00 N	26.30 E
Neath	70	51.40 N	3.48 W
Nebine Creek ≃	120	29.07 S	146.56 E
Nebit-Dag	104	39.30 N	54.22 E
Nebraska □[3]	144	41.30 N	100.00 W
Nebraska City	148	40.41 N	95.52 W
Nechako ≃	148	53.56 N	122.42 W
Neckar ≃	72	49.12 N	9.13 E
Neckarsulm	72	49.11 N	9.13 E
Necocea	140	38.34 S	58.45 W
Nederland	158	29.58 N	93.60 W
Nedstrand	68	59.21 N	5.51 E
Needham Market	70	52.09 N	1.03 W
Needle Range ↗	164	38.25 N	113.55 W
Needles	168	34.51 N	114.37 W
Needmore	158	35.57 N	78.09 W
Neembucú □[5]	140	27.00 S	58.00 W
Neenah	154	44.11 N	88.28 W
Neepawa	142	50.13 N	99.29 W
Neftečala	100	39.23 N	49.16 E
Negage	110	7.45 S	15.16 E
Negaunee	154	46.30 N	87.36 W
Negele	108	5.20 N	39.36 E
Negombo	100	7.13 N	79.50 E
Negotin	80	44.14 N	22.32 E
Negra, Cordillera ↗	134	9.30 S	77.30 W
Negra, Punta ↣	134	6.06 S	81.10 W
Negritos	134	4.42 S	81.19 W
Negro ≃, Arg.	140	41.02 S	62.47 W
Negro ≃, Bol.	134	14.11 S	63.07 W
Negro ≃, S.A.	134	3.06 S	59.52 W
Negro ≃, S.A.	140	33.24 S	58.22 W
Negros I	98	10.00 N	123.00 E
Nehbandān	104	31.32 N	60.02 E
Nehelm-Hüsten	72	51.27 N	7.57 E
Neiges, Piton des ∧	117c	21.05 S	55.29 E
Neijiang	88	29.35 N	105.03 E
Neillsville	154	44.34 N	90.36 W
Neimenggu Zizhiqu (Inner Mongolia) □[4]	88	43.00 N	115.00 E
Neisse (Nysa Łużycka) (Nisa) ≃	72	52.04 N	14.46 E
Neiva	138	2.56 N	75.18 W
Neja	86	58.18 N	43.54 E
Nekemte	108	9.05 N	36.31 E
Nekoosa	154	44.19 N	89.54 W
Neklidovo	86	56.13 N	32.46 E
Neligh	162	42.08 N	98.02 W
Nel'kan	84	57.40 N	136.13 E
Nellore	100	14.26 N	79.59 E
Nel'ma	84	47.39 N	139.09 E
Nelson, B.C., Can.	148	49.29 N	117.17 W
Nelson, N.Z.	126	41.17 S	173.17 E
Nelson ≃	142	57.04 N	92.30 W
Nelson, Cape ↣	120	38.26 S	141.33 E
Nelsonville	152	39.27 N	82.14 W
Nelspruit	116	25.30 S	30.58 E
Néma	114	16.37 N	7.15 W
Nemadji ≃	154	46.41 N	92.02 W
Neman (Ragnit), S.S.S.R.	86	55.02 N	22.02 E
Neman (Nemunas) ≃, S.S.S.R.	86	55.18 N	21.23 E
Nemenčinė	86	54.51 N	25.29 E
Nemours	74	48.16 N	2.42 E
Nemuna, Bjeshkët e ↗	80	42.27 N	19.47 E
Nemunas (Neman) ≃	86	55.18 N	21.23 E
Nemuro	90a	43.20 N	145.35 E
Nemuro Strait ↵	90a	44.00 N	145.20 E
Nenagh	70	52.52 N	8.12 W
Nenana	146	64.34 N	149.07 W
Nenana ≃	146	64.34 N	149.20 W
Nenecki Nacionalnyj Okrug □[4]	66	67.30 N	54.00 E
Neoga	162	39.19 N	88.27 W
Neola	162	41.27 N	95.37 W
Neosho	158	36.52 N	94.22 W
Neosho ≃	144	35.48 N	95.18 W
Nepa ≃	84	59.16 N	108.16 E
Nepal (Nepāl) □[1]	102	28.00 N	84.00 E
Nepālganj	102	28.03 N	81.37 E
Nephi	164	39.43 N	111.50 W
Neptune	152	40.12 N	74.02 W
Neptune Beach	156	30.19 N	81.24 W
Nérac	74	44.08 N	0.20 E
Nerastro, Sarīr ╼[2]	108	24.20 N	20.37 E
Nerča ≃	84	51.56 N	116.40 E
Nerčinsk	84	51.58 N	116.35 E
Nerčinskij Zavod	84	51.19 N	119.36 E
Nerehta	86	57.28 N	40.34 E
Neringa	86	55.19 N	21.01 E
Neriquinha	110	15.50 S	21.42 E
Nerl'	86	56.40 N	40.24 E
Nérondes	74	47.00 N	2.49 E
Nerva	76	37.42 N	6.32 W
Nes, Ned.	72	53.26 N	5.45 E
Nes, Nor.	68	60.34 N	9.59 E
Nesbyen	68	60.34 N	9.09 E
Neskaupstaður	66a	65.10 N	13.43 W
Nesle	74	49.46 N	2.55 E
Ness, Loch ⊜	70	57.15 N	4.30 W
Ness City	162	38.27 N	99.54 W
Nesselrode, Mount ∧	146	58.58 N	134.18 W
Nesselwang	72	47.37 N	10.30 E
Nesterov	86	54.38 N	22.34 E
Néstos (Mesta) ≃	80	40.41 N	24.44 E
Nesttun	68	60.19 N	5.20 E
Nesvíž	86	53.13 N	26.40 E
Netanya	104	32.20 N	34.51 E
Netherlands □[1]	64	52.15 N	5.30 E
Netherlands Antilles □[2]	128	12.15 N	69.00 W
Nettiling Fiord C[2]	142	66.02 N	68.12 W
Nettilling Lake ⊜	142	66.30 N	70.40 W
Nettleton	158	34.05 N	88.44 W
Nettuno	78	41.27 N	12.39 E
Neubrandenburg	72	53.33 N	13.15 E
Neubrandenburg □[5]	72	53.33 N	13.15 E
Neuburg an der Donau	72	48.44 N	11.11 E
Neuchâtel	74	46.59 N	6.56 E
Neuchâtel, Lac de ⊜	74	46.52 N	6.50 E
Neuenhagen	72	52.32 N	13.41 E
Neuerburg	72	50.00 N	6.17 E
Neuf-Brisach	74	48.01 N	7.32 E
Neufchâteau, Bel.	72	49.50 N	5.26 E
Neufchâteau, Fr.	74	48.21 N	5.42 E
Neufchâtel-en-Bray	74	49.44 N	1.27 E
Neugersdorf	72	50.59 N	14.36 E
Neuillé-Pont-Pierre	74	47.33 N	0.33 E
Neu-Isenburg	72	50.03 N	8.41 E
Neumarkt im Hausruckkreis]	72	48.16 N	13.45 E
Neumarkt in der Oberpfalz	72	49.16 N	11.28 E
Neumarkt in Steiermark	72	47.05 N	14.26 E
Neumarkt-Sankt Veit	72	48.22 N	12.30 E
Neumünster	72	54.04 N	9.59 E
Neunburg vorm Wald	72	49.21 N	12.24 E
Neunkirchen	72	47.43 N	16.05 E
Neunkirchen/saar	72	49.20 N	7.10 E
Neuquén	140	38.57 S	68.05 W
Neuquén □[4]	140	38.59 S	68.00 W
Neuruppin	72	52.55 N	12.48 E
Neusiedler See ⊜	72	47.50 N	16.46 E
Neustadt, B.R.D.	72	47.54 N	8.13 E
Neustadt, D.D.R.	72	50.44 N	11.44 E
Neustadt [an aisch]	72	49.34 N	10.37 E
Neustadt an der Waldnaab	72	49.44 N	12.11 E
Neustadt an der Weinstrasse	72	49.21 N	8.08 E
Neustadt bei Coburg	72	50.19 N	11.07 E
Neustadt in Holstein	72	54.06 N	10.48 E
Neustettin → Szczecinek	72	53.43 N	16.42 E
Neustrelitz	72	53.21 N	13.04 E
Neutral Zone □[2]	100	29.10 N	45.30 E
Neuvic	74	45.23 N	10.01 E
Neuville-de-Poitou	74	46.41 N	0.15 E
Neuville-sur-Saône	74	45.52 N	4.51 E
Neuwied	72	50.25 N	7.27 E
Nevada, Iowa, U.S.	154	42.01 N	93.27 W
Nevada, Mo., U.S.	158	37.51 N	94.22 W
Nevada, Ohio, U.S.	152	40.49 N	83.08 W
Nevada □[3]	144	39.00 N	117.00 W
Nevada, Sierra ↗	144	38.00 N	119.15 W
Nevada City	168	39.16 N	121.01 W
Nevado, Cerro ∧	140	35.34 S	68.29 W
Nevel'	86	56.02 N	29.55 E
Nevel'sk, S.S.S.R.	84	46.40 N	141.53 E
Nevel'sk, S.S.S.R.	88	27.28 N	40.34 E
Never	84	53.58 N	124.05 E
Nevers	74	47.00 N	3.09 E
Nevertire	120	31.52 S	147.39 E
Nevesinje	80	43.15 N	18.07 E
Nevinnomyssk	100	44.38 N	41.56 E
Nevis I	132	17.10 N	62.35 W
Nevis, Ben ∧	70	56.48 N	5.01 W
Nevjansk	82	57.32 N	60.13 E
Nevlunghamn	68	58.56 N	9.52 E
New ≃, N.A.	168	33.08 N	115.44 W
New ≃, U.S.	158	38.10 N	81.12 W
New Albany, Ind., U.S.	158	38.18 N	85.49 W
New Albany, Miss., U.S.	158	34.29 N	89.00 W
New Amsterdam	138	6.17 N	57.36 W
Newark, Del., U.S.	152	39.41 N	75.45 W
Newark, N.J., U.S.	152	40.44 N	74.10 W
Newark, N.Y., U.S.	152	43.02 N	77.05 W
Newark, Ohio, U.S.	152	40.03 N	82.24 W
Newark-upon-Trent	70	53.05 N	0.49 W
Newark Valley	152	42.13 N	76.11 W
New Athens	158	38.19 N	89.53 W
Newaygo	154	43.25 N	85.48 W
New Baden	162	38.38 N	89.42 W
New Baltimore	152	42.41 N	82.44 W
New Bedford	152	41.38 N	70.56 W
Newberg	166	45.18 N	122.58 W
New Berlin, N.Y., U.S.	152	42.37 N	75.20 W
New Berlin, Wis., U.S.	154	42.58 N	88.07 W
New Bern	158	35.06 N	77.02 W
Newberry, Fla., U.S.	156	29.38 N	82.37 W
Newberry, Mich., U.S.	154	46.21 N	85.30 W
Newberry, S.C., U.S.	156	34.16 N	81.37 W
New Bethlehem	152	41.00 N	79.20 W
New Bloomfield	152	40.25 N	77.11 W
New Boston, Ohio, U.S.	152	38.45 N	82.56 W
New Boston, Tex., U.S.	158	33.27 N	94.25 W
New Braunfels	160	29.42 N	98.08 W
New Bremen	152	40.26 N	84.23 W
New Brighton	152	40.44 N	80.18 W
New Britain	152	41.40 N	72.47 W
New Brunswick	152	40.29 N	74.27 W
New Brunswick □[4]	142	46.30 N	66.15 W
New Buffalo	154	41.47 N	86.45 W
Newburgh, Ind., U.S.	158	37.57 N	87.24 W
Newburgh, N.Y., U.S.	152	41.30 N	74.01 W
Newbury	70	51.25 N	1.20 W
Newburyport	152	42.48 N	70.53 W
New Carlisle, Qué., Can.	150	48.01 N	65.20 W
New Carlisle, Ohio, U.S.	152	39.56 N	84.02 W
Newcastle, Austl.	120	32.56 S	151.46 E
Newcastle, N.B., Can.	150	47.00 N	65.34 W
Newcastle, S. Afr.	116	27.45 S	29.55 E
Newcastle, Ire., U.K.	70	54.13 N	5.54 W
Newcastle, Calif., U.S.	168	38.53 N	121.08 W
New Castle, Del., U.S.	164	39.40 N	107.32 W
New Castle, Ind., U.S.	158	39.55 N	85.22 W
New Castle, Ky., U.S.	158	38.26 N	85.10 W
New Castle, Maine, U.S.	152	44.02 N	69.32 W
New Castle, Pa., U.S.	152	41.00 N	80.21 W
New Castle, Tex., U.S.	160	33.12 N	98.44 W
New Castle, Wyo., U.S.	162	43.51 N	104.11 W
Newcastle Emlyn	70	52.02 N	4.28 W
Newcastle-under-Lyme	70	53.00 N	2.14 W
Newcastle upon Tyne	70	54.59 N	1.35 W
Newcastle West	70	52.27 N	9.03 W
New City	152	41.09 N	73.59 W
Newcomerstown	152	40.16 N	81.36 W
New Concord	152	40.01 N	81.44 W
New Cumberland	152	40.30 N	80.36 W
New Delhi	102	28.36 N	77.12 E
New Effington	162	45.51 N	96.55 W
New Egypt	152	40.04 N	74.32 W
Newell, S. Dak., U.S.	162	44.43 N	103.25 W
Newell, W. Va., U.S.	154	40.37 N	80.36 W
New Ellenton	156	33.24 N	81.42 W
Newellton	158	32.10 N	91.14 W
New England	162	46.32 N	102.52 W
New England Range ↗	120	30.00 S	151.50 E
Newfane	152	43.17 N	78.43 W
Newfound Gap ⋈	156	35.37 N	83.25 W
Newfoundland □[4]	142	52.00 N	56.00 W
Newfoundland I	142	48.30 N	56.00 W
New Franklin	162	39.01 N	92.44 W
New Freedom	152	39.44 N	76.42 W
New Galloway	70	55.05 N	4.10 W
New Georgia I	118	8.15 S	157.30 E
New Glasgow	150	45.35 N	62.39 W
New Guinea I	124	5.00 S	140.00 E
Newgulf	160	29.16 N	95.54 W
Newhalen	146	59.43 N	154.54 W
Newhall	100	34.23 N	118.31 W
New Hamburg	154	43.23 N	80.42 W
New Hampshire □[3]	144	43.35 N	71.40 W
New Hampton	154	43.03 N	92.19 W
New Harmony	158	38.08 N	87.56 W
New Hartford	152	41.53 N	72.59 W
New Haven, Conn., U.S.	152	41.18 N	72.56 W
New Haven, Ind., U.S.	158	41.04 N	85.01 W
New Haven, Mo., U.S.	158	38.37 N	91.13 W
New Holland, Ohio, U.S.	152	39.33 N	83.15 W
New Holland, Pa., U.S.	152	40.06 N	76.05 W
New Holstein	154	43.57 N	88.05 W
New Iberia	158	30.00 N	91.49 W
New Jersey □[3]	152	40.15 N	74.30 W
New Kensington	152	40.34 N	79.46 W
New Kent	156	37.31 N	76.59 W
Newkirk	158	36.53 N	97.03 W
New Lexington	152	39.43 N	82.13 W
New Liskeard	154	47.30 N	79.40 W
New London, Conn., U.S.	152	41.21 N	72.07 W
New London, Iowa, U.S.	154	40.55 N	91.24 W
New London, N.H., U.S.	152	43.25 N	71.59 W
New London, Ohio, U.S.	152	41.05 N	82.24 W
New London, Tex., U.S.	158	32.15 N	94.56 W
New London, Wis., U.S.	154	44.23 N	88.45 W
New Madrid	158	36.36 N	89.32 W
Newman	168	37.19 N	121.01 W
Newman, Mount ∧	122	23.16 S	119.33 E
Newmarket, Ont., Can.	154	44.03 N	79.28 W
Newmarket, Eng., U.K.	70	52.15 N	0.25 E
New Market, Ala., U.S.	158	34.55 N	86.26 W
New Market, N.H., U.S.	152	43.05 N	70.56 W
New Martinsville	152	39.38 N	80.51 W
New Meadows	166	44.58 N	116.32 W
New Mexico □[3]	144	34.30 N	106.00 W
New Milford	152	41.35 N	73.25 W
Newnan	156	33.23 N	84.48 W
New Norfolk	120	42.47 S	147.03 E
New Orleans	158	29.58 N	90.07 W
New Oxford	152	39.52 N	77.03 W
New Paltz	152	41.45 N	74.05 W
New Philadelphia	152	40.30 N	81.27 W
New Plymouth, N.Z.	126	39.04 S	174.04 E
New Plymouth, Idaho, U.S.	166	43.58 N	116.49 W
Newport, Eng., U.K.	70	50.42 N	1.18 W
Newport, Scot., U.K.	70	56.27 N	2.56 W
Newport, Wales, U.K.	70	52.01 N	4.51 W
Newport, Ark., U.S.	158	35.36 N	91.17 W
Newport, Ky., U.S.	158	39.06 N	84.29 W
Newport, Maine, U.S.	152	44.50 N	69.17 W
Newport, N.H., U.S.	152	43.21 N	72.09 W
Newport, Pa., U.S.	152	40.29 N	77.08 W
Newport, R.I., U.S.	152	41.29 N	71.18 W
Newport, Tenn., U.S.	156	35.58 N	83.11 W
Newport, Vt., U.S.	152	44.57 N	72.12 W
Newport, Wash., U.S.	148	0.00 N	0.00 W
Newport Beach	168	33.37 N	117.56 W
Newport News	156	37.04 N	76.24 W
New Port Richey	156	28.14 S	82.43 W
New Prague	154	44.32 N	93.34 W
Newquay, Eng., U.K.	70	50.25 N	5.05 W
New Quay, Wales, U.K.	70	52.13 N	4.22 W
New Richland	154	43.54 N	93.29 W
New Richmond, Qué., Can.	150	48.10 N	65.52 W
New Richmond, Ohio, U.S.	152	38.57 N	84.17 W
New Richmond, Wis., U.S.	154	45.07 N	92.32 W
New Roads	158	30.42 N	91.26 W
New Rochelle	152	40.55 N	73.47 W
New Ross	70	52.24 N	6.56 W
Newry	70	54.11 N	6.20 W
New Salem	162	46.51 N	101.25 W
New Sharon	154	41.28 N	92.39 W
New Smyrna Beach	156	29.02 N	80.56 W
New South Wales □[3]	118	33.00 S	146.00 E
New Stuyahok	146	59.28 N	157.20 W
Newton, Ala., U.S.	156	31.20 N	85.36 W
Newton, Ill., U.S.	158	38.59 N	88.10 W
Newton, Iowa, U.S.	154	41.42 N	93.03 W
Newton, Kans., U.S.	162	38.03 N	97.21 W
Newton, Mass., U.S.	152	42.21 N	71.11 W
Newton, Miss., U.S.	158	32.19 N	89.10 W
Newton, N.J., U.S.	152	41.03 N	74.45 W
Newton, N.C., U.S.	156	35.40 N	81.13 W
Newton, Tex., U.S.	158	30.51 N	93.46 W
Newton Abbot	70	50.32 N	3.36 W
Newton Stewart	70	54.57 N	4.29 W
Newtown	70	52.32 N	3.19 W
Newtownabbey	70	54.42 N	5.54 W
Newtownards	70	54.36 N	5.41 W
Newtown Saint Boswells	70	55.34 N	2.40 W
New Ulm, Minn., U.S.	162	44.18 N	94.27 W
New Ulm, Tex., U.S.	160	29.53 N	96.30 W
New Vienna	152	39.18 N	83.42 W
Newville	152	40.10 N	77.24 W
New Waterford	150	46.15 N	60.05 W
New Waverly	160	30.32 N	95.29 W
New Westminster	148	49.12 N	122.55 W
New Whiteland	158	39.33 N	86.05 W
New York	152	40.43 N	74.01 W
New York □[3]	144	43.00 N	75.00 W
New York State Barge Canal ⟂	152	43.05 N	78.43 W
New Zealand □[1]	118	41.00 S	174.00 E
Ney	152	41.23 N	84.32 W
Neyshābūr	104	36.12 N	58.50 E
Nezhin	86	51.03 N	31.54 E
Nezperce	166	46.14 N	116.14 W
Ngami, Lake ⊜	116	20.37 S	22.40 E
Ngaoundéré	108	7.19 N	13.35 E
Ngauruhoe ∧	126	39.10 S	175.38 E
Ngela Group II	118	9.05 S	160.10 E
Ng'iro, Ewaso ≃	110	0.28 N	39.55 E
Ngoko ≃	110	1.40 N	16.03 E
Nguigmi	114	14.15 N	13.07 E
Ngulu I[1]	92	8.27 N	137.29 E
Nguru	114	12.52 N	10.27 E
Nhamundá ≃	138	2.12 S	56.41 W
Nha-trang	94	12.15 N	109.11 E
Nhill	120	36.20 S	141.39 E
Niafounké	114	15.56 N	4.00 W
Niagara	154	45.46 N	88.00 W
Niagara Falls, Ont., Can.	154	43.06 N	79.04 W
Niagara Falls, N.Y., U.S.	152	43.05 N	79.04 W
Niagara-on-the-Lake	154	43.15 N	79.04 W
Niah	92	3.55 N	113.41 E
Niamey	114	13.31 N	2.07 E
Niangara	108	3.42 N	27.52 E
Niangintanggula-shanmai ↗	102	30.00 N	90.00 E
Nias, Pulau I	94	1.05 N	97.30 E
Nica	86	57.29 N	64.33 E
Nicaragua □[1]	128	13.00 N	85.00 W
Nicaragua, Lago de ⊜	128	11.35 N	85.25 W
Nicastro (Lamezia Terme)	78	38.59 N	16.20 E
Nice	74	43.42 N	7.15 E
Niceville	158	30.31 N	86.29 W
Nichinan	90	31.36 N	131.23 E
Nicholas Channel ↵	132	23.25 N	80.05 W
Nicholasville	158	37.53 N	84.34 W
Nichols Hills	160	35.33 N	97.32 W
Nicholson, Miss., U.S.	158	30.29 N	89.42 W
Nicholson, Pa., U.S.	152	41.38 N	75.47 W
Nicholson ≃, Austl.	120	17.31 S	139.36 E
Nicholson ≃, Austl.	122	27.34 S	128.38 E
Nickerson	162	38.08 N	98.05 W
Nickol Bay C	122	20.36 S	116.52 E
Nicobar Islands II	94	8.00 N	93.30 E
Nicolet	152	46.13 N	72.37 W
Nicosia, It.	78	37.45 N	14.24 E
Nicosia → Levkosia, Kípros	104	35.10 N	33.22 E
Nicotera	78	38.34 N	15.57 E
Nidže (Nítse Óros) ↗[1]	132	10.00 N	85.25 W
Nídze (Nítse Óros) ↗	80	40.58 N	21.49 E
Nidzica	72	53.22 N	20.26 E
Niederbronn-les-Bains	74	48.57 N	7.38 E
Niedermarsberg	72	51.28 N	8.50 E
Niederösterreich □[3]	72	48.20 N	15.50 E
Niedersachsen □[3]	72	52.00 N	10.00 E
Niemodlin	72	50.39 N	17.37 E
Nienburg	72	52.38 N	9.13 E
Nieszawa	72	52.50 N	18.55 E
Nieuw Amsterdam	134	5.53 S	55.05 W
Nieuw Nickerie	138	5.57 N	56.59 W
Nieuwpoort	72	51.08 N	2.45 E
Nièvre □[5]	74	47.05 N	3.30 E
Niğde	104	37.59 N	34.42 E
Niger □[1]	114	16.00 N	8.00 E
Niger ≃	114	5.33 N	6.33 E
Nigeria □[1]	108	10.00 N	8.00 E
Nigrita	80	40.55 N	23.30 E
Nihing (Nahang) ≃	104	26.00 N	62.44 E
Nihoa I[1]	90	27.55 N	139.03 E
Niihama	90	33.58 N	133.16 E
Niinisalo	68	61.50 N	22.29 E
Nijkerk	72	52.13 N	5.30 E
Nijmegen	72	51.50 N	5.50 E
Nikel'	66	69.24 N	30.12 E
Nikishka	146	60.42 N	151.19 W
Nikkō	90	36.45 N	139.37 E
Nikolajev	86	46.58 N	32.00 E
Nikolajevsk-na-Amure	84	53.08 N	140.44 E
Nikol'sk, S.S.S.R.	84	59.30 N	45.27 E
Nikol'sk, S.S.S.R.	86	53.45 N	46.05 E
Nikolski	146	52.56 N	168.52 W
Nikol'skoje	84	55.12 N	166.00 E
Nikopol	86	47.35 N	34.25 E
Nikšić	80	42.46 N	18.56 E
Nila, Pulau I	124	6.44 S	129.31 E
Niland	168	33.14 N	115.31 W
Nile (Nahr an-Nīl) ≃	108	30.10 N	31.06 E
Niles, Mich., U.S.	154	41.50 N	86.15 W
Niles, Ohio, U.S.	152	41.11 N	80.45 W
Nilsiä	68	63.12 N	28.05 E
Nimach	102	24.28 N	74.52 E
Nimba, Mont ∧	114	7.37 N	8.25 W
Nimba Mountains ↗	108	7.30 N	8.30 W
Nîmes	74	43.50 N	4.21 E
Nimmitabel	120	36.31 S	149.16 E
Nimule	108	3.36 N	32.03 E
Nina Bang Lake ⊜	142	70.51 N	79.07 W
Nindigully	120	28.21 S	148.49 E
Nine Degree Channel ↵	100	9.00 N	72.50 E
Ninety Mile Beach ↗[2]	120	38.13 S	147.23 E
Ninety Six	156	34.11 N	82.01 W
Ningbo	88	29.52 N	121.31 E
Ningcheng	88	41.33 N	119.20 E
Ningdu	88	26.31 N	115.58 E
Ningming	94	22.07 N	107.09 E
Ningsia → Yinchuan	88	38.28 N	106.18 E
Ningwu	88	39.01 N	112.13 E
Ningxia Huizu Zizhiqu □[4]	88	37.00 N	106.00 E
Ninh-binh	94	20.15 N	105.59 E
Ninh Islands II	114	3.30 N	14.15 E
Ninilchik	146	60.03 N	151.41 W
Ninove	72	50.50 N	4.01 E
Nioaque	134	21.08 S	55.48 W
Niobrara	162	42.45 N	98.00 W
Niobrara ≃	144	42.46 N	98.03 W
Niono	114	14.15 N	6.00 W
Nioro du Sahel	114	15.15 N	9.35 W
Niort	74	46.19 N	0.27 W
Nipan	120	24.47 S	150.01 E
Nipawin	142	53.22 N	104.00 W
Nipigon	154	49.01 N	88.16 W
Nipigon, Lake ⊜	142	49.50 N	88.30 W
Nipissing, Lake ⊜	142	46.17 N	80.00 W
Niquero	132	20.03 N	77.35 W
Nīr	104	38.02 N	47.59 E
Niš	80	43.19 N	21.54 E
Nisa	76	39.31 N	7.39 W
Niša (Neisse) (Nysa Łużycka) ≃	72	52.04 N	14.46 E
Nišava ≃	80	43.22 N	21.46 E
Nishinomiya	90	34.43 N	135.20 E
Nisiros I	80	36.36 N	27.09 E
Niski	72	51.18 N	14.58 E
Niterói	134	22.53 S	43.07 W
Nitro	152	38.25 N	81.50 W
Nitse Óros (Nidže) ∧	80	40.58 N	21.49 E
Nittedal	68	60.04 N	10.53 E
Niut, Gunung ∧	92	0.55 N	109.59 E
Nivala	68	63.55 N	24.58 E
Nivelles	72	50.36 N	4.20 E
Nivernais □[9]	74	47.00 N	3.30 E
Nivskij	66	67.25 N	32.52 E
Nixa	158	37.03 N	93.18 W
Nixon	160	29.16 N	97.46 W
Nizāmābād	100	18.40 N	78.07 E
Nizankovići	72	49.40 N	22.47 E
Nizke Beskydy ↗	72	49.25 N	21.30 E
Nizká Omra	66	66.43 N	55.46 E
Nižn'aja Peša	66	66.45 N	47.40 E
Nižn'aja Tunguska ≃	84	65.48 N	88.04 E
Nižneilimsk	84	56.57 N	103.16 E
Nižneudinsk	84	54.54 N	99.03 E
Nižni Lomov	86	53.32 N	43.40 E
Nižnij P'andž	82	37.14 N	68.35 E
Nižnij Tagil	82	57.55 N	59.57 E
Nizwá	100	22.55 N	57.32 E
Njazidja I	117b	11.35 S	43.20 E
Njombe	110	9.20 S	34.46 E
Nkhata Bay	110	11.36 S	34.18 E
Nkhota Kota	110	12.55 S	34.18 E
Nmai ≃	94	25.42 N	97.30 E
Noākhāli	102	22.49 N	91.06 E
Noatak	146	67.34 N	162.59 W
Nobeoka	90	32.35 N	131.40 E
Noblesville	158	40.02 N	86.01 W
Noboribetsu	90a	42.26 N	141.11 E
Nocatee	156	27.09 N	81.53 W
Nocera [Inferiore]	78	40.44 N	14.38 E
Noci	78	40.48 N	17.08 E
Nockatunga	120	27.43 S	142.43 E
Nocona	160	33.47 N	97.44 W
Nodaway ≃	158	39.54 N	94.58 W
Nogales, Méx.	130	31.20 N	110.56 W
Nogales, Ariz., U.S.	164	31.20 N	110.56 W
Nogaro	74	43.46 N	0.02 W
Nogent-le-Rotrou	74	48.19 N	0.50 E
Nogent-sur-Seine	74	48.29 N	3.30 E
Noginsk	86	55.51 N	38.27 E
Nogoa ≃	120	23.33 S	148.32 E
Nogoyá	140	32.23 S	59.49 W
Nógrád □[6]	72	48.00 N	19.35 E
Noirétable	74	45.49 N	3.46 E
Noirmoutier	74	47.00 N	2.14 W
Noirmoutier, Île de I	74	47.00 N	2.15 W
Nokomis, Fla., U.S.	156	27.07 N	82.27 W
Nokomis, Ill., U.S.	158	39.18 N	89.18 W
Nola	78	40.55 N	14.33 E
Nolichucky ≃	156	36.23 N	83.14 W
Nolinsk	66	57.33 N	49.57 E
Nombre de Dios	130	23.51 N	104.14 W
Nomgon	88	42.57 N	104.55 E
Nonacho Lake ⊜	142	61.42 N	109.40 W
Nonancourt	74	48.46 N	1.12 E
Nonburg	66	65.36 N	50.40 E
Nondalton	146	60.00 N	154.49 W
Nong'an	88	44.25 N	125.10 E
Nong Khai	94	17.52 N	102.45 E
Nonoava	130	27.28 N	106.44 W
Noonamah	122	12.38 S	131.04 E
Noonan	162	48.54 N	103.01 W
Noordwijk aan Zee	72	52.14 N	4.26 E
Noormarkku	68	61.35 N	21.52 E
Nootka Island I	148	49.32 N	126.42 W
Nóqui	110	5.51 S	13.25 E
Nora	68	59.31 N	15.02 E
Nora Springs	154	43.08 N	93.00 W
Noranda	154	48.16 N	79.02 W
Norborne	158	39.18 N	93.40 W
Norcia	78	42.48 N	13.05 E
Norcross	156	33.57 N	84.13 W
Nord □[5]	74	50.20 N	3.40 E
Norden	72	53.36 N	7.12 E
Nordenham	72	53.29 N	8.28 E
Nordenšel'da, Archipelag II	84	76.50 N	96.00 E
Nordfjordeid	68	61.54 N	6.00 E
Nordhausen	72	51.30 N	10.47 E
Nordheim	160	28.55 N	97.36 W
Nordkapp ↣	66	71.11 N	25.48 E
Nordland □[6]	66	67.00 N	14.00 E
Nördlingen	72	48.51 N	10.30 E
Nordre Strømfjord C[2]	142	67.50 N	52.00 W
Nordrhein-Westfalen □[3]	72	51.30 N	7.30 E
Nord-Trøndelag □[6]	66	64.25 N	12.00 E
Nordvik	84	74.02 N	111.32 E
Nore ≃	70	52.25 N	6.58 W
Norfolk, Nebr., U.S.	162	42.01 N	97.25 W
Norfolk, Va., U.S.	156	36.50 N	76.18 W
Norfolk □[6]	70	52.40 N	1.00 E
Norfork Lake ⊜[1]	158	36.25 N	92.10 W
Norheimsund	68	60.22 N	6.08 E
Noril'sk	84	69.20 N	88.06 E
Normal, Ala., U.S.	158	34.47 N	86.34 W
Normal, Ill., U.S.	154	40.30 N	88.59 W
Norman	160	35.13 N	97.26 W
Norman ≃	120	17.28 S	140.49 E
Normandie □[9]	74	49.00 N	0.05 W
Normandie, Collines de ↗[2]	74	48.50 N	1.00 W
Normandy → Normandie □[9]	74	49.00 N	0.05 W
Normangee	160	31.02 N	96.07 W
Normanton	120	17.40 S	141.05 E
Norman Wells	146	65.17 N	126.51 W
Norquay	142	51.53 N	102.05 W
Norquincó	140	41.51 S	70.55 W
Norrahammar	68	57.42 N	14.06 E
Norra Kvarken (Merenkurkku) ↵	68	63.36 N	20.43 E
Norrbottens Län □[6]	66	66.45 N	23.00 E
Nørresundby	68	57.04 N	9.55 E
Norris	156	36.13 N	84.04 W
Norristown	152	40.07 N	75.21 W
Norrköping	68	58.36 N	16.11 E
Norrsundet	68	60.56 N	17.08 E
Norrtälje	68	59.46 N	18.42 E
Norseman	122	32.12 S	121.46 E
Norsk	84	52.20 N	129.55 E
Norte, Canal do ↵	134	0.30 N	50.30 W
Norte, Serra do ↗[1]	134	11.20 S	59.00 W
North ≃	138	57.30 N	73.00 W
North, Cape ↣[2]	142	47.02 N	60.25 W
North Adams, Mass., U.S.	152	42.41 N	73.07 W
North Adams, Mich., U.S.	154	41.58 N	84.32 W
Northallerton	70	54.20 N	1.26 W
Northam, Austl.	122	31.39 S	116.40 E
Northam, Eng., U.K.	70	51.02 N	4.13 W
Northampton, Austl.	122	28.21 S	114.37 E
Northampton, Eng., U.K.	70	52.14 N	0.54 W
Northampton, Mass., U.S.	152	42.19 N	72.38 W
Northampton, Pa., U.S.	152	40.41 N	75.29 W
Northamptonshire □[6]	70	52.20 N	0.55 W
North Andaman I	94	13.15 N	92.55 E
North Anson	152	44.52 N	69.54 W
North Atlanta	156	33.52 N	84.21 W
North Augusta	156	33.30 N	81.58 W
North Aulatsivik Island I	142	59.50 N	64.00 W
North Baltimore	152	41.11 N	83.40 W
North Battleford	142	52.47 N	108.17 W
North Bay	154	46.19 N	79.28 W
North Bend, Nebr., U.S.	162	41.28 N	96.47 W
North Bend, Oreg., U.S.	166	43.24 N	124.14 W
North Berwick, Scot., U.K.	70	56.04 N	2.44 W
North Berwick, Maine, U.S.	152	43.17 N	70.45 W
North Bourke	120	30.03 S	145.55 E
North Branch	154	45.30 N	92.58 W
North Canadian ≃	144	35.17 N	95.31 W
North Canton	152	40.52 N	81.23 W
North Caribou Lake ⊜	142	52.48 N	90.40 W
North Carolina □[3]	144	35.30 N	80.00 W
North Charleston	156	32.53 N	79.58 W
North Chicago	154	42.19 N	87.50 W
North College Hill	152	39.13 N	84.33 W
North Collins	152	42.35 N	78.56 W
North Conway	152	44.03 N	71.07 W
North Dakota □[3]	144	47.30 N	100.15 W
North East	152	42.12 N	79.50 W
North English	154	41.31 N	92.04 W
Northern Indian Lake ⊜	142	57.20 N	97.20 W
Northern Ireland □[8]	70	54.40 N	6.45 W
Northern Territory □[8]	118	20.00 S	134.00 E
North Fabius ≃	158	39.54 N	91.30 W
Northfield, Mass., U.S.	152	42.41 N	72.27 W
Northfield, Minn., U.S.	154	44.27 N	93.09 W
North Flinders Ranges ↗	120	31.00 S	139.00 E
North Fond du Lac	154	43.49 N	88.28 W
North Fork ≃	156	36.13 N	92.17 W
North Fort Myers	156	26.40 N	81.54 W
North Freedom	154	43.27 N	89.52 W
North Frisian Islands II	66	54.50 N	8.12 E
North Havre	166	48.36 N	109.41 W
North Henik Lake ⊜	142	61.45 N	97.40 W
North Highlands	168	38.40 N	121.23 W
North Kingsville	152	41.54 N	80.41 W
North Knife Lake ⊜	142	58.05 N	97.05 W
North Korea → Korea, North □[1]	88	40.00 N	127.00 E
North Ladder Creek ≃	162	38.40 N	101.34 W
North Las Vegas	168	36.12 N	115.07 W
North Little Rock	158	34.46 N	92.14 W
North Manchester	158	41.00 N	85.46 W
North Mankato	154	44.10 N	94.01 W
North Miami	156	25.54 N	80.11 W
North Miami Beach	156	25.56 N	80.09 W
North Milk ≃	166	49.08 N	112.23 W
North Mount Lofty Ranges ↗	120	33.50 S	138.32 E
North Muskegon	154	43.15 N	86.17 W
North Ogden	164	41.18 N	111.57 W
North Palm Beach	156	26.49 N	80.04 W
North Park ≃	164	40.40 N	106.20 W
North Platte	162	41.08 N	100.46 W
North Platte ≃	144	41.15 N	100.45 W
North Pole	146	64.40 N	147.07 W
Northport, Ala., U.S.	158	33.14 N	87.35 W
Northport, Mich., U.S.	154	45.08 N	85.37 W
Northport, Wash., U.S.	148	48.55 N	117.48 W
North Richland Hills	160	32.51 N	97.12 W
North Rustico	150	46.27 N	63.19 W
North Salt Lake	164	40.50 N	111.55 W
North Santiam ≃	166	44.41 N	123.00 W
North Saskatchewan ≃	142	53.15 N	105.06 W
North Sea ╼[2]	64	55.20 N	3.00 E
North Shreveport	158	32.35 N	93.48 W
North Spicer Island I	142	68.30 N	78.55 W
North Stradbroke Island I	120	27.35 S	153.28 E
North Sunderland	70	55.35 N	1.39 W
North Sydney	150	46.13 N	60.15 W
North Thompson ≃	148	50.41 N	120.21 W
North Troy	152	45.00 N	72.24 W
Northumberland □[6]	70	55.12 N	2.00 W
Northumberland Islands II	120	21.40 S	150.00 E
Northumberland Strait ↵	150	46.00 N	63.30 W
North Vancouver	148	49.19 N	123.04 W
North Vassalboro	152	44.29 N	69.47 W
North Vernon	158	39.00 N	85.37 W
North Vietnam → Vietnam, North □[1]	92	22.00 N	105.00 E
Northville	152	43.13 N	74.11 W
North Wabasha	162	52.50 N	1.24 E
North West □[5]	138	7.30 N	59.50 W
North West Cape ↣, Austl.	122	21.45 S	114.10 E
Northwest Cape ↣, Alaska, U.S.	146	63.47 N	171.45 W
North West River	142	53.32 N	60.08 W
Northwest Territories □[4]	142	70.00 N	100.00 W
North Wilkesboro	156	36.09 N	81.08 W
North Windham	152	43.50 N	70.26 W
North Wyocena	158	43.25 N	91.52 W
North Yorkshire □[6]	70	54.15 N	1.30 W
North Zulch	160	30.54 N	96.07 W
Norton, Kans., U.S.	162	39.50 N	99.53 W
Norton, Va., U.S.	156	36.56 N	82.38 W
Nort-sur-Erdre	74	47.26 N	1.30 W
Norwalk, Conn., U.S.	152	41.07 N	73.27 W
Norwalk, Iowa, U.S.	154	41.29 N	93.41 W
Norwalk, Ohio, U.S.	152	41.15 N	82.37 W
Norway, Maine, U.S.	152	44.13 N	70.32 W
Norway, Mich., U.S.	154	45.47 N	87.55 W
Norway □[1]	64	62.00 N	10.00 E
Norway Bay C	142	71.08 N	104.35 W
Norway House	142	53.59 N	97.50 W
Norwegian Sea ╼[2]	66	70.00 N	2.00 E
Norwich, Eng., U.K.	70	52.38 N	1.18 E
Norwich, Conn., U.S.	152	41.31 N	72.05 W
Norwich, Kans., U.S.	162	37.27 N	97.51 W
Norwich, N.Y., U.S.	152	42.31 N	75.31 W
Norwood, Colo., U.S.	164	38.08 N	108.20 W
Norwood, Mass., U.S.	152	42.11 N	71.12 W
Norwood, N.Y., U.S.	152	44.45 N	75.00 W
Norwoodville	158	41.43 N	93.33 W
Noshiro	90	40.12 N	140.02 E
Nossob (Nosop) ≃	116	26.55 S	20.37 E
Nosy Varika	117b	20.35 S	48.32 E
Notikewin ≃	148	57.15 N	117.05 W
Notodden	68	59.34 N	9.17 E
Noto-hantō ↣[1]	90	37.20 N	137.00 E
Notre Dame, Monts ↗	150	48.10 N	69.00 W
Notre Dame Bay C	142	49.45 N	55.15 W
Notrees	160	31.55 N	102.45 W
Nottaway ≃	142	51.22 N	79.55 W
Nottingham	70	52.58 N	1.10 W
Nottingham Island I	142	63.20 N	77.55 W
Nottinghamshire □[6]	70	53.10 N	1.00 W
Nottoway ≃	156	37.08 N	76.56 W
Nouadhibou	114	20.54 N	17.04 W
Nouakchott	114	18.06 N	15.57 W
Nouamrhar	114	19.22 N	16.31 W
Nouméa	118	22.16 S	166.27 E
Noupoort	116	31.10 S	24.57 E
Nouveau-Québec, Cratère du ⊜[6]	142	61.17 N	73.40 W
Nouvelle-Anvers	110	1.36 N	19.07 E
Nouvelle-France, Cap de ↣	142	62.27 N	73.42 W
Nova Caipemba	110	7.23 S	14.38 E
Nova Chaves	110	10.34 S	21.17 E
Nova Cruz	134	6.28 S	35.26 W
Nova Friburgo	134	22.16 S	42.32 W
Nova Gaia	110	10.05 S	17.35 E
Nova Iguaçu	134	22.45 S	43.27 W
Nova Kachovka	86	46.45 N	33.23 E
Nova Ladoga	86	60.05 N	32.16 E
Novaja Sibir', Ostrov I	84	75.00 N	149.00 E
Novaja Zeml'a II	84	74.00 N	57.00 E
Nova Lima	134	19.59 S	43.51 W
Nova Lisboa → Huambo	110	12.44 S	15.47 E
Nova Mambone	116	20.59 S	35.00 E
Novara	78	45.28 N	8.38 E
Nova Scotia □[4]	142	45.00 N	63.00 W
Nova Sofala	116	20.09 S	34.42 E
Nova Varoš	80	43.28 N	19.49 E
Nova Zagora	80	42.29 N	26.01 E
Nové Město nad ...	72	49.46 N	17.49 E
Nové Zámky	72	47.59 N	18.11 E
Novgorod	86	58.31 N	31.17 E
Novice	160	31.59 N	99.37 W
Novi Ligure	78	44.46 N	8.47 E
Novi Pazar, Blg.	80	43.21 N	27.12 E
Novi Pazar, Jugo.	80	43.08 N	20.31 E
Noviodunum ...	78	44.50 N	9.32 E
Novi Sad	80	45.15 N	19.48 E
Novoaltajsk	84	53.24 N	83.58 E
Novoannaninskij	82	50.32 N	42.41 E

Name	Page	Lat	Long
Novo Aripuanã	138	5.08 S	60.22 W
Novočerkassk	64	47.25 N	40.06 E
Novograd-Volynskij	82	50.36 N	27.36 E
Novogrudok	86	53.36 N	25.50 E
Novoje Leušino	86	56.48 N	40.32 E
Novokašírsk	86	54.51 N	38.15 E
Novokazalinsk	82	45.50 N	62.10 E
Novokujbyšévsk	66	53.07 N	49.58 E
Novokuzneck	84	53.45 N	87.06 E
Novol'vovsk	86	53.55 N	38.47 E
Novo Mesto	78	45.48 N	15.10 E
Novomoskovsk	86	54.05 N	38.13 E
Novopetrovskoje	86	55.59 N	36.28 E
Novopiscovo	86	57.19 N	41.54 E
Novo Redondo	110	11.13 S	13.50 E
Novorossijsk	64	43.45 N	37.45 E
Novošáchtinsk	64	47.47 N	39.56 E
Novosibirsk	84	55.02 N	82.55 E
Novosibirskije Ostrova II	84	75.00 N	142.00 E
Novosibirskoje Vodochranílišče ⊞1	84	54.35 N	82.35 E
Novotroick	82	51.12 N	58.20 E
Novozensk	82	50.28 N	48.08 E
Novov'azník	86	56.12 N	42.10 E
Novov'azniki	86	56.12 N	42.10 E
Novovolynsk	82	50.50 N	24.05 E
Novozavidovskij	86	56.32 N	36.30 E
Novozybkov	86	52.33 N	31.56 E
Novy Bohumín	72	49.56 N	18.20 E
Novyje Gorki	86	56.42 N	41.06 E
Novyj Jičín	72	49.36 N	18.00 E
Novyj Port		67.40 N	72.52 E
Nowa Ruda	72	50.35 N	16.31 E
Nowa Sól (Neusalz)	72	51.48 N	15.44 E
Nowata	160	36.42 N	95.38 W
Nowgong	102	26.21 N	92.40 E
Nowitna ≃	146	65.55 N	154.17 W
Nowra	120	34.53 S	150.36 E
Nowshāk ∧	102	36.26 N	71.50 E
Nowshera	102	34.01 N	71.59 E
Nowy Dwór Mazowiecki	72	52.26 N	20.43 E
Nowy Sącz	72	49.38 N	20.42 E
Nowy Targ	72	49.29 N	20.02 E
Noxen	152	41.25 N	76.03 W
Noxon	166	48.01 N	115.47 W
Noyant	74	47.31 N	0.08 E
Noyon	74	49.35 N	3.00 E
Nozay	74	47.34 N	1.38 W
Nsanje	110	16.55 S	35.12 E
Nsawam	114	5.50 N	0.20 W
Nsukka	114	6.52 N	7.24 E
Ntem ≃	106	2.15 N	9.55 E
Nuanetsi	116	21.22 S	30.45 E
Nuanetsi ≃	116	22.40 S	31.50 E
Nūbah, Jibāl an-	112	12.00 N	30.45 E
Nubian Desert ✦2	112	20.30 N	33.00 E
Ñuble	140	36.35 S	71.50 W
Nucla	166	38.16 N	108.33 W
Nudlung Fiord C2	66	63.27 N	46.28 E
Nueces ≃	160	27.50 N	97.30 W
Nueltin Lake	66	60.20 N	99.50 W
Nueva, Isla I	136	55.13 S	66.30 W
Nueva Casas Grandes	130	30.25 N	107.55 W
Nueva Esparta □3	138	11.00 N	64.00 W
Nueva Gerona	132	21.53 N	82.48 W
Nueva Imperial	140	38.44 S	72.57 W
Nueva Italia de Ruiz	130	19.01 N	102.06 W
Nueva Rosita	130	27.57 N	101.13 W
Nueve de Julio	140	35.30 S	60.50 W
Nuevitas	132	21.33 N	77.16 W
Nuevo, Golfo C	136	42.42 S	64.35 W
Nuevo Laredo	130	27.30 N	99.31 W
Nuevo Mundo, Cerro ∧	140	21.55 S	66.53 W
Nûgssuaq >1	142	71.43 N	53.00 W
Nuits-Saint-Georges	74	47.08 N	4.57 E
N'uja	84	60.32 N	116.14 E
N'uja ≃	84	60.32 N	116.20 E
Nukey Bluff ±4	120	32.33 S	135.40 E
Nukus	82	42.50 N	59.29 E
Nulato	146	64.43 N	158.06 W
Nules	76	39.51 N	0.09 W
Nullagine	122	21.53 S	120.06 E
Nullarbor Plain ≃	122	31.00 S	129.00 E
Numazu	90	35.06 N	138.52 E
Numfoor, Pulau I	124	1.03 S	134.54 E
Numila	170b	21.54 N	159.34 W
Numto	84	63.40 N	71.20 E
Numurkah	120	36.06 S	145.26 E
Nunapitchuk	146	60.54 N	162.29 W
Nunda	152	42.35 N	77.57 W
Nuneaton	70	52.32 N	1.28 W
Nunivak Island	146	60.00 N	166.30 W
Nunjiang	88	49.10 N	125.11 E
Nunjiang ≃	88	45.25 N	124.40 E
Nunkompita	82	32.16 S	134.19 E
Nunnelly	158	35.52 N	87.28 W
Nuomine	158	40.06 N	124.26 E
Nuoro	78	40.19 N	9.20 E
Nura ≃	82	50.30 N	69.59 E
N'urba	84	63.17 N	118.20 E
Nuremberg → Nürnberg	72	49.27 N	11.04 E
Nuriat	66	54.26 N	50.46 E
Nurmes	68	63.33 N	29.07 E
Nurmijärvi	68	60.28 N	24.48 E
Nürnberg	72	49.27 N	11.04 E
Nurri	78	39.42 N	9.14 E
Nurri, Mount ∧	120	31.42 S	146.02 E
Nushan ∧	94	26.50 N	99.03 E
Nushki	100	29.33 N	66.01 E
Nutter Fort	152	39.16 N	80.19 W
Nutwood Downs	124	15.49 S	134.10 E
N'uvčim	66	61.22 N	50.42 E
Nuwara-Eliya	100	6.58 N	80.46 E
Nuweveldberge ∧	116	32.13 S	21.40 E
Nuyts Archipelago II	122	32.35 S	133.17 E
Nyabing	122	33.32 S	118.09 E
Nyack	152	41.05 N	73.55 W
Nyah West	120	35.11 S	143.22 E
Nyala	112	12.03 N	24.53 E
Nyanza	110	2.21 S	29.45 E
Nyasa, Lake	110	12.00 S	34.30 E
Nybergsund	68	61.16 N	12.19 E
Nyborg	68	55.19 N	10.48 E
Nybro	68	56.45 N	15.54 E
Nyda	84	66.36 N	72.54 E
Nyeri	106	3.17 N	9.54 E
Nyíregyháza	72	47.59 N	21.43 E
Nykarleby	68	63.31 N	22.32 E
Nykøbing, Dan.	68	56.48 N	8.52 E
Nykøbing, Dan.	68	54.46 N	11.53 E
Nyköping	68	58.45 N	17.00 E
Nylstroom	116	24.42 S	28.20 E
Nymburk	72	50.11 N	15.03 E
Nynäshamn	68	58.54 N	17.57 E
Nyngan	120	31.34 S	147.11 E
Nyon	74	46.23 N	6.14 E
Nyong ≃	106	3.17 N	9.54 E
Nyons	74	44.22 N	5.08 E
Nysa	72	50.29 N	17.20 E
Nysa Łużycka (Neisse) (Nisa) ≃	72	52.04 N	14.46 E
Nyssa	166	43.53 N	117.00 W
Nytva	66	57.56 N	55.20 E
Nzérékoré	114	7.45 N	8.49 W
Nzi ≃	114	5.57 N	4.50 W

O

Name	Page	Lat	Long
Oacoma	162	43.48 N	99.24 W
Oahe, Lake ⊞1	144	45.30 N	100.25 W
Oahe Reservoir ⊞1	144	45.30 N	100.25 W
Oakbank	120	33.04 S	140.36 E
Oak Bay	148	48.27 N	123.18 W
Oak City	164	39.22 N	112.20 W
Oak Creek	164	40.16 N	106.57 W
Oak Creek ≃, U.S.	164	45.39 N	100.31 W
Oak Creek ≃, Kans., U.S.	162	39.29 N	98.28 W
Oakdale, Austl.	122	34.26 S	119.00 E
Oakdale, Calif., U.S.	168	37.46 N	120.51 W
Oakdale, La., U.S.	158	30.49 N	92.40 W
Oakey	120	27.26 S	151.43 E
Oakfield, Maine, U.S.	152	46.06 N	68.10 W
Oakfield, N.Y., U.S.	152	43.04 N	78.16 W
Oak Grove	158	32.52 N	91.23 W
Oakham	70	52.40 N	0.43 W
Oak Harbor, Ohio, U.S.	154	41.30 N	83.09 W
Oak Harbor, Wash., U.S.	166	48.18 N	122.39 W
Oak Hill, Fla., U.S.	156	28.52 N	80.51 W
Oak Hill, Mich., U.S.	154	44.13 N	86.19 W
Oak Hill, Ohio, U.S.	154	38.54 N	82.34 W
Oak Hill, Tenn., U.S.	158	36.05 N	86.48 W
Oak Hill, W. Va., U.S.	152	37.59 N	81.09 W
Oakhurst	168	37.47 N	119.40 W
Oakland, Calif., U.S.	168	37.47 N	122.13 W
Oakland, Iowa, U.S.	162	41.19 N	95.23 W
Oakland, Maine, U.S.	152	44.33 N	69.43 W
Oakland, Nebr., U.S.	162	41.50 N	96.28 W
Oakland, Oreg., U.S.	166	43.25 N	123.18 W
Oakland Md., U.S.	152	39.25 N	79.24 W
Oakland Park	156	26.12 N	80.07 W
Oak Lawn, Ill., U.S.	154	41.43 N	87.45 W
Oaklawn, Kans., U.S.	162	37.36 N	97.18 W
Oakley, Idaho, U.S.	166	42.15 N	113.53 W
Oakley, Kans., U.S.	162	39.08 N	100.51 W
Oak Park	154	41.53 N	87.48 W
Oakridge, Oreg., U.S.	166	43.45 N	122.28 W
Oak Ridge, Tenn., U.S.	156	36.01 N	84.16 W
Oak View	168	34.24 N	119.18 W
Oakville	154	41.06 N	84.23 W
Oakwood	154	41.06 N	84.23 W
Oamaru	126	45.06 S	170.58 E
Oatlands	120	42.18 S	147.21 E
Oaxaca [de Juárez]	130	17.03 N	96.43 W
Ob' ≃	84	66.45 N	69.32 E
Oban, Austl.	120	21.14 S	139.03 E
Oban, Scot., U.K.	70	56.25 N	5.29 W
Obbia	108	5.20 N	48.38 E
Oberá	140	27.30 S	55.07 W
Oberdrauburg	72	46.45 N	12.58 E
Obergurgl	72	46.52 N	11.01 E
Oberhausen	72	51.28 N	6.50 E
Oberlin, Kans., U.S.	162	39.49 N	100.32 W
Oberlin, La., U.S.	158	30.37 N	92.46 W
Oberlin, Ohio, U.S.	154	41.17 N	82.13 W
Obernai	74	48.28 N	7.28 E
Obernburg am Main	72	49.50 N	9.08 E
Oberon	120	33.43 S	149.52 E
Oberösterreich □3	72	48.15 N	14.00 E
Oberpullendorf	72	47.30 N	16.31 E
Oberursel	72	50.11 N	8.35 E
Obervellach	72	46.56 N	13.12 E
Oberviechtach	72	49.28 N	12.25 E
Oberwart	72	47.17 N	16.13 E
Oberwölz Stadt	72	47.13 N	14.17 E
Obi, Kepulauan II	124	1.23 S	127.45 E
Obi, Pulau I	124	1.30 S	127.45 E
Óbidos	134	1.55 S	55.31 W
Obihiro	90a	42.55 N	143.12 E
Obilatu, Pulau I	124	1.25 S	127.20 E
Obing	72	48.00 N	12.24 E
Obion	158	36.16 N	89.12 W
Oblong	154	39.00 N	87.55 W
Obluč'je	84	49.03 N	131.04 E
Obock	108	11.59 N	43.16 E
Oborniki	72	52.39 N	16.51 E
Oboz'orskij	66	63.28 N	40.18 E
Obščij Syrt ∧	64	52.00 N	51.30 E
Observatoire, Caye de l' I	118	21.25 S	158.50 E
Obskaja Guba C	84	69.00 N	73.00 E
Obuasi	118	6.14 N	1.39 W
Ocala	156	29.11 N	82.07 W
Ocaña	138	8.15 N	73.20 W
Occidental, Cordillera ∧, Perú	134	14.00 S	74.00 W
Occidental, Cordillera ∧, Col.	134	5.00 N	76.00 W
Ocean Cape >	142	59.30 N	139.45 W
Ocean City	152	39.16 N	74.34 W
Ocean Falls	148	52.21 N	127.40 W
Oceano	168	35.06 N	120.37 W
Oceanside	168	33.12 N	117.23 W
Ocean Springs	158	30.25 N	88.50 W
Oceanway	156	30.28 N	81.38 W
Očer	66	57.53 N	54.42 E
Ocha	84	53.34 N	142.56 E
Ocheyedan	162	43.08 N	95.09 W
Ochlockonee ≃	156	29.58 N	84.21 W
Ochota ≃	84	59.20 N	143.04 E
Ochotsk	84	59.20 N	143.18 E
Ochsenfurt	72	49.40 N	10.03 E
Ochtrup	72	52.12 N	7.11 E
Ocilla	156	31.36 N	83.15 W
Ockelbo	68	60.53 N	16.43 E
Ocoee	156	28.35 N	81.33 W
Ocoña	134	16.26 S	73.08 W
Oconomowoc	154	43.07 N	88.30 W
Oconto	154	44.53 N	87.52 W
Oconto Falls	154	44.52 N	88.08 W
Ocotal	132	13.37 N	86.31 W
Ocotlán	130	20.21 N	102.46 W
Ocotlán de Morelos	130	16.48 N	96.40 W
Ocozocoautla [de Espinosa]	130	16.46 N	93.22 W
Ocracoke Island	156	35.09 N	75.53 W
Ocumare del Tuy	138	10.07 N	66.46 W
Ocussi	124	9.12 S	124.21 E
Oda	114	5.55 N	0.59 W
Oda, Jabal ∧	112	20.21 N	36.39 E
Ōdawara	90	35.15 N	139.10 E
Odda	68	60.04 N	6.33 E
Odebolt	162	42.19 N	95.15 W
Ödemiş	30	38.13 N	27.59 E
Odemira	76	37.36 N	8.38 W
Odendaalsrus	116	27.48 S	26.45 E
Odense	68	55.24 N	10.23 E
Odenton	152	39.05 N	76.42 W
Oder (Odra) ≃	72	53.32 N	14.38 E
Oderberg	72	52.52 N	14.02 E
Oderhaff (Zalew Szczeciński) C	72	53.47 N	14.19 E
Oderzo	78	45.47 N	12.29 E
Ödeshög	68	58.14 N	14.39 E
Odessa, S.S.S.R.	64	46.28 N	30.44 E
Odessa, Mo., U.S.	158	39.00 N	93.57 W
Odessa, Tex., U.S.	160	31.51 N	102.22 W
Odessa, Wash., U.S.	166	47.20 N	118.41 W
Odesskoje	84	54.13 N	72.58 E
Odienné	114	9.30 N	7.34 W
Odin, Mount ∧	148	50.33 N	118.08 W
Odincovo	86	55.41 N	37.17 E
Odojev	86	53.56 N	36.41 E
Odonnell	160	32.58 N	101.50 W
Odorheiu Secuiesc	72	46.18 N	25.18 E
Oeiras	134	7.01 S	42.08 W
Oelde	72	51.49 N	8.08 E
Oelsnitz	72	50.24 N	12.10 E
Oelwein	162	42.41 N	91.55 W
Oenpelli Mission	124	12.20 S	133.04 E
Oettingen in Bayern	72	48.57 N	10.36 E
Oetz	72	47.12 N	10.54 E
Offaly □6	70	53.20 N	7.30 W
Offenbach	72	50.06 N	8.46 E
Offenburg	72	48.28 N	7.57 E
Ōgaki	90	35.21 N	136.37 E
Ogallala	162	41.08 N	101.43 W
Ogbomosho	114	8.08 N	4.15 E
Ogden, Iowa, U.S.	162	42.02 N	94.02 W
Ogden, Utah, U.S.	164	41.14 N	111.58 W
Ogden, Mount ∧	146	58.26 N	133.42 E
Ogdensburg	152	44.42 N	75.29 W
Ogilvie Mountains ∧	146	65.00 N	139.30 W
Oglala	162	43.17 N	102.44 W
Oglesby, Ill., U.S.	154	41.18 N	89.04 W
Oglesby, Tex., U.S.	160	31.25 N	97.31 W
Oglethorpe	156	32.18 N	84.04 W
Ogmore	120	22.37 S	149.40 E
Ogoja	114	6.40 N	8.48 E
Ogoki ≃	142	51.38 N	85.57 W
Ogooué ≃	110	0.49 S	9.00 E
Ogre	86	56.51 N	24.36 E
Ogulin	78	45.16 N	15.14 E
Ohakune	126	39.25 S	175.25 E
Ohanet	106	28.45 N	8.55 E
O'Higgins □4	136	34.15 S	70.45 W
O'Higgins, Lago (Lago San Martín)	136	49.00 S	72.40 W
Ohio □3	144	40.15 N	82.45 W
Ohio ≃	144	36.59 N	89.08 W
Ohio City	152	40.46 N	84.37 W
Ohře ≃	72	50.32 N	14.08 E
Ohrid	80	41.07 N	20.47 E
Ohrid, Lake	80	41.02 N	20.43 E
Öhringen	72	49.12 N	9.29 E
Oildale	168	35.25 N	119.01 W
Oil City	152	41.26 N	79.42 W
Oilmont	166	48.44 N	111.51 W
Oilton, Okla., U.S.	160	36.05 N	96.35 W
Oilton, Tex., U.S.	160	27.33 N	98.59 W
Oise □5	74	49.30 N	2.30 E
Oise ≃	74	49.00 N	2.04 E
Oisemont	74	49.57 N	1.46 E
Oissel	74	49.20 N	1.06 E
Ojai	168	34.27 N	119.15 W
Oja ≃	90		
Ojinaga	130	29.34 N	104.25 W
Ojm'akon	84	63.28 N	142.49 E
Ojocaliente	130	22.34 N	102.15 W
Ojos del Salado, Cerro ∧	140	27.06 S	68.32 W
Oka ≃, S.S.S.R.	84	55.15 N	102.10 E
Oka ≃, S.S.S.R.	86	56.20 N	43.59 E
Okaba	124	8.06 S	139.42 E
Okahandja	116	21.59 S	16.58 E
Okanagan (Okanogan) ≃	148	48.06 N	119.43 W
Okanagan Lake	148	50.00 N	119.28 W
Okanogan ≃	148	48.22 N	119.35 W
Okanogan	148	48.22 N	119.43 W
Okanogan Range (Okanagan Range) ∧	148	49.00 N	120.00 W
Okāra	102	30.49 N	73.27 E
Okarche	160	35.44 N	97.58 W
Okaukuejo	116	19.10 S	15.54 E
Okavango (Cubango) ≃	110	18.50 S	22.25 E
Okavango Swamp 🠵	110	18.45 S	22.45 E
Okaya	90	36.03 N	138.03 E
Okayama	90	34.39 N	133.55 E
Okazaki	90	34.57 N	137.10 E
Okeechobee	156	27.15 N	80.50 W
Okeechobee, Lake	156	26.55 N	80.45 W
Okefenokee Swamp 🠵	156	30.42 N	82.20 W
Okehampton	70	50.44 N	4.00 W
Okemah	160	35.26 N	96.19 W
Okemos	154	42.43 N	84.26 W
Okene	114	7.33 N	6.15 E
Okhotsk, Sea of (Ochotskoje More)	84	53.00 N	150.00 E
Okiep	116	29.39 S	17.53 E
Oki-guntō II	90	36.15 N	133.15 E
Okinawa-jima I	91b	26.30 N	128.00 E
Okino-Daitō-jima I	91b	24.28 N	131.11 E
Okino-Erabu-shima I	91b	27.22 N	128.35 E
Okino-Tori-Shima II	91b	20.25 N	136.05 E
Oklahoma □3	144	35.30 N	98.00 W
Oklahoma City	160	35.30 N	97.30 W
Okmulgee	160	35.37 N	95.58 W
Okolona, Ky., U.S.	154	38.08 N	85.41 W
Okolona, Miss., U.S.	158	34.00 N	88.45 W
Okpara ≃	114	7.40 N	2.35 E
Oksbøl	68	55.38 N	8.17 E
Okt'abr'	84	57.50 N	37.26 E
Okt'abr'sk	82	53.11 N	48.40 E
Okt'abr'skij, S.S.S.R.	66	54.28 N	53.28 E
Okt'abr'skij, S.S.S.R.	86	54.14 N	38.18 E
Okt'abr'skoje	84	52.38 N	156.14 E
Okt'abr'skoj Revol'ucii, Ostrov I	84	79.30 N	97.00 E
Okushiri-tō I	90a	42.10 N	139.27 E
Ólafsfjörður	66a	66.06 N	18.39 W
Olancha	168	36.17 N	118.01 W
Olanchito	132	15.30 N	86.35 W
Öland I	68	56.45 N	16.38 E
Olary	122	32.17 S	140.19 E
Olathe, Colo., U.S.	164	38.36 N	107.59 W
Olathe, Kans., U.S.	158	38.53 N	94.49 W
Olavarría	140	36.53 S	60.20 W
Oława	72	50.57 N	17.17 E
Olching	72	48.12 N	11.20 E
Olcott	152	43.20 N	78.43 W
Ol'chon, Ostrov I	84	53.09 N	107.24 E
Old Bahama Channel U	132	22.33 N	78.05 W
Oldcastle	70	53.46 N	7.10 W
Old Crow	146	67.35 N	139.50 W
Oldebroek	72	52.26 N	5.54 E
Olden, Nor.	68	61.50 N	6.49 E
Olden, Tex., U.S.	160	32.25 N	98.45 W
Oldenburg	72	53.08 N	8.13 E
Oldenburg □9	72	53.00 N	8.00 E
Oldenburg [in Holstein]	72	54.17 N	10.52 E
Oldenzaal	72	52.19 N	6.56 E
Old Forge	152	41.22 N	75.44 W
Oldham	70	53.33 N	2.07 W
Old Harbor	146	57.12 N	153.19 W
Old Hickory	158	36.16 N	86.39 W
Old Hometown	154	41.41 N	88.00 W
Oldmeldrum	70	57.20 N	2.19 W
Old Orchard Beach	152	43.31 N	70.23 W
Olds	148	51.47 N	114.06 W
Old Saybrook	152	41.17 N	72.22 W
Old Town	152	44.56 N	68.39 W
Old Wives Lake	148	50.06 N	106.00 W
Olean	152	42.05 N	78.25 W
Olecko	72	54.03 N	22.30 E
Olekma ≃	84	60.22 N	120.42 E
Olenegorsk	66	68.09 N	33.15 E
Olenij, Ostrov I	84	72.25 N	77.45 E
Olen'ok	84	68.28 N	112.18 E
Olen'ok ≃	84	73.00 N	120.00 E
Oléron, Île d' I	74	45.56 N	1.15 W
Ol'ga	84	43.45 N	135.18 E
Olga, Mount ∧	122	25.19 S	130.46 E
Ölgij	88	48.58 N	89.57 E
Ölgod	68	55.49 N	8.37 E
Oli ≃	114	7.37 N	2.17 E
Olifants (Rio dos Elefantes) ≃, Afr.	116	24.10 S	32.40 E
Olifants ≃, S. Afr.	116	31.42 S	18.12 E
Ólimarao I	92	7.41 N	145.52 E
Ólimbos ∧, Ellás	80	40.05 N	22.21 E
Ólimbos ∧, Kípros	104	34.56 N	32.52 E
Olímpia	134	20.44 S	48.54 W
Olin	162	42.00 N	91.09 W
Olinda	134	8.01 S	34.51 W
Olio	120	22.54 S	143.12 E
Oliva, Arg.	140	32.05 S	63.35 W
Oliva, Esp.	76	38.55 N	0.07 W
Oliva de la Frontera	76	38.16 N	6.55 W
Olive Hill	152	38.18 N	83.10 W
Olivehurst	168	39.06 N	121.34 W
Oliveira	134	20.41 S	44.49 W
Oliver	148	49.11 N	119.33 W
Oliver Springs	156	36.03 N	84.20 W
Olivet	154	42.27 N	84.56 W
Olivia	162	44.46 N	94.59 W
Ollagüe	136	21.14 S	68.16 W
Olmos	134	5.59 S	79.46 W
Olmos Park	160	29.28 N	98.29 W
Olney, Ill., U.S.	158	38.44 N	88.05 W
Olney, Mont., U.S.	148	48.33 N	114.35 W
Olney, Tex., U.S.	160	33.22 N	98.45 W
Olofström	68	56.16 N	14.30 E
Oloj ≃	84	66.29 N	159.29 E
Ol'okma ≃	84	60.22 N	120.42 E
Ol'okminsk	84	60.20 N	120.24 E
Olomouc	72	49.36 N	17.16 E
Olonec	66	61.00 N	32.57 E
Olongapo	92	14.49 N	120.17 E
Oloron-Sainte-Marie	74	43.12 N	0.36 W
Olot	76	42.11 N	2.29 E
Olov'annaja, S.S.S.R.	84	50.56 N	115.35 E
Olov'annaja, S.S.S.R.	84	50.56 N	178.59 E
Olpe	72	51.02 N	7.52 E
Olsztyn (Allenstein)	72	53.48 N	20.29 E
Olsztynek	72	53.36 N	20.17 E
Olt □4	80	44.20 N	24.30 E
Olt ≃	80	43.43 N	24.51 E
Olten	74	47.21 N	7.54 E
Olteniţa	80	44.05 N	26.39 E
Olton	160	34.11 N	102.08 W
Oluan Pi >	88	21.54 N	120.51 E
Olustee, Fla., U.S.	156	30.12 N	82.26 W
Olustee, Okla., U.S.	160	34.33 N	99.25 W
Ol'utorskij, Mys >	84	59.55 N	170.27 E
Ol'utorskij Zaliv C	84	59.55 N	170.27 E
Olympia	166	47.03 N	122.53 W
Olympic Mountains ∧	166	47.50 N	123.45 W
Olympus, Mount → Ólimbos ∧, Ellás	80	40.05 N	22.21 E
Olympus, Mount ∧, Ky., U.S.	156	38.03 N	83.39 W
Olympus, Mount ∧, Wash., U.S.	166	47.48 N	123.43 W
Om' ≃	84	54.59 N	73.22 E
Omagh	70	54.36 N	7.18 W
Omaha	162	41.16 N	95.57 W
Omak	166	48.24 N	119.31 W
Oman □1	100	22.00 N	58.00 E
Oman, Gulf of C	100	24.30 N	58.30 E
Omaruru	116	21.26 S	15.56 E
Ombai Strait U	124	8.30 S	125.00 E
Omboué	110	1.34 S	9.15 E
Omčak	84	61.10 N	147.55 E
Omegna	78	45.53 N	8.24 E
Omemee	152	44.18 N	78.33 W
Ometepe, Isla de I	132	11.30 N	85.35 W
Ometepec	130	16.41 N	98.25 W
Omineca ≃	148	56.05 N	124.30 W
Omineca Mountains ∧	148	56.05 N	124.30 W
Omiš	78	43.27 N	16.42 E
Ōmiya	90	35.54 N	139.38 E
Ommaney, Cape >	146	56.10 N	134.40 W
Ommanney Bay C	142	73.07 N	100.11 W
Ommen	72	52.31 N	6.25 E
Omo ≃	108	4.32 N	36.04 E
Omoloj ≃	84	71.10 N	132.08 E
Omolon	84	68.42 N	158.36 E
Omro	154	44.02 N	88.44 W
Ōmsk	84	55.00 N	73.24 E
Omsukčan	84	62.32 N	155.48 E
Ōmuta	90	33.02 N	130.27 E
Omutninsk	66	58.40 N	52.12 E
Ona	162	62.52 N	6.34 E
Onaga	162	39.29 N	96.10 W
Onalaska	154	43.53 N	91.14 W
Onamia	162	46.04 N	93.40 W
Onawa	162	42.02 N	96.06 W
Onaway	154	45.21 N	84.14 W
Onda	76	39.58 N	0.15 W
Ondangua	116	17.55 S	16.00 E
Ondo	114	7.04 N	4.47 E
Ondörchaan	88	47.19 N	110.39 E
Oneco	156	27.27 N	82.33 W
Onega	66	63.58 N	37.55 E
Onega ≃	66	63.58 N	37.55 E
Onega, Lake → Onežskoje Ozero	66	61.30 N	35.45 E
One Hundred and Two, West Fork ≃	158	40.26 N	94.49 W
Onehunga	126	36.55 S	174.47 E
Oneida, N.Y., U.S.	152	43.06 N	75.39 W
Oneida, Tenn., U.S.	156	36.30 N	84.31 W
O'Neill	162	42.27 N	98.39 W
Onekotan, Ostrov I	84	49.25 N	154.45 E
Oneonta, Ala., U.S.	158	33.57 N	86.28 W
Oneonta, N.Y., U.S.	152	42.27 N	75.04 W
Onežskoje Ozero (Lake Onega)	66	61.30 N	35.45 E
Ongerup	122	33.58 S	118.29 E
Ongole	100	15.30 N	80.03 E
Onida	162	44.42 N	100.04 W
Onitsha	114	6.09 N	6.47 E
Onomichi	90	34.25 N	133.12 E
Onon ≃	84	51.42 N	115.50 E
Onset	152	41.45 N	70.39 W
Onslow	122	21.39 S	115.06 E
Ontario, Calif., U.S.	168	34.04 N	117.39 W
Ontario, Ohio, U.S.	154	40.46 N	82.36 W
Ontario, Oreg., U.S.	166	44.01 N	116.58 W
Ontario □4	142	51.00 N	85.00 W
Ontario, Lake	154	43.45 N	78.00 W
Onteniente	76	38.49 N	0.37 W
Ontonagon	154	46.52 N	89.19 W
Oodnadatta	122	27.33 S	135.28 E
Ooldea	122	30.27 S	131.50 E
Ooratippra	124	21.45 S	135.26 E
Oostburg	154	43.37 N	87.48 W
Oostende (Ostende)	72	51.13 N	2.55 E
Oosterhout	72	51.38 N	4.51 E
Oost-Vlieland	72	53.18 N	5.04 E
Ootacamund → Udagamandalam	100	11.25 N	76.43 E
Ootsa Lake	148	53.49 N	126.18 W
Opala	110	0.37 S	24.21 E
Oparino	66	59.51 N	48.17 E
Opatów	72	50.49 N	21.26 E
Opava	72	49.56 N	17.54 E
Opelika	156	32.39 N	85.23 W
Opelousas	158	30.32 N	92.05 W
Opequon Creek ≃	152	39.25 N	78.00 W
Opheim	166	48.51 N	106.24 W
Opinaca ≃	142	52.14 N	78.02 W
Opiscotéo, Lac	142	53.10 N	68.10 W
Opobo	114	4.34 N	7.27 E
Opočka	86	56.43 N	28.38 E
Opoczno	72	51.23 N	20.17 E
Opole (Oppeln)	72	50.41 N	17.55 E
Opotiki	126	38.00 S	177.17 E
Oppdal	68	62.36 N	9.40 E
Oppland □6	68	61.10 N	9.30 E
Opportunity, Mont., U.S.	166	46.08 N	112.49 W
Opportunity, Wash., U.S.	166	47.39 N	117.15 W
Opunake	126	39.27 S	173.52 E
Opuwo	116	18.04 S	13.50 E
Ora	78	46.21 N	11.18 E
Ora Banda	122	30.22 S	121.04 E
Oracle	164	32.37 N	110.46 W
Oradea	72	47.04 N	21.57 E
Oræfajökull ∧1	66a	64.00 N	16.39 W
Orai	102	25.59 N	79.28 E
Oran, Alg.	106	35.43 N	0.43 W
Oran, Austl.	120	33.17 S	149.06 E
Orange, Austl.	120	33.17 S	149.06 E
Orange, Fr.	74	44.08 N	4.48 E
Orange, Mass., U.S.	152	42.35 N	72.19 W
Orange, Tex., U.S.	158	30.05 N	93.44 W
Orange, Va., U.S.	152	38.14 N	78.06 W
Orange (Oranje) ≃	116	28.41 S	16.28 E
Orange, Cabo >	134	4.24 N	51.33 W
Orangeburg	156	33.30 N	80.52 W
Orange City, Fla., U.S.	156	28.57 N	81.17 W
Orange City, Iowa, U.S.	162	43.00 N	96.03 W
Orange Cove	168	36.37 N	119.19 W
Orange Park	156	30.10 N	81.42 W
Orangeville, Ont., Can.	154	43.55 N	80.06 W
Orangeville, Utah, U.S.	164	39.13 N	111.03 W
Oranienburg	72	52.45 N	13.14 E
Oranje Gebergte ∧	134	3.15 N	54.50 W
Oranjemund	116	28.38 S	16.24 E
Oranjestad	132	12.33 N	70.06 W
Orăştie	80	45.50 N	23.12 E
Orbe	74	46.43 N	6.31 E
Orbetello	78	42.27 N	11.13 E
Orbost	120	37.42 S	148.27 E
Örbyhus	68	60.14 N	17.42 E
Orcera	76	38.19 N	2.39 W
Orchard Avenue	166	47.40 N	117.18 W
Orchard Homes	166	46.55 N	114.04 W
Orchard Park	152	42.43 N	78.45 W
Orchard Valley	164	41.06 N	104.19 W
Orchies	74	50.28 N	3.14 E
Orchon ≃	88	50.21 N	106.05 E
Ord	162	41.36 N	98.56 W
Ord River	122	17.23 S	128.51 E
Ordu	104	41.00 N	37.53 E
Ordway	164	38.13 N	103.46 W
Ordžonikidze	64	43.03 N	44.40 E
Örebro	68	59.17 N	15.13 E
Örebro Län □6	68	59.30 N	15.00 E
Orechovo-Zujevo	86	55.49 N	38.59 E
Orechovsk	86	54.41 N	30.30 E
Ore City	158	32.48 N	94.43 W
Oregon, Ill., U.S.	154	42.01 N	89.20 W
Oregon, Ohio, U.S.	154	41.38 N	83.28 W
Oregon □3	144	44.00 N	121.00 W
Oregon City	166	45.21 N	122.36 W
Orem	164	40.19 N	111.42 W
Orenburg	64	51.54 N	55.06 E
Orense	76	42.20 N	7.51 W
Orestiás	80	41.30 N	26.31 E
Orfordville	154	42.38 N	89.16 W
Orgelet	74	46.31 N	5.37 E
Orgtrud	86	56.12 N	40.37 E
Orick	168	41.17 N	124.04 W
Oriental, Cordillera ∧, Col.	138	6.00 N	73.00 W
Oriental, Cordillera ∧, Perú	134	13.00 S	72.00 W
Orihuela	76	38.05 N	0.57 W
Orillia	154	44.37 N	79.25 W
Orinoco ≃	138	8.37 N	62.15 W
Orion	154	41.21 N	90.23 W
Oriskany	152	43.09 N	75.20 W
Orivesi	68	61.41 N	24.21 E
Oriximiná	134	1.45 S	55.52 W
Orizaba	130	18.51 N	97.06 W
Ørje	68	59.29 N	11.39 E
Orkanger	68	63.19 N	9.52 E
Orkney	116	27.00 S	26.39 E
Orkney Islands II	70	59.00 N	3.00 W
Orkney Islands Area □8	70	59.00 N	3.00 W
Orland	168	39.45 N	122.11 W
Orlando	156	28.32 N	81.23 W
Orléanais □9	74	48.00 N	2.00 E
Orléans, Ont., Can.	152	45.28 N	75.31 W
Orléans, Fr.	74	47.55 N	1.54 E
Orleans, Calif., U.S.	168	41.18 N	123.32 W
Orlik	84	52.30 N	99.55 E
Orlov	66	58.37 N	48.53 E
Orlová	72	49.51 N	18.24 E
Ormoc	92	11.00 N	124.37 E
Ormond Beach	156	29.17 N	81.02 W
Ormstown	152	45.07 N	74.00 W
Orne □5	74	48.40 N	0.05 E
Ornes	68	61.18 N	12.24 E
Örnsköldsvik	68	63.18 N	18.43 E
Oro ≃	84	66.23 N	136.20 E
Oro, Río de ≃	134	17.59 N	94.00 W
Orocué	138	4.48 N	71.20 W
Orofino	166	46.29 N	116.15 W
Oro Grande	168	34.36 N	117.20 W
Oromocto	152	45.51 N	66.29 W
Oron	114	4.48 N	8.14 E
Orono	152	44.53 N	68.40 W
Oronsay I	70	56.01 N	6.14 W
Orosháza	72	46.34 N	20.40 E
Oroszlány	72	47.30 N	18.19 E
Oroville, Calif., U.S.	168	39.30 N	121.33 W
Oroville, Wash., U.S.	148	48.56 N	119.26 W
Orroroo	122	32.44 S	138.37 E
Orr's Island	152	43.46 N	69.57 W
Orša, S.S.S.R.	86	54.30 N	30.24 E
Orsa, Sve.	68	61.07 N	14.37 E
Orsières	74	46.02 N	7.09 E
Orsk	82	51.12 N	58.34 E
Ørsta	68	62.12 N	6.09 E
Orta Nova	78	41.19 N	15.42 E
Ortegal, Cabo >	76	43.46 N	7.52 W
Orthez	74	43.29 N	0.46 W
Ortisei	78	46.34 N	11.40 E
Ortona	78	42.21 N	14.24 E
Ortonville	162	45.18 N	96.26 W
Orto-Tokoj	82	42.20 N	76.01 E
Ortrand	72	51.23 N	13.47 E
Orümiyeh	104	37.33 N	45.04 E
Orümiyeh, Daryacheh-ye	104	37.40 N	45.30 E
Oruro	134	17.59 S	67.09 W
Orvieto	78	42.43 N	12.07 E
Orrville	152	40.47 N	81.46 W
Orwell	152	43.48 N	73.18 W
Ōs, Nor.	68	60.11 N	5.28 E
Os, Nor.	68	62.30 N	11.12 E
Oša ≃	84	56.00 N	73.00 E
Osa, Peninsula de >1	132	8.35 N	83.33 W
Ōsaka	90	34.40 N	135.30 E
Osakis	162	45.52 N	95.09 W
Osawatomie	158	38.31 N	94.57 W
Osborne	162	39.26 N	98.42 W
Osburn	166	47.30 N	116.00 W
Osceola, Ark., U.S.	158	35.42 N	89.58 W
Osceola, Iowa, U.S.	162	41.02 N	93.46 W
Osceola, Mo., U.S.	158	38.03 N	93.42 W
Osceola, Nebr., U.S.	162	41.11 N	97.33 W
Osceola Mills	152	40.51 N	78.16 W
Oschatz	72	51.17 N	13.07 E
Oschersleben	72	52.01 N	11.13 E
Oscoda	154	44.25 N	83.20 W
Osečina	80	44.22 N	19.36 E
Osen	68	64.17 N	10.31 E
Osgood	154	39.07 N	85.18 W
Osh	82	40.33 N	72.48 E
Oshawa	154	43.54 N	78.51 W
Ō-shima I	90	34.44 N	139.22 E
Oshkosh, Nebr., U.S.	162	41.24 N	102.21 W
Oshkosh, Wis., U.S.	154	44.01 N	88.32 W
Oshogbo	114	7.47 N	4.34 E
Oshwe	110	3.23 S	19.30 E
Osijek	80	45.33 N	18.41 E
Osimo	78	43.29 N	13.29 E
Osinki	66	52.52 N	47.32 E
Osinniki	84	53.37 N	87.21 E
Osintorf	86	54.37 N	30.55 E
Osipoviči	86	53.18 N	28.38 E
Oskaloosa	162	41.17 N	92.38 W
Oskarshamn	68	57.16 N	16.26 E
Oskarström	68	56.48 N	12.58 E
Oskol ≃	64	49.06 N	37.25 E
Oslo	68	59.55 N	10.45 E
Osljanka ∧	66	59.11 N	58.31 E
Ošmjany	86	54.25 N	25.56 E
Osmānābād	100	18.10 N	76.03 E
Osmānīye	104	37.05 N	36.14 E
Osnabrück	72	52.16 N	8.02 E
Osogovske Planine ∧	80	42.10 N	22.30 E
Osório	140	29.53 S	50.17 W
Osorno	140	40.34 S	73.09 W
Osoyoos Lake	148	48.59 N	119.26 W
Osøyra	68	60.11 N	5.30 E
Osprey Reef ⚬2	124	13.55 S	146.38 E
Ossa, Mount ∧	120	41.54 S	146.01 E
Osse ≃	114	6.10 N	5.20 E
Ossian	154	43.09 N	91.46 W
Ossining	152	41.10 N	73.52 W
Ossipee	152	43.41 N	71.07 W
Ossokmanuan Lake	142	54.20 N	65.00 W
Ossora	84	59.20 N	163.13 E
Ošta	66	60.49 N	35.32 E
Oštaškov	86	57.09 N	33.06 E
Ost-Berlin	72	52.31 N	13.25 E
Østby	68	61.15 N	12.32 E
Östergötland □9	68	58.24 N	15.34 E
Östergötlands Län □6	68	58.25 N	15.45 E
Osterholz-Scharmbeck	72	53.14 N	8.47 E
Osterode	72	51.44 N	10.11 E
Östersund	72	63.11 N	14.39 E
Osterwieck	72	51.58 N	10.42 E
Østfold □9	68	59.15 N	11.30 E
Ostfriesische Inseln II	72	53.44 N	7.25 E
Ostfriesland □9	72	53.20 N	7.40 E
Ostrava	72	49.50 N	18.17 E
Ostróda	72	53.43 N	19.59 E
Ostrogožsk	82	50.52 N	39.05 E
Ostroleka	72	53.06 N	21.34 E
Ostrov, Česko.	72	50.17 N	12.57 E
Ostrov, S.S.S.R.	86	57.20 N	28.22 E
Ostrovnoe	66	54.37 N	25.57 E
Ostrov-Zalit	66	58.11 N	28.04 E
Ostrowiec Świętokrzyski	72	50.57 N	21.23 E
Ostrów Mazowiecka	72	52.49 N	21.54 E
Ostrów Wielkopolski	72	51.39 N	17.49 E
Ostrzeszów	72	51.25 N	17.57 E
Ostuni	78	40.44 N	17.35 E
Ōsumi-shotō II	91b	30.30 N	130.00 E
Osuna	76	37.14 N	5.07 W
Osveja	86	56.01 N	28.06 E
Oswego, Ill., U.S.	154	41.41 N	88.21 W
Oswego, Kans., U.S.	162	37.10 N	95.06 W
Oswego, N.Y., U.S.	152	43.27 N	76.31 W
Oswestry	70	52.52 N	3.04 W
Oświęcim	72	50.03 N	19.12 E
Otago □	126	45.20 S	169.20 E
Otahuhu	126	36.57 S	174.50 E
Otaru	90a	43.13 N	141.00 E
Otava ≃	72	49.26 N	14.12 E
Otavi	116	19.39 S	17.20 E
Otepää	86	58.03 N	26.30 E
Othello	166	46.50 N	119.10 W
Otis	162	39.54 N	102.58 W
Otish, Monts ∧	142	52.22 N	70.30 W
Otjiwarongo	116	20.29 S	16.36 E
Otnes	68	61.45 N	11.14 E
Otočac	78	44.52 N	15.14 E
Otorohanga	126	38.11 S	175.12 E
Otoskwin ≃	142	52.13 N	88.06 W
Otra ≃	68	58.09 N	8.00 E
Otradnyj	66	53.22 N	51.21 E
Otranto	78	40.09 N	18.30 E
Otranto, Strait of U	78	40.00 N	19.00 E
Otrokovice	72	49.13 N	17.31 E
Otsego	154	42.27 N	85.42 W
Ōtsu	90	35.00 N	135.52 E
Ottawa, Ont., Can.	152	45.25 N	75.42 W
Ottawa, Ill., U.S.	154	41.21 N	88.51 W
Ottawa, Kans., U.S.	162	38.37 N	95.16 W
Ottawa, Ohio, U.S.	154	41.01 N	84.03 W
Ottawa ≃	142	45.20 N	73.58 W
Ottawa Islands II	142	59.30 N	80.10 W
Öttingen in Bayern	72	48.57 N	10.36 E
Ottobrunn	72	48.04 N	11.40 E
Ottumwa	162	41.01 N	92.25 W
Otway, Cape >	120	38.52 S	143.31 E
Otwock	72	52.06 N	21.16 E
Otz	72	47.12 N	10.54 E
Ötztaler Alpen ∧	74	46.45 N	10.55 E
Ou ≃	94	19.18 N	102.13 E
Ou, Lao	94	20.04 N	102.13 E
Ouachita ≃	158	31.38 N	91.49 W
Ouachita Mountains ∧	158	34.40 N	94.25 W
Ouadda	108	8.04 N	22.24 E
Ouadou ≃	114	15.40 N	9.53 W
Ouagadougou	114	12.22 N	1.31 W
Ouaka ≃	108	4.59 N	19.56 E
Ouanda Djallé	108	8.54 N	22.48 E
Ouanary	134	4.13 N	51.40 W
Ouarane ≃1	114	21.00 N	10.20 W
Ouargla	106	31.59 N	5.20 E
Ouarzazate	106	30.55 N	6.54 W
Ouassoulou ≃	114	11.24 N	8.11 W
Oubangui (Ubangi) ≃	108	1.15 N	17.50 E
Oucques	74	47.49 N	1.18 E
Oudenaarde	72	50.51 N	3.36 E
Oudtshoorn	116	33.35 S	22.14 E
Ouémé ≃	114	6.29 N	2.32 E
Ouessant, Île d' I	74	48.28 N	5.05 W
Ouesso	110	1.37 N	16.04 E
Ouezzane	106	34.52 N	5.35 W
Ouidah	114	6.22 N	2.05 E
Ouistreham	74	49.17 N	0.15 W
Oujda	106	34.41 N	1.45 W
Oulainen	68	64.16 N	24.48 E
Oulu	68	65.01 N	25.28 E
Oulujärvi	68	64.20 N	27.15 E
Oulujoki ≃	68	65.01 N	25.25 E
Oulun lääni □4	68	65.00 N	27.00 E
Oum Chalouba	108	15.48 N	20.46 E
Oum er Rbia, Oued ≃	106	33.19 N	8.21 W
Ounas ≃	68	66.31 N	25.40 E
Ounianga Kébir	108	19.04 N	20.29 E
Ourinhos	134	22.59 S	49.52 W
Ouro Prêto	134	20.23 S	43.30 W
Outardes, Rivière aux ≃	142	49.04 N	68.28 W
Outjo	116	20.08 S	16.08 E
Outlook	148	51.30 N	107.03 W
Ouyen	120	35.04 S	142.20 E
Ouzouer-le-Marché	74	47.55 N	1.32 E
Ovalle	140	30.36 S	71.12 W
Ovamboland □9	116	18.30 S	16.00 E
Ovar	76	40.52 N	8.38 W
Overflakkee I	72	51.45 N	4.10 E
Overland Park	158	38.59 N	94.40 W
Overton, Nebr., U.S.	162	40.44 N	99.32 W
Overton, Tex., U.S.	160	32.16 N	94.59 W
Ovid	152	42.41 N	76.49 W
Oviedo	76	43.22 N	5.50 W
Øvre Årdal	68	61.19 N	7.48 E
Øvre Rendal	68	61.53 N	11.05 E
Owasso	160	36.16 N	95.51 W
Owatonna	162	44.05 N	93.14 W
Owego	152	42.06 N	76.15 W
Owen Sound	154	44.34 N	80.56 W
Owen Stanley Range ∧	124	9.20 S	147.55 E
Owensville	158	38.20 N	91.30 W
Owenton	154	38.32 N	84.50 W
Owerri	114	5.29 N	7.02 E
Owl Creek ≃	164	43.48 N	108.21 W
Owo	114	7.15 N	5.37 E
Owosso	154	43.00 N	84.10 W
Øyeren	68	59.48 N	11.14 E
Owyhee	166	41.57 N	116.06 W
Owyhee ≃	166	43.46 N	117.02 W
Owyhee, South Fork ≃	166	42.26 N	116.53 W

Name	Page	Lat	Long
Oxbow	162	49.14 N	102.11 W
Oxelösund	68	58.40 N	17.06 E
Oxford, N.S., Can.	150	45.44 N	63.52 W
Oxford, N.Z.	126	43.18 S	172.11 E
Oxford, Eng., U.K.	70	51.46 N	1.15 W
Oxford, Ga., U.S.	158	33.37 N	85.50 W
Oxford, Ga., U.S.	158	33.37 N	83.52 W
Oxford, Ind., U.S.	158	40.31 N	87.15 W
Oxford, Iowa, U.S.	154	41.43 N	91.47 W
Oxford, Maine, U.S.	152	44.08 N	70.30 W
Oxford, Mich., U.S.	152	42.49 N	83.16 W
Oxford, Miss., U.S.	158	34.22 N	89.32 W
Oxford, Nebr., U.S.	162	40.15 N	99.38 W
Oxford, N.C., U.S.	156	36.19 N	78.35 W
Oxford, N.Y., U.S.	152	42.27 N	75.36 W
Oxford, Ohio, U.S.	152	39.30 N	84.44 W
Oxford, Pa., U.S.	152	39.47 N	75.59 W
Oxford Lake	142	54.51 N	95.37 W
Oxfordshire □6	70	51.50 N	1.15 W
Oxley	120	34.12 S	144.06 E
Oxnard	168	34.12 N	119.11 W
Oyapock (Oiapoque) ≃	134	4.08 N	51.40 W
Oyem	110	1.37 N	11.35 E
Oyo	114	7.51 N	3.56 E
Oyonnax	74	46.15 N	5.40 E
Oyster Bay C	120	42.11 S	148.11 E
Øystese	68	60.23 N	6.13 E
Ozamiz	92	8.09 N	123.51 E
Ozariči	86	52.28 N	29.16 E
Ozark, Ala., U.S.	158	31.28 N	85.38 W
Ozark, Ark., U.S.	158	35.29 N	93.50 W
Ozark, Mo., U.S.	158	37.01 N	93.12 W
Ozark Escarpment ⋌4	158	36.15 N	91.15 W
Ozark Plateau ⋌1	158	37.00 N	93.00 W
Ozarks, Lake of the ⊜1	158	38.10 N	92.50 W
Ózd	72	48.14 N	20.18 E
Ožerelje	86	54.48 N	38.17 E
Ozernovskij	84	51.30 N	156.31 E
Ozery	86	54.51 N	38.34 E
Ozieri	78	40.35 N	9.00 E
Ožogino, Ozero ⊜	84	69.16 N	146.36 E
Ozona	160	30.43 N	101.12 W
Ozorków	72	51.58 N	19.19 E
Oz'ornyj	86	57.10 N	40.59 E
Oz'orsk	72	54.25 N	22.01 E

P

Name	Page	Lat	Long
Pa-an	94	16.53 N	97.38 E
Paarl	116	33.45 S	18.56 E
Pabianice	72	51.40 N	19.22 E
Pābna	102	24.00 N	89.15 E
Pabradé	68	54.59 N	25.44 E
Pacaás Novos, Serra dos ⋀	134	10.45 S	64.15 W
Pacasmayo	134	7.20 S	79.35 W
Pachačā	84	60.34 N	169.03 E
Pachino	134	36.42 N	15.06 E
Pachitea ≃	134	8.46 S	74.33 W
Pachmarhi	102	22.28 N	78.26 E
Pachuca [de Soto]	130	20.07 N	98.44 W
Pacific	158	38.29 N	90.45 W
Pacifica	168	37.38 N	122.29 W
Pacific Grove	168	36.38 N	121.56 W
Pacific Islands Trust Territory □2	92	10.00 N	143.00 E
Pacific Ocean ⫪1	92	10.00 N	135.00 E
Pacy-sur-Eure	74	49.01 N	1.23 E
Padang	96	0.57 S	100.21 E
Padangpandjang	96	0.27 S	100.25 E
Padangsidempuan	94	1.23 N	99.16 E
Padany	86	63.17 N	33.22 E
Padasjoki	68	61.21 N	25.17 E
Paddle Prairie	142	57.57 N	117.29 W
Paden City	158	39.36 N	80.56 W
Paderborn	72	51.43 N	8.45 E
Padloping Island I	142	67.07 N	62.35 W
Padova	76	45.25 N	11.53 E
Padstow	70	50.33 N	4.56 W
Padua → Padova	76	45.25 N	11.53 E
Paducah, Ky., U.S.	158	37.05 N	88.36 W
Paducah, Tex., U.S.	160	34.01 N	100.18 W
Paektu-san ⋀	88	42.00 N	128.03 E
Pafúri	116	22.27 S	31.21 E
Pag	78	44.27 N	15.04 E
Pag I	78	44.30 N	14.50 E
Pagai Selatan, Pulau I	96	3.00 S	100.20 E
Pagai Utara, Pulau I	96	2.42 S	100.07 E
Pagalu I	110	1.25 S	5.36 E
Pagan I	92	18.07 N	145.46 E
Page	96	36.57 N	111.27 W
Pagégiai	68	55.09 N	21.54 E
Pageland	156	34.46 N	80.24 W
Paget, Mount ⋀	136	54.26 S	36.33 W
Pagosa Springs	164	37.16 N	107.01 W
Paguate	164	35.08 N	107.23 W
Pahang ≃	96	3.32 N	103.28 E
Pahaska	164	44.30 N	109.58 W
Pahoa	170d	19.28 N	154.51 W
Pahokee	156	26.49 N	80.40 W
Paia	170a	20.54 N	156.22 W
Paide	86	58.54 N	25.33 E
Paige	160	30.13 N	97.07 W
Paignton	70	50.26 N	3.34 W
Paimboeuf	74	47.17 N	2.02 W
Paimio	68	60.27 N	22.42 E
Painesdale	154	47.02 N	88.41 W
Painesville	152	41.43 N	81.15 W
Painted Desert ⫶2	164	36.00 N	111.20 W
Paint Rock	160	31.30 N	99.55 W
Paintsville	156	37.49 N	82.48 W
Paisley, Scot., U.K.	70	55.50 N	4.26 W
Paisley, Oreg., U.S.	166	42.42 N	120.32 W
Paita	134	5.05 S	81.10 W
Paj	84	61.13 N	34.24 E
Pajakumbuh	96	0.14 S	100.37 E
Paj-Choj ⋀2	82	69.00 N	63.00 E
Pajjer, Gora ⋀	82	66.42 N	64.25 E
Pakanbaru	96	0.32 N	101.27 E
Pakaraima Mountains ⋀	138	5.30 N	60.40 W
Pakhoi → Beihai	94	21.29 N	109.05 E
Pakistan (Pākistān) □1	100	30.00 N	70.00 E
Pakistan, East → Bangladesh □1	100	24.00 N	90.00 E
Paklay	94	18.12 N	101.25 E
Pakokku	94	21.20 N	95.05 E
Pakruojis	68	55.58 N	23.52 E
Paks	72	46.39 N	18.53 E
Pakše	94	15.07 N	105.47 E
P'akupur ≃	84	64.30 N	77.48 E
Pala	84	9.22 N	14.54 E
Palacios	160	28.42 N	96.13 W
Palagonia	78	37.19 N	14.45 E
Palagruža, Otoci I	78	42.24 N	16.15 E
Palaiseau	74	48.43 N	2.15 E
Palana	84	59.07 N	159.58 E
Palanga	86	55.55 N	21.03 E
Palanpur	102	24.10 N	72.26 E
Palapye	116	22.16 S	27.07 E
Palata, S.S.S.R.	84	60.06 N	150.54 E
Palatka, Fla., U.S.	156	29.39 N	81.38 W
Palau Islands II	92	7.30 N	134.30 E
Palawan I	96	9.30 N	118.30 E
Pālayankottai	100	8.43 N	77.44 E
Palazzolo [Acreide]	78	37.04 N	14.54 E
Paldiski	86	59.20 N	24.06 E
Palech	86	56.48 N	41.51 E
Palembang	96	3.00 S	104.45 E
Palena	136	43.38 S	14.08 W
Palencia	76	42.01 N	4.32 W
Palen Lake	168	33.46 N	115.12 W
Palermo	78	38.07 N	13.21 E
Palestine, Ill., U.S.	158	39.00 N	87.37 W
Palestine, Tex., U.S.	160	31.46 N	95.38 W
Palestrina	78	41.50 N	12.53 E
Paletwa	94	21.18 N	92.51 E
Pálghāt	100	10.46 N	76.40 E
Palgrave, Mount ⋀	122	23.22 S	115.58 E
Pali	102	25.46 N	73.20 E
Palinges	74	46.33 N	4.13 E
Palisade	164	39.07 N	108.21 W
Palisades	166	43.21 N	111.13 W
Palisades Reservoir ⊜1	166	43.15 N	111.05 W
Palitána	100	21.31 N	71.49 E
Pálkáne	68	61.20 N	24.16 E
Palkino	86	57.32 N	28.01 E
Palk Strait ⋃	100	10.00 N	79.45 E
Pallinup ≃	122	34.29 S	118.54 E
Palluau	74	46.48 N	1.37 W
Palma	116	10.46 S	40.29 E
Palma del Río	76	37.42 N	5.17 W
Palma di Montechiaro	78	37.11 N	13.46 E
Palma [de Mallorca]	76	39.34 N	2.39 E
Palmas	134	26.30 S	52.00 W
Palmas, Cape ⟩	114	4.22 N	7.44 W
Palma Soriano	132	20.13 N	76.00 W
Palm Bay	156	28.02 N	80.35 W
Palm Beach	156	26.42 N	80.02 W
Palmdale	168	34.35 N	118.07 W
Palmeira dos Índios	134	9.25 S	36.37 W
Palmer, Alaska, U.S.	146	61.36 N	149.07 W
Palmer, Mass., U.S.	152	42.09 N	72.20 W
Palmer, Mich., U.S.	154	46.27 N	87.35 W
Palmer, Tenn., U.S.	156	35.21 N	85.34 W
Palmer, Tex., U.S.	160	32.26 N	96.40 W
Palmer Crossing	156	31.16 N	89.15 W
Palmerston, Cape ⟩	120	21.32 S	149.29 E
Palmerston North	126	40.21 S	175.37 E
Palmerton	152	40.48 N	75.37 W
Palmetto, Fla., U.S.	156	27.31 N	82.35 W
Palmetto, Ga., U.S.	156	33.31 N	84.40 W
Palmi	78	38.21 N	15.51 E
Palm Springs	168	33.50 N	116.33 W
Palmyra → Tudmur, Sūriy.	104	34.33 N	38.17 E
Palmyra, Mo., U.S.	158	39.48 N	91.31 W
Palmyra, N.Y., U.S.	152	43.04 N	77.14 W
Palmyra, Pa., U.S.	152	40.18 N	76.36 W
Palmyra, Va., U.S.	152	37.51 N	78.16 W
Palo Alto	168	37.27 N	122.09 W
Palo Duro Creek ≃	160	35.39 N	100.58 W
Paloich	112	6.45 N	30.08 E
Palo Negro	138	10.11 N	67.33 W
Palo Pinto	160	32.46 N	98.18 W
Palos, Cabo de ⟩	76	37.38 N	0.41 W
Palouse	166	46.55 N	117.04 W
Palouse ≃	166	46.35 N	118.13 W
Palpalá	140	24.15 S	65.15 W
Pålsboda	68	59.04 N	15.20 E
Paltamo	68	64.25 N	27.50 E
Pamekasan	96	7.10 S	113.28 E
Pamiers	76	43.07 N	1.36 E
Pamlico Sound ⋃	156	35.20 N	75.55 W
Pampa	160	35.32 N	100.58 W
Pampas ⋀	134	13.24 S	73.12 W
Pampas ⫪1	140	35.00 S	63.00 W
Pamplona, Col.	138	7.23 N	72.39 W
Pamplona, Esp.	76	42.49 N	1.38 W
Panaca	168	37.47 N	114.23 W
Panaji (Panjim)	100	15.29 N	73.50 E
Panamá (Panama)	132	8.58 N	79.31 W
Panama, Okla., U.S.	158	35.10 N	94.40 W
Panamá (Panamá) □1	132	9.00 N	80.00 W
Panama, Bay of C	132	8.50 N	79.20 W
Panama, Isthmus of ⫶3	132	9.20 N	79.30 W
Panama City	156	30.10 N	85.41 W
Panama Gulf C	132	8.00 N	79.30 W
Panay I	96	11.10 N	122.30 E
Pančevo	80	44.52 N	20.39 E
Pandėlys	68	56.01 N	25.13 E
Pando	134	34.43 S	55.57 W
P'andž (Panj) ≃	84	37.06 N	68.20 E
Panevéžys	86	55.44 N	24.21 E
Panfilov	82	44.10 N	80.01 E
Pangala	110	3.19 S	14.34 E
Pangani	110	5.26 S	38.58 E
Pangani ≃	110	5.26 S	38.58 E
Pangfou → Bangbu	88	32.58 N	117.24 E
Pangi	110	3.11 S	26.38 E
Pangkalanbuun	96	2.41 S	111.37 E
Pangkalpinang	96	2.08 S	106.08 E
Pangnirtung	142	66.08 N	65.44 W
Pangutaran Group II	96	6.15 N	120.35 E
Panhandle	160	35.21 N	101.23 W
Pānīpat	102	29.23 N	76.58 E
Panj (P'andž) ≃	102	37.06 N	68.20 E
Panjim → Panaji	100	15.29 N	73.50 E
Panna	102	24.43 N	80.12 E
Pantar, Pulau I	96	8.25 S	124.07 E
Pantelleria, Isola di I	78	36.47 N	12.00 E
Pánuco	130	22.03 N	98.11 W
Panyam	114	9.25 N	9.13 E
Paola, It.	78	39.22 N	16.03 E
Paola, Kans., U.S.	158	38.35 N	94.53 W
Paoli	158	38.33 N	86.28 W
Paotou → Baotou	88	40.40 N	109.59 E
Pápa	72	47.19 N	17.28 E
Papaikou	170d	19.47 N	155.06 W
Papantla [de Olarte]	130	20.27 N	97.19 W
Papatoetoe	126a	36.59 S	174.52 E
Paphos → Néa Páfos	104	34.45 N	32.26 E
Papillion	162	41.09 N	96.03 W
Papua, Gulf of C	120	8.30 S	145.00 E
Papuanewguinea □1	120	6.00 S	147.00 E
Papun	94	18.04 N	97.27 E
Papuri ≃	138	0.36 N	69.11 W
Pará □3	134	4.00 S	52.00 W
Pará ≃	134	1.30 S	48.55 W
Parabel'	84	58.43 N	81.31 E
Paracatu	134	17.13 S	46.52 W
Paracel Islands II	92	16.35 N	112.00 E
Parachinar	102	33.54 N	70.06 E
Paradise, Calif., U.S.	168	39.45 N	121.37 W
Paradise, Tex., U.S.	160	33.09 N	97.41 W
Paradise Valley, Ariz., U.S.	164	33.32 N	111.57 W
Paragonah	164	37.53 N	112.46 W
Paragould	158	36.03 N	90.29 W
Paraguaçu ≃, Bol.	134	13.34 S	51.53 W
Paraguaçu	134	12.45 S	38.58 W
Paraguaçu Paulista	140	22.25 S	50.34 W
Paraguay, Peninsula de ⟩1	134	11.55 N	70.00 W
Paraguari □5	140	26.00 S	57.09 W
Paraguay ≃	140	27.18 S	58.38 W
Paraíba do Sul ≃	140	21.37 S	41.03 W
Paraiso	130	18.24 N	93.14 W
Parakou	114	9.21 N	2.37 E
Paramaribo ⋀	138	5.50 N	55.10 W
Paramillo ⋀	138	7.04 N	75.55 W
Paramirim	134	13.26 S	42.15 W
Paramus	152	40.57 N	74.04 W
Paramušir, Ostrov I	84	50.25 N	155.50 E
Paraná, Arg.	140	31.45 S	60.30 W
Paraná, Bra.	134	12.33 S	47.52 W
Paraná □3	140	24.00 S	51.00 W
Paraná ≃	140	33.43 S	59.15 W
Paranaguá, Baía de C	140	25.31 S	48.30 W
Paranaíba	134	19.40 S	51.11 W
Paranaíba ≃	134	19.40 S	51.11 W
Paranam	138	5.35 N	55.10 W
Paranapanema ≃	140	22.40 S	53.09 W
Paranavaí	140	23.04 S	52.28 W
Parangaba	134	3.45 S	38.33 W
Paray-le-Monial	74	46.27 N	4.07 E
Pārbati ≃	102	25.51 N	76.36 E
Parbhani	100	19.16 N	76.47 E
Parchim	72	53.25 N	11.51 E
Parchment	154	42.19 N	85.33 W
Parczew	72	51.39 N	22.54 E
Pardo ≃, Bra.	134	15.39 S	38.57 W
Pardo ≃, Bra.	134	21.46 S	52.09 W
Pardubice	72	50.02 N	15.47 E
Parece Vela I	92	20.25 N	136.00 E
Parecis, Serra dos ⋀	134	13.00 S	60.00 W
Paredón	130	25.56 N	100.58 W
Paren'	84	62.28 N	163.05 E
Paren' ≃	84	62.25 N	163.10 E
Parent	142	47.55 N	74.37 W
Parentis-en-Born	74	44.21 N	1.05 W
Parfino	86	57.58 N	31.41 E
Pargolovo	86	60.04 N	30.18 E
Paria, Gulf of C	138	10.20 N	62.00 W
Pariaman	96	0.38 S	100.08 E
Pariči	86	52.48 N	29.25 E
Parícutin ⋀1	130	19.28 N	102.15 W
Parika	138	6.51 N	58.26 W
Parima, Sierra ⋀	138	2.30 N	64.00 W
Pariñas, Punta ⟩	134	4.40 S	81.20 W
Parintins	134	2.36 S	56.44 W
Paris, Ont., Can.	154	43.12 N	80.23 W
Paris, Fr.	74	48.52 N	2.20 E
Paris, Ark., U.S.	158	35.18 N	93.44 W
Paris, Idaho, U.S.	166	42.13 N	111.24 W
Paris, Ill., U.S.	158	39.36 N	87.42 W
Paris, Ky., U.S.	152	38.12 N	84.14 W
Paris, Maine, U.S.	152	44.16 N	70.30 W
Paris, Mo., U.S.	158	39.29 N	92.00 W
Paris, Tenn., U.S.	158	36.18 N	88.19 W
Pariz □5	74	48.52 N	2.20 E
Park City, Kans., U.S.	162	37.45 N	97.19 W
Park City, Utah, U.S.	164	40.39 N	111.30 W
Parkdale, P.E.I., Can.	150	46.14 N	63.10 W
Parkdale, Oreg., U.S.	166	45.31 N	121.36 W
Parker, Ariz., U.S.	164	34.09 N	114.17 W
Parker, S. Dak., U.S.	162	43.24 N	97.08 W
Parker, Cape ⟩	142	75.04 N	79.40 W
Parker Dam	168	34.17 N	114.09 W
Parker Range ⋀	122	31.38 S	119.35 E
Parkersburg, Iowa, U.S.	154	42.35 N	92.47 W
Parkersburg, W. Va., U.S.	152	39.16 N	81.32 W
Parkes	120	33.08 S	148.11 E
Park Falls	154	45.56 N	90.27 W
Park Forest	154	41.28 N	87.38 W
Parkland	166	47.09 N	122.26 W
Park Rapids	154	46.55 N	95.04 W
Parkrose	166	45.34 N	122.33 W
Parksley	152	37.47 N	75.39 W
Parksville	148	49.19 N	124.19 W
Parkville, Md., U.S.	152	39.23 N	76.32 W
Parkville, Mo., U.S.	158	39.11 N	94.41 W
Parlâkimidi	100	18.46 N	84.06 E
Parma, It.	78	44.48 N	10.20 E
Parma, Idaho, U.S.	166	43.47 N	116.57 W
Parma, Mich., U.S.	154	42.16 N	84.36 W
Parma, Mo., U.S.	158	36.37 N	89.48 W
Parma, Ohio, U.S.	152	41.23 N	81.43 W
Parnaguá	134	10.13 S	44.38 W
Parnaíba	134	2.54 S	41.47 W
Parnaíba ≃	134	3.00 S	41.50 W
Parnassós ⋀	80	38.32 N	22.35 E
Páros I	80	37.08 N	25.12 E
Parowan	164	37.50 N	112.50 W
Parpaillon ⋀	74	44.30 N	6.40 E
Parral, Chile	140	36.09 S	71.50 W
Parral → Hidalgo del Parral, Méx.	130	26.56 N	105.40 W
Parramatta	120	33.49 S	151.00 E
Parras de la Fuente	130	25.25 N	102.11 W
Parrish, Ala., U.S.	158	33.44 N	87.17 W
Parrish, Fla., U.S.	156	27.35 N	82.25 W
Parry, Cape ⟩	142	70.12 N	124.24 W
Parry Sound	154	45.21 N	80.02 W
Parsnip ≃	148	55.10 N	123.00 W
Parsons, Kans., U.S.	158	37.20 N	95.15 W
Parsons, Tenn., U.S.	158	35.38 N	88.07 W
Parsons, W. Va., U.S.	152	39.06 N	79.41 W
Parsons Range ⋀	120	13.30 S	135.15 E
Partanna	78	37.43 N	12.53 E
Parthenay	74	46.39 N	0.15 W
Particnico	78	38.03 N	13.07 E
Paru ≃	134	1.33 S	52.38 W
Parys	116	27.04 S	27.16 E
Pasadena, Calif., U.S.	168	34.09 N	118.09 W
Pasadena, Tex., U.S.	160	29.42 N	95.13 W
Pa Sak ≃	94	14.21 N	100.35 E
Pascagoula	158	30.21 N	88.33 W
Pascagoula ≃	158	30.21 N	88.31 W
Pasco	166	46.14 N	119.06 W
Pas-de-Calais □5	74	50.30 N	2.20 E
Pasewalk	72	53.30 N	14.00 E
Pasing →8	72	48.09 N	11.27 E
P'asino, Ozero ⊜	84	69.43 N	87.00 E
P'asinskij Zaliv C	84	74.00 N	86.00 E
Pasirpengarajan	96	0.51 N	100.16 E
Pasley, Cape ⟩	122	33.57 S	123.31 E
Pasni	100	25.16 N	63.28 E
Paso de los Libres	140	29.45 S	57.05 W
Paso de los Toros	140	32.49 S	56.31 W
Paso Robles	168	35.38 N	120.41 W
Passaic	152	40.51 N	74.07 W
Passage West	70	51.52 N	8.20 W
Passau	72	48.35 N	13.28 E
Passero, Capo ⟩	78	36.40 N	15.09 E
Passo Fundo	140	28.15 S	52.24 W
Passos	134	20.43 S	46.37 W
Pastaza □4	138	2.00 S	77.00 W
Pastaza ≃	138	4.50 S	76.25 W
Pasto	138	1.13 N	77.17 W
Pasuruan	96	7.38 S	112.54 E
Pasvalys	68	56.04 N	24.24 E
Pászto	72	47.55 N	19.42 E
Patagonia	164	31.33 N	110.45 W
Patagonia ⫪1	136	44.00 S	68.00 W
Pátan	102	23.50 N	72.07 E
Patargán, Daqq-e ⊜	104	33.30 N	60.40 E
Patchewollock	120	35.23 S	142.11 E
Patchogue	152	40.46 N	73.00 W
Patea	126	39.45 S	174.28 E
Pate Island I	110	2.07 S	41.03 E
Paterna	76	39.30 N	0.26 W
Paternion	72	46.43 N	13.38 E
Paterno	78	37.34 N	14.54 E
Paterson	152	40.55 N	74.10 W
Pathánkot	102	32.17 N	75.39 E
Pathfinder Reservoir ⊜1	164	42.30 N	106.50 W
Patiála	102	30.19 N	76.24 E
P'atigorsk	82	44.03 N	43.04 E
Pátkai Range ⋀	102	27.00 N	96.00 E
Patna	102	25.36 N	85.07 E
Pato Branco	140	26.13 S	52.40 W
Patoka ≃	158	38.45 N	89.06 W
Patos	134	7.01 S	37.16 W
Patos, Lagoa dos C	140	31.06 S	51.15 W
Patos de Minas	134	18.35 S	46.32 W
Patquia	140	30.02 S	66.55 W
Pátrai	80	38.15 N	21.44 E
Patricio Lynch, Isla I	136	48.35 S	75.30 W
Patrocinio	134	18.57 S	46.59 W
Patroon	160	31.38 N	93.59 W
Pattada	78	40.35 N	9.07 E
Pattani	94	6.51 N	101.16 E
Patten	150	46.01 N	68.27 W
Patterson, Calif., U.S.	168	37.28 N	121.07 W
Patterson, La., U.S.	158	29.42 N	91.18 W
Patterson, Mount ⋀	146	64.04 N	134.39 W
Patti	78	38.08 N	14.58 E
Patton	152	40.38 N	78.39 W
Patuca ≃	132	15.50 N	84.18 W
Pátzcuaro	130	19.31 N	101.36 W
Pau	74	43.18 N	0.22 W
Pauini ≃	138	1.42 S	62.50 W
Pauk	92	21.27 N	94.27 E
Paul	166	42.36 N	113.47 W
Paulding	152	41.08 N	84.35 W
Paulhan	74	43.32 N	3.27 E
Paulicéia	140	21.17 S	51.51 W
Pauline, Mount ⋀	148	53.33 N	119.54 W
Paulistana	134	8.09 S	41.09 W
Paulo Afonso	134	9.21 S	38.14 W
Paulof Harbor (Pavlof Harbor)	146	54.27 N	162.42 W
Pauls Valley	160	34.44 N	97.13 W
Paungde	94	18.29 N	95.30 E
Pavia	78	45.10 N	9.10 E
Pavilion	74	43.15 N	108.42 W
Pavlodar	82	52.18 N	76.57 E
Pavlovo	66	55.58 N	43.04 E
Pavlovsk	86	59.41 N	30.27 E
Pawan ≃	96	1.51 S	109.57 E
Pawhuska	160	36.40 N	96.20 W
Pawnee	160	36.20 N	96.48 W
Pawnee City	162	40.07 N	96.09 W
Pawnee Rock	162	38.16 N	99.01 W
Paw Paw, Mich., U.S.	154	42.13 N	85.53 W
Paw Paw, W. Va., U.S.	152	39.32 N	78.27 W
Paw Paw Lake	154	42.12 N	86.15 W
Pawtucket	152	41.53 N	71.23 W
Paxton	154	40.27 N	88.06 W
Payerne	74	46.49 N	6.56 E
Payette	166	44.05 N	116.56 W
Payne	152	41.04 N	84.44 W
Payne, Bassin C	142	60.00 N	70.00 W
Payne, Lac C	142	59.25 N	74.00 W
Paynesville	154	45.23 N	94.43 W
Paysandú	140	32.19 S	58.05 W
Payson, Ariz., U.S.	164	34.14 N	111.20 W
Payson, Utah, U.S.	164	40.03 N	111.44 W
Pazardžik	80	42.12 N	24.20 E
Paz de Río	138	5.59 N	72.47 W
Pazin	78	45.14 N	13.56 E
Pea ≃	158	31.01 N	85.51 W
Peabody, Kans., U.S.	162	38.10 N	97.07 W
Peabody, Mass., U.S.	152	42.32 N	70.55 W
Peace ≃	142	59.00 N	111.25 W
Peace River	142	56.14 N	117.17 W
Peach Creek	156	37.53 N	81.50 W
Peacock Hills ⋀2	142	66.05 N	110.45 W
Peak Hill, Austl.	120	32.44 S	148.12 E
Peak Hill, Austl.	122	25.38 S	118.43 E
Peale, Mount ⋀	164	38.26 N	109.14 W
Pearisburg	152	37.19 N	80.44 W
Pearl ≃	158	30.11 N	89.32 W
Pearl City	170d	21.24 N	157.59 W
Pearl Peak ⋀	168	40.14 N	115.32 W
Pearl River, La., U.S.	158	30.23 N	89.45 W
Pearl River, N.Y., U.S.	152	41.04 N	74.02 W
Pearsall	160	28.53 N	99.06 W
Pearson	156	31.18 N	82.51 W
Pebane	116	17.10 S	38.08 E
Peć	80	42.40 N	20.19 E
Pecan Gap	160	33.26 N	95.51 W
Pecatonica	154	42.18 N	89.21 W
Pecatonica ≃	154	42.28 N	89.44 W
Pečenga	66	69.33 N	31.07 E
Peck	152	43.15 N	82.49 W
Pečora	66	65.10 N	57.11 E
Pečora ≃	66	68.13 N	54.15 E
Pečorskaja Guba C	66	68.40 N	54.45 E
Pečorskoje More ⫪2	66	70.00 N	54.00 E
Pečory	66	57.49 N	27.36 E
Pecos, N. Mex., U.S.	164	35.34 N	105.41 W
Pecos, Tex., U.S.	160	31.25 N	103.30 W
Pecos ≃	160	29.42 N	101.22 W
Pécs	72	46.05 N	18.13 E
Pedernales	132	18.02 N	71.44 W
Pedra Azul	134	16.01 S	41.17 W
Pedras Salgadas	76	41.32 N	7.36 W
Pedreiras	134	4.30 S	44.35 W
Pedro Afonso	134	8.59 S	48.11 W
Pedro de Valdivia	140	22.36 S	69.40 W
Pedrógão Grande	76	39.55 N	8.09 W
Pedro II	134	4.25 S	41.28 W
Pedro Juan Caballero	140	22.34 S	55.37 W
Peebinga	120	34.56 S	140.56 E
Peebles, Scot., U.K.	70	55.39 N	3.12 W
Peebles, Ohio, U.S.	152	38.57 N	83.24 W
Pee Dee ≃	156	33.21 N	79.16 W
Peekskill	152	41.17 N	73.55 W
Peel ≃	146	67.37 N	134.40 W
Peel Point ⟩	142	73.22 N	114.35 W
Peel Sound ⋃	142	73.00 N	96.30 W
Pego	76	38.51 N	0.07 W
Pegu	94	17.20 N	96.29 E
Pegu Yoma ⋀	94	19.00 N	95.50 E
Pegyš	66	63.26 N	53.20 E
Pehčevo	80	41.46 N	22.54 E
Peixe	134	12.01 S	48.32 W
Peixe, Rio do ≃	140	16.12 S	49.11 W
Peixian	88	34.44 N	116.56 E
Pekalongan	96	6.53 S	109.40 E
Pekan	96	3.30 N	103.24 E
Pekin	154	40.34 N	89.38 W
Peking → Beijing	88	39.55 N	116.25 E
Pelahatchie	158	32.19 N	89.48 W
Pelčyce	72	53.09 N	15.26 E
Pelée, Mount ⋀1	132	14.49 N	61.10 W
Peleliu I	92	7.01 N	134.15 E
Peleng, Pulau I	96	1.20 S	123.10 E
Pelham	156	31.08 N	84.09 W
Pelhřimov	72	49.26 N	15.13 E
Pelican Lake ⊜	154	46.34 N	96.05 W
Pelican Rapids	154	46.34 N	96.05 W
Pella	162	41.25 N	92.55 W
Pell City	158	33.35 N	86.17 W
Pelly ≃	146	62.47 N	137.19 W
Pelly Bay C	142	68.53 N	89.51 W
Pelly Crossing	146	62.49 N	136.35 W
Pelly Lake ⊜	142	65.59 N	101.12 W
Pelly Mountains ⋀	146	62.00 N	133.00 W
Pelopónnisos ⫪1	80	37.30 N	22.00 E
Pelotas	140	31.46 S	52.20 W
Pelotas ≃	140	27.28 S	51.55 W
Pemadumcook Lake ⊜	152	45.40 N	69.15 W
Pemalang	96	6.54 S	109.22 E
Pemanggil, Pulau I	96	2.53 N	104.17 E
Pemba Island I	110	5.10 S	39.48 E
Pembina ≃, Alta., Can.	148	54.45 N	114.15 W
Pembina ≃, N.A.	162	49.00 N	98.12 W
Pembina Mountains ⋀2	162	49.00 N	98.05 W
Pembroke, Ont., Can.	154	45.49 N	77.07 W
Pembroke, Wales, U.K.	70	51.41 N	4.55 W
Pembroke, Va., U.S.	152	37.19 N	80.38 W
Pembroke, Cape ⟩	136	52.09 N	57.40 W
Pembrokeshire Coast National Park ♦	70	51.47 N	5.06 W
Pembuang ≃	96	3.26 S	112.33 E
Peñafiel	76	41.12 N	8.17 W
Penang → Pinang	96	5.24 N	100.19 E
Pen Argyl	152	40.52 N	75.16 W
Peñarroya-Pueblonuevo	76	38.18 N	5.16 W
Peñas, Golfo de C	136	47.20 S	75.00 W
Penasco	164	36.10 N	105.41 W
Pender	162	42.07 N	96.42 W
Pendembu	114	9.06 N	12.12 W
Pendleton, Ind., U.S.	158	40.00 N	85.45 W
Pendleton, Oreg., U.S.	166	45.40 N	118.47 W
Pendleton, S.C., U.S.	156	34.39 N	82.47 W
Pend Oreille ≃	166	49.04 N	117.37 W
Pend Oreille, Lake ⊜	166	48.10 N	116.10 W
Penedo	134	10.17 S	36.36 W
Penedono	76	40.59 N	7.24 W
Penela	76	40.02 N	8.23 W
Penetanguishene	154	44.47 N	79.55 W
Penfield	152	41.13 N	78.34 W
Penganga ≃	100	19.53 N	79.09 E
P'enghu	88	23.34 N	119.43 E
P'enghu Liehtao II	88	23.30 N	119.30 E
Penglai	88	37.48 N	120.42 E
Pengshui	88	29.18 N	108.09 E
Penguin	120	41.07 S	146.04 E
Pengxian	88	31.03 N	103.57 E
Penicuik	70	55.26 N	3.14 W
Penitas	160	26.17 N	98.27 W
Penju, Kepulauan II	96	5.22 S	127.06 E
Penn Hills	152	40.28 N	79.53 W
Pennines, Alpes ⋀	74	46.05 N	7.50 E
Pennington Gap	156	36.45 N	83.02 W
Penns Grove	152	39.43 N	75.28 W
Pennsylvania □3	144	40.45 N	77.30 W
Penn Yan	152	42.40 N	77.03 W
Penny Strait ⋃	142	76.30 N	97.00 W
Peno	86	56.55 N	32.45 E
Penobscot ≃	152	44.30 N	68.50 W
Penola	120	37.23 S	140.50 E
Penong	122	31.55 S	133.01 E
Penonomé	132	8.31 N	80.21 W
Penrith, Austl.	120	33.45 S	150.42 E
Penrith, Eng., U.K.	70	54.40 N	2.44 W
Pensacola	158	30.25 N	87.13 W
Pentagon Mountain ⋀	166	47.56 N	113.07 W
Penticton	148	49.30 N	119.35 W
Pentland	120	20.32 S	145.24 E
Pentland Firth ⋃	70	58.44 N	3.13 W
Penwell	160	31.44 N	102.35 W
Penza	64	53.13 N	45.00 E
Penzance	70	50.07 N	5.33 W
Penzberg	72	47.45 N	11.23 E
Penžina ≃	84	62.28 N	165.18 E
Penžinskaja Guba C	84	61.00 N	163.00 E
Penžinskij Chrebet ⋀	84	62.30 N	167.00 E
Peoria, Ariz., U.S.	164	33.35 N	112.14 W
Peoria, Ill., U.S.	154	40.41 N	89.35 W
Peotone	154	41.20 N	87.47 W
Pepin, Lake ⊜	154	44.30 N	92.15 W
Perabumulih	96	3.27 S	104.15 E
Perak ≃	96	3.58 N	100.53 E
Peralta	164	34.50 N	106.41 W
Percé	150	48.31 N	64.13 W
Perchtoldsdorf	72	48.07 N	16.17 E
Percy Islands II	120	21.39 S	150.16 E
Perdido ≃	158	30.21 N	87.26 W
Perdido Bay C	158	30.19 N	87.26 W
Pereira	138	4.49 N	75.42 W
Pereira de Eça	116	17.03 S	15.47 E
Perene ≃	134	11.09 S	74.14 W
Perenjori	122	29.26 S	116.17 E
Pereslavl'-Zalesskij	86	56.44 N	38.51 E
Pergamino	140	33.53 S	60.34 W
Pergine Valsugana	78	46.04 N	11.14 E
Perham	154	46.36 N	95.34 W
Perho	68	63.13 N	24.25 E
Péribonca ≃	150	48.45 N	72.05 W
Péribonka	150	48.46 N	71.48 W
Périers	74	49.11 N	1.25 W
Périgueux	74	45.11 N	0.43 E
Perijá, Sierra de ⋀	138	10.00 N	73.00 W
Perleberg	72	53.04 N	11.51 E
Perm'	64	58.00 N	56.15 E
Permas	66	59.49 N	47.01 E
Pernik	80	42.36 N	23.02 E
Péronne	74	49.56 N	2.57 E
Perote	130	19.34 N	97.14 W
Perow	148	54.35 N	126.52 W
Perpignan	74	42.41 N	2.53 E
Perros-Guirec	74	48.48 N	3.26 W
Perris	168	33.47 N	117.14 W
Perry, Fla., U.S.	156	30.07 N	83.34 W
Perry, Ga., U.S.	156	32.27 N	83.43 W
Perry, Iowa, U.S.	154	41.50 N	94.06 W
Perry, Mich., U.S.	154	42.49 N	84.13 W
Perry, N.Y., U.S.	152	42.42 N	78.00 W
Perry, Okla., U.S.	160	36.17 N	97.17 W
Perryopolis	152	40.04 N	79.45 W
Perrysburg	152	41.33 N	83.37 W
Perryton	160	36.24 N	100.48 W
Perryville, Alaska, U.S.	146	55.54 N	159.09 W
Perryville, Mo., U.S.	158	37.43 N	89.52 W
Persia → Iran □1	100	32.00 N	53.00 E
Persian Gulf C	104	27.00 N	51.00 E
Perstorp	68	56.08 N	13.23 E
Perth, Austl.	122	31.56 S	115.50 E
Perth, Ont., Can.	154	44.54 N	76.15 W
Perth, Scot., U.K.	70	56.24 N	3.28 W
Perth Amboy	152	40.31 N	74.16 W
Perth-Andover	150	46.45 N	67.42 W
Pertuis	74	43.41 N	5.30 E
Peru, Ill., U.S.	154	41.20 N	89.08 W
Peru, Ind., U.S.	158	40.45 N	86.04 W
Peru, Nebr., U.S.	162	40.29 N	95.44 W
Peru, N.Y., U.S.	152	44.35 N	73.32 W
Peru (Perú) □1	134	10.00 S	76.00 W
Perugia	78	43.08 N	12.22 E
Perugorria	140	29.21 S	58.36 W
Pervoavgustovskij	86	52.14 N	35.03 E
Pervomajsk	66	54.53 N	43.49 E
Pervomajsk	86	64.26 N	40.47 E
Pervoural'sk	82	56.54 N	59.58 E
Pervyj Kuril'skij Proliv ⋃	84	50.50 N	156.36 E
Peš' ≃	86	65.55 N	34.19 E
Pesaro	78	43.54 N	12.55 E
Pescadores → P'enghu Liehtao II	88	23.30 N	119.30 E
Pešcanoje	82	53.12 N	45.35 E
Pescara	78	42.28 N	14.13 E
Pescia	78	43.54 N	10.41 E
Peshāwar	102	34.01 N	71.33 E
Peshtigo	154	45.03 N	87.45 W
Peski	86	56.13 N	38.46 E
Pesmes	74	47.17 N	5.34 E
Pesočenskij	86	54.10 N	36.06 E
Pesočnoje	86	58.01 N	39.10 E
Pesočnyj	86	60.07 N	30.08 E
Peso da Régua	76	41.10 N	7.47 W
Pesqueira	134	8.22 S	36.42 W
Pessac	74	44.48 N	0.38 W
Pest □6	72	47.25 N	19.20 E
Pešera	82	40.02 N	24.18 E
Petah Tiqwa	104	32.05 N	34.53 E
Petal	158	31.21 N	89.17 W
Petaluma	168	38.14 N	122.39 W
Petare	138	10.29 N	66.49 W
Petatlán	130	17.31 N	101.16 W
Petawawa	154	45.54 N	77.17 W
Peterborough, Austl.	120	32.58 S	138.50 E
Peterborough, Ont., Can.	154	44.18 N	78.19 W
Peterborough, Eng., U.K.	70	52.35 N	0.15 W
Peterborough, N.H., U.S.	152	42.53 N	71.57 W
Peterculter	70	57.05 N	2.16 W
Peterhead	70	57.30 N	1.49 W
Peter Lake ⊜	142	63.08 N	92.48 W
Peterlee	70	54.46 N	1.19 W
Petermann Ranges ⋀	122	25.00 S	129.46 E
Peter Pond Lake ⊜	142	55.55 N	108.44 W
Petersburg, Alaska, U.S.	146	56.50 N	132.59 W
Petersburg, Ill., U.S.	154	40.01 N	89.51 W
Petersburg, Ind., U.S.	158	38.30 N	87.17 W
Petersburg, Mich., U.S.	154	41.54 N	83.43 W
Petersburg, Tenn., U.S.	156	35.19 N	86.38 W
Petersburg, Va., U.S.	156	37.13 N	77.24 W
Petersburg, W. Va., U.S.	152	39.00 N	79.07 W
Pétervására	72	48.01 N	20.06 E
Petilia Policastro	78	39.07 N	16.47 E
Petit Bois Island I	158	30.12 N	88.26 W
Petite Rivière de la Baleine ≃	142	56.00 N	76.45 W
Petit-Mécatina, Rivière ≃	142	50.40 N	59.35 W
Petitot ≃	142	60.14 N	123.29 W
Petit-Saint-Bernard, Col du ⋋	74	45.41 N	6.53 E
Petitsikapau Lake ⊜	142	54.45 N	66.25 W
Petlád	102	22.48 N	72.48 E
Petone	126	41.15 S	174.47 E
Petoskey	154	45.22 N	84.57 W
Petra Velikogo, Zaliv C	84	42.40 N	132.00 E
Petric	80	41.24 N	23.13 E
Petrila	80	45.27 N	23.25 E
Petrograd → Leningrad	86	59.55 N	30.15 E
Petrolia, Ont., Can.	154	42.52 N	82.09 W
Petrolia, Tex., U.S.	160	34.01 N	98.14 W
Petrolina	134	9.24 S	40.30 W
Petropavlovsk	82	54.54 N	69.06 E
Petropavlovsk-Kamčatskij	84	53.01 N	158.39 E
Petrópolis	134	22.31 S	43.10 W
Petrosani	80	45.25 N	23.22 E
Petrovsk	64	52.19 N	45.23 E
Petrovsk-Zabajkal'skij	84	51.17 N	108.50 E
Petrozavodsk	66	61.47 N	34.20 E
Petuchovo	82	55.06 N	67.58 E
Petuški	86	55.56 N	39.28 E
Peuerbach	72	48.21 N	13.46 E
Pevek	84	69.42 N	170.17 E
Peykjahldt	66a	65.40 N	16.50 W
Peyruis	74	44.01 N	5.56 E
Pézenas	74	43.28 N	3.25 E
Pezinok	72	48.18 N	17.17 E
Pfaffenhofen an der Ilm	72	48.32 N	11.31 E
Pfarrkirchen	72	48.25 N	12.56 E
Pforzheim	72	48.54 N	8.42 E
Pfronten	72	47.34 N	10.33 E
Pfungstadt	72	49.48 N	8.36 E
Phalsbourg	74	48.46 N	7.16 E
Phangan, Ko I	94	9.45 N	100.04 E
Phangnga	94	8.28 N	98.32 E
Phan Rang	94	11.34 N	108.59 E
Phan-thiet	94	10.56 N	108.06 E
Pharr	160	26.12 N	98.11 W
Phelps	152	42.57 N	77.03 W
Phenix City	156	32.29 N	85.01 W
Phet Buri	94	13.06 N	99.56 E
Phetchabun, Thiu Khao ⋀	94	16.20 N	100.55 E
Philadelphia, Miss., U.S.	158	32.46 N	89.07 W
Philadelphia, Tenn., U.S.	156	35.41 N	84.24 W
Philadelphia, Pa., U.S.	152	39.57 N	75.07 W
Philippeville	114	36.53 N	6.54 E
Philippi	152	39.09 N	80.02 W
Philippine Sea ⫪2	92	20.00 N	135.00 E
Philippines □1	92	13.00 N	122.00 E
Philippsburg	72	49.14 N	8.27 E
Philip Smith Mountains ⋀	146	68.00 N	148.00 W
Philo, Ill., U.S.	154	40.00 N	88.09 W
Philo, Ohio, U.S.	152	39.52 N	81.55 W
Philomath	166	44.32 N	123.22 W
Philpots Island I	142	74.48 N	80.00 W
Phimai	94	15.13 N	102.30 E
Phitsanulok	94	16.49 N	100.15 E
Phnom Penh → Phnum Pénh	94	11.33 N	104.55 E
Phoenix, Ariz., U.S.	164	33.27 N	112.04 W
Phoenix, N.Y., U.S.	152	43.14 N	76.18 W
Phoenix, Oreg., U.S.	166	42.16 N	122.49 W
Phoenixville	152	40.08 N	75.31 W
Phong Saly	94	21.41 N	102.06 E
Phrae	94	18.07 N	100.11 E

Symbols in the index entries are identified on page 203.

Name	Page	Lat	Long
Phra Nakhon Si Ayutthaya	94	14.21 N	100.33 E
Phuket	94	7.54 N	98.24 E
Phuket, Ko I	94	8.00 N	98.22 E
Phu-ly	94	20.32 N	105.56 E
Phumĭ Svay Riĕng	92	11.05 N	105.48 E
Phuoc-le	92	10.30 N	107.10 E
Phu-quoc, Dao I	94	10.13 N	104.00 E
Piacenza	78	45.01 N	9.40 E
Pialba	120	25.17 S	152.51 E
Piana	78	42.14 N	8.38 E
Pian Creek ≈	120	30.02 S	148.12 E
Pianoro	78	44.22 N	11.20 E
Piaseczno	72	52.05 N	21.01 E
Piatra-Neamţ	80	46.56 N	26.22 E
Pibor ≈	112	8.26 N	33.13 E
Pibor Post	112	6.48 N	33.08 E
Picacho	164	32.43 N	111.30 W
Picardie □9	74	50.00 N	3.30 E
Picayune	158	30.26 N	89.41 W
Picharal	140	23.02 N	105.12 E
Picher	160	36.59 N	94.50 W
Pichilemu	140	34.23 S	72.02 W
Pichincha □4	138	0.10 S	78.40 W
Pickens, Miss., U.S.	158	32.53 N	89.58 W
Pickens, S.C., U.S.	158	34.53 N	82.42 W
Pickens, W. Va., U.S.	152	38.39 N	80.13 W
Pickering, Ont., Can.	154	43.52 N	79.02 W
Pickering, Eng., U.K.	70	54.14 N	0.46 W
Pickford	154	46.10 N	84.22 W
Pickton	158	33.02 N	95.24 W
Pickwick Lake ⊜1	158	35.00 N	88.10 W
Picos	134	7.05 S	41.28 W
Picquigny	74	49.57 N	2.09 E
Picton, Austl.	120	34.11 S	150.36 E
Picton, Ont., Can.	154	44.00 N	77.08 W
Picton, N.Z.	126	41.16 S	174.00 E
Picton, I.	136	55.02 S	66.57 W
Pictou	150	45.41 N	62.43 W
Picturalagala ∧	100	7.00 N	80.46 E
Piedecuesta	138	6.59 N	73.03 W
Piedicroce	74	42.23 N	9.23 E
Piedmont, Ala., U.S.	158	33.55 N	85.37 W
Piedmont, Mo., U.S.	158	37.09 N	90.42 W
Piedmont, S.C., U.S.	158	34.42 N	82.28 W
Piedmont, W. Va., U.S.	152	39.29 N	79.02 W
Piedra del Águila	136	40.02 S	70.04 W
Piedras Negras	130	28.42 N	100.31 W
Pieksämäki	68	62.18 N	27.08 E
Pielavesi	68	63.14 N	26.45 E
Piemonte □4	78	45.00 N	8.00 E
Pienza	78	43.04 N	11.41 E
Pierce, Idaho, U.S.	166	46.29 N	115.48 W
Pierce, Nebr., U.S.	162	42.12 N	97.32 W
Pierce City	158	36.57 N	94.01 W
Pierpont	152	45.30 N	97.50 W
Pierre	162	44.22 N	100.21 W
Pierre-Buffière	74	45.42 N	1.21 E
Pierre ≈	162	42.50 N	104.05 W
Pierson	156	29.14 N	81.28 W
Piešťany	72	48.36 N	17.50 E
Pietarsaari	68	63.40 N	22.42 E
Pietermaritzburg	116	29.37 S	30.16 E
Pietersburg	116	23.54 S	29.25 E
Pietrasanta	78	43.57 N	10.14 E
Piet Retief	116	27.01 S	30.50 E
Pigeon	154	43.50 N	83.16 W
Pigeon ≈, N.A.	154	48.00 N	89.34 W
Pigeon ≈, U.S.	156	41.46 N	85.47 W
Piggott	158	36.23 N	90.11 W
Pigna	78	43.56 N	7.40 E
Pigüé	140	37.40 S	62.24 W
Pilar de Goiás	134	14.41 S	49.27 W
Pilcomayo ≈	140	25.21 S	57.42 W
Pilibhit	102	28.38 N	79.48 E
Pilot Grove	158	38.53 N	92.55 W
Pilot Mountain	156	36.23 N	80.28 W
Pilot Peak ∧	168	38.52 N	117.19 W
Pilot Point	160	33.24 N	96.58 W
Pilot Rock	166	45.29 N	118.50 W
Pilot Station	146	61.56 N	162.54 W
Pilpah Range ⋌	120	20.23 S	138.34 E
Pilsen → Plzeň			
Piltene	86	57.13 N	21.40 E
Pirn ≈	86	61.18 N	71.57 E
Pima	164	32.54 N	109.50 W
Pimental	134	6.45 S	79.55 W
Pina	76	41.29 N	0.32 W
Pinang (George Town)	96	5.24 N	100.19 E
Pinang I	92	5.24 N	100.19 E
Pinar del Río	132	22.25 N	83.42 W
Pinardville	152	42.59 N	71.33 W
Pinas	140	31.12 S	65.28 W
Pincher Creek	148	49.29 N	113.57 W
Pinckney	154	42.27 N	83.57 W
Pinckneyville	158	38.05 N	89.23 W
Pinconning	154	43.51 N	83.58 W
Pinczów	72	50.32 N	20.35 E
Pindar	122	28.29 S	115.48 E
Pindaré ≈	134	3.17 S	44.47 W
Pindhos Óros ⋌	80	39.49 N	21.14 E
Pindus Mountains → Pindhos Óros			
Pine ≈	80	39.49 N	21.14 E
Pine	148	56.08 N	120.41 W
Pine Bluffs	158	34.13 N	92.01 W
Pine Castle	162	41.11 N	104.04 W
Pine City	156	28.28 N	81.22 W
Pine Creek	154	45.50 N	92.59 W
Pinedale, Calif., U.S.	124	13.49 S	131.49 E
Pinedale, Wyo., U.S.	168	36.50 N	119.48 W
Pine Falls	142	50.35 N	96.15 W
Pinega ≈	66	64.08 N	41.54 E
Pine Hills	156	28.35 N	81.27 W
Pinehouse Lake ⊜	142	55.32 N	106.35 W
Pinehurst	166	47.32 N	116.14 W
Pine Island	156	26.36 N	82.07 W
Pineland	158	31.15 N	93.58 W
Pinellas Park	156	27.51 N	82.43 W
Pine Mountain ∧	156	36.55 N	83.20 W
Pine Ridge	162	43.02 N	102.33 W
Pinerolo	78	44.53 N	7.21 E
Pinetops	156	35.48 N	77.38 W
Pineville, Ky., U.S.	156	36.46 N	83.42 W
Pineville, La., U.S.	158	31.19 N	92.26 W
Pineville, N.C., U.S.	156	35.05 N	80.53 W
Pinewood	156	33.44 N	80.27 W
Piney	160	32.40 N	4.20 E
Piney Buttes ∧	162	47.30 N	107.00 W
Ping ≈	94	15.40 N	100.09 E
Pingaring	122	32.45 S	118.37 E
Pingdingshan	88	33.44 N	113.18 E
Pingdu	88	36.47 N	119.54 E
Pingjiang	88	28.44 N	113.34 E
Pingliang	88	35.27 N	107.10 E
Pingnan	88	23.32 S	118.31 E
Pingup	122	33.32 S	118.32 E
Pinhal	88	32.25 N	46.45 W
Pinhal Novo	76	38.38 N	8.55 W
Pinheiro	134	2.31 S	45.05 W
Pinhel	76	40.46 N	7.04 W
Pini, Pulau I	94	0.07 N	98.42 E

Name	Page	Lat	Long
Pinjarra I	122	32.37 S	115.53 E
Pinnacle Island I	146	60.12 N	172.40 W
Pinnaroo	120	35.16 S	140.55 E
Pinneberg	72	53.40 N	9.47 E
Pinos, Isla de (Isle of Pines) I	132	21.40 N	82.50 W
Pinsk	86	52.07 N	26.04 E
Pinson	158	33.41 N	86.41 W
Pin'ug	66	60.15 N	47.48 E
Pioche	168	37.55 N	114.27 W
Piombino	78	42.55 N	10.32 E
Pioneer, Austl.	122	31.48 S	121.43 E
Pioneer, Ohio, U.S.	152	41.41 N	84.33 W
Pioner, Ostrov I	84	79.50 N	92.30 E
Pionerskij (Neukuhren)	72	54.57 N	20.20 E
Pionki	72	51.30 N	21.27 E
Piorini ≈	138	3.23 S	63.30 W
Piotrków Trybunalski	72	51.25 N	19.42 E
Pipestone	162	43.58 N	96.19 W
Pipestone Creek ≈, Can.	142	52.53 N	89.23 W
Pipestone Creek ≈, U.S.	162	49.42 N	100.45 W
Pipinas	140	35.30 S	57.19 W
Pipmuacan, Réservoir ⊜1	150	49.35 N	70.30 W
Pipriac	70	47.49 N	1.57 W
Piqua	152	40.09 N	84.15 W
Piquiri ≈	140	24.03 S	54.14 W
Piracicaba	140	22.43 S	47.38 W
Piraeus → Piraiévs	80	37.57 N	23.38 E
Piraí do Sul	140	24.31 S	49.56 W
Piraiévs (Piraeus)	80	37.57 N	23.38 E
Piraju	140	23.12 S	49.23 W
Pirajuí	140	21.59 S	49.29 W
Piran	78	45.32 N	13.34 E
Pirapora	134	25.44 S	59.07 W
Prenópolis	134	15.51 S	48.57 W
Pires do Rio	134	17.18 S	48.17 W
Pirgos	80	37.41 N	21.28 E
Piriápolis	140	34.54 S	55.17 W
Pirmasens	72	49.12 N	7.36 E
Pirot	80	43.09 N	22.35 E
Pir Panjāl Range ⋌	102	33.37 N	74.32 E
Pirtleville	164	31.22 N	109.34 W
Piru	78	3.03 S	128.12 E
Pisa	78	43.43 N	10.23 E
Pisagua	134	19.36 S	70.13 W
Pisco	138	13.42 S	76.13 W
Piscovo	86	57.11 N	40.32 E
Písek	72	49.19 N	14.10 E
Pishan	102	37.37 N	78.18 E
Pishīn Lora (Lowrah) ≈	102	29.09 N	64.55 E
Pissos	74	44.19 N	0.47 W
Pisticci	78	40.23 N	16.33 E
Pistoia	78	43.55 N	10.54 E
Pisz	72	53.38 N	21.49 E
Pit ≈	168	40.45 N	122.22 W
Pitalito	138	1.51 N	76.02 W
Pitanga	140	24.46 S	51.44 W
Piteå	68	65.20 N	21.30 E
Piteälven ≈	68	65.14 N	21.32 E
Piteşti	80	44.52 N	24.52 E
Pithara	122	30.24 S	116.40 E
Pithiviers	74	48.10 N	2.15 E
Pitigliano	78	42.38 N	11.40 E
Pitlochry	70	56.43 N	3.45 W
Pitt Island I	148	53.35 N	129.45 W
Pittsboro	156	35.43 N	79.11 W
Pittsburg, Kans., U.S.	162	37.25 N	94.42 W
Pittsburg, Tex., U.S.	160	33.00 N	94.58 W
Pittsburgh	152	40.26 N	80.00 W
Pittsfield, Ill., U.S.	158	39.36 N	90.48 W
Pittsfield, Maine, U.S.	152	44.47 N	69.23 W
Pittsfield, Mass., U.S.	152	42.27 N	73.15 W
Pittsfield, N.H., U.S.	152	43.18 N	71.19 W
Pittston	152	41.19 N	75.47 W
Pittsworth	120	27.43 S	151.38 E
Piu, Cerro ∧	132	13.38 N	84.52 W
Pium	134	10.27 S	49.11 W
Piura	134	5.12 S	80.36 W
Pivan'	84	50.29 N	137.06 E
Pivijay	138	10.28 N	74.37 W
Pixley	168	35.58 N	119.17 W
Pizzo	78	38.44 N	16.10 E
Placentia	150	47.14 N	53.58 W
Placentia Bay ⊂	150	47.15 N	54.30 W
Placerville	168	38.43 N	120.48 W
Placetas	132	22.19 N	79.40 W
Plain City, Ohio, U.S.	152	40.06 N	83.16 W
Plain City, Utah, U.S.	166	41.18 N	112.06 W
Plainfield, Conn., U.S.	152	41.41 N	71.55 W
Plainfield, Ind., U.S.	158	39.42 N	86.24 W
Plainfield, N.J., U.S.	152	40.37 N	74.24 W
Plains, Mont., U.S.	166	47.27 N	114.53 W
Plains, Tex., U.S.	160	33.11 N	102.50 W
Plainview, Minn., U.S.	154	44.10 N	92.10 W
Plainview, Nebr., U.S.	162	42.21 N	97.47 W
Plainview, Tex., U.S.	160	34.11 N	101.43 W
Plainville	154	43.11 N	83.16 W
Plainwell	154	42.27 N	85.38 W
Plaistow	152	42.50 N	71.06 W
Planada	168	37.18 N	120.19 W
Planeta Rica	138	8.25 N	75.36 W
Plano, Ill., U.S.	154	41.40 N	88.32 W
Plano, Tex., U.S.	160	33.01 N	96.42 W
Plantation	156	26.07 N	80.14 W
Plant City	156	28.01 N	82.08 W
Plantsite	164	33.04 N	109.21 W
Plaquemine	158	30.17 N	91.14 W
Plasencia	76	40.02 N	6.05 W
Plast	82	54.22 N	60.50 E
Plaster City	168	32.47 N	115.51 W
Plata, Río de la ⊂1	140	35.00 S	57.00 W
Plato	138	9.47 N	74.47 W
Platte	162	43.23 N	98.50 W
Platte City	158	39.22 N	94.47 W
Platte Island I	110	5.52 S	55.23 E
Platteville, Colo., U.S.	162	40.13 N	104.49 W
Platteville, Wis., U.S.	154	42.44 N	90.29 W
Plattling	72	48.47 N	12.53 E
Plattsburg	158	39.34 N	94.27 W
Plattsburgh	152	44.41 N	73.28 W
Plattsmouth	162	41.01 N	95.53 W
Plau	72	53.27 N	12.16 E
Plauen	72	50.30 N	12.08 E
Plav	80	42.36 N	19.56 E
Plavinas	86	56.37 N	25.43 E
Plavsk	86	53.43 N	37.18 E
Playgreen Lake ⊜	142	54.00 N	98.10 W
Pleasant Gap	152	40.52 N	77.45 W
Pleasant Grove	158	33.30 N	86.58 W
Pleasant Hill, Calif., U.S.	168	37.56 N	122.04 W
Pleasant Hill, Ill., U.S.	158	39.27 N	90.52 W
Pleasant Hill, Mo., U.S.	158	38.47 N	94.16 W
Pleasanton, Tex., U.S.	160	28.58 N	98.29 W
Pleasantville, Iowa, U.S.	154	41.23 N	93.18 W
Pleasantville, N.J., U.S.	152	39.23 N	74.31 W
Pléaux	74	45.08 N	2.14 E
Plechanovo	86	54.14 N	37.33 E
Pleiku	94	13.59 N	108.01 E
Plénée-Jugon	70	48.36 N	2.24 W
Plentywood	162	48.46 N	104.34 W
Pleseck	66	62.43 N	40.20 E
Plessisville	150	46.13 N	71.47 W
Pleszew	72	51.54 N	17.48 E
Plétipi, Lac ⊜	150	51.44 N	70.06 W
Pleven	80	43.25 N	24.37 E
Plevlja	80	43.21 N	19.21 E
Ploaghe	78	40.40 N	8.44 E
Płock	72	52.33 N	19.43 E
Plöckenpass)(	72	46.36 N	12.58 E
Ploërmel	70	47.56 N	2.24 W

Name	Page	Lat	Long
Plogastel-Saint-Germain	70	47.59 N	4.16 W
Ploieşti	80	44.56 N	26.02 E
Plombières-les-Bains	74	47.58 N	6.29 E
Plomer, Point >	120	31.19 S	152.58 E
Plön	72	54.09 N	10.25 E
Płońsk	72	52.38 N	20.23 E
Pl'os	86	57.27 N	41.31 E
Plouay	74	47.55 N	3.20 W
Ploudalmézeau	74	48.32 N	4.39 W
Plouescat	74	48.40 N	4.10 W
Plouguenast	74	48.17 N	2.43 W
Plouha	74	48.41 N	2.56 W
Plovdiv	80	42.09 N	24.45 E
Plummer	166	47.20 N	116.53 W
Plumridge Lakes ⊜	122	29.30 S	125.25 E
Plumtree	116	20.30 S	27.50 E
Pluvigner	70	47.46 N	3.01 W
Plymouth, Monts.	130	16.42 N	62.13 W
Plymouth, Eng., U.K.	70	50.23 N	4.10 W
Plymouth, Calif., U.S.	168	38.29 N	120.51 W
Plymouth, Ind., U.S.	158	41.21 N	86.19 W
Plymouth, Mass., U.S.	152	41.58 N	70.41 W
Plymouth, N.H., U.S.	152	43.45 N	71.41 W
Plymouth, N.C., U.S.	156	35.52 N	76.43 W
Plymouth, Ohio, U.S.	152	40.59 N	82.40 W
Plymouth, Pa., U.S.	152	41.14 N	75.58 W
Plymouth, Wis., U.S.	154	43.45 N	87.58 W
Plzeň	72	49.45 N	13.23 E
Po ≈	78	44.57 N	12.04 E
Pobeda, Gora ∧	84	65.12 N	146.12 E
Pobedino	84	49.51 N	142.49 E
Pobedy, Pik ∧	82	42.02 N	80.05 E
Pocahontas, Ark., U.S.	158	36.16 N	90.58 W
Pocahontas, Ill., U.S.	158	38.50 N	89.33 W
Pocahontas, Iowa, U.S.	162	42.44 N	94.40 W
Počep	86	52.56 N	33.27 E
Pöchlarn	72	48.12 N	15.13 E
Pochutla	130	15.44 N	96.28 W
Pochvistnevo	66	53.38 N	52.08 E
Pocomoke ≈	152	37.58 N	75.39 W
Pocomoke City	152	38.05 N	75.34 W
Poços de Caldas	140	21.48 S	46.34 W
Poděbrady	72	50.08 N	15.07 E
Podensac	74	44.39 N	0.22 W
Podkamennaja Tunguska ≈	84	61.36 N	90.09 E
Podkamennaja Tunguska ≈	84	61.36 N	90.18 E
Podol'sk	86	55.26 N	37.33 E
Podor	114	16.40 N	14.57 W
Podoz'orskij	86	57.14 N	40.20 E
Podporoze	66	60.53 N	34.07 E
Podravska Slatina	80	45.42 N	17.42 E
Pofadder	116	29.10 S	19.22 E
Pogar	86	52.33 N	33.16 E
Poggibonsi	78	43.28 N	11.09 E
Pograničnyj, S.S.S.R.	84	44.19 N	131.24 E
Pograničnyj, S.S.S.R.	84	46.57 N	45.46 E
P'ohang	88	36.03 N	129.20 E
Pohjois-Karjalan lääni □4	68	63.00 N	30.00 E
Point	160	32.56 N	95.52 W
Point Arena	168	38.55 N	123.41 W
Point Cloates	122	22.43 S	113.41 E
Point Comfort	160	28.41 N	96.33 W
Pointe-à-Pitre	132	16.14 N	61.32 W
Point Edward	154	43.00 N	82.24 W
Pointe-Noire	110	4.48 S	11.51 E
Point Fortin	132	10.11 N	61.41 W
Point Hope	146	68.21 N	166.41 W
Point Lake ⊜	142	65.15 N	113.04 W
Point Marion	152	39.44 N	79.53 W
Point Pleasant	152	40.05 N	74.04 W
Point Samson	122	20.36 S	117.12 E
Poissonnet Point >	120	19.57 S	119.11 E
Poissy	74	48.56 N	2.03 E
Poitiers	74	46.35 N	0.20 E
Poitou □9	74	46.30 N	0.30 W
Poix	74	49.47 N	1.59 E
Pojoaque Valley	164	35.53 N	105.59 W
Pokhara	102	28.14 N	83.59 E
Pokrov	86	55.55 N	39.10 E
Pokrovsk	84	61.29 N	129.06 E
Pokur	84	61.02 N	75.26 E
Pola de Lena	76	43.10 N	5.49 W
Poland □1	64	52.00 N	19.00 E
Polanów	72	54.08 N	16.39 E
Pol'arnyj	66	69.12 N	33.22 E
Polatli	30	39.34 N	32.08 E
Polesella	78	52.10 N	28.00 E
Polesje ◦1	86	52.00 N	26.20 E
Polessk (Labiau)	72	54.52 N	21.05 E
Polevskoj	82	56.26 N	60.11 E
Polgár	72	47.52 N	21.08 E
Police	72	53.33 N	14.35 E
Poligny	74	46.50 N	5.43 E
Polillo Islands II	98	38.25 N	16.05 E
Polistena	78	38.25 N	16.05 E
Polk	152	41.22 N	79.56 W
Pol'kino	84	71.10 N	99.13 E
Polla	78	40.30 N	15.30 E
Pollāchi	100	10.40 N	77.01 E
Pollock	162	45.53 N	100.17 W
Polo	154	41.59 N	89.35 W
Polock	86	55.31 N	28.46 E
Polonnaruwa	100	7.56 N	81.00 E
Polotn'anyj	86	55.44 N	36.00 E
Poltava	64	49.35 N	34.34 E
Pöltsamaa	86	58.39 N	25.58 E
Poluj ≈	84	66.31 N	66.33 E
Polunočnoje	82	60.52 N	60.25 E
Polysajevo	84	54.35 N	86.14 E
Pomabamba	134	8.50 S	77.25 W
Pombal	76	39.55 S	8.38 W
Pomerania □9	72	54.00 N	14.15 E
Pomeroy, Ohio, U.S.	152	39.02 N	82.02 W
Pomeroy, Wash., U.S.	166	46.28 N	117.36 W
Pomona, Calif., U.S.	168	34.04 N	117.45 W
Pomona, Kans., U.S.	168	38.21 N	95.27 W
Pomona Reservoir ⊜1	158	38.31 N	95.36 W
Pompano Beach	156	26.14 N	80.07 W
Pompei	78	40.45 N	14.30 E
Pompton Lakes	152	41.00 N	74.17 W
Ponca City	160	36.42 N	97.05 W
Ponca Creek ≈	162	42.57 N	98.02 W
Ponchatoula	158	30.26 N	90.26 W
Ponderay	166	48.18 N	116.32 W
Pond Inlet ⊂	142	72.41 N	78.00 W
Pondosa	166	41.10 N	117.38 W
Ponferrada	76	42.33 N	6.35 W
Pongola ≈	116	26.48 S	32.23 E
Poni ≈	66	65.21 N	41.07 E
Ponoj	66	66.59 N	41.17 E
Ponoka	148	52.42 S	113.35 W
Ponorogo	96	7.52 S	111.27 E
Pons, Fr.	74	45.35 N	0.33 W
Ponta Grossa	140	25.05 S	50.09 W
Pont-à-Marcq	74	50.31 N	3.07 E
Pont-à-Mousson	74	48.54 N	6.04 E
Pontarlier	74	46.54 N	6.22 E
Pontassieve	78	43.46 N	11.26 E
Pont-Audemer	74	49.21 N	0.31 E
Pontaumur	74	45.52 N	2.40 E
Pont-Aven	74	47.51 N	3.45 W
Pont Canavese	78	45.25 N	7.36 E
Pontchâteau	74	47.26 N	2.05 W
Pont-Croix	74	48.02 N	4.29 W

Name	Page	Lat	Long
Pont-d'Ain	74	46.03 N	5.20 E
Pont-de-Salars	74	44.17 N	2.44 E
Pont-de-Vaux	74	46.26 N	4.56 E
Pontebba	78	46.30 N	13.18 E
Ponte da Barca	76	41.48 N	8.25 W
Pontedera	78	43.40 N	10.38 E
Ponte de Sor	76	39.15 N	8.01 W
Ponte Nova	134	20.24 S	42.54 W
Ponte do Lima	76	41.46 N	8.35 W
Pontevedra	76	42.26 N	8.38 W
Pontgibaud	74	46.50 N	2.51 E
Ponthierville → Ubundi	110	0.21 S	25.29 E
Pontiac, Ill., U.S.	154	40.53 N	88.38 W
Pontiac, Mich., U.S.	154	42.37 N	83.18 W
Pontianak	96	0.02 S	109.20 E
Pontivy	74	48.04 N	2.59 W
Pont-l'Abbé	74	47.52 N	4.13 W
Pont-l'Évêque	74	49.18 N	0.11 E
Pontoise	74	49.03 N	2.06 E
Pontorson	74	48.33 N	1.31 W
Pontremoli	78	44.22 N	9.53 E
Pontresina	74	46.28 N	9.53 E
Pont-Scorff	74	47.50 N	3.24 W
Pont-sur-Yonne	74	48.17 N	3.12 E
Pontvallain	74	47.45 N	0.12 E
Pontypool	70	51.43 N	3.02 W
Pontypridd	70	51.37 N	3.22 W
Ponziane, Isole I	78	40.55 N	12.57 E
Poole	70	50.43 N	1.59 W
Poole, Mount ∧	120	29.37 S	141.46 E
Pooler	156	32.07 N	81.15 W
Poona → Pune	100	18.32 N	73.52 E
Poopelloe Lake ⊜	120	31.39 S	144.00 E
Poopó, Lago de ⊜	134	18.45 S	67.07 W
Popayán	138	2.27 N	76.36 W
Poperinge	72	50.51 N	2.43 E
Popham Bay ⊂	142	64.10 N	110.47 E
Popigaj	84	72.54 N	106.36 E
Popigaj ≈	84	72.49 N	110.27 E
Popilta, Lake ⊜	120	33.10 S	141.43 E
Poplar	162	48.07 N	105.12 W
Poplar ≈, Can.	142	53.00 N	97.19 W
Poplar ≈, N.A.	162	48.05 N	105.11 W
Poplar Bluff	158	36.45 N	90.23 W
Poplarville	158	30.51 N	89.32 W
Popocatépetl, Volcán ∧1	130	19.02 N	98.38 W
Popokabaka	110	5.42 S	16.35 E
Popoli	78	42.10 N	13.50 E
Popomanasiu, Mount ∧	118	9.42 S	160.03 E
Popondetta	124	8.45 S	148.15 E
Porbandar	102	21.38 N	69.36 E
Porcher Island I	148	53.57 N	130.30 W
Porchov	86	57.46 N	29.34 E
Porcupine ≈	146	66.35 N	145.15 W
Porcupine Creek ≈	162	48.01 N	106.20 W
Porcupine Dome ∧	146	65.31 N	145.31 W
Porcupine Mountains ⋌	154	46.40 N	89.40 W
Pordenone	78	45.57 N	12.39 E
Porečje-Rybnoje	86	57.06 N	39.25 E
Pori	68	61.29 N	21.47 E
Porirua	126	41.08 S	174.51 E
Porkkala	68	59.59 N	24.26 E
Porlamar	138	10.57 N	63.51 W
Pornic	74	47.07 N	2.06 W
Porokylä	68	63.40 N	29.00 E
Poronaisk	84	49.14 N	143.04 E
Porozovo	86	52.56 N	24.22 E
Porrentruy	74	47.25 N	7.05 E
Porsgrunn	68	59.09 N	9.40 E
Portachuelo	134	17.21 S	63.24 W
Port Adelaide	120	34.51 S	138.30 E
Portadown	70	54.26 N	6.27 W
Portage, Mich., U.S.	154	42.12 N	85.35 W
Portage, Utah, U.S.	166	41.59 N	112.14 W
Portage, Wis., U.S.	154	43.33 N	89.28 W
Portage ≈	152	41.20 N	83.39 W
Portage-la-Prairie	142	49.59 N	98.18 W
Portageville	158	36.26 N	89.42 W
Port Alberni	148	49.14 N	124.48 W
Portalegre	76	39.17 N	7.26 W
Port-Alfred, Qué., Can.	150	48.19 N	70.53 W
Port-Alfred (Kowie), S. Afr.	116	33.36 S	26.55 E
Port Alice	148	50.23 N	127.27 W
Port Allegany	152	41.48 N	78.17 W
Port Angeles	166	48.06 N	123.26 W
Port Antonio	132	18.10 N	76.28 W
Port Arthur, Austl.	120	43.09 S	147.51 E
Port Arthur → Thunder Bay, Ont., Can.	154	48.23 N	89.15 W
Port Arthur, Tex., U.S.	158	29.54 N	93.55 W
Port Augusta	120	32.30 S	137.46 E
Port-au-Prince	132	18.32 N	72.20 W
Port Austin	154	44.02 N	82.59 W
Port Barre	158	30.33 N	91.57 W
Port Blair	94	11.36 N	92.45 E
Port Borden	150	46.15 N	63.42 W
Port Broughton	120	33.36 S	137.56 E
Port Byron	154	41.36 N	90.20 W
Port-Cartier-Ouest	150	50.01 N	66.52 W
Port Chalmers	126	45.49 S	170.37 E
Port Charlotte	156	26.59 N	82.06 W
Port Chester	152	41.00 N	73.40 W
Port Clinton	152	41.30 N	82.56 W
Port Colborne	154	42.53 N	79.14 W
Port Coquitlam	148	49.16 N	122.46 W
Port Credit	154	43.33 N	79.35 W
Port-de-Paix	132	19.57 N	72.50 W
Port Dickson	96	2.31 N	101.48 E
Port Dover	154	42.47 N	80.12 W
Port Edwards	154	44.21 N	89.52 W
Portel, Port.	76	38.18 N	7.42 W
Portel, Bra.	134	1.57 S	50.49 W
Port Elgin	154	44.26 N	81.24 W
Port Elizabeth	116	33.58 S	25.40 E
Port Ellen	70	55.38 N	6.12 W
Porter	160	35.52 N	95.31 W
Porter Creek	162	40.43 N	119.01 W
Porterville	168	36.04 N	119.01 W
Port Fairy	120	38.23 S	142.14 E
Port Gentil	110	0.43 S	8.47 E
Port Germein	120	33.02 S	138.00 E
Port Gibson	158	31.57 N	90.59 W
Port Graham	146	59.21 N	151.50 W
Port Harcourt	114	4.43 N	7.05 E
Port Hawkesbury	150	45.37 N	61.21 W
Port Hedland	122	20.19 S	118.34 E
Port Hope	154	43.57 N	78.18 W
Port Huron	154	42.58 N	82.27 W
Portimão	76	37.08 N	8.32 W
Port Isabel	160	26.04 N	97.13 W
Port Jefferson	152	40.57 N	73.04 W
Port Jervis	152	41.22 N	74.41 W
Port Kembla	120	34.28 S	150.54 E
Port Kenny	122	33.10 S	134.42 E
Portland, Austl.	120	38.21 S	141.36 E
Portland, Ind., U.S.	158	40.26 N	84.59 W

Name	Page	Lat	Long
Portland, Maine, U.S.	152	43.39 N	70.17 W
Portland, Mich., U.S.	154	42.52 N	84.54 W
Portland, Oreg., U.S.	166	45.33 N	122.36 W
Portland, Tenn., U.S.	158	36.35 N	86.31 W
Portland, Tex., U.S.	160	27.53 N	97.20 W
Portland, Cape >	120	40.45 S	147.57 E
Portland Canal C	146	55.10 N	130.08 W
Portland Bay C	120	38.19 S	141.47 E
Powers	154	53.02 N	7.17 W
Powers Lake	162	48.34 N	102.39 W
Powhatan, Ark., U.S.	158	36.05 N	91.07 W
Powhatan, Va., U.S.	152	37.33 N	77.55 W
Powhatan Point	152	39.52 N	80.49 W
Powys □6	70	52.17 N	3.20 W
Poxoreu	134	15.50 S	54.23 W
Poyang	88	29.00 N	116.55 E
Poynette	154	43.24 N	89.24 W
Požarevac	80	44.37 N	21.11 E
Poza Rica de Hidalgo	130	20.33 N	97.27 W
Poznań	72	52.25 N	16.55 E
Pozoblanco	76	38.22 N	4.51 W
Pozzuoli	78	40.49 N	14.07 E
Prachin Buri	94	14.03 N	101.25 E
Prachuap Khiri Khan	92	11.49 N	99.47 E
Pradera	138	3.25 N	76.15 W
Prades	74	42.37 N	2.26 E
Prado	134	17.21 S	39.13 W
Præstø	68	55.07 S	12.03 E
Prague → Praha, Česko.	72	50.05 N	14.26 E
Prague, Okla., U.S.	160	35.29 N	96.41 W
Praha (Prague)	72	50.05 N	14.26 E
Prahova □4	80	45.00 N	26.00 E
Praia	114a	14.55 N	23.31 W
Prainha	134	7.16 S	60.23 W
Prairie City	166	44.28 N	118.43 W
Prairie du Chien	154	43.03 N	91.09 W
Prairie Grove	158	35.59 N	94.19 W
Prairies, Coteau des ∧2	162	44.30 N	96.45 W
Prairie View	160	30.04 N	96.00 W
Prairie Village	158	38.59 N	94.38 W
Praja	96	8.42 S	116.17 E
Praslin Islands II	110	4.19 S	55.44 E
Prat de Llobregat	76	41.20 N	2.06 E
Prato	78	43.53 N	11.06 E
Pratt	162	37.39 N	98.44 W
Prattville, Ala., U.S.	158	32.28 N	86.29 W
Prattville, Okla., U.S.	160	36.32 N	95.07 W
Pravdinsk	86	56.32 N	43.34 E
Pravdinskij	86	56.04 N	37.51 E
Pr'aža	66	61.42 N	33.35 E
Predazzo	78	46.19 N	11.36 E
Preditz [-Turrach]	72	47.04 N	13.55 E
Pré-en-Pail	74	48.27 N	0.12 W
Preetz	72	54.14 N	10.16 E
Pregarten	72	48.21 N	14.32 E
Préméry	74	47.10 N	3.20 E
Premnitz	72	52.32 N	12.19 E
Premont	160	27.22 N	98.08 W
Prentice	154	45.33 N	90.17 W
Prentiss	158	31.36 N	89.52 W
Prenzlau	72	53.19 N	13.52 E
Preparis Island I	94	14.52 N	93.41 E
Preparis North Channel ⥾	94	15.27 N	94.05 E
Preparis South Channel ⥾	94	14.40 N	94.00 E
Přerov	72	49.27 N	17.27 E
Prescott, Ont., Can.	154	44.43 N	75.31 W
Prescott, Ariz., U.S.	164	34.33 N	112.28 W
Prescott, Ark., U.S.	158	33.48 N	93.23 W
Prescott, Wis., U.S.	154	44.45 N	92.48 W
Presho	162	43.54 N	100.04 W
Presidencia Roca	140	26.08 S	59.36 W
Presidencia Roque Sáenz Peña	140	26.50 S	60.30 W
Presidente Epitácio	140	21.46 S	52.06 W
Presidente Hayes □5	140	24.00 S	59.00 W
Presidente Prudente	140	22.07 S	51.22 W
Presidio	160	29.33 N	104.23 W
Prešov	72	49.00 N	21.15 E
Prespa, Lake ⊜	80	40.55 N	21.00 E
Presque Isle	150	46.41 N	68.01 W
Presque Isle >1	154	42.09 N	80.06 W
Presto	162	43.54 N	100.04 W
Preston, Eng., U.K.	70	53.46 N	2.42 W
Preston, Idaho, U.S.	166	42.06 N	111.53 W
Preston, Minn., U.S.	154	43.40 N	92.05 W
Prestonsburg	156	37.40 N	82.46 W
Prestranda	68	59.06 N	9.04 E
Prestwick	70	55.30 N	4.37 W
Pretoria	116	25.45 S	28.10 E
Pretty Prairie	162	37.47 N	98.01 W
Préveza	80	38.57 N	20.44 E
Pribilof Islands II	146	57.00 N	170.00 W
Pribram	72	49.42 N	14.01 E
Price, Tex., U.S.	160	32.28 N	94.59 W
Price, Utah, U.S.	168	39.36 N	110.48 W
Prichard	158	30.44 N	88.07 W
Priddy	160	31.40 N	98.31 W
Priego de Córdoba	76	37.26 N	4.11 W
Prien	72	47.51 N	12.21 E
Prieska	116	29.40 S	22.42 E
Priest River	166	48.11 N	116.55 W
Prievidza	72	48.46 N	18.37 E
Prijedor	78	44.59 N	16.43 E
Prikaspijskaja Nizmennosť ≊	64	48.00 N	52.00 E
Prikumsk	64	44.46 N	44.09 E
Prilep	80	41.20 N	21.33 E
Priluki	64	50.36 N	32.24 E
Primghar	162	43.05 N	95.38 W
Primorsk	66	60.14 N	27.43 E
Primorsk, S.S.S.R.	86	54.44 N	20.00 E
Primorsk, S.S.S.R.	84	60.22 N	28.36 E
Primrose Lake ⊜	142	54.55 N	109.45 W
Prince Albert	142	53.12 N	105.46 W
Prince Albert Sound ⥾	142	70.25 N	115.00 W
Prince Charles Island I	142	67.50 N	76.00 W
Prince Edward Island □4	150	46.20 N	63.20 W
Prince George, B.C., Can.	148	53.55 N	122.45 W
Prince George, Va., U.S.	156	37.13 N	77.17 W
Prince Leopold Island I	142	74.02 N	89.55 W
Prince of Wales Island I, Austl.	124	10.40 S	142.10 E
Prince of Wales Island I, N.W. Ter., Can.	142	72.40 N	99.00 W
Prince of Wales Island I, Alaska, U.S.	146	55.47 N	132.50 W
Prince of Wales Strait ⥾	142	73.00 N	117.00 W
Prince Regent Inlet C	142	73.00 N	90.30 W
Princes Town	132	10.16 N	61.23 W
Princess Anne	152	38.12 N	75.41 W
Princess Charlotte Bay C	124	14.25 S	144.00 E
Princess Royal Island I	148	52.57 N	128.49 W
Princeton, B.C., Can.	148	49.27 N	120.31 W
Princeton, Calif., U.S.	168	39.24 N	122.01 W
Princeton, Ill., U.S.	154	41.22 N	89.28 W
Princeton, Iowa, U.S.	154	41.40 N	90.36 W
Princeton, Maine, U.S.	152	45.13 N	67.34 W
Princeton, Mich., U.S.	154	46.11 N	87.33 W
Princeton, Minn., U.S.	154	45.34 N	93.35 W

Name	Page	Lat	Long
Princeton, Mo., U.S.	158	40.24 N	93.35 W
Princeton, N.J., U.S.	152	40.21 N	74.40 W
Princeton, W. Va., U.S.	156	37.22 N	81.06 W
Princeville, Qué., Can.	152	46.10 N	71.53 W
Princeville, Ill., U.S.	158	40.45 N	89.45 W
Prince William Sound ⊔	146	60.40 N	147.00 W
Príncipe I	110	1.37 N	7.25 E
Príncipe da Beira	134	12.25 S	64.25 W
Prineville	166	44.18 N	120.51 W
Prinzapolca	132	13.20 N	83.35 W
Prior, Cabo >	76	43.34 N	8.19 W
Prip'at' ≃	64	51.21 N	30.09 E
Pripet → Prip'at' ≃	64	51.21 N	30.09 E
Priština	80	42.39 N	21.10 E
Pritzwalk	72	53.09 N	12.10 E
Privas	74	44.44 N	4.36 E
Priverno	78	41.28 N	13.11 E
Privodino	66	61.05 N	46.28 E
Privolžsk	86	57.23 N	41.17 E
Privolžskaja Vozvyšennost' ⚡¹	66	52.00 N	46.00 E
Privolžskij	82	51.24 N	46.02 E
Prizren	80	42.12 N	20.44 E
Prizzi	78	37.43 N	13.26 E
Probolinggo	92	7.45 S	113.13 E
Probstzella	72	50.32 N	11.22 E
Prochladnyj	82	43.46 N	44.00 E
Proctor, Minn., U.S.	154	46.45 N	92.13 W
Proctor, Vt., U.S.	152	43.40 N	73.02 W
Proddatūr	100	14.44 N	78.33 E
Proença-a-Nova	76	39.45 N	7.55 W
Professor Dr. Ir. W.J. Van Blommestein Meer ⚡¹	134	4.45 N	55.00 W
Progreso	130	21.17 N	89.40 W
Project City	168	40.41 N	122.21 W
Prokopjevsk	84	53.53 N	86.45 E
Proleplje	80	43.14 N	21.36 E
Proletarij	86	58.26 N	31.44 E
Pronsk	86	54.07 N	39.37 E
Prophetstown	154	41.40 N	89.56 W
Prophet ≃	142	58.45 N	122.45 W
Propriá	134	10.13 S	36.51 W
Propriano	78	41.40 N	8.55 E
Proserpine	120	20.24 S	148.34 E
Proskurov → Chmel'nickij	82	49.25 N	27.00 E
Prosser	166	46.12 N	119.46 W
Prostějov	72	49.29 N	17.07 E
Proston	120	26.10 S	151.36 E
Protection	160	37.12 N	99.29 W
Provadija	80	43.11 N	27.26 E
Provence ☐⁹	74	44.00 N	6.00 E
Providence, Ky., U.S.	158	37.24 N	87.39 W
Providence, R.I., U.S.	152	41.50 N	71.25 W
Providence Island I	110	9.14 S	51.02 E
Providencia, Isla de I	130	13.21 N	81.22 W
Providenija	146	64.23 N	173.18 W
Provincetown	152	42.03 N	70.11 W
Provins	74	48.33 N	3.18 E
Provo	166	40.14 N	111.39 W
Prudhoe Bay ⌐	146	70.20 N	148.20 W
Prudhoe Island I	120	21.19 S	149.40 E
Prudnik	72	50.19 N	17.34 E
Prüm	72	50.12 N	6.25 E
Pruszków	72	52.11 N	20.48 E
Prut ≃	82	45.27 N	28.12 E
Prutz	74	47.05 N	10.40 E
Pružany	86	52.33 N	24.28 E
Pryor	160	36.19 N	95.19 W
Przasnysz	72	53.01 N	20.55 E
Przedbórz	72	51.06 N	19.53 E
Przemyśl	72	49.47 N	22.47 E
Przeworsk	72	50.05 N	22.29 E
Prževal'sk	82	42.29 N	78.24 E
Pskov	86	57.50 N	28.20 E
Pszczyna	72	49.59 N	18.57 E
Pszów	72	50.03 N	18.24 E
Ptolemais	80	40.31 N	21.41 E
Ptuj	78	46.25 N	15.52 E
Pucallpa	134	8.20 S	74.30 W
Pučež	86	56.59 N	43.11 E
Pucheng	88	27.55 N	118.31 E
Puck	72	54.44 N	18.27 E
Pudož	66	61.48 N	36.32 E
Pudukkottai	100	10.24 N	78.49 E
Puebla de Don Fadrique	76	37.58 N	2.26 W
Puebla de Don Rodrigo	76	39.05 N	4.37 W
Puebla de Trives	76	42.20 N	7.15 W
Puebla [de Zaragoza]	130	19.03 N	98.12 W
Pueblo	162	38.16 N	104.37 W
Pueblo Hundido	140	26.23 S	70.03 W
Puente-Genil	76	37.23 N	4.47 W
Puerto Acosta	134	15.32 S	69.15 W
Puerto Aisén	136	45.24 S	72.42 W
Puerto Ángel	130	15.40 N	96.29 W
Puerto Armuelles	138	8.18 N	82.52 W
Puerto Asís	138	0.30 N	76.31 W
Puerto Ayacucho	138	5.40 N	67.35 W
Puerto Barrios	130	15.43 N	88.36 W
Puerto Belgrano	136	38.54 S	62.05 W
Puerto Berrío	138	6.29 N	74.24 W
Puerto Cabello	138	10.28 N	68.01 W
Puerto Cabezas	132	14.02 N	83.24 W
Puerto Carreño	138	6.12 N	67.22 W
Puerto Casado	140	22.20 S	57.55 W
Puerto Chicama	134	7.42 S	79.27 W
Puerto Cortés, C.R.	138	8.58 N	83.32 W
Puerto Cortés, Hond.	130	15.48 N	87.56 W
Puerto de Nutrias	138	8.05 N	69.18 W
Puerto de San José	138	13.55 N	90.49 W
Puerto Deseado	136	47.45 S	65.55 W
Puerto Juárez	130	21.11 N	86.49 W
Puerto la Cruz	138	10.13 N	64.38 W
Puertollano	76	38.41 N	4.07 W
Puerto Lobos	136	42.01 S	65.04 W
Puerto Madryn	136	42.46 S	65.02 W
Puerto Maldonado	134	12.36 S	69.11 W
Puerto Montt	136	41.28 S	72.57 W
Puerto Morazán	130	12.50 N	87.11 W
Puerto Natales	136	51.44 S	72.31 W
Puerto Páez	138	6.13 N	67.28 W
Puerto Peñasco	130	31.20 N	113.33 W
Puerto Pinasco	140	22.43 S	57.50 W
Puerto Pirámides	136	42.35 S	64.15 W
Puerto Plata	132	19.48 N	70.41 W
Puerto Princesa	98	9.44 N	118.44 E
Puerto Real	76	36.32 N	6.11 W
Puerto Rico	132	11.05 S	67.38 W
Puerto Rico ☐²	128	18.15 N	66.30 W
Puerto Sastre	140	22.06 S	57.55 W
Puerto Suárez	134	18.57 S	57.51 W
Puerto Tejada	138	3.14 N	76.24 W
Puerto Vallarta	130	20.37 N	105.15 W
Puerto Varas	136	41.19 S	72.59 W
Puerto Wilches	138	7.21 N	73.54 W
Pueyrredón, Lago (Lago Cochrane) ≋	136	47.20 S	72.00 W
Pugačov	66	52.01 N	48.50 E
Puget Sound ⊔	166	47.50 N	122.30 W
Puglia ☐⁹	78	41.15 N	16.15 E
Puigcerdá	76	42.25 N	1.56 E
Puigmal ∧	76	42.23 N	2.07 E
Pukch'ŏng	88	40.15 N	128.20 E
Pukekohe	126	37.12 S	174.54 E
Pukou	88	32.07 N	118.43 E
Puksoozero	66	62.38 N	40.32 E
Pula	78	44.52 N	13.50 E
Pulacayo	134	20.25 S	66.41 W
Pulan	100	30.16 N	81.14 E
Pulanzong	100	30.16 N	81.14 E
Pulaski, N.Y., U.S.	152	43.34 N	76.08 W
Pulaski, Va., U.S.	156	37.03 N	80.47 W
Puławy	72	51.25 N	21.57 E
Pulkkila	68	64.16 N	25.52 E
Pullman	166	46.44 N	117.10 W
Pullo	134	15.10 S	73.48 W
Pulo Anna I	92	4.40 N	131.58 E
Pulog, Mount ∧	98	16.35 N	120.54 E
Pulsano	78	40.23 N	17.22 E
Pultusk	72	52.43 N	21.05 E
Puná, Isla I	138	2.50 S	80.08 W
Punakha	100	27.37 N	89.52 E
Pune (Poona)	100	18.32 N	73.52 E
Púngoè ≃	116	19.50 S	34.48 E
Punia	110	1.28 S	26.27 E
Punitaqui	140	30.50 S	71.16 W
Puno	134	15.50 S	70.02 W
Punta Alta	140	38.53 S	62.04 W
Punta Arenas	136	53.09 S	70.55 W
Punta Cardón	138	11.38 N	70.14 W
Punta del Este	140	34.58 S	54.57 W
Punta Delgada	136	42.43 S	63.38 W
Punta Gorda	156	26.56 N	82.03 W
Punta Moreno	136	2.36 S	78.54 W
Punta Negra, Salar de ≃	140	24.35 S	69.00 W
Puntarenas	132	9.58 N	84.50 W
Punto Fijo	138	11.42 N	70.13 W
Punxsutawney	152	40.57 N	78.59 W
Puqi	88	29.43 N	113.53 E
Puquio	134	14.43 S	74.17 W
Pur ≃	84	67.31 N	77.55 E
Purcell	160	35.01 N	97.22 W
Purcell Mountains ⚡	166	50.00 N	115.40 W
Purcellville	152	39.08 N	77.43 W
Puri	100	19.48 N	85.51 E
Purkersdorf	72	48.12 N	16.11 E
Purley	160	51.21 N	95.16 W
Purnea	100	25.47 N	87.31 E
Purūlia	102	23.20 N	86.22 E
Purus (Purús) ≃	134	3.42 S	61.28 W
Purvis	158	31.09 N	89.25 W
Purwakarta	96	6.34 S	107.26 E
Purwokerto	96	7.25 S	109.14 E
Pusan	88	35.06 N	129.03 E
Pushkar	100	26.28 N	74.36 E
Puškin	86	59.43 N	30.25 E
Puškino	86	56.01 N	37.51 E
Puškinskije Gory	86	57.01 N	28.54 E
Püspökladány	72	47.19 N	21.07 E
Pustoška	86	56.20 N	29.22 E
Putaru	126	38.03 S	175.47 E
Puting, Tandjung ⌐	96	3.35 S	111.46 E
Putnam	152	41.55 N	71.55 W
Putorana, Plato ⚡¹	84	69.00 N	95.00 E
Puttalam	100	8.02 N	79.49 E
Puttgarden	72	54.30 N	11.13 E
Putumayo ☐⁸	138	0.30 N	76.00 W
Putumayo (Içá) ≃	138	3.07 S	67.58 W
Puurmala	68	58.23 N	28.11 E
Puyallup	166	47.11 N	122.18 W
Puy-de-Dôme ☐⁵	74	45.45 N	3.05 E
Puy de Sancy ∧	74	45.32 N	2.49 E
Puylaurens	74	43.34 N	2.01 E
Puy l'Évêque	74	44.30 N	1.08 E
Puyo	138	1.28 S	77.59 W
Pwllheli	70	52.53 N	4.25 W
Pyé (Prome)	94	18.49 N	95.13 E
Pye Islands II	146	59.22 N	150.25 W
Pyhäselkä	68	62.26 N	29.58 E
Pyinmana	94	19.44 N	96.13 E
Pymatuning Reservoir ≋	152	41.37 N	80.30 W
P'yŏngyang	88	39.01 N	125.45 E
Pyramid Lake ≋	168	40.00 N	119.35 W
Pyrenees ⚡	76	42.40 N	1.00 E
Pyrénées-Atlantiques ☐⁵	74	43.15 N	0.50 W
Pyrénées-Orientales ☐⁵	74	42.30 N	2.20 E
Pyrzyce	72	53.10 N	14.55 E
Pyskowice	72	50.24 N	18.38 E
Pytalovo	86	57.04 N	27.56 E

Q

Name	Page	Lat	Long
Qalāt	102	32.07 N	66.54 E
Qal'at Bishah	102	20.01 N	42.36 E
Qal'ah-ye Kānsī	100	32.15 N	65.15 E
Qallābāt	112	12.43 N	23.26 E
Qalyūb	112	30.11 N	31.12 E
Qamar, Ghubbat al- ≃	100	16.00 N	52.30 E
Qandahār	102	31.32 N	65.30 E
Qandala	108	11.23 N	49.53 E
Qārūn, Birkat ≋	112	29.28 N	30.40 E
Qāsh, Nahr al- (Gash) ≃	112	16.48 N	35.51 E
Qasr al-Burayqah	112	30.25 N	19.34 E
Qasr al-Farāfirah	112	27.03 N	27.58 E
Qasr Banī Walīd	112	31.45 N	14.01 E
Qatar (Qatar) ☐¹	100	25.00 N	51.10 E
Qattara Depression → Qaṭṭārah, Munkhafaḍ al- ⚋⁷	112	30.00 N	27.30 E
Qaṭṭārah, Munkhafaḍ al- ⚋⁷	112	30.00 N	27.30 E
Qāyen	100	33.44 N	59.11 E
Qegertaq	142		
Qeshm I	104	26.45 N	55.45 E
Qeys, Jazīreh-ye I	104	26.32 N	53.56 E
Qezel Owzan ≃	104	36.45 N	49.22 E
Qiemo	88	38.08 N	85.32 E
Qilianshan ∧	88	29.02 N	106.39 E
Qilianshanmai (Nanshan) ⚡	88	38.57 N	99.07 E
Qilinhu	102	31.50 N	89.00 E
Qinà	112	26.10 N	32.43 E
Qingdao (Tsingtao)	88	36.06 N	120.19 E
Qinghai ☐⁴	88	36.00 N	96.00 E
Qinghai	88	36.50 N	100.20 E
Qinglong	88	25.00 N	105.10 E
Qingshuihe	88	37.30 N	105.02 E
Qingyang	88	24.14 N	119.51 E
Qingyuan	88	24.35 N	108.05 E
Qinhuangdao	88	39.56 N	119.36 E
Qinlingshanmai ⚡	88	34.00 N	108.00 E
Qinshui	88	35.42 N	112.12 E
Qinxian (Qinzhou)	88	21.59 N	108.36 E
Qionglai	88	30.26 N	103.27 E
Qiongshan	88	20.01 N	110.21 E
Qiongzhou haixia ◡	88	20.10 N	110.15 E
Qiqihar (Tsitsihar)	88	47.19 N	123.55 E
Qishn	100	15.25 N	51.40 E
Qizān	100	16.54 N	42.29 E
Qom	104	34.39 N	50.54 E
Qomdo	88	31.11 N	97.13 E
Qondūz	102	37.45 N	68.51 E
Qu ≃	88	30.00 N	106.16 E
Quairading	122	32.00 S	117.24 E
Quakenbrück	72	52.40 N	7.57 E
Quakertown	152	40.26 N	75.21 W
Quanah	160	35.18 N	99.44 W
Quang-ngai	94	15.07 N	108.48 E
Quang-tri	94	16.45 N	107.13 E
Quan-long (Ca-mau)	94	9.11 N	105.08 E
Quanzhou	88	24.54 N	118.35 E
Qu'Appelle ≃	142	50.26 N	101.20 W
Quarai (Quaraim) ≃	140	30.12 N	57.36 W
Quarry Hill	168	34.39 N	118.13 W
Quartz Lake ≋	166	30.56 N	80.33 W
Qu'chan	104	37.06 N	58.30 E
Quartu Sant'Elena	78	39.14 N	9.11 E
Quebec	150	46.49 N	71.14 W
Québec (Québec) ☐⁴	142	52.00 N	72.00 W
Quedlinburg	72	51.48 N	11.09 E
Queen Charlotte Islands II	148	53.00 N	132.00 W
Queen Charlotte Sound ⊔	148	51.30 N	129.30 W
Queen Charlotte Strait ⊔	148	50.50 N	127.25 W
Queen Maud Gulf ⌐	148	68.25 N	102.30 W
Queens Channel ⊔	124	14.46 S	129.24 E
Queenscliff	120	38.16 S	144.40 E
Queensland ☐³	118	22.00 S	145.00 E
Queenstown, Austl.	120	42.05 S	145.33 E
Queenstown, N.Z.	126	45.02 S	168.40 E
Queenstown, S. Afr.	116	31.52 S	26.52 E
Quelimane	116	17.53 S	36.51 E
Quelpart Island → Cheju-do I	88	33.20 N	126.30 E
Quemado	164	34.20 N	108.30 W
Que Que	116	18.55 S	29.49 E
Quercy ☐⁹	74	44.30 N	1.25 E
Querétaro	130	20.36 N	100.23 W
Quesada	76	37.51 N	3.04 W
Quesnel	148	52.59 N	122.30 W
Quesnel Lake ≋	148	52.32 N	121.05 W
Questa	164	36.42 N	105.36 W
Questembert	74	47.40 N	2.27 W
Quetta	102	30.12 N	67.00 E
Quevedo	138	1.02 S	79.29 W
Quezaltenango	130	14.50 N	91.31 W
Quezon City	92	14.38 N	121.00 E
Qufu	88	35.36 N	117.02 E
Quibdó	138	5.42 N	76.40 W
Quiberon	74	47.29 N	3.07 W
Quilá	130	24.23 N	107.13 W
Quillacollo	134	17.26 S	66.17 W
Quillan	74	42.52 N	2.11 E
Quillota	140	32.53 S	71.16 W
Quilon	100	8.53 N	76.36 E
Quilpie	120	26.37 S	144.15 E
Quilpué	140	33.03 S	71.27 W
Quimilí	140	27.40 S	62.30 W
Quimper	74	48.00 N	4.06 W
Quimperlé	74	47.52 N	3.33 W
Quincemil	134	13.15 S	70.40 W
Quincy, Calif., U.S.	168	39.56 N	120.57 W
Quincy, Ill., U.S.	158	39.56 N	91.23 W
Quincy, Mass., U.S.	152	42.15 N	71.01 W
Quincy, Mich., U.S.	154	41.57 N	84.53 W
Quincy, Wash., U.S.	166	47.14 N	119.51 W
Quindío ☐⁵	138	5.20 N	75.40 W
Quines	140	32.14 S	65.48 W
Quinga	110	15.49 S	40.15 E
Quinhagak	146	59.45 N	161.43 W
Qui-nhon	94	13.46 N	109.14 E
Quinn ≃	168	39.55 N	119.00 W
Quintin	74	48.24 N	2.55 W
Quinton	160	35.07 N	95.22 W
Quirihue	140	36.17 S	72.32 W
Quirindi	120	31.31 S	150.41 E
Quiroga, Esp.	76	42.29 N	7.16 W
Quiroga, Méx.	130	19.40 N	101.32 W
Quissanga	110	12.25 S	40.29 E
Quitman, Ga., U.S.	156	30.47 N	83.33 W
Quitman, Miss., U.S.	158	32.03 N	88.43 W
Quito	138	0.13 S	78.30 W
Quixadá	134	4.58 S	39.01 W
Qujing	94	25.32 N	103.41 E
Qumalai (Sewugou)	88	35.36 N	95.27 E
Quobba Point ⌐	122	24.23 S	113.24 E
Quoich ≃	142	64.00 N	93.40 W
Quorn	120	32.21 S	138.03 E
Qutdligssat	142	70.04 N	53.01 W
Quthing	116	30.30 S	27.36 E
Quxian	88	28.58 N	118.52 E

R

Name	Page	Lat	Long
Raab (Rába) ≃	72	47.42 N	17.38 E
Raahe	68	64.41 N	24.29 E
Rääkkylä	68	62.19 N	29.37 E
Raalte	72	52.24 N	6.16 E
Raba	96	8.27 S	118.46 E
Rába (Raab) ≃	72	47.42 N	17.38 E
Rabat, Magreb	106	34.02 N	6.51 W
Rabat, Malta → Victoria, Malta	78	35.52 N	14.25 E
Rabaul	124	4.12 S	152.12 E
Râbigh	102	22.48 N	39.01 E
Rabka	72	49.36 N	19.56 E
RaboČeostrovsk	64	64.02 N	34.46 E
Race, Cape ⌐	150	46.40 N	53.10 W
Rach-gia	94	10.00 N	105.04 E
Racibórz (Ratibor)	72	50.06 N	18.13 E
Racine	154	42.43 N	87.48 W
Răckeve	72	47.10 N	18.56 E
Rădăuti	80	47.50 N	25.56 E
Radcliff	158	37.51 N	85.57 W
Rade	68	59.21 N	10.53 E
Radeberg	72	51.06 N	13.55 E
Radebeul	72	51.06 N	13.40 E
Radevormwald	72	51.12 N	7.21 E
Radford	156	37.08 N	80.34 W
Radhanpur	102	23.50 N	71.36 E
Radom	72	51.25 N	21.10 E
Radomsko	72	51.05 N	19.25 E
Radoviš	80	41.38 N	22.28 E
Radstadt	72	47.23 N	13.27 E
Radstock, Cape ⌐	122	33.12 S	134.20 E
Rae	142	62.50 N	116.03 W
Rae Bareli	102	26.14 N	81.15 E
Raeford	156	34.59 N	79.13 W
Rae Isthmus ⚋³	142	66.55 N	87.30 W
Raeside, Lake ≋	122	29.30 S	122.00 E
Rae Strait ⊔	142	68.40 N	95.00 W
Raetihi	126	39.26 S	175.16 E
Rafaela	140	31.17 S	61.30 W
Raffadali	78	37.24 N	13.33 E
Rafsanjān	104	30.23 N	55.59 E
Raft ≃	166	42.37 N	113.15 W
Raga	112	8.28 N	25.41 E
Ragay Gulf ⌐	98	13.40 N	122.40 E
Ragland	158	33.45 N	86.09 W
Ragusa	78	36.55 N	14.44 E
Rahad, Nahr ar- (Rahad) ≃	112	14.28 N	33.31 E
Rahīmyār Khān	102	28.25 N	70.18 E
Rahway	152	40.36 N	74.17 W
Räichür	100	16.12 N	77.21 E
Raiford	156	30.04 N	82.14 W
Raigarh	102	21.54 N	83.24 E
Raiton	72	52.13 N	14.25 E
Rainelle	152	37.58 N	80.46 W
Rainier, Mount ∧	166	46.52 N	121.46 W
Rainy ≃	154	48.50 N	94.41 W
Rainy Lake ≋	154	48.40 N	93.10 W
Rainy River	154	48.43 N	94.29 W
Raipur	102	21.14 N	81.38 E
Raja, Bukit ∧	96	0.01 S	112.41 E
Rajahmundry	100	17.00 N	81.47 E
Rajamäki	68	60.31 N	24.46 E
Rajang ≃	96	2.04 N	111.12 E
Rājapālaiyam	100	9.27 N	77.33 E
Rajčichinsk	84	49.46 N	129.25 E
Rajkot	102	22.18 N	70.47 E
Räj-Nändgaon	102	21.06 N	81.02 E
Räjshähi	102	24.22 N	88.36 E
Rakamaz	72	48.07 N	21.28 E
Rakaposhi ∧	102	36.10 N	74.30 E
Rakkestad	68	59.25 N	11.21 E
Rakvåg	68	50.05 N	13.43 E
Rakvere	68	59.21 N	26.21 E
Raleigh	156	35.47 N	78.39 W
Ralston	162	41.12 N	96.03 W
Ramacca	78	37.23 N	14.42 E
Ramah	160	35.08 N	108.30 W
Ramasucha	86	52.46 N	33.33 E

Name	Page	Lat	Long
Ramervillers	74	48.21 N	6.38 E
Rambouillet	74	48.39 N	1.50 E
Ramenskoje	86	55.34 N	38.14 E
Rāmeswaram	100	9.17 N	79.19 E
Ramingstein	72	47.04 N	13.50 E
Ramlo ∧	112	29.35 N	35.24 E
Ramm, Jabal ∧	112	29.35 N	35.24 E
Ramona, Calif., U.S.	168	33.08 N	116.52 W
Ramona, Okla., U.S.	160	36.32 N	95.55 W
Ramona, S. Dak., U.S.	162	44.07 N	97.13 W
Rampart	146	65.30 N	150.10 W
Ramparts ≃	142	66.11 N	129.03 W
Rāmpur	102	28.49 N	79.02 E
Ramree Island I	94	19.06 N	93.48 E
Ramsey, I. of Man	70	54.20 N	4.21 W
Ramsey, Ill., U.S.	158	39.08 N	89.06 W
Ramsgate	70	51.20 N	1.25 E
Ramu ≃	124	5.00 S	144.40 E
Ramvik	68	62.49 N	17.51 E
Ramygala	68	55.31 N	24.18 E
Rānāghāt	102	23.11 N	88.35 E
Ranau	96	5.57 N	116.40 E
Rancagua	140	34.10 S	70.45 W
Ranches of Taos	164	36.22 N	105.37 W
Ranchester	166	44.54 N	107.16 W
Rānchī	102	23.21 N	85.20 E
Rancho Cordova	168	38.36 N	121.17 W
Randers	68	56.28 N	10.03 E
Randfontein	116	26.11 S	27.42 E
Randleman	156	35.49 N	79.48 W
Randlett	160	34.11 N	98.28 W
Randolph, Ariz., U.S.	164	32.55 N	111.31 W
Randolph, Maine, U.S.	152	44.19 N	69.46 W
Randolph, Mass., U.S.	152	42.10 N	71.03 W
Randolph, Utah, U.S.	164	41.40 N	111.11 W
Randolph, Vt., U.S.	152	43.55 N	72.40 W
Rangāmati	102	22.38 N	92.12 E
Rangeley	152	44.58 N	70.39 W
Rangely	164	40.05 N	108.48 W
Ranger	160	32.28 N	98.41 W
Rangiora	126	43.18 S	172.35 E
Rangoon	94	16.47 N	96.10 E
Rangpur	102	25.45 N	89.15 E
Rānīkhet	102	29.38 N	79.26 E
Ranken ≃	120	20.31 S	137.36 E
Ranken Store	120	20.35 S	137.36 E
Rankin	158	31.13 N	101.56 W
Rankin Inlet	142	62.45 N	92.10 W
Ranlo	156	35.17 N	81.07 W
Rann of Kutch ≃	100	24.00 N	70.00 E
Ransiki	124	1.30 S	134.10 E
Ranson	152	39.18 N	77.52 W
Rantasalmi	68	62.04 N	28.18 E
Rantauprapat	94	2.06 N	99.50 E
Rantekombola, Bulu ∧	96	3.21 S	120.01 E
Rantoul	158	40.19 N	88.09 W
Rantsila	68	64.31 N	25.39 E
Ranua	68	65.55 N	26.32 E
Rapallo	78	44.21 N	9.14 E
Rapid City	162	44.05 N	103.14 W
Rappahannock ≃	156	37.34 N	76.18 W
Rapperswil	74	47.14 N	8.50 E
Räpina	68	58.06 N	27.28 E
Rāpti ≃	102	26.18 N	83.41 E
Rapulo ≃	134	13.43 S	65.32 W
Ras Dashen ∧	108	13.10 N	38.26 E
Raseiniai	86	55.24 N	23.07 E
Rashid	112	31.24 N	30.25 E
Rashīd, Maşabb ≃¹	112	31.22 N	30.20 E
Rasht	104	37.16 N	49.36 E
Raška	80	43.17 N	20.37 E
Rasskazovo	86	52.40 N	41.53 E
Rassua, Ostrov I	84	47.45 N	153.01 E
Rastatt	72	48.51 N	8.12 E
Rastede	72	53.15 N	8.11 E
Rat ≃	142	56.10 N	99.04 W
Rathdrum	166	47.48 N	116.53 W
Rathenow	72	52.36 N	12.20 E
Rathkeale	70	52.32 N	8.56 W
Rath Luirc (Charleville)	70	52.21 N	8.41 W
Ratingen	72	51.18 N	6.51 E
Ratlām	102	23.19 N	75.04 E
Ratnāgiri	100	16.59 N	73.17 E
Ratnapura	100	6.41 N	80.24 E
Raton	160	36.54 N	104.24 W
Ratz, Mount ∧	146	57.23 N	132.19 W
Ratzeburg	72	53.42 N	10.46 E
Rauch	140	36.47 S	59.05 W
Raufarhöfn	66a	66.30 N	15.57 W
Raufoss	68	60.43 N	10.37 E
Rauma	68	61.08 N	21.30 E
Rauma ≃	68	62.33 N	7.43 E
Raurkela	102	22.13 N	84.53 E
Rautalampi	68	62.38 N	26.50 E
Rautavaara	68	63.29 N	28.18 E
Ravanusa	78	37.16 N	13.58 E
Ravena	152	42.28 N	73.49 W
Ravenna, It.	78	44.25 N	12.12 E
Ravenna, Mich., U.S.	154	43.11 N	85.56 W
Ravenna, Nebr., U.S.	162	41.02 N	98.55 W
Ravenna, Ohio, U.S.	152	41.09 N	81.15 W
Ravensburg	72	47.47 N	9.37 E
Ravenshoe	120	17.37 S	145.29 E
Ravensthorpe	122	33.35 S	120.02 E
Ravenswood	156	38.57 N	81.46 W
Rāvi ≃	102	30.35 N	71.48 E
Rāwalpindi	102	33.36 N	73.04 E
Rawa Mazowiecka	72	51.46 N	20.16 E
Rawändüz	104	36.38 N	44.32 E
Rawicz	72	51.37 N	16.52 E
Rawlinna	122	30.58 S	125.28 E
Rawlins	166	41.47 N	107.14 W
Rawlinson, Mount ∧	122	25.58 S	127.28 E
Rawlinson Range ⚡	122	24.51 S	128.00 E
Rawson	136	43.18 S	65.06 W
Raxaul	102	34.40 N	84.51 E
Ray	162	48.21 N	103.10 W
Ray, Cape ⌐	150	47.40 N	59.18 W
Raymond, Alta., Can.	166	49.27 N	112.39 W
Raymond, Ill., U.S.	158	39.19 N	89.34 W
Raymond, Miss., U.S.	158	32.15 N	90.25 W
Raymond, Wash., U.S.	166	46.41 N	123.44 W
Raymond Terrace	120	32.46 S	151.44 E
Raymondville	160	26.29 N	97.47 W
Rayne	158	30.14 N	92.16 W
Raytown	158	39.00 N	94.28 W
Rayville	158	32.28 N	91.45 W
R'azan'	86	54.38 N	39.44 E
R'azancevo	86	56.54 N	39.42 E
Ražanj	86	53.43 N	40.04 E
Razgrad	80	43.32 N	26.31 E
R'ažsk	86	53.42 N	40.04 E
Ré, Île de I	74	46.12 N	1.25 W
Reading, Eng., U.K.	70	51.28 N	0.59 W
Reading, Mich., U.S.	154	41.50 N	84.45 W
Reading, Pa., U.S.	152	40.20 N	75.56 W
Real, Cordillera ⚡	140	17.00 S	67.10 W
Realicó	140	35.02 S	64.14 W
Réalmont	74	43.47 N	2.12 E
Reardan	166	47.40 N	118.01 W
Reay	70	58.33 N	3.47 W
Rebun-jima I	90a	45.23 N	141.02 E
Recanati	78	43.24 N	13.32 E
Recherche, Archipelago of the II	122	34.05 S	122.45 E
Rečica	86	52.22 N	30.24 E
Recife	134	8.03 S	34.54 W
Recklinghausen	72	51.36 N	7.13 E
Reconquista	140	29.10 S	59.40 W
Recreo	140	29.20 S	65.04 W
Rector	158	36.16 N	90.17 W
Red (Hong) (Yuanjiang) ≃, As.	94	20.17 N	106.34 E
Red ≃, U.S.	158	31.00 N	91.40 W
Red ≃, Ky., U.S.	158	37.54 N	83.54 W
Red, Elm Fork ≃	160	34.24 N	99.14 W
Red, North Fork ≃	160	34.24 N	99.14 W
Red, Salt Fork ≃	160	34.27 N	99.37 W
Red, South Fork ≃	158	36.41 N	86.56 W

Name	Page	Lat	Long
Redang, Pulau I	96	5.47 N	103.00 E
Red Bank, N.J., U.S.	152	40.21 N	74.03 W
Red Bank, Tenn., U.S.	158	35.07 N	85.17 W
Red Bay, Ala., U.S.	158	34.27 N	88.09 W
Redbay, Fla., U.S.	158	30.35 N	85.57 W
Red Bluff	168	40.11 N	122.15 W
Red Bluff Reservoir ≋	160	31.57 N	103.56 W
Red Boiling Springs	158	36.32 N	85.51 W
Red Bud	158	38.13 N	89.59 W
Red Canyon V	162	43.18 N	103.49 W
Redcar	70	54.37 N	1.04 W
Redcliff	162	50.06 N	110.47 W
Redcliffe	120	27.14 S	153.07 E
Redcliffe, Mount ∧	122	28.25 S	121.32 E
Red Cliffs	120	34.19 S	142.11 E
Red Cloud	162	40.05 N	98.32 W
Red Deer	142	52.16 N	113.48 W
Red Deer ≃, Can.	142	50.56 N	109.54 W
Red Deer ≃, Can.	142	52.53 N	101.01 W
Red Deer Lake ≋, Ont., Can.	142	51.01 N	94.05 W
Red Deer Lake ≋, S. Dak., Can.	162	52.56 N	101.20 W
Red Devil	146	61.46 N	157.18 W
Redding	168	40.35 N	122.24 W
Redfield, Iowa, U.S.	154	41.35 N	94.12 W
Redfield, S. Dak., U.S.	162	44.53 N	98.31 W
Red Hook	152	41.59 N	73.53 W
Redkey	152	40.21 N	85.09 W
Red Lake ≋, Ont., Can.	142	51.01 N	93.49 W
Red Lake ≋, S. Dak., Can.	162		
Red Lake Falls	162	47.53 N	96.16 W
Redlands	168	34.03 N	117.11 W
Red Lion	152	39.54 N	76.36 W
Red Lodge	166	45.11 N	109.15 W
Redmond, Oreg., U.S.	166	44.16 N	121.11 W
Redmond, Wash., U.S.	166	47.40 N	122.07 W
Red Mountain	168	35.22 N	117.40 W
Red Oak, Iowa, U.S.	154	41.01 N	95.14 W
Red Oak, Okla., U.S.	160	34.57 N	95.05 W
Redon	74	47.39 N	2.05 W
Redondo	76	38.39 N	7.33 W
Redondo Beach	168	33.50 N	118.23 W
Red Point Rock I²	122	32.13 S	127.32 E
Red River Valley V	162	47.00 N	96.55 W
Redruth	70	50.13 N	5.14 W
Red Sea ≃²	108	20.00 N	38.00 E
Redstone ≃	142	64.00 N	124.33 W
Redwater	142	24.00 N	103.51 W
Redwillow ≃	148	55.04 N	119.21 W
Red Wing	154	44.34 N	92.31 W
Redwood City	168	37.29 N	122.13 W
Redwood Falls	154	44.32 N	95.07 W
Redwood Valley	168	39.16 N	123.12 W
Rhyl [Ree, Lough ≋]	70	53.35 N	7.58 W
Reedley	168	36.36 N	119.27 W
Reedsburg	154	43.32 N	90.00 W
Reedsport	166	43.42 N	124.06 W
Reefton	126	42.07 S	171.52 E
Rees	72	51.45 N	6.23 E
Reese ≃	168	40.39 N	117.04 W
Reese Village			
Reform	158	33.23 N	88.01 W
Refugio	160	28.18 N	97.17 W
Regensburg	72	49.01 N	12.06 E
Reggane	106	26.42 N	0.10 E
Reggello	78	43.41 N	11.32 E
Reggio di Calabria	78	38.06 N	15.39 E
Reggio nell'Emilia	78	44.43 N	10.36 E
Regina, Sask., Can.	142	50.25 N	104.39 W
Regina, Guy. fr.	134	4.19 N	52.08 W
Reguengos de Monsaraz	76	38.25 N	7.32 W
Rehau	72	50.15 N	12.02 E
Rehoboth	116	23.18 S	17.03 E
Rehoboth Beach	152	38.43 N	75.05 W
Rehovot	104	31.54 N	34.49 E
Reichenbach	72	50.37 N	12.18 E
Reid, Mount ∧	146	55.42 N	131.15 W
Reidsville, Ga., U.S.	156	32.06 N	82.07 W
Reidsville, N.C., U.S.	156	36.21 N	79.40 W
Reigate	70	51.14 N	0.13 W
Reims	74	49.15 N	4.02 E
Reinbeck	154	42.19 N	92.36 W
Reindeer Lake ≋	142	57.15 N	102.40 W
Reinosa	76	43.00 N	4.08 W
Reisterstown	152	39.28 N	76.50 W
Reliance	166	41.40 N	109.12 W
Remada	106	32.19 N	10.24 E
Remagen	72	50.34 N	7.13 E
Remanso	134	9.41 S	42.04 W
Remarkable, Mount ∧	120	32.48 S	138.10 E
Remiremont	74	48.01 N	6.35 E
Remoulins	74	43.56 N	4.34 E
Remscheid	72	51.11 N	7.11 E
Remsen	154	42.49 N	95.58 W
Rena	68	61.08 N	11.22 E
Rende	78	39.20 N	16.11 E
Rendova I	124	8.33 S	157.17 E
Rendsburg	72	54.18 N	9.40 E
Renfrew	72	45.28 N	76.41 W
Rengat	96	0.24 S	102.33 E
Rengo	140	34.25 S	70.52 W
Renko	68	60.54 N	24.18 E
Renkum	72	51.58 N	5.45 E
Renmark	120	34.10 S	140.45 E
Rennell Island I	118	11.40 S	160.10 E
Rennes	74	48.05 N	1.41 W
Reno	168	39.31 N	119.48 W
Reno ≃	78	44.38 N	12.17 E
Renovo	152	41.19 N	77.44 W
Rensselaer, Ind., U.S.	158	40.56 N	87.09 W
Rensselaer, N.Y., U.S.	152	42.39 N	73.45 W
Renton	166	47.29 N	122.13 W
Réo	106	12.19 N	2.28 W
Repetek	100	38.35 N	63.11 E
Repino	86	60.10 N	29.52 E
Reposaari	68	61.37 N	21.27 E
Republic, Mich., U.S.	154	46.25 N	87.59 W
Republic, Wash., U.S.	166	48.38 N	118.44 W
Republican, South Fork ≃	162	40.03 N	101.33 W
Republican ≃	162	39.03 N	96.48 W
Repulse Bay	142	66.32 N	86.15 W
Repulse Bay ⌐	120	20.36 S	148.43 E
Requena	76	39.29 N	1.06 W
Reschenpass ⋊	72	46.50 N	10.30 E
Reserve, La., U.S.	158	30.03 N	90.33 W
Reserve, N. Mex., U.S.	164	33.43 N	108.45 W
Resia, Passo di ⋊	78	46.50 N	10.30 E
Resistencia	140	27.30 S	58.59 W
Reşiţa	80	45.17 N	21.55 E
Resolute	142	74.41 N	94.54 W
Resolution Island I	142	61.30 N	65.00 W
Restigouche ≃	150	48.04 N	66.20 W
Reston	152	38.57 N	77.20 W
Retalhuleu	130	14.32 N	91.41 W
Rethel	74	49.31 N	4.22 E
Réthimnon	80	35.22 N	24.28 E
Retz	72	48.45 N	15.58 E
Reus	76	41.09 N	1.07 E
Reutlingen	72	48.29 N	9.12 E
Rev'akino	86	54.17 N	37.40 E
Reval → Tallinn	86	59.25 N	24.45 E
Revda, S.S.S.R.	66	67.55 N	34.33 E
Revda, S.S.S.R.	82	56.48 N	59.57 E
Revelstoke	148	50.59 N	118.12 W

Name	Page	Lat	Long
Reventazón	134	6.10 S	80.58 W
Revigny-sur-Ornain	74	48.50 N	4.59 E
Revillagigedo, Islas de II	130	19.00 N	111.30 W
Revillagigedo Island I	146	55.35 N	131.23 W
Revin	74	49.56 N	4.38 E
Revúe ≃	116	19.49 S	34.00 E
Rewa	102	24.32 N	81.18 E
Rewāri	102	28.11 N	76.37 E
Rexburg	166	43.49 N	111.47 W
Rexford	166	48.53 N	115.13 W
Rey	104	35.35 N	51.25 E
Rey, Isla del I	138	8.22 N	78.52 W
Reyes	134	14.19 S	67.23 W
Reyes, Point ⌐	168	38.00 N	123.01 W
Reykjavík	66a	64.09 N	21.51 W
Reynolds, Ga., U.S.	156	32.34 N	84.06 W
Reynolds, N. Dak., U.S.	162	47.41 N	97.07 W
Reynoldsville	152	41.05 N	78.53 W
Reynosa	130	26.07 N	98.18 W
Rež	82	57.23 N	61.24 E
Reza, Gora (Kūh-e Rīzeh) ∧	104	41.35 N	58.05 E
Rezā'īyeh	104	37.33 N	45.04 E
Rezā'īyeh, Daryācheh-ye ≋	104	37.40 N	45.30 E
Rēzekne	86	56.30 N	27.19 E
Rēze	74	47.11 N	1.34 W
Rezovska (Rezve) ≃	80	41.59 N	28.01 E
Rezve (Rezovska) ≃	80	41.59 N	28.01 E
Rhaetian Alps ⚡	74	46.30 N	10.00 E
Rheda-Wiedenbrück	72	51.50 N	8.18 E
Rheims → Reims	74	49.15 N	4.02 E
Rheine	72	52.17 N	7.26 E
Rheinfelden, B.R.D.	72	47.33 N	7.47 E
Rheinfelden, Schw.	74	47.33 N	7.48 E
Rheinhausen	72	51.24 N	6.44 E
Rheinland-Pfalz ☐³	72	50.00 N	7.00 E
Rheydt	72	51.10 N	6.25 E
Rhine (Rhein) (Rhin) ≃	72	51.52 N	6.02 E
Rhinebeck	152	41.56 N	73.55 W
Rhinelander	154	45.38 N	89.25 W
Rhir, Cap ⌐	106	30.38 N	9.55 W
Rho	78	45.32 N	9.02 E
Rhode Island ☐³	144	41.40 N	71.30 W
Rhode Island Sound ≃	152	41.25 N	71.25 W
Rhodes → Ródhos	80	36.26 N	28.13 E
Rhodesia ☐¹	110	20.00 S	30.00 E
Rhodope Mountains ⚡	80	41.30 N	24.30 E
Rhondda	70	51.40 N	3.27 W
Rhône ≃	74	43.20 N	4.50 E
Rhyl	70	53.19 N	3.29 W
Riachão	134	7.22 S	46.37 W
Riaño	76	42.58 N	5.01 W
Riau, Kepulauan II	96	1.00 N	104.30 E
Ribadeo	76	43.32 N	7.02 W
Ribas do Rio Pardo	134	20.27 S	53.46 W
Ribe	68	55.21 N	8.46 E
Ribeauville	74	48.12 N	7.19 E
Ribeirão Prêto	134	21.10 S	47.48 W
Ribemont	74	49.48 N	3.28 E
Ribera	78	37.30 N	13.16 E
Ribérac	74	45.15 N	0.20 E
Riberalta	134	10.59 S	66.06 W
Ribnitz-Damgarten	72	54.15 N	12.28 E
Ricardo	160	27.25 N	97.51 W
Riccarton	126	43.32 S	172.35 E
Riccia	78	41.29 N	14.50 E
Riccione	78	43.59 N	12.39 E
Rice	154	45.45 N	94.13 W
Rice Lake	154	45.30 N	91.44 W
Riceville	154	43.22 N	92.33 W
Richard Collinson Inlet ⌐	142	72.45 N	113.45 W
Richards	160	30.32 N	95.51 W
Richard's Bay ⌐	116	28.50 S	32.06 E
Richards Island I	142	69.20 N	134.30 W
Richardson	160	32.57 N	96.44 W
Richardson, Mount ∧	122	28.49 S	130.37 E
Richardson Mountains ⚡	146	67.15 N	136.30 W
Riche, Pointe ⌐	150	50.42 N	57.25 W
Richelieu	152	47.01 N	73.16 W
Richey	162	47.38 N	105.04 W
Richfield, Idaho, U.S.	166	43.03 N	114.09 W
Richfield, Minn., U.S.	154	44.53 N	93.17 W
Richfield, Utah, U.S.	164	38.46 N	112.05 W
Richford	152	45.00 N	72.40 W
Rich Hill	158	38.05 N	94.22 W
Richland, Ga., U.S.	156	32.05 N	84.39 W
Richland, Mo., U.S.	158	37.51 N	92.26 W
Richland, Wash., U.S.	166	46.17 N	119.18 W
Richland Center	154	43.20 N	90.23 W
Richlands, N.C., U.S.	156	34.54 N	77.34 W
Richlands, Va., U.S.	156	37.05 N	81.47 W
Richmond, Austl.	120	20.44 S	143.08 E
Richmond, B.C., Can.	148	49.09 N	123.06 W
Richmond, Ont., Can.	152	45.11 N	75.50 W
Richmond, Qué., Can.	152	45.40 N	72.09 W
Richmond, N.Z.	126	41.21 S	173.11 E
Richmond, Eng., U.K.	70	54.24 N	1.44 W
Richmond, Calif., U.S.	168	37.57 N	122.22 W
Richmond, Ind., U.S.	158	39.50 N	84.53 W
Richmond, Ky., U.S.	156	37.44 N	84.17 W
Richmond, Maine, U.S.	152	44.05 N	69.48 W
Richmond, Mich., U.S.	154	42.49 N	82.45 W
Richmond, Mo., U.S.	158	39.16 N	93.58 W
Richmond, Tex., U.S.	160	29.35 N	95.45 W
Richmond, Utah, U.S.	164	41.55 N	111.48 W
Richmond, Va., U.S.	156	37.33 N	77.27 W
Richmond, Vt., U.S.	152	44.24 N	72.59 W
Richmond Beach	166	47.46 N	122.23 W
Richmond Heights	158	38.38 N	90.19 W
Richmond Hill	152	43.52 N	79.26 W
Rich Square	156	36.16 N	77.17 W
Richton	158	31.20 N	88.56 W
Richwood, Ohio, U.S.	152	40.25 N	83.18 W
Richwood, W. Va., U.S.	152	38.14 N	80.32 W
Rico	164	37.41 N	108.02 W
Riddle	166	42.57 N	123.22 W
Ridgecrest	168	35.37 N	117.40 W
Ridgefield	166	45.49 N	122.44 W
Ridgeland	156	32.29 N	80.59 W
Ridgetown	154	42.26 N	81.54 W
Ridgeville	156	33.05 N	80.19 W
Ridgway, Colo., U.S.	164	38.09 N	107.45 W
Ridgway, Pa., U.S.	152	41.25 N	78.43 W
Ridotta Capuzzo	112	31.35 N	25.00 E
Ried im Innkreis	72	48.13 N	13.30 E
Riesa	72	51.18 N	13.17 E
Riesco, Isla I	136	52.55 S	72.55 W
Rieti	78	42.24 N	12.51 E
Rif ∧	106	35.00 N	4.00 W
Rift Valley V	110	0.30 N	36.00 E
Riga	86	56.57 N	24.06 E
Riga, Gulf of ≃	86	57.30 N	23.35 E
Rīgas Jūras Līcis (Riga, Gulf of) ≃	86	57.30 N	23.35 E
Rigby	166	43.40 N	111.55 W
Rīgestān ⚋¹	102	31.00 N	65.00 E
Riggins	166	45.25 N	116.19 W
Rigi ∧	74	47.05 N	8.19 E
Rigolet	142	54.10 N	58.25 W
Riihimäki	68	60.45 N	24.46 E
Rijeka	78	45.20 N	14.27 E
Rijssen	72	52.18 N	6.31 E
Rikaze	88	29.17 N	88.52 E
Rikuzen-takata	90	39.01 N	141.37 E
Rima ≃	114	13.04 N	5.10 E
Rimavská Sobota	72	48.23 N	20.02 E
Rimbo	68	59.45 N	18.22 E

Symbols in the index entries are identified on page 203.

Name	Page	Lat	Long
Rimini	78	44.04 N	12.34 E
Rîmnicu-Sărat	80	45.23 N	27.03 E
Rîmnicu-Vîlcea	80	45.06 N	24.22 E
Rimouski	150	48.26 N	68.33 W
Rincon, Ga., U.S.	156	32.18 N	81.14 W
Rincon, N. Mex., U.S.	164	32.40 N	107.04 W
Rinconada	140	22.26 S	66.10 W
Rincón de Romos	130	22.14 N	102.18 W
Rindal	68	63.03 N	9.13 E
Rindjani, Gunung ⋀	96	8.24 S	116.28 E
Ringe	68	55.14 N	10.29 E
Ringgold	156	34.55 N	85.07 W
Ringling	160	34.10 N	97.36 W
Ringvassøya I	66	69.55 N	19.15 E
Rinteln	72	52.11 N	9.04 E
Rintja, Pulau I	96	8.41 S	119.42 E
Riobamba	138	1.40 S	78.38 W
Rio Benito	110	1.35 N	9.37 E
Rio Bravo	134	9.58 N	60.02 W
Rio Claro	134	25.59 N	98.06 W
Rio Claro	140	22.24 S	47.33 W
Rio Colorado	140	39.01 S	64.05 W
Rio Cuarto	140	33.08 S	64.20 W
Rio de Janeiro	134	22.54 S	43.15 W
Rio Dell	168	40.30 N	124.07 W
Rio do Sul	140	27.13 S	49.39 W
Rio Gallegos	136	51.37 S	69.10 W
Rio Grande, Arg.	136	53.50 S	67.40 W
Rio Grande, Bra.	140	32.02 S	52.05 W
Rio Grande, Méx.	130	23.50 N	103.02 W
Rio Grande do Sul □3	140	30.00 S	54.00 W
Riohacha	138	11.33 N	72.55 W
Rioja	134	6.03 S	77.05 W
Rio Largo	134	9.29 S	35.51 W
Riom	74	45.54 N	3.07 E
Rio Mayo	136	45.40 S	70.15 W
Rio Negro, Bra.	140	26.06 S	49.48 W
Rionegro, Col.	138	6.09 N	75.22 W
Rio Negro, Embalse del ⊜1	140	32.45 S	56.00 W
Rionero in Vulture	78	40.56 N	15.41 E
Rio Pardo	140	29.59 S	52.22 W
Rio Pardo de Minas	134	15.37 S	42.33 W
Rioscucio	138	5.25 N	75.42 W
Rio Tercero	140	32.10 S	64.05 W
Rio Tinto	134	6.48 S	35.05 W
Rioverde, Méx.	130	21.56 N	99.59 W
Rio Verde, Bra.	134	17.43 S	50.56 W
Rio Vista	168	38.10 N	121.42 W
Rioz	74	47.26 N	6.04 E
Ripley, Miss., U.S.	158	34.44 N	88.57 W
Ripley, N.Y., U.S.	152	42.16 N	79.43 W
Ripley, Tenn., U.S.	158	35.45 N	89.32 W
Ripley, W. Va., U.S.	152	38.49 N	81.43 W
Ripon, Eng., U.K.	70	54.08 N	1.31 W
Ripon, Calif., U.S.	168	37.44 N	121.07 W
Ripon, Wis., U.S.	154	43.51 N	88.50 W
Riposto	78	45.45 N	15.12 E
Ririe	166	43.38 N	111.46 W
Risaralda □5	138	5.00 N	76.10 W
Riscle	74	43.40 N	0.05 W
Rishiri-tō I	90a	45.11 N	141.15 E
Rising Sun	158	38.43 N	84.51 W
Risør	68	58.43 N	9.14 E
Ristiina	68	61.30 N	27.16 E
Rittman	152	40.58 N	81.47 W
Ritzville	166	47.08 N	118.23 W
Riva	78	45.53 N	10.50 E
Rive-de-Gier	74	45.32 N	4.37 E
Rivera	140	30.54 S	55.31 W
Riverbank	168	37.44 N	120.56 W
River Cess	114	5.28 N	9.32 W
Riverdale, Calif., U.S.	168	36.26 N	119.52 W
Riverdale, N. Dak., U.S.	162	47.30 N	101.22 W
River Falls	154	44.52 N	92.38 W
Rivergaro	78	44.55 N	9.36 E
Riverhead	152	40.55 N	72.40 W
Riverina ⊶1	120	35.30 S	145.30 E
Riverland Terrace	156	32.47 N	80.02 W
Rivers	142	50.02 N	100.12 W
Riverside, Calif., U.S.	168	33.57 N	117.24 W
Riverside, Wash., U.S.	148	48.30 N	119.31 W
Rivers Inlet	148	51.41 N	127.15 W
Riverton, Ill., U.S.	158	39.51 N	89.33 W
Riverton, Utah, U.S.	164	40.31 N	111.56 W
Riverton, Wyo., U.S.	164	43.02 N	108.23 W
River View, Ala., U.S.	158	32.54 N	85.07 W
Riverview, Fla., U.S.	156	27.52 N	82.20 W
Rives	158	36.21 N	89.04 W
Rivesaltes	74	42.46 N	2.52 E
Rivesville	152	39.32 N	80.07 W
Riviera Beach	156	26.46 N	80.04 W
Rivière-du-Loup	150	47.50 N	69.32 W
Rivière-du-Moulin	150	48.26 N	71.02 W
Rivière-Trois-Pistoles	150	48.07 N	69.11 W
Rivoli	78	45.04 N	7.31 E
Rivoli Bay C	120	37.32 S	140.04 E
Rize	100	41.02 N	40.31 E
Rizeh, Küh-e (Gora Reza) ⋀	104	37.47 N	58.05 E
Rizhao	88	35.27 N	119.29 E
Rižskij Zaliv C	86	57.30 N	23.35 E
Rjukan	68	59.52 N	8.34 E
Roa	68	60.17 N	10.37 E
Road Town	132	18.27 N	64.37 W
Roan Cliffs ⋀4	164	39.20 N	109.40 W
Roan Mountain	156	36.12 N	82.05 W
Roanne	74	46.02 N	4.04 E
Roanoke, Ala., U.S.	156	33.09 N	85.22 W
Roanoke, Ill., U.S.	154	40.48 N	89.12 W
Roanoke, Va., U.S. (Staunton)	156	37.16 N	79.57 W
Roanoke Rapids	156	36.56 N	76.43 W
Roan Plateau ⋀1	164	39.30 N	110.00 W
Roatán, Isla de I	132	16.23 N	86.26 W
Robbins, N.C., U.S.	156	35.26 N	79.35 W
Robbins, Tenn., U.S.	156	36.21 N	84.34 W
Robbins Island I	120	40.41 S	144.57 E
Robe, Mount ⋀	120	31.40 S	141.20 E
Röbel	72	53.23 N	12.35 E
Roberts Creek Mountain ⋀	168	39.52 N	116.18 W
Robertsdale, Ala., U.S.	156	30.33 N	87.43 W
Robertsdale, Pa., U.S.	152	40.11 N	78.07 W
Robert S. Kerr Lake ⊜1	160	35.25 N	95.00 W
Robertson Range ⋀	122	23.10 S	121.00 E
Roberts Peak ⋀	148	55.21 N	120.32 W
Robert Williams	114	6.45 N	11.22 W
Robinson, Ill., U.S.	158	39.00 N	87.44 W
Robinson, Kans., U.S.	162	39.49 N	95.25 W
Robinson, Tex., U.S.	160	31.31 N	97.06 W
Róbinson Crusoe, Isla (Isla Más A Tierra) I	136	33.38 S	78.52 W
Robinson Ranges ⋀2	122	25.45 S	119.00 E
Robinvale	120	34.35 S	142.47 E
Roblin	142	51.14 N	101.21 W
Roboré	134	18.20 S	59.45 W
Robson, Mount ⋀	148	53.07 N	119.09 W
Roby	160	32.45 N	100.23 W
Roçadas	110	16.43 S	15.11 E
Roca Partida, Isla I	130	19.01 N	112.02 W
Rocas, Atol das I1	134	3.52 S	33.33 W
Rocha	140	34.29 S	54.20 W
Rochdale	70	53.38 N	2.09 W
Rochechouart	74	45.50 N	0.50 E
Rochefort, Bel.	72	50.10 N	5.13 E
Rochefort, Fr.	74	45.56 N	0.58 W
Rochefort-Montagne	74	45.41 N	2.48 E
Rochelle, Ga., U.S.	156	31.57 N	83.27 W
Rochelle, Ill., U.S.	154	41.56 N	89.04 W
Rochester, Eng., U.K.	70	51.24 N	0.30 E
Rochester, Ind., U.S.	158	41.04 N	86.13 W
Rochester, Mich., U.S.	154	42.41 N	83.08 W
Rochester, Minn., U.S.	154	44.02 N	92.29 W
Rochester, N.H., U.S.	152	43.18 N	70.59 W
Rochester, N.Y., U.S.	152	43.10 N	77.36 W
Rochester, Tex., U.S.	160	33.19 N	99.51 W
Rochlitz	72	51.03 N	12.47 E
Rock	154	46.04 N	87.10 W
Rock ⌁, U.S.	154	41.29 N	90.37 W
Rock ⌁, U.S.	162	43.05 N	96.27 W
Rock Creek ⌁, N.A.	166	48.25 N	107.05 W
Rock Creek ⌁, Nev., U.S.	168	40.39 N	116.54 W
Rockdale, Ill., U.S.	154	41.30 N	88.06 W
Rockdale, Tex., U.S.	160	30.39 N	97.00 W
Rockenhausen	72	49.38 N	7.49 E
Rock Falls	154	41.47 N	89.41 W
Rockford, Ill., U.S.	154	42.16 N	89.06 W
Rockford, Iowa, U.S.	154	43.03 N	92.57 W
Rockford, Ohio, U.S.	152	40.42 N	84.39 W
Rock Hall	152	39.08 N	76.14 W
Rockhampton	120	23.23 S	150.31 E
Rockhampton Downs	122	18.57 S	135.01 E
Rock Hill	156	34.56 N	81.01 W
Rockingham	156	34.56 N	79.46 W
Rockingham Bay C	120	18.10 S	146.05 E
Rock Island	154	41.30 N	90.34 W
Rockland, Ont., Can.	152	45.33 N	75.17 W
Rockland, Idaho, U.S.	166	42.34 N	112.53 W
Rockland, Maine, U.S.	152	44.06 N	69.06 W
Rockland, Mass., U.S.	152	42.08 N	70.55 W
Rockland, Mich., U.S.	154	46.41 N	89.11 W
Rocklands Reservoir ⊜1	120	37.15 S	142.00 E
Rockledge	156	28.20 N	80.43 W
Rocklin	168	38.48 N	121.14 W
Rockmart	156	34.00 N	85.02 W
Rockport, Maine, U.S.	152	44.11 N	69.06 W
Rockport, Mass., U.S.	152	42.39 N	70.36 W
Rock Port, Mo., U.S.	162	40.25 N	95.31 W
Rockport, N.Y., U.S.	158	40.25 N	85.57 W
Rock Rapids	162	43.26 N	96.10 W
Rock River	162	41.44 N	105.58 W
Rocksprings, Tex., U.S.	160	30.01 N	100.13 W
Rock Springs, Wyo., U.S.	164	41.35 N	109.13 W
Rockstone	138	5.59 N	58.32 W
Rockton	154	42.27 N	89.04 W
Rock Valley	162	43.12 N	96.18 W
Rockville, Ind., U.S.	158	39.46 N	87.14 W
Rockville, Md., U.S.	152	39.05 N	77.09 W
Rockwall	156	32.56 N	96.28 W
Rockwell City	162	42.24 N	94.38 W
Rockwood	156	35.52 N	84.41 W
Rocky Cape ⊁	120	40.51 S	145.30 E
Rocky Ford	162	38.03 N	103.43 W
Rocky Mount, N.C., U.S.	156	35.56 N	77.48 W
Rocky Mount, Va., U.S.	156	37.00 N	79.54 W
Rocky Mountain House	142	52.22 N	114.55 W
Rocky Mountains ⋀	144	48.00 N	116.00 W
Rodalben	72	49.14 N	8.58 E
Rødberg	68	60.16 N	8.58 E
Rødby	68	54.42 N	11.24 E
Rødbyhavn	68	54.39 N	11.21 E
Rodeo, Arg.	140	30.13 S	69.08 W
Rodeo, N. Mex., U.S.	164	31.50 N	109.02 W
Roderick ⌁	122	25.27 S	115.13 E
Rodewisch	72	50.32 N	12.24 E
Rodez	74	44.21 N	2.35 E
Ródhos (Rhodes)	80	36.26 N	28.13 E
Ródhos I	80	36.10 N	28.00 E
Rodi Garganico	78	41.55 N	15.53 E
Roding	72	49.12 N	12.32 E
Rodney	152	42.34 N	81.41 W
Rodniki	86	57.06 N	41.44 E
Rødven	68	62.38 N	7.33 E
Roebourne	122	20.47 S	117.09 E
Roeland Park	162	39.02 N	94.37 W
Roermond	72	51.12 N	6.00 E
Roeselare	72	50.57 N	3.08 E
Roes Welcome Sound ⋃	142	64.00 N	88.00 W
Rogačov	86	53.05 N	30.03 E
Rogagua, Lago ⊜	134	13.43 S	66.54 W
Rogaland □6	68	58.50 N	6.15 E
Rogatica	78	43.48 N	19.00 E
Rogers	158	36.20 N	94.07 W
Rogers, Ark., U.S.	158	36.20 N	94.07 W
Rogers, Tex., U.S.	160	30.56 N	97.14 W
Rogers, Mount ⋀	156	36.39 N	81.33 W
Rogers City	154	45.25 N	83.49 W
Rogersville	156	36.25 N	83.02 W
Roggiano	78	42.57 N	9.25 E
Rogoaguado, Lago ⊜	134	12.52 S	65.43 W
Rogožno	72	52.46 N	17.00 E
Rogue ⌁	166	42.26 N	124.25 W
Rogue River	166	42.26 N	123.10 W
Rohtak	102	28.54 N	76.34 E
Roisel	72	49.57 N	3.06 E
Rojas	140	34.11 S	60.44 W
Rokan ⌁	96	2.00 N	100.52 E
Rokiškis	86	55.58 N	25.35 E
Rokycany	72	49.45 N	13.36 E
Rolândia	140	23.18 S	51.22 W
Røldal	68	59.49 N	6.48 E
Rolla, Kans., U.S.	162	37.07 N	101.38 W
Rolla, Mo., U.S.	158	37.57 N	91.46 W
Rolla, N. Dak., U.S.	162	48.52 N	99.37 W
Rolle	74	46.28 N	6.20 E
Rolleston	120	24.28 S	148.37 E
Rolling Fork	158	32.55 N	90.52 W
Rolling Hills	120	19.03 S	146.24 E
Rollingstone	120	19.03 S	146.24 E
Roma, Austl.	120	26.35 S	148.47 E
Romagna □9	78	44.00 N	12.00 E
Romaine ⌁	142	50.18 N	63.47 W
Roman	80	46.55 N	26.56 E
Roman, Pulau I	96	7.35 S	127.26 E
Romania (România) □1	64	46.00 N	25.30 E
Roman-Koš, Gora ⋀	64	44.37 N	34.15 E
Romano, Cayo I	132	22.15 N	78.00 W
Romanshorn	74	47.34 N	9.22 E
Romans[-sur-Isère]	74	45.03 N	5.03 E
Rome → Roma, It.	78	41.54 N	12.29 E
Rome, Ga., U.S.	156	34.16 N	85.11 W
Rome, N.Y., U.S.	152	43.13 N	75.27 W
Romeo	154	42.48 N	83.01 W
Romilly-sur-Seine	74	48.31 N	3.43 E
Romney	152	39.20 N	78.45 W
Romny	82	50.45 N	33.33 E
Romont	74	46.42 N	6.55 E
Romorantin-Lanthenay	74	47.22 N	1.45 E
Røn	68	61.03 N	9.03 E
Ron, Mui ⊁	94	18.07 N	106.22 E
Ronan	166	47.32 N	114.06 W
Roncador, Serra do ⋀1	134	12.00 S	52.00 W
Ronchamp	74	47.42 N	6.39 E
Ronda	76	36.44 N	5.10 W
Rondônia □3	134	11.00 S	63.00 W
Rondonópolis	134	16.28 S	54.38 W
Ronge, Lac la ⊜	142	55.10 N	104.55 W
Rønne	68	55.06 N	14.42 E
Ronneby	68	56.12 N	15.18 E
Ronse	72	50.45 N	3.36 E
Roodhouse	158	39.29 N	90.22 W
Rooibokaagte ⌁	116	20.50 S	21.00 E
Roorkee	102	29.52 N	77.53 E
Roosendaal	72	51.32 N	4.28 E
Roosevelt	164	40.18 N	109.59 W
Roosevelt ⌁	134	7.35 S	60.20 W
Roper ⌁	124	14.43 S	135.27 E
Roper Valley	124	15.36 S	134.00 E
Ropesville	160	33.26 N	102.09 W
Roquefort	74	44.02 N	0.19 W
Roquemaure	74	44.04 N	4.47 E
Roraima, Mount ⋀	138	5.12 N	60.44 W
Røros	68	62.35 N	11.20 E
Rorschach	74	47.29 N	9.30 E
Rosal'	86	54.55 N	39.51 E
Rosalia	166	47.14 N	117.22 W
Rosalind Bank ⊶4	132	16.30 N	80.30 W
Rosamond	168	34.52 N	118.10 W
Rosans	74	44.23 N	5.28 E
Rosario, Arg.	140	32.57 S	60.40 W
Rosário, Bra.	134	2.57 S	44.14 W
Rosario, Para.	140	24.27 S	57.03 W
Rosario, Méx.	130	23.00 N	105.52 W
Rosario Bank ⊶4	132	18.30 N	84.00 W
Rosario de la Frontera	140	25.50 S	64.55 W
Rosario de Lerma	140	24.59 S	65.32 W
Rosário do Sul	140	30.15 S	54.55 W
Rosário Oeste	134	14.50 S	56.25 W
Roscoe, S. Dak., U.S.	162	45.27 N	99.20 W
Roscoe, Tex., U.S.	160	32.27 N	100.32 W
Roscommon, Eire	70	53.38 N	8.11 W
Roscommon, Mich., U.S.	154	44.30 N	84.35 W
Roscommon □6	70	53.40 N	8.30 W
Roscrea	70	52.57 N	7.47 W
Roseau, Dom.	132	15.18 N	61.24 W
Roseau, Minn., U.S.	162	48.51 N	95.46 W
Roseau ⌁	162	49.08 N	97.15 W
Rosebery	120	41.46 S	145.32 E
Rosebud, Austl.	120	38.21 S	144.54 E
Rosebud, Tex., U.S.	160	31.04 N	96.59 W
Rose City	154	44.25 N	84.07 W
Rose Creek ⌁	162	40.04 N	97.07 W
Rosedale, Austl.	120	24.38 S	151.55 E
Rosedale, Miss., U.S.	158	33.51 N	91.02 W
Rosehearty	70	57.42 N	2.07 W
Rose Hill, Maus.	117c	20.14 S	57.27 E
Rose Hill, N.C., U.S.	156	34.49 N	78.02 W
Rose Hill, Va., U.S.	156	36.40 N	83.22 W
Roseland	158	39.46 N	90.31 W
Rosenberg	160	29.33 N	95.48 W
Rosendal	68	59.59 N	6.01 E
Rosenheim	72	47.51 N	12.07 E
Rose River Mission	124	14.18 S	135.44 E
Rosetown	142	51.33 N	108.00 W
Rosetta → Rashid	112	31.24 N	30.25 E
Rosetta Mouth → Rashid, Maşabb ≽1	112	31.30 N	30.20 E
Roseville, Calif., U.S.	168	38.45 N	121.17 W
Roseville, Ill., U.S.	154	40.44 N	90.40 W
Roseville, Mich., U.S.	154	42.30 N	82.56 W
Roseville, Minn., U.S.	154	45.01 N	93.09 W
Roseville, Ohio, U.S.	152	39.49 N	82.05 W
Rosewood, S. Dak., U.S.	162	45.52 N	96.44 W
Rosholt, Wis., U.S.	154	44.38 N	89.18 W
Rosignano Marittimo	78	43.24 N	10.28 E
Rosignol	138	6.16 N	57.32 W
Roşiori-de-Vede	80	44.07 N	25.00 E
Roskilde	68	55.39 N	12.05 E
Roslags-Näsby	68	59.26 N	18.04 E
Roslavl'	86	53.57 N	32.52 E
Rosporden	74	47.58 N	3.50 W
Ross	120	42.02 S	147.29 E
Ross ⌁	146	61.59 N	132.26 W
Rossano	78	39.35 N	16.39 E
Rossford	152	41.37 N	83.33 W
Ross River	146	61.59 N	132.27 W
Rossville, Ga., U.S.	156	34.59 N	85.16 W
Rossville, Ill., U.S.	158	40.23 N	87.40 W
Rossville, Ind., U.S.	158	40.25 N	86.36 W
Rossville, Kans., U.S.	162	39.08 N	95.57 W
Roxo, Cap ⊁	114	12.20 N	16.43 W
Roxton	160	33.33 N	95.44 W
Roy	166	41.10 N	112.02 W
Royal	162	42.56 N	95.09 W
Royal Leamington Spa	70	52.18 N	1.31 W
Royale, Isle I	154	48.00 N	89.00 W
Royal Oak	154	42.30 N	83.08 W
Royan	74	45.37 N	1.01 W
Roye	74	49.42 N	2.48 E
Royse City	160	32.59 N	96.20 W
Royston	156	34.17 N	83.06 W
Rožňava	72	48.40 N	20.32 E
Rtiščevo	82	52.16 N	43.47 E
Ruabon	70	52.59 N	3.02 W
Ruacana Falls ⌁	116	17.22 S	14.12 E
Rubcovsk	84	51.33 N	81.10 E
Rubeženoje	82	49.01 N	38.23 E
Rubidoux	168	34.00 N	117.25 W
Rubio	138	7.43 N	72.22 W
Ruby	166	64.44 N	155.30 W
Ruby Mountains ⋀	168	40.25 N	115.35 W
Rudall	120	33.41 S	136.16 E
Ruda Śląska	72	50.18 N	18.51 E
Rudensk	86	53.36 N	27.52 E
Rüdersdorf	72	52.29 N	13.47 E
Rüdesheim	72	49.59 N	7.56 E
Rudn'a	86	54.57 N	31.06 E
Rudo	78	43.37 N	19.22 E
Rudolf, Lake ⊜	108	3.30 N	36.00 E
Rudolstadt	72	50.43 N	11.20 E
Rudyard	154	46.14 N	84.36 W
Rue	74	50.16 N	1.40 E
Ruen	80	42.10 N	22.31 E
Rufā'ah	112	14.46 N	33.22 E
Ruffec	74	46.02 N	0.12 E
Ruffieux	74	45.51 N	5.50 E
Ruffin	156	33.00 N	80.49 W
Rufino	140	34.16 S	62.40 W
Rufisque	114	14.43 N	17.17 W
Rufus	166	45.42 N	120.44 W
Rugao	88	32.25 N	120.36 E
Rugby, Eng., U.K.	70	52.23 N	1.15 W
Rugby, N. Dak., U.S.	162	48.22 N	100.00 W
Rügen I	66	54.25 N	13.24 E
Ruhpolding	72	47.45 N	12.38 E
Ruian	88	27.49 N	120.38 E
Ruidosa	160	30.00 N	104.40 W
Ruidoso	164	33.20 N	105.40 W
Ruijin	88	25.50 N	116.00 E
Ruiz	130	21.57 N	105.09 W
Rukwa, Lake ⊜	110	8.00 S	32.25 E
Rule	160	33.11 N	99.54 W
Ruleville	158	33.43 N	90.33 W
Ruma	80	45.00 N	19.49 E
Rumbek	108	6.48 N	29.41 E
Rum Cay I	132	23.40 N	74.50 W
Rumford	154	44.33 N	70.33 W
Rumia	72	54.35 N	18.25 E
Rumigny	74	49.48 N	4.16 E
Rum Jungle	122	13.01 S	131.00 E
Rumoi	90a	43.56 N	141.39 E
Rumuna	126	42.24 S	171.15 E
Runanga	126	42.24 S	171.15 E
Rundvik	68	63.32 N	19.26 E
Runge	160	28.53 N	97.43 W
Rungwa	110	6.57 S	33.31 E
Running Water Draw ⌁	160	33.58 N	101.30 W
Ruokolahti	68	61.17 N	28.50 E
Ruoqiang	88	38.30 N	88.05 E
Ruoshui ⌁	88	41.00 N	100.10 E
Ruovesi	68	61.59 N	24.05 E
Rupert, Idaho, U.S.	166	42.37 N	113.40 W
Rupert, W. Va., U.S.	152	37.58 N	80.41 W
Rupert ⌁	142	51.29 N	78.45 W
Rupert, Rivière de ⌁	142	51.30 N	78.45 W
Rupert House	142	51.30 N	78.45 W
Rupununi ⌁	138	4.00 N	58.30 W
Rusape	110	18.32 S	32.07 E
Ruşayriş, Khazzān ar- ⊜1	112	11.40 N	34.20 E
Ruse	80	43.50 N	25.57 E
Rush City	154	45.41 N	92.58 W
Rushford	154	43.49 N	91.46 W
Rushville, Ill., U.S.	158	40.07 N	90.34 W
Rushville, Ind., U.S.	158	39.37 N	85.27 W
Rushville, Nebr., U.S.	162	42.43 N	102.28 W
Rusk	160	31.48 N	95.09 W
Ruskin	156	27.43 N	82.26 W
Russas	134	4.56 S	37.58 W
Russell, Man., Can.	142	50.47 N	101.15 W
Russell, Kans., U.S.	162	38.53 N	98.51 W
Russell, Ky., U.S.	152	38.31 N	82.42 W
Russell, Pa., U.S.	152	41.56 N	79.08 W
Russell, Cape ⊁	146	75.17 N	117.35 W
Russell Island	142	73.55 N	98.25 W
Russell Islands II	127a	9.04 S	159.12 E
Russell Point ⊁	146	73.30 N	115.00 W
Russell Springs	162	38.55 N	101.10 W
Russellville, Ala., U.S.	158	34.30 N	87.44 W
Russellville, Ark., U.S.	158	35.17 N	93.08 W
Russellville, Ky., U.S.	158	36.51 N	86.53 W
Rüsselsheim	72	50.00 N	8.25 E
Russian ⌁	168	38.27 N	123.08 W
Russkaja Gavan'	84	76.10 N	62.35 E
Russkij, Ostrov I	84	77.00 N	96.00 E
Rust	72	47.48 N	16.42 E
Rustavi	82	41.33 N	45.02 E
Rustburg	156	37.17 N	79.06 W
Rustenburg	116	25.40 S	27.08 E
Ruston	158	32.32 N	92.38 W
Rute	76	37.19 N	4.22 W
Ruteng	96	8.36 S	120.27 E
Ruth	168	39.17 N	114.59 W
Rutherfordton	156	35.22 N	81.57 W
Ruthin	70	53.07 N	3.18 W
Rutland, B.C., Can.	148	49.53 N	119.24 W
Rutland, Vt., U.S.	152	43.36 N	72.59 W
Rutledge	156	34.36 N	83.37 W
Rutshuru	110	1.11 S	29.27 E
Ruukki	68	64.40 N	25.06 E
Ruza	86	55.42 N	36.12 E
Ruzajevka	82	54.04 N	44.57 E
Ružany	72	52.52 N	24.53 E
Ružomberok	72	49.05 N	19.18 E
Rwanda □1	110	2.30 S	30.00 E
Rybači, Poluostrov ⊁1	66	69.45 N	32.30 E
Rybači [Rossitten]	72	55.09 N	20.51 E
Rybačje, S.S.S.R.	84	46.27 N	81.32 E
Rybačje, S.S.S.R.	100	42.26 N	76.12 E
Rybinsk	86	58.03 N	38.52 E
Rybinskoje Vodochranilišče ⊜1	86	58.30 N	38.25 E
Rybkino	86	54.36 N	43.46 E
Rybnik	72	50.06 N	18.32 E
Rybnoje	86	54.44 N	39.30 E
Ryd	68	56.28 N	14.41 E
Ryde	70	50.44 N	1.10 W
Ryder	162	47.55 N	101.40 W
Ryfoss	68	61.08 N	8.48 E
Rygge	68	59.23 N	10.45 E
Ryggestad	68	59.16 N	7.29 E
Rymań	72	54.04 N	15.52 E
Rymanów	72	49.34 N	21.51 E
Rypin	72	53.05 N	19.25 E
Rysy ⋀	72	49.12 N	20.04 E
Ryukyu Islands → Nansei-shotō II	91b	26.30 N	128.00 E
Rzanica	86	53.26 N	33.55 E
Rzeszów	72	50.03 N	22.00 E
Ržev	86	56.16 N	34.20 E

S

Name	Page	Lat	Long
Saale ⌁	72	51.57 N	11.55 E
Saales	74	48.21 N	7.07 E
Saalfeld	72	50.39 N	11.22 E
Saar (Sarre) ⌁	72	49.42 N	6.34 E
Saarbrücken	72	49.14 N	6.59 E
Saarburg	72	49.36 N	6.33 E
Saaremaa I	86	58.25 N	22.30 E
Saarland □3	72	49.20 N	7.00 E
Saarlouis	72	49.21 N	6.45 E
Sab, Tônlé ⊜	94	12.50 N	104.00 E
Šabac	80	44.45 N	19.42 E
Sabadell	76	41.33 N	2.06 E
Šabani	110	20.20 S	30.04 E
Sabana de la Mar	132	19.04 N	69.24 W
Sabanalarga	138	10.38 N	74.55 W
Sabang, Indon.	96	5.54 N	95.20 E
Sabang, Indon.	92	0.11 N	119.51 E
Sabará	134	19.53 S	43.48 W
Sabaudia	78	41.18 N	13.01 E
Sābarmati ⌁	102	22.18 N	72.22 E
Sabetha	162	39.54 N	95.48 W
Sabhah	106	27.03 N	14.26 E
Sabie (Save) ⌁	110	21.00 S	35.02 E
Sabie (Sábié) ⌁	116	25.10 S	32.18 E
Sabile	86	57.03 N	22.35 E
Sabina	152	39.29 N	83.38 W
Sabinal	160	29.19 N	99.28 W
Sabinas	130	27.51 N	101.07 W
Sabinas Hidalgo	130	26.30 N	100.10 W
Sabine ⌁	144	29.42 N	93.45 W
Sabine Bay C	142	75.35 N	109.30 W
Sabine Lake ⊜	158	29.50 N	93.50 W
Sabine Pass	158	29.44 N	93.52 W
Sabine Peninsula ⊁1	142	76.20 N	109.30 W
Sable, Cape ⊁, N.S., Can.	150	43.25 N	65.35 W
Sable, Cape ⊁, Fla., U.S.	156	25.12 N	81.05 W
Sable, Rivière du ⌁	150	55.30 N	68.21 W
Sable Island I	150	43.55 N	59.50 W
Sablé-sur-Sarthe	74	47.50 N	0.20 W
Sabres	74	44.09 N	0.44 W
Sabugal	76	40.21 N	7.05 W
Sabula	154	42.04 N	90.10 W
Sabzevār	104	36.13 N	57.42 E
Sacaton	164	33.05 N	111.44 W
Sac City	162	42.25 N	95.00 W
Săcele	80	45.37 N	25.42 E
Sachalin, Ostrov (Sakhalin) I	84	51.00 N	143.00 E
Sachigo ⌁	142	55.06 N	88.58 W
Šachovskaja	86	56.02 N	35.29 E
Šachrisabz, S.S.S.R.	100	39.03 N	66.50 E
Šachrisabz, S.S.S.R.	104	39.03 N	66.50 E
Sachs Harbour	146	72.00 N	125.00 W
Šachty	82	47.42 N	40.13 E
Šachunja	86	57.40 N	46.37 E
Sackville	150	45.54 N	64.22 W
Saco	152	43.30 N	70.27 W
Sacramento ⌁	168	38.03 N	121.56 W
Sacramento	168	38.35 N	121.29 W
Sacramento Mountains ⋀	164	33.10 N	105.50 W
Sacramento Valley ⌵	168	39.15 N	122.00 W
Sá da Bandeira	110	14.55 S	13.30 E
Şa'dah	106	16.52 N	43.37 E
Sadiya	102	27.50 N	95.40 E
Sado ⌁	76	38.00 N	8.30 W
Sado, Nihon	90	38.00 N	138.25 E
Šadrinsk	84	55.33 N	63.39 E
Sæby	68	57.20 N	10.32 E
Safi	106	32.20 N	9.17 W
Safid Küh, Selseleh-ye ⋀	104	34.30 N	65.00 E
Safonovo, S.S.S.R.	86	55.06 N	33.14 E
Safonovo, S.S.S.R.	66	65.40 N	47.39 E
Saga, Nihon	90	33.15 N	130.18 E
Saga, Zhg.	102	29.30 N	85.22 E
Sagaing	94	21.52 N	95.59 E
Sagamihara	90	35.32 N	139.23 E
Saganaga Lake ⊜	154	48.14 N	90.52 W
Saganthit Kyun I	94	11.56 N	98.29 E
Sāgar	102	23.50 N	78.45 E
Sage Creek ⌁	166	48.58 N	108.26 W
Saginaw	154	43.25 N	83.56 W
Saginaw ⌁	154	43.39 N	83.51 W
Saginaw Bay C	154	43.50 N	83.40 W
Saglek Bay C	142	58.30 N	63.00 W
Saglouc	142	62.14 N	75.38 W
Sagonar	84	51.32 N	92.48 E
Sagra ⋀	76	37.57 N	2.33 W
Sagres	76	37.00 N	8.56 W
Sagua la Grande	132	22.49 N	80.05 W
Saguache	164	38.05 N	106.08 W
Sagua de Tánamo	132	20.35 N	75.14 W
Sagunto	76	39.41 N	0.16 W
Sahagún, Col.	138	8.57 N	75.27 W
Sahagún, Esp.	76	42.23 N	5.02 W
Sahara ⌄	106	26.00 N	13.00 E
Saharanpur	102	29.58 N	77.33 E
Sāhīwāl (Montgomery)	102	30.40 N	73.06 E
Sahuaripa	130	29.03 N	109.14 W
Sahuarita	164	31.57 N	110.58 W
Sahuayo	130	20.04 N	102.43 W
Saïbai I	124	9.24 S	142.41 E
Saïda, Alg.	106	34.50 N	0.09 E
Sa'idābād → Sīrjān	104	29.27 N	55.41 E
Sai Buri	94	6.42 N	101.37 E
Saidpur	102	25.47 N	88.54 E
Saïdu	102	34.45 N	72.21 E
Sai-gon → Thanh-Pho Ho Chi Minh	94	10.45 N	106.40 E
Saïllans	74	44.42 N	5.11 E
Sailor Creek ⌁	166	42.56 N	115.29 W
Saimaa ⊜	68	61.15 N	28.15 E
Saimaa Canal ⌆	68	61.05 N	28.18 E
St. → Saint, Sankt, Sint			
Ste. → Sainte			
Saint-Agathe-des-Monts	152	46.03 N	74.17 W
Saint-Agrève	74	45.01 N	4.24 E
Saint Alban's, Newf., Can.	150	47.52 N	55.51 W
Saint Albans, Eng., U.K.	70	51.46 N	0.21 W
Saint Albans, Vt., U.S.	152	44.49 N	73.05 W
Saint Albans, W. Va., U.S.	152	38.23 N	81.49 W
Saint Albert	142	53.38 N	113.38 W
Saint-Amand-les-Eaux	74	50.27 N	3.26 E
Saint-Amand-Mont-Rond	74	46.44 N	2.30 E
Saint-Ambroix	74	44.15 N	4.12 E
Saint-Amour	74	46.26 N	5.21 E
Saint-André, Cap ⊁	117b	16.11 S	44.27 E
Saint-André-de-Cubzac	74	45.01 N	0.27 W
Saint-André-les-Alpes	74	43.58 N	6.30 E
Saint Andrews, Scot., U.K.	70	56.20 N	2.48 W
Saint Andrews, S.C., U.S.	156	32.47 N	80.00 W
Sainte-Anne-des-Monts	150	49.08 N	66.30 W
Saint Ann's Bay	132	18.26 N	77.15 W
Saint Ansgar	154	43.23 N	92.55 W
Saint Anthony, Newf., Can.	150	51.22 N	55.35 W
Saint Anthony, Idaho, U.S.	166	43.58 N	111.41 W
Saint-Antonin	74	44.09 N	1.45 E
Saint Arnaud	120	36.37 S	143.15 E
Saint-Astier	74	45.09 N	0.32 E
Saint-Auban	74	43.51 N	6.44 E
Saint-Aubin-d'Aubigné	74	48.15 N	1.36 W
Saint-Augustin	142	51.14 N	58.41 W
Saint-Augustin-Saguenay	150	51.14 N	58.39 W
Saint Augustine	156	29.54 N	81.19 W
Saint-Aulaye	74	45.12 N	0.08 E
Saint Austell	70	50.20 N	4.48 W
Saint-Avold	72	49.06 N	6.42 E
Saint-Barthélemy I	132	17.55 N	62.50 W
Saint-Basile	150	47.20 N	57.47 W
Saint-Béat	74	42.55 N	0.42 E
Saint-Benoît-du-Sault	74	46.26 N	1.23 E
Saint-Bonnet-de-Joux	74	46.29 N	4.27 E
Saint-Bonnet-en-Champsaur	74	44.41 N	6.05 E
Saint-Brieuc	74	48.31 N	2.47 W
Saint-Calais	74	47.55 N	0.45 E
Saint Catharines	154	43.10 N	79.15 W
Saint-Céré	74	44.52 N	1.53 E
Saint-Chamond	74	45.28 N	4.30 E
Saint Charles, Idaho, U.S.	166	42.07 N	111.23 W
Saint Charles, Ill., U.S.	154	41.54 N	88.19 W
Saint Charles, Minn., U.S.	154	43.58 N	92.04 W
Saint Charles, Mo., U.S.	158	38.47 N	90.29 W
Saint-Chély-d'Apcher	74	44.48 N	3.17 E
Saint Christopher (Saint Kitts) I	132	17.21 N	62.48 W
Saint-Ciers-sur-Gironde	74	45.18 N	0.37 W
Saint Clair, Mich., U.S.	154	42.49 N	82.30 W
Saint Clair ⌁	154	42.38 N	82.31 W
Saint Clair, Lake ⊜	154	42.25 N	82.41 W
Saint Clair Shores	154	42.29 N	82.54 W
Saint Clairsville	152	40.05 N	80.54 W
Saint-Claud	74	45.53 N	0.23 E
Saint-Claude	74	46.23 N	5.52 E
Saint Cloud, Fla., U.S.	156	28.15 N	81.17 W
Saint Cloud, Minn., U.S.	154	45.33 N	94.10 W
Sainte-Croix	74	46.49 N	6.31 E
Saint Croix ⌁, N.A.	152	45.35 N	67.10 W
Saint Croix ⌁	154	44.45 N	92.38 W
Saint Croix Falls	154	45.24 N	92.38 W
Saint-Cyprien	74	44.52 N	1.02 E
Saint David, Ariz., U.S.	164	31.54 N	110.13 W
Saint David's, U.S.	166	43.10 N	90.03 W
Saint David's	70	51.54 N	5.16 W
Saint David's Head ⊁	70	51.55 N	5.19 W
Saint-Denis, Fr.	74	48.56 N	2.22 E
Saint-Denis, Réu.	117c	20.52 S	55.28 E
Saint-Dié	74	48.17 N	6.57 E
Saint-Dizier	74	48.38 N	4.57 E
Saint Eleanor's	150	46.25 N	63.49 W
Saint Elias, Cape ⊁	146	59.52 N	144.30 W
Saint Elias, Mount ⋀	146	60.18 N	140.55 W
Saint Elias Mountains ⋀	146	60.30 N	139.30 W
Saint-Élie	134	4.49 N	53.17 W
Saint Elmo	158	39.02 N	88.51 W
Sainte-Énimie	74	44.22 N	3.26 E
Saint-Étienne-du-Rouvray	74	49.23 N	1.06 E
Saint-Fargeau	74	47.38 N	3.04 E
Saint-Félicien	150	48.39 N	72.26 W
Saint-Florentin	74	48.00 N	3.44 E
Saint-Florent-sur-Cher	74	46.59 N	2.15 E
Saint-Foy	74	45.02 N	3.05 E
Saint-Foy-la-Grande	74	44.50 N	0.13 E
Saint Francis, Kans., U.S.	162	39.46 N	101.48 W
Saint Francis, S. Dak., U.S.	162	43.09 N	100.54 W
Saint Francis, Wis., U.S.	154	42.57 N	87.52 W
Saint Francis ⌁, N.A.	158	34.38 N	90.35 W
Saint Francis, Cape ⊁	116	34.14 S	24.49 E
Saint Francisville	158	30.47 N	91.23 W
Saint-Gabriel	150	46.17 N	73.23 W
Saint-Gaudens	74	43.07 N	0.44 E
Saint-Gaultier	74	46.38 N	1.25 E
Sainte Genevieve	158	37.59 N	90.03 W
Saint-Genis-de-Saintonge	74	45.29 N	0.34 W
Saint George, Austl.	120	28.02 S	148.35 E
Saint George, Alaska, U.S.	146	56.36 N	169.32 W
Saint George, Utah, U.S.	164	37.06 N	113.35 W
Saint George Head ⊁	120	35.12 S	150.42 E
Saint George's, Newf., Can.	150	48.26 N	58.29 W
Saint George's, Guy. fr.	134	3.54 N	51.48 W
Saint George's Bay C	150	45.52 N	59.00 W
Saint George's Channel ⌵	70	52.00 N	6.00 W
Saint-Germain	74	48.54 N	2.05 E
Saint-Germain-du-Bois	74	46.45 N	5.15 E
Saint-Germain-Lembron	74	45.28 N	3.14 E
Saint-Germain-l'Herm	74	45.28 N	3.33 E
Saint-Gervais-les-Bains	74	46.02 N	6.43 E
Saint-Gilles-croix-de-Vie	74	46.42 N	1.57 W
Saint-Girons	74	42.59 N	1.09 E
Saint Helena	110	15.55 S	5.42 W
Saint Helena Bay C	110	32.43 S	18.05 E
Saint Helen's, Austl.	120	41.20 S	148.15 E
Saint Helens, Eng., U.K.	70	53.28 N	2.44 W
Saint Helens, Oreg., U.S.	166	45.52 N	122.48 W
Saint Helens, Mount ⋀	166	46.12 N	122.11 W
Saint Helier	74	49.12 N	2.07 W
Sainte-Hermine	74	46.33 N	1.04 W
Saint-Hilaire-du-Harcouët	74	48.35 N	1.06 W
Saint-Hippolyte	74	47.19 N	6.49 E
Saint-Hippolyte-du-Fort	74	43.58 N	3.51 E
Saint-Hyacinthe	152	45.37 N	72.57 W
Saint Ignace	154	45.52 N	84.43 W
Saint Ignace Island I	154	48.48 N	87.55 W
Saint Ignatius	166	47.19 N	114.06 W
Saint Ives	70	50.12 N	5.29 W
Saint James, Minn., U.S.	162	43.58 N	94.38 W
Saint James, Mo., U.S.	158	38.00 N	91.37 W
Saint James, Cape ⊁	148	51.56 N	131.01 W
Saint-Jean	150	45.19 N	73.16 W
Saint-Jean, Lac ⊜	142	48.35 N	72.05 W
Saint-Jean-d'Angély	74	45.57 N	0.31 W
Saint-Jean-de-Bournay	74	45.30 N	5.08 E
Saint-Jean-de-Losne	74	47.06 N	5.15 E
Saint-Jean-de-Luz	74	43.23 N	1.40 W
Saint-Jean-de-Maurienne	74	45.17 N	6.21 E
Saint-Jean-de-Monts	74	46.48 N	2.03 W
Saint-Jean-du-Gard	74	44.06 N	3.53 E

Name	Page	Lat °′	Long °′
Saint-Jean-en-Royans	74	45.01 N	5.18 E
Saint-Jean-Pied-de-Port	74	43.10 N	1.14 W
Saint-Jérôme	152	45.46 N	74.00 W
Saint John, N.B., Can.	150	45.16 N	66.03 W
Saint John, Wash., U.S.	166	47.05 N	117.35 W
Saint John ≃	150	45.15 N	66.04 W
Saint John, Cape ➤	150	50.00 N	55.32 W
Saint Johns, Antig.	132	17.06 N	61.51 W
Saint John's, Newf., Can.	150	47.34 N	52.43 W
Saint Johns, Ariz., U.S.	164	34.30 N	109.22 W
Saint Johns, Mich., U.S.	154	43.00 N	84.33 W
Saint Johnsbury	152	44.25 N	72.01 W
Saint-Joseph, Qué., Can.	152	45.37 N	72.55 W
Saint Joseph, Ill., U.S.	158	40.07 N	88.02 W
Saint Joseph, La., U.S.	158	31.55 N	91.14 W
Saint Joseph, Mich., U.S.	154	42.06 N	86.29 W
Saint Joseph, Mo., U.S.	158	39.46 N	94.51 W
Saint Joseph ≃, U.S.	154	41.05 N	85.08 W
Saint Joseph ≃, U.S.	154	42.07 N	86.29 W
Saint Joseph, Lake ⊜	142	51.05 N	90.35 W
Saint-Joseph-de-Beauce	150	46.18 N	70.53 W
Saint-Jovite	152	46.07 N	74.36 W
Saint-Julien-en-Born	74	44.04 N	1.14 W
Saint-Julien-en-Genevois	74	46.08 N	6.05 E
Saint-Junien	74	45.53 N	0.54 E
Saint-Just-en-Chaussée	74	49.30 N	2.26 E
Saint-Just-en-Chevalet	74	45.55 N	3.50 E
Saint Kilda	126	45.54 S	170.31 E
Saint Kilda I	70	57.49 N	8.36 W
Saint Kitts-Nevis □2	128	17.15 N	62.45 W
Saint-Lambert	152	45.30 N	73.30 W
Saint-Laurent-du-Maroni	134	5.30 N	54.02 W
Saint-Laurent-et-Benon	74	45.09 N	0.49 W
Saint Lawrence, Austl.	120	22.21 S	149.31 E
Saint Lawrence, Newf., Can.	150	46.55 N	55.24 W
Saint Lawrence ≃	142	49.30 N	67.00 W
Saint Lawrence, Gulf of C	150	48.00 N	62.00 W
Saint Lawrence Island I	146	63.30 N	170.30 W
Saint-Léonard-de-Noblat	74	45.50 N	1.29 E
Saint-Lô	74	49.07 N	1.05 W
Saint-Louis, Sén.	114	16.02 N	16.30 W
Saint Louis, Mich., U.S.	154	43.25 N	84.36 W
Saint Louis, Mo., U.S.	158	38.38 N	90.11 W
Saint Louis ≃	154	46.45 N	92.06 W
Saint Louis Park	154	44.56 N	93.22 W
Saint-Loup-sur-Semouse	74	47.53 N	6.16 E
Saint Lucia □2	128	13.53 N	60.58 W
Saint Lucia, Lake ⊜	116	28.05 S	32.26 E
Saint Lucia Channel ʯ	132	14.15 N	61.00 W
Sainte-Lucie	78	41.42 N	9.22 E
Saint-Malo	74	48.39 N	2.01 W
Saint-Malo, Golfe de C	74	48.45 N	2.00 W
Saint-Marc	132	19.07 N	72.42 W
Saint-Marcellin	74	45.09 N	5.19 E
Sainte-Marguerite ≃	150	50.09 N	66.36 W
Sainte-Marie, Cap ➤	117b	25.36 S	45.08 E
Sainte-Marie, Île I	117b	16.50 S	49.55 E
Sainte-Marie-aux-Mines	74	48.15 N	7.11 E
Saint Maries	166	47.19 N	116.35 W
Saint Marks	156	30.09 N	84.12 W
Saint-Martin (Sint Maarten) I	132	18.04 N	63.04 W
Saint Martin, Lake ⊜	142	51.37 N	98.29 W
Saint-Martin-de-Londres	74	43.47 N	3.44 E
Saint-Martin-Vésubie	74	44.04 N	7.15 E
Saint Martinville	158	30.07 N	91.50 W
Saint Mary ≃	148	49.37 N	112.52 W
Saint Mary Peak ∧	120	31.30 S	138.33 E
Saint Marys, Austl.	120	41.35 S	148.10 E
Saint Mary's, Ont., Can.	154	43.16 N	81.08 W
Saint Marys, Alaska, U.S.	146	62.04 N	163.10 W
Saint Marys, Ga., U.S.	156	30.44 N	81.33 W
Saint Marys, Kans., U.S.	162	39.12 N	96.04 W
Saint Marys, Ohio, U.S.	152	40.33 N	84.23 W
Saint Marys, Pa., U.S.	152	41.26 N	78.34 W
Saint Marys, W. Va., U.S.	152	39.23 N	81.12 W
Saint Marys ≃, U.S.	152	41.05 N	85.08 W
Saint Marys ≃, U.S.	156	30.43 N	81.27 W
Saint Mary's, Cape ➤	150	46.49 N	54.12 W
Saint Marys, North Prong ≃	156	30.22 N	82.06 W
Saint Mary's Bay C	150	46.50 N	53.47 W
Saint-Mathieu	74	45.42 N	0.46 E
Saint Matthew Island I	146	60.30 N	172.45 W
Saint Matthews, Ky., U.S.	158	38.15 N	85.39 W
Saint Matthews, S.C., U.S.	156	33.40 N	80.46 W
Saint-Maur [-des-Fossés]	74	48.48 N	2.30 E
Sainte-Maure-du-Touraine	74	47.07 N	0.37 E
Saint-Maurice ≃	142	46.21 N	72.31 W
Sainte-Maxime	74	43.18 N	6.38 E
Saint-Méen-le-Grand	74	48.11 N	2.12 W
Sainte-Menehould	74	49.05 N	4.54 E
Sainte-Mère-Église	74	49.25 N	1.19 W
Saint Michael	146	63.29 N	162.02 W
Saint Michaels	152	38.47 N	76.14 W
Saint-Mihiel	74	48.54 N	5.33 E
Saint-Moritz → Sankt Moritz	74	46.30 N	9.50 E
Saint-Nazaire	74	47.17 N	2.12 W
Saint Neots	70	52.14 N	0.17 W
Saint-Omer	74	50.45 N	2.15 E
Saintonge □9	74	45.30 N	0.30 W
Saint-Pamphile	150	46.58 N	69.47 W
Saint-Pascal	150	47.32 N	69.49 W
Saint Paul, Alta., Can.	148	53.59 N	111.17 W
Saint-Paul, Fr.	74	43.42 N	7.07 E
Saint-Paul, Réu.	117c	21.00 S	55.16 E
Saint Paul, Ind., U.S.	158	39.26 N	85.38 W
Saint Paul, Minn., U.S.	154	44.58 N	93.07 W
Saint Paul, Nebr., U.S.	162	41.13 N	98.27 W
Saint Paul, Va., U.S.	156	36.54 N	82.19 W
Saint-Paul ≃, Can.	142	51.26 N	57.40 W
Saint Paul ≃, Liber.	114	7.10 N	10.00 W
Saint-Paulien	74	45.08 N	3.49 E
Saint Paul Island	146	57.07 N	170.17 W
Saint Pauls	156	34.48 N	78.58 W
Saint Peter	154	44.17 N	93.57 W
Saint Peter Island I	122	32.17 S	133.35 E
Saint Peter Port	74	49.27 N	2.32 W
Saint Petersburg → Leningrad, S.S.S.R.	86	59.55 N	30.15 E
Saint Petersburg, Fla., U.S.	156	27.46 N	82.38 W
Saint-Pierre, Mart.	132	14.45 N	61.11 W
Saint-Pierre, Réu.	117c	21.19 S	55.29 E
Saint-Pierre, St. P./M.	150	46.40 N	56.00 W
Saint Pierre and Miquelon □2	142	46.55 N	56.15 W
Saint-Pierre-Église	74	49.40 N	1.24 W
Saint Pierre Island I	110	9.19 S	50.43 E
Saint Pierre-le-Moûtier	74	46.48 N	3.07 E
Saint-Pierre-sur-Dives	70	49.01 N	0.02 W
Saint-Pierreville	74	44.49 N	4.29 E
Saint-Pol-de-Léon	74	48.41 N	3.59 W
Saint-Pol-sur-Ternoise	74	50.23 N	2.20 E
Saint-Pons	74	43.29 N	2.46 E
Saint-Pourçain-sur-Sioule	74	46.19 N	3.17 E
Saint-Quentin, N.B., Can.	150	47.30 N	67.23 W
Saint-Quentin, Fr.	74	49.51 N	3.17 E
Saint-Raphaël	74	43.25 N	6.46 E
Saint Regis Falls	152	44.40 N	74.33 W
Saint-Rémy-de-Provence	74	43.47 N	4.50 E
Saint-Renan	74	48.26 N	4.37 W
Saint-Romuald-d'Etchemin	150	46.45 N	71.14 W
Saintes	74	45.45 N	0.52 W
Saint-Sauveur-sur-Tinée	74	44.05 N	7.06 E
Saint-Savin	74	46.34 N	0.52 E
Saint-Savinien	74	45.53 N	0.41 W
Saint-Sébastien, Cap ➤	110	12.26 S	48.44 E
Saint-Seine-l'Abbaye	74	47.26 N	4.47 E
Saint Simons Island	156	31.08 N	81.24 W
Saintes-Maries-de-la-Mer	74	43.27 N	4.26 E
Saint Stephen	150	45.12 N	67.17 W
Saint-Sulpice-les-Feuilles	74	46.19 N	1.22 E
Saint-Symphorien	74	44.26 N	0.30 W
Sainte-Thérèse-de-Blainville	152	45.39 N	73.49 W
Saint Thomas, Ont., Can.	154	42.47 N	81.12 W
Saint Thomas → Charlotte Amalie, Vir. Is. U.S.	132	18.21 N	64.56 W
Saint Thomas I	132	18.21 N	64.55 W
Saint-Tropez	74	43.16 N	6.38 E
Saint-Valéry-en-Caux	74	49.52 N	0.44 E
Saint-Valéry-sur-Somme	74	50.11 N	1.38 E
Saint-Vallier	74	45.10 N	4.49 E
Saint-Vallier-de-Thiey	74	43.42 N	6.51 E
Saint-Varent	74	46.53 N	0.14 W
Saint Vincent □2	128	13.15 N	61.12 W
Saint-Vincent, Cap ➤	110	21.57 S	43.16 E
Saint Vincent, Cape ➤	120	43.18 S	145.50 E
Saint Vincent, Gulf C	120	35.00 S	138.05 E
Saint Vincent Cape → São Vicente, Cabo de ➤	76	37.01 N	9.00 W
Saint-Vincent-de-Tyrosse	74	43.40 N	1.18 W
Saint Vincent Passage ʯ	132	13.30 N	61.00 W
Saint-Vith	72	50.17 N	6.08 E
Saint-Vivien-de-Médoc	74	45.26 N	1.02 W
Saint-Yrieix-la-Perche	74	45.31 N	1.12 E
Saipan I	92	15.10 N	145.45 E
Sairecábur, Cerro ∧	140	22.43 S	67.54 W
Saishu-to → Cheju-do I	88	33.20 N	126.30 E
Saitula	88	36.21 N	78.02 E
Sajama, Nevado ∧	134	18.06 S	68.54 W
Sajia	88	28.55 N	88.05 E
Sajnšand	88	44.55 N	110.11 E
Sajó ≃	72	47.56 N	21.08 E
Sajószentpéter	72	48.13 N	20.44 E
Sak ≃	116	30.52 S	20.25 E
Sakai	90	34.35 N	135.28 E
Sakākah	104	29.59 N	40.06 E
Sakakawea, Lake ⊜1	162	47.50 N	102.20 W
Sakami ≃	142	53.40 N	76.40 W
Sakami, Lac ⊜	142	53.15 N	76.45 W
Sakania	110	12.45 S	28.34 E
Sakarya ≃	64	41.07 N	30.39 E
Sakata	90	38.55 N	139.50 E
Šakiai	86	54.57 N	23.03 E
Sakishima-guntō II	88	24.46 N	124.00 E
Sal I	114a	16.45 N	22.55 W
Sal ≃	64	47.31 N	40.45 E
Sala	68	59.55 N	16.36 E
Salacgrīva	86	57.45 N	24.21 E
Saladas	140	28.15 S	58.38 W
Saladillo	140	35.38 S	59.48 W
Salado ≃, Arg.	140	31.40 S	60.41 W
Salado ≃, Méx.	130	26.50 N	99.17 W
Salaguolehe ≃	88	40.28 N	94.30 E
Sălaj □4	80	47.15 N	23.00 E
Šalakuša	66	62.15 N	40.17 E
Şalālah	100	17.00 N	54.06 E
Salamanca, Chile	140	31.47 S	70.58 W
Salamanca, Esp.	76	40.58 N	5.39 W
Salamanca, Méx.	130	20.34 N	101.12 W
Salamanca, N.Y., U.S.	152	42.09 N	78.43 W
Salamina	138	5.25 N	75.29 W
Salamís	80	37.59 N	23.28 E
Salantai	86	56.04 N	21.32 E
Salatiga	96	7.19 S	110.30 E
Salavat	64	53.21 N	55.55 E
Salaverry	134	8.14 S	78.58 W
Salawati I	124	1.07 S	130.52 E
Salazar	110	9.18 S	14.54 E
Salcombe	70	50.13 N	3.47 W
Saldanha	116	33.00 S	17.56 E
Sale, Austl.	120	38.06 S	147.04 E
Salé, Magreb	106	34.04 N	6.50 W
Salebabu, Pulau I	92	3.55 N	126.40 E
Salechard	84	66.33 N	66.40 E
Sale Creek	158	35.23 N	85.07 W
Salem, Bhārat	100	11.39 N	78.10 E
Salem, Ark., U.S.	158	36.22 N	91.49 W
Salem, Ill., U.S.	158	38.38 N	88.57 W
Salem, Ind., U.S.	158	38.36 N	86.06 W
Salem, Mass., U.S.	152	42.31 N	70.55 W
Salem, Mo., U.S.	158	37.39 N	91.32 W
Salem, N.H., U.S.	152	42.47 N	71.12 W
Salem, N.J., U.S.	152	39.34 N	75.28 W
Salem, N.Y., U.S.	152	43.10 N	73.20 W
Salem, Ohio, U.S.	152	40.54 N	80.52 W
Salem, Oreg., U.S.	166	44.57 N	123.01 W
Salem, S. Dak., U.S.	162.	43.44 N	97.23 W
Salem, Utah, U.S.	164	40.03 N	111.40 W
Salem, Va., U.S.	156	37.17 N	80.03 W
Salem, W. Va., U.S.	152	39.17 N	80.34 W
Salemi	78	37.49 N	12.49 E
Salerno	78	40.41 N	14.47 E
Salers	74	45.08 N	2.30 E
Salford	70	53.28 N	2.18 W
Salgótarján	72	48.07 N	19.48 E
Salida	164	38.32 N	106.00 W
Salies-de-Béarn	74	43.29 N	0.55 W
Salignac-Eyvignes	74	44.59 N	1.19 E
Salima	110	13.47 S	34.26 E
Salīmah, Wāḥat ⍑4	112	21.22 N	29.19 E
Salina, Kans., U.S.	162	38.50 N	97.37 W
Salina, Utah, U.S.	164	38.58 N	111.51 W
Salina Cruz	130	16.10 N	95.12 W
Salinas, Ec.	138	2.13 S	80.58 W
Salinas, Calif., U.S.	168	36.40 N	121.39 W
Salinas ≃	168	36.45 N	121.48 W
Salinas de Hidalgo	130	22.38 N	101.43 W
Saline	154	41.59 N	83.37 W
Salisbury, Austl.	120	34.46 S	138.38 E
Salisbury, Rh.	116	17.50 S	31.03 E
Salisbury, Eng., U.K.	70	51.05 N	1.48 W
Salisbury, Md., U.S.	152	38.22 N	75.36 W
Salisbury, Mo., U.S.	158	39.25 N	92.48 W
Salisbury, N.C., U.S.	156	35.40 N	80.29 W
Salisbury, Pa., U.S.	152	39.45 N	79.05 W
Salisbury Island I, Austl.	122	34.21 S	123.32 E
Salisbury Island I, N.W. Ter., Can.	142	63.30 N	77.00 W
Saljany	104	39.34 N	48.58 E
Sallanches	74	45.56 N	6.38 E
Salles-Curan	74	44.11 N	2.47 E
Sallisaw	160	35.28 N	94.47 W
Sallūm, Khalīj as- C	112	31.41 N	25.21 E
Sallyāna	100	28.22 N	82.10 E
Salmon	166	45.11 N	113.54 W
Salmon ≃, N.A.	152	45.02 N	74.31 W
Salmon ≃, Calif., U.S.	168	41.23 N	41.29 W
Salmon ≃, Idaho, U.S.	166	45.51 N	116.46 W
Salmon Arm	148	50.42 N	119.16 W
Salmon Falls Creek ≃	166	42.43 N	114.51 W
Salmon Mountains ⛰	168	41.00 N	123.00 W
Salmon River Mountains ⛰	166	44.45 N	115.30 W
Salò, It.	78	45.36 N	10.31 E
Salo, Suomi	68	60.23 N	23.08 E
Salome	164	33.47 N	113.37 W
Salon-de-Provence	74	43.38 N	5.06 E
Salonta	80	46.48 N	21.40 E
Salop □6	70	52.40 N	2.40 W
Saloum ≃	114	13.50 N	16.45 W
Salsilgo, Qawz ⍑8	112	10.49 N	22.54 E
Sal'sk	64	46.28 N	41.33 E
Salsomaggiore Terme	78	44.49 N	9.59 E
Salt ≃, U.S.	166	43.08 N	111.02 W
Salt ≃, Ariz., U.S.	164	33.23 N	112.18 W
Salta	140	24.47 S	65.24 W
Salta □4	140	25.00 S	64.30 W
Saltash	70	50.24 N	4.12 W
Saltcoats	70	55.38 N	4.47 W
Salt Creek ≃	168	36.15 N	116.49 W
Saltillo	130	25.25 N	101.00 W
Salt Lake City	164	40.46 N	111.53 W
Salto	140	31.23 S	57.58 W
Salto Grande	140	22.54 S	49.59 W
Salton Sea ⊜	168	33.19 N	115.50 W
Saltville	156	36.53 N	81.46 W
Saluda	156	34.00 N	81.46 W
Saluzzo	78	44.39 N	7.29 E
Salvador	134	12.59 S	38.31 W
Salvaterra de Magos	76	39.01 N	8.48 W
Salvatierra	130	20.13 N	100.53 W
Salvator, Lake ⊜	120	24.43 S	147.11 E
Salviac	74	44.41 N	1.16 E
Salwā, Baḥr as- C	104	25.30 N	50.40 E
Salween (Nujiang) ≃	94	16.31 N	97.37 E
Salyer	168	40.54 N	123.35 W
Salyersville	156	37.45 N	83.04 W
Salzach ≃	72	48.12 N	12.56 E
Salzburg	72	47.48 N	13.02 E
Salzburg □3	72	47.25 N	13.15 E
Salzgitter	72	52.10 N	10.25 E
Salzgitter-Bad	72	52.04 N	10.23 E
Salzwedel	72	52.51 N	11.09 E
Samālūt	112	28.18 N	30.42 E
Samar I	98	12.00 N	125.00 E
Samara ≃	64	53.10 N	50.04 E
Samaria	166	42.07 N	112.20 W
Samarinda	96	0.30 S	117.09 E
Samarkand	100	39.40 N	66.48 E
Sāmarrā'	104	34.12 N	43.52 E
Sambalpur	102	21.27 N	83.58 E
Sambas	96	1.20 N	109.15 E
Sambava	117b	14.16 S	50.10 E
Sambhal	102	28.35 N	78.33 E
Sāmbhar	100	26.55 N	75.12 E
Sambor	72	49.32 N	23.11 E
Sambre ≃	74	50.28 N	4.52 E
Samch'ŏk	88	37.27 N	129.10 E
Samch'ŏnp'o	88	34.57 N	128.03 E
Same	110	4.04 S	37.44 E
Samer	70	50.38 N	1.45 E
Samneua	94	20.25 N	104.02 E
Samoded	66	63.38 N	40.29 E
Samokov	80	42.20 N	23.33 E
Sámos □5	80	37.48 N	26.44 E
Sámos I	80	37.48 N	26.44 E
Samoset	156	27.28 N	82.33 W
Samosir, Pulau I	94	2.35 N	98.48 E
Samothrace → Samothráki I	80	40.30 N	25.32 E
Samothráki I	80	40.30 N	25.32 E
S'amozero	66	61.54 N	33.18 E
Sampit	96	2.32 S	112.57 E
Sam Rayburn Reservoir ⊜1	158	31.27 N	94.37 W
Samson	158	31.07 N	86.09 W
Samsun	64	41.17 N	36.20 E
Samtown	158	31.20 N	92.26 W
Samui, Ko I	94	9.30 N	100.04 E
Samut Prakan	94	13.35 N	100.40 E
Samut Sakhon	94	13.31 N	100.15 E
S'amža	66	60.01 N	41.02 E
San	114	13.18 N	4.54 W
San ≃, As.	94	13.32 N	105.58 E
San ≃, Eur.	72	50.45 N	21.51 E
Saña	134	6.54 S	79.36 W
Sanaga ≃	106	3.35 N	9.38 E
San Agustin, Cape ➤	98	6.16 N	126.11 E
San Ambrosio, Isla I	136	26.21 S	79.52 W
Sanana, Pulau I	96	2.12 S	125.55 E
Sanandaj	104	35.19 N	47.00 E
San Andreas	168	38.12 N	120.41 W
San Andrés	138	6.49 N	72.52 W
San Andrés, Isla de I	132	12.33 N	81.42 W
San Andrés Tuxtla	130	18.27 N	95.13 W
San Andrés y Providencia □8	132	13.00 N	81.30 W
San Angelo	160	31.28 N	100.26 W
San Anselmo	168	37.59 N	122.34 W
San Antonio, Chile	140	27.53 S	70.03 W
San Antonio, Tex., U.S.	160	29.28 N	98.31 W
San Antonio, Cabo ➤, Arg.	140	36.40 S	56.42 W
San Antonio, Cabo ➤, Cuba	132	21.52 N	84.57 W
San Antonio, Rio ≃	164	37.11 N	105.55 W
San Antonio de Areco	140	34.16 S	59.30 W
San Antonio de los Cobres	140	24.15 S	66.20 W
San Antonio del Táchira	138	7.50 N	72.27 W
San Antonio Oeste	136	40.44 S	64.57 W
San Augustine	158	31.32 N	94.07 W
Şan'ā'yaman	100	15.23 N	44.12 E
San Baudilio de Llobregat	76	41.21 N	2.03 E
San Benedetto del Tronto	78	42.57 N	13.53 E
San Benedicto, Isla I	130	19.18 N	110.49 W
San Benito, Guat.	130	16.55 N	89.54 W
San Benito, Tex., U.S.	160	26.08 N	97.38 W
San Benito ≃	168	36.53 N	121.34 W
San Benito Mountain ∧	168	36.22 N	120.38 W
San Bernardino	168	34.06 N	117.17 W
San Bernardino Mountains ⛰	168	34.10 N	117.00 W
San Bernardino Strait ʯ	98	12.37 N	124.12 E
San Bernardo	140	33.36 S	70.43 W
San Blas, Méx.	130	26.05 N	108.46 W
San Blas, Méx.	130	21.31 N	105.16 W
San Blas, Cape ➤	156	29.40 N	85.22 W
San Borja	134	14.49 S	66.51 W
Sanborn	162	43.11 N	95.39 W
San Bruno	168	37.37 N	122.25 W
San Buenaventura	130	27.05 N	101.32 W
Sanbuzhen	88	22.23 N	112.35 E
San Carlos, Chile	140	36.25 S	71.58 W
San Carlos, Gui. Ecu.	114	3.27 N	8.33 E
San Carlos, Pil.	92	10.29 N	123.25 E
San Carlos, Pil.	92	15.56 N	120.21 E
San Carlos, Ariz., U.S.	164	33.21 N	110.27 W
San Carlos, Calif., U.S.	168	37.31 N	122.16 W
San Carlos, Ur.	140	34.48 S	54.55 W
San Carlos, Ven.	138	9.40 N	68.36 W
San Carlos de Bariloche	136	41.08 S	71.15 W
San Carlos del Zulia	138	9.01 N	71.55 W
San Carlos de Río Negro	138	1.55 N	67.04 W
San Cataldo	78	37.29 N	14.04 E
Sancergues	74	47.09 N	2.55 E
Sancerre	74	47.20 N	2.51 E
Sánchez	132	19.14 N	69.36 W
San Clemente, Esp.	76	39.24 N	2.26 W
San Clemente, Calif., U.S.	168	33.26 N	117.37 W
San Clemente Island I	168	32.54 N	118.29 W
Sancoins	74	46.50 N	2.55 E
San Cristóbal, Arg.	140	30.20 S	61.15 W
San Cristóbal, Ven.	138	7.46 N	72.14 W
San Cristóbal las Casas	130	16.45 N	92.38 W
Sancti-Spíritus	132	21.56 N	79.27 W
Sand	68	59.29 N	6.15 E
Sandakan	96	5.53 N	118.05 E
Sandane	68	61.46 N	6.13 E
Sand Creek ≃	164	41.13 N	105.43 W
Sandefjord	68	59.08 N	10.14 E
Sanders	164	35.13 N	109.20 W
Sanderson	160	30.09 N	102.24 W
Sandersville, Ga., U.S.	156	32.59 N	82.48 W
Sandersville, Miss., U.S.	158	31.47 N	89.02 W
Sandgate	120	27.20 S	153.05 E
Sandhamn	68	59.17 N	18.55 E
Sandia	134	14.14 S	69.25 W
San Diego, Calif., U.S.	168	32.43 N	117.09 W
San Diego, Tex., U.S.	160	27.46 N	98.14 W
San Diego ≃	168	32.46 N	117.13 W
San Diego, Cabo ➤	136	54.38 S	65.05 W
Sandnes	68	58.51 N	5.44 E
Sandoa	110	9.41 S	22.52 E
Sandomierz	72	50.41 N	21.45 E
San Donà di Piave	78	45.38 N	12.34 E
Sandoval	158	38.37 N	89.07 W
Sandoway	94	18.28 N	94.22 E
Sandown	70	50.39 N	1.09 W
Sandpoint	166	48.16 N	116.33 W
Sandringham	70	52.50 N	0.30 W
Sand Springs	160	36.09 N	96.07 W
Sandston	156	37.31 N	77.19 W
Sandstone, Austl.	122	27.59 S	119.17 E
Sandstone, Minn., U.S.	154	46.08 N	92.52 W
Sandusky, Mich., U.S.	154	43.25 N	82.50 W
Sandusky, Ohio, U.S.	152	41.27 N	82.42 W
Sandvig	68	55.17 N	14.47 E
Sandvika	68	59.54 N	10.31 E
Sandviken	68	60.37 N	16.46 E
Sandwich, Ill., U.S.	154	41.39 N	88.37 W
Sandwich, Mass., U.S.	152	41.46 N	70.30 W
Sandwich Bay C	142	53.35 N	57.15 W
Sandwīp	92	22.29 N	91.26 E
Sandy	166	45.24 N	122.16 W
Sandy Arroyo Creek ≃	160	37.29 N	101.29 W
Sandy Cape ➤, Austl.	120	41.25 S	144.45 E
Sandy Cape ➤, Austl.	120	24.42 S	153.17 E
Sandy Creek ≃	160	36.50 N	98.10 W
Sandy Islet I	118	14.03 S	121.49 E
Sandykači	100	36.33 N	62.34 E
Sandy Lake ⊜	142	53.00 N	93.07 W
Sandy Springs	156	33.55 N	84.23 W
San Elizario	164	31.35 N	106.16 W
San Felipe, Chile	140	32.45 S	70.44 W
San Felipe, Col.	138	1.55 N	67.06 W
San Felipe, Méx.	130	31.00 N	114.52 W
San Felipe, Méx.	130	21.29 N	101.13 W
San Felipe, N. Mex., U.S.	164	35.27 N	106.28 W
San Felipe, Ven.	138	10.20 N	68.44 W
San Felipe Creek ≃	168	33.09 N	115.46 W
San Felíu de Guixols	76	41.47 N	3.02 E
San Félix, Isla I	136	26.17 S	80.05 W
San Fernando, Chile	140	34.35 S	71.00 W
San Fernando, Esp.	76	36.28 N	6.12 W
San Fernando, Méx.	128	31.16 N	110.36 W
San Fernando, Pil.	98	15.02 N	120.41 E
San Fernando, Trin.	132	10.17 N	61.28 W
San Fernando, Calif., U.S.	168	34.17 N	118.26 W
San Fernando de Apure	138	7.54 N	67.28 W
San Fernando de Atabapo	138	4.03 N	67.42 W
Sanford, Colo., U.S.	164	37.16 N	105.54 W
Sanford, Fla., U.S.	156	28.48 N	81.16 W
Sanford, Maine, U.S.	152	43.26 N	70.46 W
Sanford, Mich., U.S.	154	43.40 N	84.23 W
Sanford, N.C., U.S.	156	35.29 N	79.10 W
Sanford, Tex., U.S.	160	35.42 N	101.32 W
San Francisco, Arg.	140	31.27 S	62.05 W
San Francisco, Calif., U.S.	168	37.48 N	122.24 W
San Francisco ≃	164	32.59 N	109.22 W
San Francisco, Cabo de ➤	138	0.40 N	80.05 W
San Francisco, Paso de)(	140	26.53 S	68.19 W
San Francisco del Oro	130	26.52 N	105.51 W
San Francisco del Rincón	130	21.01 N	101.51 W
San Francisco de Macorís	132	19.18 N	70.15 W
San Francisco Mountains ⛰	164	33.45 N	109.00 W
San Francisco Peaks ⛰	164	35.20 N	111.45 W
San Gabriel	138	0.36 N	77.49 W
San Gabriel Chilac	130	18.19 N	97.21 W
San Gabriel Mountains ⛰	168	34.20 N	118.00 W
Sang'angqu	88	29.15 N	96.59 E
Sangar	84	63.55 N	127.31 E
Sangay, Volcán ∧1	138	2.00 S	78.20 W
Sangayán, Isla de I	134	13.51 S	76.28 W
Sangeang, Pulau I	96	8.12 S	119.04 E
Sanger, Calif., U.S.	168	36.42 N	119.27 W
Sanger, Tex., U.S.	160	33.22 N	97.10 W
Sangerhausen	72	51.28 N	11.17 E
San Germán	132	18.05 N	67.03 W
Sangerville	152	45.10 N	69.21 W
Sangganhe ≃	88	40.21 N	115.21 E
Sangha ≃	110	1.13 S	16.49 E
Sangihe, Kepulauan II	96	3.00 N	125.30 E
Sangihe, Pulau I	96	3.35 N	125.32 E
San Gil	138	6.33 N	73.08 W
San Gimignano	78	43.28 N	11.02 E
San Giovanni in Fiore	78	39.16 N	16.42 E
San Giovanni in Persiceto	78	44.38 N	11.11 E
San Giovanni Rotondo	78	41.42 N	15.44 E
San Giovanni Valdarno	78	43.34 N	11.32 E
Sāngli	100	16.52 N	74.34 E
Sangolquí	138	0.19 S	78.27 W
San Gorgonio Mountain ∧	168	34.06 N	116.50 W
San Gottardo, Passo del)(	74	46.33 N	8.34 E
Sangre de Cristo Mountains ⛰	164	37.30 N	105.15 W
San Gregorio	140	32.37 S	55.40 W
Sangre Grande	132	10.35 N	61.07 W
Sangue, Rio do ≃	134	11.01 S	58.39 W
San Ignacio, Arg.	140	27.15 S	55.30 W
San Ignacio, Bol.	134	16.23 S	60.59 W
San Ignacio, Bol.	134	14.53 S	65.36 W
San Ignacio, Méx.	128	23.55 N	106.25 W
San Ildefonso o La Granja	76	40.54 N	4.00 W
San Isidro, Arg.	140	28.28 S	65.44 W
San Isidro, C.R.	132	9.22 N	83.42 W
San Isidro, Tex., U.S.	160	26.43 N	98.27 W
San Jacinto	168	33.47 N	116.57 W
San Jacinto ≃	168	33.43 N	117.16 W
San Javier, Arg.	140	27.55 S	55.05 W
San Javier, Bol.	134	16.20 S	62.38 W
Sanjō	90	37.37 N	138.57 E
San Joaquín	134	13.04 S	64.49 W
San Joaquin Valley V	168	36.50 N	120.10 W
San Jorge, Golfo C	136	46.00 S	66.50 W
San José, C.R.	132	9.56 N	84.05 W
San Jose, Pil.	92	12.27 N	121.03 E
San Jose, Calif., U.S.	168	37.20 N	121.53 W
San Jose, Fla., U.S.	156	30.15 N	81.36 W
San Jose, Ill., U.S.	158	40.18 N	89.36 W
San José, Isla I	130	25.00 N	110.38 W
San José de Chiquitos	134	17.51 S	60.47 W
San José de Feliciano	140	30.25 S	58.45 W
San José de Guanipa	138	8.54 N	64.09 W
San José del Cabo	130	23.03 N	109.41 W
San José del Guaviare	138	2.35 N	72.38 W
San José de Mayo	140	34.20 S	56.42 W
San Juan, Arg.	140	31.30 S	68.30 W
San Juan, P.R.	132	18.28 N	66.07 W
San Juan □4	140	30.50 S	69.00 W
San Juan ≃, Arg.	140	32.20 S	67.25 W
San Juan ≃, N.A.	132	10.56 N	83.42 W
San Juan ≃, S.A.	138	1.11 N	78.33 W
San Juan ≃, U.S.	164	37.18 N	110.28 W
San Juan Bautista, Para.	140	26.38 S	57.10 W
San Juan Bautista, Calif., U.S.	168	36.51 N	121.32 W
San Juan Creek ≃	168	35.40 N	120.22 W
San Juan de Colón	138	8.02 N	72.16 W
San Juan [de la Maguana]	132	18.48 N	71.14 W
San Juan del Norte	132	10.56 N	83.42 W
San Juan de los Morros	138	9.55 N	67.21 W
San Juan del Río	130	20.23 N	100.00 W
San Juan del Sur	132	11.15 N	85.52 W
San Juan Mountains ⛰	164	37.35 N	107.10 W
San Juan Nepomuceno	138	9.57 N	75.05 W
San Julián	136	49.19 S	67.40 W
San Justo	140	30.47 S	60.35 W
Sankarani ≃	114	12.01 N	8.19 W
Sankosh ≃	102	26.48 N	89.56 E
Sankt Aegyd am Neuwalde	72	47.52 N	15.35 E
Sankt Anton [am Arlberg]	72	47.08 N	10.16 E
Sankt Gallen, Öst.	72	47.41 N	14.37 E
Sankt Gallen, Schw.	74	47.25 N	9.23 E
Sankt Gilgen	72	47.46 N	13.22 E
Sankt Goar	72	50.09 N	7.43 E
Sankt Goarshausen	72	50.09 N	7.44 E
Sankt Ingbert	72	49.17 N	7.06 E
Sankt Johann am Tauern	72	47.22 N	14.29 E
Sankt Johann im Pongau	72	47.21 N	13.12 E
Sankt Johann in Tirol	72	47.31 N	12.26 E
Sankt Moritz	74	46.30 N	9.50 E
Sankt Niklaus	74	46.11 N	7.48 E
Sankt Paul [im Lavanttal]	72	46.42 N	14.52 E
Sankt Peter	72	54.18 N	8.38 E
Sankt Pölten	72	48.12 N	15.37 E
Sankt Valentin	72	48.10 N	14.32 E
Sankt Veit an der Glan	72	46.46 N	14.21 E
Sankt Wendel	72	49.28 N	7.10 E
Sankt Wolfgang [im Salzkammergut]	72	47.44 N	13.27 E
Sankuru ≃	110	4.17 S	20.25 E
San Lázaro, Cabo ➤	130	24.50 N	112.18 W
San Leandro	168	37.43 N	122.09 W
San Lorenzo, Arg.	140	32.45 S	60.44 W
San Lorenzo, Ec.	138	1.17 N	78.50 W
San Lorenzo, Isla I	134	12.06 S	77.14 W
Sanlúcar de Barrameda	76	36.47 N	6.21 W
San Lucas	134	20.06 S	65.07 W
San Lucas, Cabo ➤	130	22.50 N	109.55 W
San Luis, Arg.	140	33.20 S	66.20 W
San Luis, Guat.	130	16.14 N	89.27 W
San Luis, Colo., U.S.	164	37.12 N	105.25 W
San Luis □4	140	34.00 S	66.00 W
San Luis, Lago de ⊜	134	13.45 S	64.00 W
San Luis de la Paz	130	21.18 N	100.31 W
San Luis Obispo	168	35.17 N	120.40 W
San Luis Potosí	130	22.09 N	100.59 W
San Luis Río Colorado	130	32.29 N	114.48 W
Sanluri	78	39.33 N	8.54 E
San Manuel	164	32.36 N	110.38 W
San Marcos, Col.	138	8.39 N	75.08 W
San Marcos, Méx.	130	16.48 N	99.21 W
San Marcos, Tex., U.S.	160	29.53 N	97.57 W
San Marino	78	43.55 N	12.28 E
San Marino □1	64	43.56 N	12.25 E
San Martín, Arg.	140	33.10 S	68.25 W
San Martín, Col.	138	3.42 N	73.42 W
San Martín ≃	134	13.08 S	63.43 W
San Martín de los Andes	136	40.10 S	71.20 W
San Martín Texmelucan	130	19.17 N	98.26 W
San Mateo, Calif., U.S.	168	37.35 N	122.19 W
San Mateo, Fla., U.S.	156	29.36 N	81.35 W
San Mateo, N. Mex., U.S.	164	35.20 N	107.39 W
San Matías, Golfo C	136	41.30 S	64.20 W
Sanmenxia	88	34.45 N	111.05 E
San Miguel, El Sal.	128	13.29 N	88.11 W
San Miguel, Calif., U.S.	168	35.45 N	120.42 W
San Miguel ≃	134	13.52 S	63.56 W
San Miguel de Allende	130	20.55 N	100.45 W
San Miguel del Monte	140	35.25 S	58.49 W
San Miguel de Tucumán	140	26.49 S	65.13 W
San Miguel el Alto	130	21.01 N	102.21 W
San Miniato	78	43.41 N	10.51 E
Sannār	112	13.33 N	33.38 E
Sannicandro Garganico	78	41.50 N	15.34 E
San Nicolás de los Arroyos	140	33.20 S	60.13 W
San Nicolas Island I	168	33.15 N	119.31 W
Sannikova, Proliv ʯ	84	74.30 N	140.00 E
Sanniquellie	114	7.22 N	8.43 W
Sanok	72	49.34 N	22.13 E
San Pablo	98	14.04 N	121.19 E
San Pablo, Punta ➤	130	27.12 N	114.30 W
San Pedro, Arg.	140	24.14 S	64.50 W
San Pedro, Arg.	140	33.40 S	59.41 W
San Pedro, Para.	140	24.07 S	56.59 W
San Pedro, Tex., U.S.	160	27.48 N	97.41 W
San Pedro □5	140	24.15 S	56.30 W
San Pedro ≃	164	33.00 N	110.50 W
San Pedro, Punta ➤	140	25.30 S	70.38 W
San Pedro, Volcán ∧1	140	21.53 S	68.25 W
San Pedro Channel ʯ	168	33.35 N	118.25 W
San Pedro de las Colonias	130	25.45 N	102.59 W
San Pedro de Macorís	132	18.27 N	69.18 W
San Pedro Mártir, Sierra ⛰	130	30.45 N	115.13 W
San Pedro Peaks ⛰	164	36.07 N	106.49 W
San Pedro Sula	130	15.27 N	88.02 W
Sanquhar	70	55.22 N	3.56 W
San Quintín, Cabo ➤	130	30.21 N	116.00 W
San Rafael, Arg.	140	34.40 S	68.21 W
San Rafael, Calif., U.S.	168	37.59 N	122.31 W
San Rafael, N. Mex., U.S.	164	35.06 N	107.53 W
San Rafael, Ven.	138	10.58 N	71.44 W
San Rafael Mountains ⛰	168	34.45 N	119.50 W
San Ramón, Bol.	134	13.17 S	64.43 W
San Ramón, C.R.	132	10.06 N	84.28 W
San Ramón de la Nueva Orán	140	23.08 S	64.20 W
San Remo	78	43.49 N	7.46 E
San Rosendo	140	37.16 S	72.43 W
San Saba	160	31.12 N	98.43 W
San Salvador	128	13.42 N	89.12 W
San Salvador (Watling Island) I	132	24.00 N	74.30 W
San Salvador de Jujuy	140	24.10 S	65.20 W
Sansanné-Mango	114	10.21 N	0.28 E
San Sebastián	76	43.19 N	1.59 W
Sansepolcro	78	43.34 N	12.08 E
San Severo	78	41.41 N	15.23 E
Sanshawan C	88	26.35 N	119.50 E
Sanshui	88	23.11 N	112.53 E
San Simon	164	32.16 N	109.14 W
Sans Souci	156	34.53 N	82.24 W
Santa ≃	134	8.58 S	78.39 W
Santa Ana, Bol.	134	15.31 S	67.30 W
Santa Ana, Bol.	134	13.45 S	65.35 W
Santa Ana, El Sal.	128	13.59 N	89.34 W
Santa Ana, Méx.	130	30.33 N	111.07 W
Santa Ana, Calif., U.S.	168	33.43 N	117.54 W
Santa Ana, Cuchilla de (Coxilna de Santana ⛰2	140	30.50 S	55.35 W
Santa Ana Mountains ⛰	168	33.45 N	117.35 W
Santa Bárbara, Méx.	130	26.48 N	105.49 W
Santa Barbara, Calif., U.S.	168	34.25 N	119.42 W
Santa Barbara Channel ʯ	168	34.15 N	119.55 W
Santa Catalina, Gulf of C	168	33.20 N	117.45 W
Santa Catalina Island I	168	33.23 N	118.26 W
Santa Catarina, Ilha de I	140	27.36 S	48.30 W
Santa Clara, Cuba	132	22.24 N	79.58 W
Santa Clara, Calif., U.S.	168	37.21 N	121.57 W
Santa Clara, Utah, U.S.	164	37.08 N	113.39 W
Santa Clara, Isla I	136	33.00 S	80.00 W
Santa Clara Valley V	168	37.10 N	121.40 W
Santa Comba Dão	76	40.24 N	8.08 W
Santa Cruz, Arg.	136	50.00 S	68.32 W
Santa Cruz, Bol.	134	17.48 S	63.10 W
Santa Cruz, Calif., U.S.	168	36.58 N	122.01 W
Santa Cruz ≃	136	50.10 S	68.20 W
Santa Cruz de la Palma	106	28.41 N	17.45 W
Santa Cruz del Sur	132	20.43 N	78.00 W
Santa Cruz de Tenerife	106	28.27 N	16.14 W
Santa Cruz do Rio Pardo	140	22.55 S	49.37 W
Santa Cruz do Sul	140	29.43 S	52.26 W
Santa Cruz Island I	168	34.01 N	119.45 W
Santa Eugenia	76	42.33 N	9.00 W
Santa Eulalia	76	40.34 N	1.19 W
Santa Eulalia del Río	76	38.59 N	1.31 E
Santa Fe, Arg.	140	31.40 S	60.40 W
Santa Fe, N. Mex., U.S.	164	35.42 N	106.57 W
Santa Fe □4	140	31.15 S	61.00 W
Santa Fe Baldy ∧	164	35.50 N	105.46 W
Santa Filomena	134	9.07 S	45.56 W
Santai	88	31.10 N	105.02 E
Santa Inés, Isla I	136	53.40 S	73.00 W
Santa Isabel, Arg.	140	36.15 S	66.55 W
Santa Isabel → Malabo, Gui. Ecu.	114	3.45 N	8.47 E
Santa Isabel I	118	8.00 S	159.00 E
Santa Lucía	140	34.27 S	56.24 W
Santa Lucia Range ⛰	168	36.00 N	121.20 W
Santa Luzia	76	37.44 N	8.24 W
Santa Luzia I	114a	16.46 N	24.45 W
Santa Magdalena, Isla I	130	24.50 N	112.15 W
Santa Margarita	168	35.23 N	120.37 W
Santa Margarita, Isla de I	130	24.25 N	111.50 W
Santa Margherita Ligure	78	44.20 N	9.12 E
Santa María, Arg.	140	26.40 S	66.02 W
Santa Maria, Bra.	140	29.41 S	53.48 W
Santa Maria, Calif., U.S.	168	34.57 N	120.26 W
Santa Maria ≃	168	34.58 N	120.38 W
Santa Maria, Cabo de ➤	110	13.25 S	12.32 E
Santa Maria Capua Vetere	78	41.05 N	14.15 E
Santa-Maria-Siché	78	41.52 N	8.59 E
Santa Marinella	78	42.02 N	11.51 E
Santa Marta	132	11.15 N	74.13 W
Santa Monica	168	34.01 N	118.30 W
Santa Monica Bay C	168	33.54 N	118.25 W
Santana, Coxilha de (Cuchilla De Santa Ana ⛰2	140	30.50 S	55.35 W
Santana do Livramento	140	30.53 S	55.31 W
Santander, Esp.	76	43.28 N	3.48 W
Santander, Pil.	92	9.25 N	123.20 E
Santander □5	138	7.00 N	73.15 W
Santa Paula	168	34.21 N	119.04 W
Santaquin	164	39.59 N	111.47 W
Santarém, Bra.	134	2.26 S	54.42 W
Santarém	76	39.14 N	8.41 W
Santa Rita, Hond.	130	15.09 N	87.53 W
Santa Rita, N. Mex., U.S.	164	32.48 N	108.04 W
Santa Rita, Ven.	138	10.32 N	71.32 W
Santa Rosa, Arg.	140	36.40 S	64.15 W
Santa Rosa, Arg.	140	32.20 S	65.10 W
Santa Rosa, Bra.	140	27.52 S	54.29 W
Santa Rosa, Ec.	138	3.27 S	79.58 W
Santa Rosa, Calif., U.S.	168	38.26 N	122.43 W
Santa Rosa, N. Mex., U.S.	160	34.57 N	104.41 W
Santa Rosa de Cabal	138	4.52 N	75.38 W
Santa Rosa [de Copán]	130	14.47 N	88.46 W
Santa Rosa Island I	168	33.58 N	120.06 W
Santa Rosalía	130	27.19 N	112.17 W
Šantarskije Ostrova II	84	55.00 N	137.36 E
Santa Susana	168	34.16 N	118.43 W
Santa Sylvina	140	27.50 S	61.10 W
Santa Teresa, Embalse de ⊜1	76	40.40 N	5.30 W
Santa Vitória do Palmar	140	33.31 S	53.21 W
Santa Ynez ≃	168	35.41 N	120.36 W
Santee	168	32.50 N	116.58 W
Santhià	78	45.22 N	8.10 E
Santiago, Bra.	140	29.11 S	54.53 W
Santiago, Chile	140	33.27 S	70.40 W
Santiago, Pan.	138	8.05 N	80.59 W
Santiago □4	140	33.30 S	70.50 W
Santiago ≃	138	4.27 S	77.38 W
Santiago de Compostela	76	42.53 N	8.33 W
Santiago de Cuba	132	20.01 N	75.49 W
Santiago del Estero	140	27.50 S	64.15 W
Santiago del Estero □4	140	27.40 S	63.15 W
Santiago [de los Caballeros]	132	19.27 N	70.42 W
Santiago do Cacém	76	38.01 N	8.42 W
Santiago Ixcuintla	130	21.49 N	105.13 W
Santiago Papasquiaro	130	25.03 N	105.25 W
Santiam Pass)(	166	44.25 N	121.51 W
Sāntipur	102	23.15 N	88.26 E
Säntis ∧	74	47.15 N	9.21 E
Santo	160	32.36 N	98.13 W
Santo Amaro	134	12.32 S	38.43 W
Santo Ângelo	140	28.18 S	54.16 W
Santo Antão I	114a	17.05 N	25.10 W
Santo António	110	1.39 N	7.26 E
Santo Antônio de Jesus	134	12.58 S	39.16 W
Santo Antônio do Içá	138	3.05 S	67.57 W
Santo António do Zaire	110	6.07 S	12.18 E
Santo Domingo	132	18.28 N	69.54 W
Santo Domingo de los Colorados	138	0.15 S	79.09 W
Santo Domingo Pueblo	164	35.31 N	106.22 W
Santos	140	23.57 S	46.20 W
Santos Dumont	136	21.28 S	43.34 W
Santo Tirso	76	41.21 N	8.28 W
Santo Tomé	140	28.35 S	56.05 W
San Vicente	128	13.38 N	88.48 W
San Vicente de Baracaldo	76	43.18 N	2.59 W
San Vicente del Caguán	138	2.07 N	74.46 W
San Vincenzo	78	43.06 N	10.32 E
San Vito	78	39.27 N	9.32 E
San Vito dei Normanni	78	40.39 N	17.42 E
San Ygnacio	160	27.03 N	99.27 W
Sanyuan	88	34.35 N	108.54 E
Sanza Pombo	110	7.19 S	15.59 E
São Bento	138	3.02 N	60.30 W
São Borja	140	28.39 S	56.00 W
São Brás de Alportel	76	37.09 N	7.53 W
São Carlos	140	22.01 S	47.54 W
São Cristóvão	134	11.01 S	37.12 W
São Domingos	140	26.34 S	52.32 W
São Francisco	134	15.57 S	44.52 W
São Francisco ≃	140	24.40 S	54.20 W
São Francisco do Sul	140	26.14 S	48.39 W
São Gabriel	140	30.20 S	54.19 W
Sao Hill	110	8.20 S	35.12 E
São Jerônimo	140	29.58 S	51.43 W
São João da Barra	136	21.38 S	41.03 W
São João da Boa Vista	140	21.58 S	46.47 W

Symbols in the index entries are identified on page 203.

Name	Page	Lat	Long
São João da Madeira	76	40.54 N	8.30 W
São João del Rei	134	21.09 S	44.16 W
São Joaquim da Barra	134	20.35 S	47.53 W
São José do Rio Prêto	140	20.48 S	49.23 W
São José dos Campos	140	23.11 S	45.53 W
São José dos Pinhais	134	25.31 S	49.13 W
São Leopoldo	140	29.46 S	51.09 W
São Lourenço ≊	134	17.53 S	57.27 W
São Lourenço, Pantanal de ≊	134	17.30 S	56.30 W
São Lourenço do Sul	134	31.22 S	51.58 W
São Luís	134	2.31 S	44.16 W
São Luís Gonzaga	140	28.24 S	54.58 W
São Manuel	140	22.44 S	48.34 W
São Mateus	134	18.44 S	39.51 W
Saône ≊	74	45.44 N	4.50 E
Saône-et-Loire □5	74	46.42 N	4.45 E
São Nicolau I	114a	16.35 N	24.15 W
São Paulo	136	23.32 S	46.37 W
São Paulo □3	140	22.00 S	49.00 W
São Paulo de Olivença	138	3.27 S	68.48 W
São Pedro do Sul	76	40.45 N	8.04 W
São Raimundo Nonato	134	9.01 S	42.42 W
São Roque, Cabo de ➤	134	5.29 S	35.16 W
Saorre, Mount ⋀	142	64.27 N	84.30 W
São Salvador do Congo	110	6.16 S	14.15 E
São Sebastião, Ilha de I	140	23.50 S	45.18 W
São Sebastião, Ponta ➤	116	22.07 S	35.30 E
São Sebastião do Paraíso	134	20.55 S	47.00 W
São Tiago I	114a	15.05 N	23.40 W
São Tomé I	110	0.20 N	6.44 E
São Tomé I	110	0.12 N	6.39 E
São Tomé, Cabo de ➤	136	21.59 S	40.59 W
São Tomé, Pico de ⋀	110	0.16 N	6.33 E
Sao Tome and Principe □1	111	1.00 N	7.00 E
São Vicente	140	23.58 S	46.23 W
São Vicente I	114a	16.50 N	25.00 W
São Vicente, Cabo de ➤	76	37.01 N	9.00 W
Sapé	134	7.06 S	35.13 W
Sapele	114	5.54 N	5.41 E
Sapitwa ⋀	110	15.57 S	35.36 E
Sappa Creek ≊	162	40.07 N	99.38 W
Sappington	158	38.32 N	90.23 W
Sapporo	90a	43.03 N	141.21 E
Sapri	78	40.04 N	15.38 E
Sapt Kosi ≊	102	26.31 N	86.58 E
Sapulpa	160	36.00 N	96.06 W
Saqqez	104	36.14 N	46.16 E
Sarāb	104	37.56 N	47.32 E
Sara Buri	94	14.30 N	100.55 E
Saragosa	160	31.01 N	103.39 W
Saragossa → Zaragoza	76	41.38 N	0.53 W
Sarai	86	53.44 N	45.59 E
Sārāisniemi	68	64.27 N	26.47 E
Sarajevo	80	43.52 N	18.25 E
Sarakhs	100	36.32 N	61.11 E
Saraland	158	30.49 N	88.04 W
Saran'	84	49.46 N	72.52 E
Saranac	154	42.56 N	85.13 W
Saranac Lake	152	44.20 N	74.08 W
Sarangani Islands II	98	5.25 N	125.25 E
Saranpaul'	66	64.14 N	60.53 E
Saransk	66	54.11 N	45.11 E
Sarasota	156	27.20 N	82.34 W
Saratoga, Calif., U.S.	168	37.16 N	122.02 W
Saratoga, Tex., U.S.	160	30.17 N	94.31 W
Saratoga, Wyo., U.S.	166	41.27 N	106.48 W
Saratoga Springs	152	43.05 N	73.47 W
Saratov	64	51.34 N	46.02 E
Saravane	94	15.43 N	106.25 E
Sárbogárd	72	46.53 N	18.38 E
Sarcoxie	158	37.03 N	94.07 W
Sarda (Kāli) ≊	102	27.22 N	81.23 E
Sardalas	108	25.46 N	10.34 E
Sardegna □4	78	40.00 N	9.00 E
Sardegna ≊	78	40.00 N	9.00 E
Sardinia → Sardegna I	78	40.00 N	9.00 E
Sardis	158	34.26 N	89.55 W
Sarera, Teluk ⊂	124	2.30 S	135.20 E
Sargans	74	47.03 N	9.26 E
Sargodha	102	32.05 N	72.40 E
Sarh	108	9.09 N	18.23 E
Sarigan I	124	16.42 N	145.47 E
Sarina	120	21.26 S	149.13 E
Sariñena	76	41.48 N	0.10 W
Sarita	160	27.13 N	97.47 W
Sariwŏn	88	38.31 N	125.44 E
Sarja	86	58.21 N	45.30 E
Sark I	70	49.26 N	2.21 W
Sarkad	72	46.44 N	21.23 E
Sarlat-la-Canéda	74	44.53 N	1.13 E
Sármellék	72	46.44 N	17.10 E
Sarmi	124	1.51 S	138.44 E
Sarmiento	136	45.35 S	69.05 W
Sarmiento, Monte ⋀	136	54.25 S	70.50 W
Sarnen	74	46.54 N	8.15 E
Sarnia	154	42.58 N	82.23 W
Sarno	78	40.49 N	14.37 E
Saronno	72	45.38 N	9.02 E
Sárospatak	72	48.19 N	21.34 E
Sarpsborg	68	59.17 N	11.07 E
Sarralbe	74	49.00 N	7.01 E
Sarrebourg	74	48.44 N	7.03 E
Sarreguemines	74	49.06 N	7.03 E
Sarre-Union	74	48.56 N	7.05 E
Sartang ≊	84	67.44 N	133.12 E
Sartell	154	45.37 N	94.12 W
Sartène	78	41.37 N	8.59 E
Sarthe □5	74	48.00 N	0.05 E
Sartilly	74	48.45 N	1.27 W
Sárvár	72	47.15 N	16.57 E
Saryg-Sep	84	51.30 N	95.36 E
Sarykol'skij Chrebet ⋀	102	38.00 N	74.30 E
Sarysu ≊	82	45.12 N	64.06 E
Sary-Tas	100	39.44 N	73.15 E
Saryžaz ≊	82	42.55 N	79.38 E
Sarzana	78	44.07 N	9.58 E
Sarzeau	74	47.32 N	2.46 W
Sasakwa	160	34.57 N	96.31 W
Sasarám	102	24.57 N	84.02 E
Sásd	72	46.15 N	18.06 E
Sasebo	90	33.10 N	129.43 E
Saskatchewan □4	142	54.00 N	105.00 W
Saskatchewan ≊	142	53.12 N	99.16 W
Saskatoon	142	52.07 N	106.38 W
Saslyč	86	54.24 N	41.54 E
Sasovo	86	54.21 N	41.54 E
Saspamco	160	29.14 N	98.18 W
Sassandra	114	4.58 N	6.05 W
Sassandra ≊	114	4.58 N	6.05 W
Sassari	78	40.44 N	8.33 E
Sasso Marconi	78	44.24 N	11.15 E
Sassoferrato	78	43.26 N	12.51 E
S'as'stroj	86	60.37 N	33.30 E
Sassnitz	72	54.31 N	13.38 E
Sasstown	114	4.33 N	8.26 W
Sata-misaki ➤	90	30.59 N	130.40 E
Satanta	162	37.26 N	100.59 W
Sātāra	100	17.41 N	73.59 E
Satellite Beach	156	28.11 N	80.36 W
Säter	68	60.21 N	15.45 E
Satit (Tekeze) ≊	112	14.20 N	35.50 E
Satka	64	55.03 N	59.01 E
Satna	102	24.35 N	80.50 E
Sátoraljaújhely	72	48.24 N	21.39 E
Satpura Range ⋀	100	22.00 N	78.00 E
Satsuma	158	30.51 N	88.03 W
Satsunan-shotō II	91b	29.00 N	130.00 E
Sattahip	94	12.41 N	100.54 E
Satu Mare	80	47.48 N	22.53 E
Satu Mare □5	80	47.50 N	23.00 E
Satura	86	55.34 N	39.32 E
Sauce	140	30.05 S	58.45 W
Saucillo	130	28.01 N	105.17 W
Sauda	68	59.39 N	6.20 E
Saudi Arabia □1	100	25.00 N	45.00 E
Saugatuck	154	42.40 N	86.12 W
Saugerties	152	42.05 N	73.57 W
Saujon	74	45.40 N	0.56 W
Sauk Centre	162	45.44 N	94.57 W
Sauk City	154	43.17 N	89.43 W
Sauk Rapids	154	45.34 N	94.09 W
Saukville	154	43.23 N	87.55 W
Saul	134	3.37 N	53.12 W
Saulgau	72	48.01 N	9.30 E
Saulieu	74	47.16 N	4.14 E
Sault Sainte Marie	144	46.31 N	84.20 W
Sault Sainte Marie, Mich., U.S.	154	46.30 N	84.21 W
Saumarez Reef ≋2	121	21.50 S	153.40 E
Saumlaki	124	7.57 S	131.19 E
Saumur	74	47.16 N	0.05 W
Saunders, Point ⋀	122	27.52 S	125.38 E
Sausalito	168	37.51 N	122.29 W
Sauveterre-de-Béarn	74	43.29 N	0.06 W
Sauveterre-de-Guyenne	74	44.42 N	0.05 W
Sava, It.	78	40.24 N	17.34 E
S'ava, S.S.S.R.	66	58.01 N	46.22 E
Sava ≊	80	44.50 N	20.26 E
Savage	152	39.08 N	76.49 W
Savanna, Ill., U.S.	154	42.05 N	90.08 W
Savanna, Okla., U.S.	160	34.50 N	95.50 W
Savannah, Ga., U.S.	158	32.04 N	81.05 W
Savannah, Mo., U.S.	158	39.56 N	94.50 W
Savannah, Tenn., U.S.	158	35.14 N	88.14 W
Savannah ≊	156	32.02 N	80.53 W
Savannakhet	94	16.33 N	104.45 E
Savanna-la-Mar	132	18.13 N	78.08 W
Save ≊	114	8.02 N	2.29 E
Save (Sabi) ≊	116	21.00 S	35.02 E
Sāveh	104	35.01 N	50.20 E
Savelli	78	39.19 N	16.47 E
Savenay	74	47.22 N	1.57 W
Saverdun	74	43.14 N	1.35 E
Saverne	74	48.44 N	7.22 E
Savigliano	78	44.38 N	7.40 E
Savigny-sur-Braye	74	47.53 N	0.49 E
Savinskij	86	54.35 N	41.13 E
Savitaipale	68	61.12 N	27.42 E
Savnik	80	42.57 N	19.05 E
Savoie □5	74	45.30 N	6.25 E
Savona	78	44.17 N	8.30 E
Savonranta	68	62.11 N	29.12 E
Savu Sea → Sawu, Laut ≋2	96	9.40 S	122.00 E
Sawahlunto	96	0.40 S	100.47 E
Sawai Mādhopur	102	26.00 N	76.39 E
Sawākin	112	19.07 N	37.20 E
Sawdā', Jabal as- ⋀2	108	28.40 N	15.30 E
Sawhāj	112	26.33 N	31.42 E
Sawknah	108	29.04 N	15.47 E
Sawqarah, Dawhat ⊂	100	18.35 N	57.15 E
Sawu, Laut (Savu Sea) ≋2	96	9.40 S	122.00 E
Sawu, Pulau I	96	10.30 S	121.54 E
Sawyer	154	41.53 N	86.35 W
Saxby ≊	120	18.25 S	140.53 E
Saxis	152	37.55 N	75.43 W
Saxmundham	70	52.13 N	1.29 E
Saxon, Schw.	74	46.09 N	7.11 E
Saxon, S.C., U.S.	156	34.57 N	81.57 W
Saxon, Wis., U.S.	154	46.29 N	90.25 W
Sayaboury	94	19.15 N	101.45 E
Sayan Mountains (Sajany) ⋀	82	52.45 N	96.00 E
Saybrook	158	40.26 N	88.32 W
Şaydā (Sidon)	104	33.33 N	35.22 E
Sayhūt	100	15.12 N	51.14 E
Sayre, Okla., U.S.	160	35.18 N	99.38 W
Sayre, Pa., U.S.	152	41.59 N	76.32 W
Sayreville	152	40.28 N	74.21 W
Sayula, Méx.	130	19.52 N	103.37 W
Sayula, Méx.	130	29.22 N	111.33 W
Say'ūn	100	15.56 N	48.47 E
Sazonovo	86	59.04 N	35.14 E
Scaër	74	48.02 N	3.42 E
Scalea	78	39.49 N	15.48 E
Scandia	162	39.47 N	97.47 W
Scanlon	154	37.17 N	94.49 W
Scapegoat Mountain ⋀	166	47.19 N	112.50 W
Ščapino	84	55.19 N	159.25 E
Scappoose	166	45.45 N	122.53 W
Scarborough, Trin.	132	11.11 N	60.44 W
Scarborough, Eng., U.K.	70	54.17 N	0.24 W
Scarborough Shoal ≋1	98	15.08 N	117.46 E
Scawfell Island I	120	20.52 S	149.36 E
Ščekino	86	54.01 N	37.31 E
Ščelejur	66	65.19 N	53.21 E
Ščelkovo	86	55.55 N	38.00 E
Ščerbakovo	86	65.15 N	160.30 E
Ščerbinka	86	55.31 N	37.35 E
Schaffhausen	74	47.42 N	8.38 E
Schärding	72	48.27 N	13.26 E
Scharhörn I	72	53.58 N	8.24 E
Schefferville	142	54.48 N	66.50 W
Scheibbs	72	48.00 N	15.10 E
Scheinfeld	72	49.40 N	10.27 E
Schelde (Escaut) ≊	72	51.22 N	4.15 E
Schenectady	152	42.47 N	73.53 W
Schertz	160	29.33 N	98.16 W
Schesslitz	72	49.59 N	11.02 E
Schiedam	72	51.55 N	4.24 E
Schiltigheim	74	48.36 N	7.45 E
Schio	78	45.43 N	11.21 E
Schleiden	72	50.31 N	6.28 E
Schleiz	72	50.34 N	11.49 E
Schlesien → Silesia □9	72	51.00 N	16.45 E
Schleswig	72	54.31 N	9.33 E
Schleswig-Holstein □3	72	54.00 N	10.00 E
Schleusingen	72	50.30 N	10.45 E
Schloss Neuhaus	72	51.44 N	8.43 E
Schlüchtern	72	50.22 N	9.31 E
Schmalkalden	72	50.43 N	10.26 E
Schmidmühlen	72	49.16 N	11.56 E
Schmölln	72	50.53 N	12.20 E
Schneeberg	72	50.36 N	12.38 E
Schneverdingen	72	53.07 N	9.47 E
Schoch'a	86	55.57 N	37.13 E
Schofield	154	44.54 N	89.36 W
Schoharie	152	42.40 N	74.19 W
Schönebeck	72	52.01 N	11.44 E
Schongau	72	47.49 N	10.54 E
Schoolcraft	154	42.07 N	85.38 W
Schopfheim	72	47.39 N	7.49 E
Schorndorf	72	48.48 N	9.31 E
Schouten Island I	120	42.19 S	148.17 E
Schouwen I	72	51.42 N	3.45 E
Schramberg	72	48.13 N	8.23 E
Schrobenhausen	72	48.33 N	11.17 E
Schruns	72	47.05 N	9.55 E
Schull	70	51.32 N	9.33 W
Schulenburg	160	29.41 N	96.54 W
Schultz Lake ⊜	142	64.45 N	97.30 W
Schurz	168	38.57 N	118.49 W
Schuyler, Nebr., U.S.	162	41.27 N	97.04 W
Schuyler, Va., U.S.	156	37.47 N	78.42 W
Schuylkill ≊	152	39.53 N	75.12 W
Schuylkill Haven	152	40.38 N	76.10 W
Schwabach	72	49.20 N	11.01 E
Schwaben □9	72	48.20 N	10.30 E
Schwäbisch Gmünd	72	48.48 N	9.47 E
Schwäbisch Hall	72	49.07 N	9.44 E
Schwabmünchen	72	48.11 N	10.45 E
Schwandorf in Bayern	72	49.20 N	12.08 E
Schwaner, Pegunungan ⋀	96	0.40 S	112.40 E
Schwarza	72	50.41 N	11.19 E
Schwarzach im Pongau	72	47.19 N	13.09 E
Schwarzenberg	72	50.32 N	12.47 E
Schwarzenburg	74	46.49 N	7.21 E
Schwaz	72	47.20 N	11.42 E
Schwechat	72	48.09 N	16.29 E
Schwedt	72	53.03 N	14.17 E
Schweinfurt	72	50.03 N	10.14 E
Schwerin	72	53.38 N	11.25 E
Schwerin □5	72	53.30 N	11.30 E
Schwetzingen	72	49.23 N	8.34 E
Schwyz	72	47.02 N	8.40 E
Schwyz □	72	47.05 N	8.45 E
Sciacca	78	37.30 N	13.06 E
Scicli	78	36.47 N	14.43 E
Scilla	78	38.15 N	15.44 E
Scilly, Isles of II	70	48.57 N	6.15 W
Scio	152	40.40 N	80.54 W
Scobey	162	48.47 N	105.25 W
Scofield Reservoir ⊜1	164	39.47 N	111.09 W
Ščokino	86	54.01 N	37.31 E
Scone	120	32.03 S	150.52 E
Scooba	158	32.50 N	88.29 W
Scordia	78	37.18 N	14.51 E
Scotia	152	44.54 N	73.33 W
Scotland	162	43.09 N	97.43 W
Scotland □8	70	57.00 N	4.00 W
Scotland Neck	156	36.02 N	77.32 W
Scotlandville	158	30.31 N	91.11 W
Scott ⋀	168	41.48 N	123.02 W
Scott City, Kans., U.S.	162	38.29 N	100.54 W
Scott City, Mo., U.S.	158	37.13 N	89.31 W
Scottdale, Ga., U.S.	156	33.48 N	84.16 W
Scottdale, Pa., U.S.	152	40.06 N	79.35 W
Scott Islands II	148	50.48 N	128.40 W
Scott Reef ≋2	118	14.00 S	121.50 E
Scottsbluff	162	41.52 N	103.40 W
Scottsboro	158	34.40 N	86.02 W
Scottsburg	158	38.41 N	85.46 W
Scottsdale, Austl.	120	41.10 S	147.31 E
Scottsdale, Ariz., U.S.	164	33.30 N	111.56 W
Scottsville	158	36.45 N	86.11 W
Scottville	154	43.57 N	86.17 W
Scourie	70	58.20 N	5.08 W
Scranton, N. Dak., U.S.	162	46.09 N	103.09 W
Scranton, Pa., U.S.	152	41.24 N	75.40 W
Scribner	162	41.40 N	96.40 W
Ščučin	86	53.36 N	24.45 E
Ščučinsk	82	52.56 N	70.12 E
Scunthorpe	70	53.36 N	0.38 W
Scuol	74	46.48 N	10.18 E
Scutari → Üsküdar	80	41.01 N	29.01 E
Scutari, Lake ⊜	80	42.12 N	19.18 E
Seaford	152	38.39 N	75.37 W
Seaforth	70	43.35 N	81.24 W
Seaham	70	54.52 N	1.21 W
Seahorse Point ➤	142	63.47 N	80.09 W
Seahorse Shoal ≋2	96	9.50 N	112.37 E
Sea Islands II	156	31.20 N	81.20 W
Sea Isle City	152	39.09 N	74.42 W
Seal ≊	142	59.04 N	94.48 W
Sea Lake	120	35.30 S	142.51 E
Seale	158	32.18 N	85.10 W
Seal Lake ⊜	158	54.18 N	61.40 W
Sealy	160	29.47 N	96.09 W
Searchlight	168	35.28 N	114.55 W
Searcy	158	35.15 N	91.44 W
Searsport	152	44.28 N	68.56 W
Seaside, Calif., U.S.	168	37.55 N	121.50 W
Seaside, Oreg., U.S.	166	46.02 N	123.55 W
Seaside Park	152	39.55 N	74.04 W
Seattle	166	47.36 N	122.20 W
Seattle, Mount ⋀	146	60.06 N	139.11 W
Sebago Lake ⊜	152	43.50 N	70.35 W
Šebalino, S.S.S.R.	84	51.17 N	85.40 E
Šebalino, S.S.S.R.	84	51.17 N	85.40 E
Sebastian, Cape ➤	166	42.19 N	124.26 W
Sebastián Vizcaíno, Bahia ⊂	130	28.00 N	114.30 W
Sebastopol	168	38.24 N	122.49 W
Sebatik, Pulau I	96	4.10 N	117.47 E
Sebec Lake ⊜	152	45.18 N	69.18 W
Sebeș	80	45.58 N	23.34 E
Sebeș-Körös (Crișu Repede) ≊	80	46.55 N	20.59 E
Sebewaing	154	43.44 N	83.27 W
Sebnitz	72	50.58 N	14.16 E
Sebree	158	37.36 N	87.32 W
Sebring, Fla., U.S.	156	27.29 N	81.26 W
Sebring, Ohio, U.S.	152	40.55 N	81.01 W
Sechura, Bahia de ⊂	134	5.35 S	81.00 W
Security	162	38.45 N	104.41 W
Seda	88	32.20 N	100.41 E
Sedalia	158	38.42 N	93.14 W
Sedan, Austl.	120	34.35 S	139.18 E
Sedan, Fr.	74	49.42 N	4.57 E
Sedan, Kans., U.S.	162	37.08 N	96.11 W
Sedano	76	42.43 N	3.45 W
Sedel'nikovo	84	56.30 N	75.18 E
Séderon	74	44.12 N	5.32 E
Sedgwick, Colo., U.S.	162	40.56 N	102.31 W
Sedgwick, Kans., U.S.	162	37.55 N	97.25 W
Sedini	78	40.50 N	8.49 E
Sedona	164	34.52 N	111.46 W
Sedova, Pik ⋀	82	73.29 N	54.58 E
Sedro Woolley	166	48.30 N	122.14 W
Seefeld in Tirol	72	47.20 N	11.11 E
Seeheim	116	26.50 S	17.45 E
Seelow	72	52.32 N	14.23 E
Sées	74	48.36 N	0.10 E
Seesen	72	51.53 N	10.10 E
Segamat	94	2.30 N	102.49 E
Segezha	66	63.44 N	34.19 E
Ségou	114	13.27 N	6.16 W
Segovia	76	40.57 N	4.07 W
Segré	74	47.41 N	0.53 W
Séguédine	108	20.12 N	12.59 E
Seguin	160	29.34 N	97.58 W
Segura ≊	76	38.06 N	0.54 W
Seia	76	40.25 N	7.42 W
Seiches-sur-le-Loir	74	47.34 N	0.22 W
Seilhac	74	45.22 N	1.42 E
Seiling	160	36.09 N	98.56 W
Seinäjoki	68	62.47 N	22.50 E
Seine ≊, Can.	154	48.48 N	92.10 W
Seine ≊, Fr.	74	49.26 N	0.26 E
Seine-et-Marne □5	74	48.35 N	3.01 E
Seine-Maritime □5	74	49.45 N	1.00 E
Sejm ≊	86	51.27 N	32.34 E
Séjmčan	84	62.53 N	152.26 E
Sejny	72	54.06 N	23.22 E
Seki (Nucha)	104	40.34 N	47.12 E
Sekiu	166	48.16 N	124.18 W
Šel'agskij, Mys ➤	84	70.06 N	170.26 E
Sekondi-Takoradi	114	4.53 N	1.45 W
Selah	166	46.39 N	120.32 W
Selajar, Pulau I	96	6.05 S	120.30 E
Selaru, Pulau, Tandjung ➤	124	8.11 S	131.03 E
Selassi	96	2.53 S	130.00 E
Selat Karimata (Karimata Strait) ⊔	96	2.05 S	108.40 E
Selat Makassar (Makassar Strait) ⊔	96	2.00 S	117.30 E
Selawik	146	66.37 N	160.03 W
Selb	72	50.10 N	12.08 E
Selbu	68	63.13 N	11.02 E
Selby, Eng., U.K.	70	53.48 N	1.04 W
Selby, S. Dak., U.S.	162	45.30 N	100.02 W
Seldovia	146	59.27 N	151.43 W
Selemdža ≊	84	51.42 N	128.53 E
Selenga (Selenge Mörön) ≊	84	52.16 N	106.16 E
Selenge Mörön (Selenga) ≊	84	52.16 N	106.16 E
Selenn'ach ≊	84	67.48 N	144.54 E
Sélestat	74	48.16 N	7.27 E
Seletyteniz, Ozero ⊜	82	53.15 N	73.15 E
Selfoss	66a	63.56 N	20.57 W
Sélibaby	114	15.10 N	12.11 W
Šelichova, Zaliv ⊂	84	60.00 N	158.00 E
Seligman	164	35.20 N	112.53 W
Seliger, Ozero ⊜	86	57.13 N	33.05 E
Selinsgrove	152	40.48 N	76.52 W
Selišče	86	56.53 N	33.16 E
Seližarovo	86	56.51 N	33.27 E
Selje	68	62.03 N	5.22 E
Seljord	68	59.29 N	8.37 E
Selkämeri (Bottenhavet) ⊂	68	62.00 N	20.00 E
Selkirk, Man., Can.	142	50.09 N	96.52 W
Selkirk, Scot., U.K.	70	55.33 N	2.50 W
Selkirk Mountains ⋀	166	51.00 N	117.40 W
Sellers	156	34.17 N	79.28 W
Sellersburg	158	38.24 N	85.45 W
Selles-sur-Cher	74	47.16 N	1.33 E
Selm	72	51.42 N	7.28 E
Selma, Ala., U.S.	158	32.25 N	87.01 W
Selma, Calif., U.S.	168	36.34 N	119.37 W
Selma, N.C., U.S.	156	35.32 N	78.17 W
Selmer	158	35.11 N	88.36 W
Seltz	74	48.53 N	8.06 E
Selu, Pulau I	124	7.32 S	130.54 E
Selukwe	116	19.40 S	30.00 E
Selva	140	29.50 S	62.02 W
Selvas ≊3	134	5.00 S	66.00 W
Selwyn ≊	120	21.32 S	140.30 E
Selwyn Lake ⊜	142	59.55 N	104.35 W
Selwyn Mountains ⋀	146	63.10 N	130.20 W
Selwyn Range ⋀	120	21.35 S	140.35 E
Semara	108	26.44 N	11.41 W
Semarang	96	6.58 S	110.25 E
Semau, Pulau I	96	10.13 S	123.22 E
Semeru, Gunung ⋀	96	8.06 S	112.55 E
Semibratovo	86	57.18 N	39.32 E
Seminole, Okla., U.S.	160	35.14 N	96.41 W
Seminole, Tex., U.S.	160	32.43 N	102.39 W
Seminole, Lake ⊜1	158	30.45 N	84.50 W
Seminole Draw ≊1	160	32.26 N	102.10 W
Semipalatinsk	84	50.28 N	80.13 E
Semliki ≊	110	1.14 S	30.28 E
Semnān	104	35.33 N	53.24 E
Šemonaicha	84	50.39 N	81.54 E
Semporna	96	4.28 N	118.36 E
Semur-en-Auxois	74	47.29 N	4.20 E
Sena	110	17.27 S	35.00 E
Senador Pompeu	134	5.35 S	39.22 W
Sena Madureira	134	9.04 S	68.40 W
Senanga	110	16.06 S	23.16 E
Senath	158	36.08 N	90.10 W
Senatobia	158	34.39 N	89.58 W
Sendai	88	38.15 N	140.53 E
Seneca (Crotty), Ill., U.S.	154	41.19 N	88.36 W
Seneca, Kans., U.S.	162	39.50 N	96.04 W
Seneca, Mo., U.S.	158	36.50 N	94.37 W
Seneca, S.C., U.S.	156	34.41 N	82.57 W
Seneca Falls	152	42.55 N	76.48 W
Seneca Lake ⊜	152	42.40 N	76.57 W
Senegal (Sénégal) □1	114	14.00 N	14.00 W
Sénégal ≊	114	15.48 N	16.32 W
Senekal	116	28.20 S	27.36 E
Senftenberg	72	51.32 N	14.00 E
Senhor do Bonfim	134	10.27 S	40.11 W
Senica	72	48.41 N	17.22 E
Senigallia	78	43.43 N	13.13 E
Senise	78	40.09 N	16.18 E
Senja I	68	69.20 N	17.30 E
Senkursk	66	62.08 N	42.53 E
Senlis	74	49.12 N	2.35 E
Sennestadt	72	51.59 N	8.37 E
Senneterre	144	48.23 N	77.15 W
Sennori	78	40.48 N	8.34 E
Sens	74	48.12 N	3.17 E
Senta	80	45.56 N	20.04 E
Sentinel	160	35.09 N	99.10 W
Seoni	102	22.06 N	79.32 E
Seoul → Sŏul	88	37.33 N	126.58 E
Sępólno Krajeńskie	72	53.28 N	17.32 E
Sept-Iles (Seven Islands)	142	50.12 N	66.23 W
Sepulga ≊	158	31.11 N	86.46 W
Sequeros	76	40.31 N	6.01 W
Serafimovič	64	49.36 N	42.43 E
Seraing	72	50.36 N	5.29 E
Seram, Laut ≋2	92	2.30 S	128.00 E
Serang	96	6.07 S	106.09 E
Serbia → Srbija □3	80	44.00 N	21.00 E
Serdobsk	64	52.28 N	44.13 E
Sered'	72	48.17 N	17.44 E
Seredka	86	58.12 N	28.15 E
Serednikovo	86	56.01 N	37.14 E
Seremban	94	2.44 N	101.56 E
Serengeti Plain ≊	110	2.50 S	35.00 E
Serenje	110	13.15 S	30.14 E
Sergač	64	55.32 N	45.28 E
Sergeja Kirova, Ostrova II	84	77.12 N	89.30 E
Sergejevka, S.S.S.R.	84	77.11 N	133.22 E
Sergejevka, S.S.S.R.	88	44.10 N	133.22 E
Seria	96	4.39 N	114.23 E
Serian	96	1.10 N	110.34 E
Sérifos I	80	37.09 N	24.30 E
Sérigny ≊	142	56.47 N	66.00 W
Seringapatam	100	12.25 N	76.42 E
Šerlovaja Gora	84	50.34 N	116.15 E
Sermata, Kepulauan II	124	8.10 S	128.40 E
Serock	72	52.31 N	21.03 E
Serov	82	59.29 N	60.31 E
Serowe	116	22.25 S	26.44 E
Serpa	76	37.56 N	7.36 W
Serpa Pinto	110	14.36 S	17.48 E
Serpents Mouth ⊔	132	10.00 N	62.00 W
Serpuchov	86	54.55 N	37.25 E
Serra do Navio	134	0.59 N	52.03 W
Sérrai	80	41.05 N	23.32 E
Serra Talhada	134	7.59 S	38.18 W
Serres	74	44.26 N	5.43 E
Serrezuela	140	30.40 S	65.20 W
Sertã	76	39.48 N	8.06 W
Sertânia	134	8.04 S	37.16 W
Serua, Pulau I	124	6.18 S	130.01 E
Serui	124	1.53 S	136.14 E
Sesayap ≊	96	3.36 N	117.15 E
Sesfontein	116	19.07 S	13.39 E
Sesheke	110	17.29 S	24.18 E
Sessa Aurunca	78	41.14 N	13.56 E
Sestao	76	43.18 N	3.00 W
Sesto San Giovanni	78	45.32 N	9.14 E
Sestri Levante	78	44.16 N	9.24 E
Sestroreck	86	60.06 N	29.58 E
Sète	74	43.24 N	3.41 E
Sete Lagoas	134	19.27 S	44.14 W
Sete Quedas, Salto das (Salto do Guaíra) ⋤	140	24.02 S	54.16 W
Sétif	108	36.09 N	5.26 E
Seto	90	35.14 N	137.06 E
Seto-naikai ≋2	90	34.10 N	133.20 E
Settat	108	33.04 N	7.37 W
Sette Cama	110	2.32 S	9.45 E
Sette-Daban, Chrebet ⋀	84	62.00 N	138.00 E
Setúbal	76	38.32 N	8.54 W
Seul, Lac ⊜	142	50.20 N	92.30 W
Seurre	74	47.00 N	5.09 E
Sevagram	100	20.45 N	78.30 E
Sevastopol'	64	44.36 N	33.32 E
Sevan, Ozero ⊜	104	40.20 N	45.20 E
Severn ≊, Can.	142	56.02 N	87.36 W
Severn ≊, Eng., U.K.	70	51.35 N	2.40 W
Severnaja Dvina ≊	66	64.32 N	40.30 E
Severnaja Sos'va ≊	66	64.10 N	65.28 E
Severnaja Zeml'a II	84	79.30 N	98.00 E
Severnyj	66	67.38 N	64.06 E
Severnyj Ural ⋀2	66	60.00 N	60.00 E
Severočeský Kraj □4	72	50.35 N	14.15 E
Severo-Jenisejskij	84	60.22 N	93.01 E
Severo-Kuril'sk	84	50.40 N	156.08 E
Severomorsk	66	69.05 N	33.24 E
Severo-Sibirskaja Nizmennost' ≊	84	73.00 N	100.00 E
Severoural'sk	82	60.09 N	59.57 E
Severo-Zadonsk	86	54.04 N	38.23 E
Severskij Donec ≊	64	48.20 N	40.15 E
Sevier ≊	164	39.04 N	113.06 W
Sevier Bridge Reservoir ⊜1	164	39.21 N	111.57 W
Sevier Lake ⊜	164	38.55 N	113.09 W
Sevierville	156	35.52 N	83.34 W
Sevilla, Col.	138	4.16 N	75.57 W
Sevilla, Esp.	76	37.23 N	5.59 W
Seville → Sevilla, Esp.	76	37.23 N	5.59 W
Seville, Fla., U.S.	156	29.19 N	81.30 W
Sevlievo	80	43.01 N	25.06 E
Sevsk	86	52.09 N	34.30 E
Seward, Alaska, U.S.	146	60.06 N	149.26 W
Seward, Nebr., U.S.	162	40.55 N	97.06 W
Seward Glacier ⋤	146	60.22 N	140.15 W
Seward Peninsula ⋗1	146	65.00 N	164.00 W
Sewell	140	34.05 S	70.23 W
Seychelles □1	110	4.53 S	55.40 E
Seyches	74	44.33 N	0.18 E
Seydisfjördur	66	65.16 N	14.00 W
Seymour, Austl.	120	37.02 S	145.08 E
Seymour, Conn., U.S.	152	41.24 N	73.04 W
Seymour, Ind., U.S.	158	38.58 N	85.53 W
Seymour, Iowa, U.S.	158	40.44 N	93.07 W
Seymour, Mo., U.S.	158	37.09 N	92.46 W
Seymour, Tex., U.S.	160	33.35 N	99.16 W
Seymour, Wis., U.S.	154	44.31 N	88.20 W
Seyne	74	44.21 N	6.21 E
Seyssel	74	45.57 N	5.49 E
Sézanne	74	48.44 N	3.43 E
Sezimbra	76	38.26 N	9.06 W
Sfax	108	34.44 N	10.46 E
Sfîntu-Gheorghe	80	45.52 N	25.47 E
's-Gravenhage (The Hague)	72	52.06 N	4.18 E
Shabani	116	20.20 S	30.02 E
Shadyside	152	39.58 N	80.45 W
Shafter	168	35.29 N	119.16 W
Shaftesbury	70	51.01 N	2.12 W
Shag Rocks II1	136	53.33 S	42.02 W
Shahdād, Namakzār-e ≊	100	30.30 N	58.30 E
Shahdol	102	23.20 N	81.21 E
Shāhi	88	36.45 N	52.53 E
Shahjahānpur	102	27.53 N	79.55 E
Shahrezā	104	32.01 N	51.52 E
Shāhrūd	104	36.25 N	55.01 E
Shakawe	110	18.23 S	21.50 E
Shaker Heights	152	41.29 N	81.36 W
Shakhty → Šachty	64	47.42 N	40.13 E
Shakopee	154	44.48 N	93.32 W
Shaktoolik	146	64.20 N	161.09 W
Shala, Lake ⊜	112	7.35 N	38.30 E
Shaler Mountains ⋀	142	71.55 N	110.45 W
Shām, Bādiyat ash- ≊	104	32.00 N	40.00 E
Shām, Jabal ash- ⋀	100	23.13 N	57.16 E
Shamattawa	142	55.52 N	92.05 W
Shamo, Lake ⊜	112	5.45 N	37.30 E
Shamokin	152	40.47 N	76.34 W
Shamrock	160	35.12 N	100.14 W
Shandi	112	16.42 N	33.26 E
Shandong □4	88	36.00 N	118.00 E
Shandongbandao ⋗1	88	37.00 N	121.00 E
Shangani ≊	116	18.41 S	27.10 E
Shanghai	88	31.14 N	121.28 E
Shangqiu	88	34.26 N	115.42 E
Shangrao	88	28.26 N	117.58 E
Shangshui	88	33.33 N	114.39 E
Shangxian	88	33.52 N	109.57 E
Shangzhi	88	45.13 N	127.59 E
Shanhaiguan	88	40.01 N	119.45 E
Shannon ≊	70	52.36 N	9.41 W
Shannon, Ill., U.S.	154	42.09 N	89.44 W
Shannon, Miss., U.S.	158	34.07 N	88.43 W
Shantou (Swatow)	88	23.23 N	116.41 E
Shantung Peninsula → Shandongbandao ⋗1	88	37.00 N	121.00 E
Shānxi □4 → Shānxi □4, Zhg.	88	35.00 N	109.00 E
Shānxi □4, Zhg.	88	35.00 N	109.00 E
Shānxi □4, Zhg.	88	37.00 N	112.00 E
Shanyin	88	39.35 N	112.49 E
Shaoguan	88	24.50 N	113.37 E
Shaowu	88	27.20 N	117.28 E
Shaoxing	88	30.00 N	120.35 E
Shaoyang	88	27.06 N	111.25 E
Shark Bay ⊂	118	25.30 S	113.30 E
Sharktooth Mountain ⋀	142	58.35 N	127.57 W
Sharon	152	41.14 N	80.31 W
Sharon Springs	162	38.54 N	101.45 W
Sharpe, Lake ⊜1	162	44.30 N	99.45 W
Sharqi, Jabal ash- ⋀	104	33.26 N	35.51 E
Shashi	88	30.19 N	112.15 E
Sheffield, Ala., U.S.	158	34.46 N	87.40 W
Sheffield, Ill., U.S.	154	41.21 N	89.44 W
Sheffield, Pa., U.S.	152	41.42 N	79.02 W
Sheffield, Tex., U.S.	160	30.41 N	101.49 W
Shekhūpura	102	31.42 N	73.59 E
Shelagyote Peak ⋀	148	55.58 N	127.12 W
Shelbina	158	39.47 N	92.02 W
Shelburn	158	39.11 N	87.24 W
Shelburne, N.S., Can.	150	43.46 N	65.19 W
Shelburne, Ont., Can.	154	44.04 N	80.12 W
Shelburne Falls	152	42.36 N	72.44 W
Shelby, Mich., U.S.	154	43.37 N	86.22 W
Shelby, Miss., U.S.	158	33.57 N	90.46 W
Shelby, Mont., U.S.	166	48.30 N	111.51 W
Shelby, N.C., U.S.	156	35.17 N	81.32 W
Shelby, Ohio, U.S.	152	40.53 N	82.40 W
Shelbyville, Ill., U.S.	158	39.24 N	88.47 W
Shelbyville, Ind., U.S.	158	39.31 N	85.46 W
Shelbyville, Ky., U.S.	158	38.12 N	85.13 W
Shelbyville, Tenn., U.S.	158	35.29 N	86.27 W
Sheldon	162	43.10 N	95.50 W
Shelikof Strait ⊔	146	57.30 N	155.00 W
Shell Beach	168	35.09 N	120.40 W
Shellbrook	142	53.13 N	106.24 W
Shell Creek ≊	164	40.56 N	108.37 W
Shelley	166	43.23 N	112.07 W
Shellharbour	120	34.35 S	150.52 E
Shell Rock	154	42.43 N	92.35 W
Shell Rock ≊	154	42.38 N	92.30 W
Shellsburg	154	42.06 N	91.52 W
Shelton, Conn., U.S.	152	41.19 N	73.05 W
Shelton, Wash., U.S.	166	47.13 N	123.06 W
Shemya Station	146	52.43 N	174.05 E
Shenandoah, Iowa, U.S.	162	40.46 N	95.22 W
Shenandoah, Pa., U.S.	152	40.49 N	76.12 W
Shenandoah ≊	152	39.19 N	77.44 W
Shengfang	88	39.04 N	116.42 E
Shensi → Shānxi □4	88	35.00 N	109.00 E
Shenton, Mount ⋀	122	28.00 S	123.22 E
Shenyang (Mukden)	88	41.48 N	123.27 E
Shenzha	88	30.57 N	88.38 E
Shepherd, Mich., U.S.	154	43.32 N	84.41 W
Shepherd Bay ⊂	142	68.56 N	93.40 W
Shepherdstown	152	39.26 N	77.48 W
Shepherdsville	158	37.59 N	85.43 W
Shepparton	120	36.23 S	145.25 E
Sherard, Cape ➤	142	74.36 N	80.25 W
Sherborne	70	50.57 N	2.31 W
Sherbro Island I	114	7.45 N	12.55 W
Sherbrooke	152	45.24 N	71.54 W
Sherburne	152	42.41 N	75.30 W
Sheridan, Ark., U.S.	158	34.19 N	92.24 W
Sheridan, Ind., U.S.	158	40.08 N	86.13 W
Sheridan, Oreg., U.S.	166	45.06 N	123.24 W
Sheridan, Wyo., U.S.	166	44.47 N	106.57 W
Sheringham Cromer	70	52.57 N	1.12 E
Sherman, Miss., U.S.	158	34.22 N	88.57 W
Sherman, Tex., U.S.	160	33.38 N	96.36 W
Sherman Station	152	45.54 N	68.26 W
Sherrard	154	41.19 N	90.31 W
Sherridon	142	55.07 N	101.05 W
Sherrill	154	42.36 N	90.45 W
's-Hertogenbosch	72	51.41 N	5.19 E
Sherwood, P.E.I., Can.	150	46.17 N	63.08 W
Sherwood, N. Dak., U.S.	162	48.58 N	101.38 W
Sherwood, Tenn., U.S.	158	35.05 N	85.56 W
Sherwood Park	148	53.31 N	113.19 W
Shetland Islands II	70	60.30 N	1.30 W
Shetland Islands Area □4	70	60.30 N	0.15 W
Shexian	88	29.53 N	118.26 E
Sheyenne ≊	162	47.05 N	96.50 W
Sheykh 'Oyeb, Jazīreh-ye I	100	26.48 N	53.15 E
Shibin al-Kawm	112	30.33 N	31.01 E
Shicheng	88	26.22 N	116.22 E
Shickshinny	152	41.09 N	76.09 W
Shidao	88	36.53 N	122.23 E
Shijiazhuang	88	38.03 N	114.28 E
Shijushan	88	39.20 N	106.50 E
Shikarpur	102	27.57 N	68.38 E
Shikoku I	90	33.45 N	133.30 E
Shiliguri	102	26.42 N	88.26 E
Shilka → Šilka	84	53.57 N	115.48 E
Shillelagh	70	52.45 N	6.32 W
Shillington	152	40.18 N	75.58 W
Shillong	102	25.34 N	91.53 E
Shilovo	86	54.19 N	40.51 E
Shimabara	90	32.48 N	130.22 E
Shimizu	90	35.01 N	138.29 E
Shimoda	90	34.40 N	138.57 E
Shimoga	100	13.56 N	75.35 E
Shimonoseki	90	33.57 N	130.57 E
Shimpuru Rapids ⌣	116	17.50 S	19.56 E
Shinano ≊	90	37.57 N	139.00 E
Shinglehouse	152	41.58 N	78.12 W
Shingū	90	33.44 N	135.59 E
Shinkolobwe	110	11.02 S	26.35 E
Shinnston	152	39.23 N	80.18 W
Shinyanga	110	3.40 S	33.26 E
Shiogama	90a	38.19 N	141.01 E
Shiono-misaki ➤	90	33.26 N	135.45 E
Shiping	88	23.47 N	102.30 E
Shippegan	150	47.45 N	64.42 W
Shippensburg	152	40.03 N	77.31 W
Shiprock	164	36.47 N	108.41 W
Shīrāz	104	29.36 N	52.32 E
Shire ≊	110	17.42 S	35.19 E
Shiretoko-misaki ➤1	90a	44.14 N	145.17 E
Shishmaref	146	66.15 N	166.09 W
Shively	158	38.11 N	85.46 W
Shivpuri	102	25.26 N	77.39 E
Shizuoka	90	34.58 N	138.23 E
Shkodër	80	42.05 N	19.30 E
Shoal Creek ≊, U.S.	158	40.28 N	92.42 W
Shoal Creek ≊, U.S.	158	39.01 N	94.43 W
Shoal Lake	142	50.30 N	100.35 W
Shoalwater Bay ⊂	120	22.20 S	150.15 E
Sholāpur	100	17.41 N	75.55 E
Shorewood	154	43.05 N	87.53 W
Shortsville	152	42.57 N	77.14 W
Shoshone	166	42.56 N	114.24 W
Shoshone ≊	166	44.52 N	108.15 W
Shoshone Basin ≊1	166	42.20 N	108.05 W
Shoshone Mountains ⋀	168	39.15 N	117.25 W
Shoshoni	166	43.14 N	108.07 W
Show Low	164	34.15 N	110.02 W
Shreveport	160	32.30 N	93.45 W
Shrewsbury, Eng., U.K.	70	52.43 N	2.45 W
Shrewsbury, Mass., U.S.	152	42.17 N	71.43 W
Shuajingsi	88	32.10 N	103.05 E
Shuangcheng	88	45.22 N	126.18 E
Shuangliao	88	43.31 N	123.32 E
Shuangyashan	88	46.38 N	131.22 E
Shubrā al-Khaymah	112	30.06 N	31.15 E
Shufu → Kashi	88	39.29 N	75.59 E
Shukh, Mount ⋀	148	48.50 N	121.49 W
Shulehe ≊	88	40.20 N	92.50 E
Shunde	88	22.50 N	113.14 E
Shuqrah	100	13.22 N	45.44 E
Shūshtar	104	32.03 N	48.51 E
Shwebo	94	22.34 N	95.42 E
Siak ≊	96	0.48 N	102.08 E
Sialkot	102	32.30 N	74.31 E
Siam → Thailand □1	94	15.00 N	100.00 E
Siam, Gulf of → Thailand, Gulf of ⊂	94	10.00 N	101.00 E

Name	Page	Lat	Long
Sian → Xi'an	88	34.15 N	108.52 E
Sargago Island I	98	9.52 N	126.03 E
Siaskotan, Ostrov I	84	48.49 N	154.06 E
Siau, Pulau I	96	2.42 N	125.24 E
Šiauliai	64	55.56 N	23.19 E
Sibaj	64	52.42 N	58.39 E
Šibenik	78	43.44 N	15.54 E
Siberia → Sibir' →¹	84	65.00 N	110.00 E
Sibérie Occidentale, Dépression de la → Zapadno-Sibirskaja Nizm →¹	82	60.00 N	75.00 E
Siberut, Pulau I	96	1.20 S	98.55 E
Sibi	102	29.33 N	67.53 E
Sibir' (Siberia) →¹	84	65.00 N	110.00 E
Sibir'akova, Ostrov I	84	72.50 N	79.00 E
Sibiti	110	3.41 S	13.21 E
Sibiu	80	45.48 N	24.09 E
Sibiu □⁴	80	46.00 N	24.15 E
Sibley	162	43.24 N	95.45 W
Sibolga	94	1.45 N	98.46 E
Sibsagar	102	26.59 N	94.38 E
Sibu	96	2.19 N	111.51 E
Sibutu Island I	96	4.50 N	119.30 E
Sibutu Passage ⥢	98	4.50 N	119.35 E
Sibuyan Island I	98	12.25 N	122.35 E
Sibuyan Sea ⊤²	98	12.50 N	122.20 E
Siccus ≈	120	31.26 S	139.30 E
Sichote-Alin' ⩓	84	48.00 N	138.00 E
Sichuan □⁴	88	31.00 N	105.00 E
Sicilia □⁴	78	37.30 N	14.00 E
Sicilia I	78	37.30 N	14.00 E
Sicily → Sicilia I	78	37.30 N	14.00 E
Sicily, Strait of ⥢	78	37.20 N	11.20 E
Sicuani	134	14.15 S	71.15 W
Sidenreng	92	4.03 S	119.38 E
Sidhi	100	24.24 N	81.53 E
Sidi Barrâni	112	31.36 N	25.55 E
Sidi bel Abbès	106	35.13 N	0.10 W
Sidi-Bennour	106	32.39 N	8.30 W
Sidmouth	70	50.41 N	3.15 W
Sidnaw	154	46.30 N	88.43 W
Sidney, B.C., Can.	148	48.39 N	123.24 W
Sidney, Iowa, U.S.	162	40.45 N	95.39 W
Sidney, Mont., U.S.	162	47.43 N	104.09 W
Sidney, Nebr., U.S.	162	41.09 N	102.59 W
Sidney, N.Y., U.S.	152	42.19 N	75.24 W
Sidney, Ohio, U.S.	152	40.17 N	84.09 W
Sidney Lanier, Lake ⬚¹	156	34.15 N	83.57 W
Siedlce	72	52.11 N	22.16 E
Siegburg	72	50.47 N	7.12 E
Siegen	72	50.52 N	8.02 E
Siemianowice Śląskie	72	50.19 N	19.01 E
Siemiatycze	72	52.26 N	22.53 E
Siĕmréab	94	13.22 N	103.51 E
Siena	78	43.19 N	11.21 E
Sieradz	72	51.36 N	18.45 E
Sierck-les-Bains	74	49.26 N	6.21 E
Sierpc	72	52.52 N	19.41 E
Sierra Colorada	136	40.35 S	67.50 W
Sierra de Outes	76	42.51 N	8.54 W
Sierra Leone □¹	106	8.30 N	11.30 W
Sierra Vista	164	31.33 N	110.18 W
Sierre	74	46.18 N	7.32 E
Sifnos I	80	36.59 N	24.40 E
Sigean	74	43.02 N	2.59 E
Sighetul Marmaţiei	80	47.56 N	23.54 E
Sighişoara	80	46.13 N	24.48 E
Siglan	84	59.02 N	152.25 E
Sigli	96	5.22 N	95.57 E
Siglufjörður	66a	66.10 N	18.56 W
Sigmaringen	72	48.05 N	9.13 E
Signal Mountain	158	35.07 N	85.21 W
Signy-l'Abbaye	74	49.42 N	4.25 E
Sigourney	154	41.20 N	92.12 W
Sigsig	138	3.01 S	78.45 W
Sigüenza	76	41.04 N	2.38 W
Siguiri	114	11.25 N	9.10 W
Sigulda	86	57.09 N	24.51 E
Sigurd	164	38.50 N	111.58 W
Sihanoukville → Krŏng Preăh Seihanŭ	94	10.38 N	103.30 E
Siirt	104	37.56 N	41.57 E
Sikanni Chief ≈	142	59.22 N	121.50 W
Sikar	102	27.37 N	75.09 E
Sikaram ⩕	100	34.50 N	69.55 E
Sikasso	114	11.19 N	5.40 W
Sikéai	80	36.46 N	22.56 E
Sikeston	158	36.53 N	89.35 W
Siking → Xi'an	88	34.15 N	108.52 E
Sikkim □³	100	27.35 N	88.35 E
Šikotan, Ostrov (Shikotan-tō) I	84	43.47 N	146.45 E
Sikt'ach	84	69.55 N	125.02 E
Silalè	86	55.28 N	22.12 E
Silandro	78	46.38 N	10.46 E
Silao	130	20.56 N	101.26 W
Silay	92	10.48 N	122.58 E
Silchar	102	24.49 N	92.48 E
Siler City	156	35.44 N	79.28 W
Silesia □⁹	72	51.00 N	16.45 E
Siletz	166	44.43 N	123.55 W
Silhouette I	110	4.29 S	55.14 E
Silifke	104	36.22 N	33.56 E
Siliguri	102	26.42 N	88.26 E
Silistra	80	44.07 N	27.16 E
Šilka	84	51.51 N	116.02 E
Šilka ≈	84	53.22 N	121.32 E
Silkeborg	68	56.10 N	9.34 E
Sillamäe	86	59.24 N	27.45 E
Sillé-le-Guillaume	74	48.12 N	0.08 W
Sillem Island I	142	70.55 N	71.30 W
Sillian	72	46.45 N	12.25 E
Siloam Springs	158	36.11 N	94.32 W
Šilovo	86	54.19 N	40.53 E
Silsbee	158	30.21 N	94.11 W
Silvânia	134	16.42 S	48.38 W
Silva Porto	110	12.22 S	16.56 E
Silver	160	32.04 N	100.40 W
Silver Bank →⁴	132	20.40 N	70.20 W
Silver Bank Passage ⥢	132	20.40 N	70.20 W
Silver Bay	154	47.17 N	91.16 W
Silver Bell	164	32.23 N	111.30 W
Silver Bow Park	166	46.01 N	112.28 W
Silver City	164	32.46 N	108.16 W
Silver Creek	152	42.33 N	79.10 W
Silver Lake	166	43.08 N	121.03 W
Silver Peak Range ⩔	168	37.35 N	117.45 W
Silver Spring	152	39.02 N	77.03 W
Silvertip Mountain ⩕	148	49.07 N	113.15 W
Silverton, Colo., U.S.	164	37.49 N	107.40 W
Silverton, Oreg., U.S.	166	45.01 N	122.47 W
Silverton, Tex., U.S.	160	34.28 N	101.19 W
Silvi	78	42.34 N	14.05 E
Silvretta ⩕	74	46.50 N	10.10 E
Simanggang	96	1.12 N	111.32 E
Šimanovsk	84	52.00 N	127.42 E
Simao	88	22.48 N	100.58 E
Simbach	72	48.34 N	12.45 E
Simcoe	152	42.50 N	80.18 W
Simeria	80	45.51 N	23.01 E
Simeulue, Pulau I	96	2.35 N	96.05 E
Simferopol'	64	44.57 N	34.06 E
Simi	80	36.35 N	27.50 E
Simi	168	34.16 N	118.47 W
Similkameen ≈	148	49.06 N	119.26 W
Simiti	138	7.58 N	73.57 W
Simla, Bhārat	102	31.06 N	77.10 E
Simla, Colo., U.S.	162	39.09 N	104.05 W
Simmern	72	49.59 N	7.31 E
Simmesport	158	30.59 N	91.49 W
Simms	166	47.31 N	111.55 W
Simojärvi @	66	66.06 N	27.03 E
Simplon Pass)(	74	46.15 N	8.02 E
Simpson Desert ⬦²	122	25.00 S	137.00 E
Simpson Lake @	142	68.39 N	91.19 W
Simpson Peninsula ⩥	142	68.34 N	88.45 W
Simpson Strait ⥢	142	68.27 N	97.45 W
Simpsonville	156	34.44 N	82.15 W
Sims	158	38.22 N	88.32 W
Simsbury	152	41.52 N	72.48 W
Simušir, Ostrov I	84	46.58 N	152.02 E
Sinai, Mount → Mūsá, Jabal ⩕	112	28.32 N	33.59 E
Sinā', Shibh Jazīrat ⩥¹	112	29.30 N	34.00 E
Sinaia	80	45.21 N	25.33 E
Sinai Peninsula → Sinā', Shibh Jazīrat ⩥¹	112	29.30 N	34.00 E
Sin'aja ≈	84	61.06 N	126.50 E
Sinalunga	78	43.12 N	11.44 E
Sinan	88	27.54 N	108.18 E
Sinãwan	108	31.02 N	10.36 E
Sincé	138	9.15 N	75.09 W
Sincelejo	138	9.18 N	75.24 W
Sinclair	166	41.47 N	107.07 W
Sinclair, Point ⩥	122	32.06 S	133.00 E
Sindara	110	1.02 S	10.40 E
Sindelfingen	72	48.42 N	9.00 E
Sindjai	92	5.07 S	120.15 E
Sindri	100	23.45 N	86.42 E
Sinė	114	14.10 N	16.28 W
Sines	76	37.57 N	8.52 W
Sinfães	76	41.04 N	8.05 W
Singapore	92	1.17 N	103.51 E
Singapore □¹	92	1.22 N	103.48 E
Singapore Strait ⥢	92	1.12 N	104.00 E
Singaradja	96	8.07 S	115.06 E
Singen [hohentwiel]	72	47.46 N	8.50 E
Singida	110	4.49 S	34.45 E
Singkaling Hkāmti	88	26.00 N	95.42 E
Singkang	96	4.08 S	120.01 E
Singkawang	96	0.54 N	109.00 E
Singkep, Pulau I	96	0.30 S	104.25 E
Singleton	120	32.34 S	151.10 E
Singleton, Mount ⩕, Austl.	122	22.00 S	130.04 E
Singleton, Mount ⩕, Austl.	122	29.28 S	117.18 E
Singuédeze (Groot Shingwidzi) ≈	116	23.53 S	32.17 E
Sinj	78	43.42 N	16.38 E
Sinjah	112	13.09 N	33.56 E
Sinkāt	112	18.50 N	36.50 E
Sinkiang → Xinjiang Weiwuer Zizhiqu □⁴	88	40.00 N	85.00 E
Sinnai	78	39.18 N	9.12 E
Sinnamahoning	152	41.19 N	78.06 W
Sinnamary	134	5.23 N	52.57 W
Sinnes	68	58.56 N	6.57 E
Sinnicolau Mare	80	46.05 N	20.38 E
Sinnūris	112	29.25 N	30.52 E
Sinop	82	42.01 N	35.09 E
Sinsheim	72	49.15 N	8.53 E
Sintang	96	0.04 N	111.30 E
Sint Marten (Saint-Martin) I	132	18.04 N	63.04 W
Sint-Niklaas	72	51.10 N	4.08 E
Sinton	160	28.01 N	97.30 W
Sintra	76	38.48 N	9.23 W
Sint-Truiden	72	50.48 N	5.12 E
Sinú ≈	138	9.24 N	75.49 W
Sinŭiju	88	40.05 N	124.24 E
Siocon	92	7.42 N	122.09 E
Siófok	72	46.54 N	18.03 E
Sion	74	46.14 N	7.21 E
Sioux Center	162	43.05 N	96.10 W
Sioux City	162	42.30 N	96.24 W
Sioux Falls	162	43.32 N	96.44 W
Sioux Lookout	142	50.06 N	91.55 W
Sioux Rapids	162	42.53 N	95.09 W
Siping	132	10.08 N	61.30 W
Sipiwesk Lake @	142	55.05 N	97.35 W
Sipsey Creek ≈	158	33.53 N	88.17 W
Sipura, Pulau I	96	2.12 S	99.40 E
Siquia ≈	132	12.09 N	84.14 W
Siquijor Island I	92	9.12 N	123.33 E
Sira ≈	68	58.25 N	6.38 E
Siracusa	78	37.04 N	15.17 E
Sirajganj	102	24.27 N	89.43 E
Sirba ≈	114	13.46 N	1.40 E
Sir Douglas, Mount ⩕	148	50.44 N	115.20 W
Siret ≈	80	45.24 N	28.01 E
Sirevåg	68	58.30 N	5.47 E
Sirhān, Wādī as- V	104	31.00 N	38.00 E
Sir James MacBrien, Mount ⩕	146	62.07 N	127.41 W
Sir Joseph Banks Group II	122	34.32 S	136.17 E
Sirohi	102	24.53 N	72.52 E
Siros	80	37.26 N	24.54 E
Sirri, Jazīreh-ye I	104	25.55 N	54.32 E
Sir Thomas, Mount ⩕	122	27.10 S	129.45 E
Sirvān (Diyālá) ≈	104	33.14 N	44.31 E
Sirvintos	86	55.03 N	24.57 E
Sisak	78	45.29 N	16.23 E
Sisaket	94	15.07 N	104.21 E
Sisili ≈	114	10.16 N	1.15 W
Siskiyou Mountains ⩔	168	41.55 N	123.15 W
Sissach	74	47.28 N	7.49 E
Sisseton	162	45.40 N	97.03 W
Sissonne	74	49.34 N	3.54 E
Sīstān, Daryācheh-ye @	100	31.00 N	61.15 E
Sister Bay	154	45.11 N	87.07 W
Sisteron	74	44.12 N	5.56 E
Sisters	166	44.17 N	121.33 W
Sistersville	152	39.34 N	81.00 W
Sitapur	100	27.35 N	80.40 E
Siteki	116	26.27 S	31.57 E
Sitidgi Lake @	146	68.32 N	132.44 W
Sittang ≈	94	17.10 N	96.58 E
Sittard	72	51.00 N	5.53 E
Sitten → Sion	74	46.14 N	7.21 E
Sittwe (Akyab)	94	20.09 N	92.54 E
Sivas	104	39.45 N	37.02 E
Siverek	104	37.45 N	39.19 E
Siverskij	86	59.21 N	30.05 E
Sivrihisar	82	39.27 N	31.32 E
Sīwah	112	29.12 N	25.31 E
Sizun	74	48.24 N	4.05 W
Sjælland I	68	55.30 N	11.45 E
Sjenica	80	43.16 N	20.00 E
Sjøholt	68	62.29 N	6.48 E
Skærbaek	68	55.09 N	8.46 E
Skaftung	68	62.07 N	21.22 E
Skagen	68	57.44 N	10.36 E
Skagerrak ⥢	68	57.45 N	9.00 E
Skaggs Creek ≈	158	36.54 N	86.04 W
Skagway	146	59.28 N	135.19 W
Skåne □⁹	68	55.59 N	13.30 E
Skånevik	68	59.44 N	5.59 E
Skara	68	58.22 N	13.25 E
Skaraborgs Län □⁶	68	58.20 N	13.30 E
Skarð	66a	65.05 N	22.09 W
Skārdu	102	35.18 N	75.37 E
Skarnes	68	60.15 N	11.41 E
Skarżysko-Kamienna	72	51.08 N	20.53 E
Skaudville	86	55.24 N	22.35 E
Skaugum	68	59.51 N	10.26 E
Skawina	72	49.59 N	19.49 E
Skeena ≈	148	54.09 N	130.02 W
Skeena Mountains ⩔	148	56.00 N	128.00 W
Skegness	70	53.10 N	0.21 E
Skei	68	61.34 N	6.35 E
Skellefteå	66	64.46 N	20.57 E
Skellefteälven ≈	68	64.42 N	21.06 E
Skellytown	160	35.34 N	101.11 W
Ski	68	59.43 N	10.50 E
Skiatook	160	36.22 N	96.01 W
Skibbereen	70	51.33 N	9.15 W
Skidel'	86	53.34 N	24.15 E
Skien	68	59.12 N	9.36 E
Skierniewice	72	51.58 N	20.08 E
Skikda	106	36.50 N	6.58 E
Skilak Lake @	146	60.25 N	150.25 W
Skipton	120	37.41 S	143.22 E
Skive	68	56.34 N	9.02 E
Skjeberg	68	59.14 N	11.12 E
Sklad	84	71.55 N	123.33 E
Škofja Loka	78	46.10 N	14.18 E
Skokie	154	42.03 N	87.46 W
Skopin	86	53.51 N	39.33 E
Skopje	80	41.59 N	21.26 E
Skørping	68	56.50 N	9.53 E
Skotfoss	68	59.12 N	9.30 E
Skotterud	68	59.59 N	12.07 E
Skövde	68	58.24 N	13.50 E
Skovorodino	84	53.59 N	123.55 E
Skowhegan	152	44.46 N	69.43 W
Skreia	68	60.39 N	10.56 E
Skudeneshavn	68	59.09 N	5.17 E
Skultuna	68	59.43 N	16.25 E
Skye I	70	57.15 N	6.10 W
Skyland	156	35.29 N	82.31 W
Skyring, Seno ⥢	136	52.35 S	72.00 W
Slagelse	68	55.24 N	11.22 E
Slamet, Gunung ⩕	96	7.14 S	109.14 E
Slancy	86	59.06 N	28.04 E
Slaný	72	50.11 N	14.04 E
Slater, Iowa, U.S.	154	41.53 N	93.41 W
Slater, Mo., U.S.	162	39.13 N	93.04 W
Slatina	80	44.26 N	24.22 E
Slaton	160	33.26 N	101.39 W
Slautnoje	84	63.00 N	167.59 E
Slav'ansk	64	48.52 N	37.37 E
Slav'ansk-na-Kubani	64	45.15 N	38.08 E
Slave ≈	146	61.18 N	113.39 W
Slave Coast ⥥²	114	6.25 N	3.00 E
Slave Lake	148	55.17 N	114.46 W
Slavgorod, S.S.S.R.	84	53.00 N	78.40 E
Slavgorod, S.S.S.R.	86	53.27 N	31.00 E
Slavonska Požega	78	45.20 N	17.41 E
Slavonski Brod	78	45.10 N	18.01 E
Slavsk (Heinrichswalde)	86	55.03 N	21.41 E
Sławno	72	54.22 N	16.40 E
Slayton	162	43.59 N	95.45 W
Sleaford	70	53.00 N	0.24 W
Sleepy Eye	162	44.18 N	94.43 W
Slidell	158	30.17 N	89.47 W
Sliedrecht	72	51.49 N	4.45 E
Sligo	70	54.17 N	8.28 W
Sligo □⁶	70	54.10 N	8.40 W
Slippery Rock	152	41.04 N	80.03 W
Sliven	80	42.40 N	26.19 E
Sloan	162	42.14 N	96.14 W
Slobodskoj	82	58.42 N	50.12 E
Slobozia	80	44.34 N	27.23 E
Slocomb	158	31.06 N	85.36 W
Slonim	86	53.06 N	25.19 E
Slovenija □³	78	46.15 N	15.10 E
Slovenska Bistrica	78	46.23 N	15.34 E
Slovenská Socialistická Republika □³	72	48.30 N	20.00 E
Slovensko □⁹	72	48.50 N	20.00 E
Sluck	86	53.01 N	27.33 E
Sl'ud'anka	84	51.38 N	103.42 E
Slunj	78	45.07 N	15.35 E
Słupca	72	52.19 N	17.52 E
Słupsk (Stolp)	72	54.28 N	17.01 E
Smackover	158	33.22 N	92.44 W
Småland □⁹	68	57.20 N	15.00 E
Smålininkai	86	55.05 N	22.35 E
Smederevo	80	44.39 N	20.56 E
Smela	64	49.14 N	31.53 E
Smethport	152	41.49 N	78.27 W
Smethwick	70	52.30 N	1.58 W
Smidta, Ostrov I	84	81.08 N	90.48 E
Smilovici	86	53.45 N	28.01 E
Smirnovskij	82	54.31 N	69.25 E
Smith	168	38.48 N	118.20 W
Smith Arm C	146	66.15 N	124.00 W
Smith Center	162	39.47 N	98.47 W
Smithers, B.C., Can.	148	54.47 N	127.10 W
Smithers, W. Va., U.S.	152	38.11 N	81.18 W
Smithfield, N.C., U.S.	156	35.30 N	78.21 W
Smithfield, Utah, U.S.	166	41.50 N	111.50 W
Smithfield, Va., U.S.	156	36.59 N	76.38 W
Smiths	158	32.32 N	85.06 W
Smiths Falls	152	44.54 N	76.01 W
Smithton	120	40.51 S	145.07 E
Smithville, Mo., U.S.	162	39.23 N	94.35 W
Smithville, Tenn., U.S.	158	35.58 N	85.49 W
Smithville, Tex., U.S.	160	30.00 N	97.09 W
Smokey Dome ⩕	166	43.29 N	114.56 W
Smoky ≈	148	56.10 N	117.21 W
Smoky Cape ⩥	120	30.56 S	153.05 E
Smoky Hill ≈	162	39.03 N	96.48 W
Smoky Hill, North Fork ≈	162	39.28 N	98.26 W
Smoky Hills ⩓²	162	39.15 N	99.00 W
Smolensk	86	54.47 N	32.03 E
Smolevici	86	54.02 N	28.07 E
Smoljan	80	41.35 N	24.41 E
Smoot	166	42.37 N	110.55 W
Smorgon'	86	54.29 N	26.24 E
Smyrna → İzmir, Tür.	82	38.25 N	27.09 E
Smyrna, Del., U.S.	152	39.18 N	75.36 W
Smyrna, Ga., U.S.	156	33.53 N	84.31 W
Smyrna, Tenn., U.S.	158	35.59 N	86.31 W
Smythe, Mount ⩕	142	57.54 N	124.53 W
Snaefell ⩕	70	54.16 N	4.27 W
Snag	146	62.22 N	140.22 W
Snake ≈, Yukon, Can.	146	65.58 N	134.10 W
Snake ≈, U.S.	166	46.12 N	119.02 W
Snake River Plain ⊒	166	42.45 N	114.30 W
Sneads	158	30.42 N	84.55 W
Sneedville	156	36.32 N	83.13 W
Sneek	72	53.02 N	5.40 E
Snelling	168	37.31 N	120.26 W
Snina	72	48.59 N	22.09 E
Snøhetta ⩕	68	62.20 N	9.17 E
Snohomish	166	47.55 N	122.06 W
Snønuten ⩕	68	59.35 N	6.59 E
Snover	152	43.28 N	82.58 W
Snowbird Lake @	142	60.41 N	103.00 W
Snowdon ⩕	70	53.04 N	4.05 W
Snowdonia National Park ⦿	70	53.00 N	3.57 W
Snowdrift	142	62.23 N	110.47 W
Snow Hill	152	38.11 N	75.23 W
Snow Lake	142	54.53 N	100.02 W
Snowy Mountains ⩔	120	36.30 S	148.20 E
Snowy Peak ⩕	164	33.57 N	114.58 W
Snyder	160	32.44 N	100.55 W
Soacha	138	4.35 N	74.13 W
Soalala	117b	16.06 S	45.20 E
Soap Lake	166	47.23 N	119.29 W
Sobat ≈	112	9.22 N	31.33 E
Sobernheim	72	49.47 N	7.38 E
Sobrado	76	43.02 N	8.16 W
Sobral	134	3.42 S	40.21 W
Sochaczew	72	52.14 N	20.14 E
Soči	64	43.35 N	39.45 E
Social Circle	156	33.39 N	83.43 W
Society Hill	156	34.31 N	79.51 W
Socompa, Paso)(	140	24.27 S	68.18 W
Socorro, Sierra de (Sierra Madre) ⩔	130	15.30 N	92.35 W
Socorro, Cerro ⩕	138	10.28 N	70.48 W
Socorro, Col.	138	6.29 N	73.16 W
Socorro, N. Mex., U.S.	164	34.04 N	106.54 W
Socorro, Isla I	130	18.45 N	110.58 W
Socotra → Suquṭrá I	100	12.30 N	54.00 E
Soda Lake @	168	35.08 N	116.04 W
Sodankylä	66	67.29 N	26.32 E
Soda Springs	166	42.39 N	111.36 W
Soddy	158	35.17 N	85.10 W
Söderhamn	68	61.18 N	17.03 E
Södermanlands Län □⁶	68	59.15 N	16.40 E
Södertälje	68	59.12 N	17.37 E
Sodo	108	6.52 N	37.47 E
Södra Kvarken ⥢	68	60.15 N	19.05 E
Sodus	152	43.14 N	77.04 W
Soe	96	9.52 S	124.17 E
Sofia → Sofija	80	42.41 N	23.19 E
Sofia ≈	117b	15.27 S	47.23 E
Sofija (Sofia)	80	42.41 N	23.19 E
Sofrino	86	56.09 N	37.56 E
Sogamoso	138	5.43 N	72.56 W
Sognafjorden C	68	61.06 N	5.10 E
Søgne	68	58.05 N	7.49 E
Sogn og Fjordane □⁶	68	61.30 N	6.50 E
Soignies	72	50.35 N	4.04 E
Soini	68	62.52 N	24.13 E
Soissons	74	49.22 N	3.20 E
Sôjosŏn-man C	88	39.20 N	124.50 E
Sokal'skogo, Proliv ⥢	84	79.00 N	100.25 E
Sökch'o	88	38.12 N	128.36 E
Söke	82	37.45 N	27.24 E
Sokna	68	60.14 N	9.54 E
Sokol, S.S.S.R.	72	53.25 N	23.31 E
Sokol, S.S.S.R.	86	59.28 N	40.10 E
Sokołka	72	53.25 N	23.31 E
Sokolov	72	50.14 N	12.40 E
Sokołów Podlaski	72	52.25 N	22.15 E
Sokol'skoje	86	57.08 N	43.13 E
Sokoto	114	13.04 N	5.16 E
Sokoto ≈	114	11.20 N	4.10 E
Sola	156	26.57 N	82.01 W
Solbad Hall in Tirol	72	47.17 N	11.31 E
Solberg	68	63.47 N	17.38 E
Sol de Julio	140	29.33 S	63.27 W
Soldotna	146	60.29 N	151.04 W
Soledad, Col.	138	10.55 N	74.46 W
Soledad, Calif., U.S.	168	36.26 N	121.19 W
Soledad Diez Gutiérrez	130	22.12 N	100.57 W
Solenzara	74	41.51 N	9.23 E
Solhem	68	60.53 N	5.27 E
Soligalič	86	59.05 N	42.17 E
Solihull	70	52.25 N	1.45 W
Solikamsk	66	59.39 N	56.47 E
Sol-Ileck	82	51.10 N	54.59 E
Solingen	72	51.10 N	7.05 E
Sollentuna	68	59.22 N	18.01 E
Solna	68	59.22 N	18.01 E
Solnečnogorsk	86	56.11 N	36.59 E
Sologne →¹	74	47.40 N	2.00 E
Sologoncy	84	66.13 N	114.14 E
Solok	94	0.48 S	100.39 E
Solomon	164	32.49 N	109.38 W
Solomon ≈	162	39.19 N	97.22 W
Solomon Sea ⊤²	118	8.00 S	155.00 E
Solon, Maine, U.S.	152	44.57 N	69.52 W
Solon Springs	154	46.22 N	91.48 W
Solopaca	78	41.11 N	14.33 E
Solotča	86	54.48 N	39.51 E
Solovjevsk	84	49.55 N	115.42 E
Sol'oy	68	59.09 N	11.19 E
Solsona	76	42.00 N	1.31 E
Solt	72	46.48 N	19.00 E
Soltau	72	52.59 N	9.49 E
Solvang	168	34.36 N	120.08 W
Solvay	152	43.04 N	76.12 W
Solway Firth C¹	70	54.50 N	3.35 W
Solwezi	110	12.11 S	26.25 E
Somalia → Somalia □¹	108	10.00 N	49.00 E
Sombor	80	45.46 N	19.07 E
Sombrerete	130	23.38 N	103.39 W
Somerset, Ky., U.S.	156	37.05 N	84.36 W
Somerset, Mass., U.S.	152	41.45 N	71.09 W
Somerset □⁶	70	51.10 N	3.00 W
Somerset East	116	32.42 S	25.35 E
Somerset Island I	142	73.15 N	93.30 W
Somers Point	152	39.18 N	74.36 W
Somerton	164	32.36 N	114.43 W
Somerville	152	40.34 N	74.37 W
Somes (Szamos) ≈	74	49.55 N	2.30 E
Sömmerda	72	51.10 N	11.07 E
Somogy □⁶	132	46.25 N	11.13 E
Somport, Puerto de)(	76	42.48 N	0.31 W
Sompuis	74	48.41 N	4.23 E
Son ≈	100	25.42 N	84.52 E
Sønderborg	68	54.55 N	9.47 E
Sønder Omme	68	55.50 N	8.54 E
Sondershausen	72	51.22 N	10.52 E
Søndre Strømfjord	142	66.59 N	50.40 W
Søndre Strømfjord C²	142	67.30 N	52.00 W
Sondrio	78	46.10 N	9.52 E
Sonepur	100	20.50 N	83.54 E
Songea	110	10.41 S	35.39 E
Songhuahu @¹	88	43.20 N	127.07 E
Songhuajiang ≈	88	47.42 N	132.30 E
Songjiang	88	31.01 N	121.14 E
Songkhla	94	7.13 N	100.34 E
Songnim	88	38.44 N	125.38 E
Songo	110	7.22 S	14.51 E
Songzong	88	29.45 N	96.10 E
Sonipat	100	28.59 N	77.01 E
Sonmiāni Bay C	102	25.15 N	66.30 E
Sonneberg	72	50.22 N	11.10 E
Sonoma	168	38.17 N	122.27 W
Sonora, Ariz., U.S.	164	33.10 N	111.00 W
Sonora, Calif., U.S.	168	37.59 N	120.23 W
Sonora, Tex., U.S.	160	30.34 N	100.39 W
Sonora □³	130	29.50 N	111.00 W
Sonora ≈	130	28.48 N	111.33 W
Sonora Desert ⬦²	130	33.00 N	114.00 W
Sonsonate	132	13.43 N	89.44 W
Sonsorol Islands II	92	5.20 N	132.13 E
Son-tay	88	21.08 N	105.30 E
Sonthofen	72	47.31 N	10.17 E
Soo → Sault Sainte Marie	154	46.30 N	84.21 W
Soochow → Suzhou	88	31.18 N	120.37 E
Sopchoppy	156	30.04 N	84.29 W
Soperton	156	32.22 N	82.35 W
Sopot	72	54.28 N	18.34 E
Sopron	72	47.41 N	16.36 E
Sop's Arm	150	49.47 N	56.55 W
Sora	78	41.43 N	13.37 E
Sorata	138	15.46 S	68.39 W
Sorel	152	46.02 N	73.07 W
Sorell	120	42.47 S	147.34 E
Sorell, Cape ⩥	120	42.12 S	145.10 E
Sorgono	78	40.01 N	9.06 E
Sorgues	74	44.01 N	4.52 E
Soria	76	41.46 N	2.28 W
Sorl ≈	68	62.29 N	17.17 E
Soro	68	55.26 N	11.34 E
Sorocaba	140	23.29 S	47.27 W
Soročinsk	82	52.26 N	53.10 E
Sorol I¹	92	8.08 N	140.23 E
Sorong	124	0.53 S	131.15 E
Soroti	108	1.43 N	33.37 E
Sørøya I	66	70.36 N	22.46 E
Sorrento, It.	78	40.37 N	14.22 E
Sorrento, La., U.S.	158	30.11 N	90.51 W
Sorsakoski	68	62.27 N	27.39 E
Sorsogon	92	12.58 N	124.00 E
Sortavala	66	61.42 N	30.41 E
Sør-Trøndelag □⁶	68	63.00 N	10.40 E
Šoška	66	62.42 N	50.40 E
Sosnogorsk	66	63.37 N	53.51 E
Sosnovka	86	53.16 N	51.17 E
Sosnovo-Oz'orskoje	84	52.31 N	111.32 E
Sosnovskij Bor	72	55.48 N	43.10 E
Sosnovyj Bor	86	59.55 N	29.07 E
Sospel	74	43.53 N	7.27 E
Šostka	64	51.52 N	33.30 E
Sos'va, S.S.S.R.	66	64.08 N	28.25 E
Sos'va, S.S.S.R.	82	59.10 N	61.50 E
Sotkamo	68	64.08 N	28.25 E
Sotteville	74	49.25 N	1.06 E
Soudan	154	47.49 N	92.10 W
Souderton	152	40.19 N	75.19 W
Souillac	74	44.54 N	1.29 E
Souilly	74	49.01 N	5.17 E
Souk Ahras	78	36.23 N	8.00 E
Sŏul (Seoul)	88	37.33 N	126.58 E
Soulac-sur-Mer	74	45.31 N	1.07 W
Sources, Mount aux ⩕	116	28.46 S	28.52 E
Soure	76	40.03 N	8.38 W
Souris	142	49.39 N	99.34 W
Souris ≈	162	49.39 N	99.34 W
Sourlake	158	30.09 N	94.25 W
Sourou ≈	114	12.45 N	3.25 E
Sousa	134	6.45 S	38.14 W
Sousel	134	38.57 N	7.40 W
Sousse	106	35.49 N	10.38 E
South Africa □¹	116	30.00 S	26.00 E
Southampton, Ont., Can.	154	44.29 N	81.23 W
Southampton, Eng., U.K.	70	50.55 N	1.25 W
Southampton, N.Y., U.S.	152	40.53 N	72.24 W
Southampton, Cape ⩥	142	62.09 N	83.40 W
Southampton Island I	142	64.20 N	84.40 W
South Andaman I	94	11.45 N	92.45 E
South Australia □³	118	30.00 S	135.00 E
South Bay	156	26.40 N	80.43 W
South Bay C	142	63.58 N	83.30 W
South Beloit	154	42.29 N	89.02 W
South Bend, Ind., U.S.	154	41.41 N	86.15 W
South Bend, Wash., U.S.	166	46.39 N	123.48 W
South Boston	156	36.42 N	78.54 W
Southbridge	152	42.05 N	72.02 W
South Bruny I	120	43.23 S	147.17 E
South Burlington	152	44.28 N	73.13 W
South Carolina □³	144	34.00 N	81.00 W
South Charleston	152	38.22 N	81.44 W
South China Sea ⊤²	92	10.00 N	113.00 E
South Dakota □³	144	44.15 N	100.00 W
South Deerfield	152	42.29 N	72.37 W
South East Cape ⩥	120	43.39 S	146.50 E
South East Point ⩥	120	39.00 S	146.20 E
Southend-on-Sea	70	51.33 N	0.43 E
Southern Alps ⩔	126	43.30 S	170.30 E
Southern Cross	122	31.13 S	119.19 E
Southern Indian Lake @	142	57.10 N	98.40 W
Southern Pines	156	35.11 N	79.23 W
Southern Yemen → Yemen, People's Democratic Republic of □¹	100	15.00 N	48.00 E
South Esk ≈	70	56.43 N	2.31 W
South Fallsburg	152	41.43 N	74.38 W
Southfield	154	42.28 N	83.17 W
Southgate	154	42.12 N	83.13 W
South Georgia I	136	54.15 S	36.45 W
South Glamorgan □⁶	70	51.30 N	3.25 W
South Greenwood	156	34.10 N	82.09 W
South Hadley Falls	152	42.14 N	72.36 W
South Haven, Kans., U.S.	162	37.03 N	97.24 W
South Haven, Mich., U.S.	154	42.24 N	86.16 W
South Henik Lake @	142	61.30 N	97.30 W
South Hero	152	44.39 N	73.19 W
South Hill	156	36.43 N	78.08 W
South Holston Lake @¹	156	36.35 N	82.00 W
South Houston	160	29.40 N	95.14 W
South Indian Lake	142	56.46 N	98.57 W
South International Falls	154	48.35 N	93.15 W
South Island I, Kenya	108	2.38 N	36.36 E
South Island I, N.Z.	126	43.50 S	171.00 E
South Korea → Korea, South □¹	88	36.30 N	128.00 E
South Lake Tahoe	168	38.57 N	119.59 W
South Llano ≈	160	30.28 N	99.46 W
South Lyon	154	42.27 N	83.39 W
South Miami	156	25.42 N	80.17 W
South Molton	70	51.01 N	3.50 W
South Nahanni ≈	146	61.03 N	123.20 W
South Naknek	146	58.43 N	157.00 W
South Ogden	166	41.12 N	111.59 W
South Paris	152	44.13 N	70.30 W
South Pekin	154	40.30 N	89.39 W
South Pittsburg	158	35.01 N	85.42 W
South Platte ≈	162	41.07 N	100.42 W
South Porcupine	154	48.28 N	81.13 W
Southport, Austl.	120	27.58 S	153.25 E
Southport, Eng., U.K.	70	53.39 N	3.01 W
Southport, N.C., U.S.	156	33.55 N	78.01 W
Southport, N.Y., U.S.	152	42.03 N	76.49 W
South Portland	152	43.38 N	70.15 W
South River	152	40.27 N	74.22 W
South Rockwood	154	42.04 N	83.16 W
South Salt Lake	166	40.43 N	111.53 W
South San Francisco	168	37.39 N	122.24 W
South Saskatchewan ≈	142	53.15 N	105.05 W
South Shields	70	55.00 N	1.25 W
South Sioux City	162	42.28 N	96.24 W
South Spicer Island I	142	68.08 N	79.13 W
South Superior	166	41.45 N	108.58 W
South Trail	160	28.12 N	97.18 W
South Tucson	164	32.12 N	110.56 W
South Ventana Cone ⩕	168	36.17 N	121.38 W
South Vietnam → Vietnam, South	94	13.00 N	108.00 E
South West Africa □²	116	22.00 S	17.00 E
South West Cape ⩥	126	47.17 S	167.28 E
South West City	162	36.31 N	94.37 W
South West Fargo	162	46.52 N	96.54 W
South Williamson	156	37.40 N	82.17 W
South Windham	152	43.44 N	70.26 W
Sovetsk (Tilsit)	86	55.05 N	21.53 E
Sovetsk, S.S.S.R.	66	57.37 N	48.58 E
Sovetskaja Gavan'	84	48.58 N	140.18 E
Sovetskij	86	60.32 N	28.41 E
Soviet Union → Union of Soviet Socialist Republics □¹	82	60.00 N	80.00 E
Søvik	68	62.33 N	6.18 E
Spa	72	50.30 N	5.52 E
Spain □¹	64	40.00 N	4.00 W
Spalding	70	52.47 N	0.10 W
Spaniard's Bay	150	47.37 N	53.17 W
Spanish	154	46.12 N	82.21 W
Spanish Fork	164	40.07 N	111.39 W
Spanish North Africa □²	106	35.53 N	5.19 W
Spanish Peak ⩕	166	44.24 N	119.46 W
Spanish Sahara → Western Sahara □²	106	24.30 N	13.00 W
Spanish Town	132	18.00 N	76.57 W
Sparks, Ga., U.S.	156	31.11 N	83.26 W
Sparks, Nev., U.S.	168	39.32 N	119.45 W
Sparland	154	41.02 N	89.26 W
Sparlingville	154	42.58 N	82.30 W
Sparrows Point	152	39.13 N	76.29 W
Sparta → Spárti, Ellás	80	37.05 N	22.27 E
Sparta, Ga., U.S.	156	33.17 N	82.58 W
Sparta, Ill., U.S.	158	38.07 N	89.42 W
Sparta, Mich., U.S.	154	43.10 N	85.42 W
Sparta, N.J., U.S.	152	41.01 N	74.39 W
Sparta, N.C., U.S.	156	36.30 N	81.07 W
Sparta, Tenn., U.S.	158	35.56 N	85.29 W
Sparta, Wis., U.S.	154	43.57 N	90.47 W
Spartanburg	156	34.57 N	81.55 W
Spárti (Sparta)	80	37.05 N	22.27 E
Spartivento, Capo ⩥	78	38.53 N	8.50 E
Spas-Demensk	86	54.25 N	34.01 E
Spas-Klepiki	84	40.00 N	40.13 E
Spassk-Dal'nij	84	44.35 N	132.48 E
Spearfish	162	44.30 N	103.52 W
Spearman	160	36.12 N	101.12 W
Spednic Lake @	150	45.36 N	67.35 W
Speedway	158	39.47 N	86.15 W
Spello	78	42.59 N	12.40 E
Spenard	146	61.11 N	149.55 W
Spencer Bay	142	69.32 N	93.31 W
Spencer, Iowa, U.S.	162	43.09 N	95.09 W
Spencer, Mass., U.S.	152	42.15 N	71.60 W
Spencer, N.C., U.S.	156	35.37 N	80.26 W
Spencer, S. Dak., U.S.	162	43.44 N	97.36 W
Spencer, W. Va., U.S.	152	38.48 N	81.21 W
Spencer Bay ⩥	120	35.18 S	136.53 E
Spencer Gulf C	120	34.00 S	137.00 E
Spencerville	152	40.42 N	84.21 W
Speyer	72	49.19 N	8.26 E
Spezia → La Spezia	78	44.07 N	9.50 E
Spiez	74	46.41 N	7.39 E
Spinazzola	78	40.58 N	16.06 E
Spincourt	74	49.20 N	5.40 E
Spindale	156	35.22 N	81.55 W
Spirit Lake, Idaho, U.S.	166	47.58 N	116.52 W
Spirit Lake, Iowa, U.S.	162	43.25 N	95.06 W
Spišská Nová Ves	72	48.57 N	20.34 E
Spittal an der Drau	72	46.48 N	13.30 E
Spitz	72	48.22 N	15.25 E
Split	78	43.31 N	16.27 E
Split Lake @	142	56.08 N	96.15 W
Split Rock Creek ≈	162	43.44 N	96.35 W
Splügen	74	46.33 N	9.20 E
Spofford	160	29.11 N	100.25 W
Spokane ≈	166	47.40 N	117.23 W
Spokane	166	47.40 N	117.25 W
Spoleto	78	42.44 N	12.44 E
Spooner	154	45.50 N	91.53 W
Sporoje	84	62.20 N	151.03 E
Spratly Island I	96	8.38 N	111.55 E
Spray	166	44.50 N	119.48 W
Spremberg	72	51.34 N	14.22 E
Spring, South Fork ≈	158	36.26 N	91.30 W
Spring ≈	162	39.43 N	91.10 W
Spring City, Tenn., U.S.	156	35.42 N	84.52 W
Spring City, Utah, U.S.	164	39.29 N	111.30 W
Spring Creek, Austl.	120	18.00 S	137.55 E
Spring Creek ≈	158	40.40 N	87.46 W
Springdale, Newf., Can.	150	49.30 N	56.04 W
Springdale, Ark., U.S.	158	36.11 N	94.08 W
Springe	72	52.12 N	9.32 E
Springerville	164	34.08 N	109.17 W
Springfield, Colo., U.S.	160	37.24 N	102.37 W
Springfield, Fla., U.S.	156	30.09 N	85.37 W
Springfield, Ill., U.S.	154	39.48 N	89.40 W
Springfield, Ky., U.S.	156	37.41 N	85.13 W
Springfield, Mass., U.S.	152	42.06 N	72.35 W
Springfield, Minn., U.S.	162	44.14 N	94.59 W
Springfield, Mo., U.S.	158	37.13 N	93.17 W
Springfield, Ohio, U.S.	152	39.55 N	83.48 W
Springfield, Oreg., U.S.	166	44.03 N	123.01 W
Springfield, S. Dak., U.S.	162	42.51 N	97.54 W
Springfield, Tenn., U.S.	158	36.31 N	86.52 W
Springfield, Vt., U.S.	152	43.18 N	72.29 W
Springfontein	116	30.19 S	25.36 E
Spring Garden	156	36.27 N	79.47 W
Spring Glen	164	39.41 N	110.51 W
Spring Green	154	43.11 N	90.04 W
Spring Grove, Minn., U.S.	154	43.33 N	91.38 W
Spring Grove, Pa., U.S.	152	39.52 N	76.51 W
Springhill, N.S., Can.	150	45.39 N	64.03 W
Spring Hill, Tenn., U.S.	158	35.45 N	86.56 W
Spring Mountains ⩔	168	36.10 N	115.40 W
Springs	116	26.13 S	28.25 E
Springsure	120	24.07 S	148.05 E
Spring Valley, Calif., U.S.	168	32.45 N	116.59 W
Spring Valley, Ill., U.S.	154	41.20 N	89.12 W
Spring Valley, N.Y., U.S.	152	41.07 N	74.03 W
Spring Valley Creek ≈	152	40.54 N	76.28 W
Springville, Iowa, U.S.	154	42.03 N	91.27 W
Springville, N.Y., U.S.	152	42.31 N	78.40 W
Springville, Utah, U.S.	164	40.10 N	111.37 W
Spruce Grove	148	53.33 N	113.55 W
Spruce Knob ⩕	152	38.42 N	79.32 W
Spruce Pine	156	35.55 N	82.04 W
Squamish	148	49.42 N	123.09 W
Squires, Mount ⩕	122	26.12 S	127.28 E
Srbija □⁹	80	44.00 N	21.00 E
Srbobran	80	45.33 N	19.48 E
Sredinnyj Chrebet ⩔	84	56.00 N	158.00 E
Sredkolymsk	84	67.27 N	153.41 E
Srednesibirskoje Ploskogor'e ⩓¹	82	65.00 N	105.00 E
Vozvyšennost' ⩓¹	82	52.00 N	38.00 E
Srem	80	52.06 N	17.01 E
Sremska Mitrovica	80	44.58 N	19.37 E
Sremski Karlovci	80	45.12 N	19.57 E
Sri Gangānagar	102	29.55 N	73.53 E
Sri Lanka □¹	100	7.00 N	81.00 E

Symbols in the index entries are identified on page 203.

Name	Page	Lat	Long
Srinagar	102	34.05 N	74.49 E
Środa Wielkopolski	72	52.14 N	17.17 E
Stade	72	53.36 N	9.28 E
Stadl-Paura	72	48.05 N	13.53 E
Stadskanaal	72	53.00 N	6.55 E
Stadt Haag	72	48.07 N	14.34 E
Stadthagen	72	52.19 N	9.13 E
Stadtildenhof	72	51.53 N	9.37 E
Staffelstein	72	50.06 N	11.00 E
Stafford, Eng., U.K.	70	52.48 N	2.07 W
Stafford, Conn., U.S.	162	37.58 N	98.36 W
Stafford, Kans., U.S.	152	41.03 N	73.32 W
Stafford, Tex., U.S.	160	29.37 N	95.34 W
Staffordshire □6	70	52.50 N	2.00 W
Stafford Springs	152	41.57 N	72.18 W
Staines	70	51.26 N	0.31 W
Stainz	72	46.54 N	15.16 E
Staked Plain → Estacado, Llano ≃	160	33.30 N	102.40 W
Staheim	68	60.50 N	6.40 E
Stalin (Kuçevë)	80	40.48 N	19.54 E
Stalingorsk → Novomoskovsk	86	54.05 N	38.13 W
Stalowa Wola	72	50.35 N	22.02 E
Stambaugh	154	46.04 N	88.38 W
Stamford, Austl.	120	21.16 S	143.49 E
Stamford, Eng., U.K.	70	52.39 N	0.29 W
Stamford, Conn., U.S.	152	41.03 N	73.32 W
Stamford, N.Y., U.S.	152	42.25 N	74.37 W
Stamford, Tex., U.S.	160	32.57 N	99.48 W
Stamps	158	33.22 N	93.30 W
Stanberry	158	40.13 N	94.35 W
Standard	146	64.47 N	148.32 W
Standerton	116	26.58 S	29.07 E
Standish	154	43.59 N	83.57 W
Stanfield, Ariz., U.S.	164	32.53 N	111.58 W
Stanfield, Oreg., U.S.	166	45.47 N	119.13 W
Stanford	156	37.32 N	84.40 W
Stange	68	60.43 N	11.11 E
Stanislaus	168	37.40 N	121.14 W
Stanke Dimitrov	80	42.16 N	23.07 E
Stanley, Falk. Is.	136	51.42 S	57.51 W
Stanley, N.C., U.S.	156	35.21 N	81.06 W
Stanley, Wis., U.S.	154	44.58 N	90.56 W
Stanley Falls ⇃	110	0.15 N	25.30 E
Stanleyville → Kisangani	110	0.30 N	25.12 E
Stann Creek	130	16.58 N	88.13 W
Stanovoj Chrebet ⋌	84	56.20 N	126.00 E
Stanovoje Nagorje (Stanovoy Mountains) ⋌	84	56.00 N	114.00 E
Stanovoy Mountains → Stanovoje Nagorje ⋌	84	56.00 N	114.00 E
Stanthorpe	120	28.39 S	151.57 E
Stanton, Ky., U.S.	156	37.54 N	83.52 W
Stanton, Mich., U.S.	154	43.18 N	85.05 W
Stanton, Nebr., U.S.	162	41.57 N	97.14 W
Stanton, Tex., U.S.	160	32.08 N	101.48 W
Staples	162	46.21 N	94.48 W
Starachowice	72	51.03 N	21.04 E
Staraja Russa	86	58.00 N	31.23 E
Staraja Vičuga	86	57.16 N	41.53 E
Stara Pazova	80	44.59 N	20.10 E
Stara Planina (Balkan Mountains) ⋌	80	43.15 N	25.00 E
Stara Zagora	80	42.25 N	25.38 E
Starbuck, Minn., U.S.	162	45.37 N	95.32 W
Starbuck, Wash., U.S.	166	47.31 N	118.08 W
Star City	158	33.56 N	91.51 W
Stargard Szczeciński (Stargard in Pommern)	72	53.20 N	15.02 E
Stargo	164	33.04 N	109.21 W
Starica	86	56.30 N	34.56 E
Starke	156	29.57 N	82.07 W
Starkville	158	33.28 N	88.48 W
Starnberg	72	48.00 N	11.20 E
Starobin	86	52.44 N	27.28 E
Starodub	86	52.35 N	32.46 E
Starogard Gdański	72	53.59 N	18.33 E
Staryj Oskol	82	51.19 N	37.51 E
Stassfurt	72	51.51 N	11.34 E
Staszów	72	50.34 N	21.40 E
State Center	154	42.01 N	93.10 W
State College, Miss., U.S.	158	33.26 N	88.47 W
State College, Pa., U.S.	152	40.48 N	77.52 W
Stateline	168	38.57 N	119.57 W
Statesboro	156	32.26 N	81.47 W
Statesville	156	35.47 N	80.53 W
Station Peak ⋀	122	21.10 S	118.11 E
Staunton, Ill., U.S.	158	39.01 N	89.47 W
Staunton, Va., U.S.	152	38.09 N	79.04 W
Stavanger	68	58.58 N	5.45 E
Stavenhagen	72	53.42 N	12.53 E
Staveren	72	52.53 N	5.22 E
Stavern	68	59.00 N	10.02 E
Stavropol'	82	45.02 N	41.59 E
Stawell	120	37.04 S	142.46 E
Stawiszyn	72	51.55 N	18.07 E
Stayton	166	44.48 N	122.48 W
Steamboat Springs	164	40.29 N	106.50 W
Stebbins	146	63.32 N	162.18 W
Steele, Mo., U.S.	158	36.05 N	89.50 W
Steele, N. Dak., U.S.	162	46.51 N	99.55 W
Steeleville	158	38.00 N	89.40 W
Steelton	152	40.14 N	76.49 W
Steelville	158	37.58 N	91.22 W
Steenbergen	72	51.35 N	4.19 E
Steenkool	124	2.07 S	133.32 E
Steenwijk	72	52.47 N	6.08 E
Steep Point ⊁	122	26.08 S	113.08 E
Stefansson Island I	142	73.17 N	106.45 W
Stege	68	54.59 N	12.18 E
Stegeborg	68	58.26 N	16.35 E
Stehekin	148	48.19 N	120.39 W
Steiermark □3	72	47.10 N	15.10 E
Steinach	72	49.32 N	11.28 E
Steinbach	162	49.32 N	96.41 W
Steinkjer	68	64.01 N	11.30 E
Steinshamn	68	62.47 N	6.29 E
Stellarton	150	45.34 N	62.40 W
Stellenbosch	116	33.58 S	18.50 E
Stenay	74	49.29 N	5.11 E
Stendal	72	52.36 N	11.51 E
Stepanakert	104	39.49 N	46.44 E
Stephen	162	48.27 N	96.53 W
Stephens	158	33.25 N	93.04 W
Stephens, Port ⊂	120	32.45 S	152.05 E
Stephenville, Newf., Can.	150	48.33 N	58.35 W
Stephenville, Tex., U.S.	160	32.13 N	98.12 W
Stephenville Crossing	150	48.30 N	58.26 W
Stepn'ak	82	52.50 N	70.50 E
Sterkstroom	116	31.32 S	26.32 E
Sterling, Alaska, U.S.	146	60.28 N	150.08 W
Sterling, Colo., U.S.	162	40.37 N	103.13 W
Sterling, Ill., U.S.	154	41.48 N	89.42 W
Sterling, Kans., U.S.	162	38.13 N	98.12 W
Sterling, Okla., U.S.	160	34.45 N	98.10 W
Sterling City	160	31.50 N	100.59 W
Sterlington	158	32.42 N	92.06 W
Šterltamak	64	53.37 N	55.58 E
Šternberk	72	49.44 N	17.18 E
Stettin → Szczecin	72	53.24 N	14.32 E
Stettler	148	52.19 N	112.43 W
Steubenville	152	40.22 N	80.37 W
Stevenage	70	51.55 N	0.14 W
Stevenson	166	45.42 N	121.53 W
Stevens Point	154	44.31 N	89.34 W
Stevens Village	146	66.01 N	149.05 W
Stevensville	166	46.30 N	114.05 W
Stewardson	158	39.16 N	88.38 W
Stewart, B.C., Can.	148	55.56 N	129.59 W
Stewart, Minn., U.S.	162	44.44 N	94.29 W
Stewart, Nev., U.S.	168	39.07 N	119.45 W
Stewart ⇃	146	63.19 N	139.25 W
Stewart Island I	126	47.00 S	167.52 E
Stewarton	70	55.41 N	4.31 W
Stewartstown	152	39.45 N	76.35 W
Stewartville	154	43.51 N	92.29 W
Steyr	72	48.03 N	14.25 E
Stigler	160	35.15 N	95.08 W
Stikine ≃, B.C., Can.	142	57.00 N	131.50 W
Stikine ≃, N.A.	146	56.40 N	132.30 W
Stikine Ranges ⋌	146	58.45 N	130.00 W
Stiklestad	68	63.48 N	11.33 E
Stillwater, Minn., U.S.	154	45.04 N	92.49 W
Stillwater, Okla., U.S.	160	36.07 N	97.04 W
Stilwell	158	35.49 N	94.38 W
Stinnett	160	35.50 N	101.27 W
Stirling	70	56.07 N	3.57 W
Stirling City	168	39.54 N	121.32 W
Stirling Range ⋌	122	34.23 S	117.50 E
Stittsville	154	45.15 N	75.55 W
Stjerdalshalsen	68	63.28 N	10.56 E
Stjordal	68	63.28 N	10.55 E
Stockach	72	47.51 N	9.00 E
Stockbridge, Ga., U.S.	156	33.33 N	84.14 W
Stockbridge, Mich., U.S.	154	42.27 N	84.11 W
Stockdale	160	29.14 N	97.58 W
Stockerau	72	48.23 N	16.13 E
Stockholm, Sve.	68	59.20 N	18.03 E
Stockholm, Maine, U.S.	154	47.04 N	68.08 W
Stockholms Län □6	68	59.30 N	18.20 E
Stockport	70	53.25 N	2.10 W
Stockton, Calif., U.S.	168	37.57 N	121.17 W
Stockton, Ill., U.S.	154	42.21 N	90.01 W
Stockton, Kans., U.S.	162	39.26 N	99.16 W
Stockton, Mo., U.S.	158	37.42 N	93.48 W
Stockton, Utah, U.S.	164	40.27 N	112.22 W
Stockton Plateau ⋌1	160	30.30 N	102.30 W
Stockton-upon-Tees	70	54.34 N	1.19 W
Stoeceng Trêng	94	13.31 N	105.58 E
Stoke-on-Trent	70	53.00 N	2.10 W
Stokes Point ⊁	122	40.10 S	143.56 E
Stokes Range ⋌2	124	15.46 S	130.57 E
Stolac	78	43.05 N	17.58 E
Stolberg	72	50.46 N	6.13 E
Stolbovoj, Ostrov I	84	74.05 N	136.00 E
Stollberg	72	50.42 N	12.47 E
Stolp → Słupsk	72	54.28 N	17.01 E
Stonehaven	70	56.58 N	2.13 W
Stonehenge	120	24.22 S	143.17 E
Stone Mountain	156	33.49 N	84.10 W
Stonewall, Man., Can.	142	50.09 N	97.21 W
Stonewall, Miss., U.S.	158	32.08 N	88.47 W
Stonewall, Okla., U.S.	160	34.39 N	96.31 W
Stoney Creek	154	43.13 N	79.46 W
Stonington, Ill., U.S.	158	39.44 N	89.12 W
Stonington, Maine, U.S.	154	44.09 N	68.40 W
Stony Lake	142	58.51 N	98.35 W
Stony Plain	148	53.32 N	114.00 W
Stony Point	156	35.52 N	81.03 W
Stony Rapids	142	59.16 N	105.50 W
Stora Le	68	59.10 N	11.53 E
Storby	68	60.13 N	19.34 E
Store Heddinge	68	55.19 N	12.25 E
Storen	68	63.02 N	10.18 E
Storkerson Bay ⊂	142	73.00 N	124.50 W
Storkerson Peninsula ⊁1	142	72.30 N	106.30 W
Storlien	68	63.19 N	12.06 E
Storm Bay ⊂	120	43.10 S	147.32 E
Storm Lake	162	42.39 N	95.13 W
Stornoway	70	58.12 N	6.23 W
Storrs	152	41.48 N	72.15 W
Storsjön ⊜	68	63.12 N	14.18 E
Storsvarts gruve	68	62.38 N	11.31 E
Story City	154	42.11 N	93.36 W
Stoughton, Mass., U.S.	152	42.07 N	71.06 W
Stoughton, Wis., U.S.	154	42.55 N	89.13 W
Stow	152	41.10 N	81.27 W
Stowe	152	44.28 N	72.41 W
Stowmarket	70	52.11 N	1.00 E
Strabane	70	54.49 N	7.27 W
Stradella	78	45.05 N	9.18 E
Strahan	120	42.09 S	145.19 E
Strakonice	74	49.16 N	13.55 E
Stralsund	72	54.19 N	13.05 E
Stranda	68	62.19 N	6.54 E
Strangways, Mount ⋀	122	23.02 S	133.51 E
Stranraer	70	54.55 N	5.02 W
Strasbourg	74	48.35 N	7.45 E
Strasburg, D.D.R.	72	53.30 N	13.44 E
Strasburg, N. Dak., U.S.	162	46.08 N	100.10 W
Strasburg, Pa., U.S.	152	39.59 N	76.11 W
Strasburg, Va., U.S.	152	38.59 N	78.22 W
Strasswalchen	72	47.59 N	13.15 E
Stratford, Ont., Can.	154	43.22 N	80.57 W
Stratford, N.Z.	126	39.21 S	174.18 E
Stratford, Calif., U.S.	168	36.11 N	119.49 W
Stratford, Conn., U.S.	152	41.11 N	73.07 W
Stratford, Okla., U.S.	160	34.48 N	96.58 W
Stratford, Tex., U.S.	160	36.20 N	102.04 W
Stratford, Wis., U.S.	154	44.48 N	90.04 W
Stratford-upon-Avon	70	52.12 N	1.41 W
Strathalbyn	120	35.15 S	138.54 E
Strathclyde □3	70	56.00 N	5.15 W
Strathmore	168	36.09 N	119.04 W
Strathroy	154	42.57 N	81.38 W
Stratton	72	48.00 N	10.32 E
Straubing	72	48.53 N	12.34 E
Straumen	68	63.52 N	11.19 E
Strausberg	72	52.35 N	13.53 E
Strawberry	164	34.10 N	110.24 W
Strawberry Daniels Pass ⋋	164	40.19 N	111.15 W
Strawberry Point	154	42.41 N	91.32 W
Strawberry Reservoir ⊜1	164	40.11 N	111.08 W
Strawn	160	32.33 N	98.30 W
Streaky Bay	120	32.48 S	134.13 E
Streaky Bay ⊂	120	32.36 S	134.18 E
Streator	154	41.07 N	88.50 W
Středočeský Kraj □4	72	49.55 N	14.30 E
Středoslovenský Kraj □4	72	48.50 N	19.10 E
Streetman	160	31.53 N	96.19 W
Streetsboro	152	41.14 N	81.21 W
Strehaia	80	44.37 N	23.12 E
Strelka-Čun'a	84	61.53 N	102.48 E
Strel'na	84	66.03 N	38.53 E
Strenči	86	57.37 N	25.41 E
Stresa	78	45.53 N	8.32 E
Strešin	86	52.43 N	30.05 E
Stretensk	84	52.15 N	117.43 E
Strimón (Struma) ≃	80	40.47 N	23.51 E
Stromboli I	78	38.48 N	15.13 E
Stromeferry	70	57.21 N	5.34 W
Stromness	70	58.57 N	3.18 W
Strömstad	162	41.07 N	97.36 W
Strömsund	68	63.51 N	15.35 E
Strong City	158	38.24 N	96.32 W
Stronghurst	154	40.45 N	90.55 W
Stroud, Eng., U.K.	70	51.45 N	2.12 W
Stroud, Okla., U.S.	160	35.45 N	96.40 W
Stroud Road	120	32.20 S	151.58 E
Stroudsburg	152	40.59 N	75.12 W
Struer	68	56.29 N	8.37 E
Struga	80	41.11 N	20.40 E
Struga-Krasnyji	86	58.17 N	29.06 E
Struma (Strimón) ≃	80	40.47 N	23.51 E
Strumble Head ⊁	70	52.02 N	5.04 W
Strumica	80	41.26 N	22.38 E
Struthers	152	41.04 N	80.35 W
Stryj	82	49.15 N	23.51 E
Stryn	68	61.55 N	6.47 E
Strzegom	72	50.57 N	16.21 E
Strzelce Opolskie	72	50.31 N	18.19 E
Strzelecki Creek ≃	120	29.37 S	139.59 E
Strzelin	72	50.47 N	17.03 E
Stuart, Fla., U.S.	156	27.11 N	80.15 W
Stuart, Iowa, U.S.	154	41.30 N	94.19 W
Stuart, Va., U.S.	156	36.38 N	80.16 W
Stuart ≃	168	54.00 N	123.32 W
Stuart Lake	148	54.32 N	124.35 W
Stuart Range ⋌	122	29.10 S	134.56 E
Stugudal	68	62.54 N	11.52 E
Stupino	86	54.53 N	38.05 E
Sturgeon Bay	154	44.50 N	87.23 W
Sturgeon Falls	154	46.22 N	79.55 W
Sturgis, Ky., U.S.	158	37.33 N	87.59 W
Sturgis, Mich., U.S.	154	41.48 N	85.25 W
Sturgis, S. Dak., U.S.	162	44.25 N	103.31 W
Sturt Creek ≃	122	19.10 S	128.10 E
Sturt Desert ⋌2	120	28.30 S	141.00 E
Sturtevant	154	42.42 N	87.54 W
Stuttgart, B.R.D.	72	48.46 N	9.11 E
Stuttgart, Ark., U.S.	158	34.30 N	91.33 W
Stykkishólmur	66a	65.06 N	22.48 W
Suakin Archipelago II	112	18.42 N	38.30 E
Subansiri ≃	102	26.48 N	93.50 E
Subarnarekha ≃	102	21.33 N	87.12 E
Subiaco	78	41.55 N	13.06 E
Sublette	162	37.29 N	100.50 W
Subotica	80	46.06 N	19.39 E
Sučan	84	43.08 N	133.09 E
Sucarnoochee ≃	158	32.25 N	88.02 W
Suceava	80	47.39 N	26.19 E
Suceava □4	80	47.30 N	25.45 E
Sucha [beskidzka]	72	49.44 N	19.36 E
Suchana	84	68.45 N	118.00 E
Sūchbaatar	88	50.17 N	106.10 E
Suchinicí	86	54.06 N	35.20 E
Suchona ≃	66	60.46 N	46.24 E
Suzhou → Suzhou	88	31.18 N	120.37 E
Suchoverkovo	86	56.37 N	35.35 E
Suchumi	82	43.01 N	41.02 E
Sucre	134	19.02 S	65.17 W
Sucre □3	138	10.25 N	63.30 W
Sucre □5	138	9.00 N	75.00 W
Suda ≃	86	59.24 N	37.33 E
Sudan ≃	160	34.04 N	102.32 W
Sudan □1	108	15.00 N	30.00 E
Sudan □1	108	10.00 N	20.00 E
Sudbury, Ont., Can.	154	46.30 N	81.00 W
Sudbury, Eng., U.K.	70	50.02 N	0.44 E
Sudety ⋌	72	50.30 N	16.00 E
Sudislavl'	86	57.51 N	41.43 E
Sudogda	86	55.57 N	40.50 E
Sue ≃	112	7.41 N	28.03 E
Sueca	76	39.12 N	0.19 W
Suez → As-Suways	112	29.58 N	32.33 E
Suez, Gulf of → Suways, Khalīj as- C	108	29.00 N	32.50 E
Suez Canal → Suways, Qanāt as- ⛧	108	29.00 N	32.20 E
Suffolk	156	36.44 N	76.35 W
Suffolk □6	70	52.10 N	1.00 E
Sufu → Kashi	88	39.29 N	75.59 E
Sugar ≃	154	42.26 N	89.12 W
Sugar City	164	43.52 N	111.45 W
Sugar Creek ≃	158	39.27 N	87.26 W
Sugar Hill	156	34.07 N	84.02 W
Sugar Land	160	29.37 N	95.38 W
Sugarloaf Mountain ⋀	152	45.01 N	70.22 W
Sugarloaf Point ⊁	120	32.26 S	152.33 E
Sugoj ≃	84	64.15 N	154.29 E
Şuḩār	104	24.22 N	56.45 E
Suḩl	104	50.37 N	10.41 E
Suhl	72	50.36 N	10.41 E
Suhl □5	72	50.35 N	10.40 E
Suide	88	37.33 N	110.04 E
Suifenhe	88	44.24 N	131.10 E
Suihua	88	46.38 N	127.00 E
Suining	88	30.31 N	105.34 E
Suippes	74	49.08 N	4.32 E
Suixian	88	31.42 N	113.20 E
Suizhong	88	40.20 N	120.19 E
Šuja	86	56.51 N	41.23 E
Sukabumi	96	6.55 S	106.56 E
Sukarno, Pegunungan → Djaja, Puntjak ⋀	124	4.05 S	137.11 E
Sukeva	68	63.52 N	27.26 E
Sukhothai	94	17.01 N	99.49 E
Sukkertoppen	142	65.25 N	52.53 W
Sukkozero	66	63.11 N	32.18 E
Sukkur	102	27.42 N	68.52 E
Sul, Canal do ⛧	134	0.10 S	49.30 W
Sula, Kepulauan II	96	1.52 S	125.22 E
Sulaiman Range ⋌	102	30.00 N	70.10 E
Sulawesi (Celebes) I	96	2.00 S	121.00 E
Sulechów	72	52.06 N	15.47 E
Sulejówek	72	52.14 N	21.17 E
Sulingen	72	52.41 N	8.47 E
Sulitelma ⋀	66	67.08 N	16.24 E
Sulkava	68	61.47 N	28.23 E
Sullana	138	4.53 S	80.42 W
Sulligent	158	33.54 N	88.08 W
Sullivan, Ill., U.S.	158	39.36 N	88.36 W
Sullivan, Mo., U.S.	158	38.13 N	91.10 W
Sully	74	47.46 N	2.22 E
Sulmona	78	42.03 N	13.55 E
Sulphur, La., U.S.	158	30.14 N	93.23 W
Sulphur, Okla., U.S.	160	34.31 N	96.58 W
Sulphur ≃	158	33.07 N	93.52 W
Sulphur Springs	160	33.08 N	95.36 W
Sulphur Springs Draw ≃	160	32.12 N	101.36 W
Sultan	166	47.52 N	121.49 W
Sultan Archipelago II	96	5.30 N	121.30 E
Suluq	108	31.39 N	20.15 E
Sulu Sea ⋍2	96	8.00 N	120.00 E
Sulusi	80	43.08 N	95.08 E
Sulzbach	72	49.18 N	7.07 E
Sulzbach-Rosenberg	72	49.30 N	11.45 E
Sumas	148	49.00 N	122.13 W
Sumatra (Sumatera) I	96	0.05 S	102.00 E
Sumatra → Sumatera I	96	0.05 S	102.00 E
Sumba I	96	10.00 S	120.00 E
Sumbawa I	96	8.40 S	118.00 E
Sumbawa Besar	96	8.30 S	117.26 E
Sumbawanga	110	7.58 S	31.37 E
Sümber	88	46.21 N	108.25 E
Sumbilla	76	43.10 N	1.40 W
Šumen	80	43.16 N	26.55 E
Sümeg	72	46.59 N	17.17 E
Sumenep	96	7.01 S	113.52 E
Šumerl'a	66	55.30 N	46.26 E
Sumgait	82	40.36 N	49.38 E
Šumicha	82	55.14 N	63.19 E
Sümisu-jima I	90	31.27 N	140.03 E
Summerland	148	49.39 N	119.33 W
Summerside	150	46.24 N	63.47 W
Summersville	152	38.17 N	80.51 W
Summerton	156	33.37 N	80.21 W
Summerville, Ga., U.S.	156	34.29 N	85.21 W
Summerville, S.C., U.S.	156	33.01 N	80.10 W
Summit	162	45.18 N	97.02 W
Summit Lake	148	54.17 N	122.38 W
Summit Mountain ⋀	168	39.23 N	116.28 W
Sumner, Iowa, U.S.	154	42.51 N	92.05 W
Sumner, Wash., U.S.	166	47.12 N	122.14 W
Šumperk	72	49.58 N	16.58 E
Sumqayıt	82	40.36 N	49.38 E
Sumrall	158	31.25 N	89.33 W
Sumter	156	33.55 N	80.20 W
Sumy	82	50.55 N	34.45 E
Sunbright	156	36.15 N	84.40 W
Sunburst	166	48.53 N	111.54 W
Sunbury, Austl.	120	37.35 S	144.44 E
Sunbury, Ohio, U.S.	152	40.14 N	82.52 W
Sunbury, Pa., U.S.	152	40.51 N	76.47 W
Sunchales	140	30.57 S	61.35 W
Sunch'ŏn	88	34.57 N	127.29 E
Sun City	164	33.36 N	112.17 W
Suncook	152	43.08 N	71.27 W
Sunda, Selat ⛧	96	6.00 S	105.45 E
Sundance	162	44.24 N	104.23 W
Sundarbans ⇃1	102	22.00 N	89.00 E
Sunda Strait → Sunda, Selat ⛧	96	6.00 S	105.45 E
Sunderland	70	54.55 N	1.23 W
Sundown	160	33.27 N	102.29 W
Sundsvall	68	62.23 N	17.18 E
Sungaipenuh	96	2.05 S	101.23 E
Sungikou	88	42.32 N	112.58 E
Sunland Park	164	32.15 N	106.45 W
Sunndalsøra	68	62.40 N	8.33 E
Sunnyside, Utah, U.S.	164	39.33 N	110.24 W
Sunnyside, Wash., U.S.	166	46.20 N	120.00 W
Sunnyvale	168	37.23 N	122.01 W
Sun Prairie	154	43.11 N	89.13 W
Sunray	160	36.01 N	101.49 W
Sunset, Utah, U.S.	164	41.08 N	112.02 W
Sunset, Tex., U.S.	160	33.27 N	97.46 W
Suntar	84	62.10 N	117.40 E
Suntar-Chajata, Chrebet ⋌	84	62.00 N	143.00 E
Suntrana	146	63.52 N	148.51 W
Sun Valley	166	43.42 N	114.21 W
Sunyani	114	7.20 N	2.20 W
Suoche (Yarkand)	102	38.25 N	77.16 E
Suoguohu	88	42.18 N	101.08 E
Suojarvi	66	62.05 N	32.21 E
Suomussalmi	68	64.53 N	29.07 E
Suonenjoki	68	62.37 N	27.08 E
Suordach	84	66.43 N	132.04 E
Suoxian	100	31.50 N	93.45 E
Suozong	88	31.50 N	93.45 E
Superior, Ariz., U.S.	164	33.18 N	111.06 W
Superior, Mont., U.S.	166	47.12 N	114.53 W
Superior, Nebr., U.S.	162	40.01 N	98.04 W
Superior, Wis., U.S.	154	46.44 N	92.05 W
Superior, Wyo., U.S.	164	41.46 N	108.58 W
Superior, Lake ⊜	154	48.00 N	88.00 W
Superior Upland ⋌1	154	46.00 N	90.30 W
Suphan Buri	94	14.29 N	100.10 E
Suqutrā I	100	12.30 N	54.00 E
Sūr (Tyre), Lubnān	104	33.16 N	35.11 E
Şūr, 'Umān	100	22.35 N	59.31 E
Şūra ≃	66	56.06 N	46.00 E
Surabaja	96	7.15 S	112.45 E
Surakarta	96	7.35 S	110.50 E
Surat	102	21.10 N	72.50 E
Surat Thani (Ban Don)	94	9.06 N	99.20 E
Suraž	86	55.25 N	30.44 E
Surdulica	80	42.41 N	22.10 E
Surendranagar	102	22.42 N	71.41 E
Surfers Paradise	120	28.00 S	153.26 E
Surgères	74	46.07 N	0.45 W
Surgut	84	61.14 N	73.20 E
Surgao	96	9.48 N	125.30 E
Surinam □1	134	4.00 N	56.00 W
Suring	154	44.59 N	88.22 W
Sūrmaq	104	31.03 N	52.48 E
Surnadalsøra	68	62.59 N	8.39 E
Surprise	164	33.38 N	112.20 W
Surprise □6	75	57.10 N	0.02 E
Sursee	74	47.10 N	8.06 E
Surt	108	31.12 N	16.35 E
Surt, Khalīj ⊂	108	31.30 N	18.00 E
Surtainville	70	49.25 N	1.50 W
Surtsey I	66a	63.16 N	20.32 W
Suruд Ad ⋀	100	10.41 N	47.18 E
Šūrýškary	84	65.54 N	65.22 E
Susa	78	45.08 N	7.03 E
Susanville	168	40.25 N	120.39 W
Šušenskoje	84	53.20 N	91.56 E
Susitna ≃	146	61.16 N	150.30 W
Susoh	96	3.43 N	96.48 E
Susquehanna	152	41.57 N	75.36 W
Susquehanna ≃	152	39.33 N	76.05 W
Susques	140	23.25 S	66.30 W
Sussex, N.B., Can.	150	45.43 N	65.31 W
Sussex, N.J., U.S.	152	41.13 N	74.36 W
Sussex, Va., U.S.	156	36.55 N	77.17 W
Sussex, East ⊡	70	50.55 N	0.15 E
Susten Pass)(	74	46.44 N	8.27 E
Susuman	84	62.47 N	148.10 E
Sutherland, S. Afr.	116	32.24 S	20.40 E
Sutherland, Iowa, U.S.	162	42.58 N	95.29 W
Sutherlin	166	43.25 N	123.19 W
Sutlej (Satluj) ≃	102	29.23 N	71.02 E
Sutlej (Langchuhe) ≃	102	29.23 N	71.02 E
Sutter	168	39.10 N	121.45 W
Sutter Creek	168	38.23 N	120.48 W
Sutton, Alaska, U.S.	146	61.43 N	148.53 W
Sutton, Nebr., U.S.	162	40.36 N	97.52 W
Sutton-in-Ashfield	70	53.08 N	1.15 W
Suttons Bay	154	44.59 N	85.39 W
Sutton West	154	44.18 N	79.22 W
Suttor ≃	120	21.36 S	147.02 E
Suure-Jaani	86	58.33 N	25.28 E
Suwa	90	36.02 N	138.08 E
Suwałki	72	54.07 N	22.56 E
Suwannee ≃	156	29.18 N	83.09 W
Suwanose-jima I	91b	29.38 N	129.43 E
Suways, Khalīj as- C	108	29.55 N	32.33 E
Suways, Qanāt as- ⛧	108	29.55 N	32.20 E
Suwŏn	88	37.17 N	127.01 E
Suxian	88	33.38 N	116.58 E
Suzak	82	44.08 N	68.28 E
Suzhou	88	31.18 N	120.37 E
Suz'omka	86	52.19 N	34.25 E
Suzuka	90	34.51 N	136.35 E
Svaneke	68	55.08 N	15.09 E
Svartenhuk ⊁1	142	71.55 N	55.00 W
Svartisen ⊞	66	66.40 N	14.00 E
Sv'atoj Nos, Mys ⊁, S.S.S.R.	66	68.10 N	39.45 E
Sv'atoj Nos, Mys ⊁, S.S.S.R.	84	72.52 N	140.42 E
Sveg	68	62.02 N	14.21 E
Svelgen	68	61.47 N	5.15 E
Svelvik	68	59.37 N	10.24 E
Švenčioneliai	86	55.09 N	26.01 E
Švenčionys	86	55.10 N	26.10 E
Svendborg	68	55.03 N	10.37 E
Sverdlovsk, S.S.S.R.	84	48.05 N	39.40 E
Sverdlovsk, S.S.S.R.	82	56.51 N	60.36 E
Sverdrup, Ostrov I	84	74.30 N	79.00 E
Svetlogorsk	86	52.38 N	29.46 E
Svetlovodsk	82	49.03 N	33.15 E
Svetlyj	82	54.40 N	62.20 E
Svilajnac	80	44.14 N	21.13 E
Svilengrad	80	41.46 N	26.12 E
Svir ≃	86	60.30 N	32.48 E
Svirica	86	60.28 N	32.51 E
Svir'stroj	86	60.48 N	33.43 E
Svišlov'	86	53.26 N	24.06 E
Svištov	80	43.37 N	25.20 E
Svobodnyj, S.S.S.R.	84	51.24 N	128.08 E
Svobodnyj, S.S.S.R.	86	52.26 N	40.04 E
Svolvær	66	68.14 N	14.34 E
Svorkmo	68	63.03 N	9.45 E
Svullrya	68	60.36 N	12.25 E
Swaffham	70	52.39 N	0.41 E
Swain Reefs ⋍2	120	21.40 S	152.15 E
Swainsboro	156	32.35 N	82.19 W
Swakopmund	116	22.41 S	14.34 E
Swale ≃	70	54.05 N	1.20 W
Swan ≃	122	32.03 S	115.45 E
Swan Hill	120	35.21 S	143.34 E
Swan Lake	142	52.30 N	100.45 W
Swan River	142	52.06 N	101.16 W
Swansea, Austl.	120	42.08 S	148.04 E
Swansea, Wales, U.K.	70	51.38 N	3.57 W
Swansea, S.C., U.S.	156	33.44 N	81.06 W
Swanton, Ohio, U.S.	152	41.35 N	83.53 W
Swanton, Vt., U.S.	152	44.55 N	73.07 W
Swartz Creek	154	42.57 N	83.49 W
Swarzędz	72	52.26 N	17.05 E
Swatow → Shantou	88	23.23 N	116.41 E
Swaziland □1	110	26.30 S	31.30 E
Sweden □1	64	62.00 N	15.00 E
Sweeny	160	29.02 N	95.42 W
Sweet Briar	156	37.33 N	79.04 W
Sweet Home, Oreg., U.S.	166	44.24 N	122.44 W
Sweet Home, Tex., U.S.	160	29.21 N	97.04 W
Sweet Springs	158	38.58 N	93.25 W
Sweetwater, Tenn., U.S.	156	35.36 N	84.28 W
Sweetwater, Tex., U.S.	160	32.28 N	100.25 W
Sweetwater Creek ≃	160	35.18 N	99.57 W
Swellendam	116	34.02 S	20.26 E
Świdnica (Schweidnitz)	72	50.51 N	16.29 E
Świdnik	72	51.14 N	22.41 E
Świdwin	72	53.47 N	15.47 E
Świebodzice	72	50.52 N	16.19 E
Świebodzin	72	52.15 N	15.32 E
Świecie	72	53.25 N	18.28 E
Swift Current	142	50.17 N	107.50 W
Swinburne, Cape ⊁	142	71.14 N	98.34 W
Swindon	70	51.34 N	1.47 W
Swinford	70	53.57 N	8.57 W
Świnoujście (Swinemünde)	72	53.53 N	14.14 E
Switzerland □1	64	47.00 N	8.00 E
Swords	70	53.28 N	6.13 W
Swords Range ⋌	120	21.57 S	141.32 E
Syalach	84	66.12 N	124.00 E
Sycamore	154	41.59 N	88.41 W
Syčovka	86	55.50 N	34.17 E
Sydney, Austl.	120	33.52 S	151.13 E
Sydney, N.S., Can.	150	46.09 N	60.11 W
Sydney Mines	150	46.14 N	60.14 W
Syke	72	52.54 N	8.49 E
Sykesville, Md., U.S.	152	39.22 N	76.58 W
Sykesville, Pa., U.S.	152	41.03 N	78.49 W
Sykkylven	68	62.24 N	6.35 E
Sylacauga	158	33.10 N	86.15 W
Sylarna ⋀	68	63.02 N	12.13 E
Sylhet	102	24.54 N	91.52 E
Sylva	156	35.23 N	83.13 W
Sylvan Grove	162	39.00 N	98.24 W
Sylvan Hills	158	34.51 N	92.12 W
Sylvania, Ga., U.S.	156	32.45 N	81.38 W
Sylvania, Ohio, U.S.	154	41.43 N	83.42 W
Sylvan Lake	148	52.19 N	114.05 W
Sylvester	156	31.31 N	83.49 W
Sylvia Grinnell Lake ⊜	142	64.10 N	69.25 W
Sym ≃	84	60.20 N	88.23 E
Syracuse → Siracusa, It.	78	37.04 N	15.17 E
Syracuse, Kans., U.S.	162	37.59 N	101.45 W
Syracuse, Nebr., U.S.	162	40.39 N	96.11 W
Syracuse, N.Y., U.S.	144	43.02 N	76.09 W
Syrdarja	82	40.52 N	68.38 E
Syrdarya (Syr-Darya) ≃	82	46.03 N	61.00 E
Syria □1	100	35.00 N	38.00 E
Syrian Desert → Shām, Bādiyat ash- ⋌2	104	32.00 N	40.00 E
Sysma	68	61.30 N	25.41 E
Syzran'	66	53.09 N	48.27 E
Szabolcs-Szatmár □6	72	47.50 N	22.10 E
Szamos (Someş) ≃	80	48.07 N	22.20 E
Szamotuły	72	52.37 N	16.35 E
Szczecin (Stettin)	72	53.25 N	14.32 E
Szczecinek (Neustettin)	72	53.43 N	16.42 E
Szczeciński, Zalew (Oderhaff C	72	53.46 N	14.14 E
Szczuczyn	72	53.34 N	22.18 E
Szczytno	72	53.34 N	21.00 E
Szechwan → Sichuan □4	88	31.00 N	105.00 E
Szécsény	72	48.06 N	19.31 E
Szeged	72	46.15 N	20.09 E
Szeghalom	72	47.02 N	21.11 E
Székesfehérvár	72	47.12 N	18.25 E
Szekszárd	72	46.21 N	18.42 E
Szentendre	72	47.40 N	19.05 E
Szentes	72	46.39 N	20.16 E
Szentgotthárd	72	46.57 N	16.17 E
Szerencs	72	48.10 N	21.12 E
Szob	72	47.50 N	18.52 E
Szolnok	72	47.10 N	20.12 E
Szolnok □6	72	47.10 N	20.30 E
Szombathely	72	47.14 N	16.38 E
Szprotawa	72	51.34 N	15.33 E
Szubin	72	53.00 N	17.44 E

T

Name	Page	Lat	Long
Taavetti	68	60.55 N	27.34 E
Tabas	100	33.36 N	56.54 E
Tabatinga, Serra da ⋌	134	10.25 S	44.00 W
Tabelbala	106	29.25 N	3.15 W
Taber	148	49.47 N	112.08 W
Taberg	68	57.41 N	14.05 E
Tabernes de Valldigna	76	39.04 N	0.16 W
Tablas Island I	96	12.24 N	122.02 E
Table Rock Lake ⊜1	158	36.35 N	93.30 W
Tábor, Česko.	72	49.25 N	14.41 E
Tabor, Iowa, U.S.	162	40.54 N	95.40 W
Tabora	110	5.01 S	32.48 E
Tabory	82	58.31 N	64.34 E
Tabou	114	4.25 N	7.21 W
Tabrīz	100	38.05 N	46.18 E
Tabuaço	76	41.07 N	7.34 W
Tabūk	100	28.23 N	36.35 E
Täby	68	59.26 N	18.03 E
Tacámbaro de Codallos	130	19.14 N	101.28 W
Tacaná, Volcán ⋀1	130	15.08 N	92.05 W
Tache, Lac ⊜	142	64.00 N	120.00 W
Tachiatš ≃	84	66.45 N	82.57 E
Tachikawa	90	35.42 N	139.25 E
Tachov	72	49.48 N	12.38 E
Tachtamygda	84	54.06 N	123.34 E
Tacloban	96	11.15 N	125.00 E
Tacna	134	18.01 S	70.15 W
Tacoma	166	47.15 N	122.27 W
Taconic Range ⋌	152	43.00 N	73.15 W
Tacuarembó	140	31.44 S	55.59 W
Tadoule Lake ⊜	142	58.36 N	98.20 W
Tadoussac	150	48.09 N	69.43 W
Tad Park	164	40.29 N	112.21 W
Tădpatri	100	14.55 N	78.01 E
Tadzhik Soviet Socialist Republic → Tadžikskaja Sovetskaja Socialističeskaja Respublika □3	82	39.00 N	71.00 E
Tadžikskaja Sovetskaja Socialističeskaja Respublika □3	82	39.00 N	71.00 E
Taegu	88	35.52 N	128.35 E
Taejŏn	88	36.19 N	127.26 E
Tafalla	76	42.31 N	1.40 W
Tafí Viejo	140	26.44 S	65.16 W
Taft, Calif., U.S.	168	35.08 N	119.27 W
Taft, Okla., U.S.	160	35.46 N	95.32 W
Taft, Tex., U.S.	160	27.58 N	97.23 W
Taga	127c	13.46 S	172.28 W
Taganrog	82	47.12 N	38.56 E
Tagawa	90	33.38 N	130.48 E
Tagaytay	92	14.06 N	120.56 E
Tagbilaran	96	9.39 N	123.51 E
Tagish Lake	146	59.45 N	134.15 W
Taguatinga	134	12.25 S	46.26 W
Taguke	88	32.07 N	84.35 E
Tagula Island I	118	11.30 S	153.30 E
Tagus (Tejo) (Tajo) ≃	76	38.40 N	9.24 W
Tahat ⋀	96	23.18 N	5.47 E
Tahiruyak Lake ⊜	142	70.56 N	112.20 W
Tahlequah	160	35.55 N	94.58 W
Tahoe, Lake ⊜	168	38.58 N	120.00 W
Tahoe City	168	39.10 N	120.08 W
Tahoe Lake ⊜	142	70.15 N	108.45 W
Tahoe Valley	168	38.55 N	120.00 W
Tahoka	160	33.10 N	101.48 W
Tahoua	114	14.54 N	5.16 E
Tahtā	112	26.46 N	31.30 E
Tahulandang, Pulau I	96	2.21 N	125.24 E
Tahuna	92	3.37 N	125.29 E
Tabashshan ⋌	88	33.54 N	107.46 E
T'aichung	88	24.09 N	120.41 E
Taihangshan ⋌	88	36.00 N	113.35 E
Taihape	126	39.41 S	175.47 E
Taihu	88	31.15 N	120.10 E
Tailai	88	46.23 N	123.27 E
Tailem Bend	120	35.16 S	139.27 E
Tamba ≃	84	60.18 N	98.58 E
Tain	70	57.48 N	4.04 W
T'ainan	88	23.00 N	120.11 E
Tainaron, Ákra ⊁	80	36.22 N	22.30 E
Taining	88	26.51 N	117.09 E
T'aipei	88	25.03 N	121.30 E
Taiping	96	4.51 N	100.44 E
Taisetsu-zan ⋀	90	43.30 N	142.57 E
Taishun	88	27.33 N	119.43 E
Taitao, Península de ⊁1	136	46.30 S	74.25 W
T'aitung	88	22.45 N	121.09 E
Taiwan (T'aiwan) □1	88	23.30 N	121.00 E
Taiwan (Formosa) I	88	23.30 N	121.00 E
Taiyuan	88	37.55 N	112.30 E
Taizhou	88	32.30 N	119.58 E
Ta'izz	100	13.38 N	44.04 E
Tajbola	66	68.26 N	33.19 E
Tajga	84	56.04 N	85.37 E
Tajgonos, Poluostrov ⊁1	84	61.20 N	161.00 E
Tajmura ≃	84	63.46 N	98.01 E
Tajmyr, Ozero ⊜	84	74.30 N	102.30 E
Tajmyr, Poluostrov ⊁1	84	76.00 N	104.00 E
Tajšet	84	55.57 N	98.00 E
Tajumulco, Volcán ⋀1	130	15.02 N	91.50 W
Tak	94	16.52 N	99.08 E
Takada	90	37.06 N	138.15 E
Takalar	96	5.28 S	119.24 E
Takamatsu	90	34.20 N	134.03 E
Takaoka	90	36.45 N	137.01 E
Takapuna	126	36.47 S	174.46 E
Takasaki	90	36.20 N	139.01 E
Takatsuki	90	34.51 N	135.37 E
Takefu	90	35.54 N	136.10 E
Takêv	94	10.59 N	104.47 E
Ta Khli	94	15.16 N	100.20 E
Takijug Lake ⊜	142	66.15 N	113.05 W
Takingeun	96	4.38 N	96.50 E
Takla Lake ⊜	148	55.25 N	125.53 W
Takla Makan → Talimupendi ≃2	88	39.00 N	83.00 E
Taku	88	33.16 N	133.59 W
Taku ≃	146	58.25 N	133.59 W
Takutu (Tacutu) ≃	138	3.01 N	60.29 W
Tala	130	20.39 N	103.42 W
Talagante	140	33.40 S	70.56 W
Talara	138	4.35 S	81.25 W
Talas	82	42.32 N	72.14 E
Talata Mafara	114	12.35 N	6.04 E
Talavera, Kepulauan II	96	7.30 S	131.00 E
Talavera de la Reina	76	39.57 N	4.50 W
Talawanta	120	18.38 S	140.16 E
Talawdi	108	10.38 N	30.23 E
Talbot Islands II	124	9.15 S	142.08 E
Talbotton	156	32.41 N	84.32 W
Talbragar ≃	120	32.12 S	148.37 E
Talca	140	35.26 S	71.40 W
Talca □4	140	35.30 S	71.10 W
Talcahuano	140	36.43 S	73.07 W
Talco	160	33.22 N	95.06 W
Taldom	86	56.44 N	37.32 E
Taldy-Kurgan	82	45.00 N	78.23 E
Talent	166	42.15 N	122.47 W
Talgar	82	43.18 N	77.18 E
Taliabu, Pulau I	96	1.45 S	124.48 E
Talica, S.S.S.R.	66	58.01 N	51.30 E
Talica, S.S.S.R.	82	57.00 N	63.43 E
Talimuhe ≃	88	41.05 N	86.40 E
Talimupendi (Takla Makan) ≃2	102	39.00 N	83.00 E
Talisay	92	10.45 N	122.58 E
Talish Mountains → (Kūhhā-ye Tavālesh) ⋌	104	38.42 N	48.18 E
Talladega	158	33.26 N	86.06 W
Tallahassee	156	30.25 N	84.16 W
Tallangatta	120	36.13 S	147.15 E
Tallapoosa	156	33.45 N	85.17 W
Tallard	74	44.28 N	6.03 E
Tallassee	158	32.32 N	85.54 W
Tallinn	86	59.25 N	24.45 E
Tallmadge	152	41.06 N	81.27 W
Tallowan	122	32.25 N	91.11 W
Tallulah	158	32.25 N	91.11 W
Tal'menka	84	53.51 N	83.35 E
Talnoye	82	48.53 N	30.42 E
Taloda	102	21.34 N	74.13 E
Talovaja	66	51.07 N	40.44 E
Talsi	86	57.15 N	22.36 E
Taltson ≃	142	61.24 N	112.45 W
Talwood	120	28.29 S	149.30 E
Tamacuari, Pico ⋀	138	1.13 N	64.42 W
Tamale	114	9.25 N	0.50 W
Tamanrasset	106	22.56 N	5.30 E
Tamaqua	152	40.48 N	75.58 W
Tamar ≃	70	50.22 N	4.11 W
Tâmāsi	72	46.40 N	18.18 E
Tamaulipas □3	130	24.00 N	98.40 E
Tamazula de Gordiano	130	19.41 N	103.15 W
Tamazunchale	130	21.16 N	98.46 W
Tambacounda	114	13.47 N	13.40 W
Tambelan, Kepulauan II	96	1.00 N	107.30 E
Tambo, Austl.	120	24.53 S	146.15 E
Tambo, Perú	138	17.30 S	71.29 W
Tambohorano	117b	17.30 S	43.58 E
Tamboritha, Mount ⋀	120	37.22 S	146.40 E
Tambov	66	52.43 N	41.25 E
Tamchaket	114	17.15 N	10.40 W
Tame ≃	70	52.43 N	1.45 W
Tamel Aike	136	47.00 S	70.47 W
Tamiahua	130	21.16 N	97.27 W
Tamiahua, Laguna de C	130	21.35 N	97.35 W
Tamiment	152	41.09 N	75.02 W
Tamis (Timiş) ≃	80	44.51 N	20.38 E
Tam-ky	94	15.34 N	108.29 E
Tampa	156	27.57 N	82.27 W
Tampa Bay ⊂	156	27.45 N	82.35 W
Tampere	68	61.30 N	23.45 E
Tampico	130	22.13 N	97.51 W
Tamsagbulag	88	47.14 N	117.21 E
Tamsweg	72	47.08 N	13.49 E
Tamworth, Austl.	120	31.05 S	150.55 E
Tana ≃, Eur.	66	70.30 N	28.23 E
Tana ≃, Kenya	110	2.32 S	40.31 E
Tana, Lake ⊜	108	12.00 N	37.20 E

Name	Page	Lat	Long
Tanabe	90	33.44 N	135.22 E
Tanacross	146	63.23 N	143.21 W
Tanahbala, Pulau I	94	0.25 S	98.25 E
Tanahdjampea, Pulau I	96	7.05 S	120.42 E
Tanahmasa, Pulau I	94	0.12 S	98.25 E
Tanahmerah	122	19.59 S	129.43 E
Tanami	122	19.59 S	129.43 E
Tanami Desert 2	122	20.00 S	129.30 E
Tanana	146	65.10 N	152.05 W
Tanana	146	65.09 N	151.55 W
Tananarive (Antananarivo)	117b	18.55 S	47.31 E
Tanchoj	84	51.33 N	105.07 E
Tanch'ŏn	88	40.27 N	128.54 E
Tandag	92	9.05 N	126.12 E
Tandil	140	37.20 S	59.05 W
Tandjungbalai	96	2.58 N	99.47 E
Tandjungkarang	96	5.25 S	105.16 E
Tandjungpandan	96	2.45 S	107.39 E
Tandjungpinang	96	0.55 N	104.27 E
Tandjungselor	96	2.51 N	117.22 E
Tando Ādam	102	25.46 N	68.40 E
Tandou Lake	120	32.38 S	142.05 E
Tanega-shima I	90	30.40 N	131.00 E
Taneytown	152	39.40 N	77.10 W
Tanezrouft 2	106	24.00 N	0.45 W
Tanga	110	5.04 S	39.06 E
Tanganyika, Lake	110	6.00 S	29.30 E
Tanger (Tangier)	106	35.48 N	5.45 W
Tangerhütte	72	52.26 N	11.48 E
Tangermünde	72	52.32 N	11.58 E
Tanggu	88	39.01 N	117.40 E
Tanggulashanmai	102	31.00 N	86.20 E
Tangier → Tanger, Magreb	106	35.48 N	5.45 W
Tangier, Va., U.S.	156	37.19 N	75.59 W
Tangipahoa	158	30.20 N	90.18 W
Tangshan	88	39.38 N	118.11 E
Tanimbar, Kepulauan I	124	7.30 S	131.30 E
Taninges	74	46.07 N	6.36 E
Tannila	68	65.29 N	25.59 E
Tannu-Ola, Chrebet	68	51.00 N	94.00 E
Tannūrah, Ra's at-	104	26.40 N	50.30 E
Tano	114	5.07 N	2.56 W
Tanout	114	14.58 N	8.53 E
Tanta	112	30.47 N	31.00 E
Tantoyuca	130	21.21 N	98.14 W
Tanzania 1	110	6.00 S	35.00 E
Taoerhe	88	45.42 N	124.05 E
Taohe	88	32.52 N	103.16 E
Taormina	78	37.52 N	15.17 E
Taos	164	36.24 N	105.34 W
Taoudenni	106	22.40 N	4.00 W
T'aoyüan	86	25.00 N	121.18 E
Tapa	86	59.16 N	25.58 E
Tapachula	130	14.54 N	92.17 W
Tapajós	138	2.24 S	54.41 W
Tapanahoni	134	4.20 S	54.25 W
Tāpi	102	21.06 N	72.41 E
Tapiche	134	5.03 S	73.51 W
Tapolca	72	46.53 N	17.27 E
Tappahannock	152	37.56 N	76.52 W
Tapuruucara	138	0.24 S	65.02 W
Taqātu' Hayyā	112	18.20 N	36.22 E
Taquara	140	29.39 S	50.47 W
Taquari	134	19.15 S	57.17 W
Tara, Austl.	120	27.17 S	150.28 E
Tara, S.S.S.R.	84	56.54 N	74.22 E
Taraba	106	8.30 N	10.15 E
Ṭarābulus (Tripoli), Libiya	112	32.54 N	13.11 E
Ṭarābulus (Tripoli), Lubnān	104	34.26 N	35.51 E
Ṭarābulus (Tripolitania) 1	108	31.00 N	15.00 E
Taradale	126	39.32 S	176.51 E
Tarakan	96	3.18 N	117.38 E
Taranto	78	40.28 N	17.15 E
Taranto, Golfo di	78	40.10 N	17.20 E
Tarapoto	134	6.30 S	76.20 W
Taraquá	138	0.06 N	68.28 W
Tarare	74	45.54 N	4.26 E
Tarata	134	17.37 S	66.01 W
Tarauacá	134	8.10 S	70.46 W
Tarauacá	134	6.42 S	69.48 W
Tarbagataj, Chrebet	76	41.54 N	1.44 W
Tarbert	70	57.54 N	6.49 W
Tarbes	74	43.14 N	0.05 E
Tarboro	156	35.54 N	77.32 W
Tarbu	108	26.02 N	15.10 E
Tarcento	78	46.13 N	13.13 E
Tarcoola	122	30.41 S	134.33 E
Tardajos	76	42.21 N	3.49 W
Tardoki-Jani, Gora	84	48.55 N	138.04 E
Taree	120	31.54 S	152.28 E
Tarfa, Wâdī aţ 1	112	28.36 N	30.50 E
Tärgovište	80	43.15 N	26.34 E
Tarhūnah	108	32.26 N	13.38 E
Tari	124	5.53 S	143.00 E
Tarifa	76	36.01 N	5.36 W
Tarija	134	21.31 S	64.45 W
Tariku	124	3.04 S	138.09 E
Taritatu	124	2.54 S	138.27 E
Tarkastad	116	32.00 S	26.16 E
Tarkio	158	40.27 N	95.23 W
Tarkio	162	40.43 N	95.26 W
Tarko-Sale	84	64.55 N	77.49 E
Tarkwa	114	5.19 N	1.59 W
Tarlac	92	15.29 N	120.35 E
Tarm	68	55.55 N	8.32 E
Tarma	134	11.25 S	75.43 W
Tarn 5	74	43.50 N	2.00 E
Tarn-et-Garonne 5	74	44.05 N	1.20 E
Tarnobrzeg	72	50.35 N	21.41 E
Tarnów	72	50.01 N	21.00 E
Tarnowskie Góry	72	50.27 N	18.52 E
Taro	158	40.27 N	95.23 W
Tarouca	76	41.00 N	7.40 W
Tarpon Springs	156	28.09 N	82.45 W
Tarragona	76	41.07 N	1.15 E
Tarraleah	120	42.18 S	146.27 E
Tarran Hills 2	120	32.27 S	146.27 E
Tarrant	158	33.34 N	86.46 W
Tarrasa	76	41.34 N	2.01 E
Tarsus	104	36.55 N	34.53 E
Tartagal	140	22.32 S	63.50 W
Tartu	86	58.23 N	26.43 E
Ţarţūs	104	34.53 N	35.53 E
Tarusa	86	54.43 N	37.11 E
Tarutung	94	2.01 N	98.57 E
Tarvisio	78	46.30 N	13.35 E
Tarzan	160	32.18 N	101.58 W
Tasejeva	84	58.06 N	94.01 E
Tasejevo	84	57.12 N	94.54 E
Ţashk, Daryācheh-ye 1	104	29.45 N	53.35 E
Taškent → Taškent	82	41.20 N	69.18 E
Tāshkurghān	102	36.41 N	67.41 E
Tasikmalaja	96	7.20 S	108.12 E
Täsjö	68	64.13 N	16.14 E
Taškepri	100	36.21 N	62.38 E
Tasmania 3	120	43.00 S	147.00 E
Tasmania I	120	42.00 S	147.00 E
Tasman Peninsula 1	120	43.05 S	147.50 E
Tasman Sea 2	126	39.00 S	170.00 E
Tassiaouac, Lac 1	154	53.00 N	74.00 W
Taštagol	84	52.47 N	87.53 E
Tata	72	47.39 N	18.18 E
Tatabánya	72	47.34 N	18.26 E
Tata Mailau, Monte	96	8.55 S	125.30 E
Tatarsk	84	53.16 N	28.48 E
Tatarskij Proliv U	84	55.13 N	75.58 E
Tatar Strait → Tatarskij Proliv U	84	50.00 N	141.15 E
Tate	120	17.22 S	143.44 E
Tathlina Lake	142	60.32 N	117.32 W
Tatitlek	146	60.52 N	146.41 W
Tatnam, Cape	142	57.16 N	91.00 W
Tatta	102	24.45 N	67.55 E
Tatum, N. Mex., U.S.	160	33.16 N	103.19 W
Tatum, Tex., U.S.	158	32.19 N	94.31 W
Tat'ung → Datong	88	40.08 N	113.13 E
Tatvan	100	38.30 N	42.16 E
Tau	68	59.04 N	5.54 E
Tauberbischofsheim	72	49.37 N	9.40 E
Taučik	82	44.21 N	51.19 E
Taujskaja Guba C	84	59.20 N	150.20 E
Taumarunui	126	38.53 S	175.17 E
Taunggyi	94	20.47 N	97.02 E
Taunton, Eng., U.K.	70	51.01 N	3.06 W
Taunton, Mass., U.S.	152	41.54 N	71.06 W
Taupo	126	38.41 S	176.05 E
Taupo, Lake	126	38.48 S	175.55 E
Tauragé	86	55.15 N	22.17 E
Tauranga	126	37.42 S	176.10 E
Taurianova	78	38.21 N	16.01 E
Taurus Mountains → Toros Dağları	64	37.00 N	33.00 E
Tauste	76	41.55 N	1.15 W
Tavares	156	28.48 N	81.44 W
Tavda	82	58.03 N	65.15 E
Tavda	82	59.20 N	63.28 E
Taverot	156	25.01 N	80.31 W
Tavira	76	37.07 N	7.39 W
Tavistock	154	43.19 N	80.50 W
Tavolžan	82	52.44 N	77.27 E
Tavoy	94	14.05 N	98.12 E
Tawa	126	41.10 S	174.50 E
Tawas City	154	44.17 N	83.31 W
Tawau	96	4.17 N	117.54 E
Tawitawi Island I	98	5.12 N	120.00 E
Tawkar	112	18.33 N	37.44 E
Taxco de Alarcón	130	18.33 N	99.36 W
Tay-chang, Deo X	94	21.07 N	103.00 E
Taylor, Ariz., U.S.	160	34.28 N	110.05 W
Taylor, Tex., U.S.	160	30.34 N	97.25 W
Taylors	156	34.55 N	82.18 W
Taylorsville	158	31.50 N	89.32 W
Taylorville	158	39.33 N	89.18 W
Taymá'	112	27.38 N	38.29 E
Taymyra Peninsula → Tajmyr, Poluostrov	84	76.00 N	104.00 E
Tayside Region 4	70	56.30 N	3.30 W
Taytay	98	10.49 N	119.31 E
Taz	84	67.32 N	78.40 E
Taza	106	34.16 N	4.01 W
Tazewell	152	37.07 N	81.31 W
Tazin	142	59.47 N	109.03 W
Tazin Lake	142	60.26 N	110.45 W
Tazovskaja Guba C	84	69.05 N	76.00 E
Tazovskij	82	67.28 N	78.42 E
Tazovskij Poluostrov	84	68.35 N	76.00 E
Tbilisi	82	41.43 N	44.49 E
Tchibanga	110	2.51 S	11.02 E
Tchien	114	6.04 N	8.08 W
Tczew	72	54.06 N	18.47 E
Teague	158	31.38 N	96.17 W
Te Anau, Lake	126	45.15 S	167.46 E
Teano	78	41.15 N	14.04 E
Teapa	130	17.33 N	92.57 W
Te Aroha	126	37.33 S	175.43 E
Te Awamutu	126	38.01 S	175.19 E
Teba	76	36.58 N	4.56 W
Tébessa	106	35.28 N	8.09 E
Tebingtinggi, Pulau	96	3.36 S	103.05 E
Tecamachalco	130	18.53 N	97.44 W
Tecka	140	43.29 S	70.48 W
Tecklenburg	72	52.13 N	7.48 E
Tecomán	130	18.55 N	103.53 W
Tecopa	160	35.51 N	116.13 W
Tecpan de Galeana	130	17.15 N	100.41 W
Tecuala	130	22.23 N	105.27 W
Tecuci	80	45.50 N	27.26 E
Tecumseh, Mich., U.S.	154	42.00 N	83.57 W
Tecumseh, Nebr., U.S.	162	40.22 N	96.11 W
Tecumseh, Okla., U.S.	160	35.15 N	96.56 W
Tedžen, S.S.S.R.	100	37.23 N	60.31 E
Tedžen, S.S.S.R.	100	37.24 N	60.31 E
Tedžen (Harīrūd)	104	37.24 N	60.38 E
Teesside → Middlesbrough	70	54.35 N	1.14 W
Tefé	138	3.22 S	64.42 W
Tefé	138	3.35 S	64.47 W
Tegal	96	6.52 S	109.08 E
Tegucigalpa	132	14.06 N	87.13 W
Tehachapi	168	35.08 N	118.27 W
Tehek Lake	142	64.55 N	95.30 W
Teheran → Tehrān	104	35.40 N	51.26 E
Tehrān	104	35.40 N	51.26 E
Tehuacan	130	18.27 N	97.23 W
Tehuantepec	130	16.20 N	95.14 W
Tehuantepec, Golfo de	130	16.00 N	94.50 W
Tehuantepec, Istmo de	130	17.00 N	94.30 W
Teide, Pico de ʌ	106	28.16 N	16.38 W
Teifi	70	52.07 N	4.42 W
Teignmouth	70	50.33 N	3.30 W
Teixeira da Silva	110	12.13 S	15.52 E
Teixeira de Sousa	110	10.42 S	22.12 E
Tejkovo	86	56.52 N	40.34 E
Tejo → Tagus	76	38.40 N	9.24 W
Tekamah	162	41.47 N	96.13 W
Tekax de Álvaro Obregón	130	20.12 N	89.17 W
Tekeli	82	44.48 N	78.57 E
Tekeze (Satīt)	112	14.20 N	35.50 E
Tekirdağ	80	40.59 N	27.31 E
Tekirdağ 4	80	41.00 N	27.31 E
Tekoa	166	47.14 N	117.04 W
Tekonsha	154	42.05 N	84.60 W
Te Kuiti	126	38.20 S	175.10 E
Telanaipura (Djambi)	96	1.36 S	103.37 E
Tel Aviv-Yafo	104	32.04 N	34.46 E
Telavåg	68	60.16 N	4.49 E
Teleckoje, Ozero	82	51.35 N	87.40 E
Telefomin	124	5.10 S	141.35 E
Telegraph Creek	142	57.56 N	131.10 W
Telemark 6	68	59.30 N	8.40 E
Telén	140	36.15 S	65.31 W
Teleorman 4	80	44.00 N	25.12 E
Telertheba, Djebel ʌ	106	24.10 N	6.51 E
Teles Pires	138	7.21 S	58.03 W
Telfs	72	47.18 N	11.04 E
Tell City	158	37.57 N	86.46 W
Telluride	164	37.56 N	107.48 W
Telok Anson	96	4.00 N	101.02 E
Teloloapan	130	18.21 N	99.51 W
Telsen	140	42.25 S	67.00 W
Telšiai	86	55.59 N	22.15 E
Telti	78	40.52 N	9.21 E
Teltow	72	52.23 N	13.16 E
Telukbetung	96	5.27 S	105.16 E
Temagami, Lake	154	47.00 N	80.05 W
Temax	130	21.09 N	88.56 W
Tembenči	84	64.36 N	99.58 E
Tembesi	96	1.43 S	103.06 E
Tembleque	76	39.42 N	3.30 W
Temecula	168	33.16 N	117.09 W
Teminabuan	124	1.26 S	132.01 E
Temir	82	49.08 N	57.06 E
Temirtau, S.S.S.R.	82	50.05 N	72.56 E
Temirtau, S.S.S.R.	84	53.08 N	87.28 E
Témiscaming	154	46.43 N	79.06 W
Temora	120	34.26 S	147.32 E
Temperance	154	41.47 N	83.34 W
Tempe	160	33.25 N	111.56 W
Tempio Pausania	78	40.54 N	9.07 E
Temple	160	31.06 N	97.21 W
Templemore	70	52.48 N	7.50 W
Templeton	120	18.26 S	142.28 E
Templeton	120	21.14 S	138.13 E
Templin	72	53.07 N	13.30 E
Temr'uk	82	45.17 N	37.23 E
Temuco	140	38.44 S	72.36 W
Tenabo	130	20.03 N	90.14 W
Tenaha	158	31.57 N	94.15 W
Tenakee Springs	146	57.47 N	135.13 W
Tenāli	100	16.14 N	80.40 E
Tenasserim	94	12.05 N	99.01 E
Tendaho	108	11.48 N	40.52 E
Tende	74	44.05 N	7.36 E
Tende, Col de X	74	44.09 N	7.34 E
Ten Degree Channel U	94	10.00 N	93.00 E
Ténéré	106	19.00 N	10.30 E
Tenerife I	106	28.19 N	16.34 W
Tengchong	94	25.04 N	98.29 E
Tengiz, Ozero	82	50.24 N	68.57 E
Tengxian	88	35.08 N	117.10 E
Tenke	110	10.35 S	26.07 E
Tenkodogo	114	11.47 N	0.22 W
Tennant Creek	122	19.40 S	134.10 E
Tennessee 3	144	35.50 N	86.30 W
Tennessee	144	37.04 N	88.33 W
Tennille	156	32.56 N	82.48 W
Tenom	92	5.08 N	115.55 E
Tenosique de Pino Suárez	130	17.29 N	91.26 W
Ten Sleep	166	44.02 N	107.27 W
Tenterfield	120	29.03 S	152.01 E
Teocaltiche	130	21.26 N	102.35 W
Tepa	130	7.52 S	129.31 E
Tepatitlán [de Morelos]	130	20.49 N	102.44 W
Tepeaca	130	18.58 N	97.54 W
Tepehuanes	130	25.21 N	105.44 W
Tepic	130	21.30 N	104.54 W
Teplice	72	50.39 N	13.48 E
Te Puke	126	37.47 S	176.19 E
Tequendama, Salto de ᴸ	138	4.35 N	74.18 W
Téra	114	14.01 N	0.45 E
Tera	76	41.54 N	5.44 W
Teramo	78	42.39 N	13.42 E
Terang	120	38.14 S	142.55 E
Tercero	140	32.55 S	62.19 W
Terechovka	86	52.13 N	31.27 E
Terek	82	43.44 N	46.33 E
Teresina	138	5.05 S	42.49 W
Teresópolis	138	22.26 S	42.59 W
Terespol	72	52.05 N	23.36 E
Teressa Island I	94	8.15 N	93.10 E
Terib'orka	68	69.08 N	35.08 E
Termez	102	37.14 N	67.16 E
Termini Imerese	78	37.59 N	13.42 E
Términos, Laguna de C	130	18.35 N	91.30 W
Termoli	78	42.00 N	15.00 E
Ternate	124	0.48 N	127.24 E
Ternberg	72	47.58 N	14.22 E
Terneuzen	72	51.20 N	3.50 E
Terni	78	42.34 N	12.37 E
Ternitz	72	47.44 N	16.03 E
Ternopol'	64	49.34 N	25.36 E
Terpenija, Mys ⟩	84	48.39 N	144.44 E
Terpenija, Zaliv C	84	49.00 N	143.30 E
Terra Bella	168	35.58 N	119.03 W
Terrace	142	54.31 N	128.35 W
Terracina	78	41.17 N	13.15 E
Terralba	78	39.43 N	8.38 E
Terrasson-la-Villedieu	74	45.08 N	1.18 E
Terre Haute	158	39.28 N	87.24 W
Terrell	160	32.44 N	96.17 W
Terrell Hills	160	29.29 N	98.27 W
Terry	166	46.47 N	105.19 W
Tervola	68	66.05 N	24.48 E
Teslić	78	44.37 N	17.51 E
Teslin	146	60.10 N	132.45 W
Teslin	146	61.34 N	134.54 W
Teslin Lake	146	60.15 N	132.57 W
Tessaoua	114	13.45 N	7.59 E
Tessik Lake	142	64.53 N	75.25 W
Tessy-sur-Vire	74	48.58 N	1.04 W
Tetbury	70	51.39 N	2.10 W
Tete	110	16.13 S	33.35 E
Teterow	72	53.46 N	12.34 E
Teton	166	47.56 N	110.31 W
Tetonia	166	43.49 N	111.10 W
Tétouan	106	35.34 N	5.23 W
Tetovo	80	42.01 N	20.58 E
Tet'uche	84	44.22 N	135.35 E
Tet'uši	86	54.57 N	48.50 E
Teuco	140	25.35 S	60.11 W
Teulada	78	38.58 N	8.46 E
Teun, Pulau I	124	6.59 S	129.08 E
Teutopolis	158	39.08 N	88.29 W
Teuva	68	62.29 N	21.44 E
Tevere (Tiberias)	78	41.44 N	12.14 E
Teverya (Tiberias)	104	32.47 N	35.32 E
Texarkana, Ark., U.S.	158	33.26 N	94.02 W
Texarkana, Tex., U.S.	160	33.26 N	94.03 W
Texas 3	144	31.30 N	99.00 W
Texas City	160	29.23 N	94.54 W
Texico	160	34.23 N	103.03 W
Texline	160	36.23 N	103.01 W
Texoma, Lake 1	160	34.00 N	96.37 W
Teziutlán	130	19.49 N	97.21 W
Tezpur	102	26.38 N	92.48 E
Tha-anne	142	60.31 N	94.37 W
Thabana Ntlenyana ʌ	110	29.28 S	29.17 E
Thabazimbi	110	24.41 S	27.21 E
Thailand 1	94	15.00 N	100.00 E
Thailand, Gulf of C	94	10.00 N	101.00 E
Thai-nguyen	94	21.36 N	105.50 E
Thale	72	51.45 N	11.02 E
Thalia	160	34.07 N	99.34 W
Thames	126	37.08 S	175.33 E
Thamesville	154	42.33 N	81.58 W
Thann	74	47.49 N	7.05 E
Thaon-les-Vosges	74	48.15 N	6.25 E
Thar Desert (Great Indian Desert) 2	102	27.00 N	71.00 E
Thargomindah	122	28.00 S	143.49 E
Tharrawaddy	94	17.39 N	95.48 E
Thásos I	80	40.41 N	24.47 E
Thatcher	160	32.51 N	109.46 W
Thaton	94	16.55 N	97.22 E
Thaungyin	94	17.50 N	97.42 E
Thaya (Dyje)	72	48.37 N	16.56 E
Thayer	158	36.31 N	91.33 W
Thayetmyo	94	19.19 N	95.11 E
Thazi	94	20.51 N	96.05 E
The Alberga	122	27.06 S	135.33 E
The Big Warrambool ᴸ	120	30.05 S	147.33 E
The Black Sugarloaf ʌ	120	31.20 S	151.33 E
The Brothers II	100	12.09 N	53.12 E
The Dalles	166	45.36 N	121.10 W
The English Company's Islands II	122	11.50 S	136.32 E
The Everglades ᴸ	156	26.00 N	81.00 W
The Frome ᴸ	120	29.09 S	137.52 E
The Hague → 's-Gravenhage	72	52.06 N	4.18 E
The Johnston Lakes ᴸ	122	32.25 S	120.30 E
Thelon	142	64.16 N	96.05 W
The Margaret ᴸ	120	29.26 S	137.07 E
The Minch U	70	58.05 N	5.55 W
Thénezay	74	46.43 N	0.02 W
Theodore	120	24.57 S	150.05 E
The Pas	142	53.50 N	101.15 W
The Pilot ʌ	120	36.45 S	148.13 E
The Rand → Witwatersrand ᴸ	116	26.00 S	27.00 E
Thermopolis	164	43.39 N	108.13 W
The Rock	120	35.16 S	147.07 E
The Round Mountain ʌ	120	32.30 S	146.51 E
Thesiger Bay C	142	71.30 N	124.05 W
The Sisters ʌ 2	120	26.17 S	126.40 E
The Sound U	68	55.50 N	12.40 E
Thessalon	154	46.15 N	83.34 W
Thessaloniki (Salonika)	80	40.38 N	22.56 E
The Terraces ᴸ 4	122	28.40 S	121.20 E
Thetford	70	52.25 N	0.45 E
Thetford Mines	152	46.05 N	71.18 W
The Treuer ᴸ	120	27.52 S	137.12 E
The Valley	132	18.13 N	63.04 W
The Village	160	35.35 N	97.33 W
The Warburton ᴸ	120	27.55 S	137.28 E
The Yellow Mountain ʌ	120	32.30 S	146.51 E
Thibodaux	158	29.48 N	90.49 W
Thief River Falls	162	48.07 N	96.10 W
Thielsen, Mount ʌ	166	43.09 N	122.04 W
Thiene	78	45.42 N	11.29 E
Thies	114	14.48 N	16.56 W
Thika	110	1.03 S	37.05 E
Thimbu	100	27.28 N	89.39 E
Thingvellir	66a	64.17 N	21.06 W
Thionville	74	49.22 N	6.10 E
Thíra I	80	36.26 N	25.29 E
Thirsk	70	54.14 N	1.20 W
Thisted	68	56.57 N	8.42 E
Thistle Island I	120	35.00 S	136.09 E
Thívai (Thebes)	80	38.21 N	23.19 E
Thiviers	74	45.25 N	0.56 E
Thlewiaza	142	60.30 N	109.47 W
Thoa	142	60.31 N	109.47 W
Thomaston, Conn., U.S.	152	41.40 N	73.04 W
Thomaston, Ga., U.S.	156	32.53 N	84.19 W
Thomaston, Maine, U.S.	152	44.05 N	69.10 W
Thomastown	70	52.31 N	7.08 W
Thomasville, Ala., U.S.	158	31.55 N	87.51 W
Thomasville, Ga., U.S.	156	30.50 N	83.59 W
Thomasville, N.C., U.S.	156	35.53 N	80.05 W
Thompson	142	55.45 N	97.45 W
Thompson	158	39.45 N	93.36 W
Thompson Creek	166	30.46 N	104.25 W
Thompson Falls	166	47.36 N	115.21 W
Thompsonville, Conn., U.S.	152	42.00 N	72.36 W
Thompsonville, Mich., U.S.	154	44.31 N	85.56 W
Thomsen	142	74.08 N	119.35 W
Thomson	156	33.28 N	82.30 W
Thomson	120	25.11 S	142.53 E
Thon Buri	94	13.43 N	100.29 E
Thonon-les-Bains	74	46.22 N	6.29 E
Thorlákshöfn	66a	63.53 N	21.18 W
Thornbury	70	51.37 N	2.31 W
Thorndale	160	30.37 N	97.12 W
Thornhill	70	55.15 N	3.46 W
Thornton, Ark., U.S.	158	33.46 N	92.29 W
Thornton, Colo., U.S.	164	39.55 N	104.59 W
Thornton, Tex., U.S.	160	31.24 N	96.34 W
Thorsby	158	32.55 N	86.43 W
Thorshavn → Tórshavn	64	62.00 N	6.46 W
Thórshöfn	66a	66.13 N	15.17 W
Thouars	74	46.59 N	0.13 W
Thouin, Cape ⟩	122	20.20 S	118.12 E
Thousand Oaks	168	34.10 N	118.50 W
Thousand Springs Creek ᴸ	164	41.17 N	113.51 W
Thrace 9	80	41.20 N	26.45 E
Three Fingered Jack ʌ	166	44.29 N	121.50 W
Three Forks	166	45.54 N	111.33 W
Three Hummock Island I	120	40.26 S	144.55 E
Three Oaks	154	41.48 N	86.36 W
Three Pagodas Pass X	94	15.18 N	98.23 E
Three Points, Cape ⟩	114	4.45 N	2.06 W
Three Rivers, Mich., U.S.	154	41.56 N	85.38 W
Three Rivers, Tex., U.S.	160	28.28 N	98.11 W
Three Sisters ʌ	166	44.10 N	121.46 W
Three Springs	122	29.32 S	115.45 E
Throckmorton	160	33.11 N	99.11 W
Throssell Range ʌ 2	122	22.03 S	121.43 E
Thueyts	74	44.41 N	4.13 E
Thuin	72	50.20 N	4.17 E
Thun	74	46.45 N	7.37 E
Thunder Bay	154	48.23 N	89.15 W
Thunderbolt	156	32.02 N	81.03 W
Thunder Butte	162	45.19 N	101.53 W
Thunder Knoll ⁴	132	16.21 N	80.20 W
Thüringen	72	47.13 N	9.56 E
Thüringen 9	72	50.40 N	11.00 E
Thurles	70	52.41 N	7.49 W
Thurmont	152	39.37 N	77.25 W
Thursday Island I	124	10.35 S	142.13 E
Thurso	70	58.35 N	3.32 W
Thury-Harcourt	74	48.59 N	0.29 W
Thusis	74	46.42 N	9.26 E
Thysville → Mbanza-Ngungu	110	5.14 S	14.52 E
Tiancang	88	41.09 N	100.17 E
Tiandong	94	23.48 N	106.57 E
Tianjin (Tientsin)	88	39.08 N	117.12 E
Tianjun	88	37.18 N	99.01 E
Tianmen	88	30.39 N	113.08 E
Tianmushan ʌ	88	30.20 N	119.30 E
Tiantai	88	29.09 N	121.02 E
Tiantaishan ʌ	88	29.10 N	121.08 E
Tianzhu	88	37.14 N	102.59 E
Tiaret	106	35.28 N	1.21 E
Tibagi	140	24.30 S	50.24 W
Tibati, Sarīr 2	108	24.30 S	50.24 W
Tiberias → Teverya	104	32.47 N	35.32 E
Tibesti ʌ	108	21.00 N	17.30 E
Tibet → Xizang 3	102	32.00 N	90.00 E
Tiburón, Cabo ⟩	138	8.42 N	77.24 W
Tiburón, Isla I	130	29.00 N	112.20 W
Tice	156	26.41 N	81.49 W
Tichit	106	18.26 N	9.30 W
Tichoreck	82	45.51 N	40.09 E
Tichvin	86	59.39 N	33.31 E
Ticino 3	74	46.20 N	8.45 E
Ticino	78	45.09 N	9.14 E
Tickfaw	158	30.30 N	90.28 W
Ticonderoga	152	43.51 N	73.26 W
Ticul	130	20.24 N	89.32 W
Tidioute	152	41.41 N	79.24 W
Tidjikdja	114	18.33 N	11.25 W
Tidore	92	0.40 N	127.26 E
Tidra, Île I	114	19.44 N	16.24 W
Tiel	72	51.54 N	5.25 E
Tielelihu	88	44.30 N	85.15 E
Tieli	84	46.59 N	128.02 E
Tieling	88	42.18 N	123.49 E
Tielt	72	51.00 N	3.19 E
Tienen	72	50.48 N	4.57 E
Tien Shan ʌ	102	42.00 N	80.00 E
Tierra Amarilla	164	36.42 N	106.33 W
Tierra Blanca	130	18.27 N	96.21 W
Tierra Blanca Creek	160	34.46 N	102.56 W
Tierra del Fuego, Isla Grande de I	136	54.00 S	69.00 W
Tie Siding	164	41.05 N	105.31 W
Tieté	140	20.40 S	51.35 W
Tiffin	152	41.07 N	83.11 W
Tifton	156	31.27 N	83.31 W
Tigil	84	57.48 N	158.40 E
Tigre	138	4.30 S	74.10 W
Tigris (Dicle) (Dijlah)	104	31.00 N	47.25 E
Tiguentourine	106	27.50 N	9.18 E
Tijesno	78	43.48 N	15.39 E
Tijuana	168	32.32 N	117.01 W
Tijuana	168	32.33 N	117.08 W
Tiko	106	4.05 N	9.22 E
Tikrit	104	34.36 N	43.42 E
Tiksi	84	71.36 N	128.48 E
Tilburg	72	51.34 N	5.05 E
Tilbury	154	42.16 N	82.26 W
Tilden, Nebr., U.S.	162	42.03 N	97.50 W
Tilden, Tex., U.S.	160	28.28 N	98.33 W
Tilemsi, Vallée du V	114	16.15 N	0.02 E
Tillabéry	114	14.13 N	1.27 E
Tillamook	166	45.27 N	123.51 W
Tillanchong Island I	94	8.30 N	93.37 E
Tillberga	68	59.41 N	16.37 E
Tillmans Corner	158	30.34 N	88.08 W
Tillsonburg	154	42.51 N	80.44 W
Tilton, Ill., U.S.	158	40.06 N	87.38 W
Tilton, N.H., U.S.	152	43.27 N	71.35 W
Tiltonsville	152	40.10 N	80.42 W
Tīmā	104	26.54 N	31.26 E
Timanskij Kr'až ʌ	66	65.00 N	51.00 E
Timaru	126	44.24 S	171.15 E
Timbédra	114	16.15 N	8.10 W
Timber Lake	162	45.26 N	101.04 W
Timboon	120	38.29 S	142.59 E
Timbuktu → Tombouctou	106	16.46 N	3.01 W
Timimoun	106	29.14 N	0.16 E
Tîmiş (Tamiš)	80	44.51 N	20.39 E
Timiskaming, Lake	154	47.35 N	79.35 W
Timişoara	80	45.45 N	21.13 E
Timmendorfer Strand	72	54.00 N	10.46 E
Timmins	154	48.28 N	81.20 W
Timmonsville	156	34.08 N	79.57 W
Timor I	124	9.00 S	125.00 E
Timor → Portuguese Timor 2	124	8.50 S	126.00 E
Timor Sea 2	124	11.00 S	128.00 E
Timpson	158	31.54 N	94.24 W
Timpton	84	58.43 N	127.12 E
Timšér	72	62.06 N	54.40 E
Tinaquillo	138	9.55 N	68.18 W
Tindouf	106	27.40 N	8.09 W
Tingha	120	29.57 S	151.13 E
Tinglev	68	54.56 N	9.15 E
Tingo Maria	134	9.09 S	75.56 W
Tingvoll	68	62.54 N	8.12 E
Tinharé, Ilha de I	138	13.30 S	38.58 W
Tinkisso	114	11.21 N	9.10 W
Tinnoset	68	59.43 N	9.02 E
Tinogasta	140	28.04 S	67.34 W
Tínos I	80	37.38 N	25.10 E
Tinrhert, Plateau du 1	106	29.00 N	9.00 E
Tinsukia	102	27.56 N	95.22 E
Tinta	134	14.08 S	71.24 W
Tioga	152	41.54 N	77.08 W
Tioga	120	42.09 S	145.53 E
Tioman, Pulau I	96	2.48 N	104.10 E
Tionesta	152	41.30 N	79.27 W
Tioro, Selat U	124	4.42 S	122.05 E
Tippah	158	34.44 N	88.51 W
Tipperary, Austl.	124	13.44 S	131.02 E
Tipperary	70	52.29 N	8.10 W
Tipperary 6	70	52.40 N	8.00 W
Tipton, Calif., U.S.	168	36.04 N	119.19 W
Tipton, Ind., U.S.	158	40.16 N	86.02 W
Tipton, Iowa, U.S.	154	41.46 N	91.08 W
Tipton, Mo., U.S.	158	38.39 N	92.47 W
Tiptonville	158	36.22 N	89.28 W
Tip Top Mountain ʌ	154	48.16 N	85.59 W
Tiracambu, Serra do ʌ 1	138	3.15 S	46.30 W
Tirân, Jazīrat I	112	27.56 N	34.28 E
Tirân, Madiq U	112	28.00 N	34.28 E
Tirana	80	41.20 N	19.50 E
Tirano	78	46.13 N	10.10 E
Tiraspol'	80	46.51 N	29.38 E
Tire	80	38.04 N	27.45 E
Tiree I	70	56.31 N	6.49 W
Tîrgovişte	80	44.56 N	25.27 E
Tîrgu-Jiu	80	45.03 N	23.17 E
Tîrgu Mureş	80	46.33 N	24.33 E
Tîrgu-Neamţ	80	47.12 N	26.22 E
Tîrgu-Ocna	80	46.17 N	26.37 E
Tirich Mīr ʌ	102	36.15 N	71.50 E
Tîrnăveni	80	46.20 N	24.17 E
Tírnavos	80	39.45 N	22.17 E
Tirol 4	72	47.15 N	11.20 E
Tirschenreuth	72	49.53 N	12.21 E
Tiruchirāppalli	100	10.49 N	78.41 E
Tirunelveli	100	8.44 N	77.41 E
Tiruppur	100	11.06 N	77.21 E
Tisa (Tisza)	80	45.15 N	20.17 E
Tisdale	142	52.51 N	104.04 W
Tishomingo	160	34.14 N	96.41 W
Tista	102	26.44 N	89.43 E
Tisza (Tisa)	72	45.15 N	20.17 E
Tiszaföldvár	72	46.59 N	20.15 E
Tiszavasvári	72	47.58 N	21.21 E
Tit-Ary	84	71.58 N	127.01 E
Titicaca, Lago	134	15.50 S	69.20 W
Titograd	80	42.26 N	19.14 E
Titovo Užice	80	43.52 N	19.51 E
Titov Veles	80	41.41 N	21.48 E
Titran	68	63.40 N	8.19 E
Tittling	72	48.44 N	13.23 E
Titule	108	3.17 N	25.32 E
Titusville, Fla., U.S.	156	28.37 N	80.49 W
Titusville, Pa., U.S.	152	41.38 N	79.40 W
Tiverton	70	50.55 N	3.29 W
Tivoli	78	41.58 N	12.48 E
Tivoli, Tex., U.S.	160	28.27 N	96.53 W
Tizimín	130	21.10 N	88.10 W
Tizi-Ouzou	106	36.44 N	4.03 E
Tjepu	96	7.09 S	111.35 E
Tjiandjur	96	6.49 S	107.08 E
Tjilatjap	96	7.44 S	109.00 E
Tjirebon	96	6.44 S	108.34 E
Tlacolula [de Matamoros]	130	16.57 N	96.29 W
Tlacotalpan	130	18.37 N	95.40 W
Tlalnepantla	130	19.33 N	99.12 W
Tlaxcala [de Xicoténcatl]	130	19.19 N	98.14 W
Tlaxiaco	130	17.16 N	97.41 W
Tlemcen	106	34.52 N	1.15 W
Toast	156	36.30 N	80.38 W
Toba, Danau	96	2.35 N	98.50 E
Tobago I	132	11.15 N	60.40 W
Toba Kākar Range ʌ	102	31.15 N	68.00 E
Tobelo	92	1.44 N	128.01 E
Tobermory	154	45.15 N	81.40 W
Tobermory, Scot., U.K.	70	56.37 N	6.05 W
Tobi I	92	3.00 N	131.10 E
Tobol	82	52.40 N	62.39 E
Tobol	82	58.10 N	68.12 E
Tobol'sk	82	58.12 N	68.16 E
Tobruk → Ţubruq	112	32.05 N	23.59 E
Tocantínia	138	9.33 S	48.22 W
Tocantinópolis	138	6.20 S	47.25 W
Tocantins	138	1.45 S	49.10 W
Toccoa	156	34.35 N	83.19 W
Toco	132	10.49 N	60.57 W
Toconao	140	23.11 S	68.01 W
Tocopilla	140	22.05 S	69.35 W
Tocorpuri, Cerro de ʌ	140	22.26 S	67.55 W
Tocumwal	120	35.49 S	145.34 E
Todi	78	42.47 N	12.24 E
Todmorden	122	27.08 S	134.48 E
Todos Santos	130	23.27 N	110.13 W
Todtnau	72	47.50 N	7.56 E
Tofte	68	59.33 N	10.34 E
Togiak	146	59.04 N	160.24 W
Togian, Kepulauan II	96	0.20 S	122.00 E
Togo 1	114	8.00 N	1.10 E
Toguçin	84	55.16 N	84.23 E
Toholampi	68	63.46 N	24.15 E
Toijala	68	61.10 N	23.52 E
Toiyabe Dome ʌ	168	38.51 N	117.22 W
Toiyabe Range ʌ 2	168	39.10 N	117.10 W
Tokat	104	40.19 N	36.34 E
Tokko	84	59.56 N	88.08 E
Tokmak, S.S.S.R.	82	42.55 N	75.18 E
Tokmak, S.S.S.R.	86	47.15 N	35.43 E
Toko Range ʌ	120	23.05 S	138.20 E
Tokoroa	126	38.13 S	175.52 E
Toksook Bay	146	60.32 N	165.06 W
Toksovo	86	60.09 N	30.31 E
Tokuno-shima I	91b	27.45 N	128.58 E
Tokushima	90	34.04 N	134.34 E
Tokuyama	90	34.03 N	131.49 E
Tōkyō	90	35.42 N	139.46 E
Tolbuhin	80	43.34 N	27.50 E
Toledo, Bra.	140	24.44 S	53.45 W
Toledo, Col.	138	7.19 N	72.29 W
Toledo, Esp.	76	39.52 N	4.01 W
Toledo, Iowa, U.S.	154	42.00 N	92.35 W
Toledo, Ohio, U.S.	152	41.39 N	83.32 W
Toledo, Oreg., U.S.	166	44.37 N	123.56 W
Toledo Bend Reservoir 1	158	31.30 N	93.45 W
Tolentino	78	43.12 N	13.17 E
Tolga	68	62.25 N	11.00 E
Tolima 5	138	4.00 N	75.15 W
Tolima, Nevado del ʌ	138	4.40 N	75.19 W
Tolitoli	96	1.02 N	120.49 E
Toljatti	82	53.31 N	49.26 E
Tol'ka	84	64.02 N	81.55 E
Tolleson	160	33.27 N	112.16 W
Tolmačovo	86	58.52 N	29.55 E
Tolmezzo	78	46.24 N	13.01 E
Tolna	72	46.26 N	18.46 E
Tolna 6	72	46.30 N	18.35 E
Tolo, Teluk C	96	2.00 S	122.30 E
Toločin	86	54.25 N	29.42 E
Tolono	158	39.59 N	88.16 W
Tolosa	76	43.08 N	2.04 W
Tolstoj, Mys ⟩	84	59.10 N	155.12 E
Toltén	140	39.13 S	73.14 W
Tolú	138	9.31 N	75.35 W
Toluca [de Lerdo]	130	19.17 N	99.40 W
Tom'	84	56.50 N	84.27 E
Tomah	154	43.59 N	90.30 W
Tomahawk	154	45.28 N	89.44 W
Tomakomai	90a	42.38 N	141.36 E
Tomar	76	39.36 N	8.25 W
Tomaszów Lubelski	72	50.28 N	23.25 E
Tomaszów Mazowiecki	72	51.32 N	20.01 E
Tombador, Serra do ʌ 1	138	12.00 S	57.40 W
Tombigbee	158	31.04 N	87.58 W
Tombouctou (Timbuktu)	114	16.46 N	3.01 W
Tombstone	160	31.43 N	110.04 W
Tombstone Mountain ʌ	146	64.25 N	138.30 W
Tomé	140	36.37 S	72.57 W
Tomelloso	76	39.10 N	3.01 W
Tomini	96	0.31 N	120.30 E
Tomini, Teluk C	96	0.20 S	121.00 E
Tommot	84	58.58 N	126.19 E
Tomo	138	5.20 N	67.48 W
Tompkinsville	158	36.42 N	85.41 W
Tomptokan	84	57.06 N	133.59 E
Toms River	152	39.57 N	74.11 W
Tomsk	84	56.30 N	84.58 E
Tonalá	130	16.04 N	93.45 W
Tonantins	138	2.52 S	67.48 W
Tonasket	166	48.42 N	119.26 W
Tonawanda	152	43.01 N	78.52 W
Tonbridge	70	51.12 N	0.16 E
Tønder	68	54.56 N	8.54 E
Tongaat	116	29.35 S	31.07 E
Tonga 1	58	20.00 S	175.00 W
Tonganoxie	162	39.07 N	95.05 W
Tongatapu Group II	62	21.10 S	175.10 W
Tongbai	88	32.22 N	113.24 E
Tongchuan	88	35.01 N	109.01 E
Tongeren	72	50.47 N	5.28 E
Tonghua	88	41.50 N	125.55 E
Tongjosŏn-man C	88	39.30 N	128.00 E
Tongling	88	30.56 N	117.48 E
Tongren	88	27.42 N	109.11 E
Tongue	166	46.24 N	105.52 W
Tongue of the Ocean U	132	24.00 N	77.20 W
Tonk	102	26.09 N	75.48 E
Tonkawa	160	36.41 N	97.18 W
Tonkin, Gulf of C	94	20.00 N	108.00 E
Tonle Sap → Sab, Tônlé	94	12.50 N	104.00 E
Tonnay-Boutonne	74	45.58 N	0.42 W
Tonneins	74	44.23 N	0.19 E
Tönning	72	54.19 N	8.56 E
Tonopah	168	38.04 N	117.14 W
Tønsberg	68	59.17 N	10.25 E
Toodyay	122	31.33 S	116.28 E
Tooele	164	40.32 N	112.18 W
Toompine	120	27.13 S	144.22 E
Toora-Chem	84	52.28 N	96.17 E
Toowoomba	120	27.33 S	151.57 E
Topeka	162	39.03 N	95.41 W

Symbols in the index entries are identified on page 203.

Name	Page	Lat	Long
Topka, Gora ▲	84	57.08 N	137.24 E
Topki	84	55.16 N	85.36 E
Topol'čany	72	48.34 N	18.10 E
Topolobampo	130	25.36 N	109.03 W
Toppenish	166	46.23 N	120.19 W
Tops, Mount ▲	122	21.50 S	134.00 E
Topsham	152	43.56 N	69.58 W
Torawitan, Tandjung ➤	96	1.46 N	124.58 E
Torbat-e Heydarīyeh	104	35.16 N	59.13 E
Torbat-e Jām	104	35.14 N	60.36 E
Torbay, Newf., Can.	150	47.40 N	52.44 W
Torbay → Torquay, Eng., U.K.	70	50.28 N	3.30 W
Torbay Head ➤	122	35.08 S	117.39 E
Torbejevo	86	54.05 N	43.15 E
Torch ≃	142	53.50 N	103.05 W
Tordesillas	76	41.30 N	5.00 W
Toreno	76	42.42 N	6.30 W
Torez	64	48.01 N	38.37 E
Torgau	72	51.34 N	13.00 E
Torgelow	72	53.37 N	14.00 E
Torhout	72	51.04 N	3.06 E
Torino (Turin)	78	45.03 N	7.40 E
Torit	108	4.24 N	32.34 E
Torment, Point ➤	122	17.02 S	123.36 E
Tornado Mountain ▲	148	49.58 N	114.39 W
Torneälven ≃	66	65.48 N	24.08 E
Torneträsk ⊜	66	68.20 N	19.10 E
Torngat Mountains ⋏	142	59.00 N	64.00 W
Tornio	68	65.51 N	24.08 E
Tornquist	140	38.06 S	62.14 W
Toro	76	41.31 N	5.24 W
Toro, Cerro del ▲	140	29.08 S	69.48 W
Törökszentmiklós	72	47.11 N	20.25 E
Toronto, Ont., Can.	154	43.39 N	79.23 W
Toronto, Ohio, U.S.	152	40.28 N	80.36 W
Toronto, S. Dak., U.S.	158	44.34 N	96.39 W
Toropec	86	56.30 N	31.39 E
Tororo	110	0.42 N	34.11 E
Torpo	68	60.40 N	8.43 E
Torquay (Torbay)	70	50.28 N	3.30 W
Torrance	168	33.50 N	118.19 W
Torrão	76	38.18 N	8.13 W
Torre Annunziata	78	40.45 N	14.27 E
Torre Baja	76	40.07 N	1.15 W
Torre de Moncorvo	76	41.10 N	7.03 W
Torredonjimeno	76	37.46 N	3.57 W
Torrejón de Ardoz	76	40.27 N	3.29 W
Torrelavega	76	43.21 N	4.03 W
Torremaggiore	78	41.41 N	15.17 E
Torrens, Lake ⊜	120	31.00 S	137.50 E
Torrente	76	39.26 N	0.28 W
Torreón	130	25.33 N	103.26 W
Torres Novas	76	39.29 N	8.32 W
Torres Strait ⋃	134	10.25 S	142.10 E
Torres Vedras	76	39.06 N	9.16 W
Torridon	70	57.33 N	5.31 W
Torriglia	78	44.31 N	9.10 E
Torrijos	76	39.59 N	4.17 W
Torrington, Conn., U.S.	152	41.48 N	73.08 W
Torrington, Wyo., U.S.	162	42.04 N	104.11 W
Torsås	68	56.24 N	16.00 E
Torsby	68	60.08 N	13.00 E
Tórshavn	64	62.01 N	6.46 W
Tortola ⚊	132	18.26 N	64.37 W
Tortoli	78	39.55 N	9.39 E
Tortona	78	44.54 N	8.52 E
Tortosa	76	40.48 N	0.31 E
Tortue, Île de la ⚊	132	20.01 N	72.50 W
Toruń	72	53.02 N	18.35 E
Torup	68	56.58 N	13.05 E
Toržok	86	57.03 N	34.58 E
Toscana □⁴	78	43.25 N	11.00 E
Tosno	86	59.33 N	30.53 E
T'osovskij	86	58.57 N	31.14 E
T'osovskij	86	58.48 N	30.52 E
Tostado	140	29.15 S	61.45 W
Toteng	116	20.22 S	22.58 E
Tôtes	74	49.41 N	1.03 E
Tot'ma	86	59.57 N	42.45 E
Totness	138	5.53 N	56.19 W
Tototlán	130	20.33 N	102.48 W
Totson Mountain ▲	146	64.26 N	157.15 W
Tottenham, Austl.	120	32.14 S	147.21 E
Tottenham, Ont., Can.	154	44.01 N	79.49 W
Tottori	90	35.30 N	134.14 E
Touba	114	8.17 N	7.41 W
Toubkal, Jbel ▲	106	31.05 N	7.55 W
Toucy	74	47.44 N	3.18 E
Tougan	114	13.04 N	3.04 W
Touggourt	106	33.10 N	6.00 E
Toul	74	48.41 N	5.54 E
Toulnustouc ≃	150	49.35 N	68.24 W
Toulon	74	43.07 N	5.56 E
Toulon-sur-Arroux	74	46.42 N	4.08 E
Toulouse	74	43.36 N	1.26 E
Toungoo	94	18.56 N	96.26 E
Touques ≃	74	49.22 N	0.06 E
Touraine □⁹	152	45.34 N	75.47 W
Tourcoing	74	50.43 N	3.09 E
Tournai	72	50.36 N	3.23 E
Tournon	74	45.04 N	4.50 E
Tournus	74	46.34 N	4.54 E
Tours	74	47.23 N	0.41 E
Toury	74	48.12 N	1.56 E
Touside, Pic ▲	108	21.02 N	16.25 E
Tovar	138	8.20 N	71.46 W
Tovarkovskij	86	53.40 N	38.14 E
Towanda, Kans., U.S.	158	37.48 N	97.02 W
Towanda, Pa., U.S.	152	41.46 N	76.26 W
Towcester	70	52.08 N	1.00 W
Tower	154	47.48 N	92.17 W
Townsend	162	46.19 N	111.31 W
Townsend, Mount ▲	120	36.25 S	148.15 E
Townshend ⚊	120	22.15 S	150.30 E
Townshend Island ⚊	120	22.16 S	150.30 E
Townsville	120	19.16 S	146.48 E
Towson	152	39.24 N	76.36 W
Towuti, Danau ⊜	96	2.45 S	121.31 E
Toyah	160	31.19 N	103.47 W
Toyama	90	36.41 N	137.13 E
Toyohashi	90	34.46 N	137.23 E
Toyonaka	90	34.47 N	135.28 E
Toyota	90	35.05 N	137.09 E
Tozer, Mount ▲	124	12.45 S	143.13 E
Tozeur	106	33.55 N	8.08 E
Trabzon	64	41.00 N	39.43 E
Tracy, Calif., U.S.	168	37.44 N	121.25 W
Tracy, Minn., U.S.	154	44.14 N	95.37 W
Traer	154	42.12 N	92.28 W
Traid	76	40.40 N	1.49 W
Traiguén	140	38.15 S	72.41 W
Trail	148	49.06 N	117.42 W
Traira (Taraira) ≃	138	1.04 S	69.26 W
Trakai	86	54.38 N	24.56 E
Tralee	70	52.16 N	9.42 W
Trammel	156	37.01 N	82.18 W
Trammel Creek ≃	156	36.45 N	86.23 W
Tramore	70	52.10 N	7.10 W
Trancas	140	28.20 S	65.20 W
Trancoso	76	40.47 N	7.21 W
Tranebjerg	68	55.51 N	10.36 E
Tranemo	68	57.29 N	13.21 E
Trang	94	7.33 N	99.36 E
Trangan, Pulau ⚊	124	6.35 S	134.20 E
Trangie	120	32.02 S	147.59 E
Trani	78	41.17 N	16.26 E
Transkei □⁹	78	31.20 S	29.00 E
Transvaal □⁹	116	24.45 S	29.00 E
Transylvanian Alps → Carpații Meridionali ⋏	72	45.30 N	24.15 E
Trapani	78	38.01 N	12.31 E
Traralgon	120	38.12 S	146.32 E
Trasacco	78	41.57 N	13.32 E
Trás-os-Montes □⁹	76	41.30 N	7.07 W
Traun	72	48.13 N	14.14 E
Traunstein	72	47.52 N	12.38 E
Travellers Lake ⊜	120	33.18 S	142.00 E
Traverse, Lake ⊜	162	45.43 N	96.40 W
Traverse City	154	44.46 N	85.37 W
Travnik	78	44.14 N	17.40 E
Trayning	122	31.07 S	117.48 E
Trbovlje	78	46.10 N	15.03 E
Třebíč	72	49.13 N	15.53 E
Trebinje	80	42.43 N	18.20 E
Trebisacce	78	39.52 N	16.32 E
Trebišov	72	48.40 N	21.47 E
Trecate	78	45.26 N	8.44 E
Treene ≃	54	54.22 N	9.05 E
Tregosse Islets ⚊⚊	120	17.41 S	150.43 E
Treinta y Tres	140	33.14 S	54.23 W
Trélazé	74	47.27 N	0.28 W
Trelew	136	43.15 S	65.20 W
Trelleborg	68	55.22 N	13.10 E
Tremblant, Mont ▲	152	46.16 N	74.35 W
Tremonton	166	41.43 N	112.10 W
Trenčín	72	48.54 N	18.04 E
Trenque Lauquen	140	35.58 S	62.44 W
Trent → Trento	78	46.04 N	11.08 E
Trentino-Alto Adige □⁴	78	46.30 N	11.20 E
Trento	78	46.04 N	11.08 E
Trenton, N.S., Can.	150	45.37 N	62.38 W
Trenton, Ont., Can.	154	44.06 N	77.35 W
Trenton, Fla., U.S.	156	29.37 N	82.49 W
Trenton, Ga., U.S.	156	34.52 N	85.31 W
Trenton, Ill., U.S.	158	38.36 N	89.41 W
Trenton, Mo., U.S.	158	40.05 N	93.37 W
Trenton, N.J., U.S.	152	40.13 N	74.45 W
Trenton, Tenn., U.S.	158	35.59 N	88.56 W
Trenton, Tex., U.S.	160	33.26 N	96.20 W
Trentwood	166	47.42 N	117.13 W
Tres Arroyos	140	38.22 S	60.15 W
Tres Esquinas	138	0.43 N	75.16 W
Tres Lagoas	134	20.48 S	51.43 W
Três Marias, Islas ⚊⚊	130	21.25 N	106.28 W
Três Marias, Reprêsa ⊜¹	134	18.12 S	45.15 W
Tres Passos	140	27.27 S	53.56 W
Três Picos, Cerro ▲	140	38.09 S	61.57 W
Tres Puntas, Cabo ➤	136	47.05 S	65.50 W
Tretten	68	61.19 N	10.19 E
Treuchtlingen	72	48.57 N	10.54 E
Treuen	72	50.32 N	12.18 E
Treuenbrietzen	72	52.06 N	12.52 E
Treviglio	78	45.31 N	9.35 E
Treviso	78	45.40 N	12.15 E
Trevorton	152	40.47 N	76.41 W
Trevose	152	40.09 N	74.59 W
Trévoux	74	45.56 N	4.46 E
Triabunna	120	42.30 S	147.55 E
Trianda	80	36.24 N	28.10 E
Triangle	152	38.32 N	77.20 W
Triberg	72	48.08 N	8.13 E
Tribune	162	38.28 N	101.45 W
Tricase	78	39.56 N	18.22 E
Trichūr	100	10.31 N	76.13 E
Trieben	72	47.29 N	14.30 E
Trier	72	49.45 N	6.38 E
Trieste	78	45.40 N	13.46 E
Triglav ▲	78	46.23 N	13.50 E
Trikala	80	39.34 N	21.46 E
Trikora, Puntjak ▲	124	4.15 S	138.45 E
Trilby	156	28.28 N	82.12 W
Trim	70	53.34 N	6.47 W
Trincat Island ⚊	92	8.05 N	93.35 E
Trincomalee	100	8.34 N	81.14 E
Trindade	136	20.31 S	29.19 W
Třinec ≃	138	49.41 N	18.40 E
Trinidad, Bol.	134	14.47 S	64.47 W
Trinidad, Col.	138	5.25 N	71.40 W
Trinidad, Cuba	132	21.48 N	79.59 W
Trinidad, Colo., U.S.	162	37.10 N	104.31 W
Trinidad, Tex., U.S.	160	32.09 N	96.06 W
Trinidad, Ur.	140	33.32 S	56.54 W
Trinidad ⚊	132	10.30 N	61.15 W
Trinidad and Tobago □¹	128	11.00 N	61.00 W
Trinity ≃¹	130	30.57 N	95.22 W
Trinity, Tex., U.S.	160	29.47 N	94.42 W
Trinity Bay C	150	48.00 N	53.40 W
Trinity Mountains ⋏	168	41.00 N	122.30 W
Trinkat Island ⚊	94	8.05 N	93.30 E
Trino	78	45.12 N	8.18 E
Trion	156	34.33 N	85.19 W
Tripoli → Ṭarābulus, Libiya	108	32.54 N	13.11 E
Tripoli → Ṭarābulus, Lubnān	104	34.26 N	35.51 E
Tripoli, Iowa, U.S.	154	42.48 N	92.16 W
Tripolis	80	37.31 N	22.21 E
Tripolitania → Ṭarābulus □⁹¹	108	31.00 N	15.00 E
Tripp	162	43.13 N	97.58 W
Tristao, Îles ⚊⚊	114	10.53 N	14.58 W
Triton Island ⚊	92	15.47 N	111.12 E
Triumph	158	29.20 N	89.30 W
Trivandrum	100	8.29 N	76.57 E
Trnava	72	48.23 N	17.35 E
Troarn	74	49.11 N	0.11 W
Trobriand Islands ⚊⚊	124	8.35 S	151.05 E
Trogir	78	43.31 N	16.15 E
Troia	78	41.22 N	15.18 E
Troick	82	54.06 N	61.35 E
Troicko-Pečorsk	66	62.44 N	56.06 E
Troina	78	37.47 N	14.37 E
Troisdorf	72	50.49 N	7.08 E
Trois-Rivières	152	46.21 N	72.33 W
Trollhättan	88	58.16 N	12.18 E
Tromelin ⚊	110	15.52 S	54.25 E
Troms □⁶	66	69.15 N	19.40 E
Tromsø	66	69.40 N	18.58 E
Trona	168	35.46 N	117.22 W
Tronador, Monte ▲	136	41.10 S	71.54 W
Trondheim	68	63.25 N	10.25 E
Troon	70	55.32 N	4.40 W
Tropea	78	38.41 N	15.54 E
Trotwood	152	39.48 N	84.18 W
Troup	160	32.09 N	95.07 W
Trout ≃	142	61.19 N	119.51 W
Trout Lake ⊜, N.W. Ter., Can.	142	60.35 N	121.10 W
Trout Lake ⊜, Ont., Can.	142	51.13 N	93.20 W
Trouville-[-sur-Mer]	74	49.22 N	0.05 E
Trowbridge	70	51.20 N	2.13 W
Troy, Calif., U.S.	168	37.44 N	121.25 W
Troy, Idaho, U.S.	166	46.44 N	116.46 W
Troy, Kans., U.S.	158	39.47 N	95.05 W
Troy, Mo., U.S.	158	38.59 N	90.59 W
Troy, Mont., U.S.	166	48.28 N	115.53 W
Troy, N.H., U.S.	152	42.50 N	72.11 W
Troy, N.C., U.S.	156	35.22 N	79.53 W
Troy, N.Y., U.S.	152	42.43 N	73.40 W
Troy, Ohio, U.S.	152	40.02 N	84.13 W
Troyes	74	48.18 N	4.05 E
Troy Peak ▲	168	38.19 N	115.30 W
Trstenik	80	43.37 N	21.00 E
Truchas	164	36.03 N	105.49 W
Trucial States → United Arab Emirates □¹	100	24.00 N	54.00 E
Truckee ≃	168	39.51 N	119.24 W
Trujillo, Esp.	76	39.28 N	5.53 W
Trujillo, Hond.	132	15.55 N	86.00 W
Trujillo, Perú	134	8.10 S	79.02 W
Trujillo, Ven.	138	9.22 N	70.26 W
Truman	154	43.49 N	94.26 W
Trumann	158	35.41 N	90.31 W
Trumansburg	152	42.33 N	76.40 W
Trumbull	120	41.15 S	173.17 E
Trundle	120	32.55 S	147.43 E
Truro, N.S., Can.	150	45.22 N	63.16 W
Truro, Eng., U.K.	70	50.16 N	5.03 W
Truth or Consequences (Hot Springs)	164	33.08 N	107.15 W
Trutnov	72	50.34 N	15.55 E
Trysil	68	61.19 N	12.16 E
Trysilelva (Klarälven) ≃	68	59.23 N	13.32 E
Trzcianka	72	53.03 N	16.28 E
Trzebież	72	53.42 N	14.31 E
Trzebinia	72	50.10 N	19.18 E
Tsaratanana	117b	14.00 S	49.00 E
Tsaratanana, Massif du ⋏	117b	16.47 S	47.39 E
Tsau	116	20.12 S	22.22 E
Tsavo	110	2.59 S	38.28 E
Tshabong	116	26.03 S	22.29 E
Tshane	116	24.05 S	21.54 E
Tshangalele, Lac ⊜	110	4.59 S	12.56 E
Tshela	110	4.59 S	12.56 E
Tshikapa	110	6.25 S	20.48 E
Tshofa	110	5.14 S	25.15 E
Tshuapa ≃	110	0.14 S	20.42 E
Tshwaane	116	22.29 S	22.03 E
Tsiafajavona ▲	117b	19.21 S	47.15 E
Tsihombe	117b	25.18 S	45.29 E
Tsiribihina ≃	117b	19.42 S	44.31 E
Tsiroanomandidy	117b	18.46 S	46.02 E
Tsu	90	34.43 N	136.31 E
Tsuchiura	90	36.05 N	140.12 E
Tsugaru-kaikyō ⋃	90a	41.35 N	141.00 E
Tsumeb	116	19.13 S	17.42 E
Tsumis Park	116	23.45 S	17.30 E
Tsuni → Zunyi	88	27.39 N	106.57 E
Tsuruga	90	35.39 N	136.04 E
Tsuruoka	90	38.44 N	139.50 E
Tsushima ⚊⚊	90	34.30 N	129.22 E
Tsuyama	90	35.03 N	134.00 E
Tua ≃	124	6.25 S	144.40 E
Tuakau	126	37.16 S	174.57 E
Tual	124	5.40 S	132.44 E
Tuam	70	53.31 N	8.50 W
Tuapse	64	44.07 N	39.05 E
Tubarão	140	28.30 S	49.01 W
Tübingen	72	48.31 N	9.02 E
Tubruq (Tobruk)	108	32.05 N	23.59 E
Tucacas	138	10.48 N	68.19 W
Tucano	134	10.58 S	38.48 W
Tuchola	72	53.35 N	17.50 E
Tuckanarra	122	27.07 S	118.05 E
Tuckerman	158	35.44 N	91.12 W
Tuckerton	152	39.36 N	74.20 W
Tucumán □⁴	140	32.13 S	110.58 W
Tucumcari	160	35.10 N	103.43 W
Tucupita	138	9.04 N	62.03 W
Tucuruí	134	3.42 S	49.27 W
Tudela	76	42.05 N	1.36 W
Tudmur (Palmyra)	104	34.33 N	38.17 E
Tugela ≃	116	29.14 S	31.31 E
Tugidak Island ⚊	146	56.30 N	154.36 W
Tuguegarao	98	17.37 N	121.44 E
Tugur	84	53.48 N	136.48 E
Tujmazy	82	54.36 N	53.42 E
T'ukalinsk	82	55.52 N	72.12 E
Tuktoyaktuk	146	69.27 N	133.02 W
Tukwila	166	47.29 N	122.16 W
Tula, Méx.	130	23.00 N	99.43 W
Tula, S.S.S.R.	86	54.12 N	37.37 E
Tulagi	118	9.06 S	160.09 E
Tulancingo	130	20.05 N	98.22 W
Tulangbawang ≃	96	4.24 S	105.50 E
Tulare, Calif., U.S.	168	36.13 N	119.21 W
Tulare, S. Dak., U.S.	162	44.44 N	98.31 W
Tularosa	164	33.04 N	106.01 W
Tulbagh	116	33.17 S	19.09 E
Tulcea	80	45.10 N	28.48 E
Tulcea □⁴	80	45.00 N	29.00 E
Tulia	160	34.32 N	101.46 W
Tulja'n	82	52.22 N	56.12 E
Tuli	116	21.59 S	29.15 E
Tullahoma	158	35.22 N	86.11 W
Tullamore, Austl.	120	32.38 S	147.34 E
Tullamore, Eire	70	53.16 N	7.30 W
Tulle	74	45.16 N	1.46 E
Tullibigeal	120	33.25 S	146.44 E
Tullins	74	45.18 N	5.29 E
Tully	120	17.56 S	145.56 E
Tulsa	160	36.09 N	95.58 W
Tulsequah	142	58.35 S	133.35 W
Tuluá	138	4.06 N	76.11 W
Tulufan	88	42.54 N	89.10 E
Tuluksak	146	61.06 N	160.58 W
Tulun	84	54.35 N	100.33 E
Tulungagung	96	8.04 S	111.54 E
Tuma ≃	130	12.39 N	85.25 W
Tumaco	138	1.49 N	78.46 W
Tuman-gang ≃	88	42.18 N	130.41 E
Tumany	84	60.58 N	155.56 E
Tumba	68	59.12 N	17.49 E
Tumba, Lac ⊜	110	0.50 S	18.00 E
Tumbarumba	120	35.47 S	148.01 E
Tumbes	138	3.30 S	80.25 W
Tumbotino	86	55.59 N	43.02 E
Tumby Bay	120	34.22 S	136.06 E
Tumd Zuoqi	88	66.36 N	30.48 E
T'umen', S.S.S.R.	82	57.09 N	65.32 E
Tumen, Zhg.	88	42.58 N	129.49 E
Tumeremo	138	7.18 N	61.30 W
Tumkūr	100	13.21 N	77.06 E
Tumtotegi	146	22.40 N	14.10 E
Tumucumaque, Serra ⋏ (Tumuc-Humac Mountains)	134	2.20 N	55.00 W
Tumut	120	35.18 S	148.13 E
Tumwater	166	47.01 N	122.54 W
Tunbridge Wells	70	51.08 N	0.16 E
Tunca (Tundža) ≃	80	41.40 N	26.34 E
Tunduru	110	11.07 S	37.21 E
Tundža (Tunca) ≃	80	41.40 N	26.34 E
T'ung ≃	84	63.46 N	121.35 E
Tunga ≃	108	9.30 N	10.48 E
Tungabhadra ≃	100	15.57 N	78.15 E
Tungurahua □⁴	138	1.15 S	78.35 W
Tunis	106	36.48 N	10.11 E
Tunis, Golfe de C	78	37.00 N	10.30 E
Tunisia □¹	106	34.00 N	9.00 E
Tunja	138	5.31 N	73.22 W
Tunkhannock	152	41.32 N	75.57 W
Tuntutuliak	146	60.22 N	162.38 W
Tununak	146	60.35 N	165.16 W
Tunuyán	140	33.35 S	69.00 W
Tunuyán ≃	140	33.33 S	67.30 W
Tunxi	88	29.44 N	118.18 E
Tuobuja	84	62.32 N	111.18 E
Tuoj-Chaja	84	62.28 N	111.18 E
Tuojiang ≃	88	28.57 N	105.27 E
Tuokusidawanling ▲	102	37.14 N	85.47 E
Tupã	134	21.56 S	50.30 W
Tupaciretã	140	29.05 S	53.51 W
Tupelo, Miss., U.S.	158	34.15 N	88.42 W
Tupelo, Okla., U.S.	160	34.36 N	96.25 W
Tupiza	134	21.27 S	65.43 W
Tupper Lake	152	44.13 N	74.29 W
Tupungato, Cerro ▲	140	33.22 S	69.47 W
Tuquerres ≃	138	1.05 N	77.37 W
Tura, Bhārat	100	25.31 N	90.13 E
Tura, S.S.S.R.	84	64.17 N	100.15 E
Turan	84	52.08 N	93.55 E
Turbaco	138	10.20 N	75.25 W
Turbat	100	25.59 N	63.04 E
Turbo	138	8.06 N	76.43 W
Turda	72	46.34 N	23.47 E
Turek	72	52.02 N	18.30 E
Tureński	68	60.55 N	24.38 E
Turfan Depression → Tulufanpendi ⋤⁷	88	42.40 N	89.10 E
Turgaj	82	49.38 N	63.28 E
Turgaj ≃	82	48.01 N	62.45 E
Turgajskaja Dolina ⋁	82	51.00 N	64.30 E
Turgajskaja Stolovaja Strana ⋏¹	82	51.00 N	64.00 E
Turginovo	86	56.30 N	36.00 E
Turgutlu	80	38.30 N	27.43 E
Türi	86	58.48 N	25.26 E
Turia ≃	76	39.27 N	0.19 W
Turin → Torino	78	45.03 N	7.40 E
Turinsk	82	58.03 N	63.42 E
Turkestan	82	43.18 N	68.15 E
Türkeve	72	47.06 N	20.45 E
Turkey □¹, As.	64	39.00 N	35.00 E
Turkey □¹, Eur.	64	39.00 N	35.00 E
Turkey Creek	124	17.02 S	128.12 E
Turkey Creek ≃	162	39.58 N	96.02 W
Turkmenskaja Sovetskaja Socialističeskaja Respublika □³	82	40.00 N	60.00 E
Turkmen Soviet Socialist Republic → Turkmenskaja Sovetskaja Socialističeskaja Respublika □³	82	40.00 N	60.00 E
Turks and Caicos Islands □²	128	21.45 N	71.35 W
Turks Islands ⚊⚊	132	21.24 N	71.07 W
Turku (Åbo)	68	60.27 N	22.17 E
Turkwel ≃	110	3.06 N	36.06 E
Turley	160	36.14 N	95.58 W
Turlock	168	37.30 N	120.51 W
Turnagain ≃	142	59.06 N	127.35 W
Turnagain Arm C	146	61.00 N	150.00 W
Turneffe Islands ⚊⚊	132	17.22 N	87.51 W
Turner, Austl.	122	17.50 S	128.17 E
Turner, Oreg., U.S.	166	44.51 N	122.57 W
Turners Falls	152	42.36 N	72.33 W
Turnhout	72	51.19 N	4.57 E
Türnitz	72	47.57 N	15.30 E
Turnor Lake ⊜	142	56.32 N	108.38 W
Turnov	72	50.35 N	15.10 E
Turnu-Măgurele	80	43.45 N	24.53 E
Turon	162	37.48 N	98.26 W
Turquino, Pico ▲	132	19.59 N	76.51 W
Turriff	70	57.32 N	2.28 W
Turtle Lake	154	45.24 N	92.08 W
Turu ≃	84	64.38 N	100.00 E
Turuchan ≃	84	65.56 N	87.42 E
Turuchansk	84	65.49 N	87.59 E
Tuscaloosa	158	33.11 N	87.33 W
Tuscola	158	39.48 N	88.17 W
Tuscumbia	158	34.44 N	87.42 W
Tushar Mountains ⋏	164	38.20 N	112.30 W
Tuskegee	158	32.26 N	85.42 W
Tustumena Lake ⊜	146	60.12 N	150.50 W
Tutajev	86	57.53 N	39.32 E
Tuticorin	100	8.50 N	78.09 E
Tutóia	134	2.45 S	42.16 W
Tutrakan	80	44.03 N	26.37 E
Tuttle Creek Reservoir ⊜¹	162	39.22 N	96.40 W
Tutupaca, Volcán ▲¹	134	17.02 S	70.22 W
Tutzing	72	47.54 N	11.17 E
Tuusniemi	68	62.49 N	28.30 E
Tuwayq, Jabal ⋏	100	23.00 N	46.00 E
Tuxedo	152	41.12 N	74.11 W
Tuxpan de Rodríguez Cano	130	20.57 N	97.24 W
Tuxtepec	130	18.06 N	96.07 W
Tuxtla Gutiérrez	130	16.45 N	93.07 W
Tuya ≃	142	59.07 N	130.50 W
Tuz Gölü ⊜	64	38.45 N	33.25 E
Tuzla	80	44.33 N	18.41 E
Tvedestrand	68	58.37 N	8.55 E
Tveitsund	68	59.01 N	8.32 E
Tweed ≃	70	55.46 N	2.00 W
Tweed Heads	120	28.10 S	153.31 E
Twentynine Palms	168	34.08 N	116.03 W
Twin Bridges	166	45.33 N	112.20 W
Twin City	156	32.35 N	82.10 W
Twin Falls	166	42.34 N	114.28 W
Twin Lakes	156	28.48 N	81.48 W
Twinsburg	152	41.19 N	81.27 W
Twisp	166	48.22 N	120.07 W
Twitya ≃	146	64.10 N	128.12 W
Twofold Bay C	120	37.06 S	149.55 E
Two Harbors	154	47.01 N	91.40 W
Two Rivers	154	44.09 N	87.34 W
Tychy	72	50.09 N	18.59 E
Tydal	68	63.04 N	11.34 E
Tyler, Minn., U.S.	154	44.17 N	96.08 W
Tyler, Tex., U.S.	160	32.21 N	95.18 W
Tylertown	158	31.07 N	90.09 W
Tym ≃	84	59.29 N	80.04 E
Tyndinskij	84	55.10 N	124.43 E
Tynemouth	70	55.01 N	1.24 W
Tynset	68	62.17 N	10.47 E
Tyonek	146	61.02 N	151.17 W
Tyre → Ṣūr	104	33.16 N	35.11 E
Tyrma	84	50.03 N	132.12 E
Tyrone, Okla., U.S.	160	36.57 N	101.04 W
Tyrone, Pa., U.S.	152	40.40 N	78.14 W
Tyrrell, Lake ⊜	120	35.21 S	142.50 E
Tyrrhenian Sea (Mare Tirreno) ⋿²	78	40.00 N	12.00 E
Tysse	68	60.22 N	5.45 E
Tyssedal	68	60.07 N	6.34 E
Tytuvénai	86	55.36 N	23.12 E
Tywyn	70	52.35 N	4.05 W
Tzaneen	116	23.50 S	30.09 E

U

Name	Page	Lat	Long
Uatumã ≃	138	2.26 S	57.37 W
Uaupés	138	0.08 S	67.05 W
Uaupés (Vaupés) ≃	138	1.15 S	66.51 W
Ubá	134	21.07 S	42.56 W
Ubangi (Oubangui) ≃	108	1.15 N	17.50 E
Ubayyiḍ, Wādī al- ⋁	104	32.04 N	43.48 E
Ube	90	33.56 N	131.15 E
Úbeda	76	38.01 N	3.22 W
Uberaba	134	19.45 S	47.55 W
Uberlândia	134	18.56 S	48.18 W
Ubly	154	43.42 N	82.56 W
Ubon Ratchathani	94	15.15 N	104.54 E
Ubundu	110	0.21 S	25.29 E
Učami	84	62.32 N	96.29 E
Ucayali ≃	134	4.30 S	73.30 W
Uchiura-wan C	90a	42.20 N	140.40 E
Ucholovo	86	53.48 N	40.53 E
Uchta ≃	66	63.33 N	53.38 E
Uckermark □⁹	72	53.15 N	13.50 E
Ucon	166	43.36 N	111.58 W
Učur ≃	84	58.48 N	130.35 E
Uda ≃, S.S.S.R.	84	54.42 N	135.14 E
Uda ≃, S.S.S.R.	84	51.47 N	107.33 E
Udaipur	100	24.35 N	73.41 E
Udall	162	37.23 N	97.06 W
Udbina	78	44.32 N	15.46 E
Uddevalla	68	58.21 N	11.55 E
Uddjaur ⊜	66	65.56 N	17.50 E
Udine	78	46.03 N	13.14 E
Udipi	100	13.20 N	74.45 E
Udmurtskaja A.S.S.R. □³	66	57.00 N	53.00 E
Udomľa	86	57.52 N	35.01 E
Udon Thani	94	17.26 N	102.46 E
Udor, Mount ▲	122	23.30 S	131.01 E
Udskaja Guba C	84	54.50 N	135.45 E
Udža	84	71.14 N	117.10 E
Uele ≃	108	4.09 N	22.26 E
Uelen	146	66.10 N	169.48 W
Uel'kal'	84	65.32 N	179.17 E
Uelzen	72	52.58 N	10.33 E
Uere ≃	106	3.42 N	25.24 E
Uetersen	72	53.41 N	9.39 E
Ufa	64	54.44 N	55.56 E
Uffenheim	72	49.32 N	10.14 E
Ugalla ≃	110	5.08 S	30.42 E
Uganda □¹	110	1.00 N	32.00 E
Ugine	74	45.45 N	6.25 E
Uglegorsk, S.S.S.R.	84	49.02 N	142.03 E
Uglegorsk, S.S.S.R.	84	49.05 N	38.17 E
Uglič	86	57.32 N	38.19 E
Uglovka	86	58.14 N	33.31 E
Ugoma ⋏	110	4.00 S	28.45 E
Uh (Už) ≃	72	48.34 N	22.00 E
Uijŏngbu	88	37.44 N	127.02 E
Uinta Mountains ⋏	164	40.45 N	110.05 W
Uitenhage	116	33.40 S	25.28 E
Uithuizermeeden	72	53.24 N	6.42 E
Uji	90	34.17 N	64.58 E
Ujandina ≃	84	68.23 N	145.50 E
Ujar	84	55.48 N	94.20 E
Ujedinenija, Ostrov ⚊	84	77.28 N	82.28 E
Újfehértó	72	47.48 N	21.40 E
Ujjain	100	23.11 N	75.46 E
Uka	84	57.50 N	162.06 E
Ukerewe Island ⚊	110	2.03 S	33.00 E
Ukiah	168	39.09 N	123.13 W
Ukmergé	86	55.15 N	24.45 E
Ukrainian Soviet Socialist Republic → Ukrainskaja Sovetskaja Socialističeskaja Respublika □³	64	49.00 N	32.00 E
Ukrainskaja Sovetskaja Socialističeskaja Respublika □³	64	49.00 N	32.00 E
Ukyr	84	49.28 N	108.52 E
Ulaanbaatar → Ulaangom	88	49.58 N	92.02 E
Ulan Bator → Ulaanbaatar	88	47.55 N	106.53 E
Ulan-Ude	84	51.50 N	107.37 E
Ulazów	72	50.17 N	23.00 E
Ulcinj	80	41.55 N	19.11 E
Ulefoss	68	59.17 N	9.16 E
Ulhasnagar	100	19.13 N	73.07 E
Uliastaj	88	47.45 N	96.49 E
Ulindi ≃	110	1.43 S	25.52 E
Ulithi ⚊¹	92	9.58 N	139.40 E
Ulja ≃	84	58.51 N	141.50 E
Uljanovsk	64	54.20 N	48.24 E
Ulla ≃	86	55.10 N	29.17 E
Ulladulla	120	35.21 S	150.29 E
Ullapool	70	57.54 N	5.10 W
Ullŭng-do ⚊	90	37.29 N	130.52 E
Ulm	72	48.24 N	10.00 E
Ulmarra	120	29.37 S	153.02 E
Ulrum	72	53.22 N	6.20 E
Ulsan	88	35.34 N	129.19 E
Ulsteinvik	68	62.20 N	5.53 E
Ulster □⁹	70	54.35 N	7.00 W
Ulu	84	60.19 N	127.24 E
Uluguru Mountains ⋏	110	7.10 S	37.40 E
Ulverstone	120	41.09 S	146.10 E
Ulysses	162	37.35 N	101.22 W
Umán, Méx.	130	20.53 N	89.45 W
Uman', S.S.S.R.	64	48.44 N	30.14 E
Umanak Fjord C²	142	70.55 N	53.00 W
Umarkot	100	25.22 N	69.44 E
Umatilla, Fla., U.S.	156	28.55 N	81.40 W
Umatilla, Oreg., U.S.	166	45.55 N	119.21 W
Umba ≃	66	66.40 N	34.15 E
Umbertide	78	43.18 N	12.20 E
Umbria □⁴	78	42.50 N	12.30 E
Umeå	66	63.50 N	20.15 E
Umeälven ≃	66	63.47 N	20.16 E
Umfuli ≃	116	17.30 S	29.23 E
Umm al-Qaywayn	100	25.35 N	55.34 E
Umm Durmān (Omdurman)	108	15.38 N	32.30 E
'Umrān	100	16.10 N	43.56 E
Umtali	116	18.58 S	32.40 E
Umtata	116	31.35 S	28.47 E
Umuarama	140	23.45 S	53.20 W
Umvuma	116	19.19 S	30.35 E
Umzinto	116	30.22 S	30.39 E
Unadilla, Ga., U.S.	156	32.16 N	83.44 W
Unadilla, N.Y., U.S.	152	42.19 N	75.19 W
Unalakleet	146	63.53 N	160.47 W
Unalaska	146	53.52 N	166.32 W
'Unayzah	100	26.06 N	43.58 E
Uncía	134	18.28 S	66.34 W
Uncompahgre Peak ▲	164	38.04 N	107.28 W
Uncompahgre Plateau ⋏¹	164	38.30 N	108.25 W
Underwood	162	47.27 N	101.08 W
Unečaja ≃	86	52.50 N	32.40 E
Ungarie	120	33.38 S	146.58 E
Ungava, Péninsule d' ⋗¹	142	60.00 N	74.00 W
Ungava Bay C	142	59.30 N	67.30 W
University Park, Tex., U.S.	160	32.52 N	96.47 W
Unna	72	51.32 N	7.41 E
Unža ≃	86	57.20 N	43.08 E
Upata	138	8.01 N	62.24 W
Upemba, Lac ⊜	110	8.36 S	26.26 E
Upernavik	142	72.47 N	56.10 W
Upham	162	48.35 N	100.44 W
Upington	116	28.25 S	21.15 E
Upolu ⚊	118	13.55 S	171.45 W
Upper Arlington	152	40.00 N	83.03 W
Upper Arrow Lake ⊜	148	50.30 N	117.55 W
Upper Hutt	126	41.08 S	175.03 E
Upper Iowa ≃	154	43.29 N	91.14 W
Upper Island Cove	150	47.40 N	53.12 W
Upper Kapuas Mountains ⋏	96	1.25 N	113.30 E
Upper Lake	168	39.10 N	122.54 W
Upper Red Lake ⊜	154	48.10 N	94.40 W
Upper Sandusky	152	40.49 N	83.16 W
Upper Volta □¹	106	13.00 N	2.00 W
Uppland □⁹	68	59.59 N	17.48 E
Uppsala	68	59.52 N	17.38 E
Uppsala Län □⁶	68	60.00 N	17.45 E
Upsala → Uppsala	68	59.52 N	17.38 E
Upstart, Cape ➤	120	19.42 S	147.45 E
Upton	162	44.06 N	104.38 W
Uraj	82	60.08 N	64.48 E
Urakawa	90a	42.09 N	142.47 E
Ural ≃	64	47.00 N	51.48 E
Uralla	120	30.39 S	151.30 E
Ural Mountains → Ural'skije Gory ⋏	64	60.00 N	60.00 E
Ural'sk	64	51.14 N	51.22 E
Ural'skije Gory (Ural Mountains) ⋏	64	60.00 N	60.00 E
Urana	120	35.20 S	146.16 E
Urandangi	120	21.36 S	138.12 E
Urangan	120	25.18 S	152.54 E
Urania	158	31.52 N	92.18 W
Uranium City	142	59.34 N	108.36 W
Uraricoera ≃	138	3.02 N	60.30 W
Ura-Tjube	100	39.55 N	68.59 E
Urawa	90	35.51 N	139.39 E
Urbana, Ill., U.S.	158	40.07 N	88.12 W
Urbana, Ohio, U.S.	152	40.06 N	83.45 W
Urbandale	154	41.38 N	93.48 W
Urbania	78	43.40 N	12.31 E
Urbino	78	43.43 N	12.38 E
Urdoma	66	61.47 N	48.32 E
Urečje	86	52.57 N	27.54 E
Uren'	66	57.28 N	45.47 E
Urfa	104	37.08 N	38.46 E
Urgenč	82	41.33 N	60.38 E
Ürgüp	80	38.38 N	34.56 E
Uriah	158	31.18 N	87.30 W
Uribia	138	11.43 N	72.16 W
Urjala	68	61.05 N	23.32 E
Uromi	114	6.44 N	6.18 E
Uroševac	80	42.22 N	21.09 E
Urrao	138	6.20 N	76.11 W
Uršel'skij	86	55.41 N	40.13 E
Ursus	72	52.12 N	20.53 E
Uruapan [del Progreso]	130	19.25 N	102.04 W
Urubamba ≃	134	10.43 S	73.48 W
Urubu ≃	138	2.55 S	58.25 W
Uruçuí, Serra do ⋏²	134	9.00 S	44.45 W
Uruguaiana	140	29.45 S	57.05 W
Uruguay □¹	136	33.00 S	56.00 W
Uruguay (Uruguai) ≃	140	34.12 S	58.18 W
Urukthapel ⚊	92	7.15 N	134.24 E
Urumchi → Wulumuqi	88	43.48 N	87.35 E
Ur'ung-Chaja	84	72.48 N	113.23 E
Urup, Ostrov ⚊	84	46.00 N	150.00 E
Usa ≃	66	65.57 N	56.55 E
Uşak	80	38.41 N	29.25 E
Usakos	116	22.01 S	15.32 E
Usedom ⚊	72	53.52 N	13.55 E
Ushuaia	136	54.47 S	68.19 W
Usingen	72	50.20 N	8.32 E
Usk	70	51.36 N	2.58 W
Usk ≃	70	51.36 N	2.58 W
Üsküdar	80	41.01 N	29.01 E
Usman'	86	52.03 N	39.44 E
Usolje	86	59.25 N	56.41 E
Usolje-Sibirskoje	84	52.47 N	103.38 E
Ussel	74	45.33 N	2.18 E
Ussuri (Wusulijiang) ≃	84	48.27 N	135.04 E
Ust'-Barguzin	84	53.27 N	109.00 E
Ust'-Belaja	84	65.30 N	173.20 E
Ust'-Bol'šereck	84	52.48 N	156.14 E
Ust'-Čaun	84	68.47 N	170.30 E
Ust'-Cil'ma	66	65.28 N	52.11 E
Ust'-Ilimsk	84	58.00 N	102.39 E
Ust'-Išim	82	57.42 N	71.10 E
Ustje	86	59.33 N	39.43 E
Ust'-Kamčatsk	84	56.15 N	162.30 E
Ust'-Kamenogorsk	82	49.58 N	82.38 E
Ust'-Katav	82	54.56 N	58.10 E
Ust'-Koksa	82	50.16 N	85.36 E
Ust'-Maja	84	60.25 N	134.32 E
Ust'-Nera	84	64.34 N	143.12 E
Ust'-N'ukža	84	56.34 N	121.37 E
Ust'-Omčug	84	61.09 N	149.38 E
Ust'-Ordynskij	84	52.48 N	104.45 E
Ust'-Ozjornoje	84	58.54 N	87.48 E
Ust'-Tym	84	59.24 N	80.06 E
Ust'urt, Plato ⋏¹	82	43.00 N	56.00 E
Ust'-Usa	66	65.57 N	56.54 E
Ust'-Užna	86	58.51 N	36.18 E
Usumacinta ≃	130	18.22 N	92.40 W
Usvjaty	86	55.44 N	30.46 E
Utah □³	164	39.30 N	111.30 W
Utah Lake ⊜	164	40.13 N	111.49 W
Ute Mountain ⋏	164	36.55 N	108.29 W
Utembo ≃	110	17.06 S	22.01 E
Utena	86	55.30 N	25.36 E
Utersum	54	54.43 N	8.24 E
Utete	110	7.59 S	38.47 E
Uthai Thani	94	15.23 N	100.02 E
Utiariti	134	13.02 S	58.17 W
Utica, Miss., U.S.	158	32.06 N	90.37 W
Utica, N.Y., U.S.	152	43.06 N	75.13 W
Utiel	76	39.34 N	1.12 W
Utinga	134	12.06 S	41.06 W
Utopia, Austl.	122	22.14 S	134.33 E
Utopia, Tex., U.S.	160	29.37 N	99.32 W
Utraula	100	27.19 N	82.25 E
Utrecht, Ned.	72	52.05 N	5.08 E
Utrecht, S. Afr.	116	27.40 S	30.20 E
Utrera	76	37.11 N	5.47 W
Utsjoki	66	69.54 N	27.01 E
Utsunomiya	90	36.33 N	139.52 E
Uttaradit	94	17.38 N	100.06 E
Uttar Pradesh □³	100	27.00 N	80.00 E
Uudenmaan lääni □⁴	68	60.30 N	25.00 E
Uusikaupunki	68	60.48 N	21.25 E
Uva □⁸	100	6.45 N	81.00 E
Uvalde	160	29.12 N	99.47 W
Uvarovo	86	51.59 N	42.14 E
Uvat	82	59.08 N	68.54 E
Uvinza	110	5.06 S	30.22 E
Uvira	110	3.24 S	29.08 E
Uvs Nuur ⊜	88	50.20 N	92.45 E
Uwajima	90	33.13 N	132.34 E
'Uwaynāt, Jabal al- ▲	112	21.54 N	24.58 E
Uxbridge	154	44.06 N	79.07 W
Uyuni	134	20.28 S	66.50 W

Name	Page	Lat	Long
Uyuni, Salar de ⇌	134	20.20 S	67.42 W
Už (Uh) ⇌	72	48.34 N	22.00 E
Uzbekskaja Sovetskaja Socialističeskaja Respublika □3			
Uzbek Soviet Socialist Republic → Uzbekskaja Sovetskaja Socialističeskaja Respublika □3	84	41.00 N	64.00 E
Uzda	86	53.27 N	27.13 E
Uzdin	80	45.12 N	20.38 E
Uzerche	74	45.26 N	1.34 E
Uzès	74	44.01 N	4.25 E
Užgorod	72	48.37 N	22.18 E
Uzlovaja	86	53.59 N	38.10 E
Uzunköprü	80	41.16 N	26.41 E
Užur	84	55.20 N	89.50 E
Užentis	86	55.47 N	22.39 E

V

Name	Page	Lat	Long
Vaajakoski	68	62.16 N	25.54 E
Vääksy	68	61.11 N	25.33 E
Vaal ⇌	116	27.40 S	26.09 E
Vaala	68	64.26 N	26.48 E
Vaasa (Vasa)	68	63.06 N	21.36 E
Vaasan lääni □4	68	63.00 N	23.00 E
Vabalninkas	86	55.58 N	24.45 E
Vác	72	47.47 N	19.08 E
Vača	86	55.48 N	42.46 E
Vacaria	140	28.30 S	50.56 W
Vacaville	168	38.21 N	121.59 W
Vaccarès, Étang de ⇌	74	43.32 N	4.34 E
Vach ⇌	84	60.45 N	76.45 E
Vachš ⇌	102	37.06 N	68.18 E
Vacoas	117c	20.18 S	57.29 E
Vadheim	68	61.13 N	5.49 E
Vado Ligure	78	44.17 N	8.27 E
Vadsø	66	70.03 N	29.55 E
Vaduz	74	47.47 N	9.31 E
Vaga ⇌	66	62.48 N	42.56 E
Vagaj	84	57.56 N	69.01 E
Vågåmo	68	61.53 N	9.06 E
Väh ⇌	72	47.55 N	18.00 E
Vaihingen	72	48.56 N	8.58 E
Vailly-sur-Aisne	74	49.25 N	3.31 E
Vaison-la-Romaine	74	44.14 N	5.04 E
Vajgač, Ostrov I	82	70.25 N	58.46 E
Vakhân ←1	102	37.00 N	73.00 E
Vaksdal	68	60.29 N	5.44 E
Valaisannes, Alpes ✗	74	46.00 N	7.30 E
Valašské Meziříčí	72	49.28 N	17.58 E
Valatie	152	42.25 N	73.41 W
Valbo	68	60.40 N	17.04 E
Valcheta	136	40.40 S	66.10 W
Valdagno	78	45.39 N	11.18 E
Valdaj	82	57.59 N	33.14 E
Valdajskaja Vozvyšennost' ✗2	86	57.00 N	33.30 E
Val-de-Marne □5	74	48.47 N	2.29 E
Valdemärpils	86	57.22 N	22.35 E
Valdepeñas	76	38.46 N	3.23 W
Valdés, Peninsula >1	136	42.30 S	64.00 W
Valdese	116	35.44 N	81.34 W
Valdez	146	61.07 N	146.16 W
Val-d'Isère	74	45.27 N	6.59 E
Valdivia	136	39.48 S	73.14 W
Valdobbiadene	78	45.54 N	12.00 E
Val-d'Oise □5	74	49.10 N	2.10 E
Val-d'Or	154	48.07 N	77.47 W
Valdosta	150	30.50 N	83.17 W
Vale	166	43.59 N	117.15 W
Valença, Bra.	134	13.22 S	39.05 W
Valença, Port.	76	42.02 N	8.38 W
Valençay	74	47.09 N	1.34 E
Valence	74	44.56 N	4.54 E
Valencia, Esp.	76	39.28 N	0.22 W
Valencia, Ven.	138	10.11 N	68.00 W
Valencia □4	76	39.30 N	0.40 W
Valencia de Alcántara	76	39.25 N	7.14 W
Valenciennes	74	50.21 N	3.32 E
Valentine	162	42.52 N	100.33 W
Valenza	78	45.01 N	8.38 E
Våler	68	60.40 N	11.50 E
Valera	138	9.19 N	70.37 W
Valga	86	57.47 N	26.02 E
Valka	86	57.47 N	26.00 E
Valkeakoski	68	61.16 N	24.02 E
Valkenburg	72	50.52 N	5.50 E
Valkenswaard	72	51.21 N	5.28 E
Valladolid, Esp.	76	41.39 N	4.43 W
Valladolid, Méx.	130	20.41 N	88.12 W
Valladolid □4	76	41.35 N	4.45 W
Valldal	68	62.20 N	7.21 E
Vall de Uxó	76	39.49 N	0.14 W
Valle □4	138	13.34 N	4.18 W
Valle d'Aosta □4	78	45.45 N	7.25 E
Valle de la Pascua	138	9.13 N	66.00 W
Valle del Yaqui	130	27.19 N	110.01 W
Valle de Santiago	130	20.23 N	101.12 W
Valledupar	138	10.29 N	73.15 W
Valle Hermoso	160	25.39 N	97.52 W
Vallejo	168	38.29 N	122.14 W
Vallenar	140	28.35 S	70.46 W
Vallet	74	47.10 N	1.16 W
Valletta	78	35.54 N	14.31 E
Valley	70	53.17 N	4.34 W
Valley City	162	46.55 N	97.59 W
Valley Falls	162	39.21 N	95.28 W
Valley Mills	160	31.39 N	97.28 W
Valley Springs	158	43.35 N	96.28 W
Valley Station	158	38.06 N	85.52 W
Valleyview	148	55.04 N	117.17 W
Vallon-Pont-d'Arc	74	44.24 N	4.24 E
Vallorbe	74	46.43 N	6.22 E
Valls	76	41.17 N	1.15 E
Valmiera	86	57.33 N	25.24 E
Valognes	74	49.31 N	1.28 W
Valonga	86	41.11 N	8.30 W
Valparai	100	10.19 N	76.58 E
Valparaíso, Chile	140	33.02 S	71.38 W
Valparaíso, Méx.	130	22.46 N	103.34 W
Valparaiso, Fla., U.S.	150	30.30 N	86.30 W
Valparaiso, Ind., U.S.	158	41.28 N	87.03 W
Valréas	74	44.23 N	4.59 E
Vals, Tandjung >1	124	8.25 S	137.38 E
Valsbaai C	116	34.12 S	18.40 E
Valsetz	166	44.50 N	123.39 W
Valujki	86	50.13 N	38.06 E
Valverde del Camino	76	37.34 N	6.45 W
Vam-co-dong ⇌	94	10.30 N	106.33 E
Vam-co-tay ⇌	94	10.30 N	106.33 E
Vammala	68	61.20 N	22.54 E
Van, Tür.	104	38.28 N	43.20 E
Van, Tex., U.S.	160	32.31 N	95.38 W
Van Alstyne	160	33.25 N	96.34 W
Van Buren, Ark., U.S.	158	35.26 N	94.21 W
Van Buren, Maine, U.S.	152	47.09 N	67.56 W
Van Buren, Mo., U.S.	158	37.00 N	91.01 W
Vanč	86		
Vanceburg	152	38.36 N	83.19 W
Vancouver, B.C., Can.	148		
Vancouver, Wash., U.S.	166	45.39 N	122.40 W
Vancouver, Cape >1, Austl.	122	35.01 S	118.12 E
Vancouver, Cape >1, Alaska, U.S.	146	60.33 N	165.27 W
Vancouver, Mount ▲	146	60.20 N	139.41 W
Vancouver Island I	148	49.45 N	126.00 W
Vandalia, Ill., U.S.	158	38.58 N	89.06 W

Name	Page	Lat	Long
Vandalia, Mo., U.S.	158	39.19 N	91.29 W
Vandalia, Ohio, U.S.	152	39.53 N	84.12 W
Vanderbijlpark	116	26.42 S	27.54 E
Vanderbilt, Mich., U.S.	154	45.09 N	84.40 W
Vanderbilt, Tex., U.S.	160	28.49 N	96.37 W
Vandergrift	152	40.36 N	79.34 W
Vanderhoof	148	54.01 N	124.01 W
Van Diemen Island I	124	15.44 S	137.02 E
Van Diemen, Cape >	124	11.10 S	130.23 E
Van Diemen Gulf C	124	11.50 S	132.00 E
Vänern ⇌	68	58.55 N	13.30 E
Vänersborg	68	58.22 N	12.19 E
Vangaindrano	117b	23.21 S	47.36 E
Van Gölü ⇌	104	38.33 N	42.46 E
Vangsnes	68	61.11 N	6.38 E
Vangunu I	118	8.40 S	158.05 E
Vangviang	92	19.45 N	102.27 E
Van Horn	160	31.03 N	104.50 W
Vanier	152	45.26 N	75.40 W
Vanimo	124	2.40 S	141.20 E
Vanino	84	49.05 N	140.15 E
Vankarem	84	67.51 N	175.50 W
Vankleek Hill	152	45.31 N	74.39 W
Vannes	74	47.39 N	2.46 E
Van Rees, Pegunungan ✗	124	2.30 S	138.00 E
Vanrhynsdorp	116	31.36 S	18.44 E
Vansittart Island I	142	65.50 N	84.00 W
Van Wert	152	40.52 N	84.35 W
Van Winkle	158	32.17 N	90.15 W
Var ⇌	74	43.39 N	7.12 E
Var □5	74	43.30 N	6.20 E
Vara	68	58.16 N	12.57 E
Varades	74	47.23 N	1.02 W
Vārānasi (Benares)	102	25.20 N	83.00 E
Varazze	78	44.22 N	8.34 E
Varberg	68	57.06 N	12.15 E
Vardar (Axiós) ⇌	80	40.31 N	22.43 E
Varde	68	55.38 N	8.29 E
Vardø	66	70.21 N	31.02 E
Varel	72	53.22 N	8.10 E
Varennes-sur-Allier	74	46.19 N	3.24 E
Vareš	80	44.09 N	18.19 E
Varese	78	45.48 N	8.48 E
Varginha	134	21.33 S	45.25 W
Varkaus	68	62.19 N	27.55 E
Värmland □9	68	59.48 N	13.03 E
Värmlands Län □6	68	59.45 N	13.15 E
Varna	68	43.13 N	27.55 E
Värnamo	68	57.11 N	14.02 E
Varnhem	68	58.23 N	13.39 E
Varnsdorf	72	50.55 N	14.37 E
Várpalota	72	47.12 N	18.09 E
Varzy	74	47.22 N	3.23 E
Vas □6	72	47.10 N	16.40 E
Vasconcelos	134	18.30 S	40.30 W
Vasil'evičí	86	52.14 N	29.49 E
Vasil'evskij Moch	86	57.01 N	35.55 E
Vaslui	80	46.38 N	27.44 E
Vaslui □4	80	46.30 N	27.45 E
Vassar	154	43.22 N	83.35 W
Västeräs	68	59.37 N	16.33 E
Västerbottens Län □6	68	64.00 N	17.30 E
Västergötland □9	68	58.01 N	13.00 E
Västernorrlands Län □6	68	63.00 N	17.30 E
Västervik	68	57.45 N	16.38 E
Västmanland □9	68	59.45 N	16.20 E
Västmanlands Län □6	68	59.45 N	16.20 E
Vasto	78	42.07 N	14.42 E
Vas'ugan ⇌	84	59.07 N	80.46 E
Vas'ugan ⌐	84	58.00 N	77.00 E
Vasvár	72	47.03 N	16.49 E
Vatan	74	47.05 N	1.48 E
Vathi	80	37.45 N	26.59 E
Vatican City (Città del Vaticano) □1	78	41.54 N	12.27 E
V'atka ⇌	66	55.36 N	51.30 E
Vatnajökull ⧈	66a	64.25 N	16.50 W
Vatneyri	66a	65.38 N	23.57 W
Vatomandry	117b	19.20 S	48.59 E
Vatra Dornei	80	47.21 N	25.21 E
Vatskije Pol'any	66	56.14 N	51.04 E
Vätten	68	58.24 N	14.36 E
Vaucluse □5	74	44.00 N	5.10 E
Vaucouleurs	74	48.36 N	5.40 E
Vaughan	154	43.47 N	79.36 W
Vaughn	164	34.36 N	105.13 W
Vaupés □8	138	1.00 N	71.00 W
Vaupés (Uaupés) ⇌	138	0.02 N	67.16 W
Vauvert	74	43.42 N	4.17 E
Växjö	68	56.52 N	14.49 E
V'azemskij	84	47.32 N	134.48 E
V'az'ma	86	55.13 N	34.18 E
Veazie	152	44.51 N	68.42 W
Vechta	72	52.43 N	8.16 E
Vecsés	72	47.25 N	19.16 E
Veedersburg	158	40.07 N	87.16 W
Veendam	72	53.06 N	6.58 E
Veenendaal	72	52.02 N	5.34 E
Vega	160	35.15 N	102.26 W
Vega I	66	65.39 N	11.50 E
Veghel	72	51.37 N	5.33 E
Veglie	78	40.20 N	17.58 E
Veguita	132	20.08 N	76.48 W
Veintecinco de Mayo	140	35.25 S	60.11 W
Veisiejai	86	54.06 N	23.42 E
Vejen	68	55.29 N	9.09 E
Vejer de la Frontera	76	36.15 N	5.58 W
Vejle	68	55.42 N	9.32 E
Velbert	72	51.20 N	7.02 E
Velden	72	48.19 N	12.16 E
Veldhoven	72	51.24 N	5.24 E
Veleka ⇌	80	42.04 N	27.58 E
Velenje	78	46.22 N	15.07 E
Velet'ma	86	55.20 N	42.25 E
Vélez-Málaga	76	36.47 N	4.06 W
Vel'gija	86	58.23 N	33.59 E
Velhas, Rio das ⇌	134	17.13 S	44.49 W
Velikaja ⇌, S.S.S.R.	84	64.40 N	176.20 E
Velikaja ⇌, S.S.S.R.	86	57.48 N	28.20 E
Velika Plana	80	44.20 N	21.04 E
Velike Lašče	78	45.50 N	14.33 E
Velikije Luki	86	56.20 N	30.32 E
Velikij-ust'ug	66	60.46 N	46.18 E
Velikodvorskij	86	55.15 N	40.41 E
Veliko Gradište	80	44.45 N	21.32 E
Veliko Tărnovo	80	43.04 N	25.39 E
Velingara	114	13.09 N	14.07 W
Veliž	86	55.38 N	31.12 E
Vella Lavella I	118	7.45 S	156.40 E
Velletri	78	41.41 N	12.47 E
Vellore	100	12.56 N	79.09 E
Velsen	72	52.27 N	4.40 E
Vel'sk	66	61.04 N	42.05 E
Velten	72	52.41 N	13.11 E
Venado	130	22.56 N	101.06 W
Venado Tuerto	140	33.46 S	61.58 W
Venaria	78	45.08 N	7.38 E
Venarey	74	47.33 N	4.27 E
Venčany	86	44.20 N	20.40 E
Vendas Novas	76	38.41 N	8.28 W
Vendée □5	74	46.40 N	1.20 W
Vendeuvre-sur-Barse	74	48.14 N	4.28 E
Vendôme	74	47.48 N	1.04 E
Veneto □4	78	45.30 N	12.00 E
Venezia (Venice)	78	45.27 N	12.21 E
Venezia, Golfo di C	78	45.15 N	13.00 E
Venezuela □1	138	8.00 N	66.00 W
Venezuela, Golfo de C	138	11.30 N	71.00 W
Veniaminof, Mount ▲	146	56.13 N	159.18 W
Venice → Venezia, It.	78	45.27 N	12.21 E
Venice, Fla., U.S.	156	27.06 N	82.27 W
Venice, Gulf of C → Venezia, Golfo di	78	45.15 N	13.00 E
Venlo	72	51.24 N	6.10 E
Vennesla	68	58.17 N	7.59 E
Venosa	78	40.57 N	15.49 E
Venray	72	51.32 N	5.59 E
Ventimiglia	78	43.47 N	7.36 E
Ventnor	70	50.36 N	1.11 W
Ventspils	86	57.24 N	21.33 E

Name	Page	Lat	Long
Ventuari ⇌	138	3.58 N	67.02 W
Ventura	168	34.17 N	119.18 W
Venturia	162	46.00 N	99.33 W
Veracruz [Llave]	130	19.12 N	96.08 W
Veráraval	102	20.54 N	70.22 E
Verbania	78	45.56 N	8.33 E
Verbilki	86	56.32 N	37.36 E
Verbovskij	86	55.32 N	42.00 E
Vercelli	78	45.19 N	8.25 E
Vercel [-Villedieu-le-Camp]	74	47.11 N	6.24 E
Verchn'aja Amga	84	59.30 N	126.08 E
Verchn'aja Inta	66	66.00 N	60.20 E
Verchn'aja Salda	82	58.02 N	60.33 E
Verchn'aja Tajmyra ⇌	82	74.15 N	99.48 E
Verchneimbatskoje	84	63.11 N	87.58 E
Verchnevil'ujsk	84	63.27 N	120.18 E
Verchnij Baskunčak	82	48.14 N	46.44 E
Verchnij Ufalej	82	56.04 N	60.14 E
Verchojansk	84	67.35 N	133.27 E
Verchojanskij Chrebet ✗	84	67.00 N	129.00 E
Verchoturje	82	58.52 N	60.48 E
Verchovje	86	52.49 N	37.14 E
Vercors □9	74	44.57 N	5.25 E
Verdalsøra	68	63.48 N	11.29 E
Verde, Mesa ▲	134	21.12 S	51.53 W
Verden, B.R.D.	72	52.55 N	9.13 E
Verden, Okla., U.S.	160	35.05 N	98.05 W
Verdi	168	39.31 N	119.59 W
Verdun, Qué., Can.	152	45.27 N	73.34 W
Verdun, Fr.	74	49.10 N	5.23 E
Verdun, Fr.	74	44.00 N	1.14 E
Verdun-sur-le-Doubs	74	46.54 N	5.01 E
Vereeniging	116	26.38 S	27.57 E
Vereja	86	55.21 N	36.11 E
Veresčagino, S.S.S.R.	66	58.05 N	54.40 E
Veresčagino, S.S.S.R.	84	64.14 N	87.37 E
Vergennes	152	44.10 N	73.15 W
Vergt	74	45.02 N	0.43 E
Verín	76	41.56 N	7.26 W
Verisimo Sarmento	110	8.10 S	20.39 E
Vermenton	74	47.40 N	3.44 E
Vermilion, Alta., Can.	148	53.22 N	110.51 W
Vermilion, Ohio, U.S.	152	41.25 N	82.22 W
Vermilion ⇌	158	39.53 N	87.22 W
Vermilion Bluffs ✗4	164	40.50 N	108.30 W
Vermilion Creek ⇌	164	40.06 N	108.53 W
Vermillion	162	42.47 N	96.56 W
Vermont □3	144	43.50 N	72.45 W
Vernal	164	40.27 N	109.32 W
Verneuil	74	46.25 N	0.56 E
Verneukpan ⇌	116	29.58 S	21.10 E
Vernon, B.C., Can.	148	50.16 N	119.16 W
Vernon, Fr.	74	47.48 N	1.38 E
Vernon, Ala., U.S.	158	33.45 N	88.07 W
Vernon, Conn., U.S.	152	41.52 N	72.27 W
Vernon, Ind., U.S.	158	38.59 N	85.36 W
Vernon, Tex., U.S.	160	34.09 N	99.17 W
Vernon, Utah, U.S.	164	40.06 N	112.26 W
Vernonia	166	45.52 N	123.11 W
Verny	74	49.01 N	6.12 E
Vero Beach	156	27.38 N	80.24 W
Verona, It.	78	45.27 N	11.00 E
Verona, Wis., U.S.	158	42.59 N	89.32 W
Versailles, Fr.	74	48.48 N	2.08 E
Versailles, Ky., U.S.	158	38.03 N	84.44 W
Versailles, Mo., U.S.	158	38.26 N	92.51 W
Versailles, Ohio, U.S.	152	40.13 N	84.29 W
Vert, Cap >	114	14.43 N	17.30 W
Verteillac	74	45.21 N	0.22 E
Vertientes	132	21.16 N	78.09 W
Vertou	74	47.10 N	1.29 W
Vertus	74	48.54 N	4.00 E
Verviers	72	50.35 N	5.52 E
Vervins	74	49.50 N	3.54 E
Verzy	74	49.09 N	4.10 E
Vesanto	68	62.56 N	26.25 E
Vescovato	74	42.30 N	9.26 E
Vesegonsk	86	58.40 N	37.16 E
Veselí	72	48.57 N	17.01 E
Vest-Agder □6	68	58.30 N	7.10 E
Vestavia Hills	158	33.27 N	86.47 W
Vestby	68	59.36 N	10.45 E
Vestfold □6	68	59.15 N	10.10 E
Vestmannaeyjar	66a	63.26 N	20.12 W
Vesuvio ▲1	78	40.49 N	14.26 E
Vesuvius → Vesuvio ▲1	78	40.49 N	14.26 E
Veszprém	72	47.06 N	17.55 E
Veszprém □6	72	47.05 N	17.55 E
Vésztő	72	46.55 N	21.16 E
Vetlanda	68	57.26 N	15.04 E
Vetluga	86	57.51 N	45.47 E
Vetralla	78	42.19 N	12.03 E
Vetrino	72	51.47 N	14.04 E
Vetschau	72	51.47 N	14.04 E
Veurne	72	51.04 N	2.40 E
Vevey	74	46.28 N	6.51 E
Veynes	74	44.32 N	5.49 E
Viacha	134	16.39 S	68.18 W
Viadana	78	45.00 N	10.31 E
Viana do Alentejo	76	38.20 N	7.54 W
Viana do Castelo	76	41.42 N	8.50 W
Viareggio	78	43.52 N	10.14 E
Viborg	158	43.20 N	96.56 W
Vibo Valentia	78	38.40 N	16.06 E
Vibraye	74	48.03 N	0.44 E
Vic-en-Bigorre	74	43.23 N	0.05 E
Vicente López	140	34.31 S	58.28 W
Vicenza	78	45.33 N	11.33 E
Vich	76	41.56 N	2.15 E
Vichada □8	138	4.55 N	69.30 W
Vichada ⇌	138	4.55 N	67.50 W
Vichuga	86	57.13 N	41.53 E
Vichy	74	46.08 N	3.26 E
Vici	160	36.09 N	99.18 W
Vicksburg, Mich., U.S.	154	42.07 N	85.32 W
Vicksburg, Miss., U.S.	158	32.14 N	90.56 W
Victor, Idaho, U.S.	166	43.36 N	111.07 W
Victor, Iowa, U.S.	154	41.44 N	92.18 W
Victor Harbour	122	35.34 S	138.37 E
Victoria, Arg.	140	32.37 S	60.10 W
Victoria, Cam.	106	4.01 N	9.12 E
Victoria, B.C., Can.	148	48.25 N	123.22 W
Victoria, Chile	140	38.13 S	72.20 W
Victoria (Xianggang), H.K.	88	22.17 N	114.09 E
Victoria, Malay.	92	5.18 N	115.14 E
Victoria, Sey.	110	4.38 S	55.27 E
Victoria → Rabat, Malta	78	36.02 N	14.14 E
Victoria, Kans., U.S.	162	38.52 N	99.09 W
Victoria, Tex., U.S.	160	28.48 N	96.59 W
Victoria □3	120	38.00 S	145.00 E
Victoria ⇌	146	69.30 N	100.25 W
Victoria, Lake ⇌, Afr.	110	1.00 S	33.00 E
Victoria, Lake ⇌, Austl.	120	34.00 S	141.16 E
Victoria, Lake ⇌	114	5.30 N	9.53 E
Victoria de las Tunas	132	20.58 N	76.57 W
Victoria Falls ⬙	116	17.55 S	25.51 E
Victoria Harbour	154	44.45 N	79.46 W
Victoria Island I	146	71.00 N	114.00 W
Victoria Nile ⇌	110	2.14 N	31.26 E
Victoria Peak ▲	130	16.47 N	88.36 W
Victoria River Downs	124	16.24 S	131.00 E
Victoria Strait ⇌	142	69.15 N	100.30 W
Victoriaville	154	46.03 N	71.58 W
Victoria West	116	31.25 S	23.04 E
Vicuña	140	30.02 S	70.44 W
Vicuña Mackenna	140	33.55 S	64.25 W

Name	Page	Lat	Long
Vidalia, Ga., U.S.	156	32.13 N	82.25 W
Vidalia, La., U.S.	158	31.34 N	91.26 W
Vidauban, Fr.	74	43.26 N	6.26 E
Vidauban, Fr.	74	43.26 N	6.26 E
Videbaek	68	56.05 N	8.38 E
Vidigueira	76	38.13 N	7.48 W
Vidin	80	43.59 N	22.52 E
Vidisha	102	23.32 N	77.49 E
Vidor	158	30.07 N	94.01 W
Vidzy	86	55.24 N	26.38 E
Viechtach	72	49.05 N	12.53 E
Viedma	136	40.50 S	63.00 W
Viedma, Lago ⇌	136	49.40 S	72.30 W
Vieira do Minho	76	41.39 N	8.09 W
Viella	76	42.42 N	0.48 E
Vienna → Wien, Öst.	72	48.13 N	16.20 E
Vienna, Ga., U.S.	156	32.06 N	83.47 W
Vienna, Mo., U.S.	158	38.11 N	91.57 W
Vienna, W. Va., U.S.	152	39.19 N	81.26 W
Vienne	74	45.31 N	4.52 E
Vienne □5	74	46.35 N	0.30 E
Vienne ⇌	74	47.13 N	0.05 E
Vientiane	94	17.58 N	102.36 E
Vieques, Isla de I	132	18.08 N	65.25 W
Vieremä	68	63.45 N	27.01 E
Viersen	72	51.15 N	6.23 E
Vierwaldstätter See ⇌	74	47.00 N	8.28 E
Vierzon	74	47.13 N	2.05 E
Vieste	78	41.53 N	16.10 E
Vietnam □1	94	21.00 N	105.00 E
Vietnam, North □1	94	21.00 N	106.00 E
Vietnam, South □1	94	13.00 N	108.00 E
Vievis	86	54.46 N	24.48 E
Vif	74	45.03 N	5.40 E
Vigan	94	17.35 N	120.23 E
Vigeland	68	58.05 N	7.18 E
Vigevano	78	45.19 N	8.51 E
Vignelles-lès-Hattonchâtel	74	48.59 N	5.43 E
Vignola	78	44.29 N	11.00 E
Vigo	76	42.14 N	8.43 W
Vigrestad	68	58.34 N	5.42 E
Vihanti	68	64.29 N	25.00 E
Vihiers	74	47.09 N	0.32 W
Vihti	68	60.25 N	24.20 E
Viipurijärvi ⇌	68	62.39 N	29.14 E
Vijāpur	100	23.34 N	72.45 E
Vijayapuri	100	16.32 N	79.35 E
Vijayawāda	100	16.31 N	80.37 E
Vijoše (Aóös) ⇌	80	40.37 N	19.20 E
Viken	68	56.09 N	12.34 E
Vikna	68	59.40 N	10.02 E
Vikna I	66	64.57 N	10.58 E
Vikramasingapuram	100	8.43 N	77.24 E
Viksøyri	68	61.06 N	6.35 E
vil'a	86	55.15 N	42.13 E
Vila Arriaga	110	14.46 S	13.21 E
Vila Cabral	110	13.18 S	35.14 E
Vila Coutinho	110	14.53 S	34.19 E
Vila de João Belo	110	25.02 S	33.34 E
Vila de Manica	116	18.56 S	32.53 E
Vila do Bispo	76	37.05 N	8.55 W
Vila do Conde	76	41.21 N	8.45 W
Vila Flor	76	41.18 N	7.09 W
Vilafranca del Panadés	76	41.21 N	1.42 E
Vila Franca de Xira	76	38.57 N	8.59 W
Vilaka	86	57.11 N	27.41 E
Vilanculos	116	22.01 S	35.19 E
Vila Nova de Famalicão	76	41.25 N	8.32 W
Vila Nova de Foz Côa	76	41.05 N	7.12 W
Vila Nova de Gaia	76	41.08 N	8.37 W
Vila Novo de Ourém	76	39.39 N	8.35 W
Vila Pery	116	19.08 S	33.29 E
Vila Real	76	41.18 N	7.45 W
Vila Real de Santo António	76	37.12 N	7.25 W
Vilar Formoso	76	40.37 N	6.50 W
Vila Velha de Ródão	76	39.38 N	7.40 W
Vila Verde	76	41.39 N	8.26 W
Vila Viçosa	76	38.47 N	7.25 W
Vilcabamba, Cordillera ✗	134	13.00 S	73.00 W
Vilcea □4	80	45.19 N	24.00 E
Vilhelmina	68	64.37 N	16.39 E
Viljandi	86	58.22 N	25.36 E
Vil'kickogo, Ostrov I, S.S.S.R.	84	73.29 N	75.50 E
Vil'kickogo, Ostrov I, S.S.S.R.	84	75.55 N	137.00 E
Vil'kickogo, Proliv ⨆	84	77.55 N	103.00 E
Villa Ahumada	130	30.37 N	106.31 W
Villa Angela	140	27.35 S	60.43 W
Villa Bella	134	10.23 S	65.24 W
Villacañas	76	39.38 N	3.20 W
Villa Carlos Paz	140	31.25 S	64.30 W
Villacarrillo	76	38.07 N	3.05 W
Villa Cisneros	114	23.43 N	15.57 W
Villacidro	78	39.27 N	8.44 E
Villa Colón (Caucete)	140	31.40 S	68.20 W
Villa Constitución	140	33.14 S	60.20 W
Villada	76	42.15 N	4.58 W
Villa de Cura	138	10.02 N	67.29 W
Villa de García	160	25.49 N	100.35 W
Villa del Rosario	138	10.19 N	72.19 W
Villadiego	76	42.31 N	4.01 W
Villa Dolores	140	31.58 S	65.12 W
Villafranca de los Barros	76	38.34 N	6.20 W
Villafranca di Verona	78	45.21 N	10.50 E
Villa Frontera	130	26.56 N	101.27 W
Villa Grove	158	39.51 N	88.10 W
Villaguay	140	31.52 S	59.01 W
Villa Hayes	140	25.05 S	57.34 W
Villahermosa	130	17.59 N	92.55 W
Villaines-la-Juhel	74	48.21 N	0.17 W
Villa Juárez	130	27.37 N	109.50 W
Villa María	140	32.25 S	63.15 W
Villa Montes	134	21.15 S	63.30 W
Villandraut	74	44.28 N	0.22 W
Villanueva de Córdoba	76	38.20 N	4.37 W
Villanueva de la Serana	76	38.58 N	5.48 W
Villanueva del Río y Minas	76	37.39 N	5.42 W
Villa Ocampo	140	28.30 S	59.20 W
Villa Ranchero	130	25.49 N	103.10 W
Villard-de-Lans	74	45.04 N	5.33 E
Villa Rica	156	33.43 N	84.55 W
Villarrica, Chile	136	39.16 S	72.13 W
Villarrica, Para.	140	25.45 S	56.26 W
Villarrobledo	76	39.16 N	2.36 W
Villas	152	39.01 N	74.56 W
Villasasyas	76	41.21 N	2.37 W
Villasimíus	78	39.08 N	9.31 E
Villasor	78	39.23 N	8.57 E
Villa Unión, Arg.	140	29.20 S	68.13 W
Villa Unión, Méx.	130	23.11 N	106.14 W
Villa Vicente Guerrero	130	23.43 N	103.59 W
Villaviciosa	76	43.29 N	5.26 W
Villazón	134	22.06 S	65.36 W
Villé	74	48.20 N	7.18 E
Villefort	74	44.26 N	3.56 E
Villefranche-de-Rouergue	74	44.21 N	2.02 E
Villefranche-du-Périgord	74	44.38 N	1.05 E
Ville-Marie	154	47.19 N	79.26 W
Villena	76	38.38 N	0.52 W
Villenauxe-la-Grande	74	48.35 N	3.33 E
Villeneuve-de-Berg	74	44.33 N	4.30 E

Name	Page	Lat	Long
Villeneuve-Saint-Georges	74	48.44 N	2.27 E
Villeneuve-sur-Lot	74	44.25 N	0.42 E
Villeneuve-sur-Yonne	74	48.05 N	3.18 E
Ville Platte	158	30.42 N	92.16 W
Villers-Bocage, Fr.	74	49.05 N	0.39 W
Villers-Bocage, Fr.	74	49.59 N	2.20 E
Villers-Cotterêts	74	49.15 N	3.05 E
Villersexel	74	47.33 N	6.26 E
Villerupt	74	49.28 N	5.56 E
Ville-Saint-Georges	152	46.07 N	70.40 W
Villeurbanne	74	45.46 N	4.53 E
Villingen-Schwenningen	72	48.04 N	8.28 E
Vilnius	86	54.41 N	25.19 E
Vilsbiburg	72	48.27 N	12.12 E
Vilshofen	72	48.39 N	13.12 E
Vil'uj ⇌	84	64.24 N	126.26 E
Vil'ujsk	84	63.45 N	121.35 E
Vimianzo	76	43.07 N	9.02 W
Vimoutiers	74	48.55 N	0.12 E
Vimpeli	68	63.09 N	23.48 E
Vina ⇌	106	7.45 N	15.36 E
Viña del Mar	140	33.02 S	71.34 W
Vinalhaven	152	44.03 N	68.50 W
Vinaroz	76	40.28 N	0.29 E
Vincennes	74	48.51 N	2.26 E
Vincent	158	33.23 N	86.25 W
Vindeln	68	64.12 N	19.44 E
Vindhya Range ✗	102	23.00 N	77.00 E
Vine Grove	158	37.49 N	85.59 W
Vineland	152	39.29 N	75.02 W
Vineyard Haven	152	41.27 N	70.36 W
Vinh	94	18.40 N	105.40 E
Vinh-loi	94	9.17 N	105.43 E
Vinh-long	94	10.15 N	105.58 E
Vinita	160	36.39 N	95.09 W
Vinkovci	80	45.17 N	18.49 E
Vinnica	64	49.14 N	28.29 E
Vinstra	68	61.36 N	9.45 E
Vinton, Iowa, U.S.	154	42.10 N	92.01 W
Vinton, Va., U.S.	156	37.17 N	80.01 W
Viny	74	47.09 N	0.32 W
Viola	154	43.31 N	90.40 W
Vipiteno	78	46.54 N	11.26 E
Virac	94	13.35 N	124.14 E
Viramgām	100	23.07 N	72.02 E
Virbalis	86	54.38 N	22.49 E
Virden, Man., Can.	162	49.51 N	100.55 W
Virden, Ill., U.S.	158	39.30 N	89.46 W
Vire	74	48.50 N	0.53 W
Virgin ⇌	164	36.31 N	114.20 W
Virginia, S. Afr.	116	28.12 S	26.49 E
Virginia, Minn., U.S.	154	47.31 N	92.32 W
Virginia □3	144	37.30 N	78.45 W
Virginia Beach	156	36.51 N	75.58 W
Virginia City	168	39.19 N	119.39 W
Virginia Falls ⇌	146	61.38 N	125.42 W
Virgin Islands ⌐	132	18.20 N	64.50 W
Virieu-le-Grand	74	45.51 N	5.39 E
Virkie	70	59.53 N	1.18 W
Virkkala	68	60.12 N	24.01 E
Viroqua	154	43.34 N	90.53 W
Virovitica	80	45.50 N	17.23 E
Virrat	68	62.14 N	23.47 E
Virton	72	49.34 N	5.32 E
Virtsu	86	58.34 N	23.31 E
Vis	80	43.03 N	16.12 E
Vis, Otok I	80	43.02 N	16.11 E
Visalia	168	36.20 N	119.18 W
Visby	68	57.38 N	18.18 E
Viscount Melville Sound ⇌	142	74.10 N	113.00 W
Viseu	76	40.39 N	7.55 W
Vishākhapatnam	100	17.43 N	83.19 E
Vislinskij Zaliv C	72	54.27 N	19.40 E
Visnagar	102	23.42 N	72.33 E
Visoko	80	44.00 N	18.10 E
Visp	74	46.18 N	7.53 E
Visselhövede	72	52.59 N	9.35 E
Vista	168	33.12 N	117.15 W
Vistula → Wisła ⇌	72	54.22 N	18.55 E
Vitarte	134	12.02 S	76.54 W
Vitebsk	86	55.12 N	30.11 E
Viterbo	78	42.25 N	12.06 E
Vitim ⇌	84	59.26 N	112.34 E
Vitim	84	59.28 N	112.35 E
Vitória, Bra.	134	20.19 S	40.21 W
Vitória da Conquista	134	14.51 S	40.51 W
Vitré	74	48.08 N	1.12 W
Vitteaux	74	47.24 N	4.32 E
Vittel	74	48.13 N	5.57 E
Vittoria	78	36.57 N	14.32 E
Vittorio Veneto	78	45.59 N	12.18 E
Viver	76	39.55 N	0.36 W
Vivi ⇌	84	63.53 N	97.47 E
Vivian	158	32.53 N	93.59 W
Viviers	74	44.29 N	4.41 E
Vivonne	74	46.26 N	0.16 E
Vizcachas, Meseta de las ✗1	136	50.35 S	71.55 W
Vizcaya □4	76	43.15 N	2.45 W
Vize, Ostrov I	82	79.30 N	77.00 E
Vizianagaram	100	18.07 N	83.25 E
Vizille	74	45.05 N	5.46 E
Vizzini	78	37.10 N	14.45 E
Vlaardingen	72	51.54 N	4.21 E
Vladimir	86	56.10 N	40.25 E
Vladivostok	84	43.10 N	131.56 E
Vlasenica	80	44.11 N	18.56 E
Vlasotince	80	42.58 N	22.08 E
Vlissingen (Flushing)	72	51.27 N	3.35 E
Vlorë	80	40.27 N	19.30 E
Vltava (Moldau) ⇌	72	50.21 N	14.30 E
Vnukovo	86	55.39 N	37.16 E
Vochtoga	86	58.48 N	41.07 E
Vöcklabruck	72	48.01 N	13.39 E
Vodnjany	72	49.09 N	14.11 E
Vodosalma	66	64.29 N	30.44 E
Voghera	78	44.59 N	9.01 E
Vohenstrauss	72	49.37 N	12.20 E
Voi	117b	3.23 S	38.34 E
Voikkaa	68	60.52 N	26.45 E
Voiotia □5	80	38.20 N	23.07 E
Voitsberg	72	47.03 N	15.09 E
Vojens	68	55.15 N	9.18 E
vojvodina □9	80	45.00 N	20.00 E
Volborg	162	45.51 N	105.41 W
Volchov ⇌	86	60.08 N	32.20 E
Volda	68	62.09 N	6.06 E
Volga ⇌	64	45.55 N	47.52 E
Volgodonsk	64	47.33 N	42.08 E
Volgograd (Stalingrad)	64	48.44 N	44.25 E
Volgogradskoje Vodochranilišče ⌐1	64	49.20 N	45.00 E
Volkach	72	49.52 N	10.13 E
Volketswil	74	47.23 N	8.42 E
Völkermarkt	72	46.40 N	14.38 E
Volkovysk	86	53.10 N	24.28 E
Volksrust	116	27.24 S	29.53 E
Volčanka	84	71.00 N	94.28 E
Volčin	86	52.29 N	23.27 E
Vologda	86	59.12 N	39.55 E
Volokolamsk	86	56.02 N	35.58 E
Volokovaja	66	66.28 N	48.10 E

Name	Page	Lat	Long
Volonne	74	44.07 N	6.01 E
Volos	80	39.21 N	22.56 E
Vološin	86	54.05 N	26.32 E
Vol'sk	64	52.02 N	47.23 E
Volta, Lake ⌐1	114	7.30 N	0.15 E
Volta Blanche (White Volta) ⇌	114	9.10 N	1.15 W
Volta Noire (Black Volta) ⇌	114	8.38 N	1.40 W
Volta Redonda	134	22.32 S	44.07 W
Volta Rouge ⇌	114	10.34 N	0.30 W
Volterra	78	43.24 N	10.51 E
Vol'teva	64	84.30 N	44.12 E
Voltri	78	44.26 N	8.45 E
Volžsk	86	55.53 N	48.21 E
Volžskij	64	48.50 N	44.44 E
Vondanka	66	59.07 N	45.49 E
Voria Spórades II	80	39.17 N	23.23 E
Vorkuta	66	67.27 N	63.58 E
Vorona ⇌	86	51.40 N	39.10 E
Voronež	64	51.40 N	39.10 E
Voronovo	86	54.09 N	25.19 E
Vorošilovgrad	64	48.34 N	39.20 E
Vorošilovsk → Kommunarsk, S.S.S.R.	64	48.30 N	38.47 E
Vorošilovsk → Stavropol', S.S.S.R.	64	48.30 N	38.47 E
Vorpommern □9	72	53.40 N	13.45 E
Vorsma	86	55.59 N	43.16 E
Võru	86	57.50 N	27.01 E
Vosges □5	74	48.10 N	6.20 E
Voskresensk	86	55.19 N	38.42 E
Voss	68	60.39 N	6.26 E
Vostočno-Sibirskoje More (East Siberian Sea) ⇌2	84	74.00 N	166.00 E
Vostočnyj Sajan ✗	84	53.00 N	97.00 E
Votkinsk	66	57.03 N	53.59 E
Votuporanga	134	20.24 S	49.59 W
Vouga ⇌	76	40.41 N	8.40 W
Vouillé	74	46.39 N	0.10 E
Vouziers	74	49.24 N	4.42 E
Voves	74	48.16 N	1.38 E
Vožega	86	60.29 N	40.12 E
Vozneseňsk	64	47.34 N	31.20 E
Vozneseňskoje	86	54.54 N	42.46 E
Vraca	80	43.12 N	23.33 E
Vrådal	68	59.20 N	8.25 E
Vrancea □4	80	45.45 N	27.00 E
Vrangel'a, Ostrov I	84	71.00 N	179.30 E
Vranje	80	42.33 N	21.54 E
Vrbas ⇌	80	45.15 N	19.39 E
Vrbas	80	45.34 N	17.51 E
Vrchlabí	72	50.38 N	15.37 E
Vrede	116	27.24 S	29.06 E
Vríndávan	102	27.35 N	77.42 E
Vrondádhes	80	38.25 N	26.08 E
Vršac	80	45.07 N	21.18 E
Vryburg	116	26.55 S	24.45 E
Vryheid	116	27.46 S	30.48 E
Vsetín	72	49.21 N	17.59 E
Vsevoložsk	86	60.01 N	30.40 E
Vught	72	51.39 N	5.17 E
Vukovar	80	45.21 N	19.00 E
Vulcan, Rom.	80	45.23 N	23.17 E
Vulcan, Mich., U.S.	154	45.47 N	87.53 W
Vung-tau	92	10.21 N	107.04 E
Vuohijärvi	68	61.05 N	26.48 E
Vuoksenniska	68	61.13 N	28.49 E
Vyborg	68	60.42 N	28.45 E
Vyčegda ⇌	66	61.18 N	46.36 E
Východočeský Kraj □4	72	50.10 N	16.00 E
Východoslovenský Kraj □4	72	49.00 N	21.15 E
Vygoniči	86	53.08 N	34.05 E
Vygozero, Ozero ⌐	86	63.35 N	34.45 E
Vyksa	86	55.18 N	42.11 E
Vypolzovo	86	57.53 N	33.42 E
Vyrica	86	59.25 N	30.21 E
Vyšnij Voloček	86	57.35 N	34.34 E
Vysock	86	60.40 N	28.34 E
Vysokiči	86	54.54 N	36.55 E
Vysokoje	86	52.22 N	23.22 E
Vysokovsk	86	56.19 N	36.33 E
Vytegra	66	61.00 N	36.24 E

W

Name	Page	Lat	Long
Wa	114	10.03 N	2.29 W
Waalwijk	72	51.42 N	5.04 E
Wabag	124	5.30 S	143.40 E
Wabana	154	47.38 N	52.57 W
Wabasca	148	56.00 N	113.53 W
Wabasca ⇌	148	58.22 N	115.20 W
Wabash	152	40.47 N	85.49 W
Wabash ⇌	158	37.46 N	88.02 W
Wabasso	154	44.25 N	95.15 W
Wabeno	154	45.26 N	88.40 W
Wabrzežno	72	53.17 N	18.57 E
Waccamaw ⇌	156	33.21 N	79.16 W
Waco	160	31.33 N	97.08 W
Waconia	154	44.51 N	93.47 W
Waddington, Mount ▲	148	51.23 N	125.15 W
Wadena, Sask., Can.	162	51.57 N	103.47 W
Wadena, Minn., U.S.	154	46.26 N	95.08 W
Wädenswil	74	47.14 N	8.40 E
Wadesboro	156	34.58 N	80.04 W
Wadhams	148	51.30 N	127.30 W
Wadley, Ala., U.S.	156	33.07 N	85.34 W
Wadley, Ga., U.S.	156	32.52 N	82.24 W
Wad Madani	112	14.24 N	33.32 E
Wadowice	72	49.53 N	19.30 E
Wadsworth, Nev., U.S.	168	39.38 N	119.17 W
Wadsworth, Ohio, U.S.	152	41.02 N	81.44 W
Wageningen	72	51.58 N	5.40 E
Wager Bay C	142	65.26 N	88.40 W
Wagga Wagga	122	35.07 S	147.22 E
Waging am See	72	47.56 N	12.44 E
Wagoner	160	35.57 N	95.22 W
Wagon Mound	164	36.01 N	104.42 W
Wagrowiec	72	52.49 N	17.11 E
Waha	112	28.16 N	19.54 E
Wahai	124	2.48 S	129.30 E
Wahiawa	170c	21.30 N	158.01 W
Wahoo	162	41.12 N	96.37 W
Wahpeton	162	46.16 N	96.36 W
Waialua	170c	21.34 N	158.08 W
Waianae	170c	21.26 N	158.11 W
Waiblingen	72	48.50 N	9.19 E
Waidhofen an der Thaya	72	48.49 N	15.18 E
Waidhofen an der Ybbs	72	47.58 N	14.46 E
Waigeo, Pulau I	124	0.14 S	130.45 E
Waihi	126	37.23 S	175.51 E
Waikabubak	96	9.38 S	119.25 E
Waikari	126	42.58 S	172.41 E
Waikerie	122	34.11 S	139.59 E
Wailuku	170c	20.53 N	156.30 W
Waimanalo	170c	21.21 N	157.42 W
Waimate	126	44.45 S	171.03 E
Waimea	170b	21.57 N	159.40 W
Wainganga ⇌	100	18.50 N	79.55 E
Waingapu	96	9.39 S	120.16 E
Wainwright, Alta., Can.	148	52.49 N	110.52 W
Wainwright, Alaska, U.S.	146	70.38 N	160.01 W
Waipahu	170c	21.23 N	158.00 W
Waipio Acres	170c	21.28 N	158.01 W
Waipukurau	126	39.59 S	176.33 E
Wairoa	126	39.02 S	177.25 E

Symbols in the index entries are identified on page 203.

Name	Page	Lat °′	Long °′
Waitara	126	39.00 S	174.14 E
Waite Park	154	45.33 N	94.14 W
Waitsburg	166	46.16 N	118.09 W
Wajabula	92	2.17 N	128.12 E
Wajir	108	1.45 N	40.04 E
Waka, Tex., U.S.	160	36.17 N	101.03 W
Waka, Yai.	108	7.07 N	37.26 E
Wakayama	90	34.13 N	135.11 E
Wa Keeney	162	39.01 N	99.53 W
Wakefield, Eng., U.K.	70	53.42 N	1.29 W
Wakefield, Kans., U.S.	162	39.13 N	97.01 W
Wakefield, R.I., U.S.	152	41.26 N	71.30 W
Wakefield, Va., U.S.	156	36.58 N	76.59 W
Wake Forest	156	35.59 N	78.30 W
Wake Village	158	33.26 N	94.07 W
Wakita	160	36.53 N	97.55 W
Wakkanai	90a	45.25 N	141.40 E
Wałbrzych (Waldenburg)	72	50.46 N	16.17 E
Walcha	120	30.59 S	151.36 E
Wałcz	72	53.17 N	16.28 E
Waldbröl	72	50.53 N	7.37 E
Waldeck	72	51.12 N	9.04 E
Walden, Colo., U.S.	164	40.44 N	106.17 W
Walden, N.Y., U.S.	152	41.34 N	74.11 W
Walden Ridge ∧	158	35.30 N	85.15 W
Waldkirchen	72	48.44 N	13.37 E
Waldmünchen	72	49.23 N	12.43 E
Waldo	158	33.21 N	93.18 W
Waldoboro	152	44.06 N	69.23 W
Waldorf	152	38.37 N	76.54 W
Waldport	166	44.26 N	124.04 W
Waldron, Ark., U.S.	158	34.54 N	94.05 W
Waldron, Mich., U.S.	154	41.44 N	84.25 W
Waldshut	72	47.37 N	8.13 E
Walenstadt	74	47.07 N	9.19 E
Wales	146	65.36 N	168.05 W
Wales ☐8	70	52.30 N	3.30 W
Wales Island I, N.W. Ter., Can.	142	61.50 N	72.05 W
Wales Island I, N.W. Ter., Can.	142	68.00 N	86.43 W
Walgett	120	30.01 S	148.07 E
Walhalla, N. Dak., U.S.	162	48.55 N	97.55 W
Walhalla, S.C., U.S.	156	34.46 N	83.04 W
Walker, Iowa, U.S.	154	42.17 N	91.47 W
Walker, Minn., U.S.	154	47.06 N	94.35 W
Walker Lake ⊜	168	38.44 N	118.43 W
Walkersville	152	39.29 N	77.21 W
Walkerton, Ont., Can.	154	44.07 N	81.09 W
Walkerton, Ind., U.S.	158	41.28 N	86.29 W
Walkerville	166	46.01 N	112.30 W
Wallaby Island I	124	16.28 S	139.41 E
Wallace, Idaho, U.S.	166	47.28 N	115.56 W
Wallace, N.C., U.S.	156	34.44 N	77.59 W
Wallaceburg	154	42.36 N	82.23 W
Wallachia ☐9	80	44.00 N	25.00 E
Walland	156	35.44 N	83.49 W
Wallangarra	120	28.56 S	151.56 E
Wallaroo	120	33.56 S	137.38 E
Wallasey	70	53.26 N	3.03 W
Walla Walla	166	46.08 N	118.20 W
Wallingford, Conn., U.S.	152	41.27 N	72.50 W
Wallingford, Vt., U.S.	152	43.28 N	72.59 W
Wallis	160	29.38 N	96.04 W
Wall Lake	162	42.16 N	95.05 W
Wallowa	166	45.34 N	117.32 W
Walnut Cove	156	36.18 N	80.09 W
Walnut Grove	162	44.13 N	95.28 W
Walnut Ridge	158	36.04 N	90.57 W
Walpeup	120	35.08 S	142.02 E
Walpole, Austl.	122	34.57 S	116.44 E
Walpole, N.H., U.S.	152	43.05 N	72.26 W
Walsall	70	52.35 N	1.58 W
Walsenburg	164	37.37 N	104.47 W
Walsh, Austl.	124	16.39 S	143.54 E
Walsh, Colo., U.S.	162	37.23 N	102.17 W
Walsrode	72	52.52 N	9.35 E
Walterboro	156	32.55 N	80.39 W
Walter F George Reservoir ⊜1	156	31.49 N	85.08 W
Walters	160	34.22 N	98.19 W
Waltershausen	72	50.53 N	10.33 E
Waltham	152	42.23 N	71.14 W
Walthill	162	42.09 N	96.30 W
Walton, Ky., U.S.	152	38.52 N	84.37 W
Walton, N.Y., U.S.	152	42.10 N	75.08 W
Walvisbaai (Walvis Bay)	116	22.59 S	14.31 E
Walworth	154	42.32 N	88.36 W
Wamba ≃	110	3.56 S	17.12 E
Wamego	162	39.12 N	96.18 W
Wami ≃	110	6.08 S	38.49 E
Wampum	152	40.54 N	80.21 W
Wamsutter	166	41.40 N	107.58 W
Wanaaring	120	29.42 S	144.09 E
Wanaka	126	44.42 S	169.09 E
Wanbi	120	34.46 S	140.19 E
Wandana	122	32.04 S	133.49 E
Wandoan	120	26.09 S	149.51 E
Wanfoxia	88	40.04 N	95.55 E
Wanganui	126	39.56 S	175.02 E
Wanganui ≃	126	39.57 S	174.59 E
Wangaratta	120	36.22 S	146.20 E
Wangary	120	34.33 S	135.29 E
Wangen [im Allgäu]	72	47.41 N	9.50 E
Wangiwangi, Pulau I	96	5.20 S	123.35 E
Wankie	116	18.22 S	26.29 E
Wanne-Eickel	72	51.32 N	7.09 E
Wansbeck	70	55.08 N	1.35 W
Wanxian	88	30.52 N	108.22 E
Wanzai	88	28.06 N	114.27 E
Wanzleben	72	52.03 N	11.26 E
Wapakoneta	152	40.34 N	84.12 W
Wapato	166	46.27 N	120.25 W
Wapello	154	41.11 N	91.11 W
Wapiti ≃	148	55.08 N	118.18 W
Wappingers Falls	152	41.36 N	73.55 W
Wapsipinicon ≃	154	41.44 N	90.20 W
War	156	37.18 N	81.41 W
Warangal	100	18.00 N	79.35 E
Waratah	120	41.27 S	145.32 E
Waratah Bay C	120	38.51 S	146.04 E
Warbreccan	120	24.18 S	142.51 E
Warburg	72	51.29 N	9.08 E
Warburton	120	37.46 S	145.41 E
Warburton Bay C	142	63.50 N	111.30 W
Warburton Range ⋀	122	26.09 S	126.38 E
Ward ≃	120	26.32 S	146.06 E
Ward Cove	148	55.24 N	131.43 W
Warden	166	46.58 N	119.02 W
Wardha	100	20.45 N	78.36 E
Wardha ≃	100	19.36 N	79.48 E
Ware	152	42.16 N	72.15 W
Wareham, Eng., U.K.	70	50.41 N	2.07 W
Wareham, Mass., U.S.	152	41.46 N	70.43 W
Waremme	72	50.41 N	5.15 E
Waren, D.D.R.	72	53.31 N	12.40 E
Waren, Indon.	124	2.16 S	136.20 E
Warendorf	72	51.57 N	7.59 E
Ware Shoals	156	34.24 N	82.15 W
Warialda	120	29.32 S	150.34 E
Warmbad, S. Afr.	116	24.55 S	28.15 E
Warmbad, S.W. Afr.	116	28.29 S	18.41 E
Warminster	70	51.13 N	2.12 W
Warm Springs	166	44.46 N	121.16 W
Warner Mountains ⋀	168	41.40 N	120.20 W
Warner Robins	156	32.37 N	83.36 W
Warracknabeal	120	36.15 S	142.24 E
Warr Acres	160	35.31 N	97.37 W
Warragul	120	38.10 S	145.56 E
Warratta ≃	120	29.49 S	142.17 E
Warrego ≃	120	30.24 S	145.21 E
Warrego Range ⋀	120	25.00 S	145.45 E
Warren, Austl.	120	31.42 S	147.50 E
Warren, Ark., U.S.	158	33.37 N	92.04 W
Warren, Mich., U.S.	154	42.28 N	83.01 W
Warren, Minn., U.S.	162	48.12 N	96.46 W
Warren, Ohio, U.S.	152	41.14 N	80.52 W
Warren, Pa., U.S.	152	41.51 N	79.08 W
Warrenpoint	70	54.06 N	6.15 W
Warrensburg, Mo., U.S.	158	38.46 N	93.44 W
Warrensburg, N.Y., U.S.	152	43.30 N	73.46 W
Warrenton, S. Afr.	116	28.09 S	24.47 E
Warrenton, Ga., U.S.	156	33.24 N	82.40 W
Warrenton, Oreg., U.S.	166	46.10 N	123.56 W
Warrenton, Va., U.S.	152	38.43 N	77.48 W
Warri	114	5.31 N	5.45 E
Warrina	120	28.12 S	135.50 E
Warriners ≃	120	29.25 S	137.07 E
Warrington, Eng., U.K.	70	53.24 N	2.37 W
Warrington, Fla., U.S.	158	30.23 N	87.16 W
Warrior	158	33.49 N	86.49 W
Warrior Reefs ⊹2	124	9.35 S	143.10 E
Warrnambool	120	38.23 S	142.29 E
Warroad	162	48.54 N	95.19 W
Warsaw → Warszawa, Port.	72	52.15 N	21.00 E
Warsaw, Ill., U.S.	154	40.22 N	91.26 W
Warsaw, Ind., U.S.	158	41.14 N	85.51 W
Warsaw, Mo., U.S.	158	38.15 N	93.23 W
Warsaw, N.C., U.S.	156	35.00 N	78.05 W
Warsaw, N.Y., U.S.	152	42.44 N	78.08 W
Warsaw, Ohio, U.S.	152	40.20 N	82.00 W
Warszawa (Warsaw)	72	52.15 N	21.00 E
Wartburg	156	36.06 N	84.36 W
Wartrace	158	35.32 N	86.19 W
Warwick, Austl.	120	28.13 S	152.02 E
Warwick, Qué., Can.	152	45.56 N	71.59 W
Warwick, Eng., U.K.	70	52.17 N	1.34 W
Warwick, R.I., U.S.	152	41.43 N	71.28 W
Warwick Channel ⊔	124	13.51 S	136.16 E
Warwickshire ☐6	70	52.13 N	1.37 W
Wasatch Range ⋀	164	41.15 N	111.30 W
Wasco, Calif., U.S.	168	35.36 N	119.20 W
Wasco, Oreg., U.S.	166	45.35 N	120.42 W
Waseca	154	44.05 N	93.30 W
Washburn, Ill., U.S.	154	40.55 N	89.17 W
Washburn, Maine, U.S.	150	46.47 N	68.09 W
Washburn Lake ⊜	142	70.03 N	106.50 W
Washington, D.C., U.S.	152	38.54 N	77.01 W
Washington, Ga., U.S.	156	33.44 N	82.44 W
Washington, Ill., U.S.	154	40.42 N	89.24 W
Washington, Ind., U.S.	158	38.40 N	87.10 W
Washington, Iowa, U.S.	154	41.18 N	91.42 W
Washington, Kans., U.S.	162	39.49 N	97.03 W
Washington, La., U.S.	158	30.37 N	92.03 W
Washington, Mo., U.S.	158	38.33 N	91.01 W
Washington, N.C., U.S.	156	35.33 N	77.03 W
Washington, Pa., U.S.	152	40.10 N	80.15 W
Washington, Tex., U.S.	160	30.20 N	96.10 W
Washington, Va., U.S.	152	38.43 N	78.10 W
Washington ☐3	144	47.30 N	120.30 W
Washington, Mount ∧	152	44.15 N	71.15 W
Washington Court House	152	39.32 N	83.26 W
Washington D.C. → District of Columbia ☐3	144	38.54 N	77.01 W
Washington Island	154	45.23 N	86.55 W
Washington Island I	154	45.23 N	86.55 W
Washington Terrace	166	41.12 N	111.59 W
Washita ≃	160	34.12 N	96.50 W
Washoe Lake ⊜	168	39.15 N	119.47 W
Wasilków	72	53.12 N	23.12 E
Wasilla	146	61.35 N	149.26 W
Wasior	124	2.42 S	134.30 E
Waskom	158	32.29 N	94.04 W
Wassen	74	46.42 N	8.36 E
Wasseralfingen	72	48.52 N	10.06 E
Wasserburg am Inn	72	48.04 N	12.13 E
Wassy	74	48.30 N	4.57 E
Watampone (Bone)	96	4.32 S	120.20 E
Watansoppeng	96	4.21 S	119.53 E
Waterbury, Conn., U.S.	152	41.33 N	73.02 W
Waterbury, Vt., U.S.	152	44.20 N	72.46 W
Waterdown	154	43.20 N	79.53 W
Waterford, Ont., Can.	154	42.56 N	80.17 W
Waterford, Eire	70	52.15 N	7.06 W
Waterford, Calif., U.S.	168	37.38 N	120.46 W
Waterford, Wis., U.S.	154	42.46 N	88.13 W
Waterford ☐6	70	52.10 N	7.40 W
Waterhen Lake ⊜	142	52.06 N	99.34 W
Waterloo, Austl.	124	16.38 S	129.18 E
Waterloo, Bel.	72	50.43 N	4.23 E
Waterloo, Ont., Can.	154	43.28 N	80.31 W
Waterloo, Qué., Can.	152	45.21 N	72.31 W
Waterloo, Ill., U.S.	158	38.20 N	90.09 W
Waterloo, Iowa, U.S.	154	42.30 N	92.20 W
Waterloo, N.Y., U.S.	152	42.54 N	76.52 W
Waterloo, Wis., U.S.	154	43.11 N	88.59 W
Waterman	154	41.46 N	88.46 W
Waterproof	158	31.48 N	91.23 W
Watersmeet	154	46.13 N	89.11 W
Watertown, Fla., U.S.	156	30.11 N	82.36 W
Watertown, N.Y., U.S.	152	43.59 N	75.55 W
Watertown, S. Dak., U.S.	162	44.54 N	97.07 W
Watertown, Wis., U.S.	154	43.12 N	88.43 W
Water Valley	158	34.09 N	89.38 W
Waterville, Kans., U.S.	162	39.42 N	96.45 W
Waterville, Maine, U.S.	152	44.33 N	69.38 W
Waterville, Minn., U.S.	154	44.13 N	93.34 W
Waterville, Ohio, U.S.	152	41.30 N	83.43 W
Waterville, Wash., U.S.	166	47.39 N	120.04 W
Watervliet	152	42.44 N	73.42 W
Watford	70	51.40 N	0.25 W
Watford City	162	47.48 N	103.17 W
Wathaman ≃	142	57.16 N	102.52 W
Watkins Glen	152	42.23 N	76.52 W
Watonga	160	35.51 N	98.25 W
Watrous, Sask., Can.	142	51.40 N	105.28 W
Watrous, N. Mex., U.S.	164	35.48 N	104.59 W
Watseka	154	40.47 N	87.44 W
Watson Lake	146	60.07 N	128.48 W
Watsontown	152	41.05 N	76.52 W
Watsonville	168	36.55 N	121.45 W
Wattens	72	47.17 N	11.36 E
Wattenscheid	72	51.29 N	7.08 E
Wattiwarriganna ≃	122	28.57 S	136.10 E
Wattsville, Ala., U.S.	158	33.40 N	86.17 W
Wattsville, S.C., U.S.	156	34.31 N	82.02 W
Wattwil	74	47.18 N	9.06 E
Watubela, Kepulauan II	124	4.24 S	131.35 E
Wauchope, Austl.	120	31.27 S	152.44 E
Wauchope, Austl.	122	20.36 S	134.15 E
Wauchula	156	27.33 N	81.49 W
Wauconda	148	48.44 N	118.59 W
Waugh Mountain ∧	166	45.29 N	114.47 W
Waukaringa	120	32.18 S	139.26 E
Waukegan	154	42.22 N	87.50 W
Waukesha	154	43.01 N	88.14 W
Waukon	154	43.16 N	91.29 W
Waunakee	154	43.11 N	89.27 W
Waupaca	154	44.21 N	89.05 W
Waupun	154	43.38 N	88.44 W
Wausau	154	44.59 N	89.39 W
Wauseon	152	41.33 N	84.09 W
Wautoma	154	44.04 N	89.17 W
Wauwatosa	154	43.03 N	88.00 W
Wauzeka	154	43.05 N	90.52 W
Wave Hill	122	17.29 S	130.57 E
Waveland	158	30.16 N	89.29 W
Waverly, Ill., U.S.	158	39.36 N	89.57 W
Waverly, Iowa, U.S.	154	42.44 N	92.29 W
Waverly, Minn., U.S.	154	45.04 N	93.57 W
Waverly, Mo., U.S.	158	39.12 N	93.31 W
Waverly, N.Y., U.S.	152	42.00 N	76.32 W
Waverly, Ohio, U.S.	152	39.07 N	82.59 W
Waverly, Tenn., U.S.	158	36.05 N	87.48 W
Waverly, Va., U.S.	156	37.02 N	77.06 W
Wavre	74	50.43 N	4.37 E
Wāw	112	7.42 N	28.00 E
Wawa	154	47.59 N	84.47 W
Waxahachie	160	32.24 N	96.51 W
Waycross	156	31.13 N	82.21 W
Wayland, Iowa, U.S.	154	41.08 N	91.40 W
Wayland, Mich., U.S.	154	42.40 N	85.39 W
Wayland, N.Y., U.S.	152	42.34 N	77.35 W
Wayne, Mich., U.S.	154	42.17 N	83.23 W
Wayne, Nebr., U.S.	162	42.14 N	97.01 W
Wayne, N.J., U.S.	152	40.55 N	74.17 W
Wayne, W. Va., U.S.	152	38.13 N	82.27 W
Waynesboro, Ga., U.S.	156	33.06 N	82.01 W
Waynesboro, Miss., U.S.	158	31.40 N	88.39 W
Waynesboro, Pa., U.S.	152	39.45 N	77.35 W
Waynesboro, Tenn., U.S.	158	35.19 N	87.45 W
Waynesboro, Va., U.S.	152	38.04 N	78.53 W
Waynesburg, Ohio, U.S.	152	40.40 N	81.16 W
Waynesburg, Pa., U.S.	152	39.54 N	80.11 W
Waynesville, Mo., U.S.	158	37.50 N	92.12 W
Waynesville, N.C., U.S.	156	35.29 N	83.00 W
We, Pulau I	94	5.51 N	95.18 E
Wearyan ≃	124	15.57 S	136.51 E
Weatherford, Okla., U.S.	160	35.32 N	98.42 W
Weatherford, Tex., U.S.	160	32.46 N	97.48 W
Weaver	158	33.45 N	85.49 W
Weaverville	168	40.44 N	122.56 W
Webb City	158	37.09 N	94.28 W
Weber City	156	36.37 N	82.34 W
Webster, Mass., U.S.	152	42.03 N	71.53 W
Webster, N.Y., U.S.	152	43.13 N	77.26 W
Webster, S. Dak., U.S.	162	45.20 N	97.31 W
Webster, Wis., U.S.	154	45.53 N	92.22 W
Webster City	154	42.28 N	93.49 W
Weda	92	0.21 N	127.52 E
Wedderburn, Austl.	120	36.25 S	143.37 E
Wedderburn, Oreg., U.S.	166	42.26 N	124.25 W
Wedel	72	53.35 N	9.41 E
Wedowee	158	33.19 N	85.29 W
Weed	168	41.25 N	122.23 W
Weedsport	152	43.03 N	76.34 W
Weedville	152	41.17 N	78.30 W
Weeks	158	29.48 N	91.49 W
Weeping Water	162	40.52 N	96.08 W
Weert	72	51.15 N	5.43 E
Wee Waa	120	30.14 S	149.26 E
Węgrów	72	52.25 N	22.01 E
Wegscheid	72	48.36 N	13.48 E
Weida	72	50.45 N	12.04 E
Weiden in der Oberpfalz	72	49.41 N	12.10 E
Weifang	88	36.42 N	19.04 E
Weihai	88	37.28 N	122.07 E
Weihe ≃	88	34.30 N	110.20 E
Weilburg	72	50.29 N	8.15 E
Weilheim	72	47.50 N	11.08 E
Weimar, D.D.R.	72	50.59 N	11.19 E
Weimar, Tex., U.S.	160	29.42 N	96.47 W
Weinan	88	34.29 N	109.29 E
Weinheim	72	49.33 N	8.39 E
Weipa	124	12.41 S	141.52 E
Weir	162	37.19 N	94.46 W
Weir ≃	120	28.50 S	149.06 E
Weirton	152	40.25 N	80.35 W
Weiser	166	44.15 N	116.58 W
Weissenburg in Bayern	72	49.01 N	10.58 E
Weissenfels	72	51.12 N	11.58 E
Weiss Reservoir ⊜1	156	34.15 N	85.35 W
Weisswasser	72	51.30 N	14.38 E
Weitra	72	48.42 N	14.54 E
Weiz	72	47.13 N	15.37 E
Wejherowo	72	54.37 N	18.15 E
Welch, Okla., U.S.	160	36.52 N	95.06 W
Welch, W. Va., U.S.	156	37.25 N	81.31 W
Welcome, Minn., U.S.	162	43.40 N	94.37 W
Welcome, S.C., U.S.	156	34.49 N	82.26 W
Weldon	156	36.25 N	77.36 W
Weldon ≃	158	40.06 N	93.38 W
Weleetka	160	35.20 N	96.08 W
Welkom	116	27.59 S	26.45 E
Welland	154	42.59 N	79.15 W
Wellesley Islands II	120	16.42 S	139.30 E
Wellingborough	70	52.19 N	0.42 W
Wellington, Austl.	120	32.33 S	148.57 E
Wellington, N.Z.	126	41.18 S	174.46 E
Wellington, Eng., U.K.	70	52.43 N	2.31 W
Wellington, Colo., U.S.	164	40.42 N	105.00 W
Wellington, Kans., U.S.	162	37.16 N	97.24 W
Wellington, Mo., U.S.	158	39.08 N	93.59 W
Wellington, Ohio, U.S.	152	41.10 N	82.13 W
Wellington, Tex., U.S.	160	34.51 N	100.13 W
Wellington, Utah, U.S.	164	39.32 N	110.44 W
Wellington, Isla I	136	49.20 S	74.40 W
Wellington Bay C	142	69.30 N	106.30 W
Wellington Channel ⊔	142	75.00 N	93.00 W
Wellman	154	41.28 N	91.50 W
Wells, Eng., U.K.	70	51.13 N	2.39 W
Wells, Mich., U.S.	154	45.47 N	87.04 W
Wells, Minn., U.S.	154	43.44 N	93.44 W
Wells, Nev., U.S.	168	41.07 N	114.58 W
Wells, Lake ⊜	122	26.43 S	123.10 E
Wellsboro	152	41.45 N	77.18 W
Wellsburg, Iowa, U.S.	154	42.26 N	92.56 W
Wellsburg, W. Va., U.S.	152	40.16 N	80.37 W
Wells-next-the-Sea	70	52.58 N	0.51 W
Wellston	152	39.07 N	82.32 W
Wellsville, Kans., U.S.	162	38.43 N	95.05 W
Wellsville, N.Y., U.S.	152	42.07 N	77.57 W
Wellsville, Ohio, U.S.	152	40.36 N	80.39 W
Wellsville, Utah, U.S.	166	41.38 N	111.56 W
Wellton	164	32.40 N	114.08 W
Wels	72	48.10 N	14.02 E
Welsh	158	30.14 N	92.49 W
Welshpool	70	52.40 N	3.09 W
Wembere ≃	110	4.10 S	34.11 E
Wenatchee	166	47.25 N	120.19 W
Wenatchee Mountains ⋀	166	47.20 N	120.45 W
Wendell, Idaho, U.S.	166	42.46 N	114.42 W
Wendell, N.C., U.S.	156	35.47 N	78.22 W
Wendover	168	40.44 N	114.02 W
Wenlock ≃	124	12.02 S	141.55 E
Wenona	154	41.03 N	89.03 W
Wenshan	94	23.30 N	104.20 E
Wentworth, Austl.	120	34.07 S	141.55 E
Wentworth, S. Dak., U.S.	162	44.00 N	96.58 W
Wentzville	158	38.49 N	90.51 W
Wenzhou	88	28.01 N	120.39 E
Werdau	72	50.44 N	12.22 E
Werder	72	52.23 N	12.56 E
Werdohl	72	51.16 N	7.46 E
Werl	72	51.33 N	7.54 E
Werne [an der Lippe]	72	51.40 N	7.38 E
Wernigerode	72	51.50 N	10.47 E
Werra ≃	72	51.26 N	9.39 E
Werribee	120	37.54 S	144.40 E
Werris Creek	120	31.21 S	150.39 E
Wertheim	72	49.46 N	9.31 E
Wertingen	72	48.34 N	10.41 E
Wervik	74	50.47 N	3.02 E
Wesconnett	156	30.14 N	81.44 W
Wesel	72	51.40 N	6.38 E
Weslaco	160	26.09 N	97.59 W
Wesley	154	43.05 N	93.59 W
Wesleyville	152	42.08 N	80.01 W
Wessel, Cape ≻	124	10.59 S	136.46 E
Wessington	162	44.27 N	98.42 W
Wessington Springs	162	44.05 N	98.34 W
Wesson	158	31.42 N	90.23 W
West	160	31.48 N	97.06 W
Westall, Point ≻	122	32.55 S	134.04 E
West Allis	154	43.01 N	88.00 W
West Bend, Iowa, U.S.	162	42.57 N	94.27 W
West Bend, Wis., U.S.	154	43.25 N	88.11 W
West Berbice ☐5	138	6.20 N	57.55 W
West-Berlin	72	52.30 N	13.20 E
West Branch, Iowa, U.S.	154	41.40 N	91.20 W
West Branch, Mich., U.S.	154	44.17 N	84.14 W
West Bridgford	70	52.56 N	1.08 W
Westbrook, Maine, U.S.	152	43.41 N	70.21 W
Westbrook, Minn., U.S.	162	44.03 N	95.26 W
West Burlington	154	40.49 N	91.09 W
Westby	154	43.39 N	90.51 W
West Chester	152	39.58 N	75.36 W
Westcliffe	164	38.08 N	105.28 W
West Columbia, S.C., U.S.	156	34.00 N	81.04 W
West Columbia, Tex., U.S.	160	29.09 N	95.39 W
West Concord	154	44.09 N	92.54 W
West Cote Blanche Bay C	158	29.40 N	91.45 W
West Demerara ☐5	138	5.25 N	58.35 W
West Des Moines	154	41.35 N	93.43 W
Westerland	72	54.54 N	8.18 E
Westerly	152	41.22 N	71.50 W
Western ≃	120	22.22 S	142.25 E
Western Australia ☐3	118	25.00 S	122.00 E
Western Desert → Aṣ-Ṣaḥrā' al-Gharbīyah ⌁2	108	27.00 N	27.00 E
Western Ghāts ⋀	100	14.00 N	75.00 E
Western Isles Islands Region ☐4	70	57.40 N	7.00 W
Westernport	152	39.29 N	79.03 W
Western Port C	120	38.22 S	145.20 E
Western Sahara ☐2	106	24.30 N	13.00 W
Westerstede	72	53.15 N	7.55 E
Westerville	152	40.08 N	82.56 W
West Falkland I	136	51.40 S	60.00 W
West Farmington	152	44.40 N	70.10 W
Westfield, Mass., U.S.	152	42.08 N	72.45 W
Westfield, N.J., U.S.	152	40.39 N	74.21 W
Westfield, N.Y., U.S.	152	42.19 N	79.35 W
West Fiord C2	142	76.02 N	90.00 W
West Frankfort	158	37.54 N	88.55 W
Westgate, Austl.	120	26.35 S	146.12 E
Westgate, Fla., U.S.	156	26.47 N	80.06 W
West Germany → Germany, Federal Republic of ☐1	64	51.00 N	9.00 E
West Glamorgan ☐6	70	51.35 N	3.35 W
West Hamlin	152	38.17 N	82.12 W
West Harbour	126	45.52 S	170.33 E
West Hartford	152	41.46 N	72.45 W
West Haven	152	41.16 N	72.57 W
West Helena	158	34.33 N	90.39 W
West Hollywood	156	25.59 N	80.11 W
West Indies II	128	19.00 N	70.00 W
West Irian → Irian Barat ☐4	124	5.00 S	138.00 E
West Island I	124	15.36 S	136.34 E
West Jefferson	152	39.57 N	83.16 W
West Junction	158	35.04 N	90.05 W
West Lafayette	158	40.27 N	86.55 W
Westlake	158	30.15 N	93.15 W
West Las Vegas	160	35.35 N	105.14 W
West Liberty, Iowa, U.S.	154	41.34 N	91.16 W
West Liberty, Ky., U.S.	156	37.55 N	83.16 W
Westmeath ☐6	70	53.30 N	7.30 W
West Melbourne	156	28.04 N	80.38 W
West Memphis	158	35.08 N	90.11 W
West Mifflin	152	40.22 N	79.52 W
Westminster, Colo., U.S.	164	39.50 N	105.02 W
Westminster, Md., U.S.	152	39.35 N	77.00 W
Westminster, S.C., U.S.	156	34.40 N	83.06 W
West Monroe	158	32.31 N	92.09 W
Westmont	152	40.19 N	78.57 W
Westmoreland, Kans., U.S.	162	39.24 N	96.25 W
Westmoreland, Tenn., U.S.	158	36.34 N	86.15 W
Westmorland	168	33.02 N	115.37 W
West Nicholson	116	21.06 S	29.25 E
West Nishnabotna ≃	162	40.39 N	95.37 W
Weston, Idaho, U.S.	166	42.02 N	111.59 W
Weston, Mo., U.S.	158	39.25 N	94.54 W
Weston, Oreg., U.S.	166	45.49 N	118.26 W
Weston, W. Va., U.S.	152	39.02 N	80.28 W
Weston-super-Mare	70	51.21 N	2.59 W
West Orange	158	30.05 N	93.46 W
Westover	152	39.38 N	79.58 W
West Palm Beach	156	26.43 N	80.04 W
West Paris	152	44.20 N	70.35 W
West Pembroke	152	44.57 N	67.11 W
West Pensacola	158	30.27 N	87.15 W
Westphalia	162	38.11 N	95.29 W
West Plains	158	36.44 N	91.51 W
West Point, Calif., U.S.	168	38.24 N	120.32 W
West Point, Ga., U.S.	156	32.52 N	85.10 W
West Point, Iowa, U.S.	154	40.43 N	91.27 W
West Point, Ky., U.S.	158	37.59 N	85.57 W
West Point, Miss., U.S.	158	33.36 N	88.39 W
West Point, Nebr., U.S.	162	41.51 N	96.43 W
West Point, N.Y., U.S.	152	41.23 N	73.57 W
West Point, Va., U.S.	156	37.32 N	77.06 W
Westport, Eire	70	53.48 N	9.32 W
Westport, N.Z.	126	41.45 S	171.36 E
Westport, Conn., U.S.	152	41.09 N	73.22 W
West Rutland	152	43.36 N	73.03 W
West Sacramento	168	38.34 N	121.32 W
West Salem, Ill., U.S.	158	38.31 N	88.01 W
West Salem, Ohio, U.S.	152	40.58 N	82.06 W
West Salem, Wis., U.S.	154	43.54 N	91.05 W
West Siberian Plain → Zapadno-Sibirskaja Nizmennost' ≍	82	60.00 N	75.00 E
West Slope	166	45.31 N	122.46 W
West Spanish Peak ∧	164	37.23 N	105.00 W
West Sussex ☐6	70	50.55 N	0.35 W
West Terre Haute	158	39.28 N	87.27 W
West Union, Iowa, U.S.	154	42.57 N	91.49 W
West Union, W. Va., U.S.	152	39.18 N	80.47 W
West University Place	160	29.43 N	95.26 W
West Vancouver	148	49.22 N	123.12 W
West View Park	156	36.33 N	82.35 W
Westville, N.S., Can.	150	45.34 N	62.43 W
Westville, Okla., U.S.	158	35.59 N	94.34 W
West Virginia ☐3	144	38.45 N	80.30 W
West Walker ≃	168	38.53 N	119.10 W
West Warwick	152	41.42 N	71.32 W
Westwego	158	29.55 N	90.09 W
Westwood	168	40.18 N	121.00 W
West Wyalong	120	33.55 S	147.13 E
West Yellowstone	166	44.30 N	111.05 W
Wetar, Pulau I	96	7.48 S	126.18 E
Wetar Strait ⊔	96	8.20 S	126.30 E
Wetaskiwin	148	52.58 N	113.22 W
Wete	110	5.04 S	39.43 E
Wethersfield	152	41.43 N	72.40 W
Wetmore	162	39.38 N	95.49 W
Wetumka	160	35.14 N	96.15 W
Wetumpka	158	32.27 N	86.13 W
Wetzlar	72	50.33 N	8.29 E
Wewahitchka	156	30.07 N	85.12 W
Wewak	124	3.35 S	143.40 E
Wewoka	160	35.09 N	96.30 W
Wexford	70	52.20 N	6.27 W
Wexford ☐6	70	52.20 N	6.40 W
Weyanoke	156	38.48 N	77.09 W
Weyburn	162	49.41 N	103.52 W
Weyer Markt	72	47.52 N	14.41 E
Weyib ≃	108	4.11 N	42.09 E
Weymouth	152	42.13 N	70.58 W
Whakatane	126	37.58 S	177.00 E
Whaleyville	156	36.37 N	76.41 W
Whangarei	126	35.43 S	174.20 E
Wharton, Tex., U.S.	160	29.19 N	96.06 W
Wharton, W. Va., U.S.	156	37.55 N	81.40 W
Wharton Lake ⊜	142	64.00 N	99.55 W
What Cheer	154	41.24 N	92.21 W
Wheatland, Calif., U.S.	168	39.01 N	121.25 W
Wheatland, Iowa, U.S.	154	41.50 N	90.51 W
Wheatland, Wyo., U.S.	164	42.03 N	104.57 W
Wheatland Reservoir ⊜1	162	41.52 N	105.36 W
Wheaton, Ill., U.S.	158	41.52 N	88.06 W
Wheaton, Md., U.S.	152	39.03 N	77.03 W
Wheaton, Minn., U.S.	162	45.48 N	96.30 W
Wheat Ridge	164	39.46 N	105.07 W
Wheeler ≃	142	57.02 N	67.13 W
Wheeler Peak ∧	164	36.34 N	105.25 W
Wheeling	152	40.05 N	80.42 W
Wheelwright	156	37.20 N	82.43 W
Whelan, Mount ∧2	120	23.25 S	138.54 E
Whidbey Islands II	122	34.45 S	135.04 E
Whinham, Mount ∧	122	26.04 S	130.15 E
Whiskey Peak ∧	166	42.18 N	107.35 W
Whitby, Ont., Can.	154	43.52 N	78.56 W
Whitby, Eng., U.K.	70	54.29 N	0.37 W
Whitchurch-Stouffville	154	43.58 N	79.15 W
White	162	44.26 N	96.39 W
White ≃, N.A.	146	63.11 N	139.36 W
White ≃, U.S.	158	33.53 N	91.03 W
White ≃, U.S.	162	43.45 N	99.30 W
White Bay C	150	50.00 N	56.30 W
White Bear Lake	154	45.05 N	93.01 W
White Bluff	158	36.06 N	87.13 W
White Castle	158	30.10 N	91.09 W
White City	162	38.48 N	96.44 W
White Clay Creek ≃	162	43.12 N	102.48 W
White Cliffs, Austl.	120	30.51 S	143.05 E
White Cliffs, Austl.	122	28.26 S	122.57 E
White Cloud	154	43.33 N	85.46 W
Whitecourt	148	54.09 N	115.41 W
Whitefield	152	44.22 N	71.36 W
Whitefish	166	48.25 N	114.20 W
Whitefish Bay	154	43.07 N	87.55 W
Whitefish Bay C	154	46.40 N	84.50 W
Whitefish Lake ⊜	142	62.41 N	106.48 W
White Hall, Ill., U.S.	158	39.26 N	90.24 W
Whitehall, Mich., U.S.	154	43.24 N	86.21 W
Whitehall, Mont., U.S.	166	45.52 N	112.06 W
Whitehall, N.Y., U.S.	152	43.33 N	73.25 W
Whitehaven, Eng., U.K.	70	54.33 N	3.35 W
White Haven, Pa., U.S.	152	41.04 N	75.47 W
Whitehaven, Tenn., U.S.	158	35.01 N	90.01 W
White Hills ⋀	164	37.15 N	109.05 W
Whitehorse	146	60.43 N	135.03 W
White Island I	142	65.50 N	84.50 W
White Lake, S. Dak., U.S.	162	43.44 N	98.43 W
White Lake, Wis., U.S.	154	45.09 N	88.46 W
Whitemark	120	40.07 S	148.01 E
White Mountain	146	64.40 N	162.12 W
White Mountains ⋀, U.S.	168	37.30 N	118.15 W
White Mountains ⋀, Alaska, U.S.	146	65.30 N	147.00 W
White Nile (Al-Baḥr al-Abyaḍ) ≃	112	15.38 N	32.31 E
White Oak	158	32.32 N	94.52 W
White Pass)(	146	59.38 N	135.05 W
White Pigeon	154	41.48 N	85.38 W
White Pine	156	36.07 N	83.17 W
White Plains	152	41.02 N	73.46 W
Whiteriver, Ariz., U.S.	164	33.50 N	109.58 W
White River, S. Dak., U.S.	162	43.34 N	100.45 W
White River Junction	152	43.39 N	72.19 W
White Rock	148	49.02 N	122.49 W
White Rocks ∧	156	36.40 N	83.27 W
Whitesboro	160	33.39 N	96.54 W
Whitesburg	156	37.07 N	82.49 W
White Sea → Beloje More ⊤2	66	65.30 N	38.00 E
White Settlement	160	32.45 N	97.27 W
White Sulphur Springs, Mont., U.S.	166	46.33 N	110.54 W
White Sulphur Springs, W. Va., U.S.	156	37.48 N	80.18 W
Whitesville	156	37.59 N	81.32 W
Whiteville, N.C., U.S.	156	34.20 N	78.42 W
Whiteville, Tenn., U.S.	158	35.20 N	89.11 W
White Volta (Volta Blanche) ≃	114	9.10 N	1.15 W
Whitewater, Kans., U.S.	162	37.58 N	97.09 W
Whitewater, Wis., U.S.	154	42.50 N	88.44 W
Whitewater ≃	158	39.10 N	84.47 W
Whitewater Creek ≃	166	48.30 N	107.11 W
Whitewoman Creek ≃	162	38.25 N	100.54 W
Whitewood	120	21.28 S	143.36 E
Whithorn	70	54.44 N	4.25 W
Whiting	162	39.35 N	95.37 W
Whitley Bay	70	55.03 N	1.25 W
Whitley City	156	36.43 N	84.28 W
Whitman	152	42.05 N	70.56 W
Whitmire	156	34.30 N	81.37 W
Whitmore Village	170c	21.31 N	158.01 W
Whitnel	156	35.53 N	81.31 W
Whitney	160	31.57 N	97.19 W
Whitney, Mount ∧	168	36.35 N	118.18 W
Whitney Point	152	42.20 N	75.58 W
Whitsunday Island I	120	20.17 S	148.59 E
Whittemore, Iowa, U.S.	162	43.04 N	94.25 W
Whittemore, Mich., U.S.	154	44.14 N	83.48 W
Whittier	146	60.46 N	148.41 W
Whittle, Cap ≻	150	50.11 N	60.08 W
Whittlesea	120	37.31 S	145.07 E
Wholdaia Lake ⊜	142	60.43 N	104.10 W
Whyalla	120	33.02 S	137.35 E
Wiarton	154	44.45 N	81.09 W
Wibaux	162	46.59 N	104.11 W
Wichita	162	37.41 N	97.20 W
Wichita Falls	160	33.54 N	98.30 W
Wick	70	58.26 N	3.06 W
Wickenburg	164	33.58 N	112.44 W
Wickepin	122	32.46 S	117.30 E
Wickett	160	31.34 N	102.59 W
Wickham, Cape ≻	120	39.36 S	143.57 E
Wicklow	70	52.59 N	6.03 W
Wicklow ☐6	70	53.00 N	6.30 W
Widgiemooltha	122	31.30 S	121.34 E
Widnes	70	53.22 N	2.44 W
Wiehl	72	50.57 N	7.31 E
Wiek	72	54.37 N	13.17 E
Wieliczka	72	49.59 N	20.04 E
Wieluń	72	51.14 N	18.34 E
Wien (Vienna)	72	48.13 N	16.20 E
Wiener Neustadt	72	47.49 N	16.15 E
Wierden	72	52.22 N	6.35 E
Wiesbaden	72	50.05 N	8.14 E
Wieselburg	72	48.08 N	15.09 E
Wiesloch	72	49.17 N	8.42 E
Wietze	72	52.39 N	9.50 E
Wigan	70	53.33 N	2.38 W
Wiggins	158	30.51 N	89.08 W
Wight, Isle of I	64	50.40 N	1.20 W
Wigtown	70	54.52 N	4.26 W
Wil	74	47.27 N	9.03 E
Wilber	162	40.29 N	96.58 W
Wilberforce Falls ⌊	142	67.07 N	108.47 W
Wilbur	166	47.46 N	118.42 W
Wilburton	160	34.55 N	95.19 W
Wilcannia	120	31.34 S	143.23 E
Wilder	166	43.40 N	116.55 W
Wildhorse Creek ≃	162	44.39 N	106.08 W
Wildon	72	46.53 N	15.31 E
Wildwood	152	38.59 N	74.49 W
Wilhelm, Mount ∧	124	5.45 S	145.05 E
Wilhelmina Gebergte ⋀	138	3.45 N	56.30 W
Wilhelmina Peak → Trikora, Puntjak ∧	124	4.15 S	138.45 E
Wilhelm-Pieck-Stadt Guben	72	51.57 N	14.43 E
Wilhelmshaven	72	53.31 N	8.08 E
Wilkes-Barre	152	41.14 N	75.53 W
Wilkesboro	156	36.09 N	81.09 W
Wilkie	142	52.25 N	108.43 W
Wilkinsburg	152	40.27 N	79.53 W
Willacoochee	156	31.20 N	83.03 W
Willamette ≃	166	45.39 N	122.46 W
Willamina	166	45.05 N	123.29 W
Willard, N. Mex., U.S.	164	34.36 N	106.02 W
Willard, Ohio, U.S.	152	41.03 N	82.44 W
Willard, Utah, U.S.	166	41.25 N	112.02 W
Willcox	164	32.15 N	109.50 W
Willemstad	132	12.06 N	68.56 W
Willeroo	124	15.17 S	131.35 E
William, Mount ∧	120	37.17 S	142.36 E
William Creek	120	28.55 S	136.21 E
Williams, Ariz., U.S.	164	35.15 N	112.11 W
Williams, Calif., U.S.	168	39.09 N	122.09 W
Williams ≃	120	20.04 S	141.08 E
Williamsburg, Iowa, U.S.	154	41.40 N	92.01 W
Williamsburg, Ky., U.S.	156	36.44 N	84.10 W
Williamsburg, Va., U.S.	156	37.16 N	76.43 W
Williams Lake	148	52.08 N	122.09 W
Williams Mountain ∧	158	34.15 N	94.33 W
Williamson, N.Y., U.S.	152	43.13 N	77.11 W
Williamson, W. Va., U.S.	156	37.41 N	82.17 W
Williamsport, Ind., U.S.	158	40.17 N	87.17 W
Williamsport, Pa., U.S.	152	41.14 N	77.00 W
Williamston, Mich., U.S.	154	42.41 N	84.17 W
Williamston, S.C., U.S.	156	34.37 N	82.29 W
Williamstown, Ky., U.S.	152	38.38 N	84.34 W
Williamstown, Mass., U.S.	152	42.43 N	73.12 W
Williamstown, N.J., U.S.	152	39.41 N	74.60 W
Williamstown, Vt., U.S.	152	44.07 N	72.33 W
Williamstown, W. Va., U.S.	152	39.24 N	81.27 W
Williamsville, Ill., U.S.	158	39.57 N	89.33 W
Williamsville, Mo., U.S.	158	36.58 N	90.33 W
Willich	74	51.16 N	6.33 E
Willimantic	152	41.43 N	72.13 W
Willingboro	152	40.03 N	74.53 W
Willis Islets II	124	16.18 S	150.00 E
Williston, Fla., U.S.	156	29.23 N	82.27 W
Williston, N. Dak., U.S.	162	48.09 N	103.37 W
Williston, S.C., U.S.	156	33.24 N	81.25 W
Williston Basin ≍1	162	48.15 N	105.00 W
Williston Lake ⊜1	148	56.00 N	124.00 W
Willits	168	39.25 N	123.21 W
Willmar	162	45.07 N	95.03 W
Willoughby	152	41.38 N	81.25 W
Willoughby, Cape ≻	120	35.51 S	138.07 E
Willowick	152	41.38 N	81.28 W
Willow Lake ⊜	142	62.11 N	119.10 W
Willowlake ≃	142	62.52 N	123.08 W
Willowmore	116	33.17 S	23.29 E
Willowra	122	21.15 S	132.35 E
Willows	168	39.31 N	122.12 W
Willow Springs	158	36.59 N	91.58 W
Willshire	152	40.45 N	84.48 W
Wills Point	160	32.43 N	96.01 W
Willunga	120	35.17 S	138.33 E
Wilmer	160	32.35 N	96.41 W
Wilmette	154	42.04 N	87.43 W
Wilmington, Austl.	120	32.39 S	138.07 E
Wilmington, Del., U.S.	152	39.44 N	75.33 W
Wilmington, Ill., U.S.	154	41.18 N	88.09 W
Wilmington, N.C., U.S.	156	34.13 N	77.55 W
Wilmington, Ohio, U.S.	152	39.27 N	83.50 W
Wilmore	156	37.52 N	84.40 W
Wilna → Vilnius	86	54.41 N	25.19 E
Wilson, Austl.	120	32.00 S	138.22 E
Wilson, Ark., U.S.	158	35.34 N	90.03 W
Wilson, Kans., U.S.	162	38.50 N	98.29 W
Wilson, N.C., U.S.	156	35.44 N	77.55 W
Wilson, N.Y., U.S.	152	43.19 N	78.50 W
Wilson, Okla., U.S.	160	34.10 N	97.26 W
Wilson, Tex., U.S.	160	33.19 N	101.44 W
Wilson ≃, Austl.	120	27.38 S	141.24 E
Wilson ≃, Austl.	124	16.47 S	128.17 E
Wilson, Cape ≻	142	66.59 N	81.28 W
Wilson, Mount ∧, Calif., U.S.	168	34.13 N	118.04 W
Wilson, Mount ∧, Nev., U.S.	168	38.15 N	114.23 W
Wilson Range ⋀	122	28.50 S	124.25 E
Wilsons Promontory ≻	120	38.55 S	146.20 E
Wilton, Eng., U.K.	70	51.05 N	1.52 W
Wilton, Maine, U.S.	152	44.35 N	70.14 W
Wilton, N.H., U.S.	152	42.51 N	71.44 W
Wilton, N. Dak., U.S.	162	47.10 N	100.47 W
Wilton Junction	158	41.35 N	91.01 W
Wilton Manors	156	26.10 N	80.07 W
Wiltshire ☐6	70	51.15 N	1.50 W
Wiluna	122	26.36 S	120.13 E
Wimberley	160	30.00 N	98.06 W
Wimbledon	162	47.10 N	98.28 W
Winamac	158	41.03 N	86.36 W
Winchendon	152	42.41 N	72.03 W
Winchester, Eng., U.K.	70	51.04 N	1.19 W
Winchester, Ill., U.S.	158	39.38 N	90.27 W
Winchester, Ind., U.S.	158	40.10 N	84.59 W
Winchester, Ky., U.S.	156	37.59 N	84.11 W
Winchester, N.H., U.S.	152	42.46 N	72.23 W
Winchester, Tenn., U.S.	158	35.10 N	86.01 W
Winchester, Va., U.S.	152	39.11 N	78.10 W
Wind ≃	146	65.49 N	135.18 W
Windber	152	40.14 N	78.50 W
Winder	156	32.59 N	83.43 W
Windermere	70	54.23 N	2.54 W
Windhoek	116	22.34 S	17.06 E
Windischgarsten	72	47.44 N	14.20 E
Wind Lake	154	42.50 N	88.09 W
Windom	162	43.52 N	95.07 W
Windorah	120	25.26 S	142.39 E
Windsor, Austl.	120	33.37 S	150.49 E
Windsor, N.S., Can.	150	44.59 N	64.08 W
Windsor, Ont., Can.	154	42.18 N	83.01 W
Windsor, Qué., Can.	152	45.34 N	72.00 W
Windsor, Eng., U.K.	70	51.29 N	0.38 W
Windsor, Colo., U.S.	164	40.29 N	104.54 W
Windsor, Conn., U.S.	152	41.51 N	72.39 W
Windsor, Mo., U.S.	158	38.32 N	93.31 W
Windsor, N.C., U.S.	156	36.00 N	76.57 W
Windsor, Vt., U.S.	152	43.29 N	72.23 W
Windsor Heights	154	41.36 N	93.42 W
Windsor Locks	152	41.56 N	72.38 W
Windward Islands II	132	13.00 N	61.00 W
Windward Passage ⊔	132	20.00 N	73.50 W
Winfield, Ala., U.S.	158	33.56 N	87.49 W
Winfield, Iowa, U.S.	154	41.07 N	91.26 W
Winfield, Kans., U.S.	162	37.15 N	96.59 W
Winfield, Mo., U.S.	158	39.00 N	90.44 W
Winfield, W. Va., U.S.	152	38.32 N	81.53 W
Wingate	156	34.59 N	80.27 W
Wingate Mountains ⋀	124	14.29 S	130.42 E
Wingham, Austl.	120	31.52 S	152.22 E
Wingham, Ont., Can.	154	43.53 N	81.19 W
Winisk	142	55.15 N	85.12 W
Winisk ≃	142	55.17 N	85.05 W
Winisk Lake ⊜	142	52.55 N	87.22 W
Wink	160	31.45 N	103.09 W
Winkelman	164	32.59 N	110.46 W
Winkler	162	49.11 N	97.56 W
Winklern	72	46.52 N	12.52 E
Winneba	114	5.25 N	0.36 W
Winnebago	154	43.46 N	94.10 W
Winnebago, Lake ⊜	154	44.00 N	88.25 W
Winneconne	154	44.07 N	88.43 W
Winnemucca	168	40.58 N	117.44 W
Winner	162	43.22 N	99.51 W
Winnetka	154	42.07 N	87.44 W
Winnfield	158	31.55 N	92.38 W
Winnie	158	29.49 N	94.23 W
Winning	122	23.09 S	114.32 E
Winnipeg	162	49.53 N	97.09 W
Winnipeg ≃	142	50.38 N	96.19 W
Winnipeg, Lake ⊜	142	52.00 N	97.00 W
Winnipegosis, Lake ⊜	142	52.30 N	100.00 W
Winnsboro, La., U.S.	158	32.10 N	91.43 W
Winnsboro, S.C., U.S.	156	34.22 N	81.05 W
Winnsboro, Tex., U.S.	160	32.58 N	95.17 W
Winnsboro Mills	156	34.22 N	81.06 W
Winona, Kans., U.S.	162	39.04 N	101.15 W
Winona, Minn., U.S.	154	44.03 N	91.39 W
Winona, Miss., U.S.	158	33.29 N	89.44 W
Winona Lake	158	41.14 N	85.49 W
Winooski	152	44.29 N	73.11 W
Winschoten	72	53.08 N	7.02 E
Winsen	72	53.22 N	10.12 E
Winslow, Ariz., U.S.	164	35.01 N	110.42 W
Winslow, Maine, U.S.	152	44.32 N	69.38 W
Winsted, Conn., U.S.	152	41.55 N	73.04 W
Winsted, Minn., U.S.	154	44.58 N	94.03 W
Winston, Fla., U.S.	156	28.02 N	82.01 W
Winston, Oreg., U.S.	166	45.07 N	123.25 W

Symbols in the index entries are identified on page 203.

Name	Page	Lat ° ′	Long ° ′
Winston-Salem	156	36.06 N	80.15 W
Winter Garden	156	28.34 N	81.35 W
Winter Harbor	152	44.24 N	68.05 W
Winterhaven, Calif., U.S.	168	32.44 N	114.38 W
Winter Haven, Fla., U.S.	156	28.01 N	81.44 W
Winter Island I	142	66.14 N	83.04 W
Winter Park	156	28.36 N	81.20 W
Winterport	152	44.38 N	68.51 W
Winters, Calif., U.S.	168	38.31 N	121.58 W
Winters, Tex., U.S.	160	31.57 N	99.58 W
Winterset	154	41.20 N	94.01 W
Winterswijk	72	51.58 N	6.44 E
Winterthur	74	47.30 N	8.43 E
Winterville	156	35.32 N	77.24 W
Winthrop, Iowa, U.S.	154	42.28 N	91.44 W
Winthrop, Maine, U.S.	152	44.18 N	69.59 W
Winthrop, Minn., U.S.	154	44.32 N	94.22 W
Winthrop Harbor	154	42.29 N	87.49 W
Wintinna	122	27.44 S	134.07 E
Winton, Austl.	120	22.23 S	143.02 E
Winton, N.Z.	126	46.09 S	168.19 E
Wipperfürth	72	51.07 N	7.23 E
Wirral ≻[1]	70	53.20 N	3.03 W
Wirraminna	120	31.12 S	136.15 E
Wisbech	70	52.40 N	0.10 E
Wiscasset	152	44.00 N	69.40 W
Wisconsin □[3]	144	44.45 N	89.30 W
Wisconsin ≃	154	43.00 N	91.15 W
Wisconsin Dells	154	43.38 N	89.46 W
Wisconsin Rapids	154	44.23 N	89.49 W
Wise	156	36.59 N	82.34 W
Wishek	162	46.16 N	99.33 W
Wisła ≃	72	54.22 N	18.55 E
Wismar, D.D.R.	72	53.53 N	11.28 E
Wismar, Guy.	138	5.59 N	58.18 W
Wisner, La., U.S.	158	31.59 N	91.39 W
Wisner, Nebr., U.S.	162	41.59 N	96.55 W
Wissembourg	74	49.02 N	7.57 E
Wisznice	72	51.48 N	23.12 E
Witbank	116	25.56 S	29.07 E
Withlacoochee ≃	156	30.24 N	83.10 W
Witney	70	51.48 N	1.29 W
Wittabrinna Creek ≃	120	29.20 S	142.43 E
Witten	72	51.26 N	7.20 E
Wittenberg	72	51.52 N	12.39 E
Wittenberge	72	53.00 N	11.44 E
Wittenburg	72	53.31 N	11.04 E
Wittenoom	122	22.17 S	118.19 E
Wittingen	72	52.43 N	10.44 E
Wittlich	72	49.59 N	6.53 E
Wittmund	72	53.34 N	7.47 E
Wittstock	72	53.10 N	12.29 E
Witwatersrand ⊸[1]	116	26.00 S	27.00 E
Witzenhausen	72	51.20 N	9.51 E
Wiżajny	72	54.23 N	22.51 E
Włocławek	72	52.39 N	19.02 E
Włoszczowa	72	50.52 N	19.59 E
Woburn	152	42.31 N	71.12 W
Wodonga	120	36.07 S	146.54 E
Wokam, Pulau I	124	5.37 S	134.30 E
Woking	70	51.20 N	0.34 W
Wokingham Creek ≃	120	22.19 S	142.30 E
Wolcott	152	43.13 N	76.49 W
Woleai I[1]	92	7.21 N	143.52 E
Wolf ≃	158	35.09 N	90.04 W
Wolfach	72	48.17 N	8.13 E
Wolf Creek	166	42.42 N	123.24 W
Wolf Creek ≃	160	36.35 N	99.30 W
Wolfeboro	152	43.35 N	71.12 W
Wolfen	72	51.40 N	12.16 E
Wolfenbüttel	72	52.10 N	10.32 E
Wolfforth	160	33.30 N	102.01 W
Wolfhagen	72	51.19 N	9.10 E
Wolf Lake	154	43.14 N	86.10 W
Wolf Point	166	48.05 N	105.39 W
Wolfratshausen	72	47.54 N	11.25 E
Wolfsberg	72	46.51 N	14.51 E
Wolfsburg	72	52.25 N	10.47 E
Wolfville	150	45.05 N	64.22 W
Wolgast	72	54.03 N	13.46 E
Wollaston, Cape ≻	142	71.04 N	118.07 W
Wollaston, Islas II	136	55.45 S	67.40 W
Wollaston Lake ⊜	142	58.15 N	103.20 W
Wollaston Peninsula ≻[1]	142	70.00 N	115.00 W
Wollogorang	120	17.13 S	137.57 E
Wollongong	120	34.25 S	150.54 E
Wołomin	72	52.21 N	21.14 E
Wolseley	142	50.25 N	103.19 W
Wolsztyn	72	52.08 N	16.06 E
Wolverhampton	70	52.36 N	2.08 W
Wolverine	154	45.16 N	84.36 W
Wonarah	122	19.55 S	136.20 E
Wondai	120	26.19 S	151.52 E
Wŏnju	88	37.22 N	127.58 E
Wonotobo Fall ⌞	138	4.22 N	57.55 W
Wŏnsan	88	39.09 N	127.25 E
Wonthaggi	120	38.36 S	145.35 E
Woodbine, Iowa, U.S.	162	41.44 N	95.43 W
Woodbine, N.J., U.S.	152	39.14 N	74.49 W
Woodbridge	70	52.06 N	1.19 E
Woodburn	166	45.09 N	122.51 W
Woodbury, Conn., U.S.	152	41.33 N	73.13 W
Woodbury, Ga., U.S.	156	32.59 N	84.35 W
Woodbury, N.J., U.S.	152	39.50 N	75.10 W
Wooded Bluff ⩋[4]	120	29.22 S	153.22 E
Woodenbong	120	28.23 S	152.37 E
Woodlake	168	36.25 N	119.06 W
Woodland, Calif., U.S.	168	38.41 N	121.46 W
Woodland, Maine, U.S.	152	45.09 N	67.24 W
Woodland Park	164	39.00 N	105.03 W
Woodlark Island I	124	9.05 S	152.50 E
Woodridge, Mount ∧	120	23.13 S	137.39 E
Wood River	158	38.52 N	90.05 W
Woodroffe ≃	120	21.28 S	137.58 E
Woodroffe, Mount ∧	122	26.20 S	131.45 E
Woodruff, Ariz., U.S.	164	34.47 N	110.03 W
Woodruff, S.C., U.S.	156	34.45 N	82.02 W
Woodruff, Wis., U.S.	154	45.54 N	89.42 W
Woods, Lake of the ⊜	142	49.15 N	94.45 W
Woodsboro	160	28.14 N	97.20 W
Woodsfield	152	39.46 N	81.07 W
Woodside	120	38.31 S	146.52 E
Woodstock, N.B., Can.	150	46.09 N	67.34 W
Woodstock, Ont., Can.	154	43.08 N	80.45 W
Woodstock, Eng., U.K.	70	51.52 N	1.21 W
Woodstock, Ill., U.S.	154	42.19 N	88.27 W
Woodstock, Vt., U.S.	152	43.37 N	72.31 W
Woodstock, Va., U.S.	152	38.53 N	78.31 W
Woodsville	152	44.09 N	72.02 W
Woodville, N.Z.	126	40.20 S	175.52 E
Woodville, Miss., U.S.	158	31.01 N	91.18 W
Woodville, Tex., U.S.	158	30.46 N	94.25 W
Woodward, Iowa, U.S.	154	41.51 N	93.55 W
Woodward, Okla., U.S.	160	36.26 N	99.24 W
Woody Island	146	57.47 N	152.22 W
Woolgoolga	120	30.07 S	153.12 E
Woomera	120	31.31 S	137.10 E
Woonsocket	152	42.00 N	71.31 W
Woorabinda	120	24.08 S	149.28 E
Wooramel	122	25.44 S	114.17 E
Wooramel ≃	122	25.47 S	114.10 E
Wooster	152	40.48 N	81.56 W
Worb	74	46.56 N	7.34 E
Worcester, S. Afr.	116	33.39 S	19.27 E
Worcester, Eng., U.K.	70	52.11 N	2.13 W
Worcester, Mass., U.S.	152	42.16 N	71.48 W
Worden	158	38.56 N	89.50 W
Wörgl	72	47.29 N	12.04 E
Workington	70	54.39 N	3.35 W
Worksop	70	53.18 N	1.07 W
Worland	166	44.01 N	107.57 W
Worms	72	49.38 N	8.22 E
Wortham	160	31.47 N	96.28 W
Worthing	70	50.48 N	0.23 W
Worthington, Ind., U.S.	158	39.07 N	86.59 W
Worthington, Minn., U.S.	162	43.37 N	95.36 W
Worthington, Ohio, U.S.	152	40.05 N	83.01 W
Worthington Peak ∧	168	37.55 N	115.37 W
Wowan	120	23.55 S	150.12 E
Wowoni, Pulau I	96	4.08 S	123.06 E
Woy Woy	120	33.30 S	151.20 E
Wrangel Island → Vrangel'a, Ostrov I	84	71.00 N	179.30 W
Wrangell	146	56.28 N	132.23 W
Wrangell, Mount ∧	146	62.00 N	144.06 W
Wrangell Island I	146	56.15 N	132.10 W
Wrangell Mountains ⛰	146	62.00 N	143.00 W
Wrath, Cape ≻	70	58.37 N	5.01 W
Wray	162	40.05 N	102.13 W
Wreck Reefs ⊹[2]	120	22.13 S	155.17 E
Wrens	156	33.12 N	82.23 W
Wrexham	70	53.03 N	3.00 W
Wright, Mount ∧, Austl.	120	31.12 S	142.26 E
Wright, Mount ∧, Mont., U.S.	166	47.58 N	112.49 W
Wright City	158	38.50 N	91.01 W
Wrightsville	156	32.44 N	82.43 W
Wrightwood	168	34.21 N	117.38 W
Wrigley	146	63.16 N	123.37 W
Wrocław (Breslau)	72	51.06 N	17.00 E
Września	72	52.20 N	17.34 E
Wuchin → Changzhou	88	31.47 N	119.57 E
Wuchuan	94	21.25 N	110.40 E
Wudangshan ⛰	88	32.30 N	110.50 E
Wudinna	120	33.03 S	135.28 E
Wudu	88	33.21 N	105.00 E
Wuershunhe ≃	88	49.00 N	117.41 E
Wugang	88	26.40 N	110.31 E
Wugongshan ⛰	88	27.21 N	113.50 E
Wuhan	88	30.36 N	114.17 E
Wuhsing → Huzhou	88	30.52 N	120.06 E
Wuhu	88	31.21 N	118.22 E
Wulanhaote	88	46.05 N	122.05 E
Wuliangshan ⛰	94	24.30 N	100.45 E
Wuliaru, Pulau I	124	7.27 S	131.04 E
Wulumuqi (Urumchi)	88	43.48 N	87.35 E
Wulunguhe ≃	88	46.59 N	87.27 E
Wunnummin Lake ⊜	142	52.55 N	89.10 W
Wunstorf	72	52.25 N	9.26 E
Wuppertal	72	51.16 N	7.11 E
Würzburg	72	49.48 N	9.56 E
Wurzen	72	51.22 N	12.44 E
Wushan	88	31.05 N	109.48 E
Wushenqi	88	38.58 N	109.01 E
Wusu	88	44.27 N	84.37 E
Wusulijiang (Ussuri) ≃	84	48.27 N	135.04 E
Wutai	88	38.44 N	113.17 E
Wutaishan ∧	88	39.04 N	113.35 E
Wutongqiao	88	29.26 N	103.51 E
Wuvulu I	124	1.45 S	142.50 E
Wuxi	88	31.35 N	120.18 E
Wuyishan ⛰	88	27.52 N	117.40 E
Wuyuan	88	41.06 N	108.29 E
Wuzhishan ∧	94	18.57 N	109.43 E
Wuzhong	88	37.57 N	106.10 E
Wuzhou (Wuchow)	94	23.30 N	111.27 E
Wyaaba ≃	124	16.27 S	141.35 E
Wyaconda	158	40.24 N	91.55 W
Wyalkatchem	122	31.10 S	117.22 E
Wyalusing	152	41.40 N	76.16 W
Wyandotte	154	42.12 N	83.10 W
Wyandra	120	27.15 S	145.59 E
Wyangala Reservoir ⊜[1]	120	33.58 S	148.55 E
Wycheproof	120	36.05 S	143.14 E
Wyeville	154	44.01 N	90.23 W
Wyk	72	54.42 N	8.34 E
Wylie	160	33.01 N	96.32 W
Wymondham	70	52.34 N	1.07 E
Wymore	162	40.07 N	96.40 W
Wyndham	124	15.28 S	128.06 E
Wynne	158	35.14 N	90.47 W
Wynnewood	160	34.39 N	97.10 W
Wynniatt Bay C	142	72.55 N	110.30 W
Wynyard, Austl.	120	40.59 S	145.41 E
Wynyard, Sask., Can.	142	51.47 N	104.10 W
Wyodak	162	44.18 N	105.24 W
Wyoming, Ill., U.S.	154	41.04 N	89.47 W
Wyoming, Iowa, U.S.	154	42.04 N	91.00 W
Wyoming, Mich., U.S.	154	42.54 N	85.42 W
Wyoming □[3]	144	43.00 N	107.30 W
Wyoming Peak ∧	166	42.36 N	110.37 W
Wyoming Ranges ⛰	164	42.00 N	111.00 W
Wyong	120	33.17 S	151.25 E
Wysokie Mazowieckie	72	52.56 N	22.32 E
Wyszków	72	52.36 N	21.28 E
Wytheville	156	36.57 N	81.05 W

X

Name	Page	Lat ° ′	Long ° ′
Xánthi	80	41.08 N	24.53 E
Xapuri	134	10.39 S	68.31 W
Xenia, Ill., U.S.	158	38.38 N	88.38 W
Xenia, Ohio, U.S.	152	39.41 N	83.56 W
Xertigny	74	48.03 N	6.24 E
Xiaguan	88	33.37 N	111.46 E
Xiahe	88	35.06 N	102.40 E
Xiamen (Amoy)	88	24.28 N	118.07 E
Xi'an (Sian)	88	34.15 N	108.52 E
Xiangfan	88	32.03 N	112.01 E
Xiangjiang ≃	88	29.00 N	112.56 E
Xiangkhoang	94	19.20 N	103.22 E
Xiangride	88	36.02 N	98.08 E
Xiangtan	88	27.51 N	112.54 E
Xianyang	88	34.23 N	108.40 E
Xianyou	88	25.23 N	118.40 E
Xiaogan	88	30.55 N	113.54 E
Xiaoxing'anlingshanmai ⛰	88	48.45 N	127.00 E
Xiapu	88	26.52 N	120.01 E
Xichang	88	27.58 N	102.13 E
Xihe ≃	88	41.44 N	121.30 E
Xijiang ≃	94	22.25 N	113.23 E
Xilinhaote	88	43.58 N	116.04 E
Xinavane	116	25.02 S	32.47 E
Xincheng	88	39.15 N	115.59 E
Xingan	88	25.37 N	110.31 E
Xinghe	88	40.48 N	113.58 E
Xinghua	88	32.57 N	119.50 E
Xingkathu (Ozero Chanka) ⊜	84	45.00 N	132.24 E
Xingtai	88	37.04 N	114.29 E
Xingu ≃	134	1.30 S	51.53 W
Xingyi	94	25.06 N	104.58 E
Xinhailian	88	34.39 N	119.16 E
Xinhua	88	27.37 N	111.02 E
Xining	88	36.38 N	101.55 E
Xinjiang	88	35.40 N	111.11 E
Xinjiang Weiwuer Zizhiqu (Sinkiang) □[4]	88	40.00 N	85.00 E
Xinxiang	88	35.20 N	113.51 E
Xinyang	88	32.19 N	114.01 E
Xique-Xique	134	10.50 S	42.44 W
Xizang Zizhiqu □[4]	88	32.00 N	88.00 E
Xuancheng	88	30.58 N	118.45 E
Xuanhua	88	40.37 N	115.03 E
Xuchang	88	34.03 N	113.49 E
Xuefengshan ⛰	88	27.44 N	111.00 E
Xuwen	94	20.21 N	110.11 E
Xuyong	88	28.10 N	105.24 E
Xuzhou	88	34.16 N	117.11 E

Y

Name	Page	Lat ° ′	Long ° ′
Yaan	88	30.03 N	103.02 E
Yablonovy Range → Jablonovyj Chrebet ⛰	84	53.30 N	115.00 E
Yacuiba	140	22.02 S	63.45 W
Yadkinville	156	36.08 N	80.39 W
Yadong	88	27.29 N	88.55 E
Yafran	108	32.04 N	12.31 E
Yagoua	106	10.20 N	15.14 E
Yaguajay	132	22.19 N	79.14 W
Yaguarón (Jaguarão) ≃	140	32.39 S	53.12 W
Yaheladazeshan ∧	102	35.12 N	95.20 E
Yahualica	130	21.08 N	102.51 W
Yaizu	90	34.52 N	138.20 E
Yakima	166	46.36 N	120.31 W
Yakobi Island I	146	58.00 N	136.30 W
Yakoma	108	4.05 N	22.27 E
Yaku-shima I	91b	30.20 N	130.30 E
Yakutat	146	59.33 N	139.44 W
Yakutat Bay C	146	59.45 N	140.45 W
Yakutsk → Jakutsk	84	62.13 N	129.49 E
Yale	154	43.08 N	82.48 W
Yalgoo	122	28.20 S	116.41 E
Yalinga	108	6.31 N	23.15 E
Yalleroi	120	24.04 S	145.45 E
Yalongjiang ≃	88	30.01 N	101.07 E
Yalta → Jalta	64	44.30 N	34.10 E
Yalujiang (Amnok-kang) ≃	88	39.55 N	124.22 E
Yamagata	90	38.15 N	140.15 E
Yamaguchi	90	34.10 N	131.29 E
Yamba	120	29.26 S	153.22 E
Yambio	108	4.34 N	28.23 E
Y'Ami Island I	92	21.07 N	121.57 E
Yampa	164	40.09 N	106.55 W
Yampa Plateau ⛰[1]	164	40.25 N	109.00 W
Yampi Sound	118	15.15 S	123.30 E
Yamuna ≃	102	25.25 N	81.50 E
Yanac	120	36.08 S	141.26 E
Yanam	100	16.40 N	82.10 E
Yan'an	88	36.41 N	109.19 E
Yanbu'	104	24.05 N	38.03 E
Yanceyville	156	36.24 N	79.20 W
Yanchang	88	36.35 N	110.15 E
Yancheng	88	33.24 N	120.09 E
Yanchi	88	37.52 N	107.22 E
Yanco	120	34.36 S	146.25 E
Yandal	122	27.33 S	121.07 E
Yangjiang	88	21.51 N	111.56 E
Yangquan	88	37.52 N	113.36 E
Yangtze → Changjiang ≃	88	31.48 N	121.10 E
Yangzhou	88	32.24 N	119.26 E
Yangzhuoyonghu ⊜	102	28.58 N	90.44 E
Yanji	88	42.57 N	129.32 E
Yankton	162	42.53 N	97.23 W
Yanna	120	26.56 S	146.03 E
Yanqi	88	42.00 N	86.15 E
Yantabulla	120	29.21 S	145.00 E
Yantai (Chefoo)	88	37.33 N	121.20 E
Yanzhou	88	35.33 N	116.50 E
Yaoundé	106	3.52 N	11.31 E
Yap I	92	9.31 N	138.06 E
Yappar ≃	120	18.22 S	141.16 E
Yaqui ≃	130	27.37 N	110.39 W
Yaracuy □[3]	138	10.20 N	69.10 W
Yaraka	120	24.53 S	144.04 E
Yardea	120	32.23 S	135.32 E
Yarí ≃	138	0.23 S	72.16 W
Yarīm	100	14.29 N	44.21 E
Yaritagua	138	10.05 N	69.08 W
Yarkand → Suoche	102	38.25 N	77.16 E
Yarmouth, N.S., Can.	150	43.50 N	66.07 W
Yarmouth, Maine, U.S.	152	43.48 N	70.12 W
Yarra ≃	120	37.51 S	144.54 E
Yarram	120	38.33 S	146.41 E
Yarraman	120	26.50 S	151.59 E
Yarrawonga	120	36.01 S	146.00 E
Yarumal	138	6.58 N	75.24 W
Yass	120	34.50 S	148.55 E
Yata ≃	134	10.29 S	65.26 W
Yatesboro	152	40.48 N	79.20 W
Yates Center	162	37.53 N	95.44 W
Yates City	154	40.47 N	90.01 W
Yathkyed Lake ⊜	142	62.41 N	98.00 W
Yatsushiro	90	32.30 N	130.36 E
Yatta Plateau ⛰[1]	110	2.00 S	38.00 E
Yauco	132	18.02 N	66.51 W
Yavarí (Javari) ≃	134	4.21 S	70.02 W
Yaví, Cerro ∧	138	5.32 N	65.59 W
Yaxian	94	18.20 N	109.30 E
Yazd	104	31.53 N	54.25 E
Yazoo ≃	158	32.22 N	91.00 W
Yazoo City	158	32.51 N	90.28 W
Ybbs an der Donau	72	48.11 N	15.05 E
Ydstebøhavn	68	59.08 N	5.15 E
Ye	94	15.15 N	97.51 E
Yecheng	102	37.54 N	77.25 E
Yecla	76	38.37 N	1.07 W
Yeeda River	122	17.36 S	123.39 E
Yeelanna	120	34.09 S	135.45 E
Yeelirrie	122	27.17 S	120.06 E
Yeerqianghe (Yarkand) ≃	102	40.28 N	80.52 E
Yei ≃	112	6.15 N	30.13 E
Yelarbon	120	28.34 S	150.45 E
Yélimané	114	15.08 N	10.34 W
Yellow ≃, U.S.	158	30.33 N	87.00 W
Yellow → Huanghe ≃, Zhg.	88	37.32 N	118.19 E
Yellow Creek ≃	158	33.34 N	88.20 W
Yellowdine	122	31.18 S	119.39 E
Yellowhead Pass)(	148	52.53 N	118.28 W
Yellowknife	142	62.27 N	114.21 W
Yellowknife ≃	142	62.31 N	114.19 W
Yellow Sea ⊤[2]	88	36.00 N	123.00 E
Yellowstone ≃	144	47.58 N	103.59 W
Yellowstone, Clarks Fork ≃	166	45.39 N	108.43 W
Yellowstone Falls ⌞	166	44.43 N	110.30 W
Yellowstone Lake ⊜	166	44.25 N	110.22 W
Yellowstone National Park	166	44.58 N	110.42 W
Yellowtail Reservoir ⊜[1]	166	45.06 N	108.08 W
Yellville	158	36.14 N	92.41 W
Yelma	122	26.30 S	121.40 E
Yelvertoft	120	20.13 S	138.53 E
Yemassee	156	32.41 N	80.51 W
Yemen □[1]	100	15.00 N	44.00 E
Yemen, People's Democratic Republic of □[1]	100	15.00 N	48.00 E
Yenangyaung	94	20.28 N	94.52 E
Yen-bai	94	21.42 N	104.52 E
Yenda	120	34.15 S	146.11 E
Yendi	114	9.26 N	0.01 W
Yeoval	120	32.45 S	148.40 E
Yeovil	70	50.57 N	2.39 W
Yeppoon	120	23.08 S	150.45 E
Yerevan → Jerevan	104	40.11 N	44.30 E
Yerington	168	38.59 N	119.10 W
Yermo	168	34.54 N	116.50 W
Yerupajá, Nevado ∧	134	10.16 S	76.54 W
Yerushalayim (Jerusalem)	104	31.46 N	35.14 E
Yesa, Embalse de ⊜[1]	76	42.36 N	1.09 W
Yeso	160	34.26 N	104.37 W
Yeste	76	38.22 N	2.18 W
Yetman	120	28.54 S	150.46 E
Ye-u	92	22.46 N	95.26 E
Yeu, Île d' I	74	46.42 N	2.20 W
Yian	88	47.55 N	125.20 E
Yiannitsá	80	40.48 N	22.25 E
Yibin	88	28.47 N	104.38 E
Yichang	88	30.42 N	111.11 E
Yichun, Zhg.	88	47.42 N	128.55 E
Yichun, Zhg.	88	27.50 N	114.23 E
Yilan	88	46.19 N	129.34 E
Yiliang	94	24.58 N	103.07 E
Yinchuan	88	38.30 N	106.18 E
Yindarlgooda, Lake ⊜	122	30.45 S	121.55 E
Yinghe ≃	88	32.30 N	116.32 E
Yingjisha	88	38.57 N	76.03 E
Yingkou	88	40.40 N	122.14 E
Yingtan	88	28.14 N	117.00 E
Yining (Kuldja)	88	43.55 N	81.14 E
Yinkanie	120	34.20 S	140.19 E
Yinnietharra	122	24.39 S	116.11 E
Yirga Alem	108	6.52 N	38.22 E
Yirrkala Mission	124	12.14 S	136.56 E
Yishan	94	24.40 N	108.35 E
Yishui	88	35.50 N	118.41 E
Yitulihe	88	50.38 N	121.57 E
Yiyang	88	28.36 N	112.20 E
Yläne	68	60.53 N	22.55 E
Ylistaro	68	62.57 N	22.31 E
Ylöjärvi	68	61.33 N	23.36 E
Ynykčanskij	84	60.15 N	137.43 E
Yoakum	160	29.17 N	97.09 W
Yokkaichi	90	34.58 N	136.37 E
Yokohama	90	35.27 N	139.39 E
Yokosuka	90	35.18 N	139.40 E
Yola	106	9.12 N	12.29 E
Yom ≃	94	16.40 N	100.14 E
Yonago	90	35.26 N	133.20 E
Yoncalla	166	43.36 N	123.17 W
Yonezawa	90	37.55 N	140.07 E
Yongan	88	25.58 N	117.22 E
Yongdeng	88	36.48 N	103.14 E
Yongding	88	24.46 N	116.43 E
Yongdinghe ≃	88	39.39 N	116.13 E
Yongdingzhen	88	26.08 N	101.40 E
Yongfeng	88	27.19 N	115.24 E
Yongshan	88	28.15 N	103.24 E
Yonkers	152	41.00 N	73.52 W
Yonne □[5]	74	47.55 N	3.45 E
York, Austl.	122	31.53 S	116.46 E
York, Eng., U.K.	70	53.58 N	1.05 W
York, Ala., U.S.	158	32.29 N	88.18 W
York, Nebr., U.S.	162	40.52 N	97.36 W
York, N. Dak., U.S.	162	48.19 N	99.34 W
York, Pa., U.S.	152	39.58 N	76.44 W
York, S.C., U.S.	156	35.00 N	81.14 W
York, Cape ≻	124	10.42 S	142.31 E
Yorke Peninsula ≻[1]	120	35.00 S	137.30 E
York Factory	142	57.00 N	92.18 W
York Sound ⩌	118	14.50 S	125.05 E
Yorkton	142	51.13 N	102.28 W
Yorktown, Tex., U.S.	160	28.59 N	97.30 W
Yorktown, Va., U.S.	156	37.14 N	76.30 W
Yorkville, Ill., U.S.	154	41.38 N	88.27 W
Yorkville, N.Y., U.S.	152	43.07 N	75.16 W
Yoro	132	15.09 N	87.07 W
Yoron-jima I	91b	27.02 N	128.26 E
Yosemite Falls ⌞	168	37.45 N	119.37 W
Yosemite National Park	168	37.45 N	119.35 W
Yŏsu	88	34.46 N	127.44 E
Youanmi	122	28.37 S	118.49 E
Youghal	70	51.51 N	7.50 W
Youjiang ≃	94	22.50 N	108.06 E
Young	120	34.19 S	148.18 E
Younghusband Peninsula ≻[1]	120	36.00 S	139.30 E
Youngstown, N.Y., U.S.	152	43.15 N	79.03 W
Youngstown, Ohio, U.S.	152	41.06 N	80.39 W
Youngsville, N. Mex., U.S.	164	36.11 N	106.34 W
Youngsville, Pa., U.S.	152	41.51 N	79.19 W
Yountville	168	38.24 N	122.22 W
Youssoufia	106	32.16 N	8.33 W
Youyang	88	28.58 N	108.41 E
Yoweragabbie	122	28.13 S	117.39 E
Ypres → Ieper	72	50.51 N	2.53 E
Ypsilanti	154	42.15 N	83.36 W
Yreka	166	41.44 N	122.38 W
Yssingeaux	74	45.08 N	4.07 E
Ystad	68	55.25 N	13.49 E
Ystwyth ≃	70	52.24 N	4.05 W
Ytre Arna	68	60.26 N	5.30 E
Yuanling	88	28.20 N	110.16 E
Yuanmou	94	25.38 N	101.54 E
Yuba City	168	39.08 N	121.37 W
Yūbari	90a	43.04 N	141.59 E
Yucaipa	168	34.02 N	117.02 W
Yucatan Channel ⩌	132	21.45 N	85.45 W
Yucatan Peninsula ≻[1]	130	19.30 N	89.00 W
Yucca Lake ⊜	168	36.59 N	116.01 W
Yuci	88	37.45 N	112.41 E
Yueyang	88	29.23 N	113.06 E
Yugoslavia □[1]	64	44.00 N	19.00 E
Yujiang ≃	94	23.24 N	110.16 E
Yukon □[4]	142	64.00 N	135.00 W
Yukon ≃	146	62.33 N	163.59 W
Yulin, Zhg.	88	38.20 N	109.29 E
Yulin, Zhg.	94	22.36 N	110.07 E
Yuma, Ariz., U.S.	164	32.43 N	114.37 W
Yuma, Colo., U.S.	162	40.08 N	102.43 W
Yumbo	138	3.35 N	76.28 W
Yumen	88	39.56 N	97.51 E
Yuncheng	88	35.00 N	110.59 E
Yunhe (Grand Canal) ⌅	88	32.12 N	119.31 E
Yunnan □[4]	88	24.00 N	101.00 E
Yunta	120	32.35 S	139.33 E
Yunxian	88	32.49 N	110.49 E
Yupanyang C	88	30.30 N	121.46 E
Yurimaguas	134	5.54 S	76.05 W
Yuriria	130	20.12 N	101.09 W
Yushu	88	33.28 N	96.18 E
Yutian	102	36.51 N	81.40 E
Yuty	140	26.32 S	56.18 W
Yuxian	88	34.10 N	113.28 E
Yvelines □[5]	74	48.50 N	1.50 E
Yverdon	74	46.47 N	6.39 E
Yvetot	74	49.37 N	0.46 E

Z

Name	Page	Lat ° ′	Long ° ′
Zaandam	72	52.26 N	4.49 E
Zabajkal'sk	84	49.38 N	117.19 E
Žabari	80	44.21 N	21.13 E
Zabarjad, Jazīrat I	112	23.37 N	36.12 E
Zabīd	100	14.10 N	43.17 E
Žabinka	86	52.12 N	24.01 E
Ząbkowice Śląskie	72	50.36 N	16.53 E
Žabljak	80	43.09 N	19.07 E
Zābol	104	31.02 N	61.30 E
Zabrze	72	50.18 N	18.46 E
Zacapa	130	14.58 N	89.32 W
Zacapu	130	19.50 N	101.43 W
Zacatecas	130	22.47 N	102.35 W
Zacatlán	130	19.56 N	97.58 W
Zachary	158	30.39 N	91.09 W
Zacoalco de Torres	130	20.14 N	103.35 W
Zadar	78	44.07 N	15.14 E
Zadetkyi Kyun I	94	9.58 N	98.13 E
Zadonsk	86	52.23 N	38.57 E
Zafra	76	38.25 N	6.25 W
Żagań	72	51.37 N	15.19 E
Žagarė	86	56.21 N	23.15 E
Zagorsk	86	56.18 N	38.08 E
Zagreb	78	45.48 N	15.58 E
Zāgros, Kūhhā-ye ⛰	104	33.40 N	47.00 E
Zagros Mountains → Zāgros, Kūhhā-ye ⛰	104	33.40 N	47.00 E
Žagubica	80	44.13 N	21.48 E
Zāhedān	104	29.30 N	60.52 E
Zaḥlah	104	33.51 N	35.53 E
Záhony	72	48.14 N	22.10 E
Zaire □[1]	110	4.00 S	25.00 E
Zaječar	80	43.54 N	22.17 E
Zajsan	84	47.28 N	84.55 E
Zajsan, Ozero ⊜	84	48.00 N	84.00 E
Zakamensk	84	50.23 N	103.17 E
Zákinthos	80	37.47 N	20.53 E
Zákinthos I	80	37.52 N	20.44 E
Zakopane	72	49.19 N	19.57 E
Zala □[6]	72	46.45 N	16.50 E
Zalaegerszeg	72	46.51 N	16.51 E
Zalalövő	72	46.51 N	16.35 E
Zalaszentgrót	72	46.59 N	17.02 E
Zalău	80	47.11 N	23.03 E
Zalegošč'	86	52.56 N	36.53 E
Žaltyr	82	51.40 N	69.50 E
Zambezi (Zambeze) ≃	110	18.55 S	36.04 E
Zambia □[1]	110	15.00 S	30.00 E
Zamboanga	96	6.54 N	122.05 E
Zambrów	72	53.00 N	22.15 E
Zamfara ≃	114	12.05 N	4.02 E
Zamora	76	41.30 N	5.45 W
Zamora-Chinchipe □[4]	138	4.15 S	78.50 W
Zamora de Hidalgo	130	19.59 N	102.16 W
Zamość	72	50.44 N	23.15 E
Zanaga	110	2.51 S	13.50 E
Zandvoort	72	52.22 N	4.32 E
Zanesville	152	39.56 N	82.01 W
Zanjān	104	36.40 N	48.29 E
Zanjón ≃	140	31.16 S	67.41 W
Žannetty, Ostrov I	84	76.43 N	158.00 E
Zanzibar	110	6.10 S	39.11 E
Zanzibar Island I	110	6.10 S	39.20 E
Zaouia el Kahla	106	28.09 N	6.43 E
Zaoz'ornyj	84	55.58 N	94.42 E
Zapadnaja Dvina (Daugava) ≃	86	57.04 N	24.03 E
Zapadno-Sibirskaja Nizmennost' ⩸	82	60.00 N	75.00 E
Zapadnyj Sajan ⛰	84	53.00 N	94.00 E
Západočeský Kraj □[4]	72	49.45 N	13.00 E
Západoslovenský Kraj □[4]	72	48.20 N	18.00 E
Zapala	140	38.55 S	70.05 W
Zapata	160	26.52 N	99.19 W
Zapl'usje	86	58.26 N	29.43 E
Zapol'arnyj	66	69.26 N	30.48 E
Zapolje	86	58.23 N	29.41 E
Zaporožje	64	47.50 N	35.10 E
Zapotlanejo	130	20.38 N	103.04 W
Zaprudn'a	86	56.34 N	37.26 E
Zaragosa □[4]	74	42.30 N	1.00 W
Zaragoza, Esp.	76	41.38 N	0.53 W
Zaragoza, Méx.	130	28.29 N	100.55 W
Zarajsk	86	54.46 N	38.53 E
Zaranj	104	31.06 N	61.53 E
Zárate	140	34.05 S	59.02 W
Zarauz	76	43.17 N	2.10 W
Zaraza	138	9.21 N	65.19 W
Zard Kūh ∧	104	32.22 N	50.04 E
Zareb (Agram)	78	45.48 N	15.58 E
Zarembo Island I	146	56.20 N	132.50 W
Zarghūn Shahr	102	32.51 N	68.25 E
Zaria	114	11.07 N	7.44 E
Žarma	84	48.48 N	80.50 E
Żary (Sorau)	72	51.38 N	15.09 E
Zarzal	138	4.24 N	76.04 W
Zāskār Mountains ⛰	102	33.00 N	78.00 E
Zasulje	66	64.41 N	47.48 E
Žatec	72	50.18 N	13.32 E
Zavidovići	80	44.27 N	18.09 E
Zavitinsk	84	50.07 N	129.27 E
Zavolžsk	86	57.30 N	42.10 E
Zawiercie	72	50.30 N	19.25 E
Zāwiyat al-Bayḍā'	108	32.46 N	21.43 E
Ždanov	64	47.06 N	37.33 E
Zduńska Wola	72	51.36 N	18.57 E
Zebulon	156	35.49 N	78.19 W
Zedang	88	29.16 N	91.46 E
Zeehan	120	41.53 S	145.20 E
Zeeland, Mich., U.S.	154	42.49 N	86.01 W
Zeeland, N. Dak., U.S.	162	45.58 N	99.50 W
Zeerust	116	25.33 S	26.06 E
Zehdenick	72	52.59 N	13.20 E
Zeigler	158	37.54 N	89.03 W
Zeila	108	11.21 N	43.30 E
Zeist	72	52.05 N	5.15 E
Zeitz	72	51.03 N	12.08 E
Zeja	84	53.45 N	127.15 E
Zeja ≃	84	50.13 N	127.35 E
Zele	72	51.04 N	4.02 E
Żelechów	72	51.49 N	21.54 E
Zelenogorsk	86	60.12 N	29.42 E
Zelenogradsk	86	54.58 N	20.29 E
Železnodorožnyj	86	54.22 N	21.19 E
Železnogorsk	86	52.22 N	35.23 E
Železnogorsk-Ilimskij	84	56.37 N	104.08 E
Zelienople	152	40.48 N	80.08 W
Zell	72	50.01 N	7.10 E
Zella-Mehlis	72	50.39 N	10.39 E
Zell am See	72	47.19 N	12.47 E
Zell am Ziller	72	47.14 N	11.53 E
Zel'onodol'sk	66	55.51 N	48.33 E
Zelów	72	51.28 N	19.13 E
Želudok	86	53.36 N	24.59 E
Zel'va	86	53.08 N	24.48 E
Zemetčino	86	53.30 N	42.38 E
Zenica	80	44.12 N	17.55 E
Zephyrhills	156	28.14 N	82.11 W
Zeravšan ≃	82	39.22 N	63.45 E
Zerbst	72	51.58 N	12.04 E
Žerdevka	86	51.51 N	41.28 E
Zereh, Gowd-e ⊜	104	29.45 N	61.50 E
Zermatt	74	46.02 N	7.45 E
Zernograd	82	46.50 N	40.19 E
Zeulenroda	72	50.39 N	11.58 E
Zeven	72	53.18 N	9.16 E
Zevenaar	72	51.56 N	6.05 E
Zgierz	72	51.52 N	19.25 E
Zhalinghu ⊜	88	34.53 N	97.58 E
Zhalinhu ⊜	102	31.10 N	88.15 E
Zhalutegi	88	44.37 N	120.58 E
Zhangguangcailing ⛰	88	45.25 N	129.20 E
Zhangjiakou (Kalgan)	88	40.50 N	114.53 E
Zhangping	88	25.19 N	117.25 E
Zhangye	88	38.57 N	100.37 E
Zhangzhou	88	24.33 N	117.39 E
Zhanjiang	94	21.16 N	110.28 E
Zhanyi	88	25.38 N	103.43 E
Zhaoan	88	23.44 N	116.11 E
Zhaoqing	88	23.03 N	112.27 E
Zhaotong	88	27.19 N	103.48 E
Zhaxigang	88	32.32 N	79.41 E
Zhejiang □[4]	88	29.00 N	120.00 E
Zhengding	88	38.10 N	114.34 E
Zhengzhou	88	34.48 N	113.39 E
Zhenjiang	88	32.13 N	119.26 E
Zhenping	88	33.08 N	112.19 E
Zhenyuan	88	26.53 N	108.19 E
Zhide	88	30.04 N	116.58 E
Zhob ≃	102	32.04 N	69.50 E
Zhongba	88	29.54 N	83.40 E
Zhongdian	88	27.50 N	99.40 E
Zhongning	88	37.27 N	105.38 E
Zhongshan	88	22.31 N	113.22 E
Zhongxiang	88	31.11 N	112.33 E
Zhoucun	88	36.47 N	117.48 E
Zhoushan	88	30.02 N	122.06 E
Zhoushanqundao II	88	30.00 N	122.00 E
Zhuangaerpendi ⩸[1]	88	45.00 N	88.00 E
Zhujiangkou C	88	23.36 N	113.44 E
Zhungeerqi	88	39.49 N	111.10 E
Zhuoxian	88	39.30 N	115.58 E
Zhushan	88	32.10 N	110.19 E
Zhuzhou	88	27.50 N	113.09 E
Žiar nad Hronom	72	48.36 N	18.52 E
Zibo	88	36.47 N	118.01 E
Ziegenhain	72	50.55 N	9.15 E
Ziel, Mount ∧	122	23.24 S	132.23 E
Zielona Góra (Grünberg)	72	51.56 N	15.31 E
Zierikzee	72	51.38 N	3.55 E
Ziesar	72	52.16 N	12.17 E
Ziftā	112	30.43 N	31.15 E
Žigalovo	84	54.48 N	105.08 E
Zigana Dağları ⛰	100	40.37 N	39.30 E
Žigansk	84	66.45 N	123.20 E
Zigong	88	29.24 N	104.47 E
Ziguinchor	114	12.35 N	16.16 W
Žigulevsk	66	53.25 N	49.27 E
Zihuatanejo	130	17.38 N	101.33 W
Žilina	72	49.14 N	18.46 E
Zillah, Lībīya	108	28.33 N	17.35 E
Zillah, Wash., U.S.	166	46.24 N	120.16 W
Zillertaler Alpen ⛰	72	47.00 N	11.55 E
Žil'ovo	86	54.59 N	38.02 E
Zilwaukee	154	43.28 N	83.55 W
Zima	84	53.55 N	102.04 E
Zimnicea	80	43.39 N	25.21 E
Zinder	114	13.48 N	8.59 E
Zinkgruvan	68	58.49 N	15.05 E
Zinnowitz	72	54.04 N	13.55 E
Zion	154	42.27 N	87.50 W
Zionsville	158	39.57 N	86.16 W
Zipaquirá	138	5.02 N	74.00 W
Zishui ≃	88	28.45 N	112.25 E
Žitomir	64	50.16 N	28.40 E
Zittau	72	50.54 N	14.47 E
Ziway, Lake ⊜	108	8.00 N	38.50 E
Ziyun	88	25.43 N	106.05 E
Zizhong	88	29.48 N	104.50 E
Zlatar	78	46.06 N	16.05 E
Zlatoust	64	55.10 N	59.40 E
Zlītan	108	32.28 N	14.34 E
Žlobin	86	52.54 N	30.03 E
Złotoryja	72	51.08 N	15.55 E
Złotów	72	53.22 N	17.02 E
Zmeinogorsk	84	51.10 N	82.13 E
Znamenka	82	48.43 N	32.40 E
Znamenskoje	84	57.08 N	73.55 E
Znojmo	72	48.52 N	16.02 E
Žochova, Ostrov I	84	76.04 N	152.40 E
Žodino	86	54.06 N	28.21 E
Zogno	78	45.48 N	9.40 E
Zolfo Springs	156	27.30 N	81.48 W
Zolotkovo	86	55.32 N	41.06 E
Žoltyje Vody	82	48.21 N	33.31 E
Žolymbet	82	51.45 N	71.44 E
Zomba	110	15.23 S	35.18 E
Zonguldak	64	41.27 N	31.49 E
Zorita	76	39.17 N	5.42 W
Zouar	108	20.27 N	16.32 E
Zrenjanin	80	45.23 N	20.24 E
Zubcov	86	56.10 N	34.34 E
Zubova Pol'ana	86	54.04 N	42.51 E
Zudañez	134	19.06 S	64.44 W
Zuera	76	41.52 N	0.47 W
Zug	74	47.10 N	8.31 E
Zugdidi	64	42.30 N	41.53 E
Zugspitze ∧	72	47.25 N	10.59 E
Zuiderzee → IJsselmeer ⊤[2]	72	52.45 N	5.25 E
Zujevka	66	58.25 N	51.10 E
Žukovskij	86	55.35 N	38.08 E
Zulia □[3]	138	10.00 N	72.10 W
Zulia ≃	138	9.04 N	72.18 W
Zululand □[9]	110	28.10 S	32.00 E
Zumbo	110	15.36 S	30.25 E
Zumbrota	154	44.17 N	92.40 W
Zuni	164	35.04 N	108.51 W
Zuni ≃	164	34.39 N	109.40 W
Zunyi	88	27.39 N	106.57 E
Zuqar, Jazīrat I	100	14.00 N	42.45 E
Zürich	74	47.23 N	8.32 E
Zürichsee ⊜	74	47.13 N	8.45 E
Zutphen	72	52.08 N	6.12 E
Zuwārah	108	32.56 N	12.06 E
Zvolen	72	48.35 N	19.08 E
Zvornik	80	44.23 N	19.06 E
Zweibrücken	72	49.15 N	7.21 E
Zweisimmen	74	46.33 N	7.22 E
Zwettl	72	48.37 N	15.10 E
Zwickau	72	50.44 N	12.29 E
Zwiesel	72	49.01 N	13.14 E
Zwischenahn	72	53.11 N	8.00 E
Zwolle, Ned.	72	52.30 N	6.05 E
Zwolle, La., U.S.	158	31.38 N	93.38 W
Zyr'anka	84	65.45 N	150.51 E
Zyr'anovsk	84	49.43 N	84.20 E
Żywiec	72	49.41 N	19.12 E

Symbols in the index entries are identified on page 203.